KEY TO WORLD MAP PAGES

ASIA 26–27

32–33

34–35

30–31

40–41

42–43

38–39

36–37

PACIFIC OCEAN 64–65

INDIAN OCEAN

60–61

62–63

59

59

AUSTRALIA AND OCEANIA

PHILIP'S

WORLD ATLAS

The World in Focus
Cartography by Philip's

Picture Acknowledgements
Page 14
Science Photo Library/NOAA

Illustrations
Stefan Chabluk

CONSULTANTS

Philip's are grateful to the following people for acting as specialist geography consultants on 'The World in Focus' front section:

Professor D. Brunsden, Kings College, University of London, UK
Dr C. Clarke, Oxford University, UK
Dr I. S. Evans, Durham University, UK
Professor P. Haggett, University of Bristol, UK
Professor K. McLachlan, University of London, UK
Professor M. Monmonier, Syracuse University, New York, USA
Professor M-L. Hsu, University of Minnesota, Minnesota, USA
Professor M. J. Tooley, University of St Andrews, UK
Dr T. Unwin, Royal Holloway, University of London, UK

Published in Great Britain in 2000
by George Philip Limited,
a division of Octopus Publishing Group Limited,
2–4 Heron Quays, London E14 4JP

Copyright © 2000 George Philip Limited

Cartography by Philip's

ISBN 0–540–07890–5

A CIP catalogue record for this book is available from the British Library.

Printed in China

Details of other Philip's titles and services can be found on our website at: www.philips-maps.co.uk

Philip's is proud to announce that its World Atlases are now published in association with The Royal Geographical Society (with The Institute of British Geographers).

The Society was founded in 1830 and given a Royal Charter in 1859 for 'the advancement of geographical science'. It holds historical collections of national and international importance, many of which relate to the Society's association with and support for scientific exploration and research from the 19th century onwards. It was pivotal in establishing geography as a teaching and research discipline in British universities close to the turn of the century, and has played a key role in geographical and environmental education ever since.

Today the Society is a leading world centre for geographical learning – supporting education, teaching, research and expeditions, and promoting public understanding of the subject.

The Society welcomes those interested in geography as members. For further information, please visit the website at: www.rgs.org

PHILIP'S

WORLD ATLAS

TENTH EDITION

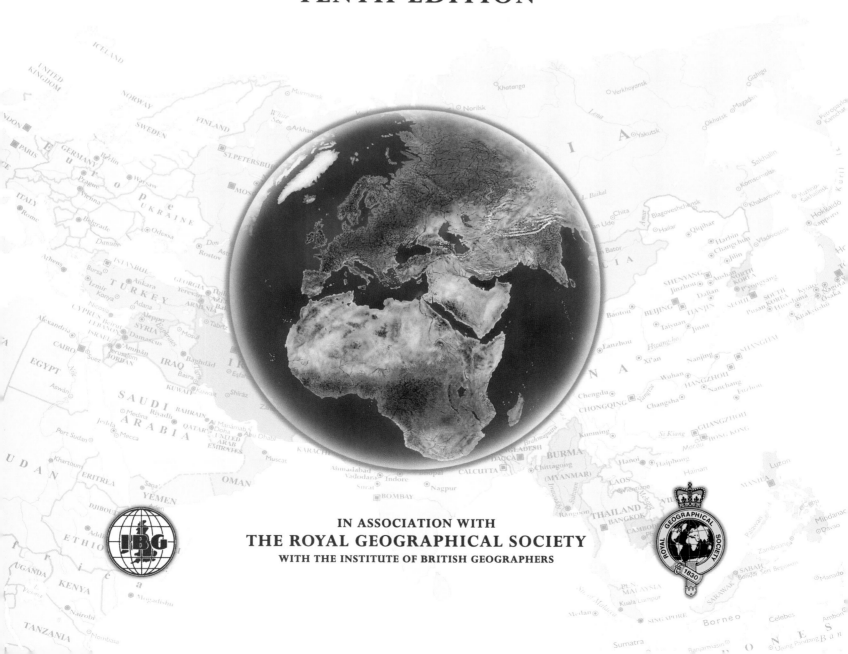

IN ASSOCIATION WITH
THE ROYAL GEOGRAPHICAL SOCIETY
WITH THE INSTITUTE OF BRITISH GEOGRAPHERS

Contents

v

World Statistics: Countries

This alphabetical list includes all the countries and territories of the world. If a territory is not completely independent, then the country it is associated with is named. The area figures give the total area of land, inland water and ice. The population figures are 2000 estimates. The annual income is the Gross National Product per capita in US dollars. The figures are the latest available, usually 1998.

Country/Territory	Area km² Thousands	Area miles² Thousands	Population Thousands	Capital	Annual Income US $
Afghanistan	652	252	26,511	Kabul	800
Albania	28.8	11.1	3,795	Tirana	810
Algeria	2,382	920	32,904	Algiers	1,550
American Samoa (US)	0.20	0.08	39	Pago Pago	2,600
Andorra	0.45	0.17	49	Andorra La Vella	18,000
Angola	1,247	481	13,295	Luanda	340
Anguilla (UK)	0.1	0.04	8	The Valley	6,800
Antigua & Barbuda	0.44	0.17	79	St John's	8,300
Argentina	2,767	1,068	36,238	Buenos Aires	8,970
Armenia	29.8	11.5	3,968	Yerevan	480
Aruba (Netherlands)	0.19	0.07	58	Oranjestad	22,000
Australia	7,687	2,968	18,855	Canberra	20,300
Austria	83.9	32.4	7,613	Vienna	26,850
Azerbaijan	86.6	33.4	8,324	Baku	490
Azores (Portugal)	2.2	0.87	238	Ponta Delgada	–
Bahamas	13.9	5.4	295	Nassau	20,100
Bahrain	0.68	0.26	683	Manama	7,660
Bangladesh	144	56	150,589	Dhaka	350
Barbados	0.43	0.17	265	Bridgetown	7,890
Belarus	207.6	80.1	10,697	Minsk	2,200
Belgium	30.5	11.8	9,832	Brussels	25,380
Belize	23	8.9	230	Belmopan	2,610
Benin	113	43	6,369	Porto-Novo	380
Bermuda (UK)	0.05	0.02	62	Hamilton	34,000
Bhutan	47	18.1	1,906	Thimphu	1,000
Bolivia	1,099	424	9,724	La Paz/Sucre	1,000
Bosnia-Herzegovina	51	20	4,601	Sarajevo	1,720
Botswana	582	225	1,822	Gaborone	3,600
Brazil	8,512	3,286	179,487	Brasília	4,570
Brunei	5.8	2.2	333	Bandar Seri Begawan	24,000
Bulgaria	111	43	9,071	Sofia	1,230
Burkina Faso	274	106	12,092	Ouagadougou	240
Burma (= Myanmar)	677	261	51,129	Rangoon	1,200
Burundi	27.8	10.7	7,358	Bujumbura	140
Cambodia	181	70	10,046	Phnom Penh	280
Cameroon	475	184	16,701	Yaoundé	610
Canada	9,976	3,852	28,488	Ottawa	20,020
Canary Is. (Spain)	7.3	2.8	1,494	Las Palmas/Santa Cruz	–
Cape Verde Is.	4	1.6	515	Praia	1,060
Cayman Is. (UK)	0.26	0.10	35	George Town	20,000
Central African Republic	623	241	4,074	Bangui	300
Chad	1,284	496	7,337	Ndjaména	230
Chile	757	292	15,272	Santiago	4,810
China	9,597	3,705	1,299,180	Beijing	750
Colombia	1,139	440	39,397	Bogotá	2,600
Comoros	2.2	0.86	670	Moroni	370
Congo	342	132	3,167	Brazzaville	690
Congo (Dem. Rep. of the)	2,345	905	49,190	Kinshasa	110
Cook Is. (NZ)	0.24	0.09	17	Avarua	900
Costa Rica	51.1	19.7	3,711	San José	2,780
Croatia	56.5	21.8	4,960	Zagreb	4,520
Cuba	111	43	11,504	Havana	1,560
Cyprus	9.3	3.6	762	Nicosia	13,000
Czech Republic	78.9	30.4	10,500	Prague	5,040
Denmark	43.1	16.6	5,153	Copenhagen	33,260
Djibouti	23.2	9	552	Djibouti	1,200
Dominica	0.75	0.29	87	Roseau	3,010
Dominican Republic	48.7	18.8	8,621	Santo Domingo	1,770
Ecuador	284	109	13,319	Quito	1,530
Egypt	1,001	387	64,210	Cairo	1,290
El Salvador	21	8.1	6,739	San Salvador	1,850
Equatorial Guinea	28.1	10.8	455	Malabo	1,500
Eritrea	94	36	4,523	Asmara	200
Estonia	44.7	17.3	1,647	Tallinn	3,390
Ethiopia	1,128	436	61,841	Addis Ababa	100
Faroe Is. (Denmark)	1.4	0.54	49	Tórshavn	16,000
Fiji	18.3	7.1	883	Suva	2,110
Finland	338	131	5,077	Helsinki	24,110
France	552	213	58,145	Paris	24,940
French Guiana (France)	90	34.7	130	Cayenne	6,000
French Polynesia (France)	4	1.5	268	Papeete	10,800
Gabon	268	103	1,612	Libreville	3,950
Gambia, The	11.3	4.4	1,119	Banjul	340
Georgia	69.7	26.9	5,777	Tbilisi	930
Germany	357	138	76,962	Berlin	25,850
Ghana	239	92	20,564	Accra	390
Gibraltar (UK)	0.007	0.003	32	Gibraltar Town	5,000
Greece	132	51	10,193	Athens	11,650
Greenland (Denmark)	2,176	840	60	Nuuk (Godthåb)	16,100
Grenada	0.34	0.13	83	St George's	3,170
Guadeloupe (France)	1.7	0.66	365	Basse-Terre	9,200
Guam (US)	0.55	0.21	128	Agana	19,000
Guatemala	109	42	12,222	Guatemala City	1,640
Guinea	246	95	7,830	Conakry	540
Guinea-Bissau	36.1	13.9	1,197	Bissau	160
Guyana	215	83	891	Georgetown	770
Haiti	27.8	10.7	8,003	Port-au-Prince	410
Honduras	112	43	6,846	Tegucigalpa	730
Hong Kong (China)	1.1	0.40	6,336	–	23,670
Hungary	93	35.9	10,531	Budapest	4,510
Iceland	103	40	274	Reykjavik	28,010
India	3,288	1,269	1,041,543	New Delhi	430
Indonesia	1,905	735	218,661	Jakarta	680
Iran	1,648	636	68,759	Tehran	1,770
Iraq	438	169	26,339	Baghdad	2,400
Ireland	70.3	27.1	4,086	Dublin	18,340
Israel	27	10.3	5,321	Jerusalem	15,940
Italy	301	116	57,195	Rome	20,250
Ivory Coast (Côte d'Ivoire)	322	125	17,600	Yamoussoukro	700
Jamaica	11	4.2	2,735	Kingston	1,680
Japan	378	146	128,470	Tokyo	32,380
Jordan	89.2	34.4	5,558	Amman	1,520
Kazakstan	2,717	1,049	19,006	Astana	1,310
Kenya	580	224	35,060	Nairobi	330
Kiribati	0.72	0.28	72	Tarawa	1,180
Korea, North	121	47	26,117	Pyŏngyang	1,000
Korea, South	99	38.2	46,403	Seoul	7,970
Kuwait	17.8	6.9	2,639	Kuwait City	22,700
Kyrgyzstan	198.5	76.6	5,403	Bishkek	350
Laos	237	91	5,463	Vientiane	330
Latvia	65	25	2,768	Riga	2,430
Lebanon	10.4	4	3,327	Beirut	3,560
Lesotho	30.4	11.7	2,370	Maseru	570
Liberia	111	43	3,575	Monrovia	1,000
Libya	1,760	679	6,500	Tripoli	6,700
Liechtenstein	0.16	0.06	28	Vaduz	50,000
Lithuania	65.2	25.2	3,935	Vilnius	2,440
Luxembourg	2.6	1	377	Luxembourg	43,570
Macau (China)	0.02	0.006	656	Macau	16,000
Macedonia (F.Y.R.O.M.)	25.7	9.9	2,157	Skopje	1,290
Madagascar	587	227	16,627	Antananarivo	260
Madeira (Portugal)	0.81	0.31	253	Funchal	–
Malawi	118	46	12,458	Lilongwe	200
Malaysia	330	127	21,983	Kuala Lumpur	3,600
Maldives	0.30	0.12	283	Malé	1,230
Mali	1,240	479	12,685	Bamako	250
Malta	0.32	0.12	366	Valletta	9,440
Marshall Is.	0.18	0.07	70	Dalap-Uliga-Darrit	1,540
Martinique (France)	1.1	0.42	362	Fort-de-France	10,700
Mauritania	1,030	412	2,702	Nouakchott	410
Mauritius	2.0	0.72	1,201	Port Louis	3,700
Mayotte (France)	0.37	0.14	141	Mamoundzou	1,430
Mexico	1,958	756	107,233	Mexico City	3,970
Micronesia, Fed. States of	0.70	0.27	110	Palikir	1,800
Moldova	33.7	13	4,707	Chişinău	410
Monaco	0.002	0.0001	30	Monaco	25,000
Mongolia	1,567	605	2,847	Ulan Bator	400
Montserrat (UK)	0.10	0.04	13	Plymouth	4,500
Morocco	447	172	31,559	Rabat	1,250
Mozambique	802	309	20,493	Maputo	210
Namibia	825	318	2,437	Windhoek	1,940
Nauru	0.02	0.008	10	Yaren District	10,000
Nepal	141	54	24,084	Katmandu	210
Netherlands	41.5	16	15,829	Amsterdam/The Hague	24,760
Netherlands Antilles (Neths)	0.99	0.38	203	Willemstad	11,500
New Caledonia (France)	18.6	7.2	195	Nouméa	11,400
New Zealand	269	104	3,662	Wellington	14,700
Nicaragua	130	50	5,261	Managua	390
Niger	1,267	489	10,752	Niamey	190
Nigeria	924	357	105,000	Abuja	300
Northern Mariana Is. (US)	0.48	0.18	50	Saipan	9,300
Norway	324	125	4,331	Oslo	34,330
Oman	212	82	2,176	Muscat	7,900
Pakistan	796	307	162,409	Islamabad	480
Palau	0.46	0.18	18	Koror	8,800
Panama	77.1	29.8	2,893	Panama City	3,080
Papua New Guinea	463	179	4,845	Port Moresby	890
Paraguay	407	157	5,538	Asunción	1,760
Peru	1,285	496	26,276	Lima	2,460
Philippines	300	116	77,473	Manila	1,050
Poland	313	121	40,366	Warsaw	3,900
Portugal	92.4	35.7	10,587	Lisbon	10,690
Puerto Rico (US)	9	3.5	3,836	San Juan	9,000
Qatar	11	4.2	499	Doha	17,100
Réunion (France)	2.5	0.97	692	Saint-Denis	4,800
Romania	238	92	24,000	Bucharest	1,390
Russia	17,075	6,592	155,096	Moscow	2,300
Rwanda	26.3	10.2	10,200	Kigali	230
St Kitts & Nevis	0.36	0.14	44	Basseterre	6,130
St Lucia	0.62	0.24	177	Castries	3,410
St Vincent & Grenadines	0.39	0.15	128	Kingstown	2,420
Samoa	2.8	1.1	171	Apia	1,020
San Marino	0.06	0.02	25	San Marino	20,000
São Tomé & Príncipe	0.96	0.37	151	São Tomé	280
Saudi Arabia	2,150	830	20,697	Riyadh	9,000
Senegal	197	76	8,716	Dakar	530
Seychelles	0.46	0.18	75	Victoria	6,450
Sierra Leone	71.7	27.7	5,437	Freetown	140
Singapore	0.62	0.24	3,000	Singapore	30,060
Slovak Republic	49	18.9	5,500	Bratislava	3,700
Slovenia	20.3	7.8	2,055	Ljubljana	9,760
Solomon Is.	28.9	11.2	429	Honiara	750
Somalia	638	246	9,736	Mogadishu	600
South Africa	1,220	471	43,666	C. Town/Pretoria/Bloem.	2,880
Spain	505	195	40,667	Madrid	14,080
Sri Lanka	65.6	25.3	19,416	Colombo	810
Sudan	2,506	967	33,625	Khartoum	290
Surinam	163	63	497	Paramaribo	1,660
Swaziland	17.4	6.7	1,121	Mbabane	1,400
Sweden	450	174	8,560	Stockholm	25,620
Switzerland	41.3	15.9	6,762	Bern	40,080
Syria	185	71	17,826	Damascus	1,020
Taiwan	36	13.9	22,000	Taipei	12,400
Tajikistan	143.1	55.2	7,041	Dushanbe	350
Tanzania	945	365	39,639	Dodoma	210
Thailand	513	198	63,670	Bangkok	2,200
Togo	56.8	21.9	4,861	Lomé	330
Tonga	0.75	0.29	92	Nuku'alofa	1,690
Trinidad & Tobago	5.1	2	1,484	Port of Spain	4,430
Tunisia	164	63	9,924	Tunis	2,050
Turkey	779	301	66,789	Ankara	3,160
Turkmenistan	488.1	188.5	4,585	Ashkhabad	1,630
Turks & Caicos Is. (UK)	0.43	0.17	12	Cockburn Town	5,000
Tuvalu	0.03	0.01	11	Fongafale	600
Uganda	236	91	26,958	Kampala	320
Ukraine	603.7	233.1	52,558	Kiev	850
United Arab Emirates	83.6	32.3	1,951	Abu Dhabi	18,220
United Kingdom	243.3	94	58,393	London	21,400
United States of America	9,373	3,619	266,096	Washington, DC	29,340
Uruguay	177	68	3,274	Montevideo	6,180
Uzbekistan	447.4	172.7	26,044	Tashkent	870
Vanuatu	12.2	4.7	206	Port-Vila	1,270
Venezuela	912	352	24,715	Caracas	350
Vietnam	332	127	82,427	Hanoi	330
Virgin Is. (UK)	0.15	0.06	15	Road Town	–
Virgin Is. (US)	0.34	0.13	135	Charlotte Amalie	12,500
Wallis & Futuna Is. (France)	0.20	0.08	26	Mata-Utu	–
Western Sahara	266	103	228	El Aaiún	300
Yemen	528	204	13,219	Sana	300
Yugoslavia	102.3	39.5	10,761	Belgrade	2,300
Zambia	753	291	12,267	Lusaka	330
Zimbabwe	391	151	13,123	Harare	610

World Statistics: Physical Dimensions

Each topic list is divided into continents and within a continent the items are listed in order of size. The bottom part of many of the lists is selective in order to give examples from as many different countries as possible. The order of the continents is the same as in the atlas, beginning with Europe and ending with South America. The figures are rounded as appropriate.

World, Continents, Oceans

	km²	miles²	%
The World	509,450,000	196,672,000	–
Land	149,450,000	57,688,000	29.3
Water	360,000,000	138,984,000	70.7
Asia	44,500,000	17,177,000	29.8
Africa	30,302,000	11,697,000	20.3
North America	24,241,000	9,357,000	16.2
South America	17,793,000	6,868,000	11.9
Antarctica	14,100,000	5,443,000	9.4
Europe	9,957,000	3,843,000	6.7
Australia & Oceania	8,557,000	3,303,000	5.7
Pacific Ocean	179,679,000	69,356,000	49.9
Atlantic Ocean	92,373,000	35,657,000	25.7
Indian Ocean	73,917,000	28,532,000	20.5
Arctic Ocean	14,090,000	5,439,000	3.9

Ocean Depths

Atlantic Ocean	m	ft
Puerto Rico (Milwaukee) Deep	9,220	30,249
Cayman Trench	7,680	25,197
Gulf of Mexico	5,203	17,070
Mediterranean Sea	5,121	16,801
Black Sea	2,211	7,254
North Sea	660	2,165

Indian Ocean	m	ft
Java Trench	7,450	24,442
Red Sea	2,635	8,454

Pacific Ocean	m	ft
Mariana Trench	11,022	36,161
Tonga Trench	10,882	35,702
Japan Trench	10,554	34,626
Kuril Trench	10,542	34,587

Arctic Ocean	m	ft
Molloy Deep	5,608	18,399

Mountains

Europe		m	ft
Elbrus	*Russia*	5,642	18,510
Mont Blanc	*France/Italy*	4,807	15,771
Monte Rosa	*Italy/Switzerland*	4,634	15,203
Dom	*Switzerland*	4,545	14,911
Liskamm	*Switzerland*	4,527	14,852
Weisshorn	*Switzerland*	4,505	14,780
Taschorn	*Switzerland*	4,490	14,730
Matterhorn/Cervino	*Italy/Switzerland*	4,478	14,691
Mont Maudit	*France/Italy*	4,465	14,649
Dent Blanche	*Switzerland*	4,356	14,291
Nadelhorn	*Switzerland*	4,327	14,196
Grandes Jorasses	*France/Italy*	4,208	13,806
Jungfrau	*Switzerland*	4,158	13,642
Grossglockner	*Austria*	3,797	12,457
Mulhacén	*Spain*	3,478	11,411
Zugspitze	*Germany*	2,962	9,718
Olympus	*Greece*	2,917	9,570
Triglav	*Slovenia*	2,863	9,393
Gerlachovka	*Slovak Republic*	2,655	8,711
Galdhöpiggen	*Norway*	2,468	8,100
Kebnekaise	*Sweden*	2,117	6,946
Ben Nevis	*UK*	1,343	4,406

Asia		m	ft
Everest	*China/Nepal*	8,850	29,035
K2 (Godwin Austen)	*China/Kashmir*	8,611	28,251
Kanchenjunga	*India/Nepal*	8,598	28,208
Lhotse	*China/Nepal*	8,516	27,939
Makalu	*China/Nepal*	8,481	27,824
Cho Oyu	*China/Nepal*	8,201	26,906
Dhaulagiri	*Nepal*	8,172	26,811
Manaslu	*Nepal*	8,156	26,758
Nanga Parbat	*Kashmir*	8,126	26,660
Annapurna	*Nepal*	8,078	26,502
Gasherbrum	*China/Kashmir*	8,068	26,469
Broad Peak	*China/Kashmir*	8,051	26,414
Xixabangma	*China*	8,012	26,286
Kangbachen	*India/Nepal*	7,902	25,925
Trivor	*Pakistan*	7,720	25,328
Pik Kommunizma	*Tajikistan*	7,495	24,590
Demavend	*Iran*	5,604	18,386
Ararat	*Turkey*	5,165	16,945
Gunong Kinabalu	*Malaysia (Borneo)*	4,101	13,455
Fuji-San	*Japan*	3,776	12,388

Africa		m	ft
Kilimanjaro	*Tanzania*	5,895	19,340
Mt Kenya	*Kenya*	5,199	17,057
Ruwenzori (Margherita)	*Ug./Congo (D.R.)*	5,109	16,762
Ras Dashan	*Ethiopia*	4,620	15,157
Meru	*Tanzania*	4,565	14,977
Karisimbi	*Rwanda/Congo (D.R.)*	4,507	14,787
Mt Elgon	*Kenya/Uganda*	4,321	14,176
Batu	*Ethiopia*	4,307	14,130
Toubkal	*Morocco*	4,165	13,665
Mt Cameroon	*Cameroon*	4,070	13,353

Oceania		m	ft
Puncak Jaya	*Indonesia*	5,029	16,499
Puncak Trikora	*Indonesia*	4,750	15,584
Puncak Mandala	*Indonesia*	4,702	15,427
Mt Wilhelm	*Papua New Guinea*	4,508	14,790
Mauna Kea	*USA (Hawaii)*	4,205	13,796
Mauna Loa	*USA (Hawaii)*	4,169	13,681
Mt Cook (Aoraki)	*New Zealand*	3,753	12,313
Mt Kosciuszko	*Australia*	2,237	7,339

North America		m	ft
Mt McKinley (Denali)	*USA (Alaska)*	6,194	20,321
Mt Logan	*Canada*	5,959	19,551
Citlaltepetl	*Mexico*	5,700	18,701
Mt St Elias	*USA/Canada*	5,489	18,008
Popocatepetl	*Mexico*	5,452	17,887
Mt Foraker	*USA (Alaska)*	5,304	17,401
Ixtaccihuatl	*Mexico*	5,286	17,342
Lucania	*Canada*	5,227	17,149
Mt Steele	*Canada*	5,073	16,644
Mt Bona	*USA (Alaska)*	5,005	16,420
Mt Whitney	*USA*	4,418	14,495
Tajumulco	*Guatemala*	4,220	13,845
Chirripó Grande	*Costa Rica*	3,837	12,589
Pico Duarte	*Dominican Rep.*	3,175	10,417

South America		m	ft
Aconcagua	*Argentina*	6,960	22,834
Bonete	*Argentina*	6,872	22,546
Ojos del Salado	*Argentina/Chile*	6,863	22,516
Pissis	*Argentina*	6,779	22,241
Mercedario	*Argentina/Chile*	6,770	22,211
Huascaran	*Peru*	6,768	22,204
Llullaillaco	*Argentina/Chile*	6,723	22,057
Nudo de Cachi	*Argentina*	6,720	22,047
Yerupaja	*Peru*	6,632	21,758
Sajama	*Bolivia*	6,542	21,463
Chimborazo	*Ecuador*	6,267	20,561
Pico Colon	*Colombia*	5,800	19,029
Pico Bolivar	*Venezuela*	5,007	16,427

Antarctica		m	ft
Vinson Massif		4,897	16,066
Mt Kirkpatrick		4,528	14,855

Rivers

Europe		km	miles
Volga	*Caspian Sea*	3,700	2,300
Danube	*Black Sea*	2,850	1,770
Ural	*Caspian Sea*	2,535	1,575
Dnepr (Dnipro)	*Black Sea*	2,285	1,420
Kama	*Volga*	2,030	1,260
Don	*Black Sea*	1,990	1,240
Petchora	*Arctic Ocean*	1,790	1,110
Oka	*Volga*	1,480	920
Dnister (Dniester)	*Black Sea*	1,400	870
Vyatka	*Kama*	1,370	850
Rhine	*North Sea*	1,320	820
N. Dvina	*Arctic Ocean*	1,290	800
Elbe	*North Sea*	1,145	710

Asia		km	miles
Yangtze	*Pacific Ocean*	6,380	3,960
Yenisey–Angara	*Arctic Ocean*	5,550	3,445
Huang He	*Pacific Ocean*	5,464	3,395
Ob–Irtysh	*Arctic Ocean*	5,410	3,360
Mekong	*Pacific Ocean*	4,500	2,795
Amur	*Pacific Ocean*	4,400	2,730
Lena	*Arctic Ocean*	4,400	2,730
Irtysh	*Ob*	4,250	2,640
Yenisey	*Arctic Ocean*	4,090	2,540
Ob	*Arctic Ocean*	3,680	2,285
Indus	*Indian Ocean*	3,100	1,925
Brahmaputra	*Indian Ocean*	2,900	1,800
Syrdarya	*Aral Sea*	2,860	1,775
Salween	*Indian Ocean*	2,800	1,740
Euphrates	*Indian Ocean*	2,700	1,675
Amudarya	*Aral Sea*	2,540	1,575

Africa		km	miles
Nile	*Mediterranean*	6,670	4,140
Congo	*Atlantic Ocean*	4,670	2,900
Niger	*Atlantic Ocean*	4,180	2,595
Zambezi	*Indian Ocean*	3,540	2,200
Oubangi/Uele	*Congo (D.R.)*	2,250	1,400
Kasai	*Congo (D.R.)*	1,950	1,210
Shaballe	*Indian Ocean*	1,930	1,200
Orange	*Atlantic Ocean*	1,860	1,155
Cubango	*Okavango Swamps*	1,800	1,120
Limpopo	*Indian Ocean*	1,600	995
Senegal	*Atlantic Ocean*	1,600	995

Australia		km	miles
Murray–Darling	*Indian Ocean*	3,750	2,330
Darling	*Murray*	3,070	1,905
Murray	*Indian Ocean*	2,575	1,600
Murrumbidgee	*Murray*	1,690	1,050

North America		km	miles
Mississippi–Missouri	*Gulf of Mexico*	6,020	3,740
Mackenzie	*Arctic Ocean*	4,240	2,630
Mississippi	*Gulf of Mexico*	3,780	2,350
Missouri	*Mississippi*	3,780	2,350
Yukon	*Pacific Ocean*	3,185	1,980
Rio Grande	*Gulf of Mexico*	3,030	1,880
Arkansas	*Mississippi*	2,340	1,450
Colorado	*Pacific Ocean*	2,330	1,445
Red	*Mississippi*	2,040	1,270
Columbia	*Pacific Ocean*	1,950	1,210
Saskatchewan	*Lake Winnipeg*	1,940	1,205

South America		km	miles
Amazon	*Atlantic Ocean*	6,450	4,010
Paraná–Plate	*Atlantic Ocean*	4,500	2,800
Purus	*Amazon*	3,350	2,080
Madeira	*Amazon*	3,200	1,990
São Francisco	*Atlantic Ocean*	2,900	1,800
Paraná	*Plate*	2,800	1,740
Tocantins	*Atlantic Ocean*	2,750	1,710
Paraguay	*Paraná*	2,550	1,580
Orinoco	*Atlantic Ocean*	2,500	1,550
Pilcomayo	*Paraná*	2,500	1,550
Araguaia	*Tocantins*	2,250	1,400

Lakes

Europe		km²	miles²
Lake Ladoga	*Russia*	17,700	6,800
Lake Onega	*Russia*	9,700	3,700
Saimaa system	*Finland*	8,000	3,100
Vänern	*Sweden*	5,500	2,100

Asia		km²	miles²
Caspian Sea	*Asia*	371,800	143,550
Lake Baykal	*Russia*	30,500	11,780
Aral Sea	*Kazakstan/Uzbekistan*	28,687	11,086
Tonlé Sap	*Cambodia*	20,000	7,700
Lake Balqash	*Kazakstan*	18,500	7,100

Africa		km²	miles²
Lake Victoria	*East Africa*	68,000	26,000
Lake Tanganyika	*Central Africa*	33,000	13,000
Lake Malawi/Nyasa	*East Africa*	29,600	11,430
Lake Chad	*Central Africa*	25,000	9,700
Lake Turkana	*Ethiopia/Kenya*	8,500	3,300
Lake Volta	*Ghana*	8,500	3,300

Australia		km²	miles²
Lake Eyre	*Australia*	8,900	3,400
Lake Torrens	*Australia*	5,800	2,200
Lake Gairdner	*Australia*	4,800	1,900

North America		km²	miles²
Lake Superior	*Canada/USA*	82,350	31,800
Lake Huron	*Canada/USA*	59,600	23,010
Lake Michigan	*USA*	58,000	22,400
Great Bear Lake	*Canada*	31,800	12,280
Great Slave Lake	*Canada*	28,500	11,000
Lake Erie	*Canada/USA*	25,700	9,900
Lake Winnipeg	*Canada*	24,400	9,400
Lake Ontario	*Canada/USA*	19,500	7,500
Lake Nicaragua	*Nicaragua*	8,200	3,200

South America		km²	miles²
Lake Titicaca	*Bolivia/Peru*	8,300	3,200
Lake Poopo	*Peru*	2,800	1,100

Islands

Europe		km²	miles²
Great Britain	*UK*	229,880	88,700
Iceland	*Atlantic Ocean*	103,000	39,800
Ireland	*Ireland/UK*	84,400	32,600
Novaya Zemlya (N.)	*Russia*	48,200	18,600
Sicily	*Italy*	25,500	9,800
Corsica	*France*	8,700	3,400

Asia		km²	miles²
Borneo	*Southeast Asia*	744,360	287,400
Sumatra	*Indonesia*	473,600	182,860
Honshu	*Japan*	230,500	88,980
Sulawesi (Celebes)	*Indonesia*	189,000	73,000
Java	*Indonesia*	126,700	48,900
Luzon	*Philippines*	104,700	40,400
Hokkaido	*Japan*	78,400	30,300

Africa		km²	miles²
Madagascar	*Indian Ocean*	587,040	226,660
Socotra	*Indian Ocean*	3,600	1,400
Réunion	*Indian Ocean*	2,500	965

Oceania		km²	miles²
New Guinea	*Indonesia/Papua NG*	821,030	317,000
New Zealand (S.)	*Pacific Ocean*	150,500	58,100
New Zealand (N.)	*Pacific Ocean*	114,700	44,300
Tasmania	*Australia*	67,800	26,200
Hawaii	*Pacific Ocean*	10,450	4,000

North America		km²	miles²
Greenland	*Atlantic Ocean*	2,175,600	839,800
Baffin Is.	*Canada*	508,000	196,100
Victoria Is.	*Canada*	212,200	81,900
Ellesmere Is.	*Canada*	212,000	81,800
Cuba	*Caribbean Sea*	110,860	42,800
Hispaniola	*Dominican Rep./Haiti*	76,200	29,400
Jamaica	*Caribbean Sea*	11,400	4,400
Puerto Rico	*Atlantic Ocean*	8,900	3,400

South America		km²	miles²
Tierra del Fuego	*Argentina/Chile*	47,000	18,100
Falkland Is. (E.)	*Atlantic Ocean*	6,800	2,600

Philip's World Maps

The reference maps which form the main body of this atlas have been prepared in accordance with the highest standards of international cartography to provide an accurate and detailed representation of the Earth. The scales and projections used have been carefully chosen to give balanced coverage of the world, while emphasizing the most densely populated and economically significant regions. A hallmark of Philip's mapping is the use of hill shading and relief colouring to create a graphic impression of landforms: this makes the maps exceptionally easy to read. However, knowledge of the key features employed in the construction and presentation of the maps will enable the reader to derive the fullest benefit from the atlas.

Map sequence

The atlas covers the Earth continent by continent: first Europe; then its land neighbour Asia (mapped north before south, in a clockwise sequence), then Africa, Australia and Oceania, North America and South America. This is the classic arrangement adopted by most cartographers since the 16th century. For each continent, there are maps at a variety of scales. First, physical relief and political maps of the whole continent; then a series of larger-scale maps of the regions within the continent, each followed, where required, by still larger-scale maps of the most important or densely populated areas. The governing principle is that by turning the pages of the atlas, the reader moves steadily from north to south through each continent, with each map overlapping its neighbours. A key map showing this sequence, and the area covered by each map, can be found on the endpapers of the atlas.

Map presentation

With very few exceptions (e.g. for the Arctic and Antarctica), the maps are drawn with north at the top, regardless of whether they are presented upright or sideways on the page. In the borders will be found the map title; a locator diagram showing the area covered and the page numbers for maps of adjacent areas; the scale; the projection used; the degrees of latitude and longitude; and the letters and figures used in the index for locating place names and geographical features. Physical relief maps also have a height reference panel identifying the colours used for each layer of contouring.

Map symbols

Each map contains a vast amount of detail which can only be conveyed clearly and accurately by the use of symbols. Points and circles of varying sizes locate and identify the relative importance of towns and cities; different styles of type are employed for administrative, geographical and regional place names. A variety of pictorial symbols denote features such as glaciers and marshes, as well

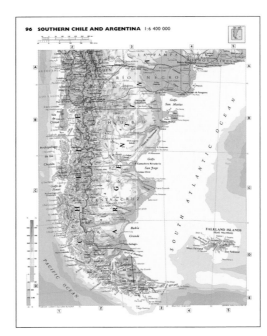

as man-made structures including roads, railways, airports and canals. International borders are shown by red lines. Where neighbouring countries are in dispute, for example in the Middle East, the maps show the *de facto* boundary between nations, regardless of the legal or historical situation. The symbols are explained on the first page of the World Maps section of the atlas.

Map scales

The scale of each map is given in the numerical form known as the 'representative fraction'. The first figure is always one, signifying one unit of distance on the map; the second figure, usually in millions, is the number by which the map unit must be multiplied to give the equivalent distance on the Earth's surface. Calculations can easily be made in centimetres and kilometres, by dividing the Earth units figure by 100 000 (i.e. deleting the last five 0s). Thus 1:1 000 000 means 1 cm = 10 km. The calculation for inches and miles is more laborious, but 1 000 000 divided by 63 360 (the number of inches in a mile) shows that the ratio 1:1 000 000 means approximately 1 inch = 16 miles. The table below provides distance equivalents for scales down to 1:50 000 000.

LARGE SCALE		
1:1 000 000	1 cm = 10 km	1 inch = 16 miles
1:2 500 000	1 cm = 25 km	1 inch = 39.5 miles
1:5 000 000	1 cm = 50 km	1 inch = 79 miles
1:6 000 000	1 cm = 60 km	1 inch = 95 miles
1:8 000 000	1 cm = 80 km	1 inch = 126 miles
1:10 000 000	1 cm = 100 km	1 inch = 158 miles
1:15 000 000	1 cm = 150 km	1 inch = 237 miles
1:20 000 000	1 cm = 200 km	1 inch = 316 miles
1:50 000 000	1 cm = 500 km	1 inch = 790 miles
SMALL SCALE		

Measuring distances

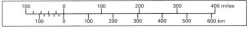

Although each map is accompanied by a scale bar, distances cannot always be measured with confidence because of the distortions involved in portraying the curved surface of the Earth on a flat page. As a general rule, the larger the map scale (i.e. the lower the number of Earth units in the representative fraction), the more accurate and reliable will be the distance measured. On small-scale maps such as those of the world and of entire continents, measurement may only be accurate along the 'standard parallels', or central axes, and should not be attempted without considering the map projection.

Latitude and longitude

Accurate positioning of individual points on the Earth's surface is made possible by reference to the geometrical system of latitude and longitude. Latitude *parallels* are drawn west–east around the Earth and numbered by degrees north and south of the Equator, which is designated 0° of latitude. Longitude *meridians* are drawn north–south and numbered by degrees east and west of the *prime meridian*, 0° of longitude, which passes through Greenwich in England. By referring to these co-ordinates and their subdivisions of minutes ($^1/_{60}$th of a degree) and seconds ($^1/_{60}$th of a minute), any place on Earth can be located to within a few hundred metres. Latitude and longitude are indicated by blue lines on the maps; they are straight or curved according to the projection employed. Reference to these lines is the easiest way of determining the relative positions of places on different maps, and for plotting compass directions.

Name forms

For ease of reference, both English and local name forms appear in the atlas. Oceans, seas and countries are shown in English throughout the atlas; country names may be abbreviated to their commonly accepted form (e.g. Germany, not The Federal Republic of Germany). Conventional English forms are also used for place names on the smaller-scale maps of the continents. However, local name forms are used on all large-scale and regional maps, with the English form given in brackets only for important cities – the large-scale map of Russia and Central Asia thus shows Moskva (Moscow). For countries which do not use a Roman script, place names have been transcribed according to the systems adopted by the British and US Geographic Names Authorities. For China, the Pin Yin system has been used, with some more widely known forms appearing in brackets, as with Beijing (Peking). Both English and local names appear in the index, the English form being cross-referenced to the local form.

The
WORLD IN
FOCUS

Planet Earth

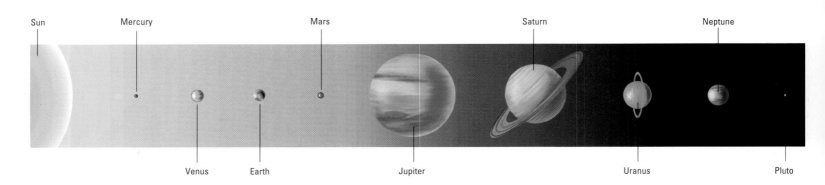

Sun · Mercury · Mars · Saturn · Neptune · Venus · Earth · Jupiter · Uranus · Pluto

The Solar System

A minute part of one of the billions of galaxies (collections of stars) that comprises the Universe, the Solar System lies some 27,000 light-years from the centre of our own galaxy, the 'Milky Way'. Thought to be over 4,700 million years old, it consists of a central sun with nine planets and their moons revolving around it, attracted by its gravitational pull. The planets orbit the Sun in the same direction – anti-clockwise when viewed from the Northern Heavens – and almost in the same plane. Their orbital paths, however, vary enormously.

The Sun's diameter is 109 times that of Earth, and the temperature at its core – caused by continuous thermonuclear fusions of hydrogen into helium – is estimated to be 15 million degrees Celsius. It is the Solar System's only source of light and heat.

Profile of the Planets

	Mean distance from Sun (million km)	Mass (Earth = 1)	Period of orbit (Earth years)	Period of rotation (Earth days)	Equatorial diameter (km)	Number of known satellites
Mercury	57.9	0.055	0.24 years	58.67	4,878	0
Venus	108.2	0.815	0.62 years	243.00	12,104	0
Earth	149.6	1.0	1.00 years	1.00	12,756	1
Mars	227.9	0.107	1.88 years	1.03	6,787	2
Jupiter	778.3	317.8	11.86 years	0.41	142,800	16
Saturn	1,427	95.2	29.46 years	0.43	120,000	20
Uranus	2,871	14.5	84.01 years	0.75	51,118	15
Neptune	4,497	17.1	164.80 years	0.80	49,528	8
Pluto	5,914	0.002	248.50 years	6.39	2,320	1

All planetary orbits are elliptical in form, but only Pluto and Mercury follow paths that deviate noticeably from a circular one. Near perihelion – its closest approach to the Sun – Pluto actually passes inside the orbit of Neptune, an event that last occurred in 1983. Pluto did not regain its station as outermost planet until February 1999.

The Seasons

Seasons occur because the Earth's axis is tilted at a constant angle of 23½°. When the northern hemisphere is tilted to a maximum extent towards the Sun, on 21 June, the Sun is overhead at the Tropic of Cancer (latitude 23½° North). This is midsummer, or the summer solstice, in the northern hemisphere.

On 22 or 23 September, the Sun is overhead at the Equator, and day and night are of equal length throughout the world. This is the autumn equinox in the northern hemisphere. On 21 or 22 December, the Sun is overhead at the Tropic of Capricorn (23½° South), the winter solstice in the northern hemisphere. The overhead Sun then tracks north until, on 21 March, it is overhead at the Equator. This is the spring (vernal) equinox in the northern hemisphere.

In the southern hemisphere, the seasons are the reverse of those in the north.

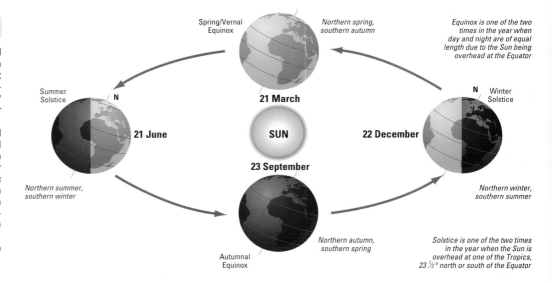

Spring/Vernal Equinox — Northern spring, southern autumn — Equinox is one of the two times in the year when day and night are of equal length due to the Sun being overhead at the Equator

Summer Solstice — N — 21 March — N Winter Solstice

21 June — SUN — 22 December

23 September

Northern summer, southern winter — Northern winter, southern summer

Northern autumn, southern spring

Autumnal Equinox — Solstice is one of the two times in the year when the Sun is overhead at one of the Tropics, 23½° north or south of the Equator

Day and Night

The Sun appears to rise in the east, reach its highest point at noon, and then set in the west, to be followed by night. In reality, it is not the Sun that is moving but the Earth rotating from west to east. The moment when the Sun's upper limb first appears above the horizon is termed sunrise; the moment when the Sun's upper limb disappears below the horizon is sunset.

At the summer solstice in the northern hemisphere (21 June), the Arctic has total daylight and the Antarctic total darkness. The opposite occurs at the winter solstice (21 or 22 December). At the Equator, the length of day and night are almost equal all year.

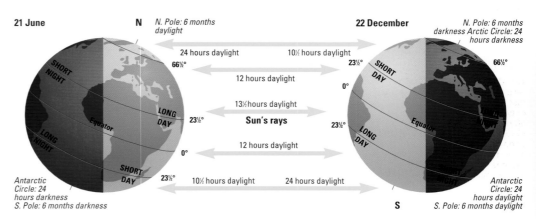

21 June — N. Pole: 6 months daylight — 22 December — N. Pole: 6 months darkness Arctic Circle: 24 hours darkness

24 hours daylight — 10½ hours daylight — 23½° — 66½°

66½° — SHORT NIGHT — SHORT DAY — 12 hours daylight — 0°

LONG DAY — 23½° — 13½ hours daylight — Sun's rays — 23½° — Equator

Equator — 0° — 12 hours daylight — 23½° — LONG DAY

LONG NIGHT — 23½° — 10½ hours daylight — 24 hours daylight — SHORT DAY

Antarctic Circle: 24 hours darkness — SHORT DAY — S. Pole: 6 months darkness — Antarctic Circle: 24 hours daylight — S — S. Pole: 6 months daylight

Time

Year: The time taken by the Earth to revolve around the Sun, or 365.24 days.

Leap Year: A calendar year of 366 days, 29 February being the additional day. It offsets the difference between the calendar and the solar year.

Month: The approximate time taken by the Moon to revolve around the Earth. The 12 months of the year in fact vary from 28 (29 in a Leap Year) to 31 days.

Week: An artificial period of 7 days, not based on astronomical time.

Day: The time taken by the Earth to complete one rotation on its axis.

Hour: 24 hours make one day. Usually the day is divided into hours AM (ante meridiem or before noon) and PM (post meridiem or after noon), although most timetables now use the 24-hour system, from midnight to midnight.

Sunrise

Sunset

The Moon

The Moon rotates more slowly than the Earth, making one complete turn on its axis in just over 27 days. Since this corresponds to its period of revolution around the Earth, the Moon always presents the same hemisphere or face to us, and we never see 'the dark side'. The interval between one full Moon and the next (and between new Moons) is about 29½ days – a lunar month. The apparent changes in the shape of the Moon are caused by its changing position in relation to the Earth; like the planets, it produces no light of its own and shines only by reflecting the rays of the Sun.

Phases of the Moon

Distance from Earth: 356,410 km – 406,685 km; Mean diameter: 3,475.1 km;
Mass: approx. 1/81 that of Earth; Surface gravity: one-sixth of Earth's;
Daily range of temperature at lunar equator: 200°C; Average orbital speed: 3,683 km/h

| New Moon | Crescent | First quarter | Gibbous | Full Moon | Gibbous | Last quarter | Crescent | New Moon |

Eclipses

When the Moon passes between the Sun and the Earth it causes a partial eclipse of the Sun (1) if the Earth passes through the Moon's outer shadow (P), or a total eclipse (2) if the inner cone shadow crosses the Earth's surface. In a lunar eclipse, the Earth's shadow crosses the Moon and, again, provides either a partial or total eclipse.

Eclipses of the Sun and the Moon do not occur every month because of the 5° difference between the plane of the Moon's orbit and the plane in which the Earth moves. In the 1990s only 14 lunar eclipses were possible, for example, seven partial and seven total; each was visible only from certain, and variable, parts of the world. The same period witnessed 13 solar eclipses – six partial (or annular) and seven total.

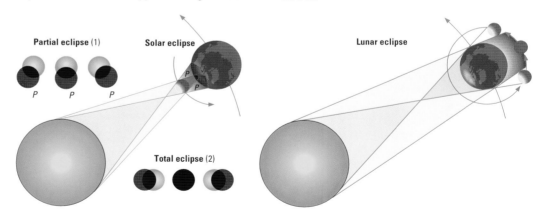

Partial eclipse (1)

Solar eclipse

Lunar eclipse

Total eclipse (2)

Tides

The daily rise and fall of the ocean's tides are the result of the gravitational pull of the Moon and that of the Sun, though the effect of the latter is only 46.6% as strong as that of the Moon. This effect is greatest on the hemisphere facing the Moon and causes a tidal 'bulge'. When the Sun, Earth and Moon are in line, tide-raising forces are at a maximum and Spring tides occur: high tide reaches the highest values, and low tide falls to low levels. When lunar and solar forces are least coincidental with the Sun and Moon at an angle (near the Moon's first and third quarters), Neap tides occur, which have a small tidal range.

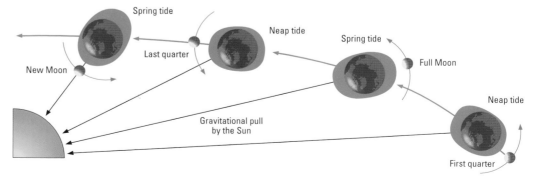

Spring tide

Neap tide

Spring tide

New Moon

Last quarter

Full Moon

Neap tide

Gravitational pull by the Sun

First quarter

Restless Earth

The Earth's Structure

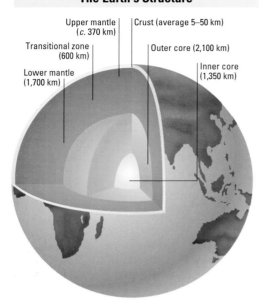

Upper mantle (c. 370 km)
Crust (average 5–50 km)
Transitional zone (600 km)
Outer core (2,100 km)
Lower mantle (1,700 km)
Inner core (1,350 km)

Continental Drift

About 200 million years ago the original Pangaea landmass began to split into two continental groups, which further separated over time to produce the present-day configuration.

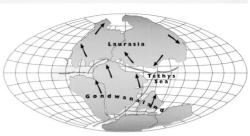

180 million years ago

135 million years ago

Trench
Rift
New ocean floor
Zones of slippage

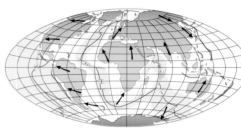

Present day

Notable Earthquakes Since 1900

Year	Location	Richter Scale	Deaths
1906	San Francisco, USA	8.3	503
1906	Valparaiso, Chile	8.6	22,000
1908	Messina, Italy	7.5	83,000
1915	Avezzano, Italy	7.5	30,000
1920	Gansu (Kansu), China	8.6	180,000
1923	Yokohama, Japan	8.3	143,000
1927	Nan Shan, China	8.3	200,000
1932	Gansu (Kansu), China	7.6	70,000
1933	Sanriku, Japan	8.9	2,990
1934	Bihar, India/Nepal	8.4	10,700
1935	Quetta, India (now Pakistan)	7.5	60,000
1939	Chillan, Chile	8.3	28,000
1939	Erzincan, Turkey	7.9	30,000
1960	Agadir, Morocco	5.8	12,000
1962	Khorasan, Iran	7.1	12,230
1968	N.E. Iran	7.4	12,000
1970	N. Peru	7.7	66,794
1972	Managua, Nicaragua	6.2	5,000
1974	N. Pakistan	6.3	5,200
1976	Guatemala	7.5	22,778
1976	Tangshan, China	8.2	255,000
1978	Tabas, Iran	7.7	25,000
1980	El Asnam, Algeria	7.3	20,000
1980	S. Italy	7.2	4,800
1985	Mexico City, Mexico	8.1	4,200
1988	N.W. Armenia	6.8	55,000
1990	N. Iran	7.7	36,000
1993	Maharashtra, India	6.4	30,000
1994	Los Angeles, USA	6.6	51
1995	Kobe, Japan	7.2	5,000
1995	Sakhalin Is., Russia	7.5	2,000
1997	N.E. Iran	7.1	2,500
1998	Takhar, Afghanistan	6.1	4,200
1998	Rostaq, Afghanistan	7.0	5,000
1999	Izmit, Turkey	7.4	15,000
1999	Taipei, Taiwan	7.6	1,700

Earthquakes

Earthquake magnitude is usually rated according to either the Richter or the Modified Mercalli scale, both devised by seismologists in the 1930s. The Richter scale measures absolute earthquake power with mathematical precision: each step upwards represents a tenfold increase in shockwave amplitude. Theoretically, there is no upper limit, but the largest earthquakes measured have been rated at between 8.8 and 8.9. The 12–point Mercalli scale, based on observed effects, is often more meaningful, ranging from I (earthquakes noticed only by seismographs) to XII (total destruction); intermediate points include V (people awakened at night; unstable objects overturned), VII (collapse of ordinary buildings; chimneys and monuments fall) and IX (conspicuous cracks in ground; serious damage to reservoirs).

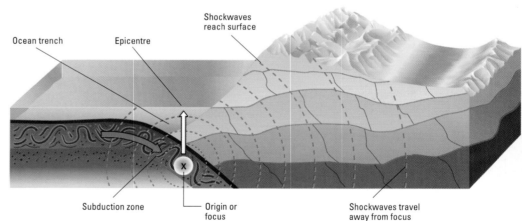

Shockwaves reach surface
Ocean trench
Epicentre
Subduction zone
Origin or focus
Shockwaves travel away from focus

Structure and Earthquakes

Mobile land areas
Submarine zones of mobile land areas
Stable land platforms
Submarine extensions of stable land platforms
Mid-oceanic volcanic ridges
Oceanic platforms

1976○ Principal earthquakes and dates

Earthquakes are a series of rapid vibrations originating from the slipping or faulting of parts of the Earth's crust when stresses within build up to breaking point. They usually happen at depths varying from 8 km to 30 km. Severe earthquakes cause extensive damage when they take place in populated areas, destroying structures and severing communications. Most initial loss of life occurs due to secondary causes such as falling masonry, fires and flooding.

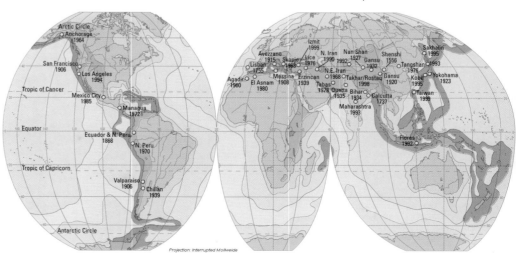

Projection: Interrupted Mollweide

Plate Tectonics

Plate boundaries   PACIFIC   Major plates

➤ Direction of plate movements and rate of movement (cm/year)

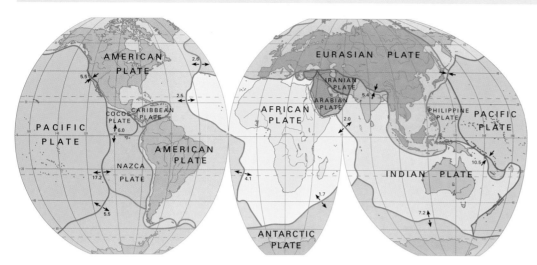

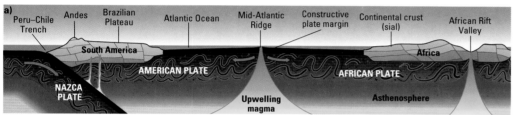

a) Peru–Chile Trench — Andes — Brazilian Plateau — Atlantic Ocean — Mid-Atlantic Ridge — Constructive plate margin — Continental crust (sial) — African Rift Valley — South America — Africa — AMERICAN PLATE — AFRICAN PLATE — NAZCA PLATE — Upwelling magma — Asthenosphere

The drifting of the continents is a feature that is unique to Planet Earth. The complementary, almost jigsaw-puzzle fit of the coastlines on each side of the Atlantic Ocean inspired Alfred Wegener's theory of continental drift in 1915. The theory suggested that the ancient super-continent, which Wegener named Pangaea, incorporated all of the Earth's landmasses and gradually split up to form today's continents.

The original debate about continental drift was a prelude to a more radical idea: plate tectonics. The basic theory is that the Earth's crust is made up of a series of rigid plates which float on a soft layer of the mantle and are moved about by continental convection currents within the Earth's interior. These plates diverge and converge along margins marked by seismic activity. Plates diverge from mid-ocean ridges where molten lava pushes upwards and forces the plates apart at rates of up to 40 mm [1.6 in] a year.

The three diagrams, left, give some examples of plate boundaries from around the world. Diagram (a) shows sea-floor spreading at the Mid-Atlantic Ridge as the American and African plates slowly diverge. The same thing is happening in (b) where sea-floor spreading at the Mid-Indian Ocean Ridge is forcing the Indian plate to collide into the Eurasian plate. In (c) oceanic crust (sima) is being subducted beneath lighter continental crust (sial).

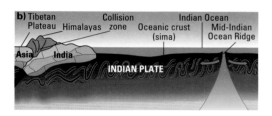

b) Tibetan Plateau — Himalayas — Collision zone — Indian Ocean — Oceanic crust (sima) — Mid-Indian Ocean Ridge — Asia — India — INDIAN PLATE

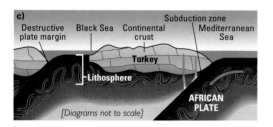

c) Destructive plate margin — Black Sea — Continental crust — Subduction zone — Mediterranean Sea — Turkey — Lithosphere — [Diagrams not to scale] — AFRICAN PLATE

Volcanoes

Volcanoes occur when hot liquefied rock beneath the Earth's crust is pushed up by pressure to the surface as molten lava. Some volcanoes erupt in an explosive way, throwing out rocks and ash, whilst others are effusive and lava flows out of the vent. There are volcanoes which are both, such as Mount Fuji. An accumulation of lava and cinders creates cones of variable size and shape. As a result of many eruptions over centuries, Mount Etna in Sicily has a circumference of more than 120 km [75 miles].

Climatologists believe that volcanic ash, if ejected high into the atmosphere, can influence temperature and weather for several years afterwards. The 1991 eruption of Mount Pinatubo in the Philippines ejected more than 20 million tonnes of dust and ash 32 km [20 miles] into the atmosphere and is believed to have accelerated ozone depletion over a large part of the globe.

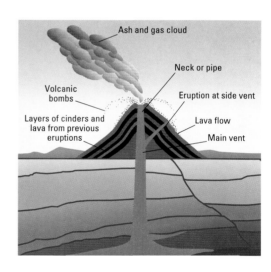

Ash and gas cloud — Neck or pipe — Volcanic bombs — Eruption at side vent — Layers of cinders and lava from previous eruptions — Lava flow — Main vent

Distribution of Volcanoes

Volcanoes today may be the subject of considerable scientific study but they remain both dramatic and unpredictable: in 1991 Mount Pinatubo, 100 km [62 miles] north of the Philippines capital Manila, suddenly burst into life after lying dormant for more than six centuries. Most of the world's active volcanoes occur in a belt around the Pacific Ocean, on the edge of the Pacific plate, called the 'ring of fire'. Indonesia has the greatest concentration with 90 volcanoes, 12 of which are active. The most famous, Krakatoa, erupted in 1883 with such force that the resulting tidal wave killed 36,000 people and tremors were felt as far away as Australia.

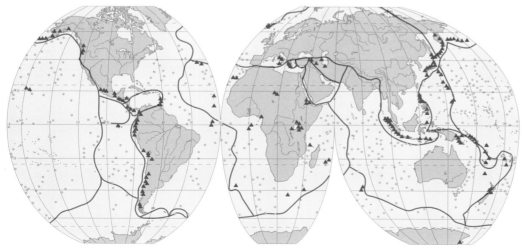

⬤ Submarine volcanoes

▲ Land volcanoes active since 1700

— Boundaries of tectonic plates

Landforms

The Rock Cycle

James Hutton first proposed the rock cycle in the late 1700s after he observed the slow but steady effects of erosion.

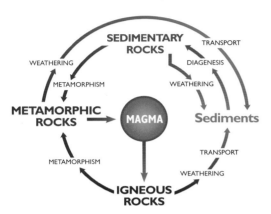

Above and below the surface of the oceans, the features of the Earth's crust are constantly changing. The phenomenal forces generated by convection currents in the molten core of our planet carry the vast segments or 'plates' of the crust across the globe in an endless cycle of creation and destruction. A continent may travel little more than 25 mm [1 in] per year, yet in the vast span of geological time this process throws up giant mountain ranges and creates new land.

Destruction of the landscape, however, begins as soon as it is formed. Wind, water, ice and sea, the main agents of erosion, mount a constant assault that even the most resistant rocks cannot withstand. Mountain peaks may dwindle by as little as a few millimetres each year, but if they are not uplifted by further movements of the crust they will eventually be reduced to rubble and transported away.

Water is the most powerful agent of erosion – it has been estimated that 100 billion tonnes of sediment are washed into the oceans every year. Three Asian rivers account for 20% of this total, the Huang He, in China, and the Brahmaputra and Ganges in Bangladesh.

Rivers and glaciers, like the sea itself, generate much of their effect through abrasion – pounding the land with the debris they carry with them. But as well as destroying they also create new landforms, many of them spectacular: vast deltas like those of the Mississippi and the Nile, or the deep fjords cut by glaciers in British Columbia, Norway and New Zealand.

Geologists once considered that landscapes evolved from 'young', newly uplifted mountainous areas, through a 'mature' hilly stage, to an 'old age' stage when the land was reduced to an almost flat plain, or peneplain. This theory, called the 'cycle of erosion', fell into disuse when it became evident that so many factors, including the effects of plate tectonics and climatic change, constantly interrupt the cycle, which takes no account of the highly complex interactions that shape the surface of our planet.

Mountain Building

Mountains are formed when pressures on the Earth's crust caused by continental drift become so intense that the surface buckles or cracks. This happens where oceanic crust is subducted by continental crust or, more dramatically, where two tectonic plates collide: the Rockies, Andes, Alps, Urals and Himalayas resulted from such impacts. These are all known as fold mountains because they were formed by the compression of the rocks, forcing the surface to bend and fold like a crumpled rug. The Himalayas are formed from the folded former sediments of the Tethys Sea which was trapped in the collision zone between the Indian and Eurasian plates.

The other main mountain-building process occurs when the crust fractures to create faults, allowing rock to be forced upwards in large blocks; or when the pressure of magma within the crust forces the surface to bulge into a dome, or erupts to form a volcano. Large mountain ranges may reveal a combination of those features; the Alps, for example, have been compressed so violently that the folds are fragmented by numerous faults and intrusions of molten igneous rock.

Over millions of years, even the greatest mountain ranges can be reduced by the agents of erosion (most notably rivers) to a low rugged landscape known as a peneplain.

Types of faults: Faults occur where the crust is being stretched or compressed so violently that the rock strata break in a horizontal or vertical movement. They are classified by the direction in which the blocks of rock have moved. A normal fault results when a vertical movement causes the surface to break apart; compression causes a reverse fault. Horizontal movement causes shearing, known as a strike-slip fault. When the rock breaks in two places, the central block may be pushed up in a horst fault, or sink (creating a rift valley) in a graben fault.

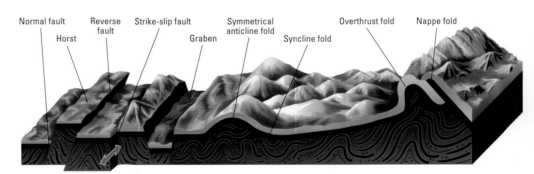

Normal fault — Horst — Reverse fault — Strike-slip fault — Symmetrical anticline fold — Graben — Syncline fold — Overthrust fold — Nappe fold

Types of fold: Folds occur when rock strata are squeezed and compressed. They are common therefore at destructive plate margins and where plates have collided, forcing the rocks to buckle into mountain ranges. Geographers give different names to the degrees of fold that result from continuing pressure on the rock. A simple fold may be symmetric, with even slopes on either side, but as the pressure builds up, one slope becomes steeper and the fold becomes asymmetric. Later, the ridge or 'anticline' at the top of the fold may slide over the lower ground or 'syncline' to form a recumbent fold. Eventually, the rock strata may break under the pressure to form an overthrust and finally a nappe fold.

Continental Glaciation

Ice sheets were at their greatest extent about 200,000 years ago. The maximum advance of the last Ice Age was about 18,000 years ago, when ice covered virtually all of Canada and reached as far south as the Bristol Channel in Britain.

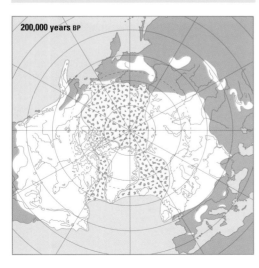

200,000 years BP

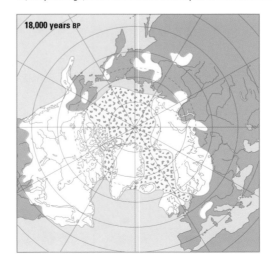

18,000 years BP

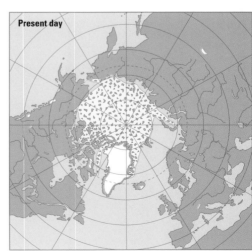

Present day

Natural Landforms

A stylized diagram to show a selection of landforms found in the mid-latitudes.

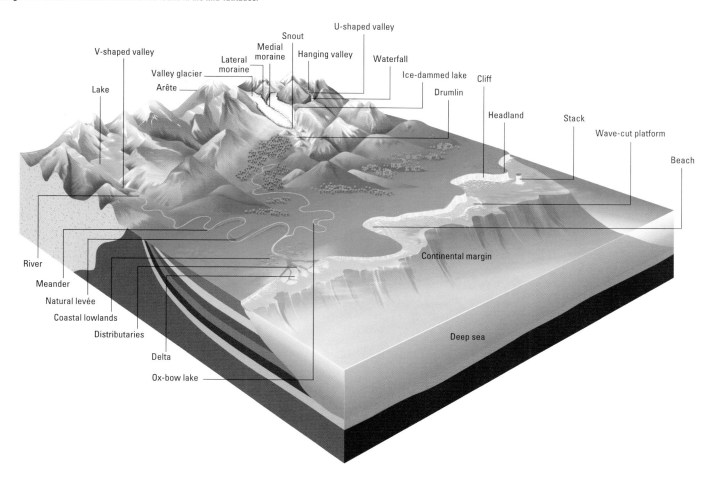

V-shaped valley · Lake · Arête · Valley glacier · Lateral moraine · Medial moraine · Snout · Hanging valley · U-shaped valley · Waterfall · Ice-dammed lake · Cliff · Drumlin · Headland · Stack · Wave-cut platform · Beach · Continental margin · Deep sea · River · Meander · Natural levée · Coastal lowlands · Distributaries · Delta · Ox-bow lake

Desert Landscapes

The popular image that deserts are all huge expanses of sand is wrong. Despite harsh conditions, deserts contain some of the most varied and interesting landscapes in the world. They are also one of the most extensive environments – the hot and cold deserts together cover almost 40% of the Earth's surface.

The three types of hot desert are known by their Arabic names: sand desert, called *erg*, covers only about one-fifth of the world's desert; the rest is divided between *hammada* (areas of bare rock) and *reg* (broad plains covered by loose gravel or pebbles).

In areas of *erg*, such as the Namib Desert, the shape of the dunes reflects the character of local winds. Where winds are constant in direction, crescent-shaped *barchan* dunes form. In areas of bare rock, wind-blown sand is a major agent of erosion. The erosion is mainly confined to within 2 m [6.5 ft] of the surface, producing characteristic, mushroom-shaped rocks.

Erg

Hammada

Reg

Surface Processes

Catastrophic changes to natural landforms are periodically caused by such phenomena as avalanches, landslides and volcanic eruptions, but most of the processes that shape the Earth's surface operate extremely slowly in human terms. One estimate, based on a study in the United States, suggested that 1 m [3 ft] of land was removed from the entire surface of the country, on average, every 29,500 years. However, the time-scale varies from 1,300 years to 154,200 years depending on the terrain and climate.

In hot, dry climates, mechanical weathering, a result of rapid temperature changes, causes the outer layers of rock to peel away, while in cold mountainous regions, boulders are prised apart when water freezes in cracks in rocks. Chemical weathering, at its greatest in warm, humid regions, is responsible for hollowing out limestone caves and decomposing granites.

The erosion of soil and rock is greatest on sloping land and the steeper the slope, the greater the tendency for mass wasting – the movement of soil and rock downhill under the influence of gravity. The mechanisms of mass wasting (ranging from very slow to very rapid) vary with the type of material, but the presence of water as a lubricant is usually an important factor.

Running water is the world's leading agent of erosion and transportation. The energy of a river depends on several factors, including its velocity and volume, and its erosive power is at its peak when it is in full flood. Sea waves also exert tremendous erosive power during storms when they hurl pebbles against the shore, undercutting cliffs and hollowing out caves.

Glacier ice forms in mountain hollows and spills out to form valley glaciers, which transport rocks shattered by frost action. As glaciers move, rocks embedded into the ice erode steep-sided, U-shaped valleys. Evidence of glaciation in mountain regions includes cirques, knife-edged ridges, or arêtes, and pyramidal peaks.

Oceans

The Great Oceans

Relative sizes of the world's oceans

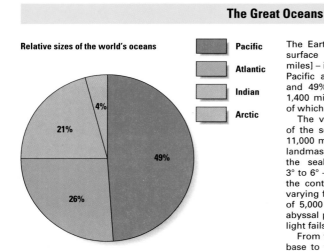

- Pacific
- Atlantic
- Indian
- Arctic

In a strict geographical sense there are only three true oceans – the Atlantic, Indian and Pacific. The legendary 'Seven Seas' would require these to be divided at the Equator and the addition of the Arctic Ocean – which accounts for less than 4% of the total sea area. The International Hydrographic Bureau does not recognize the Antarctic Ocean (even less the 'Southern Ocean') as a separate entity.

The Earth is a watery planet: more than 70% of its surface – over 360,000,000 sq km [140,000,000 sq miles] – is covered by the oceans and seas. The mighty Pacific alone accounts for nearly 36% of the total, and 49% of the sea area. Gravity holds in around 1,400 million cu. km [320 million cu. miles] of water, of which over 97% is saline.

The vast underwater world starts in the shallows of the seaside and plunges to depths of more than 11,000 m [36,000 ft]. The continental shelf, part of the landmass, drops gently to around 200 m [650 ft]; here the seabed falls away suddenly at an angle of 3° to 6° – the continental slope. The third stage, called the continental rise, is more gradual with gradients varying from 1 in 100 to 1 in 700. At an average depth of 5,000 m [16,500 ft] there begins the aptly-named abyssal plain – massive submarine depths where sunlight fails to penetrate and few creatures can survive.

From these plains rise volcanoes which, taken from base to top, rival and even surpass the tallest continental mountains in height. Mount Kea, on Hawaii, reaches a total of 10,203 m [33,400 ft], some 1,355 m [4,500 ft] more than Mount Everest, though scarcely 40% is visible above sea level.

In addition, there are underwater mountain chains up to 1,000 km [600 miles] across, whose peaks sometimes appear above sea level as islands such as Iceland and Tristan da Cunha.

The Ocean Depths

Average and maximum depths of the world's great oceans, in metres

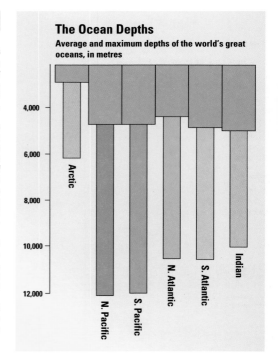

Ocean Currents

January temperatures and ocean currents

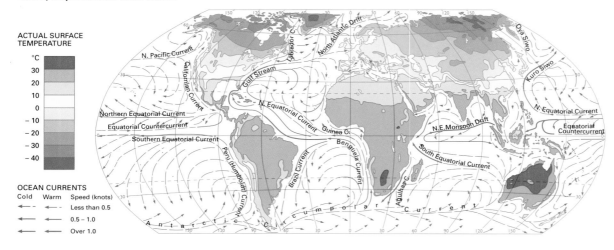

ACTUAL SURFACE TEMPERATURE

°C
- 30
- 20
- 10
- 0
- −10
- −20
- −30
- −40

OCEAN CURRENTS

Cold	Warm	Speed (knots)
		Less than 0.5
		0.5 – 1.0
		Over 1.0

July temperatures and ocean currents

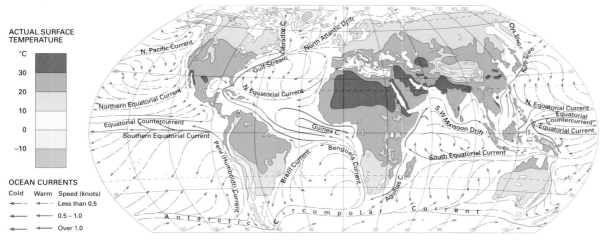

ACTUAL SURFACE TEMPERATURE

°C
- 30
- 20
- 10
- 0
- −10

OCEAN CURRENTS

Cold	Warm	Speed (knots)
		Less than 0.5
		0.5 – 1.0
		Over 1.0

Moving immense quantities of energy as well as billions of tonnes of water every hour, the ocean currents are a vital part of the great heat engine that drives the Earth's climate. They themselves are produced by a twofold mechanism. At the surface, winds push huge masses of water before them; in the deep ocean, below an abrupt temperature gradient that separates the churning surface waters from the still depths, density variations cause slow vertical movements.

The pattern of circulation of the great surface currents is determined by the displacement known as the Coriolis effect. As the Earth turns beneath a moving object – whether it is a tennis ball or a vast mass of water – it appears to be deflected to one side. The deflection is most obvious near the Equator, where the Earth's surface is spinning eastwards at 1,700 km/h [1,050 mph]; currents moving polewards are curved clockwise in the northern hemisphere and anti-clockwise in the southern.

The result is a system of spinning circles known as gyres. The Coriolis effect piles up water on the left of each gyre, creating a narrow, fast-moving stream that is matched by a slower, broader returning current on the right. North and south of the Equator, the fastest currents are located in the west and in the east respectively. In each case, warm water moves from the Equator and cold water returns to it. Cold currents often bring an upwelling of nutrients with them, supporting the world's most economically important fisheries.

Depending on the prevailing winds, some currents on or near the Equator may reverse their direction in the course of the year – a seasonal variation on which Asian monsoon rains depend, and whose occasional failure can bring disaster to millions.

World Fishing Areas

Main commercial fishing areas (numbered FAO regions)

Catch by top marine fishing areas, thousand tonnes (1992)

1. Pacific, NW	[61]	24,199	29.3%
2. Pacific, SE	[87]	13,899	16.8%
3. Atlantic, NE	[27]	11,073	13.4%
4. Pacific, WC	[71]	7,710	9.3%
5. Indian, W	[51]	3,747	4.5%
6. Indian, E	[57]	3,262	4.0%
7. Atlantic, EC	[34]	3,259	3.9%
8. Pacific, NE	[67]	3,149	3.8%

Principal fishing areas

Leading fishing nations

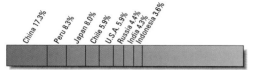

China 17.3% Peru 8.3% Japan 8.0% Chile 5.9% U.S.A. 5.9% Russia 4.4% India 4.3% Indonesia 3.6%

World total (1993): 101,417,500 tonnes
(Marine catch 83.1% Inland catch 16.9%)

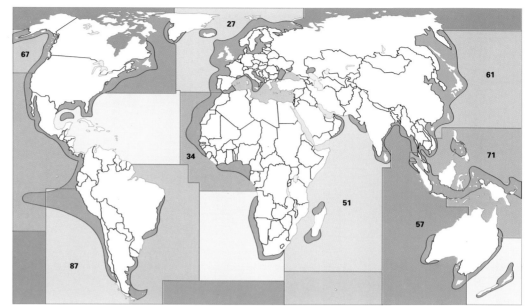

Marine Pollution

Sources of marine oil pollution (latest available year)

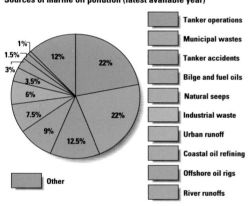

1%, 1.5%, 12%, 22%, 3%, 3.5%, 6%, 22%, 7.5%, 9%, 12.5%

- Tanker operations
- Municipal wastes
- Tanker accidents
- Bilge and fuel oils
- Natural seeps
- Industrial waste
- Urban runoff
- Coastal oil refining
- Offshore oil rigs
- River runoffs

Other

Oil Spills

Major oil spills from tankers and combined carriers

Year	Vessel	Location	Spill (barrels)**	Cause
1979	Atlantic Empress	West Indies	1,890,000	collision
1983	Castillo De Bellver	South Africa	1,760,000	fire
1978	Amoco Cadiz	France	1,628,000	grounding
1991	Haven	Italy	1,029,000	explosion
1988	Odyssey	Canada	1,000,000	fire
1967	Torrey Canyon	UK	909,000	grounding
1972	Sea Star	Gulf of Oman	902,250	collision
1977	Hawaiian Patriot	Hawaiian Is.	742,500	fire
1979	Independenta	Turkey	696,350	collision
1993	Braer	UK	625,000	grounding
1996	Sea Empress	UK	515,000	grounding

Other sources of major oil spills

1983	Nowruz oilfield	The Gulf	4,250,000†	war
1979	Ixtoc 1 oilwell	Gulf of Mexico	4,200,000	blow-out
1991	Kuwait	The Gulf	2,500,000†	war

** 1 barrel = 0.136 tonnes/159 lit./35 Imperial gal./42 US gal. † estimated

River Pollution

Sources of river pollution, USA (latest available year)

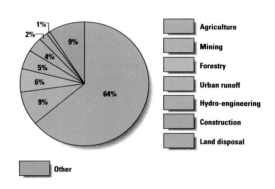

1%, 2%, 9%, 4%, 5%, 6%, 64%, 9%

- Agriculture
- Mining
- Forestry
- Urban runoff
- Hydro-engineering
- Construction
- Land disposal

Other

Water Pollution

- Severely polluted sea areas and lakes
- Polluted sea areas and lakes
- Areas of frequent oil pollution by shipping
- ◤ Major oil tanker spills
- ▲ Major oil rig blow-outs
- ▼ Offshore dumpsites for industrial and municipal waste
- —— Severely polluted rivers and estuaries

The most notorious tanker spillage of the 1980s occurred when the *Exxon Valdez* ran aground in Prince William Sound, Alaska, in 1989, spilling 267,000 barrels of crude oil close to shore in a sensitive ecological area. This rates as the world's 28th worst spill in terms of volume.

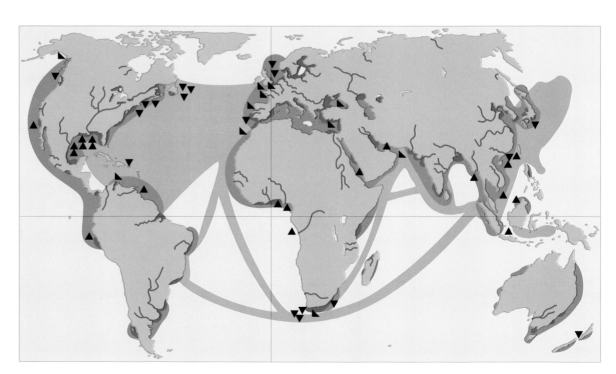

Climate

Climatic Regions

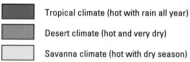

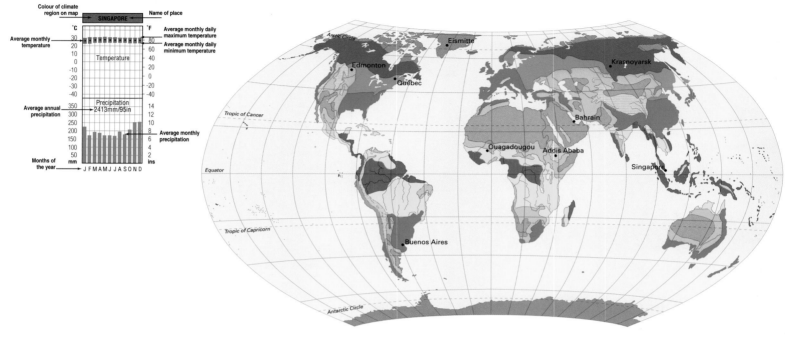

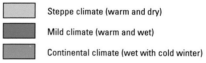

Tropical climate (hot with rain all year)	

Steppe climate (warm and dry)

Subarctic climate (very cold winter)

Desert climate (hot and very dry)

Mild climate (warm and wet)

Polar climate (very cold and dry)

Savanna climate (hot with dry season)

Continental climate (wet with cold winter)

Mountainous climate (altitude affects climate)

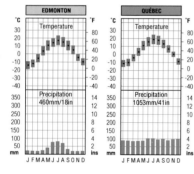

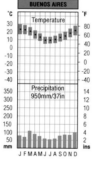

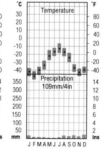

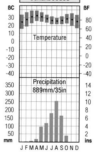

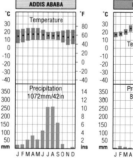

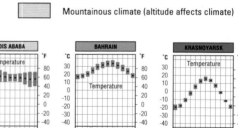

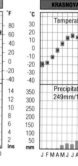

Climate Records

Temperature

Highest recorded shade temperature: Al Aziziyah, Libya, 58°C [136.4°F], 13 September 1922.

Highest mean annual temperature: Dallol, Ethiopia, 34.4°C [94°F], 1960–66.

Longest heatwave: Marble Bar, W. Australia, 162 days over 38°C [100°F], 23 October 1923 to 7 April 1924.

Lowest recorded temperature (outside poles): Verkhoyansk, Siberia, –68°C [–90°F], 6 February 1933.

Lowest mean annual temperature: Plateau Station, Antarctica, –56.6°C [–72.0°F]

Pressure

Longest drought: Calama, N. Chile, no recorded rainfall in 400 years to 1971.

Wettest place (12 months): Cherrapunji, Meghalaya, N. E. India, 26,470 mm [1,040 in], August 1860 to August 1861. Cherrapunji also holds the record for the most rainfall in one month: 2,930 mm [115 in], July 1861.

Wettest place (average): Mawsynram, India, mean annual rainfall 11,873 mm [467.4 in].

Wettest place (24 hours): Cilaos, Réunion, Indian Ocean, 1,870 mm [73.6 in], 15–16 March 1952.

Heaviest hailstones: Gopalganj, Bangladesh, up to 1.02 kg [2.25 lb], 14 April 1986 (killed 92 people).

Heaviest snowfall (continuous): Bessans, Savoie, France, 1,730 mm [68 in] in 19 hours, 5–6 April 1969.

Heaviest snowfall (season/year): Paradise Ranger Station, Mt Rainier, Washington, USA, 31,102 mm [1,224.5 in], 19 February 1971 to 18 February 1972.

Pressure and winds

Highest barometric pressure: Agata, Siberia (at 262 m [862 ft] altitude), 1,083.8 mb, 31 December 1968.

Lowest barometric pressure: Typhoon Tip, Guam, Pacific Ocean, 870 mb, 12 October 1979.

Highest recorded wind speed: Mt Washington, New Hampshire, USA, 371 km/h [231 mph], 12 April 1934. This is three times as strong as hurricane force on the Beaufort Scale.

Windiest place: Commonwealth Bay, Antarctica, where gales frequently reach over 320 km/h [200 mph].

Climate

Climate is weather in the long term: the seasonal pattern of hot and cold, wet and dry, averaged over time (usually 30 years). At the simplest level, it is caused by the uneven heating of the Earth. Surplus heat at the Equator passes towards the poles, levelling out the energy differential. Its passage is marked by a ceaseless churning of the atmosphere and the oceans, further agitated by the Earth's diurnal spin and the motion it imparts to moving air and water. The heat's means of transport – by winds and ocean currents, by the continual evaporation and recondensation of water molecules – is the weather itself. There are four basic types of climate, each of which can be further subdivided: tropical, desert (dry), temperate and polar.

Composition of Dry Air

Nitrogen	78.09%	Sulphur dioxide	trace
Oxygen	20.95%	Nitrogen oxide	trace
Argon	0.93%	Methane	trace
Water vapour	0.2–4.0%	Dust	trace
Carbon dioxide	0.03%	Helium	trace
Ozone	0.00006%	Neon	trace

El Niño

In a normal year, south-easterly trade winds drive surface waters westwards off the coast of South America, drawing cold, nutrient-rich water up from below. In an El Niño year (which occurs every 2–7 years), warm water from the west Pacific suppresses up-welling in the east, depriving the region of nutrients. The water is warmed by as much as 7°C [12°F], disturbing the tropical atmospheric circulation. During an intense El Niño, the south-east trade winds change direction and become equatorial westerlies, resulting in climatic extremes in many regions of the world, such as drought in parts of Australia and India, and heavy rainfall in south-eastern USA. An intense El Niño occurred in 1997–8, with resultant freak weather conditions across the entire Pacific region.

Normal year

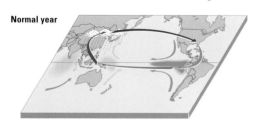

El Niño event

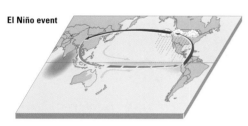

Beaufort Wind Scale

Named after the 19th-century British naval officer who devised it, the Beaufort Scale assesses wind speed according to its effects. It was originally designed as an aid for sailors, but has since been adapted for use on the land.

Scale	Wind speed		Effect
	km/h	mph	
0	0–1	0–1	**Calm**
			Smoke rises vertically
1	1–5	1–3	**Light air**
			Wind direction shown only by smoke drift
2	6–11	4–7	**Light breeze**
			Wind felt on face; leaves rustle; vanes moved by wind
3	12–19	8–12	**Gentle breeze**
			Leaves and small twigs in constant motion; wind extends small flag
4	20–28	13–18	**Moderate**
			Raises dust and loose paper; small branches move
5	29–38	19–24	**Fresh**
			Small trees in leaf sway; wavelets on inland waters
6	39–49	25–31	**Strong**
			Large branches move; difficult to use umbrellas
7	50–61	32–38	**Near gale**
			Whole trees in motion; difficult to walk against wind
8	62–74	39–46	**Gale**
			Twigs break from trees; walking very difficult
9	75–88	47–54	**Strong gale**
			Slight structural damage
10	89–102	55–63	**Storm**
			Trees uprooted; serious structural damage
11	103–117	64–72	**Violent storm**
			Widespread damage
12	118+	73+	**Hurricane**

Conversions
°C = (°F − 32) × 5/9; °F = (°C × 9/5) + 32; 0°C = 32°F
1 in = 25.4 mm; 1 mm = 0.0394 in; 100 mm = 3.94 in

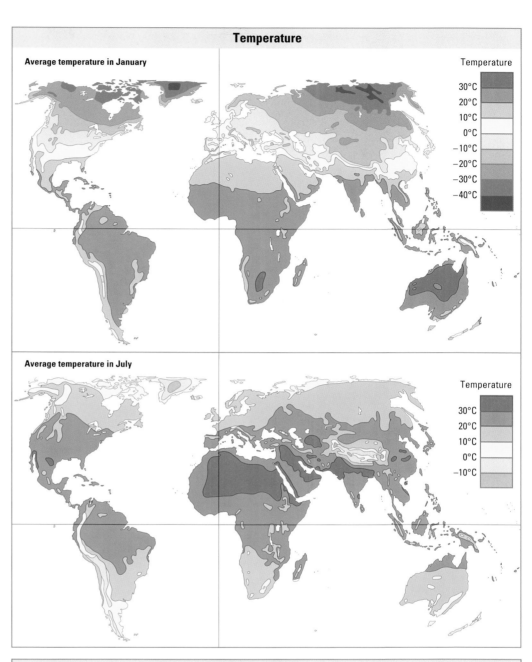

Temperature

Average temperature in January

Temperature
30°C
20°C
10°C
0°C
−10°C
−20°C
−30°C
−40°C

Average temperature in July

Temperature
30°C
20°C
10°C
0°C
−10°C

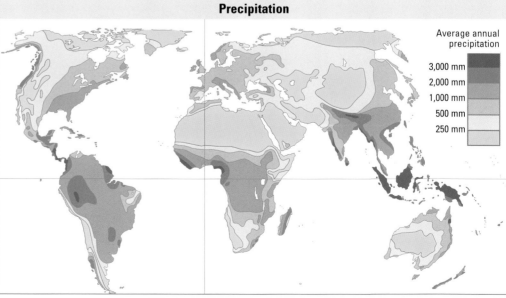

Precipitation

Average annual precipitation
3,000 mm
2,000 mm
1,000 mm
500 mm
250 mm

Water and Vegetation

The Hydrological Cycle

The world's water balance is regulated by the constant recycling of water between the oceans, atmosphere and land. The movement of water between these three reservoirs is known as the hydrological cycle. The oceans play a vital role in the hydrological cycle: 74% of the total precipitation falls over the oceans and 84% of the total evaporation comes from the oceans.

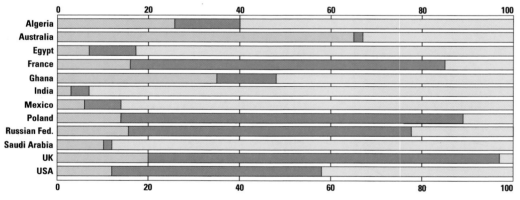

Water Distribution

The distribution of planetary water, by percentage. Oceans and ice-caps together account for more than 99% of the total; the breakdown of the remainder is estimated.

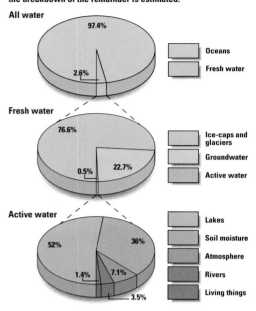

All water
97.4%
2.6%
- Oceans
- Fresh water

Fresh water
76.6%
0.5%
22.7%
- Ice-caps and glaciers
- Groundwater
- Active water

Active water
52%
36%
1.4%
7.1%
3.5%
- Lakes
- Soil moisture
- Atmosphere
- Rivers
- Living things

Water Utilization

- Domestic
- Industrial
- Agriculture

The percentage breakdown of water usage by sector, selected countries (1996)

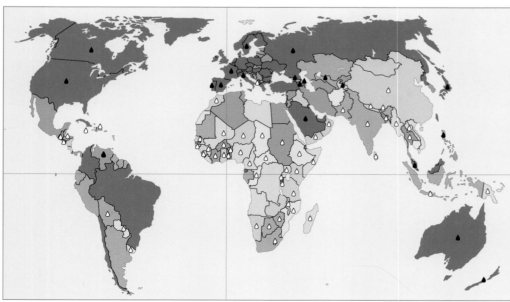

Algeria
Australia
Egypt
France
Ghana
India
Mexico
Poland
Russian Fed.
Saudi Arabia
UK
USA

Water Usage

Almost all the world's water is 3,000 million years old, and all of it cycles endlessly through the hydrosphere, though at different rates. Water vapour circulates over days, even hours, deep ocean water circulates over millennia, and ice-cap water remains solid for millions of years.

Fresh water is essential to all terrestrial life. Humans cannot survive more than a few days without it, and even the hardiest desert plants and animals could not exist without some water. Agriculture requires huge quantities of fresh water: without large-scale irrigation most of the world's people would starve. In the USA, agriculture uses 42% and industry 45% of all water withdrawals.

The United States is one of the heaviest users of water in the world. According to the latest figures the average American uses 380 litres a day and the average household uses 415,000 litres a year. This is two to four times more than in Western Europe.

Water Supply

Percentage of total population with access to safe drinking water (1995)

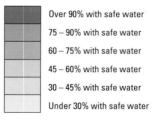

- Over 90% with safe water
- 75 – 90% with safe water
- 60 – 75% with safe water
- 45 – 60% with safe water
- 30 – 45% with safe water
- Under 30% with safe water

△ Under 80 litres per person per day domestic water consumption

▲ Over 320 litres per person per day domestic water consumption

NB: 80 litres of water a day is considered necessary for a reasonable quality of life.

Least well-provided countries

Paraguay	8%	Central Afr. Rep	18%
Afghanistan	10%	Bhutan	21%
Cambodia	13%	Congo (D. Rep.)	25%

12

CARTOGRAPHY BY PHILIP'S. COPYRIGHT GEORGE PHILIP LTD

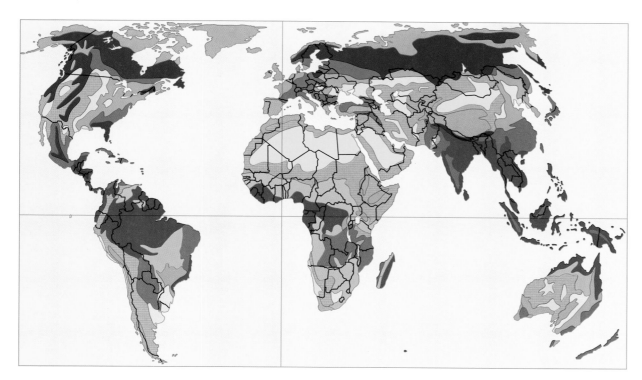

Natural Vegetation

Regional variation in vegetation

- Tundra and mountain vegetation
- Needleleaf evergreen forest
- Mixed needleleaf evergreen & broadleaf deciduous trees
- Broadleaf deciduous woodland
- Mid-latitude grassland
- Evergreen broadleaf and deciduous trees & shrubs
- Semi-desert scrub
- Desert
- Tropical grassland (savanna)
- Tropical broadleaf rainforest and monsoon forest
- Subtropical broadleaf and needleleaf forest

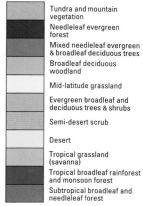

The map shows the natural 'climax vegetation' of regions, as dictated by climate and topography. In most cases, however, agricultural activity has drastically altered the vegetation pattern. Western Europe, for example, lost most of its broadleaf forest many centuries ago, while irrigation has turned some natural semi-desert into productive land.

Land Use by Continent

- Forest
- Permanent pasture and rough grazing
- Permanent crops and plantations
- Arable
- Non-productive

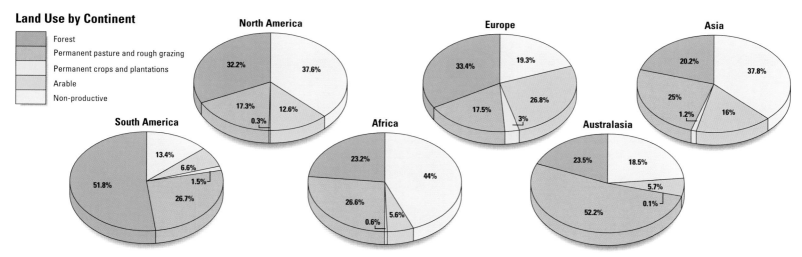

North America
37.6% / 32.2% / 17.3% / 0.3% / 12.6%

Europe
19.3% / 33.4% / 17.5% / 3% / 26.8%

Asia
37.8% / 20.2% / 25% / 1.2% / 16%

South America
13.4% / 6.6% / 1.5% / 51.8% / 26.7%

Africa
44% / 23.2% / 26.6% / 0.6% / 5.6%

Australasia
18.5% / 23.5% / 5.7% / 0.1% / 52.2%

Forestry: Production

	Forest and woodland (million hectares)	Annual production (1996, million cubic metres)	
		Fuelwood and charcoal	Industrial roundwood*
World	*3,987.9*	*1,864.8*	*1,489.5*
S. America	829.3	193.0	129.9
N. & C. America	709.8	155.4	600.4
Africa	684.6	519.9	67.9
Asia	131.8	905.2	280.2
Europe	157.3	82.4	369.7
Australasia	157.2	8.7	41.5

Paper and Board

Top producers (1996)**		Top exporters (1996)**	
USA	85,173	Canada	13,393
China	30,253	USA	9,113
Japan	30,014	Finland	8,529
Canada	18,414	Sweden	7,483
Germany	14,733	Germany	6,319

* roundwood is timber as it is felled
** in thousand tonnes

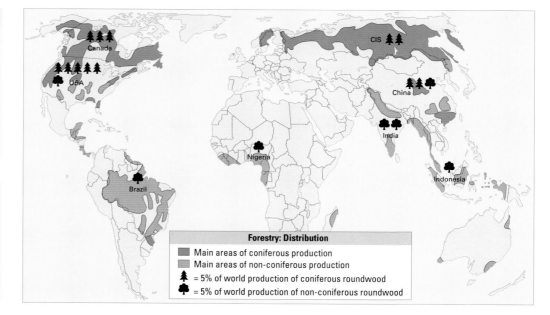

Forestry: Distribution

- Main areas of coniferous production
- Main areas of non-coniferous production
- 🌲 = 5% of world production of coniferous roundwood
- 🌳 = 5% of world production of non-coniferous roundwood

Environment

Humans have always had a dramatic effect on their environment, at least since the development of agriculture almost 10,000 years ago. Generally, the Earth has accepted human interference without obvious ill effects: the complex systems that regulate the global environment have been able to absorb substantial damage while maintaining a stable and comfortable home for the planet's trillions of lifeforms. But advancing human technology and the rapidly-expanding populations it supports are now threatening

to overwhelm the Earth's ability to compensate.

Industrial wastes, acid rainfall, desertification and large-scale deforestation all combine to create environmental change at a rate far faster than the great slow cycles of planetary evolution can accommodate. As a result of overcultivation, overgrazing and overcutting of groundcover for firewood, desertification is affecting as much as 60% of the world's croplands. In addition, with fire and chain-saws, humans are destroying more forest in a day than their ancestors could

have done in a century, upsetting the balance between plant and animal, carbon dioxide and oxygen, on which all life ultimately depends.

The fossil fuels that power industrial civilization have pumped enough carbon dioxide and other so-called greenhouse gases into the atmosphere to make climatic change a near-certainty. As a result of the combination of these factors, the Earth's average temperature has risen by approximately 0.5°C [1°F] since the beginning of the 20th century, and it is still rising.

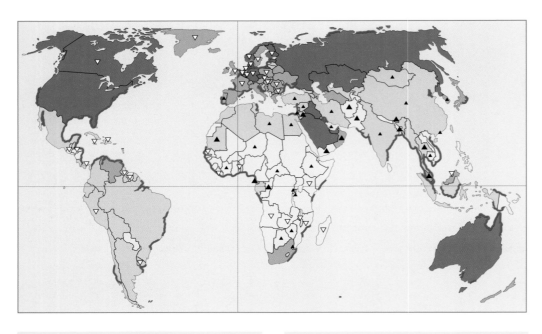

Global Warming

Carbon dioxide emissions in tonnes per person per year (1995)

- Over 10 tonnes of CO_2
- 5 – 10 tonnes of CO_2
- 1 – 5 tonnes of CO_2
- Under 1 tonne of CO_2

Changes in CO_2 emissions 1980–90

- ▲ Over 100% increase in emissions
- ▲ 50–100% increase in emissions
- ▽ Reduction in emissions
- — Coastal areas in danger of flooding from rising sea levels caused by global warming

High atmospheric concentrations of heat-absorbing gases, especially carbon dioxide, appear to be causing a steady rise in average temperatures worldwide – up to 1.5°C [3°F] by the year 2020, according to some estimates. Global warming is likely to bring with it a rise in sea levels that may flood some of the Earth's most densely populated coastal areas.

Greenhouse Power

Relative contributions to the Greenhouse Effect by the major heat-absorbing gases in the atmosphere.

The chart combines greenhouse potency and volume. Carbon dioxide has a greenhouse potential of only 1, but its concentration of 350 parts per million makes it predominate. CFC 12, with 25,000 times the absorption capacity of CO_2, is present only as 0.00044 ppm.

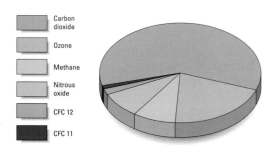

- Carbon dioxide
- Ozone
- Methane
- Nitrous oxide
- CFC 12
- CFC 11

Ozone Layer

The ozone 'hole' over the northern hemisphere on 12 March 1995.

The colours represent Dobson Units (DU). The ozone 'hole' is seen as the dark blue and purple patch in the centre, where ozone values are around 120 DU or lower. Normal levels are around 280 DU. The ozone 'hole' over Antarctica is much larger.

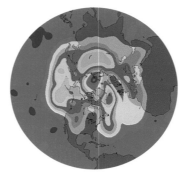

Carbon Dioxide

Carbon dioxide released in millions of tonnes (1992)

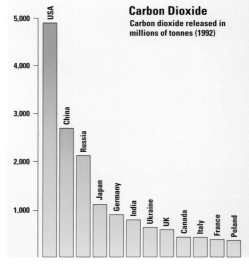

The Greenhouse Effect

Carbon dioxide is increased by burning fossil fuels and cutting forests

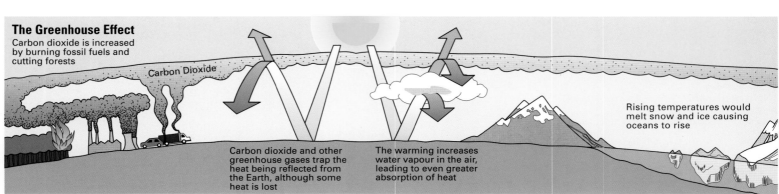

Carbon Dioxide

Carbon dioxide and other greenhouse gases trap the heat being reflected from the Earth, although some heat is lost

The warming increases water vapour in the air, leading to even greater absorption of heat

Rising temperatures would melt snow and ice causing oceans to rise

Desertification

- Existing deserts
- Areas with a high risk of desertification
- Areas with a moderate risk of desertification
- Former areas of rainforest
- Existing rainforest

Forest Clearance

Thousands of hectares of forest cleared annually, tropical countries surveyed 1981–85 and 1987–90. Loss as a percentage of remaining stocks is shown in figures on each column.

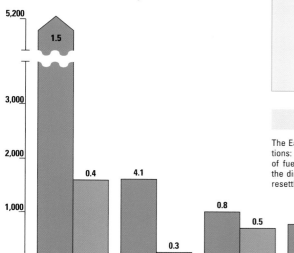

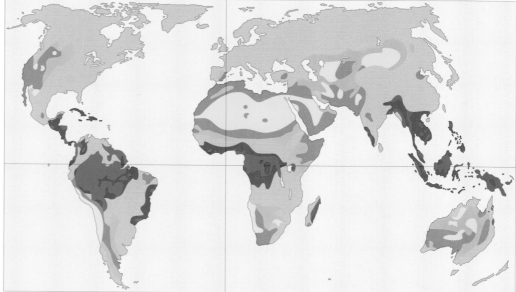

Deforestation

The Earth's remaining forests are under attack from three directions: expanding agriculture, logging, and growing consumption of fuelwood, often in combination. Sometimes deforestation is the direct result of government policy, as in the efforts made to resettle the urban poor in some parts of Brazil; just as often,

it comes about despite state attempts at conservation. Loggers, licensed or unlicensed, blaze a trail into virgin forest, often destroying twice as many trees as they harvest. Landless farmers follow, burning away most of what remains to plant their crops, completing the destruction.

■ 1987–90   ■ 1981–85

Ozone Depletion

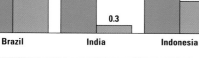

The ozone layer, 25–30 km [15–18 miles] above sea level, acts as a barrier to most of the Sun's harmful ultra-violet radiation, protecting us from the ionizing radiation that can cause skin cancer and cataracts. In recent years, however, two holes in the ozone layer have been observed during winter: one over the Arctic and the other, the size of the USA, over Antarctica. By 1996, ozone had been reduced to around a half of its 1970 amount. The ozone (O_3) is broken down by chlorine released into the atmosphere as CFCs (chlorofluorocarbons) – chemicals used in refrigerators, packaging and aerosols.

Air Pollution

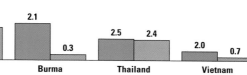

Sulphur dioxide is the main pollutant associated with industrial cities. According to the World Health Organization, at least 600 million people live in urban areas where sulphur dioxide concentrations regularly reach damaging levels. One of the world's most dangerously polluted urban areas is Mexico City, due to a combination of its enclosed valley location, 3 million cars and 60,000 factories. In May 1998, this lethal cocktail was added to by nearby forest fires and the resultant air pollution led to over 20% of the population (3 million people) complaining of respiratory problems.

Acid Rain

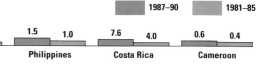

Killing trees, poisoning lakes and rivers and eating away buildings, acid rain is mostly produced by sulphur dioxide emissions from industry and volcanic eruptions. By the mid 1990s, acid rain had sterilized 4,000 or more of Sweden's lakes and left 45% of Switzerland's alpine conifers dead or dying, while the monuments of Greece were dissolving in Athens' smog. Prevailing wind patterns mean that the acids often fall many hundred kilometres from where the original pollutants were discharged. In parts of Europe acid deposition has slightly decreased, following reductions in emissions, but not by enough.

World Pollution

Acid rain and sources of acidic emissions (latest available year)

Acid rain is caused by high levels of sulphur and nitrogen in the atmosphere. They combine with water vapour and oxygen to form acids (H_2SO_4 and HNO_3) which fall as precipitation.

- Regions where sulphur and nitrogen oxides are released in high concentrations, mainly from fossil fuel combustion
- Major cities with high levels of air pollution (including nitrogen and sulphur emissions)

Areas of heavy acid deposition

pH numbers indicate acidity, decreasing from a neutral 7. Normal rain, slightly acid from dissolved carbon dioxide, never exceeds a pH of 5.6.

- pH less than 4.0 (most acidic)
- pH 4.0 to 4.5
- pH 4.5 to 5.0
- Areas where acid rain is a potential problem

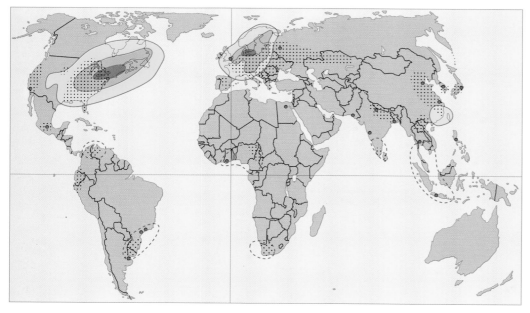

15

Population

Demographic Profiles

Developed nations such as the UK have populations evenly spread across the age groups and, usually, a growing proportion of elderly people. The great majority of the people in developing nations, however, are in the younger age groups, about to enter their most fertile years. In time, these population profiles should resemble the world profile (even Kenya has made recent progress with reducing its birth rate), but the transition will come about only after a few more generations of rapid population growth.

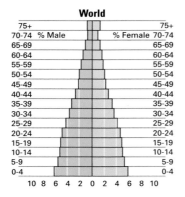

World

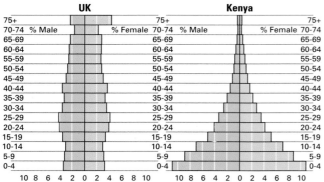

UK · Kenya

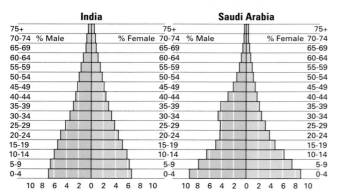

India · Saudi Arabia

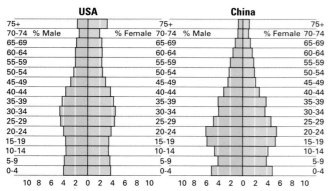

USA · China

Most Populous Nations [in millions (2000 estimates)]

1. China	1,299	9. Japan	128	17. Egypt	64
2. India	1,041	10. Mexico	107	18. Thailand	63
3. USA	266	11. Nigeria	105	19. Ethiopia	61
4. Indonesia	218	12. Vietnam	82	20. France	58
5. Brazil	179	13. Philippines	77	21. UK	58
6. Pakistan	162	14. Germany	76	22. Italy	57
7. Russia	155	15. Iran	68	23. Ukraine	52
8. Bangladesh	150	16. Turkey	66	24. Burma	51

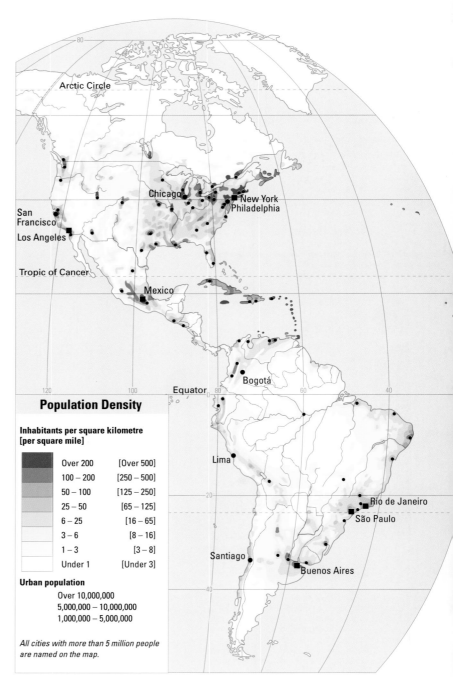

Population Density

Inhabitants per square kilometre [per square mile]

	Over 200	[Over 500]
	100 – 200	[250 – 500]
	50 – 100	[125 – 250]
	25 – 50	[65 – 125]
	6 – 25	[16 – 65]
	3 – 6	[8 – 16]
	1 – 3	[3 – 8]
	Under 1	[Under 3]

Urban population

- Over 10,000,000
- 5,000,000 – 10,000,000
- 1,000,000 – 5,000,000

All cities with more than 5 million people are named on the map.

Continental Comparisons

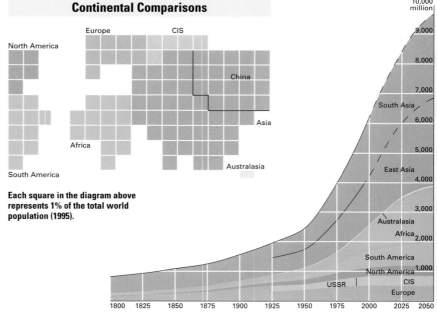

Each square in the diagram above represents 1% of the total world population (1995).

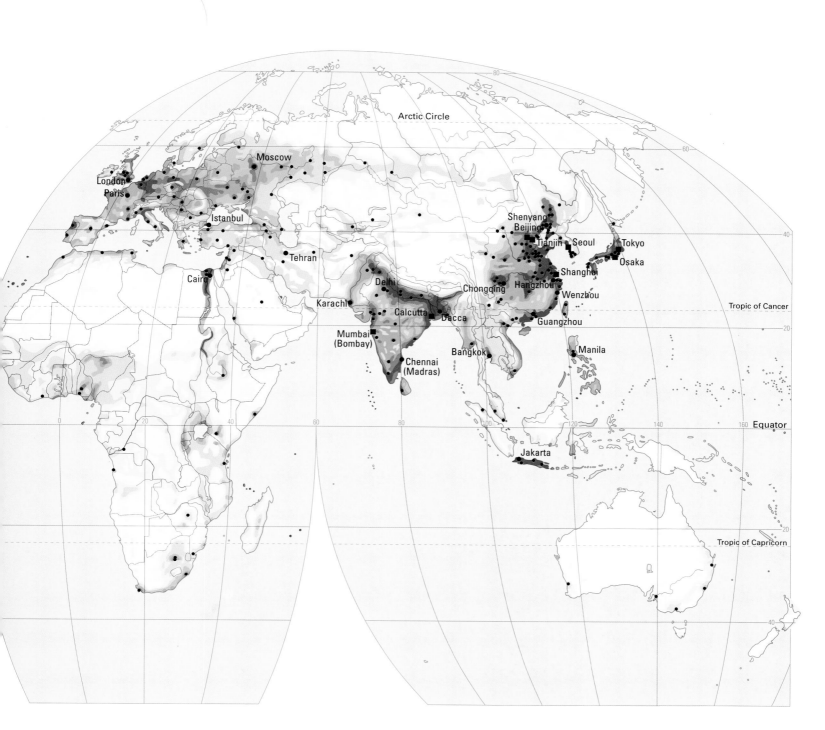

Moscow

London
Paris

Istanbul

Tehran

Cairo

Delhi

Karachi

Calcutta

Dacca

Mumbai
(Bombay)

Chennai
(Madras)

Bangkok

Shenyang

Beijing

Tianjin

Seoul

Tokyo

Osaka

Shanghai

Chongqing

Hangzhou

Wenzhou

Guangzhou

Manila

Jakarta

Arctic Circle

Tropic of Cancer

Equator

Tropic of Capricorn

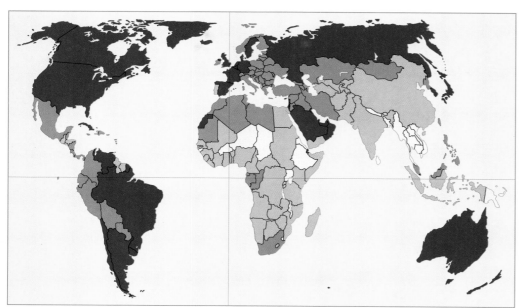

Urban Population

Percentage of total population living in towns and cities (1997)

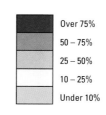

Over 75%

50 – 75%

25 – 50%

10 – 25%

Under 10%

Most urbanized

Singapore	100%
Belgium	97%
Israel	91%
Uruguay	91%
Netherlands	89%

[UK 89%]

Least urbanized

Rwanda	6%
Bhutan	8%
Burundi	8%
Nepal	11%
Swaziland	12%

The Human Family

Predominant Languages

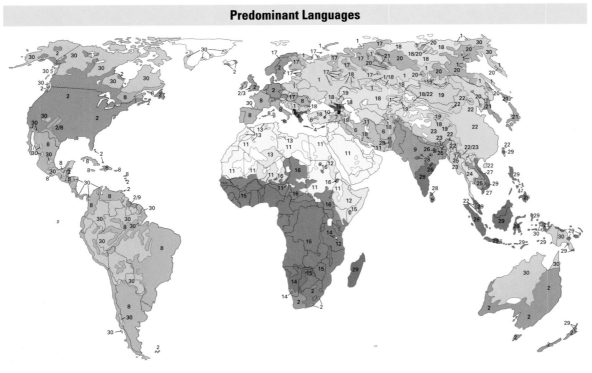

INDO-EUROPEAN FAMILY

1	Balto-Slavic group (incl. Russian, Ukrainian)
2	Germanic group (incl. English, German)
3	Celtic group
4	Greek
5	Albanian
6	Iranian group
7	Armenian
8	Romance group (incl. Spanish, Portuguese, French, Italian)
9	Indo-Aryan group (incl. Hindi, Bengali, Urdu, Punjabi, Marathi)
10	CAUCASIAN FAMILY

AFRO-ASIATIC FAMILY

11	Semitic group (incl. Arabic)
12	Kushitic group
13	Berber group
14	KHOISAN FAMILY
15	NIGER-CONGO FAMILY
16	NILO-SAHARAN FAMILY
17	URALIC FAMILY

ALTAIC FAMILY

18	Turkic group
19	Mongolian group
20	Tungus-Manchu group
21	Japanese and Korean

SINO-TIBETAN FAMILY

22	Sinitic (Chinese) languages
23	Tibetic-Burmic languages
24	TAI FAMILY

AUSTRO-ASIATIC FAMILY

25	Mon-Khmer group
26	Munda group
27	Vietnamese
28	DRAVIDIAN FAMILY (incl. Telugu, Tamil)
29	AUSTRONESIAN FAMILY (incl. Malay-Indonesian)
30	OTHER LANGUAGES

Predominant Religions

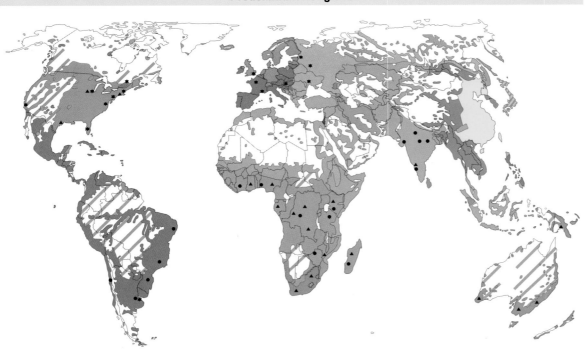

▲	Roman Catholicism
	Orthodox and other Eastern Churches
•	Protestantism
	Sunni Islam
	Shia Islam
	Buddhism
	Hinduism
	Confucianism
★	Judaism
	Shintoism
	Tribal Religions

United Nations

Created in 1945 to promote peace and co-operation and based in New York, the United Nations is the world's largest international organization, with 185 members and an annual budget of US $2.6 billion (1996–97). Each member of the General Assembly has one vote, while the permanent members of the 15-nation Security Council – USA, Russia, China, UK and France – hold a veto. The Secretariat is the UN's principal administrative arm. The 54 members of the Economic and Social Council are responsible for economic, social, cultural, educational, health and related matters. The UN has 16 specialized agencies – based in Canada, France, Switzerland and Italy, as well as the USA – which help members in fields such as education (UNESCO), agriculture (FAO), medicine (WHO) and finance (IFC). By the end of 1994, all the original 11 trust territories of the Trusteeship Council had become independent.

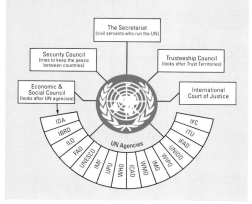

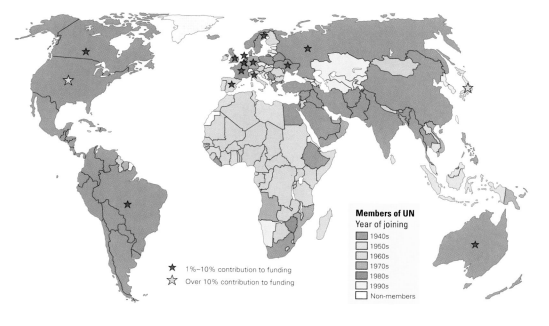

Members of UN
Year of joining
- 1940s
- 1950s
- 1960s
- 1970s
- 1980s
- 1990s
- Non-members

★ 1%–10% contribution to funding
☆ Over 10% contribution to funding

MEMBERSHIP OF THE UN In 1945 there were 51 members; by 2000 membership had increased to 188 following the admission of Kiribati, Nauru and Tonga. There are 4 independent states which are not members of the UN – Switzerland, Taiwan, Tuvalu and the Vatican City. All the successor states of the former USSR had joined by the end of 1992. The official languages of the UN are Chinese, English, French, Russian, Spanish and Arabic.

FUNDING The UN budget for 1996–97 was US $2.6 billion. Contributions are assessed by the members' ability to pay, with the maximum 25% of the total, the minimum 0.01%. Contributions for 1996 were: USA 25.0%, Japan 15.4%, Germany 9.0%, France 6.4%, UK 5.3%, Italy 5.2%, Russia 4.5%, Canada 3.1%, Spain 2.4%, Brazil 1.6%, Netherlands 1.6%, Australia 1.5%, Sweden 1.2%, Ukraine 1.1%, Belgium 1.0%.

International Organizations

EU European Union (evolved from the European Community in 1993). The 15 members – Austria, Belgium, Denmark, Finland, France, Germany, Greece, Ireland, Italy, Luxembourg, Netherlands, Portugal, Spain, Sweden and the UK – aim to integrate economies, co-ordinate social developments and bring about political union. These members of what is now the world's biggest market share agricultural and industrial policies and tariffs on trade. The original body, the European Coal and Steel Community (ECSC), was created in 1951 following the signing of the Treaty of Paris.

EFTA European Free Trade Association (formed in 1960). Portugal left the original 'Seven' in 1989 to join what was then the EC, followed by Austria, Finland and Sweden in 1995. Only 4 members remain: Norway, Iceland, Switzerland and Liechtenstein.

ACP African-Caribbean-Pacific (formed in 1963). Members have economic ties with the EU.

NATO North Atlantic Treaty Organization (formed in 1949). It continues after 1991 despite the winding up of the Warsaw Pact. The Czech Republic, Hungary and Poland were the latest members to join in 1999.

OAS Organization of American States (formed in 1948). It aims to promote social and economic co-operation between developed countries of North America and developing nations of Latin America.

ASEAN Association of South-east Asian Nations (formed in 1967). Cambodia joined in 1999.

OAU Organization of African Unity (formed in 1963). Its 53 members represent over 94% of Africa's population. Arabic, French, Portuguese and English are recognized as working languages.

LAIA Latin American Integration Association (1980). Its aim is to promote freer regional trade.

OECD Organization for Economic Co-operation and Development (formed in 1961). It comprises the 29 major Western free-market economies. Poland, Hungary and South Korea joined in 1996. 'G8' is its 'inner group' comprising Canada, France, Germany, Italy, Japan, Russia, the UK and the USA.

COMMONWEALTH The Commonwealth of Nations evolved from the British Empire; it comprises 16 Queen's realms, 32 republics and 5 indigenous monarchies, giving a total of 53.

OPEC Organization of Petroleum Exporting Countries (formed in 1960). It controls about three-quarters of the world's oil supply. Gabon left the organization in 1996.

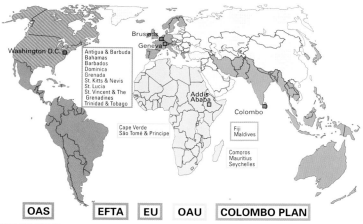

OAS   EFTA   EU   OAU   COLOMBO PLAN

ARAB LEAGUE (formed in 1945). The League's aim is to promote economic, social, political and military co-operation. There are 21 member nations.

COLOMBO PLAN (formed in 1951). Its 26 members aim to promote economic and social development in Asia and the Pacific.

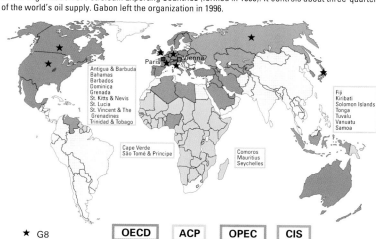

★ G8   OECD   ACP   OPEC   CIS

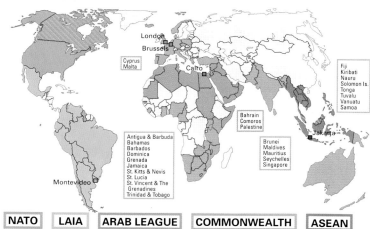

NATO   LAIA   ARAB LEAGUE   COMMONWEALTH   ASEAN

Wealth

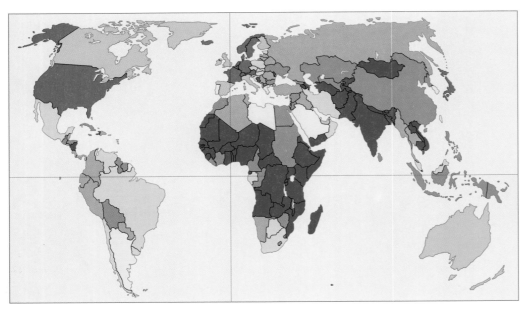

Levels of Income

Gross National Product per capita: the value of total production divided by the population (1997)

	Over 400% of world average
	200 – 400% of world average
	100 – 200% of world average

[World average wealth per person US $6,316]

	50 – 100% of world average
	25 – 50% of world average
	10 – 25% of world average
	Under 10% of world average

GNP per capita growth rate (%), selected countries, 1985–94

Thailand	8.2	Brazil	–0.4
Chile	6.9	Zimbabwe	–0.6
Japan	3.2	USA	–1.3
Germany	1.9	UK	–1.4
Australia	1.2	Armenia	–12.9

Wealth Creation

The Gross National Product (GNP) of the world's largest economies, US $ million (1998)

1. USA	7,922,651	23. Saudi Arabia	186,000
2. Japan	4,089,910	24. Denmark	176,374
3. Germany	2,122,673	25. Hong Kong	158,286
4. Italy	1,666,178	26. Norway	152,082
5. France	1,466,014	27. Poland	150,798
6. UK	1,263,777	28. Indonesia	138,501
7. China	928,950	29. Thailand	134,433
8. Botswana	758,043	30. Finland	124,293
9. Canada	612,332	31. Greece	122,880
10. Spain	553,690	32. South Africa	119,001
11. India	421,259	33. Iran	109,645
12. Netherlands	388,682	34. Portugal	106,376
13. Mexico	380,917	35. Colombia	106,090
14. Australia	380,625	36. Israel	95,179
15. South Korea	369,890	37. Singapore	95,095
16. Russia	337,914	38. Venezuela	81,347
17. Argentina	324,084	39. Malaysia	79,848
18. Switzerland	284,808	40. Egypt	79,208
19. Belgium	259,045	41. Philippines	78,896
20. Sweden	226,861	42. Chile	71,294
21. Austria	217,163	43. Ireland	67,491
22. Turkey	200,505	44. Pakistan	63,159

The Wealth Gap

The world's richest and poorest countries, by Gross National Product per capita in US $ (1998)

1. Liechtenstein	50,000	1. Ethiopia	100
2. Luxembourg	43,570	2. Congo (D. Rep.)	110
3. Switzerland	40,080	3. Burundi	140
4. Norway	34,330	4. Sierra Leone	140
5. Bermuda	34,000	5. Guinea-Bissau	160
6. Denmark	33,260	6. Niger	190
7. Japan	32,380	7. Eritrea	200
8. Singapore	30,060	8. Malawi	200
9. USA	29,340	9. Mozambique	210
10. Iceland	28,010	10. Nepal	210
11. Austria	26,850	11. Tanzania	210
12. Germany	25,850	12. Chad	230
13. Sweden	25,620	13. Rwanda	230
14. Belgium	25,380	14. Burkina Faso	240
15. Monaco	25,000	15. Mali	250
16. France	24,940	16. Madagascar	260
17. Netherlands	24,760	17. Cambodia	280
18. Finland	24,110	18. São Tomé & Príncipe	280
19. Brunei	24,000	19. Sudan	290
20. Hong Kong	23,670	20. Central African Rep.	300

GNP per capita is calculated by dividing a country's Gross National Product by its total population.

Continental Shares

Shares of population and of wealth (GNP) by continent

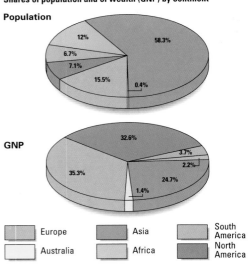

Population

GNP

Europe		Asia		South America
Australia		Africa		North America

Inflation

Average annual rate of inflation (1990–96)

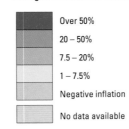

	Over 50%
	20 – 50%
	7.5 – 20%
	1 – 7.5%
	Negative inflation
	No data available

Highest average inflation

Congo (D. Rep.)	2747%
Georgia	2279%
Angola	1103%
Turkmenistan	1074%
Armenia	897%

Lowest average inflation

Oman	–3.0%
Bahrain	–0.5%
Brunei	–0.0%
Saudi Araba	1.0%
Japan	1.0%

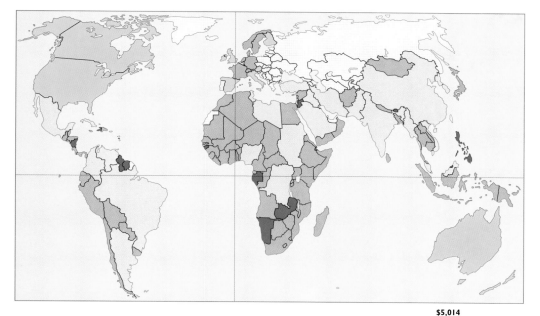

Over $100 per person
$10 – $100 per person
$0 – $10 per person
No aid given or received
$0 – $10 per person
$10 – $100 per person
Over $100 per person

Providers

Receivers

Top 5 providers per capita (1994)		Top 5 receivers per capita (1994)	
France	$279	São Tomé & P.	$378
Denmark	$260	Cape Verde	$314
Norway	$247	Djibouti	$235
Sweden	$201	Surinam	$198
Germany	$166	Mauritania	$153

Debt and Aid

International debtors and the aid they receive (1996)

Although aid grants make a vital contribution to many of the world's poorer countries, they are usually dwarfed by the burden of debt that the developing economies are expected to repay. In 1992, they had to pay US $160,000 million in debt service charges alone – more than two and a half times the amount of Official Development Assistance (ODA) the developing countries were receiving, and US $60,000 million more than total private flows of aid in the same year. In 1990, the debts of Mozambique, one of the world's poorest countries, were estimated to be 75 times its entire earnings from exports.

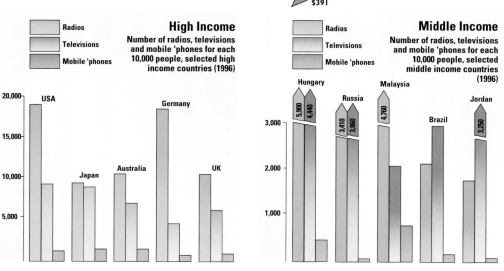

Debt, US$ per capita

Aid, US$ per capita

Distribution of Spending

Percentage share of household spending, selected countries

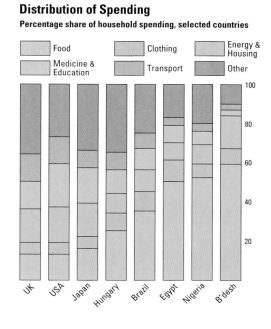

Food
Medicine & Education
Clothing
Transport
Energy & Housing
Other

UK USA Japan Hungary Brazil Egypt Nigeria B'desh

High Income

Radios
Televisions
Mobile 'phones

Number of radios, televisions and mobile 'phones for each 10,000 people, selected high income countries (1996)

USA Germany Japan Australia UK

Middle Income

Radios
Televisions
Mobile 'phones

Number of radios, televisions and mobile 'phones for each 10,000 people, selected middle income countries (1996)

Hungary Russia Malaysia Brazil Jordan

Low Income

Radios
Televisions
Mobile 'phones

Number of radios, televisions and mobile 'phones for each 10,000 people, selected low income countries (1996)

Albania Nigeria China India Laos

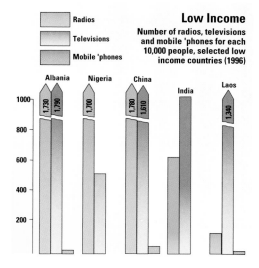

Quality of Life

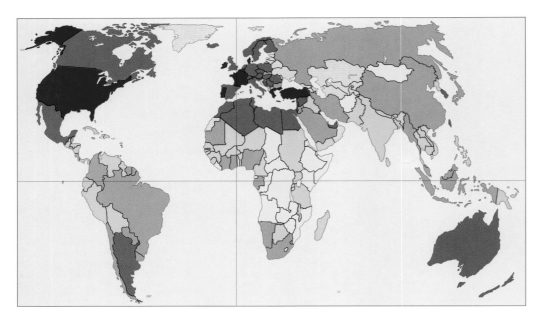

Daily Food Consumption

Average daily food intake in calories per person (1995)

■	Over 3,500 calories per person
■	3,000 – 3,500 calories per person
■	2,500 – 3,000 calories per person
■	2,000 – 2,500 calories per person
□	Under 2,000 calories per person
	No available data

Top 5 countries		**Bottom 5 countries**	
Cyprus	3,708 cal.	Congo (D.Rep.)	1,879 cal.
Denmark	3,704 cal.	Djibouti	1,831 cal.
Portugal	3,639 cal.	Togo	1,754 cal.
Ireland	3,638 cal.	Burundi	1,749 cal.
USA	3,603 cal.	Mozambique	1,678 cal.

[UK 3,149 calories]

Hospital Capacity

Hospital beds available for each 1,000 people (1996)

Highest capacity		**Lowest capacity**	
Switzerland	20.8	Benin	0.2
Japan	16.2	Nepal	0.2
Tajikistan	16.0	Afghanistan	0.3
Norway	13.5	Bangladesh	0.3
Belarus	12.4	Ethiopia	0.3
Kazakstan	12.2	Mali	0.4
Moldova	12.2	Burkina Faso	0.5
Ukraine	12.2	Niger	0.5
Latvia	11.9	Guinea	0.6
Russia	11.8	India	0.6

[UK 4.9] [USA 4.2]

Although the ratio of people to hospital beds gives a good approximation of a country's health provision, it is not an absolute indicator. Raw numbers may mask inefficiency and other weaknesses: the high availability of beds in Kazakstan, for example, has not prevented infant mortality rates over three times as high as in the United Kingdom and the United States.

Life Expectancy

Years of life expectancy at birth, selected countries (1997)

The chart shows combined data for both sexes. On average, women live longer than men worldwide, even in developing countries with high maternal mortality rates. Overall, life expectancy is steadily rising, though the difference between rich and poor nations remains dramatic.

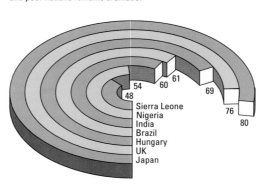

48   54   60   61   69   76   80

Sierra Leone
Nigeria
India
Brazil
Hungary
UK
Japan

Causes of Death

Causes of death for selected countries by % (1992–94)

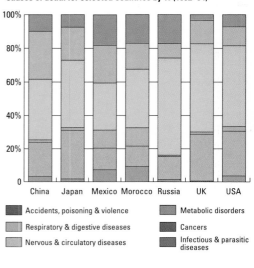

China   Japan   Mexico   Morocco   Russia   UK   USA

■ Accidents, poisoning & violence	■ Metabolic disorders
■ Respiratory & digestive diseases	■ Cancers
■ Nervous & circulatory diseases	■ Infectious & parasitic diseases

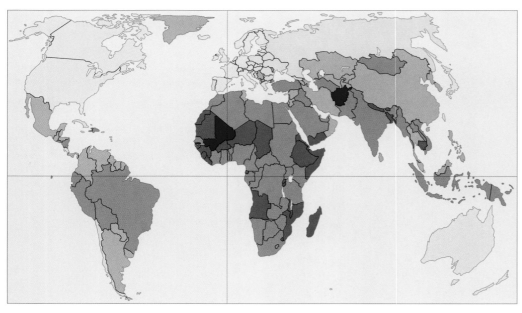

Child Mortality

Number of babies who will die under the age of one, per 1,000 births (average 1990–95)

■	Over 150 deaths per 1,000 births
■	100 – 150 deaths per 1,000 births
■	50 – 100 deaths per 1,000 births
■	20 – 50 deaths per 1,000 births
□	10 – 20 deaths per 1,000 births
□	Under 10 deaths per 1,000 births

Highest child mortality		**Lowest child mortality**	
Afghanistan	162	Hong Kong	6
Mali	159	Denmark	6
Sierra Leone	143	Japan	5
Guinea-Bissau	140	Iceland	5
Malawi	138	Finland	5

[UK 8 deaths]

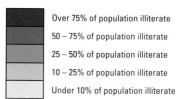

Illiteracy

Percentage of the total population unable to read or write (latest available year)

- Over 75% of population illiterate
- 50 – 75% of population illiterate
- 25 – 50% of population illiterate
- 10 – 25% of population illiterate
- Under 10% of population illiterate

Educational expenditure per person (latest available year)

Top 5 countries		Bottom 5 countries	
Sweden	$997	Chad	$2
Qatar	$989	Bangladesh	$3
Canada	$983	Ethiopia	$3
Norway	$971	Nepal	$4
Switzerland	$796	Somalia	$4

Fertility and Education

Fertility rates compared with female education, selected countries (1992–95)

Percentage of females aged 12–17 in secondary education

Fertility rate: average number of children borne per woman

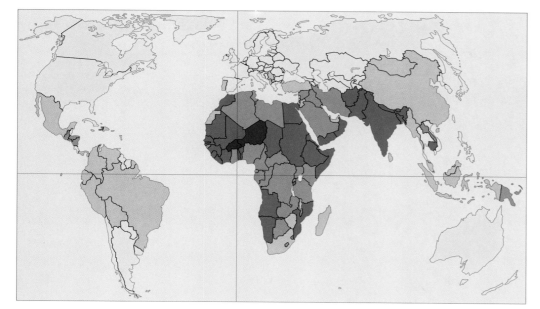

Living Standards

At first sight, most international contrasts in living standards are swamped by differences in wealth. The rich not only have more money, they have more of everything, including years of life. Those with only a little money are obliged to spend most of it on food and clothing, the basic maintenance costs of their existence; air travel and tourism are unlikely to feature on their expenditure lists. However, poverty and wealth are both relative: slum dwellers living on social security payments in an affluent industrial country have far more resources at their disposal than an average African peasant, but feel their own poverty nonetheless. A middle-class Indian lawyer cannot command a fraction of the earnings of a counterpart living in New York, London or Rome; nevertheless, he rightly sees himself as prosperous.

The rich not only live longer, on average, than the poor, they also die from different causes. Infectious and parasitic diseases, all but eliminated in the developed world, remain a scourge in the developing nations. On the other hand, more than two-thirds of the populations of OECD nations eventually succumb to cancer or circulatory disease.

Women in the Workforce

Women in paid employment as a percentage of the total workforce (latest available year)

- Over 50% are women
- 40 – 50% are women
- 30 – 40% are women
- 20 – 30% are women
- 10 – 20% are women
- Under 10% are women

Most women in the workforce		Fewest women in the workforce	
Cambodia	56%	Saudi Arabia	4%
Kazakstan	54%	Oman	6%
Burundi	53%	Afghanistan	8%
Mozambique	53%	Algeria	9%
Turkmenistan	52%	Libya	9%

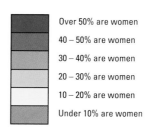

[USA 45] [UK 44]

CARTOGRAPHY BY PHILIP'S. COPYRIGHT GEORGE PHILIP LTD

Energy

Production

[Each square represents 1% of world energy production]

North America **Europe** **CIS**

Middle East

Japan

Africa **Asia**

South America **Australasia**

Consumption

[Each square represents 1% of world energy consumption]

North America **Europe** **CIS**

Middle East

Africa **Asia**

Japan

South America **Australasia**

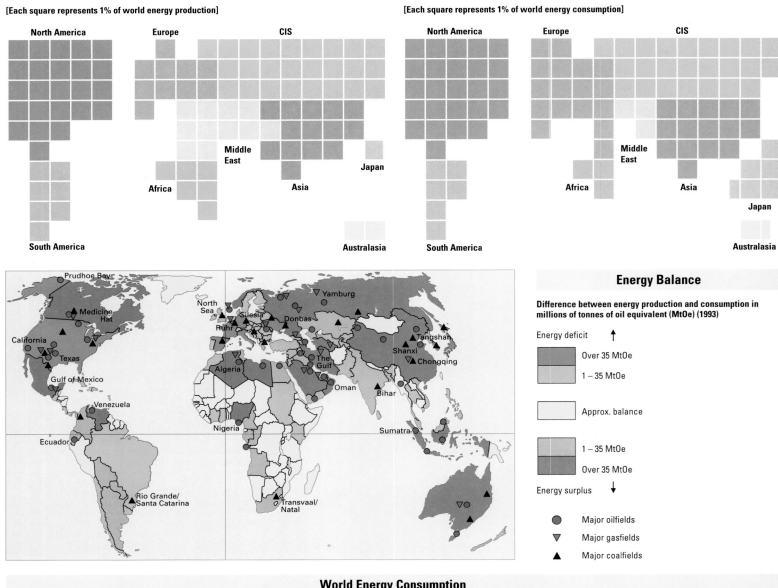

Prudhoe Bay · Medicine Hat · California · Texas · Gulf of Mexico · Venezuela · Ecuador · Rio Grande/Santa Catarina · North Sea · Ruhr · Silesia · Donbas · Algeria · Nigeria · The Gulf · Oman · Bihar · Transvaal/Natal · Yamburg · Tangshan · Shanxi · Chongqing · Sumatra

Energy Balance

Difference between energy production and consumption in millions of tonnes of oil equivalent (MtOe) (1993)

Energy deficit ↑

- Over 35 MtOe
- 1 – 35 MtOe
- Approx. balance
- 1 – 35 MtOe
- Over 35 MtOe

Energy surplus ↓

- ● Major oilfields
- ▽ Major gasfields
- ▲ Major coalfields

World Energy Consumption

Energy consumed by world regions, measured in million tonnes of oil equivalent in 1997. Total world consumption was 8,509 MtOe. Only energy from oil, gas, coal, nuclear and hydroelectric sources are included. Excluded are fuels such as wood, peat, animal waste, wind, solar and geothermal which, though important in some countries, are unreliably documented in terms of consumption statistics.

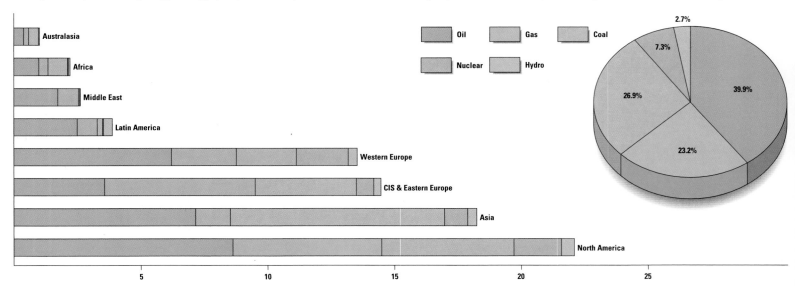

Australasia
Africa
Middle East
Latin America
Western Europe
CIS & Eastern Europe
Asia
North America

Oil Gas Coal
Nuclear Hydro

2.7%
7.3%
26.9%
39.9%
23.2%

5   10   15   20   25

Energy

Energy is used to keep us warm or cool, fuel our industries and our transport systems, and even feed us; high-intensity agriculture, with its use of fertilizers, pesticides and machinery, is heavily energy-dependent. Although we live in a high-energy society, there are vast discrepancies between rich and poor; for example, a North American consumes 13 times as much energy as a Chinese person. But even developing nations have more power at their disposal than was imaginable a century ago.

The distribution of energy supplies, most importantly fossil fuels (coal, oil and natural gas), is very uneven. In addition, the diagrams and map opposite show that the largest producers of energy are not necessarily the largest consumers. The movement of energy supplies around the world is therefore an important component of international trade. In 1995, total world movements in oil amounted to 1,815 million tonnes.

As the finite reserves of fossil fuels are depleted, renewable energy sources, such as solar, hydro-thermal, wind, tidal and biomass, will become increasingly important around the world.

Nuclear Power

Percentage of electricity generated by nuclear power stations, leading nations (1995)

1. Lithuania	85%	11. Spain	33%
2. France	77%	12. Finland	30%
3. Belgium	56%	13. Germany	29%
4. Slovak Rep.	49%	14. Japan	29%
5. Sweden	48%	15. UK	27%
6. Bulgaria	41%	16. Ukraine	27%
7. Hungary	41%	17. Czech Rep.	22%
8. Switzerland	39%	18. Canada	19%
9. Slovenia	38%	19. USA	18%
10. South Korea	33%	20. Russia	12%

Although the 1980s were a bad time for the nuclear power industry (major projects ran over budget, and fears of long-term environmental damage were heavily reinforced by the 1986 disaster at Chernobyl), the industry picked up in the early 1990s. However, whilst the number of reactors is still increasing, orders for new plants have shrunk. This is partly due to the increasingly difficult task of disposing of nuclear waste.

Hydroelectricity

Percentage of electricity generated by hydroelectric power stations, leading nations (1995)

1. Paraguay	99.9%	11. Rwanda	97.6%
2. Congo (Zaïre)	99.7%	12. Malawi	97.6%
3. Bhutan	99.6%	13. Cameroon	96.9%
4. Zambia	99.5%	14. Nepal	96.7%
5. Norway	99.4%	15. Laos	95.3%
6. Ghana	99.3%	16. Albania	95.2%
7. Congo	99.3%	17. Iceland	94.0%
8. Uganda	99.1%	18. Brazil	92.2%
9. Burundi	98.3%	19. Honduras	87.6%
10. Uruguay	98.0%	20. Tanzania	87.1%

Countries heavily reliant on hydroelectricity are usually small and non-industrial: a high proportion of hydroelectric power more often reflects a modest energy budget than vast hydroelectric resources. The USA, for instance, produces only 9% of power requirements from hydroelectricity; yet that 9% amounts to more than three times the hydropower generated by all of Africa.

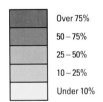

Fuel Exports

Fuels as a percentage of total value of exports (1990–94)

- Over 75%
- 50 – 75%
- 25 – 50%
- 10 – 25%
- Under 10%

Conversion Rates

1 barrel = 0.136 tonnes or 159 litres or 35 Imperial gallons or 42 US gallons

1 tonne = 7.33 barrels or 1,185 litres or 256 Imperial gallons or 261 US gallons

1 tonne oil = 1.5 tonnes hard coal or 3.0 tonnes lignite or 12,000 kWh

1 Imperial gallon = 1.201 US gallons or 4.546 litres or 277.4 cubic inches

Measurements
For historical reasons, oil is traded in 'barrels'. The weight and volume equivalents (shown right) are all based on average-density 'Arabian light' crude oil.

The energy equivalents given for a tonne of oil are also somewhat imprecise: oil and coal of different qualities will have varying energy contents, a fact usually reflected in their price on world markets.

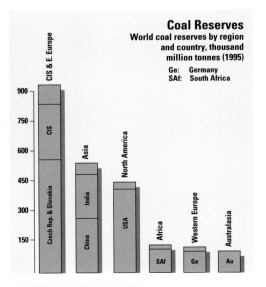

Coal Reserves
World coal reserves by region and country, thousand million tonnes (1995)

Ge: Germany
SAf: South Africa

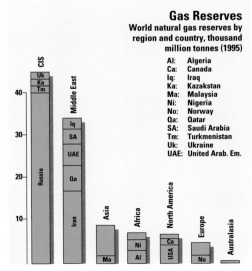

Gas Reserves
World natural gas reserves by region and country, thousand million tonnes (1995)

Al: Algeria
Ca: Canada
Iq: Iraq
Ka: Kazakstan
Ma: Malaysia
Ni: Nigeria
No: Norway
Qa: Qatar
SA: Saudi Arabia
Tm: Turkmenistan
Uk: Ukraine
UAE: United Arab. Em.

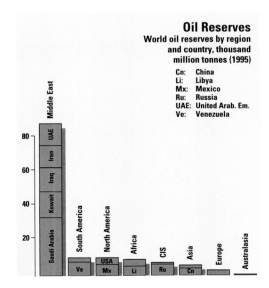

Oil Reserves
World oil reserves by region and country, thousand million tonnes (1995)

Cn: China
Li: Libya
Mx: Mexico
Ru: Russia
UAE: United Arab. Em.
Ve: Venezuela

Production

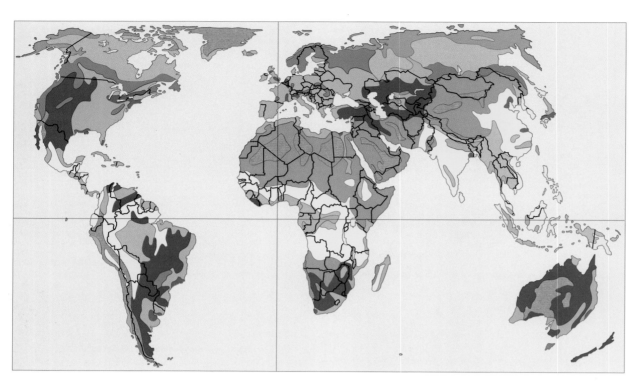

Agriculture

Predominant type of farming or land use.

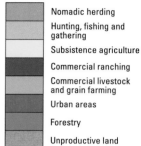

- Nomadic herding
- Hunting, fishing and gathering
- Subsistence agriculture
- Commercial ranching
- Commercial livestock and grain farming
- Urban areas
- Forestry
- Unproductive land

The development of agriculture has transformed human existence more than any other. The whole business of farming is constantly developing: due mainly to the new varieties of rice and wheat, world grain production has increased by over 70% since 1965. New machinery and modern agricultural techniques enable relatively few farmers to produce enough food for the world's 6 billion or so people.

Staple Crops

Wheat

China 18.9% | India 12.2% | USA 11.0% | France 5.7% | Russia 5.6% | Canada 4.6%

World total (1996): 584,874,000 tonnes

Maize

USA 36.4% | China 21.8% | Brazil 7.0%

World total (1996): 576,821,000 tonnes

Oats

Russia 29.7% | Canada 9.9% | USA 8.2% | Australia 6.7% | Germany 5.6%

World total (1996): 28,794,000 tonnes

Millet

India 33.2% | Nigeria 18.3% | China 16.1% | Niger 6.4%

World total (1996): 29,563,000 tonnes

Rice

China 34.0% | India 21.7% | Indonesia 9.0% | Bangladesh 4.8% | Vietnam 4.4% | Thailand 3.8%

World total (1996): 562,259,000 tonnes

Potatoes

China 16.0% | Russia 14.0% | Poland 8.7% | India 6.3% | Ukraine 5.2%

World total (1996): 294,834,000 tonnes

Soya

USA 47.1% | Brazil 20.4% | China 10.7% | Argentina 9.6%

World total (1996): 130,302,000 tonnes

Cassava

Nigeria 19.2% | Brazil 15.6% | Thailand 11.1% | Congo (Zaire) 10.7% | Indonesia 9.4% | Ghana 4.2%

World total (1996): 162,942,000 tonnes

Sugars

Sugar cane

Brazil 26.0% | India 22.2% | China 6.0% | Thailand 5.0% | Pakistan 4.0% | Mexico 3.6%

World total (1996): 1,192,555,000 tonnes

Sugar beet

France 11.5% | Ukraine 11.2% | Germany 9.8% | USA 9.6% | Russia 7.2% | Italy 5.0% | Poland 5.0% | Turkey 4.2%

World total (1996): 255,500,000 tonnes

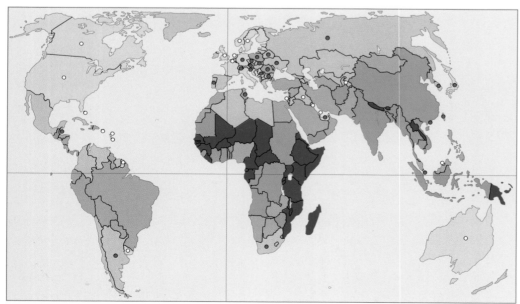

Balance of Employment

Percentage of total workforce employed in agriculture, including forestry and fishing (1990–92)

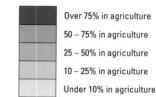

- Over 75% in agriculture
- 50 – 75% in agriculture
- 25 – 50% in agriculture
- 10 – 25% in agriculture
- Under 10% in agriculture

Employment in industry and services

- Over a third of total workforce employed in manufacturing

- Over two-thirds of total workforce employed in service industries (work in offices, shops, tourism, transport, construction and government)

Mineral Production

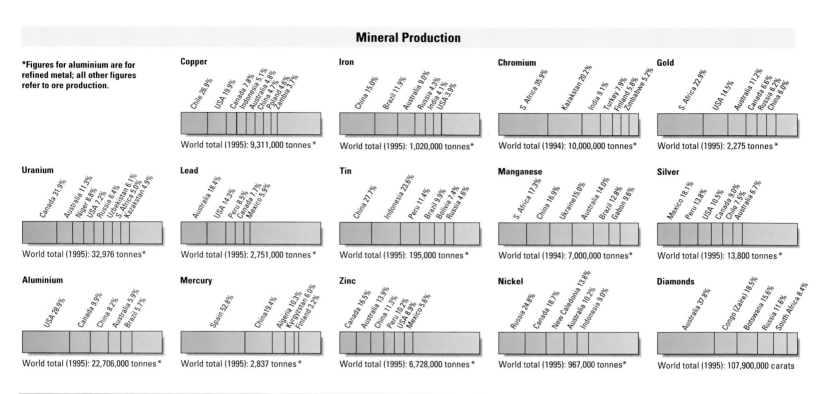

*Figures for aluminium are for refined metal; all other figures refer to ore production.

Copper
Chile 26.9% · USA 19.5% · Canada 7.8% · Indonesia 5.1% · Australia 4.8% · China 4.7% · Poland 4.6% · Zambia 3.7%
World total (1995): 9,311,000 tonnes *

Iron
China 15.0% · Brazil 11.9% · Australia 9.0% · Russia 4.3% · India 4.1% · USA 3.9%
World total (1995): 1,020,000 tonnes *

Chromium
S. Africa 35.9% · Kazakstan 20.2% · India 9.1% · Turkey 7.9% · Finland 5.8% · Zimbabwe 5.2%
World total (1994): 10,000,000 tonnes *

Gold
S. Africa 22.9% · USA 14.5% · Australia 11.2% · Canada 6.6% · Russia 6.2% · China 6.0%
World total (1995): 2,275 tonnes *

Uranium
Canada 31.9% · Australia 11.3% · Niger 8.8% · USA 7.2% · Russia 6.4% · Uzbekistan 6.1% · S. Africa 5.0% · Kazakstan 4.9%
World total (1995): 32,976 tonnes *

Lead
Australia 18.4% · USA 14.3% · Peru 8.5% · Canada 7.7% · Mexico 5.9%
World total (1995): 2,751,000 tonnes *

Tin
China 27.7% · Indonesia 23.6% · Peru 11.4% · Brazil 9.9% · Bolivia 7.4% · Russia 4.6%
World total (1995): 195,000 tonnes *

Manganese
S. Africa 17.3% · China 16.9% · Ukraine 15.0% · Australia 14.0% · Brazil 12.8% · Gabon 9.6%
World total (1994): 7,000,000 tonnes *

Silver
Mexico 18.1% · Peru 13.8% · USA 10.5% · Canada 9.0% · Chile 7.5% · Australia 6.7%
World total (1995): 13,800 tonnes *

Aluminium
USA 28.9% · Canada 9.9% · China 8.2% · Australia 5.9% · Brazil 5.7%
World total (1995): 22,706,000 tonnes *

Mercury
Spain 52.8% · China 19.4% · Algeria 10.3% · Kyrgyzstan 6.0% · Finland 3.2%
World total (1995): 2,837 tonnes *

Zinc
Canada 16.5% · Australia 13.9% · China 11.3% · Peru 10.2% · USA 8.9% · Mexico 5.6%
World total (1995): 6,728,000 tonnes *

Nickel
Russia 24.8% · Canada 18.7% · New Caledonia 13.8% · Australia 10.2% · Indonesia 9.0%
World total (1995): 967,000 tonnes *

Diamonds
Australia 37.8% · Congo (Zaire) 18.5% · Botswana 15.6% · Russia 11.6% · South Africa 8.4%
World total (1995): 107,900,000 carats

Mineral Distribution

The map shows the richest sources of the most important minerals. Major mineral locations are named.

Light metals
- ● Bauxite

Base metals
- ▢ Copper
- ▲ Lead
- ▽ Mercury
- ▽ Tin
- ◆ Zinc

Iron and ferro-alloys
- ● Iron
- ◗ Chrome
- ▲ Manganese
- ▢ Nickel

Precious metals
- ▽ Gold
- ◠ Silver

Precious stones
- ◆ Diamonds

The map does not show undersea deposits, most of which are considered inaccessible.

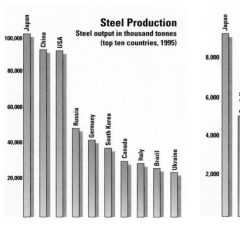

Steel Production
Steel output in thousand tonnes (top ten countries, 1995)

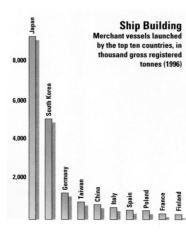

Ship Building
Merchant vessels launched by the top ten countries, in thousand gross registered tonnes (1996)

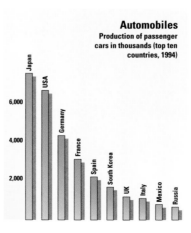

Automobiles
Production of passenger cars in thousands (top ten countries, 1994)

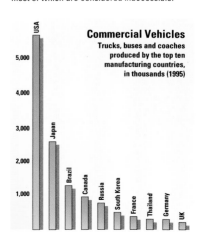

Commercial Vehicles
Trucks, buses and coaches produced by the top ten manufacturing countries, in thousands (1995)

Trade

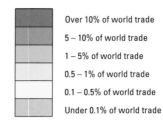

Share of World Trade

Percentage share of total world exports by value (1996)

- Over 10% of world trade
- 5 – 10% of world trade
- 1 – 5% of world trade
- 0.5 – 1% of world trade
- 0.1 – 0.5% of world trade
- Under 0.1% of world trade

International trade is dominated by a handful of powerful maritime nations. The members of 'G8', the inner circle of OECD (see page 19), and the top seven countries listed in the diagram below, account for more than half the total. The majority of nations – including all but four in Africa – contribute less than one quarter of 1% to the worldwide total of exports; the EU countries account for 40%, the Pacific Rim nations over 35%.

The Main Trading Nations

The imports and exports of the top ten trading nations as a percentage of world trade (1994). Each country's trade in manufactured goods is shown in dark blue.

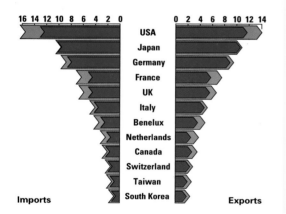

16 14 12 10 8 6 4 2 0 | **0 2 4 6 8 10 12 14**

- USA
- Japan
- Germany
- France
- UK
- Italy
- Benelux
- Netherlands
- Canada
- Switzerland
- Taiwan
- South Korea

Imports | Exports

Patterns of Trade

Thriving international trade is the outward sign of a healthy world economy, the obvious indicator that some countries have goods to sell and others the means to buy them. Global exports expanded to an estimated US $3.92 trillion in 1994, an increase due partly to economic recovery in industrial nations but also to export-led growth strategies in many developing nations and lowered regional trade barriers. International trade remains dominated, however, by the rich, industrialized countries of the Organization for Economic Development: between them, OECD members account for almost 75% of world imports and exports in most years. However, continued rapid economic growth in some developing countries is altering global trade patterns. The 'tiger economies' of South-east Asia are particularly vibrant, averaging more than 8% growth between 1992 and 1994. The size of the largest trading economies means that imports and exports usually represent only a small percentage of their total wealth. In export-concious Japan, for example, trade in goods and services amounts to less than 18% of GDP. In poorer countries, trade – often in a single commodity – may amount to 50% of GDP.

Traded Products

Top ten manufactures traded, by value in billions of US $ (latest available year)

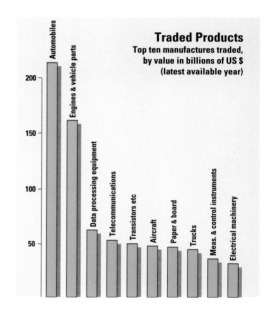

- Automobiles
- Engines & vehicle parts
- Data processing equipment
- Telecommunications
- Transistors etc
- Aircraft
- Paper & board
- Trucks
- Meas. & control instruments
- Electrical machinery

Balance of Trade

Value of exports in proportion to the value of imports (1995)

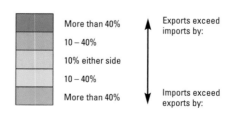

Exports exceed imports by:
- More than 40%
- 10 – 40%
- 10% either side
- 10 – 40%
- More than 40%

Imports exceed exports by:

The total world trade balance should amount to zero, since exports must equal imports on a global scale. In practice, at least $100 billion in exports go unrecorded, leaving the world with an apparent deficit and many countries in a better position than public accounting reveals. However, a favourable trade balance is not necessarily a sign of prosperity: many poorer countries must maintain a high surplus in order to service debts, and do so by restricting imports below the levels needed to sustain successful economies.

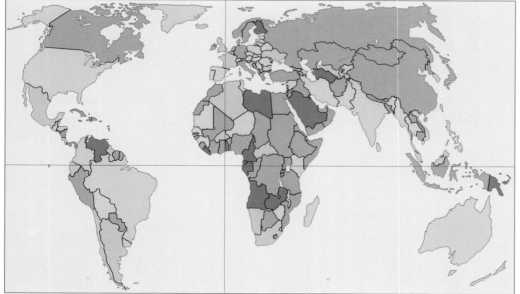

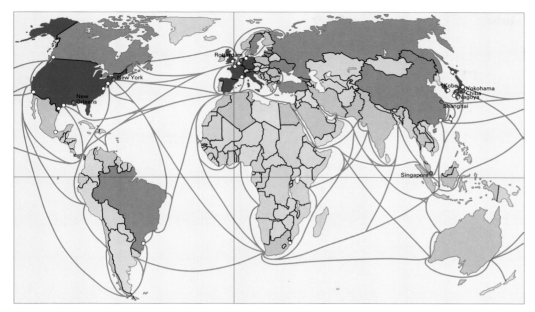

Seaborne Freight

Freight unloaded in millions of tonnes (latest available year)

- Over 100
- 50 – 100
- 10 – 50
- 5 – 10
- Under 5
- Landlocked countries

Major seaports

- ● Over 100 million tonnes per year
- ○ 50–100 million tonnes per year
- — Major shipping routes

Cargoes

Type of seaborne freight

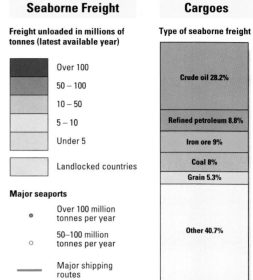

- Crude oil 28.2%
- Refined petroleum 8.8%
- Iron ore 9%
- Coal 8%
- Grain 5.3%
- Other 40.7%

Merchant Fleets

Merchant fleets in thousand gross tonnage (1996). A large number of vessels are registered in Liberia and Panama but they are not part of the national fleet.

Hong Kong, Denmark, Taiwan, Italy, Turkey, India, Germany, South Korea, Philippines, USA, Russia, China, Japan, Singapore, Norway, Cyprus, Greece, Bahamas, Liberia, Panama

20,000 · 40,000 · 60,000 · 80,000 · 100,000

The Great Ports

Total Cargo Traffic (1995) '000 tonnes

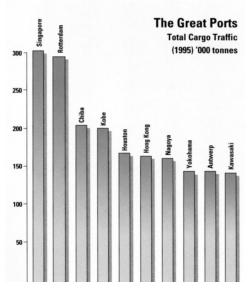

Singapore, Rotterdam, Chiba, Kobe, Houston, Hong Kong, Nagoya, Yokohama, Antwerp, Kawasaki

World Shipping

World merchant fleet by type of vessel and deadweight tonnage (latest available year)

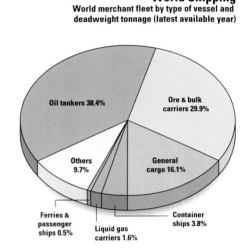

- Oil tankers 38.4%
- Ore & bulk carriers 29.9%
- General cargo 16.1%
- Others 9.7%
- Container ships 3.8%
- Liquid gas carriers 1.6%
- Ferries & passenger ships 0.5%

Dependence on Trade

Value of exports as a percentage of Gross Domestic Product (1997)

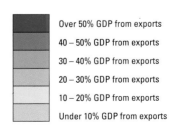

- Over 50% GDP from exports
- 40 – 50% GDP from exports
- 30 – 40% GDP from exports
- 20 – 30% GDP from exports
- 10 – 20% GDP from exports
- Under 10% GDP from exports

- ○ Most dependent on industrial exports (over 75% of total exports)
- ● Most dependent on fuel exports (over 75% of total exports)
- ● Most dependent on mineral and metal exports (over 75% of total exports)

Travel and Tourism

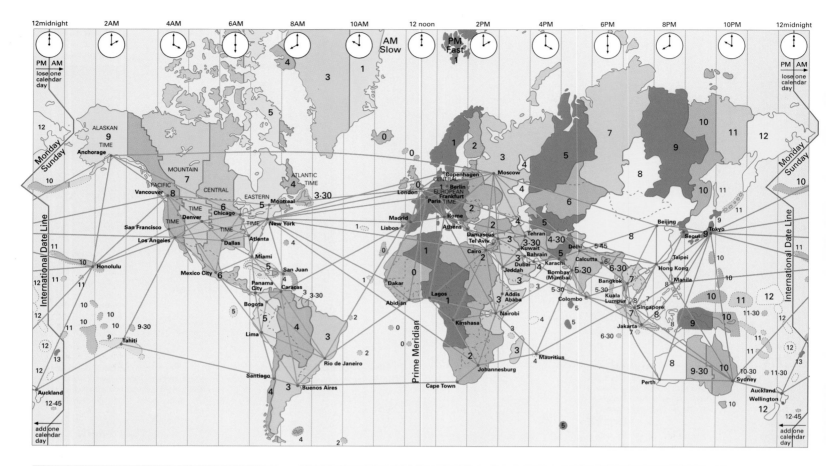

Time Zones

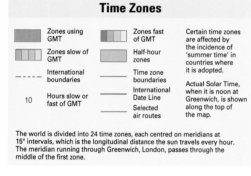

Zones using GMT	Zones fast of GMT
Zones slow of GMT	Half-hour zones
- - - International boundaries	—— Time zone boundaries
10 Hours slow or fast of GMT	—— International Date Line
	—— Selected air routes

Certain time zones are affected by the incidence of 'summer time' in countries where it is adopted.

Actual Solar Time, when it is noon at Greenwich, is shown along the top of the map.

The world is divided into 24 time zones, each centred on meridians at 15° intervals, which is the longitudinal distance the sun travels every hour. The meridian running through Greenwich, London, passes through the middle of the first zone.

Rail and Road: The Leading Nations

	Total rail network ('000 km) (1995)	Passenger km per head per year	Total road network ('000 km)	Vehicle km per head per year	Number of vehicles per km of roads
1.	USA 235.7	Japan 2,017	USA 6,277.9	USA..................12,505	Hong Kong 284
2.	Russia 87.4	Belarus...............1,880	India 2,962.5	Luxembourg 7,989	Taiwan 211
3.	India 62.7	Russia 1,826	Brazil 1,824.4	Kuwait 7,251	Singapore 152
4.	China 54.6	Switzerland 1,769	Japan 1,130.9	France 7,142	Kuwait 140
5.	Germany..............41.7	Ukraine 1,456	China 1,041.1	Sweden..............6,991	Brunei..................96
6.	Australia...............35.8	Austria 1,168	Russia 884.0	Germany..............6,806	Italy 91
7.	Argentina.............34.2	France 1,011	Canada 849.4	Denmark..............6,764	Israel 87
8.	France...................31.9	Netherlands 994	France 811.6	Austria 6,518	Thailand 73
9.	Mexico...................26.5	Latvia....................918	Australia 810.3	Netherlands 5,984	Ukraine 73
10.	South Africa..........26.3	Denmark 884	Germany 636.3	UK 5,738	UK 67
11.	Poland...................24.9	Slovak Rep. 862	Romania 461.9	Canada 5,493	Netherlands 66
12.	Ukraine 22.6	Romania 851	Turkey 388.1	Italy.....................4,852	Germany 62

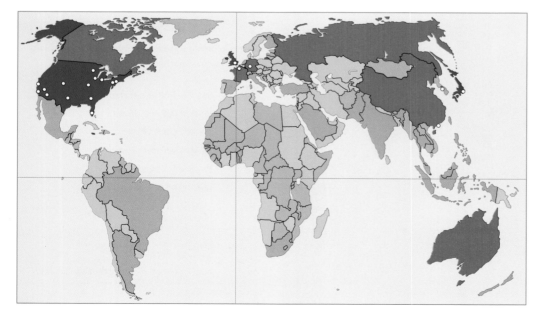

Air Travel

Passenger kilometres (the number of passengers – international and domestic – multiplied by the distance flown by each passenger from the airport of origin) (1996)

	Over 100,000 million
	50,000 – 100,000 million
	10,000 – 50,000 million
	1,000 – 10,000 million
	500 – 1,000 million
	Under 500 million
○	Major airports (handling over 25 million passengers in 1995)

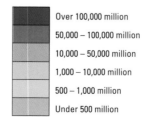

World's busiest airports (total passengers)	World's busiest airports (international passengers)
1. Chicago (O'Hare)	1. London (Heathrow)
2. Atlanta (Hatsfield)	2. London (Gatwick)
3. Dallas (Dallas/Ft Worth)	3. Frankfurt (International)
4. Los Angeles (Intern'l)	4. New York (Kennedy)
5. London (Heathrow)	5. Paris (De Gaulle)

Destinations

■	Cultural and historical centres
■	Coastal resorts
□	Ski resorts
■	Centres of entertainment
■	Places of pilgrimage
■	Places of great natural beauty
—	Popular holiday cruise routes

Visitors to the USA

Overseas travellers to the USA, thousands (1997 estimates)

1.	Canada	13,900
2.	Mexico	12,370
3.	Japan	4,640
4.	UK	3,350
5.	Germany	1,990
6.	France	1,030
7.	Taiwan	885
8.	Venezuela	860
9.	South Korea	800
10.	Brazil	785

In 1996, the USA earned the most from tourism, with receipts of more than US $75 billion.

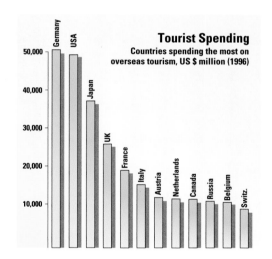

Tourist Spending
Countries spending the most on overseas tourism, US $ million (1996)

Importance of Tourism

		Arrivals from abroad (1996)	% of world total (1996)
1.	France	66,800,000	10.2%
2.	USA	49,038,000	7.5%
3.	Spain	43,403,000	6.6%
4.	Italy	34,087,000	5.2%
5.	UK	25,960,000	3.9%
6.	China	23,770,000	3.6%
7.	Poland	19,514,000	3.0%
8.	Mexico	18,667,000	2.9%
9.	Canada	17,610,000	2.7%
10.	Czech Republic	17,400,000	2.7%
11.	Hungary	17,248,000	2.6%
12.	Austria	16,642,000	2.5%

In 1996, there was a 4.6% rise, to 593 million, in the total number of people travelling abroad. Small economies in attractive areas are often completely dominated by tourism: in some West Indian islands, for example, tourist spending provides over 90% of total income.

Tourist Earning
Countries receiving the most from overseas tourism, US $ million (1996)

Tourism

Tourism receipts as a percentage of Gross National Product (1994)

■	Over 10% of GNP from tourism
■	5 – 10% of GNP from tourism
■	2.5 – 5% of GNP from tourism
■	1 – 2.5% of GNP from tourism
■	0.5 – 1% of GNP from tourism
□	Under 0.5% of GNP from tourism

Countries spending the most on promoting tourism, millions of US $ (1996)

Australia	88
Spain	79
UK	79
France	73
Singapore	54

Fastest growing tourist destinations, % change in receipts (1994–5)

South Korea	49%
Czech Republic	27%
India	21%
Russia	19%
Philippines	18%

The World In Focus: Index

WORLD MAPS

SETTLEMENTS

◾ PARIS   ◾ Berne   ◉ Livorno   ◎ Brugge   ◎ Algeciras   ○ Frejus   ○ Oberammergau   ○ Thira

Settlement symbols and type styles vary according to the scale of each map and indicate the importance
of towns on the map rather than specific population figures

∴   Ruins or Archæological Sites   Wells in Desert

ADMINISTRATION

——— International Boundaries

– – – – International Boundaries
(Undefined or Disputed)

·········· Internal Boundaries

     National Parks

Country Names
NICARAGUA

Administrative
Area Names

KENT

CALABRIA

International boundaries show the *de facto* situation where there are rival claims to territory

COMMUNICATIONS

——— Principal Roads

——— Other Roads

⊣---⊢ Road Tunnels

⤬ Passes

⊕   Airfields

——— Principal Railways

– – – Railways
Under Construction

——— Other Railways

⊣---⊢ Railway Tunnels

·········· Principal Canals

PHYSICAL FEATURES

∿ Perennial Streams

– – – Intermittent Streams

⬭ Perennial Lakes

⬭ Intermittent Lakes

Swamps and Marshes

Permanent Ice
and Glaciers

▲ 8848   Elevations in metres

▼ 8500   Sea Depths in metres

1134   Height of Lake Surface
Above Sea Level in metres

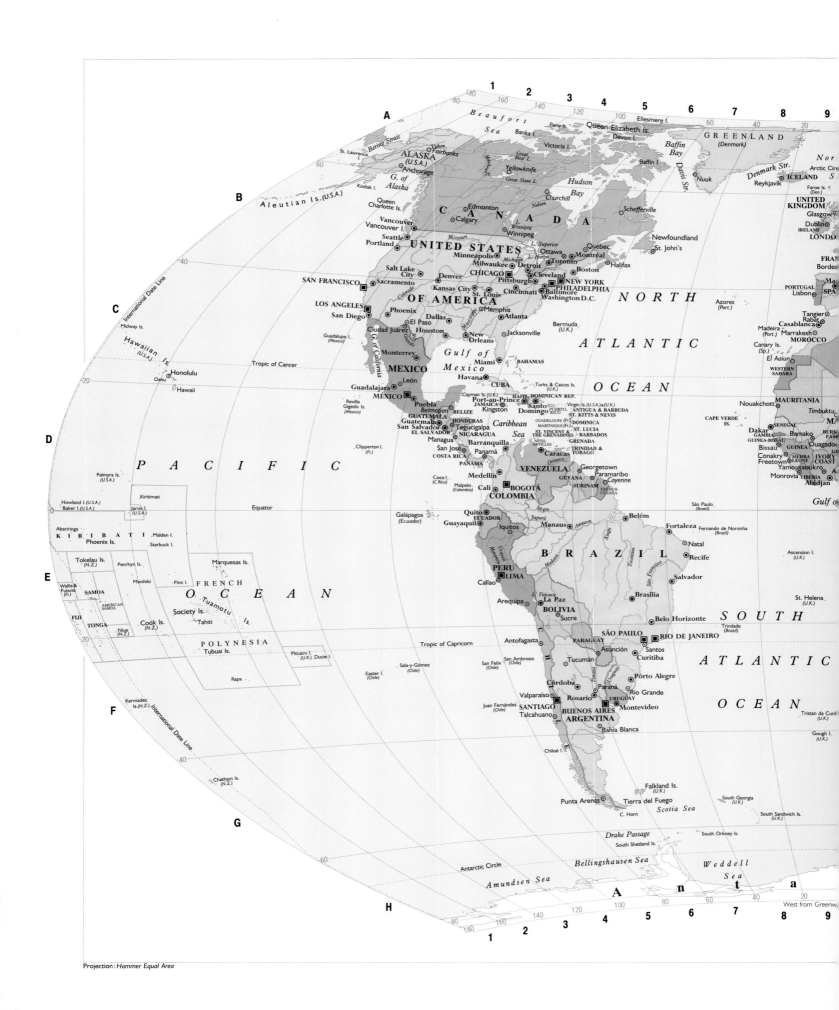

Projection: *Hammer Equal Area*

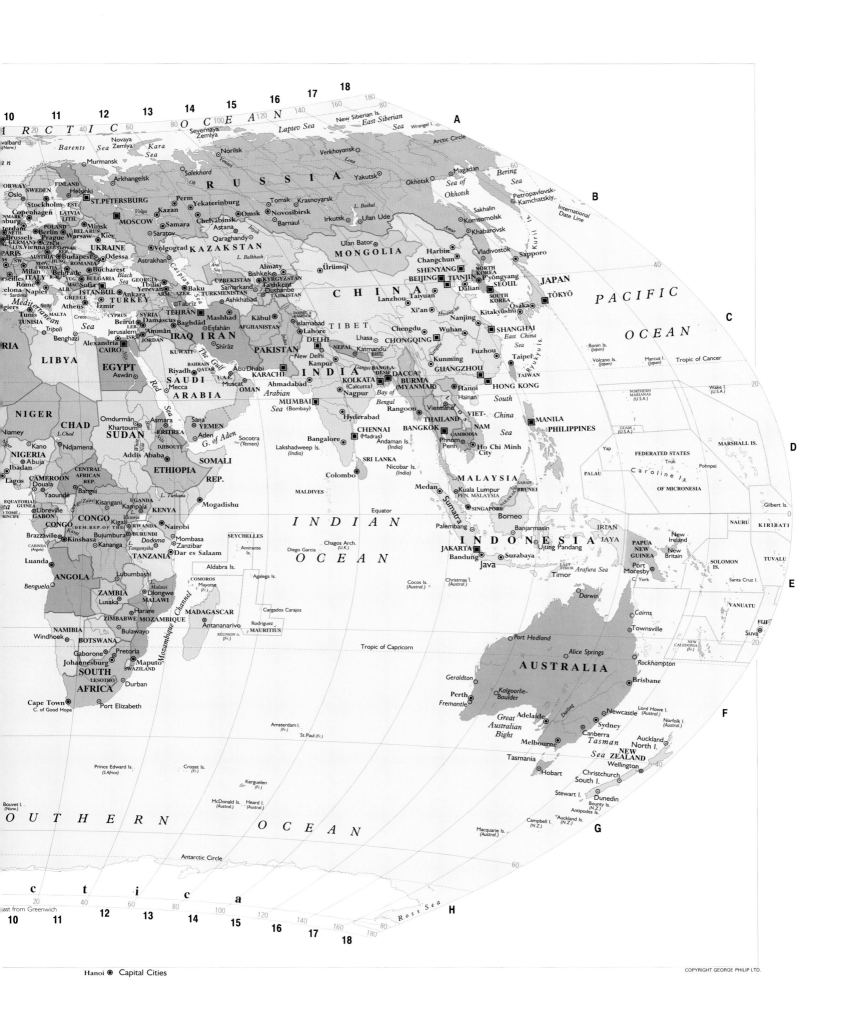

Hanoi ◉ Capital Cities

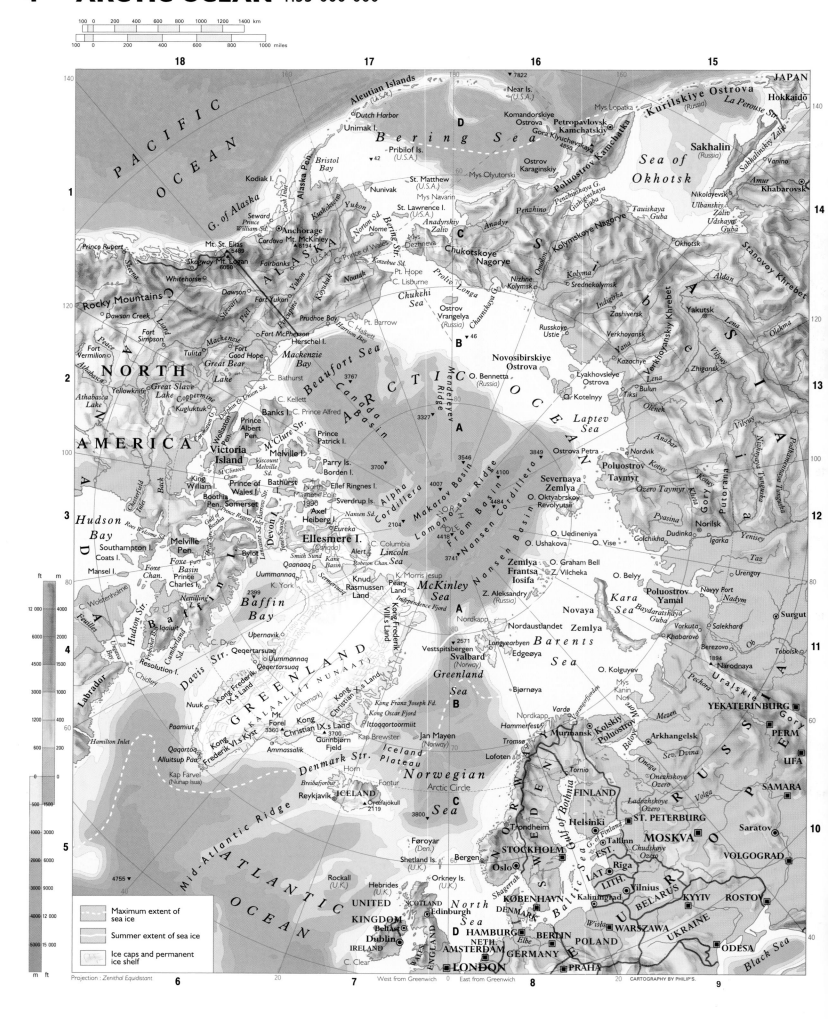

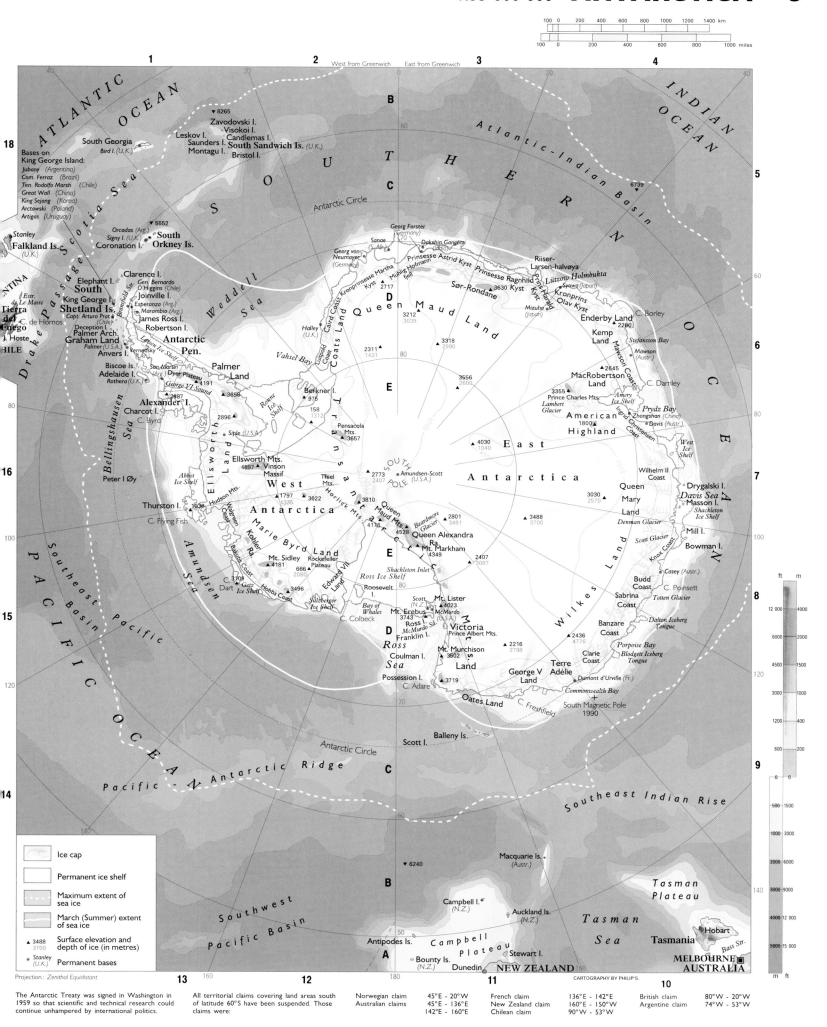

Ice cap

Permanent ice shelf

Maximum extent of
sea ice

March (Summer) extent
of sea ice

▲3488
3700 Surface elevation and
depth of ice (in metres)

• Stanley
(U.K.) Permanent bases

Projection: Zenithal Equidistant

CARTOGRAPHY BY PHILIP'S.

The Antarctic Treaty was signed in Washington in
1959 so that scientific and technical research could
continue unhampered by international politics.

All territorial claims covering land areas south
of latitude 60°S have been suspended. Those
claims were:

Norwegian claim	45°E – 20°W
Australian claims	45°E – 136°E
	142°E – 160°E

French claim	136°E – 142°E
New Zealand claim	160°E – 150°W
Chilean claim	90°W – 53°W

| British claim | 80°W – 20°W |
| Argentine claim | 74°W – 53°W |

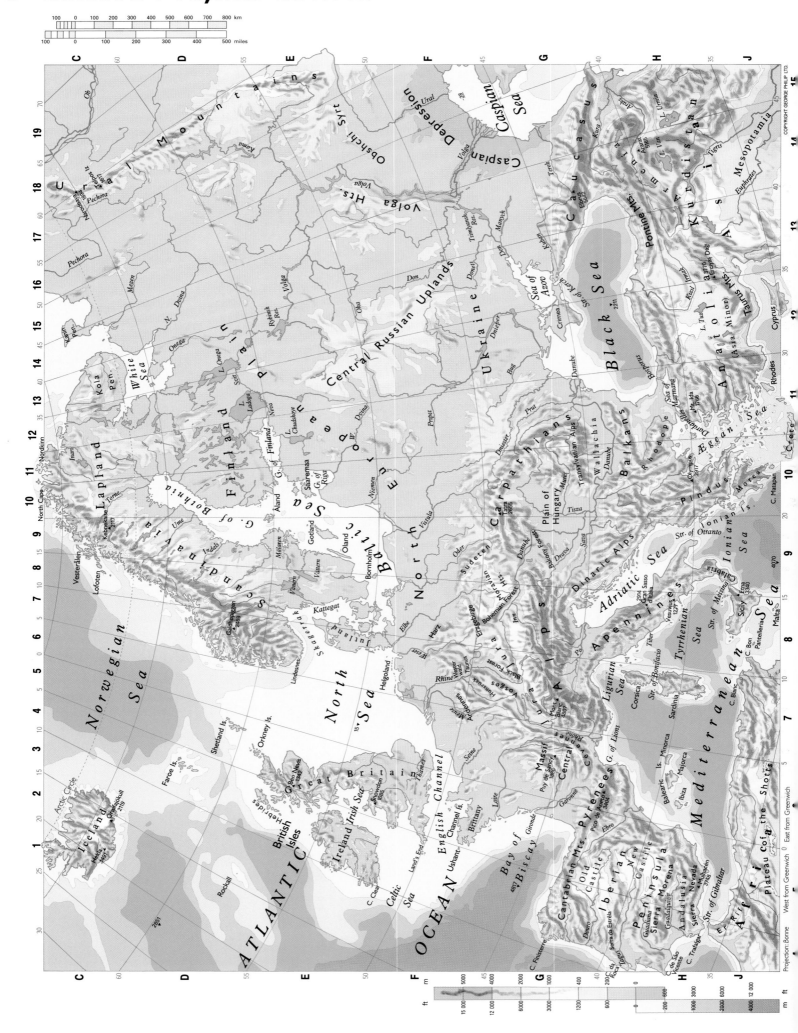

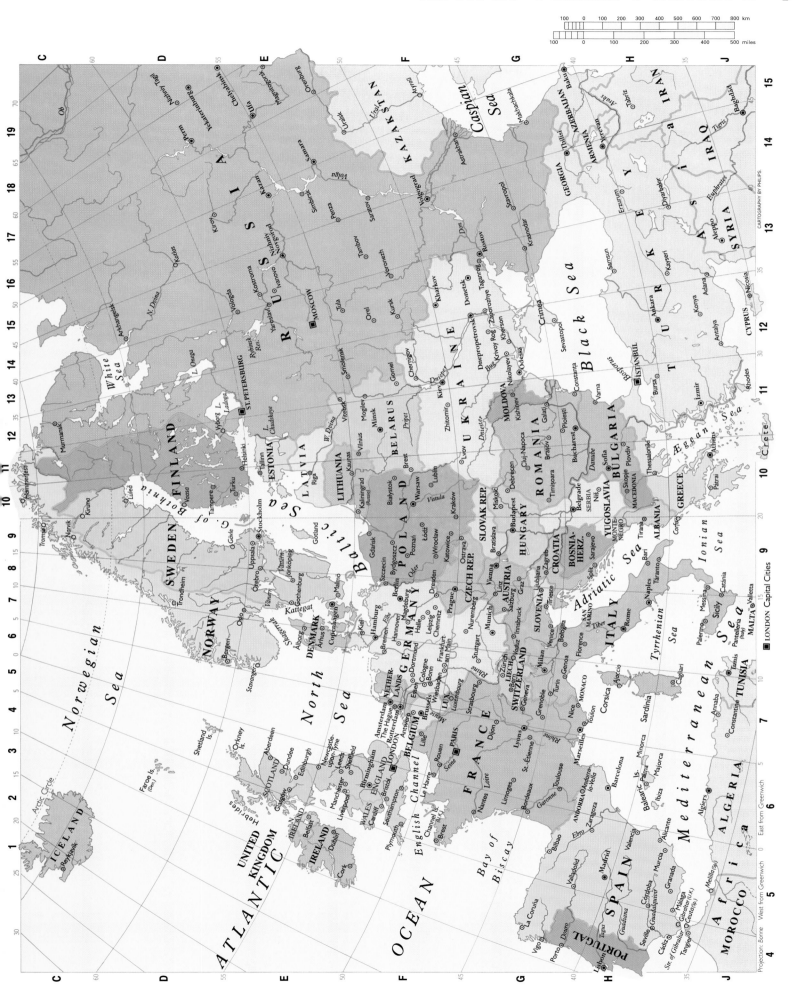

SCANDINAVIA 1:5 000 000

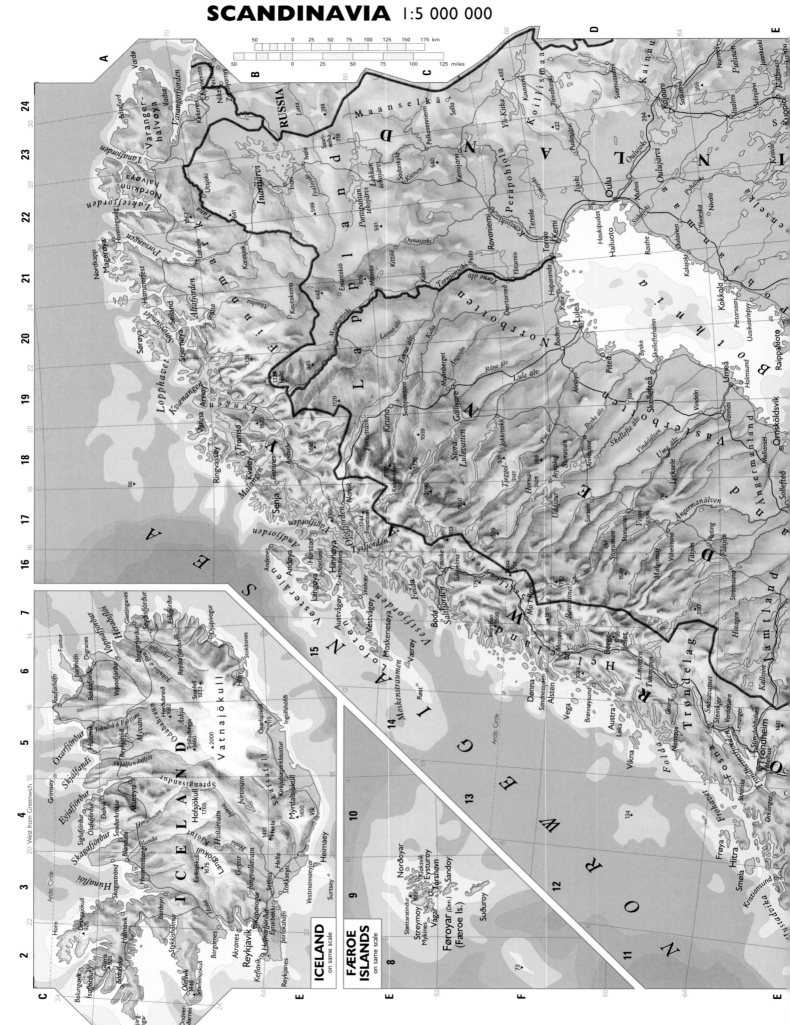

ICELAND
on same scale

FÆROE
ISLANDS
on same scale

East from Greenwich

Projection: Conical with two standard parallels

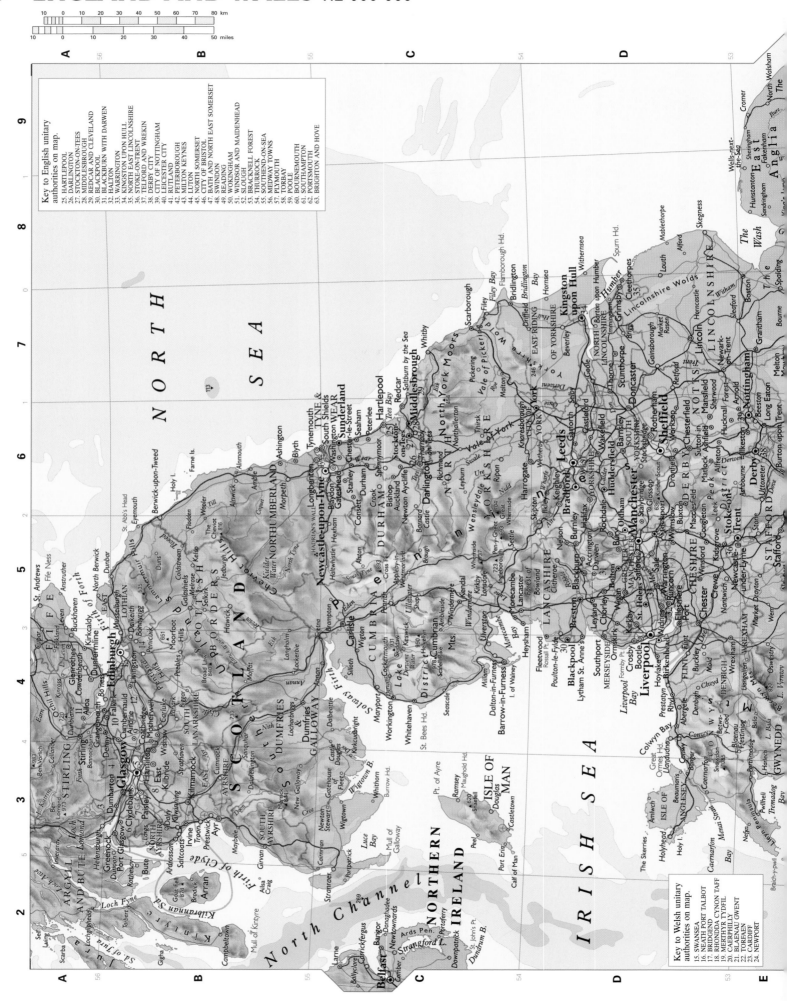

Key to English unitary authorities on map.

25. HARTLEPOOL
26. DARLINGTON
27. STOCKTON-ON-TEES
28. MIDDLESBROUGH
29. REDCAR AND CLEVELAND
30. BLACKPOOL
31. BLACKBURN WITH DARWEN
32. HALTON
33. WARRINGTON
34. KINGSTON UPON HULL
35. NORTH EAST LINCOLNSHIRE
36. STOKE-ON-TRENT
37. TELFORD AND WREKIN
38. DERBY CITY
39. CITY OF NOTTINGHAM
40. LEICESTER CITY
41. RUTLAND
42. PETERBOROUGH
43. MILTON KEYNES
44. LUTON
45. NORTH SOMERSET
46. CITY OF BRISTOL
47. BATH AND NORTH EAST SOMERSET
48. SWINDON
49. READING
50. WOKINGHAM
51. WINDSOR AND MAIDENHEAD
52. SLOUGH
53. BRACKNELL FOREST
54. SOUTHEND-ON-SEA
55. THURROCK
56. MEDWAY TOWNS
57. PLYMOUTH
58. TORBAY
59. POOLE
60. BOURNEMOUTH
61. SOUTHAMPTON
62. PORTSMOUTH
63. BRIGHTON AND HOVE

Key to Welsh unitary authorities on map.

15. SWANSEA
16. NEATH PORT TALBOT
17. BRIDGEND
18. RHONDDA CYNON TAFF
19. MERTHYR TYDFIL
20. BLAENAU GWENT
21. CAERPHILLY
22. TORFAEN
23. CARDIFF
24. NEWPORT

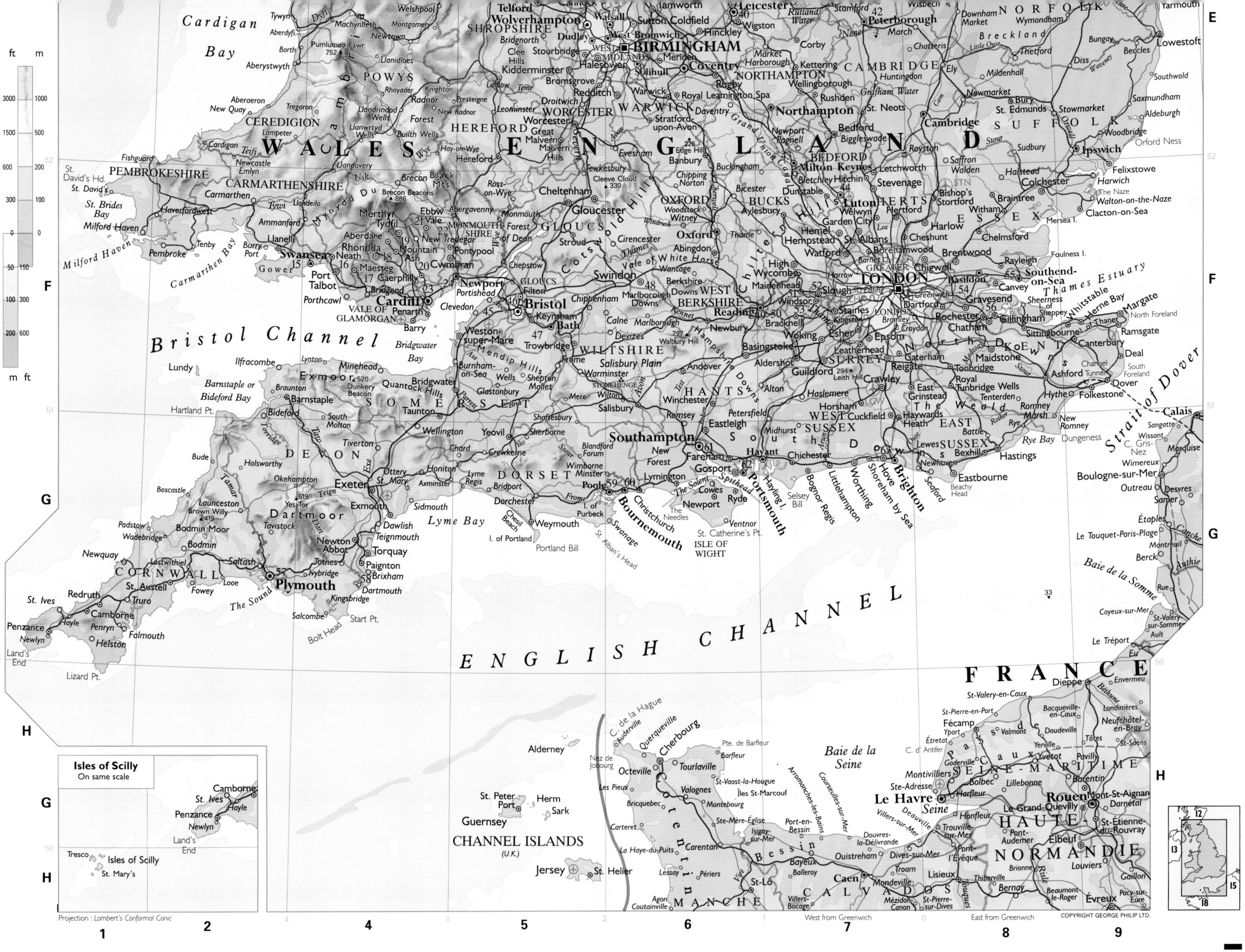

Projection : Lambert's Conformal Conic

ENGLAND

WALES

FRANCE

NORMANDIE

SEINE-MARITIME

HAUTE-NORMANDIE

CALVADOS

ENGLISH CHANNEL

Bristol Channel

Cardigan Bay

Strait of Dover

Baie de la Seine

LONDON

Birmingham

Cardiff

Bristol

Plymouth

Exeter

Portsmouth

Southampton

Bournemouth

Brighton

Hove

Le Havre

Rouen

Cherbourg

Caen

Calais

Boulogne-sur-Mer

Dieppe

Évreux

East from Greenwich

West from Greenwich

Isles of Scilly
On same scale

Isles of Scilly

St. Mary's

Tresco

ft   m
3000 1000
1500   500
600   200
300   100
0   0
       -50-150
       -100-300
       -200-600
m ft

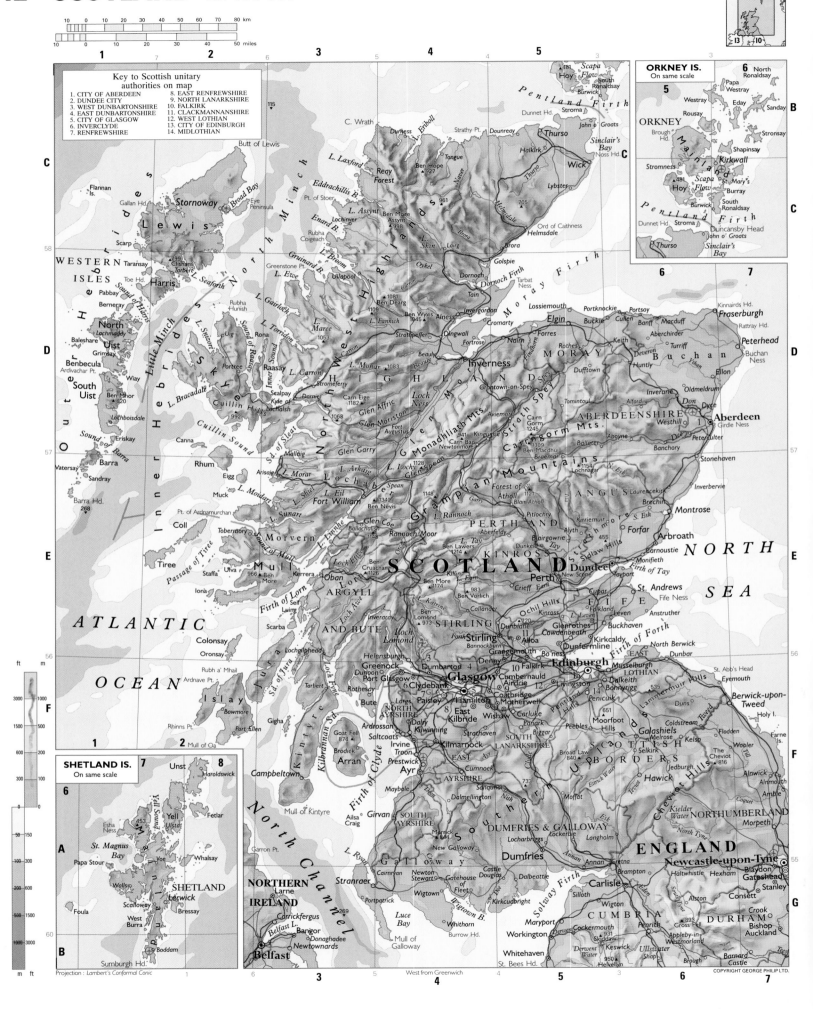

Key to Scottish unitary
authorities on map
1. CITY OF ABERDEEN   8. EAST RENFREWSHIRE
2. DUNDEE CITY   9. NORTH LANARKSHIRE
3. WEST DUNBARTONSHIRE   10. FALKIRK
4. EAST DUNBARTONSHIRE   11. CLACKMANNANSHIRE
5. CITY OF GLASGOW   12. WEST LOTHIAN
6. INVERCLYDE   13. CITY OF EDINBURGH
7. RENFREWSHIRE   14. MIDLOTHIAN

ORKNEY IS.
On same scale

SHETLAND IS.
On same scale

Projection : Lambert's Conformal Conic

West from Greenwich

COPYRIGHT GEORGE PHILIP LTD.

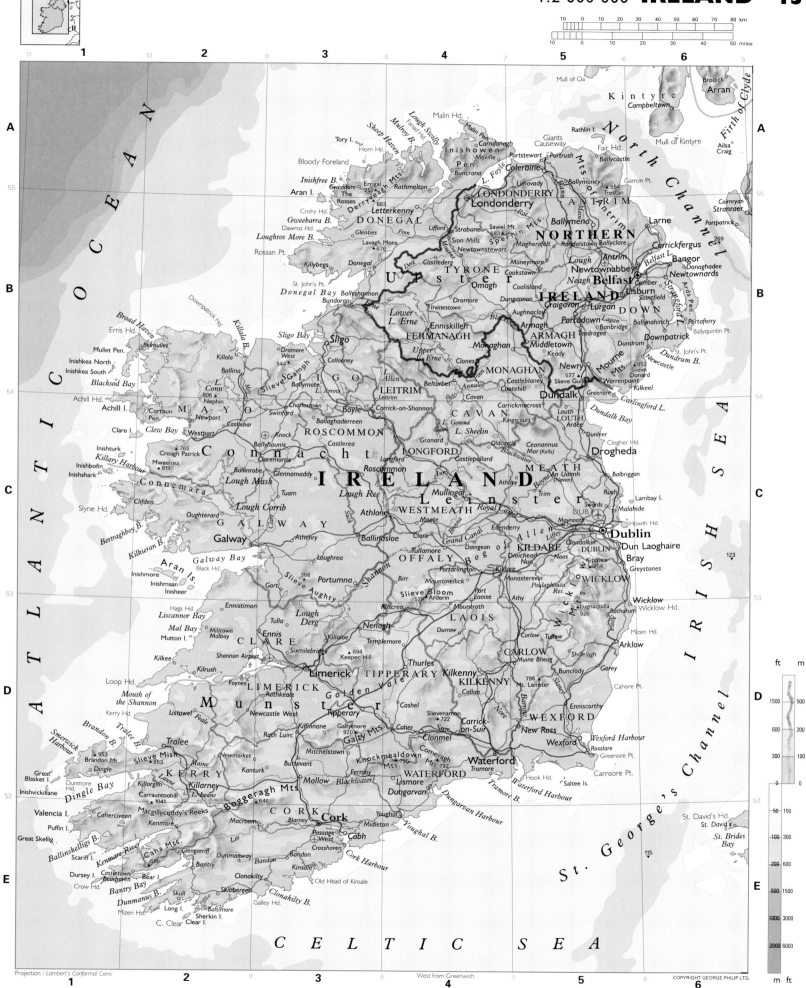

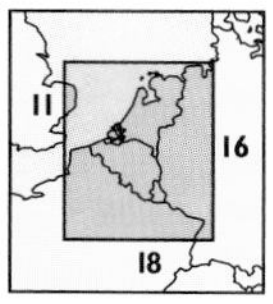

10 0 10 20 30 40 50 60 70 80 90 km
10 0 10 20 30 40 50 60 miles

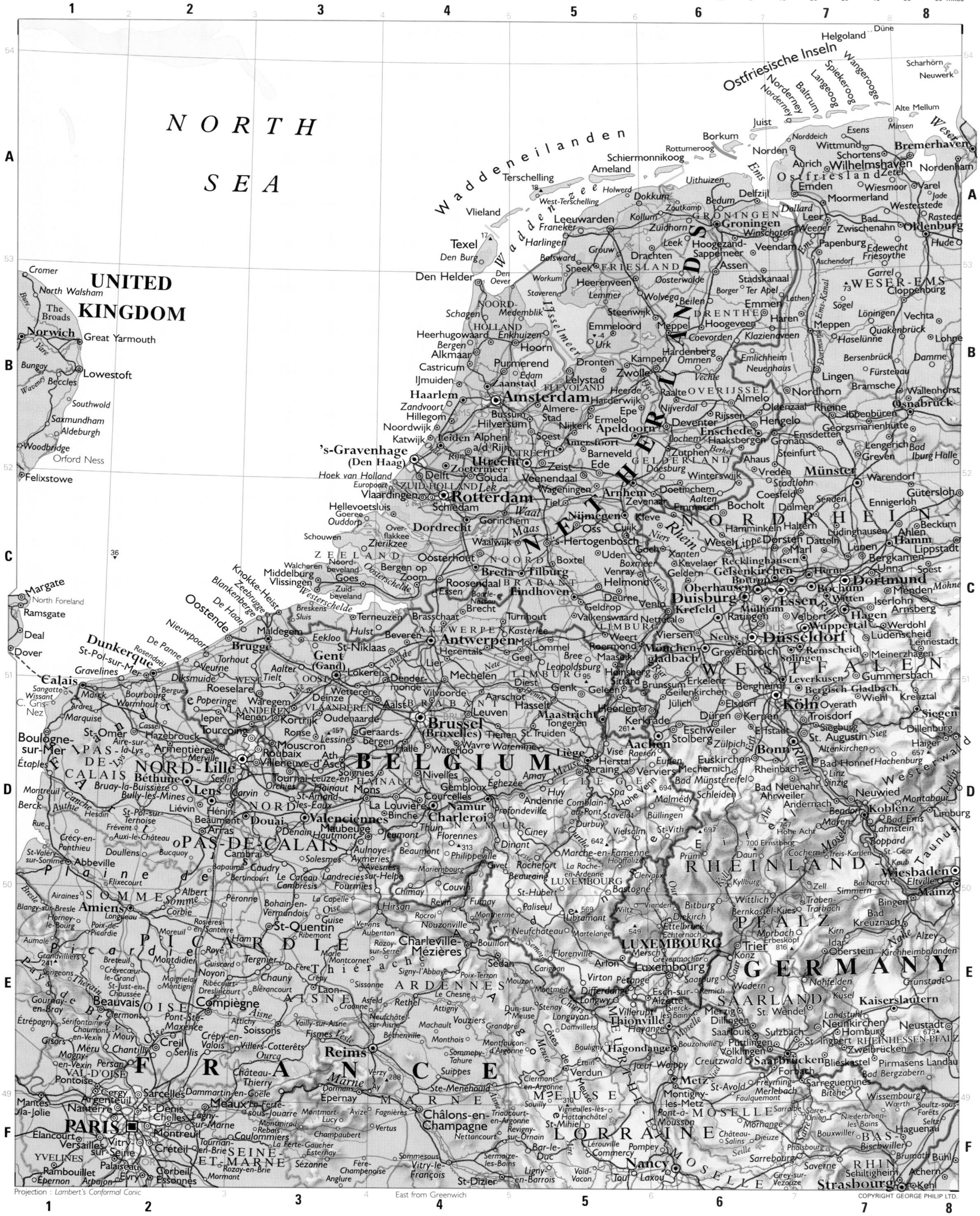

NORTH SEA

UNITED KINGDOM

Cromer
North Walsham
The Broads
Norwich · Great Yarmouth
Bungay · Lowestoft
Beccles
Southwold
Saxmundham · Aldeburgh
Woodbridge
Orford Ness
Felixstowe
Margate
North Foreland
Ramsgate
Deal
Dover
Calais
Sangatte
Wissant
C. Gris Nez
Ardres
Marquise
Boulogne-sur-Mer
Étaples
Montreuil
Berck
Rue

NETHERLANDS

Helgoland · Düne
Scharhörn · Neuwerk
Ostfriesische Inseln · Wangerooge
Norderney · Spiekeroog · Langeoog · Baltrum
Juist · Norderney
Borkum
Waddeneilanden
Schiermonnikoog
Ameland
Terschelling
West-Terschelling
Vlieland
Texel
Den Burg
Den Helder
Leeuwarden · Groningen
Harlingen · Franeker
Bolsward · Sneek · Drachten · Assen
Workum · Heerenveen
Schagen
NOORD-HOLLAND
Heerhugowaard · Hoorn
Bergen · Enkhuizen
Alkmaar
Castricum · Purmerend · Edam
IJmuiden · Zaanstad
Haarlem
Zandvoort
Hillegom
Noordwijk · Bussum · Hilversum
Katwijk · Leiden Alphen a/d Rijn · Soest
's-Gravenhage (Den Haag) · Zeist
Delft · Zoetermeer · Gouda · UTRECHT
Hoek van Holland · Utrecht
Vlaardingen · Rotterdam · Wageningen
Schiedam · Gorinchem · Arnhem
Hellevoetsluis · Dordrecht · Nijmegen
ZEELAND · Breda · Tilburg · Eindhoven
Middelburg · Vlissingen · Bergen op Zoom
Knokke-Heist · Roosendaal
Blankenberge
Oostende · De Haan

GERMANY

Bremerhaven · Nordenham
Wilhelmshaven
Wittmund · Oldenburg
Aurich · Emden
Groningen · WESER-EMS
Cloppenburg
Papenburg · Friesoythe
Lingen · Münster
Nordhorn
Osnabrück
Bocholt · Gütersloh
Wesel · Dortmund
Oberhausen · Bochum · Essen
Duisburg · Düsseldorf
Krefeld · Wuppertal
Mönchengladbach · Köln
Aachen · Bonn
Koblenz
RHEINLAND-PFALZ
Wiesbaden · Mainz
Trier
Saarbrücken
SAARLAND
Kaiserslautern

BELGIUM

Brugge · Gent (Gand) · Antwerpen
Mechelen · Brussel (Bruxelles)
Leuven · Hasselt · Maastricht
Tournai · Mons · Charleroi · Namur · Liège
Nivelles · Verviers
La Louvière · Dinant
LUXEMBOURG · Bastogne
Arlon · LUXEMBOURG
Luxembourg · Esch-sur-Alzette
Differdange · Thionville

FRANCE

Dunkerque
St-Omer
Lille · NORD
Béthune · Lens · Douai
Valenciennes · Maubeuge
Arras · Cambrai
PAS-DE-CALAIS
Abbeville
Amiens · SOMME
PICARDIE
St-Quentin
Beauvais · OISE
Compiègne
Laon · AISNE
Soissons
ARDENNES
Charleville-Mézières
Sedan
Reims · MARNE
Épernay
Châlons-en-Champagne
PARIS
Versailles · YVELINES
Meaux · SEINE-ET-MARNE
LORRAINE
Verdun · MEUSE
Metz · MOSELLE
Nancy · Toul
Strasbourg · BAS-RHIN

Projection: Lambert's Conformal Conic
East from Greenwich
COPYRIGHT GEORGE PHILIP LTD.

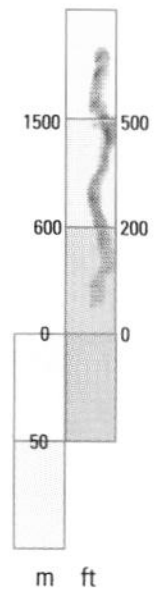

Underlined towns give their name to the administrative area in which they stand.

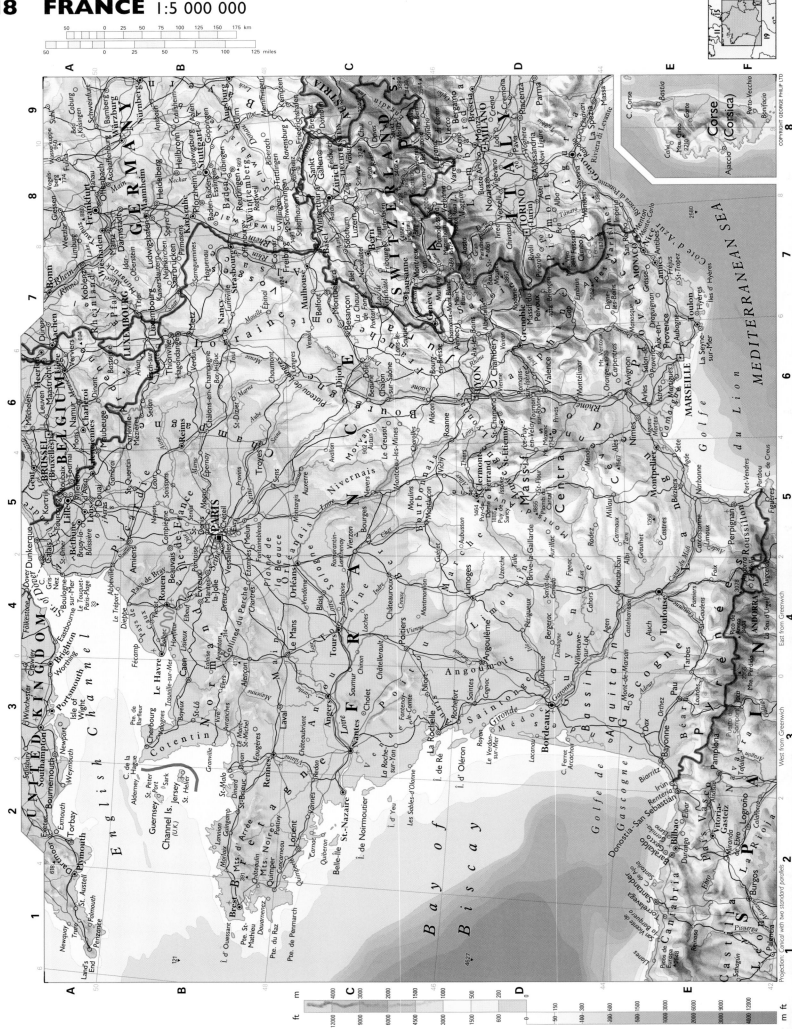

Projection: Conical with two standard parallels

COPYRIGHT GEORGE PHILIP LTD

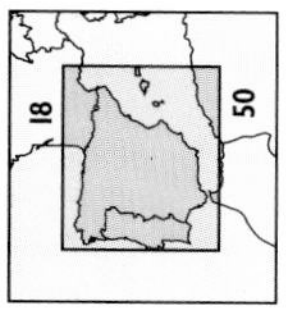

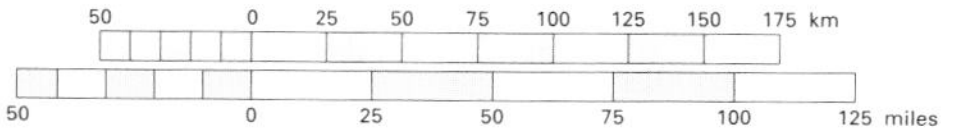

50 0 25 50 75 100 125 150 175 km
50 0 25 50 75 100 125 miles

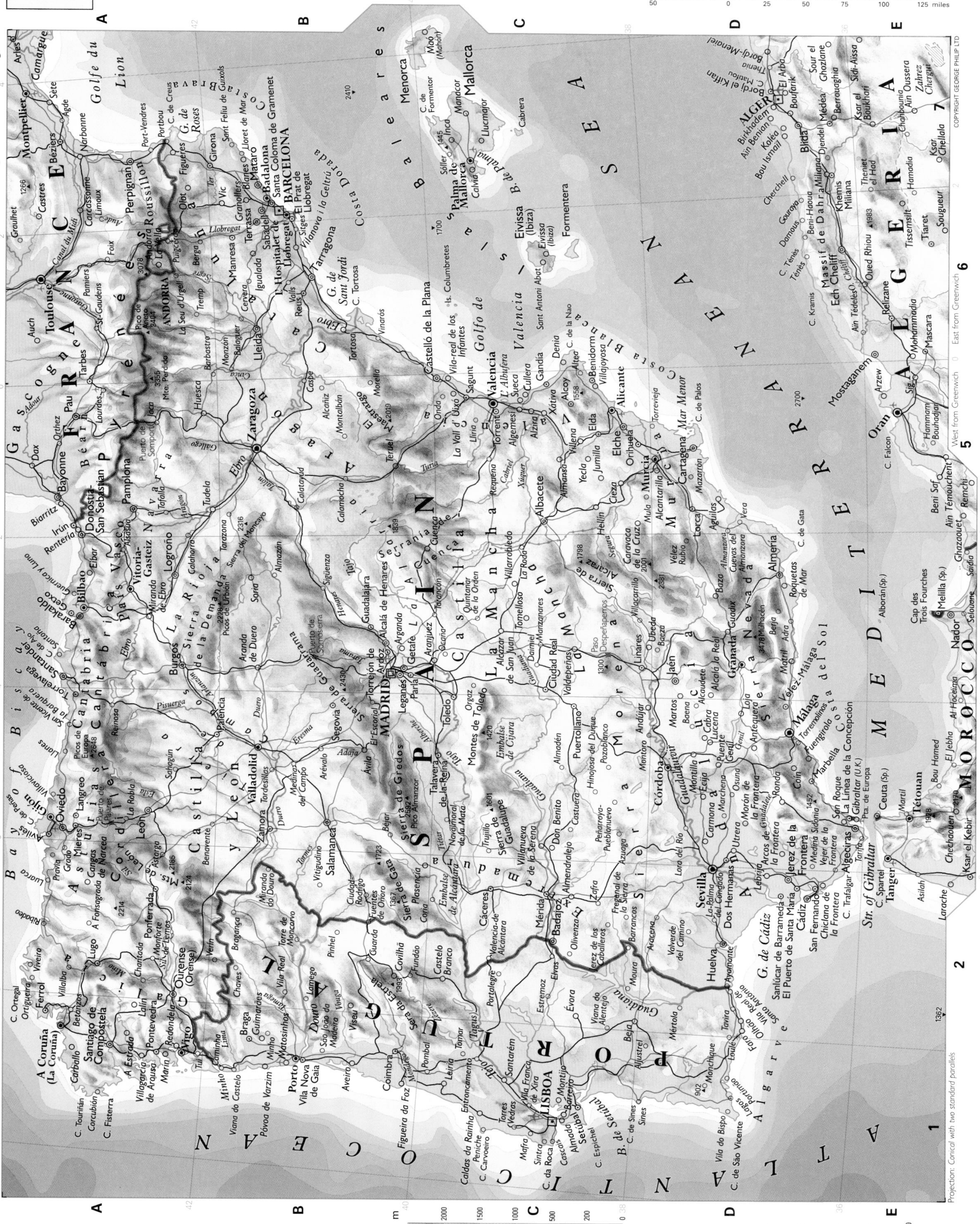

SPAIN AND PORTUGAL

Projection: Conical with two standard parallels

COPYRIGHT GEORGE PHILIP LTD

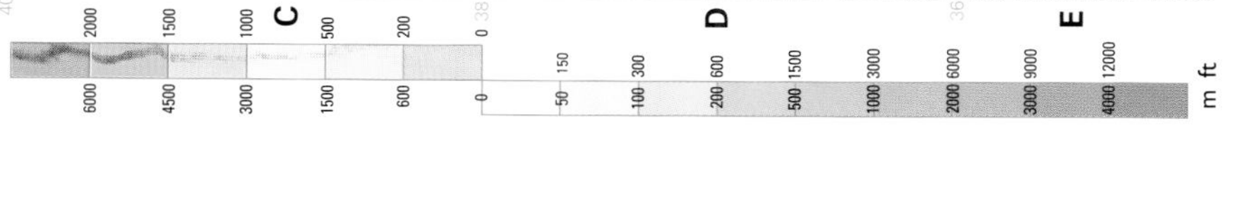

West from Greenwich 0 East from Greenwich

FRANCE

SPAIN

PORTUGAL

MOROCCO

ALGERIA

ANDORRA

Pyrenees

Golfe du Lion

Baleares

Menorca

Mallorca

Eivissa (Ibiza)

MEDITERRANEAN SEA

Costa Brava

Costa Blanca

Costa del Sol

Golfo de Valencia

BARCELONA

Zaragoza

MADRID

Valencia

Sevilla

LISBOA

Porto

Toulouse

Montpellier

Bilbao

Str. of Gibraltar

ATLANTIC OCEAN

Bay of Biscay

m ft
2000 6000
1500 4500
1000 3000
500 1500
200 600
0 0
-50 -150
-100 -300
-200 -600
-1000 -3000
-2000 -6000
-3000 -9000
-4000 -12000
m ft

Projection: Conical with two standard parallels

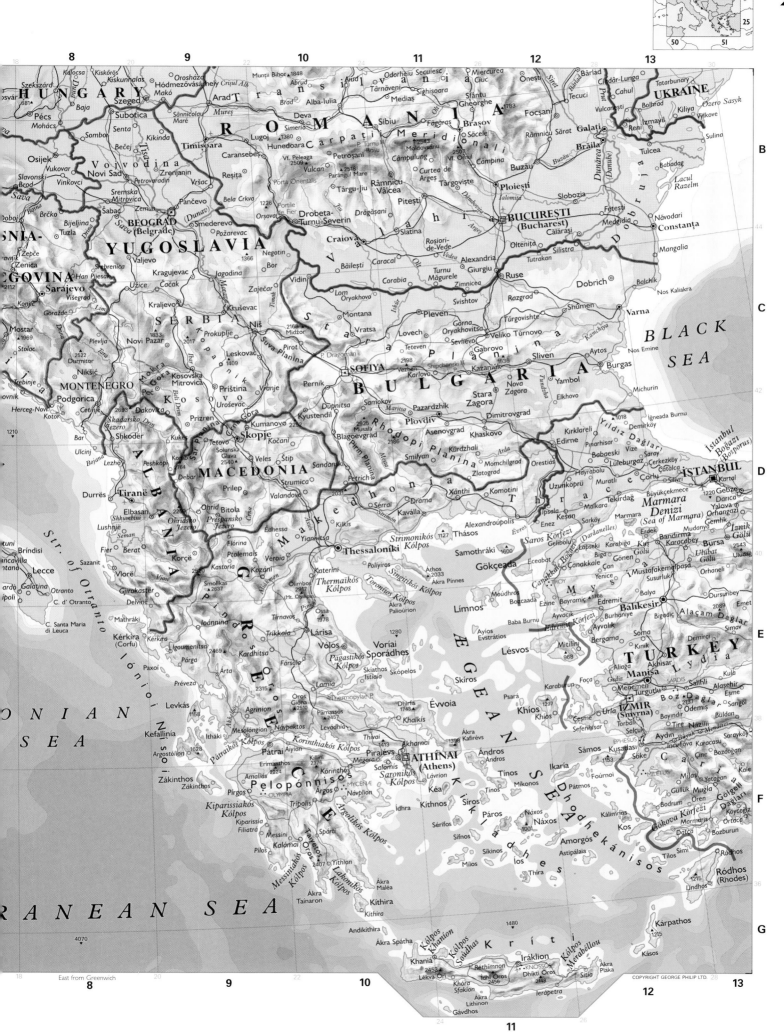

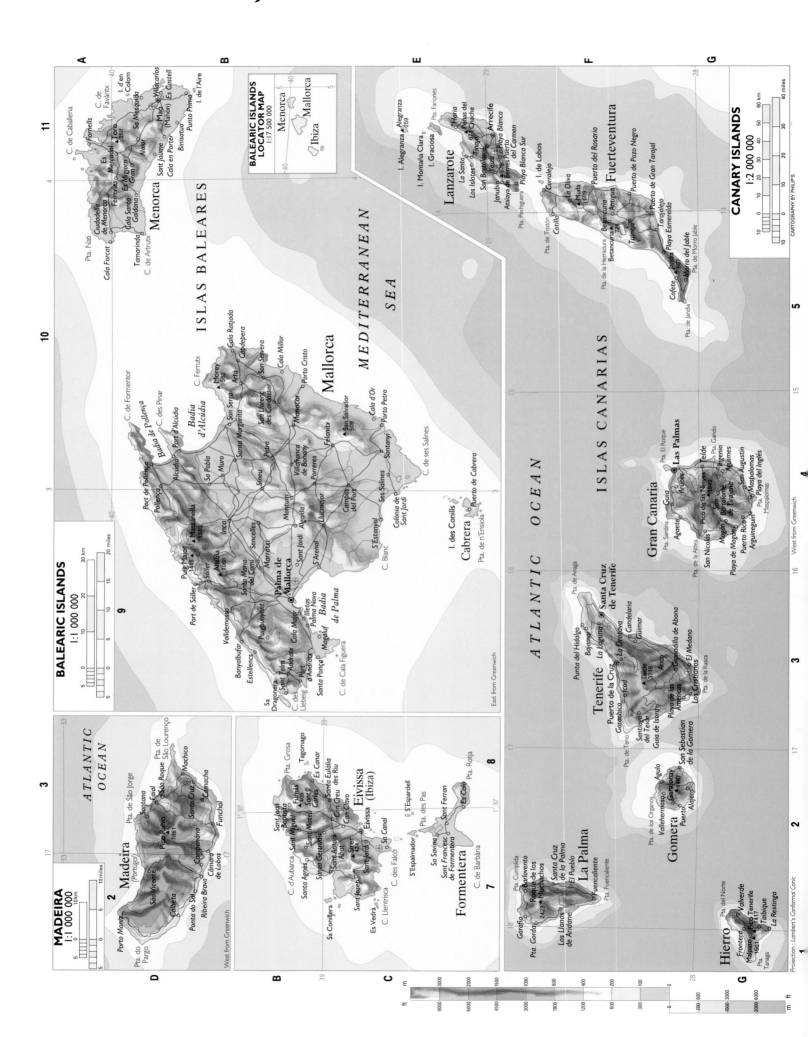

BALEARIC ISLANDS LOCATOR MAP
1:17 500 000

Menorca
Mallorca
Ibiza

CANARY ISLANDS
1:2 000 000

CARTOGRAPHY BY PHILIP'S.

ISLAS BALEARES

Menorca

MEDITERRANEAN SEA

Mallorca

Palma de Mallorca

Cabrera

ISLAS CANARIAS

Lanzarote

Fuerteventura

ATLANTIC OCEAN

Gran Canaria
Las Palmas

Tenerife
Santa Cruz de Tenerife

Gomera

La Palma

Hierro

Formentera

Eivissa (Ibiza)

MADEIRA
1:1 000 000

Madeira
(Portugal)

Funchal

ATLANTIC OCEAN

BALEARIC ISLANDS
1:1 000 000

Projection : Lambert's Conformal Conic

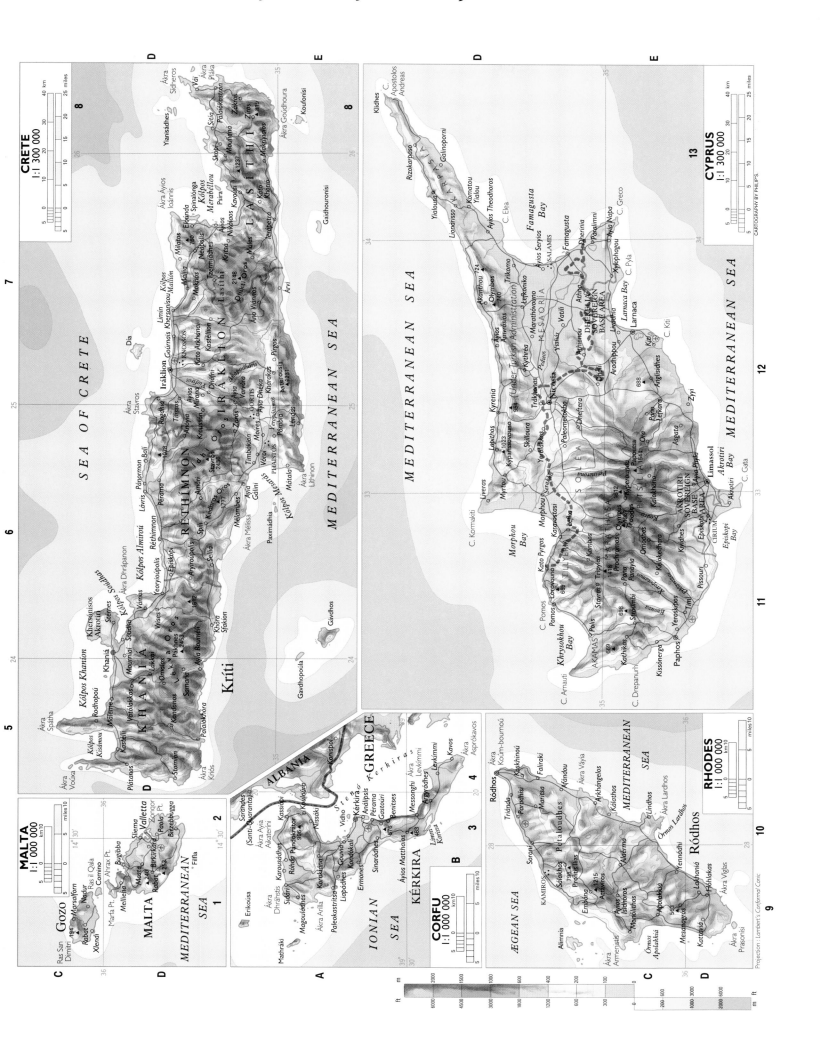

CRETE
1:1 300 000

MALTA
1:1 000 000

CORFU
1:1 000 000

RHODES
1:1 000 000

CYPRUS
1:1 300 000

CARTOGRAPHY BY PHILIP'S.

Projection: Lambert's Conformal Conic

SEA OF CRETE

MEDITERRANEAN SEA

MEDITERRANEAN SEA

MEDITERRANEAN SEA

AEGEAN SEA

IONIAN SEA

Kríti

Ródhos

Kérkira

Gozo

GREECE

ALBANIA

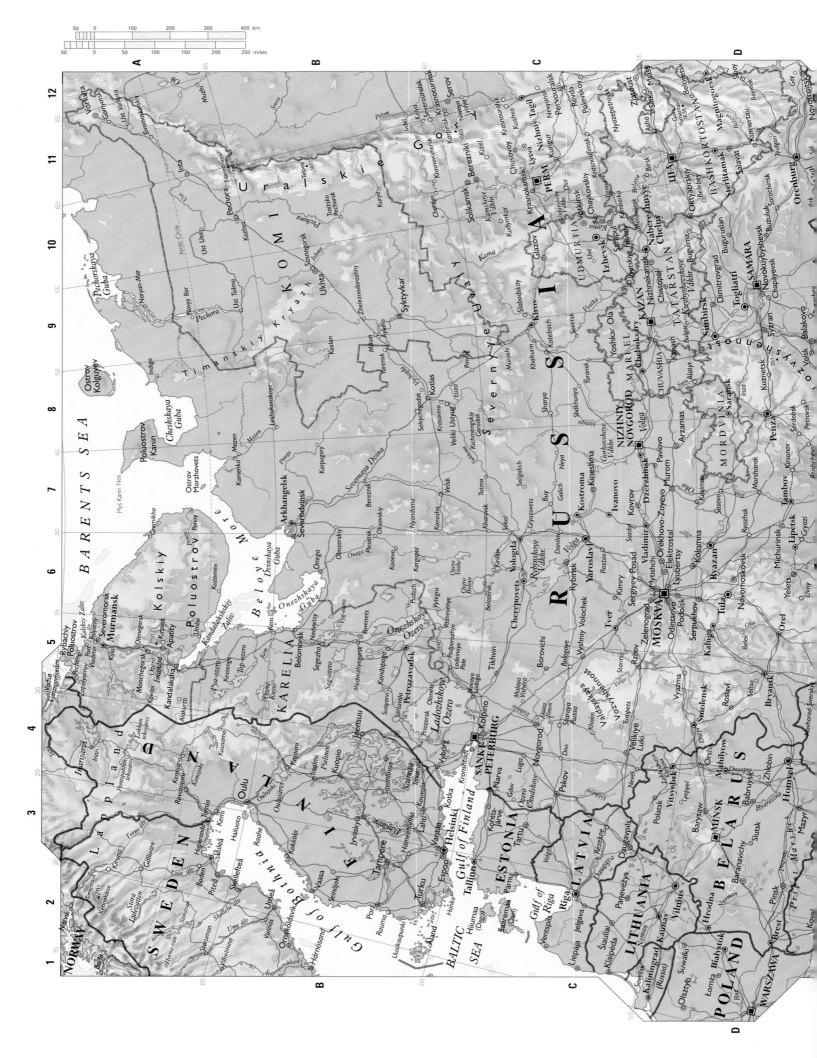

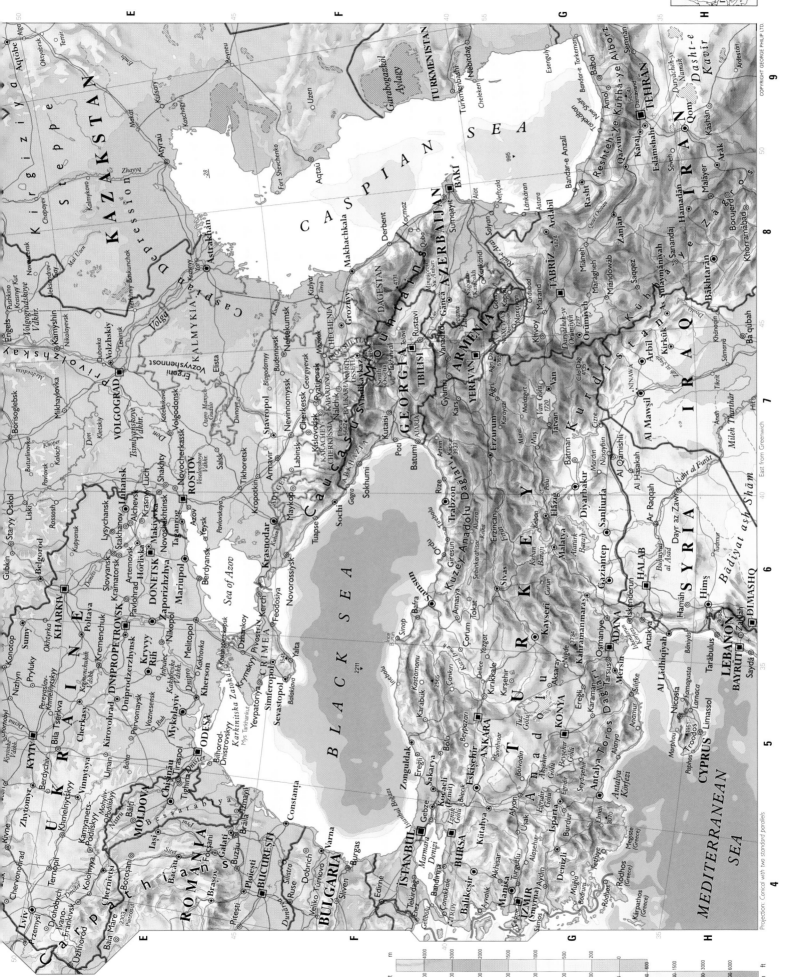

Projection: Conical with two standard parallels

East from Greenwich

C A S P I A N   S E A

B L A C K   S E A

Sea of Azov

MEDITERRANEAN SEA

KAZAKSTAN

TURKMENISTAN

IRAN

TEHRĀN

BAKU

AZERBAIJAN

ARMENIA

YEREVAN

GEORGIA

TBILISI

GEORGIA

TURKEY

ANKARA

ISTANBUL

IZMIR

BURSA

KONYA

ADANA

CYPRUS

SYRIA

DIMASHQ

LEBANON

BAYRŪT

IRAQ

UKRAINE

KYIV

KHARKIV

ROMANIA

BUCUREȘTI

MOLDOVA

BULGARIA

ODESA

VOLGOGRAD

ROSTOV

DONETSK

DNIPROPETROVSK

TABRIZ

HALAB

TARSUS

Projection: Conical Orthomorphic with two standard parallels

East from Greenwich

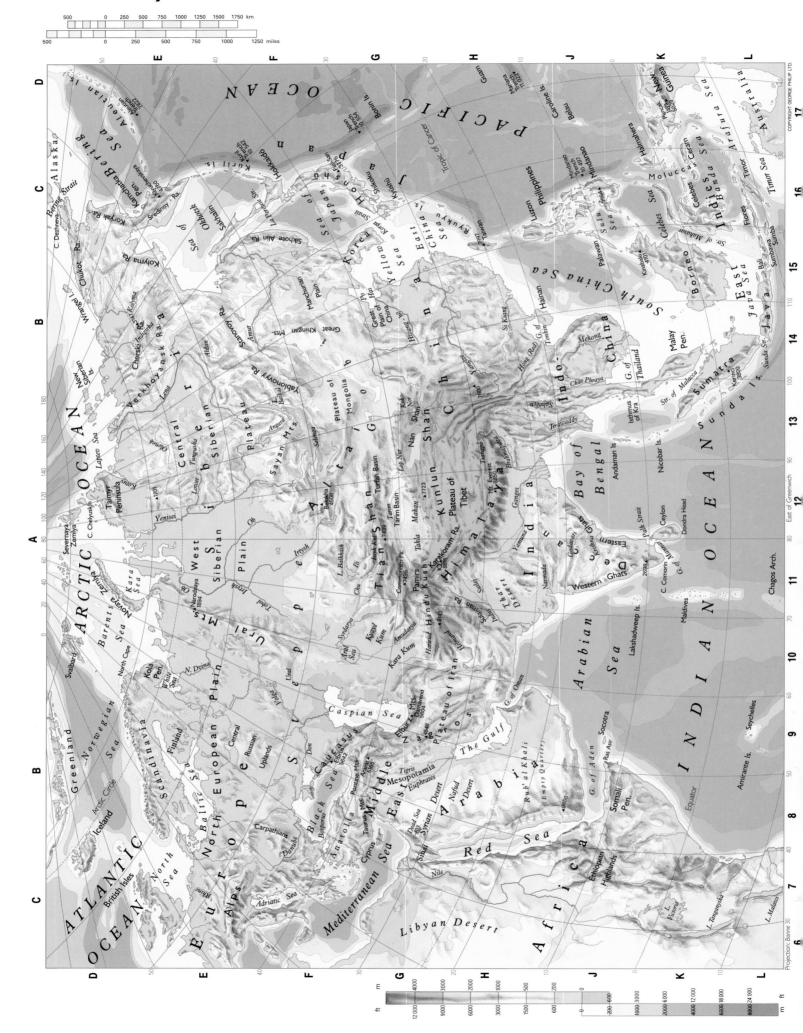

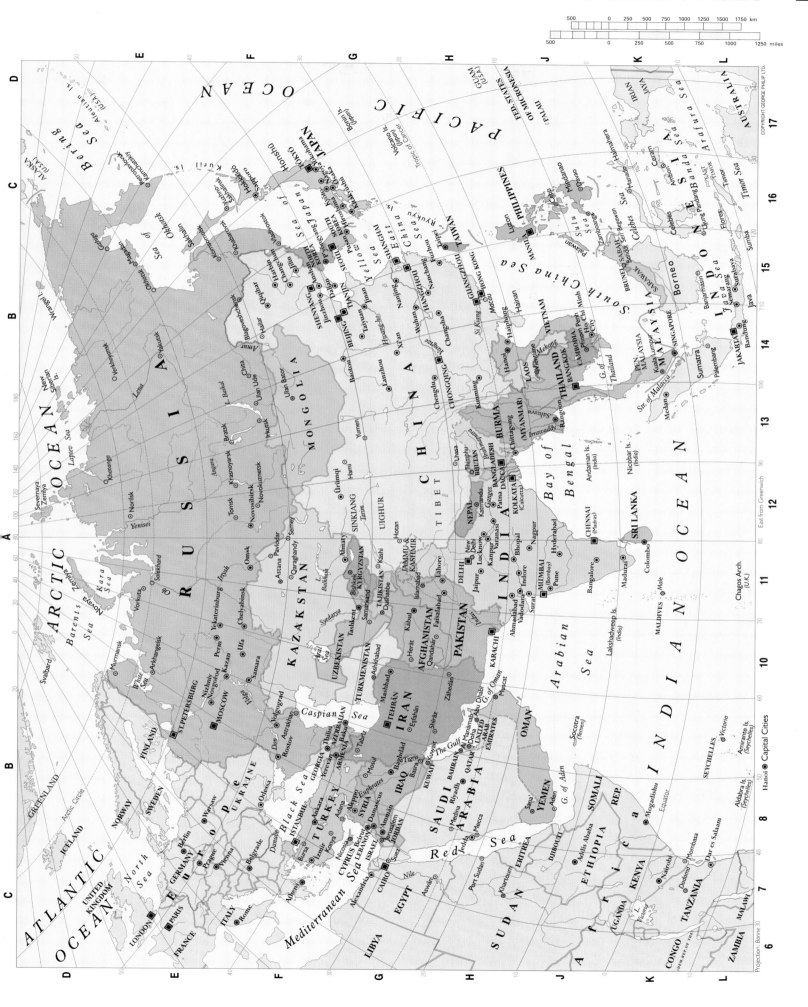

500   0   250   500   750 1000 1250 1500 1750 km

500   0   250   500   750 1000   1250 miles

JAPAN 1:5 000 000

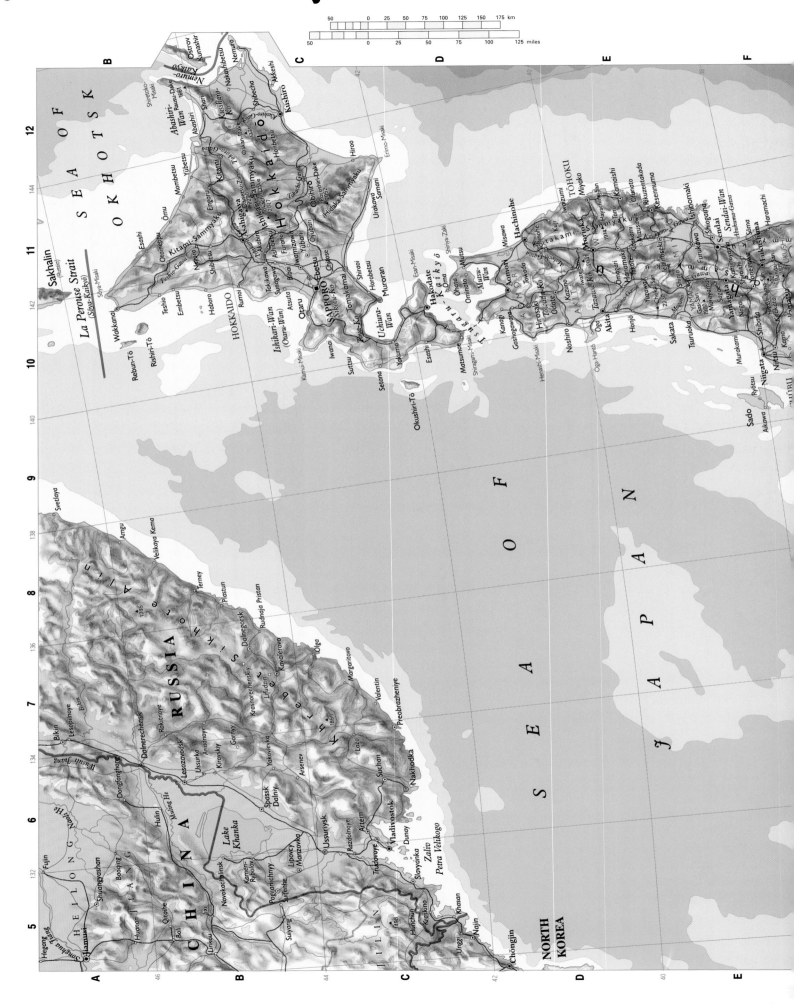

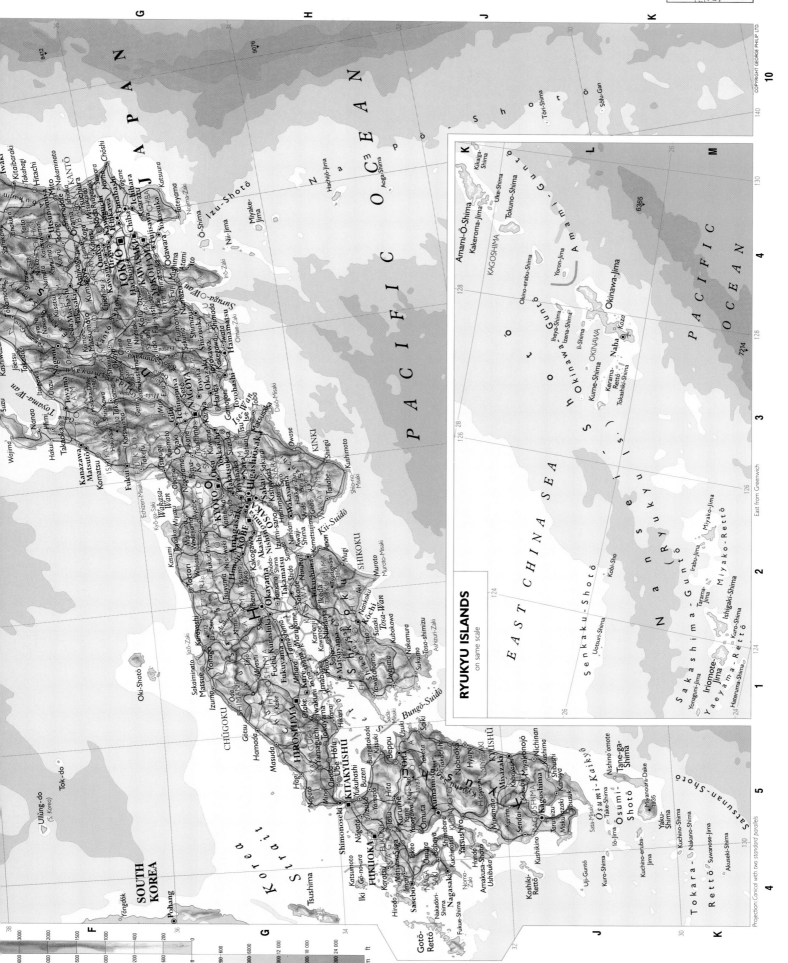

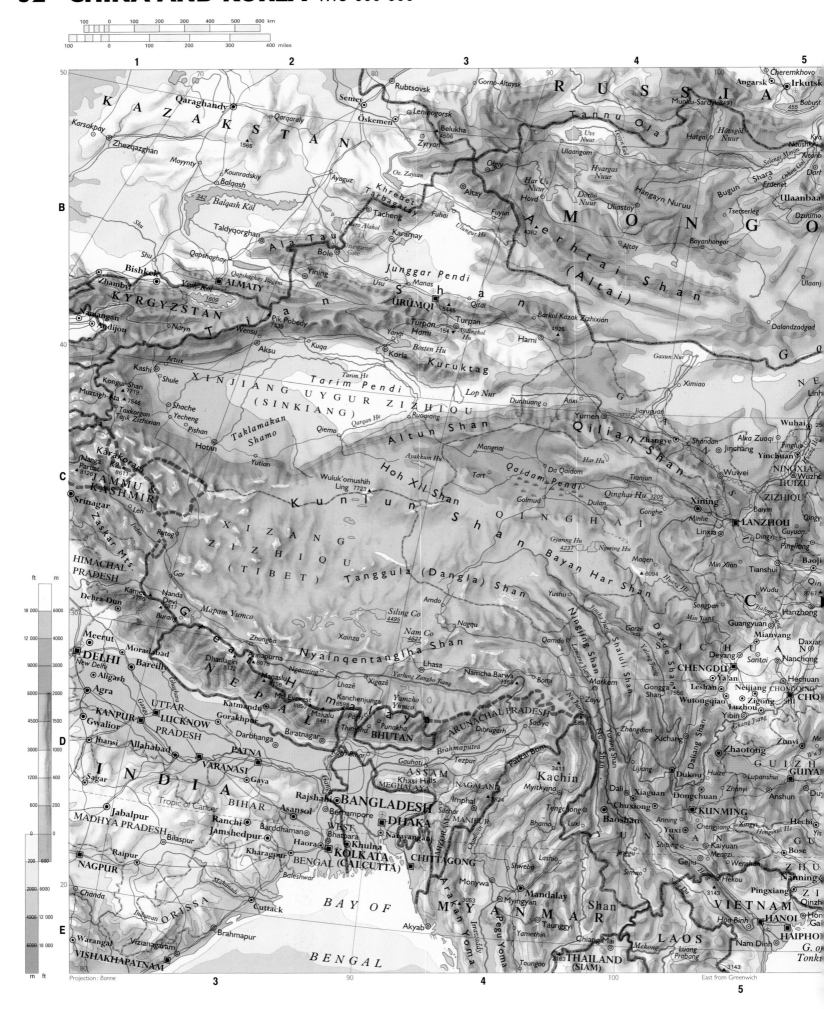

East from Greenwich

COPYRIGHT GEORGE PHILIP LTD.

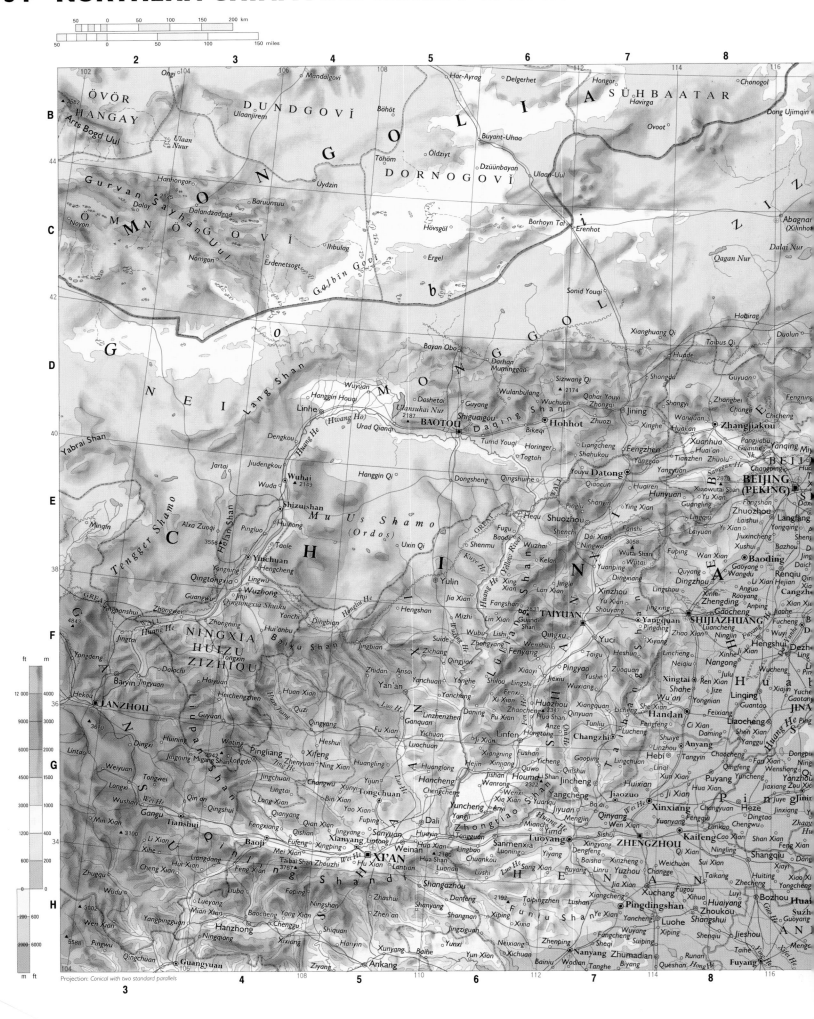

38 33
58
60 62
15 16

Luzon

Claveria · Babuyan Chan.
Bacarra · C. Engaño
Laoag · Aparri
Batac · 2048 · Tuao · Tuguegarao
Bangued · Vigan · Ilagan · Palanan Pt.
Bontoc · 2929 · Solano · Palanan
San Fernando · Baguio · Bayombong
Lingayen G. · Casiguran
Bolinao · Dagupan · Baler
Iba · Tarlac · Cabanatuan · C. San Ildefonso
Mt. Pinatubo · 1759 · Angeles · San Jose
Olongapo · San Fernando
Bataan · Malolos · Polillo Is.
QUEZON CITY · Lamon
Cavite · **MANILA** · Bay
Manila B. · Santa Cruz · Daet
Lubang Is. · Batangas · 2188 · Lucena · Catanduanes
Mindoro · Calapan · Marinduque · Virac
Mamburao · Naga · Tabaco
Sablayan · Halcon · 2586 · Mayon Volcano · Legazpi
Romblon · Masbate · Sorsogon · San Bernardino Str.
Tablas · Sibuyan · Bulan · Laoang
Sea · Masbate · Catarman
Semirara Is. · Calbayog · Oras · Samar
Pandan · Panay · 2117 · Taft
Pototan · Roxas · Borongan · General
Iloilo · Cadiz · Ormoc · MacArthur
San Carlos · Mandaue · Leyte · Guiuan
Bacolod · Cebu · Baybay
Buenavista · Talibon · Maasin · Dinagat
Guimaras G. · 2485 · Bohol · Siargao
Negros · Tanjay · Bohol · Surigao
Dumaguete · 5576 · Tagbilaran · Siquijor · Camiguin
Dipolog · L. Mainit · 2012 · Tandag
Dapitan · Oroquieta · Iligan · Lianga
Sindangan · 2425 · Malaybalay
Liloy · Cagayan · Cateel
Kabasalan · Ozamiz · de Oro · Baganga
Siocon · Pagadian · **Mindanao** · 2938 · Parang · Tagum · 2804
Sibuco · Cotabato · Mt. Apo · **Davao** · Mati
Zamboanga · Moro G. · Datu Piang · 2854
Isabela · Basilan · Lebak · Koronadal · Digos
General Santos · Makta · 2083 · C. San Agustin
Parang · Jolo · Kiamba · Tinaca Pt.
Jolo · Samales Group · Sarangani B. · Sarangani
Siasi · Tapul Group · 5824 · Is.
Tawitawi

PHILIPPINE · SULU SEA · CELEBES SEA · Mindanao Trench

10 497 · 9540

JAVA AND MADURA

1 : 7 500 000

50 | 0 | 50 | 100 | 150 | 200 | 250 | 300 km
50 | 0 | 50 | 100 | 150 | 200 miles

JAKARTA / Java

Selat Sunda · Anyer-Kidul · Merak · Serang · Karawang
Pulau Rakata · Pandeglang · Tangerang · Pamanukan
Panaitan · Labuhan · **JAKARTA** · Kandanghaur
Tanjung Guhakolak · Rangkasbitung · Purwakarta · Indramayu
Pelabuhanratu · **Bogor** · Subang · Jatibarang · Cirebon
Teluk Pelabuhan Ratu · Sukabumi · Cianjur · Sumedang · Majalengka · Brebes · Pemalang · Pekalongan · Jepara · Kudus
Pengalengan · **BANDUNG** · 3078 · Kuningan · Tegal · Kendal · **SEMARANG** · Demak
Genteng · Garut · Ciamis · Purwokerto · Slamet · Wonosobo · 3265 · Salatiga · Purwodadi · Cepu
Sindangbarang · Tasikmalaya · Banyumas · 428 · Magelang · Boyolali · Ngawi · Jambang
Cijulang · Cilacap · Karanganyar · Kebumen · **Yogyakarta** · 3142 · **Surakarta** · Madiun · Kediri
Nusa Kambangan · Wates · Bantul · Ponorogo · 2563 · Liman · Pare
Wonosari · Trenggalek · Blitar · **Malang** · 3339
Pacitan · Tulungagung · Wlingi · Semeru · 3676

Kepulauan Karimunjawa · Bawean · Sangkapura
Muria · 1602 · Rembang · Tuban · Tanjung Pangkah · Madura
Pati · Blora · Kragan · Bojonegoro · Gresik · **SURABAYA** · Bangkalan · Tambuku · 471 · Sumenep
TENGAH · Jepara · Lamongan · Sidoarjo · Pasuruan · Sampang · Pamekasan
Jombang · Mojokerto · **TIMUR** · Selat Madura
Probolinggo · Situbondo
Lumajang · Bondowoso
Jember · Banyuwangi
Nusa Barung · Pasirian · Rambipuji · Bali · Gili

PACIFIC OCEAN

FEDERATED STATES
8597 · Ulithi Atoll
OF MICRONESIA
Yap
Ngulu Atoll · Sorol Atoll
8527
PALAU · Babelthuap
Koror · 8138 · Caroline Islands
Angaur

Sonsorol Islands
Pulo-Anna · 5798
Merir
Tobi · Helen Atoll

CELEBES SEA

Kepulauan Kawio
Karakelong · Kepulauan Nanusa
Beo · Kepulauan Talaud
Salibabu
Tahuna · Kaburuang
Pulau Sanghe
Karakitang · Kepulauan Sanghe
Siau

Sopi
Doi · Biaro · Berebere · Morotai
Galela
Ibu · 1325 · Tobelo · Akelamo
Tahulandang · Bangka · Jailolo · Halmahera
Manado · 1995 · Kema · Ternate
Tolitoli · Paleleh · Kema · Tondano · Tidore · Teluk Buli · Patani
Buol · Sumalata · Kuandang · Ma · Kayoa · Weda · Teluk Weda · Gebe
Malino · 2490 · Tilamuta · Kotamobagu · Selat · Umera · Waigeo
UTARA · Gorontalo · Tanjung Flesko · Wosi · Gani · Waigeo · Dampier · Wakre
Moutong · Teluk Tomini · Labuha · Tanjung Libobo · Saonek · Salawati
Donggala · Tomini · Kepulauan Togian · Maliku · Bacan · Misool · Sailolof · Seget
Palu · 2355 · Parigi · Poh · Mandioli · 2111 · Kofiau · Lenmalu · Teminabuan
Tojo · Tokala · Luwuk · Obilatu · Bisa · Fluk · Adua
TENGAH · Poso · 2630 · Banggai · Mangole · Kawasi · Inanwatan
SULAWESI · Danau Poso · Kolonodale · Taliabu · Sanana · Obi · Sawai
(Celebes) · Kepulauan Banggai · Todeli · Kepulauan Sula · Piru · Wahai
Masamba · Danau Towuti · Todeli · Buru · 2736 · Amahai · 3019
Malili · Mondeodo · Namlea · Kayeli · Seram
Makale · 3440 · Mekongga · Manui · Wamulan · Tifu · (Ceram) · Tehoru
Rantemario · Pinrang · 2799 · Monse · Namrole · Lima
Parepare · Singkang · Kendari · Wowoni · Buru · Waru
Watampone · Pampanua · Buapinang · Pising · Raha · Wangiwangi
Sinjai · Buton · Lawele · Kepulauan Tukangbesi
Lompobatang · 2871 · Muna · Baubau · Binongko
Bantaeng · Kabaena · Batuata
Bulukumba · Benteng · Kepulauan Bonerate
Salayar · Kalaotoa
Tanahjampea · Bonerate · Kalao

MOLUCCA SEA · BANDA SEA

Kepulauan Asia
Kepulauan Ayu
Kepulauan Mapia
Raja Ampat · Batanta · Sorong · 2452 · Kwoka · Waibeem · Kaironi · Manokwari · Supiori · Biak
Selpele · Jazirah Doberai · 2926 · Warkopi · Numfoor · Warsa · Bosnik
Klamono · Klamono · Wasian · Ransiki · Number · Biak · Kumamba
Teminabuan · Bintuni · Wariap · Selat Yapen · Yapen · Bonoi · D'Urville
Teluk Berau · Babo · Wendesi · Serui · Sarmi
Tanjung Fatagar · Teluk Cenderawasih · Nuboai · Barapasi · Saberania
Fakfak · Kokas · Wenut · Susunu · Kwatisore · Pegunungan Van Rees · Genyem · Jayapura
Weri · Ibonma · Kaimana · Nabire · Waghete · Enarotali · **IRIAN JAYA** · Wamena · Sentani
Kumawa · Karufa · Uta · Pegunungan · 5029 · Jaya · **Pegunungan Maoke** · Krau
Kambrau · Adi · Tembagapura · Puncak · 4730 · Puncak · Taritatu
Manggawitu · Trikora · Sudirman · Jayawijaya · 7027 · Oksibil
Gorong · Amamapare · Uta · Mandala
Kepulauan Watubela · Yapero · PAPUA NEW GUINEA
Kepulauan Banda · Mindiptana
Bandanaira · Tual · Har · Kola · Gumzai · Wokam · Dobo · Tanahmerah
7440 · Kai Besar · Kai Kecil · Banda Elat · Wangal · Sewer · Pirimapun
Gunungapi · Nila · Serua · Kepulauan Kai · Trangan · Rebi · Koba · Kepulauan Aru · Kepi
5888 · Damar · Teun · Daya · Molu · Larat · Gomogomo · Bade · Digul
Wetar · Wesiri · Romang · Barat · Wuliaru · Tafermaar · Tanjung Ngabordamlu · Muting
Ilwaki · Kisar · Moa · Leti · Tepa · Selu · Yamdena · Okaba
Alor · Atauro · Baukau · Babar · Eliase · Kepulauan Tanimbar · Saumlaki · Pulau Dolak · Merauke
Kalabahi · Dili · Tutuala · Leti · Sermata · Masela · Adaut · Selaru · Kimaam · Pulau Komoran · Tanjung Vals

FLORES SEA / Lesser Sunda Is.

5123 · Sangeang · Ruteng
Bima · Labuhanbajo · Aimere · Maumere
Raba · 2350 · Flores
Sumba · Memboro · Mbai · Larantuka · Solor · Pantar · Adonara · Lomblen · Kalabahi
NUSA TENGGARA TIMUR · Pante · Macassar · Atapupu · 2963 · Vikeke · **EAST TIMOR**
Sumba · Waingapu · Kupang · Kefamenanu · Nikiniki
Melolo · Baing · Sawu · Raijua · Dana · Roti · Baa

ARAFURA SEA

SAWU SEA

COPYRIGHT GEORGE PHILIP LTD.

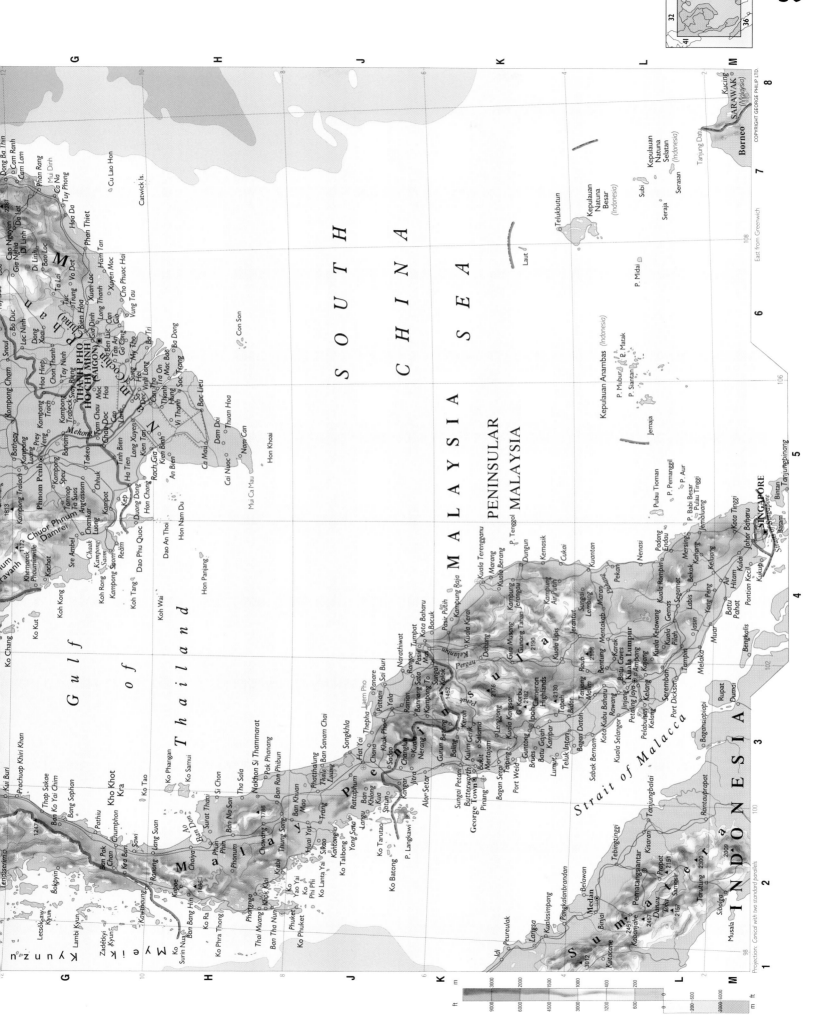

S O U T H   C H I N A   S E A

M A L A Y S I A

PENINSULAR
MALAYSIA

I N D O N E S I A

G u l f   o f   T h a i l a n d

Strait of Malacca

Borneo
SARAWAK
(Malaysia)

Phnom Penh

HO CHI MINH
THANH PHO
SAIGON

SINGAPORE

Kuala Lumpur

Projection: Conical with two standard parallels

East from Greenwich

COPYRIGHT GEORGE PHILIP LTD.

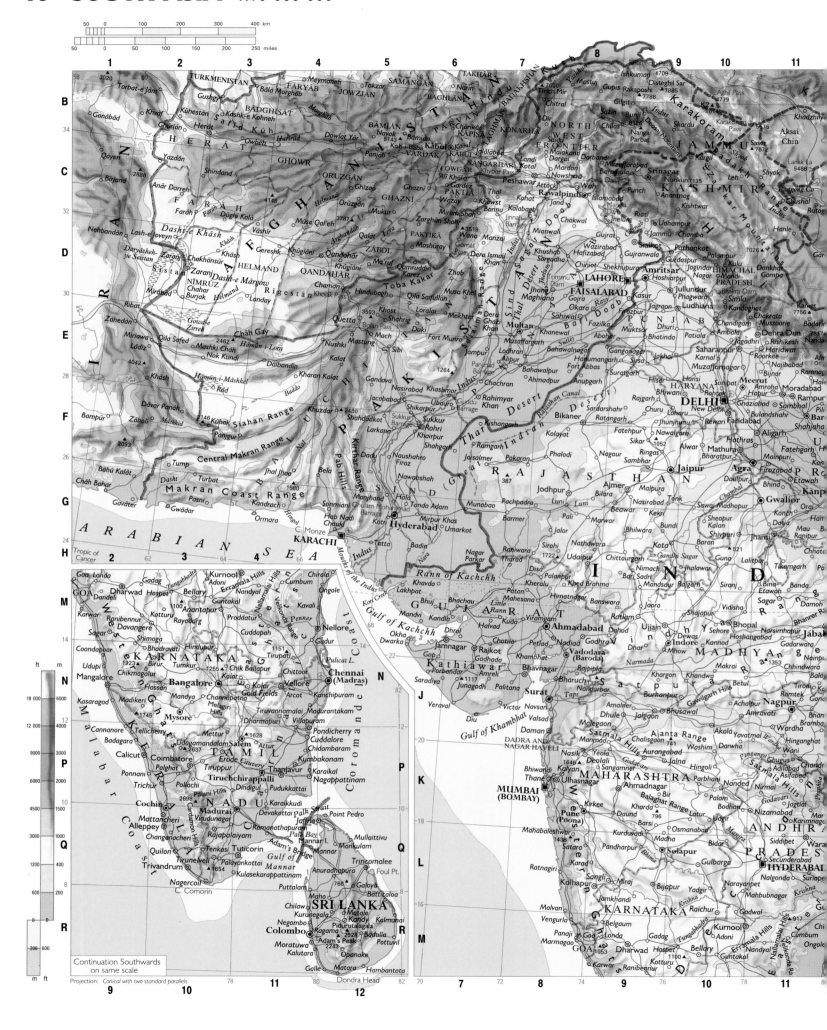

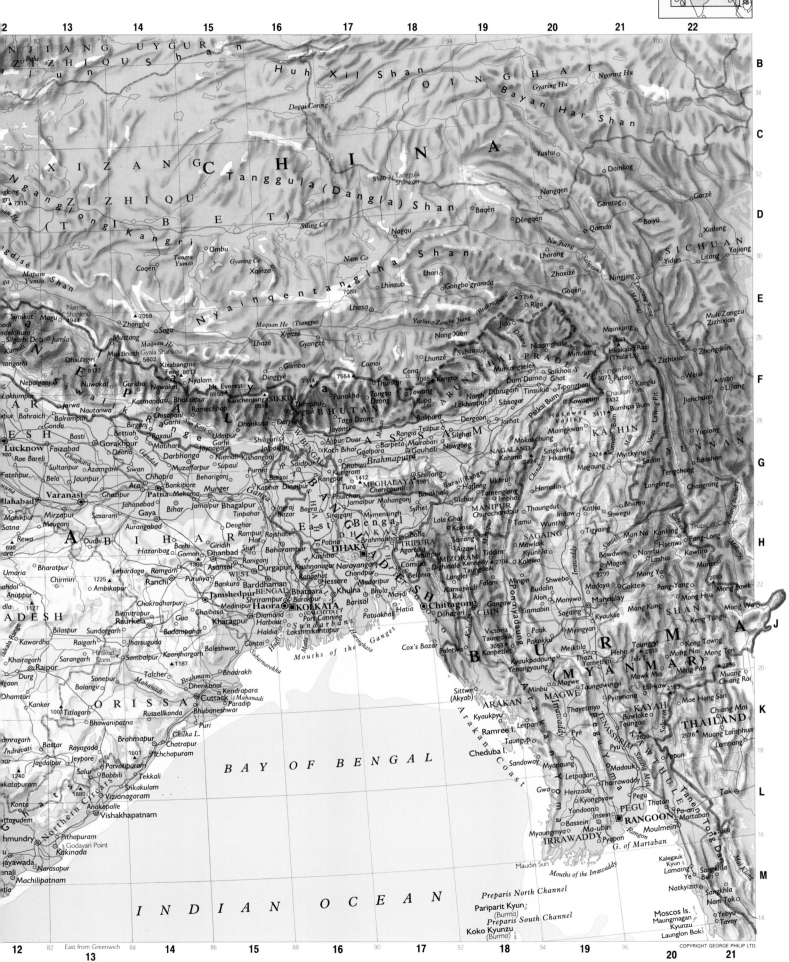

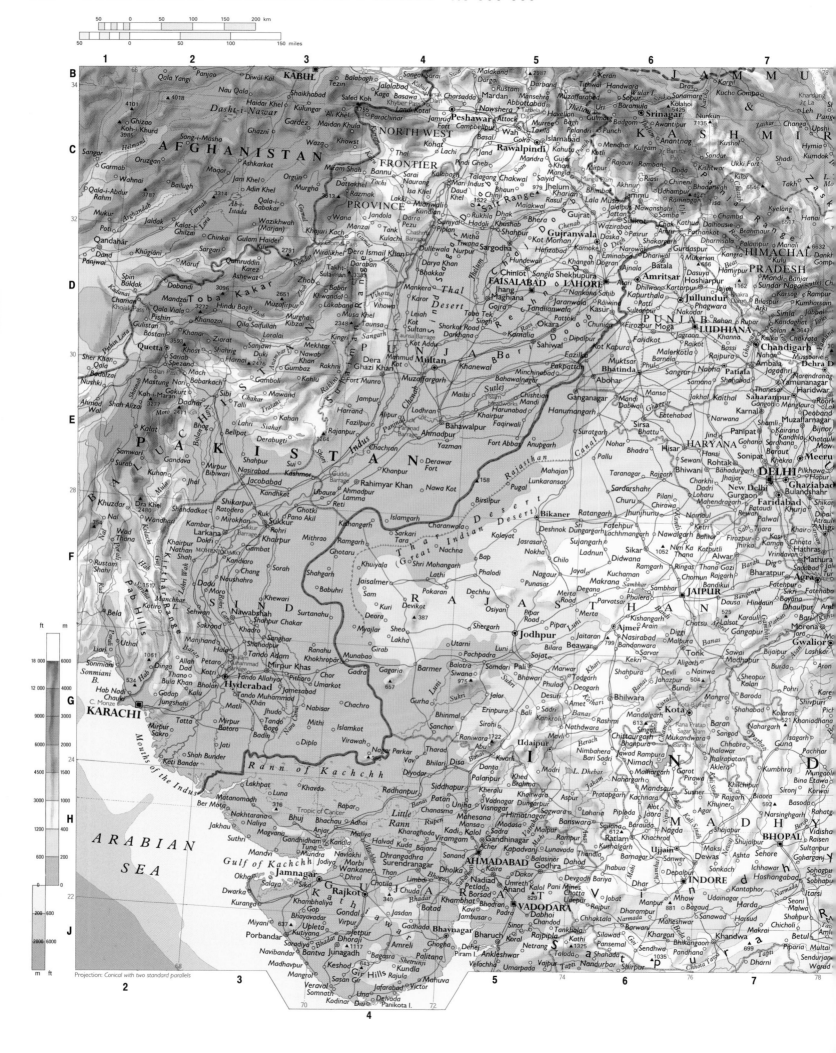

East from Greenwich

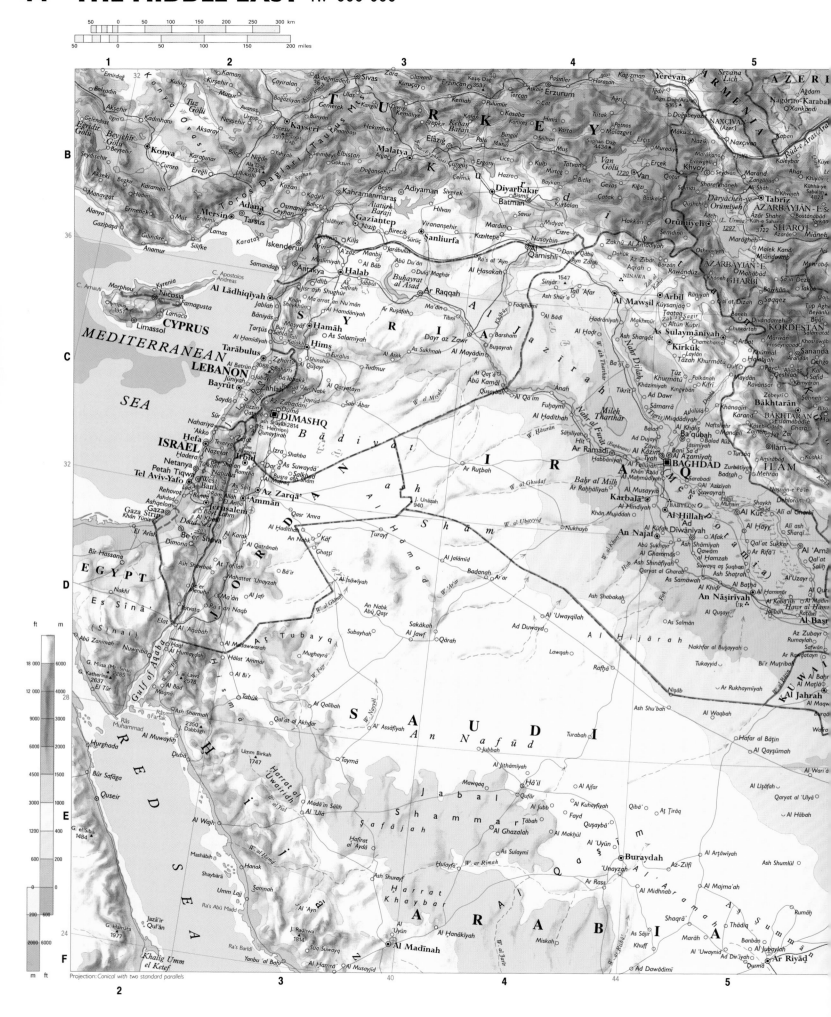

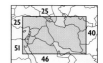

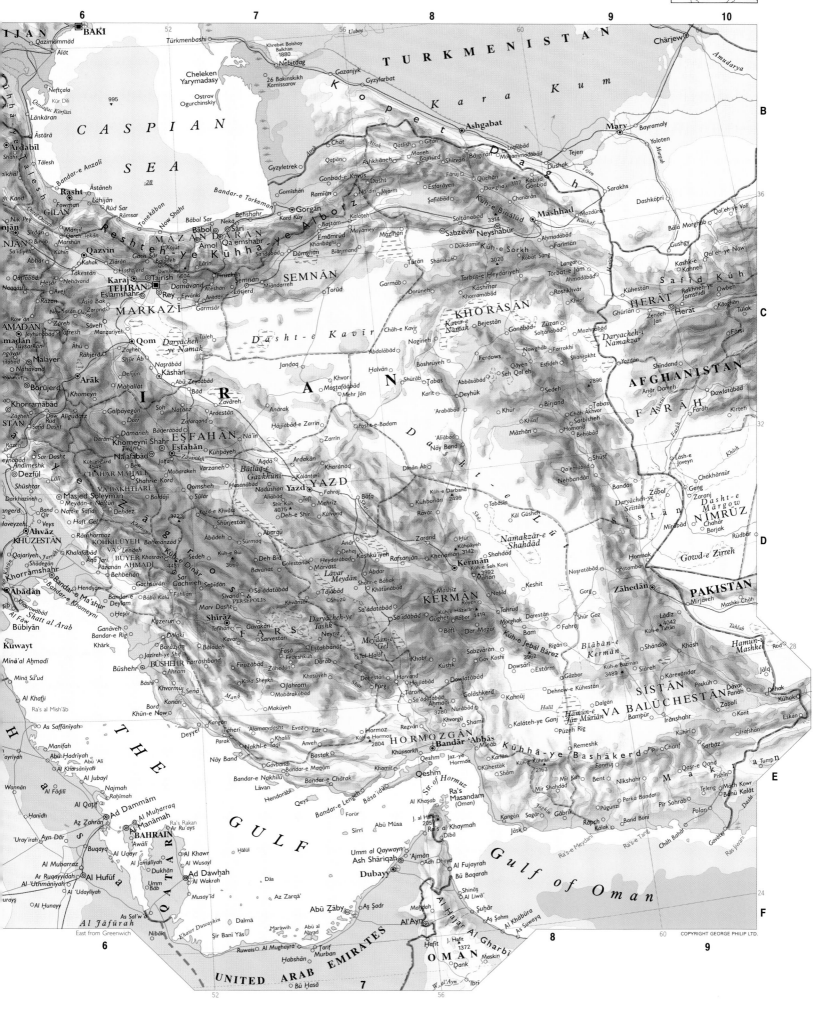

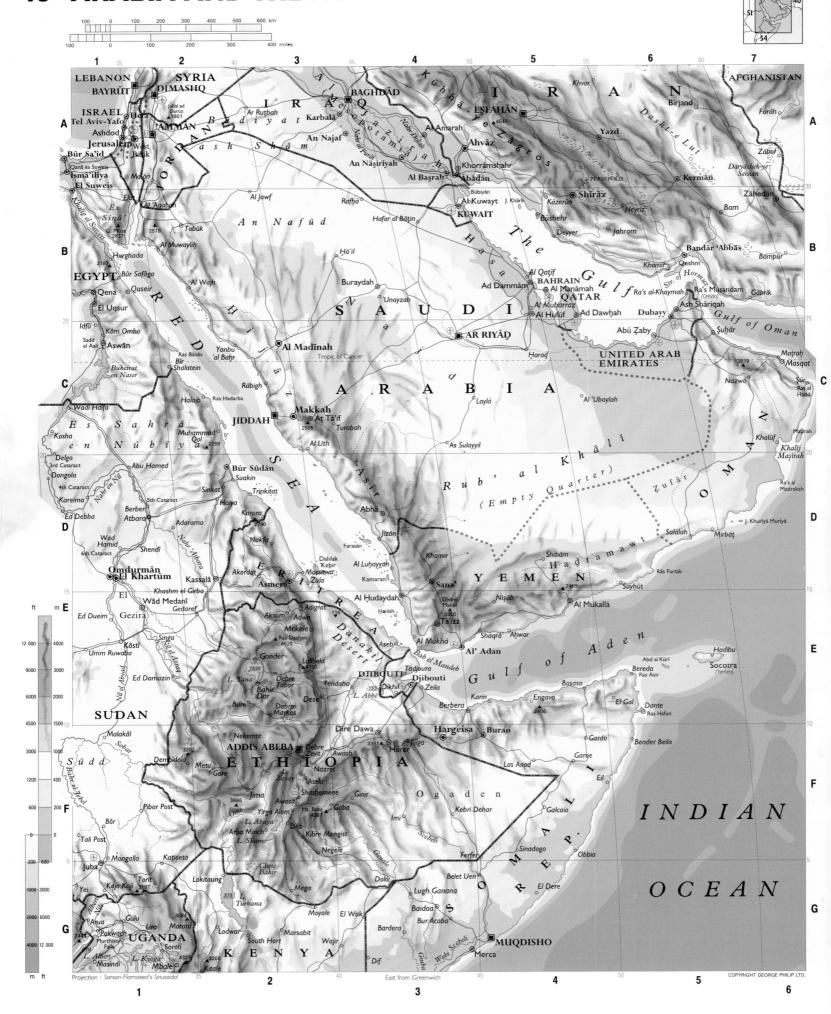

Projection: Polyconic

East from Greenwich

▬▭▭ 1974 Cease Fire Lines

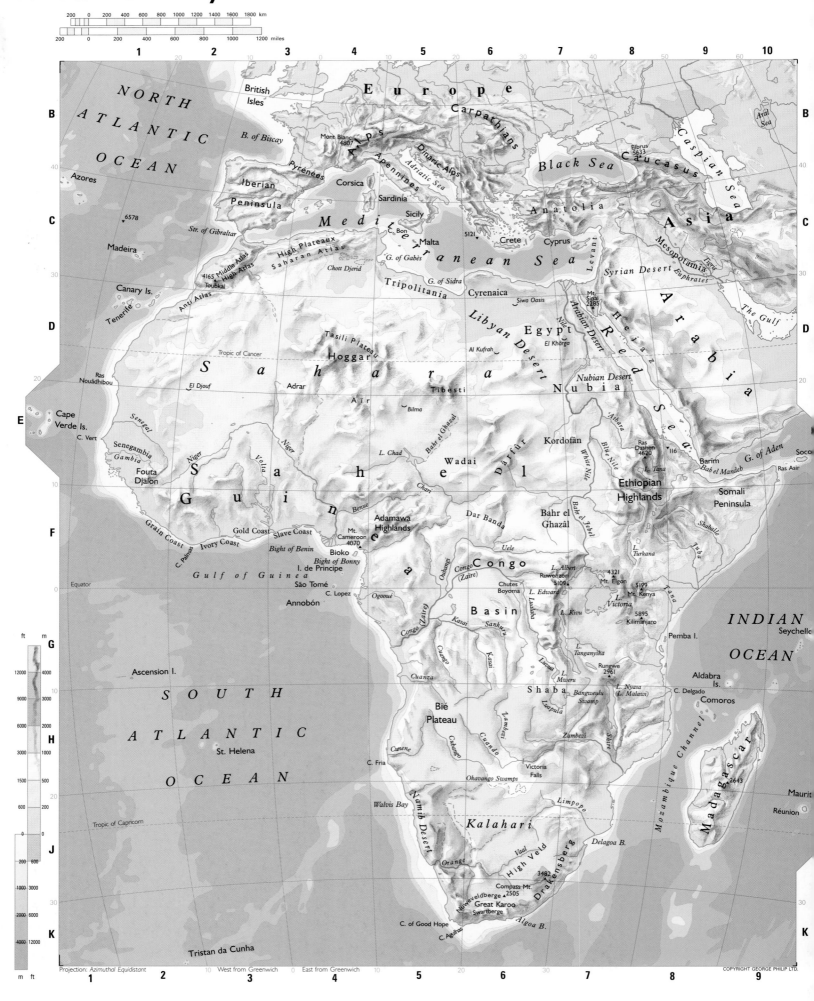

200 0 200 400 600 800 1000 1200 1400 1600 1800 km

200 0 200 400 600 800 1000 1200 miles

B

NORTH

ATLANTIC

OCEAN

Azores
(Port.)

Madeira
(Port.)

Canary Is.
(Sp.)

C. VERDE IS.

Praia

C. Vert

St-Louis

Dakar

Banjul

GAMBIA

GUINEA-
BISSAU

Bissau

Conakry

Freetown

SIERRA
LEONE

Monrovia

LIBERIA

B. of Biscay

Lisbon

PORTUGAL

Madrid

SPAIN

Rabat

Casablanca

Fès

MOROCCO

Marrakech

Tétouan

El Aaiún

WESTERN SAHARA

Fdérik

Ras
Nouâdhibou

Dakhla

MAURITANIA

Nouakchott

Tombouctou

MALI

Bamako

Senegal

Niger

Niamey

BURKINA
FASO

Bobo
Dioulasso

Ouagadougou

Kano

GUINEA

IVORY
COAST

Bouaké

GHANA

Kumasi

BENIN

TOGO

Lomé

Accra

Sekondi-
Takoradi

Abidjan

Yamoussoukro

**UNITED
KINGDOM**

London

FRANCE

Paris

NETH.

BELG.

GERMANY

SWITZ.

Vienna

AUSTRIA

CZECH REP.

Prague

POLAND

SLOVAK REP.

HUNGARY

CROATIA

**BOS.-
HERZ.**

ALB.

ITALY

Rome

Corsica

Sardinia

Sicily

MAC.

YUG.

ROMANIA

BULGARIA

GREECE

Athens

Crete

MALTA

Warsaw

Kiev

UKRAINE

Odessa

RUSSIA

Volgograd

KAZAKSTAN

Aral
Sea

Black Sea

GEORGIA

ARM.

AZER.

Baku

Caspian Sea

TURKMEN.

Ankara

TURKEY

CYPRUS

Aleppo

SYRIA

LEB.

Damascus

Tel Aviv
-Jaffa

ISRAEL

Jerusalem

JORDAN

Mosul

Tigris

Baghdad

Euphrates

IRAQ

Basra

KUWAIT

Tehrān

Eşfahān

IRAN

The Gulf

BAHRAIN

QATAR

Algiers

Annaba

Constantine

Tunis

TUNISIA

Sfax

Chott Djerid

Mediterranean Sea

Tripoli

Misrātah

Benghazi

Alexandria

Port Said

CAIRO

El Faiyûm

Suez

El Jawf

Marzûq

In Salah

ALGERIA

LIBYA

Sahara

Tropic of Cancer

EGYPT

Asyût

Aswân

Wadi Halfa

Nile

Red Sea

SAUDI

ARABIA

Medina

Riyadh

Jedda

Mecca

Port Sudan

YEMEN

Socotra
(Yemen)

Ras Asir

G. of Aden

Berbera

DJIBOUTI

Djibouti

SOMALI REP.

Mogadishu

Kismayu

NIGER

Agadès

CHAD

L. Chad

Abéché

Ndjamena

Maiduguri

NIGERIA

Abuja

Ibadan

Lagos

Porto
Novo

Enugu

Benue

Port
Harcourt

CAMEROON

Douala

Malabo

Yaoundé

**EQUATORIAL
GUINEA**

SÃO TOMÉ & PRINCIPE

Annobón

GABON

Libreville

C. Lopez

Equator

CONGO

Brazzaville

Pointe-Noire

CABINDA
(Angola)

**CENTRAL
AFRICAN REP.**

Bangui

Ubangi

Chari

El Fâsher

SUDAN

El Obeid

Malakâl

Wau

White Nile

Blue Nile

Omdurmân

Khartoum

Wâd Medani

Atbara

Atbara

ERITREA

Asmera

Mesewa

L. Tana

Addis Ababa

ETHIOPIA

Harer

Bahr el Jebel

L. Turkana

L. Albert

UGANDA

Kampala

Kisangani

Mbandaka

*Congo
(Zaïre)*

**CONGO
(DEM. REP. OF THE)**

Bahr el Ghazal

L. Edward

L. Kivu

RWANDA

Kigali

Bujumbura

BURUNDI

L. Victoria

Kisumu

KENYA

Nairobi

Mombasa

L. Kwango

INDIAN

OCEAN

SEYCHELLES

Ascension I.
(U.K.)

SOUTH

ATLANTIC

OCEAN

St. Helena
(U.K.)

C. Fria

Zaïre

Kinshasa

Matadi

Kananga

Kasai

Luanda

Lobito

ANGOLA

Huambo

Namibe

Cunene

Kwango

Cubango

Likasi

Lubumbashi

Ndola

ZAMBIA

Lusaka

L. Mweru

L. Tanganyika

Dodoma

TANZANIA

Zanzibar

Dar es Salaam

L. Malawi

MALAWI

Lilongwe

Blantyre

C. Delgado

COMOROS

Moroni

Mayotte
(Fr.)

Antsiranana

Mahajanga

Toamasina

Antananarivo

MADAGASCAR

Fianarantsoa

MAURITIUS

Port
Louis

Réunion
(Fr.)

Livingstone

Harare

Beira

ZIMBABWE

Bulawayo

Zambezi

Limpopo

Mozambique Channel

MOZAMBIQUE

Moçambique

NAMIBIA

Windhoek

BOTSWANA

Gaborone

Tropic of Capricorn

Orange

Johannesburg

Kimberley

Vaal

Pretoria

Maputo

Mbabane

SWAZ.

Maseru

LESOTHO

Durban

SOUTH AFRICA

Cape Town

C. of Good Hope

C. Agulhas

Port
Elizabeth

East
London

Tristan da Cunha
(U.K.)

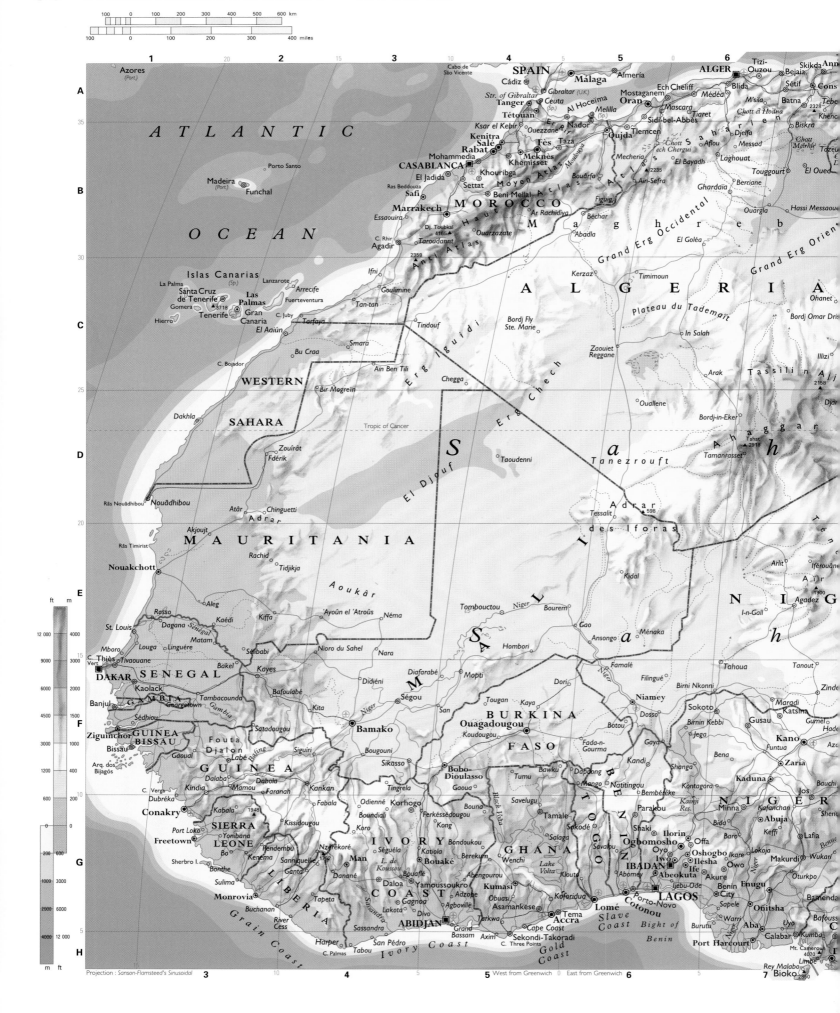

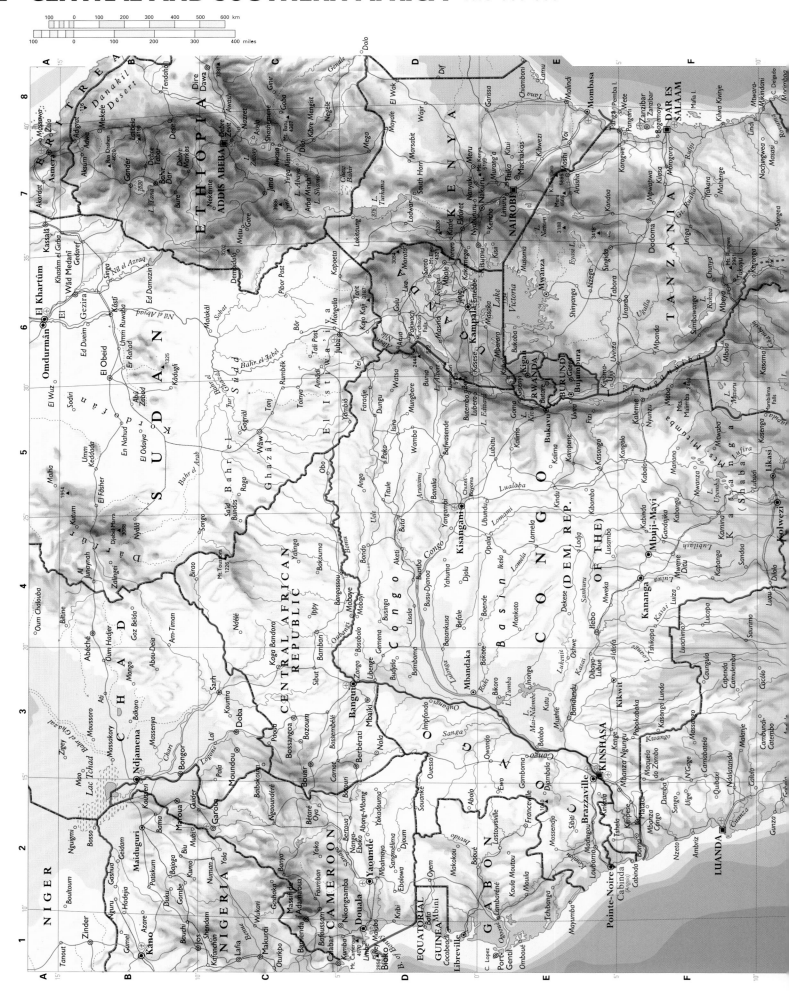

53

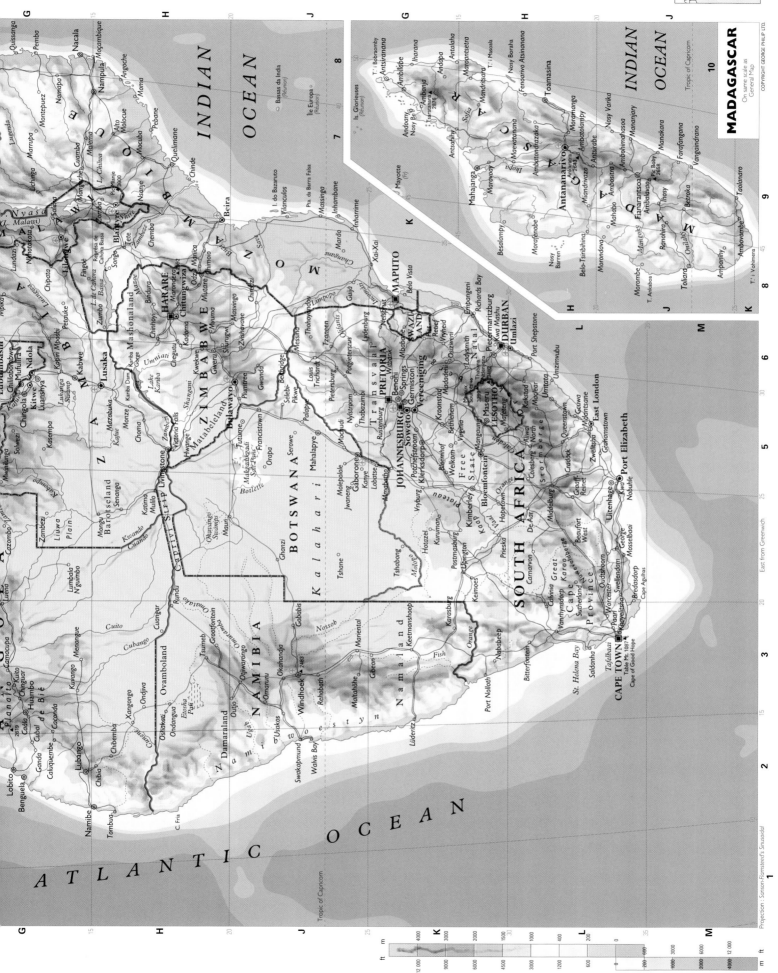

MADAGASCAR
On same scale as
General Map

COPYRIGHT GEORGE PHILIP LTD.

INDIAN OCEAN

ATLANTIC OCEAN

INDIAN OCEAN

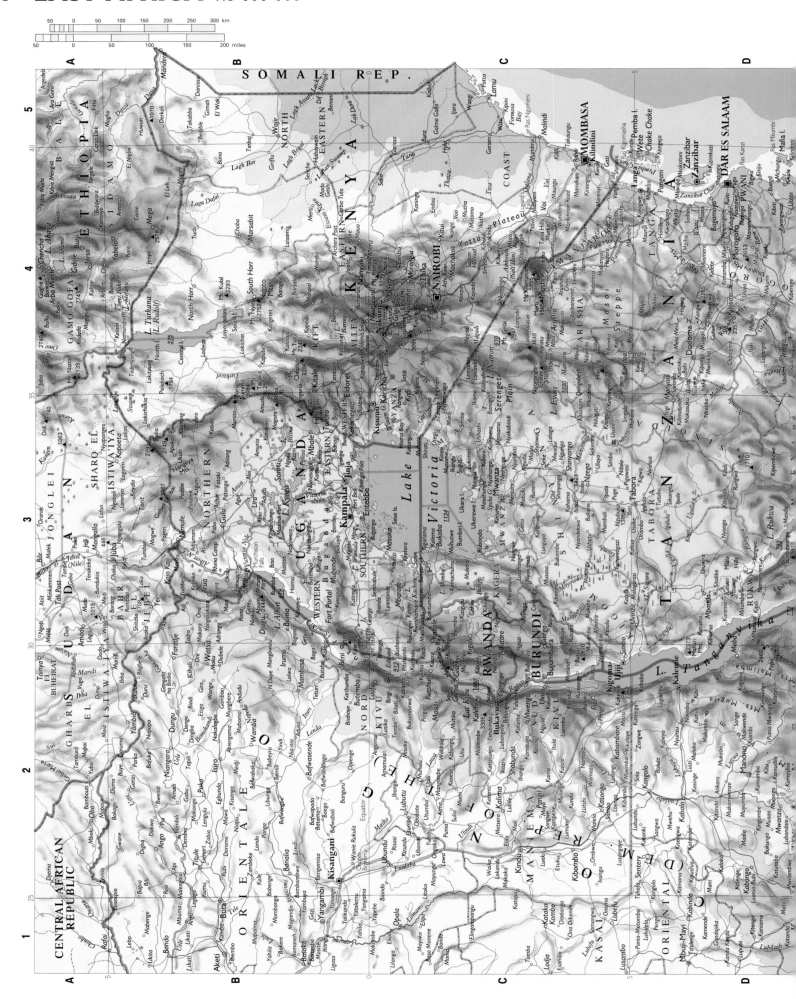

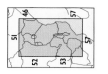

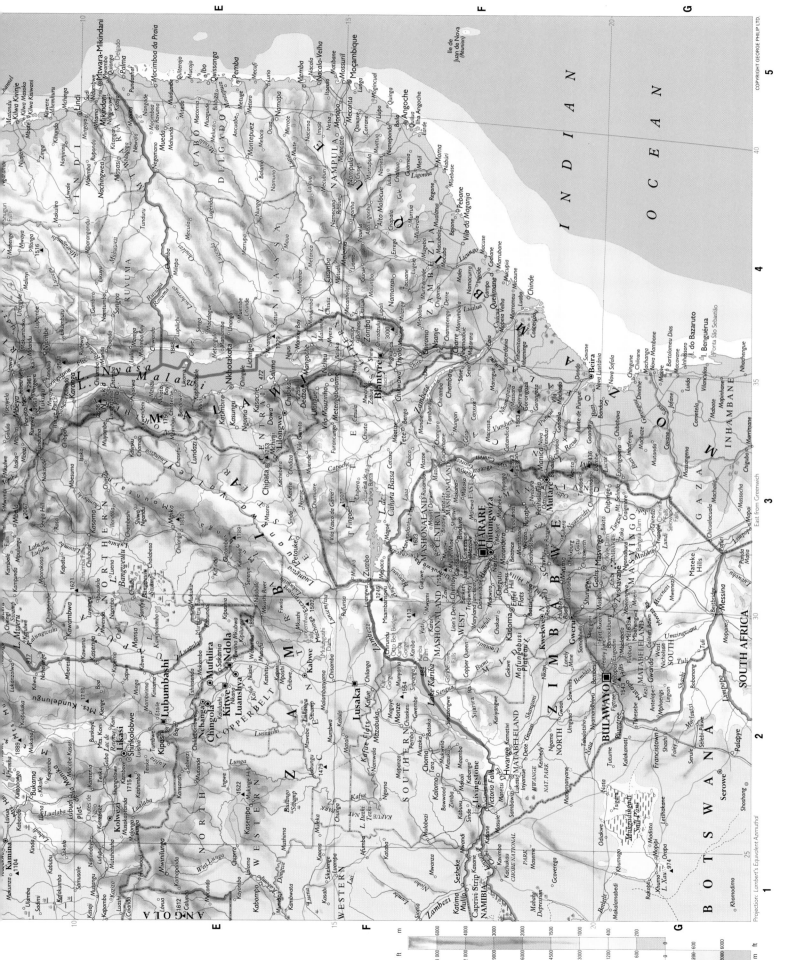

Projection: Lambert's Equivalent Azimuthal

East from Greenwich

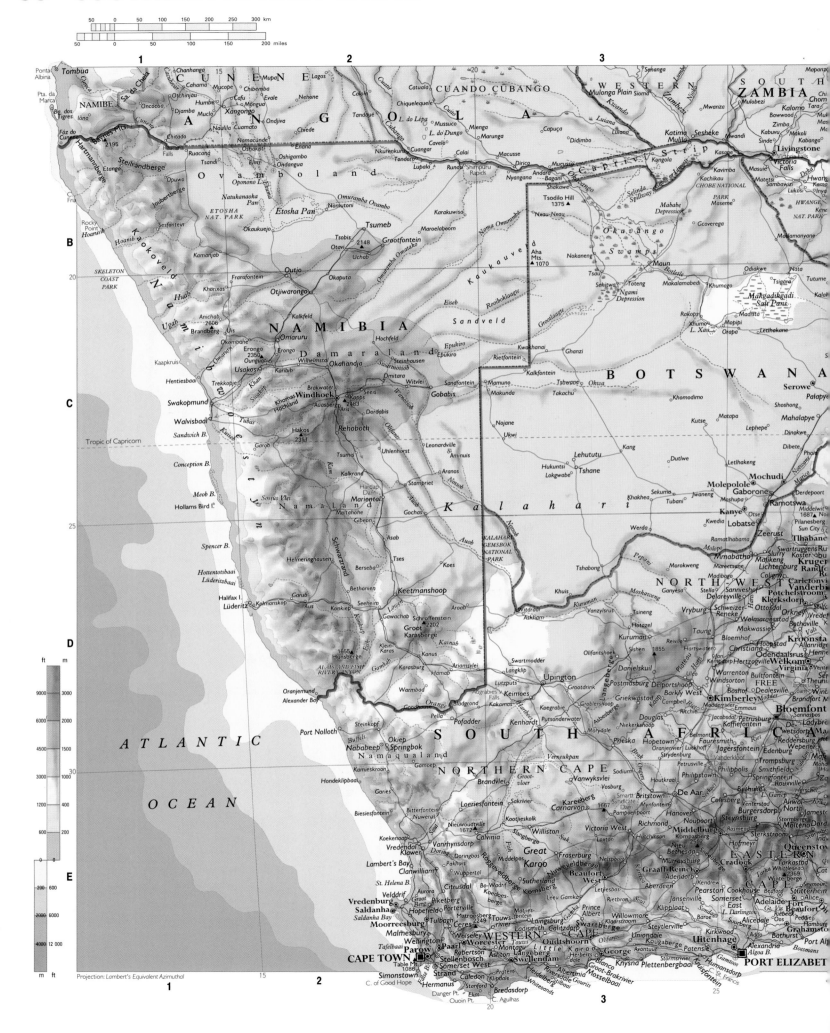

6

7

8

B

A

C

B

C

D

9

MOZAMBIQUE

CHANNEL

INDIAN

OCEAN

MOZAMBIQUE

INDIAN

OCEAN

ZIMBABWE

MOZAMBIQUE

MALAWI

ZAMBEZIA

TETE

MADAGASCAR

Antananarivo

Antsiranana

Mahajanga

Fianarantsoa

Toamasina

Toliara

HARARE

Chitungwiza

PRETORIA

JOHANNESBURG

DURBAN

Maputo

MADAGASCAR

On same scale as General Map

COPYRIGHT GEORGE PHILIP LTD.

East from Greenwich

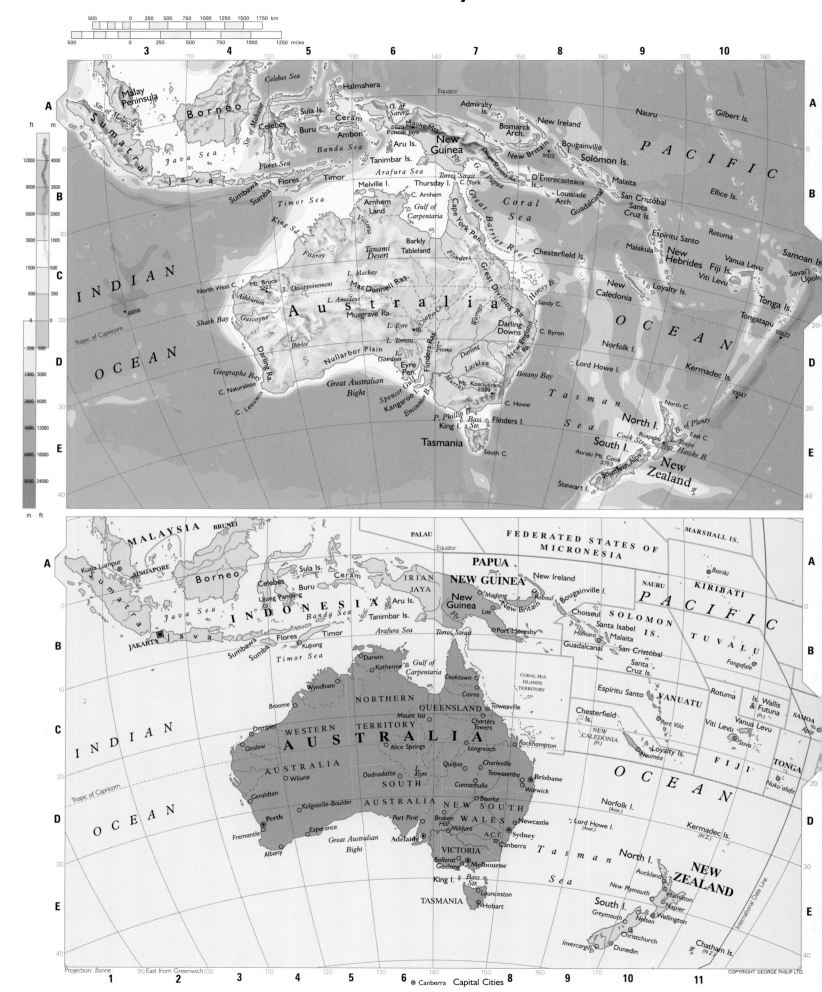

500   0   250 500 750 1000 1250 1500 1750 km

500   0   250   500   750   1000   1250 miles

Physical map labels:

Malay Peninsula · Str. of Malacca · Sumatra · Java · Borneo · Celebes Sea · Halmahera · Equator · Admiralty Is. · New Ireland · Nauru · Gilbert Is. · PACIFIC

Celebes · Sula Is. · Ceram · Buru · Ambon · Aru Is. · Maoke Mts. Puncak Jaya 5029 · New Guinea · Bismarck Arch. · New Britain 9103 · Bougainville · Solomon Is. · Malaita

Sumbawa · Sumba · Java Sea · Flores Sea · Flores · Timor · Tanimbar Is. · Arafura Sea · G. of Sarera · Owen Stanley Ra. · D'Entrecasteaux · San Cristóbal · Santa Cruz Is. · Ellice Is.

INDIAN · Timor Sea · Melville I. · Arnhem Land · C. Arnhem · Thursday I. · C. York · Torres Strait · G. of Papua · Coral Sea · Louisiade Arch. · Guadalcanal · Espíritu Santo · Rotuma · Samoan Is. · Savai'i · Upolu

King Sd. · Victoria · Gulf of Carpentaria · Cape York Pen. · Great Barrier Reef · Chesterfield Is. · Malakula · New Hebrides · Fiji Is. · Vanua Levu

Fitzroy · Barkly Tableland · Tanami Desert · Flinders · Great Dividing Ra. · New Caledonia · Viti Levu · Tonga Is.

North West C. · Mt. Bruce 1227 · L. Disappointment · L. Mackay · MacDonnell Ras. · Hervey B. · Loyalty Is. · OCEAN · Tongatapu

Ashburton · Australia · L. Amadeus · Cooper Ck. · Sandy C. · 10822

Shark Bay · Gascoyne · Musgrave Ra. · L. Eyre · Warrego · Darling Downs · C. Byron · Norfolk I.

Tropic of Capricorn · 6658 · L. Barlee · L. Torrens · L. Frome · Darling · New England · Kermadec Is.

OCEAN · Geographe Bay · Darling Ra. · Nullarbor Plain · Gairdner · Eyre Pen. · Lachlan · Murray · Botany Bay · Lord Howe I. · 10047

C. Naturaliste · Great Australian Bight · Spencer Gulf · Mt. Kosciuszko 2230 · Tasman · North C.

C. Leeuwin · Kangaroo I. · Encounter B. · C. Howe · Sea · North I. · B. of Plenty · East C.

P. Phillip B. · Bass Str. · Flinders I. · Ruapehu 2797 · Hawke B. · Cook Strait · L. Taupo

King I. · Bass Str. · Tasmania · South C. · Aoraki Mt. Cook 3753 · Southern Alps · New Zealand · South I.

Stewart I.

Elevation scale:
ft / m · 12000 / 4000 · 9000 / 3000 · 6000 / 2000 · 3000 / 1000 · 1500 / 600 · 600 / 200 · 0 · 200 / 600 · 1000 / 3000 · 2000 / 6000 · 4000 / 12000 · 6000 / 18000 · 8000 / 24000 · m ft

Political map labels:

MALAYSIA · BRUNEI · PALAU · FEDERATED STATES OF MICRONESIA · MARSHALL IS.

Kuala Lumpur · SINGAPORE · Borneo · Sula Is. · Ceram · IRIAN JAYA · PAPUA NEW GUINEA · New Ireland · NAURU · KIRIBATI · Bairiki

Sumatra · Celebes · Buru · Aru Is. · New Guinea · Madang · Rabaul · Bougainville I. · PACIFIC

Ujung Pandang · Lae · New Britain · Choiseul · SOLOMON IS. · TUVALU

INDONESIA · Java Sea · Banda Sea · Tanimbar Is. · Port Moresby · Santa Isabel · Honiara · Malaita

JAKARTA · Java · Flores · Timor · Arafura Sea · Torres Strait · Guadalcanal · San Cristóbal · Fongafale

Sumbawa · Sumba · Kupang · Timor Sea · Darwin · Katherine · Gulf of Carpentaria · Cooktown · CORAL SEA ISLANDS TERRITORY · Santa Cruz Is.

Wyndham · NORTHERN · QUEENSLAND · Cairns · Espíritu Santo · VANUATU · Rotuma · Is. Wallis & Futuna (Fr.) · SAMOA

Broome · TERRITORY · Townsville · Chesterfield Is. · Port Vila · Vanua Levu · Apia

INDIAN · Dampier · WESTERN · Mount Isa · Charters Towers · NEW CALEDONIA (Fr.) · Viti Levu · Suva · FIJI

Onslow · AUSTRALIA · Alice Springs · Longreach · Rockhampton · Loyalty Is. · Nouméa · TONGA

AUSTRALIA · L. Eyre · Quilpie · Charleville · Toowoomba · Norfolk I. (Aust.) · Nuku'alofa

Tropic of Capricorn · Oodnadatta · Wiluna · SOUTH · Cunnamulla · Warwick · Brisbane · OCEAN

Geraldton · Kalgoorlie-Boulder · AUSTRALIA · Bourke · NEW SOUTH · Lord Howe I. (Aust.) · Kermadec Is. (N.Z.)

OCEAN · Perth · Port Pirie · Broken Hill · WALES · Newcastle · North I.

Fremantle · Esperance · Mildura · A.C.T. · Sydney · Tasman · NEW ZEALAND

Albany · Great Australian Bight · Adelaide · VICTORIA · Canberra · Sea · Auckland

Ballarat · Melbourne · New Plymouth · Hamilton

Geelong · King I. · Bass Str. · Napier · Wellington

TASMANIA · Launceston · South I. · Greymouth · Nelson

Hobart · Invercargill · Christchurch · Chatham Is. (N.Z.) · Dunedin

Projection: Bonne · 90 East from Greenwich 100 · COPYRIGHT GEORGE PHILIP LTD.

⊙ Canberra   Capital Cities

50   0   50   100   150   200 km
50   0   50   100   150 miles

64

PACIFIC OCEAN

North Island

C. Reinga
C. Maria van Diemen
North C.
Houhora Heads
Rangaunu B.
Ahipara B.
Kaitaia
Doubtless B.
Tauroa Pt.
Manganui
Whangaroa Harb.
Northland
B. of Islands
Okaihau
Opua
C. Brett
Rawene
Kaikohe
Hikurangi
Hokianga Harbour
Whangarei
Donnelly's Crossing
Whangarei Harb.
Dargaville
Waipu
Bream Hd.
Bream B.
Little Barrier I.
Great Barrier I.
Warkworth
C. Rodney
C. Colville
Cuvier I.
Kaipara Harbour
Helensville
Hauraki Gulf
Coromandel
Takapuna
Devonport
Whitianga
AUCKLAND
Manukau
Papakura
Thames
Waiuku
Pukekohe
Mercer
Paeroa
Waihi
Mayor I.
Waikato
Huntly
Te Aroha
Tauranga Harb.
Morrinsville
Tauranga
White I.
C. Runaway
Raglan
Hamilton
Cambridge
Te Puke
East C.
Kawhia Harbour
Te Awamutu
Putaruru
Whakatane
Kawerau
Opotiki
Raukumara Ra.
Mc Hikurangi 1753
Otorohanga
Tokoroa
Rotorua
Tarawera
Taneatua
Waipiro
Te Kuiti
Kinleith
Kaingaroa
Murupara
Motu
Tolaga Bay
Mokau
Mokau
Waiotapu
Forest
Mokau
Wairakei
Ongarue
Taupo
Waikaremoana
Ormond
Gisborne
North Taranaki Bight
Waitara
Taumarunui
L. Taupo
Ruatahuna
Poverty Bay
New Plymouth
Inglewood
Whangamomona
Turangi
Tarawera
Nuhaka
Waikokopu
Mt. Taranaki (Mt. Egmont) 2518
Stratford
Ohakune
Ruapehu 2797
Kaimanawa Mts.
Wairoa
Mahia Pen.
C. Egmont
Opunake
Eltham
Raetihi
Waiouru
Bay View
Hawke Bay
Kapuni
Hawera
Waverley
Taihape
Ruahine Ra.
Napier
C. Kidnappers
Patea
Mangaweka
Hastings
South Taranaki Bight
Wanganui
Waipawa
Marton
Hunterville
Waipukurau
Halcombe
Feilding
Dannevirke
Bulls
Woodville
Palmerston North
Foxton
Pahiatua
Shannon
Levin
Eketahuna
C. Turnagain
Paraparaumu
Otaki
Tararua Ra.
Kapiti I.
Masterton
Upper Hutt
Carterton
Pelorus Sd.
Featherston
Greytown
Petone
Martinborough
Wellington
Lower Hutt
Eastbourne
Wairarapa

South Island

C. Farewell
Golden B.
Collingwood
D'Urville I.
Tasman B.
Takaka
Tasman Mts.
Motueka
Karamea
Nelson
Havelock
Karamea Bight
Tadmor
Richmond
Picton
Seddonville
Murchison Rotoiti
Wakefield
Blenheim
Granity
Lyell
Waiau
Seddon
Lewis
Inangahua Junction
Mt. Travers 2338
Ward
Westport
Reefton
Spenser Mts.
2885 Mt. Tapuaenuku
Blackball
Grey
Lewis Pass
Clarence
Greymouth
Runanga
Hanmer Springs
Kaikoura Ra.
Kumara
Stillwater
Amuri Pass
Waiau
Hokitika
L. Brunner
Jacksons
Kaikoura
Ross
Waikari
Hurunui
Culverden
Waiau
Arthur's Pass
Waipara
Hawarden
Okuru
Haast
Waikari
Amberley
Rangiora
Pegasus Bay
Abut Hd.
Coleridge
Oxford
Kaiapoi
Whitecliffs
Springfield
New Brighton
Aoraki/Mt. Cook 3753
Southern Alps
Methven
Christchurch
Jackson B.
Staveley
Riccarton
Lyttelton
Lincoln
Canterbury Plains
Akaroa
Banks Pen.
Mt. Aspiring 3027
Fairlie
Southbridge
Little River
Mt. Earnslaw 2818
Ohai
Tekapo
Ashburton
Pranchi L.
Pukaki L.
Temuka
Ashburton Bight
Milford Sd.
Wanaka
Hawea
Timaru
Bligh Sound
Dunstan Mts.
St. Andrews
George Sound
Arrowtown
Cromwell
Kurow
Waimate
Queenstown
Clyde
Kakanui Mts.
Ngapara
Secretary I.
Alexandra
Naseby
Maheno
Oamaru
Doubtful Sd.
Anau Kingston
Garvie Mts.
Roxburgh
Dunback
Hampden
Manapouri
Otago
Waikouaiti
Palmerston
Breaksea Sd.
Eyre Mts.
Resolution I.
Mossburn
Umbrella Mts.
Port Chalmers
Dusky Sd.
Lumsden
Lawrence
Saunders C.
Southland
Mosgiel
Otago Harbour
Edievale
Fairfield
Chalky Inlet
Ohai
Kelso
Milton
Dunedin
Preservation Inlet
Clifden
Tuatapere
Nightcaps
Winton
Gore
Clinton
Te Waewae B.
Orepuki
Hedgehope
Mataura
Kaitangata
Balclutha
Riverton
Wyndham
Owaka
Nugget Pt.
Invercargill
Tokanui
Tahakopa
Bluff
Ruapuke I.
Foveaux Str.
Halfmoon Bay
Stewart I.
Southwest C.
Port Pegasus

TASMAN SEA

Westland Bight

Projection : Conical with two standard parallels
East from Greenwich
COPYRIGHT GEORGE PHILIP LTD.

SAMOA ISLANDS
1:12 000 000

SAMOA
AMERICAN SAMOA
Savai'i
Apia
Upolu
Pago Pago
Tutuila
West from Greenwich

FIJI AND TONGA ISLANDS
1:12 000 000

Wallis & Futuna (Fr.)
Futuna
Niuafo'ou (Tonga)
Thikombia
Yasawa Group
Lambasa
Vanua Levu
Lautoka 1323
Taveuni
Koro
Vanua Mbalavu
Nandi
Levuka
Viti Levu
Ovalau
Gau
Lakemba
TONGA (Friendly Is.)
Suva
Koro Sea
Lau Group
FIJI
Moala
Vava'u
Kandavu
Vatoa
Tofua
Tongatapu
Nuku'alofa
Nuku'alofa

50   0   50   100   150   200 km
50   0   50   100   150 miles

ft   m
9000   3000
6000   2000
3000   1000
1200   400
600   200
0   0
200   600
2000   6000
4000   12 000
6000   18 000
m   ft

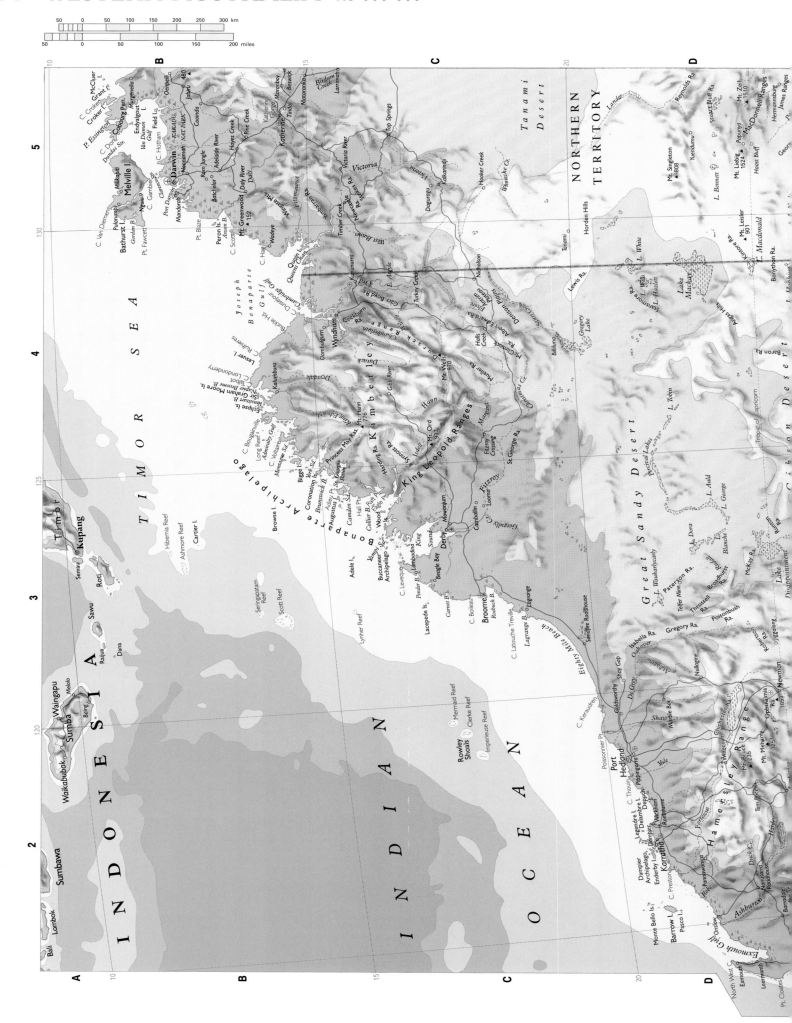

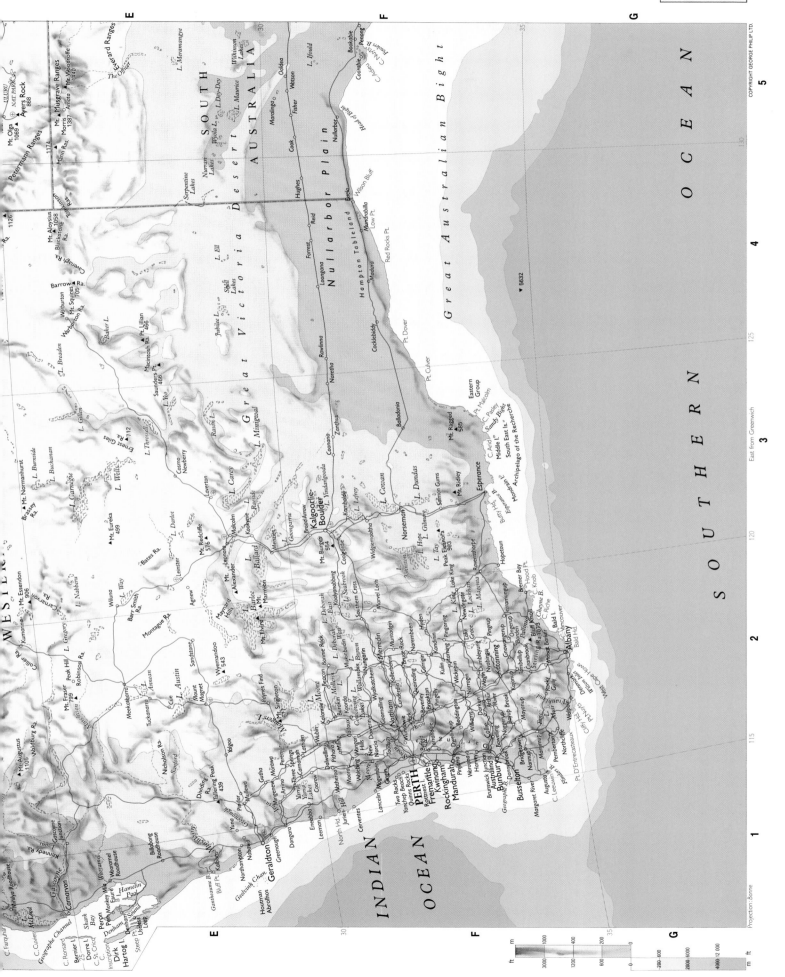

WESTERN

SOUTH
AUSTRALIA

Great Victoria Desert

Nullarbor Plain

Hampton Tableland

Great Australian Bight

INDIAN
OCEAN

SOUTHERN

OCEAN

ULURU
NAT. PARK
Ayers Rock
868

Mt. Olga
1069
Mt. Musgrave Ranges
Morris 1387 Mt. Woodroffe
Ra. 1174 Amata 1440
Petermann Ranges
The Officer

Peron
Shark Bay
Hamelin Pool

Geraldton

PERTH
Fremantle
Rockingham
Mandurah
Bunbury
Busselton

Albany

Kalgoorlie-
Boulder

Esperance

Norseman

COPYRIGHT GEORGE PHILIP LTD.

East from Greenwich

Projection: Bonne

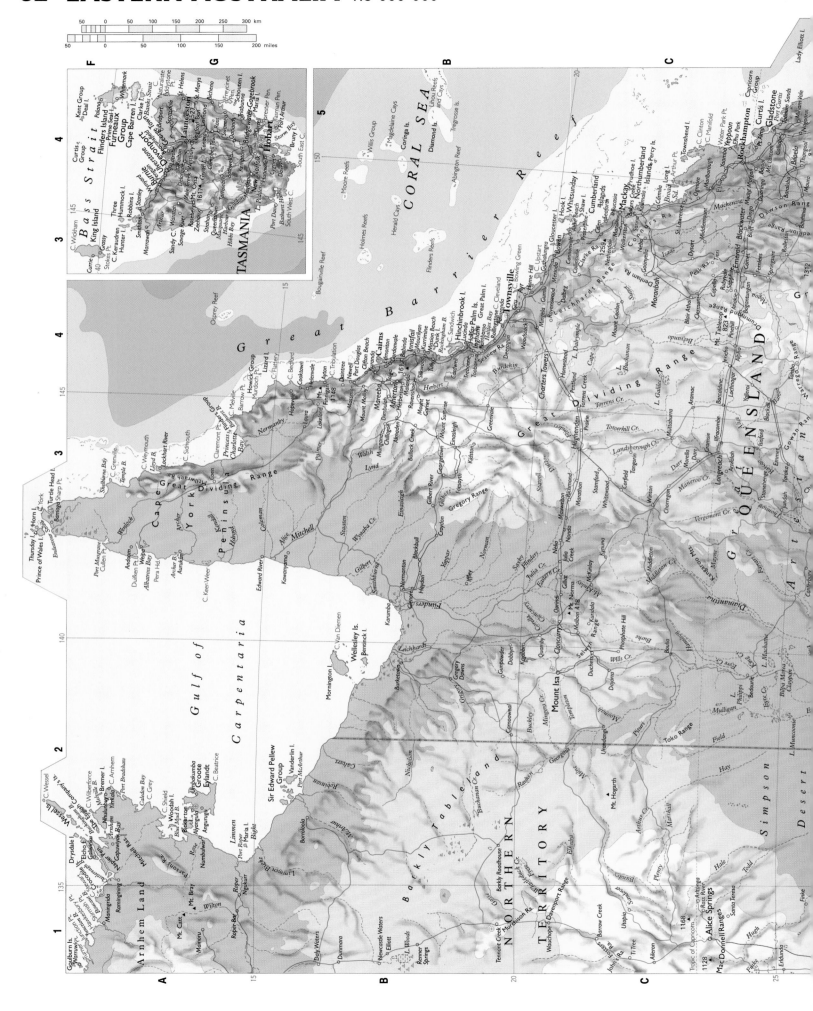

SOUTH AUSTRALIA

NEW SOUTH WALES

V I C T O R I A

T A S M A N   S E A

S O U T H E R N   O C E A N

Bass Strait

BRISBANE
Gold Coast
Tweed Heads

SYDNEY
Newcastle
Gosford
Wollongong

CANBERRA
AUSTRALIAN CAPITAL TERRITORY

ADELAIDE

MELBOURNE
Geelong

Broken Hill

Mount Gambier

King Island

Flinders Island
Furneaux
Group
Cape Barren I.

Projection: Bonne

East from Greenwich

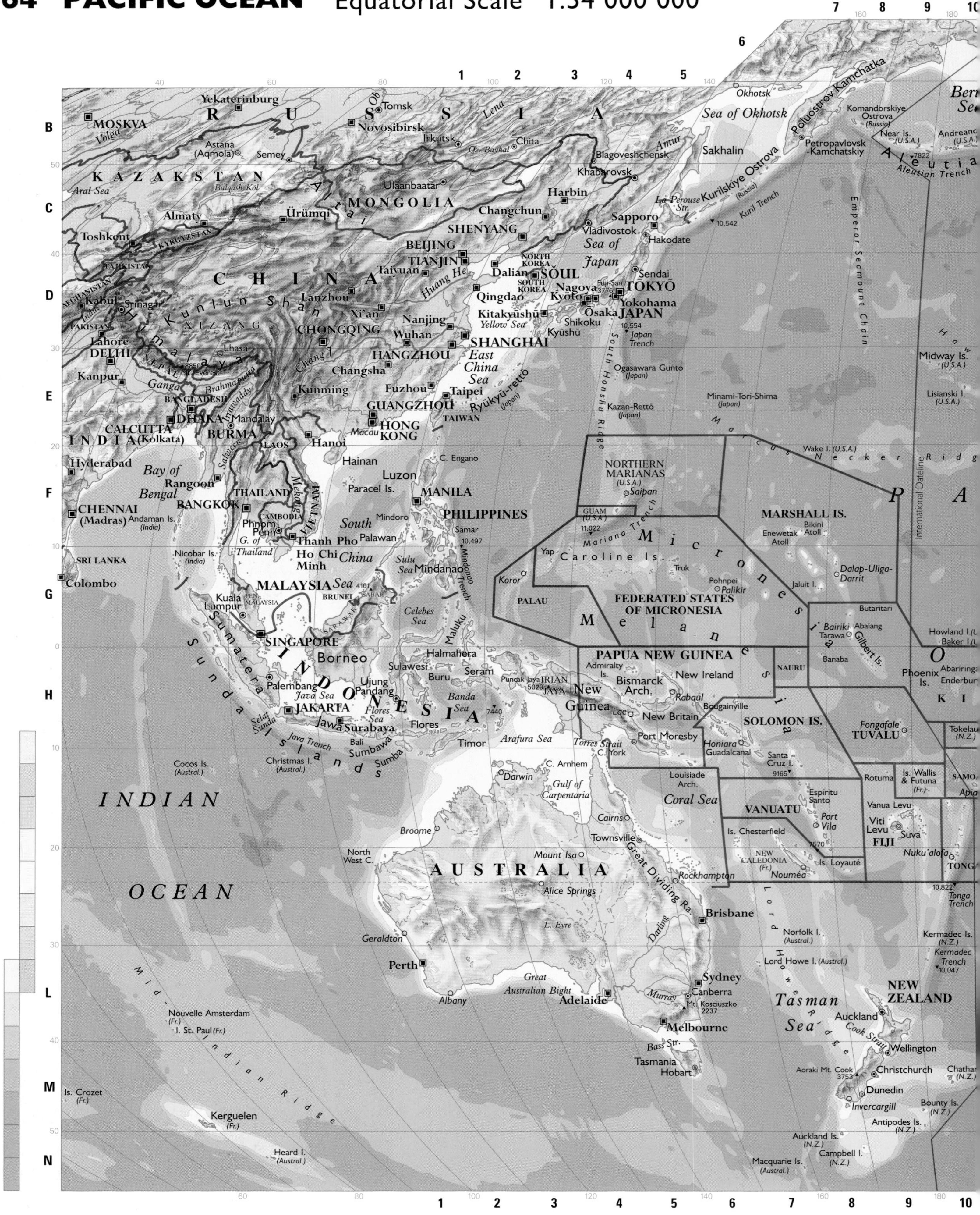

7   160   8   9   180   10

6

1   100   2   3   120   4   5   140

B MOSKVA
Volga
Yekaterinburg
Tomsk
Novosibirsk
R U S S I A
Lena
Ob
Irkutsk
Chita
Baykal
Blagoveshchensk
Amur
Khabarovsk
Okhotsk
Sea of Okhotsk
Poluostrov Kamchatka
Komandorskiye Ostrova (Russia)
Near Is.
Petropavlovsk-Kamchatskiy
Andreano (U.S.A.)
Bera
Sea

Astana (Aqmola)
Semey
KAZAKSTAN
50
Balqash Kol
Ulaanbaatar
MONGOLIA
Changchun
Harbin
Sapporo
Sakhalin
La Perouse Str.
Kurilskiye Ostrova (Russia)
Kuril Trench
10,542
Aleutia
Aleutian Trench
7822

C Aral Sea
Almaty
Ürümqi
Altai
Vladivostok
Hakodate
Sea of Japan

Toshkent
KYRGYZSTAN
SHENYANG
Emperor Seamount Chain

40
BEIJING
TIANJIN
Taiyuan
NORTH KOREA
SOUL
SOUTH KOREA
Dalian
Sendai
Fuji-San 3776
TOKYO
How

D TAJIKISTAN
Kabul
Srinagar
AFGHANISTAN
C H I N A
Kunlun Shan
Lanzhou
Xi'an
Nanjing
Qingdao
Yellow Sea
Nagoya
Kyoto
Osaka
JAPAN
Shikoku
Kyūshū
Kitakyūshū
Yokohama
10,554
Japan Trench
Midway Is. (U.S.A.)

PAKISTAN
Lahore
DELHI
XIZANG
Himalaya
8850
Everest
CHONGQING
Wuhan
SHANGHAI
East China Sea
Ogasawara Gunto (Japan)
Lisianski I. (U.S.A.)

E Kanpur
Ganga
Lhasa
Chang Jiang
HANGZHOU
Changsha
Kunming
Fuzhou
Taipei
Ryūkyū-retto (Japan)
Minami-Tori-Shima (Japan)

30
Brahmaputra
BANGLADESH
DHAKA
Mandalay
GUANGZHOU
TAIWAN
Kazan-Rettō (Japan)
South Honshu Ridge
Morcus

CALCUTTA (Kolkata)
I N D I A
BURMA
Macau
HONG KONG
Wake I. (U.S.A.)
Necker Ridge
P A

F Hyderabad
LAOS
Hanoi
Hainan
C. Engano
Luzon
Paracel Is.
MANILA
NORTHERN MARIANAS (U.S.A.)
Saipan
MARSHALL IS.
International Dateline.

Bay of Bengal
Rangoon
THAILAND
Mindoro
PHILIPPINES
Samar
GUAM (U.S.A.)
11,922
Mariana Trench
Micro
Enewetak Atoll
Bikini Atoll

CHENNAI (Madras)
Andaman Is. (India)
BANGKOK
CAMBODIA
Phnom Penh
Thanh Pho
Palawan
Yap
Caroline Is.
Truk
n e s i a
Dalap-Uliga-Darrit

10
SRI LANKA
Nicobar Is. (India)
G. of Thailand
Ho Chi Minh
South China Sea
Sulu Sea
Mindanao
10,497
Mindanao Trench
Koror
Pohnpei
Palikir
Jaluit I.

G Colombo
MALAYSIA
Celebes Sea
4101
BRUNEI
SABAH
FEDERATED STATES OF MICRONESIA
PALAU
Butaritari
Bairiki
Abaiang
Tarawa
Gilbert Is.

Kuala Lumpur
PEN. MALAYSIA
SINGAPORE
SARAWAK
Sulawesi
Halmahera
Maluku
Seram
Melanesi
NAURU
Banaba
Howland I. (U.
Baker I. (U.

Sumatera
Borneo
Buru
IRIAN JAYA
5029
PAPUA NEW GUINEA
Admiralty Is.
New Ireland
Bismarck Arch.
Phoenix Is.
Abariringa
Enderbur

H Palembang
Ujung Pandang
Banda Sea
Puncak Jaya
New Guinea
Lae
New Britain
Rabaul
Bougainville
SOLOMON IS.
Fongafale
TUVALU
KI

JAKARTA
Jawa
Surabaya
Flores Sea
7440
Flores
Port Moresby
Honiara
Guadalcanal
Tokelau (N.Z.)

Selat Sunda
Bali
Sumbawa
Timor
Arafura Sea
Torres Strait
C. York
Santa Cruz Is.
9165
Rotuma
Is. Wallis & Futuna (Fr.)
SAMO
Apia

10
Java Trench
Sunda Islands
Sumba
C. Arnhem
Gulf of Carpentaria
Coral Sea
VANUATU
Espiritu Santo
Vanua Levu
Viti Levu
Suva
FIJI

Cocos Is. (Austral.)
Christmas Island (Austral.)
Darwin
Broome
Cairns
Townsville
Is. Chesterfield
7570
Port Vila
Is. Loyauté
Nuku'alofa
TONGA

L I N D I A N
North West C.
Mount Isa
AUSTRALIA
Great Dividing Ra.
NEW CALEDONIA (Fr.)
Nouméa
10,822
Tonga Trench

20
O C E A N
Alice Springs
Rockhampton
Norfolk I. (Austral.)
Kermadec Is. (N.Z.)

Geraldton
L. Eyre
Brisbane
Lord Howe I. (Austral.)
Kermadec Trench
10,047

30
Perth
Great Australian Bight
Darling
Murray
Sydney
Canberra
Mt. Kosciuszko 2237
Tasman Sea
NEW ZEALAND
Auckland

Albany
Adelaide
Melbourne
Bass Str.
Cook Strait
Wellington
Chatham (N.Z.)

M Nouvelle Amsterdam (Fr.)
I. St. Paul (Fr.)
Mid-Indian Ridge
Tasmania
Hobart
Aoraki Mt. Cook 3753
Christchurch
Dunedin
Bounty Is. (N.Z.)

Is. Crozet (Fr.)
Invercargill
Antipodes Is. (N.Z.)

50
Kerguelen (Fr.)
Auckland Is. (N.Z.)
Campbell I. (N.Z.)

N Heard I. (Austral.)
Macquarie I. (Austral.)

60   80   100   2   120   4   140   160   180   10
1   2   3   4   5   6   7   8   9   10

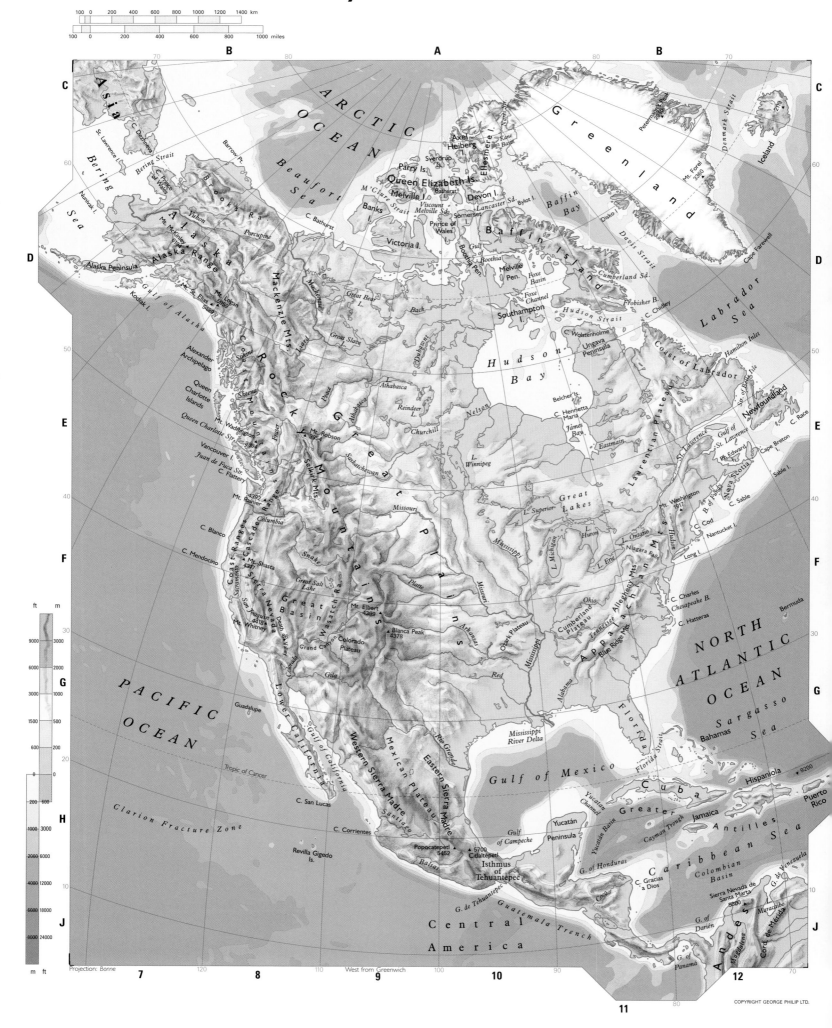

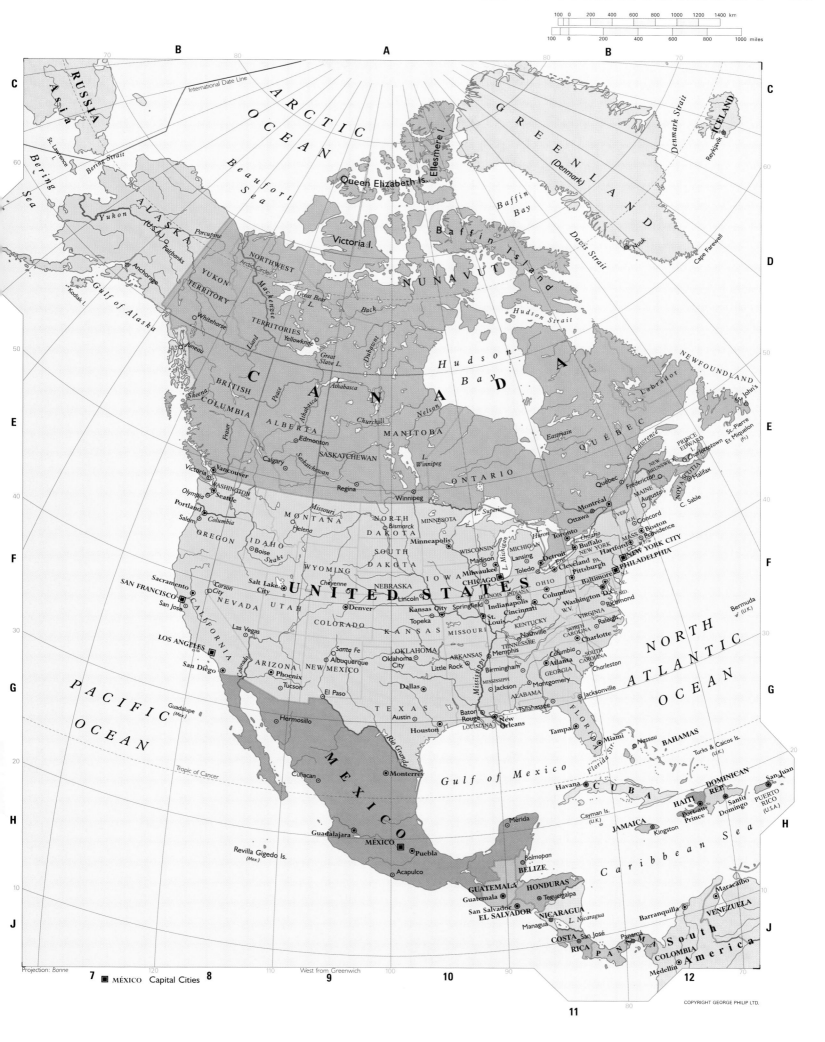

100 0 200 400 600 800 1000 1200 1400 km
100 0 200 400 600 800 1000 miles

Projection: *Bonne*

7 ■ MÉXICO Capital Cities 8

West from Greenwich

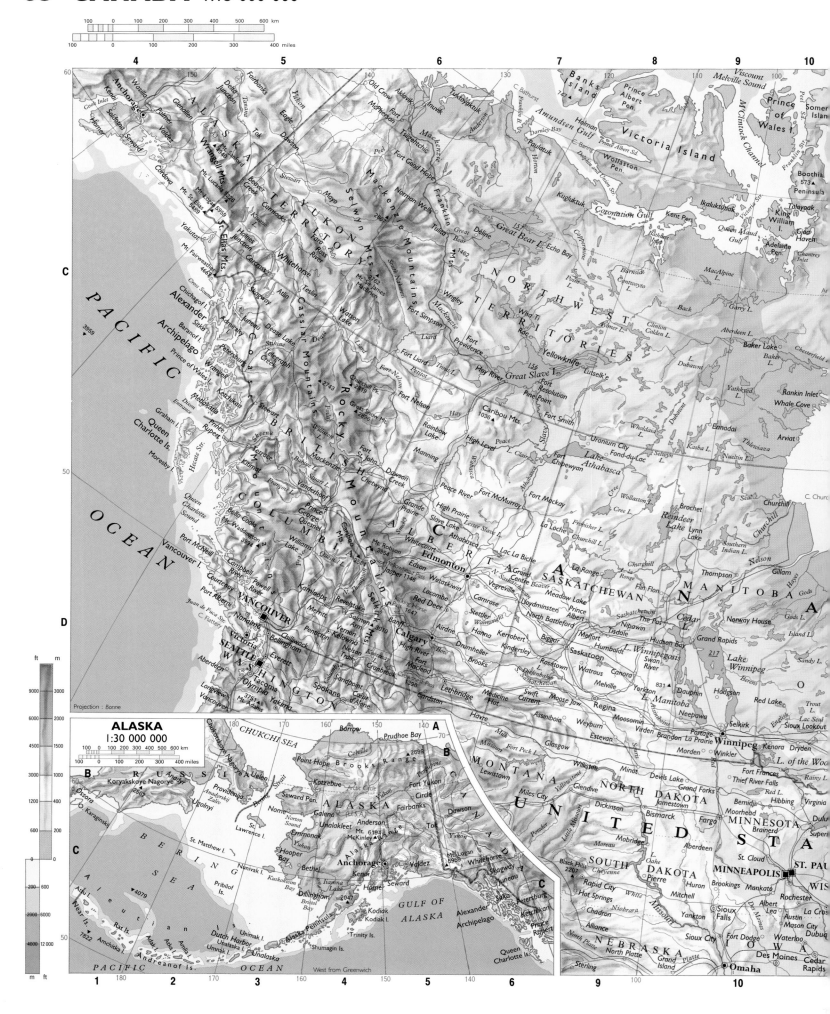

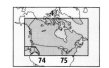

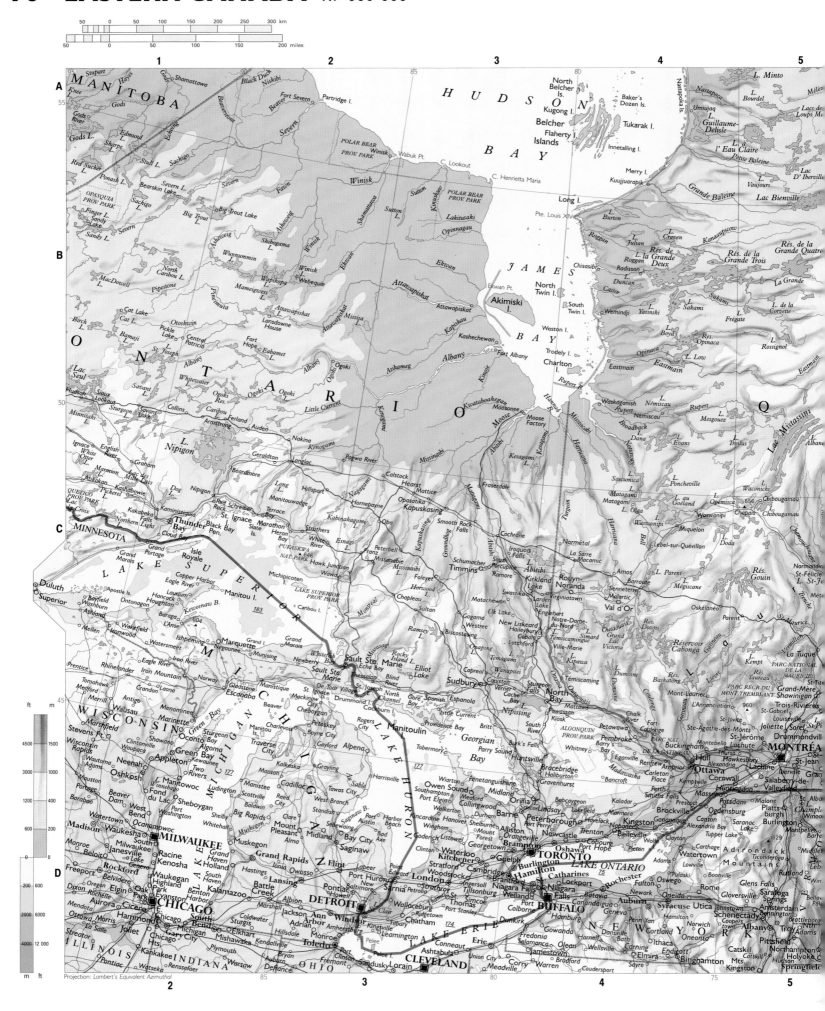

71

A

LABRADOR

SEA

N E W F O U N D L A N D

Z E
W
F
O
U
N
D
L
A
N
D

Labrador

Smallwood Reservoir

B

Labrador City
Fermont

Labrador un

Newfoundland

C

L a b r a d o r

St. Lawrence

U É B E C
Q U É B E C

Sept-Îles
Port-Cartier

Î. d'Anticosti

Dét. de Jacques-Cartier

GULF OF

ST. LAWRENCE

Corner Brook

Gander
Grand Falls
Windsor

St. John's

Pen. de Gaspé
Chic-Chocs

Gaspé

Îs. de la
Madeleine
(Québec)

Cabot Strait

ST-PIERRE
ET MIQUELON
(France)

Jonquière
La Baie
Chicoutimi
Alma

Rimouski

Rivière-du-Loup

Québec

N E W
B R U N S W I C K

Edmundston

Bathurst

Newcastle

Miramichi

PRINCE EDWARD
ISLAND

Charlottetown

Summerside

CAPE BRETON
HIGHLANDS
NAT. PARK

Sydney
Glace Bay

Cape Breton
Island

Fredericton

Moncton

Saint
John

Amherst
Truro

N O V A   S C O T I A

Halifax
Dartmouth

Bay of Fundy

Sackville

M A I N E

Sherbrooke

Bangor

Augusta
Lewiston

Portland

A T L A N T I C

Sable I.
(Nova Scotia)

N E W   H A M P S H I R E

Concord
Manchester
Nashua

BOSTON
Quincy
Brockton
Woonsocket

U N I T E D   **S T A T E S**

O C E A N

D

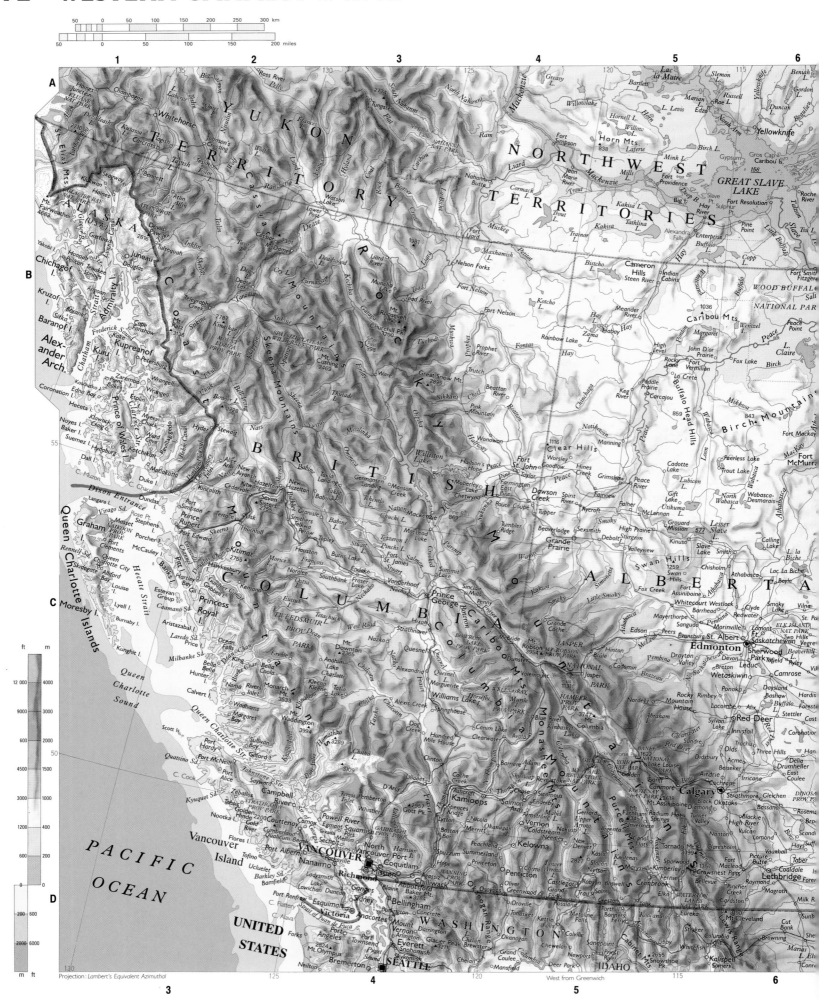

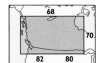

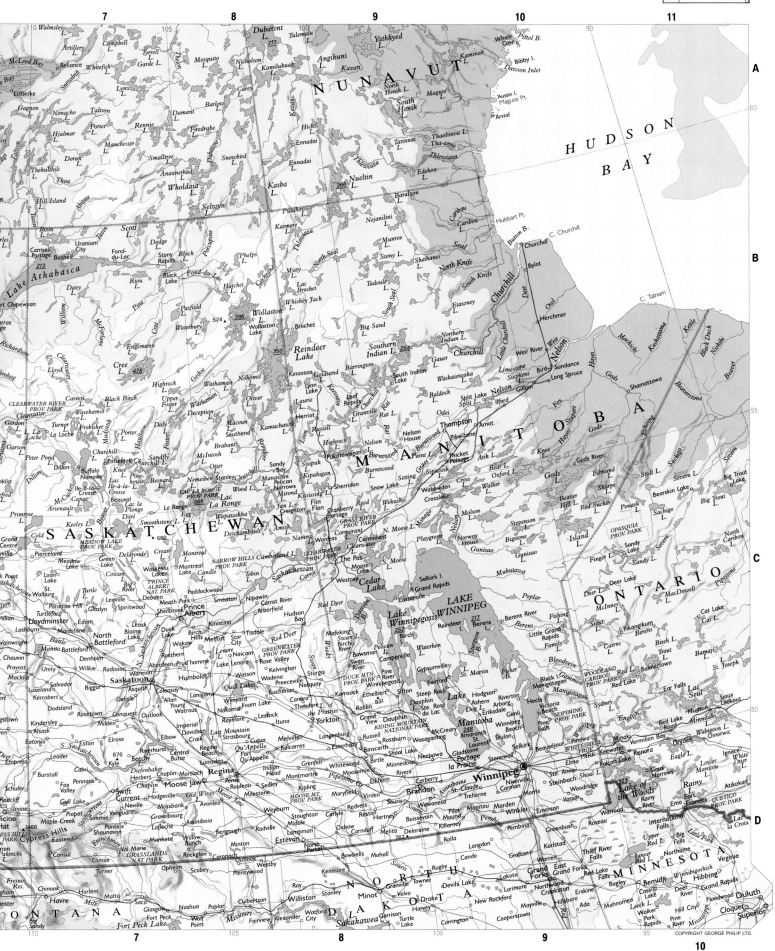

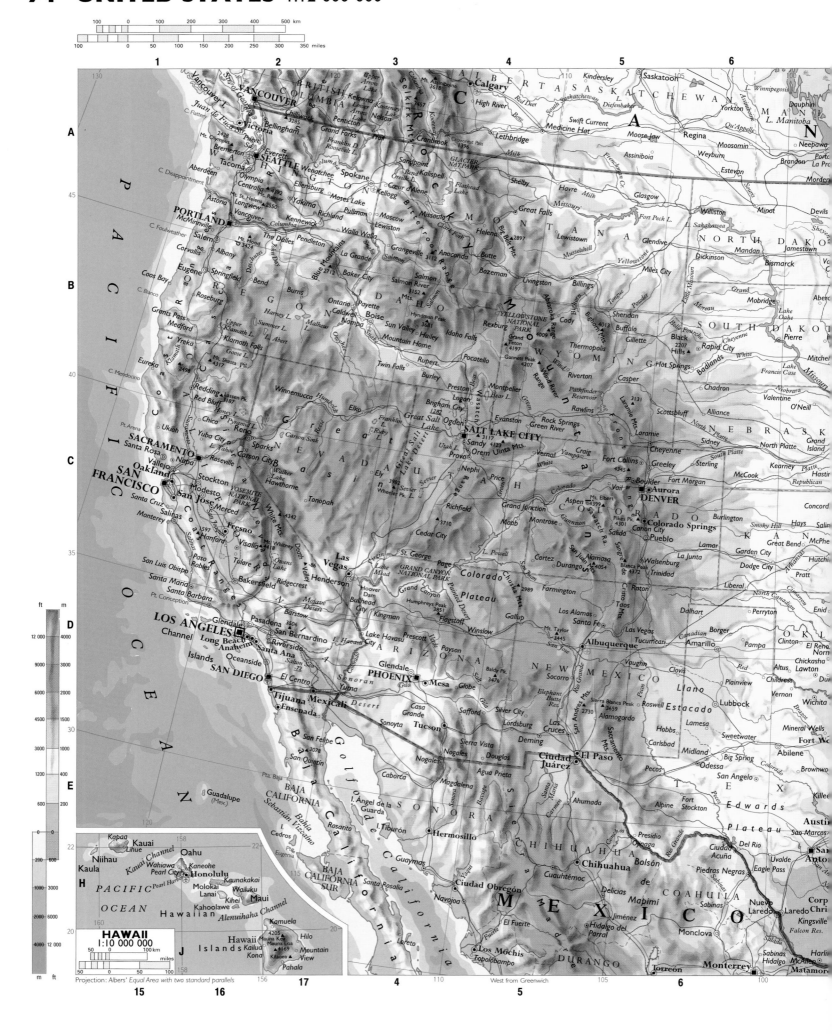

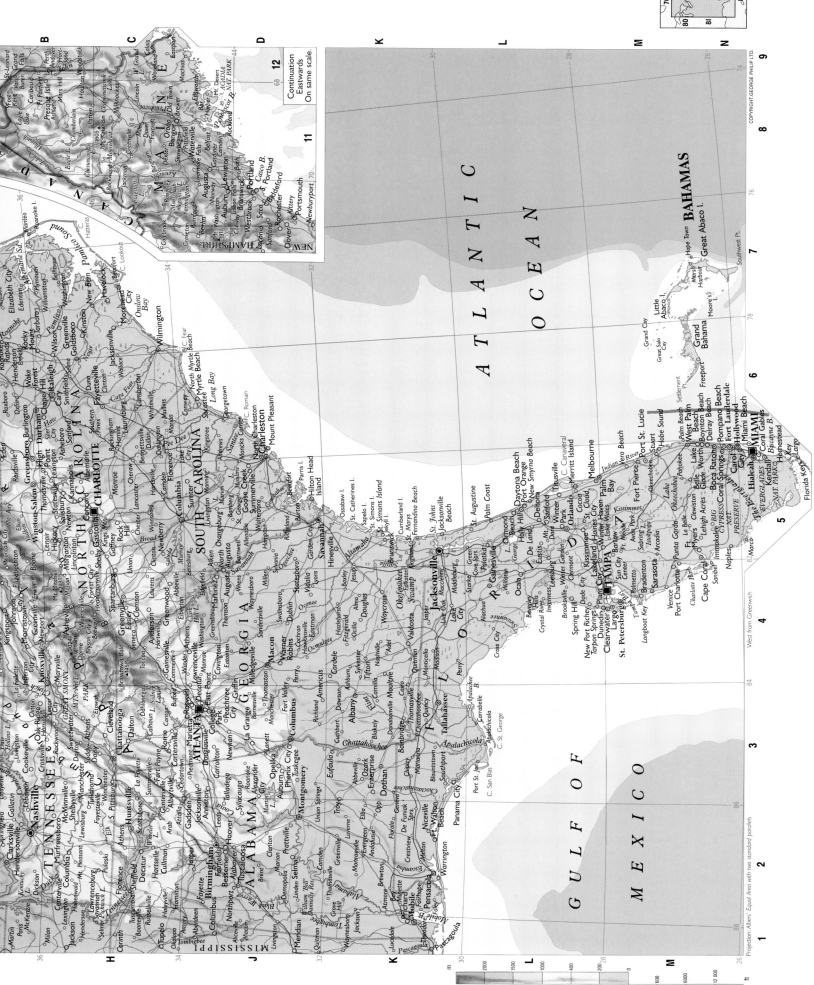

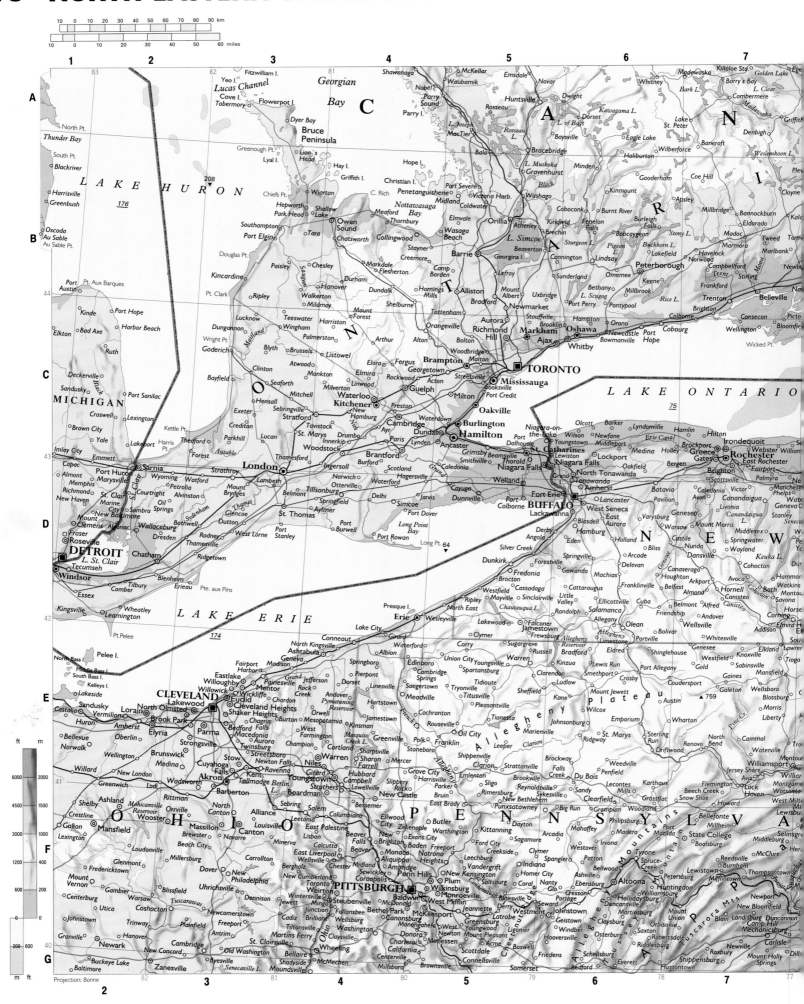

Projection: Bonne

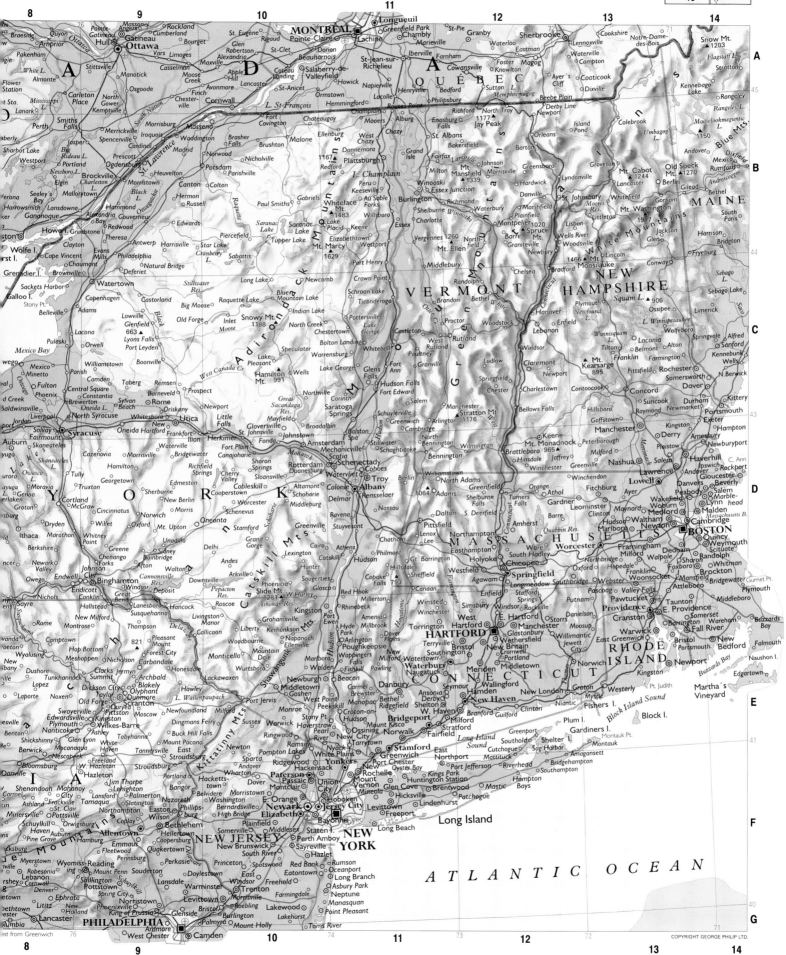

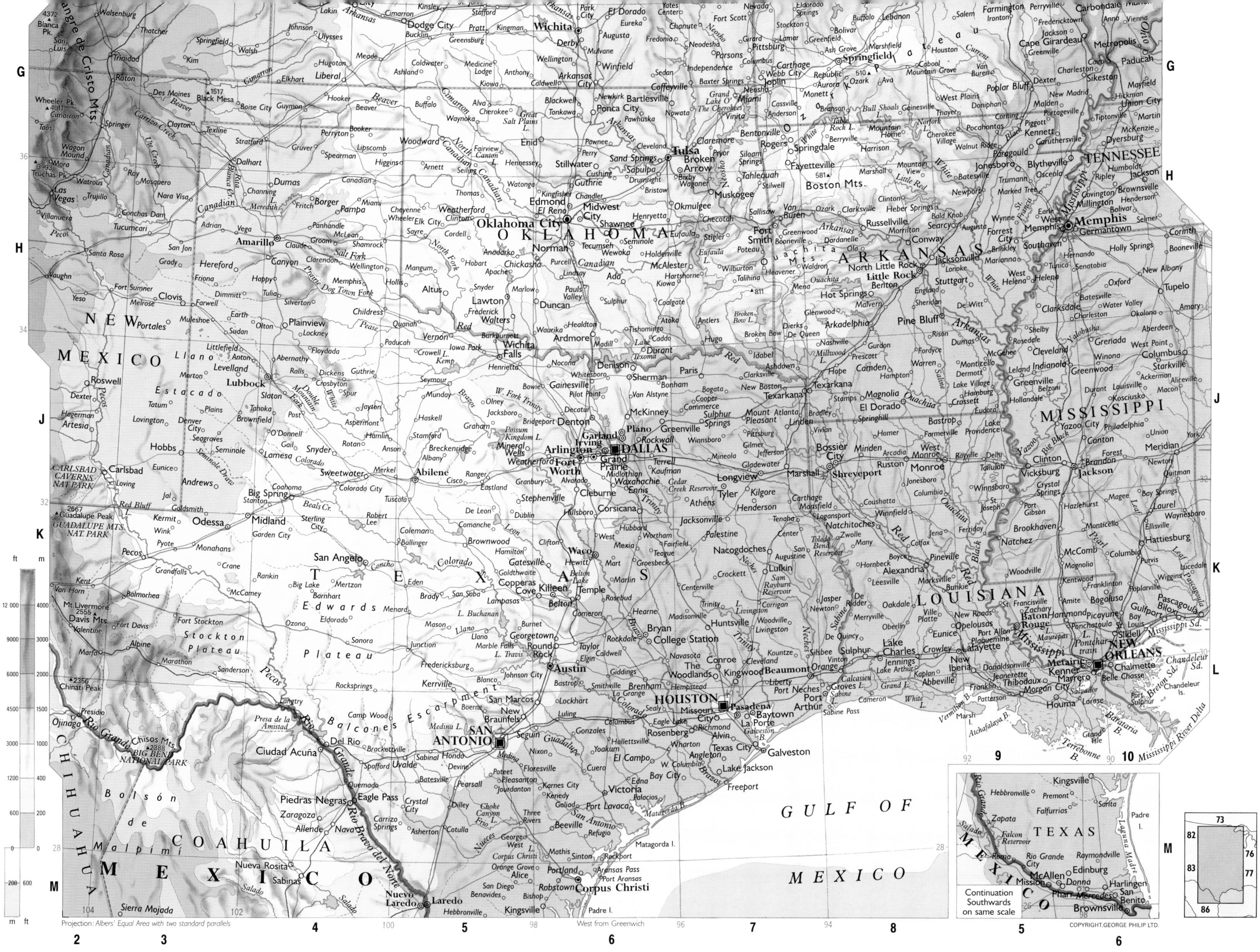

OKLAHOMA
ARKANSAS
MISSISSIPPI
TENNESSEE
LOUISIANA
TEXAS
NEW MEXICO
MEXICO
COAHUILA
CHIHUAHUA
GULF OF MEXICO
Oklahoma City
Tulsa
Wichita
Memphis
Little Rock
DALLAS
Fort Worth
HOUSTON
SAN ANTONIO
Austin
NEW ORLEANS
Shreveport
Jackson
Amarillo
Lubbock
Corpus Christi
Galveston
Laredo
Brownsville
Continuation Southwards on same scale
Projection: Albers' Equal Area with two standard parallels
West from Greenwich
COPYRIGHT.GEORGE PHILIP LTD.

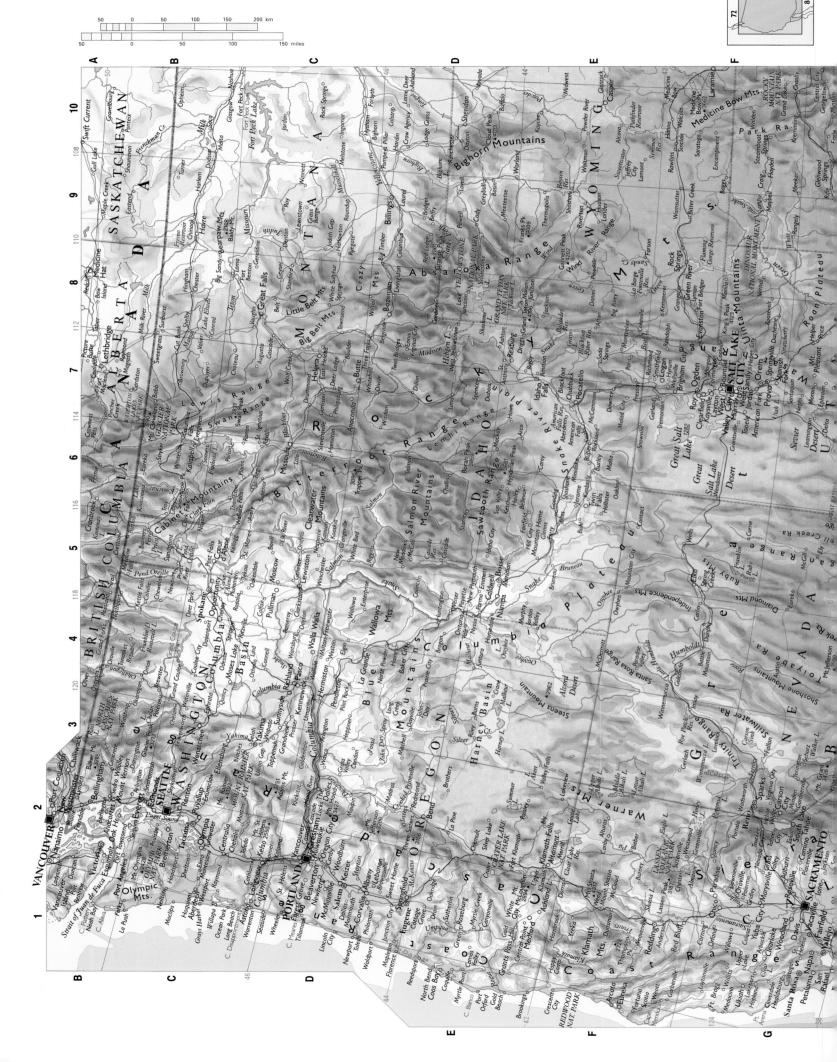

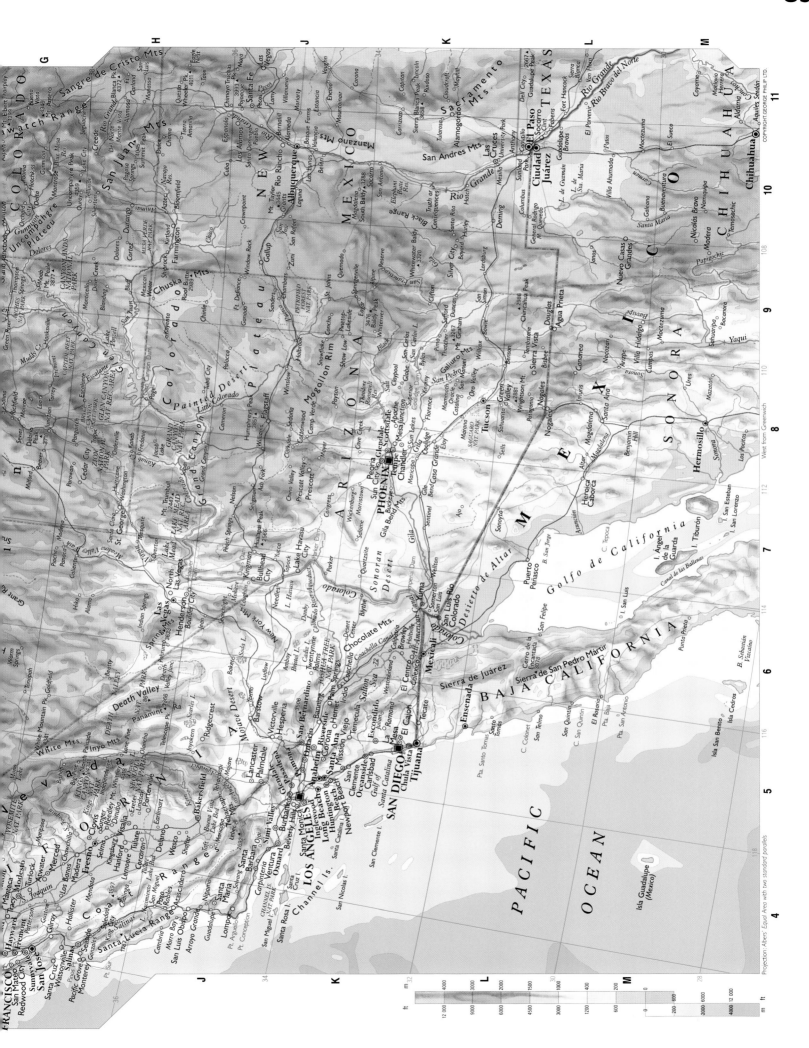

WESTERN WASHINGTON REGION
On same scale

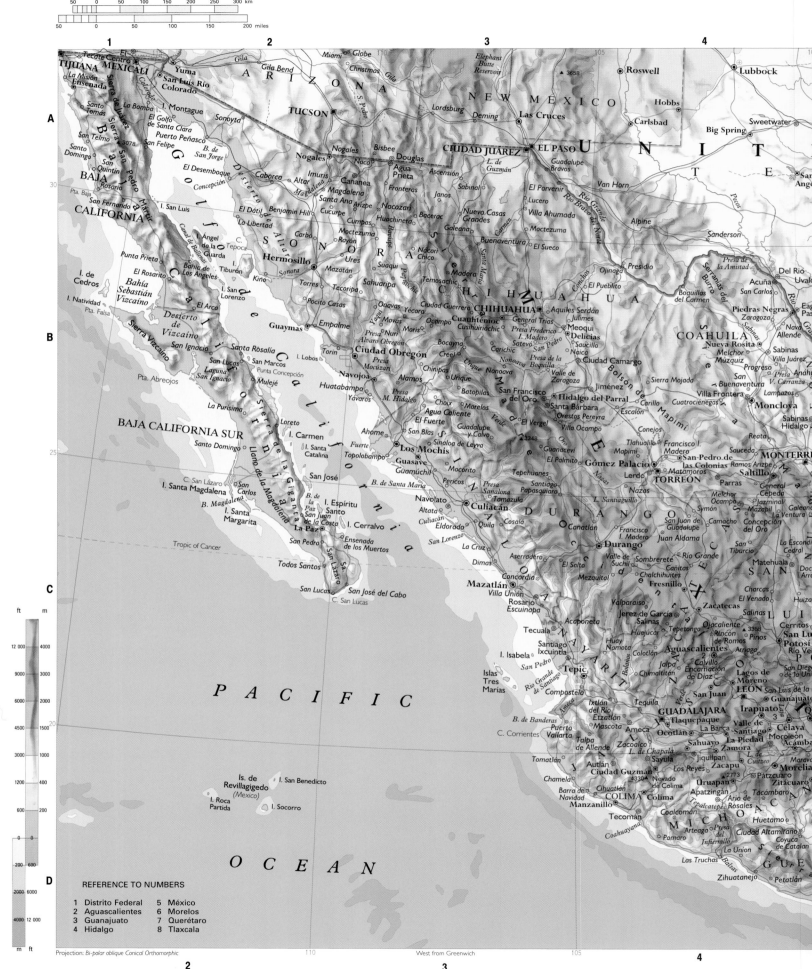

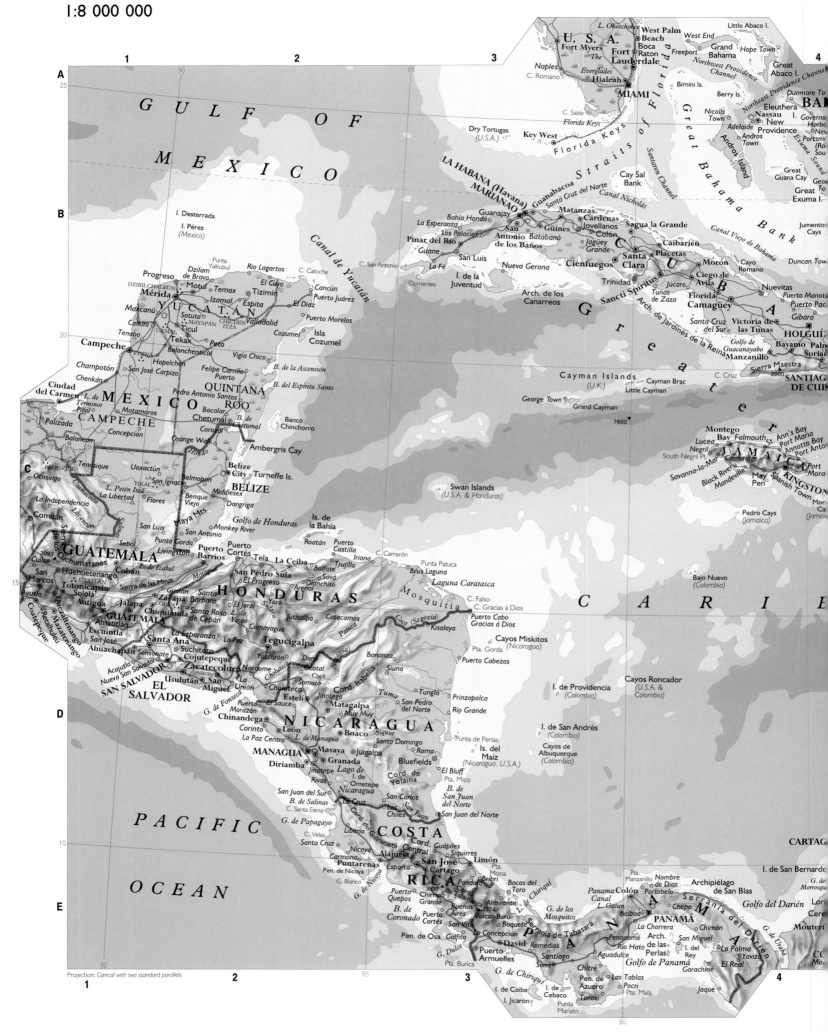

Projection: Conical with two standard parallels

100 0 200 400 600 800 1000 1200 1400 km
100 0 200 400 600 800 1000 miles

| | | | | | | 1 | | | | 2 | | | | 3 | | | 4 | | | | 5 | | | 6 | | | 7 |

Tropic of Cancer

NORTH ATLANTIC OCEAN

Yucatan Channel
Cuba
Greater Antilles
Gulf of Campeche
Yucatán Peninsula
Turks & Caicos Is.
Hispaniola
9200
Puerto Rico
Lesser Antilles
Isthmus of Tehuantepec
G. de Honduras
Jamaica
Guadeloupe
Dominica
Martinique
St. Lucia
St. Vincent
Barbados
Grenada
Tobago
Trinidad
Guatemala Trench
Coco
C. Gracias a Dios
L. Nicaragua
Panama Canal
Gulf of Panamá
G. of Darién
Caribbean Sea
C. de la Aguja
5800
Sierra Nevada de Santa Marta
L. Maracaibo
I. Margarita
Cordillera Occidental
Cordillera Central
Cordillera Oriental
Cord. de Mérida
Llanos
Meta
Orinoco
Guiana Highlands
Mt. Roraima 2810
Sierra Pacaraima
C. Orange
Guaviare
Branco
Caroní
Essequibo
Serra Tumucumaque
C. de San Francisco
Caquetá
Negro
Cotopaxi 5897
Chimborazo 6267
PACIFIC
Galapagos Is.
G. of Guayaquil
Pta. Pariñas
Pta. Negra
Marañón
Napo
Putumayo
Japurá
Amazon
Marajó I.
Equator
Amazon
Tocantins
Huascarán 6768
Ucayali
Juruá
Purus
Madeira
Iapiós
Xingu
Araguaia
Parnaíba
São Francisco
C. de São Roque
S e l v a s
Roosevelt
Aripuanã
Telês Pires
Arinos
Plat. of Borborema
Madre de Dios
Guaporé
Chincha Alta
Titicaca
Nevada Ancohuma 6550
Bolivian Plateau
L. de Poopó
Mamoré
Plateau of Mato Grosso
Brazilian Highlands
Paraguay
Abrolhos Bank
OCEAN
8050
Atacama Desert
Cerro Ojos del Salado 6863
Gran Chaco
Salado
Paraná
Serra da Mantiqueira 2890
Pico da Bandeira
C. Frio
Iguaçu Falls
Uruguay
Serra do Mar
Tropic of Capricorn
San Félix
San Ambrosio
Pilcomayo
A n d e s
Salinas Grandes
Salado
L. Mar Chiquita
Entre Ríos
Paraná
P a m p a
L. dos Patos
Mt. Aconcagua 6960
Sierra de Córdoba
Arch. de Juan Fernández
Río de la Plata
SOUTH ATLANTIC OCEAN
Colorado
Negro
Bahía Blanca
G. San Matías
6212
Chile Rise
Chiloé I.
Chonos Archipelago
Taitao Peninsula
Gulf of Penas
Wellington I.
Madre de Dios I.
Chubut
Mte. San Valentin 4058
P a t a g o n i a
Gulf of San Jorge
Valdés Peninsula
Argentine Basin
Santa Inés I.
Canal Cockburn
Magellan's Str.
Canal Beagle
C. Horn
West Falkland
East Falkland
Falkland Is.
Staten I.
Tierra del Fuego
South Georgia

ft m
20 6000
12000 4000
9000 3000
6000 2000
3000 1000
1500 500
600 200
0 0
0 0
200 600
1000 3000
2000 6000
4000 12000
6000 18000
8000 24000
m ft

Projection: Lambert's Azimuthal Equal Area

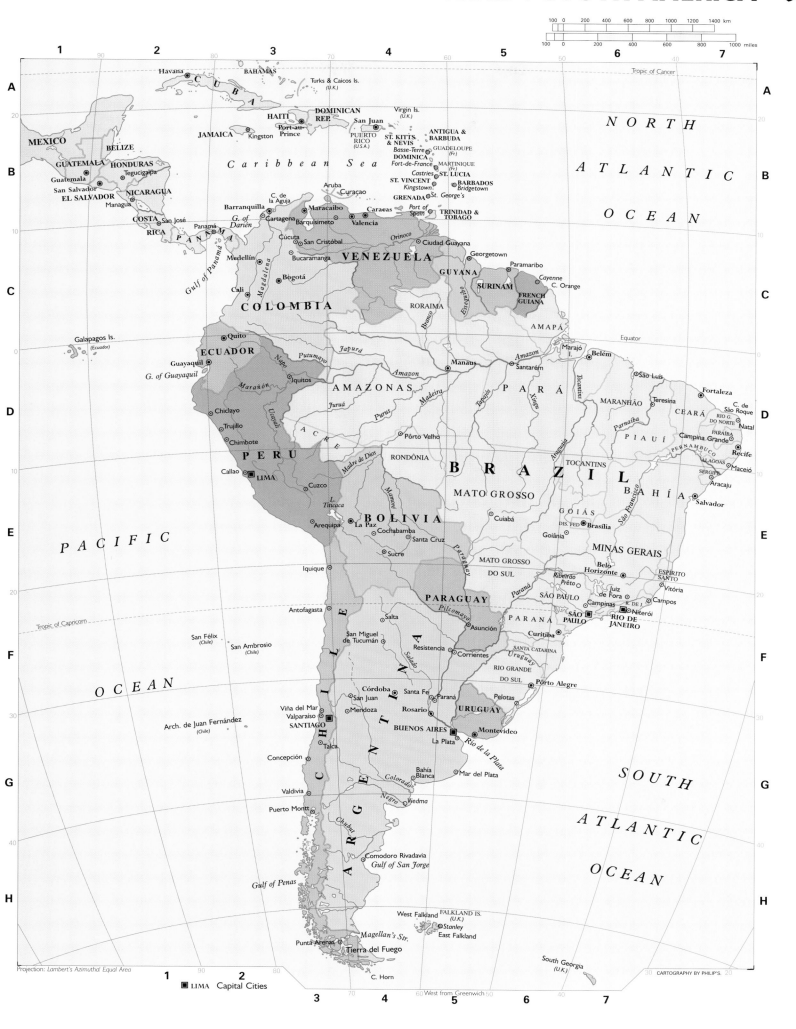

100 0   200   400   600   800   1000   1200   1400 km
100 0   200   400   600   800   1000 miles

1   90   2   80   3   70   4   60   5   6   40   7

Tropic of Cancer

Havana
BAHAMAS
CUBA
Turks & Caicos Is.
(U.K.)

NORTH

A

HAITI
JAMAICA   Kingston
Port-au-Prince
DOMINICAN REP.
San Juan
Virgin Is.
(U.K.)
PUERTO RICO
(U.S.A.)
ANTIGUA & BARBUDA
ST. KITTS & NEVIS
GUADELOUPE (Fr.)
Basse-Terre
DOMINICA
Fort-de-France
MARTINIQUE (Fr.)
Castries   ST. LUCIA
ST. VINCENT
Kingstown   BARBADOS
Bridgetown
GRENADA
St. George's

ATLANTIC

MEXICO
BELIZE
GUATEMALA
Guatemala
HONDURAS
Tegucigalpa
San Salvador
EL SALVADOR   NICARAGUA
Managua
COSTA
RICA   San José
Panamá
PANAMA

Caribbean   Sea

B

OCEAN

B

Barranquilla
C. de la Aguja
Aruba   Curaçao
Cartagena
Gulf of Darién
Maracaibo
Barquisimeto
Caracas
Valencia
Port of Spain
TRINIDAD & TOBAGO

Gulf of Panamá

Cúcuta   San Cristóbal
Orinoco
Ciudad Guayana
Georgetown
Paramaribo
Cayenne
C. Orange

Medellín
Bucaramanga
VENEZUELA
GUYANA
SURINAM
FRENCH GUIANA

C

Bogotá
Magdalena
Cali
COLOMBIA
RORAIMA
Branco
Essequibo
AMAPÁ

C

Galapagos Is.
(Ecuador)
Quito
ECUADOR
Napo
Putumayo
Japurá
Equator

PACIFIC

Guayaquil
G. of Guayaquil
Marañón
Iquitos
AMAZONAS
Amazon
Manaus
Santarém
Marajó I.
Belém
São Luís

Chiclayo
Juruá
Purus
Madeira
Tapajós
PARÁ
Xingu
Tocantins
MARANHÃO
Teresina
Fortaleza
C. de São Roque

D

Trujillo
Chimbote
Ucayali
ACRE
Pôrto Velho
RONDÔNIA
BRAZIL
PIAUÍ
CEARÁ
RIO G. DO NORTE   Natal
PARAÍBA   Campina Grande
PERNAMBUCO   Recife

D

PERU
Callao   LIMA
Cuzco
Madre de Dios
Mamoré
MATO GROSSO
Araguaia
São Francisco
TOCANTINS
BAHÍA
ALAGOAS   Maceió
SERGIPE
Aracaju
Salvador

L. Titicaca
Arequipa
La Paz
BOLIVIA
Cochabamba
Santa Cruz
Cuiabá
GOIÁS
DIS. FED   Brasília
Goiânia

E

Sucre
Paraguay
MATO GROSSO DO SUL
MINAS GERAIS
Belo Horizonte
ESPÍRITO SANTO

E

Iquique
Ribeirão Prêto
Juiz de Fora
Vitória
Campos

Tropic of Capricorn
Antofagasta
PARAGUAY
Pilcomayo
Paraná
SÃO PAULO
Campinas
R. DE J.
Niterói
RIO DE JANEIRO

San Félix
(Chile)
San Ambrosio
(Chile)
Salta
Asunción
PARANÁ
SÃO PAULO
Curitiba

F

San Miguel de Tucumán
Resistencia
Corrientes
SANTA CATARINA
Uruguay
RIO GRANDE DO SUL
Pôrto Alegre

OCEAN

F

Arch. de Juan Fernández
(Chile)
Córdoba
San Juan
Santa Fe
Paraná
Pelotas
URUGUAY
Rosario
Salado

Viña del Mar
Valparaíso
SANTIAGO
Mendoza
Buenos Aires
Montevideo

G

Talca
ARGENTINA
La Plata
Río de la Plata

G

Concepción
Bahía Blanca
Colorado
Mar del Plata

SOUTH

Valdivia
Negro   Viedma

ATLANTIC

Puerto Montt
Chubut

Comodoro Rivadavia
Gulf of San Jorge

OCEAN

H

Gulf of Penas
West Falkland   FALKLAND IS.
(U.K.)
Stanley
East Falkland

H

Magellan's Str.
Punta Arenas
Tierra del Fuego
C. Horn
South Georgia
(U.K.)

Projection: Lambert's Azimuthal Equal Area

CARTOGRAPHY BY PHILIP'S.

1   90   2   80   3   70   4   60   5   6   40   7

■ LIMA   Capital Cities

West from Greenwich

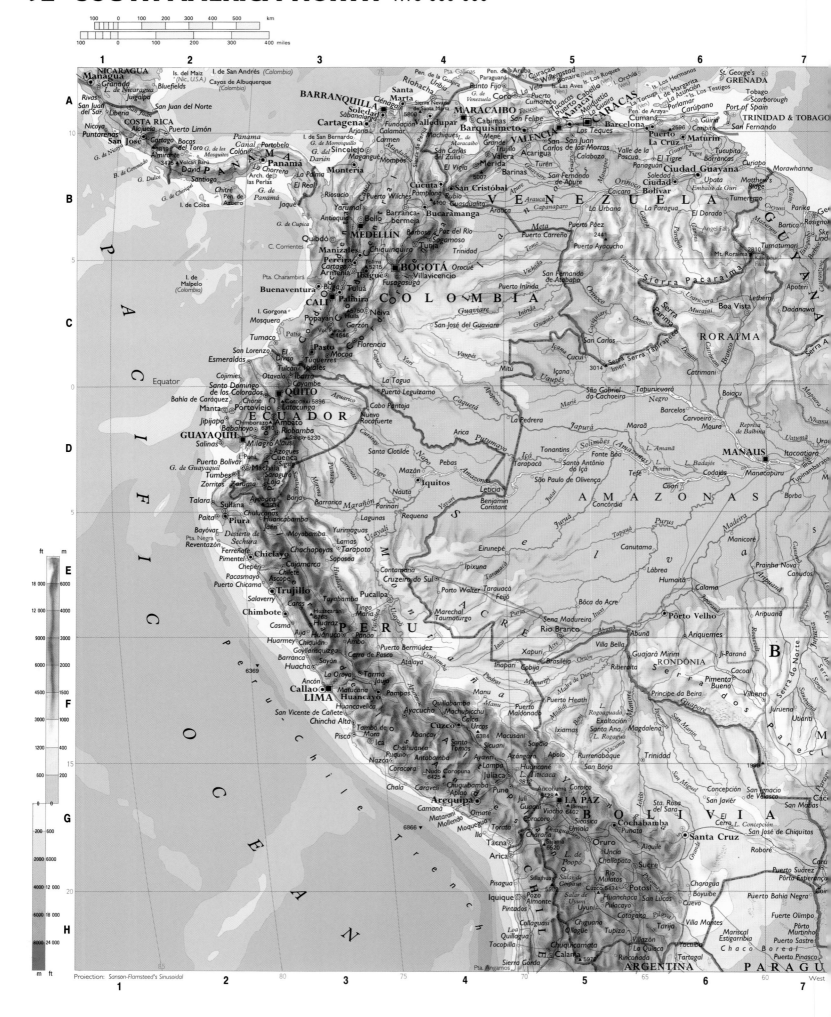

A
B
C
D
E
F
G
H

ATLANTIC

OCEAN

FRENCH GUIANA

AMAPÁ

Equator

São Paulo (Braz.)

BELÉM

São Luís

FORTALEZA

Fernando de Noronha (Braz.)

MARANHÃO

Teresina

CEARÁ

Natal

PIAUÍ

PARAÍBA

João Pessoa

Olinda

RECIFE

PERNAMBUCO

Maceió

ALAGOAS

SERGIPE

Aracaju

BAHIA

Feira de Santana

SALVADOR

TOCANTINS

BRASÍLIA

GOIÁS

Goiânia

MINAS GERAIS

BELO HORIZONTE

Vitória

ESPÍRITO SANTO

Trindade (Braz.)

SÃO PAULO

RIO DE JANEIRO

Campinas

Niterói

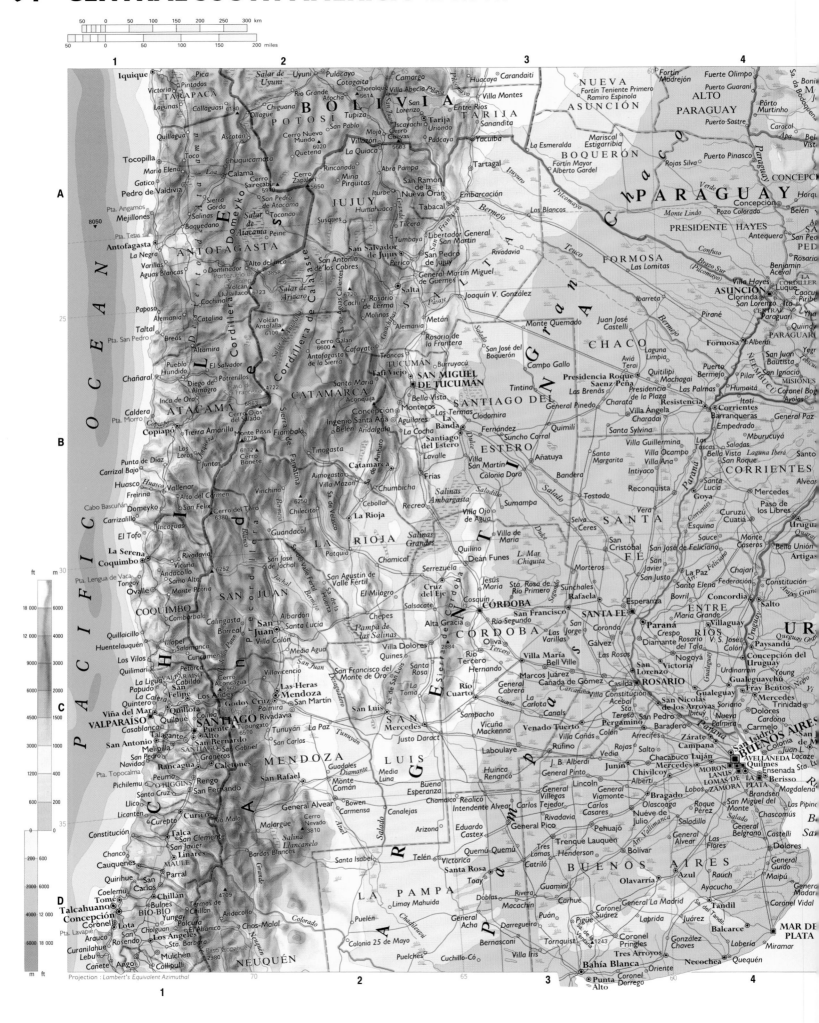

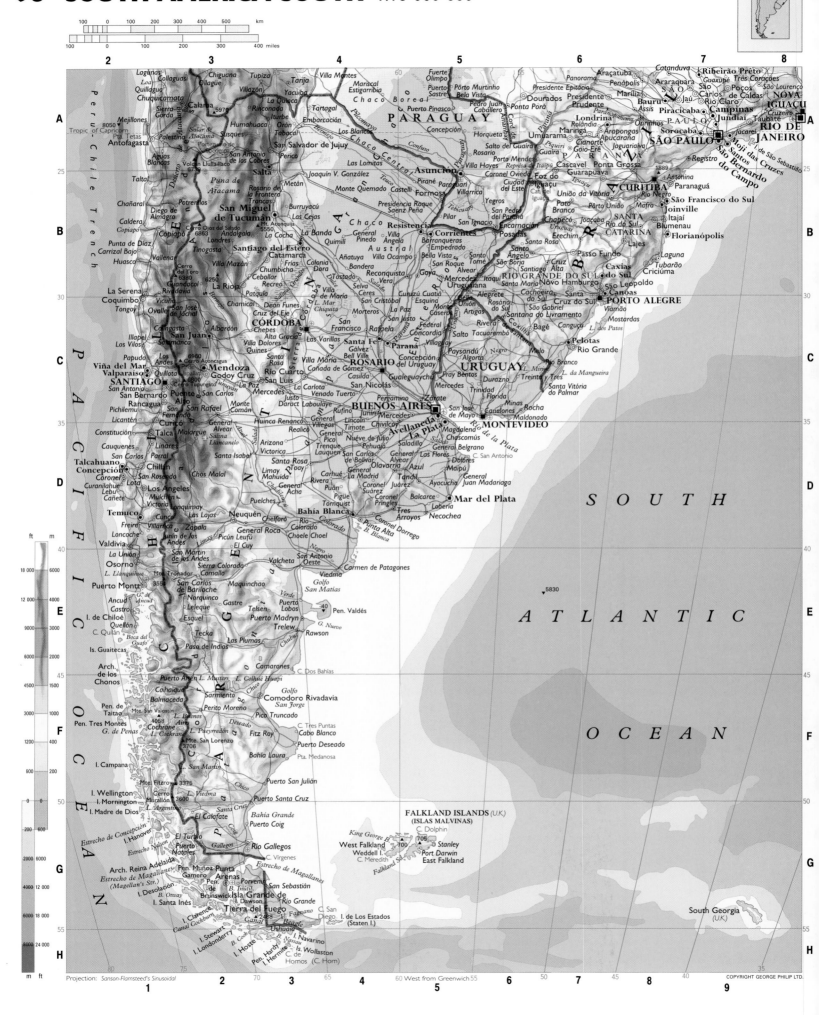

INDEX

The index contains the names of all the principal places and features shown on the World Maps. Each name is followed by an additional entry in italics giving the country or region within which it is located. The alphabetical order of names composed of two or more words is governed primarily by the first word and then by the second. This is an example of the rule:

Mīr Kūh, *Iran* . . . . **45 E8** 26 22N 58 55 E
Mīr Shahdād, *Iran* . . . . **45 E8** 26 15N 58 29 E
Mira, *Italy* . . . . **20 B5** 45 26N 12 8 E
Mira por vos Cay, *Bahamas* . **89 B5** 22 9N 74 30W
Miraj, *India* . . . . **40 L9** 16 50N 74 45 E

Physical features composed of a proper name (Erie) and a description (Lake) are positioned alphabetically by the proper name. The description is positioned after the proper name and is usually abbreviated:

Erie, L., *N. Amer.* **78 D4** 42 15N 81 0W

Where a description forms part of a settlement or administrative name however, it is always written in full and put in its true alphabetic position:

Mount Morris, *U.S.A.* **78 D7** 42 44N 77 52W

Names beginning with M' and Mc are indexed as if they were spelled Mac. Names beginning St. are alphabetised under Saint, but Sankt, Sint, Sant', Santa and San are all spelt in full and are alphabetised accordingly. If the same place name occurs two or more times in the index and all are in the same country, it is followed by the name of the administrative subdivision in which it is located. The names are placed in the alphabetical order of the subdivisions. For example:

Jackson, *Ky., U.S.A.* **76 G4** 37 33N 83 23W
Jackson, *Mich., U.S.A.* **76 D3** 42 15N 84 24W
Jackson, *Minn., U.S.A.* **80 D7** 43 37N 95 1W

The number in bold type which follows each name in the index refers to the number of the map page where that feature or place will be found. This is usually the largest scale at which the place or feature appears.

The letter and figure which are in bold type immediately after the page number give the grid square on the map page, within which the feature is situated. The letter represents the latitude and the figure the longitude.

In some cases the feature itself may fall within the specified square, while the name is outside. This is usually the case only with features which are larger than a grid square.

For a more precise location the geographical coordinates which follow the letter/figure references give the latitude and the longitude of each place. The first set of figures represent the latitude which is the distance north or south of the Equator measured as an angle at the centre of the earth. The Equator is latitude 0°, the North Pole is 90°N, and the South Pole 90°S.

The second set of figures represent the longitude, which is the distance East or West of the prime meridian, which runs through Greenwich, England. Longitude is also measured as an angle at the centre of the earth and is given East or West of the prime meridian, from 0° to 180° in either direction.

The unit of measurement for latitude and longitude is the degree, which is subdivided into 60 minutes. Each index entry states the position of a place in degrees and minutes, a space being left between the degrees and the minutes.

The latitude is followed by N(orth) or S(outh) and the longitude by E(ast) or W(est).

Rivers are indexed to their mouths or confluences, and carry the symbol → after their names. A solid square ■ follows the name of a country, while an open square □ refers to a first order administrative area.

Abbreviations used in the index

A.C.T. – Australian Capital Territory
Afghan. – Afghanistan
Ala. – Alabama
Alta. – Alberta
Amer. – America(n)
Arch. – Archipelago
Ariz. – Arizona
Ark. – Arkansas
Atl. Oc. – Atlantic Ocean
B. – Baie, Bahía, Bay, Bucht, Bugt
B.C. – British Columbia
Bangla. – Bangladesh
Barr. – Barrage
Bos.-H. – Bosnia-Herzegovina
C. – Cabo, Cap, Cape, Coast
C.A.R. – Central African Republic
C. Prov. – Cape Province
Calif. – California
Cent. – Central
Chan. – Channel
Colo. – Colorado
Conn. – Connecticut
Cord. – Cordillera
Cr. – Creek
Czech. – Czech Republic
D.C. – District of Columbia
Del. – Delaware
Dep. – Dependency
Des. – Desert
Dist. – District
Dj. – Djebel
Domin. – Dominica
Dom. Rep. – Dominican Republic
E. – East

E. Salv. – El Salvador
Eq. Guin. – Equatorial Guinea
Fla. – Florida
Falk. Is. – Falkland Is.
G. – Golfe, Golfo, Gulf, Guba, Gebel
Ga. – Georgia
Gt. – Great, Greater
Guinea-Biss. – Guinea-Bissau
H.K. – Hong Kong
H.P. – Himachal Pradesh
Hants. – Hampshire
Harb. – Harbor, Harbour
Hd. – Head
Hts. – Heights
I.(s). – Île, Ilha, Insel, Isla, Island, Isle
Ill. – Illinois
Ind. – Indiana
Ind. Oc. – Indian Ocean
Ivory C. – Ivory Coast
J. – Jabal, Jebel, Jazira
Junc. – Junction
K. – Kap, Kapp
Kans. – Kansas
Kep. – Kepulauan
Ky. – Kentucky
L. – Lac, Lacul, Lago, Lagoa, Lake, Limni, Loch, Lough
La. – Louisiana
Liech. – Liechtenstein
Lux. – Luxembourg
Mad. P. – Madhya Pradesh
Madag. – Madagascar
Man. – Manitoba
Mass. – Massachusetts

Md. – Maryland
Me. – Maine
Medit. S. – Mediterranean Sea
Mich. – Michigan
Minn. – Minnesota
Miss. – Mississippi
Mo. – Missouri
Mont. – Montana
Mozam. – Mozambique
Mt.(e) – Mont, Monte, Monti, Montaña, Mountain
N. – Nord, Norte, North, Northern, Nouveau
N.B. – New Brunswick
N.C. – North Carolina
N. Cal. – New Caledonia
N. Dak. – North Dakota
N.H. – New Hampshire
N.I. – North Island
N.J. – New Jersey
N. Mex. – New Mexico
N.S. – Nova Scotia
N.S.W. – New South Wales
N.W.T. – North West Territory
N.Y. – New York
N.Z. – New Zealand
Nebr. – Nebraska
Neths. – Netherlands
Nev. – Nevada
Nfld. – Newfoundland
Nic. – Nicaragua
O. – Oued, Ouadi
Occ. – Occidentale
Okla. – Oklahoma
Ont. – Ontario
Or. – Orientale

Oreg. – Oregon
Os. – Ostrov
Oz. – Ozero
P. – Pass, Passo, Pasul, Pulau
P.E.I. – Prince Edward Island
Pa. – Pennsylvania
Pac. Oc. – Pacific Ocean
Papua N.G. – Papua New Guinea
Pass. – Passage
Pen. – Peninsula, Péninsule
Phil. – Philippines
Pk. – Park, Peak
Plat. – Plateau
Prov. – Province, Provincial
Pt. – Point
Pta. – Ponta, Punta
Pte. – Pointe
Qué. – Québec
Queens. – Queensland
R. – Rio, River
R.I. – Rhode Island
Ra.(s). – Range(s)
Raj. – Rajasthan
Reg. – Region
Rep. – Republic
Res. – Reserve, Reservoir
S. – San, South, Sea
Si. Arabia – Saudi Arabia
S.C. – South Carolina
S. Dak. – South Dakota
S.I. – South Island
S. Leone – Sierra Leone
Sa. – Serra, Sierra
Sask. – Saskatchewan
Scot. – Scotland
Sd. – Sound

Sev. – Severnaya
Sib. – Siberia
Sprs. – Springs
St. – Saint
Sta. – Santa, Station
Ste. – Sainte
Sto. – Santo
Str. – Strait, Stretto
Switz. – Switzerland
Tas. – Tasmania
Tenn. – Tennessee
Tex. – Texas
Tg. – Tanjung
Trin. & Tob. – Trinidad & Tobago
U.A.E. – United Arab Emirates
U.K. – United Kingdom
U.S.A. – United States of America
Ut. P. – Uttar Pradesh
Va. – Virginia
Vdkhr. – Vodokhranilishche
Vf. – Vîrful
Vic. – Victoria
Vol. – Volcano
Vt. – Vermont
W. – Wadi, West
W. Va. – West Virginia
Wash. – Washington
Wis. – Wisconsin
Wlkp. – Wielkopolski
Wyo. – Wyoming
Yorks. – Yorkshire
Yug. – Yugoslavia

A Coruña

A

A Coruña, Spain 19 A1 43 20N 8 25W
A Estrada, Spain 19 A1 42 43N 8 27W
A Fonsagrada, Spain 19 A2 43 8N 7 4W
Aachen, Germany 16 C4 50 45N 6 6 E
Aalborg = Ålborg, Denmark 9 H13 57 2N 9 54 E
Aalen, Germany 16 D6 48 51N 10 6 E
Aalst, Belgium 15 D4 50 56N 4 2 E
Aalten, Neths. 15 C6 51 56N 6 35 E
Aalter, Belgium 15 C3 51 5N 3 28 E
Äänekoski, Finland 9 E21 62 36N 25 44 E
Aarau, Switz. 18 C8 47 23N 8 4 E
Aare →, Switz. 18 C8 47 33N 8 14 E
Aarhus = Århus, Denmark 9 H14 56 8N 10 11 E
Aarschot, Belgium 15 D4 50 59N 4 49 E
Aba, Dem. Rep. of the Congo 54 B3 3 58N 30 17 E
Aba, Nigeria 50 G7 5 10N 7 19 E
Ābādān, Iran 45 D6 30 22N 48 20 E
Ābādeh, Iran 45 D7 31 8N 52 40 E
Abadla, Algeria 50 B5 31 2N 2 45W
Abaetetuba, Brazil 93 D9 1 40S 48 50W
Abagnar Qi, China 34 C9 43 52N 116 2 E
Abai, Paraguay 95 B4 25 58S 55 54W
Abakan, Russia 27 D10 53 40N 91 10 E
Abancay, Peru 92 F4 13 35S 72 55W
Abariringa, Kiribati 64 H10 2 50S 171 40W
Abarqū, Iran 45 D7 31 10N 53 20 E
Abashiri, Japan 30 C12 44 0N 144 15 E
Abashiri-Wan, Japan 30 C12 44 0N 144 30 E
Abay, Kazakstan 26 E8 49 38N 72 53 E
Abaya, L., Ethiopia 46 F2 6 30N 37 50 E
Abaza, Russia 26 D10 52 39N 90 6 E
'Abbāsābād, Iran 45 C8 33 34N 58 23 E
Abbay = Nîl el Azraq →, Sudan 51 E12 15 38N 32 31 E
Abbaye, Pt., U.S.A. 76 B1 46 58N 88 8W
Abbé, L., Ethiopia 46 E3 11 8N 41 47 E
Abbeville, France 18 A4 50 6N 1 49 E
Abbeville, Ala., U.S.A. 77 K3 31 34N 85 15W
Abbeville, La., U.S.A. 81 L8 29 58N 92 8W
Abbeville, S.C., U.S.A. 77 H4 34 11N 82 23W
Abbot Ice Shelf, Antarctica 5 D16 73 0S 92 0W
Abbottabad, Pakistan 42 B5 34 10N 73 15 E
Abd al Kūrī, Ind. Oc. 46 E5 12 5N 52 20 E
Ābdar, Iran 45 D7 30 16N 55 19 E
'Abdolābād, Iran 45 C8 34 12N 56 30 E
Abdulpur, Bangla. 43 G13 24 15N 88 59 E
Abéché, Chad 51 F10 13 50N 20 35 E
Abengourou, Ivory C. 50 G5 6 42N 3 27W
Åbenrå, Denmark 9 J13 55 3N 9 25 E
Abeokuta, Nigeria 50 G6 7 3N 3 19 E
Aber, Uganda 54 B3 2 12N 32 25 E
Aberaeron, U.K. 11 E3 52 15N 4 15W
Aberayron = Aberaeron, U.K. 11 E3 52 15N 4 15W
Aberchirder, U.K. 12 D6 57 34N 2 37W
Abercorn = Mbala, Zambia 55 D3 8 46S 31 24 E
Abercorn, Australia 63 D5 25 12S 151 5 E
Aberdare, U.K. 11 F4 51 43N 3 27W
Aberdare Ra., Kenya 54 C4 0 15S 36 50 E
Aberdeen, Australia 63 E5 32 9S 150 56 E
Aberdeen, Canada 73 C7 52 20N 106 8W
Aberdeen, S. Africa 56 E3 32 28S 24 2 E
Aberdeen, U.K. 12 D6 57 9N 2 5W
Aberdeen, Ala., U.S.A. 77 J1 33 49N 88 33W
Aberdeen, Idaho, U.S.A. 82 E7 42 57N 112 50W
Aberdeen, Md., U.S.A. 76 F7 39 31N 76 10W
Aberdeen, S. Dak., U.S.A. 80 C5 45 28N 98 29W
Aberdeen, Wash., U.S.A. 84 D3 46 59N 123 50W
Aberdeen, City of □, U.K. 12 D6 57 10N 2 10W
Aberdeenshire □, U.K. 12 D6 57 17N 2 36W
Aberdovey = Aberdyfi, U.K. 11 E3 52 33N 4 3W
Aberdyfi, U.K. 11 E3 52 33N 4 3W
Aberfeldy, U.K. 12 E5 56 37N 3 51W
Abergavenny, U.K. 11 F4 51 49N 3 1W
Abergele, U.K. 10 D4 53 17N 3 35W
Abernathy, U.S.A. 81 J4 33 50N 101 51W
Abert, L., U.S.A. 82 E3 42 38N 120 14W
Aberystwyth, U.K. 11 E3 52 25N 4 5W
Abhā, Si. Arabia 46 D3 18 0N 42 34 E
Abhar, Iran 45 B6 36 9N 49 13 E
Abhayapuri, India 43 F14 26 24N 90 38 E
Abidjan, Ivory C. 50 G5 5 26N 3 58W
Abilene, Kans., U.S.A. 80 F6 38 55N 97 13W
Abilene, Tex., U.S.A. 81 J5 32 28N 99 43W
Abingdon, U.K. 11 F6 51 40N 1 17W
Abingdon, U.S.A. 77 G5 36 43N 81 59W
Abington Reef, Australia 62 B4 18 0S 149 35 E
Abitau →, Canada 73 B7 59 53N 109 3W
Abitibi →, Canada 70 B3 51 3N 80 55W
Abitibi, L., Canada 70 C4 48 40N 79 40W
Abkhaz Republic = Abkhazia □, Georgia 25 F7 43 12N 41 5 E
Abkhazia □, Georgia 25 F7 43 12N 41 5 E
Abminga, Australia 63 D1 26 8S 134 51 E
Åbo = Turku, Finland 9 F20 60 30N 22 19 E
Abohar, India 42 D6 30 10N 74 10 E
Abolo, Congo 52 D2 0 8N 14 16 E
Abomey, Benin 50 G6 7 10N 2 5 E
Abong-Mbang, Cameroon 52 D2 4 0N 13 8 E
Abou-Deïa, Chad 51 F9 11 20N 19 20 E
Aboyne, U.K. 12 D6 57 4N 2 47W
Abra Pampa, Argentina 94 A2 22 43S 65 42W
Abraham L., Canada 72 C5 52 15N 116 35W
Abreojos, Pta., Mexico 86 B2 26 50N 113 40W
Abrud, Romania 17 E12 46 19N 23 5 E
Absaroka Range, U.S.A. 82 D9 44 45N 109 50W
Abu, India 42 G5 24 41N 72 50 E
Abu al Abyad, U.A.E. 45 E7 24 11N 53 50 E
Abū al Khaşīb, Iraq 45 D6 30 25N 48 0 E
Abū 'Alī, Si. Arabia 45 E6 27 20N 49 27 E
Abū 'Alī →, Lebanon 47 A4 34 25N 35 50 E
Abu Dhabi = Abū Ẓāby, U.A.E. 45 E7 24 28N 54 22 E
Abū Du'ān, Syria 44 B3 36 25N 38 15 E
Abu el Gairi, W. →, Egypt 47 F2 29 35N 33 30 E
Abu Ga'da, W. →, Egypt 47 F1 29 15N 32 53 E
Abū Ḩadrīyah, Si. Arabia 45 E6 27 20N 48 58 E
Abu Hamed, Sudan 51 E12 19 32N 33 13 E
Abū Kamāl, Syria 44 C4 34 30N 41 0 E
Abū Madd, Ra's, Si. Arabia 44 E3 24 50N 37 7 E
Abū Mūsā, U.A.E. 45 E7 25 52N 55 3 E
Abu Şafāt, W. →, Jordan 47 E5 30 24N 36 7 E
Abu Simbel, Egypt 51 D12 22 18N 31 40 E
Abū Şukhayr, Iraq 44 D5 31 54N 44 30 E
Abū Zabad, Sudan 51 F11 12 25N 29 10 E
Abū Ẓāby, U.A.E. 45 E7 24 28N 54 22 E
Abū Zeydābād, Iran 45 C6 33 54N 51 45 E
Abuja, Nigeria 50 G7 9 16N 7 2 E
Abukuma-Gawa →, Japan 30 E10 38 6N 140 52 E
Abukuma-Sammyaku, Japan 30 F10 37 30N 140 45 E
Abunã, Brazil 92 E5 9 40S 65 20W
Abunã →, Brazil 92 E5 9 41S 65 20W
Aburo, Dem. Rep. of the Congo 54 B3 2 4N 30 53 E
Abut Hd., N.Z. 59 K3 43 7S 170 15 E
Acadia National Park, U.S.A. 77 C11 44 20N 68 13W
Açailândia, Brazil 93 D9 4 57S 47 0W
Acajutla, El Salv. 88 D2 13 36N 89 50W
Acámbaro, Mexico 86 D4 20 0N 100 40W
Acaponeta, Mexico 86 C3 22 30N 105 20W
Acapulco, Mexico 87 D5 16 51N 99 56W
Acarai, Serra, Brazil 92 C7 1 50N 57 50W
Acarigua, Venezuela 92 B5 9 33N 69 12W
Acatlán, Mexico 87 D5 18 10N 98 3W
Acayucan, Mexico 87 D6 17 59N 94 58W
Accomac, U.S.A. 76 G8 37 43N 75 40W
Accra, Ghana 50 G5 5 35N 0 6W
Accrington, U.K. 10 D5 53 45N 2 22W
Acebal, Argentina 94 C3 33 20S 60 50W
Aceh □, Indonesia 36 D1 4 15N 97 30 E
Achalpur, India 40 J10 21 22N 77 32 E
Acheng, China 35 B14 45 30N 126 58 E
Acher, India 42 H5 23 10N 72 32 E
Achill Hd., Ireland 13 C1 53 58N 10 15W
Achill I., Ireland 13 C1 53 58N 10 1W
Achinsk, Russia 27 D10 56 20N 90 20 E
Acireale, Italy 20 F6 37 37N 15 10 E
Ackerman, U.S.A. 81 J10 33 19N 89 11W
Acklins I., Bahamas 89 B5 22 30N 74 0W
Acme, Canada 72 C6 51 33N 113 30W
Acme, U.S.A. 78 F5 40 8N 79 26W
Aconcagua, Cerro, Argentina 94 C2 32 39S 70 0W
Aconquija, Mt., Argentina 94 B2 27 0S 66 0W
Açores, Is. dos = Azores, Atl. Oc. 50 A1 38 44N 29 0W
Acraman, L., Australia 63 E2 32 2S 135 23 E
Acre = 'Akko, Israel 47 C4 32 55N 35 4 E
Acre □, Brazil 92 E4 9 1S 71 0W
Acre →, Brazil 92 E5 8 45S 67 22W
Acton, Canada 78 C4 43 38N 80 3W
Acuña, Mexico 86 B4 29 18N 100 55W
Ad Dammām, Si. Arabia 45 E6 26 20N 50 5 E
Ad Dāmūr, Lebanon 47 B4 33 44N 35 27 E
Ad Dawādimī, Si. Arabia 44 E5 24 35N 44 15 E
Ad Dawḩah, Qatar 45 E6 25 15N 51 35 E
Ad Dawr, Iraq 44 C4 34 27N 43 47 E
Ad Dir'īyah, Si. Arabia 44 E5 24 44N 46 35 E
Ad Dīwānīyah, Iraq 44 D5 32 0N 45 0 E
Ad Dujayl, Iraq 44 C5 33 51N 44 14 E
Ad Duwayd, Si. Arabia 44 D4 30 15N 42 17 E
Ada, Minn., U.S.A. 80 B6 47 18N 96 31W
Ada, Okla., U.S.A. 81 H6 34 46N 96 41W
Adabiya, Egypt 47 F1 29 53N 32 28 E
Adair, C., Canada 69 A12 71 31N 71 24W
Adaja →, Spain 19 B3 41 32N 4 52W
Adak I., U.S.A. 68 C2 51 45N 176 45W
Adamaoua, Massif de l', Cameroon 52 C2 7 20N 12 20 E
Adamawa Highlands = Adamaoua, Massif de l', Cameroon 52 C2 7 20N 12 20 E
Adamello, Mte., Italy 18 C9 46 9N 10 30 E
Adaminaby, Australia 63 F4 36 0S 148 45 E
Adams, Mass., U.S.A. 79 D11 42 38N 73 7W
Adams, N.Y., U.S.A. 79 C8 43 49N 76 1W
Adams, Wis., U.S.A. 80 D10 43 57N 89 49W
Adam's Bridge, Sri Lanka 40 Q11 9 15N 79 40 E
Adams L., Canada 72 C5 51 10N 119 40W
Adams Mt., U.S.A. 84 D5 46 12N 121 30W
Adam's Peak, Sri Lanka 40 R12 6 48N 80 30 E
Adana, Turkey 25 G6 37 0N 35 16 E
Adapazarı = Sakarya, Turkey 25 F5 40 48N 30 25 E
Adarama, Sudan 51 E12 17 10N 34 52 E
Adare, C., Antarctica 5 D11 71 0S 171 0 E
Adaut, Indonesia 37 F8 8 8S 131 7 E
Adavale, Australia 63 D3 25 52S 144 32 E
Adda →, Italy 18 D8 45 8N 9 53 E
Addis Ababa = Addis Abeba, Ethiopia 46 F2 9 2N 38 42 E
Addis Abeba, Ethiopia 46 F2 9 2N 38 42 E
Addison, U.S.A. 78 D7 42 1N 77 14W
Addo, S. Africa 56 E4 33 32S 25 45 E
Ādeh, Iran 44 B5 37 42N 45 11 E
Adel, U.S.A. 77 K4 31 8N 83 25W
Adelaide, Australia 63 E2 34 52S 138 30 E
Adelaide, Bahamas 88 A4 25 4N 77 31W
Adelaide, S. Africa 56 E4 32 42S 26 20 E
Adelaide I., Antarctica 5 C17 67 15S 68 30W
Adelaide Pen., Canada 68 B10 68 15N 97 30W
Adelaide River, Australia 60 B5 13 15S 131 7 E
Adelanto, U.S.A. 85 L9 34 35N 117 22W
Adele I., Australia 60 C3 15 32S 123 9 E
Adélie, Terre, Antarctica 5 C10 68 0S 140 0 E
Adélie Land = Adélie, Terre, Antarctica 5 C10 68 0S 140 0 E
Aden = Al 'Adan, Yemen 46 E4 12 45N 45 0 E
Aden, G. of, Asia 46 E4 12 30N 47 30 E
Adendorp, S. Africa 56 E3 32 15S 24 30 E
Adh Dhayd, U.A.E. 45 E7 25 17N 55 53 E
Adhoi, India 42 H4 23 26N 70 32 E
Adi, Indonesia 37 E8 4 15S 133 30 E
Adieu, C., Australia 61 F5 32 0S 132 10 E
Adieu Pt., Australia 60 C3 15 14S 124 35 E
Adige →, Italy 20 B5 45 9N 12 20 E
Adigrat, Ethiopia 46 E2 14 20N 39 26 E
Adilabad, India 40 K11 19 33N 78 20 E
Adin Khel, Afghan. 40 C6 32 45N 68 5 E
Adirondack Mts., U.S.A. 79 C10 44 0N 74 0W
Adjumani, Uganda 54 B3 3 20N 31 50 E
Adlavik Is., Canada 71 A8 55 2N 57 45W
Admiralty G., Australia 60 B4 14 20S 125 55 E
Admiralty I., U.S.A. 72 B2 57 30N 134 30W
Admiralty Is., Papua N. G. 64 H6 2 0S 147 0 E
Adonara, Indonesia 37 F6 8 15S 123 5 E
Adoni, India 40 M10 15 33N 77 18 E
Adour →, France 18 E3 43 32N 1 32W
Adra, India 43 H12 23 30N 86 42 E
Adra, Spain 19 D4 36 43N 3 3W
Adrano, Italy 20 F6 37 40N 14 50 E
Adrar, Algeria 48 D4 27 51N 0 11 E
Adrar, Mauritania 50 D3 20 30N 7 30 E
Adrian, Mich., U.S.A. 76 E3 41 54N 84 2W
Adrian, Tex., U.S.A. 81 H3 35 16N 102 40W
Adriatic Sea, Medit. S. 20 C6 43 0N 16 0 E
Adua, Indonesia 37 E7 1 45S 129 50 E
Adwa, Ethiopia 46 E2 14 15N 38 52 E
Adygea □, Russia 25 F7 45 0N 40 0 E
Adzhar Republic = Ajaria □, Georgia 25 F7 41 30N 42 0 E
Adzopé, Ivory C. 50 G5 6 7N 3 49W
Ægean Sea, Medit. S. 21 E11 38 30N 25 0 E
Aerhtai Shan, Mongolia 32 B4 46 40N 92 45 E
'Afak, Iraq 44 C5 32 4N 45 15 E
Afándou, Greece 23 C10 36 18N 28 12 E
Afghanistan ■, Asia 40 C4 33 0N 65 0 E
Aflou, Algeria 50 B6 34 7N 2 3 E
Africa 48 E6 10 0N 20 0 E
'Afrīn, Syria 44 B3 36 32N 36 50 E
Afton, N.Y., U.S.A. 79 D9 42 14N 75 32W
Afton, Wyo., U.S.A. 82 E8 42 44N 110 56W
Afuá, Brazil 93 D8 0 15S 50 20W
'Afula, Israel 47 C4 32 37N 35 17 E
Afyon, Turkey 25 G5 38 45N 30 33 E
Afyonkarahisar = Afyon, Turkey 25 G5 38 45N 30 33 E
Agadès = Agadez, Niger 50 E7 16 58N 7 59 E
Agadez, Niger 50 E7 16 58N 7 59 E
Agadir, Morocco 50 B4 30 28N 9 55W
Agaete, Canary Is. 22 F4 28 6N 15 43W
Agar, India 42 H7 23 40N 76 2 E
Agartala, India 41 H17 23 50N 91 23 E
Agassiz, Canada 72 D4 49 14N 121 46W
Agats, Indonesia 37 F9 5 33S 138 0 E
Agawam, U.S.A. 79 D12 42 5N 72 37W
Agboville, Ivory C. 50 G5 5 55N 4 15W
Ağdam, Azerbaijan 44 B5 40 0N 46 58 E
Agde, France 18 E5 43 19N 3 28 E
Agen, France 18 D4 44 12N 0 38 E
Āgh Kand, Iran 45 B6 37 15N 48 4 E
Aginskoye, Russia 27 D12 51 6N 114 32 E
Agnew, Australia 61 E3 28 1S 120 31 E
Agori, India 43 G10 24 33N 82 57 E
Agra, India 42 F7 27 17N 77 58 E
Ağrı, Turkey 25 G7 39 44N 43 3 E
Agri →, Italy 20 D7 40 13N 16 44 E
Ağrı Dağı, Turkey 25 G7 39 50N 44 15 E
Ağrı Karakose = Ağrı, Turkey 25 G7 39 44N 43 3 E
Agrigento, Italy 20 F5 37 19N 13 34 E
Agrinion, Greece 21 E9 38 37N 21 27 E
Agua Caliente, Baja Calif., Mexico 85 N10 32 29N 116 59W
Agua Caliente, Sinaloa, Mexico 86 B3 26 30N 108 20W
Agua Caliente Springs, U.S.A. 85 N10 32 56N 116 19W
Água Clara, Brazil 93 H8 20 25S 52 45W
Agua Hechicero, Mexico 85 N10 32 26N 116 14W
Agua Prieta, Mexico 86 A3 31 20N 109 32W
Aguadilla, Puerto Rico 89 C6 18 26N 67 10W
Aguadulce, Panama 88 E3 8 15N 80 32W
Aguanga, U.S.A. 85 M10 33 27N 116 51W
Aguanish, Canada 71 B7 50 14N 62 2W
Aguanus →, Canada 71 B7 50 13N 62 5W
Aguapey →, Argentina 94 B4 29 7S 56 36W
Aguaray Guazú →, Paraguay 94 A4 24 47S 57 19W
Aguarico →, Ecuador 92 D3 0 59S 75 11W
Aguas Blancas, Chile 94 A2 24 15S 69 55W
Aguas Calientes, Sierra de, Argentina 94 B2 25 26S 66 40W
Aguascalientes, Mexico 86 C4 21 53N 102 12W
Aguascalientes □, Mexico 86 C4 22 0N 102 20W
Aguilares, Argentina 94 B2 27 26S 65 35W
Aguilas, Spain 19 D5 37 23N 1 35W
Agüimes, Canary Is. 22 G4 27 58N 15 27W
Aguja, C. de la, Colombia 90 B3 11 18N 74 12W
Agulhas, C., S. Africa 56 E3 34 52S 20 0 E
Agulo, Canary Is. 22 F2 28 11N 17 12W
Agung, Indonesia 36 F5 8 20S 115 28 E
Agur, Uganda 54 B3 2 28N 32 55 E
Agusan →, Phil. 37 C7 9 0N 125 30 E
Aha Mts., Botswana 56 B3 19 45S 21 0 E
Ahaggar, Algeria 50 D7 23 0N 6 30 E
Ahar, Iran 44 B5 38 35N 47 0 E
Ahipara B., N.Z. 59 F4 35 5S 173 5 E
Ahiri, India 40 K12 19 30N 80 0 E
Ahmad Wal, Pakistan 42 E1 29 18N 65 58 E
Ahmadabad, India 42 H5 23 0N 72 40 E
Aḩmadābād, Khorāsān, Iran 45 C9 35 3N 60 50 E
Aḩmadābād, Khorāsān, Iran 45 C8 35 49N 59 42 E
Aḩmadī, Iran 45 E8 27 56N 56 42 E
Ahmadnagar, India 40 K9 19 7N 74 46 E
Ahmadpur, Pakistan 42 E4 29 12N 71 10 E
Ahmadpur Lamma, Pakistan 42 E4 28 19N 70 3 E
Ahmedabad = Ahmadabad, India 42 H5 23 0N 72 40 E
Ahmednagar = Ahmadnagar, India 40 K9 19 7N 74 46 E
Ahome, Mexico 86 B3 25 55N 109 11W
Ahoskie, U.S.A. 77 G7 36 17N 76 59W
Ahram, Iran 45 D6 28 52N 51 16 E
Ahrax Pt., Malta 23 D1 35 59N 14 22 E
Āhū, Iran 45 C6 34 33N 50 2 E
Ahuachapán, El Salv. 88 D2 13 54N 89 52W
Ahvāz, Iran 45 D6 31 20N 48 40 E
Ahvenanmaa = Åland, Finland 9 F19 60 15N 20 0 E
Aḩwar, Yemen 46 E4 13 30N 46 40 E
Ai →, India 43 F14 26 26N 90 44 E
Aichi □, Japan 31 G8 35 0N 137 15 E
Aigua, Uruguay 95 C5 34 13S 54 46W
Aigues-Mortes, France 18 E6 43 35N 4 12 E
Aihui, China 33 A7 50 10N 127 30 E
Aija, Peru 92 E3 9 50S 77 45W
Aikawa, Japan 30 E9 38 2N 138 15 E
Aiken, U.S.A. 77 J5 33 34N 81 43W
Aileron, Australia 62 C1 22 39S 133 20 E
Aillik, Canada 71 A8 55 11N 59 18W
Ailsa Craig, U.K. 12 F3 55 15N 5 6W
'Ailūn, Jordan 47 C4 32 18N 35 47 E
Aim, Russia 27 D14 59 0N 133 55 E
Aimere, Indonesia 37 F6 8 45S 121 3 E
Aimogasta, Argentina 94 B2 28 33S 66 50W
Aïn Ben Tili, Mauritania 50 C4 25 59N 9 27W
Aïn-Sefra, Algeria 50 B5 32 47N 0 37W
'Ain Sudr, Egypt 47 F2 29 50N 33 6 E
Ainaži, Latvia 9 H21 57 50N 24 24 E
Ainsworth, U.S.A. 80 D5 42 33N 99 52W
Aiquile, Bolivia 92 G5 18 10S 65 10W
Aïr, Niger 50 E7 18 30N 8 0 E
Air Force I., Canada 69 B12 67 58N 74 5W
Air Hitam, Malaysia 39 M4 1 55N 103 11 E
Airdrie, Canada 72 C6 51 18N 114 2W
Airdrie, U.K. 12 F5 55 52N 3 57W
Aire →, U.K. 10 D7 53 43N 0 55W
Aire, I. de l', Spain 22 B11 39 48N 4 16 E
Airlie Beach, Australia 62 C4 20 16S 148 43 E
Aisne →, France 18 B5 49 26N 2 50 E
Ait, India 43 G8 25 54N 79 14 E
Aitkin, U.S.A. 80 B8 46 32N 93 42W
Aiud, Romania 17 E12 46 19N 23 44 E
Aix-en-Provence, France 18 E6 43 32N 5 27 E
Aix-la-Chapelle = Aachen, Germany 16 C4 50 45N 6 6 E
Aix-les-Bains, France 18 D6 45 41N 5 53 E
Aíyion, Greece 21 E10 38 15N 22 5 E
Aizawl, India 41 H18 23 40N 92 44 E
Aizkraukle, Latvia 9 H21 56 36N 25 11 E
Aizpute, Latvia 9 H19 56 43N 21 40 E
Aizuwakamatsu, Japan 30 F9 37 30N 139 56 E
Ajaccio, France 18 F8 41 55N 8 40 E
Ajaigarh, India 43 G9 24 52N 80 16 E
Ajalpan, Mexico 87 D5 18 22N 97 15W
Ajanta Ra., India 40 J9 20 28N 75 50 E
Ajari Rep. = Ajaria □, Georgia 25 F7 41 30N 42 0 E
Ajaria □, Georgia 25 F7 41 30N 42 0 E
Ajax, Canada 78 C5 43 50N 79 1W
Ajdâbiyah, Libya 51 B10 30 54N 20 4 E
Ajka, Hungary 17 E9 47 4N 17 31 E
'Ajmān, U.A.E. 45 E7 25 25N 55 30 E
Ajmer, India 42 F6 26 28N 74 37 E
Ajnala, India 42 D6 31 50N 74 48 E
Ajo, U.S.A. 83 K7 32 22N 112 52W
Ajo, C. de, Spain 19 A4 43 31N 3 35W
Akabira, Japan 30 C11 43 33N 142 5 E
Akamas □, Cyprus 23 D11 35 3N 32 18 E
Akanthou, Cyprus 23 D12 35 22N 33 45 E
Akaroa, N.Z. 59 K4 43 49S 172 59 E
Akashi, Japan 31 G7 34 45N 134 58 E
Akbarpur, Bihar, India 43 G10 24 39N 83 58 E
Akbarpur, Ut. P., India 43 F10 26 25N 82 32 E
Akelamo, Indonesia 37 D7 1 35N 129 40 E
Aketi, Dem. Rep. of the Congo 52 D4 2 38N 23 47 E
Akharnaí, Greece 21 E10 38 5N 23 44 E
Akhelóös →, Greece 21 E9 38 19N 21 7 E
Akhisar, Turkey 21 E12 38 56N 27 48 E
Akhnur, India 43 C6 32 52N 74 45 E
Akhtyrka = Okhtyrka, Ukraine 25 D5 50 25N 35 0 E
Aki, Japan 31 H6 33 30N 133 54 E
Akimiski I., Canada 70 B3 52 50N 81 30W
Akita, Japan 30 E10 39 45N 140 7 E
Akita □, Japan 30 E10 39 40N 140 30 E
Akjoujt, Mauritania 50 E3 19 45N 14 15W
Akkeshi, Japan 30 C12 43 2N 144 51 E
'Akko, Israel 47 C4 32 55N 35 4 E
Aklavik, Canada 68 B6 68 12N 135 0W
Aklera, India 42 G7 24 26N 76 32 E
Akmolinsk = Astana, Kazakstan 26 D8 51 10N 71 30 E
Akō, Japan 31 G7 34 45N 134 24 E
Akola, India 40 J10 20 42N 77 2 E
Akordat, Eritrea 46 D2 15 30N 37 40 E
Akpatok I., Canada 69 B13 60 25N 68 8W
Åkrahamn, Norway 9 G11 59 15N 5 10 E
Akranes, Iceland 8 D2 64 19N 22 5W
Akron, Colo., U.S.A. 80 E3 40 10N 103 13W
Akron, Ohio, U.S.A. 78 E3 41 5N 81 31W
Akrotiri, Cyprus 23 E11 34 36N 32 57 E
Akrotiri Bay, Cyprus 23 E12 34 35N 33 10 E
Aksai Chin, India 43 B8 35 15N 79 55 E
Aksaray, Turkey 25 G5 38 25N 34 2 E
Aksay, Kazakstan 25 D9 51 11N 53 0 E
Akşehir, Turkey 44 B1 38 18N 31 30 E
Akşehir Gölü, Turkey 25 G5 38 30N 31 25 E
Aksu, China 32 B3 41 5N 80 10 E
Aksum, Ethiopia 46 E2 14 5N 38 40 E
Aktogay, Kazakstan 26 E8 46 57N 79 40 E
Aktsyabrski, Belarus 17 B15 52 38N 28 53 E
Aktyubinsk = Aqtöbe, Kazakstan 25 D10 50 17N 57 10 E
Akure, Nigeria 50 G7 7 15N 5 5 E
Akureyri, Iceland 8 D4 65 40N 18 6W
Akuseki-Shima, Japan 31 K4 29 27N 129 37 E
Akyab = Sittwe, Burma 41 J18 20 18N 92 45 E
Al 'Adan, Yemen 46 E4 12 45N 45 0 E
Al Aḩsā = Hasa □, Si. Arabia 45 E6 25 50N 49 0 E
Al Ajfar, Si. Arabia 44 E4 27 26N 43 0 E
Al Amādīyah, Iraq 44 B4 37 5N 43 30 E
Al 'Amārah, Iraq 44 D5 31 55N 47 15 E
Al 'Aqabah, Jordan 47 F4 29 31N 35 0 E
Al Arak, Syria 44 C3 34 38N 38 35 E
Al 'Aramah, Si. Arabia 44 E5 25 30N 46 0 E
Al Arţāwīyah, Si. Arabia 44 E5 26 31N 45 20 E
Al 'Āşimah = 'Ammān □, Jordan 47 D5 31 40N 36 30 E
Al 'Assāfīyah, Si. Arabia 44 D3 28 17N 38 59 E
Al 'Ayn, Oman 45 E7 24 15N 55 45 E
Al 'Ayn, Si. Arabia 44 E3 25 4N 38 6 E
Al 'Azamīyah, Iraq 44 C5 33 22N 44 22 E
Al 'Azīzīyah, Iraq 44 C5 32 54N 45 4 E
Al Bāb, Syria 44 B3 36 23N 37 29 E
Al Bad', Si. Arabia 44 D2 28 28N 35 1 E
Al Bādī, Iraq 44 C4 35 56N 41 32 E
Al Baḩrah, Kuwait 44 D5 29 40N 47 52 E
Al Baḩral Mayyit = Dead Sea, Asia 47 D4 31 30N 35 30 E
Al Balqā' □, Jordan 47 C4 32 5N 35 45 E
Al Bārūk, J., Lebanon 47 B4 33 39N 35 40 E
Al Başrah, Iraq 44 D5 30 30N 47 50 E
Al Baţḩā, Iraq 44 D5 31 6N 45 53 E
Al Batrūn, Lebanon 47 A4 34 15N 35 40 E
Al Bayḑā, Libya 51 B10 32 50N 21 44 E
Al Biqā, Lebanon 47 A5 34 10N 36 10 E
Al Bi'r, Si. Arabia 44 D3 28 51N 36 16 E
Al Burayj, Syria 47 A5 34 15N 36 46 E
Al Faḑilī, Si. Arabia 45 E6 26 58N 49 10 E

Amadeus, L.

Al Fallūjah, Iraq 44 C4 33 20N 43 55 E
Al Fāw, Iraq 45 D6 30 0N 48 30 E
Al Fujayrah, U.A.E. 45 E8 25 7N 56 18 E
Al Ghadaf, W. →, Jordan 47 D5 31 26N 36 43 E
Al Ghammās, Iraq 44 D5 31 45N 44 37 E
Al Ghazālah, Si. Arabia 44 E4 26 48N 41 19 E
Al Hābah, Si. Arabia 44 E5 27 10N 47 0 E
Al Ḥadīthah, Iraq 44 C4 34 0N 41 13 E
Al Ḥadīthah, Si. Arabia 47 D6 31 28N 37 8 E
Al Ḥaḍr, Iraq 44 C4 35 35N 42 44 E
Al Ḥājānah, Syria 47 B5 33 20N 36 33 E
Al Hajar al Gharbi, Oman 45 E8 24 10N 56 15 E
Al Hāmad, Si. Arabia 44 D3 31 30N 39 30 E
Al Hamdānīyah, Syria 44 C3 35 25N 36 50 E
Al Ḥamīdīyah, Syria 47 A4 34 42N 35 57 E
Al Ḥammār, Iraq 44 D5 30 57N 46 51 E
Al Ḥamrā', Si. Arabia 44 E3 24 2N 38 55 E
Al Ḥanākīyah, Si. Arabia 44 E4 24 51N 40 31 E
Al Harīr, W. →, Syria 47 C4 32 44N 35 59 E
Al Ḥasā, W. →, Jordan 47 D4 31 4N 35 29 E
Al Ḥasakah, Syria 44 B4 36 35N 40 45 E
Al Haydān, W. →, Jordan 47 D4 31 29N 35 34 E
Al Ḥayy, Iraq 44 C5 32 5N 46 5 E
Al Ḥijarah, Asia 44 D4 30 0N 44 0 E
Al Ḥillah, Iraq 44 C5 32 30N 44 25 E
Al Hindīyah, Iraq 44 C5 32 30N 44 10 E
Al Hirmil, Lebanon 47 A5 34 26N 36 24 E
Al Hoceïma, Morocco 50 A5 35 8N 3 58W
Al Ḥudaydah, Yemen 46 E3 14 50N 43 0 E
Al Hufūf, Si. Arabia 45 E6 25 25N 49 45 E
Al Ḥumayḍah, Si. Arabia 44 D2 29 14N 34 56 E
Al Ḥunayy, Si. Arabia 45 E6 25 58N 48 45 E
Al Īsāwīyah, Si. Arabia 44 D3 30 43N 37 59 E
Al Jafr, Jordan 47 E5 30 18N 36 14 E
Al Jāfūrah, Si. Arabia 45 E7 25 0N 50 15 E
Al Jaghbūb, Libya 51 C10 29 42N 24 38 E
Al Jahrah, Kuwait 44 D5 29 25N 47 40 E
Al Jalāmīd, Si. Arabia 44 D3 31 20N 40 6 E
Al Jamalīyah, Qatar 45 E6 25 37N 51 5 E
Al Janūb □, Lebanon 47 B4 33 20N 35 20 E
Al Jawf, Libya 51 D10 24 10N 23 24 E
Al Jawf, Si. Arabia 44 D3 29 55N 39 40 E
Al Jazirah, Iraq 44 C5 33 30N 44 0 E
Al Jithāmīyah, Si. Arabia 44 E4 27 41N 41 43 E
Al Jubayl, Si. Arabia 45 E6 27 0N 49 50 E
Al Jubaylah, Si. Arabia 44 E5 24 55N 46 25 E
Al Jubb, Si. Arabia 44 E4 27 11N 42 17 E
Al Junaynah, Sudan 51 F10 13 27N 22 45 E
Al Kaba'ish, Iraq 44 D5 30 58N 47 0 E
Al Karak, Jordan 47 D4 31 11N 35 42 E
Al Karak □, Jordan 47 E5 31 0N 36 0 E
Al Kāzim Tyah, Iraq 44 C5 33 22N 44 12 E
Al Khābūra, Oman 45 F8 23 57N 57 5 E
Al Khafji, Si. Arabia 45 E6 28 24N 48 29 E
Al Khalīl, West Bank 47 D4 31 32N 35 6 E
Al Khāliṣ, Iraq 44 C5 33 49N 44 32 E
Al Kharsānīyah, Si. Arabia 45 E6 27 13N 49 18 E
Al Khaṣab, Oman 45 E8 26 14N 56 15 E
Al Khawr, Qatar 45 E6 25 41N 51 30 E
Al Khiḍr, Iraq 44 D5 31 12N 45 33 E
Al Khiyām, Lebanon 47 B4 33 20N 35 36 E
Al Khums, Libya 51 B8 32 40N 14 17 E
Al Kiswah, Syria 47 B5 33 23N 36 14 E
Al Kūfah, Iraq 44 C5 32 2N 44 24 E
Al Kufrah, Libya 51 D10 24 17N 23 15 E
Al Kuhayfiyah, Si. Arabia 44 E4 27 12N 43 3 E
Al Kūt, Iraq 44 C5 32 30N 46 0 E
Al Kuwayt, Kuwait 44 D5 29 30N 48 0 E
Al Labwah, Lebanon 47 A5 34 11N 36 20 E
Al Lādhiqīyah, Syria 44 C2 35 30N 35 45 E
Al Līth, Si. Arabia 46 C3 20 9N 40 15 E
Al Liwā', Oman 45 E8 24 31N 56 36 E
Al Luḥayyah, Yemen 46 D3 15 45N 42 40 E
Al Madīnah, Iraq 44 D5 30 57N 47 16 E
Al Madīnah, Si. Arabia 46 C2 24 35N 39 52 E
Al Mafraq, Jordan 47 C5 32 17N 36 14 E
Al Maḥmūdīyah, Iraq 44 C5 33 3N 44 21 E
Al Majma'ah, Si. Arabia 44 E5 25 57N 45 22 E
Al Makhruq, W. →, Jordan 47 D6 31 28N 37 0 E
Al Makḥūl, Si. Arabia 44 E4 26 37N 42 39 E
Al Manāmah, Bahrain 45 E6 26 10N 50 30 E
Al Maqwa', Kuwait 44 D5 29 10N 47 59 E
Al Marj, Libya 51 B10 32 25N 20 30 E
Al Maṭlā, Kuwait 44 D5 29 24N 47 40 E
Al Mawjib, W. →, Jordan 47 D4 31 28N 35 36 E
Al Mawṣil, Iraq 44 B4 36 15N 43 5 E
Al Mayādin, Syria 44 C4 35 1N 40 27 E
Al Mazār, Jordan 47 D4 31 4N 35 41 E
Al Midhnab, Si. Arabia 44 E5 25 50N 44 18 E
Al Minā', Lebanon 47 A4 34 24N 35 49 E
Al Miqdādīyah, Iraq 44 C5 34 0N 45 0 E
Al Mubarraz, Si. Arabia 45 E6 25 30N 49 40 E
Al Mudawwarah, Jordan 47 F5 29 19N 36 0 E
Al Mughayrā', U.A.E. 45 E7 24 5N 53 32 E
Al Muḥarraq, Bahrain 45 E6 26 15N 50 40 E
Al Mukallā, Yemen 46 E4 14 33N 49 2 E
Al Mukhā, Yemen 46 E3 13 18N 43 15 E
Al Musayjīd, Si. Arabia 44 E3 24 5N 39 5 E
Al Musayyib, Iraq 44 C5 32 49N 44 20 E
Al Muwayliḥ, Si. Arabia 44 E2 27 40N 35 30 E
Al Qā'im, Iraq 44 C4 34 21N 41 7 E
Al Qalībah, Si. Arabia 44 D3 28 24N 37 42 E
Al Qāmishli, Syria 44 B4 37 10N 41 10 E
Al Qaryatayn, Syria 47 A6 34 12N 37 13 E
Al Qaṣīm, Si. Arabia 44 E4 26 0N 43 0 E
Al Qaṭ'ā, Syria 44 C4 34 40N 40 48 E
Al Qaṭīf, Si. Arabia 45 E6 26 35N 50 0 E
Al Qatrānah, Jordan 47 D5 31 12N 36 6 E
Al Qaṭrūn, Libya 51 D9 24 56N 15 3 E
Al Qayṣūmah, Si. Arabia 44 D5 28 20N 46 7 E
Al Quds = Jerusalem, Israel 47 D4 31 47N 35 10 E
Al Qunayṭirah, Syria 47 C4 32 55N 35 45 E
Al Qurnah, Iraq 44 D5 31 1N 47 25 E
Al Quṣayr, Iraq 44 D5 30 39N 45 50 E
Al Quṣayr, Syria 47 A5 34 31N 36 34 E
Al Qutayfah, Syria 47 B5 33 44N 36 36 E
Al 'Ubaylah, Si. Arabia 46 C5 21 59N 50 57 E
Al 'Uḍaylīyah, Si. Arabia 45 E6 25 8N 49 18 E
Al 'Ulā, Si. Arabia 44 E3 26 35N 38 0 E
Al 'Uqayr, Si. Arabia 45 E6 25 40N 50 15 E
Al 'Uthmānīyah, Si. Arabia 45 E6 25 5N 49 22 E
Al 'Uwaynid, Si. Arabia 44 E5 24 50N 46 0 E
Al 'Uwayqīlah, Si. Arabia 44 D4 30 30N 42 10 E
Al 'Uyūn, Ḥijāz, Si. Arabia 44 E3 24 33N 39 35 E
Al 'Uyūn, Najd, Si. Arabia 44 E4 26 30N 43 50 E
Al 'Uzayr, Iraq 44 D5 31 19N 47 25 E
Al Wajh, Si. Arabia 44 E3 26 10N 36 30 E
Al Wakrah, Qatar 45 E6 25 10N 51 40 E
Al Wannān, Si. Arabia 45 E6 26 55N 48 24 E
Al Waqbah, Si. Arabia 44 D5 28 48N 45 33 E
Al Wari'āh, Si. Arabia 44 E5 27 51N 47 25 E
Al Wusayl, Qatar 45 E6 25 29N 51 29 E
Ala Dağ, Turkey 44 B2 37 44N 35 9 E
Ala Tau Shankou = Dzungarian Gates, Kazakstan 32 B3 45 0N 82 0 E
Alabama □, U.S.A. 77 J2 33 0N 87 0W
Alabama →, U.S.A. 77 K2 31 8N 87 57W
Alabaster, U.S.A. 77 J2 33 15N 86 49W
Alaçam Dağları, Turkey 21 E13 39 18N 28 49 E
Alachua, U.S.A. 77 L4 29 47N 82 30W
Alaérma, Greece 23 C9 36 9N 27 57 E
Alagoa Grande, Brazil 93 E11 7 3S 35 35W
Alagoas □, Brazil 93 E11 9 0S 36 0W
Alagoinhas, Brazil 93 F11 12 7S 38 20W
Alaior, Spain 22 B11 39 57N 4 8 E
Alajero, Canary Is. 22 F2 28 3N 17 13W
Alajuela, Costa Rica 88 D3 10 2N 84 8W
Alakamisy, Madag. 57 C8 21 19S 47 14 E
Alaknanda →, India 43 D8 30 8N 78 36 E
Alakurtti, Russia 24 A5 67 0N 30 30 E
Alamarvdasht, Iran 45 E7 27 37N 52 59 E
Alameda, Calif., U.S.A. 84 H4 37 46N 122 15W
Alameda, N. Mex., U.S.A. 83 J10 35 11N 106 37W
Alamo, U.S.A. 85 J11 37 22N 115 10W
Alamo Crossing, U.S.A. 85 L13 34 16N 113 33W
Alamogordo, U.S.A. 83 K11 32 54N 105 57W
Alamos, Mexico 86 B3 27 0N 109 0W
Alamosa, U.S.A. 83 H11 37 28N 105 52W
Åland, Finland 9 F19 60 15N 20 0 E
Ålands hav, Sweden 9 F18 60 0N 19 30 E
Alandur, India 40 N12 13 0N 80 15 E
Alania = North Ossetia □, Russia 25 F7 43 30N 44 30 E
Alanya, Turkey 25 G5 36 38N 32 0 E
Alaotra, Farihin', Madag. 57 B8 17 30S 48 30 E
Alapayevsk, Russia 26 D7 57 52N 61 42 E
Alaşehir, Turkey 21 E13 38 23N 28 30 E
Alaska □, U.S.A. 68 B5 64 0N 154 0W
Alaska, G. of, Pac. Oc. 68 C5 58 0N 145 0W
Alaska Peninsula, U.S.A. 68 C4 56 0N 159 0W
Alaska Range, U.S.A. 68 B4 62 50N 151 0W
Älät, Azerbaijan 25 G8 39 58N 49 25 E
Alatyr, Russia 24 D8 54 55N 46 35 E
Alausi, Ecuador 92 D3 2 0S 78 50W
Alava, C., U.S.A. 82 B1 48 10N 124 44W
Alavus, Finland 9 E20 62 35N 23 36 E
Alawoona, Australia 63 E3 34 45S 140 30 E
'Alayh, Lebanon 47 B4 33 46N 35 33 E
Alba, Italy 18 D8 44 42N 8 2 E
Alba-Iulia, Romania 17 E12 46 8N 23 39 E
Albacete, Spain 19 C5 39 0N 1 50W
Albacutya, L., Australia 63 F3 35 45S 141 58 E
Albanel, L., Canada 70 B5 50 55N 73 12W
Albania ■, Europe 21 D9 41 0N 20 0 E
Albany, Australia 61 G2 35 1S 117 58 E
Albany, Ga., U.S.A. 77 K3 31 35N 84 10W
Albany, N.Y., U.S.A. 79 D11 42 39N 73 45W
Albany, Oreg., U.S.A. 82 D2 44 38N 123 6W
Albany, Tex., U.S.A. 81 J5 32 44N 99 18W
Albany →, Canada 70 B3 52 17N 81 31W
Albardón, Argentina 94 C2 31 20S 68 30W
Albatross B., Australia 62 A3 12 45S 141 30 E
Albemarle, U.S.A. 77 H5 35 21N 80 11W
Albemarle Sd., U.S.A. 77 H7 36 5N 76 0W
Alberche →, Spain 19 C3 39 58N 4 46W
Alberdi, Paraguay 94 B4 26 14S 58 20W
Albert, L., Australia 63 F2 35 30S 139 10 E
Albert Edward Ra., Australia 60 C4 18 17S 127 57 E
Albert L., Africa 54 B3 1 30N 31 0 E
Albert Lea, U.S.A. 80 D8 43 39N 93 22W
Albert Nile →, Uganda 54 B3 3 36N 32 2 E
Albert Town, Bahamas 89 B5 22 37N 74 33W
Alberta □, Canada 72 C6 54 40N 115 0W
Alberti, Argentina 94 D3 35 1S 60 16W
Albertinia, S. Africa 56 E3 34 11S 21 34 E
Alberton, Canada 71 C7 46 50N 64 0W
Albertville = Kalemie, Dem. Rep. of the Congo 54 D2 5 55S 29 9 E
Albertville, France 18 D7 45 40N 6 22 E
Albertville, U.S.A. 77 H2 34 16N 86 13W
Albi, France 18 E5 43 56N 2 9 E
Albia, U.S.A. 80 E8 41 2N 92 48W
Albina, Surinam 93 B8 5 37N 54 15W
Albina, Ponta, Angola 56 B1 15 52S 11 44 E
Albion, Mich., U.S.A. 76 D3 42 15N 84 45W
Albion, Nebr., U.S.A. 80 E6 41 42N 98 0W
Albion, Pa., U.S.A. 78 E4 41 53N 80 22W
Alborán, Medit. S. 19 E4 35 57N 3 0W
Ålborg, Denmark 9 H13 57 2N 9 54 E
Alborz, Reshteh-ye Kūhhā-ye, Iran 45 C7 36 0N 52 0 E
Albuquerque, U.S.A. 83 J10 35 5N 106 39W
Albuquerque, Cayos de, Caribbean 88 D3 12 10N 81 50W
Alburg, U.S.A. 79 B11 44 59N 73 18W
Albury-Wodonga, Australia 63 F4 36 3S 146 56 E
Alcalá de Henares, Spain 19 B4 40 28N 3 22W
Alcalá la Real, Spain 19 D4 37 27N 3 57W
Álcamo, Italy 20 F5 37 59N 12 55 E
Alcañiz, Spain 19 B5 41 2N 0 8W
Alcântara, Brazil 93 D10 2 20S 44 30W
Alcántara, Embalse de, Spain 19 C2 39 44N 6 50W
Alcantarilla, Spain 19 D5 37 59N 1 12W
Alcaraz, Sierra de, Spain 19 C4 38 40N 2 20W
Alcaudete, Spain 19 D3 37 35N 4 5W
Alcázar de San Juan, Spain 19 C4 39 24N 3 12W
Alchevsk, Ukraine 25 E6 48 30N 38 45 E
Alcira = Alzira, Spain 19 C5 39 9N 0 30W
Alcova, U.S.A. 82 E10 42 34N 106 43W
Alcoy, Spain 19 C5 38 43N 0 30W
Alcúdia, Spain 22 B10 39 51N 3 7 E
Alcúdia, B. d', Spain 22 B10 39 47N 3 15 E
Aldabra Is., Seychelles 49 G8 9 22S 46 28 E
Aldama, Mexico 87 C5 23 0N 98 4W
Aldan, Russia 27 D13 58 40N 125 30 E
Aldan →, Russia 27 C13 63 28N 129 35 E
Aldea, Pta. de la, Canary Is. 22 G4 28 0N 15 50W
Aldeburgh, U.K. 11 E9 52 10N 1 37 E
Alder Pk., U.S.A. 84 K5 35 53N 121 22W
Alderney, U.K. 11 H5 49 42N 2 11W
Aldershot, U.K. 11 F7 51 15N 0 44W
Aledo, U.S.A. 80 E9 41 12N 90 45W
Aleg, Mauritania 50 E3 17 3N 13 55W
Alegranza, Canary Is. 22 E6 29 23N 13 32W
Alegranza, I., Canary Is. 22 E6 29 23N 13 32W
Alegre, Brazil 95 A7 20 50S 41 30W
Alegrete, Brazil 95 B4 29 40S 56 0W
Aleisk, Russia 26 D9 52 40N 83 0 E
Aleksandriya = Oleksandriya, Ukraine 17 C14 50 37N 26 19 E
Aleksandrov Gay, Russia 25 D8 50 9N 48 34 E
Aleksandrovsk-Sakhalinskiy, Russia 27 D15 50 50N 142 20 E
Além Paraíba, Brazil 95 A7 21 52S 42 41W
Alemania, Argentina 94 B2 25 40S 65 30W
Alemania, Chile 94 B2 25 10S 69 55W
Alençon, France 18 B4 48 27N 0 4 E
Alenquer, Brazil 93 D8 1 56S 54 46W
Alenuihaha Channel, U.S.A. 74 H17 20 30N 156 0W
Aleppo = Ḥalab, Syria 44 B3 36 10N 37 15 E
Alès, France 18 D6 44 9N 4 5 E
Alessándria, Italy 18 D8 44 54N 8 37 E
Ålesund, Norway 9 E12 62 28N 6 12 E
Aleutian Is., Pac. Oc. 68 C2 52 0N 175 0W
Aleutian Trench, Pac. Oc. 64 C10 48 0N 180 0 E
Alexander, U.S.A. 80 B3 47 51N 103 39W
Alexander, Mt., Australia 61 E3 28 58S 120 16 E
Alexander Arch., U.S.A. 68 C6 56 0N 136 0W
Alexander Bay, S. Africa 56 D2 28 40S 16 30 E
Alexander City, U.S.A. 77 J3 32 56N 85 58W
Alexander I., Antarctica 5 C17 69 0S 70 0W
Alexandra, Australia 63 F4 37 8S 145 40 E
Alexandra, N.Z. 59 L2 45 14S 169 25 E
Alexandra Falls, Canada 72 A5 60 29N 116 18W
Alexandria = El Iskandarîya, Egypt 51 B11 31 13N 29 58 E
Alexandria, B.C., Canada 72 C4 52 35N 122 27W
Alexandria, Ont., Canada 79 A10 45 19N 74 38W
Alexandria, Romania 17 G13 43 57N 25 24 E
Alexandria, S. Africa 56 E4 33 38S 26 28 E
Alexandria, U.K. 12 F4 55 59N 4 35W
Alexandria, La., U.S.A. 81 K8 31 18N 92 27W
Alexandria, Minn., U.S.A. 80 C7 45 53N 95 22W
Alexandria, S. Dak., U.S.A. 80 D6 43 39N 97 47W
Alexandria, Va., U.S.A. 76 F7 38 48N 77 3W
Alexandria Bay, U.S.A. 79 B9 44 20N 75 55W
Alexandrina, L., Australia 63 F2 35 25S 139 10 E
Alexandroúpolis, Greece 21 D11 40 50N 25 54 E
Alexis →, Canada 71 B8 52 33N 56 8W
Alexis Creek, Canada 72 C4 52 10N 123 20W
Alfabia, Spain 22 B9 39 44N 2 44 E
Alfenas, Brazil 95 A6 21 20S 46 10W
Alford, Aberds., U.K. 12 D6 57 14N 2 41W
Alford, Lincs., U.K. 10 D8 53 15N 0 10 E
Alfred, Maine, U.S.A. 79 C14 43 29N 70 43W
Alfred, N.Y., U.S.A. 78 D7 42 16N 77 48W
Alfreton, U.K. 10 D6 53 6N 1 24W
Alga, Kazakstan 25 E10 49 53N 57 20 E
Algaida, Spain 22 B9 39 33N 2 53 E
Ålgård, Norway 9 G11 58 46N 5 53 E
Algarve, Portugal 19 D1 36 58N 8 20W
Algeciras, Spain 19 D3 36 9N 5 28W
Algemesí, Spain 19 C5 39 11N 0 27W
Alger, Algeria 50 A6 36 42N 3 8 E
Algeria ■, Africa 50 C6 28 30N 2 0 E
Alghero, Italy 20 D3 40 33N 8 19 E
Algiers = Alger, Algeria 50 A6 36 42N 3 8 E
Algoa B., S. Africa 56 E4 33 50S 25 45 E
Algoma, U.S.A. 76 C2 44 36N 87 26W
Algona, U.S.A. 80 D7 43 4N 94 14W
Algonac, U.S.A. 78 D2 42 37N 82 32W
Algonquin Prov. Park, Canada 70 C4 45 50N 78 30W
Algorta, Uruguay 96 C5 32 25S 57 23W
Alhambra, U.S.A. 85 L8 34 8N 118 6W
Alhucemas = Al Hoceïma, Morocco 50 A5 35 8N 3 58W
'Alī al Gharbī, Iraq 44 C5 32 30N 46 45 E
'Alī ash Sharqī, Iraq 44 C5 32 7N 46 44 E
'Alī Khēl, Afghan. 42 C3 33 57N 69 43 E
'Alī Shāh, Iran 44 B5 38 9N 45 50 E
'Alīābād, Khorāsān, Iran 45 C8 32 30N 57 30 E
'Alīābād, Kordestān, Iran 44 C5 35 4N 46 58 E
'Alīābād, Yazd, Iran 45 D7 31 41N 53 49 E
Aliağa, Turkey 21 E12 38 47N 26 59 E
Aliákmon →, Greece 21 D10 40 30N 22 36 E
Alicante, Spain 19 C5 38 23N 0 30W
Alice, S. Africa 56 E4 32 48S 26 55 E
Alice, U.S.A. 81 M5 27 45N 98 5W
Alice →, Queens., Australia 62 C3 24 2S 144 50 E
Alice →, Queens., Australia 62 B3 15 35S 142 20 E
Alice Arm, Canada 72 B3 55 29N 129 31W
Alice Springs, Australia 62 C1 23 40S 133 50 E
Alicedale, S. Africa 56 E4 33 15S 26 4 E
Aliceville, U.S.A. 77 J1 33 8N 88 9W
Aliganj, India 43 F8 27 30N 79 10 E
Aligarh, Raj., India 42 G7 25 55N 76 15 E
Aligarh, Ut. P., India 42 F8 27 55N 78 10 E
Alīgūdarz, Iran 45 C6 33 25N 49 45 E
Alimnía, Greece 23 C9 36 16N 27 43 E
Alingsås, Sweden 9 H15 57 56N 12 31 E
Alipur, Pakistan 42 E4 29 25N 70 55 E
Alipur Duar, India 41 F16 26 30N 89 35 E
Aliquippa, U.S.A. 78 F4 40 37N 80 15W
Alitus = Alytus, Lithuania 9 J21 54 24N 24 3 E
Aliwal North, S. Africa 56 E4 30 45S 26 45 E
Alix, Canada 72 C6 52 24N 113 11W
Aljustrel, Portugal 19 D1 37 55N 8 10W
Alkmaar, Neths. 15 B4 52 37N 4 45 E
All American Canal, U.S.A. 83 K6 32 45N 115 15W
Allagash →, U.S.A. 77 B11 47 5N 69 3W
Allah Dad, Pakistan 42 G2 25 38N 67 34 E
Allahabad, India 43 G9 25 25N 81 58 E
Allan, Canada 73 C7 51 53N 106 4W
Allanmyo, Burma 41 K19 19 30N 95 17 E
Allanridge, S. Africa 56 D4 27 45S 26 40 E
Allegany, U.S.A. 78 D6 42 6N 78 30W
Allegheny →, U.S.A. 78 F5 40 27N 80 1W
Allegheny Mts., U.S.A. 76 G6 38 15N 80 10W
Allegheny Reservoir, U.S.A. 78 E6 41 50N 79 0W
Allen, Bog of, Ireland 13 C5 53 15N 7 0W
Allen, L., Ireland 13 B3 54 8N 8 4W
Allendale, U.S.A. 77 J5 33 1N 81 18W
Allende, Mexico 86 B4 28 20N 100 50W
Allentown, U.S.A. 79 F9 40 37N 75 29W
Alleppey, India 40 Q10 9 30N 76 28 E
Aller →, Germany 16 B5 52 56N 9 12 E
Alliance, Nebr., U.S.A. 80 D3 42 6N 102 52W
Alliance, Ohio, U.S.A. 78 F3 40 55N 81 6W
Allier →, France 18 C5 46 57N 3 4 E
Alliford Bay, Canada 72 C2 53 12N 131 58W
Alliston, Canada 78 B5 44 9N 79 52W
Alloa, U.K. 12 E5 56 7N 3 47W
Allora, Australia 63 D5 28 2S 152 0 E
Alluitsup Paa = Sydprøven, Greenland 4 C5 60 30N 45 35W
Alma, Canada 71 C5 48 35N 71 40W
Alma, Ga., U.S.A. 77 K4 31 33N 82 28W
Alma, Kans., U.S.A. 80 F6 39 1N 96 17W
Alma, Mich., U.S.A. 76 D3 43 23N 84 39W
Alma, Nebr., U.S.A. 80 E5 40 6N 99 22W
Alma Ata = Almaty, Kazakstan 26 E8 43 15N 76 57 E
Almada, Portugal 19 C1 38 40N 9 9W
Almaden, Australia 62 B3 17 22S 144 40 E
Almadén, Spain 19 C3 38 49N 4 52W
Almanor, L., U.S.A. 82 F3 40 14N 121 9W
Almansa, Spain 19 C5 38 51N 1 5W
Almanzor, Pico, Spain 19 B3 40 15N 5 18W
Almanzora →, Spain 19 D5 37 14N 1 46W
Almaty, Kazakstan 26 E8 43 15N 76 57 E
Almazán, Spain 19 B4 41 30N 2 30W
Almeirim, Brazil 93 D8 1 30S 52 34W
Almelo, Neths. 15 B6 52 22N 6 42 E
Almendralejo, Spain 19 C2 38 41N 6 26W
Almere-Stad, Neths. 15 B5 52 20N 5 15 E
Almería, Spain 19 D4 36 52N 2 27W
Almirante, Panama 88 E3 9 10N 82 30W
Almiroú, Kólpos, Greece 23 D6 35 23N 24 20 E
Almond, U.S.A. 78 D7 42 19N 77 44W
Almont, U.S.A. 78 D1 42 55N 83 3W
Almonte, Canada 79 A8 45 14N 76 12W
Almora, India 43 E8 29 38N 79 40 E
Alness, U.K. 12 D4 57 41N 4 16W
Alnmouth, U.K. 10 B6 55 24N 1 37W
Alnwick, U.K. 10 B6 55 24N 1 42W
Aloi, Uganda 54 B3 2 16N 33 10 E
Alon, Burma 41 H19 22 12N 95 5 E
Alor, Indonesia 37 F6 8 15S 124 30 E
Alor Setar, Malaysia 39 J3 6 7N 100 22 E
Alot, India 42 H6 23 56N 75 40 E
Aloysius, Mt., Australia 61 E4 26 0S 128 38 E
Alpaugh, U.S.A. 84 K7 35 53N 119 29W
Alpena, U.S.A. 76 C4 45 4N 83 27W
Alpha, Australia 62 C4 23 39S 146 37 E
Alphen aan den Rijn, Neths. 15 B4 52 7N 4 40 E
Alpine, Ariz., U.S.A. 83 K9 33 51N 109 9W
Alpine, Calif., U.S.A. 85 N10 32 50N 116 46W
Alpine, Tex., U.S.A. 81 K3 30 22N 103 40W
Alps, Europe 18 C8 46 30N 9 30 E
Alsace, France 18 B7 48 15N 7 25 E
Alsask, Canada 73 C7 51 21N 109 59W
Alsasua, Spain 19 A4 42 54N 2 10W
Alsek →, U.S.A. 72 B1 59 10N 138 12W
Alsten, Norway 8 D15 65 58N 12 40 E
Alston, U.K. 10 C5 54 49N 2 25W
Alta, Norway 8 B20 69 57N 23 10 E
Alta Gracia, Argentina 94 C3 31 40S 64 30W
Alta Sierra, U.S.A. 85 K8 35 42N 118 33W
Altaelva →, Norway 8 B20 69 54N 23 17 E
Altafjorden, Norway 8 A20 70 5N 23 5 E
Altai = Aerhtai Shan, Mongolia 32 B4 46 40N 92 45 E
Altamaha →, U.S.A. 77 K5 31 20N 81 20W
Altamira, Brazil 93 D8 3 12S 52 10W
Altamira, Chile 94 B2 25 47S 69 51W
Altamira, Mexico 87 C5 22 24N 97 55W
Altamont, U.S.A. 79 D10 42 43N 74 3W
Altamura, Italy 20 D7 40 49N 16 33 E
Altanbulag, Mongolia 32 A5 50 16N 106 30 E
Altar, Mexico 86 A2 30 40N 111 50W
Altar, Desierto de, Mexico 86 B2 30 10N 112 0W
Altata, Mexico 86 C3 24 30N 108 0W
Altavista, U.S.A. 76 G6 37 6N 79 17W
Altay, China 32 B3 47 48N 88 10 E
Altea, Spain 19 C5 38 38N 0 2W
Altiplano = Bolivian Plateau, S. Amer. 90 E4 20 0S 67 30W
Alto Araguaia, Brazil 93 G8 17 15S 53 20W
Alto Cuchumatanes = Cuchumatanes, Sierra de los, Guatemala 88 C1 15 35N 91 25W
Alto del Carmen, Chile 94 B1 28 46S 70 30W
Alto del Inca, Chile 94 A2 24 10S 68 10W
Alto Ligonha, Mozam. 55 F4 15 30S 38 11 E
Alto Molocue, Mozam. 55 F4 15 50S 37 35 E
Alto Paraguay □, Paraguay 94 A4 21 0S 58 30W
Alto Paraná □, Paraguay 95 B5 25 30S 54 50W
Alton, Canada 78 C4 43 54N 80 5W
Alton, U.K. 11 F7 51 9N 0 59W
Alton, Ill., U.S.A. 80 F9 38 53N 90 11W
Alton, N.H., U.S.A. 79 C13 43 27N 71 13W
Altoona, U.S.A. 78 F6 40 31N 78 24W
Altūn Kūprī, Iraq 44 C5 35 45N 44 9 E
Altun Shan, China 32 C3 38 30N 88 0 E
Alturas, U.S.A. 82 F3 41 29N 120 32W
Altus, U.S.A. 81 H5 34 38N 99 20W
Alucra, Turkey 25 F6 40 22N 38 47 E
Alūksne, Latvia 9 H22 57 24N 27 3 E
Alunite, U.S.A. 85 K12 35 59N 114 55W
Alusi, Indonesia 37 F8 7 35S 131 40 E
Alva, U.S.A. 81 G5 36 48N 98 40W
Alvarado, Mexico 87 D5 18 40N 95 50W
Alvarado, U.S.A. 81 J6 32 24N 97 13W
Alvaro Obregón, Presa, Mexico 86 B3 27 55N 109 52W
Alvear, Argentina 94 B4 29 5S 56 30W
Alvesta, Sweden 9 H16 56 54N 14 35 E
Alvin, U.S.A. 81 L7 29 26N 95 15W
Alvinston, Canada 78 D3 42 49N 81 52W
Älvkarleby, Sweden 9 F17 60 34N 17 26 E
Alvord Desert, U.S.A. 82 E4 42 30N 118 25W
Älvsbyn, Sweden 8 D19 65 40N 21 0 E
Alwar, India 42 F7 27 38N 76 34 E
Alxa Zuoqi, China 34 E3 38 50N 105 40 E
Alyangula, Australia 62 A2 13 55S 136 30 E
Alyata = Älät, Azerbaijan 25 G8 39 58N 49 25 E
Alyth, U.K. 12 E5 56 38N 3 13W
Alytus, Lithuania 9 J21 54 24N 24 3 E
Alzada, U.S.A. 80 C2 45 2N 104 25W
Alzira, Spain 19 C5 39 9N 0 30W
Am-Timan, Chad 51 F10 11 0N 20 10 E
Amadeus, L., Australia 61 D5 24 54S 131 0 E

Amadi

Amadi, *Dem. Rep. of the Congo* **54 B2** 3 40N 26 40 E
Amâdi, *Sudan* **51 G12** 5 29N 30 25 E
Amadjuak L., *Canada* **69 B12** 65 0N 71 8W
Amagansett, *U.S.A.* **79 F12** 40 59N 72 9W
Amagasaki, *Japan* **31 G7** 34 42N 135 20 E
Amahai, *Indonesia* **37 E7** 3 20S 128 55 E
Amakusa-Shotō, *Japan* **31 H5** 32 15N 130 10 E
Åmål, *Sweden* **9 G15** 59 3N 12 42 E
Amaliás, *Greece* **21 F9** 37 47N 21 22 E
Amalner, *India* **40 J9** 21 5N 75 5 E
Amamapare, *Indonesia* **37 E9** 4 53S 136 38 E
Amambaí, *Brazil* **95 A4** 23 5S 55 13W
Amambaí →, *Brazil* **95 A5** 23 22S 53 56W
Amambay □, *Paraguay* **95 A4** 23 0S 56 0W
Amambay, Cordillera de, *S. Amer.* **95 A4** 23 0S 55 45W
Amami-Guntō, *Japan* **31 L4** 27 16N 129 21 E
Amami-Ō-Shima, *Japan* **31 L4** 28 0N 129 0 E
Amaná, L., *Brazil* **92 D6** 2 35S 64 40W
Amanat →, *India* **43 G11** 24 7N 84 4 E
Amanda Park, *U.S.A.* **84 C3** 47 28N 123 55W
Amangeldy, *Kazakstan* **26 D7** 50 10N 65 10 E
Amapá, *Brazil* **93 C8** 2 5N 50 50W
Amapá □, *Brazil* **93 C8** 1 40N 52 0W
Amarante, *Brazil* **93 E10** 6 14S 42 50W
Amaranth, *Canada* **73 C9** 50 36N 98 43W
Amargosa →, *U.S.A.* **85 J10** 36 14N 116 51W
Amargosa Range, *U.S.A.* **85 J10** 36 20N 116 45W
Amári, *Greece* **23 D6** 35 13N 24 40 E
Amarillo, *U.S.A.* **81 H4** 35 13N 101 50W
Amarkantak, *India* **43 H9** 22 40N 81 45 E
Amaro, Mte., *Italy* **20 C6** 42 5N 14 5 E
Amarpur, *India* **43 G12** 25 5N 87 0 E
Amarwara, *India* **43 H8** 22 18N 79 10 E
Amasya □, *Turkey* **25 F6** 40 40N 35 50 E
Amata, *Australia* **61 E5** 26 9S 131 9 E
Amatikulu, *S. Africa* **57 D5** 29 3S 31 33 E
Amatitlán, *Guatemala* **88 D1** 14 29N 90 38W
Amay, *Belgium* **15 D5** 50 33N 5 19 E
Amazon = Amazonas →, *S. Amer.* **93 D9** 0 5S 50 0W
Amazonas □, *Brazil* **92 E6** 5 0S 65 0W
Amazonas →, *S. Amer.* **93 D9** 0 5S 50 0W
Ambah, *India* **42 F8** 26 43N 78 13 E
Ambahakily, *Madag.* **57 C7** 21 36S 43 41 E
Ambala, *India* **42 D7** 30 23N 76 56 E
Ambalavao, *Madag.* **57 C8** 21 50S 46 56 E
Ambanja, *Madag.* **57 A8** 13 40S 48 27 E
Ambarchik, *Russia* **27 C17** 69 40N 162 20 E
Ambarijeby, *Madag.* **57 A8** 14 56S 47 41 E
Ambaro, Helodranon', *Madag.* **57 A8** 13 23S 48 38 E
Ambato, *Ecuador* **92 D3** 1 5S 78 42W
Ambato, Sierra de, *Argentina* **94 B2** 28 25S 66 10W
Ambato Boeny, *Madag.* **57 B8** 16 28S 46 43 E
Ambatofinandrahana, *Madag.* **57 C8** 20 33S 46 48 E
Ambatolampy, *Madag.* **57 B8** 19 20S 47 35 E
Ambatondrazaka, *Madag.* **57 B8** 17 55S 48 28 E
Ambatosoratra, *Madag.* **57 B8** 17 37S 48 31 E
Ambenja, *Madag.* **57 B8** 15 17S 46 58 E
Amberg, *Germany* **16 D6** 49 26N 11 52 E
Ambergris Cay, *Belize* **87 D7** 18 0N 88 0W
Amberley, *N.Z.* **59 K4** 43 9S 172 44 E
Ambikapur, *India* **43 H10** 23 15N 83 15 E
Ambilobé, *Madag.* **57 A8** 13 10S 49 3 E
Ambinanindrano, *Madag.* **57 C8** 20 5S 48 23 E
Amble, *U.K.* **10 B6** 55 20N 1 36W
Ambleside, *U.K.* **10 C5** 54 26N 2 58W
Ambo, *Peru* **92 F3** 10 5S 76 10W
Ambodifototra, *Madag.* **57 B8** 16 59S 49 52 E
Ambodilazana, *Madag.* **57 B8** 18 6S 49 10 E
Ambohimahasoa, *Madag.* **57 C8** 21 7S 47 13 E
Ambohimanga, *Madag.* **57 C8** 20 52S 47 36 E
Ambohitra, *Madag.* **57 A8** 12 30S 49 10 E
Amboise, *France* **18 C4** 47 24N 1 2 E
Ambon, *Indonesia* **37 E7** 3 35S 128 20 E
Amboseli, L., *Kenya* **54 C4** 2 40S 37 10 E
Ambositra, *Madag.* **57 C8** 20 31S 47 25 E
Ambovombe, *Madag.* **57 D8** 25 11S 46 5 E
Amboy, *U.S.A.* **85 L11** 34 33N 115 45W
Amboyna Cay, *S. China Sea* **36 C4** 7 50N 112 50 E
Ambridge, *U.S.A.* **78 F4** 40 36N 80 14W
Ambriz, *Angola* **52 F2** 7 48S 13 8 E
Amchitka I., *U.S.A.* **68 C1** 51 32N 179 0 E
Amderma, *Russia* **26 C7** 69 45N 61 30 E
Amdhi, *India* **43 H9** 23 51N 81 27 E
Ameca, *Mexico* **86 C4** 20 30N 104 0W
Ameca →, *Mexico* **86 C3** 20 40N 105 15W
Amecameca, *Mexico* **87 D5** 19 7N 98 46W
Ameland, *Neths.* **15 A5** 53 27N 5 45 E
Amenia, *U.S.A.* **79 E11** 41 51N 73 33W
American Falls, *U.S.A.* **82 E7** 42 47N 112 51W
American Falls Reservoir, *U.S.A.* **82 E7** 42 47N 112 52W
American Fork, *U.S.A.* **82 F8** 40 23N 111 48W
American Highland, *Antarctica* **5 D6** 73 0S 75 0 E
American Samoa ■, *Pac. Oc.* **59 B13** 14 20S 170 40W
Americana, *Brazil* **95 A6** 22 45S 47 20W
Americus, *U.S.A.* **77 K3** 32 4N 84 14W
Amersfoort, *Neths.* **15 B5** 52 9N 5 23 E
Amersfoort, *S. Africa* **57 D4** 26 59S 29 53 E
Amery Ice Shelf, *Antarctica* **5 C6** 69 30S 72 0 E
Ames, *U.S.A.* **80 E8** 42 2N 93 37W
Amesbury, *U.S.A.* **79 D14** 42 51N 70 56W
Amet, *India* **42 G5** 25 18N 73 56 E
Amga, *Russia* **27 C14** 60 50N 132 0 E
Amga →, *Russia* **27 C14** 62 38N 134 32 E
Amgu, *Russia* **27 E14** 45 45N 137 15 E
Amgun →, *Russia* **27 D14** 52 56N 139 38 E
Amherst, *Burma* **41 L20** 16 2N 97 20 E
Amherst, *Canada* **71 C7** 45 48N 64 8W
Amherst, *Mass., U.S.A.* **79 D12** 42 23N 72 31W
Amherst, *N.Y., U.S.A.* **78 D6** 42 59N 78 48W
Amherst, *Ohio, U.S.A.* **78 E2** 41 24N 82 14W
Amherst I., *Canada* **79 B8** 44 8N 76 43W
Amherstburg, *Canada* **70 D3** 42 6N 83 6W
Amiata, Mte., *Italy* **20 C4** 42 53N 11 37 E
Amidon, *U.S.A.* **80 B3** 46 29N 103 19W
Amiens, *France* **18 B5** 49 54N 2 16 E
Amīrābād, *Iran* **44 C5** 33 20N 46 16 E
Amirante Is., *Seychelles* **28 K9** 6 0S 53 0 E
Amisk L., *Canada* **73 C8** 54 35N 102 15W
Amistad, Presa de la, *Mexico* **86 B4** 29 24N 101 0W
Amite, *U.S.A.* **81 K9** 30 44N 90 30W
Amla, *India* **42 J8** 21 56N 78 7 E
Amlia I., *U.S.A.* **68 C2** 52 4N 173 30W
Amlwch, *U.K.* **10 D3** 53 24N 4 20W
'Ammān, *Jordan* **47 D4** 31 57N 35 52 E
'Ammān □, *Jordan* **47 D5** 31 40N 36 30 E
Ammanford, *U.K.* **11 F4** 51 48N 3 59W
Ammassalik = Angmagssalik, *Greenland* **4 C6** 65 40N 37 20W
Ammon, *U.S.A.* **82 E8** 43 28N 111 58W
Amnat Charoen, *Thailand* **38 E5** 15 51N 104 38 E
Amnura, *Bangla.* **43 G13** 24 37N 88 25 E
Āmol, *Iran* **45 B7** 36 23N 52 20 E
Amorgós, *Greece* **21 F11** 36 50N 25 57 E
Amory, *U.S.A.* **77 J1** 33 59N 88 29W
Amos, *Canada* **70 C4** 48 35N 78 5W
Åmot, *Norway* **9 G13** 59 57N 9 54 E
Amoy = Xiamen, *China* **33 D6** 24 25N 118 4 E
Ampang, *Malaysia* **39 L3** 3 8N 101 45 E
Ampanihy, *Madag.* **57 C7** 24 40S 44 45 E
Ampasindava, Helodranon', *Madag.* **57 A8** 13 40S 48 15 E
Ampasindava, Saikanosy, *Madag.* **57 A8** 13 42S 47 55 E
Ampenan, *Indonesia* **36 F5** 8 35S 116 13 E
Amper →, *Germany* **16 D6** 48 29N 11 55 E
Ampotaka, *Madag.* **57 D7** 25 3S 44 41 E
Ampoza, *Madag.* **57 C7** 22 20S 44 44 E
Amqui, *Canada* **71 C6** 48 28N 67 27W
Amravati, *India* **40 J10** 20 55N 77 45 E
Amreli, *India* **42 J4** 21 35N 71 17 E
Amritsar, *India* **42 D6** 31 35N 74 57 E
Amroha, *India* **43 E8** 28 53N 78 30 E
Amsterdam, *Neths.* **15 B4** 52 23N 4 54 E
Amsterdam, *U.S.A.* **79 D10** 42 56N 74 11W
Amsterdam, I., *Ind. Oc.* **3 F13** 38 30S 77 30 E
Amstetten, *Austria* **16 D8** 48 7N 14 51 E
Amudarya →, *Uzbekistan* **26 E6** 43 58N 59 34 E
Amundsen Gulf, *Canada* **68 A7** 71 0N 124 0W
Amundsen Sea, *Antarctica* **5 D15** 72 0S 115 0W
Amuntai, *Indonesia* **36 E5** 2 28S 115 25 E
Amur →, *Russia* **27 D15** 52 56N 141 10 E
Amurang, *Indonesia* **37 D6** 1 5N 124 40 E
Amuri Pass, *N.Z.* **59 K4** 42 31S 172 11 E
Amursk, *Russia* **27 D14** 50 14N 136 54 E
Amyderya = Amudarya →, *Uzbekistan* **26 E6** 43 58N 59 34 E
An Bien, *Vietnam* **39 H5** 9 45N 105 0 E
An Hoa, *Vietnam* **38 E7** 15 40N 108 5 E
An Nabatīyah at Tahta, *Lebanon* **47 B4** 33 23N 35 27 E
An Nabk, *Si. Arabia* **44 D3** 31 20N 37 20 E
An Nabk, *Syria* **47 A5** 34 2N 36 44 E
An Nabk Abū Qaşr, *Si. Arabia* **44 D3** 30 21N 38 34 E
An Nafūd, *Si. Arabia* **44 D4** 28 15N 41 0 E
An Najaf, *Iraq* **44 C5** 32 3N 44 15 E
An Nāşirīyah, *Iraq* **44 D5** 31 0N 46 15 E
An Nhon, *Vietnam* **38 F7** 13 55N 109 7 E
An Nu'ayrīyah, *Si. Arabia* **45 E6** 27 30N 48 30 E
An Nuwayb'ī, W. →, *Si. Arabia* **47 F3** 29 18N 34 57 E
An Thoi, Dao, *Vietnam* **39 H5** 9 58N 104 0 E
An Uaimh, *Ireland* **13 C5** 53 39N 6 41W
Anabar →, *Russia* **27 B12** 73 8N 113 36 E
'Anabtā, *West Bank* **47 C4** 32 19N 35 7 E
Anaconda, *U.S.A.* **82 C7** 46 8N 112 57W
Anacortes, *U.S.A.* **84 B4** 48 30N 122 37W
Anadarko, *U.S.A.* **81 H5** 35 4N 98 15W
Anadolu, *Turkey* **25 G5** 39 0N 30 0 E
Anadyr, *Russia* **27 C18** 64 35N 177 20 E
Anadyr →, *Russia* **27 C18** 64 55N 176 5 E
Anadyrskiy Zaliv, *Russia* **27 C19** 64 0N 180 0 E
Anaga, Pta. de, *Canary Is.* **22 F3** 28 34N 16 9W
'Ānah, *Iraq* **44 C4** 34 25N 42 0 E
Anaheim, *U.S.A.* **85 M9** 33 50N 117 55W
Anahim Lake, *Canada* **72 C3** 52 28N 125 18W
Anáhuac, *Mexico* **86 B4** 27 14N 100 9W
Anakapalle, *India* **41 L13** 17 42N 83 6 E
Anakie, *Australia* **62 C4** 23 32S 147 45 E
Analalava, *Madag.* **57 A8** 14 35S 48 0 E
Análipsis, *Greece* **23 A3** 39 36N 19 55 E
Anambar →, *Pakistan* **42 D3** 30 15N 68 50 E
Anambas, Kepulauan, *Indonesia* **39 L6** 3 20N 106 30 E
Anambas Is. = Anambas, Kepulauan, *Indonesia* **39 L6** 3 20N 106 30 E
Anamosa, *U.S.A.* **80 D9** 42 7N 91 17W
Anamur, *Turkey* **25 G5** 36 8N 32 58 E
Anan, *Japan* **31 H7** 33 54N 134 40 E
Anand, *India* **42 H5** 22 32N 72 59 E
Anantnag, *India* **43 C6** 33 45N 75 10 E
Ananyiv, *Ukraine* **17 E15** 47 44N 29 58 E
Anapodháris →, *Greece* **23 E7** 34 59N 25 20 E
Anápolis, *Brazil* **93 G9** 16 15S 48 50W
Anapu →, *Brazil* **93 D8** 1 53S 50 53W
Anār, *Iran* **45 D7** 30 55N 55 13 E
Anārak, *Iran* **45 C7** 33 25N 53 40 E
Anas →, *India* **42 H5** 23 26N 74 0 E
Anatolia = Anadolu, *Turkey* **25 G5** 39 0N 30 0 E
Anatsogno, *Madag.* **57 C7** 23 33S 43 46 E
Añatuya, *Argentina* **94 B3** 28 20S 62 50W
Anaunethad L., *Canada* **73 A8** 60 55N 104 25W
Anbyŏn, *N. Korea* **35 E14** 39 1N 127 35 E
Ancaster, *Canada* **78 C5** 43 13N 79 59W
Anchor Bay, *U.S.A.* **84 G3** 38 48N 123 34W
Anchorage, *U.S.A.* **68 B5** 61 13N 149 54W
Anci, *China* **34 E9** 39 20N 116 40 E
Ancohuma, Nevada, *Bolivia* **92 G5** 16 0S 68 50W
Ancón, *Peru* **92 F3** 11 50S 77 10W
Ancona, *Italy* **20 C5** 43 38N 13 30 E
Ancud, *Chile* **96 E2** 42 0S 73 50W
Ancud, G. de, *Chile* **96 E2** 42 0S 73 0W
Anda, *China* **33 B7** 46 24N 125 19 E
Andacollo, *Argentina* **94 D1** 37 10S 70 42W
Andacollo, *Chile* **94 C1** 30 14S 71 6W
Andalgalá, *Argentina* **94 B2** 27 40S 66 30W
Åndalsnes, *Norway* **9 E12** 62 35N 7 43 E
Andalucía □, *Spain* **19 D3** 37 35N 5 0W
Andalusia = Andalucía □, *Spain* **19 D3** 37 35N 5 0W
Andalusia, *U.S.A.* **77 K2** 31 18N 86 29W
Andaman Is., *Ind. Oc.* **28 H13** 12 30N 92 30 E
Andaman Sea, *Ind. Oc.* **36 B1** 13 0N 96 0 E
Andamooka Opal Fields, *Australia* **63 E2** 30 27S 137 9 E
Andapa, *Madag.* **53 G9** 14 30S 49 30 E
Andara, *Namibia* **56 B3** 18 2S 21 9 E
Andenes, *Norway* **8 B17** 69 19N 16 18 E
Andenne, *Belgium* **15 D5** 50 28N 5 5 E
Anderson, *Alaska, U.S.A.* **68 B5** 64 25N 149 15W
Anderson, *Calif., U.S.A.* **82 F2** 40 27N 122 18W
Anderson, *Ind., U.S.A.* **76 E3** 40 10N 85 41W
Anderson, *Mo., U.S.A.* **81 G7** 36 39N 94 27W
Anderson, *S.C., U.S.A.* **77 H4** 34 31N 82 39W
Anderson →, *Canada* **68 B7** 69 42N 129 0W
Andes, *U.S.A.* **79 D10** 42 12N 74 47W
Andes, Cord. de los, *S. Amer.* **92 H5** 20 0S 68 0W
Andfjorden, *Norway* **8 B17** 69 10N 16 20 E
Andhra Pradesh □, *India* **40 L11** 18 0N 79 0 E
Andijon, *Uzbekistan* **26 E8** 41 10N 72 15 E
Andikíthira, *Greece* **21 G10** 35 52N 23 15 E
Andīmeshk, *Iran* **45 C6** 32 27N 48 21 E
Andizhan = Andijon, *Uzbekistan* **26 E8** 41 10N 72 15 E
Andoany, *Madag.* **57 A8** 13 25S 48 16 E
Andong, *S. Korea* **35 F15** 36 40N 128 43 E
Andongwei, *China* **35 G10** 35 6N 119 20 E
Andoom, *Australia* **62 A3** 12 25S 141 53 E
Andorra ■, *Europe* **18 E4** 42 30N 1 30 E
Andorra La Vella, *Andorra* **18 E4** 42 31N 1 32 E
Andover, *U.K.* **11 F6** 51 12N 1 29W
Andover, *Maine, U.S.A.* **79 B14** 44 38N 70 45W
Andover, *Mass., U.S.A.* **79 D13** 42 40N 71 8W
Andover, *N.J., U.S.A.* **79 F10** 40 59N 74 45W
Andover, *N.Y., U.S.A.* **78 D7** 42 10N 77 48W
Andover, *Ohio, U.S.A.* **78 E4** 41 36N 80 34W
Andøya, *Norway* **8 B16** 69 10N 15 50 E
Andradina, *Brazil* **93 H8** 20 54S 51 23W
Andrahary, Mt., *Madag.* **57 A8** 13 37S 49 17 E
Andramasina, *Madag.* **57 B8** 19 11S 47 35 E
Andranopasy, *Madag.* **57 C7** 21 17S 43 44 E
Andratx, *Spain* **22 B9** 39 39N 2 25 E
Andreanof Is., *U.S.A.* **68 C2** 51 30N 176 0W
Andrews, *S.C., U.S.A.* **77 J6** 33 27N 79 34W
Andrews, *Tex., U.S.A.* **81 J3** 32 19N 102 33W
Ándria, *Italy* **20 D7** 41 13N 16 17 E
Andriba, *Madag.* **57 B8** 17 30S 46 58 E
Androka, *Madag.* **57 C7** 24 58S 44 2 E
Andropov = Rybinsk, *Russia* **24 C6** 58 5N 38 50 E
Ándros, *Greece* **21 F11** 37 50N 24 57 E
Andros I., *Bahamas* **88 B4** 24 30N 78 0W
Andros Town, *Bahamas* **88 B4** 24 43N 77 47W
Androscoggin →, *U.S.A.* **79 C14** 43 58N 70 0W
Andselv, *Norway* **8 B18** 69 4N 18 34 E
Andújar, *Spain* **19 C3** 38 3N 4 5W
Andulo, *Angola* **52 G3** 11 25S 16 45 E
Anegada I., *Virgin Is.* **89 C7** 18 45N 64 20W
Anegada Passage, *W. Indies* **89 C7** 18 15N 63 45W
Aneto, Pico de, *Spain* **19 A6** 42 37N 0 40 E
Ang Thong, *Thailand* **38 E3** 14 35N 100 31 E
Angamos, Punta, *Chile* **94 A1** 23 1S 70 32W
Angara →, *Russia* **27 D10** 58 5N 94 20 E
Angarsk, *Russia* **27 D11** 52 30N 104 0 E
Angas Hills, *Australia* **60 D4** 23 0S 127 50 E
Angaston, *Australia* **63 E2** 34 30S 139 8 E
Angaur I., *Pac. Oc.* **37 C8** 6 54N 134 9 E
Ånge, *Sweden* **9 E16** 62 31N 15 35 E
Ángel, Salto = Angel Falls, *Venezuela* **92 B6** 5 57N 62 30W
Ángel de la Guarda, I., *Mexico* **86 B2** 29 30N 113 30W
Angel Falls, *Venezuela* **92 B6** 5 57N 62 30W
Angeles, *Phil.* **37 A6** 15 9N 120 33 E
Ängelholm, *Sweden* **9 H15** 56 15N 12 58 E
Angels Camp, *U.S.A.* **84 G6** 38 4N 120 32W
Ångermanälven →, *Sweden* **8 E17** 62 40N 18 0 E
Ångermanland, *Sweden* **8 E18** 63 36N 17 45 E
Angers, *Canada* **79 A9** 45 31N 75 29W
Angers, *France* **18 C3** 47 30N 0 35W
Ängesån →, *Sweden* **8 C20** 66 16N 22 47 E
Angikuni L., *Canada* **73 A9** 62 0N 100 0W
Angkor, *Cambodia* **38 F4** 13 22N 103 50 E
Anglesey, *U.K.* **10 D3** 53 17N 4 20W
Anglesey, Isle of □, *U.K.* **10 D3** 53 16N 4 18W
Angleton, *U.S.A.* **81 L7** 29 10N 95 26W
Anglisidhes, *Cyprus* **23 E12** 34 51N 33 27 E
Angmagssalik, *Greenland* **4 C6** 65 40N 37 20W
Ango, *Dem. Rep. of the Congo* **54 B2** 4 10N 26 5 E
Angoche, *Mozam.* **55 F4** 16 8S 39 55 E
Angoche, I., *Mozam.* **55 F4** 16 20S 39 50 E
Angol, *Chile* **94 D1** 37 56S 72 45W
Angola, *Ind., U.S.A.* **76 E3** 41 38N 85 0W
Angola, *N.Y., U.S.A.* **78 D5** 42 38N 79 2W
Angola ■, *Africa* **53 G3** 12 0S 18 0 E
Angoulême, *France* **18 D4** 45 39N 0 10 E
Angoumois, *France* **18 D3** 45 50N 0 25 E
Angra dos Reis, *Brazil* **95 A7** 23 0S 44 10W
Angren, *Uzbekistan* **26 E8** 41 1N 70 12 E
Angtassom, *Cambodia* **39 G5** 11 1N 104 41 E
Angu, *Dem. Rep. of the Congo* **54 B1** 3 25N 24 28 E
Anguang, *China* **35 B12** 45 15N 123 45 E
Anguilla ■, *W. Indies* **89 C7** 18 14N 63 5W
Anguo, *China* **34 E8** 38 28N 115 15 E
Angurugu, *Australia* **62 A2** 14 0S 136 25 E
Angus □, *U.K.* **12 E6** 56 46N 2 56W
Anhanduí →, *Brazil* **95 A5** 21 46S 52 9W
Anholt, *Denmark* **9 H14** 56 42N 11 33 E
Anhui □, *China* **33 C6** 32 0N 117 0 E
Anhwei = Anhui □, *China* **33 C6** 32 0N 117 0 E
Anichab, *Namibia* **56 C1** 21 0S 14 46 E
Animas →, *U.S.A.* **83 H9** 36 43N 108 13W
Anivorano, *Madag.* **57 B8** 18 44S 48 58 E
Anjalankoski, *Finland* **9 F22** 60 45N 26 51 E
Anjar, *India* **42 H4** 23 6N 70 10 E
Anjidiv I., *India* **40 M9** 14 40N 74 10 E
Anjou, *France* **18 C3** 47 20N 0 15W
Anjozorobe, *Madag.* **57 B8** 18 22S 47 52 E
Anju, *N. Korea* **35 E13** 39 36N 125 40 E
Ankaboa, Tanjon, *Madag.* **57 C7** 21 58S 43 20 E
Ankang, *China* **34 H5** 32 40N 109 1 E
Ankara, *Turkey* **25 G5** 39 57N 32 54 E
Ankaramena, *Madag.* **57 C8** 21 57S 46 39 E
Ankaratra, *Madag.* **53 H9** 19 25S 47 12 E
Ankazoabo, *Madag.* **57 C7** 22 18S 44 31 E
Ankazobe, *Madag.* **57 B8** 18 20S 47 10 E
Ankeny, *U.S.A.* **80 E8** 41 44N 93 36W
Ankisabe, *Madag.* **57 B8** 19 17S 46 29 E
Ankoro, *Dem. Rep. of the Congo* **54 D2** 6 45S 26 55 E
Anmyŏn-do, *S. Korea* **35 F14** 36 25N 126 25 E
Ann, C., *U.S.A.* **79 D14** 42 38N 70 35W
Ann Arbor, *U.S.A.* **76 D4** 42 17N 83 45W
Anna, *U.S.A.* **81 G10** 37 28N 89 15W
Annaba, *Algeria* **50 A7** 36 50N 7 46 E
Annalee →, *Ireland* **13 B4** 54 2N 7 24W
Annam, *Vietnam* **38 E7** 16 0N 108 0 E
Annamitique, Chaîne, *Asia* **38 D6** 17 0N 106 0 E
Annan, *U.K.* **12 G5** 54 59N 3 16W
Annan →, *U.K.* **12 G5** 54 58N 3 16W
Annapolis, *U.S.A.* **76 F7** 38 59N 76 30W
Annapolis Royal, *Canada* **71 D6** 44 44N 65 32W
Annapurna, *Nepal* **43 E10** 28 34N 83 50 E
Annean, L., *Australia* **61 E2** 26 54S 118 14 E
Annecy, *France* **18 D7** 45 55N 6 8 E
Anning, *China* **32 D5** 24 55N 102 26 E
Anniston, *U.S.A.* **77 J3** 33 39N 85 50W
Annobón, *Atl. Oc.* **49 G4** 1 25S 5 36 E
Annotto Bay, *Jamaica* **88 C4** 18 17N 76 45W
Annville, *U.S.A.* **79 F8** 40 20N 76 31W
Áno Viánnos, *Greece* **23 D7** 35 2N 25 21 E
Anorotsangana, *Madag.* **57 A8** 13 56S 47 55 E
Anóyia, *Greece* **23 D6** 35 16N 24 52 E
Anping, *Hebei, China* **34 E8** 38 15N 115 30 E
Anping, *Liaoning, China* **35 D12** 41 5N 123 30 E
Anqing, *China* **33 C6** 30 30N 117 3 E
Anqiu, *China* **35 F10** 36 25N 119 10 E
Ansai, *China* **34 F5** 36 50N 109 20 E
Ansbach, *Germany* **16 D6** 49 28N 10 34 E
Anshan, *China* **35 D12** 41 5N 122 58 E
Anshun, *China* **32 D5** 26 18N 105 57 E
Ansley, *U.S.A.* **80 E5** 41 18N 99 23W
Anson, *U.S.A.* **81 J5** 32 45N 99 54W
Anson B., *Australia* **60 B5** 13 20S 130 6 E
Ansongo, *Mali* **50 E6** 15 25N 0 35 E
Ansonia, *U.S.A.* **79 E11** 41 21N 73 5W
Anstruther, *U.K.* **12 E6** 56 14N 2 41W
Ansudu, *Indonesia* **37 E9** 2 11S 139 22 E
Antabamba, *Peru* **92 F4** 14 40S 73 0W
Antakya, *Turkey* **25 G6** 36 14N 36 10 E
Antalaha, *Madag.* **57 A9** 14 57S 50 20 E
Antalya, *Turkey* **25 G5** 36 52N 30 45 E
Antalya Körfezi, *Turkey* **25 G5** 36 15N 31 30 E
Antananarivo, *Madag.* **57 B8** 18 55S 47 31 E
Antananarivo □, *Madag.* **57 B8** 19 0S 47 0 E
Antanimbaribe, *Madag.* **57 C7** 21 30S 44 48 E
Antarctic Pen., *Antarctica* **5 C18** 67 0S 60 0W
Antarctica **5 E3** 90 0S 0 0 E
Antelope, *Zimbabwe* **55 G2** 21 2S 28 31 E
Antequera, *Paraguay* **94 A4** 24 8S 57 7W
Antequera, *Spain* **19 D3** 37 5N 4 33W
Antero, Mt., *U.S.A.* **83 G10** 38 41N 106 15W
Anthony, *Kans., U.S.A.* **81 G5** 37 9N 98 2W
Anthony, *N. Mex., U.S.A.* **83 K10** 32 0N 106 36W
Anti Atlas, *Morocco* **50 C4** 30 0N 8 30W
Anti-Lebanon = Ash Sharqi, Al Jabal, *Lebanon* **47 B5** 33 40N 36 10 E
Antibes, *France* **18 E7** 43 34N 7 6 E
Anticosti, Î. d', *Canada* **71 C7** 49 30N 63 0W
Antigo, *U.S.A.* **80 C10** 45 9N 89 9W
Antigonish, *Canada* **71 C7** 45 38N 61 58W
Antigua, *Canary Is.* **22 F5** 28 24N 14 1W
Antigua, *W. Indies* **89 C7** 17 0N 61 50W
Antigua & Barbuda ■, *W. Indies* **89 C7** 17 20N 61 48W
Antigua Guatemala, *Guatemala* **88 D1** 14 34N 90 41W
Antilla, *Cuba* **88 B4** 20 40N 75 50W
Antilles = West Indies, *Cent. Amer.* **89 D7** 15 0N 65 0W
Antioch, *U.S.A.* **84 G5** 38 1N 121 48W
Antioquia, *Colombia* **92 B3** 6 40N 75 55W
Antipodes Is., *Pac. Oc.* **64 M9** 49 45S 178 40 E
Antlers, *U.S.A.* **81 H7** 34 14N 95 37W
Antofagasta, *Chile* **94 A1** 23 50S 70 30W
Antofagasta □, *Chile* **94 A2** 24 0S 69 0W
Antofagasta de la Sierra, *Argentina* **94 B2** 26 5S 67 20W
Antofalla, *Argentina* **94 B2** 25 30S 68 5W
Antofalla, Salar de, *Argentina* **94 B2** 25 40S 67 45W
Anton, *U.S.A.* **81 J3** 33 49N 102 10W
Antongila, Helodrano, *Madag.* **57 B8** 15 30S 49 50 E
Antonibé, *Madag.* **57 B8** 15 7S 47 24 E
Antonibé, Presqu'île d', *Madag.* **57 A8** 14 55S 47 20 E
Antonina, *Brazil* **95 B6** 25 26S 48 42W
Antrim, *U.K.* **13 B5** 54 43N 6 14W
Antrim, *U.S.A.* **78 F3** 40 7N 81 21W
Antrim □, *U.K.* **13 B5** 54 56N 6 25W
Antrim, Mts. of, *U.K.* **13 A5** 55 3N 6 14W
Antrim Plateau, *Australia* **60 C4** 18 8S 128 20 E
Antsalova, *Madag.* **57 B7** 18 40S 44 37 E
Antsirabe, *Madag.* **57 B8** 19 55S 47 2 E
Antsiranana, *Madag.* **57 A8** 12 25S 49 20 E
Antsohihy, *Madag.* **57 A8** 14 50S 47 59 E
Antsohimbondrona Seranana, *Madag.* **57 A8** 13 7S 48 48 E
Antu, *China* **35 C15** 42 30N 128 20 E
Antwerp = Antwerpen, *Belgium* **15 C4** 51 13N 4 25 E
Antwerp, *U.S.A.* **79 B9** 44 12N 75 37W
Antwerpen, *Belgium* **15 C4** 51 13N 4 25 E
Antwerpen □, *Belgium* **15 C4** 51 15N 4 40 E
Anupgarh, *India* **42 E5** 29 10N 73 10 E
Anuppur, *India* **43 H9** 23 6N 81 41 E
Anuradhapura, *Sri Lanka* **40 Q12** 8 22N 80 28 E
Anveh, *Iran* **45 E7** 27 23N 54 11 E
Anvers = Antwerpen, *Belgium* **15 C4** 51 13N 4 25 E
Anvers I., *Antarctica* **5 C17** 64 30S 63 40W
Anxi, *China* **32 B4** 40 30N 95 43 E
Anxious B., *Australia* **63 E1** 33 24S 134 45 E
Anyang, *China* **34 F8** 36 5N 114 21 E
Anyer-Kidul, *Indonesia* **37 G11** 6 4S 105 53 E
Anyi, *China* **34 G6** 35 2N 111 2 E
Anza, *U.S.A.* **85 M10** 33 35N 116 39W
Anze, *China* **34 F7** 36 10N 112 12 E
Anzhero-Sudzhensk, *Russia* **26 D9** 56 10N 86 0 E
Ánzio, *Italy* **20 D5** 41 27N 12 37 E
Aoga-Shima, *Japan* **31 H9** 32 28N 139 46 E
Aomen = Macau, *China* **33 G6** 22 16N 113 35 E
Aomori, *Japan* **30 D10** 40 45N 140 45 E

Asmara

Aomori □, *Japan* **30 D10** 40 45N 140 40 E
Aonla, *India* **43 E8** 28 16N 79 11 E
Aoraki Mt. Cook, *N.Z.* **59 K3** 43 36S 170 9 E
Aosta, *Italy* **18 D7** 45 45N 7 20 E
Aouker, *Mauritania* **50 E4** 17 40N 10 0W
Aozou, *Chad* **51 D9** 21 45N 17 28 E
Apa →, *S. Amer.* **94 A4** 22 6S 58 2W
Apache, *U.S.A.* **81 H5** 34 54N 98 22W
Apache Junction, *U.S.A.* **83 K8** 33 25N 111 33W
Apalachee B., *U.S.A.* **77 L4** 30 0N 84 0W
Apalachicola, *U.S.A.* **77 L3** 29 43N 84 59W
Apalachicola →, *U.S.A.* **77 L3** 29 43N 84 58W
Apaporis →, *Colombia* **92 D5** 1 23S 69 25W
Aparri, *Phil.* **37 A6** 18 22N 121 38 E
Apatity, *Russia* **24 A5** 67 34N 33 22 E
Apatzingán, *Mexico* **86 D4** 19 0N 102 20W
Apeldoorn, *Neths.* **15 B5** 52 13N 5 57 E
Apennines = Appennini, *Italy* **20 B4** 44 0N 10 0 E
Apia, *Samoa* **59 A13** 13 50S 171 50W
Apiacás, Serra dos, *Brazil* **92 E7** 9 50S 57 0W
Apizaco, *Mexico* **87 D5** 19 26N 98 9W
Aplao, *Peru* **92 G4** 16 0S 72 40W
Apo, Mt., *Phil.* **37 C7** 6 53N 125 14 E
Apolakkiá, *Greece* **23 C9** 36 5N 27 48 E
Apolakkiá, Órmos, *Greece* **23 C9** 36 5N 27 45 E
Apollo Bay, *Australia* **63 F3** 38 45S 143 40 E
Apolo, *Bolivia* **92 F5** 14 30S 68 30W
Aporé →, *Brazil* **93 G8** 19 27S 50 57W
Apostle Is., *U.S.A.* **80 B9** 47 0N 90 40W
Apóstoles, *Argentina* **95 B4** 28 0S 56 0W
Apostolos Andreas, C., *Cyprus* **23 D13** 35 42N 34 35 E
Apoteri, *Guyana* **92 C7** 4 2N 58 32W
Appalachian Mts., *U.S.A.* **76 G6** 38 0N 80 0W
Appennini, *Italy* **20 B4** 44 0N 10 0 E
Apple Hill, *Canada* **79 A10** 45 13N 74 46W
Apple Valley, *U.S.A.* **85 L9** 34 32N 117 14W
Appleby-in-Westmorland, *U.K.* **10 C5** 54 35N 2 29W
Appleton, *U.S.A.* **76 C1** 44 16N 88 25W
Approuague →, *Fr. Guiana* **93 C8** 4 30N 51 57W
Aprília, *Italy* **20 D5** 41 36N 12 39 E
Apsley, *Canada* **78 B6** 44 45N 78 6W
Apucarana, *Brazil* **95 A5** 23 55S 51 33W
Apure →, *Venezuela* **92 B5** 7 37N 66 25W
Apurimac →, *Peru* **92 F4** 12 17S 73 56W
Āqā Jarī, *Iran* **45 D6** 30 42N 49 50 E
Aqaba = Al 'Aqabah, *Jordan* **47 F4** 29 31N 35 0 E
Aqaba, G. of, *Red Sea* **44 D2** 28 15N 33 20 E
'Aqabah, Khalīj al = Aqaba, G. of, *Red Sea* **44 D2** 28 15N 33 20 E
'Aqdā, *Iran* **45 C7** 32 26N 53 37 E
Aqmola = Astana, *Kazakstan* **26 D8** 51 10N 71 30 E
Aqrah, *Iraq* **44 B4** 36 46N 43 45 E
Aqtaū, *Kazakstan* **26 E6** 43 39N 51 12 E
Aqtöbe, *Kazakstan* **25 D10** 50 17N 57 10 E
Aquidauana, *Brazil* **93 H7** 20 30S 55 50W
Aquiles Serdán, *Mexico* **86 B3** 28 37N 105 54W
Aquin, *Haiti* **89 C5** 18 16N 73 24W
Aquitain, Bassin, *France* **18 D3** 44 0N 0 30W
Ar Rachidiya, *Morocco* **50 B5** 31 58N 4 20W
Ar Rafid, *Syria* **47 C4** 32 57N 35 52 E
Ar Raḥḥālīyah, *Iraq* **44 C4** 32 44N 43 23 E
Ar Ramādī, *Iraq* **44 C4** 33 25N 43 20 E
Ar Ramthā, *Jordan* **47 C5** 32 34N 36 0 E
Ar Raqqah, *Syria* **44 C3** 35 59N 39 8 E
Ar Rass, *Si. Arabia* **44 E4** 25 50N 43 40 E
Ar Rifā'ī, *Iraq* **44 D5** 31 50N 46 10 E
Ar Riyāḍ, *Si. Arabia* **46 C4** 24 41N 46 42 E
Ar Ru'ays, *Qatar* **45 E6** 26 8N 51 12 E
Ar Rukhaymīyah, *Iraq* **44 D5** 29 22N 45 38 E
Ar Ruqayyidah, *Si. Arabia* **45 E6** 25 21N 49 34 E
Ar Ruṣāfah, *Syria* **44 C3** 35 45N 38 49 E
Ar Ruṭbah, *Iraq* **44 C4** 33 0N 40 15 E
Ara, *India* **43 G11** 25 35N 84 32 E
Arab, *U.S.A.* **77 H2** 34 19N 86 30W
'Arab, Bahr el →, *Sudan* **51 G11** 9 0N 29 30 E
'Arabābād, *Iran* **45 C8** 33 2N 57 41 E
Arabia, *Asia* **28 G8** 25 0N 45 0 E
Arabian Desert = Es Sahrâ' Esh Sharqîya, *Egypt* **51 C12** 27 30N 32 30 E
Arabian Gulf = Gulf, The, *Asia* **45 E6** 27 0N 50 0 E
Arabian Sea, *Ind. Oc.* **29 H10** 16 0N 65 0 E
Aracaju, *Brazil* **93 F11** 10 55S 37 4W
Aracati, *Brazil* **93 D11** 4 30S 37 44W
Araçatuba, *Brazil* **95 A5** 21 10S 50 30W
Aracena, *Spain* **19 D2** 37 53N 6 38W
Araçuai, *Brazil* **93 G10** 16 52S 42 4W
'Arad, *Israel* **47 D4** 31 15N 35 12 E
Arad, *Romania* **17 E11** 46 10N 21 20 E
Arādān, *Iran* **45 C7** 35 21N 52 30 E
Aradhippou, *Cyprus* **23 E12** 34 57N 33 36 E
Arafura Sea, *E. Indies* **37 F9** 9 0S 135 0 E
Aragón □, *Spain* **19 B5** 41 25N 0 40W
Aragón →, *Spain* **19 A5** 42 13N 1 44W
Araguacema, *Brazil* **93 E9** 8 50S 49 20W
Araguaia →, *Brazil* **93 E9** 5 21S 48 41W
Araguaína, *Brazil* **93 E9** 7 12S 48 12W
Araguari, *Brazil* **93 G9** 18 38S 48 11W
Araguari →, *Brazil* **93 C9** 1 15N 49 55W
Arain, *India* **42 F6** 26 27N 75 2 E
Arak, *Algeria* **50 C6** 25 20N 3 45 E
Arāk, *Iran* **45 C6** 34 0N 49 40 E
Arakan Coast, *Burma* **41 K19** 19 0N 94 0 E
Arakan Yoma, *Burma* **41 K19** 20 0N 94 40 E
Araks = Aras, Rūd-e →, *Azerbaijan* **44 B5** 40 5N 48 29 E
Aral, *Kazakstan* **26 E7** 46 41N 61 45 E
Aral Sea, *Asia* **26 E7** 44 30N 60 0 E
Aral Tengizi = Aral Sea, *Asia* **26 E7** 44 30N 60 0 E
Aralsk = Aral, *Kazakstan* **26 E7** 46 41N 61 45 E
Aralskoye More = Aral Sea, *Asia* **26 E7** 44 30N 60 0 E
Aramac, *Australia* **62 C4** 22 58S 145 14 E
Aran I., *Ireland* **13 A3** 55 0N 8 30W
Aran Is., *Ireland* **13 C2** 53 6N 9 38W
Aranda de Duero, *Spain* **19 B4** 41 39N 3 42W
Arandān, *Iran* **44 C5** 35 23N 46 55 E
Aranjuez, *Spain* **19 B4** 40 1N 3 40W
Aranos, *Namibia* **56 C2** 24 9S 19 7 E
Aransas Pass, *U.S.A.* **81 M6** 27 55N 97 9W
Aranyaprathet, *Thailand* **38 F4** 13 41N 102 30 E
Arapahoe, *U.S.A.* **80 E5** 40 18N 99 54W
Arapey Grande →, *Uruguay* **94 C4** 30 55S 57 49W
Arapgir, *Turkey* **44 B3** 39 5N 38 30 E
Arapiraca, *Brazil* **93 E11** 9 45S 36 39W
Arapongas, *Brazil* **95 A5** 23 29S 51 28W
Ar'ar, *Si. Arabia* **44 D4** 30 59N 41 2 E
Araranguá, *Brazil* **95 B6** 29 0S 49 30W
Araraquara, *Brazil* **93 H9** 21 50S 48 0W
Ararás, Serra das, *Brazil* **95 B5** 25 0S 53 10W
Ararat, *Australia* **63 F3** 37 16S 143 0 E
Ararat, Mt. = Ağrı Dağı, *Turkey* **25 G7** 39 50N 44 15 E
Araria, *India* **43 F12** 26 9N 87 33 E
Araripe, Chapada do, *Brazil* **93 E11** 7 20S 40 0W
Araruama, L. de, *Brazil* **95 A7** 22 53S 42 12W
Aras, Rūd-e →, *Azerbaijan* **44 B5** 40 5N 48 29 E
Arauca, *Colombia* **92 B4** 7 0N 70 40W
Arauca →, *Venezuela* **92 B5** 7 24N 66 35W
Arauco, *Chile* **94 D1** 37 16S 73 25W
Araxá, *Brazil* **93 G9** 19 35S 46 55W
Araya, Pen. de, *Venezuela* **92 A6** 10 40N 64 0W
Arba Minch, *Ethiopia* **46 F2** 6 0N 37 30 E
Arbat, *Iraq* **44 C5** 35 25N 45 35 E
Árbatax, *Italy* **20 E3** 39 56N 9 42 E
Arbīl, *Iraq* **44 B5** 36 15N 44 5 E
Arborfield, *Canada* **73 C8** 53 6N 103 39W
Arborg, *Canada* **73 C9** 50 54N 97 13W
Arbroath, *U.K.* **12 E6** 56 34N 2 35W
Arbuckle, *U.S.A.* **84 F4** 39 1N 122 3W
Arcachon, *France* **18 D3** 44 40N 1 10W
Arcade, *Calif., U.S.A.* **85 L8** 34 2N 118 15W
Arcade, *N.Y., U.S.A.* **78 D6** 42 32N 78 25W
Arcadia, *Fla., U.S.A.* **77 M5** 27 13N 81 52W
Arcadia, *La., U.S.A.* **81 J8** 32 33N 92 55W
Arcadia, *Pa., U.S.A.* **78 F6** 40 47N 78 51W
Arcata, *U.S.A.* **82 F1** 40 52N 124 5W
Archangel = Arkhangelsk, *Russia* **24 B7** 64 38N 40 36 E
Archbald, *U.S.A.* **79 E9** 41 30N 75 32W
Archer →, *Australia* **62 A3** 13 28S 141 41 E
Archer B., *Australia* **62 A3** 13 20S 141 30 E
Archers Post, *Kenya* **54 B4** 0 35N 37 35 E
Arches National Park, *U.S.A.* **83 G9** 38 45N 109 25W
Arckaringa Cr. →, *Australia* **63 D2** 28 10S 135 22 E
Arco, *U.S.A.* **82 E7** 43 38N 113 18W
Arcos de la Frontera, *Spain* **19 D3** 36 45N 5 49W
Arcot, *India* **40 N11** 12 53N 79 20 E
Arctic Bay, *Canada* **69 A11** 73 1N 85 7W
Arctic Ocean, *Arctic* **4 B18** 78 0N 160 0W
Arctic Red River = Tsiigehtchic, *Canada* **68 B6** 67 15N 134 0W
Arda →, *Bulgaria* **21 D12** 41 40N 26 30 E
Ardabīl, *Iran* **45 B6** 38 15N 48 18 E
Ardakān = Sepīdān, *Iran* **45 D7** 30 20N 52 5 E
Ardakān, *Iran* **45 C7** 32 19N 53 59 E
Ardee, *Ireland* **13 C5** 53 52N 6 33W
Arden, *Canada* **78 B8** 44 43N 76 56W
Arden, *Calif., U.S.A.* **84 G5** 38 36N 121 33W
Arden, *Nev., U.S.A.* **85 J11** 36 1N 115 14W
Ardenne, *Belgium* **16 D3** 49 50N 5 5 E
Ardennes = Ardenne, *Belgium* **16 D3** 49 50N 5 5 E
Arderin, *Ireland* **13 C4** 53 2N 7 39W
Ardestān, *Iran* **45 C7** 33 20N 52 25 E
Ardivachar Pt., *U.K.* **12 D1** 57 23N 7 26W
Ardlethan, *Australia* **63 E4** 34 22S 146 53 E
Ardmore, *Okla., U.S.A.* **81 H6** 34 10N 97 8W
Ardmore, *Pa., U.S.A.* **79 G9** 39 58N 75 18W
Ardnamurchan, Pt. of, *U.K.* **12 E2** 56 43N 6 14W
Ardnave Pt., *U.K.* **12 F2** 55 53N 6 20W
Ardrossan, *Australia* **63 E2** 34 26S 137 53 E
Ardrossan, *U.K.* **12 F4** 55 39N 4 49W
Ards Pen., *U.K.* **13 B6** 54 33N 5 34W
Arecibo, *Puerto Rico* **89 C6** 18 29N 66 43W
Areia Branca, *Brazil* **93 E11** 5 0S 37 0W
Arena, Pt., *U.S.A.* **84 G3** 38 57N 123 44W
Arenal, *Honduras* **88 C2** 15 21N 86 50W
Arendal, *Norway* **9 G13** 58 28N 8 46 E
Arequipa, *Peru* **92 G4** 16 20S 71 30W
Arévalo, *Spain* **19 B3** 41 3N 4 43W
Arezzo, *Italy* **20 C4** 43 25N 11 53 E
Arga, *Turkey* **44 B3** 38 21N 37 59 E
Arganda, *Spain* **19 B4** 40 19N 3 26W
Argenta, *Canada* **72 C5** 50 11N 116 56W
Argentan, *France* **18 B3** 48 45N 0 1W
Argentário, Mte., *Italy* **20 C4** 42 24N 11 9 E
Argentia, *Canada* **71 C9** 47 18N 53 58W
Argentina ■, *S. Amer.* **96 D3** 35 0S 66 0W
Argentina Is., *Antarctica* **5 C17** 66 0S 64 0W
Argentino, L., *Argentina* **96 G2** 50 10S 73 0W
Argeș →, *Romania* **17 F14** 44 5N 26 38 E
Arghandab →, *Afghan.* **42 D1** 31 30N 64 15 E
Argolikós Kólpos, *Greece* **21 F10** 37 20N 22 52 E
Árgos, *Greece* **21 F10** 37 40N 22 43 E
Argostólion, *Greece* **21 E9** 38 12N 20 33 E
Arguello, Pt., *U.S.A.* **85 L6** 34 35N 120 39W
Arguineguín, *Canary Is.* **22 G4** 27 46N 15 41W
Argun →, *Russia* **27 D13** 53 20N 121 28 E
Argus Pk., *U.S.A.* **85 K9** 35 52N 117 26W
Argyle, L., *Australia* **60 C4** 16 20S 128 40 E
Argyll & Bute □, *U.K.* **12 E3** 56 13N 5 28W
Århus, *Denmark* **9 H14** 56 8N 10 11 E
Ariadnoye, *Russia* **30 B7** 45 8N 134 25 E
Ariamsvlei, *Namibia* **56 D2** 28 9S 19 51 E
Ariana, *Tunisia* **51 A7** 36 52N 10 12 E
Arica, *Chile* **92 G4** 18 32S 70 20W
Arica, *Colombia* **92 D4** 2 0S 71 50W
Arico, *Canary Is.* **22 F3** 28 9N 16 29W
Arid, C., *Australia* **61 F3** 34 1S 123 10 E
Arida, *Japan* **31 G7** 34 5N 135 8 E
Arílla, Ákra, *Greece* **23 A3** 39 43N 19 39 E
Arima, *Trin. & Tob.* **89 D7** 10 38N 61 17W
Arinos →, *Brazil* **92 F7** 10 25S 58 20W
Ario de Rosales, *Mexico* **86 D4** 19 12N 102 0W
Aripuanã, *Brazil* **92 E6** 9 25S 60 30W
Aripuanã →, *Brazil* **92 E6** 5 7S 60 25W
Ariquemes, *Brazil* **92 E6** 9 55S 63 6W
Arisaig, *U.K.* **12 E3** 56 55N 5 51W
Aristazabal I., *Canada* **72 C3** 52 40N 129 10W
Arivonimamo, *Madag.* **57 B8** 19 1S 47 11 E
Arizaro, Salar de, *Argentina* **94 A2** 24 40S 67 50W
Arizona, *Argentina* **94 D2** 35 45S 65 25W
Arizona □, *U.S.A.* **83 J8** 34 0N 112 0W
Arizpe, *Mexico* **86 A2** 30 20N 110 11W
Arjeplog, *Sweden* **8 D18** 66 3N 18 2 E
Arjona, *Colombia* **92 A3** 10 14N 75 22W
Arjuna, *Indonesia* **37 G15** 7 49S 112 34 E
Arka, *Russia* **27 C15** 60 15N 142 0 E
Arkadelphia, *U.S.A.* **81 H8** 34 7N 93 4W
Arkaig, L., *U.K.* **12 E3** 56 59N 5 10W
Arkalyk = Arqalyk, *Kazakstan* **26 D7** 50 13N 66 50 E
Arkansas □, *U.S.A.* **81 H8** 35 0N 92 30W
Arkansas →, *U.S.A.* **81 J9** 33 47N 91 4W
Arkansas City, *U.S.A.* **81 G6** 37 4N 97 2W
Arkaroola, *Australia* **63 E2** 30 20S 139 22 E
Arkhángelos, *Greece* **23 C10** 36 13N 28 7 E
Arkhangelsk, *Russia* **24 B7** 64 38N 40 36 E
Arki, *India* **42 D7** 31 9N 76 58 E
Arklow, *Ireland* **13 D5** 52 48N 6 10W
Arkport, *U.S.A.* **78 D7** 42 24N 77 42W
Arkticheskiy, Mys, *Russia* **27 A10** 81 10N 95 0 E
Arkville, *U.S.A.* **79 D10** 42 9N 74 37W
Arlanzón →, *Spain* **19 A3** 42 3N 4 17W
Arlbergpass, *Austria* **16 E6** 47 9N 10 12 E
Arles, *France* **18 E6** 43 41N 4 40 E
Arlington, *S. Africa* **57 D4** 28 1S 27 53 E
Arlington, *N.Y., U.S.A.* **79 E11** 41 42N 73 54W
Arlington, *Oreg., U.S.A.* **82 D3** 45 43N 120 12W
Arlington, *S. Dak., U.S.A.* **80 C6** 44 22N 97 8W
Arlington, *Tex., U.S.A.* **81 J6** 32 44N 97 7W
Arlington, *Va., U.S.A.* **76 F7** 38 53N 77 7W
Arlington, *Vt., U.S.A.* **79 C11** 43 5N 73 9W
Arlington, *Wash., U.S.A.* **84 B4** 48 12N 122 8W
Arlington Heights, *U.S.A.* **76 D2** 42 5N 87 59W
Arlit, *Niger* **50 E7** 19 0N 7 38 E
Arlon, *Belgium* **15 E5** 49 42N 5 49 E
Arltunga, *Australia* **62 C1** 23 26S 134 41 E
Armagh, *U.K.* **13 B5** 54 21N 6 39W
Armagh □, *U.K.* **13 B5** 54 18N 6 37W
Armavir, *Russia* **25 E7** 45 2N 41 7 E
Armenia, *Colombia* **92 C3** 4 35N 75 45W
Armenia ■, *Asia* **25 F7** 40 20N 45 0 E
Armenistís, Ákra, *Greece* **23 C9** 36 8N 27 42 E
Armidale, *Australia* **63 E5** 30 30S 151 40 E
Armour, *U.S.A.* **80 D5** 43 19N 98 21W
Armstrong, *B.C., Canada* **72 C5** 50 25N 119 10W
Armstrong, *Ont., Canada* **70 B2** 50 18N 89 4W
Arnarfjörður, *Iceland* **8 D2** 65 48N 23 40W
Arnaud →, *Canada* **69 C13** 60 0N 70 0W
Arnauti, C., *Cyprus* **23 D11** 35 6N 32 17 E
Arnett, *U.S.A.* **81 G5** 36 8N 99 46W
Arnhem, *Neths.* **15 C5** 51 58N 5 55 E
Arnhem, C., *Australia* **62 A2** 12 20S 137 30 E
Arnhem B., *Australia* **62 A2** 12 20S 136 10 E
Arnhem Land, *Australia* **62 A1** 13 10S 134 30 E
Arno →, *Italy* **20 C4** 43 41N 10 17 E
Arno Bay, *Australia* **63 E2** 33 54S 136 34 E
Arnold, *U.K.* **10 D6** 53 1N 1 7W
Arnold, *U.S.A.* **84 G6** 38 15N 120 20W
Arnot, *Canada* **73 B9** 55 56N 96 41W
Arnøy, *Norway* **8 A19** 70 9N 20 40 E
Arnprior, *Canada* **79 A8** 45 26N 76 21W
Arnsberg, *Germany* **16 C5** 51 24N 8 5 E
Aroab, *Namibia* **56 D2** 26 41S 19 39 E
Aron, *India* **42 G6** 25 57N 77 56 E
Arqalyk, *Kazakstan* **26 D7** 50 13N 66 50 E
Arrah = Ara, *India* **43 G11** 25 35N 84 32 E
Arran, *U.K.* **12 F3** 55 34N 5 12W
Arras, *France* **18 A5** 50 17N 2 46 E
Arrecife, *Canary Is.* **22 F6** 28 57N 13 37W
Arrecifes, *Argentina* **94 C3** 34 6S 60 9W
Arrée, Mts. d', *France* **18 B2** 48 26N 3 55W
Arriaga, *Chiapas, Mexico* **87 D6** 16 15N 93 52W
Arriaga, *San Luis Potosí, Mexico* **86 C4** 21 55N 101 23W
Arrilalah, *Australia* **62 C3** 23 43S 143 54 E
Arrino, *Australia* **61 E2** 29 30S 115 40 E
Arrow, L., *Ireland* **13 B3** 54 3N 8 19W
Arrowhead, L., *U.S.A.* **85 L9** 34 16N 117 10W
Arrowtown, *N.Z.* **59 L2** 44 57S 168 50 E
Arroyo Grande, *U.S.A.* **85 K6** 35 7N 120 35W
Ars, *Iran* **44 B5** 37 9N 47 46 E
Arsenault L., *Canada* **73 B7** 55 6N 108 32W
Arsenev, *Russia* **30 B6** 44 10N 133 15 E
Árta, *Greece* **21 E9** 39 8N 21 2 E
Artà, *Spain* **22 B10** 39 41N 3 21 E
Arteaga, *Mexico* **86 D4** 18 50N 102 20W
Artem, *Russia* **30 C6** 43 22N 132 13 E
Artemovsk, *Russia* **27 D10** 54 45N 93 35 E
Artemovsk, *Ukraine* **25 E6** 48 35N 38 0 E
Artesia = Mosomane, *Botswana* **56 C4** 24 2S 26 19 E
Artesia, *U.S.A.* **81 J2** 32 51N 104 24W
Arthur, *Canada* **78 C4** 43 50N 80 32W
Arthur →, *Australia* **62 G3** 41 2S 144 40 E
Arthur Cr. →, *Australia* **62 C2** 22 30S 136 25 E
Arthur Pt., *Australia* **62 C5** 22 7S 150 3 E
Arthur River, *Australia* **61 F2** 33 20S 117 2 E
Arthur's Pass, *N.Z.* **59 K3** 42 54S 171 35 E
Arthur's Town, *Bahamas* **89 B4** 24 38N 75 42W
Artigas, *Uruguay* **94 C4** 30 20S 56 30W
Artillery L., *Canada* **73 A7** 63 9N 107 52W
Artois, *France* **18 A5** 50 20N 2 30 E
Artrutx, C. de, *Spain* **22 B10** 39 55N 3 49 E
Artsyz, *Ukraine* **17 E15** 46 4N 29 26 E
Artvin, *Turkey* **25 F7** 41 14N 41 44 E
Aru, Kepulauan, *Indonesia* **37 F8** 6 0S 134 30 E
Aru Is. = Aru, Kepulauan, *Indonesia* **37 F8** 6 0S 134 30 E
Arua, *Uganda* **54 B3** 3 1N 30 58 E
Aruanã, *Brazil* **93 F8** 14 54S 51 10W
Aruba ■, *W. Indies* **89 D6** 12 30N 70 0W
Arucas, *Canary Is.* **22 F4** 28 7N 15 32W
Arun →, *Nepal* **43 F12** 26 55N 87 10 E
Arun →, *U.K.* **11 G7** 50 49N 0 33W
Arunachal Pradesh □, *India* **41 F19** 28 0N 95 0 E
Arusha, *Tanzania* **54 C4** 3 20S 36 40 E
Arusha □, *Tanzania* **54 C4** 4 0S 36 30 E
Arusha Chini, *Tanzania* **54 C4** 3 32S 37 20 E
Aruwimi →, *Dem. Rep. of the Congo* **54 B1** 1 13N 23 36 E
Arvada, *Colo., U.S.A.* **80 F2** 39 48N 105 5W
Arvada, *Wyo., U.S.A.* **82 D10** 44 39N 106 8W
Árvi, *Greece* **23 E7** 34 59N 25 28 E
Arviat, *Canada* **73 A10** 61 6N 93 59W
Arvidsjaur, *Sweden* **8 D18** 65 35N 19 10 E
Arvika, *Sweden* **9 G15** 59 40N 12 36 E
Arvin, *U.S.A.* **85 K8** 35 12N 118 50W
Arwal, *India* **43 G11** 25 15N 84 41 E
Arxan, *China* **33 B6** 47 11N 119 57 E
Aryirádhes, *Greece* **23 B3** 39 27N 19 58 E
Aryiroúpolis, *Greece* **23 D6** 35 17N 24 20 E
Arys, *Kazakstan* **26 E7** 42 26N 68 48 E
Arzamas, *Russia* **24 C7** 55 27N 43 55 E
Aş Şadr, *U.A.E.* **45 E7** 24 40N 54 41 E
Aş Şafā, *Syria* **47 B6** 33 10N 37 0 E
As Saffānīyah, *Si. Arabia* **45 E6** 27 55N 48 50 E
As Safīrah, *Syria* **44 B3** 36 5N 37 21 E
Aş Şahm, *Oman* **45 E8** 24 10N 56 53 E
As Sājir, *Si. Arabia* **44 E5** 25 11N 44 36 E
As Salamīyah, *Syria* **44 C3** 35 1N 37 2 E
As Salmān, *Iraq* **44 D5** 30 30N 44 32 E
As Salṭ, *Jordan* **47 C4** 32 2N 35 43 E
As Sal'w'a, *Qatar* **45 E6** 24 23N 50 50 E
As Samāwah, *Iraq* **44 D5** 31 15N 45 15 E
As Sanamayn, *Syria* **47 B5** 33 3N 36 10 E
As Sohar = Şuḥār, *Oman* **45 E8** 24 20N 56 40 E
As Sukhnah, *Syria* **44 C3** 34 52N 38 52 E
As Sulaymānīyah, *Iraq* **44 C5** 35 35N 45 29 E
As Sulaymī, *Si. Arabia* **44 E4** 26 17N 41 21 E
As Sulayyil, *Si. Arabia* **46 C4** 20 27N 45 34 E
As Summān, *Si. Arabia* **44 E5** 25 0N 47 0 E
As Suwaydā', *Syria* **47 C5** 32 40N 36 30 E
As Suwaydā' □, *Syria* **47 C5** 32 45N 36 45 E
As Suwayq, *Oman* **45 F8** 23 51N 57 26 E
As Şuwayrah, *Iraq* **44 C5** 32 55N 45 0 E
Asab, *Namibia* **56 D2** 25 30S 18 0 E
Asad, Buḥayrat al, *Syria* **44 C3** 36 0N 38 15 E
Asahi-Gawa →, *Japan* **31 G6** 34 36N 133 58 E
Asahigawa, *Japan* **30 C11** 43 46N 142 22 E
Asamankese, *Ghana* **50 G5** 5 50N 0 40W
Asan →, *India* **43 F8** 26 37N 78 24 E
Asansol, *India* **43 H12** 23 40N 87 1 E
Asbesberge, *S. Africa* **56 D3** 29 0S 23 0 E
Asbestos, *Canada* **71 C5** 45 47N 71 58W
Asbury Park, *U.S.A.* **79 F10** 40 13N 74 1W
Ascensión, *Mexico* **86 A3** 31 6N 107 59W
Ascensión, B. de la, *Mexico* **87 D7** 19 50N 87 20W
Ascension I., *Atl. Oc.* **49 G2** 8 0S 14 15W
Aschaffenburg, *Germany* **16 D5** 49 58N 9 6 E
Aschersleben, *Germany* **16 C6** 51 45N 11 29 E
Ascoli Piceno, *Italy* **20 C5** 42 51N 13 34 E
Ascope, *Peru* **92 E3** 7 46S 79 8W
Ascotán, *Chile* **94 A2** 21 45S 68 17W
Aseb, *Eritrea* **46 E3** 13 0N 42 40 E
Asela, *Ethiopia* **46 F2** 8 0N 39 0 E
Asenovgrad, *Bulgaria* **21 C11** 42 1N 24 51 E
Aserradero, *Mexico* **86 C3** 23 40N 105 43W
Asgata, *Cyprus* **23 E12** 34 46N 33 15 E
Ash Fork, *U.S.A.* **83 J7** 35 13N 112 29W
Ash Grove, *U.S.A.* **81 G8** 37 19N 93 35W
Ash Shabakah, *Iraq* **44 D4** 30 49N 43 39 E
Ash Shamāl □, *Lebanon* **47 A5** 34 25N 36 0 E
Ash Shāmīyah, *Iraq* **44 D5** 31 55N 44 35 E
Ash Shāriqah, *U.A.E.* **45 E7** 25 23N 55 26 E
Ash Sharmah, *Si. Arabia* **44 D2** 28 1N 35 16 E
Ash Sharqāt, *Iraq* **44 C4** 35 27N 43 16 E
Ash Sharqi, Al Jabal, *Lebanon* **47 B5** 33 40N 36 10 E
Ash Shaṭrah, *Iraq* **44 D5** 31 30N 46 10 E
Ash Shawbak, *Jordan* **44 D2** 30 32N 35 34 E
Ash Shawmari, J., *Jordan* **47 E5** 30 35N 36 35 E
Ash Shināfīyah, *Iraq* **44 D5** 31 35N 44 39 E
Ash Shu'bah, *Si. Arabia* **44 D5** 28 54N 44 44 E
Ash Shumlūl, *Si. Arabia* **44 E5** 26 31N 47 20 E
Ash Shūr'a, *Iraq* **44 C4** 35 58N 43 13 E
Ash Shurayf, *Si. Arabia* **44 E3** 25 43N 39 14 E
Ash Shuwayfāt, *Lebanon* **47 B4** 33 45N 35 30 E
Asha, *Russia* **24 D10** 55 0N 57 16 E
Ashau, *Vietnam* **38 D6** 16 6N 107 22 E
Ashbourne, *U.K.* **10 D6** 53 2N 1 43W
Ashburn, *U.S.A.* **77 K4** 31 43N 83 39W
Ashburton, *N.Z.* **59 K3** 43 53S 171 48 E
Ashburton →, *Australia* **60 D1** 21 40S 114 56 E
Ashcroft, *Canada* **72 C4** 50 40N 121 20W
Ashdod, *Israel* **47 D3** 31 49N 34 35 E
Ashdown, *U.S.A.* **81 J7** 33 40N 94 8W
Asheboro, *U.S.A.* **77 H6** 35 43N 79 49W
Ashern, *Canada* **73 C9** 51 11N 98 21W
Asherton, *U.S.A.* **81 L5** 28 27N 99 46W
Asheville, *U.S.A.* **77 H4** 35 36N 82 33W
Ashewat, *Pakistan* **42 D3** 31 22N 68 32 E
Asheweig →, *Canada* **70 B2** 54 17N 87 12W
Ashford, *Australia* **63 D5** 29 15S 151 3 E
Ashford, *U.K.* **11 F8** 51 8N 0 53 E
Ashgabat, *Turkmenistan* **26 F6** 38 0N 57 50 E
Ashibetsu, *Japan* **30 C11** 43 31N 142 11 E
Ashikaga, *Japan* **31 F9** 36 28N 139 29 E
Ashington, *U.K.* **10 B6** 55 11N 1 33W
Ashizuri-Zaki, *Japan* **31 H6** 32 44N 133 0 E
Ashkarkot, *Afghan.* **42 C2** 33 3N 67 58 E
Ashkhabad = Ashgabat, *Turkmenistan* **26 F6** 38 0N 57 50 E
Āshkhāneh, *Iran* **45 B8** 37 26N 56 55 E
Ashland, *Kans., U.S.A.* **81 G5** 37 11N 99 46W
Ashland, *Ky., U.S.A.* **76 F4** 38 28N 82 38W
Ashland, *Mont., U.S.A.* **82 D10** 45 36N 106 16W
Ashland, *Ohio, U.S.A.* **78 F2** 40 52N 82 19W
Ashland, *Oreg., U.S.A.* **82 E2** 42 12N 122 43W
Ashland, *Pa., U.S.A.* **79 F8** 40 45N 76 22W
Ashland, *Va., U.S.A.* **76 G7** 37 46N 77 29W
Ashland, *Wis., U.S.A.* **80 B9** 46 35N 90 53W
Ashley, *N. Dak., U.S.A.* **80 B5** 46 2N 99 22W
Ashley, *Pa., U.S.A.* **79 E9** 41 12N 75 55W
Ashmore Reef, *Australia* **60 B3** 12 14S 123 5 E
Ashmyany, *Belarus* **9 J21** 54 26N 25 52 E
Ashokan Reservoir, *U.S.A.* **79 E10** 41 56N 74 13W
Ashqelon, *Israel* **47 D3** 31 42N 34 35 E
Ashta, *India* **42 H7** 23 1N 76 43 E
Ashtabula, *U.S.A.* **78 E4** 41 52N 80 47W
Ashton, *S. Africa* **56 E3** 33 50S 20 5 E
Ashton, *U.S.A.* **82 D8** 44 4N 111 27W
Ashuanipi, L., *Canada* **71 B6** 52 45N 66 15W
Ashville, *U.S.A.* **78 F6** 40 34N 78 33W
Asia **28 E11** 45 0N 75 0 E
Āsīā Bak, *Iran* **45 C6** 35 19N 50 30 E
Asifabad, *India* **40 K11** 19 20N 79 24 E
Asinara, *Italy* **20 D3** 41 4N 8 16 E
Asinara, G. dell', *Italy* **20 D3** 41 0N 8 30 E
Asino, *Russia* **26 D9** 57 0N 86 0 E
Asipovichy, *Belarus* **17 B15** 53 19N 28 33 E
'Asīr □, *Si. Arabia* **46 D3** 18 40N 42 30 E
Asir, Ras, *Somali Rep.* **46 E5** 11 55N 51 10 E
Askersund, *Sweden* **9 G16** 58 53N 14 55 E
Askham, *S. Africa* **56 D3** 26 59S 20 47 E
Askim, *Norway* **9 G14** 59 35N 11 10 E
Askja, *Iceland* **8 D5** 65 3N 16 48W
Askøy, *Norway* **9 F11** 60 29N 5 10 E
Asmara = Asmera, *Eritrea* **46 D2** 15 19N 38 55 E

Asmera

Asmera, *Eritrea* **46 D2** 15 19N 38 55 E
Åsnen, *Sweden* **9 H16** 56 37N 14 45 E
Aspen, *U.S.A.* **83 G10** 39 11N 106 49W
Aspermont, *U.S.A.* **81 J4** 33 8N 100 14W
Aspiring, Mt., *N.Z.* **59 L2** 44 23S 168 46 E
Asprókavos, Ákra, *Greece* **23 B4** 39 21N 20 6 E
Aspur, *India* **42 H6** 23 58N 74 7 E
Asquith, *Canada* **73 C7** 52 8N 107 13W
Assam □, *India* **41 G18** 26 0N 93 0 E
Asse, *Belgium* **15 D4** 50 24N 4 10 E
Assen, *Neths.* **15 A6** 53 0N 6 35 E
Assiniboia, *Canada* **73 D7** 49 40N 105 59W
Assiniboine →, *Canada* **73 D9** 49 53N 97 8W
Assiniboine, Mt., *Canada* **72 C5** 50 52N 115 39W
Assis, *Brazil* **95 A5** 22 40S 50 20W
Assisi, *Italy* **20 C5** 43 4N 12 37 E
Assynt, L., *U.K.* **12 C3** 58 10N 5 3W
Astana, *Kazakstan* **26 D8** 51 10N 71 30 E
Āstāneh, *Iran* **45 B6** 37 17N 49 59 E
Astara, *Azerbaijan* **25 G8** 38 30N 48 50 E
Asteroúsia, *Greece* **23 E7** 34 59N 25 3 E
Asti, *Italy* **18 D8** 44 54N 8 12 E
Astipálaia, *Greece* **21 F12** 36 32N 26 22 E
Astorga, *Spain* **19 A2** 42 29N 6 8W
Astoria, *U.S.A.* **84 D3** 46 11N 123 50W
Astrakhan, *Russia* **25 E8** 46 25N 48 5 E
Asturias □, *Spain* **19 A3** 43 15N 6 0W
Asunción, *Paraguay* **94 B4** 25 10S 57 30W
Asunción Nochixtlán, *Mexico* **87 D5** 17 28N 97 14W
Aswa →, *Uganda* **54 B3** 3 43N 31 55 E
Aswân, *Egypt* **51 D12** 24 4N 32 57 E
Aswân High Dam = Sadd el Aali, *Egypt* **51 D12** 23 54N 32 54 E
Asyût, *Egypt* **51 C12** 27 11N 31 4 E
At Ṭafilah, *Jordan* **47 E4** 30 45N 35 30 E
At Tā'if, *Si. Arabia* **46 C3** 21 5N 40 27 E
Aṭ Ṭirāq, *Si. Arabia* **44 E5** 27 19N 44 33 E
Aṭ Tubayq, *Si. Arabia* **44 D3** 29 30N 37 0 E
Atacama □, *Chile* **94 B2** 27 30S 70 0W
Atacama, Desierto de, *Chile* **94 A2** 24 0S 69 20W
Atacama, Salar de, *Chile* **94 A2** 23 30S 68 20W
Atalaya, *Peru* **92 F4** 10 45S 73 50W
Atalaya de Femes, *Canary Is.* **22 F6** 28 56N 13 47W
Atami, *Japan* **31 G9** 35 5N 139 4 E
Atapupu, *Indonesia* **37 F6** 9 0S 124 51 E
Atâr, *Mauritania* **50 D3** 20 30N 13 5W
Atari, *Pakistan* **42 D6** 30 56N 74 2 E
Atascadero, *U.S.A.* **84 K6** 35 29N 120 40W
Atasu, *Kazakstan* **26 E8** 48 30N 71 0 E
Atatürk Barajı, *Turkey* **25 G6** 37 28N 38 30 E
Atauro, *Indonesia* **37 F7** 8 10S 125 30 E
Atbara, *Sudan* **51 E12** 17 42N 33 59 E
'Atbara →, *Sudan* **51 E12** 17 40N 33 56 E
Atbasar, *Kazakstan* **26 D7** 51 48N 68 20 E
Atchafalaya B., *U.S.A.* **81 L9** 29 25N 91 25W
Atchison, *U.S.A.* **80 F7** 39 34N 95 7W
Āteshān, *Iran* **45 C7** 35 35N 52 37 E
Ath, *Belgium* **15 D3** 50 38N 3 47 E
Athabasca, *Canada* **72 C6** 54 45N 113 20W
Athabasca →, *Canada* **73 B6** 58 40N 110 50W
Athabasca, L., *Canada* **73 B7** 59 15N 109 15W
Athboy, *Ireland* **13 C5** 53 37N 6 56W
Athenry, *Ireland* **13 C3** 53 18N 8 44W
Athens = Athínai, *Greece* **21 F10** 37 58N 23 46 E
Athens, *Ala., U.S.A.* **77 H2** 34 48N 86 58W
Athens, *Ga., U.S.A.* **77 J4** 33 57N 83 23W
Athens, *N.Y., U.S.A.* **79 D11** 42 16N 73 49W
Athens, *Ohio, U.S.A.* **76 F4** 39 20N 82 6W
Athens, *Pa., U.S.A.* **79 E8** 41 57N 76 31W
Athens, *Tenn., U.S.A.* **77 H3** 35 27N 84 36W
Athens, *Tex., U.S.A.* **81 J7** 32 12N 95 51W
Atherley, *Canada* **78 B5** 44 37N 79 20W
Atherton, *Australia* **62 B4** 17 17S 145 30 E
Athienou, *Cyprus* **23 D12** 35 3N 33 32 E
Athínai, *Greece* **21 F10** 37 58N 23 46 E
Athlone, *Ireland* **13 C4** 53 25N 7 56W
Athna, *Cyprus* **23 D12** 35 3N 33 47 E
Athol, *U.S.A.* **79 D12** 42 36N 72 14W
Atholl, Forest of, *U.K.* **12 E5** 56 51N 3 50W
Atholville, *Canada* **71 C6** 47 59N 66 43W
Áthos, *Greece* **21 D11** 40 9N 24 22 E
Athy, *Ireland* **13 C5** 53 0N 7 0W
Ati, *Chad* **51 F9** 13 13N 18 20 E
Atiak, *Uganda* **54 B3** 3 12N 32 2 E
Atik L., *Canada* **73 B9** 55 15N 96 0W
Atikameg →, *Canada* **70 B3** 52 30N 82 46W
Atikokan, *Canada* **70 C1** 48 45N 91 37W
Atikonak L., *Canada* **71 B7** 52 40N 64 32W
Atka, *Russia* **27 C16** 60 50N 151 48 E
Atka I., *U.S.A.* **68 C2** 52 7N 174 30W
Atkinson, *U.S.A.* **80 D5** 42 32N 98 59W
Atlanta, *Ga., U.S.A.* **77 J3** 33 45N 84 23W
Atlanta, *Tex., U.S.A.* **81 J7** 33 7N 94 10W
Atlantic, *U.S.A.* **80 E7** 41 24N 95 1W
Atlantic City, *U.S.A.* **76 F8** 39 21N 74 27W
Atlantic Ocean **2 E9** 0 0 20 0W
Atlas Mts. = Haut Atlas, *Morocco* **50 B4** 32 30N 5 0W
Atlin, *Canada* **72 B2** 59 31N 133 41W
Atlin, L., *Canada* **72 B2** 59 26N 133 45W
Atlin Prov. Park, *Canada* **72 B2** 59 10N 134 30W
Atmore, *U.S.A.* **77 K2** 31 2N 87 29W
Atoka, *U.S.A.* **81 H6** 34 23N 96 8W
Atolia, *U.S.A.* **85 K9** 35 19N 117 37W
Atrai →, *Bangla.* **43 G13** 24 7N 89 22 E
Atrak = Atrek →, *Turkmenistan* **45 B8** 37 35N 53 58 E
Atrauli, *India* **42 E8** 28 2N 78 20 E
Atrek →, *Turkmenistan* **45 B8** 37 35N 53 58 E
Atsuta, *Japan* **30 C10** 43 24N 141 26 E
Attalla, *U.S.A.* **77 H2** 34 1N 86 6W
Attapu, *Laos* **38 E6** 14 48N 106 50 E
Attáviros, *Greece* **23 C9** 36 12N 27 50 E
Attawapiskat, *Canada* **70 B3** 52 56N 82 24W
Attawapiskat →, *Canada* **70 B3** 52 57N 82 18W
Attawapiskat L., *Canada* **70 B2** 52 18N 87 54W
Attica, *Ind., U.S.A.* **76 E2** 40 18N 87 15W
Attica, *Ohio, U.S.A.* **78 E2** 41 4N 82 53W
Attikamagen L., *Canada* **71 B6** 55 0N 66 30W
Attleboro, *U.S.A.* **79 E13** 41 57N 71 17W
Attock, *Pakistan* **42 C5** 33 52N 72 20 E
Attopeu = Attapu, *Laos* **38 E6** 14 48N 106 50 E
Attu I., *U.S.A.* **68 C1** 52 55N 172 55 E
Attur, *India* **40 P11** 11 35N 78 30 E
Atuel →, *Argentina* **94 D2** 36 17S 66 50W
Åtvidaberg, *Sweden* **9 G17** 58 12N 16 0 E
Atwater, *U.S.A.* **84 H6** 37 21N 120 37W
Atwood, *Canada* **78 C3** 43 40N 81 1W
Atwood, *U.S.A.* **80 F4** 39 48N 101 3W
Atyraū, *Kazakstan* **25 E9** 47 5N 52 0 E
Au Sable, *U.S.A.* **78 B1** 44 25N 83 20W
Au Sable →, *U.S.A.* **76 C4** 44 25N 83 20W
Au Sable Forks, *U.S.A.* **79 B11** 44 27N 73 41W
Au Sable Pt., *U.S.A.* **78 B1** 44 20N 83 20W
Aubagne, *France* **18 E6** 43 17N 5 37 E
Aubarca, C. d', *Spain* **22 B7** 39 4N 1 22 E
Aube →, *France* **18 B5** 48 34N 3 43 E
Auberry, *U.S.A.* **84 H7** 37 7N 119 29W
Auburn, *Ala., U.S.A.* **77 J3** 32 36N 85 29W
Auburn, *Calif., U.S.A.* **84 G5** 38 54N 121 4W
Auburn, *Ind., U.S.A.* **76 E3** 41 22N 85 4W
Auburn, *Maine, U.S.A.* **77 C10** 44 6N 70 14W
Auburn, *N.Y., U.S.A.* **79 D8** 42 56N 76 34W
Auburn, *Nebr., U.S.A.* **80 E7** 40 23N 95 51W
Auburn, *Pa., U.S.A.* **79 F8** 40 36N 76 6W
Auburn, *Wash., U.S.A.* **84 C4** 47 18N 122 14W
Auburn Ra., *Australia* **63 D5** 25 15S 150 30 E
Aubusson, *France* **18 D5** 45 57N 2 11 E
Auch, *France* **18 E4** 43 39N 0 36 E
Auckland, *N.Z.* **59 G5** 36 52S 174 46 E
Auckland Is., *Pac. Oc.* **64 N8** 50 40S 166 5 E
Aude →, *France* **18 E5** 43 13N 3 14 E
Auden, *Canada* **70 B2** 50 14N 87 53W
Audubon, *U.S.A.* **80 E7** 41 43N 94 56W
Augathella, *Australia* **63 D4** 25 48S 146 35 E
Aughnacloy, *U.K.* **13 B5** 54 25N 6 59W
Augrabies Falls, *S. Africa* **56 D3** 28 35S 20 20 E
Augsburg, *Germany* **16 D6** 48 25N 10 52 E
Augusta, *Australia* **61 F2** 34 19S 115 9 E
Augusta, *Italy* **20 F6** 37 13N 15 13 E
Augusta, *Ark., U.S.A.* **81 H9** 35 17N 91 22W
Augusta, *Ga., U.S.A.* **77 J5** 33 28N 81 58W
Augusta, *Kans., U.S.A.* **81 G6** 37 41N 96 59W
Augusta, *Maine, U.S.A.* **69 D13** 44 19N 69 47W
Augusta, *Mont., U.S.A.* **82 C7** 47 30N 112 24W
Augustów, *Poland* **17 B12** 53 51N 23 0 E
Augustus, Mt., *Australia* **61 D2** 24 20S 116 50 E
Augustus I., *Australia* **60 C3** 15 20S 124 30 E
Aukum, *U.S.A.* **84 G6** 38 34N 120 43W
Auld, L., *Australia* **60 D3** 22 25S 123 50 E
Ault, *U.S.A.* **80 E2** 40 35N 104 44W
Aunis, *France* **18 C3** 46 5N 0 50W
Auponhia, *Indonesia* **37 E7** 1 58S 125 27 E
Aur, Pulau, *Malaysia* **39 L5** 2 35N 104 10 E
Auraiya, *India* **43 F8** 26 28N 79 33 E
Aurangabad, *Bihar, India* **43 G11** 24 45N 84 18 E
Aurangabad, *Maharashtra, India* **40 K9** 19 50N 75 23 E
Aurich, *Germany* **16 B4** 53 28N 7 28 E
Aurillac, *France* **18 D5** 44 55N 2 26 E
Aurora, *Canada* **78 C5** 44 0N 79 28W
Aurora, *S. Africa* **56 E2** 32 40S 18 29 E
Aurora, *Colo., U.S.A.* **80 F2** 39 44N 104 52W
Aurora, *Ill., U.S.A.* **76 E1** 41 45N 88 19W
Aurora, *Mo., U.S.A.* **81 G8** 36 58N 93 43W
Aurora, *N.Y., U.S.A.* **79 D8** 42 45N 76 42W
Aurora, *Nebr., U.S.A.* **80 E6** 40 52N 98 0W
Aurora, *Ohio, U.S.A.* **78 E3** 41 21N 81 20W
Aurukun, *Australia* **62 A3** 13 20S 141 45 E
Aus, *Namibia* **56 D2** 26 35S 16 12 E
Ausable →, *Canada* **78 C3** 43 19N 81 46W
Auschwitz = Oświęcim, *Poland* **17 C10** 50 2N 19 11 E
Austin, *Minn., U.S.A.* **80 D8** 43 40N 92 58W
Austin, *Nev., U.S.A.* **82 G5** 39 30N 117 4W
Austin, *Pa., U.S.A.* **78 E6** 41 38N 78 6W
Austin, *Tex., U.S.A.* **81 K6** 30 17N 97 45W
Austin, L., *Australia* **61 E2** 27 40S 118 0 E
Austin I., *Canada* **73 A10** 61 10N 94 0W
Austra, *Norway* **8 D14** 65 8N 11 55 E
Austral Is. = Tubuai Is., *Pac. Oc.* **65 K13** 25 0S 150 0W
Austral Seamount Chain, *Pac. Oc.* **65 K13** 24 0S 150 0W
Australia ■, *Oceania* **64 K5** 23 0S 135 0 E
Australian Capital Territory □, *Australia* **63 F4** 35 30S 149 0 E
Australind, *Australia* **61 F2** 33 17S 115 42 E
Austria ■, *Europe* **16 E8** 47 0N 14 0 E
Austvågøy, *Norway* **8 B16** 68 20N 14 40 E
Autlán, *Mexico* **86 D4** 19 40N 104 30W
Autun, *France* **18 C6** 46 58N 4 17 E
Auvergne, *France* **18 D5** 45 20N 3 15 E
Auvergne, Mts. d', *France* **18 D5** 45 20N 2 55 E
Auxerre, *France* **18 C5** 47 48N 3 32 E
Ava, *U.S.A.* **81 G8** 36 57N 92 40W
Avallon, *France* **18 C5** 47 30N 3 53 E
Avalon, *U.S.A.* **85 M8** 33 21N 118 20W
Avalon Pen., *Canada* **71 C9** 47 30N 53 20W
Avanos, *Turkey* **44 B2** 38 43N 34 51 E
Avaré, *Brazil* **95 A6** 23 4S 48 58W
Avawatz Mts., *U.S.A.* **85 K10** 35 40N 116 30W
Aveiro, *Brazil* **93 D7** 3 10S 55 5W
Aveiro, *Portugal* **19 B1** 40 37N 8 38W
Āvej, *Iran* **45 C6** 35 40N 49 15 E
Avellaneda, *Argentina* **94 C4** 34 50S 58 10W
Avellino, *Italy* **20 D6** 40 54N 14 47 E
Avenal, *U.S.A.* **84 K6** 36 0N 120 8W
Aversa, *Italy* **20 D6** 40 58N 14 12 E
Avery, *U.S.A.* **82 C6** 47 15N 115 49W
Aves, Is. las, *Venezuela* **89 D6** 12 0N 67 30W
Avesta, *Sweden* **9 F17** 60 9N 16 10 E
Avezzano, *Italy* **20 C5** 42 2N 13 25 E
Aviá Terai, *Argentina* **94 B3** 26 45S 60 50W
Aviemore, *U.K.* **12 D5** 57 12N 3 50W
Avignon, *France* **18 E6** 43 57N 4 50 E
Ávila, *Spain* **19 B3** 40 39N 4 43W
Avila Beach, *U.S.A.* **85 K6** 35 11N 120 44W
Avilés, *Spain* **19 A3** 43 35N 5 57W
Avis, *U.S.A.* **78 E7** 41 11N 77 19W
Avoca, *U.S.A.* **78 D7** 42 25N 77 25W
Avoca →, *Australia* **63 F3** 35 40S 143 43 E
Avoca →, *Ireland* **13 D5** 52 48N 6 10W
Avola, *Canada* **72 C5** 51 45N 119 19W
Avola, *Italy* **20 F6** 36 56N 15 7 E
Avon, *U.S.A.* **78 D7** 42 55N 77 45W
Avon →, *Australia* **61 F2** 31 40S 116 7 E
Avon →, *Bristol, U.K.* **11 F5** 51 29N 2 41W
Avon →, *Dorset, U.K.* **11 G6** 50 44N 1 46W
Avon →, *Warks., U.K.* **11 E5** 52 0N 2 8W
Avon Park, *U.S.A.* **77 M5** 27 36N 81 31W
Avondale, *Zimbabwe* **55 F3** 17 43S 30 58 E
Avonlea, *Canada* **73 D8** 50 0N 105 0W
Avonmore, *Canada* **79 A10** 45 10N 74 58W
Avranches, *France* **18 B3** 48 40N 1 20W
A'waj →, *Syria* **47 B5** 33 23N 36 20 E
Awaji-Shima, *Japan* **31 G7** 34 30N 134 50 E
'Awālī, *Bahrain* **45 E6** 26 0N 50 30 E
Awantipur, *India* **43 C6** 33 55N 75 3 E
Awasa, *Ethiopia* **46 F2** 7 3N 38 28 E
Awash, *Ethiopia* **46 F3** 9 1N 40 10 E
Awatere →, *N.Z.* **59 J5** 41 37S 174 10 E
Awbārī, *Libya* **51 C8** 26 46N 12 57 E
Awe, L., *U.K.* **12 E3** 56 17N 5 16W
Awjilah, *Libya* **51 C10** 29 8N 21 7 E
Axe →, *U.K.* **11 F5** 50 42N 3 4W
Axel Heiberg I., *Canada* **4 B3** 80 0N 90 0W
Axim, *Ghana* **50 H5** 4 51N 2 15W
Axiós →, *Greece* **21 D10** 40 57N 22 35 E
Axminster, *U.K.* **11 G4** 50 46N 3 0W
Ayabaca, *Peru* **92 D3** 4 40S 79 53W
Ayabe, *Japan* **31 G7** 35 20N 135 20 E
Ayacucho, *Argentina* **94 D4** 37 5S 58 20W
Ayacucho, *Peru* **92 F4** 13 0S 74 0W
Ayaguz, *Kazakstan* **26 E9** 48 10N 80 10 E
Ayamonte, *Spain* **19 D2** 37 12N 7 24W
Ayan, *Russia* **27 D14** 56 30N 138 16 E
Ayaviri, *Peru* **92 F4** 14 50S 70 35W
Aydın, *Turkey* **21 F12** 37 51N 27 51 E
Aydin □, *Turkey* **25 G4** 37 50N 28 0 E
Ayer, *U.S.A.* **79 D13** 42 34N 71 35W
Ayer's Cliff, *Canada* **79 A12** 45 10N 72 3W
Ayers Rock, *Australia* **61 E5** 25 23S 131 5 E
Ayia Aikateríni, Ákra, *Greece* **23 A3** 39 50N 19 50 E
Ayia Dhéka, *Greece* **23 D6** 35 3N 24 58 E
Ayia Gálini, *Greece* **23 D6** 35 6N 24 41 E
Ayia Napa, *Cyprus* **23 E13** 34 59N 34 0 E
Ayia Phyla, *Cyprus* **23 E12** 34 43N 33 1 E
Ayia Varvára, *Greece* **23 D7** 35 8N 25 1 E
Áyios Amvrósios, *Cyprus* **23 D12** 35 20N 33 35 E
Áyios Evstrátios, *Greece* **21 E11** 39 34N 24 58 E
Áyios Ioánnis, Ákra, *Greece* **23 D7** 35 20N 25 40 E
Áyios Isidhoros, *Greece* **23 C9** 36 9N 27 51 E
Áyios Matthaíos, *Greece* **23 B3** 39 30N 19 47 E
Áyios Nikólaos, *Greece* **23 D7** 35 11N 25 41 E
Áyios Seryios, *Cyprus* **23 D12** 35 12N 33 53 E
Áyios Theodhoros, *Cyprus* **23 D13** 35 22N 34 1 E
Aykino, *Russia* **24 B8** 62 15N 49 56 E
Aylesbury, *U.K.* **11 F7** 51 49N 0 49W
Aylmer, *Canada* **78 D4** 42 46N 80 59W
Aylmer, L., *Canada* **68 B8** 64 0N 110 8W
'Ayn, Wādī al, *Oman* **45 F7** 22 15N 55 28 E
Ayn Dār, *Si. Arabia* **45 E7** 25 55N 49 10 E
Ayn Zālah, *Iraq* **44 B4** 36 45N 42 35 E
Ayolas, *Paraguay* **94 B4** 27 10S 56 59W
Ayon, Ostrov, *Russia* **27 C17** 69 50N 169 0 E
'Ayoûn el 'Atroûs, *Mauritania* **50 E4** 16 40N 9 37W
Ayr, *Australia* **62 B4** 19 35S 147 25 E
Ayr, *Canada* **78 C4** 43 17N 80 27W
Ayr, *U.K.* **12 F4** 55 28N 4 38W
Ayr →, *U.K.* **12 F4** 55 28N 4 38W
Ayre, Pt. of, *U.K.* **10 C3** 54 25N 4 21W
Ayton, *Australia* **62 B4** 15 56S 145 22 E
Aytos, *Bulgaria* **21 C12** 42 42N 27 16 E
Ayu, Kepulauan, *Indonesia* **37 D8** 0 35N 131 5 E
Ayutla, *Guatemala* **88 D1** 14 40N 92 10W
Ayutla, *Mexico* **87 D5** 16 58N 99 17W
Ayvacık, *Turkey* **21 E12** 39 36N 26 24 E
Ayvalık, *Turkey* **21 E12** 39 20N 26 46 E
Az Zabadānī, *Syria* **47 B5** 33 43N 36 5 E
Aẓ Ẓāhirīyah, *West Bank* **47 D3** 31 25N 34 58 E
Aẓ Ẓahrān, *Si. Arabia* **45 E6** 26 10N 50 7 E
Az Zarqā, *Jordan* **47 C5** 32 5N 36 4 E
Az Zarqā', *U.A.E.* **45 E7** 24 53N 53 4 E
Az Zāwiyah, *Libya* **51 B8** 32 52N 12 56 E
Az Zībār, *Iraq* **44 B5** 36 52N 44 4 E
Az-Zilfī, *Si. Arabia* **44 E5** 26 12N 44 52 E
Az Zubayr, *Iraq* **44 D5** 30 26N 47 40 E
Azamgarh, *India* **43 F10** 26 5N 83 13 E
Azangaro, *Peru* **92 F4** 14 55S 70 13W
Āzār Shahr, *Iran* **44 B5** 37 45N 45 59 E
Azarān, *Iran* **44 B5** 37 25N 47 16 E
Azärbayjan = Azerbaijan ■, *Asia* **25 F8** 40 20N 48 0 E
Āzarbāyjān-e Gharbī □, *Iran* **44 B5** 37 0N 44 30 E
Āzarbāyjān-e Sharqī □, *Iran* **44 B5** 37 20N 47 0 E
Azare, *Nigeria* **50 F8** 11 55N 10 10 E
A'zāz, *Syria* **44 B3** 36 36N 37 4 E
Azbine = Aïr, *Niger* **50 E7** 18 30N 8 0 E
Azerbaijan ■, *Asia* **25 F8** 40 20N 48 0 E
Azerbaijchan = Azerbaijan ■, *Asia* **25 F8** 40 20N 48 0 E
Azimganj, *India* **43 G13** 24 14N 88 16 E
Azogues, *Ecuador* **92 D3** 2 35S 78 0W
Azores, *Atl. Oc.* **50 A1** 38 44N 29 0W
Azov, *Russia* **25 E6** 47 3N 39 25 E
Azov, Sea of, *Europe* **25 E6** 46 0N 36 30 E
Azovskoye More = Azov, Sea of, *Europe* **25 E6** 46 0N 36 30 E
Azraq ash Shīshān, *Jordan* **47 D5** 31 50N 36 49 E
Aztec, *U.S.A.* **83 H10** 36 49N 107 59W
Azúa de Compostela, *Dom. Rep.* **89 C5** 18 25N 70 44W
Azuaga, *Spain* **19 C3** 38 16N 5 39W
Azuero, Pen. de, *Panama* **88 E3** 7 30N 80 30W
Azul, *Argentina* **94 D4** 36 42S 59 43W
Azusa, *U.S.A.* **85 L9** 34 8N 117 52W

B

Ba Don, *Vietnam* **38 D6** 17 45N 106 26 E
Ba Dong, *Vietnam* **39 H6** 9 40N 106 33 E
Ba Ngoi = Cam Lam, *Vietnam* **39 G7** 11 54N 109 10 E
Ba Tri, *Vietnam* **39 G6** 10 2N 106 36 E
Ba Xian = Bazhou, *China* **34 E9** 39 8N 116 22 E
Baa, *Indonesia* **37 F6** 10 50S 123 0 E
Baarle-Nassau, *Belgium* **15 C4** 51 27N 4 56 E
Bab el Mandeb, *Red Sea* **46 E3** 12 35N 43 25 E
Baba Burnu, *Turkey* **21 E12** 39 29N 26 2 E
Bābā Kalū, *Iran* **45 D6** 30 7N 50 49 E
Babadag, *Romania* **17 F15** 44 53N 28 44 E
Babadayhan, *Turkmenistan* **26 F7** 37 42N 60 23 E
Babaeski, *Turkey* **21 D12** 41 26N 27 6 E
Babahoyo, *Ecuador* **92 D3** 1 40S 79 30W
Babai = Sarju →, *India* **43 F9** 27 21N 81 23 E
Babar, *Indonesia* **37 F7** 8 0S 129 30 E
Babar, *Pakistan* **42 D3** 31 7N 69 32 E
Babarkach, *Pakistan* **42 E3** 29 45N 68 0 E
Babb, *U.S.A.* **82 B7** 48 51N 113 27W
Babelthuap, *Pac. Oc.* **37 C8** 7 30N 134 30 E
Baberu, *India* **43 G9** 25 33N 80 43 E
Babi Besar, Pulau, *Malaysia* **39 L4** 2 25N 103 59 E
Babinda, *Australia* **62 B4** 17 20S 145 56 E
Babine, *Canada* **72 B3** 55 22N 126 37W
Babine →, *Canada* **72 B3** 55 45N 127 44W
Babine L., *Canada* **72 C3** 54 48N 126 0W
Babo, *Indonesia* **37 E8** 2 30S 133 30 E
Bābol, *Iran* **45 B7** 36 40N 52 50 E
Bābol Sar, *Iran* **45 B7** 36 45N 52 45 E
Babruysk, *Belarus* **17 B15** 53 10N 29 15 E
Babuhri, *India* **42 F3** 26 49N 69 43 E
Babusar Pass, *Pakistan* **43 B5** 35 12N 73 59 E
Babuyan Chan., *Phil.* **37 A6** 18 40N 121 30 E
Babylon, *Iraq* **44 C5** 32 34N 44 22 E
Bac Lieu, *Vietnam* **39 H5** 9 17N 105 43 E
Bac Phan, *Vietnam* **38 B5** 22 0N 105 0 E
Bacabal, *Brazil* **93 D10** 4 15S 44 45W
Bacalar, *Mexico* **87 D7** 18 50N 87 27W
Bacan, Kepulauan, *Indonesia* **37 E7** 0 35S 127 30 E
Bacarra, *Phil.* **37 A6** 18 15N 120 37 E
Bacău, *Romania* **17 E14** 46 35N 26 55 E
Bacerac, *Mexico* **86 A3** 30 18N 108 50W
Bach Long Vi, Dao, *Vietnam* **38 B6** 20 10N 107 40 E
Bachelina, *Russia* **26 D7** 57 45N 67 20 E
Bachhwara, *India* **43 G11** 25 35N 85 54 E
Back →, *Canada* **68 B9** 65 10N 104 0W
Bacolod, *Phil.* **37 B6** 10 40N 122 57 E
Bacuk, *Malaysia* **39 J4** 6 4N 102 25 E
Bād, *Iran* **45 C7** 33 41N 52 1 E
Bad →, *U.S.A.* **80 C4** 44 21N 100 22W
Bad Axe, *U.S.A.* **78 C2** 43 48N 83 0W
Bad Ischl, *Austria* **16 E7** 47 44N 13 38 E
Bad Kissingen, *Germany* **16 C6** 50 11N 10 4 E
Bad Lands, *U.S.A.* **80 D3** 43 40N 102 10W
Bada Barabil, *India* **43 H11** 22 7N 85 24 E
Badagara, *India* **40 P9** 11 35N 75 40 E
Badajós, L., *Brazil* **92 D6** 3 15S 62 50W
Badajoz, *Spain* **19 C2** 38 50N 6 59W
Badalona, *Spain* **19 B7** 41 26N 2 15 E
Badalzai, *Afghan.* **42 E1** 29 50N 65 35 E
Badampahar, *India* **41 H15** 22 10N 86 10 E
Badanah, *Si. Arabia* **44 D4** 30 58N 41 30 E
Badarinath, *India* **43 D8** 30 45N 79 30 E
Badas, Kepulauan, *Indonesia* **36 D3** 0 45N 107 5 E
Baddo →, *Pakistan* **40 F4** 28 0N 64 20 E
Bade, *Indonesia* **37 F9** 7 10S 139 35 E
Baden, *Austria* **16 D9** 48 1N 16 13 E
Baden, *U.S.A.* **78 F4** 40 38N 80 14W
Baden-Baden, *Germany* **16 D5** 48 44N 8 13 E
Baden-Württemberg □, *Germany* **16 D5** 48 20N 8 40 E
Badgastein, *Austria* **16 E7** 47 7N 13 9 E
Badger, *Canada* **71 C8** 49 0N 56 4W
Badger, *U.S.A.* **84 J7** 36 38N 119 1W
Bādghīsāt □, *Afghan.* **40 B3** 35 0N 63 0 E
Badgom, *India* **43 B6** 34 1N 74 45 E
Badin, *Pakistan* **42 G3** 24 38N 68 54 E
Badlands National Park, *U.S.A.* **80 D3** 43 38N 102 56W
Badrah, *Iraq* **44 C5** 33 6N 45 58 E
Badrinath, *India* **43 D8** 30 44N 79 29 E
Badulla, *Sri Lanka* **40 R12** 7 1N 81 7 E
Baena, *Spain* **19 D3** 37 37N 4 20W
Baeza, *Spain* **19 D4** 37 57N 3 25W
Baffin B., *Canada* **4 B4** 72 0N 64 0W
Baffin I., *Canada* **69 B12** 68 0N 75 0W
Bafing →, *Mali* **50 F3** 13 49N 10 50W
Bafliyūn, *Syria* **44 B3** 36 37N 36 59 E
Bafoulabé, *Mali* **50 F3** 13 50N 10 55W
Bafoussam, *Cameroon* **52 C2** 5 28N 10 25 E
Bāfq, *Iran* **45 D7** 31 40N 55 25 E
Bafra, *Turkey* **25 F6** 41 34N 35 54 E
Bāft, *Iran* **45 D8** 29 15N 56 38 E
Bafwasende, *Dem. Rep. of the Congo* **54 B2** 1 3N 27 5 E
Bagamoyo, *Tanzania* **54 D4** 6 28S 38 55 E
Bagan Datoh, *Malaysia* **39 L3** 3 59N 100 47 E
Bagan Serai, *Malaysia* **39 K3** 5 1N 100 32 E
Baganga, *Phil.* **37 C7** 7 34N 126 33 E
Bagani, *Namibia* **56 B3** 18 7S 21 41 E
Bagansiapiapi, *Indonesia* **36 D2** 2 12N 100 50 E
Bagasra, *India* **42 J4** 21 30N 71 0 E
Bagaud, *India* **42 H6** 22 19N 75 53 E
Bagdad, *U.S.A.* **85 L11** 34 35N 115 53W
Bagdarin, *Russia* **27 D12** 54 26N 113 36 E
Bagé, *Brazil* **95 C5** 31 20S 54 15W
Bagenalstown = Muine Bheag, *Ireland* **13 D5** 52 42N 6 58W
Baggs, *U.S.A.* **82 F10** 41 2N 107 39W
Bagh, *Pakistan* **43 C5** 33 59N 73 45 E
Baghain →, *India* **43 G9** 25 32N 81 1 E
Baghdād, *Iraq* **44 C5** 33 20N 44 30 E
Bagheria, *Italy* **20 E5** 38 5N 13 30 E
Baghlān, *Afghan.* **40 A6** 32 12N 69 0 E
Bagley, *U.S.A.* **80 B7** 47 32N 95 24W
Bagodar, *India* **43 G11** 24 5N 85 52 E
Bagrationovsk, *Russia* **9 J19** 54 23N 20 39 E
Baguio, *Phil.* **37 A6** 16 26N 120 34 E
Bah, *India* **43 F8** 26 53N 78 36 E
Bahadurganj, *India* **43 F12** 26 16N 87 49 E
Bahadurgarh, *India* **42 E7** 28 40N 76 57 E
Bahama, Canal Viejo de, *W. Indies* **88 B4** 22 10N 77 30W
Bahamas ■, *N. Amer.* **89 B5** 24 0N 75 0W
Baharampur, *India* **43 G13** 24 2N 88 27 E
Bahawalnagar, *Pakistan* **42 E5** 30 0N 73 15 E
Bahawalpur, *Pakistan* **42 E4** 29 24N 71 40 E
Baheri, *India* **43 E8** 28 45N 79 34 E
Bahgul →, *India* **43 F8** 27 45N 79 36 E
Bahi, *Tanzania* **54 D4** 5 58S 35 21 E
Bahi Swamp, *Tanzania* **54 D4** 6 10S 35 0 E
Bahía = Salvador, *Brazil* **93 F11** 13 0S 38 30W
Bahía □, *Brazil* **93 F10** 12 0S 42 0W
Bahía, Is. de la, *Honduras* **88 C2** 16 45N 86 15W
Bahía Blanca, *Argentina* **94 D3** 38 35S 62 13W
Bahía de Caráquez, *Ecuador* **92 D2** 0 40S 80 27W
Bahía Honda, *Cuba* **88 B3** 22 54N 83 10W
Bahía Laura, *Argentina* **96 F3** 48 10S 66 30W
Bahía Negra, *Paraguay* **92 H7** 20 5S 58 5W

Bardstown

Bahir Dar, Ethiopia 46 E2 11 37N 37 10 E
Bahmanzād, Iran 45 D6 31 15N 51 47 E
Bahr el Ghazâl □, Sudan 51 G11 7 0N 28 0 E
Bahraich, India 43 F9 27 38N 81 37 E
Bahrain ■, Asia 45 E6 26 0N 50 35 E
Bahror, India 42 F7 27 51N 76 20 E
Bāhū Kalāt, Iran 45 E9 25 43N 61 25 E
Bai Bung, Mui = Ca Mau, Mui, Vietnam 39 H5 8 38N 104 44 E
Bai Duc, Vietnam 38 C5 18 3N 105 49 E
Bai Thuong, Vietnam 38 C5 19 54N 105 23 E
Baia Mare, Romania 17 E12 47 40N 23 35 E
Baião, Brazil 93 D9 2 40S 49 40W
Baïbokoum, Chad 51 G9 7 46N 15 43 E
Baicheng, China 35 B12 45 38N 122 42 E
Baidoa, Somali Rep. 46 G3 3 8N 43 30 E
Baie Comeau, Canada 71 C6 49 12N 68 10W
Baie-St-Paul, Canada 71 C5 47 28N 70 32W
Baie Trinité, Canada 71 C6 49 25N 67 20W
Baie Verte, Canada 71 C8 49 55N 56 12W
Baihar, India 43 H9 22 6N 80 33 E
Baihe, China 34 H6 32 50N 110 5 E
Ba'iji, Iraq 44 C4 35 0N 43 30 E
Baijnath, India 43 E8 29 55N 79 37 E
Baikal, L. = Baykal, Oz., Russia 27 D11 53 0N 108 0 E
Baikunthpur, India 43 H10 23 15N 82 33 E
Baile Atha Cliath = Dublin, Ireland 13 C5 53 21N 6 15W
Băileşti, Romania 17 F12 44 1N 23 20 E
Bainbridge, Ga., U.S.A. 77 K3 30 55N 84 35W
Bainbridge, N.Y., U.S.A. 79 D9 42 18N 75 29W
Baing, Indonesia 37 F6 10 14S 120 34 E
Bainiu, China 34 H7 32 50N 112 15 E
Bā'ir, Jordan 47 E5 30 45N 36 55 E
Bairiki, Kiribati 64 G9 1 30N 173 0 E
Bairin Youqi, China 35 C10 43 30N 118 35 E
Bairin Zuoqi, China 35 C10 43 58N 119 15 E
Bairnsdale, Australia 63 F4 37 48S 147 36 E
Baisha, China 34 G7 34 20N 112 32 E
Baitadi, Nepal 43 E9 29 35N 80 25 E
Baiyin, China 34 F3 36 45N 104 14 E
Baiyu Shan, China 34 F4 37 15N 107 30 E
Baj Baj, India 43 H13 22 30N 88 5 E
Baja, Hungary 17 E10 46 12N 18 59 E
Baja, Pta., Mexico 86 B1 29 50N 116 0W
Baja California, Mexico 86 A1 31 10N 115 12W
Baja California □, Mexico 86 B2 30 0N 115 0W
Baja California Sur □, Mexico 86 B2 25 50N 111 50W
Bajag, India 43 H9 22 40N 81 21 E
Bajamar, Canary Is. 22 F3 28 33N 16 20W
Bajana, India 42 H4 23 7N 71 49 E
Bājgirān, Iran 45 B8 37 36N 58 24 E
Bajimba, Mt., Australia 63 D5 29 17S 152 6 E
Bajo Nuevo, Caribbean 88 C4 15 40N 78 50W
Bajoga, Nigeria 51 F8 10 57N 11 20 E
Bajool, Australia 62 C5 23 40S 150 35 E
Bakel, Senegal 50 F3 14 56N 12 20W
Baker, Calif., U.S.A. 85 K10 35 16N 116 4W
Baker, Mont., U.S.A. 80 B2 46 22N 104 17W
Baker, L., Canada 68 B10 64 0N 96 0W
Baker City, U.S.A. 82 D5 44 47N 117 50W
Baker I., Pac. Oc. 64 G10 0 10N 176 35W
Baker I., U.S.A. 72 B2 55 20N 133 40W
Baker L., Australia 61 E4 26 54S 126 5 E
Baker Lake, Canada 68 B10 64 20N 96 3W
Baker Mt., U.S.A. 82 B3 48 50N 121 49W
Bakers Creek, Australia 62 C4 21 13S 149 7 E
Baker's Dozen Is., Canada 70 A4 56 45N 78 45W
Bakersfield, Calif., U.S.A. 85 K8 35 23N 119 1W
Bakersfield, Vt., U.S.A. 79 B12 44 45N 72 48W
Bākhtarān, Iran 44 C5 34 23N 47 0 E
Bākhtarān □, Iran 44 C5 34 0N 46 30 E
Bakı, Azerbaijan 25 F8 40 29N 49 56 E
Bakkafjörður, Iceland 8 C6 66 2N 14 48W
Bakony, Hungary 17 E9 47 10N 17 30 E
Bakony Forest = Bakony, Hungary 17 E9 47 10N 17 30 E
Bakouma, C.A.R. 52 C4 5 40N 22 56 E
Bakswaho, India 43 G8 24 15N 79 18 E
Baku = Bakı, Azerbaijan 25 F8 40 29N 49 56 E
Bakutis Coast, Antarctica 5 D15 74 0S 120 0W
Baky = Bakı, Azerbaijan 25 F8 40 29N 49 56 E
Bala, Canada 78 A5 45 1N 79 37W
Bala, U.K. 10 E4 52 54N 3 36W
Bala, L., U.K. 10 E4 52 53N 3 37W
Balabac I., Phil. 36 C5 8 0N 117 0 E
Balabac Str., E. Indies 36 C5 7 53N 117 5 E
Balabagh, Afghan. 42 B4 34 25N 70 12 E
Ba'labakk, Lebanon 47 B5 34 0N 36 10 E
Balabalangan, Kepulauan, Indonesia 36 E5 2 20S 117 30 E
Balad, Iraq 44 C5 34 1N 44 9 E
Balad Rūz, Iraq 44 C5 33 42N 45 5 E
Bālādeh, Fārs, Iran 45 D6 29 17N 51 56 E
Bālādeh, Māzandaran, Iran 45 B6 36 12N 51 48 E
Balaghat, India 40 J12 21 49N 80 12 E
Balaghat Ra., India 40 K10 18 50N 76 30 E
Balaguer, Spain 19 B6 41 50N 0 50 E
Balaklava, Ukraine 25 F5 44 30N 33 30 E
Balakovo, Russia 24 D8 52 4N 47 55 E
Balamau, India 43 F9 27 10N 80 21 E
Balancán, Mexico 87 D6 17 48N 91 32W
Balashov, Russia 25 D7 51 30N 43 10 E
Balasinor, India 42 H5 22 57N 73 23 E
Balasore = Baleshwar, India 41 J15 21 35N 87 3 E
Balaton, Hungary 17 E9 46 50N 17 40 E
Balbina, Reprêsa de, Brazil 92 D7 2 0S 59 30W
Balboa, Panama 88 E4 8 57N 79 34W
Balbriggan, Ireland 13 C5 53 37N 6 11W
Balcarce, Argentina 94 D4 38 0S 58 10W
Balcarres, Canada 73 C8 50 50N 103 35W
Balchik, Bulgaria 21 C13 43 28N 28 11 E
Balclutha, N.Z. 59 M2 46 15S 169 45 E
Balcones Escarpment, U.S.A. 81 L5 29 30N 99 15W
Bald Hd., Australia 61 G2 35 6S 118 1 E
Bald I., Australia 61 F2 34 57S 118 27 E
Bald Knob, U.S.A. 81 H9 35 19N 91 34W
Baldock L., Canada 73 B9 56 33N 97 57W
Baldwin, Mich., U.S.A. 76 D3 43 54N 85 51W
Baldwin, Pa., U.S.A. 78 F5 40 23N 79 59W
Baldwinsville, U.S.A. 79 C8 43 10N 76 20W
Baldy Mt., U.S.A. 82 B9 48 9N 109 39W
Baldy Peak, U.S.A. 83 K9 33 54N 109 34W
Baleares, Is., Spain 22 B10 39 30N 3 0 E
Balearic Is. = Baleares, Is., Spain 22 B10 39 30N 3 0 E
Baleine = Whale →, Canada 71 A6 58 15N 67 40W
Baler, Phil. 37 A6 15 46N 121 34 E
Baleshare, U.K. 12 D1 57 31N 7 22W
Baleshwar, India 41 J15 21 35N 87 3 E
Balfate, Honduras 88 C2 15 48N 86 25W
Balí, Greece 23 D6 35 25N 24 47 E
Bali, India 42 G5 25 11N 73 17 E
Bali □, Indonesia 36 F5 8 20S 115 0 E
Bali, Selat, Indonesia 37 H16 8 18S 114 25 E
Baliapal, India 43 J12 21 40N 87 17 E
Balikeşir, Turkey 21 E12 39 39N 27 53 E
Balikpapan, Indonesia 36 E5 1 10S 116 55 E
Balimbing, Phil. 37 C5 5 5N 119 58 E
Baling, Malaysia 39 K3 5 41N 100 55 E
Balipara, India 41 F18 26 50N 92 45 E
Balkan Mts. = Stara Planina, Bulgaria 21 C10 43 15N 23 0 E
Balkhash = Balqash, Kazakstan 26 E8 46 50N 74 50 E
Balkhash, Ozero = Balqash Köl, Kazakstan 26 E8 46 0N 74 50 E
Balla, Bangla. 41 G17 24 10N 91 35 E
Ballachulish, U.K. 12 E3 56 41N 5 8W
Balladonia, Australia 61 F3 32 27S 123 51 E
Ballaghaderreen, Ireland 13 C3 53 55N 8 34W
Ballarat, Australia 63 F3 37 33S 143 50 E
Ballard, L., Australia 61 E3 29 20S 120 40 E
Ballater, U.K. 12 D5 57 3N 3 3W
Ballenas, Canal de, Mexico 86 B2 29 10N 113 45W
Balleny Is., Antarctica 5 C11 66 30S 163 0 E
Ballia, India 43 G11 25 46N 84 12 E
Ballina, Australia 63 D5 28 50S 153 31 E
Ballina, Ireland 13 B2 54 7N 9 9W
Ballinasloe, Ireland 13 C3 53 20N 8 13W
Ballinger, U.S.A. 81 K5 31 45N 99 57W
Ballinrobe, Ireland 13 C2 53 38N 9 13W
Ballinskelligs B., Ireland 13 E1 51 48N 10 13W
Ballston Spa, U.S.A. 79 D11 43 0N 73 51W
Ballycastle, U.K. 13 A5 55 12N 6 15W
Ballyclare, U.K. 13 B5 54 46N 6 0W
Ballyhaunis, Ireland 13 C3 53 46N 8 46W
Ballymena, U.K. 13 B5 54 52N 6 17W
Ballymoney, U.K. 13 A5 55 5N 6 31W
Ballymote, Ireland 13 B3 54 5N 8 31W
Ballynahinch, U.K. 13 B6 54 24N 5 54W
Ballyquintin Pt., U.K. 13 B6 54 20N 5 30W
Ballyshannon, Ireland 13 B3 54 30N 8 11W
Balmaceda, Chile 96 F2 46 0S 71 50W
Balmertown, Canada 73 C10 51 4N 93 41W
Balmoral, Australia 63 F3 37 15S 141 48 E
Balmorhea, U.S.A. 81 K3 30 59N 103 45W
Balonne →, Australia 63 D4 28 47S 147 56 E
Balotra, India 42 G5 25 50N 72 14 E
Balqash, Kazakstan 26 E8 46 50N 74 50 E
Balqash Köl, Kazakstan 26 E8 46 0N 74 50 E
Balrampur, India 43 F10 27 30N 82 20 E
Balranald, Australia 63 E3 34 38S 143 33 E
Balsas, Mexico 87 D5 18 0N 99 40W
Balsas →, Brazil 93 E9 7 15S 44 35W
Balsas →, Mexico 86 D4 17 55N 102 10W
Balston Spa, U.S.A. 79 D11 43 0N 73 52W
Balta, Ukraine 17 D15 48 2N 29 45 E
Bălţi, Moldova 17 E14 47 48N 27 58 E
Baltic Sea, Europe 9 H18 57 0N 19 0 E
Baltimore, Ireland 13 E2 51 29N 9 22W
Baltimore, Md., U.S.A. 76 F7 39 17N 76 37W
Baltimore, Ohio, U.S.A. 78 G2 39 51N 82 36W
Baltit, Pakistan 43 A6 36 15N 74 40 E
Baltiysk, Russia 9 J18 54 41N 19 58 E
Baluchistan □, Pakistan 40 F4 27 30N 65 0 E
Balurghat, India 43 G13 25 15N 88 44 E
Balvi, Latvia 9 H22 57 8N 27 15 E
Balya, Turkey 21 E12 39 44N 27 35 E
Bam, Iran 45 D8 29 7N 58 14 E
Bama, Nigeria 51 F8 11 33N 13 41 E
Bamaga, Australia 62 A3 10 50S 142 25 E
Bamaji L., Canada 70 B1 51 9N 91 25W
Bamako, Mali 50 F4 12 34N 7 55W
Bambari, C.A.R. 52 C4 5 40N 20 35 E
Bambaroo, Australia 62 B4 18 50S 146 10 E
Bamberg, Germany 16 D6 49 54N 10 54 E
Bamberg, U.S.A. 77 J5 33 18N 81 2W
Bambili, Dem. Rep. of the Congo 54 B2 3 40N 26 0 E
Bamenda, Cameroon 52 C1 5 57N 10 11 E
Bamfield, Canada 72 D3 48 45N 125 10W
Bāmīān □, Afghan. 40 B5 35 0N 67 0 E
Bamiancheng, China 35 C13 43 15N 124 2 E
Bampūr, Iran 45 E9 27 15N 60 21 E
Ban Ban, Laos 38 C4 19 31N 103 30 E
Ban Bang Hin, Thailand 39 H2 9 32N 98 35 E
Ban Chiang Klang, Thailand 38 C3 19 25N 100 55 E
Ban Chik, Laos 38 D4 17 15N 102 22 E
Ban Choho, Thailand 38 E4 15 2N 102 9 E
Ban Dan Lan Hoi, Thailand 38 D2 17 0N 99 35 E
Ban Don = Surat Thani, Thailand 39 H2 9 6N 99 20 E
Ban Don, Vietnam 38 F6 12 53N 107 48 E
Ban Don, Ao →, Thailand 39 H2 9 20N 99 25 E
Ban Dong, Thailand 38 C3 19 30N 100 59 E
Ban Hong, Thailand 38 C2 18 18N 98 50 E
Ban Kaeng, Thailand 38 D3 17 29N 100 7 E
Ban Kantang, Thailand 39 J2 7 25N 99 31 E
Ban Keun, Laos 38 C4 18 22N 102 35 E
Ban Khai, Thailand 38 F3 12 46N 101 18 E
Ban Kheun, Laos 38 B3 20 13N 101 7 E
Ban Khlong Kua, Thailand 39 J3 6 57N 100 8 E
Ban Khuan Mao, Thailand 39 J2 7 50N 99 37 E
Ban Ko Yai Chim, Thailand 39 G2 11 17N 99 26 E
Ban Kok, Thailand 38 D4 16 40N 103 40 E
Ban Laem, Thailand 38 F2 13 13N 99 59 E
Ban Lao Ngam, Laos 38 E6 15 28N 106 10 E
Ban Le Kathe, Thailand 38 E2 15 49N 98 53 E
Ban Mae Chedi, Thailand 38 C2 19 11N 99 31 E
Ban Mae Laeng, Thailand 38 B2 20 1N 99 17 E
Ban Mae Sariang, Thailand 38 C1 18 10N 97 56 E
Ban Mê Thuôt = Buon Ma Thuot, Vietnam 38 F7 12 40N 108 3 E
Ban Mi, Thailand 38 E3 15 3N 100 32 E
Ban Muong Mo, Laos 38 C4 19 4N 103 58 E
Ban Na Mo, Laos 38 D5 17 7N 105 40 E
Ban Na San, Thailand 39 H2 8 53N 99 52 E
Ban Na Tong, Laos 38 B3 20 56N 101 47 E
Ban Nam Bac, Laos 38 B4 20 38N 102 20 E
Ban Nam Ma, Laos 38 A3 22 2N 101 37 E
Ban Ngang, Laos 38 E6 15 59N 106 11 E
Ban Nong Bok, Laos 38 D5 17 5N 104 48 E
Ban Nong Boua, Laos 38 E6 15 40N 106 33 E
Ban Nong Pling, Thailand 38 E3 15 40N 100 10 E
Ban Pak Chan, Thailand 39 G2 10 32N 98 51 E
Ban Phai, Thailand 38 D4 16 4N 102 44 E
Ban Pong, Thailand 38 F2 13 50N 99 55 E
Ban Ron Phibun, Thailand 39 H2 8 9N 99 51 E
Ban Sanam Chai, Thailand 39 J3 7 33N 100 25 E
Ban Sangkha, Thailand 38 E4 14 37N 103 52 E
Ban Tak, Thailand 38 D2 17 2N 99 4 E
Ban Tako, Thailand 38 E4 14 5N 102 40 E
Ban Tha Dua, Thailand 38 D2 17 59N 98 39 E
Ban Tha Li, Thailand 38 D3 17 37N 101 25 E
Ban Tha Nun, Thailand 39 H2 8 12N 98 18 E
Ban Thahine, Laos 38 E5 14 12N 105 33 E
Ban Xien Kok, Laos 38 B3 20 54N 100 39 E
Ban Yen Nhan, Vietnam 38 B6 20 57N 106 2 E
Banaba, Kiribati 64 H8 0 45S 169 50 E
Banalia, Dem. Rep. of the Congo 54 B2 1 32N 25 5 E
Banam, Cambodia 39 G5 11 20N 105 17 E
Bananal, I. do, Brazil 93 F8 11 30S 50 30W
Banaras = Varanasi, India 43 G10 25 22N 83 0 E
Banas →, Gujarat, India 42 H4 23 45N 71 25 E
Banas →, Mad. P., India 43 G9 24 15N 81 30 E
Bânâs, Ras, Egypt 51 D13 23 57N 35 59 E
Banbān, Si. Arabia 44 E5 25 1N 46 35 E
Banbridge, U.K. 13 B5 54 22N 6 16W
Banbury, U.K. 11 E6 52 4N 1 20W
Banchory, U.K. 12 D6 57 3N 2 29W
Bancroft, Canada 78 A7 45 3N 77 51W
Band Bonī, Iran 45 E8 25 30N 59 33 E
Band Qīr, Iran 45 D6 31 39N 48 53 E
Banda, India 43 G9 25 30N 80 26 E
Banda, Mad. P., India 43 G8 24 3N 78 57 E
Banda, Kepulauan, Indonesia 37 E7 4 37S 129 50 E
Banda Aceh, Indonesia 36 C1 5 35N 95 20 E
Banda Banda, Mt., Australia 63 E5 31 10S 152 28 E
Banda Elat, Indonesia 37 F8 5 40S 133 5 E
Banda Is. = Banda, Kepulauan, Indonesia 37 E7 4 37S 129 50 E
Banda Sea, Indonesia 37 F8 6 0S 130 0 E
Bandai-San, Japan 30 F10 37 36N 140 4 E
Bandān, Iran 45 D9 31 23N 60 44 E
Bandanaira, Indonesia 37 E7 4 32S 129 54 E
Bandanwara, India 42 F6 26 9N 74 38 E
Bandar = Machilipatnam, India 41 L12 16 12N 81 8 E
Bandār 'Abbās, Iran 45 E8 27 15N 56 15 E
Bandar-e Anzalī, Iran 45 B6 37 30N 49 30 E
Bandar-e Bushehr = Būshehr, Iran 45 D6 28 55N 50 55 E
Bandar-e Chārak, Iran 45 E7 26 45N 54 20 E
Bandar-e Deylam, Iran 45 D6 30 5N 50 10 E
Bandar-e Khomeynı, Iran 45 D6 30 30N 49 5 E
Bandar-e Lengeh, Iran 45 E7 26 35N 54 58 E
Bandar-e Maqām, Iran 45 E7 26 56N 53 29 E
Bandar-e Ma'shur, Iran 45 D6 30 35N 49 10 E
Bandar-e Nakhīlū, Iran 45 E7 26 58N 53 30 E
Bandar-e Rīg, Iran 45 D6 29 29N 50 38 E
Bandar-e Torkeman, Iran 45 B7 37 0N 54 10 E
Bandar Maharani = Muar, Malaysia 39 L4 2 3N 102 34 E
Bandar Penggaram = Batu Pahat, Malaysia 39 M4 1 50N 102 56 E
Bandar Seri Begawan, Brunei 36 D5 4 52N 115 0 E
Bandar Sri Aman, Malaysia 36 D4 1 15N 111 32 E
Bandawe, Malawi 55 E3 11 58S 34 5 E
Bandeira, Pico da, Brazil 95 A7 20 26S 41 47W
Bandera, Argentina 94 B3 28 55S 62 20W
Banderas, B. de, Mexico 86 C3 20 40N 105 30W
Bandhogarh, India 43 H9 23 40N 81 2 E
Bandi →, India 42 F6 26 12N 75 47 E
Bandikui, India 42 F7 27 3N 76 34 E
Bandırma, Turkey 21 D13 40 20N 28 0 E
Bandon, Ireland 13 E3 51 44N 8 44W
Bandon →, Ireland 13 E3 51 43N 8 37W
Bandula, Mozam. 55 F3 19 0S 33 7 E
Bandundu, Dem. Rep. of the Congo 52 E3 3 15S 17 22 E
Bandung, Indonesia 37 G12 6 54S 107 36 E
Bāneh, Iran 44 C5 35 59N 45 53 E
Banes, Cuba 89 B4 21 0N 75 42W
Banff, Canada 72 C5 51 10N 115 34W
Banff, U.K. 12 D6 57 40N 2 33W
Banff Nat. Park, Canada 72 C5 51 30N 116 15W
Bang Fai →, Laos 38 D5 16 57N 104 45 E
Bang Hieng →, Laos 38 D5 16 10N 105 10 E
Bang Krathum, Thailand 38 D3 16 34N 100 18 E
Bang Lamung, Thailand 38 F3 13 3N 100 56 E
Bang Mun Nak, Thailand 38 D3 16 2N 100 23 E
Bang Pa In, Thailand 38 E3 14 14N 100 35 E
Bang Rakam, Thailand 38 D3 16 45N 100 7 E
Bang Saphan, Thailand 39 G2 11 14N 99 28 E
Bangaduni I., India 43 J13 21 34N 88 52 E
Bangala Dam, Zimbabwe 55 G3 21 7S 31 25 E
Bangalore, India 40 N10 12 59N 77 40 E
Banganga →, India 42 F6 27 6N 77 25 E
Bangaon, India 43 H13 23 0N 88 47 E
Bangassou, C.A.R. 52 D4 4 55N 23 7 E
Banggai, Indonesia 37 E6 1 34S 123 30 E
Banggai, Kepulauan, Indonesia 37 E6 1 40S 123 30 E
Banggai Arch. = Banggai, Kepulauan, Indonesia 37 E6 1 40S 123 30 E
Banggi, Malaysia 36 C5 7 17N 117 12 E
Banghāzī, Libya 51 B10 32 11N 20 3 E
Bangka, Sulawesi, Indonesia 37 D7 1 50N 125 5 E
Bangka, Sumatera, Indonesia 36 E3 2 0S 105 50 E
Bangka, Selat, Indonesia 36 E3 2 30S 105 30 E
Bangkalan, Indonesia 37 G15 7 2S 112 46 E
Bangkinang, Indonesia 36 D2 0 18N 101 5 E
Bangko, Indonesia 36 E2 2 5S 102 9 E
Bangkok, Thailand 38 F3 13 45N 100 35 E
Bangladesh ■, Asia 41 H17 24 0N 90 0 E
Bangong Co, India 43 B8 35 50N 79 20 E
Bangor, Down, U.K. 13 B6 54 40N 5 40W
Bangor, Gwynedd, U.K. 10 D3 53 14N 4 8W
Bangor, Maine, U.S.A. 69 D13 44 48N 68 46W
Bangor, Pa., U.S.A. 79 F9 40 52N 75 13W
Bangued, Phil. 37 A6 17 40N 120 37 E
Bangui, C.A.R. 52 D3 4 23N 18 35 E
Banguru, Dem. Rep. of the Congo 54 B2 0 30N 27 10 E
Bangweulu, L., Zambia 55 E3 11 0S 30 0 E
Bangweulu Swamp, Zambia 55 E3 11 20S 30 15 E
Bani, Dom. Rep. 89 C5 18 16N 70 22W
Banī Sa'd, Iraq 44 C5 33 34N 44 32 E
Banihal Pass, India 43 C6 33 30N 75 12 E
Bāniyās, Syria 44 C3 35 10N 36 0 E
Banja Luka, Bos.-H. 20 B7 44 49N 17 11 E
Banjar, India 42 D7 31 38N 77 21 E
Banjar →, India 43 H9 22 36N 80 22 E
Banjarmasin, Indonesia 36 E4 3 20S 114 35 E
Banjul, Gambia 50 F2 13 28N 16 40W
Banka, India 43 G12 24 53N 86 55 E
Banket, Zimbabwe 55 F3 17 27S 30 19 E
Bankipore, India 41 G14 25 35N 85 10 E
Banks I., B.C., Canada 72 C3 53 20N 130 0W
Banks I., N.W.T., Canada 68 A7 73 15N 121 30W
Banks Pen., N.Z. 59 K4 43 45S 173 15 E
Banks Str., Australia 62 G4 40 40S 148 10 E
Bankura, India 43 H12 23 11N 87 18 E
Banmankhi, India 43 G12 25 53N 87 11 E
Bann →, Arm., U.K. 13 B5 54 30N 6 31W
Bann →, L'derry., U.K. 13 A5 55 8N 6 41W
Bannang Sata, Thailand 39 J3 6 16N 101 16 E
Banning, U.S.A. 85 M10 33 56N 116 53W
Banningville = Bandundu, Dem. Rep. of the Congo 52 E3 3 15S 17 22 E
Bannockburn, Canada 78 B7 44 39N 77 33W
Bannockburn, U.K. 12 E5 56 5N 3 55W
Bannockburn, Zimbabwe 55 G2 20 17S 29 48 E
Bannu, Pakistan 40 C7 33 0N 70 18 E
Bano, India 43 H11 22 40N 84 55 E
Bansgaon, India 43 F10 26 33N 83 21 E
Banská Bystrica, Slovak Rep. 17 D10 48 46N 19 14 E
Banswara, India 42 H6 23 32N 74 24 E
Bantaeng, Indonesia 37 F5 5 32S 119 56 E
Bantry, Ireland 13 E2 51 41N 9 27W
Bantry B., Ireland 13 E2 51 37N 9 44W
Bantul, Indonesia 37 G14 7 55S 110 19 E
Bantva, India 42 J4 21 29N 70 12 E
Banu, Afghan. 40 B6 35 35N 69 5 E
Banyak, Kepulauan, Indonesia 36 D1 2 10N 97 10 E
Banyalbufar, Spain 22 B9 39 42N 2 31 E
Banyo, Cameroon 52 C2 6 52N 11 45 E
Banyumas, Indonesia 37 G13 7 32S 109 18 E
Banyuwangi, Indonesia 37 H16 8 13S 114 21 E
Banzare Coast, Antarctica 5 C9 68 0S 125 0 E
Banzyville = Mobayi, Dem. Rep. of the Congo 52 D4 4 15N 21 8 E
Bao Lac, Vietnam 38 A5 22 57N 105 40 E
Bao Loc, Vietnam 39 G6 11 32N 107 48 E
Baocheng, China 34 H4 33 12N 106 56 E
Baode, China 34 E6 39 1N 111 5 E
Baodi, China 35 E9 39 38N 117 20 E
Baoding, China 34 E8 38 50N 115 28 E
Baoji, China 34 G4 34 20N 107 5 E
Baoshan, China 32 D4 25 10N 99 5 E
Baotou, China 34 D6 40 32N 110 2 E
Baoying, China 35 H10 33 17N 119 20 E
Bap, India 42 F5 27 23N 72 18 E
Bapatla, India 41 M12 15 55N 80 30 E
Bāqerābād, Iran 45 C6 33 2N 51 58 E
Ba'qūbah, Iraq 44 C5 33 45N 44 50 E
Baquedano, Chile 94 A2 23 20S 69 52W
Bar, Montenegro, Yug. 21 C8 42 8N 19 6 E
Bar, Ukraine 17 D14 49 4N 27 40 E
Bar Bigha, India 43 G11 25 21N 85 47 E
Bar Harbor, U.S.A. 77 C11 44 23N 68 13W
Bar-le-Duc, France 18 B6 48 47N 5 10 E
Bara, India 43 G9 25 16N 81 43 E
Bara Banki, India 43 F9 26 55N 81 12 E
Barabai, Indonesia 36 E5 2 32S 115 34 E
Baraboo, U.S.A. 80 D10 43 28N 89 45W
Baracoa, Cuba 89 B5 20 20N 74 30W
Baradā →, Syria 47 B5 33 33N 36 34 E
Baradero, Argentina 94 C4 33 52S 59 29W
Baradine, Australia 63 E4 30 56S 149 4 E
Baraga, U.S.A. 80 B10 46 47N 88 30W
Barah →, India 42 F6 27 42N 77 5 E
Barahona, Dom. Rep. 89 C5 18 13N 71 7W
Barail Range, India 41 G18 25 15N 93 20 E
Barakaldo, Spain 19 A4 43 18N 2 59W
Barakar →, India 43 G12 24 7N 86 14 E
Barakhola, India 41 G18 25 0N 92 45 E
Barakot, India 43 J11 21 33N 84 59 E
Barakpur, India 43 H13 22 44N 88 30 E
Baralaba, Australia 62 C4 24 13S 149 50 E
Baralzon L., Canada 73 B9 60 0N 98 3W
Baramula, India 43 B6 34 15N 74 20 E
Baran, India 42 G7 25 9N 76 40 E
Baran →, Pakistan 42 G3 25 13N 68 17 E
Baranavichy, Belarus 17 B14 53 10N 26 0 E
Baranof, U.S.A. 72 B2 57 5N 134 50W
Baranof I., U.S.A. 68 C6 57 0N 135 0W
Barapasi, Indonesia 37 E9 2 15S 137 5 E
Barasat, India 43 H13 22 46N 88 31 E
Barat Daya, Kepulauan, Indonesia 37 F7 7 30S 128 0 E
Barataria B., U.S.A. 81 L10 29 20N 89 55W
Barauda, India 42 H6 23 33N 75 15 E
Baraut, India 42 E7 29 13N 77 7 E
Barbacena, Brazil 95 A7 21 15S 43 56W
Barbados ■, W. Indies 89 D8 13 10N 59 30W
Barbària, C. de, Spain 22 C7 38 39N 1 24 E
Barbastro, Spain 19 A6 42 2N 0 5 E
Barberton, S. Africa 57 D5 25 42S 31 2 E
Barberton, U.S.A. 78 E3 41 0N 81 39W
Barbosa, Colombia 92 B4 5 57N 73 37W
Barbourville, U.S.A. 77 G4 36 52N 83 53W
Barbuda, W. Indies 89 C7 17 30N 61 40W
Barcaldine, Australia 62 C4 23 43S 145 6 E
Barcellona Pozzo di Gotto, Italy 20 E6 38 9N 15 13 E
Barcelona, Spain 19 B7 41 21N 2 10 E
Barcelona, Venezuela 92 A6 10 10N 64 40W
Barcelos, Brazil 92 D6 1 0S 63 0W
Barcoo →, Australia 62 D3 25 30S 142 50 E
Bardaï, Chad 51 D9 21 25N 17 0 E
Bardas Blancas, Argentina 94 D2 35 49S 69 45W
Barddhaman, India 43 H12 23 14N 87 39 E
Bardejov, Slovak Rep. 17 D11 49 18N 21 15 E
Bardera, Somali Rep. 46 G3 2 20N 42 27 E
Bardīyah, Libya 51 B10 31 45N 25 5 E
Bardsey I., U.K. 10 E3 52 45N 4 47W
Bardstown, U.S.A. 76 G3 37 49N 85 28W

Big Timber

Belfast, Maine, U.S.A. 77 C11 44 26N 69 1W
Belfast, N.Y., U.S.A. 78 D6 42 21N 78 7W
Belfast L., U.K. 13 B6 54 40N 5 50W
Belfield, U.S.A. 80 B3 46 53N 103 12W
Belfort, France 18 C7 47 38N 6 50 E
Belfry, U.S.A. 82 D9 45 9N 109 1W
Belgaum, India 40 M9 15 55N 74 35 E
Belgium ■, Europe 15 D4 50 30N 5 0 E
Belgorod, Russia 25 D6 50 35N 36 35 E
Belgorod-Dnestrovskiy = Bilhorod-Dnistrovskyy, Ukraine 25 E5 46 11N 30 23 E
Belgrade = Beograd, Serbia, Yug. 21 B9 44 50N 20 37 E
Belgrade, U.S.A. 82 D8 45 47N 111 11W
Belhaven, U.S.A. 77 H7 35 33N 76 37W
Beli Drim →, Europe 21 C9 42 6N 20 25 E
Belinyu, Indonesia 36 E3 1 35S 105 50 E
Beliton Is. = Belitung, Indonesia 36 E3 3 10S 107 50 E
Belitung, Indonesia 36 E3 3 10S 107 50 E
Belize ■, Cent. Amer. 87 D7 17 0N 88 30W
Belize City, Belize 87 D7 17 25N 88 0W
Belkovskiy, Ostrov, Russia 27 B14 75 32N 135 44 E
Bell →, Canada 70 C4 49 48N 77 38W
Bell I., Canada 71 B8 50 46N 55 35W
Bell-Irving →, Canada 72 B3 56 12N 129 5W
Bell Peninsula, Canada 69 B11 63 50N 82 0W
Bell Ville, Argentina 94 C3 32 40S 62 40W
Bella Bella, Canada 72 C3 52 10N 128 10W
Bella Coola, Canada 72 C3 52 25N 126 40W
Bella Unión, Uruguay 94 C4 30 15S 57 40W
Bella Vista, Corrientes, Argentina 94 B4 28 33S 59 0W
Bella Vista, Tucuman, Argentina 94 B2 27 10S 65 25W
Bellaire, U.S.A. 78 F4 40 1N 80 45W
Bellary, India 40 M10 15 10N 76 56 E
Bellata, Australia 63 D4 29 53S 149 46 E
Belle-Chasse, U.S.A. 81 L10 29 51N 89 59W
Belle Fourche, U.S.A. 80 C3 44 40N 103 51W
Belle Fourche →, U.S.A. 80 C3 44 26N 102 18W
Belle Glade, U.S.A. 77 M5 26 41N 80 40W
Belle-Île, France 18 C2 47 20N 3 10W
Belle Isle, Canada 71 B8 51 57N 55 25W
Belle Isle, Str. of, Canada 71 B8 51 30N 56 30W
Belle Plaine, U.S.A. 80 E8 41 54N 92 17W
Bellefontaine, U.S.A. 76 E4 40 22N 83 46W
Bellefonte, U.S.A. 78 F7 40 55N 77 47W
Belleoram, Canada 71 C8 47 31N 55 25W
Belleville, Canada 78 B7 44 10N 77 23W
Belleville, Ill., U.S.A. 80 F10 38 31N 89 59W
Belleville, Kans., U.S.A. 80 F6 39 50N 97 38W
Belleville, N.Y., U.S.A. 79 C8 43 46N 76 10W
Bellevue, Canada 72 D6 49 35N 114 22W
Bellevue, Idaho, U.S.A. 82 E6 43 28N 114 16W
Bellevue, Nebr., U.S.A. 80 E7 41 8N 95 53W
Bellevue, Ohio, U.S.A. 78 E2 41 17N 82 51W
Bellevue, Wash., U.S.A. 84 C4 47 37N 122 12W
Bellin = Kangirsuk, Canada 69 C13 60 0N 70 0W
Bellingen, Australia 63 E5 30 25S 152 50 E
Bellingham, U.S.A. 68 D7 48 46N 122 29W
Bellingshausen Sea, Antarctica 5 C17 66 0S 80 0W
Bellinzona, Switz. 18 C8 46 11N 9 1 E
Bello, Colombia 92 B3 6 20N 75 33W
Bellows Falls, U.S.A. 79 C12 43 8N 72 27W
Bellpat, Pakistan 42 E3 29 0N 68 5 E
Belluno, Italy 20 A5 46 9N 12 13 E
Bellwood, U.S.A. 78 F6 40 36N 78 20W
Belmont, Canada 78 D3 42 53N 81 5W
Belmont, S. Africa 56 D3 29 28S 24 22 E
Belmont, U.S.A. 78 D6 42 14N 78 2W
Belmonte, Brazil 93 G11 16 0S 39 0W
Belmopan, Belize 87 D7 17 18N 88 30W
Belmullet, Ireland 13 B2 54 14N 9 58W
Belo Horizonte, Brazil 93 G10 19 55S 43 56W
Belo-sur-Mer, Madag. 57 C7 20 42S 44 0 E
Belo-Tsiribihina, Madag. 57 B7 19 40S 44 30 E
Belogorsk, Russia 27 D13 51 0N 128 20 E
Beloha, Madag. 57 D8 25 10S 45 3 E
Beloit, Kans., U.S.A. 80 F5 39 28N 98 6W
Beloit, Wis., U.S.A. 80 D10 42 31N 89 2W
Belokorovichi, Ukraine 17 C15 51 7N 28 2 E
Belomorsk, Russia 24 B5 64 35N 34 54 E
Belonia, India 41 H17 23 15N 91 30 E
Beloretsk, Russia 24 D10 53 58N 58 24 E
Belorussia = Belarus ■, Europe 17 B14 53 30N 27 0 E
Belovo, Russia 26 D9 54 30N 86 0 E
Beloye, Ozero, Russia 24 B6 60 10N 37 35 E
Beloye More, Russia 24 A6 66 30N 38 0 E
Belozersk, Russia 24 B6 60 1N 37 45 E
Belpre, U.S.A. 76 F5 39 17N 81 34W
Belrain, India 43 E9 28 23N 80 55 E
Belt, U.S.A. 82 C8 47 23N 110 55W
Beltana, Australia 63 E2 30 48S 138 25 E
Belterra, Brazil 93 D8 2 45S 55 0W
Belton, U.S.A. 81 K6 31 3N 97 28W
Belton L., U.S.A. 81 K6 31 8N 97 32W
Beltsy = Bălţi, Moldova 17 E14 47 48N 27 58 E
Belturbet, Ireland 13 B4 54 6N 7 26W
Belukha, Russia 26 E9 49 50N 86 50 E
Beluran, Malaysia 36 C5 5 48N 117 35 E
Belvidere, Ill., U.S.A. 80 D10 42 15N 88 50W
Belvidere, N.J., U.S.A. 79 F9 40 50N 75 5W
Belyando →, Australia 62 C4 21 38S 146 50 E
Belyy, Ostrov, Russia 26 B8 73 30N 71 0 E
Belyy Yar, Russia 26 D9 58 26N 84 39 E
Belzoni, U.S.A. 81 J9 33 11N 90 29W
Bemaraha, Lembalemban' i, Madag. 57 B7 18 40S 44 45 E
Bemarivo, Madag. 57 C7 21 45S 44 45 E
Bemarivo →, Madag. 57 B8 15 27S 47 40 E
Bemavo, Madag. 57 C8 21 33S 45 25 E
Bembéréke, Benin 50 F6 10 11N 2 43 E
Bembesi, Zimbabwe 55 G2 20 0S 28 58 E
Bembesi →, Zimbabwe 55 F2 18 57S 27 47 E
Bemetara, India 43 J9 21 42N 81 32 E
Bemidji, U.S.A. 80 B7 47 28N 94 53W
Ben, Iran 45 C6 32 32N 50 45 E
Ben Cruachan, U.K. 12 E3 56 26N 5 8W
Ben Dearg, U.K. 12 D4 57 47N 4 56W
Ben Hope, U.K. 12 C4 58 25N 4 36W
Ben Lawers, U.K. 12 E4 56 32N 4 14W
Ben Lomond, N.S.W., Australia 63 E5 30 1S 151 43 E
Ben Lomond, Tas., Australia 62 G4 41 38S 147 42 E
Ben Lomond, U.K. 12 E4 56 11N 4 38W
Ben Luc, Vietnam 39 G6 10 39N 106 29 E
Ben Macdhui, U.K. 12 D5 57 4N 3 40W
Ben Mhor, U.K. 12 D1 57 15N 7 18W
Ben More, Arg. & Bute, U.K. 12 E2 56 26N 6 1W
Ben More, Stirl., U.K. 12 E4 56 23N 4 32W
Ben More Assynt, U.K. 12 C4 58 8N 4 52W
Ben Nevis, U.K. 12 E3 56 48N 5 1W
Ben Quang, Vietnam 38 D6 17 3N 106 55 E
Ben Vorlich, U.K. 12 E4 56 21N 4 14W
Ben Wyvis, U.K. 12 D4 57 40N 4 35W
Bena, Nigeria 50 F7 11 20N 5 50 E
Benalla, Australia 63 F4 36 30S 146 0 E
Benares = Varanasi, India 43 G10 25 22N 83 0 E
Benavente, Spain 19 A3 42 2N 5 43W
Benavides, U.S.A. 81 M5 27 36N 98 25W
Benbecula, U.K. 12 D1 57 26N 7 21W
Benbonyathe, Australia 63 E2 30 25S 139 11 E
Bend, U.S.A. 82 D3 44 4N 121 19W
Bendemeer, Australia 63 E5 30 53S 151 8 E
Bender Beila, Somali Rep. 46 F5 9 30N 50 48 E
Bendery = Tighina, Moldova 17 E15 46 50N 29 30 E
Bendigo, Australia 63 F3 36 40S 144 15 E
Benē Beraq, Israel 47 C3 32 6N 34 51 E
Benenitra, Madag. 57 C8 23 27S 45 5 E
Benevento, Italy 20 D6 41 8N 14 45 E
Benga, Mozam. 55 F3 16 11S 33 40 E
Bengal, Bay of, Ind. Oc. 41 M17 15 0N 90 0 E
Bengbu, China 35 H9 32 58N 117 20 E
Benghazi = Banghāzī, Libya 51 B10 32 11N 20 3 E
Bengkalis, Indonesia 36 D2 1 30N 102 10 E
Bengkulu, Indonesia 36 E2 3 50S 102 12 E
Bengkulu □, Indonesia 36 E2 3 48S 102 16 E
Bengough, Canada 73 D7 49 25N 105 10W
Benguela, Angola 53 G2 12 37S 13 25 E
Benguérua, I., Mozam. 57 C6 21 58S 35 28 E
Beni, Dem. Rep. of the Congo 54 B2 0 30N 29 27 E
Beni →, Bolivia 92 F5 10 23S 65 24W
Beni Mellal, Morocco 50 B4 32 21N 6 21W
Beni Suef, Egypt 51 C12 29 5N 31 6 E
Beniah L., Canada 72 A6 63 23N 112 17W
Benicia, U.S.A. 84 G4 38 3N 122 9W
Benidorm, Spain 19 C5 38 33N 0 9W
Benin ■, Africa 50 G6 10 0N 2 0 E
Benin, Bight of, W. Afr. 50 H6 5 0N 3 0 E
Benin City, Nigeria 50 G7 6 20N 5 31 E
Benitses, Greece 23 A3 39 32N 19 55 E
Benjamin Aceval, Paraguay 94 A4 24 58S 57 34W
Benjamin Constant, Brazil 92 D4 4 40S 70 15W
Benjamin Hill, Mexico 86 A2 30 10N 111 10W
Benkelman, U.S.A. 80 E4 40 3N 101 32W
Bennett, Canada 72 B2 59 56N 134 53W
Bennett, L., Australia 60 D5 22 50S 131 2 E
Bennetta, Ostrov, Russia 27 B15 76 21N 148 56 E
Bennettsville, U.S.A. 77 H6 34 37N 79 41W
Bennington, N.H., U.S.A. 79 D11 43 0N 71 55W
Bennington, Vt., U.S.A. 79 D11 42 53N 73 12W
Benoni, S. Africa 57 D4 26 11S 28 18 E
Benque Viejo, Belize 87 D7 17 5N 89 8W
Benson, Ariz., U.S.A. 83 L8 31 58N 110 18W
Benson, Minn., U.S.A. 80 C7 45 19N 95 36W
Bent, Iran 45 E8 26 20N 59 31 E
Benteng, Indonesia 37 F6 6 10S 120 30 E
Bentinck I., Australia 62 B2 17 3S 139 35 E
Bento Gonçalves, Brazil 95 B5 29 10S 51 31W
Benton, Ark., U.S.A. 81 H8 34 34N 92 35W
Benton, Calif., U.S.A. 84 H8 37 48N 118 32W
Benton, Ill., U.S.A. 80 G10 38 0N 88 55W
Benton, Pa., U.S.A. 79 E8 41 12N 76 23W
Benton Harbor, U.S.A. 76 D2 42 6N 86 27W
Bentonville, U.S.A. 81 G7 36 22N 94 13W
Bentung, Malaysia 39 L3 3 31N 101 55 E
Benue →, Nigeria 50 G7 7 48N 6 46 E
Benxi, China 35 D12 41 20N 123 48 E
Beo, Indonesia 37 D7 4 25N 126 50 E
Beograd, Serbia, Yug. 21 B9 44 50N 20 37 E
Beppu, Japan 31 H5 33 15N 131 30 E
Beqaa Valley = Al Biqā, Lebanon 47 A5 34 10N 36 10 E
Ber Mota, India 42 H3 23 27N 68 34 E
Berach →, India 42 G6 25 15N 75 2 E
Berati, Albania 21 D8 40 43N 19 59 E
Berau, Teluk, Indonesia 37 E8 2 30S 132 30 E
Berber, Sudan 51 E12 18 0N 34 0 E
Berbera, Somali Rep. 46 E4 10 30N 45 2 E
Berbérati, C.A.R. 52 D3 4 15N 15 40 E
Berbice →, Guyana 92 B7 6 20N 57 32W
Berdichev = Berdychiv, Ukraine 17 D15 49 57N 28 30 E
Berdsk, Russia 26 D9 54 47N 83 2 E
Berdyansk, Ukraine 25 E6 46 45N 36 50 E
Berdychiv, Ukraine 17 D15 49 57N 28 30 E
Berea, U.S.A. 76 G3 37 34N 84 17W
Berebere, Indonesia 37 D7 2 25N 128 45 E
Bereda, Somali Rep. 46 E5 11 45N 51 0 E
Berehove, Ukraine 17 D12 48 15N 22 35 E
Berekum, Ghana 50 G5 7 29N 2 34W
Berens →, Canada 73 C9 52 25N 97 2W
Berens I., Canada 73 C9 52 18N 97 18W
Berens River, Canada 73 C9 52 25N 97 0W
Beresford, U.S.A. 80 D6 43 5N 96 47W
Berestechko, Ukraine 17 C13 50 22N 25 5 E
Berevo, Mahajanga, Madag. 57 B7 17 14S 44 17 E
Berevo, Toliara, Madag. 57 B7 19 44S 44 58 E
Bereza, Belarus 17 B13 52 31N 24 51 E
Berezhany, Ukraine 17 D13 49 26N 24 58 E
Berezina = Byarezina →, Belarus 17 B16 52 33N 30 14 E
Bereznik, Russia 24 B7 62 51N 42 40 E
Berezniki, Russia 24 C10 59 24N 56 46 E
Berezovo, Russia 26 C7 64 0N 65 0 E
Berga, Spain 19 A6 42 6N 1 48 E
Bergama, Turkey 21 E12 39 8N 27 11 E
Bérgamo, Italy 18 D8 45 41N 9 43 E
Bergen, Neths. 15 B4 52 40N 4 43 E
Bergen, Norway 9 F11 60 20N 5 20 E
Bergen, U.S.A. 78 C7 43 5N 77 57W
Bergen op Zoom, Neths. 15 C4 51 28N 4 18 E
Bergerac, France 18 D4 44 51N 0 30 E
Bergholz, U.S.A. 78 F4 40 31N 80 53W
Bergisch Gladbach, Germany 15 D7 50 59N 7 8 E
Bergville, S. Africa 57 D4 28 52S 29 18 E
Berhala, Selat, Indonesia 36 E2 1 0S 104 15 E
Berhampore = Baharampur, India 43 G13 24 2N 88 27 E
Berhampur = Brahmapur, India 41 K14 19 15N 84 54 E
Bering Sea, Pac. Oc. 68 C1 58 0N 171 0 E
Bering Strait, Pac. Oc. 68 B3 65 30N 169 0W
Beringovskiy, Russia 27 C18 63 3N 179 19 E
Berisso, Argentina 94 C4 34 56S 57 50W
Berja, Spain 19 D4 36 50N 2 56W
Berkeley, U.S.A. 84 H4 37 52N 122 16W
Berkner I., Antarctica 5 D18 79 30S 50 0W
Berkshire, U.S.A. 79 D8 42 19N 76 11W
Berkshire Downs, U.K. 11 F6 51 33N 1 29W
Berlin, Germany 16 B7 52 30N 13 25 E
Berlin, Md., U.S.A. 76 F8 38 20N 75 13W
Berlin, N.H., U.S.A. 79 B13 44 28N 71 11W
Berlin, N.Y., U.S.A. 79 D11 42 42N 73 23W
Berlin, Wis., U.S.A. 76 D1 43 58N 88 57W
Berlin L., U.S.A. 78 E4 41 3N 81 0W
Bermejo →, Formosa, Argentina 94 B4 26 51S 58 23W
Bermejo →, San Juan, Argentina 94 C2 32 30S 67 30W
Bermen, L., Canada 71 B6 53 35N 68 55W
Bermuda ■, Atl. Oc. 66 F13 32 45N 65 0W
Bern, Switz. 18 C7 46 57N 7 28 E
Bernalillo, U.S.A. 83 J10 35 18N 106 33W
Bernardo de Irigoyen, Argentina 95 B5 26 15S 53 40W
Bernardo O'Higgins □, Chile 94 C1 34 15S 70 45W
Bernardsville, U.S.A. 79 F10 40 43N 74 34W
Bernasconi, Argentina 94 D3 37 55S 63 44W
Bernburg, Germany 16 C6 51 47N 11 44 E
Berne = Bern, Switz. 18 C7 46 57N 7 28 E
Berneray, U.K. 12 D1 57 43N 7 11W
Bernier I., Australia 61 D1 24 50S 113 12 E
Bernina, Piz, Switz. 18 C8 46 20N 9 54 E
Beroroha, Madag. 57 C8 21 40S 45 10 E
Beroun, Czech Rep. 16 D8 49 57N 14 5 E
Berri, Australia 63 E3 34 14S 140 35 E
Berriane, Algeria 50 B6 32 50N 3 46 E
Berrigan, Australia 63 F4 35 38S 145 49 E
Berry, Australia 63 E5 34 46S 150 43 E
Berry, France 18 C5 46 50N 2 0 E
Berry Is., Bahamas 88 A4 25 40N 77 50W
Berryessa L., U.S.A. 84 G4 38 31N 122 6W
Berryville, U.S.A. 81 G8 36 22N 93 34W
Bershad, Ukraine 17 D15 48 22N 29 31 E
Berthold, U.S.A. 80 A4 48 19N 101 44W
Berthoud, U.S.A. 80 E2 40 19N 105 5W
Bertoua, Cameroon 52 D2 4 30N 13 45 E
Bertraghboy B., Ireland 13 C2 53 22N 9 54W
Berwick, U.S.A. 79 E8 41 3N 76 14W
Berwick-upon-Tweed, U.K. 10 B6 55 46N 2 0W
Berwyn Mts., U.K. 10 E4 52 54N 3 26W
Besal, Pakistan 43 B5 35 4N 73 56 E
Besalampy, Madag. 57 B7 16 43S 44 29 E
Besançon, France 18 C7 47 15N 6 2 E
Besar, Indonesia 36 E5 2 40S 116 0 E
Besnard L., Canada 73 B7 55 25N 106 0W
Besni, Turkey 44 B3 37 41N 37 52 E
Besor, N. →, Egypt 47 D3 31 28N 34 22 E
Bessarabiya, Moldova 17 E15 47 0N 28 10 E
Bessarabka = Basarabeasca, Moldova 17 E15 46 21N 28 58 E
Bessemer, Ala., U.S.A. 77 J2 33 24N 86 58W
Bessemer, Mich., U.S.A. 80 B9 46 29N 90 3W
Bessemer, Pa., U.S.A. 78 F4 40 59N 80 30W
Beswick, Australia 60 B5 14 34S 132 53 E
Bet She'an, Israel 47 C4 32 30N 35 30 E
Bet Shemesh, Israel 47 D4 31 44N 35 0 E
Betafo, Madag. 57 B8 19 50S 46 51 E
Betancuria, Canary Is. 22 F5 28 25N 14 3W
Betanzos, Spain 19 A1 43 15N 8 12W
Bétaré Oya, Cameroon 52 C2 5 40N 14 5 E
Bethal, S. Africa 57 D4 26 27S 29 28 E
Bethanien, Namibia 56 D2 26 31S 17 8 E
Bethany, Canada 78 B6 44 11N 78 34W
Bethany, U.S.A. 80 E7 40 16N 94 2W
Bethel, Alaska, U.S.A. 68 B3 60 48N 161 45W
Bethel, Conn., U.S.A. 79 E11 41 22N 73 25W
Bethel, Maine, U.S.A. 79 B14 44 25N 70 47W
Bethel, Vt., U.S.A. 79 C12 43 50N 72 38W
Bethel Park, U.S.A. 78 F4 40 20N 80 1W
Bethlehem = Bayt Lahm, West Bank 47 D4 31 43N 35 12 E
Bethlehem, S. Africa 57 D4 28 14S 28 18 E
Bethlehem, U.S.A. 79 F9 40 37N 75 23W
Bethulie, S. Africa 56 E4 30 30S 25 59 E
Béthune, France 18 A5 50 30N 2 38 E
Betioky, Madag. 57 C7 23 48S 44 20 E
Betong, Thailand 39 K3 5 45N 101 5 E
Betoota, Australia 62 D3 25 45S 140 42 E
Betroka, Madag. 57 C8 23 16S 46 0 E
Betsiamites, Canada 71 C6 48 56N 68 40W
Betsiamites →, Canada 71 C6 48 56N 68 38W
Betsiboka →, Madag. 57 B8 16 3S 46 36 E
Bettendorf, U.S.A. 80 E9 41 32N 90 30W
Bettiah, India 43 F11 26 48N 84 33 E
Betul, India 40 J10 21 58N 77 59 E
Betung, Malaysia 36 D4 1 24N 111 31 E
Betws-y-Coed, U.K. 10 D4 53 5N 3 48W
Beulah, Mich., U.S.A. 76 C2 44 38N 86 6W
Beulah, N. Dak., U.S.A. 80 B4 47 16N 101 47W
Beveren, Belgium 15 C4 51 12N 4 16 E
Beverley, Australia 61 F2 32 9S 116 56 E
Beverley, U.K. 10 D7 53 51N 0 26W
Beverley Hills, U.S.A. 77 L4 28 56N 82 28W
Beverly, U.S.A. 79 D14 42 33N 70 53W
Beverly Hills, U.S.A. 85 L8 34 4N 118 25W
Bewas →, India 43 H8 23 59N 79 21 E
Bexhill, U.K. 11 G8 50 51N 0 29 E
Beyānlū, Iran 44 C5 36 0N 47 51 E
Beyneu, Kazakstan 25 E10 45 18N 55 9 E
Beypazarı, Turkey 25 F5 40 10N 31 56 E
Beyşehir Gölü, Turkey 25 G5 37 41N 31 33 E
Béziers, France 18 E5 43 20N 3 12 E
Bezwada = Vijayawada, India 41 L12 16 31N 80 39 E
Bhabua, India 43 G10 25 3N 83 37 E
Bhachau, India 40 H7 23 20N 70 16 E
Bhadar →, Gujarat, India 42 H5 22 17N 72 20 E
Bhadar →, Gujarat, India 42 J3 21 27N 69 47 E
Bhadarwah, India 43 C6 32 58N 75 46 E
Bhadohi, India 43 G10 25 25N 82 34 E
Bhadra, India 42 E6 29 8N 75 14 E
Bhadrakh, India 41 J15 21 10N 86 30 E
Bhadran, India 42 H5 22 19N 72 6 E
Bhadravati, India 40 N9 13 49N 75 40 E
Bhag, Pakistan 42 E2 29 2N 67 49 E
Bhagalpur, India 43 G12 25 10N 87 0 E
Bhagirathi →, Ut. P., India 43 D8 30 8N 78 35 E
Bhagirathi →, W. Bengal, India 43 H13 23 25N 88 23 E
Bhakkar, Pakistan 42 D4 31 40N 71 5 E
Bhakra Dam, India 42 D7 31 30N 76 45 E
Bhamo, Burma 41 G20 24 15N 97 15 E
Bhandara, India 40 J11 21 5N 79 42 E
Bhanpura, India 42 G6 24 31N 75 44 E
Bhanrer Ra., India 43 H8 23 40N 79 45 E
Bhaptiahi, India 43 F12 26 19N 86 44 E
Bharat = India ■, Asia 40 K11 20 0N 78 0 E
Bharatpur, Mad. P., India 43 H9 23 44N 81 46 E
Bharatpur, Raj., India 42 F7 27 15N 77 30 E
Bharno, India 43 H11 23 14N 84 53 E
Bhatinda, India 42 D6 30 15N 74 57 E
Bhatpara, India 43 H13 22 50N 88 25 E
Bhattu, India 42 E6 29 36N 75 19 E
Bhaun, Pakistan 42 C5 32 55N 72 40 E
Bhaunagar = Bhavnagar, India 40 J8 21 45N 72 10 E
Bhavnagar, India 40 J8 21 45N 72 10 E
Bhawanipatna, India 41 K12 19 55N 80 10 E
Bhawari, India 42 G5 25 42N 73 4 E
Bhayavadar, India 42 J4 21 51N 70 15 E
Bhera, Pakistan 42 C5 32 29N 72 57 E
Bhikangaon, India 42 J6 21 52N 75 57 E
Bhilsa = Vidisha, India 42 H7 23 28N 77 53 E
Bhilwara, India 42 G6 25 25N 74 38 E
Bhima →, India 40 L10 16 25N 77 17 E
Bhimavaram, India 41 L12 16 30N 81 30 E
Bhimbar, Pakistan 43 C6 32 59N 74 3 E
Bhind, India 43 F8 26 30N 78 46 E
Bhinga, India 43 F9 27 43N 81 56 E
Bhinmal, India 42 G5 25 0N 72 15 E
Bhiwandi, India 40 K8 19 20N 73 0 E
Bhiwani, India 42 E7 28 50N 76 9 E
Bhogava →, India 42 H5 22 26N 72 20 E
Bhola, Bangla. 41 H17 22 45N 90 35 E
Bholari, Pakistan 42 G3 25 19N 68 13 E
Bhopal, India 42 H7 23 20N 77 30 E
Bhubaneshwar, India 41 J14 20 15N 85 50 E
Bhuj, India 42 H3 23 15N 69 49 E
Bhusaval, India 40 J9 21 3N 75 46 E
Bhutan ■, Asia 41 F17 27 25N 90 30 E
Biafra, B. of = Bonny, Bight of, Africa 52 D1 3 30N 9 20 E
Biak, Indonesia 37 E9 1 10S 136 6 E
Biała Podlaska, Poland 17 B12 52 4N 23 6 E
Białogard, Poland 16 A8 54 2N 15 58 E
Białystok, Poland 17 B12 53 10N 23 10 E
Biaora, India 42 H7 23 56N 76 56 E
Bīārjmand, Iran 45 B7 36 6N 55 53 E
Biaro, Indonesia 37 D7 2 5N 125 26 E
Biarritz, France 18 E3 43 29N 1 33W
Bibai, Japan 30 C10 43 19N 141 52 E
Bibby I., Canada 73 A10 61 55N 93 0W
Biberach, Germany 16 D5 48 5N 9 47 E
Bibungwa, Dem. Rep. of the Congo 54 C2 2 40S 28 15 E
Bic, Canada 71 C6 48 20N 68 41W
Bicester, U.K. 11 F6 51 54N 1 9W
Bicheno, Australia 62 G4 41 52S 148 18 E
Bichia, India 43 H9 22 27N 80 42 E
Bickerton I., Australia 62 A2 13 45S 136 10 E
Bida, Nigeria 50 G7 9 3N 5 58 E
Bidar, India 40 L10 17 55N 77 35 E
Biddeford, U.S.A. 77 D10 43 30N 70 28W
Bideford, U.K. 11 F3 51 1N 4 13W
Bideford Bay, U.K. 11 F3 51 5N 4 20W
Bidhuna, India 43 F8 26 49N 79 31 E
Bidor, Malaysia 39 K3 4 6N 101 15 E
Bié, Planalto de, Angola 53 G3 12 0S 16 0 E
Bieber, U.S.A. 82 F3 41 7N 121 8W
Biel, Switz. 18 C7 47 8N 7 14 E
Bielefeld, Germany 16 B5 52 1N 8 33 E
Biella, Italy 18 D8 45 34N 8 3 E
Bielsk Podlaski, Poland 17 B12 52 47N 23 12 E
Bielsko-Biała, Poland 17 D10 49 50N 19 2 E
Bien Hoa, Vietnam 39 G6 10 57N 106 49 E
Bienne = Biel, Switz. 18 C7 47 8N 7 14 E
Bienville, L., Canada 70 A5 55 5N 72 40W
Biesiesfontein, S. Africa 56 E2 30 57S 17 58 E
Big →, Canada 71 B8 54 50N 58 55W
Big B., Canada 71 A7 55 43N 60 35W
Big Bear City, U.S.A. 85 L10 34 16N 116 51W
Big Bear Lake, U.S.A. 85 L10 34 15N 116 56W
Big Belt Mts., U.S.A. 82 C8 46 30N 111 25W
Big Bend, Swaziland 57 D5 26 50S 31 58 E
Big Bend National Park, U.S.A. 81 L3 29 20N 103 5W
Big Black →, U.S.A. 81 K9 32 3N 91 4W
Big Blue →, U.S.A. 80 F6 39 35N 96 34W
Big Creek, U.S.A. 84 H7 37 11N 119 14W
Big Cypress National Preserve, U.S.A. 77 M5 26 0N 81 10W
Big Cypress Swamp, U.S.A. 77 M5 26 12N 81 10W
Big Falls, U.S.A. 80 A8 48 12N 93 48W
Big Fork →, U.S.A. 80 A8 48 31N 93 43W
Big Horn Mts. = Bighorn Mts., U.S.A. 82 D10 44 30N 107 30W
Big I., Canada 72 A5 61 7N 116 45W
Big Lake, U.S.A. 81 K4 31 12N 101 28W
Big Moose, U.S.A. 79 C10 43 49N 74 58W
Big Muddy Cr. →, U.S.A. 80 A2 48 8N 104 36W
Big Pine, U.S.A. 84 H8 37 10N 118 17W
Big Piney, U.S.A. 82 E8 42 32N 110 7W
Big Rapids, U.S.A. 76 D3 43 42N 85 29W
Big Rideau L., Canada 79 B8 44 40N 76 15W
Big River, Canada 73 C7 53 50N 107 0W
Big Run, U.S.A. 78 F6 40 57N 78 55W
Big Sable Pt., U.S.A. 76 C2 44 3N 86 1W
Big Salmon →, Canada 72 A2 61 52N 134 55W
Big Sand L., Canada 73 B9 57 45N 99 45W
Big Sandy, U.S.A. 82 B8 48 11N 110 7W
Big Sandy →, U.S.A. 76 F4 38 25N 82 36W
Big Sandy Cr. →, U.S.A. 80 F3 38 7N 102 29W
Big Sioux →, U.S.A. 80 D6 42 29N 96 27W
Big Spring, U.S.A. 81 J4 32 15N 101 28W
Big Stone City, U.S.A. 80 C6 45 18N 96 28W
Big Stone Gap, U.S.A. 77 G4 36 52N 82 47W
Big Stone L., U.S.A. 80 C6 45 30N 96 35W
Big Sur, U.S.A. 84 J5 36 15N 121 48W
Big Timber, U.S.A. 82 D9 45 50N 109 57W

Cárdenas

Cabora Bassa Dam = Cahora Bassa, Reprêsa de, *Mozam.* **55 F3** 15 20S 32 50 E
Caborca, *Mexico* **86 A2** 30 40N 112 10W
Cabot, Mt., *U.S.A.* **79 B13** 44 30N 71 25W
Cabot Hd., *Canada* **78 A3** 45 14N 81 17W
Cabot Str., *Canada* **71 C8** 47 15N 59 40W
Cabra, *Spain* **19 D3** 37 30N 4 28W
Cabrera, *Spain* **22 B9** 39 8N 2 57 E
Cabri, *Canada* **73 C7** 50 35N 108 25W
Cabriel →, *Spain* **19 C5** 39 14N 1 3W
Caçador, *Brazil* **95 B5** 26 47S 51 0W
Čačak, *Serbia, Yug.* **21 C9** 43 54N 20 20 E
Caçapava do Sul, *Brazil* **95 C5** 30 30S 53 30W
Cáceres, *Brazil* **92 G7** 16 5S 57 40W
Cáceres, *Spain* **19 C2** 39 26N 6 23W
Cache Bay, *Canada* **70 C4** 46 22N 80 0W
Cache Cr. →, *U.S.A.* **84 G5** 38 42N 121 42W
Cache Creek, *Canada* **72 C4** 50 48N 121 19W
Cachi, *Argentina* **94 B2** 25 5S 66 10W
Cachimbo, Serra do, *Brazil* **93 E7** 9 30S 55 30W
Cachinal de la Sierra, *Chile* **94 A2** 24 58S 69 32W
Cachoeira, *Brazil* **93 F11** 12 30S 39 0W
Cachoeira do Sul, *Brazil* **95 C5** 30 3S 52 53W
Cachoeiro de Itapemirim, *Brazil* **95 A7** 20 51S 41 7W
Cacoal, *Brazil* **92 F6** 11 32S 61 18W
Cacólo, *Angola* **52 G3** 10 9S 19 21 E
Caconda, *Angola* **53 G3** 13 48S 15 8 E
Caddo, *U.S.A.* **81 H6** 34 7N 96 16W
Cader Idris, *U.K.* **11 E4** 52 42N 3 53W
Cadereyta, *Mexico* **86 B5** 25 36N 100 0W
Cadibarrawirracanna, L., *Australia* **63 D2** 28 52S 135 27 E
Cadillac, *U.S.A.* **76 C3** 44 15N 85 24W
Cadiz, *Phil.* **37 B6** 10 57N 123 15 E
Cádiz, *Spain* **19 D2** 36 30N 6 20W
Cadiz, *Calif., U.S.A.* **85 L11** 34 30N 115 28W
Cadiz, *Ohio, U.S.A.* **78 F4** 40 22N 81 0W
Cádiz, G. de, *Spain* **19 D2** 36 40N 7 0W
Cadiz L., *U.S.A.* **83 J6** 34 18N 115 24W
Cadney Park, *Australia* **63 D1** 27 55S 134 3 E
Cadomin, *Canada* **72 C5** 53 2N 117 20W
Cadotte Lake, *Canada* **72 B5** 56 26N 116 23W
Cadoux, *Australia* **61 F2** 30 46S 117 7 E
Caen, *France* **18 B3** 49 10N 0 22W
Caernarfon, *U.K.* **10 D3** 53 8N 4 16W
Caernarfon B., *U.K.* **10 D3** 53 4N 4 40W
Caernarvon = Caernarfon, *U.K.* **10 D3** 53 8N 4 16W
Caerphilly, *U.K.* **11 F4** 51 35N 3 13W
Caerphilly □, *U.K.* **11 F4** 51 37N 3 12W
Caesarea, *Israel* **47 C3** 32 30N 34 53 E
Caetité, *Brazil* **93 F10** 13 50S 42 32W
Cafayate, *Argentina* **94 B2** 26 2S 66 0W
Cafu, *Angola* **56 B2** 16 30S 15 8 E
Cagayan de Oro, *Phil.* **37 C6** 8 30N 124 40 E
Cagayan Is., *Phil.* **37 C5** 9 40N 121 16 E
Cágliari, *Italy* **20 E3** 39 13N 9 7 E
Cágliari, G. di, *Italy* **20 E3** 39 8N 9 11 E
Caguán →, *Colombia* **92 D4** 0 8S 74 18W
Caguas, *Puerto Rico* **89 C6** 18 14N 66 2W
Caha Mts., *Ireland* **13 E2** 51 45N 9 40W
Cahama, *Angola* **56 B1** 16 17S 14 19 E
Caher, *Ireland* **13 D4** 52 22N 7 56W
Caherciveen, *Ireland* **13 E1** 51 56N 10 14W
Cahora Bassa, Reprêsa de, *Mozam.* **55 F3** 15 20S 32 50 E
Cahore Pt., *Ireland* **13 D5** 52 33N 6 12W
Cahors, *France* **18 D4** 44 27N 1 27 E
Cahul, *Moldova* **17 F15** 45 50N 28 15 E
Cai Nuoc, *Vietnam* **39 H5** 8 56N 105 1 E
Caia, *Mozam.* **55 F4** 17 51S 35 24 E
Caianda, *Angola* **55 E1** 11 2S 23 31 E
Caibarién, *Cuba* **88 B4** 22 30N 79 30W
Caicara, *Venezuela* **92 B5** 7 38N 66 10W
Caicó, *Brazil* **93 E11** 6 20S 37 0W
Caicos Is., *W. Indies* **89 B5** 21 40N 71 40W
Caicos Passage, *W. Indies* **89 B5** 22 45N 72 45W
Caird Coast, *Antarctica* **5 D1** 75 0S 25 0W
Cairn Gorm, *U.K.* **12 D5** 57 7N 3 39W
Cairngorm Mts., *U.K.* **12 D5** 57 6N 3 42W
Cairnryan, *U.K.* **12 G3** 54 59N 5 1W
Cairns, *Australia* **62 B4** 16 57S 145 45 E
Cairns L., *Canada* **73 C10** 51 42N 94 30W
Cairo = El Qâhira, *Egypt* **51 B12** 30 1N 31 14 E
Cairo, *Ga., U.S.A.* **77 K3** 30 52N 84 13W
Cairo, *Ill., U.S.A.* **81 G10** 37 0N 89 11W
Cairo, *N.Y., U.S.A.* **79 D11** 42 18N 74 0W
Caithness, Ord of, *U.K.* **12 C5** 58 8N 3 36W
Cajamarca, *Peru* **92 E3** 7 5S 78 28W
Cajàzeiras, *Brazil* **93 E11** 6 52S 38 30W
Cala d'Or, *Spain* **22 B10** 39 23N 3 14 E
Cala en Porter, *Spain* **22 B11** 39 52N 4 8 E
Cala Figuera, C. de, *Spain* **22 B9** 39 27N 2 31 E
Cala Forcat, *Spain* **22 B10** 40 0N 3 47 E
Cala Major, *Spain* **22 B9** 39 33N 2 37 E
Cala Mezquida = Sa Mesquida, *Spain* **22 B11** 39 55N 4 16 E
Cala Millor, *Spain* **22 B10** 39 35N 3 22 E
Cala Ratjada, *Spain* **22 B10** 39 43N 3 27 E
Cala Santa Galdana, *Spain* **22 B10** 39 56N 3 58 E
Calabar, *Nigeria* **50 H7** 4 57N 8 20 E
Calabogie, *Canada* **79 A8** 45 18N 76 43W
Calabozo, *Venezuela* **92 B5** 9 0N 67 28W
Calábria □, *Italy* **20 E7** 39 0N 16 30 E
Calafate, *Argentina* **96 G2** 50 19S 72 15W
Calahorra, *Spain* **19 A5** 42 18N 1 59W
Calais, *France* **18 A4** 50 57N 1 56 E
Calais, *U.S.A.* **77 C12** 45 11N 67 17W
Calalaste, Cord. de, *Argentina* **94 B2** 25 0S 67 0W
Calama, *Brazil* **92 E6** 8 0S 62 50W
Calama, *Chile* **94 A2** 22 30S 68 55W
Calamar, *Colombia* **92 A4** 10 15N 74 55W
Calamian Group, *Phil.* **37 B5** 11 50N 119 55 E
Calamocha, *Spain* **19 B5** 40 50N 1 17W
Calang, *Indonesia* **36 D1** 4 37N 95 37 E
Calapan, *Phil.* **37 B6** 13 25N 121 7 E
Călăraşi, *Romania* **17 F14** 44 12N 27 20 E
Calatayud, *Spain* **19 B5** 41 20N 1 40W
Calauag, *Phil.* **37 B6** 13 55N 122 15 E
Calavite, C., *Phil.* **37 B6** 13 26N 120 20 E
Calbayog, *Phil.* **37 B6** 12 4N 124 38 E
Calca, *Peru* **92 F4** 13 22S 72 0W
Calcasieu L., *U.S.A.* **81 L8** 29 55N 93 18W
Calcutta = Kolkata, *India* **43 H13** 22 36N 88 24 E
Calcutta, *U.S.A.* **78 F4** 40 40N 80 34W
Caldas da Rainha, *Portugal* **19 C1** 39 24N 9 8W
Calder →, *U.K.* **10 D6** 53 44N 1 22W
Caldera, *Chile* **94 B1** 27 5S 70 55W
Caldwell, *Idaho, U.S.A.* **82 E5** 43 40N 116 41W
Caldwell, *Kans., U.S.A.* **81 G6** 37 2N 97 37W
Caldwell, *Tex., U.S.A.* **81 K6** 30 32N 96 42W
Caledon, *S. Africa* **56 E2** 34 14S 19 26 E
Caledon →, *S. Africa* **56 E4** 30 31S 26 5 E
Caledon B., *Australia* **62 A2** 12 45S 137 0 E
Caledonia, *Canada* **78 C5** 43 7N 79 58W
Caledonia, *U.S.A.* **78 D7** 42 58N 77 51W
Calemba, *Angola* **56 B2** 16 0S 15 44 E
Calen, *Australia* **62 C4** 20 56S 148 48 E
Caletones, *Chile* **94 C1** 34 6S 70 27W
Calexico, *U.S.A.* **85 N11** 32 40N 115 30W
Calf of Man, *U.K.* **10 C3** 54 3N 4 48W
Calgary, *Canada* **72 C6** 51 0N 114 10W
Calheta, *Madeira* **22 D2** 32 44N 17 11W
Calhoun, *U.S.A.* **77 H3** 34 30N 84 57W
Cali, *Colombia* **92 C3** 3 25N 76 35W
Calicut, *India* **40 P9** 11 15N 75 43 E
Caliente, *U.S.A.* **83 H6** 37 37N 114 31W
California, *Mo., U.S.A.* **80 F8** 38 38N 92 34W
California, *Pa., U.S.A.* **78 F5** 40 4N 79 54W
California □, *U.S.A.* **84 H7** 37 30N 119 30W
California, Baja, *Mexico* **86 A1** 32 10N 115 12W
California, Baja, T.N. = Baja California □, *Mexico* **86 B2** 30 0N 115 0W
California, Baja, T.S. = Baja California Sur □, *Mexico* **86 B2** 25 50N 111 50W
California, G. de, *Mexico* **86 B2** 27 0N 111 0W
California City, *U.S.A.* **85 K9** 35 10N 117 55W
California Hot Springs, *U.S.A.* **85 K8** 35 51N 118 41W
Calingasta, *Argentina* **94 C2** 31 15S 69 30W
Calipatria, *U.S.A.* **85 M11** 33 8N 115 31W
Calistoga, *U.S.A.* **84 G4** 38 35N 122 35W
Calitzdorp, *S. Africa* **56 E3** 33 33S 21 42 E
Callabonna, L., *Australia* **63 D3** 29 40S 140 5 E
Callan, *Ireland* **13 D4** 52 32N 7 24W
Callander, *U.K.* **12 E4** 56 15N 4 13W
Callao, *Peru* **92 F3** 12 0S 77 0W
Calles, *Mexico* **87 C5** 23 2N 98 42W
Callicoon, *U.S.A.* **79 E9** 41 46N 75 3W
Calling Lake, *Canada* **72 B6** 55 15N 113 12W
Calliope, *Australia* **62 C5** 24 0S 151 16 E
Calne, *U.K.* **11 F6** 51 26N 2 0W
Calola, *Angola* **56 B2** 16 25S 17 48 E
Caloundra, *Australia* **63 D5** 26 45S 153 10 E
Calpella, *U.S.A.* **84 F3** 39 14N 123 12W
Calpine, *U.S.A.* **84 F6** 39 40N 120 27W
Calstock, *Canada* **70 C3** 49 47N 84 9W
Caltagirone, *Italy* **20 F6** 37 14N 14 31 E
Caltanissetta, *Italy* **20 F6** 37 29N 14 4 E
Calulo, *Angola* **52 G2** 10 1S 14 56 E
Caluquembe, *Angola* **53 G2** 13 47S 14 44 E
Calvert →, *Australia* **62 B2** 16 17S 137 44 E
Calvert I., *Canada* **72 C3** 51 30N 128 0W
Calvert Ra., *Australia* **60 D3** 24 0S 122 30 E
Calvi, *France* **18 E8** 42 34N 8 45 E
Calvià, *Spain* **19 C7** 39 34N 2 31 E
Calvillo, *Mexico* **86 C4** 21 51N 102 43W
Calvinia, *S. Africa* **56 E2** 31 28S 19 45 E
Calwa, *U.S.A.* **84 J7** 36 42N 119 46W
Cam →, *U.K.* **11 E8** 52 21N 0 16 E
Cam Lam, *Vietnam* **39 G7** 11 54N 109 10 E
Cam Ranh, *Vietnam* **39 G7** 11 54N 109 12 E
Cam Xuyen, *Vietnam* **38 C6** 18 15N 106 0 E
Camabatela, *Angola* **52 F3** 8 20S 15 26 E
Camacha, *Madeira* **22 D3** 32 41N 16 49W
Camacho, *Mexico* **86 C4** 24 25N 102 18W
Camacupa, *Angola* **53 G3** 11 58S 17 22 E
Camagüey, *Cuba* **88 B4** 21 20N 78 0W
Camaná, *Peru* **92 G4** 16 30S 72 50W
Camanche Reservoir, *U.S.A.* **84 G6** 38 14N 121 1W
Camaquã, *Brazil* **95 C5** 30 51S 51 49W
Camaquã →, *Brazil* **95 C5** 31 17S 51 47W
Câmara de Lobos, *Madeira* **22 D3** 32 39N 16 59W
Camargo, *Mexico* **87 B5** 26 19N 98 50W
Camargue, *France* **18 E6** 43 34N 4 34 E
Camarillo, *U.S.A.* **85 L7** 34 13N 119 2W
Camarón, C., *Honduras* **88 C2** 16 0N 85 5W
Camarones, *Argentina* **96 E3** 44 50S 65 40W
Camas, *U.S.A.* **84 E4** 45 35N 122 24W
Camas Valley, *U.S.A.* **82 E2** 43 2N 123 40W
Camballin, *Australia* **60 C3** 17 59S 124 12 E
Cambará, *Brazil* **95 A5** 23 2S 50 5W
Cambay = Khambhat, *India* **42 H5** 22 23N 72 33 E
Cambay, G. of = Khambhat, G. of, *India* **40 J8** 20 45N 72 30 E
Cambodia ■, *Asia* **38 F5** 12 15N 105 0 E
Camborne, *U.K.* **11 G2** 50 12N 5 19W
Cambrai, *France* **18 A5** 50 11N 3 14 E
Cambria, *U.S.A.* **84 K5** 35 34N 121 5W
Cambrian Mts., *U.K.* **11 E4** 52 3N 3 57W
Cambridge, *Canada* **78 C4** 43 23N 80 15W
Cambridge, *Jamaica* **88 C4** 18 18N 77 54W
Cambridge, *N.Z.* **59 G5** 37 54S 175 29 E
Cambridge, *U.K.* **11 E8** 52 12N 0 8 E
Cambridge, *Mass., U.S.A.* **79 D13** 42 22N 71 6W
Cambridge, *Md., U.S.A.* **75 C11** 38 34N 76 5W
Cambridge, *Minn., U.S.A.* **80 C8** 45 34N 93 13W
Cambridge, *N.Y., U.S.A.* **79 C11** 43 2N 73 22W
Cambridge, *Nebr., U.S.A.* **80 E4** 40 17N 100 10W
Cambridge, *Ohio, U.S.A.* **78 F3** 40 2N 81 35W
Cambridge Bay = Ikaluktutiak, *Canada* **68 B9** 69 10N 105 0W
Cambridge G., *Australia* **60 B4** 14 55S 128 15 E
Cambridge Springs, *U.S.A.* **78 E4** 41 48N 80 4W
Cambridgeshire □, *U.K.* **11 E7** 52 25N 0 7W
Cambuci, *Brazil* **95 A7** 21 35S 41 55W
Cambundi-Catembo, *Angola* **52 G3** 10 10S 17 35 E
Camden, *Ala., U.S.A.* **77 K2** 31 59N 87 17W
Camden, *Ark., U.S.A.* **81 J8** 33 35N 92 50W
Camden, *Maine, U.S.A.* **77 C11** 44 13N 69 4W
Camden, *N.J., U.S.A.* **79 G9** 39 56N 75 7W
Camden, *N.Y., U.S.A.* **79 C9** 43 20N 75 45W
Camden, *S.C., U.S.A.* **77 H5** 34 16N 80 36W
Camden Sd., *Australia* **60 C3** 15 27S 124 25 E
Camdenton, *U.S.A.* **81 F8** 38 1N 92 45W
Cameron, *Ariz., U.S.A.* **83 J8** 35 53N 111 25W
Cameron, *La., U.S.A.* **81 L8** 29 48N 93 20W
Cameron, *Mo., U.S.A.* **80 F7** 39 44N 94 14W
Cameron, *Tex., U.S.A.* **81 K6** 30 51N 96 59W
Cameron Highlands, *Malaysia* **39 K3** 4 27N 101 22 E
Cameron Hills, *Canada* **72 B5** 59 48N 118 0W
Cameroon ■, *Africa* **52 C2** 6 0N 12 30 E
Cameroun, Mt., *Cameroon* **52 D1** 4 13N 9 10 E
Cametá, *Brazil* **93 D9** 2 12S 49 30W
Camiguin I., *Phil.* **37 C6** 18 56N 121 55 E
Camilla, *U.S.A.* **77 K3** 31 14N 84 12W
Caminha, *Portugal* **19 B1** 41 50N 8 50W
Camino, *U.S.A.* **84 G6** 38 44N 120 41W
Camira Creek, *Australia* **63 D5** 29 15S 152 58 E
Cammal, *U.S.A.* **78 E7** 41 24N 77 28W
Camocim, *Brazil* **93 D10** 2 55S 40 50W
Camooweal, *Australia* **62 B2** 19 56S 138 7 E
Camopi, *Fr. Guiana* **93 C8** 3 12N 52 17W
Camp Borden, *Canada* **78 B5** 44 18N 79 56W
Camp Hill, *U.S.A.* **78 F8** 40 14N 76 55W
Camp Nelson, *U.S.A.* **85 J8** 36 8N 118 39W
Camp Pendleton, *U.S.A.* **85 M9** 33 16N 117 23W
Camp Verde, *U.S.A.* **83 J8** 34 34N 111 51W
Camp Wood, *U.S.A.* **81 L5** 29 40N 100 1W
Campana, *Argentina* **94 C4** 34 10S 58 55W
Campana, I., *Chile* **96 F1** 48 20S 75 20W
Campanário, *Madeira* **22 D2** 32 39N 17 2W
Campânia □, *Italy* **20 D6** 41 0N 14 30 E
Campbell, *S. Africa* **56 D3** 28 48S 23 44 E
Campbell, *Calif., U.S.A.* **84 H5** 37 17N 121 57W
Campbell, *Ohio, U.S.A.* **78 E4** 41 5N 80 37W
Campbell I., *Pac. Oc.* **64 N8** 52 30S 169 0 E
Campbell L., *Canada* **73 A7** 63 14N 106 55W
Campbell River, *Canada* **72 C3** 50 5N 125 20W
Campbell Town, *Australia* **62 G4** 41 52S 147 30 E
Campbellford, *Canada* **78 B7** 44 18N 77 48W
Campbellpur, *Pakistan* **42 C5** 33 46N 72 26 E
Campbellsville, *U.S.A.* **76 G3** 37 21N 85 20W
Campbellton, *Canada* **71 C6** 47 57N 66 43W
Campbelltown, *Australia* **63 E5** 34 4S 150 49 E
Campbeltown, *U.K.* **12 F3** 55 26N 5 36W
Campeche, *Mexico* **87 D6** 19 50N 90 32W
Campeche □, *Mexico* **87 D6** 19 50N 90 32W
Campeche, Golfo de, *Mexico* **87 D6** 19 30N 93 0W
Camperdown, *Australia* **63 F3** 38 14S 143 9 E
Camperville, *Canada* **73 C8** 51 59N 100 9W
Câmpina, *Romania* **17 F13** 45 10N 25 45 E
Campina Grande, *Brazil* **93 E11** 7 20S 35 47W
Campinas, *Brazil* **95 A6** 22 50S 47 0W
Campo Grande, *Brazil* **93 H8** 20 25S 54 40W
Campo Maíor, *Brazil* **93 D10** 4 50S 42 12W
Campo Mourão, *Brazil* **95 A5** 24 3S 52 22W
Campobasso, *Italy* **20 D6** 41 34N 14 39 E
Campos, *Brazil* **95 A7** 21 50S 41 20W
Campos Belos, *Brazil* **93 F9** 13 10S 47 3W
Campos del Puerto, *Spain* **22 B10** 39 26N 3 1 E
Campos Novos, *Brazil* **95 B5** 27 21S 51 50W
Camptonville, *U.S.A.* **84 F5** 39 27N 121 3W
Camptown, *U.S.A.* **79 E8** 41 44N 76 14W
Câmpulung, *Romania* **17 F13** 45 17N 25 3 E
Camrose, *Canada* **72 C6** 53 0N 112 50W
Camsell Portage, *Canada* **73 B7** 59 37N 109 15W
Çan, *Turkey* **21 D12** 40 2N 27 3 E
Can Clavo, *Spain* **22 C7** 38 57N 1 27 E
Can Creu, *Spain* **22 C7** 38 58N 1 28 E
Can Gio, *Vietnam* **39 G6** 10 25N 106 58 E
Can Tho, *Vietnam* **39 G5** 10 2N 105 46 E
Canaan, *U.S.A.* **79 D11** 42 2N 73 20W
Canada ■, *N. Amer.* **68 C10** 60 0N 100 0W
Cañada de Gómez, *Argentina* **94 C3** 32 40S 61 30W
Canadian, *U.S.A.* **81 H4** 35 55N 100 23W
Canadian →, *U.S.A.* **81 H7** 35 28N 95 3W
Canajoharie, *U.S.A.* **79 D10** 42 54N 74 35W
Çanakkale, *Turkey* **21 D12** 40 8N 26 24 E
Çanakkale Boğazı, *Turkey* **21 D12** 40 17N 26 32 E
Canal Flats, *Canada* **72 C5** 50 10N 115 48W
Canalejas, *Argentina* **94 D2** 35 15S 66 34W
Canals, *Argentina* **94 C3** 33 35S 62 53W
Canandaigua, *U.S.A.* **78 D7** 42 54N 77 17W
Canandaigua L., *U.S.A.* **78 D7** 42 47N 77 19W
Cananea, *Mexico* **86 A2** 31 0N 110 20W
Canarias, Is., *Atl. Oc.* **22 F4** 28 30N 16 0W
Canarreos, Arch. de los, *Cuba* **88 B3** 21 35N 81 40W
Canary Is. = Canarias, Is., *Atl. Oc.* **22 F4** 28 30N 16 0W
Canaseraga, *U.S.A.* **78 D7** 42 27N 77 45W
Canatlán, *Mexico* **86 C4** 24 31N 104 47W
Canaveral, C., *U.S.A.* **77 L5** 28 27N 80 32W
Canavieiras, *Brazil* **93 G11** 15 39S 39 0W
Canberra, *Australia* **63 F4** 35 15S 149 8 E
Canby, *Calif., U.S.A.* **82 F3** 41 27N 120 52W
Canby, *Minn., U.S.A.* **80 C6** 44 43N 96 16W
Canby, *Oreg., U.S.A.* **84 E4** 45 16N 122 42W
Cancún, *Mexico* **87 C7** 21 8N 86 44W
Candelaria, *Argentina* **95 B4** 27 29S 55 44W
Candelaria, *Canary Is.* **22 F3** 28 22N 16 22W
Candelo, *Australia* **63 F4** 36 47S 149 43 E
Candia = Iráklion, *Greece* **23 D7** 35 20N 25 12 E
Candle L., *Canada* **73 C7** 53 50N 105 18W
Candlemas I., *Antarctica* **5 B1** 57 3S 26 40W
Cando, *U.S.A.* **80 A5** 48 32N 99 12W
Canea = Khaniá, *Greece* **23 D6** 35 30N 24 4 E
Canelones, *Uruguay* **95 C4** 34 32S 56 17W
Cañete, *Chile* **94 D1** 37 50S 73 30W
Cañete, *Peru* **92 F3** 13 8S 76 30W
Cangas de Narcea, *Spain* **19 A2** 43 10N 6 32W
Canguaretama, *Brazil* **93 E11** 6 20S 35 5W
Canguçu, *Brazil* **95 C5** 31 22S 52 43W
Canguçu, Serra do, *Brazil* **95 C5** 31 20S 52 40W
Cangzhou, *China* **34 E9** 38 19N 116 52 E
Caniapiscau →, *Canada* **71 A6** 56 40N 69 30W
Caniapiscau Rés. de, *Canada* **71 B6** 54 10N 69 55W
Canicattì, *Italy* **20 F5** 37 21N 13 51 E
Canim Lake, *Canada* **72 C4** 51 47N 120 54W
Canindeyu □, *Paraguay* **95 A5** 24 10S 55 0W
Canisteo, *U.S.A.* **78 D7** 42 16N 77 36W
Canisteo →, *U.S.A.* **78 D7** 42 7N 77 8W
Cañitas, *Mexico* **86 C4** 23 36N 102 43W
Çankırı, *Turkey* **25 F5** 40 40N 33 37 E
Cankuzo, *Burundi* **54 C3** 3 10S 30 31 E
Canmore, *Canada* **72 C5** 51 7N 115 18W
Cann River, *Australia* **63 F4** 37 35S 149 7 E
Canna, *U.K.* **12 D2** 57 3N 6 33W
Cannanore, *India* **40 P9** 11 53N 75 27 E
Cannes, *France* **18 E7** 43 32N 7 1 E
Canning Town = Port Canning, *India* **43 H13** 22 23N 88 40 E
Cannington, *Canada* **78 B5** 44 20N 79 2W
Cannock, *U.K.* **11 E5** 52 41N 2 1W
Cannon Ball →, *U.S.A.* **80 B4** 46 20N 100 38W
Cannondale Mt., *Australia* **62 D4** 25 13S 148 57 E
Cannonsville Reservoir, *U.S.A.* **79 D9** 42 4N 75 22W
Cannonvale, *Australia* **62 C4** 20 17S 148 43 E
Canoas, *Brazil* **95 B5** 29 56S 51 11W
Canoe L., *Canada* **73 B7** 55 10N 108 15W
Canon City, *U.S.A.* **80 F2** 38 27N 105 14W
Canora, *Canada* **73 C8** 51 40N 102 30W
Canowindra, *Australia* **63 E4** 33 35S 148 38 E
Canso, *Canada* **71 C7** 45 20N 61 0W
Cantabria □, *Spain* **19 A4** 43 10N 4 0W
Cantabrian Mts. = Cantábrica, Cordillera, *Spain* **19 A3** 43 0N 5 10W
Cantábrica, Cordillera, *Spain* **19 A3** 43 0N 5 10W
Cantal, Plomb du, *France* **18 D5** 45 3N 2 45 E
Canterbury, *Australia* **62 D3** 25 23S 141 53 E
Canterbury, *U.K.* **11 F9** 51 16N 1 6 E
Canterbury □, *N.Z.* **59 K3** 43 45S 171 19 E
Canterbury Bight, *N.Z.* **59 L3** 44 16S 171 55 E
Canterbury Plains, *N.Z.* **59 K3** 43 55S 171 22 E
Cantil, *U.S.A.* **85 K9** 35 18N 117 58W
Canton = Guangzhou, *China* **33 D6** 23 5N 113 10 E
Canton, *Ga., U.S.A.* **77 H3** 34 14N 84 29W
Canton, *Ill., U.S.A.* **80 E9** 40 33N 90 2W
Canton, *Miss., U.S.A.* **81 J9** 32 37N 90 2W
Canton, *Mo., U.S.A.* **80 E9** 40 8N 91 32W
Canton, *N.Y., U.S.A.* **79 B9** 44 36N 75 10W
Canton, *Ohio, U.S.A.* **78 F3** 40 48N 81 23W
Canton, *Pa., U.S.A.* **78 E8** 41 39N 76 51W
Canton, *S. Dak., U.S.A.* **80 D6** 43 18N 96 35W
Canton L., *U.S.A.* **81 G5** 36 6N 98 35W
Canudos, *Brazil* **92 E7** 7 13S 58 5W
Canumã →, *Brazil* **92 D7** 3 55S 59 10W
Canutama, *Brazil* **92 E6** 6 30S 64 20W
Canutillo, *U.S.A.* **83 L10** 31 55N 106 36W
Canvey, *U.K.* **11 F8** 51 31N 0 37 E
Canyon, *U.S.A.* **81 H4** 34 59N 101 55W
Canyonlands National Park, *U.S.A.* **83 G9** 38 15N 110 0W
Canyonville, *U.S.A.* **82 E2** 42 56N 123 17W
Cao He →, *China* **35 D13** 40 10N 124 32 E
Cao Lanh, *Vietnam* **39 G5** 10 27N 105 38 E
Cao Xian, *China* **34 G8** 34 50N 115 35 E
Cap-aux-Meules, *Canada* **71 C7** 47 23N 61 52W
Cap-Chat, *Canada* **71 C6** 49 6N 66 40W
Cap-de-la-Madeleine, *Canada* **70 C5** 46 22N 72 31W
Cap-Haïtien, *Haiti* **89 C5** 19 40N 72 20W
Capac, *U.S.A.* **78 C2** 43 1N 82 56W
Capanaparo →, *Venezuela* **92 B5** 7 1N 67 7W
Cape →, *Australia* **62 C4** 20 59S 146 51 E
Cape Barren I., *Australia* **62 G4** 40 25S 148 15 E
Cape Breton Highlands Nat. Park, *Canada* **71 C7** 46 50N 60 40W
Cape Breton I., *Canada* **71 C7** 46 0N 60 30W
Cape Charles, *U.S.A.* **76 G8** 37 16N 76 1W
Cape Coast, *Ghana* **50 G5** 5 5N 1 15W
Cape Coral, *U.S.A.* **77 M5** 26 33N 81 57W
Cape Dorset, *Canada* **69 B12** 64 14N 76 32W
Cape Fear →, *U.S.A.* **77 H6** 33 53N 78 1W
Cape Girardeau, *U.S.A.* **81 G10** 37 19N 89 32W
Cape May, *U.S.A.* **76 F8** 38 56N 74 56W
Cape May Point, *U.S.A.* **75 C12** 38 56N 74 58W
Cape Province □, *S. Africa* **53 L3** 32 0S 23 0 E
Cape Tormentine, *Canada* **71 C7** 46 8N 63 47W
Cape Town, *S. Africa* **56 E2** 33 55S 18 22 E
Cape Verde Is. ■, *Atl. Oc.* **49 E1** 17 10N 25 20W
Cape Vincent, *U.S.A.* **79 B8** 44 8N 76 20W
Cape York Peninsula, *Australia* **62 A3** 12 0S 142 30 E
Capela, *Brazil* **93 F11** 10 30S 37 0W
Capella, *Australia* **62 C4** 23 2S 148 1 E
Capenda Camulemba, *Angola* **52 F3** 9 24S 18 27 E
Capim →, *Brazil* **93 D9** 1 40S 47 47W
Capitan, *U.S.A.* **83 K11** 33 35N 105 35W
Capitol Reef National Park, *U.S.A.* **83 G8** 38 15N 111 10W
Capitola, *U.S.A.* **84 J5** 36 59N 121 57W
Capoche →, *Mozam.* **55 F3** 15 35S 33 0 E
Capraia, *Italy* **18 E8** 43 2N 9 50 E
Capreol, *Canada* **70 C3** 46 43N 80 56W
Capri, *Italy* **20 D6** 40 33N 14 14 E
Capricorn Group, *Australia* **62 C5** 23 30S 151 55 E
Capricorn Ra., *Australia* **60 D2** 23 20S 116 50 E
Caprivi Strip, *Namibia* **56 B3** 18 0S 23 0 E
Captain's Flat, *Australia* **63 F4** 35 35S 149 27 E
Caquetá →, *Colombia* **92 D5** 1 15S 69 15W
Caracal, *Romania* **17 F13** 44 8N 24 22 E
Caracas, *Venezuela* **92 A5** 10 30N 66 55W
Caracol, *Brazil* **94 A4** 22 18S 57 1W
Caracol, *Piauí, Brazil* **93 E10** 9 15S 43 22W
Carajas, *Brazil* **93 E8** 6 5S 50 23W
Carajás, Serra dos, *Brazil* **93 E8** 6 0S 51 30W
Carangola, *Brazil* **95 A7** 20 44S 42 5W
Caransebeş, *Romania* **17 F12** 45 28N 22 18 E
Caraquet, *Canada* **71 C6** 47 48N 64 57W
Caras, *Peru* **92 E3** 9 3S 77 47W
Caratasca, L., *Honduras* **88 C3** 15 20N 83 40W
Caratinga, *Brazil* **93 G10** 19 50S 42 10W
Caraúbas, *Brazil* **93 E11** 5 43S 37 33W
Caravaca = Caravaca de la Cruz, *Spain* **19 C5** 38 8N 1 52W
Caravaca de la Cruz, *Spain* **19 C5** 38 8N 1 52W
Caravelas, *Brazil* **93 G11** 17 45S 39 15W
Caraveli, *Peru* **92 G4** 15 45S 73 25W
Caràzinho, *Brazil* **95 B5** 28 16S 52 46W
Carballo, *Spain* **19 A1** 43 13N 8 41W
Carberry, *Canada* **73 D9** 49 50N 99 25W
Carbó, *Mexico* **86 B2** 29 42N 110 58W
Carbonara, C., *Italy* **20 E3** 39 6N 9 31 E
Carbondale, *Colo., U.S.A.* **82 G10** 39 24N 107 13W
Carbondale, *Ill., U.S.A.* **81 G10** 37 44N 89 13W
Carbondale, *Pa., U.S.A.* **79 E9** 41 35N 75 30W
Carbonear, *Canada* **71 C9** 47 42N 53 13W
Carbónia, *Italy* **20 E3** 39 10N 8 30 E
Carcajou, *Canada* **72 B5** 57 47N 117 6W
Carcarana →, *Argentina* **94 C3** 32 27S 60 48W
Carcasse, C., *Haiti* **89 C5** 18 30N 74 28W
Carcassonne, *France* **18 E5** 43 13N 2 20 E
Carcross, *Canada* **72 A2** 60 13N 134 45W
Cardamon Hills, *India* **40 Q10** 9 30N 77 15 E
Cárdenas, *Cuba* **88 B3** 23 0N 81 30W
Cárdenas, *Mexico* **87 C5** 22 0N 99 41W

Cárdenas

Cárdenas, Tabasco, Mexico 87 D6 17 59N 93 21W
Cardiff, U.K. 11 F4 51 29N 3 10W
Cardiff □, U.K. 11 F4 51 31N 3 12W
Cardiff-by-the-Sea, U.S.A. 85 M9 33 1N 117 17W
Cardigan, U.K. 11 E3 52 5N 4 40W
Cardigan B., U.K. 11 E3 52 30N 4 30W
Cardinal, Canada 79 B9 44 47N 75 23W
Cardona, Uruguay 94 C4 33 53S 57 18W
Cardoso, Ilha do, Brazil 95 B5 25 8S 47 58W
Cardston, Canada 72 D6 49 15N 113 20W
Cardwell, Australia 62 B4 18 14S 146 2 E
Careen L., Canada 73 B7 57 0N 108 11W
Carei, Romania 17 E12 47 40N 22 29 E
Careme = Ciremai, Indonesia 37 G13 6 55S 108 27 E
Carey, U.S.A. 82 E7 43 19N 113 57W
Carey, L., Australia 61 E3 29 0S 122 15 E
Carey L., Canada 73 A8 62 12N 102 55W
Carhué, Argentina 94 D3 37 10S 62 50W
Caria, Turkey 21 F13 37 20N 28 10 E
Cariacica, Brazil 93 H10 20 16S 40 25W
Caribbean Sea, W. Indies 89 D5 15 0N 75 0W
Cariboo Mts., Canada 72 C4 53 0N 121 0W
Caribou, U.S.A. 77 B12 46 52N 68 1W
Caribou →, Man., Canada 73 B10 59 20N 94 44W
Caribou →, N.W.T., Canada 72 A3 61 27N 125 45W
Caribou I., Canada 70 C2 47 22N 85 49W
Caribou Is., Canada 72 A6 61 55N 113 15W
Caribou L., Man., Canada 73 B9 59 21N 96 10W
Caribou L., Ont., Canada 70 B2 50 25N 89 5W
Caribou Mts., Canada 72 B5 59 12N 115 40W
Carichic, Mexico 86 B3 27 56N 107 3W
Carillo, Mexico 86 B4 26 50N 103 55W
Carinda, Australia 63 E4 30 28S 147 41 E
Carinhanha, Brazil 93 F10 14 15S 44 46W
Carinhanha →, Brazil 93 F10 14 20S 43 47W
Carinthia = Kärnten □, Austria 16 E8 46 52N 13 30 E
Caripito, Venezuela 92 A6 10 8N 63 6W
Carleton, Mt., Canada 71 C6 47 23N 66 53W
Carleton Place, Canada 79 A8 45 8N 76 9W
Carletonville, S. Africa 56 D4 26 23S 27 22 E
Carlin, U.S.A. 82 F5 40 43N 116 7W
Carlingford L., U.K. 13 B5 54 3N 6 9W
Carlinville, U.S.A. 80 F10 39 17N 89 53W
Carlisle, U.K. 10 C5 54 54N 2 56W
Carlisle, U.S.A. 78 F7 40 12N 77 12W
Carlos Casares, Argentina 94 D3 35 32S 61 20W
Carlos Tejedor, Argentina 94 D3 35 25S 62 25W
Carlow, Ireland 13 D5 52 50N 6 56W
Carlow □, Ireland 13 D5 52 43N 6 50W
Carlsbad, Calif., U.S.A. 85 M9 33 10N 117 21W
Carlsbad, N. Mex., U.S.A. 81 J2 32 25N 104 14W
Carlsbad Caverns National Park, U.S.A. 81 J2 32 10N 104 35W
Carluke, U.K. 12 F5 55 45N 3 50W
Carlyle, Canada 73 D8 49 40N 102 20W
Carmacks, Canada 68 B6 62 5N 136 16W
Carman, Canada 73 D9 49 30N 98 0W
Carmarthen, U.K. 11 F3 51 52N 4 19W
Carmarthen B., U.K. 11 F3 51 40N 4 30W
Carmarthenshire □, U.K. 11 F3 51 55N 4 13W
Carmaux, France 18 D5 44 3N 2 10 E
Carmel, U.S.A. 79 E11 41 26N 73 41W
Carmel-by-the-Sea, U.S.A. 84 J5 36 33N 121 55W
Carmel Valley, U.S.A. 84 J5 36 29N 121 43W
Carmelo, Uruguay 94 C4 34 0S 58 20W
Carmen, Colombia 92 B3 9 43N 75 8W
Carmen, Paraguay 95 B4 27 13S 56 12W
Carmen →, Mexico 86 A3 30 42N 106 29W
Carmen, I., Mexico 86 B2 26 0N 111 20W
Carmen de Patagones, Argentina 96 E4 40 50S 63 0W
Carmensa, Argentina 94 D2 35 15S 67 40W
Carmi, Canada 72 D5 49 36N 119 8W
Carmi, U.S.A. 76 F1 38 5N 88 10W
Carmichael, U.S.A. 84 G5 38 38N 121 19W
Carmila, Australia 62 C4 21 55S 149 24 E
Carmona, Costa Rica 88 E2 10 0N 85 15W
Carmona, Spain 19 D3 37 28N 5 42W
Carn Ban, U.K. 12 D4 57 7N 4 15W
Carn Eige, U.K. 12 D3 57 17N 5 8W
Carnac, France 18 C2 47 35N 3 6W
Carnamah, Australia 61 E2 29 41S 115 53 E
Carnarvon, Australia 61 D1 24 51S 113 42 E
Carnarvon, S. Africa 56 E3 30 56S 22 8 E
Carnarvon Ra., Queens., Australia 62 D4 25 15S 148 30 E
Carnarvon Ra., W. Austral., Australia 61 E3 25 20S 120 45 E
Carnation, U.S.A. 84 C5 47 39N 121 55W
Carndonagh, Ireland 13 A4 55 16N 7 15W
Carnduff, Canada 73 D8 49 10N 101 50W
Carnegie, U.S.A. 78 F4 40 24N 80 5W
Carnegie, L., Australia 61 E3 26 5S 122 30 E
Carnic Alps = Karnische Alpen, Europe 16 E7 46 36N 13 0 E
Carniche Alpi = Karnische Alpen, Europe 16 E7 46 36N 13 0 E
Carnot, C.A.R. 52 D3 4 59N 15 56 E
Carnot, C., Australia 63 E2 34 57S 135 38 E
Carnot B., Australia 60 C3 17 20S 122 15 E
Carnoustie, U.K. 12 E6 56 30N 2 42W
Carnsore Pt., Ireland 13 D5 52 10N 6 22W
Caro, U.S.A. 76 D4 43 29N 83 24W
Carol City, U.S.A. 77 N5 25 56N 80 16W
Carolina, Brazil 93 E9 7 10S 47 30W
Carolina, Puerto Rico 89 C6 18 23N 65 58W
Carolina, S. Africa 57 D5 26 5S 30 6 E
Caroline I., Kiribati 65 H12 9 15S 150 3W
Caroline Is., Micronesia 28 J17 8 0N 150 0 E
Caroni →, Venezuela 92 B6 8 21N 62 43W
Caronie = Nébrodi, Monti, Italy 20 F6 37 54N 14 35 E
Caroona, Australia 63 E5 31 24S 150 26 E
Carpathians, Europe 17 D11 49 30N 21 0 E
Carpații Meridionali, Romania 17 F13 45 30N 25 0 E
Carpentaria, G. of, Australia 62 A2 14 0S 139 0 E
Carpentras, France 18 D6 44 3N 5 2 E
Carpi, Italy 20 B4 44 47N 10 53 E
Carpinteria, U.S.A. 85 L7 34 24N 119 31W
Carr Boyd Ra., Australia 60 C4 16 15S 128 35 E
Carrabelle, U.S.A. 77 L3 29 51N 84 40W
Carranza, Presa V., Mexico 86 B4 27 20N 100 50W
Carrara, Italy 18 D9 44 5N 10 6 E
Carrauntoohill, Ireland 13 D2 52 0N 9 45W
Carrick-on-Shannon, Ireland 13 C3 53 57N 8 5W
Carrick-on-Suir, Ireland 13 D4 52 21N 7 24W
Carrickfergus, U.K. 13 B6 54 43N 5 49W
Carrickmacross, Ireland 13 C5 53 59N 6 43W
Carrieton, Australia 63 E2 32 25S 138 31 E
Carrington, U.S.A. 80 B5 47 27N 99 8W
Carrizal Bajo, Chile 94 B1 28 5S 71 20W
Carrizalillo, Chile 94 B1 29 5S 71 30W
Carrizo Cr. →, U.S.A. 81 G3 36 55N 103 55W
Carrizo Springs, U.S.A. 81 L5 28 31N 99 52W
Carrizozo, U.S.A. 83 K11 33 38N 105 53W
Carroll, U.S.A. 80 D7 42 4N 94 52W
Carrollton, Ga., U.S.A. 77 J3 33 35N 85 5W
Carrollton, Ill., U.S.A. 80 F9 39 18N 90 24W
Carrollton, Ky., U.S.A. 76 F3 38 41N 85 11W
Carrollton, Mo., U.S.A. 80 F8 39 22N 93 30W
Carrollton, Ohio, U.S.A. 78 F3 40 34N 81 5W
Carron →, U.K. 12 D4 57 53N 4 22W
Carron, L., U.K. 12 D3 57 22N 5 35W
Carrot →, Canada 73 C8 53 50N 101 17W
Carrot River, Canada 73 C8 53 17N 103 35W
Carruthers, Canada 73 C7 52 52N 109 16W
Carson, Calif., U.S.A. 85 M8 33 48N 118 17W
Carson, N. Dak., U.S.A. 80 B4 46 25N 101 34W
Carson →, U.S.A. 84 F8 39 45N 118 40W
Carson City, U.S.A. 84 F7 39 10N 119 46W
Carson Sink, U.S.A. 82 G4 39 50N 118 25W
Cartagena, Colombia 92 A3 10 25N 75 33W
Cartagena, Spain 19 D5 37 38N 0 59W
Cartago, Colombia 92 C3 4 45N 75 55W
Cartago, Costa Rica 88 E3 9 50N 83 55W
Cartersville, U.S.A. 77 H3 34 10N 84 48W
Carterton, N.Z. 59 J5 41 2S 175 31 E
Carthage, Tunisia 51 A8 36 50N 10 21 E
Carthage, Ill., U.S.A. 80 E9 40 25N 91 8W
Carthage, Mo., U.S.A. 81 G7 37 11N 94 19W
Carthage, N.Y., U.S.A. 76 D8 43 59N 75 37W
Carthage, Tex., U.S.A. 81 J7 32 9N 94 20W
Cartier I., Australia 60 B3 12 31S 123 29 E
Cartwright, Canada 71 B8 53 41N 56 58W
Caruaru, Brazil 93 E11 8 15S 35 55W
Carúpano, Venezuela 92 A6 10 39N 63 15W
Caruthersville, U.S.A. 81 G10 36 11N 89 39W
Carvoeiro, Brazil 92 D6 1 30S 61 59W
Carvoeiro, C., Portugal 19 C1 39 21N 9 24W
Cary, U.S.A. 77 H6 35 47N 78 46W
Casa Grande, U.S.A. 83 K8 32 53N 111 45W
Casablanca, Chile 94 C1 33 20S 71 25W
Casablanca, Morocco 50 B4 33 36N 7 36W
Cascade, Idaho, U.S.A. 82 D5 44 31N 116 2W
Cascade, Mont., U.S.A. 82 C8 47 16N 111 42W
Cascade Locks, U.S.A. 84 E5 45 40N 121 54W
Cascade Ra., U.S.A. 84 D5 47 0N 121 30W
Cascade Reservoir, U.S.A. 82 D5 44 32N 116 3W
Cascais, Portugal 19 C1 38 41N 9 25W
Cascavel, Brazil 95 A5 24 57S 53 28W
Cáscina, Italy 20 C4 43 41N 10 33 E
Casco B., U.S.A. 77 D10 43 45N 70 0W
Caserta, Italy 20 D6 41 4N 14 20 E
Cashel, Ireland 13 D4 52 30N 7 53W
Casiguran, Phil. 37 A6 16 22N 122 7 E
Casilda, Argentina 94 C3 33 10S 61 10W
Casino, Australia 63 D5 28 52S 153 3 E
Casiquiare →, Venezuela 92 C5 2 1N 67 7W
Casma, Peru 92 E3 9 30S 78 20W
Casmalia, U.S.A. 85 L6 34 50N 120 32W
Caspe, Spain 19 B5 41 14N 0 1W
Casper, U.S.A. 82 E10 42 51N 106 19W
Caspian Depression, Eurasia 25 E8 47 0N 48 0 E
Caspian Sea, Eurasia 25 F9 43 0N 50 0 E
Cass Lake, U.S.A. 80 B7 47 23N 94 37W
Cassadaga, U.S.A. 78 D5 42 20N 79 19W
Casselman, Canada 79 A9 45 19N 75 5W
Casselton, U.S.A. 80 B6 46 54N 97 13W
Cassiar, Canada 72 B3 59 16N 129 40W
Cassiar Mts., Canada 72 B2 59 30N 130 30W
Cassino, Italy 20 D5 41 30N 13 49 E
Cassville, U.S.A. 81 G8 36 41N 93 52W
Castaic, U.S.A. 85 L8 34 30N 118 38W
Castalia, U.S.A. 78 E2 41 24N 82 49W
Castanhal, Brazil 93 D9 1 18S 47 55W
Castellammare di Stábia, Italy 20 D6 40 42N 14 29 E
Castelli, Argentina 94 D4 36 7S 57 47W
Castelló de la Plana, Spain 19 C5 39 58N 0 3W
Castelo, Brazil 95 A7 20 33S 41 14W
Castelo Branco, Portugal 19 C2 39 50N 7 31W
Castelsarrasin, France 18 E4 44 2N 1 7 E
Castelvetrano, Italy 20 F5 37 41N 12 47 E
Casterton, Australia 63 F3 37 30S 141 30 E
Castile, U.S.A. 78 D6 42 38N 78 3W
Castilla-La Mancha □, Spain 19 C4 39 30N 3 30W
Castilla y Leon □, Spain 19 B3 42 0N 5 0W
Castillos, Uruguay 95 C5 34 12S 53 52W
Castle Dale, U.S.A. 82 G8 39 13N 111 1W
Castle Douglas, U.K. 12 G5 54 56N 3 56W
Castle Rock, Colo., U.S.A. 80 F2 39 22N 104 51W
Castle Rock, Wash., U.S.A. 84 D4 46 17N 122 54W
Castlebar, Ireland 13 C2 53 52N 9 18W
Castleblaney, Ireland 13 B5 54 7N 6 44W
Castlederg, U.K. 13 B4 54 42N 7 35W
Castleford, U.K. 10 D6 53 43N 1 21W
Castlegar, Canada 72 D5 49 20N 117 40W
Castlemaine, Australia 63 F3 37 2S 144 12 E
Castlepollard, Ireland 13 C4 53 41N 7 19W
Castlerea, Ireland 13 C3 53 46N 8 29W
Castlereagh →, Australia 63 E4 30 12S 147 32 E
Castlereagh B., Australia 62 A2 12 10S 135 10 E
Castleton, U.S.A. 79 C11 43 37N 73 11W
Castletown, U.K. 10 C3 54 5N 4 38W
Castletown Bearhaven, Ireland 13 E2 51 39N 9 55W
Castor, Canada 72 C6 52 15N 111 50W
Castor →, Canada 70 B4 53 24N 78 58W
Castorland, U.S.A. 79 C9 43 53N 75 31W
Castres, France 18 E5 43 37N 2 13 E
Castricum, Neths. 15 B4 52 33N 4 40 E
Castries, St. Lucia 89 D7 14 2N 60 58W
Castro, Brazil 95 A6 24 45S 50 0W
Castro, Chile 96 E2 42 30S 73 50W
Castro Alves, Brazil 93 F11 12 46S 39 33W
Castroville, U.S.A. 84 J5 36 46N 121 45W
Castuera, Spain 19 C3 38 43N 5 37W
Cat Ba, Dao, Vietnam 38 B6 20 50N 107 0 E
Cat I., Bahamas 89 B4 24 30N 75 30W
Cat L., Canada 70 B1 51 40N 91 50W
Cat Lake, Canada 70 B1 51 40N 91 50W
Catacamas, Honduras 88 D2 14 54N 85 56W
Cataguases, Brazil 95 A7 21 23S 42 39W
Catalão, Brazil 93 G9 18 10S 47 57W
Çatalca, Turkey 21 D13 41 8N 28 27 E
Catalina, Canada 71 C9 48 31N 53 4W
Catalina, Chile 94 B2 25 13S 69 43W
Catalina, U.S.A. 83 K8 32 30N 110 50W
Catalonia = Cataluña □, Spain 19 B6 41 40N 1 15 E
Cataluña □, Spain 19 B6 41 40N 1 15 E
Catamarca, Argentina 94 B2 28 30S 65 50W
Catamarca □, Argentina 94 B2 27 0S 65 50W
Catanduanes, Phil. 37 B6 13 50N 124 20 E
Catanduva, Brazil 95 A6 21 5S 48 58W
Catánia, Italy 20 F6 37 30N 15 6 E
Catanzaro, Italy 20 E7 38 54N 16 35 E
Catarman, Phil. 37 B6 12 28N 124 35 E
Cateel, Phil. 37 C7 7 47N 126 24 E
Caterham, U.K. 11 F7 51 15N 0 4W
Cathcart, S. Africa 56 E4 32 18S 27 10 E
Cathlamet, U.S.A. 84 D3 46 12N 123 23W
Catlettsburg, U.S.A. 76 F4 38 25N 82 36W
Catoche, C., Mexico 87 C7 21 40N 87 8W
Catriló, Argentina 94 D3 36 26S 63 24W
Catrimani, Brazil 92 C6 0 27N 61 41W
Catrimani →, Brazil 92 C6 0 28N 61 44W
Catskill, U.S.A. 79 D11 42 14N 73 52W
Catskill Mts., U.S.A. 79 D10 42 10N 74 25W
Catt, Mt., Australia 62 A1 13 49S 134 23 E
Cattaraugus, U.S.A. 78 D6 42 22N 78 52W
Catuala, Angola 56 B2 16 25S 19 2 E
Catur, Mozam. 55 E4 13 45S 35 30 E
Catwick Is., Vietnam 39 H7 10 0N 109 0 E
Cauca →, Colombia 92 B4 8 54N 74 28W
Caucaia, Brazil 93 D11 3 40S 38 35W
Caucasus Mountains, Eurasia 25 F7 42 50N 44 0 E
Caungula, Angola 52 F3 8 26S 18 38 E
Cauquenes, Chile 94 D1 36 0S 72 22W
Caura →, Venezuela 92 B6 7 38N 64 53W
Cauresi →, Mozam. 55 F3 17 8S 33 0 E
Causapscal, Canada 71 C6 48 19N 67 12W
Cauvery →, India 40 P11 11 9N 78 52 E
Caux, Pays de, France 18 B4 49 38N 0 35 E
Cavalier, U.S.A. 80 A6 48 48N 97 37W
Cavalleria, C. de, Spain 22 A11 40 5N 4 5 E
Cavan, Ireland 13 B4 54 0N 7 22W
Cavan □, Ireland 13 C4 54 1N 7 16W
Cave Creek, U.S.A. 83 K7 33 50N 111 57W
Cavenagh Ra., Australia 61 E4 26 12S 127 55 E
Cavendish, Australia 63 F3 37 31S 142 2 E
Caviana, I., Brazil 93 C8 0 10N 50 10W
Cavite, Phil. 37 B6 14 29N 120 55 E
Cawndilla L., Australia 63 E3 32 30S 142 15 E
Cawnpore = Kanpur, India 43 F9 26 28N 80 20 E
Caxias, Brazil 93 D10 4 55S 43 20W
Caxias do Sul, Brazil 95 B5 29 10S 51 10W
Cay Sal Bank, Bahamas 88 B4 23 45N 80 0W
Cayambe, Ecuador 92 C3 0 3N 78 8W
Cayenne, Fr. Guiana 93 B8 5 5N 52 18W
Cayman Brac, Cayman Is. 88 C4 19 43N 79 49W
Cayman Is. ■, W. Indies 88 C3 19 40N 80 30W
Cayo Romano, Cuba 88 B4 22 0N 78 0W
Cayuga, Canada 78 D5 42 59N 79 50W
Cayuga, U.S.A. 79 D8 42 54N 76 44W
Cayuga L., U.S.A. 79 D8 42 41N 76 41W
Cazenovia, U.S.A. 79 D9 42 56N 75 51W
Cazombo, Angola 53 G4 11 54S 22 56 E
Ceanannus Mor, Ireland 13 C5 53 44N 6 53W
Ceará = Fortaleza, Brazil 93 D11 3 45S 38 35W
Ceará □, Brazil 93 E11 5 0S 40 0W
Ceará Mirim, Brazil 93 E11 5 38S 35 25W
Cebaco, I. de, Panama 88 E3 7 33N 81 9W
Cebollar, Argentina 94 B2 29 10S 66 35W
Cebu, Phil. 37 B6 10 18N 123 54 E
Cecil Plains, Australia 63 D5 27 30S 151 11 E
Cedar →, U.S.A. 80 E9 41 17N 91 21W
Cedar City, U.S.A. 83 H7 37 41N 113 4W
Cedar Creek Reservoir, U.S.A. 81 J6 32 11N 96 4W
Cedar Falls, Iowa, U.S.A. 80 D8 42 32N 92 27W
Cedar Falls, Wash., U.S.A. 84 C5 47 25N 121 45W
Cedar L., Canada 73 C9 53 10N 100 0W
Cedar Rapids, U.S.A. 80 E9 41 59N 91 40W
Cedartown, U.S.A. 77 H3 34 1N 85 15W
Cedarvale, Canada 72 B3 55 1N 128 22W
Cedarville, S. Africa 57 E4 30 23S 29 3 E
Cedral, Mexico 86 C4 23 50N 100 42W
Cedro, Brazil 93 E11 6 34S 39 3W
Cedros, I. de, Mexico 86 B1 28 10N 115 20W
Ceduna, Australia 63 E1 32 7S 133 46 E
Cefalù, Italy 20 E6 38 2N 14 1 E
Cegléd, Hungary 17 E10 47 11N 19 47 E
Celaya, Mexico 86 C4 20 31N 100 37W
Celebes = Sulawesi □, Indonesia 37 E6 2 0S 120 0 E
Celebes Sea, Indonesia 37 D6 3 0N 123 0 E
Celina, U.S.A. 76 E3 40 33N 84 35W
Celje, Slovenia 16 E8 46 16N 15 18 E
Celle, Germany 16 B6 52 37N 10 4 E
Cenderwasih, Teluk, Indonesia 37 E9 3 0S 135 20 E
Center, N. Dak., U.S.A. 80 B4 47 7N 101 18W
Center, Tex., U.S.A. 81 K7 31 48N 94 11W
Centerburg, U.S.A. 78 F2 40 18N 82 42W
Centerville, Calif., U.S.A. 84 J7 36 44N 119 30W
Centerville, Iowa, U.S.A. 80 E8 40 44N 92 52W
Centerville, Pa., U.S.A. 78 F5 40 3N 79 59W
Centerville, Tenn., U.S.A. 77 H2 35 47N 87 28W
Centerville, Tex., U.S.A. 81 K7 31 16N 95 59W
Central □, Kenya 54 C4 0 30S 37 30 E
Central □, Malawi 55 E3 13 30S 33 30 E
Central □, Zambia 55 E2 14 25S 28 50 E
Central, Cordillera, Colombia 92 C4 5 0N 75 0W
Central, Cordillera, Costa Rica 88 D3 10 10N 84 5W
Central, Cordillera, Dom. Rep. 89 C5 19 15N 71 0W
Central African Rep. ■, Africa 52 C4 7 0N 20 0 E
Central America, America 66 H11 12 0N 85 0W
Central Butte, Canada 73 C7 50 48N 106 31W
Central City, Colo., U.S.A. 82 G11 39 48N 105 31W
Central City, Ky., U.S.A. 76 G2 37 18N 87 7W
Central City, Nebr., U.S.A. 80 E6 41 7N 98 0W
Central I., Kenya 54 B4 3 30N 36 0 E
Central Makran Range, Pakistan 40 F4 26 30N 64 15 E
Central Patricia, Canada 70 B1 51 30N 90 9W
Central Point, U.S.A. 82 E2 42 23N 122 55W
Central Russian Uplands, Europe 6 E13 54 0N 36 0 E
Central Siberian Plateau, Russia 28 C14 65 0N 105 0 E
Central Square, U.S.A. 79 C8 43 17N 76 9W
Centralia, Ill., U.S.A. 80 F10 38 32N 89 8W
Centralia, Mo., U.S.A. 80 F8 39 13N 92 8W
Centralia, Wash., U.S.A. 84 D4 46 43N 122 58W
Cephalonia = Kefallinía, Greece 21 E9 38 20N 20 30 E
Cepu, Indonesia 37 G14 7 9S 111 35 E
Ceram = Seram, Indonesia 37 E7 3 10S 129 0 E
Ceram Sea = Seram Sea, Indonesia 37 E7 2 30S 128 30 E
Ceredigion □, U.K. 11 E3 52 16N 4 15W
Ceres, Argentina 94 B3 29 55S 61 55W
Ceres, S. Africa 56 E2 33 21S 19 18 E
Ceres, U.S.A. 84 H6 37 35N 120 57W
Cerignola, Italy 20 D6 41 17N 15 53 E
Cerigo = Kíthira, Greece 21 F10 36 8N 23 0 E
Çerkezköy, Turkey 21 D12 41 17N 28 0 E
Cerralvo, I., Mexico 86 C3 24 20N 109 45W
Cerritos, Mexico 86 C4 22 27N 100 20W
Cerro Chato, Uruguay 95 C4 33 6S 55 8W
Cerventes, Australia 61 F2 30 31S 115 3 E
Cervera, Spain 19 B6 41 40N 1 16 E
Cesena, Italy 20 B5 44 8N 12 15 E
Cēsis, Latvia 9 H21 57 18N 25 15 E
České Budějovice, Czech Rep. 16 D8 48 55N 14 25 E
Českomoravská Vrchovina, Czech Rep. 16 D8 49 30N 15 40 E
Çeşme, Turkey 21 E12 38 20N 26 23 E
Cessnock, Australia 63 E5 32 50S 151 21 E
Cetinje, Montenegro, Yug. 21 C8 42 23N 18 59 E
Cetraro, Italy 20 E6 39 31N 15 55 E
Ceuta, N. Afr. 19 E3 35 52N 5 18W
Cévennes, France 18 D5 44 10N 3 50 E
Ceyhan, Turkey 44 B2 37 4N 35 47 E
Ceylon = Sri Lanka ■, Asia 40 R12 7 30N 80 50 E
Cha-am, Thailand 38 F2 12 48N 99 58 E
Cha Pa, Vietnam 38 A4 22 20N 103 47 E
Chacabuco, Argentina 94 C3 34 40S 60 27W
Chachapoyas, Peru 92 E3 6 15S 77 50W
Chachoengsao, Thailand 38 F3 13 42N 101 5 E
Chachran, Pakistan 40 E7 28 55N 70 30 E
Chachro, Pakistan 42 G4 25 5N 70 15 E
Chaco □, Argentina 94 B3 26 30S 61 0W
Chaco □, Paraguay 94 B4 26 0S 60 0W
Chaco →, U.S.A. 83 H9 36 46N 108 39W
Chaco Austral, S. Amer. 96 B4 27 0S 61 30W
Chaco Boreal, S. Amer. 92 H6 22 0S 60 0W
Chaco Central, S. Amer. 96 A4 24 0S 61 0W
Chacon, C., U.S.A. 72 C2 54 42N 132 0W
Chad ■, Africa 51 F8 15 0N 17 15 E
Chad, L. = Tchad, L., Chad 51 F8 13 30N 14 30 E
Chadan, Russia 27 D10 51 17N 91 35 E
Chadileuvú →, Argentina 94 D2 37 46S 66 0W
Chadiza, Zambia 55 E3 14 45S 32 27 E
Chadron, U.S.A. 80 D3 42 50N 103 0W
Chadyr-Lunga = Ciadâr-Lunga, Moldova 17 E15 46 3N 28 51 E
Chae Hom, Thailand 38 C2 18 43N 99 35 E
Chaem →, Thailand 38 C2 18 11N 98 38 E
Chaeryŏng, N. Korea 35 E13 38 24N 125 36 E
Chagai Hills, Afghan. 40 E3 29 30N 63 0 E
Chagda, Russia 27 D14 58 45N 130 38 E
Chagos Arch., Ind. Oc. 29 K11 6 0S 72 0 E
Chagrin Falls, U.S.A. 78 E3 41 26N 81 24W
Chāh Ākhvor, Iran 45 C8 32 41N 59 40 E
Chāh Bahār, Iran 45 E9 25 20N 60 40 E
Chāh-e Kavīr, Iran 45 C8 34 29N 56 52 E
Chahar Burjak, Afghan. 40 D3 30 15N 62 0 E
Chahār Mahāll va Bakhtīarī □, Iran 45 C6 32 0N 49 0 E
Chaibasa, India 41 H14 22 42N 85 49 E
Chainat, Thailand 38 E3 15 11N 100 8 E
Chaiya, Thailand 39 H2 9 23N 99 14 E
Chaj Doab, Pakistan 42 C5 32 15N 73 0 E
Chajari, Argentina 94 C4 30 42S 58 0W
Chak Amru, Pakistan 42 C6 32 22N 75 11 E
Chakar →, Pakistan 42 E3 29 29N 68 2 E
Chake Chake, Tanzania 54 D4 5 15S 39 45 E
Chakhānsūr, Afghan. 40 D3 31 10N 62 0 E
Chakonipau, L., Canada 71 A6 56 18N 68 30W
Chakradharpur, India 43 H11 22 45N 85 40 E
Chakrata, India 42 D7 30 42N 77 51 E
Chakwal, Pakistan 42 C5 32 56N 72 53 E
Chala, Peru 92 G4 15 48S 74 20W
Chalchihuites, Mexico 86 C4 23 29N 103 53W
Chalcis = Khalkís, Greece 21 E10 38 27N 23 42 E
Chaleur B., Canada 71 C6 47 55N 65 30W
Chalfant, U.S.A. 84 H8 37 32N 118 21W
Chalhuanca, Peru 92 F4 14 15S 73 15W
Chalisgaon, India 40 J9 20 30N 75 10 E
Chalk River, Canada 70 C4 46 1N 77 27W
Chalky Inlet, N.Z. 59 M1 46 3S 166 31 E
Challapata, Bolivia 92 G5 18 53S 66 50W
Challis, U.S.A. 82 D6 44 30N 114 14W
Chalmette, U.S.A. 81 L10 29 56N 89 58W
Chalon-sur-Saône, France 18 C6 46 48N 4 50 E
Châlons-en-Champagne, France 18 B6 48 58N 4 20 E
Chalyaphum, Thailand 38 E4 15 48N 102 2 E
Cham, Cu Lao, Vietnam 38 E7 15 57N 108 30 E
Chama, U.S.A. 83 H10 36 54N 106 35W
Chamaicó, Argentina 94 D3 35 3S 64 58W
Chaman, Pakistan 40 D5 30 58N 66 25 E
Chamba, India 42 C7 32 35N 76 10 E
Chamba, Tanzania 55 E4 11 37S 37 0 E
Chambal →, India 43 F8 26 29N 79 15 E
Chamberlain, U.S.A. 80 D5 43 49N 99 20W
Chamberlain →, Australia 60 C4 15 30S 127 54 E
Chamberlain L., U.S.A. 77 B11 46 14N 69 19W
Chambers, U.S.A. 83 J9 35 11N 109 26W
Chambersburg, U.S.A. 76 F7 39 56N 77 40W
Chambéry, France 18 D6 45 34N 5 55 E
Chambeshi →, Zambia 52 G6 11 53S 29 48 E
Chambly, Canada 79 A11 45 27N 73 17W
Chambord, Canada 71 C5 48 25N 72 6W
Chamchamal, Iraq 44 C5 35 32N 44 50 E
Chamela, Mexico 86 D3 19 32N 105 5W

Desolación, I.

Dalton, Mass., U.S.A. 79 D11 42 28N 73 11W
Dalton, Nebr., U.S.A. 80 E3 41 25N 102 58W
Dalton Iceberg Tongue, Antarctica .... 5 C9 66 15S 121 30 E
Dalton-in-Furness, U.K. ... 10 C4 54 10N 3 11W
Dalvík, Iceland 8 D4 65 58N 18 32W
Dalwallinu, Australia ...... 61 F2 30 17S 116 40 E
Daly →, Australia .... 60 B5 13 35S 130 19 E
Daly City, U.S.A. 84 H4 37 42N 122 28W
Daly L., Canada 73 B7 56 32N 105 39W
Daly River, Australia ...... 60 B5 13 46S 130 42 E
Daly Waters, Australia .... 62 B1 16 15S 133 24 E
Dam Doi, Vietnam .... 39 H5 8 50N 105 12 E
Dam Ha, Vietnam .... 38 B6 21 21N 107 36 E
Daman, India .... 40 J8 20 25N 72 57 E
Dāmaneh, Iran .... 45 C6 33 1N 50 29 E
Damanhûr, Egypt .... 51 B12 31 0N 30 30 E
Damant L., Canada 73 A7 61 45N 105 5W
Damanzhuang, China ..... 34 E9 38 5N 116 35 E
Damar, Indonesia .... 37 F7 7 7S 128 40 E
Damaraland, Namibia ..... 56 C2 20 0S 15 0 E
Damascus = Dimashq, Syria 47 B5 33 30N 36 18 E
Damāvand, Iran .... 45 C7 35 47N 52 0 E
Damāvand, Qolleh-ye, Iran 45 C7 35 56N 52 10 E
Damba, Angola .... 52 F3 6 44S 15 20 E
Dâmboviţa →, Romania . 17 F14 44 12N 26 26 E
Dame Marie, Haiti 89 C5 18 36N 74 26W
Dāmghān, Iran .... 45 B7 36 10N 54 17 E
Damiel, Spain 19 C4 39 4N 3 37W
Damietta = Dumyât, Egypt 51 B12 31 24N 31 48 E
Daming, China .... 34 F8 36 15N 115 6 E
Damīr Qābū, Syria .... 44 B4 36 58N 41 51 E
Dammam = Ad Dammām, Si. Arabia .... 45 E6 26 20N 50 5 E
Damodar →, India ...... 43 H12 23 17N 87 35 E
Damoh, India .... 43 H8 23 50N 79 28 E
Dampier, Australia .... 60 D2 20 41S 116 42 E
Dampier, Selat, Indonesia . 37 E8 0 40S 131 0 E
Dampier Arch., Australia .. 60 D2 20 38S 116 32 E
Damrei, Chuor Phnum, Cambodia .... 39 G4 11 30N 103 0 E
Dan Xian, China .... 38 C7 19 31N 109 33 E
Dana, Indonesia .... 37 F6 11 0S 122 52 E
Dana, L., Canada 70 B4 50 53N 77 20W
Dana, Mt., U.S.A. 84 H7 37 54N 119 12W
Danakil Depression, Ethiopia 46 E3 12 45N 41 0 E
Danané, Ivory C. 50 G4 7 16N 8 9W
Danau Poso, Indonesia .... 37 E6 1 52S 120 35 E
Danbury, U.S.A. 79 E11 41 24N 73 28W
Danby L., U.S.A. 83 J6 34 13N 115 5W
Dand, Afghan. .... 42 D1 31 28N 65 32 E
Dandeldhura, Nepal ...... 43 E9 29 20N 80 35 E
Dandeli, India .... 40 M9 15 5N 74 30 E
Dandenong, Australia ..... 63 F4 38 0S 145 15 E
Dandong, China .... 35 D13 40 10N 124 20 E
Danfeng, China .... 34 H6 33 45N 110 25 E
Danger Is. = Pukapuka, Cook Is. 65 J11 10 53S 165 49W
Danger Pt., S. Africa ..... 56 E2 34 40S 19 17 E
Dangla Shan = Tanggula Shan, China .... 32 C4 32 40N 92 10 E
Dangrek, Phnom, Thailand 38 E5 14 15N 105 0 E
Dangriga, Belize 87 D7 17 0N 88 13W
Dangshan, China .... 34 G9 34 27N 116 22 E
Daniel, U.S.A. 82 E8 42 52N 110 4W
Daniel's Harbour, Canada . 71 B8 50 13N 57 35W
Danielskuil, S. Africa ..... 56 D3 28 11S 23 33 E
Danielson, U.S.A. 79 E13 41 48N 71 53W
Danilov, Russia .... 24 C7 58 16N 40 13 E
Daning, China .... 34 F6 36 28N 110 45 E
Danissa, Kenya .... 54 B5 3 15N 40 58 E
Dank, Oman .... 45 F8 23 33N 56 16 E
Dankhar Gompa, India .... 40 C11 32 10N 78 10 E
Danlí, Honduras 88 D2 14 4N 86 35W
Dannemora, U.S.A. 79 B11 44 43N 73 44W
Dannevirke, N.Z. .... 59 J6 40 12S 176 8 E
Dannhauser, S. Africa .... 57 D5 28 0S 30 3 E
Dansville, U.S.A. 78 D7 42 34N 77 42W
Danta, India .... 42 G5 24 11N 72 46 E
Dantan, India .... 43 J12 21 57N 87 20 E
Dante, Somali Rep. .... 46 E5 10 25N 51 16 E
Danube = Dunărea →, Europe .... 17 F15 45 20N 29 40 E
Danvers, U.S.A. 79 D14 42 34N 70 56W
Danville, Ill., U.S.A. 76 E2 40 8N 87 37W
Danville, Ky., U.S.A. 76 G3 37 39N 84 46W
Danville, Pa., U.S.A. 79 F8 40 58N 76 37W
Danville, Va., U.S.A. 77 G6 36 36N 79 23W
Danville, Vt., U.S.A. 79 B12 44 25N 72 9W
Danzig = Gdańsk, Poland . 17 A10 54 22N 18 40 E
Dapaong, Togo .... 50 F6 10 55N 0 16 E
Daqing Shan, China ...... 34 D6 40 40N 111 0 E
Dar Banda, Africa .... 48 F6 8 0N 23 0 E
Dar el Beida = Casablanca, Morocco 50 B4 33 36N 7 36W
Dar es Salaam, Tanzania .. 54 D4 6 50S 39 12 E
Dar Mazār, Iran .... 45 D8 29 14N 57 20 E
Dar'ā, Syria .... 47 C5 32 36N 36 7 E
Dar'ā □, Syria .... 47 C5 32 55N 36 10 E
Dārāb, Iran .... 45 D7 28 50N 54 30 E
Daraban, Pakistan .... 42 D4 31 44N 70 20 E
Daraj, Libya .... 51 B8 30 10N 10 28 E
Dārān, Iran .... 45 C6 32 59N 50 24 E
Dārayyā, Syria .... 47 B5 33 28N 36 15 E
Darband, Pakistan .... 42 B5 34 20N 72 50 E
Darband, Kūh-e, Iran ..... 45 D8 31 34N 57 8 E
Darbhanga, India .... 43 F11 26 15N 85 55 E
D'Arcy, Canada 72 C4 50 27N 122 35W
Dardanelle, Ark., U.S.A. ... 81 H8 35 13N 93 9W
Dardanelle, Calif., U.S.A. .. 84 G7 38 20N 119 50W
Dardanelles = Çanakkale Boğazı, Turkey .... 21 D12 40 17N 26 32 E
Dārestān, Iran .... 45 D8 29 9N 58 42 E
Dârfûr, Sudan .... 51 F10 13 40N 24 0 E
Dargai, Pakistan .... 42 B4 34 25N 71 55 E
Dargan Ata, Uzbekistan ... 26 E7 40 29N 62 10 E
Dargaville, N.Z. .... 59 F4 35 57S 173 52 E
Darhan, Mongolia .... 32 B5 49 37N 106 21 E
Darhan Muminggan Lianheqi, China .... 34 D6 41 40N 110 28 E
Darıca, Turkey .... 21 D13 40 45N 29 23 E
Darién, G. del, Colombia .. 92 B3 9 0N 77 0W
Dariganga = Ovoot, Mongolia .... 34 B7 45 21N 113 45 E
Darjeeling = Darjiling, India 43 F13 27 3N 88 18 E
Darjiling, India .... 43 F13 27 3N 88 18 E
Darkan, Australia .... 61 F2 33 20S 116 43 E
Darkhana, Pakistan .... 42 D5 30 39N 72 11 E
Darkhazīneh, Iran .... 45 D6 31 54N 48 39 E
Darkot Pass, Pakistan .... 43 A5 36 45N 73 26 E
Darling →, Australia ..... 63 E3 34 4S 141 54 E
Darling Downs, Australia .. 63 D5 27 30S 150 30 E
Darling Ra., Australia ..... 61 F2 32 30S 116 0 E
Darlington, U.K. 10 C6 54 32N 1 33W
Darlington, U.S.A. 77 H6 34 18N 79 52W
Darlington □, U.K. 10 C6 54 32N 1 33W
Darlington, L., S. Africa ... 56 E4 33 10S 25 9 E
Darlington Point, Australia . 63 E4 34 37S 146 1 E
Darlot, L., Australia .... 61 E3 27 48S 121 35 E
Darłowo, Poland .... 16 A9 54 25N 16 25 E
Darmstadt, Germany ..... 16 D5 49 51N 8 39 E
Darnah, Libya .... 51 B10 32 45N 22 45 E
Darnall, S. Africa .... 57 D5 29 23S 31 18 E
Darnley, C., Antarctica .... 5 C6 68 0S 69 0 E
Darnley B., Canada 68 B7 69 30N 123 30W
Darr →, Australia .... 62 C3 23 39S 143 50 E
Darra Pezu, Pakistan ..... 42 C4 32 19N 70 44 E
Darrequeira, Argentina 94 D3 37 42S 63 10W
Darrington, U.S.A. 82 B3 48 15N 121 36W
Dart →, U.K. 11 G4 50 24N 3 39W
Dart, C., Antarctica 5 D14 73 6S 126 20W
Dartford, U.K. .... 11 F8 51 26N 0 13 E
Dartmoor, U.K. 11 G4 50 38N 3 57W
Dartmouth, Canada 71 D7 44 40N 63 30W
Dartmouth, U.K. 11 G4 50 21N 3 36W
Dartmouth, L., Australia ... 63 D4 26 4S 145 18 E
Dartuch, C. = Artrutx, C. de, Spain .... 22 B10 39 55N 3 49 E
Darvaza, Turkmenistan .... 26 E6 40 11N 58 24 E
Darvel, Teluk = Lahad Datu, Teluk, Malaysia .... 37 D5 4 50N 118 20 E
Darwen, U.K. 10 D5 53 42N 2 29W
Darwha, India .... 40 J10 20 15N 77 45 E
Darwin, Australia .... 60 B5 12 25S 130 51 E
Darwin, U.S.A. 85 J9 36 15N 117 35W
Darya Khan, Pakistan ..... 42 D4 31 48N 71 6 E
Daryoi Amu = Amudarya →, Uzbekistan .... 26 E6 43 58N 59 34 E
Dās, U.A.E. .... 45 E7 25 20N 53 30 E
Dashetai, China .... 34 D5 41 0N 109 5 E
Dashhowuz, Turkmenistan . 26 E6 41 49N 59 58 E
Dashköpri, Turkmenistan .. 45 B9 36 16N 62 8 E
Dasht, Iran .... 45 B8 37 17N 56 7 E
Dasht →, Pakistan .... 40 G2 25 10N 61 40 E
Dasht-e Mārgow, Afghan. .. 40 D3 30 40N 62 30 E
Dasht-i-Nawar, Afghan. .... 42 C3 33 52N 68 0 E
Daska, Pakistan .... 42 C6 32 20N 74 20 E
Dasuya, India .... 42 D6 31 49N 75 38 E
Datça, Turkey .... 21 F12 36 46N 27 40 E
Datia, India .... 43 G8 25 39N 78 27 E
Datong, China .... 34 D7 40 6N 113 18 E
Dattakhel, Pakistan .... 42 C3 32 54N 69 46 E
Datu, Tanjung, Indonesia ... 36 D3 2 5N 109 39 E
Datu Piang, Phil. .... 37 C6 7 2N 124 30 E
Daud Khel, Pakistan .... 42 C4 32 53N 71 34 E
Daudnagar, India .... 43 G11 25 2N 84 24 E
Daugava →, Latvia .... 9 H21 57 4N 24 3 E
Daugavpils, Latvia .... 9 J22 55 53N 26 32 E
Daulpur, India .... 42 F7 26 45N 77 59 E
Dauphin, Canada 73 C8 51 9N 100 5W
Dauphin, U.S.A. 78 F8 40 22N 76 56W
Dauphin L., Canada 73 C9 51 20N 99 45W
Dauphiné, France .... 18 D6 45 15N 5 25 E
Dausa, India .... 42 F7 26 52N 76 20 E
Davangere, India .... 40 M9 14 25N 75 55 E
Davao, Phil. .... 37 C7 7 0N 125 40 E
Davao, G. of, Phil. .... 37 C7 6 30N 125 48 E
Dāvar Panāh, Iran .... 45 E9 27 25N 62 15 E
Davenport, Calif., U.S.A. .. 84 H4 37 1N 122 12W
Davenport, Iowa, U.S.A. ... 80 E9 41 32N 90 35W
Davenport, Wash., U.S.A. .. 82 C4 47 39N 118 9W
Davenport Ra., Australia .. 62 C1 20 28S 134 0 E
Daventry, U.K. 11 E6 52 16N 1 10W
David, Panama 88 E3 8 30N 82 30W
David City, U.S.A. 80 E6 41 15N 97 8W
David Gorodok = Davyd Haradok, Belarus .... 17 B14 52 4N 27 8 E
Davidson, Canada 73 C7 51 16N 105 59W
Davis, U.S.A. 84 G5 38 33N 121 44W
Davis Dam, U.S.A. 85 K12 35 11N 114 34W
Davis Inlet, Canada 71 A7 55 50N 60 59W
Davis Mts., U.S.A. 81 K2 30 50N 103 55W
Davis Sea, Antarctica ..... 5 C7 66 0S 92 0 E
Davis Str., N. Amer. 69 B14 65 0N 58 0W
Davos, Switz. .... 18 C8 46 48N 9 49 E
Davy L., Canada 73 B7 58 53N 108 18W
Davyd Haradok, Belarus ... 17 B14 52 4N 27 8 E
Dawei, Burma .... 38 E2 14 2N 98 12 E
Dawes Ra., Australia ...... 62 C5 24 40S 150 40 E
Dawlish, U.K. 11 G4 50 35N 3 28W
Dawros Hd., Ireland 13 B3 54 50N 8 33W
Dawson, Canada 68 B6 64 10N 139 30W
Dawson, U.S.A. 77 K3 31 46N 84 27W
Dawson, I., Chile 96 G2 53 50S 70 50W
Dawson B., Canada 73 C8 52 53N 100 49W
Dawson Creek, Canada 72 B4 55 45N 120 15W
Dawson Inlet, Canada 73 A10 61 50N 93 25W
Dawson Ra., Australia ..... 62 C4 24 30S 149 48 E
Dax, France 18 E3 43 44N 1 3W
Daxian, China .... 32 C5 31 15N 107 23 E
Daxindian, China .... 35 F11 37 30N 120 50 E
Daxinggou, China .... 35 C15 43 25N 129 40 E
Daxue Shan, China .... 32 C5 30 30N 101 30 E
Daylesford, Australia ...... 63 F3 37 21S 144 9 E
Dayr az Zawr, Syria .... 44 C4 35 20N 40 5 E
Daysland, Canada 72 C6 52 50N 112 20W
Dayton, Nev., U.S.A. 84 F7 39 14N 119 36W
Dayton, Ohio, U.S.A. 76 F3 39 45N 84 12W
Dayton, Pa., U.S.A. 78 F5 40 53N 79 15W
Dayton, Tenn., U.S.A. 77 H3 35 30N 85 1W
Dayton, Wash., U.S.A. 82 C4 46 19N 117 59W
Dayton, Wyo., U.S.A. 82 D10 44 53N 107 16W
Daytona Beach, U.S.A. 77 L5 29 13N 81 1W
Dayville, U.S.A. 82 D4 44 28N 119 32W
De Aar, S. Africa .... 56 E3 30 39S 24 0 E
De Funiak Springs, U.S.A. . 77 K2 30 43N 86 7W
De Grey →, Australia .... 60 D2 20 12S 119 13 E
De Haan, Belgium .... 15 C3 51 16N 3 2 E
De Kalb, U.S.A. 80 E10 41 56N 88 46W
De Land, U.S.A. 77 L5 29 2N 81 18W
De Leon, U.S.A. 81 J5 32 7N 98 32W
De Panne, Belgium .... 15 C2 51 6N 2 34 E
De Pere, U.S.A. 76 C1 44 27N 88 4W
De Queen, U.S.A. 81 H7 34 2N 94 21W
De Quincy, U.S.A. 81 K8 30 27N 93 26W
De Ridder, U.S.A. 81 K8 30 51N 93 17W
De Smet, U.S.A. 80 C6 44 23N 97 33W
De Soto, U.S.A. 80 F9 38 8N 90 34W
De Tour Village, U.S.A. ... 76 C4 46 0N 83 56W
De Witt, U.S.A. 81 H9 34 18N 91 20W
Dead Sea, Asia .... 47 D4 31 30N 35 30 E
Deadwood, U.S.A. 80 C3 44 23N 103 44W
Deadwood L., Canada 72 B3 59 10N 128 30W
Deal, U.K. .... 11 F9 51 13N 1 25 E
Deal I., Australia .... 62 F4 39 30S 147 20 E
Dealesville, S. Africa ..... 56 D4 28 41S 25 44 E
Dean →, Canada 72 C3 52 49N 126 58W
Dean, Forest of, U.K. 11 F5 51 45N 2 33W
Dean Chan., Canada 72 C3 52 30N 127 15W
Deán Funes, Argentina 94 C3 30 20S 64 20W
Dease →, Canada 72 B3 59 56N 128 32W
Dease L., Canada 72 B2 58 40N 130 5W
Dease Lake, Canada 72 B2 58 25N 130 6W
Death Valley, U.S.A. 85 J10 36 15N 116 50W
Death Valley Junction, U.S.A. 85 J10 36 20N 116 25W
Death Valley National Park, U.S.A. 85 J10 36 45N 117 15W
Debar, Macedonia .... 21 D9 41 31N 20 30 E
Debden, Canada 73 C7 53 30N 106 50W
Dębica, Poland .... 17 C11 50 2N 21 25 E
Debolt, Canada 72 B5 55 12N 118 1W
Deborah East, L., Australia 61 F2 30 45S 119 0 E
Deborah West, L., Australia 61 F2 30 45S 118 50 E
Debre Markos, Ethiopia ... 46 E2 10 20N 37 40 E
Debre Tabor, Ethiopia .... 46 E2 11 50N 38 26 E
Debre Zeyit, Ethiopia ..... 46 F2 11 48N 38 30 E
Debrecen, Hungary .... 17 E11 47 33N 21 42 E
Decatur, Ala., U.S.A. 77 H2 34 36N 86 59W
Decatur, Ga., U.S.A. 77 J3 33 47N 84 18W
Decatur, Ill., U.S.A. 80 F10 39 51N 88 57W
Decatur, Ind., U.S.A. 76 E3 40 50N 84 56W
Decatur, Tex., U.S.A. 81 J6 33 14N 97 35W
Deccan, India .... 40 L11 18 0N 79 0 E
Deception Bay, Australia .. 63 D5 27 10S 153 5 E
Deception L., Canada 73 B8 56 33N 104 13W
Dechhu, India .... 42 F5 26 46N 72 20 E
Děčín, Czech Rep. .... 16 C8 50 47N 14 12 E
Deckerville, U.S.A. 78 C2 43 32N 82 44W
Decorah, U.S.A. 80 D9 43 18N 91 48W
Dedéagach = Alexandroúpolis, Greece 21 D11 40 50N 25 54 E
Dedham, U.S.A. 79 D13 42 15N 71 10W
Dedza, Malawi .... 55 E3 14 20S 34 20 E
Dee →, Aberds., U.K. 12 D6 57 9N 2 5W
Dee →, Dumf. & Gall., U.K. 12 G4 54 51N 4 3W
Dee →, Wales, U.K. 10 D4 53 22N 3 17W
Deep B., Canada 72 A5 61 15N 116 35W
Deepwater, Australia ..... 63 D5 29 25S 151 51 E
Deer →, Canada 73 B10 58 23N 94 13W
Deer L., Canada 73 C10 52 40N 94 20W
Deer Lake, Nfld., Canada .. 71 C8 49 11N 57 27W
Deer Lake, Ont., Canada .. 73 C10 52 36N 94 20W
Deer Lodge, U.S.A. 82 C7 46 24N 112 44W
Deer Park, U.S.A. 82 C5 47 57N 117 28W
Deer River, U.S.A. 80 B8 47 20N 93 48W
Deeragun, Australia ...... 62 B4 19 16S 146 33 E
Deerdepoort, S. Africa .... 56 C4 24 37S 26 27 E
Deferiet, U.S.A. 79 B9 44 2N 75 41W
Defiance, U.S.A. 76 E3 41 17N 84 22W
Degana, India .... 42 F6 26 50N 74 20 E
Dégelis, Canada 71 C6 47 30N 68 35W
Deggendorf, Germany .... 16 D7 48 50N 12 57 E
Degh →, Pakistan .... 42 D5 31 3N 73 21 E
Deh Bīd, Iran .... 45 D7 30 39N 53 11 E
Deh-e Shīr, Iran .... 45 D7 31 29N 53 45 E
Dehaj, Iran .... 45 D7 30 42N 54 53 E
Dehak, Iran .... 45 E9 27 11N 62 37 E
Dehdez, Iran .... 45 D6 31 43N 50 17 E
Dehej, India .... 42 J5 21 44N 72 40 E
Dehestān, Iran .... 45 D7 28 30N 55 35 E
Dehgolān, Iran .... 44 C5 35 17N 47 25 E
Dehi Titan, Afghan. .... 40 C3 33 45N 63 50 E
Dehibat, Tunisia .... 51 B8 32 0N 10 47 E
Dehlorān, Iran .... 44 C5 32 41N 47 16 E
Dehnow-e Kūhestān, Iran .. 45 E8 27 58N 58 32 E
Dehra Dun, India .... 42 D8 30 20N 78 4 E
Dehri, India .... 43 G11 24 50N 84 15 E
Dehui, China .... 35 B13 44 30N 125 40 E
Deinze, Belgium .... 15 D3 50 59N 3 32 E
Dej, Romania .... 17 E12 47 10N 23 52 E
Dekese, Dem. Rep. of the Congo . 52 E4 3 24S 21 24 E
Del Mar, U.S.A. 85 N9 32 58N 117 16W
Del Norte, U.S.A. 83 H10 37 41N 106 21W
Del Rio, U.S.A. 81 L4 29 22N 100 54W
Delambre I., Australia .... 60 D2 20 26S 117 5 E
Delano, U.S.A. 85 K7 35 46N 119 15W
Delano Peak, U.S.A. 83 G7 38 22N 112 22W
Delareyville, S. Africa .... 56 D4 26 41S 25 26 E
Delaronde L., Canada 73 C7 54 3N 107 3W
Delavan, U.S.A. 80 D10 42 38N 88 39W
Delaware, U.S.A. 76 E4 40 18N 83 4W
Delaware □, U.S.A. 76 F8 39 0N 75 20W
Delaware →, U.S.A. 79 G9 39 15N 75 20W
Delaware B., U.S.A. 76 F8 39 0N 75 10W
Delay →, Canada 71 A5 56 56N 71 28W
Delegate, Australia .... 63 F4 37 4S 148 56 E
Delevan, U.S.A. 78 D6 42 29N 78 29W
Delft, Neths. .... 15 B4 52 1N 4 22 E
Delfzijl, Neths. .... 15 A6 53 20N 6 55 E
Delgado, C., Mozam. ...... 55 E5 10 45S 40 40 E
Delgerhet, Mongolia ...... 34 B6 45 50N 110 30 E
Delgo, Sudan .... 51 D12 20 6N 30 40 E
Delhi, Canada 78 D4 42 51N 80 30W
Delhi, India .... 42 E7 28 38N 77 17 E
Delhi, La., U.S.A. 81 J9 32 28N 91 30W
Delhi, N.Y., U.S.A. 79 D10 42 17N 74 55W
Delia, Canada 72 C6 51 38N 112 23W
Delice, Turkey .... 25 G5 39 54N 34 2 E
Delicias, Mexico 86 B3 28 10N 105 30W
Delījān, Iran .... 45 C6 33 59N 50 40 E
Déline, Canada 68 B7 65 10N 123 30W
Delisle, Canada 73 C7 51 55N 107 8W
Dell City, U.S.A. 83 L11 31 56N 105 12W
Dell Rapids, U.S.A. 80 D6 43 50N 96 43W
Delmar, U.S.A. 79 D11 42 37N 73 47W
Delmenhorst, Germany .... 16 B5 53 3N 8 37 E
Delong, Ostrova, Russia .. 27 B15 76 40N 149 20 E
Deloraine, Australia ...... 62 G4 41 30S 146 40 E
Deloraine, Canada 73 D8 49 15N 100 29W
Delphi, U.S.A. 76 E2 40 36N 86 41W
Delphos, U.S.A. 76 E3 40 51N 84 21W
Delportshoop, S. Africa ... 56 D3 28 22S 24 20 E
Delray Beach, U.S.A. 77 M5 26 28N 80 4W
Delta, Colo., U.S.A. 83 G9 38 44N 108 4W
Delta, Utah, U.S.A. 82 G7 39 21N 112 35W
Delta Junction, U.S.A. 68 B5 64 2N 145 44W
Deltona, U.S.A. 77 L5 28 54N 81 16W
Delungra, Australia .... 63 D5 29 39S 150 51 E
Delvada, India .... 42 J4 20 46N 71 2 E
Delvinë, Albania .... 21 E9 39 59N 20 6 E
Demak, Indonesia .... 37 G14 6 53S 110 38 E
Demanda, Sierra de la, Spain 19 A4 42 15N 3 0W
Demavand = Damāvand, Iran .... 45 C7 35 47N 52 0 E
Dembia, Dem. Rep. of the Congo . 54 B2 3 33N 25 48 E
Dembidolo, Ethiopia ...... 46 F1 8 34N 34 50 E
Demchok, India .... 43 C8 32 42N 79 29 E
Demer →, Belgium ...... 15 D4 50 57N 4 42 E
Deming, N. Mex., U.S.A. .. 83 K10 32 16N 107 46W
Deming, Wash., U.S.A. ... 84 B4 48 50N 122 13W
Demini →, Brazil 92 D6 0 46S 62 56W
Demirci, Turkey .... 21 E13 39 2N 28 38 E
Demirköy, Turkey .... 21 D12 41 49N 27 45 E
Demopolis, U.S.A. 77 J2 32 31N 87 50W
Dempo, Indonesia .... 36 E2 4 2S 103 15 E
Den Burg, Neths. .... 15 A4 53 3N 4 47 E
Den Chai, Thailand .... 38 D3 17 59N 100 4 E
Den Haag = 's-Gravenhage, Neths. .... 15 B4 52 7N 4 17 E
Den Helder, Neths. .... 15 B4 52 57N 4 45 E
Den Oever, Neths. .... 15 B5 52 56N 5 2 E
Denair, U.S.A. 84 H6 37 32N 120 48W
Denau, Uzbekistan .... 26 F7 38 16N 67 54 E
Denbigh, Canada 78 A7 45 8N 77 15W
Denbigh, U.K. 10 D4 53 12N 3 25W
Denbighshire □, U.K. 10 D4 53 8N 3 22W
Dendang, Indonesia ...... 36 E3 3 7S 107 56 E
Dendermonde, Belgium ... 15 C4 51 2N 4 5 E
Dengfeng, China .... 34 G7 34 25N 113 2 E
Dengkou, China .... 34 D4 40 18N 106 55 E
Denham, Australia .... 61 E1 25 56S 113 31 E
Denham Ra., Australia .... 62 C4 21 55S 147 46 E
Denham Sd., Australia .... 61 E1 25 45S 113 15 E
Denholm, Canada 73 C7 52 39N 108 1W
Denia, Spain .... 19 C6 38 49N 0 8 E
Denial B., Australia .... 63 E1 32 14S 133 32 E
Deniliquin, Australia ...... 63 F3 35 30S 144 58 E
Denison, Iowa, U.S.A. 80 E7 42 1N 95 21W
Denison, Tex., U.S.A. 81 J6 33 45N 96 33W
Denison Plains, Australia . 60 C4 18 35S 128 0 E
Denizli, Turkey .... 25 G4 37 42N 29 2 E
Denman Glacier, Antarctica 5 C7 66 45S 99 25 E
Denmark, Australia .... 61 F2 34 59S 117 25 E
Denmark ■, Europe ...... 9 J13 55 45N 10 0 E
Denmark Str., Atl. Oc. 4 C6 66 0N 30 0W
Dennison, U.S.A. 78 F3 40 24N 81 19W
Denny, U.K. 12 E5 56 1N 3 55W
Denpasar, Indonesia ...... 36 F5 8 45S 115 14 E
Denton, Mont., U.S.A. 82 C9 47 19N 109 57W
Denton, Tex., U.S.A. 81 J6 33 13N 97 8W
D'Entrecasteaux, Pt., Australia .... 61 F2 34 50S 115 57 E
Denver, Colo., U.S.A. 80 F2 39 44N 104 59W
Denver, Pa., U.S.A. 79 F8 40 14N 76 8W
Denver City, U.S.A. 81 J3 32 58N 102 50W
Deoband, India .... 42 E7 29 42N 77 43 E
Deogarh, India .... 42 G5 25 32N 73 54 E
Deoghar, India .... 43 G12 24 30N 86 42 E
Deolali, India .... 40 K8 19 58N 73 50 E
Deoli = Devli, India ...... 42 G6 25 50N 75 20 E
Deora, India .... 42 F4 26 22N 70 55 E
Deori, India .... 43 H8 23 24N 79 1 E
Deoria, India .... 43 F10 26 31N 83 48 E
Deosai Mts., Pakistan .... 43 B6 35 40N 75 0 E
Deosri, India .... 43 F14 26 46N 90 29 E
Depalpur, India .... 42 H6 22 51N 75 33 E
Deping, China .... 35 F9 37 25N 116 58 E
Deposit, U.S.A. 79 D9 42 4N 75 25W
Depuch I., Australia ...... 60 D2 20 37S 117 44 E
Deputatskiy, Russia ...... 27 C14 69 18N 139 54 E
Dera Ghazi Khan, Pakistan 42 D4 30 5N 70 43 E
Dera Ismail Khan, Pakistan 42 D4 31 50N 70 50 E
Derabugti, Pakistan ...... 42 E3 29 2N 69 9 E
Derawar Fort, Pakistan ... 42 E4 28 46N 71 20 E
Derbent, Russia .... 25 F8 42 5N 48 15 E
Derby, Australia .... 60 C3 17 18S 123 38 E
Derby, U.K. 10 E6 52 56N 1 28W
Derby, Conn., U.S.A. 79 E11 41 19N 73 5W
Derby, Kans., U.S.A. 81 G6 37 33N 97 16W
Derby, N.Y., U.S.A. 78 D6 42 41N 78 58W
Derby City □, U.K. 10 E6 52 56N 1 28W
Derby Line, U.S.A. 79 B12 45 0N 72 6W
Derbyshire □, U.K. 10 D6 53 11N 1 38W
Derg →, U.K. 13 B4 54 44N 7 26W
Derg, L., Ireland 13 D3 53 0N 8 20W
Dergaon, India .... 41 F19 26 45N 94 0 E
Dermott, U.S.A. 81 J9 33 32N 91 26W
Derry = Londonderry, U.K. 13 B4 55 0N 7 20W
Derry = Londonderry □, U.K. 13 B4 55 0N 7 20W
Derry, N.H., U.S.A. 79 D13 42 53N 71 19W
Derry, Pa., U.S.A. 78 F5 40 20N 79 18W
Derryveagh Mts., Ireland . 13 B3 54 56N 8 11W
Derwent →, Cumb., U.K. . 10 C4 54 39N 3 33W
Derwent →, Derby, U.K. . 10 E6 52 57N 1 28W
Derwent →, N. Yorks., U.K. 10 D7 53 45N 0 58W
Derwent Water, U.K. 10 C4 54 35N 3 9W
Des Moines, Iowa, U.S.A. . 80 E8 41 35N 93 37W
Des Moines, N. Mex., U.S.A. 81 G3 36 46N 103 50W
Des Moines →, U.S.A. ... 80 E9 40 23N 91 25W
Desaguadero →, Argentina 94 C2 34 30S 66 46W
Desaguadero →, Bolivia . 92 G5 16 35S 69 5W
Descanso, Pta., Mexico ... 85 N9 32 21N 117 3W
Deschaillons, Canada 71 C5 46 32N 72 7W
Deschambault L., Canada . 73 C8 54 50N 103 30W
Deschutes →, U.S.A. 82 D3 45 38N 120 55W
Dese, Ethiopia .... 46 E2 11 5N 39 40 E
Deseado →, Argentina ... 96 F3 47 45S 65 54W
Desert Center, U.S.A. 85 M11 33 43N 115 24W
Desert Hot Springs, U.S.A. 85 M10 33 58N 116 30W
Deshnok, India .... 42 F5 27 48N 73 21 E
Desna →, Ukraine .... 17 C16 50 33N 30 32 E
Desolación, I., Chile 96 G2 53 0S 74 0W

Eddystone Pt.

Dowerin, Australia 61 F2 31 12S 117 2 E
Dowgha'i, Iran 45 B8 36 54N 58 32 E
Dowlatābād, Iran 45 D8 28 20N 56 40 E
Down □, U.K. 13 B5 54 23N 6 2W
Downey, Calif., U.S.A. 85 M8 33 56N 118 7W
Downey, Idaho, U.S.A. 82 E7 42 26N 112 7W
Downham Market, U.K. 11 E8 52 37N 0 23 E
Downieville, U.S.A. 84 F6 39 34N 120 50W
Downpatrick, U.K. 13 B6 54 20N 5 43W
Downpatrick Hd., Ireland 13 B2 54 20N 9 21W
Downsville, U.S.A. 79 D10 42 5N 74 50W
Downton, Mt., Canada 72 C4 52 42N 124 52W
Dowsārī, Iran 45 D8 28 25N 57 59 E
Doyle, U.S.A. 84 E6 40 2N 120 6W
Doylestown, U.S.A. 79 F9 40 21N 75 10W
Dozois, Rés., Canada 70 C4 47 30N 77 5W
Dra Khel, Pakistan 42 F2 27 58N 66 45 E
Drachten, Neths. 15 A6 53 7N 6 5 E
Drăgăşani, Romania 17 F13 44 39N 24 17 E
Dragichyn, Belarus 17 B13 52 15N 25 8 E
Dragoman, Prokhod, Bulgaria 21 C10 42 58N 22 53 E
Draguignan, France 18 E7 43 32N 6 27 E
Drain, U.S.A. 82 E2 43 40N 123 19W
Drake, U.S.A. 80 B4 47 55N 100 23W
Drake Passage, S. Ocean 5 B17 58 0S 68 0W
Drakensberg, S. Africa 57 E4 31 0S 28 0 E
Dráma, Greece 21 D11 41 9N 24 10 E
Drammen, Norway 9 G14 59 42N 10 12 E
Drangajökull, Iceland 8 C2 66 9N 22 15W
Dras, India 43 B6 34 25N 75 48 E
Drau = Drava →, Croatia 21 B8 45 33N 18 55 E
Drava →, Croatia 21 B8 45 33N 18 55 E
Drayton Valley, Canada 72 C6 53 12N 114 58W
Drenthe □, Neths. 15 B6 52 52N 6 40 E
Drepanum, C., Cyprus 23 E11 34 54N 32 19 E
Dresden, Canada 78 D2 42 35N 82 11W
Dresden, Germany 16 C7 51 3N 13 44 E
Dreux, France 18 B4 48 44N 1 23 E
Driffield, U.K. 10 C7 54 0N 0 26W
Driftwood, U.S.A. 78 E6 41 20N 78 8W
Driggs, U.S.A. 82 E8 43 44N 111 6W
Drina →, Bos.-H. 21 B8 44 53N 19 21 E
Drini →, Albania 21 C8 42 1N 19 38 E
Drøbak, Norway 9 G14 59 39N 10 39 E
Drochia, Moldova 17 D14 48 2N 27 48 E
Drogheda, Ireland 13 C5 53 43N 6 22W
Drogichin = Dragichyn, Belarus 17 B13 52 15N 25 8 E
Drogobych = Drohobych, Ukraine 17 D12 49 20N 23 30 E
Drohobych, Ukraine 17 D12 49 20N 23 30 E
Droichead Atha = Drogheda, Ireland 13 C5 53 43N 6 22W
Droichead Nua, Ireland 13 C5 53 11N 6 48W
Droitwich, U.K. 11 E5 52 16N 2 8W
Dromedary, C., Australia 63 F5 36 17S 150 10 E
Dromore, U.K. 13 B4 54 31N 7 28W
Dromore West, Ireland 13 B3 54 15N 8 52W
Dronfield, U.K. 10 D6 53 19N 1 27W
Dronten, Neths. 15 B5 52 32N 5 43 E
Drumbo, Canada 78 C4 43 16N 80 35W
Drumheller, Canada 72 C6 51 25N 112 40W
Drummond, U.S.A. 82 C7 46 40N 113 9W
Drummond I., U.S.A. 76 C4 46 1N 83 39W
Drummond Pt., Australia 63 E2 34 9S 135 16 E
Drummond Ra., Australia 62 C4 23 45S 147 10 E
Drummondville, Canada 70 C5 45 55N 72 25W
Drumright, U.S.A. 81 H6 35 59N 96 36W
Druskininkai, Lithuania 9 J20 54 3N 23 58 E
Drut →, Belarus 17 B16 53 8N 30 5 E
Druzhina, Russia 27 C15 68 14N 145 18 E
Dry Tortugas, U.S.A. 88 B3 24 38N 82 55W
Dryden, Canada 73 D10 49 47N 92 50W
Dryden, U.S.A. 79 D8 42 30N 76 18W
Drygalski I., Antarctica 5 C7 66 0S 92 0 E
Drysdale →, Australia 60 B4 13 59S 126 51 E
Drysdale I., Australia 62 A2 11 41S 136 0 E
Du Bois, U.S.A. 78 E6 41 8N 78 46W
Du Gué →, Canada 70 A5 57 21N 70 45W
Du Quoin, U.S.A. 80 G10 38 1N 89 14W
Duanesburg, U.S.A. 79 D10 42 45N 74 11W
Duaringa, Australia 62 C4 23 42S 149 42 E
Ḑubā, Si. Arabia 44 E2 27 10N 35 40 E
Dubai = Dubayy, U.A.E. 45 E7 25 18N 55 20 E
Dubăsari, Moldova 17 E15 47 15N 29 10 E
Dubăsari Vdkhr., Moldova 17 E15 47 30N 29 0 E
Dubawnt →, Canada 73 A8 64 33N 100 6W
Dubawnt, L., Canada 73 A8 63 4N 101 42W
Dubayy, U.A.E. 45 E7 25 18N 55 20 E
Dubbo, Australia 63 E4 32 11S 148 35 E
Dubele, Dem. Rep. of the Congo 54 B2 2 56N 29 35 E
Dublin, Ireland 13 C5 53 21N 6 15W
Dublin, Ga., U.S.A. 77 J4 32 32N 82 54W
Dublin, Tex., U.S.A. 81 J5 32 5N 98 21W
Dublin □, Ireland 13 C5 53 24N 6 20W
Dubno, Ukraine 17 C13 50 25N 25 45 E
Dubois, U.S.A. 82 D7 44 10N 112 14W
Dubossary = Dubăsari, Moldova 17 E15 47 15N 29 10 E
Dubossary Vdkhr. = Dubăsari Vdkhr., Moldova 17 E15 47 30N 29 0 E
Dubovka, Russia 25 E7 49 5N 44 50 E
Dubrajpur, India 43 H12 23 48N 87 25 E
Dubréka, Guinea 50 G3 9 46N 13 31W
Dubrovitsa = Dubrovytsya, Ukraine 17 C14 51 31N 26 35 E
Dubrovnik, Croatia 21 C8 42 39N 18 6 E
Dubrovytsya, Ukraine 17 C14 51 31N 26 35 E
Dubuque, U.S.A. 80 D9 42 30N 90 41W
Duchesne, U.S.A. 82 F8 40 10N 110 24W
Duchess, Australia 62 C2 21 20S 139 50 E
Ducie I., Pac. Oc. 65 K15 24 40S 124 48W
Duck →, U.S.A. 77 G2 36 2N 87 52W
Duck Cr. →, Australia 60 D2 22 37S 116 53 E
Duck Lake, Canada 73 C7 52 50N 106 16W
Duck Mountain Prov. Park, Canada 73 C8 51 45N 101 0W
Duckwall, Mt., U.S.A. 84 H6 37 58N 120 7W
Dudhi, India 41 G13 24 15N 83 10 E
Dudinka, Russia 27 C9 69 30N 86 13 E
Dudley, U.K. 11 E5 52 31N 2 5W
Dudwa, India 43 E9 28 30N 80 41 E
Duero = Douro →, Europe 19 B1 41 8N 8 40W
Dufftown, U.K. 12 D5 57 27N 3 8W
Dugi Otok, Croatia 16 G8 44 0N 15 3 E
Duifken Pt., Australia 62 A3 12 33S 141 38 E
Duisburg, Germany 16 C4 51 26N 6 45 E
Duiwelskloof, S. Africa 57 C5 23 42S 30 10 E
Dūkdamīn, Iran 45 C8 35 59N 57 43 E
Dukelský Průsmyk, Slovak Rep. 17 D11 49 25N 21 42 E
Dukhān, Qatar 45 E6 25 25N 50 50 E
Duki, Pakistan 40 D6 30 14N 68 25 E
Duku, Nigeria 51 F8 10 43N 10 43 E
Dulce, U.S.A. 83 H10 36 56N 107 0W
Dulce →, Argentina 94 C3 30 32S 62 33W
Dulce, G., Costa Rica 88 E3 8 40N 83 20W
Dulf, Iraq 44 C5 35 7N 45 51 E
Dulit, Banjaran, Malaysia 36 D4 3 15N 114 30 E
Duliu, China 34 E9 39 2N 116 55 E
Dullewala, Pakistan 42 D4 31 50N 71 25 E
Dulq Maghār, Syria 44 B3 36 22N 38 39 E
Duluth, U.S.A. 80 B8 46 47N 92 6W
Dum Dum, India 43 H13 22 39N 88 33 E
Dum Duma, India 41 F19 27 40N 95 40 E
Dūmā, Syria 47 B5 33 34N 36 24 E
Dumaguete, Phil. 37 C6 9 17N 123 15 E
Dumai, Indonesia 36 D2 1 35N 101 28 E
Dumaran, Phil. 37 B5 10 33N 119 50 E
Dumas, Ark., U.S.A. 81 J9 33 53N 91 29W
Dumas, Tex., U.S.A. 81 H4 35 52N 101 58W
Ḑumayr, Syria 47 B5 33 39N 36 42 E
Dumbarton, U.K. 12 F4 55 57N 4 33W
Dumbleyung, Australia 61 F2 33 17S 117 42 E
Dumfries, U.K. 12 F5 55 4N 3 37W
Dumfries & Galloway □, U.K. 12 F5 55 9N 3 58W
Dumka, India 43 G12 24 12N 87 15 E
Dumoine →, Canada 70 C4 46 13N 77 51W
Dumoine, L., Canada 70 C4 46 55N 77 55W
Dumraon, India 43 G11 25 33N 84 8 E
Dumyât, Egypt 51 B12 31 24N 31 48 E
Dún Dealgan = Dundalk, Ireland 13 B5 54 1N 6 24W
Dun Laoghaire, Ireland 13 C5 53 17N 6 8W
Duna = Dunărea →, Europe 17 F15 45 20N 29 40 E
Dunagiri, India 43 D8 30 31N 79 52 E
Dunaj = Dunărea →, Europe 17 F15 45 20N 29 40 E
Dunakeszi, Hungary 17 E10 47 37N 19 8 E
Dunărea →, Europe 17 F15 45 20N 29 40 E
Dunaújváros, Hungary 17 E10 46 58N 18 57 E
Dunav = Dunărea →, Europe 17 F15 45 20N 29 40 E
Dunay, Russia 30 C6 42 52N 132 22 E
Dunback, N.Z. 59 L3 45 23S 170 36 E
Dunbar, U.K. 12 E6 56 0N 2 31W
Dunblane, U.K. 12 E5 56 11N 3 58W
Duncan, Canada 72 D4 48 45N 123 40W
Duncan, Ariz., U.S.A. 83 K9 32 43N 109 6W
Duncan, Okla., U.S.A. 81 H6 34 30N 97 57W
Duncan, L., Canada 70 B4 53 29N 77 58W
Duncan L., Canada 72 A6 62 51N 113 58W
Duncan Town, Bahamas 88 B4 22 15N 75 45W
Duncannon, U.S.A. 78 F7 40 23N 77 2W
Duncansby Head, U.K. 12 C5 58 38N 3 1W
Duncansville, U.S.A. 78 F6 40 25N 78 26W
Dundalk, Canada 78 B4 44 10N 80 24W
Dundalk, Ireland 13 B5 54 1N 6 24W
Dundalk, U.S.A. 76 F7 39 16N 76 32W
Dundalk Bay, Ireland 13 C5 53 55N 6 15W
Dundas, Canada 78 C5 43 17N 79 59W
Dundas, L., Australia 61 F3 32 35S 121 50 E
Dundas I., Canada 72 C2 54 30N 130 50W
Dundas Str., Australia 60 B5 11 15S 131 35 E
Dundee, S. Africa 57 D5 28 11S 30 15 E
Dundee, U.K. 12 E6 56 28N 2 59W
Dundee, U.S.A. 78 D8 42 32N 76 59W
Dundee City □, U.K. 12 E6 56 30N 2 58W
Dundgovĭ □, Mongolia 34 B4 45 10N 106 0 E
Dundrum, U.K. 13 B6 54 16N 5 52W
Dundrum B., U.K. 13 B6 54 13N 5 47W
Dunedin, N.Z. 59 L3 45 50S 170 33 E
Dunedin, U.S.A. 77 L4 28 1N 82 47W
Dunedoo, Australia 63 E4 32 0S 149 25 E
Dunfermline, U.K. 12 E5 56 5N 3 27W
Dungannon, Canada 78 C3 43 51N 81 36W
Dungannon, U.K. 13 B5 54 31N 6 46W
Dungarpur, India 42 H5 23 52N 73 45 E
Dungarvan, Ireland 13 D4 52 5N 7 37W
Dungarvan Harbour, Ireland 13 D4 52 4N 7 35W
Dungeness, U.K. 11 G8 50 54N 0 59 E
Dungo, L. do, Angola 56 B2 17 15S 19 0 E
Dungog, Australia 63 E5 32 22S 151 46 E
Dungu, Dem. Rep. of the Congo 54 B2 3 40N 28 32 E
Dungun, Malaysia 39 K4 4 45N 103 25 E
Dunhua, China 35 C15 43 20N 128 14 E
Dunhuang, China 32 B4 40 8N 94 36 E
Dunk I., Australia 62 B4 17 59S 146 29 E
Dunkeld, Australia 63 E4 33 25S 149 29 E
Dunkeld, U.K. 12 E5 56 34N 3 35W
Dunkerque, France 18 A5 51 2N 2 20 E
Dunkery Beacon, U.K. 11 F4 51 9N 3 36W
Dunkirk = Dunkerque, France 18 A5 51 2N 2 20 E
Dunkirk, U.S.A. 78 D5 42 29N 79 20W
Dúnleary = Dun Laoghaire, Ireland 13 C5 53 17N 6 8W
Dunleer, Ireland 13 C5 53 50N 6 24W
Dunmanus B., Ireland 13 E2 51 31N 9 50W
Dunmanway, Ireland 13 E2 51 43N 9 6W
Dunmara, Australia 62 B1 16 42S 133 25 E
Dunmore, U.S.A. 79 E9 41 25N 75 38W
Dunmore Hd., Ireland 13 D1 52 10N 10 35W
Dunmore Town, Bahamas 88 A4 25 30N 76 39W
Dunn, U.S.A. 77 H6 35 19N 78 37W
Dunnet Hd., U.K. 12 C5 58 40N 3 21W
Dunning, U.S.A. 80 E4 41 50N 100 6W
Dunnville, Canada 78 D5 42 54N 79 36W
Dunolly, Australia 63 F3 36 51S 143 44 E
Dunoon, U.K. 12 F4 55 57N 4 56W
Dunphy, U.S.A. 82 F5 40 42N 116 31W
Duns, U.K. 12 F6 55 47N 2 20W
Dunseith, U.S.A. 80 A4 48 50N 100 3W
Dunsmuir, U.S.A. 82 F2 41 13N 122 16W
Dunstable, U.K. 11 F7 51 53N 0 32W
Dunstan Mts., N.Z. 59 L2 44 53S 169 35 E
Dunster, Canada 72 C5 53 8N 119 50W
Dunvegan L., Canada 73 A7 60 8N 107 10W
Duolun, China 34 C9 42 12N 116 28 E
Duong Dong, Vietnam 39 G4 10 13N 103 58 E
Dupree, U.S.A. 80 C4 45 4N 101 35W
Dupuyer, U.S.A. 82 B7 48 13N 112 30W
Duque de Caxias, Brazil 95 A7 22 45S 43 19W
Durack →, Australia 60 C4 15 33S 127 52 E
Durack Ra., Australia 60 C4 16 50S 127 40 E
Durance →, France 18 E6 43 55N 4 45 E
Durand, U.S.A. 80 C9 44 38N 91 58W
Durango, Mexico 86 C4 24 3N 104 39W
Durango, U.S.A. 83 H10 37 16N 107 53W
Durango □, Mexico 86 C4 25 0N 105 0W
Durant, Miss., U.S.A. 81 J10 33 4N 89 51W
Durant, Okla., U.S.A. 81 J6 33 59N 96 25W
Durazno, Uruguay 94 C4 33 25S 56 31W
Durazzo = Durrësi, Albania 21 D8 41 19N 19 28 E
Durban, S. Africa 57 D5 29 49S 31 1 E
Durbuy, Belgium 15 D5 50 21N 5 28 E
Düren, Germany 16 C4 50 48N 6 29 E
Durg, India 41 J12 21 15N 81 22 E
Durgapur, India 43 H12 23 30N 87 20 E
Durham, Canada 78 B4 44 10N 80 49W
Durham, U.K. 10 C6 54 47N 1 34W
Durham, Calif., U.S.A. 84 F5 39 39N 121 48W
Durham, N.C., U.S.A. 77 H6 35 59N 78 54W
Durham, N.H., U.S.A. 79 C14 43 8N 70 56W
Durham □, U.K. 10 C6 54 42N 1 45W
Ḑurmā, Si. Arabia 44 E5 24 37N 46 8 E
Durmitor, Montenegro, Yug. 21 C8 43 10N 19 0 E
Durness, U.K. 12 C4 58 34N 4 45W
Durrësi, Albania 21 D8 41 19N 19 28 E
Durrow, Ireland 13 D4 52 51N 7 24W
Dursey I., Ireland 13 E1 51 36N 10 12W
Dursunbey, Turkey 21 E13 39 35N 28 37 E
Duru, Dem. Rep. of the Congo 54 B2 4 14N 28 50 E
Durūz, Jabal ad, Jordan 47 C5 32 35N 36 40 E
D'Urville, Tanjung, Indonesia 37 E9 1 28S 137 54 E
D'Urville I., N.Z. 59 J4 40 50S 173 55 E
Duryea, U.S.A. 79 E9 41 20N 75 45W
Dushak, Turkmenistan 26 F7 37 13N 60 1 E
Dushanbe, Tajikistan 26 F7 38 33N 68 48 E
Dushore, U.S.A. 79 E8 41 31N 76 24W
Dusky Sd., N.Z. 59 L1 45 47S 166 30 E
Dussejour, C., Australia 60 B4 14 45S 128 13 E
Düsseldorf, Germany 16 C4 51 14N 6 47 E
Dutch Harbor, U.S.A. 68 C3 53 53N 166 32W
Dutlwe, Botswana 56 C3 23 58S 23 46 E
Dutton, Canada 78 D3 42 39N 81 30W
Dutton →, Australia 62 C3 20 44S 143 10 E
Duwayhin, Khawr, U.A.E. 45 E6 24 20N 51 25 E
Duyun, China 32 D5 26 18N 107 29 E
Duzdab = Zāhedān, Iran 45 D9 29 30N 60 50 E
Dvina, Severnaya →, Russia 24 B7 64 32N 40 30 E
Dvinsk = Daugavpils, Latvia 9 J22 55 53N 26 32 E
Dvinskaya Guba, Russia 24 B6 65 0N 39 0 E
Dwarka, India 42 H3 22 18N 69 8 E
Dwellingup, Australia 61 F2 32 43S 116 4 E
Dwight, Canada 78 A5 45 20N 79 1W
Dwight, U.S.A. 76 E1 41 5N 88 26W
Dyatlovo = Dzyatlava, Belarus 17 B13 53 28N 25 28 E
Dyce, U.K. 12 D6 57 13N 2 12W
Dyer, C., Canada 69 B13 66 40N 61 0W
Dyer Bay, Canada 78 A3 45 10N 81 20W
Dyer Plateau, Antarctica 5 D17 70 45S 65 30W
Dyersburg, U.S.A. 81 G10 36 3N 89 23W
Dyfi →, U.K. 11 E3 52 32N 4 3W
Dymer, Ukraine 17 C16 50 47N 30 18 E
Dysart, Australia 62 C4 22 32S 148 23 E
Dzamin Üüd = Borhoyn Tal, Mongolia 34 C6 43 50N 111 58 E
Dzerzhinsk, Russia 24 C7 56 14N 43 30 E
Dzhalinda, Russia 27 D13 53 26N 124 0 E
Dzhambul = Zhambyl, Kazakstan 26 E8 42 54N 71 22 E
Dzhankoy, Ukraine 25 E5 45 40N 34 20 E
Dzhezkazgan = Zhezqazghan, Kazakstan 26 E7 47 44N 67 40 E
Dzhizak = Jizzakh, Uzbekistan 26 E7 40 6N 67 50 E
Dzhugdzur, Khrebet, Russia 27 D14 57 30N 138 0 E
Dzhungarskiye Vorota = Dzungarian Gates, Kazakstan 32 B3 45 0N 82 0 E
Działdowo, Poland 17 B11 53 15N 20 15 E
Dzibilchaltun, Mexico 87 C7 21 5N 89 36W
Dzierżoniów, Poland 17 C9 50 45N 16 39 E
Dzilam de Bravo, Mexico 87 C7 21 24N 88 53W
Dzungaria = Junggar Pendi, China 32 B3 44 30N 86 0 E
Dzungarian Gates, Kazakstan 32 B3 45 0N 82 0 E
Dzuumod, Mongolia 32 B5 47 45N 106 58 E
Dzyarzhynsk, Belarus 17 B14 53 40N 27 1 E
Dzyatlava, Belarus 17 B13 53 28N 25 28 E

E

Eabamet L., Canada 70 B2 51 30N 87 46W
Eads, U.S.A. 80 F3 38 29N 102 47W
Eagar, U.S.A. 83 J9 34 6N 109 17W
Eagle, Alaska, U.S.A. 68 B5 64 47N 141 12W
Eagle, Colo., U.S.A. 82 G10 39 39N 106 50W
Eagle →, Canada 71 B8 53 36N 57 26W
Eagle Butte, U.S.A. 80 C4 45 0N 101 10W
Eagle Grove, U.S.A. 80 D8 42 40N 93 54W
Eagle L., Canada 73 D10 49 42N 93 13W
Eagle L., Calif., U.S.A. 82 F3 40 39N 120 45W
Eagle L., Maine, U.S.A. 77 B11 46 20N 69 22W
Eagle Lake, Canada 78 A6 45 8N 78 29W
Eagle Lake, Maine, U.S.A. 77 B11 47 3N 68 36W
Eagle Lake, Tex., U.S.A. 81 L6 29 35N 96 20W
Eagle Mountain, U.S.A. 85 M11 33 49N 115 27W
Eagle Nest, U.S.A. 83 H11 36 33N 105 16W
Eagle Pass, U.S.A. 81 L4 28 43N 100 30W
Eagle Pk., U.S.A. 84 G7 38 10N 119 25W
Eagle Pt., Australia 60 C3 16 11S 124 23 E
Eagle River, Mich., U.S.A. 76 B1 47 24N 88 18W
Eagle River, Wis., U.S.A. 80 C10 45 55N 89 15W
Eaglehawk, Australia 63 F3 36 44S 144 15 E
Eagles Mere, U.S.A. 79 E8 41 25N 76 33W
Ealing, U.K. 11 F7 51 31N 0 20W
Ear Falls, Canada 73 C10 50 38N 93 13W
Earle, U.S.A. 81 H9 35 16N 90 28W
Earlimart, U.S.A. 85 K7 35 53N 119 16W
Earn →, U.K. 12 E5 56 21N 3 18W
Earn, L., U.K. 12 E4 56 23N 4 13W
Earnslaw, Mt., N.Z. 59 L2 44 32S 168 27 E
Earth, U.S.A. 81 H3 34 14N 102 24W
Easley, U.S.A. 77 H4 34 50N 82 36W
East Anglia, U.K. 10 E9 52 30N 1 0 E
East Angus, Canada 71 C5 45 30N 71 40W
East Aurora, U.S.A. 78 D6 42 46N 78 37W
East Ayrshire □, U.K. 12 F4 55 26N 4 11W
East Bengal, Bangla. 41 H17 24 0N 90 0 E
East Beskids = Vychodné Beskydy, Europe 17 D11 49 20N 22 0 E
East Brady, U.S.A. 78 F5 40 59N 79 36W
East C., N.Z. 59 G7 37 42S 178 35 E
East Chicago, U.S.A. 76 E2 41 38N 87 27W
East China Sea, Asia 33 D7 30 0N 126 0 E
East Coulee, Canada 72 C6 51 23N 112 27W
East Dereham, U.K. 11 E8 52 41N 0 57 E
East Dunbartonshire □, U.K. 12 F4 55 57N 4 13W
East Falkland, Falk. Is. 96 G5 51 30S 58 30W
East Grand Forks, U.S.A. 80 B6 47 56N 97 1W
East Greenwich, U.S.A. 79 E13 41 40N 71 27W
East Grinstead, U.K. 11 F8 51 7N 0 0W
East Hartford, U.S.A. 79 E12 41 46N 72 39W
East Helena, U.S.A. 82 C8 46 35N 111 56W
East Indies, Asia 28 K15 0 0 120 0 E
East Kilbride, U.K. 12 F4 55 47N 4 11W
East Lansing, U.S.A. 76 D3 42 44N 84 29W
East Liverpool, U.S.A. 78 F4 40 37N 80 35W
East London, S. Africa 57 E4 33 0S 27 55 E
East Lothian □, U.K. 12 F6 55 58N 2 44W
East Main = Eastmain, Canada 70 B4 52 10N 78 30W
East Northport, U.S.A. 79 F11 40 53N 73 20W
East Orange, U.S.A. 79 F10 40 46N 74 13W
East Pacific Ridge, Pac. Oc. 65 J17 15 0S 110 0W
East Palestine, U.S.A. 78 F4 40 50N 80 33W
East Pine, Canada 72 B4 55 48N 120 12W
East Point, U.S.A. 77 J3 33 41N 84 27W
East Providence, U.S.A. 79 E13 41 49N 71 23W
East Pt., Canada 71 C7 46 27N 61 58W
East Renfrewshire □, U.K. 12 F4 55 46N 4 21W
East Retford = Retford, U.K. 10 D7 53 19N 0 56W
East Riding of Yorkshire □, U.K. 10 D7 53 55N 0 30W
East Rochester, U.S.A. 78 C7 43 7N 77 29W
East St. Louis, U.S.A. 80 F9 38 37N 90 9W
East Schelde = Oosterschelde →, Neths. 15 C4 51 33N 4 0 E
East Siberian Sea, Russia 27 B17 73 0N 160 0 E
East Stroudsburg, U.S.A. 79 E9 41 1N 75 11W
East Sussex □, U.K. 11 G8 50 56N 0 19 E
East Tawas, U.S.A. 76 C4 44 17N 83 29W
East Timor □, Indonesia 37 F7 9 0S 125 0 E
East Toorale, Australia 63 E4 30 27S 145 28 E
East Walker →, U.S.A. 84 G7 38 52N 119 10W
East Windsor, U.S.A. 79 F10 40 17N 74 34W
Eastbourne, N.Z. 59 J5 41 19S 174 55 E
Eastbourne, U.K. 11 G8 50 46N 0 18 E
Eastend, Canada 73 D7 49 32N 108 50W
Easter I. = Pascua, I. de, Pac. Oc. 65 K17 27 0S 109 0W
Eastern □, Kenya 54 C4 0 0 38 30 E
Eastern □, Uganda 54 B3 1 50N 33 45 E
Eastern Cape □, S. Africa 56 E4 32 0S 26 0 E
Eastern Cr. →, Australia 62 C3 20 40S 141 35 E
Eastern Ghats, India 40 N11 14 0N 78 50 E
Eastern Group = Lau Group, Fiji 59 C9 17 0S 178 30W
Eastern Group, Australia 61 F3 33 30S 124 30 E
Eastern Transvaal = Mpumalanga □, S. Africa 57 B5 26 0S 30 0 E
Easterville, Canada 73 C9 53 8N 99 49W
Easthampton, U.S.A. 79 D12 42 16N 72 40W
Eastlake, U.S.A. 78 E3 41 40N 81 26W
Eastland, U.S.A. 81 J5 32 24N 98 49W
Eastleigh, U.K. 11 G6 50 58N 1 21W
Eastmain, Canada 70 B4 52 10N 78 30W
Eastmain →, Canada 70 B4 52 27N 78 26W
Eastman, Canada 79 A12 45 18N 72 19W
Eastman, U.S.A. 77 J4 32 12N 83 11W
Easton, Md., U.S.A. 76 F7 38 47N 76 5W
Easton, Pa., U.S.A. 79 F9 40 41N 75 13W
Easton, Wash., U.S.A. 84 C5 47 14N 121 11W
Eastpointe, U.S.A. 78 D2 42 27N 82 56W
Eastport, U.S.A. 77 C12 44 56N 67 0W
Eastsound, U.S.A. 84 B4 48 42N 122 55W
Eaton, U.S.A. 80 E2 40 32N 104 42W
Eatonia, Canada 73 C7 51 13N 109 25W
Eatonton, U.S.A. 77 J4 33 20N 83 23W
Eatontown, U.S.A. 79 F10 40 19N 74 4W
Eatonville, U.S.A. 84 D4 46 52N 122 16W
Eau Claire, U.S.A. 80 C9 44 49N 91 30W
Eau Claire, L. à l', Canada 70 A5 56 10N 74 25W
Ebbw Vale, U.K. 11 F4 51 46N 3 12W
Ebeltoft, Denmark 9 H14 56 12N 10 41 E
Ebensburg, U.S.A. 78 F6 40 29N 78 44W
Eberswalde-Finow, Germany 16 B7 52 50N 13 49 E
Ebetsu, Japan 30 C10 43 7N 141 34 E
Ebolowa, Cameroon 52 D2 2 55N 11 10 E
Ebro →, Spain 19 B6 40 43N 0 54 E
Eceabat, Turkey 21 D12 40 11N 26 21 E
Ech Cheliff, Algeria 50 A6 36 10N 1 20 E
Echigo-Sammyaku, Japan 31 F9 36 50N 139 50 E
Echizen-Misaki, Japan 31 G7 35 59N 135 57 E
Echo Bay, N.W.T., Canada 68 B8 66 5N 117 55W
Echo Bay, Ont., Canada 70 C3 46 29N 84 4W
Echoing →, Canada 70 B1 55 51N 92 5W
Echternach, Lux. 15 E6 49 49N 6 25 E
Echuca, Australia 63 F3 36 10S 144 20 E
Ecija, Spain 19 D3 37 30N 5 10W
Eclipse Is., Australia 60 B4 13 54S 126 19 E
Eclipse Sd., Canada 69 A11 72 38N 79 0W
Ecuador ■, S. Amer. 92 D3 2 0S 78 0W
Ed Damazin, Sudan 51 F12 11 46N 34 21 E
Ed Debba, Sudan 51 E12 18 0N 30 51 E
Ed Dueim, Sudan 51 F12 14 0N 32 10 E
Edam, Canada 73 C7 53 11N 108 46W
Edam, Neths. 15 B5 52 31N 5 3 E
Eday, U.K. 12 B6 59 11N 2 47W
Eddrachillis B., U.K. 12 C3 58 17N 5 10W
Eddystone Pt., Australia 62 G4 40 59S 148 20 E

Felipe Carrillo Puerto

Felipe Carrillo Puerto, Mexico **87 D7** 19 38N 88 3W
Felixstowe, U.K. **11 F9** 51 58N 1 23 E
Felton, U.S.A. **84 H4** 37 3N 122 4W
Femer Bælt = Fehmarn Bælt, Europe **9 J14** 54 35N 11 20 E
Femunden, Norway **9 E14** 62 10N 11 53 E
Fen He →, China **34 G6** 35 36N 110 42 E
Fenelon Falls, Canada **78 B6** 44 32N 78 45W
Feng Xian, Jiangsu, China **34 G9** 34 43N 116 35 E
Feng Xian, Shaanxi, China **34 H4** 33 54N 106 40 E
Fengcheng, China **35 D13** 40 28N 124 5 E
Fengfeng, China **34 F8** 36 28N 114 8 E
Fengjie, China **33 C5** 31 5N 109 36 E
Fengning, China **34 D9** 41 10N 116 33 E
Fengqiu, China **34 G8** 35 2N 114 25 E
Fengrun, China **35 E10** 39 48N 118 8 E
Fengtai, China **34 E9** 39 50N 116 18 E
Fengxiang, China **34 G4** 34 29N 107 25 E
Fengyang, China **35 H9** 32 51N 117 29 E
Fengzhen, China **34 D7** 40 25N 113 2 E
Fenoarivo Afovoany, Madag. **57 B8** 18 26S 46 34 E
Fenoarivo Atsinanana, Madag. **57 B8** 17 22S 49 25 E
Fens, The, U.K. **10 E7** 52 38N 0 2W
Fenton, U.S.A. **76 D4** 42 48N 83 42W
Fenxi, China **34 F6** 36 40N 111 31 E
Fenyang, China **34 F6** 37 18N 111 48 E
Feodosiya, Ukraine **25 E6** 45 2N 35 16 E
Ferdows, Iran **45 C8** 33 58N 58 2 E
Ferfer, Somali Rep. **46 F4** 5 4N 45 9 E
Fergana = Farghona, Uzbekistan **26 E8** 40 23N 71 19 E
Fergus, Canada **78 C4** 43 43N 80 24W
Fergus Falls, U.S.A. **80 B6** 46 17N 96 4W
Ferkéssédougou, Ivory C. **50 G4** 9 35N 5 6W
Ferland, Canada **70 B2** 50 19N 88 27W
Fermanagh □, U.K. **13 B4** 54 21N 7 40W
Fermo, Italy **20 C5** 43 9N 13 43 E
Fermont, Canada **71 B6** 52 47N 67 5W
Fermont, Qué., Canada **69 C13** 50 28N 67 29W
Fermoy, Ireland **13 D3** 52 9N 8 16W
Fernández, Argentina **94 B3** 27 55S 63 50W
Fernandina Beach, U.S.A. **77 K5** 30 40N 81 27W
Fernando de Noronha, Brazil **93 D12** 4 0S 33 10W
Fernando Póo = Bioko, Eq. Guin. **52 D1** 3 30N 8 40 E
Ferndale, U.S.A. **84 B4** 48 51N 122 36W
Fernie, Canada **72 D5** 49 30N 115 5W
Fernlees, Australia **62 C4** 23 51S 148 7 E
Fernley, U.S.A. **82 G4** 39 36N 119 15W
Ferozepore = Firozpur, India **42 D6** 30 55N 74 40 E
Ferrara, Italy **20 B4** 44 50N 11 35 E
Ferreñafe, Peru **92 E3** 6 42S 79 50W
Ferrerías, Spain **22 B11** 39 59N 4 1 E
Ferret, C., France **18 D3** 44 38N 1 15W
Ferriday, U.S.A. **81 K9** 31 38N 91 33W
Ferrol, Spain **19 A1** 43 29N 8 15W
Ferron, U.S.A. **83 G8** 39 5N 111 8W
Ferrutx, C., Spain **22 B10** 39 47N 3 21 E
Ferryland, Canada **71 C9** 47 2N 52 53W
Fertile, U.S.A. **80 B6** 47 32N 96 17W
Fès, Morocco **50 B5** 34 0N 5 0W
Fessenden, U.S.A. **80 B5** 47 39N 99 38W
Festus, U.S.A. **80 F9** 38 13N 90 24W
Feteşti, Romania **17 F14** 44 22N 27 51 E
Fethiye, Turkey **25 G4** 36 36N 29 6 E
Fetlar, U.K. **12 A8** 60 36N 0 52W
Feuilles →, Canada **69 C12** 58 47N 70 4W
Fez = Fès, Morocco **50 B5** 34 0N 5 0W
Fezzan, Libya **51 C8** 27 0N 13 0 E
Fiambalá, Argentina **94 B2** 27 45S 67 37W
Fianarantsoa, Madag. **57 C8** 21 26S 47 5 E
Fianarantsoa □, Madag. **57 B8** 19 30S 47 0 E
Ficksburg, S. Africa **57 D4** 28 51S 27 53 E
Field →, Australia **62 C2** 23 48S 138 0 E
Field I., Australia **60 B5** 12 5S 132 23 E
Fieri, Albania **21 D8** 40 43N 19 33 E
Fife □, U.K. **12 E5** 56 16N 3 1W
Fife Ness, U.K. **12 E6** 56 17N 2 35W
Fifth Cataract, Sudan **51 E12** 18 23N 33 47 E
Figeac, France **18 D5** 44 37N 2 2 E
Figtree, Zimbabwe **55 G2** 20 22S 28 20 E
Figueira da Foz, Portugal **19 B1** 40 7N 8 54W
Figueres, Spain **19 A7** 42 18N 2 58 E
Figuig, Morocco **50 B5** 32 5N 1 11W
Fihaonana, Madag. **57 B8** 18 36S 47 12 E
Fiherenana, Madag. **57 B8** 18 29S 48 24 E
Fiherenana →, Madag. **57 C7** 23 19S 43 37 E
Fiji ■, Pac. Oc. **59 C8** 17 20S 179 0 E
Filey, U.K. **10 C7** 54 12N 0 18W
Filey B., U.K. **10 C7** 54 12N 0 15W
Filfla, Malta **23 D1** 35 47N 14 24 E
Filiatrá, Greece **21 F9** 37 9N 21 35 E
Filingué, Niger **50 F6** 14 21N 3 22 E
Filipstad, Sweden **9 G16** 59 43N 14 9 E
Fillmore, Calif., U.S.A. **85 L8** 34 24N 118 55W
Fillmore, Utah, U.S.A. **83 G7** 38 58N 112 20W
Finch, Canada **79 A9** 45 11N 75 7W
Findhorn →, U.K. **12 D5** 57 38N 3 38W
Findlay, U.S.A. **76 E4** 41 2N 83 39W
Finger L., Canada **70 B1** 53 33N 93 30W
Finger Lakes, U.S.A. **79 D8** 42 40N 76 30W
Fingoè, Mozam. **55 E3** 14 55S 31 50 E
Finisterre, C. = Fisterra, C., Spain **19 A1** 42 50N 9 19W
Finke, Australia **62 D1** 25 34S 134 35 E
Finland ■, Europe **8 E22** 63 0N 27 0 E
Finland, G. of, Europe **9 G21** 60 0N 26 0 E
Finlay →, Canada **72 B3** 57 0N 125 10W
Finley, Australia **63 F4** 35 38S 145 35 E
Finley, U.S.A. **80 B6** 47 31N 97 50W
Finn →, Ireland **13 B4** 54 51N 7 28W
Finnigan, Mt., Australia **62 B4** 15 49S 145 17 E
Finniss, C., Australia **63 E1** 33 8S 134 51 E
Finnmark, Norway **8 B20** 69 37N 23 57 E
Finnsnes, Norway **8 B18** 69 14N 18 0 E
Finspång, Sweden **9 G16** 58 43N 15 47 E
Fiora →, Italy **20 C4** 42 20N 11 34 E
Fiq, Syria **47 C4** 32 46N 35 41 E
Firat = Furāt, Nahr al →, Asia **44 D5** 31 0N 47 25 E
Firebag →, Canada **73 B6** 57 45N 111 21W
Firebaugh, U.S.A. **84 J6** 36 52N 120 27W
Firedrake L., Canada **73 A8** 61 25N 104 30W
Firenze, Italy **20 C4** 43 46N 11 15 E
Firk →, Iraq **44 D5** 30 59N 44 34 E
Firozabad, India **43 F8** 27 10N 78 25 E
Firozpur, India **42 D6** 30 55N 74 40 E
Firozpur-Jhirka, India **42 F7** 27 48N 76 57 E
Fīrūzābād, Iran **45 D7** 28 52N 52 35 E
Fīrūzkūh, Iran **45 C7** 35 50N 52 50 E
Firvale, Canada **72 C3** 52 27N 126 13W
Fish →, Namibia **56 D2** 28 7S 17 10 E
Fish →, S. Africa **56 E3** 31 30S 20 16 E
Fisher, Australia **61 F5** 30 30S 131 0 E
Fisher B., Canada **73 C9** 51 35N 97 13W
Fishers I., U.S.A. **79 E13** 41 15N 72 0W
Fishguard, U.K. **11 E3** 52 0N 4 58W
Fishing L., Canada **73 C9** 52 10N 95 24W
Fishkill, U.S.A. **79 E11** 41 32N 73 53W
Fisterra, C., Spain **19 A1** 42 50N 9 19W
Fitchburg, U.S.A. **79 D13** 42 35N 71 48W
Fitz Roy, Argentina **96 F3** 47 0S 67 0W
Fitzgerald, Canada **72 B6** 59 51N 111 36W
Fitzgerald, U.S.A. **77 K4** 31 43N 83 15W
Fitzmaurice →, Australia **60 B5** 14 45S 130 5 E
Fitzroy →, Queens., Australia **62 C5** 23 32S 150 52 E
Fitzroy →, W. Austral., Australia **60 C3** 17 31S 123 35 E
Fitzroy, Mte., Argentina **96 F2** 49 17S 73 5W
Fitzroy Crossing, Australia **60 C4** 18 9S 125 38 E
Fitzwilliam I., Canada **78 A3** 45 30N 81 45W
Fiume = Rijeka, Croatia **16 F8** 45 20N 14 21 E
Five Points, U.S.A. **84 J6** 36 26N 120 6W
Fizi, Dem. Rep. of the Congo **54 C2** 4 17S 28 55 E
Flagstaff, U.S.A. **83 J8** 35 12N 111 39W
Flagstaff L., Maine, U.S.A. **77 C10** 45 12N 70 19W
Flagstaff L., Maine, U.S.A. **79 A14** 45 12N 70 18W
Flaherty I., Canada **70 A4** 56 15N 79 15W
Flåm, Norway **9 F12** 60 50N 7 7 E
Flambeau →, U.S.A. **80 C9** 45 18N 91 14W
Flamborough Hd., U.K. **10 C7** 54 7N 0 5W
Flaming Gorge Reservoir, U.S.A. **82 F9** 41 10N 109 25W
Flamingo, Teluk, Indonesia **37 F9** 5 30S 138 0 E
Flanders = Flandre, Europe **18 A5** 50 50N 2 30 E
Flandre, Europe **18 A5** 50 50N 2 30 E
Flandre Occidentale = West-Vlaanderen □, Belgium **15 D2** 51 0N 3 0 E
Flandre Orientale = Oost-Vlaanderen □, Belgium **15 C3** 51 5N 3 50 E
Flandreau, U.S.A. **80 C6** 44 3N 96 36W
Flanigan, U.S.A. **84 E7** 40 10N 119 53W
Flannan Is., U.K. **12 C1** 58 9N 7 52W
Flåsjön, Sweden **8 D16** 64 5N 15 40 E
Flat →, Canada **72 A3** 61 33N 125 18W
Flathead L., U.S.A. **82 C7** 47 51N 114 8W
Flattery, C., Australia **62 A4** 14 58S 145 21 E
Flattery, C., U.S.A. **84 B2** 48 23N 124 29W
Flatwoods, U.S.A. **76 F4** 38 31N 82 43W
Fleetwood, U.K. **10 D4** 53 55N 3 1W
Fleetwood, U.S.A. **79 F9** 40 27N 75 49W
Flekkefjord, Norway **9 G12** 58 18N 6 39 E
Flemington, U.S.A. **78 E7** 41 7N 77 28W
Flensburg, Germany **16 A5** 54 47N 9 27 E
Flers, France **18 B3** 48 47N 0 33W
Flesherton, Canada **78 B4** 44 16N 80 33W
Flesko, Tanjung, Indonesia **37 D6** 0 29N 124 30 E
Fleurieu Pen., Australia **63 F2** 35 40S 138 5 E
Flevoland □, Neths. **15 B5** 52 30N 5 30 E
Flin Flon, Canada **73 C8** 54 46N 101 53W
Flinders →, Australia **62 B3** 17 36S 140 36 E
Flinders B., Australia **61 F2** 34 19S 115 19 E
Flinders Group, Australia **62 A3** 14 11S 144 15 E
Flinders I., S. Austral., Australia **63 E1** 33 44S 134 41 E
Flinders I., Tas., Australia **62 G4** 40 0S 148 0 E
Flinders Ranges, Australia **63 E2** 31 30S 138 30 E
Flinders Reefs, Australia **62 B4** 17 37S 148 31 E
Flint, U.K. **10 D4** 53 15N 3 8W
Flint, U.S.A. **76 D4** 43 1N 83 41W
Flint →, U.S.A. **77 K3** 30 57N 84 34W
Flint I., Kiribati **65 J12** 11 26S 151 48W
Flintshire □, U.K. **10 D4** 53 17N 3 17W
Flodden, U.K. **10 B5** 55 37N 2 8W
Floodwood, U.S.A. **80 B8** 46 55N 92 55W
Flora, U.S.A. **76 F1** 38 40N 88 29W
Florala, U.S.A. **77 K2** 31 0N 86 20W
Florence = Firenze, Italy **20 C4** 43 46N 11 15 E
Florence, Ala., U.S.A. **77 H2** 34 48N 87 41W
Florence, Ariz., U.S.A. **83 K8** 33 2N 111 23W
Florence, Colo., U.S.A. **80 F2** 38 23N 105 8W
Florence, Oreg., U.S.A. **82 E1** 43 58N 124 7W
Florence, S.C., U.S.A. **77 H6** 34 12N 79 46W
Florence, L., Australia **63 D2** 28 53S 138 9 E
Florencia, Colombia **92** 1 36N 75 36W
Florennes, Belgium **15 D4** 50 15N 4 35 E
Florenville, Belgium **15 E5** 49 40N 5 19 E
Flores, Guatemala **88 C2** 16 59N 89 50W
Flores, Indonesia **37 F6** 8 35S 121 0 E
Flores I., Canada **72 D3** 49 20N 126 10W
Flores Sea, Indonesia **37 F6** 6 30S 120 0 E
Floreşti, Moldova **17 E15** 47 53N 28 17 E
Floresville, U.S.A. **81 L5** 29 8N 98 10W
Floriano, Brazil **93 E10** 6 50S 43 0W
Florianópolis, Brazil **95 B6** 27 30S 48 30W
Florida, Cuba **88 B4** 21 32N 78 14W
Florida, Uruguay **95 C4** 34 7S 56 10W
Florida □, U.S.A. **77 L5** 28 0N 82 0W
Florida, Straits of, U.S.A. **88 B4** 25 0N 80 0W
Florida B., U.S.A. **88 B3** 25 0N 80 45W
Florida Keys, U.S.A. **77 N5** 24 40N 81 0W
Flórina, Greece **21 D9** 40 48N 21 26 E
Florø, Norway **9 F11** 61 35N 5 1 E
Flower Station, Canada **79 A8** 45 10N 76 41W
Flowerpot I., Canada **78 A3** 45 18N 81 38W
Floydada, U.S.A. **81 J4** 33 59N 101 20W
Fluk, Indonesia **37 E7** 1 42S 127 44 E
Flushing = Vlissingen, Neths. **15 C3** 51 26N 3 34 E
Flying Fish, C., Antarctica **5 D15** 72 6S 102 29W
Foam Lake, Canada **73 C8** 51 40N 103 32W
Foča, Turkey **21 E12** 38 39N 26 46 E
Focşani, Romania **17 F14** 45 41N 27 15 E
Fóggia, Italy **20 D6** 41 27N 15 34 E
Fogo, Canada **71 C9** 49 43N 54 17W
Fogo I., Canada **71 C9** 49 40N 54 5W
Föhr, Germany **16 A5** 54 43N 8 30 E
Foix, France **18 E4** 42 58N 1 38 E
Folda, Nord-Trøndelag, Norway **8 D14** 64 32N 10 30 E
Folda, Nordland, Norway **8 C16** 67 38N 14 50 E
Foley, U.S.A. **77 K2** 30 24N 87 41W
Foleyet, Canada **70 C3** 48 15N 82 25W
Folgefonni, Norway **9 F12** 60 3N 6 23 E
Foligno, Italy **20 C5** 42 57N 12 42 E
Folkestone, U.K. **11 F9** 51 5N 1 12 E
Folkston, U.S.A. **77 K5** 30 50N 82 0W
Follansbee, U.S.A. **78 F4** 40 19N 80 35W
Folsom L., U.S.A. **84 G5** 38 42N 121 9W
Fond-du-Lac, Canada **73 B7** 59 19N 107 12W
Fond du Lac, U.S.A. **80 D10** 43 47N 88 27W
Fond-du-Lac →, Canada **73 B7** 59 17N 106 0W
Fonda, U.S.A. **79 D10** 42 57N 74 22W
Fondi, Italy **20 D5** 41 21N 13 25 E
Fongafale, Tuvalu **64 H9** 8 31S 179 13 E
Fonsagrada = A Fonsagrada, Spain **19 A2** 43 8N 7 4W
Fonseca, G. de, Cent. Amer. **88 D2** 13 10N 87 40W
Fontainebleau, France **18 B5** 48 24N 2 40 E
Fontana, U.S.A. **85 L9** 34 6N 117 26W
Fontas →, Canada **72 B4** 58 14N 121 48W
Fonte Boa, Brazil **92 D5** 2 33S 66 0W
Fontenay-le-Comte, France **18 C3** 46 28N 0 48W
Fontenelle Reservoir, U.S.A. **82 E8** 42 1N 110 3W
Fontur, Iceland **8 C6** 66 23N 14 32W
Foochow = Fuzhou, China **33 D6** 26 5N 119 16 E
Foping, China **34 H5** 33 41N 108 0 E
Forbes, Australia **63 E4** 33 22S 148 0 E
Forbesganj, India **43 F12** 26 17N 87 18 E
Ford City, Calif., U.S.A. **85 K7** 35 9N 119 27W
Ford City, Pa., U.S.A. **78 F5** 40 46N 79 32W
Førde, Norway **9 F11** 61 27N 5 53 E
Ford's Bridge, Australia **63 D4** 29 41S 145 29 E
Fordyce, U.S.A. **81 J8** 33 49N 92 25W
Forel, Mt., Greenland **4 C6** 66 52N 36 55W
Foremost, Canada **72 D6** 49 26N 111 34W
Forest, Canada **78 C3** 43 6N 82 0W
Forest, U.S.A. **81 J10** 32 22N 89 29W
Forest City, Iowa, U.S.A. **80 D8** 43 16N 93 39W
Forest City, N.C., U.S.A. **77 H5** 35 20N 81 52W
Forest City, Pa., U.S.A. **79 E9** 41 39N 75 28W
Forest Grove, U.S.A. **84 E3** 45 31N 123 7W
Forestburg, Canada **72 C6** 52 35N 112 1W
Foresthill, U.S.A. **84 F6** 39 1N 120 49W
Forestier Pen., Australia **62 G4** 43 0S 148 0 E
Forestville, Canada **71 C6** 48 48N 69 2W
Forestville, Calif., U.S.A. **84 G4** 38 28N 122 54W
Forestville, N.Y., U.S.A. **78 D5** 42 28N 79 10W
Forfar, U.K. **12 E6** 56 39N 2 53W
Forks, U.S.A. **84 C2** 47 57N 124 23W
Forksville, U.S.A. **79 E8** 41 29N 76 35W
Forlì, Italy **20 B5** 44 13N 12 3 E
Forman, U.S.A. **80 B6** 46 7N 97 38W
Formby Pt., U.K. **10 D4** 53 33N 3 6W
Formentera, Spain **22 C7** 38 43N 1 27 E
Formentor, C. de, Spain **22 B10** 39 58N 3 13 E
Former Yugoslav Republic of Macedonia = Macedonia ■, Europe **21 D9** 41 53N 21 40 E
Fórmia, Italy **20 D5** 41 15N 13 37 E
Formosa = Taiwan ■, Asia **33 D7** 23 30N 121 0 E
Formosa, Argentina **94 B4** 26 15S 58 10W
Formosa, Brazil **93 G9** 15 32S 47 20W
Formosa □, Argentina **94 B4** 25 0S 60 0W
Formosa, Serra, Brazil **93 F8** 12 0S 55 0W
Formosa Bay, Kenya **54 C5** 2 40S 40 20 E
Fornells, Spain **22 A11** 40 3N 4 7 E
Føroyar, Atl. Oc. **8 F9** 62 0N 7 0W
Forres, U.K. **12 D5** 57 37N 3 37W
Forrest, Australia **61 F4** 30 51S 128 6 E
Forrest, Mt., Australia **61 D4** 24 48S 127 45 E
Forrest City, U.S.A. **81 H9** 35 1N 90 47W
Forsayth, Australia **62 B3** 18 33S 143 34 E
Forssa, Finland **9 F20** 60 49N 23 38 E
Forst, Germany **16 C8** 51 45N 14 37 E
Forsyth, U.S.A. **82 C10** 46 16N 106 41W
Fort Abbas, Pakistan **42 E5** 29 12N 72 52 E
Fort Albany, Canada **70 B3** 52 15N 81 35W
Fort Ann, U.S.A. **79 C11** 43 25N 73 30W
Fort Assiniboine, Canada **72 C6** 54 20N 114 45W
Fort Augustus, U.K. **12 D4** 57 9N 4 42W
Fort Beaufort, S. Africa **56 E4** 32 46S 26 40 E
Fort Benton, U.S.A. **82 C8** 47 49N 110 40W
Fort Bragg, U.S.A. **82 G2** 39 26N 123 48W
Fort Bridger, U.S.A. **82 F8** 41 19N 110 23W
Fort Chipewyan, Canada **73 B6** 58 42N 111 8W
Fort Collins, U.S.A. **80 E2** 40 35N 105 5W
Fort-Coulonge, Canada **70 C4** 45 50N 76 45W
Fort Covington, U.S.A. **79 B10** 44 59N 74 29W
Fort Davis, U.S.A. **81 K3** 30 35N 103 54W
Fort-de-France, Martinique **89 D7** 14 36N 61 2W
Fort Defiance, U.S.A. **83 J9** 35 45N 109 5W
Fort Dodge, U.S.A. **80 D7** 42 30N 94 11W
Fort Edward, U.S.A. **79 C11** 43 16N 73 35W
Fort Erie, Canada **78 D6** 42 54N 78 56W
Fort Fairfield, U.S.A. **77 B12** 46 46N 67 50W
Fort Frances, Canada **73 D10** 48 36N 93 24W
Fort Garland, U.S.A. **83 H11** 37 26N 105 26W
Fort George = Chisasibi, Canada **70 B4** 53 50N 79 0W
Fort Good-Hope, Canada **68 B7** 66 14N 128 40W
Fort Hancock, U.S.A. **83 L11** 31 18N 105 51W
Fort Hertz = Putao, Burma **41 F20** 27 28N 97 30 E
Fort Hope, Canada **70 B2** 51 30N 88 0W
Fort Irwin, U.S.A. **85 K10** 35 16N 116 34W
Fort Jameson = Chipata, Zambia **55 E3** 13 38S 32 28 E
Fort Kent, U.S.A. **77 B11** 47 15N 68 36W
Fort Klamath, U.S.A. **82 E3** 42 42N 122 0W
Fort-Lamy = Ndjamena, Chad **51 F8** 12 10N 14 59 E
Fort Laramie, U.S.A. **80 D2** 42 13N 104 31W
Fort Lauderdale, U.S.A. **77 M5** 26 7N 80 8W
Fort Liard, Canada **72 A4** 60 14N 123 30W
Fort Liberté, Haiti **89 C5** 19 42N 71 51W
Fort Lupton, U.S.A. **80 E2** 40 5N 104 49W
Fort Mackay, Canada **72 B6** 57 12N 111 41W
Fort Macleod, Canada **72 D6** 49 45N 113 30W
Fort McMurray, Canada **72 B6** 56 44N 111 7W
Fort McPherson, Canada **68 B6** 67 30N 134 55W
Fort Madison, U.S.A. **80 E9** 40 38N 91 27W
Fort Meade, U.S.A. **77 M5** 27 45N 81 48W
Fort Morgan, U.S.A. **80 E3** 40 15N 103 48W
Fort Munro, Pakistan **42 E3** 29 54N 69 58 E
Fort Myers, U.S.A. **77 M5** 26 39N 81 52W
Fort Nelson, Canada **72 B4** 58 50N 122 44W
Fort Nelson →, Canada **72 B4** 59 32N 124 0W
Fort Norman = Tulita, Canada **68 B7** 64 57N 125 30W
Fort Payne, U.S.A. **77 H3** 34 26N 85 43W
Fort Peck, U.S.A. **82 B10** 48 1N 106 27W
Fort Peck Dam, U.S.A. **82 C10** 48 0N 106 26W
Fort Peck L., U.S.A. **82 C10** 48 0N 106 26W
Fort Pierce, U.S.A. **77 M5** 27 27N 80 20W
Fort Pierre, U.S.A. **80 C4** 44 21N 100 22W
Fort Plain, U.S.A. **79 D10** 42 56N 74 37W
Fort Portal, Uganda **54 B3** 0 40N 30 20 E
Fort Providence, Canada **72 A5** 61 3N 117 40W
Fort Qu'Appelle, Canada **73 C8** 50 45N 103 50W
Fort Resolution, Canada **72 A6** 61 10N 113 40W
Fort Rixon, Zimbabwe **55 G2** 20 2S 29 17 E
Fort Rosebery = Mansa, Zambia **55 E2** 11 13S 28 55 E
Fort Ross, U.S.A. **84 G3** 38 32N 123 13W
Fort Rousset = Owando, Congo **52 E3** 0 29S 15 55 E
Fort Rupert = Waskaganish, Canada **70 B4** 51 30N 78 40W
Fort St. James, Canada **72 C4** 54 30N 124 10W
Fort St. John, Canada **72 B4** 56 15N 120 50W
Fort Sandeman = Zhob, Pakistan **42 D3** 31 20N 69 31 E
Fort Saskatchewan, Canada **72 C6** 53 40N 113 15W
Fort Scott, U.S.A. **81 G7** 37 50N 94 42W
Fort Severn, Canada **70 A2** 56 0N 87 40W
Fort Shevchenko, Kazakstan **25 F9** 44 35N 50 23 E
Fort Simpson, Canada **72 A4** 61 45N 121 15W
Fort Smith, Canada **72 B6** 60 0N 111 51W
Fort Smith, U.S.A. **81 H7** 35 23N 94 25W
Fort Stockton, U.S.A. **81 K3** 30 53N 102 53W
Fort Sumner, U.S.A. **81 H2** 34 28N 104 15W
Fort Thompson, U.S.A. **80 C5** 44 3N 99 26W
Fort Trinquet = Bir Mogreïn, Mauritania **50 C3** 25 10N 11 25W
Fort Valley, U.S.A. **77 J4** 32 33N 83 53W
Fort Vermilion, Canada **72 B5** 58 24N 116 0W
Fort Walton Beach, U.S.A. **77 K2** 30 25N 86 36W
Fort Wayne, U.S.A. **76 E3** 41 4N 85 9W
Fort William, U.K. **12 E3** 56 49N 5 7W
Fort Worth, U.S.A. **81 J6** 32 45N 97 18W
Fort Yates, U.S.A. **80 B4** 46 5N 100 38W
Fort Yukon, U.S.A. **68 B5** 66 34N 145 16W
Fortaleza, Brazil **93 D11** 3 45S 38 35W
Forteau, Canada **71 B8** 51 28N 56 58W
Fortescue →, Australia **60 D2** 21 0S 116 4 E
Forth →, U.K. **12 E5** 56 9N 3 50W
Forth, Firth of, U.K. **12 E6** 56 5N 2 55W
Fortrose, U.K. **12 D4** 57 35N 4 9W
Fortuna, Calif., U.S.A. **82 F1** 40 36N 124 9W
Fortuna, N. Dak., U.S.A. **80 A3** 48 55N 103 47W
Fortune, Canada **71 C8** 47 4N 55 50W
Fortune B., Canada **71 C8** 47 30N 55 22W
Forūr, Iran **45 E7** 26 17N 54 32 E
Foshan, China **33 D6** 23 4N 113 5 E
Fosna, Norway **8 E14** 63 50N 10 20 E
Fosnavåg, Norway **9 E11** 62 22N 5 38 E
Fossano, Italy **18 D7** 44 33N 7 43 E
Fossil, U.S.A. **82 D3** 45 0N 120 9W
Foster, Australia **63 F4** 38 40S 146 15 E
Foster, Canada **79 A12** 45 17N 72 30W
Foster →, Canada **73 B7** 55 47N 105 49W
Fosters Ra., Australia **62 C1** 21 35S 133 48 E
Fostoria, U.S.A. **76 E4** 41 10N 83 25W
Fougères, France **18 B3** 48 21N 1 14W
Foul Pt., Sri Lanka **40 Q12** 8 35N 81 18 E
Foula, U.K. **12 A6** 60 10N 2 5W
Foulness I., U.K. **11 F8** 51 36N 0 55 E
Foulpointe, Madag. **57 B8** 17 41S 49 31 E
Foulweather, C., U.S.A. **74 B2** 44 50N 124 5W
Foumban, Cameroon **52 C2** 5 45N 10 50 E
Fountain, U.S.A. **80 F2** 38 41N 104 42W
Fountain Springs, U.S.A. **85 K8** 35 54N 118 51W
Fouriesburg, S. Africa **56 D4** 28 38S 28 14 E
Foúrnoi, Greece **21 F12** 37 36N 26 32 E
Fourth Cataract, Sudan **51 E12** 18 47N 32 3 E
Fouta Djalon, Guinea **50 F3** 11 20N 12 10W
Foux, Cap-à-, Haiti **89 C5** 19 43N 73 27W
Foveaux Str., N.Z. **59 M2** 46 42S 168 10 E
Fowey, U.K. **11 G3** 50 20N 4 39W
Fowler, Calif., U.S.A. **84 J7** 36 38N 119 41W
Fowler, Colo., U.S.A. **80 F3** 38 8N 104 2W
Fowlers B., Australia **61 F5** 31 59S 132 34 E
Fowman, Iran **45 B6** 37 13N 49 19 E
Fox →, Canada **73 B10** 56 3N 93 18W
Fox Creek, Canada **72 C5** 54 24N 116 48W
Fox Lake, Canada **72 B6** 58 28N 114 31W
Fox Valley, Canada **73 C7** 50 30N 109 25W
Foxboro, U.S.A. **79 D13** 42 4N 71 16W
Foxe Basin, Canada **69 B12** 66 0N 77 0W
Foxe Chan., Canada **69 B12** 65 0N 80 0W
Foxe Pen., Canada **69 B12** 65 0N 76 0W
Foxton, N.Z. **59 J5** 40 29S 175 18 E
Foyle, Lough, U.K. **13 A4** 55 7N 7 4W
Foynes, Ireland **13 D2** 52 37N 9 7W
Fóz do Cunene, Angola **56 B1** 17 15S 11 48 E
Foz do Iguaçu, Brazil **95 B5** 25 30S 54 30W
Frackville, U.S.A. **79 F8** 40 47N 76 14W
Fraile Muerto, Uruguay **95 C5** 32 31S 54 32W
Framingham, U.S.A. **79 D13** 42 17N 71 25W
Franca, Brazil **93 H9** 20 33S 47 30W
Francavilla Fontana, Italy **21 D7** 40 32N 17 35 E
France ■, Europe **18 C5** 47 0N 3 0 E
Frances, Australia **63 F3** 36 41S 140 55 E
Frances →, Canada **72 A3** 60 16N 129 10W
Frances L., Canada **72 A3** 61 23N 129 30W
Franceville, Gabon **52 E2** 1 40S 13 32 E
Franche-Comté, France **18 C6** 46 50N 5 55 E
Francis Case, L., U.S.A. **80 D5** 43 4N 98 34W
Francisco Beltrão, Brazil **95 B5** 26 5S 53 4W
Francisco I. Madero, Coahuila, Mexico **86 B4** 25 48N 103 18W
Francisco I. Madero, Durango, Mexico **86 C4** 24 32N 104 22W
Francistown, Botswana **57 C4** 21 7S 27 33 E
François, Canada **71 C8** 47 35N 56 45W
François L., Canada **72 C3** 54 0N 125 30W
Franeker, Neths. **15 A5** 53 12N 5 33 E
Frankford, Canada **78 B7** 44 12N 77 36W
Frankfort, S. Africa **57 D4** 27 17S 28 30 E
Frankfort, Ind., U.S.A. **76 E2** 40 17N 86 31W
Frankfort, Kans., U.S.A. **80 F6** 39 42N 96 25W
Frankfort, Ky., U.S.A. **76 F3** 38 12N 84 52W
Frankfort, N.Y., U.S.A. **79 C9** 43 2N 75 4W

Gatton

Frankfurt, *Brandenburg, Germany* **16 B8** 52 20N 14 32 E
Frankfurt, *Hessen, Germany* **16 C5** 50 7N 8 41 E
Fränkische Alb, *Germany* **16 D6** 49 10N 11 23 E
Frankland →, *Australia* **61 G2** 35 0S 116 48 E
Franklin, *Ky., U.S.A.* **77 G2** 36 43N 86 35W
Franklin, *La., U.S.A.* **81 L9** 29 48N 91 30W
Franklin, *Mass., U.S.A.* **79 D13** 42 5N 71 24W
Franklin, *N.H., U.S.A.* **79 C13** 43 27N 71 39W
Franklin, *Nebr., U.S.A.* **80 E5** 40 6N 98 57W
Franklin, *Pa., U.S.A.* **78 E5** 41 24N 79 50W
Franklin, *Va., U.S.A.* **77 G7** 36 41N 76 56W
Franklin, *W. Va., U.S.A.* **76 F6** 38 39N 79 20W
Franklin B., *Canada* **68 B7** 69 45N 126 0W
Franklin D. Roosevelt L., *U.S.A.* **82 B4** 48 18N 118 9W
Franklin I., *Antarctica* **5 D11** 76 10S 168 30 E
Franklin L., *U.S.A.* **82 F6** 40 25N 115 22W
Franklin Mts., *Canada* **68 B7** 65 0N 125 0W
Franklin Str., *Canada* **68 A10** 72 0N 96 0W
Franklinton, *U.S.A.* **81 K9** 30 51N 90 9W
Franklinville, *U.S.A.* **78 D6** 42 20N 78 27W
Franks Pk., *U.S.A.* **82 E9** 43 58N 109 18W
Frankston, *Australia* **63 F4** 38 8S 145 8 E
Frantsa Iosifa, Zemlya, *Russia* **26 A6** 82 0N 55 0 E
Franz, *Canada* **70 C3** 48 25N 84 30W
Franz Josef Land = Frantsa Iosifa, Zemlya, *Russia* **26 A6** 82 0N 55 0 E
Fraser, *U.S.A.* **78 D2** 42 32N 82 57W
Fraser →, *B.C., Canada* **72 D4** 49 7N 123 11W
Fraser →, *Nfld., Canada* **71 A7** 56 39N 62 10W
Fraser, Mt., *Australia* **61 E2** 25 35S 118 20 E
Fraser I., *Australia* **63 D5** 25 15S 153 10 E
Fraser Lake, *Canada* **72 C4** 54 0N 124 50W
Fraserburg, *S. Africa* **56 E3** 31 55S 21 30 E
Fraserburgh, *U.K.* **12 D6** 57 42N 2 1W
Fraserdale, *Canada* **70 C3** 49 55N 81 37W
Fray Bentos, *Uruguay* **94 C4** 33 10S 58 15W
Fredericia, *Denmark* **9 J13** 55 34N 9 45 E
Frederick, *Md., U.S.A.* **76 F7** 39 25N 77 25W
Frederick, *Okla., U.S.A.* **81 H5** 34 23N 99 1W
Frederick, *S. Dak., U.S.A.* **80 C5** 45 50N 98 31W
Fredericksburg, *Pa., U.S.A.* **79 F8** 40 27N 76 26W
Fredericksburg, *Tex., U.S.A.* **81 K5** 30 16N 98 52W
Fredericksburg, *Va., U.S.A.* **76 F7** 38 18N 77 28W
Fredericktown, *Mo., U.S.A.* **81 G9** 37 34N 90 18W
Fredericktown, *Ohio, U.S.A.* **78 F2** 40 29N 82 33W
Frederico I. Madero, Presa, *Mexico* **86 B3** 28 7N 105 40W
Frederico Westphalen, *Brazil* **95 B5** 27 22S 53 24W
Fredericton, *Canada* **71 C6** 45 57N 66 40W
Fredericton Junction, *Canada* **71 C6** 45 41N 66 40W
Frederikshåb, *Greenland* **4 C5** 62 0N 49 43W
Frederikshavn, *Denmark* **9 H14** 57 28N 10 31 E
Frederiksted, *Virgin Is.* **89 C7** 17 43N 64 53W
Fredonia, *Ariz., U.S.A.* **83 H7** 36 57N 112 32W
Fredonia, *Kans., U.S.A.* **81 G7** 37 32N 95 49W
Fredonia, *N.Y., U.S.A.* **78 D5** 42 26N 79 20W
Fredrikstad, *Norway* **9 G14** 59 13N 10 57 E
Free State □, *S. Africa* **56 D4** 28 30S 27 0 E
Freehold, *U.S.A.* **79 F10** 40 16N 74 17W
Freel Peak, *U.S.A.* **84 G7** 38 52N 119 54W
Freeland, *U.S.A.* **79 E9** 41 1N 75 54W
Freels, C., *Canada* **71 C9** 49 15N 53 30W
Freeman, *Calif., U.S.A.* **85 K9** 35 35N 117 53W
Freeman, *S. Dak., U.S.A.* **80 D6** 43 21N 97 26W
Freeport, *Bahamas* **88 A4** 26 30N 78 47W
Freeport, *Ill., U.S.A.* **80 D10** 42 17N 89 36W
Freeport, *N.Y., U.S.A.* **79 F11** 40 39N 73 35W
Freeport, *Ohio, U.S.A.* **78 F3** 40 12N 81 15W
Freeport, *Pa., U.S.A.* **78 F5** 40 41N 79 41W
Freeport, *Tex., U.S.A.* **81 L7** 28 57N 95 21W
Freetown, *S. Leone* **50 G3** 8 30N 13 17W
Frégate, L., *Canada* **70 B5** 53 15N 74 45W
Fregenal de la Sierra, *Spain* **19 C2** 38 10N 6 39W
Freibourg = Fribourg, *Switz.* **18 C7** 46 49N 7 9 E
Freiburg, *Germany* **16 E4** 47 59N 7 51 E
Freire, *Chile* **96 D2** 38 54S 72 38W
Freirina, *Chile* **94 B1** 28 30S 71 10W
Freising, *Germany* **16 D6** 48 24N 11 45 E
Freistadt, *Austria* **16 D8** 48 30N 14 30 E
Fréjus, *France* **18 E7** 43 25N 6 44 E
Fremantle, *Australia* **61 F2** 32 7S 115 47 E
Fremont, *Calif., U.S.A.* **84 H4** 37 32N 121 57W
Fremont, *Mich., U.S.A.* **76 D3** 43 28N 85 57W
Fremont, *Nebr., U.S.A.* **80 E6** 41 26N 96 30W
Fremont, *Ohio, U.S.A.* **76 E4** 41 21N 83 7W
Fremont →, *U.S.A.* **83 G8** 38 24N 110 42W
French Camp, *U.S.A.* **84 H5** 37 53N 121 16W
French Creek →, *U.S.A.* **78 E5** 41 24N 79 50W
French Guiana ■, *S. Amer.* **93 C8** 4 0N 53 0W
French Pass, *N.Z.* **59 J4** 40 55S 173 55 E
French Polynesia ■, *Pac. Oc.* **65 K13** 20 0S 145 0W
Frenchman Cr. →, *N. Amer.* **82 B10** 48 31N 107 10W
Frenchman Cr. →, *U.S.A.* **80 E4** 40 14N 100 50W
Fresco →, *Brazil* **93 E8** 7 15S 51 30W
Freshfield, C., *Antarctica* **5 C10** 68 25S 151 10 E
Fresnillo, *Mexico* **86 C4** 23 10N 103 0W
Fresno, *U.S.A.* **84 J7** 36 44N 119 47W
Fresno Reservoir, *U.S.A.* **82 B9** 48 36N 109 57W
Frew →, *Australia* **62 C2** 20 0S 135 38 E
Frewsburg, *U.S.A.* **78 D5** 42 3N 79 10W
Freycinet Pen., *Australia* **62 G4** 42 10S 148 25 E
Fria, C., *Namibia* **56 B1** 18 0S 12 0 E
Friant, *U.S.A.* **84 J7** 36 59N 119 43W
Frías, *Argentina* **94 B2** 28 40S 65 5W
Fribourg, *Switz.* **18 C7** 46 49N 7 9 E
Friday Harbor, *U.S.A.* **84 B3** 48 32N 123 1W
Friedens, *U.S.A.* **78 F6** 40 3N 78 59W
Friedrichshafen, *Germany* **16 E5** 47 39N 9 30 E
Friendly Is. = Tonga ■, *Pac. Oc.* **59 D11** 19 50S 174 30W
Friendship, *U.S.A.* **78 D6** 42 12N 78 8W
Friesland □, *Neths.* **15 A5** 53 5N 5 50 E
Frio →, *U.S.A.* **81 L5** 28 26N 98 11W
Frio, C., *Brazil* **90 F6** 22 50S 41 50W
Friona, *U.S.A.* **81 H3** 34 38N 102 43W
Fritch, *U.S.A.* **81 H4** 35 38N 101 36W
Frobisher B., *Canada* **69 B13** 62 30N 66 0W
Frobisher Bay = Iqaluit, *Canada* **69 B13** 63 44N 68 31W
Frobisher L., *Canada* **73 B7** 56 20N 108 15W
Frohavet, *Norway* **8 E13** 64 0N 9 30 E
Frome, *U.K.* **11 F5** 51 14N 2 19W
Frome →, *U.K.* **11 G5** 50 41N 2 6W
Frome, L., *Australia* **63 E2** 30 45S 139 45 E
Front Range, *U.S.A.* **74 C5** 40 25N 105 45W
Front Royal, *U.S.A.* **76 F6** 38 55N 78 12W
Frontera, *Canary Is.* **22 G2** 27 47N 17 59W
Frontera, *Mexico* **87 D6** 18 30N 92 40W
Fronteras, *Mexico* **86 A3** 30 56N 109 31W
Frosinone, *Italy* **20 D5** 41 38N 13 19 E
Frostburg, *U.S.A.* **76 F6** 39 39N 78 56W
Frostisen, *Norway* **8 B17** 68 14N 17 10 E
Frøya, *Norway* **8 E13** 63 43N 8 40 E
Frunze = Bishkek, *Kyrgyzstan* **26 E8** 42 54N 74 46 E
Frutal, *Brazil* **93 H9** 20 0S 49 0W
Frýdek-Místek, *Czech Rep.* **17 D10** 49 40N 18 20 E
Fryeburg, *U.S.A.* **79 B14** 44 1N 70 59W
Fu Xian = Wafangdian, *China* **35 E11** 39 38N 121 58 E
Fu Xian, *China* **34 G5** 36 0N 109 20 E
Fucheng, *China* **34 F9** 37 50N 116 10 E
Fuchou = Fuzhou, *China* **33 D6** 26 5N 119 16 E
Fuchū, *Japan* **31 G6** 34 34N 133 14 E
Fuencaliente, *Canary Is.* **22 F2** 28 28N 17 50W
Fuencaliente, Pta., *Canary Is.* **22 F2** 28 27N 17 51W
Fuengirola, *Spain* **19 D3** 36 32N 4 41W
Fuentes de Oñoro, *Spain* **19 B2** 40 33N 6 52W
Fuerte →, *Mexico* **86 B3** 25 50N 109 25W
Fuerte Olimpo, *Paraguay* **94 A4** 21 0S 57 51W
Fuerteventura, *Canary Is.* **22 F6** 28 30N 14 0W
Fufeng, *China* **34 G5** 34 22N 108 0 E
Fugou, *China* **34 G8** 34 3N 114 25 E
Fugu, *China* **34 E6** 39 2N 111 3 E
Fuhai, *China* **32 B3** 47 2N 87 25 E
Fuḩaymī, *Iraq* **44 C4** 34 16N 42 10 E
Fuji, *Japan* **31 G9** 35 9N 138 39 E
Fuji-San, *Japan* **31 G9** 35 22N 138 44 E
Fuji-yoshida, *Japan* **31 G9** 35 30N 138 46 E
Fujian □, *China* **33 D6** 26 0N 118 0 E
Fujinomiya, *Japan* **31 G9** 35 10N 138 40 E
Fujisawa, *Japan* **31 G9** 35 22N 139 29 E
Fujiyama, Mt. = Fuji-San, *Japan* **31 G9** 35 22N 138 44 E
Fukien = Fujian □, *China* **33 D6** 26 0N 118 0 E
Fukuchiyama, *Japan* **31 G7** 35 19N 135 9 E
Fukue-Shima, *Japan* **31 H4** 32 40N 128 45 E
Fukui, *Japan* **31 F8** 36 5N 136 10 E
Fukui □, *Japan* **31 G8** 36 0N 136 12 E
Fukuoka, *Japan* **31 H5** 33 39N 130 21 E
Fukuoka □, *Japan* **31 H5** 33 30N 131 0 E
Fukushima, *Japan* **30 F10** 37 44N 140 28 E
Fukushima □, *Japan* **30 F10** 37 30N 140 15 E
Fukuyama, *Japan* **31 G6** 34 35N 133 20 E
Fulda, *Germany* **16 C5** 50 32N 9 40 E
Fulda →, *Germany* **16 C5** 51 25N 9 39 E
Fulford Harbour, *Canada* **84 B3** 48 47N 123 27W
Fullerton, *Calif., U.S.A.* **85 M9** 33 53N 117 56W
Fullerton, *Nebr., U.S.A.* **80 E6** 41 22N 97 58W
Fulongquan, *China* **35 B13** 44 20N 124 42 E
Fulton, *Mo., U.S.A.* **80 F9** 38 52N 91 57W
Fulton, *N.Y., U.S.A.* **79 C8** 43 19N 76 25W
Funabashi, *Japan* **31 G10** 35 45N 140 0 E
Funchal, *Madeira* **22 D3** 32 38N 16 54W
Fundación, *Colombia* **92 A4** 10 31N 74 11W
Fundão, *Portugal* **19 B2** 40 8N 7 30W
Fundy, B. of, *Canada* **71 D6** 45 0N 66 0W
Funing, *Hebei, China* **35 E10** 39 53N 119 12 E
Funing, *Jiangsu, China* **35 H10** 33 45N 119 50 E
Funiu Shan, *China* **34 H7** 33 30N 112 20 E
Funtua, *Nigeria* **50 F7** 11 30N 7 18 E
Fuping, *Hebei, China* **34 E8** 38 48N 114 12 E
Fuping, *Shaanxi, China* **34 G5** 34 42N 109 10 E
Furano, *Japan* **30 C11** 43 21N 142 23 E
Furāt, Nahr al →, *Asia* **44 D5** 31 0N 47 25 E
Fūrg, *Iran* **45 D7** 28 18N 55 13 E
Furnás, *Spain* **22 B8** 39 3N 1 32 E
Furnas, Reprêsa de, *Brazil* **95 A6** 20 50S 45 30W
Furneaux Group, *Australia* **62 G4** 40 10S 147 50 E
Furqlus, *Syria* **47 A6** 34 36N 37 8 E
Fürstenwalde, *Germany* **16 B8** 52 22N 14 3 E
Fürth, *Germany* **16 D6** 49 28N 10 59 E
Furukawa, *Japan* **30 E10** 38 34N 140 58 E
Fury and Hecla Str., *Canada* **69 B11** 69 56N 84 0W
Fusagasuga, *Colombia* **92 C4** 4 21N 74 22W
Fushan, *Shandong, China* **35 F11** 37 30N 121 15 E
Fushan, *Shanxi, China* **34 G6** 35 58N 111 51 E
Fushun, *China* **35 D12** 41 50N 123 56 E
Fusong, *China* **35 C14** 42 20N 127 15 E
Futuna, *Wall. & F. Is.* **59 B8** 14 25S 178 20 E
Fuxin, *China* **35 C11** 42 5N 121 48 E
Fuyang, *China* **34 H8** 33 0N 115 48 E
Fuyang He →, *China* **34 E9** 38 12N 117 0 E
Fuyu, *China* **35 B13** 45 12N 124 43 E
Fuzhou, *China* **33 D6** 26 5N 119 16 E
Fylde, *U.K.* **10 D5** 53 50N 2 58W
Fyn, *Denmark* **9 J14** 55 20N 10 30 E
Fyne, L., *U.K.* **12 F3** 55 59N 5 23W

G

Gabela, *Angola* **52 G2** 11 0S 14 24 E
Gabès, *Tunisia* **51 B8** 33 53N 10 2 E
Gabès, G. de, *Tunisia* **51 B8** 34 0N 10 30 E
Gabon ■, *Africa* **52 E2** 0 10S 10 0 E
Gaborone, *Botswana* **56 C4** 24 45S 25 57 E
Gabriels, *U.S.A.* **79 B10** 44 26N 74 12W
Gābrīk, *Iran* **45 E8** 25 44N 58 28 E
Gabrovo, *Bulgaria* **21 C11** 42 52N 25 19 E
Gāch Sār, *Iran* **45 B6** 36 7N 51 19 E
Gachsārān, *Iran* **45 D6** 30 15N 50 45 E
Gadag, *India* **40 M9** 15 30N 75 45 E
Gadap, *Pakistan* **42 G2** 25 5N 67 28 E
Gadarwara, *India* **43 H8** 22 50N 78 50 E
Gadhada, *India* **42 J4** 22 0N 71 35 E
Gadra, *Pakistan* **42 G4** 25 40N 70 38 E
Gadsden, *U.S.A.* **77 H3** 34 1N 86 1W
Gadwal, *India* **40 L10** 16 10N 77 50 E
Gaffney, *U.S.A.* **77 H5** 35 5N 81 39W
Gafsa, *Tunisia* **50 B7** 34 24N 8 43 E
Gagaria, *India* **42 G4** 25 43N 70 46 E
Gagnoa, *Ivory C.* **50 G4** 6 56N 5 16W
Gagnon, *Canada* **71 B6** 51 50N 68 5W
Gagnon, L., *Canada* **73 A6** 62 3N 110 27W
Gahini, *Rwanda* **54 C3** 1 50S 30 30 E
Gahmar, *India* **43 G10** 25 27N 83 49 E
Gai Xian = Gaizhou, *China* **35 D12** 40 22N 122 20 E
Gaïdhouronísi, *Greece* **23 E7** 34 53N 25 41 E
Gail, *U.S.A.* **81 J4** 32 46N 101 27W
Gaillimh = Galway, *Ireland* **13 C2** 53 17N 9 3W
Gaines, *U.S.A.* **78 E7** 41 46N 77 35W
Gainesville, *Fla., U.S.A.* **77 L4** 29 40N 82 20W
Gainesville, *Ga., U.S.A.* **77 H4** 34 18N 83 50W
Gainesville, *Mo., U.S.A.* **81 G8** 36 36N 92 26W
Gainesville, *Tex., U.S.A.* **81 J6** 33 38N 97 8W
Gainsborough, *U.K.* **10 D7** 53 24N 0 46W
Gairdner, L., *Australia* **63 E2** 31 30S 136 0 E
Gairloch, L., *U.K.* **12 D3** 57 43N 5 45W
Gaizhou, *China* **35 D12** 40 22N 122 20 E
Gaj →, *Pakistan* **42 F2** 26 26N 67 21 E
Gakuch, *Pakistan* **43 A5** 36 7N 73 45 E
Galán, Cerro, *Argentina* **94 B2** 25 55S 66 52W
Galana →, *Kenya* **54 C5** 3 9S 40 8 E
Galápagos, *Pac. Oc.* **90 D1** 0 0 91 0W
Galashiels, *U.K.* **12 F6** 55 37N 2 49W
Galați, *Romania* **17 F15** 45 27N 28 2 E
Galatina, *Italy* **21 D8** 40 10N 18 10 E
Galax, *U.S.A.* **77 G5** 36 40N 80 56W
Galcaio, *Somali Rep.* **46 F4** 6 30N 47 30 E
Galdhøpiggen, *Norway* **9 F12** 61 38N 8 18 E
Galeana, *Mexico* **86 C4** 24 50N 100 4W
Galeana, *Nuevo León, Mexico* **86 A3** 24 50N 100 4W
Galela, *Indonesia* **37 D7** 1 50N 127 49 E
Galena, *U.S.A.* **68 B4** 64 44N 156 56W
Galera Point, *Trin. & Tob.* **89 D7** 10 8N 61 0W
Galesburg, *U.S.A.* **80 E9** 40 57N 90 22W
Galeton, *U.S.A.* **78 E7** 41 44N 77 39W
Galich, *Russia* **24 C7** 58 22N 42 24 E
Galicia □, *Spain* **19 A2** 42 43N 7 45W
Galilee = Hagalil, *Israel* **47 C4** 32 53N 35 18 E
Galilee, L., *Australia* **62 C4** 22 20S 145 50 E
Galilee, Sea of = Yam Kinneret, *Israel* **47 C4** 32 45N 35 35 E
Galinoporni, *Cyprus* **23 D13** 35 31N 34 18 E
Galion, *U.S.A.* **78 F2** 40 44N 82 47W
Galiuro Mts., *U.S.A.* **83 K8** 32 30N 110 20W
Galiwinku, *Australia* **62 A2** 12 2S 135 34 E
Gallan Hd., *U.K.* **12 C1** 58 15N 7 2W
Gallatin, *U.S.A.* **77 G2** 36 24N 86 27W
Galle, *Sri Lanka* **40 R12** 6 5N 80 10 E
Gállego →, *Spain* **19 B5** 41 39N 0 51W
Gallegos →, *Argentina* **96 G3** 51 35S 69 0W
Galley Hd., *Ireland* **13 E3** 51 32N 8 55W
Gallinas, Pta., *Colombia* **92 A4** 12 28N 71 40W
Gallipoli = Gelibolu, *Turkey* **21 D12** 40 28N 26 43 E
Gallipoli, *Italy* **21 D8** 40 3N 17 58 E
Gallipolis, *U.S.A.* **76 F4** 38 49N 82 12W
Gällivare, *Sweden* **8 C19** 67 9N 20 40 E
Galloo I., *U.S.A.* **79 C8** 43 55N 76 25W
Galloway, *U.K.* **12 F4** 55 1N 4 29W
Galloway, Mull of, *U.K.* **12 G4** 54 39N 4 52W
Gallup, *U.S.A.* **83 J9** 35 32N 108 45W
Galoya, *Sri Lanka* **40 Q12** 8 10N 80 55 E
Galt, *U.S.A.* **84 G5** 38 15N 121 18W
Galty Mts., *Ireland* **13 D3** 52 22N 8 10W
Galtymore, *Ireland* **13 D3** 52 21N 8 11W
Galva, *U.S.A.* **80 E9** 41 10N 90 3W
Galveston, *U.S.A.* **81 L7** 29 18N 94 48W
Galveston B., *U.S.A.* **81 L7** 29 36N 94 50W
Gálvez, *Argentina* **94 C3** 32 0S 61 14W
Galway, *Ireland* **13 C2** 53 17N 9 3W
Galway □, *Ireland* **13 C2** 53 22N 9 1W
Galway B., *Ireland* **13 C2** 53 13N 9 10W
Gam →, *Vietnam* **38 B5** 21 55N 105 12 E
Gamagori, *Japan* **31 G8** 34 50N 137 14 E
Gambat, *Pakistan* **42 F3** 27 17N 68 26 E
Gambhir →, *India* **42 F6** 26 58N 77 27 E
Gambia ■, *W. Afr.* **50 F2** 13 25N 16 0W
Gambia →, *W. Afr.* **50 F2** 13 28N 16 34W
Gambier, *U.S.A.* **78 F2** 40 22N 82 23W
Gambier, C., *Australia* **60 B5** 11 56S 130 57 E
Gambier Is., *Australia* **63 F2** 35 3S 136 30 E
Gambo, *Canada* **71 C9** 48 47N 54 13W
Gamboli, *Pakistan* **42 E3** 29 53N 68 24 E
Gamboma, *Congo* **52 E3** 1 55S 15 52 E
Gamlakarleby = Kokkola, *Finland* **8 E20** 63 50N 23 8 E
Gammon →, *Canada* **73 C9** 51 24N 95 44W
Gan Jiang →, *China* **33 D6** 29 15N 116 0 E
Ganado, *U.S.A.* **83 J9** 35 43N 109 33W
Gananoque, *Canada* **79 B8** 44 20N 76 10W
Ganāveh, *Iran* **45 D6** 29 35N 50 35 E
Gäncä, *Azerbaijan* **25 F8** 40 45N 46 20 E
Gancheng, *China* **38 C7** 18 51N 108 37 E
Gand = Gent, *Belgium* **15 C3** 51 2N 3 42 E
Ganda, *Angola* **53 G2** 13 3S 14 35 E
Gandajika, *Dem. Rep. of the Congo* **52 F4** 6 45S 23 57 E
Gandak →, *India* **43 G11** 25 39N 85 13 E
Gandava, *Pakistan* **42 E2** 28 32N 67 32 E
Gander, *Canada* **71 C9** 48 58N 54 35W
Gander L., *Canada* **71 C9** 48 58N 54 35W
Ganderowe Falls, *Zimbabwe* **55 F2** 17 20S 29 10 E
Gandhi Sagar, *India* **42 G6** 24 40N 75 40 E
Gandhinagar, *India* **42 H5** 23 15N 72 45 E
Gandía, *Spain* **19 C5** 38 58N 0 9W
Gando, Pta., *Canary Is.* **22 G4** 27 55N 15 22W
Ganedidalem = Gani, *Indonesia* **37 E7** 0 48S 128 14 E
Ganga →, *India* **43 H14** 23 20N 90 30 E
Ganga Sagar, *India* **43 J13** 21 38N 88 5 E
Gangan →, *India* **43 E8** 28 38N 78 58 E
Ganganagar, *India* **42 E5** 29 56N 73 56 E
Gangapur, *India* **42 F7** 26 32N 76 49 E
Gangaw, *Burma* **41 H19** 22 5N 94 5 E
Gangdisê Shan, *China* **41 D12** 31 20N 81 0 E
Ganges = Ganga →, *India* **43 H14** 23 20N 90 30 E
Ganges, *Canada* **72 D4** 48 51N 123 31W
Ganges, Mouths of the, *India* **43 J14** 21 30N 90 0 E
Gangoh, *India* **42 E7** 29 46N 77 18 E
Gangroti, *India* **43 D8** 30 50N 79 10 E
Gangtok, *India* **41 F16** 27 20N 88 37 E
Gangu, *China* **34 G3** 34 40N 105 15 E
Gangyao, *China* **35 B14** 44 12N 126 37 E
Gani, *Indonesia* **37 E7** 0 48S 128 14 E
Ganj, *India* **43 F8** 27 45N 78 57 E
Gannett Peak, *U.S.A.* **82 E9** 43 11N 109 39W
Ganquan, *China* **34 F5** 36 20N 109 20 E
Gansu □, *China* **34 G3** 36 0N 104 0 E
Ganta, *Liberia* **50 G4** 7 15N 8 59W
Gantheaume, C., *Australia* **63 F2** 36 4S 137 32 E
Gantheaume B., *Australia* **61 E1** 27 40S 114 10 E
Gantsevichi = Hantsavichy, *Belarus* **17 B14** 52 49N 26 30 E
Ganyem = Genyem, *Indonesia* **37 E10** 2 46S 140 12 E
Ganyu, *China* **35 G10** 34 50N 119 8 E
Ganzhou, *China* **33 D6** 25 51N 114 56 E
Gao, *Mali* **50 E5** 16 15N 0 5W
Gaomi, *China* **35 F10** 36 20N 119 42 E
Gaoping, *China* **34 G7** 35 45N 112 55 E
Gaotang, *China* **34 F9** 36 50N 116 15 E
Gaoua, *Burkina Faso* **50 F5** 10 20N 3 8W
Gaoual, *Guinea* **50 F3** 11 45N 13 25W
Gaoxiong = Kaohsiung, *Taiwan* **33 D7** 22 35N 120 16 E
Gaoyang, *China* **34 E8** 38 40N 115 45 E
Gaoyou Hu, *China* **35 H10** 32 45N 119 20 E
Gaoyuan, *China* **35 F9** 37 8N 117 58 E
Gap, *France* **18 D7** 44 33N 6 5 E
Gapat →, *India* **43 G10** 24 30N 82 28 E
Gapuwiyak, *Australia* **62 A2** 12 25S 135 43 E
Gar, *China* **32 C2** 32 10N 79 58 E
Garabogazköl Aylagy, *Turkmenistan* **25 F9** 41 0N 53 30 E
Garachico, *Canary Is.* **22 F3** 28 22N 16 46W
Garachiné, *Panama* **88 E4** 8 0N 78 12W
Garafia, *Canary Is.* **22 F2** 28 48N 17 57W
Garah, *Australia* **63 D4** 29 5S 149 38 E
Garajonay, *Canary Is.* **22 F2** 28 7N 17 14W
Garanhuns, *Brazil* **93 E11** 8 50S 36 30W
Garautha, *India* **43 G8** 25 34N 79 18 E
Garba Tula, *Kenya* **54 B4** 0 30N 38 32 E
Garberville, *U.S.A.* **82 F2** 40 6N 123 48W
Garbiyang, *India* **43 D9** 30 8N 80 54 E
Garda, L. di, *Italy* **20 B4** 45 40N 10 41 E
Garde L., *Canada* **73 A7** 62 50N 106 13W
Garden City, *Ga., U.S.A.* **77 J5** 32 6N 81 9W
Garden City, *Kans., U.S.A.* **81 G4** 37 58N 100 53W
Garden City, *Tex., U.S.A.* **81 K4** 31 52N 101 29W
Garden Grove, *U.S.A.* **85 M9** 33 47N 117 55W
Gardēz, *Afghan.* **42 C3** 33 37N 69 9 E
Gardiner, *Maine, U.S.A.* **77 C11** 44 14N 69 47W
Gardiner, *Mont., U.S.A.* **82 D8** 45 2N 110 22W
Gardiners I., *U.S.A.* **79 E12** 41 6N 72 6W
Gardner, *U.S.A.* **79 D13** 42 34N 71 59W
Gardner Canal, *Canada* **72 C3** 53 27N 128 8W
Gardnerville, *U.S.A.* **84 G7** 38 56N 119 45W
Gardo, *Somali Rep.* **46 F4** 9 30N 49 6 E
Garey, *U.S.A.* **85 L6** 34 53N 120 19W
Garfield, *U.S.A.* **82 C5** 47 1N 117 9W
Garforth, *U.K.* **10 D6** 53 47N 1 24W
Gargano, Mte., *Italy* **20 D6** 41 43N 15 43 E
Garibaldi Prov. Park, *Canada* **72 D4** 49 50N 122 40W
Garies, *S. Africa* **56 E2** 30 32S 17 59 E
Garigliano →, *Italy* **20 D5** 41 13N 13 45 E
Garissa, *Kenya* **54 C4** 0 25S 39 40 E
Garland, *Tex., U.S.A.* **81 J6** 32 55N 96 38W
Garland, *Utah, U.S.A.* **82 F7** 41 47N 112 10W
Garm, *Tajikistan* **26 F8** 39 0N 70 20 E
Garmāb, *Iran* **45 C8** 35 25N 56 45 E
Garmisch-Partenkirchen, *Germany* **16 E6** 47 30N 11 6 E
Garmsār, *Iran* **45 C7** 35 20N 52 25 E
Garner, *U.S.A.* **80 D8** 43 6N 93 36W
Garnett, *U.S.A.* **80 F7** 38 17N 95 14W
Garo Hills, *India* **43 G14** 25 30N 90 30 E
Garoe, *Somali Rep.* **46 F4** 8 25N 48 33 E
Garonne →, *France* **18 D3** 45 2N 0 36W
Garot, *India* **42 G6** 24 19N 75 41 E
Garoua, *Cameroon* **51 G8** 9 19N 13 21 E
Garrauli, *India* **43 G8** 25 5N 79 22 E
Garrison, *Mont., U.S.A.* **82 C7** 46 31N 112 49W
Garrison, *N. Dak., U.S.A.* **80 B4** 47 40N 101 25W
Garrison Res. = Sakakawea, L., *U.S.A.* **80 B4** 47 30N 101 25W
Garron Pt., *U.K.* **13 A6** 55 3N 5 59W
Garry →, *U.K.* **12 E5** 56 44N 3 47W
Garry, L., *Canada* **68 B9** 65 58N 100 18W
Garsen, *Kenya* **54 C5** 2 20S 40 5 E
Garson L., *Canada* **73 B6** 56 19N 110 2W
Garu, *India* **43 H11** 23 40N 84 14 E
Garub, *Namibia* **56 D2** 26 37S 16 0 E
Garut, *Indonesia* **37 G12** 7 14S 107 53 E
Garvie Mts., *N.Z.* **59 L2** 45 30S 168 50 E
Garwa = Garoua, *Cameroon* **51 G8** 9 19N 13 21 E
Garwa, *India* **43 G10** 24 11N 83 47 E
Gary, *U.S.A.* **76 E2** 41 36N 87 20W
Garzê, *China* **32 C5** 31 38N 100 1 E
Garzón, *Colombia* **92 C3** 2 10N 75 40W
Gas-San, *Japan* **30 E10** 38 32N 140 1 E
Gasan Kuli = Esenguly, *Turkmenistan* **26 F6** 37 37N 53 59 E
Gascogne, *France* **18 E4** 43 45N 0 20 E
Gascogne, G. de, *Europe* **18 D2** 44 0N 2 0W
Gascony = Gascogne, *France* **18 E4** 43 45N 0 20 E
Gascoyne →, *Australia* **61 D1** 24 52S 113 37 E
Gascoyne Junction, *Australia* **61 E2** 25 2S 115 17 E
Gashaka, *Nigeria* **51 G8** 7 20N 11 29 E
Gasherbrum, *Pakistan* **43 B7** 35 40N 76 40 E
Gashua, *Nigeria* **51 F8** 12 54N 11 0 E
Gaspé, *Canada* **71 C7** 48 52N 64 30W
Gaspé, C. de, *Canada* **71 C7** 48 48N 64 7W
Gaspé, Pén. de, *Canada* **71 C6** 48 45N 65 40W
Gaspésie, Parc de Conservation de la, *Canada* **71 C6** 48 55N 65 50W
Gasteiz = Vitoria-Gasteiz, *Spain* **19 A4** 42 50N 2 41W
Gastonia, *U.S.A.* **77 H5** 35 16N 81 11W
Gastre, *Argentina* **96 E3** 42 20S 69 15W
Gata, C., *Cyprus* **23 E12** 34 34N 33 2 E
Gata, C. de, *Spain* **19 D4** 36 41N 2 13W
Gata, Sierra de, *Spain* **19 B2** 40 20N 6 45W
Gataga →, *Canada* **72 B3** 58 35N 126 59W
Gatehouse of Fleet, *U.K.* **12 G4** 54 53N 4 12W
Gates, *U.S.A.* **78 C7** 43 9N 77 42W
Gateshead, *U.K.* **10 C6** 54 57N 1 35W
Gatesville, *U.S.A.* **81 K6** 31 26N 97 45W
Gaths, *Zimbabwe* **55 G3** 20 2S 30 32 E
Gatico, *Chile* **94 A1** 22 29S 70 20W
Gatineau, *Canada* **79 A9** 45 29N 75 38W
Gatineau →, *Canada* **70 C4** 45 27N 75 42W
Gatineau, Parc Nat. de la, *Canada* **70 C4** 45 40N 76 0W
Gatton, *Australia* **63 D5** 27 32S 152 17 E

Grenadines

Goldsworthy, *Australia* 60 D2 20 21S 119 30 E
Goldthwaite, *U.S.A.* 81 K5 31 27N 98 34W
Goleniów, *Poland* 16 B8 53 35N 14 50 E
Golestānak, *Iran* 45 D7 30 36N 54 14 E
Goleta, *U.S.A.* 85 L7 34 27N 119 50W
Golfito, *Costa Rica* 88 E3 8 41N 83 5W
Golfo Aranci, *Italy* 20 D3 40 59N 9 38 E
Goliad, *U.S.A.* 81 L6 28 40N 97 23W
Golpāyegān, *Iran* 45 C6 33 27N 50 18 E
Golra, *Pakistan* 42 C5 33 37N 72 56 E
Golspie, *U.K.* 12 D5 57 58N 3 59W
Goma,
Dem. Rep. of the Congo 54 C2 1 37S 29 10 E
Gomal Pass, *Pakistan* 42 D3 31 56N 69 20 E
Gomati →, *India* 43 G10 25 32N 83 11 E
Gombari,
Dem. Rep. of the Congo 54 B2 2 45N 29 3 E
Gombe, *Nigeria* 51 F8 10 19N 11 2 E
Gombe →, *Tanzania* 54 C3 4 38S 31 40 E
Gomel = Homyel, *Belarus* 17 B16 52 28N 31 0 E
Gomera, *Canary Is.* 22 F2 28 7N 17 14W
Gómez Palacio, *Mexico* 86 B4 25 40N 104 0W
Gomīshān, *Iran* 45 B7 37 4N 54 6 E
Gomogomo, *Indonesia* 37 F8 6 39S 134 43 E
Gomoh, *India* 41 H15 23 52N 86 10 E
Gompa = Ganta, *Liberia* 50 G4 7 15N 8 59W
Gonābād, *Iran* 45 C8 34 15N 58 45 E
Gonaïves, *Haiti* 89 C5 19 20N 72 42W
Gonâve, G. de la, *Haiti* 89 C5 19 29N 72 42W
Gonâve, I. de la, *Haiti* 89 C5 18 45N 73 0W
Gonbad-e Kāvūs, *Iran* 45 B7 37 20N 55 25 E
Gonda, *India* 43 F9 27 9N 81 58 E
Gondal, *India* 42 J4 21 58N 70 52 E
Gonder, *Ethiopia* 46 E2 12 39N 37 30 E
Gondia, *India* 40 J12 21 23N 80 10 E
Gondola, *Mozam.* 55 F3 19 10S 33 37 E
Gönen, *Turkey* 21 D12 40 6N 27 39 E
Gonghe, *China* 32 C5 36 18N 100 32 E
Gongolgon, *Australia* 63 E4 30 21S 146 54 E
Gongzhuling, *China* 35 C13 43 30N 124 40 E
Gonzales, *Calif., U.S.A.* 84 J5 36 30N 121 26W
Gonzales, *Tex., U.S.A.* 81 L6 29 30N 97 27W
González Chaves, *Argentina* 94 D3 38 2S 60 5W
Good Hope, C. of, *S. Africa* 56 E2 34 24S 18 30 E
Gooderham, *Canada* 78 B6 44 54N 78 21W
Gooding, *U.S.A.* 82 E6 42 56N 114 43W
Goodland, *U.S.A.* 80 F4 39 21N 101 43W
Goodlow, *Canada* 72 B4 56 20N 120 8W
Goodooga, *Australia* 63 D4 29 3S 147 28 E
Goodsprings, *U.S.A.* 85 K11 35 49N 115 27W
Goole, *U.K.* 10 D7 53 42N 0 53W
Goolgowi, *Australia* 63 E4 33 58S 145 41 E
Goolwa, *Australia* 63 F2 35 30S 138 47 E
Goomalling, *Australia* 61 F2 31 15S 116 49 E
Goomeri, *Australia* 63 D5 26 12S 152 6 E
Goonda, *Mozam.* 55 F3 19 48S 33 57 E
Goondiwindi, *Australia* 63 D5 28 30S 150 21 E
Goongarrie, L., *Australia* 61 F3 30 3S 121 9 E
Goonyella, *Australia* 62 C4 21 47S 147 58 E
Goose →, *Canada* 71 B7 53 20N 60 35W
Goose Creek, *U.S.A.* 77 J5 32 59N 80 2W
Goose L., *U.S.A.* 82 F3 41 56N 120 26W
Gop, *India* 40 H6 22 5N 69 50 E
Gopalganj, *India* 43 F11 26 28N 84 30 E
Göppingen, *Germany* 16 D5 48 42N 9 39 E
Gorakhpur, *India* 43 F10 26 47N 83 23 E
Goražde, *Bos.-H.* 21 C8 43 38N 18 58 E
Gorda, *U.S.A.* 84 K5 35 53N 121 26W
Gorda, Pta., *Canary Is.* 22 F2 28 45N 18 0W
Gorda, Pta., *Nic.* 88 D3 14 20N 83 10W
Gordan B., *Australia* 60 B5 11 35S 130 10 E
Gordon, *U.S.A.* 80 D3 42 48N 102 12W
Gordon →, *Australia* 62 G4 42 27S 145 30 E
Gordon L., *Alta., Canada* 73 B6 56 30N 110 25W
Gordon L., *N.W.T., Canada* 72 A6 63 5N 113 11W
Gordonvale, *Australia* 62 B4 17 5S 145 50 E
Gore, *Ethiopia* 46 F2 8 12N 35 32 E
Gore, *N.Z.* 59 M2 46 5S 168 58 E
Gore Bay, *Canada* 70 C3 45 57N 82 28W
Gorey, *Ireland* 13 D5 52 41N 6 18W
Gorg, *Iran* 45 D8 29 29N 59 43 E
Gorgān, *Iran* 45 B7 36 50N 54 29 E
Gorgona, I., *Colombia* 92 C3 3 0N 78 10W
Gorham, *U.S.A.* 79 B13 44 23N 71 10W
Goriganga →, *India* 43 E9 29 45N 80 23 E
Gorinchem, *Neths.* 15 C4 51 50N 4 59 E
Goris, *Armenia* 25 G8 39 31N 46 22 E
Gorizia, *Italy* 20 B5 45 56N 13 37 E
Gorki = Nizhniy Novgorod,
Russia 24 C7 56 20N 44 0 E
Gorkiy = Nizhniy Novgorod,
Russia 24 C7 56 20N 44 0 E
Gorkovskoye Vdkhr., *Russia* 24 C7 57 2N 43 4 E
Görlitz, *Germany* 16 C8 51 9N 14 58 E
Gorlovka = Horlivka,
Ukraine 25 E6 48 19N 38 5 E
Gorman, *U.S.A.* 85 L8 34 47N 118 51W
Gorna Dzhumayo =
Blagoevgrad, *Bulgaria* 21 C10 42 2N 23 5 E
Gorna Oryakhovitsa,
Bulgaria 21 C11 43 7N 25 40 E
Gorno-Altay □, *Russia* 26 D9 51 0N 86 0 E
Gorno-Altaysk, *Russia* 26 D9 51 50N 86 5 E
Gornyatski, *Russia* 24 A11 67 32N 64 3 E
Gornyy, *Russia* 30 B6 44 57N 133 59 E
Gorodenka = Horodenka,
Ukraine 17 D13 48 41N 25 29 E
Gorodok = Horodok,
Ukraine 17 D12 49 46N 23 32 E
Gorokhov = Horokhiv,
Ukraine 17 C13 50 30N 24 45 E
Goromonzi, *Zimbabwe* 55 F3 17 52S 31 22 E
Gorong, Kepulauan,
Indonesia 37 E8 3 59S 131 25 E
Gorongose →, *Mozam.* 57 C5 20 30S 34 40 E
Gorongoza, *Mozam.* 55 F3 18 44S 34 2 E
Gorongoza, Sa. da, *Mozam.* 55 F3 18 27S 34 2 E
Gorontalo, *Indonesia* 37 D6 0 35N 123 5 E
Gort, *Ireland* 13 C3 53 3N 8 49W
Gortis, *Greece* 23 D6 35 4N 24 58 E
Gorzów Wielkopolski,
Poland 16 B8 52 43N 15 15 E
Gosford, *Australia* 63 E5 33 23S 151 18 E
Goshen, *Calif., U.S.A.* 84 J7 36 21N 119 25W
Goshen, *Ind., U.S.A.* 76 E3 41 35N 85 50W
Goshen, *N.Y., U.S.A.* 79 E10 41 24N 74 20W
Goshogawara, *Japan* 30 D10 40 48N 140 27 E
Goslar, *Germany* 16 C6 51 54N 10 25 E
Gospič, *Croatia* 16 F8 44 35N 15 23 E
Gosport, *U.K.* 11 G6 50 48N 1 9W
Gosse →, *Australia* 62 B1 19 32S 134 37 E
Göta älv →, *Sweden* 9 H14 57 42N 11 54 E
Göta kanal, *Sweden* 9 G16 58 30N 15 58 E
Götaland, *Sweden* 9 G15 57 30N 14 30 E
Göteborg, *Sweden* 9 H14 57 43N 11 59 E
Gotha, *Germany* 16 C6 50 56N 10 42 E
Gothenburg = Göteborg,
Sweden 9 H14 57 43N 11 59 E
Gothenburg, *U.S.A.* 80 E4 40 56N 100 10W
Gotland, *Sweden* 9 H18 57 30N 18 33 E
Gotō-Rettō, *Japan* 31 H4 32 55N 129 5 E
Gotska Sandön, *Sweden* 9 G18 58 24N 19 15 E
Gōtsu, *Japan* 31 G6 35 0N 132 14 E
Gott Pk., *Canada* 72 C4 50 18N 122 16W
Göttingen, *Germany* 16 C5 51 31N 9 55 E
Gottwaldov = Zlín,
Czech Rep. 17 D9 49 14N 17 40 E
Goubangzi, *China* 35 D11 41 20N 121 52 E
Gouda, *Neths.* 15 B4 52 1N 4 42 E
Goúdhoura, Ákra, *Greece* 23 E8 34 59N 26 6 E
Gough I., *Atl. Oc.* 2 G9 40 10S 9 45W
Gouin, Rés., *Canada* 70 C5 48 35N 74 40W
Goulburn, *Australia* 63 E4 34 44S 149 44 E
Goulburn Is., *Australia* 62 A1 11 40S 133 20 E
Goulimine, *Morocco* 50 C3 28 56N 10 0W
Gourits →, *S. Africa* 56 E3 34 21S 21 52 E
Goúrnais, *Greece* 23 D7 35 19N 25 16 E
Gouverneur, *U.S.A.* 79 B9 44 20N 75 28W
Gouviá, *Greece* 23 A3 39 39N 19 50 E
Governador Valadares,
Brazil 93 G10 18 15S 41 57W
Governor's Harbour,
Bahamas 88 A4 25 10N 76 14W
Govindgarh, *India* 43 G9 24 23N 81 18 E
Gowan Ra., *Australia* 62 D4 25 0S 145 0 E
Gowanda, *U.S.A.* 78 D6 42 28N 78 56W
Gowd-e Zirreh, *Afghan.* 40 E3 29 45N 62 0 E
Gower, *U.K.* 11 F3 51 35N 4 10W
Gowna, L., *Ireland* 13 C4 53 51N 7 34W
Goya, *Argentina* 94 B4 29 10S 59 10W
Goyder Lagoon, *Australia* 63 D2 27 3S 138 58 E
Goyllarisquisga, *Peru* 92 F3 10 31S 76 24W
Goz Beïda, *Chad* 51 F10 12 10N 21 20 E
Gozo, *Malta* 23 C1 36 3N 14 13 E
Graaff-Reinet, *S. Africa* 56 E3 32 13S 24 32 E
Gračac, *Croatia* 16 F8 44 18N 15 57 E
Gracias a Dios, C., *Honduras* 88 D3 15 0N 83 10W
Graciosa, I., *Canary Is.* 22 E6 29 15N 13 32W
Grado, *Spain* 19 A2 43 23N 6 4W
Grady, *U.S.A.* 81 H3 34 49N 103 19W
Grafham Water, *U.K.* 11 E7 52 19N 0 18W
Grafton, *Australia* 63 D5 29 38S 152 58 E
Grafton, *N. Dak., U.S.A.* 80 A6 48 25N 97 25W
Grafton, *W. Va., U.S.A.* 76 F5 39 21N 80 2W
Graham, *Canada* 70 C1 49 20N 90 30W
Graham, *U.S.A.* 81 J5 33 6N 98 35W
Graham, Mt., *U.S.A.* 83 K9 32 42N 109 52W
Graham Bell, Ostrov =
Greem-Bell, Ostrov,
Russia 26 A7 81 0N 62 0 E
Graham I., *B.C., Canada* 72 C2 53 40N 132 30W
Graham I., *N.W.T., Canada* 68 C6 77 25N 90 30W
Graham Land, *Antarctica* 5 C17 65 0S 64 0W
Grahamstown, *S. Africa* 56 E4 33 19S 26 31 E
Grahamsville, *U.S.A.* 79 E10 41 51N 74 33W
Grain Coast, *W. Afr.* 50 H3 4 20N 10 0W
Grajaú, *Brazil* 93 E9 5 50S 46 4W
Grajaú →, *Brazil* 93 D10 3 41S 44 48W
Grampian, *U.S.A.* 78 F6 40 58N 78 37W
Grampian Highlands =
Grampian Mts., *U.K.* 12 E5 56 50N 4 0W
Grampian Mts., *U.K.* 12 E5 56 50N 4 0W
Grampians, The, *Australia* 63 F3 37 0S 142 20 E
Gran Canaria, *Canary Is.* 22 G4 27 55N 15 35W
Gran Chaco, *S. Amer.* 94 B3 25 0S 61 0W
Gran Paradiso, *Italy* 18 D7 45 33N 7 17 E
Gran Sasso d'Itália, *Italy* 20 C5 42 27N 13 42 E
Granada, *Nic.* 88 D2 11 58N 86 0W
Granada, *Spain* 19 D4 37 10N 3 35W
Granada, *U.S.A.* 81 F3 38 4N 102 19W
Granadilla de Abona,
Canary Is. 22 F3 28 7N 16 33W
Granard, *Ireland* 13 C4 53 47N 7 30W
Granbury, *U.S.A.* 81 J6 32 27N 97 47W
Granby, *Canada* 79 A12 45 25N 72 45W
Granby, *U.S.A.* 82 F11 40 5N 105 56W
Grand →, *Canada* 78 D5 42 51N 79 34W
Grand →, *Mo., U.S.A.* 80 F8 39 23N 93 7W
Grand →, *S. Dak., U.S.A.* 80 C4 45 40N 100 45W
Grand Bahama, *Bahamas* 88 A4 26 40N 78 30W
Grand Bank, *Canada* 71 C8 47 6N 55 48W
Grand Bassam, *Ivory C.* 50 G5 5 10N 3 49W
Grand-Bourg, *Guadeloupe* 89 C7 15 53N 61 19W
Grand Canal = Yun Ho →,
China 35 E9 39 10N 117 10 E
Grand Canyon, *U.S.A.* 83 H7 36 3N 112 9W
Grand Canyon National
Park, *U.S.A.* 83 H7 36 15N 112 30W
Grand Cayman, *Cayman Is.* 88 C3 19 20N 81 20W
Grand Centre, *Canada* 73 C6 54 25N 110 13W
Grand Coulee, *U.S.A.* 82 C4 47 57N 119 0W
Grand Coulee Dam, *U.S.A.* 82 C4 47 57N 118 59W
Grand Erg du Bilma, *Niger* 51 E8 18 30N 14 0 E
Grand Erg Occidental,
Algeria 50 B6 30 20N 1 0 E
Grand Erg Oriental, *Algeria* 50 B7 30 0N 6 30 E
Grand Falls, *Canada* 71 C6 47 3N 67 44W
Grand Falls-Windsor,
Canada 71 C8 48 56N 55 40W
Grand Forks, *Canada* 72 D5 49 0N 118 30W
Grand Forks, *U.S.A.* 80 B6 47 55N 97 3W
Grand Gorge, *U.S.A.* 79 D10 42 21N 74 29W
Grand Haven, *U.S.A.* 76 D2 43 4N 86 13W
Grand I., *Mich., U.S.A.* 76 B2 46 31N 86 40W
Grand I., *N.Y., U.S.A.* 78 D6 43 0N 78 58W
Grand Island, *U.S.A.* 80 E5 40 55N 98 21W
Grand Isle, *La., U.S.A.* 81 L9 29 14N 90 0W
Grand Isle, *Vt., U.S.A.* 79 B11 44 43N 73 18W
Grand Junction, *U.S.A.* 83 G9 39 4N 108 33W
Grand L., *N.B., Canada* 71 C6 45 57N 66 7W
Grand L., *Nfld., Canada* 71 C8 49 0N 57 30W
Grand L., *Nfld., Canada* 71 B7 53 40N 60 30W
Grand L., *U.S.A.* 81 L8 29 55N 92 47W
Grand Lake, *U.S.A.* 82 F11 40 15N 105 49W
Grand Manan I., *Canada* 71 D6 44 45N 66 52W
Grand Marais, *Canada* 80 B9 47 45N 90 25W
Grand Marais, *U.S.A.* 76 B3 46 40N 85 59W
Grand-Mère, *Canada* 70 C5 46 36N 72 40W
Grand Prairie, *U.S.A.* 81 J6 32 47N 97 0W
Grand Rapids, *Canada* 73 C9 53 12N 99 19W
Grand Rapids, *Mich., U.S.A.* 76 D2 42 58N 85 40W
Grand Rapids, *Minn., U.S.A.* 80 B8 47 14N 93 31W
Grand St-Bernard, Col du,
Europe 18 D7 45 50N 7 10 E
Grand Teton, *U.S.A.* 82 E8 43 54N 111 50W
Grand Teton National Park,
U.S.A. 82 D8 43 50N 110 50W
Grand Union Canal, *U.K.* 11 E7 52 7N 0 53W
Grand View, *Canada* 73 C8 51 10N 100 42W
Grande →, *Jujuy,*
Argentina 94 A2 24 20S 65 2W
Grande →, *Mendoza,*
Argentina 94 D2 36 52S 69 45W
Grande →, *Bolivia* 92 G6 15 51S 64 39W
Grande →, *Bahia, Brazil* 93 F10 11 30S 44 30W
Grande →, *Minas Gerais,*
Brazil 93 H8 20 6S 51 4W
Grande, B., *Argentina* 96 G3 50 30S 68 20W
Grande, Rio →, *U.S.A.* 81 N6 25 58N 97 9W
Grande Baleine, R. de
la →, *Canada* 70 A4 55 16N 77 47W
Grande Cache, *Canada* 72 C5 53 53N 119 8W
Grande-Entrée, *Canada* 71 C7 47 30N 61 40W
Grande Prairie, *Canada* 72 B5 55 10N 118 50W
Grande-Rivière, *Canada* 71 C7 48 26N 64 30W
Grande-Vallée, *Canada* 71 C6 49 14N 65 8W
Grandfalls, *U.S.A.* 81 K3 31 20N 102 51W
Grandview, *U.S.A.* 82 C4 46 15N 119 54W
Graneros, *Chile* 94 C1 34 5S 70 45W
Grangemouth, *U.K.* 12 E5 56 1N 3 42W
Granger, *U.S.A.* 82 F9 41 35N 109 58W
Grangeville, *U.S.A.* 82 D5 45 56N 116 7W
Granisle, *Canada* 72 C3 54 53N 126 13W
Granite City, *U.S.A.* 80 F9 38 42N 90 9W
Granite Falls, *U.S.A.* 80 C7 44 49N 95 33W
Granite L., *Canada* 71 C8 48 8N 57 5W
Granite Mt., *U.S.A.* 85 M10 33 5N 116 28W
Granite Pk., *U.S.A.* 82 D9 45 10N 109 48W
Graniteville, *U.S.A.* 79 B12 44 8N 72 29W
Granity, *N.Z.* 59 J3 41 39S 171 51 E
Granja, *Brazil* 93 D10 3 7S 40 50W
Granollers, *Spain* 19 B7 41 39N 2 18 E
Grant, *U.S.A.* 80 E4 40 53N 101 42W
Grant, Mt., *U.S.A.* 82 G4 38 34N 118 48W
Grant City, *U.S.A.* 80 E7 40 29N 94 25W
Grant I., *Australia* 60 B5 11 10S 132 52 E
Grant Range, *U.S.A.* 83 G6 38 30N 115 25W
Grantham, *U.K.* 10 E7 52 55N 0 38W
Grantown-on-Spey, *U.K.* 12 D5 57 20N 3 36W
Grants, *U.S.A.* 83 J10 35 9N 107 52W
Grants Pass, *U.S.A.* 82 E2 42 26N 123 19W
Grantsville, *U.S.A.* 82 F7 40 36N 112 28W
Granville, *France* 18 B3 48 50N 1 35W
Granville, *N. Dak., U.S.A.* 80 A4 48 16N 100 47W
Granville, *N.Y., U.S.A.* 79 C11 43 24N 73 16W
Granville, *Ohio, U.S.A.* 78 F2 40 4N 82 31W
Granville L., *Canada* 73 B8 56 18N 100 30W
Graskop, *S. Africa* 57 C5 24 56S 30 49 E
Grass →, *Canada* 73 B9 56 3N 96 33W
Grass Range, *U.S.A.* 82 C9 47 0N 109 0W
Grass River Prov. Park,
Canada 73 C8 54 40N 100 50W
Grass Valley, *Calif., U.S.A.* 84 F6 39 13N 121 4W
Grass Valley, *Oreg., U.S.A.* 82 D3 45 22N 120 47W
Grasse, *France* 18 E7 43 38N 6 56 E
Grassflat, *U.S.A.* 78 F6 41 0N 78 6W
Grasslands Nat. Park,
Canada 73 D7 49 11N 107 38W
Grassy, *Australia* 62 G3 40 3S 144 5 E
Graulhet, *France* 18 E4 43 45N 1 59 E
Gravelbourg, *Canada* 73 D7 49 50N 106 35W
's-Gravenhage, *Neths.* 15 B4 52 7N 4 17 E
Gravenhurst, *Canada* 78 B5 44 52N 79 20W
Gravesend, *Australia* 63 D5 29 35S 150 20 E
Gravesend, *U.K.* 11 F8 51 26N 0 22 E
Gravois, Pointe-à-, *Haiti* 89 C5 18 15N 73 56W
Grayling, *U.S.A.* 76 C3 44 40N 84 43W
Grays Harbor, *U.S.A.* 82 C1 46 59N 124 1W
Grays L., *U.S.A.* 82 E8 43 4N 111 26W
Grays River, *U.S.A.* 84 D3 46 21N 123 37W
Graz, *Austria* 16 E8 47 4N 15 27 E
Greasy L., *Canada* 72 A4 62 55N 122 12W
Great Abaco I., *Bahamas* 88 A4 26 25N 77 10W
Great Artesian Basin,
Australia 62 C3 23 0S 144 0 E
Great Australian Bight,
Australia 61 F5 33 30S 130 0 E
Great Bahama Bank,
Bahamas 88 B4 23 15N 78 0W
Great Barrier I., *N.Z.* 59 G5 36 11S 175 25 E
Great Barrier Reef, *Australia* 62 B4 18 0S 146 50 E
Great Barrington, *U.S.A.* 79 D11 42 12N 73 22W
Great Basin, *U.S.A.* 82 G5 40 0N 117 0W
Great Basin Nat. Park,
U.S.A. 82 G6 38 55N 114 14W
Great Bear →, *Canada* 68 B7 65 0N 124 0W
Great Bear L., *Canada* 68 B8 65 30N 120 0W
Great Belt = Store Bælt,
Denmark 9 J14 55 20N 11 0 E
Great Bend, *Kans., U.S.A.* 80 F5 38 22N 98 46W
Great Bend, *Pa., U.S.A.* 79 E9 41 58N 75 45W
Great Blasket I., *Ireland* 13 D1 52 6N 10 32W
Great Britain, *Europe* 6 E5 54 0N 2 15W
Great Codroy, *Canada* 71 C8 47 51N 59 16W
Great Dividing Ra., *Australia* 62 C4 23 0S 146 0 E
Great Driffield = Driffield,
U.K. 10 C7 54 0N 0 26W
Great Exuma I., *Bahamas* 88 B4 23 30N 75 50W
Great Falls, *U.S.A.* 82 C8 47 30N 111 17W
Great Fish = Groot Vis →,
S. Africa 56 E4 33 28S 27 5 E
Great Guana Cay, *Bahamas* 88 B4 24 0N 76 20W
Great Inagua I., *Bahamas* 89 B5 21 0N 73 20W
Great Indian Desert = Thar
Desert, *India* 42 F5 28 0N 72 0 E
Great Karoo, *S. Africa* 56 E3 31 55S 21 0 E
Great Lake, *Australia* 62 G4 41 50S 146 40 E
Great Lakes, *N. Amer.* 66 E11 46 0N 84 0W
Great Malvern, *U.K.* 11 E5 52 7N 2 18W
Great Miami →, *U.S.A.* 76 F3 39 20N 84 40W
Great Ormes Head, *U.K.* 10 D4 53 20N 3 52W
Great Ouse →, *U.K.* 10 E8 52 48N 0 21 E
Great Palm I., *Australia* 62 B4 18 45S 146 40 E
Great Plains, *N. Amer.* 74 A6 47 0N 105 0W
Great Ruaha →, *Tanzania* 54 D4 7 56S 37 52 E
Great Sacandaga Res.,
U.S.A. 79 C10 43 6N 74 16W
Great Saint Bernard Pass =
Grand St-Bernard, Col du,
Europe 18 D7 45 50N 7 10 E
Great Salt L., *U.S.A.* 82 F7 41 15N 112 40W
Great Salt Lake Desert,
U.S.A. 82 F7 40 50N 113 30W
Great Salt Plains L., *U.S.A.* 81 G5 36 45N 98 8W
Great Sandy Desert,
Australia 60 D3 21 0S 124 0 E
Great Sangi = Sangihe,
Pulau, *Indonesia* 37 D7 3 45N 125 30 E
Great Skellig, *Ireland* 13 E1 51 47N 10 33W
Great Slave L., *Canada* 72 A5 61 23N 115 38W
Great Smoky Mts. Nat. Park,
U.S.A. 77 H4 35 40N 83 40W
Great Snow Mt., *Canada* 72 B4 57 26N 124 0W
Great Stour = Stour →,
U.K. 11 F9 51 18N 1 22 E
Great Victoria Desert,
Australia 61 E4 29 30S 126 30 E
Great Wall, *China* 34 E5 38 30N 109 30 E
Great Whernside, *U.K.* 10 C6 54 10N 1 58W
Great Yarmouth, *U.K.* 11 E9 52 37N 1 44 E
Greater Antilles, *W. Indies* 89 C5 17 40N 74 0W
Greater London □, *U.K.* 11 F7 51 31N 0 6W
Greater Manchester □, *U.K.* 10 D5 53 30N 2 15W
Greater Sunda Is., *Indonesia* 36 F4 7 0S 112 0 E
Greco, C., *Cyprus* 23 E13 34 57N 34 5 E
Gredos, Sierra de, *Spain* 19 B3 40 20N 5 0W
Greece, *U.S.A.* 78 C7 43 13N 77 41W
Greece ■, *Europe* 21 E9 40 0N 23 0 E
Greeley, *Colo., U.S.A.* 80 E2 40 25N 104 42W
Greeley, *Nebr., U.S.A.* 80 E5 41 33N 98 32W
Greem-Bell, Ostrov, *Russia* 26 A7 81 0N 62 0 E
Green, *U.S.A.* 82 E2 43 9N 123 22W
Green →, *Ky., U.S.A.* 76 G2 37 54N 87 30W
Green →, *Utah, U.S.A.* 83 G9 38 11N 109 53W
Green B., *U.S.A.* 76 C2 45 0N 87 30W
Green Bay, *U.S.A.* 76 C2 44 31N 88 0W
Green C., *Australia* 63 F5 37 13S 150 1 E
Green Cove Springs, *U.S.A.* 77 L5 29 59N 81 42W
Green Lake, *Canada* 73 C7 54 17N 107 47W
Green Mts., *U.S.A.* 79 C12 43 45N 72 45W
Green River, *Utah, U.S.A.* 83 G8 38 59N 110 10W
Green River, *Wyo., U.S.A.* 82 F9 41 32N 109 28W
Green Valley, *U.S.A.* 83 L8 31 52N 110 56W
Greenbank, *U.S.A.* 84 B4 48 6N 122 34W
Greenbush, *Mich., U.S.A.* 78 B1 44 35N 83 19W
Greenbush, *Minn., U.S.A.* 80 A6 48 42N 96 11W
Greencastle, *U.S.A.* 76 F2 39 38N 86 52W
Greene, *U.S.A.* 79 D9 42 20N 75 46W
Greenfield, *Calif., U.S.A.* 84 J5 36 19N 121 15W
Greenfield, *Calif., U.S.A.* 85 K8 35 15N 119 0W
Greenfield, *Ind., U.S.A.* 76 F3 39 47N 85 46W
Greenfield, *Iowa, U.S.A.* 80 E7 41 18N 94 28W
Greenfield, *Mass., U.S.A.* 79 D12 42 35N 72 36W
Greenfield, *Mo., U.S.A.* 81 G8 37 25N 93 51W
Greenfield Park, *Canada* 79 A11 45 29N 73 29W
Greenland ■, *N. Amer.* 4 C5 66 0N 45 0W
Greenland Sea, *Arctic* 4 B7 73 0N 10 0W
Greenock, *U.K.* 12 F4 55 57N 4 46W
Greenore, *Ireland* 13 B5 54 2N 6 8W
Greenore Pt., *Ireland* 13 D5 52 14N 6 19W
Greenough, *Australia* 61 E1 28 58S 114 43 E
Greenough →, *Australia* 61 E1 28 51S 114 38 E
Greenough Pt., *Canada* 78 B3 44 58N 81 26W
Greenport, *U.S.A.* 79 E12 41 6N 72 22W
Greensboro, *Ga., U.S.A.* 77 J4 33 35N 83 11W
Greensboro, *N.C., U.S.A.* 77 G6 36 4N 79 48W
Greensboro, *Vt., U.S.A.* 79 B12 44 36N 72 18W
Greensburg, *Ind., U.S.A.* 76 F3 39 20N 85 29W
Greensburg, *Kans., U.S.A.* 81 G5 37 36N 99 18W
Greensburg, *Pa., U.S.A.* 78 F5 40 18N 79 33W
Greenstone Pt., *U.K.* 12 D3 57 55N 5 37W
Greenvale, *Australia* 62 B4 18 59S 145 7 E
Greenville, *Ala., U.S.A.* 77 K2 31 50N 86 38W
Greenville, *Calif., U.S.A.* 84 E6 40 8N 120 57W
Greenville, *Maine, U.S.A.* 77 C11 45 28N 69 35W
Greenville, *Mich., U.S.A.* 76 D3 43 11N 85 15W
Greenville, *Miss., U.S.A.* 81 J9 33 24N 91 4W
Greenville, *Mo., U.S.A.* 81 G9 37 8N 90 27W
Greenville, *N.C., U.S.A.* 77 H7 35 37N 77 23W
Greenville, *N.H., U.S.A.* 79 D13 42 46N 71 49W
Greenville, *N.Y., U.S.A.* 79 D10 42 25N 74 1W
Greenville, *Ohio, U.S.A.* 76 E3 40 6N 84 38W
Greenville, *Pa., U.S.A.* 78 E4 41 24N 80 23W
Greenville, *S.C., U.S.A.* 77 H4 34 51N 82 24W
Greenville, *Tenn., U.S.A.* 77 G4 36 13N 82 51W
Greenville, *Tex., U.S.A.* 81 J6 33 8N 96 7W
Greenwater Lake Prov. Park,
Canada 73 C8 52 32N 103 30W
Greenwich, *U.K.* 11 F8 51 29N 0 1 E
Greenwich, *Conn., U.S.A.* 79 E11 41 2N 73 38W
Greenwich, *N.Y., U.S.A.* 79 C11 43 5N 73 30W
Greenwich, *Ohio, U.S.A.* 78 E2 41 2N 82 31W
Greenwood, *Canada* 72 D5 49 10N 118 40W
Greenwood, *Ark., U.S.A.* 81 H7 35 13N 94 16W
Greenwood, *Ind., U.S.A.* 76 F2 39 37N 86 7W
Greenwood, *Miss., U.S.A.* 81 J9 33 31N 90 11W
Greenwood, *S.C., U.S.A.* 77 H4 34 12N 82 10W
Greenwood, Mt., *Australia* 60 B5 13 48S 130 4 E
Gregory, *U.S.A.* 80 D5 43 14N 99 20W
Gregory →, *Australia* 62 B2 17 53S 139 17 E
Gregory, L., *S. Austral.,*
Australia 63 D2 28 55S 139 0 E
Gregory, L., *W. Austral.,*
Australia 61 E2 25 38S 119 58 E
Gregory Downs, *Australia* 62 B2 18 35S 138 45 E
Gregory L., *Australia* 60 D4 20 0S 127 40 E
Gregory Ra., *Queens.,*
Australia 62 B3 19 30S 143 40 E
Gregory Ra., *W. Austral.,*
Australia 60 D3 21 20S 121 12 E
Greifswald, *Germany* 16 A7 54 5N 13 23 E
Greiz, *Germany* 16 C7 50 39N 12 10 E
Gremikha, *Russia* 24 A6 67 59N 39 47 E
Grenå, *Denmark* 9 H14 56 25N 10 53 E
Grenada, *U.S.A.* 81 J10 33 47N 89 49W
Grenada ■, *W. Indies* 89 D7 12 10N 61 40W
Grenadier I., *U.S.A.* 79 B8 44 3N 76 22W
Grenadines, *W. Indies* 89 D7 12 40N 61 20W

Grenen

Grenen, Denmark 9 H14 57 44N 10 40 E
Grenfell, Australia 63 E4 33 52S 148 8 E
Grenfell, Canada 73 C8 50 30N 102 56W
Grenoble, France 18 D6 45 12N 5 42 E
Grenville, C., Australia 62 A3 12 0S 143 13 E
Grenville Chan., Canada 72 C3 53 40N 129 46W
Gresham, U.S.A. 84 E4 45 30N 122 26W
Gresik, Indonesia 37 G15 7 13S 112 38 E
Gretna, U.K. 12 F5 55 0N 3 3W
Grevenmacher, Lux. 15 E6 49 41N 6 26 E
Grey —►, Canada 71 C8 47 34N 57 6W
Grey —►, N.Z. 59 K3 42 27S 171 12 E
Grey, C., Australia 62 A2 13 0S 136 35 E
Grey Ra., Australia 63 D3 27 0S 143 30 E
Greybull, U.S.A. 82 D9 44 30N 108 3W
Greymouth, N.Z. 59 K3 42 29S 171 13 E
Greystones, Ireland 13 C5 53 9N 6 5W
Greytown, N.Z. 59 J5 41 5S 175 29 E
Greytown, S. Africa 57 D5 29 1S 30 36 E
Gribbell I., Canada 72 C3 53 23N 129 0W
Gridley, U.S.A. 84 F5 39 22N 121 42W
Griekwastad, S. Africa 56 D3 28 49S 23 15 E
Griffin, U.S.A. 77 J3 33 15N 84 16W
Griffith, Australia 63 E4 34 18S 146 2 E
Griffith, Canada 78 A7 45 15N 77 10W
Griffith I., Canada 78 B4 44 50N 80 55W
Grimaylov = Hrymayliv, Ukraine 17 D14 49 20N 26 5 E
Grimes, U.S.A. 84 F5 39 4N 121 54W
Grimsay, U.K. 12 D1 57 29N 7 14W
Grimsby, Canada 78 C5 43 12N 79 34W
Grimsby, U.K. 10 D7 53 34N 0 5W
Grímsey, Iceland 8 C5 66 33N 17 58W
Grimshaw, Canada 72 B5 56 10N 117 40W
Grimstad, Norway 9 G13 58 20N 8 35 E
Grindstone I., Canada 79 B8 44 43N 76 14W
Grinnell, U.S.A. 80 E8 41 45N 92 43W
Gris-Nez, C., France 18 A4 50 52N 1 35 E
Groais I., Canada 71 B8 50 55N 55 35W
Groblersdal, S. Africa 57 D4 25 15S 29 25 E
Grodno = Hrodna, Belarus 17 B12 53 42N 23 52 E
Grodzyanka = Hrodzyanka, Belarus 17 B15 53 31N 28 42 E
Groesbeck, U.S.A. 81 K6 30 48N 96 31W
Grójec, Poland 17 C11 51 50N 20 58 E
Grong, Norway 8 D15 64 25N 12 8 E
Groningen, Neths. 15 A6 53 15N 6 35 E
Groningen □, Neths. 15 A6 53 16N 6 40 E
Groom, U.S.A. 81 H4 35 12N 101 6W
Groot —►, S. Africa 56 E3 33 45S 24 36 E
Groot Berg —►, S. Africa 56 E2 32 47S 18 8 E
Groot-Brakrivier, S. Africa 56 E3 34 2S 22 18 E
Groot-Kei —►, S. Africa 57 E4 32 41S 28 22 E
Groot Vis —►, S. Africa 56 E4 33 28S 27 5 E
Groote Eylandt, Australia 62 A2 14 0S 136 40 E
Grootfontein, Namibia 56 B2 19 31S 18 6 E
Grootlaagte —►, Africa 56 C3 20 55S 21 27 E
Grootvloer, S. Africa 56 E3 30 0S 20 40 E
Gros C., Canada 72 A6 61 59N 113 32W
Gros Morne Nat. Park, Canada 71 C8 49 40N 57 50W
Grossa, Pta., Spain 22 B8 39 6N 1 36 E
Grosser Arber, Germany 16 D7 49 6N 13 8 E
Grosseto, Italy 20 C4 42 46N 11 8 E
Grossglockner, Austria 16 E7 47 5N 12 40 E
Groswater B., Canada 71 B8 54 20N 57 40W
Groton, Conn., U.S.A. 79 E12 41 21N 72 5W
Groton, N.Y., U.S.A. 79 D8 42 36N 76 22W
Groton, S. Dak., U.S.A. 80 C5 45 27N 98 6W
Grouard Mission, Canada 72 B5 55 33N 116 9W
Groundhog —►, Canada 70 C3 48 45N 82 58W
Grouw, Neths. 15 A5 53 5N 5 51 E
Grove City, U.S.A. 78 E4 41 10N 80 5W
Grove Hill, U.S.A. 77 K2 31 42N 87 47W
Groveland, U.S.A. 84 H6 37 50N 120 14W
Grover City, U.S.A. 85 K6 35 7N 120 37W
Groves, U.S.A. 81 L8 29 57N 93 54W
Groveton, U.S.A. 79 B13 44 36N 71 31W
Groznyy, Russia 25 F8 43 20N 45 45 E
Grudziądz, Poland 17 B10 53 30N 18 47 E
Gruinard B., U.K. 12 D3 57 56N 5 35W
Grundy Center, U.S.A. 80 D8 42 22N 92 47W
Gruver, U.S.A. 81 G4 36 16N 101 24W
Gryazi, Russia 24 D6 52 30N 39 58 E
Gryazovets, Russia 24 C7 58 50N 40 10 E
Gua, India 41 H14 22 18N 85 20 E
Gua Musang, Malaysia 39 K3 4 53N 101 58 E
Guacanayabo, G. de, Cuba 88 B4 20 40N 77 20W
Guachípas —►, Argentina 94 B2 25 40S 65 30W
Guadalajara, Mexico 86 C4 20 40N 103 20W
Guadalajara, Spain 19 B4 40 37N 3 12W
Guadalcanal, Solomon Is. 64 H8 9 32S 160 12 E
Guadales, Argentina 94 C2 34 30S 67 55W
Guadalete —►, Spain 19 D2 36 35N 6 13W
Guadalquivir —►, Spain 19 D2 36 47N 6 22W
Guadalupe = Guadeloupe ■, W. Indies 89 C7 16 20N 61 40W
Guadalupe, Mexico 85 N10 32 4N 116 32W
Guadalupe, U.S.A. 85 L6 34 59N 120 33W
Guadalupe —►, Mexico 85 N10 32 6N 116 51W
Guadalupe —►, U.S.A. 81 L6 28 27N 96 47W
Guadalupe, Sierra de, Spain 19 C3 39 28N 5 30W
Guadalupe Bravos, Mexico 86 A3 31 20N 106 10W
Guadalupe I., Pac. Oc. 66 G8 29 0N 118 50W
Guadalupe Mts. Nat. Park, U.S.A. 81 K2 32 0N 104 30W
Guadalupe Peak, U.S.A. 81 K2 31 50N 104 52W
Guadalupe y Calvo, Mexico 86 B3 26 6N 106 58W
Guadarrama, Sierra de, Spain 19 B4 41 0N 4 0W
Guadeloupe ■, W. Indies 89 C7 16 20N 61 40W
Guadeloupe Passage, W. Indies 89 C7 16 50N 62 15W
Guadiana —►, Portugal 19 D2 37 14N 7 22W
Guadix, Spain 19 D4 37 18N 3 11W
Guafo, Boca del, Chile 96 E2 43 35S 74 0W
Guainía —►, Colombia 92 C5 2 1N 67 7W
Guaíra, Brazil 95 A5 24 5S 54 10W
Guaíra □, Paraguay 94 B4 25 45S 56 30W
Guaitecas, Is., Chile 96 E2 44 0S 74 30W
Guajará-Mirim, Brazil 92 F5 10 50S 65 20W
Guajira, Pen. de la, Colombia 92 A4 12 0N 72 0W
Gualán, Guatemala 88 C2 15 8N 89 22W
Gualeguay, Argentina 94 C4 33 10S 59 14W
Gualeguaychú, Argentina 94 C4 33 3S 59 31W
Gualequay —►, Argentina 94 C4 33 19S 59 39W
Guam ■, Pac. Oc. 64 F6 13 27N 144 45 E
Guaminí, Argentina 94 D3 37 1S 62 28W
Guamúchil, Mexico 86 B3 25 25N 108 3W
Guanabacoa, Cuba 88 B3 23 8N 82 18W
Guanacaste, Cordillera del, Costa Rica 88 D2 10 40N 85 4W
Guanaceví, Mexico 86 B3 25 40N 106 0W
Guanahani = San Salvador I., Bahamas 89 B5 24 0N 74 40W
Guanajay, Cuba 88 B3 22 56N 82 42W
Guanajuato, Mexico 86 C4 21 0N 101 20W
Guanajuato □, Mexico 86 C4 20 40N 101 20W
Guandacol, Argentina 94 B2 29 30S 68 40W
Guane, Cuba 88 B3 22 10N 84 7W
Guangdong □, China 33 D6 23 0N 113 0 E
Guangling, China 34 E8 39 47N 114 22 E
Guangrao, China 35 F10 37 5N 118 25 E
Guangwu, China 34 F3 37 48N 105 57 E
Guangxi Zhuangzu Zizhiqu □, China 33 D5 24 0N 109 0 E
Guangzhou, China 33 D6 23 5N 113 10 E
Guanipa —►, Venezuela 92 B6 9 56N 62 26W
Guannan, China 35 G10 34 8N 119 21 E
Guantánamo, Cuba 89 B4 20 10N 75 14W
Guantao, China 34 F8 36 42N 115 25 E
Guanyun, China 35 G10 34 20N 119 18 E
Guápiles, Costa Rica 88 D3 10 10N 83 46W
Guaporé, Brazil 95 B5 28 51S 51 54W
Guaporé —►, Brazil 92 F5 11 55S 65 4W
Guaqui, Bolivia 92 G5 16 41S 68 54W
Guarapari, Brazil 95 A7 20 40S 40 30W
Guarapuava, Brazil 95 B5 25 20S 51 30W
Guaratinguetá, Brazil 95 A6 22 49S 45 9W
Guaratuba, Brazil 95 B6 25 53S 48 38W
Guarda, Portugal 19 B2 40 32N 7 20W
Guardafui, C. = Asir, Ras, Somali Rep. 46 E5 11 55N 51 10 E
Guárico □, Venezuela 92 B5 8 40N 66 35W
Guarujá, Brazil 95 A6 24 2S 46 25W
Guarus, Brazil 95 A7 21 44S 41 20W
Guasave, Mexico 86 B3 25 34N 108 27W
Guasdualito, Venezuela 92 B4 7 15N 70 44W
Guatemala, Guatemala 88 D1 14 40N 90 22W
Guatemala ■, Cent. Amer. 88 C1 15 40N 90 30W
Guaviare —►, Colombia 92 C5 4 3N 67 44W
Guaxupé, Brazil 95 A6 21 10S 47 5W
Guayama, Puerto Rico 89 C6 17 59N 66 7W
Guayaquil, Ecuador 92 D3 2 15S 79 52W
Guayaquil, G. de, Ecuador 92 D2 3 10S 81 0W
Guaymas, Mexico 86 B2 27 59N 110 54W
Guba, Dem. Rep. of the Congo 55 E2 10 38S 26 27 E
Gubkin, Russia 25 D6 51 17N 37 32 E
Gudbrandsdalen, Norway 9 F14 61 33N 10 10 E
Guddu Barrage, Pakistan 40 E6 28 30N 69 50 E
Gudivada, India 41 L12 16 30N 81 3 E
Gudur, India 40 M11 14 12N 79 55 E
Guecho = Getxo, Spain 19 A4 43 21N 2 59W
Guelph, Canada 78 C4 43 35N 80 20W
Guéret, France 18 C4 46 11N 1 51 E
Guerneville, U.S.A. 84 G4 38 30N 123 0W
Guernica = Gernika-Lumo, Spain 19 A4 43 19N 2 40W
Guernsey, U.K. 11 H5 49 26N 2 35W
Guernsey, U.S.A. 80 D2 42 19N 104 45W
Guerrero □, Mexico 87 D5 17 30N 100 0W
Gügher, Iran 45 D8 29 28N 56 27 E
Guhakolak, Tanjung, Indonesia 37 G11 6 50S 105 14 E
Guia, Canary Is. 22 F4 28 8N 15 38W
Guia de Isora, Canary Is. 22 F3 28 12N 16 46W
Guia Lopes da Laguna, Brazil 95 A4 21 26S 56 7W
Guiana, S. Amer. 90 C4 5 10N 60 40W
Guider, Cameroon 51 G8 9 56N 13 57 E
Guidónia-Montecélio, Italy 20 C5 42 1N 12 45 E
Guijá, Mozam. 57 C5 24 27S 33 0 E
Guildford, U.K. 11 F7 51 14N 0 34W
Guilford, U.S.A. 79 E12 41 17N 72 41W
Guilin, China 33 D6 25 18N 110 15 E
Guillaume-Delisle L., Canada 70 A4 56 15N 76 17W
Güímar, Canary Is. 22 F3 28 18N 16 24W
Guimarães, Portugal 19 B1 41 28N 8 24W
Guimaras, Phil. 37 B6 10 35N 122 37 E
Guinda, U.S.A. 84 G4 38 50N 122 12W
Guinea, Africa 48 F4 8 0N 8 0 E
Guinea ■, W. Afr. 50 F3 10 20N 11 30W
Guinea, Gulf of, Atl. Oc. 48 F4 3 0N 2 30 E
Guinea-Bissau ■, Africa 50 F3 12 0N 15 0W
Güines, Cuba 88 B3 22 50N 82 0W
Guingamp, France 18 B2 48 34N 3 10W
Güiria, Venezuela 92 A6 10 32N 62 18W
Guiuan, Phil. 37 B7 11 5N 125 55 E
Guiyang, China 32 D5 26 32N 106 40 E
Guizhou □, China 32 D5 27 0N 107 0 E
Gujar Khan, Pakistan 42 C5 33 16N 73 19 E
Gujarat □, India 42 H4 23 20N 71 0 E
Gujranwala, Pakistan 42 C6 32 10N 74 12 E
Gujrat, Pakistan 42 C6 32 40N 74 2 E
Gulargambone, Australia 63 E4 31 20S 148 30 E
Gulbarga, India 40 L10 17 20N 76 50 E
Gulbene, Latvia 9 H22 57 8N 26 52 E
Gulf, The, Asia 45 E6 27 0N 50 0 E
Gulfport, U.S.A. 81 K10 30 22N 89 6W
Gulgong, Australia 63 E4 32 20S 149 49 E
Gulistan, Pakistan 42 D2 30 30N 66 35 E
Gull Lake, Canada 73 C7 50 10N 108 29W
Güllük, Turkey 21 F12 37 14N 27 35 E
Gulmarg, India 43 B6 34 3N 74 25 E
Gulshad, Kazakstan 26 E8 46 45N 74 25 E
Gulu, Uganda 54 B3 2 48N 32 17 E
Gulwe, Tanzania 54 D4 6 30S 36 25 E
Gumal —►, Pakistan 42 D4 31 40N 71 50 E
Gumbaz, Pakistan 42 D3 30 2N 69 0 E
Gumel, Nigeria 50 F7 12 39N 9 22 E
Gumla, India 43 H11 23 3N 84 33 E
Gumlu, Australia 62 B4 19 53S 147 41 E
Gumma □, Japan 31 F9 36 30N 138 20 E
Gumzai, Indonesia 37 F8 5 28S 134 42 E
Guna, India 42 G7 24 40N 77 19 E
Gunisao —►, Canada 73 C9 53 56N 97 53W
Gunisao L., Canada 73 C9 53 33N 96 15W
Gunjyal, Pakistan 42 C4 32 20N 71 55 E
Gunnbjørn Fjeld, Greenland 4 C6 68 55N 29 47W
Gunnedah, Australia 63 E5 30 59S 150 15 E
Gunnewin, Australia 63 D4 25 59S 148 33 E
Gunningbar Cr. —►, Australia 63 E4 31 14S 147 6 E
Gunnison, Colo., U.S.A. 83 G10 38 33N 106 56W
Gunnison, Utah, U.S.A. 82 G8 39 9N 111 49W
Gunnison —►, U.S.A. 83 G9 39 4N 108 35W
Gunpowder, Australia 62 B2 19 42S 139 22 E
Guntakal, India 40 M10 15 11N 77 27 E
Guntersville, U.S.A. 77 H2 34 21N 86 18W
Guntong, Malaysia 39 K3 4 36N 101 3 E
Guntur, India 41 L12 16 23N 80 30 E
Gunungapi, Indonesia 37 F7 6 45S 126 30 E
Gunungsitoli, Indonesia 36 D1 1 15N 97 30 E
Gunza, Angola 52 G2 10 50S 13 50 E
Guo He —►, China 35 H9 32 59N 117 10 E
Guoyang, China 34 H9 33 32N 116 12 E
Gupis, Pakistan 43 A5 36 15N 73 20 E
Gurdaspur, India 42 C6 32 5N 75 31 E
Gurdon, U.S.A. 81 J8 33 55N 93 9W
Gurgaon, India 42 E7 28 27N 77 1 E
Gurgueia —►, Brazil 93 E10 6 50S 43 24W
Gurha, India 42 G4 25 12N 71 39 E
Guri, Embalse de, Venezuela 92 B6 7 50N 62 52W
Gurkha, Nepal 43 E11 28 5N 84 40 E
Gurley, Australia 63 D4 29 45S 149 48 E
Gurnet Point, U.S.A. 79 D14 42 1N 70 34W
Gurué, Mozam. 55 F4 15 25S 36 58 E
Gurun, Malaysia 39 K3 5 49N 100 27 E
Gürün, Turkey 25 G6 38 43N 37 15 E
Gurupá, Brazil 93 D8 1 25S 51 35W
Gurupá, I. Grande de, Brazil 93 D8 1 25S 51 45W
Gurupi, Brazil 93 F9 11 43S 49 4W
Gurupi —►, Brazil 93 D9 1 13S 46 6W
Guryev = Atyraū, Kazakstan 25 E9 47 5N 52 0 E
Gusau, Nigeria 50 F7 12 12N 6 40 E
Gusev, Russia 9 J20 54 35N 22 10 E
Gushan, China 35 E12 39 50N 123 35 E
Gushgy, Turkmenistan 26 F7 35 20N 62 18 E
Gusinoozersk, Russia 27 D11 51 16N 106 27 E
Gustavus, U.S.A. 72 B1 58 25N 135 44W
Gustine, U.S.A. 84 H6 37 16N 121 0W
Güstrow, Germany 16 B7 53 47N 12 10 E
Gütersloh, Germany 16 C5 51 54N 8 24 E
Gutha, Australia 61 E2 28 58S 115 55 E
Guthalungra, Australia 62 B4 19 52S 147 50 E
Guthrie, Okla., U.S.A. 81 H6 35 53N 97 25W
Guthrie, Tex., U.S.A. 81 J4 33 37N 100 19W
Guttenberg, U.S.A. 80 D9 42 47N 91 6W
Guyana ■, S. Amer. 92 C7 5 0N 59 0W
Guyane française = French Guiana ■, S. Amer. 93 C8 4 0N 53 0W
Guyang, China 34 D6 41 0N 110 5 E
Guyenne, France 18 D4 44 30N 0 40 E
Guymon, U.S.A. 81 G4 36 41N 101 29W
Guyra, Australia 63 E5 30 15S 151 40 E
Guyuan, Hebei, China 34 D8 41 37N 115 40 E
Guyuan, Ningxia Huizu, China 34 G4 36 0N 106 20 E
Guzhen, China 35 H9 33 22N 117 18 E
Guzmán, L. de, Mexico 86 A3 31 25N 107 25W
Gvardeysk, Russia 9 J19 54 39N 21 5 E
Gwa, Burma 41 L19 17 36N 94 34 E
Gwaai, Zimbabwe 55 F2 19 15S 27 45 E
Gwabegar, Australia 63 E4 30 31S 149 0 E
Gwādar, Pakistan 40 G3 25 10N 62 18 E
Gwalior, India 42 F8 26 12N 78 10 E
Gwanda, Zimbabwe 55 G2 20 55S 29 0 E
Gwane, Dem. Rep. of the Congo 54 B2 4 45N 25 48 E
Gweebarra B., Ireland 13 B3 54 51N 8 23W
Gweedore, Ireland 13 A3 55 3N 8 13W
Gweru, Zimbabwe 55 F2 19 28S 29 45 E
Gwinn, U.S.A. 76 B2 46 19N 87 27W
Gwydir —►, Australia 63 D4 29 27S 149 48 E
Gwynedd □, U.K. 10 E3 52 52N 4 10W
Gyandzha = Gäncä, Azerbaijan 25 F8 40 45N 46 20 E
Gyaring Hu, China 32 C4 34 50N 97 40 E
Gydanskiy Poluostrov, Russia 26 C8 70 0N 78 0 E
Gympie, Australia 63 D5 26 11S 152 38 E
Gyöngyös, Hungary 17 E10 47 48N 19 56 E
Győr, Hungary 17 E9 47 41N 17 40 E
Gypsum Pt., Canada 72 A6 61 53N 114 35W
Gypsumville, Canada 73 C9 51 45N 98 40W
Gyula, Hungary 17 E11 46 38N 21 17 E
Gyumri, Armenia 25 F7 40 47N 43 50 E
Gyzylarbat, Turkmenistan 26 F6 39 4N 56 23 E
Gyzyletrek, Turkmenistan 45 B7 37 36N 54 46 E

H

Ha 'Arava —►, Israel 47 E4 30 50N 35 20 E
Ha Tien, Vietnam 39 G5 10 23N 104 29 E
Ha Tinh, Vietnam 38 C5 18 20N 105 54 E
Ha Trung, Vietnam 38 C5 19 58N 105 50 E
Haaksbergen, Neths. 15 B6 52 9N 6 45 E
Haapsalu, Estonia 9 G20 58 56N 23 30 E
Haarlem, Neths. 15 B4 52 23N 4 39 E
Haast —►, N.Z. 59 K2 43 50S 169 2 E
Haast Bluff, Australia 60 D5 23 22S 132 0 E
Hab —►, Pakistan 42 G3 24 53N 66 41 E
Hab Nadi Chauki, Pakistan 42 G2 25 0N 66 50 E
Habaswein, Kenya 54 B4 1 2N 39 30 E
Habay, Canada 72 B5 58 50N 118 44W
Ḩabbānīyah, Iraq 44 C4 33 17N 43 29 E
Haboro, Japan 30 B10 44 22N 141 42 E
Ḩabshān, U.A.E. 45 F7 23 50N 53 37 E
Hachijō-Jima, Japan 31 H9 33 5N 139 45 E
Hachinohe, Japan 30 D10 40 30N 141 29 E
Hachiōji, Japan 31 G9 35 40N 139 20 E
Hachŏn, N. Korea 35 D15 41 29N 129 2 E
Hackensack, U.S.A. 79 F10 40 53N 74 3W
Hackettstown, U.S.A. 79 F10 40 51N 74 50W
Hadali, Pakistan 42 C5 32 16N 72 11 E
Hadarba, Ras, Sudan 51 D13 22 4N 36 51 E
Hadarom □, Israel 47 E4 31 0N 35 0 E
Hadd, Ra's al, Oman 46 C6 22 35N 59 50 E
Hadejia, Nigeria 50 F7 12 30N 10 5 E
Hadera, Israel 47 C3 32 27N 34 55 E
Hadera, N. —►, Israel 47 C3 32 28N 34 52 E
Haderslev, Denmark 9 J13 55 15N 9 30 E
Hadhramaut = Ḩaḑramawt, Yemen 46 D4 15 30N 49 30 E
Hadibu, Yemen 46 E5 12 39N 54 2 E
Hadong, S. Korea 35 G14 35 5N 127 44 E
Ḩaḑramawt, Yemen 46 D4 15 30N 49 30 E
Ḩadrānīyah, Iraq 44 C4 35 38N 43 14 E
Hadrian's Wall, U.K. 10 B5 55 0N 2 30W
Haeju, N. Korea 35 E13 38 3N 125 45 E
Haenam, S. Korea 35 G14 34 34N 126 35 E
Haerhpin = Harbin, China 35 B14 45 48N 126 40 E
Hafar al Bāţin, Si. Arabia 44 D5 28 32N 45 52 E
Ḩafirat al 'Aydā, Si. Arabia 44 E3 26 26N 39 12 E
Ḩafit, Oman 45 F7 23 59N 55 49 E
Ḩafit, Jabal, Oman 45 E7 24 3N 55 46 E
Hafizabad, Pakistan 42 C5 32 5N 73 40 E
Haflong, India 41 G18 25 10N 93 5 E
Hafnarfjörður, Iceland 8 D3 64 4N 21 57W
Haft Gel, Iran 45 D6 31 30N 49 32 E
Hafun, Ras, Somali Rep. 46 E5 10 29N 51 30 E
Hagalil, Israel 47 C4 32 53N 35 18 E
Hagen, Germany 16 C4 51 21N 7 27 E
Hagerman, U.S.A. 81 J2 33 7N 104 20W
Hagerstown, U.S.A. 76 F7 39 39N 77 43W
Hagersville, Canada 78 D4 42 58N 80 3W
Hagfors, Sweden 9 F15 60 3N 13 45 E
Hagi, Japan 31 G5 34 30N 131 22 E
Hagolan, Syria 47 C4 33 0N 35 45 E
Hagondange, France 18 B7 49 16N 6 11 E
Hags Hd., Ireland 13 D2 52 57N 9 28W
Hague, C. de la, France 18 B3 49 44N 1 56W
Hague, The = 's-Gravenhage, Neths. 15 B4 52 7N 4 17 E
Haguenau, France 18 B7 48 49N 7 47 E
Haicheng, China 35 D12 40 50N 122 45 E
Haidar Khel, Afghan. 42 C3 33 58N 68 38 E
Haidargarh, India 43 F9 26 37N 81 22 E
Haifa = Ḩefa, Israel 47 C4 32 46N 35 0 E
Haikou, China 33 D6 20 1N 110 16 E
Ḩā'il, Si. Arabia 44 E4 27 28N 41 45 E
Hailar, China 33 B6 49 10N 119 38 E
Hailey, U.S.A. 82 E6 43 31N 114 19W
Haileybury, Canada 70 C4 47 30N 79 38W
Hailin, China 35 B15 44 37N 129 30 E
Hailong, China 35 C13 42 32N 125 40 E
Hailuoto, Finland 8 D21 65 3N 24 45 E
Hainan □, China 33 E5 19 0N 109 30 E
Hainaut □, Belgium 15 D4 50 30N 4 0 E
Haines, Alaska, U.S.A. 72 B1 59 14N 135 26W
Haines, Oreg., U.S.A. 82 D5 44 55N 117 56W
Haines City, U.S.A. 77 L5 28 7N 81 38W
Haines Junction, Canada 72 A1 60 45N 137 30W
Haiphong, Vietnam 32 D5 20 47N 106 41 E
Haiti ■, W. Indies 89 C5 19 0N 72 30W
Haiya, Sudan 51 E13 18 20N 36 21 E
Haiyang, China 35 F11 36 47N 121 9 E
Haiyuan, China 34 F3 36 35N 105 52 E
Haizhou, China 35 G10 34 37N 119 7 E
Haizhou Wan, China 35 G10 34 50N 119 20 E
Hajdúböszörmény, Hungary 17 E11 47 40N 21 30 E
Hajipur, India 43 G11 25 45N 85 13 E
Ḩājjī Muḩsin, Iraq 44 C5 32 35N 45 29 E
Ḩājjīābād, Iran 45 D7 28 19N 55 55 E
Ḩājjīābād-e Zarrīn, Iran 45 C7 33 9N 54 51 E
Hajnówka, Poland 17 B12 52 47N 23 35 E
Hakansson, Mts., Dem. Rep. of the Congo 55 D2 8 40S 25 45 E
Hakkâri, Turkey 44 B4 37 34N 43 44 E
Hakken-Zan, Japan 31 G7 34 10N 135 54 E
Hakodate, Japan 30 D10 41 45N 140 44 E
Haku-San, Japan 31 F8 36 9N 136 46 E
Hakui, Japan 31 F8 36 53N 136 47 E
Hala, Pakistan 40 G6 25 43N 68 20 E
Ḩalab, Syria 44 B3 36 10N 37 15 E
Ḩalabjah, Iraq 44 C5 35 10N 45 58 E
Halaib, Sudan 51 D13 22 12N 36 30 E
Hālat 'Ammār, Si. Arabia 44 D3 29 10N 36 4 E
Halbā, Lebanon 47 A5 34 34N 36 6 E
Halberstadt, Germany 16 C6 51 54N 11 3 E
Halcombe, N.Z. 59 J5 40 8S 175 30 E
Halcon, Phil. 37 B6 13 0N 121 30 E
Halden, Norway 9 G14 59 9N 11 23 E
Haldia, India 41 H16 22 5N 88 3 E
Haldwani, India 43 E8 29 31N 79 30 E
Hale —►, Australia 62 C2 24 56S 135 53 E
Haleakala Crater, U.S.A. 74 H16 20 43N 156 16W
Halesowen, U.K. 11 E5 52 27N 2 3W
Haleyville, U.S.A. 77 H2 34 14N 87 37W
Halfway —►, Canada 72 B4 56 12N 121 32W
Halia, India 43 G10 24 50N 82 19 E
Haliburton, Canada 78 A6 45 3N 78 30W
Halifax, Australia 62 B4 18 32S 146 22 E
Halifax, Canada 71 D7 44 38N 63 35W
Halifax, U.K. 10 D6 53 43N 1 52W
Halifax, U.S.A. 78 F8 40 25N 76 55W
Halifax B., Australia 62 B4 18 50S 147 0 E
Halifax I., Namibia 56 D2 26 38S 15 4 E
Halīl —►, Iran 45 E8 27 40N 58 30 E
Halkirk, U.K. 12 C5 58 30N 3 29W
Hall Beach = Sanirajak, Canada 69 B11 68 46N 81 12W
Hall Pen., Canada 69 B13 63 30N 66 0W
Hall Pt., Australia 60 C3 15 40S 124 23 E
Halland, Sweden 9 H15 57 8N 12 47 E
Halle, Belgium 15 D4 50 44N 4 13 E
Halle, Germany 16 C6 51 30N 11 56 E
Hällefors, Sweden 9 G16 59 47N 14 31 E
Hallett, Australia 63 E2 33 25S 138 55 E
Hallettsville, U.S.A. 81 L6 29 27N 96 57W
Hallim, S. Korea 35 H14 33 24N 126 15 E
Hallingdalselvi —►, Norway 9 F13 60 23N 9 35 E
Halls Creek, Australia 60 C4 18 16S 127 38 E
Hallsberg, Sweden 9 G16 59 5N 15 7 E
Hallstead, U.S.A. 79 E9 41 58N 75 45W
Halmahera, Indonesia 37 D7 0 40N 128 0 E
Halmstad, Sweden 9 H15 56 41N 12 52 E
Hälsingborg = Helsingborg, Sweden 9 H15 56 3N 12 42 E
Hälsingland, Sweden 9 F16 61 40N 16 5 E
Halstead, U.K. 11 F8 51 57N 0 40 E
Halti, Finland 8 B19 69 17N 21 18 E
Halton □, U.K. 10 D5 53 22N 2 45W
Haltwhistle, U.K. 10 C5 54 58N 2 26W
Halul, Qatar 45 E7 25 40N 52 40 E
Halvad, India 42 H4 23 1N 71 11 E
Ḩalvān, Iran 45 C8 33 57N 56 15 E
Ham Tan, Vietnam 39 G6 10 40N 107 45 E
Ham Yen, Vietnam 38 A5 22 4N 105 3 E
Hamab, Namibia 56 D2 28 7S 19 16 E
Hamada, Japan 31 G6 34 56N 132 4 E
Hamadān, Iran 45 C6 34 52N 48 32 E

125

Indore

Indore, *India* 42 H6 22 42N 75 53 E
Indramayu, *Indonesia* 37 G13 6 20S 108 19 E
Indravati →, *India* 41 K12 19 20N 80 20 E
Indre →, *France* 18 C4 47 16N 0 11 E
Indulkana, *Australia* 63 D1 26 58S 133 5 E
Indus →, *Pakistan* 42 G2 24 20N 67 47 E
Indus, Mouth of the, *Pakistan* 42 H3 24 0N 68 0 E
İnebolu, *Turkey* 25 F5 41 55N 33 40 E
Infiernillo, Presa del, *Mexico* 86 D4 18 9N 102 0W
Ingenio, *Canary Is.* 22 G4 27 55N 15 26W
Ingenio Santa Ana, *Argentina* 94 B2 27 25S 65 40W
Ingersoll, *Canada* 78 C4 43 4N 80 55W
Ingham, *Australia* 62 B4 18 43S 146 10 E
Ingleborough, *U.K.* 10 C5 54 10N 2 22W
Inglewood, *Queens., Australia* 63 D5 28 25S 151 2 E
Inglewood, *Vic., Australia* 63 F3 36 29S 143 53 E
Inglewood, *N.Z.* 59 H5 39 9S 174 14 E
Inglewood, *U.S.A.* 85 M8 33 58N 118 21W
Ingólfshöfði, *Iceland* 8 E5 63 48N 16 39W
Ingolstadt, *Germany* 16 D6 48 46N 11 26 E
Ingomar, *U.S.A.* 82 C10 46 35N 107 23W
Ingonish, *Canada* 71 C7 46 42N 60 18W
Ingraj Bazar, *India* 43 G13 24 58N 88 10 E
Ingrid Christensen Coast, *Antarctica* 5 C6 69 30S 76 0 E
Ingulec = Inhulec, *Ukraine* 25 E5 47 42N 33 14 E
Ingushetia □, *Russia* 25 E8 43 20N 44 50 E
Ingwavuma, *S. Africa* 57 D5 27 9S 31 59 E
Inhaca, I., *Mozam.* 57 D5 26 1S 32 57 E
Inhafenga, *Mozam.* 57 C5 20 36S 33 53 E
Inhambane, *Mozam.* 57 C6 23 54S 35 30 E
Inhambane □, *Mozam.* 57 C5 22 30S 34 20 E
Inhaminga, *Mozam.* 55 F4 18 26S 35 0 E
Inharrime, *Mozam.* 57 C6 24 30S 35 0 E
Inharrime →, *Mozam.* 57 C6 24 30S 35 0 E
Inhulec, *Ukraine* 25 E5 47 42N 33 14 E
Ining = Yining, *China* 26 E9 43 58N 81 10 E
Inírida →, *Colombia* 92 C5 3 55N 67 52W
Inishbofin, *Ireland* 13 C1 53 37N 10 13W
Inisheer, *Ireland* 13 C2 53 3N 9 32W
Inishfree B., *Ireland* 13 A3 55 4N 8 23W
Inishkea North, *Ireland* 13 B1 54 9N 10 11W
Inishkea South, *Ireland* 13 B1 54 7N 10 12W
Inishmaan, *Ireland* 13 C2 53 5N 9 35W
Inishmore, *Ireland* 13 C2 53 8N 9 45W
Inishowen Pen., *Ireland* 13 A4 55 14N 7 15W
Inishshark, *Ireland* 13 C1 53 37N 10 16W
Inishturk, *Ireland* 13 C1 53 42N 10 7W
Inishvickillane, *Ireland* 13 D1 52 3N 10 37W
Injune, *Australia* 63 D4 25 53S 148 32 E
Inklin →, *Canada* 72 B2 58 50N 133 10W
Inle L., *Burma* 41 J20 20 30N 96 58 E
Inlet, *U.S.A.* 79 C10 43 45N 74 48W
Inn →, *Austria* 16 D7 48 35N 13 28 E
Innamincka, *Australia* 63 D3 27 44S 140 46 E
Inner Hebrides, *U.K.* 12 E2 57 0N 6 30W
Inner Mongolia = Nei Monggol Zizhiqu □, *China* 34 D7 42 0N 112 0 E
Inner Sound, *U.K.* 12 D3 57 30N 5 55W
Innerkip, *Canada* 78 C4 43 13N 80 42W
Innetalling I., *Canada* 70 A4 56 0N 79 0W
Innisfail, *Australia* 62 B4 17 33S 146 5 E
Innisfail, *Canada* 72 C6 52 0N 113 57W
In'no-shima, *Japan* 31 G6 34 19N 133 10 E
Innsbruck, *Austria* 16 E6 47 16N 11 23 E
Inny →, *Ireland* 13 C4 53 30N 7 50W
Inongo, *Dem. Rep. of the Congo* 52 E3 1 55S 18 30 E
Inoucdjouac = Inukjuak, *Canada* 69 C12 58 25N 78 15W
Inowrocław, *Poland* 17 B10 52 50N 18 12 E
Inpundong, *N. Korea* 35 D14 41 25N 126 34 E
Inscription, C., *Australia* 61 E1 25 29S 112 59 E
Insein, *Burma* 41 L20 16 50N 96 5 E
Inta, *Russia* 24 A11 66 5N 60 8 E
Intendente Alvear, *Argentina* 94 D3 35 12S 63 32W
Interlaken, *Switz.* 18 C7 46 41N 7 50 E
Interlaken, *U.S.A.* 79 D8 42 37N 76 44W
International Falls, *U.S.A.* 80 A8 48 36N 93 25W
Intiyaco, *Argentina* 94 B3 28 43S 60 5W
Inukjuak, *Canada* 69 C12 58 25N 78 15W
Inútil, B., *Chile* 96 G2 53 30S 70 15W
Inuvik, *Canada* 68 B6 68 16N 133 40W
Inveraray, *U.K.* 12 E3 56 14N 5 5W
Inverbervie, *U.K.* 12 E6 56 51N 2 17W
Invercargill, *N.Z.* 59 M2 46 24S 168 24 E
Inverclyde □, *U.K.* 12 F4 55 55N 4 49W
Inverell, *Australia* 63 D5 29 45S 151 8 E
Invergordon, *U.K.* 12 D4 57 41N 4 10W
Inverloch, *Australia* 63 F4 38 38S 145 45 E
Invermere, *Canada* 72 C5 50 30N 116 2W
Inverness, *Canada* 71 C7 46 15N 61 19W
Inverness, *U.K.* 12 D4 57 29N 4 13W
Inverness, *U.S.A.* 77 L4 28 50N 82 20W
Inverurie, *U.K.* 12 D6 57 17N 2 23W
Investigator Group, *Australia* 63 E1 34 45S 134 20 E
Investigator Str., *Australia* 63 F2 35 30S 137 0 E
Inya, *Russia* 26 D9 50 28N 86 37 E
Inyanga, *Zimbabwe* 55 F3 18 12S 32 40 E
Inyangani, *Zimbabwe* 55 F3 18 5S 32 50 E
Inyantue, *Zimbabwe* 55 F2 18 30S 26 40 E
Inyo Mts., *U.S.A.* 84 J9 36 40N 118 0W
Inyokern, *U.S.A.* 85 K9 35 39N 117 49W
Inza, *Russia* 24 D8 53 55N 46 25 E
Iō-Jima, *Japan* 31 J5 30 48N 130 18 E
Ioánnina, *Greece* 21 E9 39 42N 20 47 E
Iola, *U.S.A.* 81 G7 37 55N 95 24W
Iona, *U.K.* 12 E2 56 20N 6 25W
Ione, *U.S.A.* 84 G6 38 21N 120 56W
Ionia, *U.S.A.* 76 D3 42 59N 85 4W
Ionian Is. = Iónioi Nísoi, *Greece* 21 E9 38 40N 20 0 E
Ionian Sea, *Medit. S.* 21 E7 37 30N 17 30 E
Iónioi Nísoi, *Greece* 21 E9 38 40N 20 0 E
Íos, *Greece* 21 F11 36 41N 25 20 E
Iowa □, *U.S.A.* 80 D8 42 18N 93 30W
Iowa →, *U.S.A.* 80 E9 41 10N 91 1W
Iowa City, *U.S.A.* 80 E9 41 40N 91 32W
Iowa Falls, *U.S.A.* 80 D8 42 31N 93 16W
Iowa Park, *U.S.A.* 81 J5 33 57N 98 40W
Ipala, *Tanzania* 54 C3 4 30S 32 52 E
Ipameri, *Brazil* 93 G9 17 44S 48 9W
Ipatinga, *Brazil* 93 G10 19 32S 42 30W
Ipiales, *Colombia* 92 C3 0 50N 77 37W
Ipin = Yibin, *China* 32 D5 28 45N 104 32 E
Ipixuna, *Brazil* 92 E4 7 0S 71 40W
Ipoh, *Malaysia* 39 K3 4 35N 101 5 E
Ippy, *C.A.R.* 52 C4 6 5N 21 7 E
İpsala, *Turkey* 21 D12 40 55N 26 23 E
Ipswich, *Australia* 63 D5 27 35S 152 40 E
Ipswich, *U.K.* 11 E9 52 4N 1 10 E
Ipswich, *Mass., U.S.A.* 79 D14 42 41N 70 50W
Ipswich, *S. Dak., U.S.A.* 80 C5 45 27N 99 2W
Ipu, *Brazil* 93 D10 4 23S 40 44W
Iqaluit, *Canada* 69 B13 63 44N 68 31W
Iquique, *Chile* 92 H4 20 19S 70 5W
Iquitos, *Peru* 92 D4 3 45S 73 10W
Irabu-Jima, *Japan* 31 M2 24 50N 125 10 E
Iracoubo, *Fr. Guiana* 93 B8 5 30N 53 10W
Īrafshān, *Iran* 45 E9 26 42N 61 56 E
Iráklion, *Greece* 23 D7 35 20N 25 12 E
Iráklion □, *Greece* 23 D7 35 10N 25 10 E
Irala, *Paraguay* 95 B5 25 55S 54 35W
Iran ■, *Asia* 45 C7 33 0N 53 0 E
Iran, Gunung-Gunung, *Malaysia* 36 D4 2 20N 114 50 E
Iran, Plateau of, *Asia* 28 F9 32 0N 55 0 E
Iran Ra. = Iran, Gunung-Gunung, *Malaysia* 36 D4 2 20N 114 50 E
Īrānshahr, *Iran* 45 E9 27 15N 60 40 E
Irapuato, *Mexico* 86 C4 20 40N 101 30W
Iraq ■, *Asia* 44 C5 33 0N 44 0 E
Irati, *Brazil* 95 B5 25 25S 50 38W
Irbid, *Jordan* 47 C4 32 35N 35 48 E
Irbid □, *Jordan* 47 C5 32 15N 36 35 E
Ireland ■, *Europe* 13 C4 53 50N 7 52W
Irhyangdong, *N. Korea* 35 D15 41 15N 129 30 E
Iri, *S. Korea* 35 G14 35 59N 127 0 E
Irian Jaya □, *Indonesia* 37 E9 4 0S 137 0 E
Iringa, *Tanzania* 54 D4 7 48S 35 43 E
Iringa □, *Tanzania* 54 D4 7 48S 35 43 E
Iriomote-Jima, *Japan* 31 M1 24 19N 123 48 E
Iriona, *Honduras* 88 C2 15 57N 85 11W
Iriri →, *Brazil* 93 D8 3 52S 52 37W
Irish Republic ■, *Europe* 13 C3 53 0N 8 0W
Irish Sea, *U.K.* 10 D3 53 38N 4 48W
Irkutsk, *Russia* 27 D11 52 18N 104 20 E
Irma, *Canada* 73 C6 52 55N 111 14W
Irō-Zaki, *Japan* 31 G9 34 36N 138 51 E
Iron Baron, *Australia* 63 E2 32 58S 137 11 E
Iron Gate = Portile de Fier, *Europe* 17 F12 44 44N 22 30 E
Iron Knob, *Australia* 63 E2 32 46S 137 8 E
Iron Mountain, *U.S.A.* 76 C1 45 49N 88 4W
Iron River, *U.S.A.* 80 B10 46 6N 88 39W
Irondequoit, *U.S.A.* 78 C7 43 13N 77 35W
Ironstone Kopje, *Botswana* 56 D3 25 17S 24 5 E
Ironton, *Mo., U.S.A.* 81 G9 37 36N 90 38W
Ironton, *Ohio, U.S.A.* 76 F4 38 32N 82 41W
Ironwood, *U.S.A.* 80 B9 46 27N 90 9W
Iroquois, *Canada* 79 B9 44 51N 75 19W
Iroquois Falls, *Canada* 70 C3 48 46N 80 41W
Irpin, *Ukraine* 17 C16 50 30N 30 15 E
Irrara Cr. →, *Australia* 63 D4 29 35S 145 31 E
Irrawaddy □, *Burma* 41 L19 17 0N 95 0 E
Irrawaddy →, *Burma* 41 M19 15 50N 95 6 E
Irricana, *Canada* 72 C6 51 19N 113 37W
Irtysh →, *Russia* 26 C7 61 4N 68 52 E
Irumu, *Dem. Rep. of the Congo* 54 B2 1 32N 29 53 E
Irún, *Spain* 19 A5 43 20N 1 52W
Irunea = Pamplona, *Spain* 19 A5 42 48N 1 38W
Irvine, *Canada* 73 D6 49 57N 110 16W
Irvine, *U.K.* 12 F4 55 37N 4 41W
Irvine, *Calif., U.S.A.* 85 M9 33 41N 117 46W
Irvine, *Ky., U.S.A.* 76 G4 37 42N 83 58W
Irvinestown, *U.K.* 13 B4 54 28N 7 39W
Irving, *U.S.A.* 81 J6 32 49N 96 56W
Irvona, *U.S.A.* 78 F6 40 46N 78 33W
Irwin →, *Australia* 61 E1 29 15S 114 54 E
Irymple, *Australia* 63 E3 34 14S 142 8 E
Isa Khel, *Pakistan* 42 C4 32 41N 71 17 E
Isaac →, *Australia* 62 C4 22 55S 149 20 E
Isabel, *U.S.A.* 80 C4 45 24N 101 26W
Isabela, I., *Mexico* 86 C3 21 51N 105 55W
Isabelia, Cord., *Nic.* 88 D2 13 30N 85 25W
Isabella, *Phil.* 37 C6 6 40N 122 10 E
Isabella Ra., *Australia* 60 D3 21 0S 121 4 E
Ísafjarðardjúp, *Iceland* 8 C2 66 10N 23 0W
Ísafjörður, *Iceland* 8 C2 66 5N 23 9W
Isagarh, *India* 42 G7 24 48N 77 51 E
Isahaya, *Japan* 31 H5 32 52N 130 2 E
Isaka, *Tanzania* 54 C3 3 56S 32 59 E
Isan →, *India* 43 F9 26 51N 80 7 E
Isana = Içana →, *Brazil* 92 C5 0 26N 67 19W
Isar →, *Germany* 16 D7 48 48N 12 57 E
Íschia, *Italy* 20 D5 40 44N 13 57 E
Isdell →, *Australia* 60 C3 16 27S 124 51 E
Ise, *Japan* 31 G8 34 25N 136 45 E
Ise-Wan, *Japan* 31 G8 34 43N 136 43 E
Iseramagazi, *Tanzania* 54 C3 4 37S 32 10 E
Isère →, *France* 18 D6 44 59N 4 51 E
Isérnia, *Italy* 20 D6 41 36N 14 14 E
Isfahan = Eşfahān, *Iran* 45 C6 32 39N 51 43 E
Ishigaki-Shima, *Japan* 31 M2 24 20N 124 10 E
Ishikari-Gawa →, *Japan* 30 C10 43 15N 141 23 E
Ishikari-Sammyaku, *Japan* 30 C11 43 30N 143 0 E
Ishikari-Wan, *Japan* 30 C10 43 25N 141 1 E
Ishikawa □, *Japan* 31 F8 36 30N 136 30 E
Ishim, *Russia* 26 D7 56 10N 69 30 E
Ishim →, *Russia* 26 D8 57 45N 71 10 E
Ishinomaki, *Japan* 30 E10 38 32N 141 20 E
Ishioka, *Japan* 31 F10 36 11N 140 16 E
Ishkuman, *Pakistan* 43 A5 36 30N 73 50 E
Ishpeming, *U.S.A.* 76 B2 46 29N 87 40W
Isil Kul, *Russia* 26 D8 54 55N 71 16 E
Isiolo, *Kenya* 54 B4 0 24N 37 33 E
Isiro, *Dem. Rep. of the Congo* 54 B2 2 53N 27 40 E
Isisford, *Australia* 62 C3 24 15S 144 21 E
İskenderun, *Turkey* 25 G6 36 32N 36 10 E
İskenderun Körfezi, *Turkey* 25 G6 36 40N 35 50 E
Iskŭr →, *Bulgaria* 21 C11 43 45N 24 25 E
Iskut →, *Canada* 72 B2 56 45N 131 49W
Isla →, *U.K.* 12 E5 56 32N 3 20W
Isla Vista, *U.S.A.* 85 L7 34 25N 119 53W
Islam Headworks, *Pakistan* 42 E5 29 49N 72 33 E
Islamabad, *Pakistan* 42 C5 33 40N 73 10 E
Islamgarh, *Pakistan* 42 F4 27 51N 70 48 E
Islamkot, *Pakistan* 42 G4 24 42N 70 13 E
Islampur, *India* 43 G11 25 9N 85 12 E
Island L., *Canada* 73 C10 53 47N 94 25W
Island Lagoon, *Australia* 63 E2 31 30S 136 40 E
Island Pond, *U.S.A.* 79 B13 44 49N 71 53W
Islands, B. of, *Canada* 71 C8 49 11N 58 15W
Islay, *U.K.* 12 F2 55 46N 6 10W
Isle →, *France* 18 D3 44 55N 0 15W
Isle aux Morts, *Canada* 71 C8 47 35N 59 0W
Isle of Wight □, *U.K.* 11 G6 50 41N 1 17W
Isle Royale, *U.S.A.* 80 B10 48 0N 88 54W
Isle Royale National Park, *U.S.A.* 80 B10 48 0N 88 55W
Isleton, *U.S.A.* 84 G5 38 10N 121 37W
Ismail = Izmayil, *Ukraine* 17 F15 45 22N 28 46 E
Ismâ'ilîya, *Egypt* 51 B12 30 37N 32 18 E
Isogstalo, *India* 43 B8 34 15N 78 46 E
Isparta, *Turkey* 25 G5 37 47N 30 30 E
Íspica, *Italy* 20 F6 36 47N 14 55 E
Israel ■, *Asia* 47 D3 32 0N 34 50 E
Issoire, *France* 18 D5 45 32N 3 15 E
Issyk-Kul = Ysyk-Köl, *Kyrgyzstan* 28 E11 42 26N 76 12 E
Issyk-Kul, Ozero = Ysyk-Köl, Ozero, *Kyrgyzstan* 26 E8 42 25N 77 15 E
İstanbul, *Turkey* 21 D13 41 0N 29 0 E
İstanbul Boğazı, *Turkey* 21 D13 41 10N 29 10 E
Istiaía, *Greece* 21 E10 38 57N 23 9 E
Istokpoga, L., *U.S.A.* 77 M5 27 23N 81 17W
Istra, *Croatia* 16 F7 45 10N 14 0 E
Istres, *France* 18 E6 43 31N 4 59 E
Istria = Istra, *Croatia* 16 F7 45 10N 14 0 E
Itá, *Paraguay* 94 B4 25 29S 57 21W
Itaberaba, *Brazil* 93 F10 12 32S 40 18W
Itabira, *Brazil* 93 G10 19 37S 43 13W
Itabirito, *Brazil* 95 A7 20 15S 43 48W
Itabuna, *Brazil* 93 F11 14 48S 39 16W
Itacaunas →, *Brazil* 93 E9 5 21S 49 8W
Itacoatiara, *Brazil* 92 D7 3 8S 58 25W
Itaipú, Represa de, *Brazil* 95 B5 25 30S 54 30W
Itaituba, *Brazil* 93 D7 4 10S 55 50W
Itajaí, *Brazil* 95 B6 27 50S 48 39W
Itajubá, *Brazil* 95 A6 22 24S 45 30W
Itaka, *Tanzania* 55 D3 8 50S 32 49 E
Italy ■, *Europe* 20 C5 42 0N 13 0 E
Itamaraju, *Brazil* 93 G11 17 5S 39 31W
Itampolo, *Madag.* 57 C7 24 41S 43 57 E
Itapecuru-Mirim, *Brazil* 93 D10 3 24S 44 20W
Itaperuna, *Brazil* 95 A7 21 10S 41 54W
Itapetininga, *Brazil* 95 A6 23 36S 48 7W
Itapeva, *Brazil* 95 A6 23 59S 48 59W
Itapicuru →, *Bahia, Brazil* 93 F11 11 47S 37 32W
Itapicuru →, *Maranhão, Brazil* 93 D10 2 52S 44 12W
Itapipoca, *Brazil* 93 D11 3 30S 39 35W
Itapuá □, *Paraguay* 95 B4 26 40S 55 40W
Itaquari, *Brazil* 95 A7 20 20S 40 25W
Itaqui, *Brazil* 94 B4 29 8S 56 30W
Itararé, *Brazil* 95 A6 24 6S 49 23W
Itarsi, *India* 42 H7 22 36N 77 51 E
Itatí, *Argentina* 94 B4 27 16S 58 15W
Itchen →, *U.K.* 11 G6 50 55N 1 22W
Itezhi Tezhi, L., *Zambia* 55 F2 15 30S 25 30 E
Ithaca = Itháki, *Greece* 21 E9 38 25N 20 40 E
Ithaca, *U.S.A.* 79 D8 42 27N 76 30W
Itháki, *Greece* 21 E9 38 25N 20 40 E
Itiquira →, *Brazil* 93 G7 17 18S 56 44W
Ito, *Japan* 31 G9 34 58N 139 5 E
Ito Aba I., *S. China Sea* 36 B4 10 23N 114 21 E
Itoigawa, *Japan* 31 F8 37 2N 137 51 E
Itonamas →, *Bolivia* 92 F6 12 28S 64 24W
Ittoqqortoormiit, *Greenland* 4 B6 70 20N 23 0W
Itu, *Brazil* 95 A6 23 17S 47 15W
Ituiutaba, *Brazil* 93 G9 19 0S 49 25W
Itumbiara, *Brazil* 93 G9 18 20S 49 10W
Ituna, *Canada* 73 C8 51 10N 103 24W
Itunge Port, *Tanzania* 55 D3 9 40S 33 55 E
Iturbe, *Argentina* 94 A2 23 0S 65 25W
Ituri →, *Dem. Rep. of the Congo* 54 B2 1 40N 27 1 E
Iturup, Ostrov, *Russia* 27 E15 45 0N 148 0 E
Ituxi →, *Brazil* 92 E6 7 18S 64 51W
Ituyuro →, *Argentina* 94 A3 22 40S 63 50W
Itzehoe, *Germany* 16 B5 53 55N 9 31 E
Ivaí →, *Brazil* 95 A5 23 18S 53 42W
Ivalo, *Finland* 8 B22 68 38N 27 35 E
Ivalojoki →, *Finland* 8 B22 68 40N 27 40 E
Ivanava, *Belarus* 17 B13 52 7N 25 29 E
Ivanhoe, *Australia* 63 E3 32 56S 144 20 E
Ivanhoe, *Calif., U.S.A.* 84 J7 36 23N 119 13W
Ivanhoe, *Minn., U.S.A.* 80 C6 44 28N 96 15W
Ivano-Frankivsk, *Ukraine* 17 D13 48 40N 24 40 E
Ivano-Frankovsk = Ivano-Frankivsk, *Ukraine* 17 D13 48 40N 24 40 E
Ivanovo = Ivanava, *Belarus* 17 B13 52 7N 25 29 E
Ivanovo, *Russia* 24 C7 57 5N 41 0 E
Ivato, *Madag.* 57 C8 20 37S 47 10 E
Ivatsevichy, *Belarus* 17 B13 52 43N 25 21 E
Ivdel, *Russia* 24 B11 60 42N 60 24 E
Ivindo →, *Gabon* 52 D2 0 9S 12 9 E
Ivinheima →, *Brazil* 95 A5 23 14S 53 42W
Ivinhema, *Brazil* 95 A5 22 10S 53 37W
Ivohibe, *Madag.* 57 C8 22 31S 46 57 E
Ivory Coast, *Africa* 50 H4 5 0N 5 0W
Ivory Coast ■, *Africa* 50 G4 7 30N 5 0W
Ivrea, *Italy* 18 D7 45 28N 7 52 E
Ivujivik, *Canada* 69 B12 62 24N 77 55W
Ivybridge, *U.K.* 11 G4 50 23N 3 56W
Iwaizumi, *Japan* 30 E10 39 50N 141 45 E
Iwaki, *Japan* 31 F10 37 3N 140 55 E
Iwakuni, *Japan* 31 G6 34 15N 132 8 E
Iwamizawa, *Japan* 30 C10 43 12N 141 46 E
Iwanai, *Japan* 30 C10 42 58N 140 30 E
Iwata, *Japan* 31 G8 34 42N 137 51 E
Iwate □, *Japan* 30 E10 39 30N 141 30 E
Iwate-San, *Japan* 30 E10 39 51N 141 0 E
Iwo, *Nigeria* 50 G6 7 39N 4 9 E
Ixiamas, *Bolivia* 92 F5 13 50S 68 5W
Ixopo, *S. Africa* 57 E5 30 11S 30 5 E
Ixtepec, *Mexico* 87 D5 16 32N 95 10W
Ixtlán del Río, *Mexico* 86 C4 21 5N 104 21W
Iyo, *Japan* 31 H6 33 45N 132 45 E
Izabal, L. de, *Guatemala* 88 C2 15 30N 89 10W
Izamal, *Mexico* 87 C7 20 56N 89 1W
Izena-Shima, *Japan* 31 L3 26 56N 127 56 E
Izhevsk, *Russia* 24 C9 56 51N 53 14 E
Izhma →, *Russia* 24 A9 65 19N 52 54 E
Izmayil, *Ukraine* 17 F15 45 22N 28 46 E
İzmir, *Turkey* 21 E12 38 25N 27 8 E
İzmit = Kocaeli, *Turkey* 25 F4 40 45N 29 50 E
İznik Gölü, *Turkey* 21 D13 40 27N 29 30 E
Izra, *Syria* 47 C5 32 51N 36 15 E
Izu-Shotō, *Japan* 31 G10 34 30N 140 0 E
Izúcar de Matamoros, *Mexico* 87 D5 18 36N 98 28W
Izumi-sano, *Japan* 31 G7 34 23N 135 18 E
Izumo, *Japan* 31 G6 35 20N 132 46 E
Izyaslav, *Ukraine* 17 C14 50 5N 26 50 E

J

Jabalpur, *India* 43 H8 23 9N 79 58 E
Jabbūl, *Syria* 44 B3 36 4N 37 30 E
Jabiru, *Australia* 60 B5 12 40S 132 53 E
Jablah, *Syria* 44 C3 35 20N 36 0 E
Jablonec nad Nisou, *Czech Rep.* 16 C8 50 43N 15 10 E
Jaboatão, *Brazil* 93 E11 8 7S 35 1W
Jaboticabal, *Brazil* 95 A6 21 15S 48 17W
Jaca, *Spain* 19 A5 42 35N 0 33W
Jacareí, *Brazil* 95 A6 23 20S 46 0W
Jacarèzinho, *Brazil* 95 A6 23 5S 49 58W
Jackman, *U.S.A.* 77 C10 45 35N 70 17W
Jacksboro, *U.S.A.* 81 J5 33 14N 98 15W
Jackson, *Ala., U.S.A.* 77 K2 31 31N 87 53W
Jackson, *Calif., U.S.A.* 84 G6 38 21N 120 46W
Jackson, *Ky., U.S.A.* 76 G4 37 33N 83 23W
Jackson, *Mich., U.S.A.* 76 D3 42 15N 84 24W
Jackson, *Minn., U.S.A.* 80 D7 43 37N 95 1W
Jackson, *Miss., U.S.A.* 81 J9 32 18N 90 12W
Jackson, *Mo., U.S.A.* 81 G10 37 23N 89 40W
Jackson, *N.H., U.S.A.* 79 B13 44 10N 71 11W
Jackson, *Ohio, U.S.A.* 76 F4 39 3N 82 39W
Jackson, *Tenn., U.S.A.* 77 H1 35 37N 88 49W
Jackson, *Wyo., U.S.A.* 82 E8 43 29N 110 46W
Jackson B., *N.Z.* 59 K2 43 58S 168 42 E
Jackson L., *U.S.A.* 82 E8 43 52N 110 36W
Jacksons, *N.Z.* 59 K3 42 46S 171 32 E
Jackson's Arm, *Canada* 71 C8 49 52N 56 47W
Jacksonville, *Ala., U.S.A.* 77 J3 33 49N 85 46W
Jacksonville, *Ark., U.S.A.* 81 H8 34 52N 92 7W
Jacksonville, *Calif., U.S.A.* 84 H6 37 52N 120 24W
Jacksonville, *Fla., U.S.A.* 77 K5 30 20N 81 39W
Jacksonville, *Ill., U.S.A.* 80 F9 39 44N 90 14W
Jacksonville, *N.C., U.S.A.* 77 H7 34 45N 77 26W
Jacksonville, *Tex., U.S.A.* 81 K7 31 58N 95 17W
Jacksonville Beach, *U.S.A.* 77 K5 30 17N 81 24W
Jacmel, *Haiti* 89 C5 18 14N 72 32W
Jacob Lake, *U.S.A.* 83 H7 36 43N 112 13W
Jacobabad, *Pakistan* 42 E3 28 20N 68 29 E
Jacobina, *Brazil* 93 F10 11 11S 40 30W
Jacques Cartier, Dét. de, *Canada* 71 C7 50 0N 63 30W
Jacques-Cartier, Mt., *Canada* 71 C6 48 57N 66 0W
Jacques Cartier, Parc Prov., *Canada* 71 C5 47 15N 71 33W
Jacuí →, *Brazil* 95 C5 30 2S 51 15W
Jacumba, *U.S.A.* 85 N10 32 37N 116 11W
Jacundá →, *Brazil* 93 D8 1 57S 50 26W
Jadotville = Likasi, *Dem. Rep. of the Congo* 55 E2 10 55S 26 48 E
Jaén, *Peru* 92 E3 5 25S 78 40W
Jaén, *Spain* 19 D4 37 44N 3 43W
Jafarabad, *India* 42 J4 20 52N 71 22 E
Jaffa = Tel Aviv-Yafo, *Israel* 47 C3 32 4N 34 48 E
Jaffa, C., *Australia* 63 F2 36 58S 139 40 E
Jaffna, *Sri Lanka* 40 Q12 9 45N 80 2 E
Jaffrey, *U.S.A.* 79 D12 42 49N 72 2W
Jagadhri, *India* 42 D7 30 10N 77 20 E
Jagadishpur, *India* 43 G11 25 30N 84 21 E
Jagdalpur, *India* 41 K13 19 3N 82 0 E
Jagersfontein, *S. Africa* 56 D4 29 44S 25 27 E
Jaghīn →, *Iran* 45 E8 27 17N 57 13 E
Jagodina, *Serbia, Yug.* 21 C9 44 5N 21 15 E
Jagraon, *India* 40 D9 30 50N 75 25 E
Jagtial, *India* 40 K11 18 50N 79 0 E
Jaguariaíva, *Brazil* 95 A6 24 10S 49 50W
Jaguaribe →, *Brazil* 93 D11 4 25S 37 45W
Jagüey Grande, *Cuba* 88 B3 22 35N 81 7W
Jahanabad, *India* 43 G11 25 13N 84 59 E
Jahazpur, *India* 42 G6 25 37N 75 17 E
Jahrom, *Iran* 45 D7 28 30N 53 31 E
Jaijon, *India* 42 D7 31 21N 76 9 E
Jailolo, *Indonesia* 37 D7 1 5N 127 30 E
Jailolo, Selat, *Indonesia* 37 D7 0 5N 129 5 E
Jaipur, *India* 42 F6 27 0N 75 50 E
Jais, *India* 43 F9 26 15N 81 32 E
Jaisalmer, *India* 42 F4 26 55N 70 54 E
Jaisinghnagar, *India* 43 H8 23 38N 78 34 E
Jaitaran, *India* 42 F5 26 12N 73 56 E
Jaithari, *India* 43 H8 23 14N 78 37 E
Jājarm, *Iran* 45 B8 36 58N 56 27 E
Jakam →, *India* 42 H6 23 54N 74 13 E
Jakarta, *Indonesia* 37 G12 6 9S 106 49 E
Jakhal, *India* 42 E6 29 48N 75 50 E
Jakhau, *India* 42 H3 23 13N 68 43 E
Jakobstad = Pietarsaari, *Finland* 8 E20 63 40N 22 43 E
Jal, *U.S.A.* 81 J3 32 7N 103 12W
Jalalabad, *Afghan.* 42 B4 34 30N 70 29 E
Jalalabad, *India* 43 F8 27 41N 79 42 E
Jalalpur Jattan, *Pakistan* 42 C6 32 38N 74 11 E
Jalama, *U.S.A.* 85 L6 34 29N 120 29W
Jalapa, *Guatemala* 88 D2 14 39N 89 59W
Jalapa Enríquez, *Mexico* 87 D5 19 32N 96 55W
Jalasjärvi, *Finland* 9 E20 62 29N 22 47 E
Jalaun, *India* 43 F8 26 8N 79 25 E
Jaldhaka →, *Bangla.* 43 F13 26 16N 89 16 E
Jalesar, *India* 42 F8 27 29N 78 19 E
Jaleswar, *Nepal* 43 F11 26 38N 85 48 E
Jalgaon, *Maharashtra, India* 40 J10 21 2N 76 31 E
Jalgaon, *Maharashtra, India* 40 J9 21 0N 75 42 E
Jalībah, *Iraq* 44 D5 30 35N 46 32 E
Jalisco □, *Mexico* 86 D4 20 0N 104 0W
Jalkot, *Pakistan* 43 B5 35 14N 73 24 E
Jalna, *India* 40 K9 19 48N 75 38 E
Jalón →, *Spain* 19 B5 41 47N 1 4W
Jalor, *India* 42 G5 25 21N 72 37 E
Jalpa, *Mexico* 86 C4 21 38N 102 58W
Jalpaiguri, *India* 41 F16 26 32N 88 46 E
Jaluit I., *Marshall Is.* 64 G8 6 0N 169 30 E

Kentucky L.

Kapuas Hulu Ra. = Kapuas Hulu, Pegunungan, *Malaysia* **36 D4** 1 30N 113 30 E
Kapulo, *Dem. Rep. of the Congo* **55 D2** 8 18S 29 15 E
Kapunda, *Australia* **63 E2** 34 20S 138 56 E
Kapuni, *N.Z.* **59 H5** 39 29S 174 8 E
Kapurthala, *India* **42 D6** 31 23N 75 25 E
Kapuskasing, *Canada* **70 C3** 49 25N 82 30W
Kapuskasing →, *Canada* **70 C3** 49 49N 82 0W
Kaputar, *Australia* **63 E5** 30 15S 150 10 E
Kaputir, *Kenya* **54 B4** 2 5N 35 28 E
Kara, *Russia* **26 C7** 69 10N 65 0 E
Kara Bogaz Gol, Zaliv = Garabogazköl Aylagy, *Turkmenistan* **25 F9** 41 0N 53 30 E
Kara Kalpak Republic = Karakalpakstan □, *Uzbekistan* **26 E6** 43 0N 58 0 E
Kara Kum, *Turkmenistan* **26 F7** 39 30N 60 0 E
Kara Sea, *Russia* **26 B8** 75 0N 70 0 E
Karabiğa, *Turkey* **21 D12** 40 23N 27 17 E
Karabük, *Turkey* **25 F5** 41 12N 32 37 E
Karaburun, *Turkey* **21 E12** 38 41N 26 28 E
Karabutak = Qarabutaq, *Kazakstan* **26 E7** 49 59N 60 14 E
Karacabey, *Turkey* **21 D13** 40 12N 28 21 E
Karacasu, *Turkey* **21 F13** 37 43N 28 35 E
Karachey-Cherkessia □, *Russia* **25 F7** 43 40N 41 30 E
Karachi, *Pakistan* **42 G2** 24 53N 67 0 E
Karad, *India* **40 L9** 17 15N 74 10 E
Karaganda = Qaraghandy, *Kazakstan* **26 E8** 49 50N 73 10 E
Karagayly, *Kazakstan* **26 E8** 49 26N 76 0 E
Karaginskiy, Ostrov, *Russia* **27 D17** 58 45N 164 0 E
Karagiye, Vpadina, *Kazakstan* **25 F9** 43 27N 51 45 E
Karagiye Depression = Karagiye, Vpadina, *Kazakstan* **25 F9** 43 27N 51 45 E
Karagola Road, *India* **43 G12** 25 29N 87 23 E
Karaikal, *India* **40 P11** 10 59N 79 50 E
Karaikkudi, *India* **40 P11** 10 5N 78 45 E
Karaj, *Iran* **45 C6** 35 48N 51 0 E
Karak, *Malaysia* **39 L4** 3 25N 102 2 E
Karakalpakstan □, *Uzbekistan* **26 E6** 43 0N 58 0 E
Karakelong, *Indonesia* **37 D7** 4 35N 126 50 E
Karakitang, *Indonesia* **37 D7** 3 14N 125 28 E
Karaklis = Vanadzor, *Armenia* **25 F7** 40 48N 44 30 E
Karakoram Pass, *Pakistan* **43 B7** 35 33N 77 50 E
Karakoram Ra., *Pakistan* **43 B7** 35 30N 77 0 E
Karalon, *Russia* **27 D12** 57 5N 115 50 E
Karama, *Jordan* **47 D4** 31 57N 35 35 E
Karaman, *Turkey* **25 G5** 37 14N 33 13 E
Karamay, *China* **32 B3** 45 30N 84 58 E
Karambu, *Indonesia* **36 E5** 3 53S 116 6 E
Karamea Bight, *N.Z.* **59 J3** 41 22S 171 40 E
Karamnasa →, *India* **43 G10** 25 31N 83 52 E
Karand, *Iran* **44 C5** 34 16N 46 15 E
Karanganyar, *Indonesia* **37 G13** 7 38S 109 37 E
Karanjia, *India* **43 J11** 21 47N 85 58 E
Karasburg, *Namibia* **56 D2** 28 0S 18 44 E
Karasino, *Russia* **26 C9** 66 50N 86 50 E
Karasjok, *Norway* **8 B21** 69 27N 25 30 E
Karasuk, *Russia* **26 D8** 53 44N 78 2 E
Karasuyama, *Japan* **31 F10** 36 39N 140 9 E
Karatau = Qarataū, *Kazakstan* **26 E8** 43 10N 70 28 E
Karatau, Khrebet, *Kazakstan* **26 E7** 43 30N 69 30 E
Karatsu, *Japan* **31 H5** 33 26N 129 58 E
Karaul, *Russia* **26 B9** 70 6N 82 15 E
Karauli, *India* **42 F7** 26 30N 77 4 E
Karavostasi, *Cyprus* **23 D11** 35 8N 32 50 E
Karawang, *Indonesia* **37 G12** 6 30S 107 15 E
Karawanken, *Europe* **16 E8** 46 30N 14 40 E
Karayazı, *Turkey* **25 G7** 39 41N 42 9 E
Karazhal, *Kazakstan* **26 E8** 48 2N 70 49 E
Karbalā', *Iraq* **44 C5** 32 36N 44 3 E
Karcag, *Hungary* **17 E11** 47 19N 20 57 E
Karcha →, *Pakistan* **43 B7** 34 45N 76 10 E
Karchana, *India* **43 G9** 25 17N 81 56 E
Kardhítsa, *Greece* **21 E9** 39 23N 21 54 E
Kärdla, *Estonia* **9 G20** 58 50N 22 40 E
Kareeberge, *S. Africa* **56 E3** 30 59S 21 50 E
Kareha →, *India* **43 G12** 25 44N 86 21 E
Kareima, *Sudan* **51 E12** 18 30N 31 49 E
Karelia □, *Russia* **24 A5** 65 30N 32 30 E
Karelian Republic = Karelia □, *Russia* **24 A5** 65 30N 32 30 E
Karera, *India* **42 G8** 25 32N 78 9 E
Kārevāndar, *Iran* **45 E9** 27 53N 60 44 E
Kargasok, *Russia* **26 D9** 59 3N 80 53 E
Kargat, *Russia* **26 D9** 55 10N 80 15 E
Kargil, *India* **43 B7** 34 32N 76 12 E
Kargopol, *Russia* **24 B6** 61 30N 38 58 E
Karhal, *India* **43 F8** 27 1N 78 57 E
Karīān, *Iran* **45 E8** 26 57N 57 14 E
Kariba, *Zimbabwe* **55 F2** 16 28S 28 50 E
Kariba, L., *Zimbabwe* **55 F2** 16 40S 28 25 E
Kariba Dam, *Zimbabwe* **55 F2** 16 30S 28 35 E
Kariba Gorge, *Zambia* **55 F2** 16 30S 28 50 E
Karibib, *Namibia* **56 C2** 22 0S 15 56 E
Karimata, Kepulauan, *Indonesia* **36 E3** 1 25S 109 0 E
Karimata, Selat, *Indonesia* **36 E3** 2 0S 108 40 E
Karimata Is. = Karimata, Kepulauan, *Indonesia* **36 E3** 1 25S 109 0 E
Karimnagar, *India* **40 K11** 18 26N 79 10 E
Karimunjawa, Kepulauan, *Indonesia* **36 F4** 5 50S 110 30 E
Karin, *Somali Rep.* **46 E4** 10 50N 45 52 E
Karīt, *Iran* **45 C8** 33 29N 56 55 E
Kariya, *Japan* **31 G8** 34 58N 137 1 E
Karkaralinsk = Qarqaraly, *Kazakstan* **26 E8** 49 26N 75 30 E
Karkheh →, *Iran* **44 D5** 31 2N 47 29 E
Karkinitska Zatoka, *Ukraine* **25 E5** 45 56N 33 0 E
Karkinitskiy Zaliv = Karkinitska Zatoka, *Ukraine* **25 E5** 45 56N 33 0 E
Karl-Marx-Stadt = Chemnitz, *Germany* **16 C7** 50 51N 12 54 E
Karlovac, *Croatia* **16 F8** 45 31N 15 36 E
Karlovo, *Bulgaria* **21 C11** 42 38N 24 47 E
Karlovy Vary, *Czech Rep.* **16 C7** 50 13N 12 51 E
Karlsbad = Karlovy Vary, *Czech Rep.* **16 C7** 50 13N 12 51 E
Karlsborg, *Sweden* **9 G16** 58 33N 14 33 E
Karlshamn, *Sweden* **9 H16** 56 10N 14 51 E
Karlskoga, *Sweden* **9 G16** 59 28N 14 33 E
Karlskrona, *Sweden* **9 H16** 56 10N 15 35 E
Karlsruhe, *Germany* **16 D5** 49 0N 8 23 E
Karlstad, *Sweden* **9 G15** 59 23N 13 30 E
Karlstad, *U.S.A.* **80 A6** 48 35N 96 31W
Karmi'el, *Israel* **47 C4** 32 55N 35 18 E
Karnak, *Egypt* **51 C12** 25 43N 32 39 E
Karnal, *India* **42 E7** 29 42N 77 2 E
Karnali →, *Nepal* **43 E9** 28 45N 81 16 E
Karnaphuli Res., *Bangla.* **41 H18** 22 40N 92 20 E
Karnaprayag, *India* **43 D8** 30 16N 79 15 E
Karnataka □, *India* **40 N10** 13 15N 77 0 E
Karnes City, *U.S.A.* **81 L6** 28 53N 97 54W
Karnische Alpen, *Europe* **16 E7** 46 36N 13 0 E
Kärnten □, *Austria* **16 E8** 46 52N 13 30 E
Karoi, *Zimbabwe* **55 F2** 16 48S 29 45 E
Karonga, *Malawi* **55 D3** 9 57S 33 55 E
Karoonda, *Australia* **63 F2** 35 1S 139 59 E
Karor, *Pakistan* **42 D4** 31 15N 70 59 E
Karora, *Sudan* **51 E13** 17 44N 38 15 E
Karpasia □, *Cyprus* **23 D13** 35 32N 34 15 E
Kárpathos, *Greece* **21 G12** 35 37N 27 10 E
Karpinsk, *Russia* **24 C11** 59 45N 60 1 E
Karpogory, *Russia* **24 B7** 64 0N 44 27 E
Karpuz Burnu = Apostolos Andreas, C., *Cyprus* **23 D13** 35 42N 34 35 E
Karratha, *Australia* **60 D2** 20 53S 116 40 E
Kars, *Turkey* **25 F7** 40 40N 43 5 E
Karsakpay, *Kazakstan* **26 E7** 47 55N 66 40 E
Karshi = Qarshi, *Uzbekistan* **26 F7** 38 53N 65 48 E
Karsiyang, *India* **43 F13** 26 56N 88 18 E
Karsog, *India* **42 D7** 31 23N 77 12 E
Kartaly, *Russia* **26 D7** 53 3N 60 40 E
Kartapur, *India* **42 D6** 31 27N 75 32 E
Karthaus, *U.S.A.* **78 E6** 41 8N 78 9W
Karufa, *Indonesia* **37 E8** 3 50S 133 20 E
Karumba, *Australia* **62 B3** 17 31S 140 50 E
Karumo, *Tanzania* **54 C3** 2 25S 32 50 E
Karumwa, *Tanzania* **54 C3** 3 12S 32 38 E
Kārūn →, *Iran* **45 D6** 30 26N 48 10 E
Karungu, *Kenya* **54 C3** 0 50S 34 10 E
Karviná, *Czech Rep.* **17 D10** 49 53N 18 31 E
Karwan →, *India* **42 F8** 27 26N 78 4 E
Karwar, *India* **40 M9** 14 55N 74 13 E
Karwi, *India* **43 G9** 25 12N 80 57 E
Kasache, *Malawi* **55 E3** 13 25S 34 20 E
Kasai →, *Dem. Rep. of the Congo* **52 E3** 3 30S 16 10 E
Kasaï-Oriental □, *Dem. Rep. of the Congo* **54 D1** 5 0S 24 30 E
Kasaji, *Dem. Rep. of the Congo* **55 E1** 10 25S 23 27 E
Kasama, *Zambia* **55 E3** 10 16S 31 9 E
Kasan-dong, *N. Korea* **35 D14** 41 18N 126 55 E
Kasane, *Namibia* **56 B3** 17 34S 24 50 E
Kasanga, *Tanzania* **55 D3** 8 30S 31 10 E
Kasaragod, *India* **40 N9** 12 30N 74 58 E
Kasba L., *Canada* **73 A8** 60 20N 102 10W
Kāseh Garān, *Iran* **44 C5** 34 5N 46 2 E
Kasempa, *Zambia* **55 E2** 13 30S 25 44 E
Kasenga, *Dem. Rep. of the Congo* **55 E2** 10 20S 28 45 E
Kasese, *Uganda* **54 B3** 0 13N 30 3 E
Kasewa, *Zambia* **55 E2** 14 28S 28 53 E
Kasganj, *India* **43 F8** 27 48N 78 42 E
Kashabowie, *Canada* **70 C1** 48 40N 90 26W
Kashaf, *Iran* **45 C9** 35 58N 61 7 E
Kāshān, *Iran* **45 C6** 34 5N 51 30 E
Kashechewan, *Canada* **70 B3** 52 18N 81 37W
Kashi, *China* **32 C2** 39 30N 76 2 E
Kashimbo, *Dem. Rep. of the Congo* **55 E2** 11 12S 26 19 E
Kashipur, *India* **43 E8** 29 15N 79 0 E
Kashiwazaki, *Japan* **31 F9** 37 22N 138 33 E
Kashk-e Kohneh, *Afghan.* **40 B3** 34 55N 62 30 E
Kashkū'īyeh, *Iran* **45 D7** 30 31N 55 40 E
Kāshmar, *Iran* **45 C8** 35 16N 58 26 E
Kashmir, *Asia* **43 C7** 34 0N 76 0 E
Kashmor, *Pakistan* **42 E3** 28 28N 69 32 E
Kashun Noerh = Gaxun Nur, *China* **32 B5** 42 22N 100 30 E
Kasiari, *India* **43 H12** 22 8N 87 14 E
Kasimov, *Russia* **24 D7** 54 55N 41 20 E
Kasinge, *Dem. Rep. of the Congo* **54 D2** 6 15S 26 58 E
Kasiruta, *Indonesia* **37 E7** 0 25S 127 12 E
Kaskaskia →, *U.S.A.* **80 G10** 37 58N 89 57W
Kaskattama →, *Canada* **73 B10** 57 3N 90 4W
Kaskinen, *Finland* **9 E19** 62 22N 21 15 E
Kaslo, *Canada* **72 D5** 49 55N 116 55W
Kasmere L., *Canada* **73 B8** 59 34N 101 10W
Kasongo, *Dem. Rep. of the Congo* **54 C2** 4 30S 26 33 E
Kasongo Lunda, *Dem. Rep. of the Congo* **52 F3** 6 35S 16 49 E
Kásos, *Greece* **21 G12** 35 20N 26 55 E
Kassalâ, *Sudan* **51 E13** 15 30N 36 0 E
Kassel, *Germany* **16 C5** 51 18N 9 26 E
Kassiópi, *Greece* **23 A3** 39 48N 19 53 E
Kasson, *U.S.A.* **80 C8** 44 2N 92 45W
Kastamonu, *Turkey* **25 F5** 41 25N 33 43 E
Kastélli, *Greece* **23 D5** 35 29N 23 38 E
Kastéllion, *Greece* **23 D7** 35 12N 25 20 E
Kasterlee, *Belgium* **15 C4** 51 15N 4 59 E
Kastoría, *Greece* **21 D9** 40 30N 21 19 E
Kasulu, *Tanzania* **54 C3** 4 37S 30 5 E
Kasumi, *Japan* **31 G7** 35 38N 134 38 E
Kasungu, *Malawi* **55 E3** 13 0S 33 29 E
Kasur, *Pakistan* **42 D6** 31 5N 74 25 E
Kataba, *Zambia* **55 F2** 16 5S 25 10 E
Katahdin, Mt., *U.S.A.* **77 C11** 45 54N 68 56W
Kataka Kombe, *Dem. Rep. of the Congo* **54 C1** 3 25S 24 20 E
Katale, *Tanzania* **54 C3** 4 52S 31 7 E
Katanda, Katanga, *Dem. Rep. of the Congo* **54 D1** 7 52S 24 13 E
Katanda, Nord-Kivu, *Dem. Rep. of the Congo* **54 C2** 0 55S 29 21 E
Katanga □, *Dem. Rep. of the Congo* **54 D2** 8 0S 25 0 E
Katangi, *India* **40 J11** 21 56N 79 50 E
Katanning, *Australia* **61 F2** 33 40S 117 33 E
Katavi Swamp, *Tanzania* **54 D3** 6 50S 31 10 E
Kateríni, *Greece* **21 D10** 40 18N 22 37 E
Katghora, *India* **43 H10** 22 30N 82 33 E
Katha, *Burma* **41 G20** 24 10N 96 30 E
Katherîna, Gebel, *Egypt* **44 D2** 28 30N 33 57 E
Katherine, *Australia* **60 B5** 14 27S 132 20 E
Katherine Gorge, *Australia* **60 B5** 14 18S 132 28 E
Kathi, *India* **42 J6** 21 47N 74 3 E
Kathiawar, *India* **42 H4** 22 20N 71 0 E
Kathikas, *Cyprus* **23 E11** 34 55N 32 25 E
Kathua, *India* **42 C6** 32 23N 75 34 E
Katihar, *India* **43 G12** 25 34N 87 36 E
Katima Mulilo, *Zambia* **56 B3** 17 28S 24 13 E
Katimbira, *Malawi* **55 E3** 12 40S 34 0 E
Katingan = Mendawai →, *Indonesia* **36 E4** 3 30S 113 0 E
Katiola, *Ivory C.* **50 G4** 8 10N 5 10W
Katmandu, *Nepal* **43 F11** 27 45N 85 20 E
Katni, *India* **43 H9** 23 51N 80 24 E
Káto Arkhánai, *Greece* **23 D7** 35 15N 25 10 E
Káto Khorió, *Greece* **23 D7** 35 3N 25 47 E
Kato Pyrgos, *Cyprus* **23 D11** 35 11N 32 41 E
Katompe, *Dem. Rep. of the Congo* **54 D2** 6 2S 26 23 E
Katonga →, *Uganda* **54 B3** 0 34N 31 50 E
Katoomba, *Australia* **63 E5** 33 41S 150 19 E
Katowice, *Poland* **17 C10** 50 17N 19 5 E
Katrine, L., *U.K.* **12 E4** 56 15N 4 30W
Katrineholm, *Sweden* **9 G17** 59 9N 16 12 E
Katsepe, *Madag.* **57 B8** 15 45S 46 15 E
Katsina, *Nigeria* **50 F7** 13 0N 7 32 E
Katsumoto, *Japan* **31 H4** 33 51N 129 42 E
Katsuura, *Japan* **31 G10** 35 10N 140 20 E
Katsuyama, *Japan* **31 F8** 36 3N 136 30 E
Kattaviá, *Greece* **23 D9** 35 57N 27 46 E
Kattegat, *Denmark* **9 H14** 56 40N 11 20 E
Katumba, *Dem. Rep. of the Congo* **54 D2** 7 40S 25 17 E
Katungu, *Kenya* **54 C5** 2 55S 40 3 E
Katwa, *India* **43 H13** 23 30N 88 5 E
Katwijk, *Neths.* **15 B4** 52 12N 4 24 E
Kauai, *U.S.A.* **74 H15** 22 3N 159 30W
Kauai Channel, *U.S.A.* **74 H15** 21 45N 158 50W
Kaufman, *U.S.A.* **81 J6** 32 35N 96 19W
Kauhajoki, *Finland* **9 E20** 62 25N 22 10 E
Kaukauna, *U.S.A.* **76 C1** 44 17N 88 17W
Kaukauveld, *Namibia* **56 C3** 20 0S 20 15 E
Kaunakakai, *U.S.A.* **74 H16** 21 6N 157 1W
Kaunas, *Lithuania* **9 J20** 54 54N 23 54 E
Kaunia, *Bangla.* **43 G13** 25 46N 89 26 E
Kautokeino, *Norway* **8 B20** 69 0N 23 4 E
Kauwapur, *India* **43 F10** 27 31N 82 18 E
Kavacha, *Russia* **27 C17** 60 16N 169 51 E
Kavalerovo, *Russia* **30 B7** 44 15N 135 4 E
Kavali, *India* **40 M12** 14 55N 80 1 E
Kavála, *Greece* **21 D11** 40 57N 24 28 E
Kavār, *Iran* **45 D7** 29 11N 52 44 E
Kavi, *India* **42 H5** 22 12N 72 38 E
Kavīr, Dasht-e, *Iran* **45 C7** 34 30N 55 0 E
Kavos, *Greece* **23 B4** 39 23N 20 3 E
Kaw, *Fr. Guiana* **93 C8** 4 30N 52 15W
Kawagama L., *Canada* **78 A6** 45 18N 78 45W
Kawagoe, *Japan* **31 G9** 35 55N 139 29 E
Kawaguchi, *Japan* **31 G9** 35 52N 139 45 E
Kawaihae, *U.S.A.* **74 H17** 20 3N 155 50W
Kawambwa, *Zambia* **55 D2** 9 48S 29 3 E
Kawanoe, *Japan* **31 G6** 34 1N 133 34 E
Kawardha, *India* **43 J9** 22 0N 81 17 E
Kawasaki, *Japan* **31 G9** 35 35N 139 42 E
Kawasi, *Indonesia* **37 E7** 1 38S 127 28 E
Kawerau, *N.Z.* **59 H6** 38 7S 176 42 E
Kawhia Harbour, *N.Z.* **59 H5** 38 5S 174 51 E
Kawio, Kepulauan, *Indonesia* **37 D7** 4 30N 125 30 E
Kawnro, *Burma* **41 H21** 22 48N 99 8 E
Kawthaung, *Burma* **39 H2** 10 5N 98 36 E
Kawthoolei = Kawthule □, *Burma* **41 L20** 18 0N 97 30 E
Kawthule □, *Burma* **41 L20** 18 0N 97 30 E
Kaya, *Burkina Faso* **50 F5** 13 4N 1 10W
Kayah □, *Burma* **41 K20** 19 15N 97 15 E
Kayan →, *Indonesia* **36 D5** 2 55N 117 35 E
Kaycee, *U.S.A.* **82 E10** 43 43N 106 38W
Kayeli, *Indonesia* **37 E7** 3 20S 127 10 E
Kayenta, *U.S.A.* **83 H8** 36 44N 110 15W
Kayes, *Mali* **50 F3** 14 25N 11 30W
Kayin = Kawthule □, *Burma* **41 L20** 18 0N 97 30 E
Kayoa, *Indonesia* **37 D7** 0 1N 127 28 E
Kayomba, *Zambia* **55 E1** 13 11S 24 2 E
Kayseri, *Turkey* **25 G6** 38 45N 35 30 E
Kaysville, *U.S.A.* **82 F8** 41 2N 111 56W
Kazachye, *Russia* **27 B14** 70 52N 135 58 E
Kazakstan ■, *Asia* **26 E8** 50 0N 70 0 E
Kazan, *Russia* **24 C8** 55 50N 49 10 E
Kazan →, *Canada* **73 A9** 64 3N 95 35W
Kazan-Rettō, *Pac. Oc.* **64 E6** 25 0N 141 0 E
Kazanlŭk, *Bulgaria* **21 C11** 42 38N 25 20 E
Kazatin = Kozyatyn, *Ukraine* **17 D15** 49 45N 28 50 E
Kāzerūn, *Iran* **45 D6** 29 38N 51 40 E
Kazi Magomed = Qazimämmäd, *Azerbaijan* **45 A6** 40 3N 49 0 E
Kazuno, *Japan* **30 D10** 40 10N 140 45 E
Kazym →, *Russia* **26 C7** 63 54N 65 50 E
Kéa, *Greece* **21 F11** 37 35N 24 22 E
Keady, *U.K.* **13 B5** 54 15N 6 42W
Kearney, *U.S.A.* **80 E5** 40 42N 99 5W
Kearny, *U.S.A.* **83 K8** 33 3N 110 55W
Kearsarge, Mt., *U.S.A.* **79 C13** 43 22N 71 50W
Keban, *Turkey* **25 G6** 38 50N 38 50 E
Keban Baraji, *Turkey* **25 G6** 38 41N 38 33 E
Kebnekaise, *Sweden* **8 C18** 67 53N 18 33 E
Kebri Dehar, *Ethiopia* **46 F3** 6 45N 44 17 E
Kebumen, *Indonesia* **37 G13** 7 42S 109 40 E
Kechika →, *Canada* **72 B3** 59 41N 127 12W
Kecskemét, *Hungary* **17 E10** 46 57N 19 42 E
Kėdainiai, *Lithuania* **9 J21** 55 15N 24 2 E
Kedarnath, *India* **43 D8** 30 44N 79 4 E
Kedgwick, *Canada* **71 C6** 47 40N 67 20W
Kédhros Óros, *Greece* **23 D6** 35 11N 24 37 E
Kedia Hill, *Botswana* **56 C3** 21 28S 24 37 E
Kediri, *Indonesia* **37 G15** 7 51S 112 1 E
Keeler, *U.S.A.* **84 J9** 36 29N 117 52W
Keeley L., *Canada* **73 C7** 54 54N 108 8W
Keeling Is. = Cocos Is., *Ind. Oc.* **64 J1** 12 10S 96 55 E
Keelung = Chilung, *Taiwan* **33 D7** 25 3N 121 45 E
Keene, *Canada* **78 B6** 44 15N 78 10W
Keene, *Calif., U.S.A.* **85 K8** 35 13N 118 33W
Keene, *N.H., U.S.A.* **79 D12** 42 56N 72 17W
Keene, *N.Y., U.S.A.* **79 B11** 44 16N 73 46W
Keeper Hill, *Ireland* **13 D3** 52 45N 8 16W
Keer-Weer, C., *Australia* **62 A3** 14 0S 141 32 E
Keeseville, *U.S.A.* **79 B11** 44 29N 73 30W
Keetmanshoop, *Namibia* **56 D2** 26 35S 18 8 E
Keewatin, *Canada* **73 D10** 49 46N 94 34W
Keewatin →, *Canada* **73 B8** 56 29N 100 46W
Kefallinía, *Greece* **21 E9** 38 20N 20 30 E
Kefamenanu, *Indonesia* **37 F6** 9 28S 124 29 E
Kefar Sava, *Israel* **47 C3** 32 11N 34 54 E
Keffi, *Nigeria* **50 G7** 8 55N 7 43 E
Keflavík, *Iceland* **8 D2** 64 2N 22 35W
Keg River, *Canada* **72 B5** 57 54N 117 55W
Kegaska, *Canada* **71 B7** 50 9N 61 18W
Keighley, *U.K.* **10 D6** 53 52N 1 54W
Keila, *Estonia* **9 G21** 59 18N 24 25 E
Keimoes, *S. Africa* **56 D3** 28 41S 20 59 E
Keitele, *Finland* **8 E22** 63 10N 26 20 E
Keith, *Australia* **63 F3** 36 6S 140 20 E
Keith, *U.K.* **12 D6** 57 32N 2 57W
Keizer, *U.S.A.* **82 D2** 44 57N 123 1W
Kejimkujik Nat. Park, *Canada* **71 D6** 44 25N 65 25W
Kejser Franz Joseph Fjord = Kong Franz Joseph Fd., *Greenland* **4 B6** 73 30N 24 30W
Kekri, *India* **42 G6** 26 0N 75 10 E
Kelan, *China* **34 E6** 38 43N 111 31 E
Kelang, *Malaysia* **39 L3** 3 2N 101 26 E
Kelantan →, *Malaysia* **39 J4** 6 13N 102 14 E
Kelkit →, *Turkey* **25 F6** 40 45N 36 32 E
Kellerberrin, *Australia* **61 F2** 31 36S 117 38 E
Kellett, C., *Canada* **4 B1** 72 0N 126 0W
Kelleys I., *U.S.A.* **78 E2** 41 36N 82 42W
Kellogg, *U.S.A.* **82 C5** 47 32N 116 7W
Kells = Ceanannus Mor, *Ireland* **13 C5** 53 44N 6 53W
Kelokedhara, *Cyprus* **23 E11** 34 48N 32 39 E
Kelowna, *Canada* **72 D5** 49 50N 119 25W
Kelseyville, *U.S.A.* **84 G4** 38 59N 122 50W
Kelso, *N.Z.* **59 L2** 45 54S 169 15 E
Kelso, *U.K.* **12 F6** 55 36N 2 26W
Kelso, *U.S.A.* **84 D4** 46 9N 122 54W
Keluang, *Malaysia* **39 L4** 2 3N 103 18 E
Kelvington, *Canada* **73 C8** 52 10N 103 30W
Kem, *Russia* **24 B5** 65 0N 34 38 E
Kem →, *Russia* **24 B5** 64 57N 34 41 E
Kema, *Indonesia* **37 D7** 1 22N 125 8 E
Kemah, *Turkey* **44 B3** 39 32N 39 5 E
Kemaman, *Malaysia* **36 D2** 4 12N 103 18 E
Kemano, *Canada* **72 C3** 53 35N 128 0W
Kemasik, *Malaysia* **39 K4** 4 25N 103 27 E
Kemerovo, *Russia* **26 D9** 55 20N 86 5 E
Kemi, *Finland* **8 D21** 65 44N 24 34 E
Kemi älv = Kemijoki →, *Finland* **8 D21** 65 47N 24 32 E
Kemijärvi, *Finland* **8 C22** 66 43N 27 22 E
Kemijoki →, *Finland* **8 D21** 65 47N 24 32 E
Kemmerer, *U.S.A.* **82 F8** 41 48N 110 32W
Kemmuna = Comino, *Malta* **23 C1** 36 2N 14 20 E
Kemp, L., *U.S.A.* **81 J5** 33 46N 99 9W
Kemp Land, *Antarctica* **5 C5** 69 0S 55 0 E
Kempsey, *Australia* **63 E5** 31 1S 152 50 E
Kempt, L., *Canada* **70 C5** 47 25N 74 22W
Kempten, *Germany* **16 E6** 47 45N 10 17 E
Kempton, *Australia* **62 G4** 42 31S 147 12 E
Kemptville, *Canada* **79 B9** 45 0N 75 38W
Ken →, *India* **43 G9** 25 13N 80 27 E
Kenai, *U.S.A.* **68 B4** 60 33N 151 16W
Kendai, *India* **43 H10** 22 45N 82 37 E
Kendal, *Indonesia* **37 G14** 6 56S 110 14 E
Kendal, *U.K.* **10 C5** 54 20N 2 44W
Kendall, *Australia* **63 E5** 31 35S 152 44 E
Kendall, *U.S.A.* **77 N5** 25 41N 80 19W
Kendall →, *Australia* **62 A3** 14 4S 141 35 E
Kendallville, *U.S.A.* **76 E3** 41 27N 85 16W
Kendari, *Indonesia* **37 E6** 3 50S 122 30 E
Kendawangan, *Indonesia* **36 E4** 2 32S 110 17 E
Kendrapara, *India* **41 J15** 20 35N 86 30 E
Kendrew, *S. Africa* **56 E3** 32 32S 24 30 E
Kene Thao, *Laos* **38 D3** 17 44N 101 10 E
Kenedy, *U.S.A.* **81 L6** 28 49N 97 51W
Kenema, *S. Leone* **50 G3** 7 50N 11 14W
Keng Kok, *Laos* **38 D5** 16 26N 105 12 E
Keng Tawng, *Burma* **41 J21** 20 45N 98 18 E
Keng Tung, *Burma* **41 J21** 21 0N 99 30 E
Kenge, *Dem. Rep. of the Congo* **52 E3** 4 50S 17 4 E
Kengeja, *Tanzania* **54 D4** 5 26S 39 45 E
Kenhardt, *S. Africa* **56 D3** 29 19S 21 12 E
Kenitra, *Morocco* **50 B4** 34 15N 6 40W
Kenli, *China* **35 F10** 37 30N 118 20 E
Kenmare, *Ireland* **13 E2** 51 53N 9 36W
Kenmare, *U.S.A.* **80 A3** 48 41N 102 5W
Kenmare River, *Ireland* **13 E2** 51 48N 9 51W
Kennebago Lake, *U.S.A.* **79 A14** 45 4N 70 40W
Kennebec, *U.S.A.* **80 D5** 43 54N 99 52W
Kennebec →, *U.S.A.* **77 D11** 43 45N 69 46W
Kennebunk, *U.S.A.* **79 C14** 43 23N 70 33W
Kennedy, *Zimbabwe* **55 F2** 18 52S 27 10 E
Kennedy Ra., *Australia* **61 D2** 24 45S 115 10 E
Kennedy Taungdeik, *Burma* **41 H18** 23 15N 93 45 E
Kenner, *U.S.A.* **81 L9** 29 59N 90 15W
Kennet →, *U.K.* **11 F7** 51 27N 0 57W
Kenneth Ra., *Australia* **61 D2** 23 50S 117 8 E
Kennett, *U.S.A.* **81 G9** 36 14N 90 3W
Kennewick, *U.S.A.* **82 C4** 46 12N 119 7W
Kenogami →, *Canada* **70 B3** 51 6N 84 28W
Kenora, *Canada* **73 D10** 49 47N 94 29W
Kenosha, *U.S.A.* **76 D2** 42 35N 87 49W
Kensington, *Canada* **71 C7** 46 28N 63 34W
Kent, *Ohio, U.S.A.* **78 E3** 41 9N 81 22W
Kent, *Tex., U.S.A.* **81 K2** 31 4N 104 13W
Kent, *Wash., U.S.A.* **84 C4** 47 23N 122 14W
Kent □, *U.K.* **11 F8** 51 12N 0 40 E
Kent Group, *Australia* **62 F4** 39 30S 147 20 E
Kent Pen., *Canada* **68 B9** 68 30N 107 0W
Kentau, *Kazakstan* **26 E7** 43 32N 68 36 E
Kentland, *U.S.A.* **76 E2** 40 46N 87 27W
Kenton, *U.S.A.* **76 E4** 40 39N 83 37W
Kentucky □, *U.S.A.* **76 G3** 37 0N 84 0W
Kentucky →, *U.S.A.* **76 F3** 38 41N 85 11W
Kentucky L., *U.S.A.* **77 G2** 37 1N 88 16W

Kentville

Kentville, *Canada* **71 C7** 45 6N 64 29W
Kentwood, *U.S.A.* **81 K9** 30 56N 90 31W
Kenya ■, *Africa* **54 B4** 1 0N 38 0 E
Kenya, Mt., *Kenya* **54 C4** 0 10S 37 18 E
Keo Neua, Deo, *Vietnam* **38 C5** 18 23N 105 10 E
Keokuk, *U.S.A.* **80 E9** 40 24N 91 24W
Keonjhargarh, *India* **43 J11** 21 28N 85 35 E
Kep, *Cambodia* **39 G5** 10 29N 104 19 E
Kep, *Vietnam* **38 B6** 21 24N 106 16 E
Kepi, *Indonesia* **37 F9** 6 32S 139 19 E
Kerala □, *India* **40 P10** 11 0N 76 15 E
Kerama-Rettō, *Japan* **31 L3** 26 5N 127 15 E
Keran, *Pakistan* **43 B5** 34 35N 73 59 E
Kerang, *Australia* **63 F3** 35 40S 143 55 E
Keraudren, C., *Australia* **60 C2** 19 58S 119 45 E
Kerava, *Finland* **9 F21** 60 25N 25 5 E
Kerch, *Ukraine* **25 E6** 45 20N 36 20 E
Kerguelen, *Ind. Oc.* **3 G13** 49 15S 69 10 E
Kericho, *Kenya* **54 C4** 0 22S 35 15 E
Kerinci, *Indonesia* **36 E2** 1 40S 101 15 E
Kerki, *Turkmenistan* **26 F7** 37 50N 65 12 E
Kérkira, *Greece* **23 A3** 39 38N 19 50 E
Kerkrade, *Neths.* **15 D6** 50 53N 6 4 E
Kermadec Is., *Pac. Oc.* **64 L10** 30 0S 178 15W
Kermadec Trench, *Pac. Oc.* **64 L10** 30 30S 176 0W
Kermān, *Iran* **45 D8** 30 15N 57 1 E
Kerman, *U.S.A.* **84 J6** 36 43N 120 4W
Kermān □, *Iran* **45 D8** 30 0N 57 0 E
Kermān, Bīābān-e, *Iran* **45 D8** 28 45N 59 45 E
Kermānshāh = Bākhtarān, *Iran* **44 C5** 34 23N 47 0 E
Kermit, *U.S.A.* **81 K3** 31 52N 103 6W
Kern →, *U.S.A.* **85 K7** 35 16N 119 18W
Kernville, *U.S.A.* **85 K8** 35 45N 118 26W
Keroh, *Malaysia* **39 K3** 5 43N 101 1 E
Kerrera, *U.K.* **12 E3** 56 24N 5 33W
Kerrobert, *Canada* **73 C7** 51 56N 109 8W
Kerrville, *U.S.A.* **81 K5** 30 3N 99 8W
Kerry □, *Ireland* **13 D2** 52 7N 9 35W
Kerry Hd., *Ireland* **13 D2** 52 25N 9 56W
Kerulen →, *Asia* **33 B6** 48 48N 117 0 E
Kerzaz, *Algeria* **50 C5** 29 29N 1 37W
Kesagami →, *Canada* **70 B4** 51 40N 79 45W
Kesagami L., *Canada* **70 B3** 50 23N 80 15W
Keşan, *Turkey* **21 D12** 40 49N 26 38 E
Kesennuma, *Japan* **30 E10** 38 54N 141 35 E
Keshit, *Iran* **45 D8** 29 43N 58 17 E
Kestell, *S. Africa* **57 D4** 28 17S 28 42 E
Kestenga, *Russia* **24 A5** 65 50N 31 45 E
Keswick, *U.K.* **10 C4** 54 36N 3 8W
Ket →, *Russia* **26 D9** 58 55N 81 32 E
Ketapang, *Indonesia* **36 E4** 1 55S 110 0 E
Ketchikan, *U.S.A.* **72 B2** 55 21N 131 39W
Ketchum, *U.S.A.* **82 E6** 43 41N 114 22W
Ketef, Khalîg Umm el, *Egypt* **44 F2** 23 40N 35 35 E
Keti Bandar, *Pakistan* **42 G2** 24 8N 67 27 E
Ketri, *India* **42 E6** 28 1N 75 50 E
Kętrzyn, *Poland* **17 A11** 54 7N 21 22 E
Kettering, *U.K.* **11 E7** 52 24N 0 43W
Kettering, *U.S.A.* **76 F3** 39 41N 84 10W
Kettle →, *Canada* **73 B11** 56 40N 89 34W
Kettle Falls, *U.S.A.* **82 B4** 48 37N 118 3W
Kettle Pt., *Canada* **78 C2** 43 13N 82 1W
Kettleman City, *U.S.A.* **84 J7** 36 1N 119 58W
Keuka L., *U.S.A.* **78 D7** 42 30N 77 9W
Keuruu, *Finland* **9 E21** 62 16N 24 41 E
Kewanee, *U.S.A.* **80 E10** 41 14N 89 56W
Kewaunee, *U.S.A.* **76 C2** 44 27N 87 31W
Keweenaw B., *U.S.A.* **76 B1** 47 0N 88 15W
Keweenaw Pen., *U.S.A.* **76 B2** 47 30N 88 0W
Keweenaw Pt., *U.S.A.* **76 B2** 47 25N 87 43W
Key Largo, *U.S.A.* **77 N5** 25 5N 80 27W
Key West, *U.S.A.* **75 F10** 24 33N 81 48W
Keynsham, *U.K.* **11 F5** 51 24N 2 29W
Keyser, *U.S.A.* **76 F6** 39 26N 78 59W
Kezhma, *Russia* **27 D11** 58 59N 101 9 E
Khabarovsk, *Russia* **27 E14** 48 30N 135 5 E
Khabr, *Iran* **45 D8** 28 51N 56 22 E
Khābūr →, *Syria* **44 C4** 35 17N 40 35 E
Khachmas = Xaçmaz, *Azerbaijan* **25 F8** 41 31N 48 42 E
Khachrod, *India* **42 H6** 23 25N 75 20 E
Khadro, *Pakistan* **42 F3** 26 11N 68 50 E
Khadzhilyangar, *India* **43 B8** 35 45N 79 20 E
Khaga, *India* **43 G9** 25 47N 81 7 E
Khagaria, *India* **43 G12** 25 30N 86 32 E
Khaipur, *Pakistan* **42 E5** 29 34N 72 17 E
Khair, *India* **42 F7** 27 57N 77 46 E
Khairabad, *India* **43 F9** 27 33N 80 47 E
Khairagarh, *India* **43 J9** 21 27N 81 2 E
Khairpur, *Pakistan* **40 F6** 27 32N 68 49 E
Khairpur, *Hyderabad, Pakistan* **42 F3** 27 32N 68 49 E
Khairpur Nathan Shah, *Pakistan* **42 F2** 27 6N 67 44 E
Khairwara, *India* **42 H5** 23 58N 73 38 E
Khaisor →, *Pakistan* **42 D3** 31 17N 68 59 E
Khajuri Kach, *Pakistan* **42 C3** 32 4N 69 51 E
Khakassia □, *Russia* **26 D9** 53 0N 90 0 E
Khakhea, *Botswana* **56 C3** 24 48S 23 22 E
Khalafābād, *Iran* **45 D6** 30 54N 49 24 E
Khalilabad, *India* **43 F10** 26 48N 83 5 E
Khalīlī, *Iran* **45 E7** 27 38N 53 17 E
Khalkhāl, *Iran* **45 B6** 37 37N 48 32 E
Khalkís, *Greece* **21 E10** 38 27N 23 42 E
Khalmer-Sede = Tazovskiy, *Russia* **26 C8** 67 30N 78 44 E
Khalmer Yu, *Russia* **26 C7** 67 58N 65 1 E
Khalturin, *Russia* **24 C8** 58 40N 48 50 E
Khalūf, *Oman* **46 C6** 20 30N 58 13 E
Kham Keut, *Laos* **38 C5** 18 15N 104 43 E
Khamaria, *India* **43 H9** 23 5N 80 48 E
Khamas Country, *Botswana* **56 C4** 21 45S 26 30 E
Khambhaliya, *India* **42 H3** 22 14N 69 41 E
Khambhat, *India* **42 H5** 22 23N 72 33 E
Khambhat, G. of, *India* **40 J8** 20 45N 72 30 E
Khamīr, *Iran* **45 E7** 26 57N 55 36 E
Khamir, *Yemen* **46 D3** 16 2N 44 0 E
Khamsa, *Egypt* **47 E1** 30 27N 32 23 E
Khān Abū Shāmat, *Syria* **47 B5** 33 39N 36 53 E
Khān Azād, *Iraq* **44 C5** 33 7N 44 22 E
Khān Mujiddah, *Iraq* **44 C4** 32 21N 43 48 E
Khān Shaykhūn, *Syria* **44 C3** 35 26N 36 38 E
Khān Yūnis, *Gaza Strip* **47 D3** 31 21N 34 18 E
Khanai, *Pakistan* **42 D2** 30 30N 67 8 E
Khānaqīn, *Iraq* **44 C5** 34 23N 45 25 E
Khānbāghī, *Iran* **45 B7** 36 10N 55 25 E
Khandwa, *India* **40 J10** 21 49N 76 22 E
Khandyga, *Russia* **27 C14** 62 42N 135 35 E
Khāneh, *Iran* **44 B5** 36 41N 45 8 E
Khanewal, *Pakistan* **42 D4** 30 20N 71 55 E
Khangah Dogran, *Pakistan* **42 D5** 31 50N 73 37 E
Khanh Duong, *Vietnam* **38 F7** 12 44N 108 44 E
Khaniá, *Greece* **23 D6** 35 30N 24 4 E
Khaniá □, *Greece* **23 D6** 35 30N 24 0 E
Khaniadhana, *India* **42 G8** 25 1N 78 8 E
Khanion, Kólpos, *Greece* **23 D5** 35 33N 23 55 E
Khanka, L., *Asia* **27 E14** 45 0N 132 24 E
Khankendy = Xankändi, *Azerbaijan* **25 G8** 39 52N 46 49 E
Khanna, *India* **42 D7** 30 42N 76 16 E
Khanozai, *Pakistan* **42 D2** 30 37N 67 19 E
Khanpur, *Pakistan* **42 E4** 28 42N 70 35 E
Khanty-Mansiysk, *Russia* **26 C7** 61 0N 69 0 E
Khapalu, *Pakistan* **43 B7** 35 10N 76 20 E
Khapcheranga, *Russia* **27 E12** 49 42N 112 24 E
Kharaghoda, *India* **42 H4** 23 11N 71 46 E
Kharagpur, *India* **43 H12** 22 20N 87 25 E
Khárakas, *Greece* **23 D7** 35 1N 25 7 E
Kharan Kalat, *Pakistan* **40 E4** 28 34N 65 21 E
Kharānaq, *Iran* **45 C7** 32 20N 54 45 E
Kharda, *India* **40 K9** 18 40N 75 34 E
Khardung La, *India* **43 B7** 34 20N 77 43 E
Khârga, El Wâhât el, *Egypt* **51 C12** 25 10N 30 35 E
Khargon, *India* **40 J9** 21 45N 75 40 E
Khari →, *India* **42 G6** 25 54N 74 31 E
Kharian, *Pakistan* **42 C5** 32 49N 73 52 E
Khārk, Jazīreh-ye, *Iran* **45 D6** 29 15N 50 28 E
Kharkiv, *Ukraine* **25 E6** 49 58N 36 20 E
Kharkov = Kharkiv, *Ukraine* **25 E6** 49 58N 36 20 E
Kharovsk, *Russia* **24 C7** 59 56N 40 13 E
Kharsawangarh, *India* **43 H11** 22 48N 85 50 E
Kharta, *Turkey* **21 D13** 40 55N 29 7 E
Khartoum = El Khartûm, *Sudan* **51 E12** 15 31N 32 35 E
Khasan, *Russia* **30 C5** 42 25N 130 40 E
Khāsh, *Iran* **40 E2** 28 15N 61 15 E
Khashm el Girba, *Sudan* **51 F13** 14 59N 35 58 E
Khaskovo, *Bulgaria* **21 D11** 41 56N 25 30 E
Khatanga, *Russia* **27 B11** 72 0N 102 20 E
Khatanga →, *Russia* **27 B11** 72 55N 106 0 E
Khatauli, *India* **42 E7** 29 17N 77 43 E
Khatra, *India* **43 H12** 22 59N 86 51 E
Khātūnābād, *Iran* **45 D7** 30 1N 55 25 E
Khatyrka, *Russia* **27 C18** 62 3N 175 15 E
Khavda, *India* **42 H3** 23 51N 69 43 E
Khaybar, Harrat, *Si. Arabia* **44 E4** 25 45N 40 0 E
Khayelitsha, *S. Africa* **53 L3** 34 5S 18 42 E
Khāzimiyah, *Iraq* **44 C4** 34 46N 43 37 E
Khe Bo, *Vietnam* **38 C5** 19 8N 104 41 E
Khe Long, *Vietnam* **38 B5** 21 29N 104 46 E
Khed Brahma, *India* **40 G8** 24 7N 73 5 E
Khekra, *India* **42 E7** 28 52N 77 20 E
Khemarak Phouminville, *Cambodia* **39 G4** 11 37N 102 59 E
Khemisset, *Morocco* **50 B4** 33 50N 6 1W
Khemmarat, *Thailand* **38 D5** 16 10N 105 15 E
Khenāmān, *Iran* **45 D8** 30 27N 56 29 E
Khenchela, *Algeria* **50 A7** 35 28N 7 11 E
Khersān →, *Iran* **45 D6** 31 33N 50 22 E
Kherson, *Ukraine* **25 E5** 46 35N 32 35 E
Khersónisos Akrotírí, *Greece* **23 D6** 35 30N 24 10 E
Kheta →, *Russia* **27 B11** 71 54N 102 6 E
Khewari, *Pakistan* **42 F3** 26 36N 68 52 E
Khilchipur, *India* **42 G7** 24 2N 76 34 E
Khilok, *Russia* **27 D12** 51 30N 110 45 E
Khíos, *Greece* **21 E12** 38 27N 26 9 E
Khirsadoh, *India* **43 H8** 22 11N 78 47 E
Khiuma = Hiiumaa, *Estonia* **9 G20** 58 50N 22 45 E
Khiva, *Uzbekistan* **26 E7** 41 30N 60 18 E
Khīyāv, *Iran* **44 B5** 38 30N 47 45 E
Khlong Khlung, *Thailand* **38 D2** 16 12N 99 43 E
Khmelnik, *Ukraine* **17 D14** 49 33N 27 58 E
Khmelnitskiy = Khmelnytskyy, *Ukraine* **17 D14** 49 23N 27 0 E
Khmelnytskyy, *Ukraine* **17 D14** 49 23N 27 0 E
Khmer Rep. = Cambodia ■, *Asia* **38 F5** 12 15N 105 0 E
Khoai, Hon, *Vietnam* **39 H5** 8 26N 104 50 E
Khodoriv, *Ukraine* **17 D13** 49 24N 24 19 E
Khodzent = Khudzhand, *Tajikistan* **26 E7** 40 17N 69 37 E
Khojak Pass, *Afghan.* **42 D2** 30 51N 66 34 E
Khok Kloi, *Thailand* **39 H2** 8 17N 98 19 E
Khok Pho, *Thailand* **39 J3** 6 43N 101 6 E
Kholm, *Russia* **24 C5** 57 10N 31 15 E
Kholmsk, *Russia* **27 E15** 47 40N 142 5 E
Khomas Hochland, *Namibia* **56 C2** 22 40S 16 0 E
Khomeyn, *Iran* **45 C6** 33 40N 50 7 E
Khomeynī Shahr, *Iran* **45 C6** 32 41N 51 31 E
Khon Kaen, *Thailand* **38 D4** 16 30N 102 47 E
Khong →, *Cambodia* **38 F5** 13 32N 105 58 E
Khong Sedone, *Laos* **38 E5** 15 34N 105 49 E
Khonuu, *Russia* **27 C15** 66 30N 143 12 E
Khoper →, *Russia* **25 D6** 49 30N 42 20 E
Khóra Sfakion, *Greece* **23 D6** 35 15N 24 9 E
Khorāsān □, *Iran* **45 C8** 34 0N 58 0 E
Khorat = Nakhon Ratchasima, *Thailand* **38 E4** 14 59N 102 12 E
Khorat, Cao Nguyen, *Thailand* **38 E4** 15 30N 102 50 E
Khorixas, *Namibia* **56 C1** 20 16S 14 59 E
Khorramābād, *Khorāsān, Iran* **45 C8** 35 6N 57 57 E
Khorramābād, *Lorestān, Iran* **45 C6** 33 30N 48 25 E
Khorramshahr, *Iran* **45 D6** 30 29N 48 15 E
Khorugh, *Tajikistan* **26 F8** 37 30N 71 36 E
Khosravī, *Iran* **45 D6** 30 48N 51 28 E
Khosrowābād, *Khuzestān, Iran* **45 D6** 30 10N 48 25 E
Khosrowābād, *Kordestān, Iran* **44 C5** 35 31N 47 38 E
Khost, *Pakistan* **42 D2** 30 13N 67 35 E
Khosūyeh, *Iran* **45 D7** 28 32N 54 26 E
Khotyn, *Ukraine* **17 D14** 48 31N 26 27 E
Khouribga, *Morocco* **50 B4** 32 58N 6 57W
Khowai, *Bangla.* **41 G17** 24 5N 91 40 E
Khowst, *Afghan.* **42 C3** 33 22N 69 58 E
Khoyniki, *Belarus* **17 C15** 51 54N 29 55 E
Khrysokhou B., *Cyprus* **23 D11** 35 6N 32 25 E
Khu Khan, *Thailand* **38 E5** 14 42N 104 12 E
Khudzhand, *Tajikistan* **26 E7** 40 17N 69 37 E
Khuff, *Si. Arabia* **44 E5** 24 55N 44 53 E
Khūgīānī, *Afghan.* **42 D1** 31 28N 65 14 E
Khuiyala, *India* **42 F4** 27 9N 70 25 E
Khujner, *India* **42 H7** 23 47N 76 36 E
Khulna, *Bangla.* **41 H16** 22 45N 89 34 E
Khulna □, *Bangla.* **41 H16** 22 25N 89 35 E
Khumago, *Botswana* **56 C3** 20 26S 24 32 E
Khūnsorkh, *Iran* **45 E8** 27 9N 56 7 E
Khunti, *India* **43 H11** 23 5N 85 17 E
Khūr, *Iran* **45 C8** 32 55N 58 18 E
Khurai, *India* **42 G8** 24 3N 78 23 E
Khurayş, *Si. Arabia* **45 E6** 25 6N 48 2 E
Khurīyā Murīyā, Jazā 'ir, *Oman* **46 D6** 17 30N 55 58 E
Khurja, *India* **42 E7** 28 15N 77 58 E
Khūrmāl, *Iraq* **44 C5** 35 18N 46 2 E
Khurr, Wādī al, *Iraq* **44 C4** 32 3N 43 52 E
Khūsf, *Iran* **45 C8** 32 46N 58 53 E
Khush, *Afghan.* **40 C3** 32 55N 62 10 E
Khushab, *Pakistan* **42 C5** 32 20N 72 20 E
Khust, *Ukraine* **17 D12** 48 10N 23 18 E
Khuzdar, *Pakistan* **42 F2** 27 52N 66 30 E
Khūzestān □, *Iran* **45 D6** 31 0N 49 0 E
Khvāf, *Iran* **45 C9** 34 33N 60 8 E
Khvājeh, *Iran* **44 B5** 38 9N 46 35 E
Khvānsār, *Iran* **45 D7** 29 56N 54 8 E
Khvor, *Iran* **45 C7** 33 45N 55 0 E
Khvorgū, *Iran* **45 E8** 27 34N 56 27 E
Khvormūj, *Iran* **45 D6** 28 40N 51 30 E
Khvoy, *Iran* **44 B5** 38 35N 45 0 E
Khyber Pass, *Afghan.* **42 B4** 34 10N 71 8 E
Kiabukwa, *Dem. Rep. of the Congo* **55 D1** 8 40S 24 48 E
Kiama, *Australia* **63 E5** 34 40S 150 50 E
Kiamba, *Phil.* **37 C6** 6 2N 124 46 E
Kiambi, *Dem. Rep. of the Congo* **54 D2** 7 15S 28 0 E
Kiambu, *Kenya* **54 C4** 1 8S 36 50 E
Kiangsi = Jiangxi □, *China* **33 D6** 27 30N 116 0 E
Kiangsu = Jiangsu □, *China* **35 H11** 33 0N 120 0 E
Kibanga Port, *Uganda* **54 B3** 0 10N 32 58 E
Kibara, *Tanzania* **54 C3** 2 8S 33 30 E
Kibare, Mts., *Dem. Rep. of the Congo* **54 D2** 8 25S 27 10 E
Kibombo, *Dem. Rep. of the Congo* **54 C2** 3 57S 25 53 E
Kibondo, *Tanzania* **54 C3** 3 35S 30 45 E
Kibre Mengist, *Ethiopia* **46 F2** 5 53N 38 59 E
Kibumbu, *Burundi* **54 C2** 3 32S 29 45 E
Kibungo, *Rwanda* **54 C3** 2 10S 30 32 E
Kibuye, *Burundi* **54 C2** 3 39S 29 59 E
Kibuye, *Rwanda* **54 C2** 2 3S 29 21 E
Kibwesa, *Tanzania* **54 D2** 6 30S 29 58 E
Kibwezi, *Kenya* **54 C4** 2 27S 37 57 E
Kichha, *India* **43 E8** 28 53N 79 30 E
Kichha →, *India* **43 E8** 28 41N 79 18 E
Kichmengskiy Gorodok, *Russia* **24 B8** 59 59N 45 48 E
Kicking Horse Pass, *Canada* **72 C5** 51 28N 116 16W
Kidal, *Mali* **50 E6** 18 26N 1 22 E
Kidderminster, *U.K.* **11 E5** 52 24N 2 15W
Kidete, *Tanzania* **54 D4** 6 25S 37 17 E
Kidnappers, C., *N.Z.* **59 H6** 39 38S 177 5 E
Kidsgrove, *U.K.* **10 D5** 53 5N 2 14W
Kidston, *Australia* **62 B3** 18 52S 144 8 E
Kidugallo, *Tanzania* **54 D4** 6 49S 38 15 E
Kiel, *Germany* **16 A6** 54 19N 10 8 E
Kiel Canal = Nord-Ostsee-Kanal, *Germany* **16 A5** 54 12N 9 32 E
Kielce, *Poland* **17 C11** 50 52N 20 42 E
Kielder Water, *U.K.* **10 B5** 55 11N 2 31W
Kieler Bucht, *Germany* **16 A6** 54 35N 10 25 E
Kien Binh, *Vietnam* **39 H5** 9 55N 105 19 E
Kien Tan, *Vietnam* **39 G5** 10 7N 105 17 E
Kienge, *Dem. Rep. of the Congo* **55 E2** 10 30S 27 30 E
Kiev = Kyyiv, *Ukraine* **17 C16** 50 30N 30 28 E
Kiffa, *Mauritania* **50 E3** 16 37N 11 24W
Kifrī, *Iraq* **44 C5** 34 45N 45 0 E
Kigali, *Rwanda* **54 C3** 1 59S 30 4 E
Kigarama, *Tanzania* **54 C3** 1 1S 31 50 E
Kigoma □, *Tanzania* **54 D3** 5 0S 30 0 E
Kigoma-Ujiji, *Tanzania* **54 C2** 4 55S 29 36 E
Kigomasha, Ras, *Tanzania* **54 C4** 4 58S 38 58 E
Kığzı, *Turkey* **44 B4** 38 18N 43 25 E
Kihei, *U.S.A.* **74 H16** 20 47N 156 28W
Kihnu, *Estonia* **9 G21** 58 9N 24 1 E
Kii-Sanchi, *Japan* **31 G8** 34 20N 136 0 E
Kii-Suidō, *Japan* **31 H7** 33 40N 134 45 E
Kikaiga-Shima, *Japan* **31 K4** 28 19N 129 59 E
Kikinda, *Serbia, Yug.* **21 B9** 45 50N 20 30 E
Kikládhes, *Greece* **21 F11** 37 0N 24 30 E
Kikwit, *Dem. Rep. of the Congo* **52 F3** 5 0S 18 45 E
Kilar, *India* **42 C7** 33 6N 76 25 E
Kilauea, *U.S.A.* **74 J14** 22 13N 159 25W
Kilauea Crater, *U.S.A.* **74 J17** 19 25N 155 17W
Kilbrannan Sd., *U.K.* **12 F3** 55 37N 5 26W
Kilchu, *N. Korea* **35 D15** 40 57N 129 25 E
Kilcoy, *Australia* **63 D5** 26 59S 152 30 E
Kildare, *Ireland* **13 C5** 53 9N 6 55W
Kildare □, *Ireland* **13 C5** 53 10N 6 50W
Kilfinnane, *Ireland* **13 D3** 52 21N 8 28W
Kilgore, *U.S.A.* **81 J7** 32 23N 94 53W
Kilifi, *Kenya* **54 C4** 3 40S 39 48 E
Kilimanjaro, *Tanzania* **54 C4** 3 7S 37 20 E
Kilimanjaro □, *Tanzania* **54 C4** 4 0S 38 0 E
Kilindini, *Kenya* **54 C4** 4 4S 39 40 E
Kilis, *Turkey* **44 B3** 36 42N 37 6 E
Kiliya, *Ukraine* **17 F15** 45 28N 29 16 E
Kilkee, *Ireland* **13 D2** 52 41N 9 39W
Kilkeel, *U.K.* **13 B5** 54 4N 6 0W
Kilkenny, *Ireland* **13 D4** 52 39N 7 15W
Kilkenny □, *Ireland* **13 D4** 52 35N 7 15W
Kilkieran B., *Ireland* **13 C2** 53 20N 9 41W
Kilkís, *Greece* **21 D10** 40 58N 22 57 E
Killala, *Ireland* **13 B2** 54 13N 9 12W
Killala B., *Ireland* **13 B2** 54 16N 9 8W
Killaloe, *Ireland* **13 D3** 52 48N 8 28W
Killaloe Sta., *Canada* **78 A7** 45 33N 77 25W
Killarney, *Australia* **63 D5** 28 20S 152 18 E
Killarney, *Canada* **73 D9** 49 10N 99 40W
Killarney, *Ireland* **13 D2** 52 4N 9 30W
Killary Harbour, *Ireland* **13 C2** 53 38N 9 52W
Killdeer, *U.S.A.* **80 B3** 47 26N 102 48W
Killeen, *U.S.A.* **81 K6** 31 7N 97 44W
Killin, *U.K.* **12 E4** 56 28N 4 19W
Killíni, *Greece* **21 F10** 37 54N 22 25 E
Killorglin, *Ireland* **13 D2** 52 6N 9 47W
Killybegs, *Ireland* **13 B3** 54 38N 8 26W
Kilmarnock, *U.K.* **12 F4** 55 37N 4 29W
Kilmore, *Australia* **63 F3** 37 25S 144 53 E
Kilondo, *Tanzania* **55 D3** 9 45S 34 20 E
Kilosa, *Tanzania* **54 D4** 6 48S 37 0 E
Kilrush, *Ireland* **13 D2** 52 38N 9 29W
Kilwa Kisiwani, *Tanzania* **55 D4** 8 58S 39 32 E
Kilwa Kivinje, *Tanzania* **55 D4** 8 45S 39 25 E
Kilwa Masoko, *Tanzania* **55 D4** 8 55S 39 30 E
Kilwinning, *U.K.* **12 F4** 55 39N 4 43W
Kim, *U.S.A.* **81 G3** 37 15N 103 21W
Kimaam, *Indonesia* **37 F9** 7 58S 138 53 E
Kimamba, *Tanzania* **54 D4** 6 45S 37 10 E
Kimba, *Australia* **63 E2** 33 8S 136 23 E
Kimball, *Nebr., U.S.A.* **80 E3** 41 14N 103 40W
Kimball, *S. Dak., U.S.A.* **80 D5** 43 45N 98 57W
Kimberley, *Australia* **60 C4** 16 20S 127 0 E
Kimberley, *Canada* **72 D5** 49 40N 115 59W
Kimberley, *S. Africa* **56 D3** 28 43S 24 46 E
Kimberly, *U.S.A.* **82 E6** 42 32N 114 22W
Kimch'aek, *N. Korea* **35 D15** 40 40N 129 10 E
Kimch'ŏn, *S. Korea* **35 F15** 36 11N 128 4 E
Kimje, *S. Korea* **35 G14** 35 48N 126 45 E
Kimmirut, *Canada* **69 B13** 62 50N 69 50W
Kimpese, *Dem. Rep. of the Congo* **52 F2** 5 35S 14 26 E
Kimry, *Russia* **24 C6** 56 55N 37 15 E
Kinabalu, Gunong, *Malaysia* **36 C5** 6 3N 116 14 E
Kinaskan L., *Canada* **72 B2** 57 38N 130 8W
Kinbasket L., *Canada* **72 C5** 52 0N 118 10W
Kincardine, *Canada* **78 B3** 44 10N 81 40W
Kincolith, *Canada* **72 B3** 55 0N 129 57W
Kinda, *Dem. Rep. of the Congo* **55 D2** 9 18S 25 4 E
Kinde, *U.S.A.* **78 C2** 43 56N 83 0W
Kinder Scout, *U.K.* **10 D6** 53 24N 1 52W
Kindersley, *Canada* **73 C7** 51 30N 109 10W
Kindia, *Guinea* **50 F3** 10 0N 12 52W
Kindu, *Dem. Rep. of the Congo* **54 C2** 2 55S 25 50 E
Kineshma, *Russia* **24 C7** 57 30N 42 5 E
Kinesi, *Tanzania* **54 C3** 1 25S 33 50 E
King, L., *Australia* **61 F2** 33 10S 119 35 E
King, Mt., *Australia* **62 D4** 25 10S 147 30 E
King City, *U.S.A.* **84 J5** 36 13N 121 8W
King Cr. →, *Australia* **62 C2** 24 35S 139 30 E
King Edward →, *Australia* **60 B4** 14 14S 126 35 E
King Frederick VI Land = Kong Frederik VI.s Kyst, *Greenland* **4 C5** 63 0N 43 0W
King George B., *Falk. Is.* **96 G4** 51 30S 60 30W
King George I., *Antarctica* **5 C18** 60 0S 60 0W
King George Is., *Canada* **69 C11** 57 20N 80 30W
King I. = Kadan Kyun, *Burma* **38 F2** 12 30N 98 20 E
King I., *Australia* **62 F3** 39 50S 144 0 E
King I., *Canada* **72 C3** 52 10N 127 40W
King Leopold Ranges, *Australia* **60 C4** 17 30S 125 45 E
King of Prussia, *U.S.A.* **79 F9** 40 5N 75 23W
King Sd., *Australia* **60 C3** 16 50S 123 20 E
King William I., *Canada* **68 B10** 69 10N 97 25W
King William's Town, *S. Africa* **56 E4** 32 51S 27 22 E
Kingaroy, *Australia* **63 D5** 26 32S 151 51 E
Kingfisher, *U.S.A.* **81 H6** 35 52N 97 56W
Kingirbān, *Iraq* **44 C5** 34 40N 44 54 E
Kingisepp = Kuressaare, *Estonia* **9 G20** 58 15N 22 30 E
Kingman, *Ariz., U.S.A.* **85 K12** 35 12N 114 4W
Kingman, *Kans., U.S.A.* **81 G5** 37 39N 98 7W
Kingoonya, *Australia* **63 E2** 30 55S 135 19 E
Kingri, *Pakistan* **42 D3** 30 27N 69 49 E
Kings →, *U.S.A.* **84 J7** 36 3N 119 50W
Kings Canyon National Park, *U.S.A.* **84 J8** 36 50N 118 40W
King's Lynn, *U.K.* **10 E8** 52 45N 0 24 E
Kings Mountain, *U.S.A.* **77 H5** 35 15N 81 20W
Kings Park, *U.S.A.* **79 F11** 40 53N 73 16W
King's Peak, *U.S.A.* **82 F8** 40 46N 110 27W
Kingsbridge, *U.K.* **11 G4** 50 17N 3 47W
Kingsburg, *U.S.A.* **84 J7** 36 31N 119 33W
Kingscote, *Australia* **63 F2** 35 40S 137 38 E
Kingscourt, *Ireland* **13 C5** 53 55N 6 48W
Kingsford, *U.S.A.* **76 C1** 45 48N 88 4W
Kingsland, *U.S.A.* **77 K5** 30 48N 81 41W
Kingsley, *U.S.A.* **80 D7** 42 35N 95 58W
Kingsport, *U.S.A.* **77 G4** 36 33N 82 33W
Kingston, *Canada* **79 B8** 44 14N 76 30W
Kingston, *Jamaica* **88 C4** 18 0N 76 50W
Kingston, *N.Z.* **59 L2** 45 20S 168 43 E
Kingston, *N.H., U.S.A.* **79 D13** 42 56N 71 3W
Kingston, *N.Y., U.S.A.* **79 E11** 41 56N 73 59W
Kingston, *Pa., U.S.A.* **79 E9** 41 16N 75 54W
Kingston, *R.I., U.S.A.* **79 E13** 41 29N 71 30W
Kingston Pk., *U.S.A.* **85 K11** 35 45N 115 54W
Kingston South East, *Australia* **63 F2** 36 51S 139 55 E
Kingston upon Hull, *U.K.* **10 D7** 53 45N 0 21W
Kingston upon Hull □, *U.K.* **10 D7** 53 45N 0 21W
Kingston-upon-Thames, *U.K.* **11 F7** 51 24N 0 17W
Kingstown, *St. Vincent* **89 D7** 13 10N 61 10W
Kingstree, *U.S.A.* **77 J6** 33 40N 79 50W
Kingsville, *Canada* **78 D2** 42 2N 82 45W
Kingsville, *U.S.A.* **81 M6** 27 31N 97 52W
Kingussie, *U.K.* **12 D4** 57 6N 4 2W
Kingwood, *U.S.A.* **81 K7** 29 54N 95 18W
Kınık, *Turkey* **21 E12** 39 6N 27 24 E
Kinistino, *Canada* **73 C7** 52 57N 105 2W
Kinkala, *Congo* **52 E2** 4 18S 14 49 E
Kinki □, *Japan* **31 H8** 33 45N 136 0 E
Kinleith, *N.Z.* **59 H5** 38 20S 175 56 E
Kinmount, *Canada* **78 B6** 44 48N 78 45W
Kinna, *Sweden* **9 H15** 57 32N 12 42 E
Kinnairds Hd., *U.K.* **12 D6** 57 43N 2 1W
Kinnarodden, *Norway* **6 A11** 71 8N 27 40 E
Kino, *Mexico* **86 B2** 28 45N 111 59W
Kinoje →, *Canada* **70 B3** 51 8N 81 25W
Kinomoto, *Japan* **31 G8** 35 30N 136 13 E
Kinoni, *Uganda* **54 C3** 0 41S 30 28 E
Kinoosao, *Canada* **73 B8** 57 5N 102 1W
Kinross, *U.K.* **12 E5** 56 13N 3 25W
Kinsale, *Ireland* **13 E3** 51 42N 8 31W

Laporte

Kyustendil, *Bulgaria* **21 C10** 42 16N 22 41 E
Kyusyur, *Russia* **27 B13** 70 19N 127 30 E
Kyyiv, *Ukraine* **17 C16** 50 30N 30 28 E
Kyyivske Vdskh., *Ukraine* **17 C16** 51 0N 30 25 E
Kyzyl, *Russia* **27 D10** 51 50N 94 30 E
Kyzyl Kum, *Uzbekistan* **26 E7** 42 30N 65 0 E
Kyzyl-Kyya, *Kyrgyzstan* **26 E8** 40 16N 72 8 E
Kzyl-Orda = Qyzylorda, *Kazakstan* **26 E7** 44 48N 65 28 E

L

La Alcarria, *Spain* **19 B4** 40 31N 2 45W
La Asunción, *Venezuela* **92 A6** 11 2N 63 53W
La Baie, *Canada* **71 C5** 48 19N 70 53W
La Banda, *Argentina* **94 B3** 27 45S 64 10W
La Barca, *Mexico* **86 C4** 20 20N 102 40W
La Barge, *U.S.A.* **82 E8** 42 16N 110 12W
La Belle, *U.S.A.* **77 M5** 26 46N 81 26W
La Biche →, *Canada* **72 B4** 59 57N 123 50W
La Biche, L., *Canada* **72 C6** 54 50N 112 5W
La Bomba, *Mexico* **86 A1** 31 53N 115 2W
La Calera, *Chile* **94 C1** 32 50S 71 10W
La Canal = Sa Canal, *Spain* **22 C7** 38 51N 1 23 E
La Carlota, *Argentina* **94 C3** 33 30S 63 20W
La Ceiba, *Honduras* **88 C2** 15 40N 86 50W
La Chaux-de-Fonds, *Switz.* **18 C7** 47 7N 6 50 E
La Chorrera, *Panama* **88 E4** 8 53N 79 47W
La Cocha, *Argentina* **94 B2** 27 50S 65 40W
La Concepción, *Panama* **88 E3** 8 31N 82 37W
La Concordia, *Mexico* **87 D6** 16 8N 92 38W
La Coruña = A Coruña, *Spain* **19 A1** 43 20N 8 25W
La Crescent, *U.S.A.* **80 D9** 43 50N 91 18W
La Crete, *Canada* **72 B5** 58 11N 116 24W
La Crosse, *Kans., U.S.A.* **80 F5** 38 32N 99 18W
La Crosse, *Wis., U.S.A.* **80 D9** 43 48N 91 15W
La Cruz, *Costa Rica* **88 D2** 11 4N 85 39W
La Cruz, *Mexico* **86 C3** 23 55N 106 54W
La Désirade, *Guadeloupe* **89 C7** 16 18N 61 3W
La Escondida, *Mexico* **86 C5** 24 6N 99 55W
La Esmeralda, *Paraguay* **94 A3** 22 16S 62 33W
La Esperanza, *Cuba* **88 B3** 22 46N 83 44W
La Esperanza, *Honduras* **88 D2** 14 15N 88 10W
La Estrada = A Estrada, *Spain* **19 A1** 42 43N 8 27W
La Fayette, *U.S.A.* **77 H3** 34 42N 85 17W
La Fé, *Cuba* **88 B3** 22 2N 84 15W
La Follette, *U.S.A.* **77 G3** 36 23N 84 7W
La Grande, *U.S.A.* **82 D4** 45 20N 118 5W
La Grande →, *Canada* **70 B5** 53 50N 79 0W
La Grande Deux, Rés., *Canada* **70 B4** 53 40N 76 55W
La Grande Quatre, Rés., *Canada* **70 B5** 54 0N 73 15W
La Grande Trois, Rés., *Canada* **70 B4** 53 40N 75 10W
La Grange, *Calif., U.S.A.* **84 H6** 37 42N 120 27W
La Grange, *Ga., U.S.A.* **77 J3** 33 2N 85 2W
La Grange, *Ky., U.S.A.* **76 F3** 38 25N 85 23W
La Grange, *Tex., U.S.A.* **81 L6** 29 54N 96 52W
La Guaira, *Venezuela* **92 A5** 10 36N 66 56W
La Habana, *Cuba* **88 B3** 23 8N 82 22W
La Independencia, *Mexico* **87 D6** 16 31N 91 47W
La Isabela, *Dom. Rep.* **89 C5** 19 58N 71 2W
La Junta, *U.S.A.* **81 F3** 37 59N 103 33W
La Laguna, *Canary Is.* **22 F3** 28 28N 16 18W
La Libertad, *Guatemala* **88 C1** 16 47N 90 7W
La Libertad, *Mexico* **86 B2** 29 55N 112 41W
La Ligua, *Chile* **94 C1** 32 30S 71 16W
La Línea de la Concepción, *Spain* **19 D3** 36 15N 5 23W
La Loche, *Canada* **73 B7** 56 29N 109 26W
La Louvière, *Belgium* **15 D4** 50 27N 4 10 E
La Malbaie, *Canada* **71 C5** 47 40N 70 10W
La Mancha, *Spain* **19 C4** 39 10N 2 54W
La Martre, L., *Canada* **72 A5** 63 15N 117 55W
La Mesa, *U.S.A.* **85 N9** 32 46N 117 3W
La Misión, *Mexico* **86 A1** 32 5N 116 50W
La Moure, *U.S.A.* **80 B5** 46 21N 98 18W
La Negra, *Chile* **94 A1** 23 46S 70 18W
La Oliva, *Canary Is.* **22 F6** 28 36N 13 57W
La Orotava, *Canary Is.* **22 F3** 28 22N 16 31W
La Oroya, *Peru* **92** 11 32S 75 54W
La Palma, *Canary Is.* **22 F2** 28 40N 17 50W
La Palma, *Panama* **88 E4** 8 15N 78 0W
La Palma del Condado, *Spain* **19 D2** 37 21N 6 38W
La Paloma, *Chile* **94 C1** 30 35S 71 0W
La Pampa □, *Argentina* **94 D2** 36 50S 66 0W
La Paragua, *Venezuela* **92 B6** 6 50N 63 20W
La Paz, *Entre Ríos, Argentina* **94 C4** 30 50S 59 45W
La Paz, *San Luis, Argentina* **94 C2** 33 30S 67 20W
La Paz, *Bolivia* **92 G5** 16 20S 68 10W
La Paz, *Honduras* **88 D2** 14 20N 87 47W
La Paz, *Mexico* **86 C2** 24 10N 110 20W
La Paz Centro, *Nic.* **88 D2** 12 20N 86 41W
La Pedrera, *Colombia* **92 D5** 1 18S 69 43W
La Pérade, *Canada* **71 C5** 46 35N 72 12W
La Perouse Str., *Asia* **30 B11** 45 40N 142 0 E
La Pesca, *Mexico* **87 C5** 23 46N 97 47W
La Piedad, *Mexico* **86 C4** 20 20N 102 1W
La Pine, *U.S.A.* **82 E3** 43 40N 121 30W
La Plata, *Argentina* **94 D4** 35 0S 57 55W
La Pocatière, *Canada* **71 C5** 47 22N 70 2W
La Porte, *Ind., U.S.A.* **76 E2** 41 36N 86 43W
La Porte, *Tex., U.S.A.* **81 L7** 29 39N 95 1W
La Purísima, *Mexico* **86 B2** 26 10N 112 4W
La Push, *U.S.A.* **84 C2** 47 55N 124 38W
La Quiaca, *Argentina* **94 A2** 22 5S 65 35W
La Restinga, *Canary Is.* **22 G2** 27 38N 17 59W
La Rioja, *Argentina* **94 B2** 29 20S 67 0W
La Rioja □, *Argentina* **94 B2** 29 30S 67 0W
La Rioja □, *Spain* **19 A4** 42 20N 2 20W
La Robla, *Spain* **19 A3** 42 50N 5 41W
La Roche-en-Ardenne, *Belgium* **15 D5** 50 11N 5 35 E
La Roche-sur-Yon, *France* **18 C3** 46 40N 1 25W
La Rochelle, *France* **18 C3** 46 10N 1 9W
La Roda, *Spain* **19 C4** 39 13N 2 15W
La Romana, *Dom. Rep.* **89 C6** 18 27N 68 57W
La Ronge, *Canada* **73 B7** 55 5N 105 20W
La Rumorosa, *Mexico* **85 N10** 32 33N 116 4W
La Sabina = Sa Savina, *Spain* **22 C7** 38 44N 1 25 E
La Salle, *U.S.A.* **80 E10** 41 20N 89 6W
La Santa, *Canary Is.* **22 E6** 29 5N 13 40W
La Sarre, *Canada* **70 C4** 48 45N 79 15W
La Scie, *Canada* **71 C8** 49 57N 55 36W
La Selva Beach, *U.S.A.* **84 J5** 36 56N 121 51W
La Serena, *Chile* **94 B1** 29 55S 71 10W
La Seu d'Urgell, *Spain* **19 A6** 42 22N 1 23 E
La Seyne-sur-Mer, *France* **18 E6** 43 7N 5 52 E
La Soufrière, *St. Vincent* **89 D7** 13 20N 61 11W
La Spézia, *Italy* **18 D8** 44 7N 9 50 E
La Tagua, *Colombia* **92 C4** 0 3N 74 40W
La Tortuga, *Venezuela* **89 D6** 11 0N 65 22W
La Tuque, *Canada* **70 C5** 47 30N 72 50W
La Unión, *Chile* **96 E2** 40 10S 73 0W
La Unión, *El Salv.* **88 D2** 13 20N 87 50W
La Unión, *Mexico* **86 D4** 17 58N 101 49W
La Urbana, *Venezuela* **92 B5** 7 8N 66 56W
La Vall d'Uixó, *Spain* **19 C5** 39 49N 0 15W
La Vega, *Dom. Rep.* **89 C5** 19 20N 70 30W
La Vela de Coro, *Venezuela* **92 A5** 11 27N 69 34W
La Venta, *Mexico* **87 D6** 18 8N 94 3W
La Ventura, *Mexico* **86 C4** 24 38N 100 54W
Labe = Elbe →, *Europe* **16 B5** 53 50N 9 0 E
Labé, *Guinea* **50 F3** 11 24N 12 16W
Laberge, L., *Canada* **72 A1** 61 11N 135 12W
Labinsk, *Russia* **25 F7** 44 40N 40 48 E
Labis, *Malaysia* **39 L4** 2 22N 103 2 E
Laboulaye, *Argentina* **94 C3** 34 10S 63 30W
Labrador, *Canada* **71 B7** 53 20N 61 0W
Labrador City, *Canada* **71 B6** 52 57N 66 55W
Labrador Sea, *Atl. Oc.* **69 C14** 57 0N 54 0W
Lábrea, *Brazil* **92 E6** 7 15S 64 51W
Labuan, *Malaysia* **36 C5** 5 20N 115 14 E
Labuan, Pulau, *Malaysia* **36 C5** 5 21N 115 13 E
Labuha, *Indonesia* **37 E7** 0 30S 127 30 E
Labuhan, *Indonesia* **37 G11** 6 22S 105 50 E
Labuhanbajo, *Indonesia* **37 F6** 8 28S 120 1 E
Labuk, Telok, *Malaysia* **36 C5** 6 10N 117 50 E
Labyrinth, L., *Australia* **63 E2** 30 40S 135 11 E
Labytnangi, *Russia* **26 C7** 66 39N 66 21 E
Lac Bouchette, *Canada* **71 C5** 48 16N 72 11W
Lac Édouard, *Canada* **70 C5** 47 40N 72 16W
Lac La Biche, *Canada* **72 C6** 54 45N 111 58W
Lac la Martre = Wha Ti, *Canada* **68 B8** 63 8N 117 16W
Lac La Ronge Prov. Park, *Canada* **73 B7** 55 9N 104 41W
Lac-Mégantic, *Canada* **71 C5** 45 35N 70 53W
Lac Seul, Res., *Canada* **70 B1** 50 25N 92 30W
Lac Thien, *Vietnam* **38 F7** 12 25N 108 11 E
Lacanau, *France* **18 D3** 44 58N 1 5W
Lacantúm →, *Mexico* **87 D6** 16 36N 90 40W
Laccadive Is. = Lakshadweep Is., *Ind. Oc.* **28 H11** 10 0N 72 30 E
Lacepede B., *Australia* **63 F2** 36 40S 139 40 E
Lacepede Is., *Australia* **60 C3** 16 55S 122 0 E
Lacerdónia, *Mozam.* **55 F4** 18 3S 35 35 E
Lacey, *U.S.A.* **84 C4** 47 7N 122 49W
Lachhmangarh, *India* **42 F6** 27 50N 75 4 E
Lachi, *Pakistan* **42 C4** 33 25N 71 20 E
Lachine, *Canada* **79 A11** 45 30N 73 40W
Lachlan →, *Australia* **63 E3** 34 22S 143 55 E
Lachute, *Canada* **70 C5** 45 39N 74 21W
Lackawanna, *U.S.A.* **78 D6** 42 50N 78 50W
Lackawaxen, *U.S.A.* **79 E10** 41 29N 74 59W
Lacolle, *Canada* **79 A11** 45 5N 73 22W
Lacombe, *Canada* **72 C6** 52 30N 113 44W
Lacona, *U.S.A.* **79 C8** 43 39N 76 10W
Laconia, *U.S.A.* **79 C13** 43 32N 71 28W
Ladakh Ra., *India* **43 C8** 34 0N 78 0 E
Ladismith, *S. Africa* **56 E3** 33 28S 21 15 E
Ladnun, *India* **42 F6** 27 38N 74 25 E
Ladoga, L. = Ladozhskoye Ozero, *Russia* **24 B5** 61 15N 30 30 E
Ladozhskoye Ozero, *Russia* **24 B5** 61 15N 30 30 E
Lady Elliott I., *Australia* **62 C5** 24 7S 152 42 E
Lady Grey, *S. Africa* **56 E4** 30 43S 27 13 E
Ladybrand, *S. Africa* **56 D4** 29 9S 27 29 E
Ladysmith, *Canada* **72 D4** 49 0N 123 49W
Ladysmith, *S. Africa* **57 D4** 28 32S 29 46 E
Ladysmith, *U.S.A.* **80 C9** 45 28N 91 12W
Lae, *Papua N. G.* **64 H6** 6 40S 147 2 E
Laem Ngop, *Thailand* **39 F4** 12 10N 102 26 E
Laem Pho, *Thailand* **39 J3** 6 55N 101 19 E
Læsø, *Denmark* **9 H14** 57 15N 11 5 E
Lafayette, *Colo., U.S.A.* **80 F2** 39 58N 105 12W
Lafayette, *Ind., U.S.A.* **76 E2** 40 25N 86 54W
Lafayette, *La., U.S.A.* **81 K9** 30 14N 92 1W
Lafayette, *Tenn., U.S.A.* **77 G2** 36 31N 86 2W
Laferte →, *Canada* **72 A5** 61 53N 117 44W
Lafia, *Nigeria* **50 G7** 8 30N 8 34 E
Lafleche, *Canada* **73 D7** 49 45N 106 40W
Lagan →, *U.K.* **13 B6** 54 36N 5 55W
Lagarfljót →, *Iceland* **8 D6** 65 40N 14 18W
Lågen →, *Oppland, Norway* **9 F14** 61 8N 10 25 E
Lågen →, *Vestfold, Norway* **9 G14** 59 3N 10 3 E
Laghouat, *Algeria* **50 B6** 33 50N 2 59 E
Lagoa Vermelha, *Brazil* **95 B5** 28 13S 51 32W
Lagonoy G., *Phil.* **37 B6** 13 50N 123 50 E
Lagos, *Nigeria* **50 G6** 6 25N 3 27 E
Lagos, *Portugal* **19 D1** 37 5N 8 41W
Lagos de Moreno, *Mexico* **86 C4** 21 21N 101 55W
Lagrange, *Australia* **60 C3** 18 45S 121 43 E
Lagrange B., *Australia* **60 C3** 18 38S 121 42 E
Laguna, *Brazil* **95 B6** 28 30S 48 50W
Laguna, *U.S.A.* **83 J10** 35 2N 107 25W
Laguna Beach, *U.S.A.* **85 M9** 33 33N 117 47W
Laguna Limpia, *Argentina* **94 B4** 26 32S 59 45W
Laguna Madre, *U.S.A.* **87 B5** 27 0N 97 20W
Lagunas, *Chile* **94 A2** 21 0S 69 45W
Lagunas, *Peru* **92 E3** 5 10S 75 35W
Lahad Datu, *Malaysia* **37 D5** 5 0N 118 20 E
Lahad Datu, Teluk, *Malaysia* **37 D5** 4 50N 118 20 E
Lahan Sai, *Thailand* **38 E4** 14 25N 102 52 E
Lahanam, *Laos* **38 D5** 16 16N 105 16 E
Lahar, *India* **43 F8** 26 12N 78 57 E
Laharpur, *India* **43 F9** 27 43N 80 56 E
Lahat, *Indonesia* **36 E2** 3 45S 103 30 E
Lahewa, *Indonesia* **36 D1** 1 22N 97 12 E
Lāhījān, *Iran* **45 B6** 37 10N 50 6 E
Lahn →, *Germany* **16 C4** 50 19N 7 37 E
Laholm, *Sweden* **9 H15** 56 30N 13 2 E
Lahore, *Pakistan* **42 D6** 31 32N 74 22 E
Lahri, *Pakistan* **42 E3** 29 11N 68 13 E
Lahti, *Finland* **9 F21** 60 58N 25 40 E
Lahtis = Lahti, *Finland* **9 F21** 60 58N 25 40 E
Laï, *Chad* **51 G9** 9 25N 16 18 E
Laila = Laylá, *Si. Arabia* **46 C4** 22 10N 46 40 E
Laingsburg, *S. Africa* **56 E3** 33 9S 20 52 E
Lainio älv →, *Sweden* **8 C20** 67 35N 22 40 E
Lairg, *U.K.* **12 C4** 58 2N 4 24W
Laishui, *China* **34 E8** 39 23N 115 45 E
Laiwu, *China* **35 F9** 36 15N 117 40 E
Laixi, *China* **35 F11** 36 50N 120 31 E
Laiyang, *China* **35 F11** 36 59N 120 45 E
Laiyuan, *China* **34 E8** 39 20N 114 40 E
Laizhou, *China* **35 F10** 37 8N 119 57 E
Laizhou Wan, *China* **35 F10** 37 30N 119 30 E
Laja →, *Mexico* **86 C4** 20 55N 100 46W
Lajes, *Brazil* **95 B5** 27 48S 50 20W
Lak Sao, *Laos* **38 C5** 18 11N 104 59 E
Lakaband, *Pakistan* **42 D3** 31 2N 69 15 E
Lake Alpine, *U.S.A.* **84 G7** 38 29N 120 0W
Lake Andes, *U.S.A.* **80 D5** 43 9N 98 32W
Lake Arthur, *U.S.A.* **81 K8** 30 5N 92 41W
Lake Cargelligo, *Australia* **63 E4** 33 15S 146 22 E
Lake Charles, *U.S.A.* **81 K8** 30 14N 93 13W
Lake City, *Colo., U.S.A.* **83 G10** 38 2N 107 19W
Lake City, *Fla., U.S.A.* **77 K4** 30 11N 82 38W
Lake City, *Mich., U.S.A.* **76 C3** 44 20N 85 13W
Lake City, *Minn., U.S.A.* **80 C8** 44 27N 92 16W
Lake City, *Pa., U.S.A.* **78 D4** 42 1N 80 21W
Lake City, *S.C., U.S.A.* **77 J6** 33 52N 79 45W
Lake Cowichan, *Canada* **72 D4** 48 49N 124 3W
Lake District, *U.K.* **10 C4** 54 35N 3 20 E
Lake Elsinore, *U.S.A.* **85 M9** 33 38N 117 20W
Lake George, *U.S.A.* **79 C11** 43 26N 73 43W
Lake Grace, *Australia* **61 F2** 33 7S 118 28 E
Lake Harbour = Kimmirut, *Canada* **69 B13** 62 50N 69 50W
Lake Havasu City, *U.S.A.* **85 L12** 34 27N 114 22W
Lake Hughes, *U.S.A.* **85 L8** 34 41N 118 26W
Lake Isabella, *U.S.A.* **85 K8** 35 38N 118 28W
Lake Jackson, *U.S.A.* **81 L7** 29 3N 95 27W
Lake Junction, *U.S.A.* **82 D8** 44 35N 110 28W
Lake King, *Australia* **61 F2** 33 5S 119 45 E
Lake Lenore, *Canada* **73 C8** 52 24N 104 59W
Lake Louise, *Canada* **72 C5** 51 30N 116 10W
Lake Mead National Recreation Area, *U.S.A.* **85 K12** 36 15N 114 30W
Lake Mills, *U.S.A.* **80 D8** 43 25N 93 32W
Lake Placid, *U.S.A.* **79 B11** 44 17N 73 59W
Lake Pleasant, *U.S.A.* **79 C10** 43 28N 74 25W
Lake Providence, *U.S.A.* **81 J9** 32 48N 91 10W
Lake St. Peter, *Canada* **78 A6** 45 18N 78 2W
Lake Superior Prov. Park, *Canada* **70 C3** 47 45N 84 45W
Lake Village, *U.S.A.* **81 J9** 33 20N 91 17W
Lake Wales, *U.S.A.* **77 M5** 27 54N 81 35W
Lake Worth, *U.S.A.* **77 M5** 26 37N 80 3W
Lakefield, *Canada* **78 B6** 44 25N 78 16W
Lakehurst, *U.S.A.* **79 F10** 40 1N 74 19W
Lakeland, *Australia* **62 B3** 15 49S 144 57 E
Lakeland, *U.S.A.* **77 M5** 28 3N 81 57W
Lakemba, *Fiji* **59 D9** 18 13S 178 47W
Lakeport, *Calif., U.S.A.* **84 F4** 39 3N 122 55W
Lakeport, *Mich., U.S.A.* **78 C2** 43 7N 82 30W
Lakes Entrance, *Australia* **63 F4** 37 50S 148 0 E
Lakeside, *Ariz., U.S.A.* **83 J9** 34 9N 109 58W
Lakeside, *Calif., U.S.A.* **85 N10** 32 52N 116 55W
Lakeside, *Nebr., U.S.A.* **80 D3** 42 3N 102 26W
Lakeside, *Ohio, U.S.A.* **78 E2** 41 32N 82 46W
Lakeview, *U.S.A.* **82 E3** 42 11N 120 21W
Lakeville, *U.S.A.* **80 C8** 44 39N 93 14W
Lakewood, *Colo., U.S.A.* **80 F2** 39 44N 105 5W
Lakewood, *N.J., U.S.A.* **79 F10** 40 6N 74 13W
Lakewood, *N.Y., U.S.A.* **78 D5** 42 6N 79 19W
Lakewood, *Ohio, U.S.A.* **78 E3** 41 29N 81 48W
Lakewood, *Wash., U.S.A.* **84 C4** 47 11N 122 32W
Lakha, *India* **42 F4** 26 9N 70 54 E
Lakhaniá, *Greece* **23 D9** 35 58N 27 54 E
Lakhimpur, *India* **43 F9** 27 57N 80 46 E
Lakhnadon, *India* **43 H8** 22 36N 79 36 E
Lakhonpheng, *Laos* **38 E5** 15 54N 105 34 E
Lakhpat, *India* **42 H3** 23 48N 68 47 E
Lakin, *U.S.A.* **81 G4** 37 57N 101 15W
Lakitusaki →, *Canada* **70 B3** 54 21N 82 25W
Lakki, *Pakistan* **42 C4** 32 36N 70 55 E
Lákkoi, *Greece* **23 D5** 35 24N 23 57 E
Lakonikós Kólpos, *Greece* **21 F10** 36 40N 22 40 E
Lakor, *Indonesia* **37 F7** 8 15S 128 17 E
Lakota, *Ivory C.* **50 G4** 5 50N 5 30W
Lakota, *U.S.A.* **80 A5** 48 2N 98 21W
Laksar, *India* **42 E8** 29 46N 78 3 E
Laksefjorden, *Norway* **8 A22** 70 45N 26 50 E
Lakselv, *Norway* **8 A21** 70 2N 25 0 E
Lakshadweep Is., *Ind. Oc.* **28 H11** 10 0N 72 30 E
Lakshmanpur, *India* **43 H10** 22 58N 83 3 E
Lakshmikantapur, *India* **43 H13** 22 5N 88 20 E
Lala Ghat, *India* **41 G18** 24 30N 92 40 E
Lala Musa, *Pakistan* **42 C5** 32 40N 73 57 E
Lalago, *Tanzania* **54 C3** 3 28S 33 58 E
Lalapanzi, *Zimbabwe* **55 F3** 19 20S 30 15 E
L'Albufera, *Spain* **19 C5** 39 20N 0 27W
Lalganj, *India* **43 G11** 25 52N 85 13 E
Lalgola, *India* **43 G13** 24 25N 88 15 E
Lālī, *Iran* **45 C6** 32 21N 49 6 E
Lalibela, *Ethiopia* **46 E2** 12 2N 39 2 E
Lalin, *China* **35 B14** 45 12N 127 0 E
Lalín, *Spain* **19 A1** 42 40N 8 5W
Lalin He →, *China* **35 B13** 45 32N 125 40 E
Lalitapur = Patan, *Nepal* **41 F14** 27 40N 85 20 E
Lalitpur, *India* **43 G8** 24 42N 78 28 E
Lalkua, *India* **43 E8** 29 5N 79 31 E
Lalsot, *India* **42 F7** 26 34N 76 20 E
Lam, *Vietnam* **38 B6** 21 21N 106 31 E
Lam Pao Res., *Thailand* **38 D4** 16 50N 103 15 E
Lamaing, *Burma* **41 M20** 15 25N 97 53 E
Lamar, *Colo., U.S.A.* **80 F3** 38 5N 102 37W
Lamar, *Mo., U.S.A.* **81 G7** 37 30N 94 16W
Lamas, *Peru* **92 E3** 6 28S 76 31W
Lambaréné, *Gabon* **52 E2** 0 41S 10 12 E
Lambasa, *Fiji* **59 C8** 16 30S 179 10 E
Lambay I., *Ireland* **13 C5** 53 29N 6 1W
Lambert Glacier, *Antarctica* **5 D6** 71 0S 70 0 E
Lamberts Bay, *S. Africa* **56 E2** 32 5S 18 17 E
Lambeth, *Canada* **78 D3** 42 54N 81 18W
Lambi Kyun, *Burma* **39 G2** 10 50N 98 20 E
Lame Deer, *U.S.A.* **82 D10** 45 37N 106 40W
Lamego, *Portugal* **19 B2** 41 5N 7 52W
Lamèque, *Canada* **71 C7** 47 45N 64 38W
Lameroo, *Australia* **63 F3** 35 19S 140 33 E
Lamesa, *U.S.A.* **81 J4** 32 44N 101 58W
Lamía, *Greece* **21 E10** 38 55N 22 26 E
Lammermuir Hills, *U.K.* **12 F6** 55 50N 2 40W
Lamoille →, *U.S.A.* **79 B11** 44 38N 73 13W
Lamon B., *Phil.* **37 B6** 14 30N 122 20 E
Lamont, *Canada* **72 C6** 53 46N 112 50W
Lamont, *Calif., U.S.A.* **85 K8** 35 15N 118 55W
Lamont, *Wyo., U.S.A.* **82 E10** 42 13N 107 29W
Lampa, *Peru* **92 G4** 15 22S 70 22W
Lampang, *Thailand* **38 C2** 18 16N 99 32 E
Lampasas, *U.S.A.* **81 K5** 31 4N 98 11W
Lampazos de Naranjo, *Mexico* **86 B4** 27 2N 100 32W
Lampedusa, *Medit. S.* **20 G5** 35 36N 12 40 E
Lampeter, *U.K.* **11 E3** 52 7N 4 4W
Lampione, *Medit. S.* **20 G5** 35 33N 12 20 E
Lampman, *Canada* **73 D8** 49 25N 102 50W
Lampung □, *Indonesia* **36 F2** 5 30S 104 30 E
Lamta, *India* **43 H9** 22 8N 80 7 E
Lamu, *Kenya* **54 C5** 2 16S 40 55 E
Lamy, *U.S.A.* **83 J11** 35 29N 105 53W
Lan Xian, *China* **34 E6** 38 15N 111 35 E
Lanai, *U.S.A.* **74 H16** 20 50N 156 55W
Lanak La, *India* **43 B8** 34 27N 79 32 E
Lanak'o Shank'ou = Lanak La, *India* **43 B8** 34 27N 79 32 E
Lanark, *Canada* **79 A8** 45 1N 76 22W
Lanark, *U.K.* **12 F5** 55 40N 3 47W
Lancang Jiang →, *China* **32 D5** 21 40N 101 10 E
Lancashire □, *U.K.* **10 D5** 53 50N 2 48W
Lancaster, *Canada* **79 A10** 45 10N 74 30W
Lancaster, *U.K.* **10 C5** 54 3N 2 48W
Lancaster, *Calif., U.S.A.* **85 L8** 34 42N 118 8W
Lancaster, *Ky., U.S.A.* **76 G3** 37 37N 84 35W
Lancaster, *N.H., U.S.A.* **79 B13** 44 29N 71 34W
Lancaster, *N.Y., U.S.A.* **78 D6** 42 54N 78 40W
Lancaster, *Ohio, U.S.A.* **76 F4** 39 43N 82 36W
Lancaster, *Pa., U.S.A.* **79 F8** 40 2N 76 19W
Lancaster, *S.C., U.S.A.* **77 H5** 34 43N 80 46W
Lancaster, *Wis., U.S.A.* **80 D9** 42 51N 90 43W
Lancaster Sd., *Canada* **69 A11** 74 13N 84 0W
Lancelin, *Australia* **61 F2** 31 0S 115 18 E
Lanchow = Lanzhou, *China* **34 F2** 36 1N 103 52 E
Lanciano, *Italy* **20 C6** 42 14N 14 23 E
Lancun, *China* **35 F11** 36 25N 120 10 E
Landeck, *Austria* **16 E6** 47 9N 10 34 E
Lander, *U.S.A.* **82 E9** 42 50N 108 44W
Lander →, *Australia* **60 D5** 22 0S 132 0 E
Landes, *France* **18 D3** 44 0N 1 0W
Landi Kotal, *Pakistan* **42 B4** 34 7N 71 6 E
Landisburg, *U.S.A.* **78 F7** 40 21N 77 19W
Land's End, *U.K.* **11 G2** 50 4N 5 44W
Landsborough Cr. →, *Australia* **62 C3** 22 28S 144 35 E
Landshut, *Germany* **16 D7** 48 34N 12 8 E
Landskrona, *Sweden* **9 J15** 55 53N 12 50 E
Lanesboro, *U.S.A.* **79 E9** 41 57N 75 34W
Lanett, *U.S.A.* **77 J3** 32 52N 85 12W
Lang Qua, *Vietnam* **38 A5** 22 16N 104 27 E
Lang Shan, *China* **34 D4** 41 0N 106 30 E
Lang Suan, *Thailand* **39 H2** 9 57N 99 4 E
La'nga Co, *China* **41 D12** 30 45N 81 15 E
Langar, *Iran* **45 C9** 35 23N 60 25 E
Langara I., *Canada* **72 C2** 54 14N 133 1W
Langdon, *U.S.A.* **80 A5** 48 45N 98 22W
Langeberg, *S. Africa* **56 E3** 33 55S 21 0 E
Langeberge, *S. Africa* **56 D3** 28 15S 22 33 E
Langeland, *Denmark* **9 J14** 54 56N 10 48 E
Langenburg, *Canada* **73 C8** 50 51N 101 43W
Langholm, *U.K.* **12 F5** 55 9N 3 0W
Langjökull, *Iceland* **8 D3** 64 39N 20 12W
Langkawi, Pulau, *Malaysia* **39 J2** 6 25N 99 45 E
Langklip, *S. Africa* **56 D3** 28 12S 20 20 E
Langkon, *Malaysia* **36 C5** 6 30N 116 40 E
Langlade, *St- P. & M.* **71 C8** 46 50N 56 20W
Langley, *Canada* **84 A4** 49 7N 122 39W
Langøya, *Norway* **8 B16** 68 45N 14 50 E
Langreo, *Spain* **19 A3** 43 18N 5 40W
Langres, *France* **18 C6** 47 52N 5 20 E
Langres, Plateau de, *France* **18 C6** 47 45N 5 3 E
Langsa, *Indonesia* **36 D1** 4 30N 97 57 E
Langtry, *U.S.A.* **81 L4** 29 49N 101 34W
Langu, *Thailand* **39 J2** 6 53N 99 47 E
Languedoc, *France* **18 E5** 43 58N 3 55 E
Langxiangzhen, *China* **34 E9** 39 43N 116 8 E
Lanigan, *Canada* **73 C7** 51 51N 105 2W
Lankao, *China* **34 G8** 34 48N 114 50 E
Länkäran, *Azerbaijan* **25 G8** 38 48N 48 52 E
Lannion, *France* **18 B2** 48 46N 3 29W
L'Annonciation, *Canada* **70 C5** 46 25N 74 55W
Lansdale, *U.S.A.* **79 F9** 40 14N 75 17W
Lansdowne, *Australia* **63 E5** 31 48S 152 30 E
Lansdowne, *Canada* **79 B8** 44 24N 76 1W
Lansdowne, *India* **43 E8** 29 50N 78 41 E
Lansdowne House, *Canada* **70 B2** 52 14N 87 53W
L'Anse, *Mich., U.S.A.* **76 B1** 46 42N 88 25W
L'Anse, *Mich., U.S.A.* **80 B10** 46 45N 88 27W
L'Anse au Loup, *Canada* **71 B8** 51 32N 56 50W
L'Anse aux Meadows, *Canada* **71 B8** 51 36N 55 32W
Lansford, *U.S.A.* **79 F9** 40 50N 75 53W
Lansing, *U.S.A.* **76 D3** 42 44N 84 33W
Lanta Yai, Ko, *Thailand* **39 J2** 7 35N 99 3 E
Lantian, *China* **34 G5** 34 11N 109 20 E
Lanus, *Argentina* **94 C4** 34 44S 58 27W
Lanusei, *Italy* **20 E3** 39 52N 9 34 E
Lanzarote, *Canary Is.* **22 F6** 29 0N 13 40W
Lanzhou, *China* **34 F2** 36 1N 103 52 E
Lao Bao, *Laos* **38 D6** 16 35N 106 30 E
Laoag, *Phil.* **37 A6** 18 7N 120 34 E
Laoang, *Phil.* **37 B7** 12 32N 125 8 E
Laoha He →, *China* **35 C11** 43 25N 120 35 E
Laois □, *Ireland* **13 D4** 52 57N 7 36W
Laon, *France* **18 B5** 49 33N 3 35 E
Laona, *U.S.A.* **76 C1** 45 34N 88 40W
Laos ■, *Asia* **38 D5** 17 45N 105 0 E
Lapa, *Brazil* **95 B6** 25 46S 49 44W
Lapeer, *U.S.A.* **76 D4** 43 3N 83 19W
Lapithos, *Cyprus* **23 D12** 35 21N 33 11 E
Lapland = Lappland, *Europe* **8 B21** 68 7N 24 0 E
Laporte, *U.S.A.* **79 E8** 41 25N 76 30W

Lappeenranta

Lappeenranta, Finland 9 F23 61 3N 28 12 E
Lappland, Europe 8 B21 68 7N 24 0 E
Laprida, Argentina 94 D3 37 34S 60 45W
Lapseki, Turkey 21 D12 40 20N 26 41 E
Laptev Sea, Russia 27 B13 76 0N 125 0 E
Lapua, Finland 8 E20 62 58N 23 0 E
L'Áquila, Italy 20 C5 42 22N 13 22 E
Lār, Āzarbājān-e Sharqī, Iran 44 B5 38 30N 47 52 E
Lār, Fārs, Iran 45 E7 27 40N 54 14 E
Laramie, U.S.A. 80 E2 41 19N 105 35W
Laramie →, U.S.A. 82 F11 42 13N 104 33W
Laramie Mts., U.S.A. 80 E2 42 0N 105 30W
Laranjeiras do Sul, Brazil 95 B5 25 23S 52 23W
Larantuka, Indonesia 37 F6 8 21S 122 55 E
Larat, Indonesia 37 F8 7 0S 132 0 E
Larde, Mozam. 55 F4 16 28S 39 43 E
Larder Lake, Canada 70 C4 48 5N 79 40W
Lardhos, Ákra = Líndhos, Ákra, Greece 23 C10 36 4N 28 10 E
Lardhos, Órmos, Greece 23 C10 36 4N 28 2 E
Laredo, U.S.A. 81 M5 27 30N 99 30W
Laredo Sd., Canada 72 C3 52 30N 128 53W
Largo, U.S.A. 77 M4 27 55N 82 47W
Largs, U.K. 12 F4 55 47N 4 52W
Lariang, Indonesia 37 E5 1 26S 119 17 E
Larimore, U.S.A. 80 B6 47 54N 97 38W
Lārīn, Iran 45 C7 35 55N 52 19 E
Lárisa, Greece 21 E10 39 36N 22 27 E
Larkana, Pakistan 42 F3 27 32N 68 18 E
Larnaca, Cyprus 23 E12 34 55N 33 38 E
Larnaca Bay, Cyprus 23 E12 34 53N 33 45 E
Larne, U.K. 13 B6 54 51N 5 51W
Larned, U.S.A. 80 F5 38 11N 99 6W
Larose, U.S.A. 81 L9 29 34N 90 23W
Larrimah, Australia 60 C5 15 35S 133 12 E
Larsen Ice Shelf, Antarctica 5 C17 67 0S 62 0W
Larvik, Norway 9 G14 59 4N 10 2 E
Las Animas, U.S.A. 80 F3 38 4N 103 13W
Las Anod, Somali Rep. 46 F4 8 26N 47 19 E
Las Aves, Is., W. Indies 89 C7 15 45N 63 55W
Las Brenãs, Argentina 94 B3 27 5S 61 7W
Las Cejas, Argentina 96 B4 26 53S 64 44W
Las Chimeneas, Mexico 85 N10 32 8N 116 5W
Las Cruces, U.S.A. 83 K10 32 19N 106 47W
Las Flores, Argentina 94 D4 36 10S 59 7W
Las Heras, Argentina 94 C2 32 51S 68 49W
Las Lajas, Argentina 96 D2 38 30S 70 25W
Las Lomitas, Argentina 94 A3 24 43S 60 35W
Las Palmas, Argentina 94 B4 27 8S 58 45W
Las Palmas, Canary Is. 22 F4 28 7N 15 26W
Las Palmas →, Mexico 85 N10 32 26N 116 54W
Las Piedras, Uruguay 95 C4 34 44S 56 14W
Las Pipinas, Argentina 94 D4 35 30S 57 19W
Las Plumas, Argentina 96 E3 43 40S 67 15W
Las Rosas, Argentina 94 C3 32 30S 61 35W
Las Tablas, Panama 88 E3 7 49N 80 14W
Las Termas, Argentina 94 B3 27 29S 64 52W
Las Toscas, Argentina 94 B4 28 21S 59 18W
Las Truchas, Mexico 86 D4 17 57N 102 13W
Las Varillas, Argentina 94 C3 31 50S 62 50W
Las Vegas, N. Mex., U.S.A. 83 J11 35 36N 105 13W
Las Vegas, Nev., U.S.A. 85 J11 36 10N 115 9W
Lascano, Uruguay 95 C5 33 35S 54 12W
Lashburn, Canada 73 C7 53 10N 109 40W
Lashio, Burma 41 H20 22 56N 97 45 E
Lashkar, India 42 F8 26 10N 78 10 E
Lasíthi, Greece 23 D7 35 11N 25 31 E
Lasíthi □, Greece 23 D7 35 5N 25 50 E
Lāsjerd, Iran 45 C7 35 24N 53 4 E
Lassen Pk., U.S.A. 82 F3 40 29N 121 31W
Lassen Volcanic National Park, U.S.A. 82 F3 40 30N 121 20W
Last Mountain L., Canada 73 C7 51 5N 105 14W
Lastchance Cr. →, U.S.A. 84 E5 40 2N 121 15W
Lastoursville, Gabon 52 E2 0 55S 12 38 E
Lastovo, Croatia 20 C7 42 46N 16 55 E
Lat Yao, Thailand 38 E2 15 45N 99 48 E
Latacunga, Ecuador 92 D3 0 50S 78 35W
Latakia = Al Lādhiqīyah, Syria 44 C2 35 30N 35 45 E
Latchford, Canada 70 C4 47 20N 79 50W
Latehar, India 43 H11 23 45N 84 30 E
Latham, Australia 61 E2 29 44S 116 20 E
Lathi, India 42 F4 27 43N 71 23 E
Lathrop Wells, U.S.A. 85 J10 36 39N 116 24W
Latina, Italy 20 D5 41 28N 12 52 E
Latium = Lazio □, Italy 20 C5 42 10N 12 30 E
Laton, U.S.A. 84 J7 36 26N 119 41W
Latouche Treville, C., Australia 60 C3 18 27S 121 49 E
Latrobe, Australia 62 G4 41 14S 146 30 E
Latrobe, U.S.A. 78 F5 40 19N 79 23W
Latvia ■, Europe 9 H20 56 50N 24 0 E
Lau Group, Fiji 59 C9 17 0S 178 30W
Lauchhammer, Germany 16 C7 51 29N 13 47 E
Laughlin, U.S.A. 83 J6 35 8N 114 35W
Laukaa, Finland 9 E21 62 24N 25 56 E
Launceston, Australia 62 G4 41 24S 147 8 E
Launceston, U.K. 11 G3 50 38N 4 22W
Laune →, Ireland 13 D2 52 7N 9 47W
Launglon Bok, Burma 38 F1 13 50N 97 54 E
Laura, Australia 62 B3 15 32S 144 32 E
Laurel, Miss., U.S.A. 81 K10 31 41N 89 8W
Laurel, Mont., U.S.A. 82 D9 45 40N 108 46W
Laurencekirk, U.K. 12 E6 56 50N 2 28W
Laurens, U.S.A. 77 H4 34 30N 82 1W
Laurentian Plateau, Canada 71 B6 52 0N 70 0W
Lauria, Italy 20 E6 40 2N 15 50 E
Laurie L., Canada 73 B8 56 35N 101 57W
Laurinburg, U.S.A. 77 H6 34 47N 79 28W
Laurium, U.S.A. 76 B1 47 14N 88 27W
Lausanne, Switz. 18 C7 46 32N 6 38 E
Laut, Indonesia 39 K6 4 45N 108 0 E
Laut, Pulau, Indonesia 36 E5 3 40S 116 10 E
Laut Kecil, Kepulauan, Indonesia 36 E5 4 45S 115 40 E
Lautoka, Fiji 59 C7 17 37S 177 27 E
Lavagh More, Ireland 13 B3 54 46N 8 6W
Laval, France 18 B3 48 4N 0 48W
Lavalle, Argentina 94 B2 28 15S 65 15W
Lavant Station, Canada 79 A8 45 3N 76 42W
Lāvar Meydān, Iran 45 D7 30 20N 54 30 E
Laverton, Australia 61 E3 28 44S 122 29 E
Lavras, Brazil 95 A7 21 20S 45 0W
Lávrion, Greece 23 F11 37 40N 24 4 E
Lávris, Greece 23 D6 35 25N 24 40 E
Lavumisa, Swaziland 57 D5 27 20S 31 55 E
Lawas, Malaysia 36 D5 4 55N 115 25 E
Lawele, Indonesia 37 F6 5 16S 123 3 E
Lawng Pit, Burma 41 G20 25 30N 97 25 E
Lawqah, Si. Arabia 44 D4 29 49N 42 45 E
Lawrence, N.Z. 59 L2 45 55S 169 41 E
Lawrence, Kans., U.S.A. 80 F7 38 58N 95 14W
Lawrence, Mass., U.S.A. 79 D13 42 43N 71 10W
Lawrenceburg, Ind., U.S.A. 76 F3 39 6N 84 52W
Lawrenceburg, Tenn., U.S.A. 77 H2 35 14N 87 20W
Lawrenceville, Ga., U.S.A. 77 J4 33 57N 83 59W
Lawrenceville, Pa., U.S.A. 78 E7 41 59N 77 8W
Laws, U.S.A. 84 H8 37 24N 118 20W
Lawton, U.S.A. 81 H5 34 37N 98 25W
Lawu, Indonesia 37 G14 7 40S 111 13 E
Laxford, L., U.K. 12 C3 58 24N 5 6W
Laylá, Si. Arabia 46 C4 22 10N 46 40 E
Laylān, Iraq 44 C5 35 18N 44 31 E
Layton, U.S.A. 82 F7 41 4N 111 58W
Laytonville, U.S.A. 82 G2 39 41N 123 29W
Lazio □, Italy 20 C5 42 10N 12 30 E
Lazo, Russia 30 C6 43 25N 133 55 E
Le Creusot, France 18 C6 46 48N 4 24 E
Le François, Martinique 89 D7 14 38N 60 57W
Le Havre, France 18 B4 49 30N 0 5 E
Le Mans, France 18 C4 48 0N 0 10 E
Le Mars, U.S.A. 80 D6 42 47N 96 10W
Le Mont-St-Michel, France 18 B3 48 40N 1 30W
Le Moule, Guadeloupe 89 C7 16 20N 61 22W
Le Puy-en-Velay, France 18 D5 45 3N 3 52 E
Le Sueur, U.S.A. 80 C8 44 28N 93 55W
Le Thuy, Vietnam 38 D6 17 14N 106 49 E
Le Touquet-Paris-Plage, France 18 A4 50 30N 1 36 E
Le Tréport, France 18 A4 50 3N 1 20 E
Le Verdon-sur-Mer, France 18 D3 45 33N 1 4W
Lea →, U.K. 11 F8 51 31N 0 1 E
Leach, Cambodia 39 F4 12 21N 103 46 E
Lead, U.S.A. 80 C3 44 21N 103 46W
Leader, Canada 73 C7 50 50N 109 30W
Leadville, U.S.A. 83 G10 39 15N 106 18W
Leaf →, U.S.A. 81 K10 30 59N 88 44W
Leaf Rapids, Canada 73 B9 56 30N 99 59W
Leamington, Canada 78 D2 42 3N 82 36W
Leamington, U.S.A. 82 G7 39 32N 112 17W
Leamington Spa = Royal Leamington Spa, U.K. 11 E6 52 18N 1 31W
Leandro Norte Alem, Argentina 95 B4 27 34S 55 15W
Leane, L., Ireland 13 D2 52 2N 9 32W
Learmonth, Australia 60 D1 22 13S 114 10 E
Leask, Canada 73 C7 53 5N 106 45W
Leatherhead, U.K. 11 F7 51 18N 0 20W
Leavenworth, Kans., U.S.A. 80 F7 39 19N 94 55W
Leavenworth, Wash., U.S.A. 82 C3 47 36N 120 40W
Lebak, Phil. 37 C6 6 32N 124 5 E
Lebam, U.S.A. 84 D3 46 34N 123 33W
Lebanon, Ind., U.S.A. 76 E2 40 3N 86 28W
Lebanon, Kans., U.S.A. 80 F5 39 49N 98 33W
Lebanon, Ky., U.S.A. 76 G3 37 34N 85 15W
Lebanon, Mo., U.S.A. 81 G8 37 41N 92 40W
Lebanon, N.H., U.S.A. 79 C12 43 39N 72 15W
Lebanon, Oreg., U.S.A. 82 D2 44 32N 122 55W
Lebanon, Pa., U.S.A. 79 F8 40 20N 76 26W
Lebanon, Tenn., U.S.A. 77 G2 36 12N 86 18W
Lebanon ■, Asia 47 B5 34 0N 36 0 E
Lebec, U.S.A. 85 L8 34 50N 118 52W
Lebel-sur-Quévillon, Canada 70 C4 49 3N 76 59W
Lebomboberge, S. Africa 57 C5 24 30S 32 0 E
Lębork, Poland 17 A9 54 33N 17 46 E
Lebrija, Spain 19 D2 36 53N 6 5W
Lebu, Chile 94 D1 37 40S 73 47W
Lecce, Italy 21 D8 40 23N 18 11 E
Lecco, Italy 18 D8 45 51N 9 23 E
Lech →, Germany 16 D6 48 43N 10 56 E
Lecontes Mills, U.S.A. 78 E6 41 5N 78 17W
Łęczyca, Poland 17 B10 52 5N 19 15 E
Ledong, China 38 C7 18 41N 109 5 E
Leduc, Canada 72 C6 53 15N 113 30W
Lee, U.S.A. 79 D11 42 19N 73 15W
Lee →, Ireland 13 E3 51 53N 8 56W
Lee Vining, U.S.A. 84 H7 37 58N 119 7W
Leech L., U.S.A. 80 B7 47 10N 94 24W
Leechburg, U.S.A. 78 F5 40 37N 79 36W
Leeds, U.K. 10 D6 53 48N 1 33W
Leeds, U.S.A. 77 J2 33 33N 86 33W
Leek, Neths. 15 A6 53 10N 6 24 E
Leek, U.K. 10 D5 53 7N 2 1W
Leeman, Australia 61 E1 29 57S 114 58 E
Leeper, U.S.A. 78 E5 41 22N 79 18W
Leer, Germany 16 B4 53 13N 7 26 E
Leesburg, U.S.A. 77 L5 28 49N 81 53W
Leesville, U.S.A. 81 K8 31 9N 93 16W
Leeton, Australia 63 E4 34 33S 146 23 E
Leetonia, U.S.A. 78 F4 40 53N 80 45W
Leeu Gamka, S. Africa 56 E3 32 47S 21 59 E
Leeuwarden, Neths. 15 A5 53 15N 5 48 E
Leeuwin, C., Australia 61 F2 34 20S 115 9 E
Leeward Is., Atl. Oc. 89 C7 16 30N 63 30W
Lefka, Cyprus 23 D11 35 6N 32 51 E
Lefkoniko, Cyprus 23 D12 35 18N 33 44 E
Lefroy, Canada 78 B5 44 16N 79 34W
Lefroy, L., Australia 61 F3 31 21S 121 40 E
Leganés, Spain 19 B4 40 19N 3 45W
Legazpi, Phil. 37 B6 13 10N 123 45 E
Legendre I., Australia 60 D2 20 22S 116 55 E
Leghorn = Livorno, Italy 20 C4 43 33N 10 19 E
Legionowo, Poland 17 B11 52 25N 20 50 E
Legnago, Italy 20 B4 45 11N 11 18 E
Legnica, Poland 16 C9 51 12N 16 10 E
Leh, India 43 B7 34 9N 77 35 E
Lehigh Acres, U.S.A. 77 M5 26 36N 81 39W
Lehighton, U.S.A. 79 F9 40 50N 75 43W
Lehututu, Botswana 56 C3 23 54S 21 55 E
Leiah, Pakistan 42 D4 30 58N 70 58 E
Leicester, U.K. 11 E6 52 38N 1 8W
Leicester City □, U.K. 11 E6 52 38N 1 8W
Leicestershire □, U.K. 11 E6 52 41N 1 17W
Leichhardt →, Australia 62 B2 17 35S 139 48 E
Leichhardt Ra., Australia 62 C4 20 46S 147 40 E
Leiden, Neths. 15 B4 52 9N 4 30 E
Leie →, Belgium 15 C3 51 2N 3 45 E
Leigh Creek, Australia 63 E2 30 38S 138 26 E
Leine →, Germany 16 B5 52 43N 9 36 E
Leinster, Australia 61 E3 27 51S 120 36 E
Leinster □, Ireland 13 C4 53 3N 7 8W
Leinster, Mt., Ireland 13 D5 52 37N 6 46W
Leipzig, Germany 16 C7 51 18N 12 22 E
Leiria, Portugal 19 C1 39 46N 8 53W
Leirvik, Norway 9 G11 59 47N 5 28 E
Leisler, Mt., Australia 60 D4 23 23S 129 20 E
Leith, U.K. 12 F5 55 59N 3 11W
Leith Hill, U.K. 11 F7 51 11N 0 22W
Leitrim, Ireland 13 B3 54 0N 8 5W
Leitrim □, Ireland 13 B4 54 8N 8 0W
Leizhou Bandao, China 33 D6 21 0N 110 0 E
Lek →, Neths. 15 C4 51 54N 4 35 E
Leka, Norway 8 D14 65 5N 11 35 E
Lékva Óros, Greece 23 D6 35 18N 24 3 E
Leland, Mich., U.S.A. 76 C3 45 1N 85 45W
Leland, Miss., U.S.A. 81 J9 33 24N 90 54W
Leleque, Argentina 96 E2 42 28S 71 0W
Lelystad, Neths. 15 B5 52 30N 5 25 E
Léman, L., Europe 18 C7 46 26N 6 30 E
Lemera, Dem. Rep. of the Congo 54 C2 3 0S 28 55 E
Lemhi Ra., U.S.A. 82 D7 44 30N 113 30W
Lemmer, Neths. 15 B5 52 51N 5 43 E
Lemmon, U.S.A. 80 C3 45 57N 102 10W
Lemon Grove, U.S.A. 85 N9 32 45N 117 2W
Lemoore, U.S.A. 84 J7 36 18N 119 46W
Lemvig, Denmark 9 H13 56 33N 8 20 E
Lena →, Russia 27 B13 72 52N 126 40 E
Léndas, Greece 23 E6 34 56N 24 56 E
Lendeh, Iran 45 D6 30 58N 50 25 E
Lenggong, Malaysia 39 K3 5 6N 100 58 E
Lengua de Vaca, Pta., Chile 94 C1 30 14S 71 38W
Leninabad = Khudzhand, Tajikistan 26 E7 40 17N 69 37 E
Leninakan = Gyumri, Armenia 25 F7 40 47N 43 50 E
Leningrad = Sankt-Peterburg, Russia 24 C5 59 55N 30 20 E
Leninogorsk, Kazakstan 26 D9 50 20N 83 30 E
Leninsk, Russia 25 E8 48 40N 45 15 E
Leninsk-Kuznetskiy, Russia 26 D9 54 44N 86 10 E
Lenkoran = Länkäran, Azerbaijan 25 G8 38 48N 48 52 E
Lenmalu, Indonesia 37 E8 1 45S 130 15 E
Lennox, U.S.A. 80 D6 43 21N 96 53W
Lennoxville, Canada 79 A13 45 22N 71 51W
Lenoir, U.S.A. 77 H5 35 55N 81 32W
Lenoir City, U.S.A. 77 H3 35 48N 84 16W
Lenore L., Canada 73 C8 52 30N 104 59W
Lenox, U.S.A. 79 D11 42 22N 73 17W
Lens, France 18 A5 50 26N 2 50 E
Lensk, Russia 27 C12 60 48N 114 55 E
Lentini, Italy 20 F6 37 17N 15 0 E
Lenwood, U.S.A. 85 L9 34 53N 117 7W
Lenya, Burma 36 B1 11 33N 98 57 E
Leoben, Austria 16 E8 47 22N 15 5 E
Leodhas = Lewis, U.K. 12 C2 58 9N 6 40W
Leola, U.S.A. 80 C5 45 43N 98 56W
Leominster, U.K. 11 E5 52 14N 2 43W
Leominster, U.S.A. 79 D13 42 32N 71 46W
León, Mexico 86 C4 21 7N 101 40W
León, Nic. 88 D2 12 20N 86 51W
León, Spain 19 A3 42 38N 5 34W
Leon, U.S.A. 80 E8 40 44N 93 45W
Leon →, U.S.A. 81 K6 31 14N 97 28W
León, Montes de, Spain 19 A2 42 30N 6 18W
Leonardtown, U.S.A. 76 F7 38 17N 76 38W
Leongatha, Australia 63 F4 38 30S 145 58 E
Leonora, Australia 61 E3 28 49S 121 19 E
Léopold II, Lac = Mai-Ndombe, L., Dem. Rep. of the Congo 52 E3 2 0S 18 20 E
Leopoldina, Brazil 95 A7 21 28S 42 40W
Leopoldsburg, Belgium 15 C5 51 7N 5 13 E
Léopoldville = Kinshasa, Dem. Rep. of the Congo 52 E3 4 20S 15 15 E
Leoti, U.S.A. 80 F4 38 29N 101 21W
Leova, Moldova 17 E15 46 28N 28 15 E
Leoville, Canada 73 C7 53 39N 107 33W
Lepel = Lyepyel, Belarus 24 D4 54 50N 28 40 E
Lépo, L. do, Angola 56 B2 17 0S 19 0 E
Leppävirta, Finland 9 E22 62 29N 27 46 E
Lerdo, Mexico 86 B4 25 32N 103 32W
Leribe, Lesotho 57 D4 28 51S 28 3 E
Lérida = Lleida, Spain 19 B6 41 37N 0 39 E
Lerwick, U.K. 12 A7 60 9N 1 9W
Les Cayes, Haiti 89 C5 18 15N 73 46W
Les Sables-d'Olonne, France 18 C3 46 30N 1 45W
Lesbos = Lésvos, Greece 21 E12 39 10N 26 20 E
Leshan, China 32 D5 29 33N 103 41 E
Leshukonskoye, Russia 24 B8 64 54N 45 46 E
Leskov I., Antarctica 5 B1 56 0S 28 0W
Leskovac, Serbia, Yug. 21 C9 43 0N 21 58 E
Lesopilnoye, Russia 30 A7 46 44N 134 20 E
Lesotho ■, Africa 57 D4 29 40S 28 0 E
Lesozavodsk, Russia 27 E14 45 30N 133 29 E
Lesse →, Belgium 15 D4 50 15N 4 54 E
Lesser Antilles, W. Indies 89 D7 15 0N 61 0W
Lesser Slave L., Canada 72 B5 55 30N 115 25W
Lesser Sunda Is., Indonesia 37 F6 7 0S 120 0 E
Lessines, Belgium 15 D3 50 42N 3 50 E
Lester, U.S.A. 84 C5 47 12N 121 29W
Lestock, Canada 73 C8 51 19N 103 59W
Lesuer I., Australia 60 B4 13 50S 127 17 E
Lésvos, Greece 21 E12 39 10N 26 20 E
Leszno, Poland 17 C9 51 50N 16 30 E
Letchworth, U.K. 11 F7 51 59N 0 13W
Lethbridge, Canada 72 D6 49 45N 112 45W
Lethem, Guyana 92 C7 3 20N 59 50W
Leti, Kepulauan, Indonesia 37 F7 8 10S 128 0 E
Leti Is. = Leti, Kepulauan, Indonesia 37 F7 8 10S 128 0 E
Letiahau →, Botswana 56 C3 21 16S 24 0 E
Leticia, Colombia 92 D5 4 9S 70 0W
Leting, China 35 E10 39 23N 118 55 E
Letjiesbos, S. Africa 56 E3 32 34S 22 16 E
Letlhakeng, Botswana 56 C3 24 0S 24 59 E
Letong, Indonesia 36 D3 2 58N 105 42 E
Letpadan, Burma 41 L19 17 45N 95 45 E
Letpan, Burma 41 K19 19 28N 94 10 E
Letsôk-aw Kyun, Burma 39 G2 11 30N 98 25 E
Letterkenny, Ireland 13 B4 54 57N 7 45W
Leucadia, U.S.A. 85 M9 33 4N 117 18W
Leuser, G., Indonesia 36 D1 3 46N 97 12 E
Leuven, Belgium 15 D4 50 52N 4 42 E
Leuze-en-Hainaut, Belgium 15 D3 50 36N 3 37 E
Levádhia, Greece 21 E10 38 27N 22 54 E
Levanger, Norway 8 E14 63 45N 11 19 E
Levelland, U.S.A. 81 J3 33 35N 102 23W
Leven, U.K. 12 E6 56 12N 3 0W
Leven, L., U.K. 12 E5 56 12N 3 22W
Leven, Toraka, Madag. 57 A8 12 30S 47 45 E
Leveque C., Australia 60 C3 16 20S 123 0 E
Levice, Slovak Rep. 17 D10 48 13N 18 35 E
Levin, N.Z. 59 J5 40 37S 175 18 E
Lévis, Canada 71 C5 46 48N 71 9W
Levis, L., Canada 72 A5 62 37N 117 58W
Levittown, N.Y., U.S.A. 79 F11 40 44N 73 31W
Levittown, Pa., U.S.A. 79 F10 40 9N 74 51W
Levkás, Greece 21 E9 38 40N 20 43 E
Levkímmi, Greece 23 B4 39 25N 20 3 E
Levkímmi, Ákra, Greece 23 B4 39 29N 20 4 E
Levkôsia = Nicosia, Cyprus 23 D12 35 10N 33 25 E
Levskigrad = Karlovo, Bulgaria 21 C11 42 38N 24 47 E
Lewes, U.K. 11 G8 50 52N 0 1 E
Lewes, U.S.A. 76 F8 38 46N 75 9W
Lewis, U.K. 12 C2 58 9N 6 40W
Lewis →, U.S.A. 84 E4 45 51N 122 48W
Lewis, Butt of, U.K. 12 C2 58 31N 6 16W
Lewis Ra., Australia 60 D4 20 3S 128 50 E
Lewis Range, U.S.A. 82 C7 48 5N 113 5W
Lewis Run, U.S.A. 78 E6 41 52N 78 40W
Lewisburg, Pa., U.S.A. 78 F8 40 58N 76 54W
Lewisburg, Tenn., U.S.A. 77 H2 35 27N 86 48W
Lewisburg, W. Va., U.S.A. 76 G5 37 48N 80 27W
Lewisporte, Canada 71 C8 49 15N 55 3W
Lewiston, Idaho, U.S.A. 82 C5 46 25N 117 1W
Lewiston, Maine, U.S.A. 77 C11 44 6N 70 13W
Lewiston, N.Y., U.S.A. 78 C5 43 11N 79 3W
Lewistown, Mont., U.S.A. 82 C9 47 4N 109 26W
Lewistown, Pa., U.S.A. 78 F7 40 36N 77 34W
Lexington, Ill., U.S.A. 80 E10 40 39N 88 47W
Lexington, Ky., U.S.A. 76 F3 38 3N 84 30W
Lexington, Mich., U.S.A. 78 C2 43 16N 82 32W
Lexington, Mo., U.S.A. 80 F8 39 11N 93 52W
Lexington, N.C., U.S.A. 77 H5 35 49N 80 15W
Lexington, N.Y., U.S.A. 79 D10 42 15N 74 22W
Lexington, Nebr., U.S.A. 80 E5 40 47N 99 45W
Lexington, Ohio, U.S.A. 78 F2 40 41N 82 35W
Lexington, Tenn., U.S.A. 77 H1 35 39N 88 24W
Lexington, Va., U.S.A. 76 G6 37 47N 79 27W
Lexington Park, U.S.A. 76 F7 38 16N 76 27W
Leyburn, U.K. 10 C6 54 19N 1 48W
Leyland, U.K. 10 D5 53 42N 2 43W
Leyte, Phil. 37 B7 11 0N 125 0 E
Lezha, Albania 21 D8 41 47N 19 39 E
Lhasa, China 32 D4 29 25N 90 58 E
Lhazê, China 32 D3 29 5N 87 38 E
Lhokkruet, Indonesia 36 D1 4 55N 95 24 E
Lhokseumawe, Indonesia 36 C1 5 10N 97 10 E
L'Hospitalet de Llobregat, Spain 19 B7 41 21N 2 6 E
Lhuntsi Dzong, India 41 F17 27 39N 91 10 E
Li, Thailand 38 D2 17 48N 98 57 E
Li Xian, Gansu, China 34 G3 34 10N 105 5 E
Li Xian, Hebei, China 34 E8 38 30N 115 35 E
Lianga, Phil. 37 C7 8 38N 126 6 E
Liangcheng, Nei Mongol Zizhiqu, China 34 D7 40 28N 112 25 E
Liangcheng, Shandong, China 35 G10 35 32N 119 37 E
Liangdang, China 34 H4 33 56N 106 18 E
Liangpran, Indonesia 36 D4 1 4N 114 23 E
Lianshanguan, China 35 D12 40 53N 123 43 E
Lianshui, China 35 H10 33 42N 119 20 E
Lianyungang, China 35 G10 34 40N 119 11 E
Liao He →, China 35 D11 41 0N 121 50 E
Liaocheng, China 34 F8 36 28N 115 58 E
Liaodong Bandao, China 35 E12 40 0N 122 30 E
Liaodong Wan, China 35 D11 40 20N 121 10 E
Liaoning □, China 35 D12 41 40N 122 30 E
Liaoyang, China 35 D12 41 15N 122 58 E
Liaoyuan, China 35 C13 42 58N 125 2 E
Liaozhong, China 35 D12 41 23N 122 50 E
Liard →, Canada 72 A4 61 51N 121 18W
Liard River, Canada 72 B3 59 25N 126 5W
Liari, Pakistan 42 G2 25 37N 66 30 E
Libau = Liepāja, Latvia 9 H19 56 30N 21 0 E
Libby, U.S.A. 82 B6 48 23N 115 33W
Libenge, Dem. Rep. of the Congo 52 D3 3 40N 18 55 E
Liberal, U.S.A. 81 G4 37 3N 100 55W
Liberec, Czech Rep. 16 C8 50 47N 15 7 E
Liberia, Costa Rica 88 D2 10 40N 85 30W
Liberia ■, W. Afr. 50 G4 6 30N 9 30W
Liberty, Mo., U.S.A. 80 F7 39 15N 94 25W
Liberty, N.Y., U.S.A. 79 E10 41 48N 74 45W
Liberty, Pa., U.S.A. 78 E7 41 34N 77 6W
Liberty, Tex., U.S.A. 81 K7 30 3N 94 48W
Lībīya, Sahrâ', Africa 51 C10 25 0N 25 0 E
Libobo, Tanjung, Indonesia 37 E7 0 54S 128 28 E
Libode, S. Africa 57 E4 31 33S 29 2 E
Libourne, France 18 D3 44 55N 0 14W
Libramont, Belgium 15 E5 49 55N 5 23 E
Libreville, Gabon 52 D1 0 25N 9 26 E
Libya ■, N. Afr. 51 C9 27 0N 17 0 E
Libyan Desert = Lībīya, Sahrâ', Africa 51 C10 25 0N 25 0 E
Licantén, Chile 94 D1 35 55S 72 0W
Licata, Italy 20 F5 37 6N 13 56 E
Licheng, China 34 F7 36 28N 113 20 E
Lichfield, U.K. 11 E6 52 41N 1 49W
Lichinga, Mozam. 55 E4 13 13S 35 11 E
Lichtenburg, S. Africa 56 D4 26 8S 26 8 E
Licking →, U.S.A. 76 F3 39 6N 84 30W
Lida, Belarus 9 K21 53 53N 25 15 E
Lidköping, Sweden 9 G15 58 31N 13 7 E
Liebig, Mt., Australia 60 D5 23 18S 131 22 E
Liechtenstein ■, Europe 18 C8 47 8N 9 35 E
Liège, Belgium 15 D5 50 38N 5 35 E
Liège □, Belgium 15 D5 50 32N 5 35 E
Liegnitz = Legnica, Poland 16 C9 51 12N 16 10 E
Lienart, Dem. Rep. of the Congo 54 B2 3 3N 25 31 E
Lienyünchiangshih = Lianyungang, China 35 G10 34 40N 119 11 E
Lienz, Austria 16 E7 46 50N 12 46 E
Liepāja, Latvia 9 H19 56 30N 21 0 E
Lier, Belgium 15 C4 51 7N 4 34 E
Lièvre →, Canada 70 C4 45 31N 75 26W
Liffey →, Ireland 13 C5 53 21N 6 13W
Lifford, Ireland 13 B4 54 51N 7 29W

137

Longview

Longview, *Wash., U.S.A.* .. **84 D4** 46 8N 122 57W
Longxi, *China* .... **34 G3** 34 53N 104 40 E
Lonoke, *U.S.A.* **81 H9** 34 47N 91 54W
Lonquimay, *Chile* **96 D2** 38 26S 71 14W
Lons-le-Saunier, *France* .. **18 C6** 46 40N 5 31 E
Looe, *U.K.* **11 G3** 50 22N 4 28W
Lookout, C., *Canada* **70 A3** 55 18N 83 56W
Lookout, C., *U.S.A.* **77 H7** 34 35N 76 32W
Loolmalasin, *Tanzania* ... **54 C4** 3 0S 35 53 E
Loon →, *Alta., Canada* .. **72 B5** 57 8N 115 3W
Loon →, *Man., Canada* .. **73 B8** 55 53N 101 59W
Loon Lake, *Canada* **73 C7** 54 2N 109 10W
Loongana, *Australia* ..... **61 F4** 30 52S 127 5 E
Loop Hd., *Ireland* **13 D2** 52 34N 9 56W
Lop Buri, *Thailand* ...... **38 E3** 14 48N 100 37 E
Lop Nor = Lop Nur, *China* . **32 B4** 40 20N 90 10 E
Lop Nur, *China* .... **32 B4** 40 20N 90 10 E
Lopatina, Gora, *Russia* ... **27 D15** 50 47N 143 10 E
Lopez, *U.S.A.* **79 E8** 41 27N 76 20W
Lopez, C., *Gabon* .... **52 E1** 0 47S 8 40 E
Lopphavet, *Norway* ...... **8 A19** 70 27N 21 15 E
Lora →, *Afghan.* .... **40 D4** 31 35N 65 50 E
Lora, Hamun-i-, *Pakistan* .. **40 E4** 29 38N 64 58 E
Lora Cr. →, *Australia* ... **63 D2** 28 10S 135 22 E
Lora del Río, *Spain* **19 D3** 37 39N 5 33W
Lorain, *U.S.A.* **78 E2** 41 28N 82 11W
Loralai, *Pakistan* .... **42 D3** 30 20N 68 41 E
Lorca, *Spain* **19 D5** 37 41N 1 42W
Lord Howe I., *Pac. Oc.* ... **64 L7** 31 33S 159 6 E
Lord Howe Ridge, *Pac. Oc.* **64 L8** 30 0S 162 30 E
Lordsburg, *U.S.A.* **83 K9** 32 21N 108 43W
Lorestan □, *Iran* .... **45 C6** 33 30N 48 40 E
Loreto, *Brazil* **93 E9** 7 5S 45 10W
Loreto, *Mexico* **86 B2** 26 1N 111 21W
Lorient, *France* **18 C2** 47 45N 3 23W
Lormi, *India* .... **43 H9** 22 17N 81 41 E
Lorn, *U.K.* **12 E3** 56 26N 5 10W
Lorn, Firth of, *U.K.* **12 E3** 56 20N 5 40W
Lorne, *Australia* .... **63 F3** 38 33S 143 59 E
Lorovouno, *Cyprus* .... **23 D11** 35 8N 32 36 E
Lorraine □, *France* .... **18 B7** 48 53N 6 0 E
Los Alamos, *Calif., U.S.A.* . **85 L6** 34 44N 120 17W
Los Alamos, *N. Mex., U.S.A.* **83 J10** 35 53N 106 19W
Los Altos, *U.S.A.* **84 H4** 37 23N 122 7W
Los Andes, *Chile* **94 C1** 32 50S 70 40W
Los Angeles, *Chile* **94 D1** 37 28S 72 23W
Los Angeles, *U.S.A.* **85 M8** 34 4N 118 15W
Los Angeles, Bahia de,
Mexico **86 B2** 28 56N 113 34W
Los Angeles Aqueduct,
U.S.A. **85 K9** 35 22N 118 5W
Los Banos, *U.S.A.* **84 H6** 37 4N 120 51W
Los Blancos, *Argentina* ... **94 A3** 23 40S 62 30W
Los Chiles, *Costa Rica* ... **88 D3** 11 2N 84 43W
Los Cristianos, *Canary Is.* .. **22 F3** 28 3N 16 42W
Los Gatos, *U.S.A.* **84 H5** 37 14N 121 59W
Los Hermanos, I., *Venezuela* **89 D7** 11 45N 64 25W
Los Islotes, *Canary Is.* **22 E6** 29 4N 13 44W
Los Llanos de Aridane,
Canary Is. **22 F2** 28 38N 17 54W
Los Loros, *Chile* **94 B1** 27 50S 70 6W
Los Lunas, *U.S.A.* **83 J10** 34 48N 106 44W
Los Mochis, *Mexico* **86 B3** 25 45N 108 57W
Los Olivos, *U.S.A.* **85 L6** 34 40N 120 7W
Los Palacios, *Cuba* **88 B3** 22 35N 83 15W
Los Reyes, *Mexico* **86 D4** 19 34N 102 30W
Los Roques Is., *Venezuela* . **89 D6** 11 50N 66 45W
Los Teques, *Venezuela* ... **92 A5** 10 21N 67 2W
Los Testigos, Is., *Venezuela* **92 A6** 11 23N 63 6W
Los Vilos, *Chile* **94 C1** 32 10S 71 30W
Lošinj, *Croatia* .... **16 F8** 44 30N 14 30 E
Lossiemouth, *U.K.* **12 D5** 57 42N 3 17W
Lostwithiel, *U.K.* **11 G3** 50 24N 4 41W
Lot →, *France* .... **18 D4** 44 18N 0 20 E
Lota, *Chile* **94 D1** 37 5S 73 10W
Loṭfābād, *Iran* .... **45 B8** 37 32N 59 20 E
Lothair, *S. Africa* .... **57 D5** 26 22S 30 27 E
Loubomo, *Congo* .... **52 E2** 4 9S 12 47 E
Loudonville, *U.S.A.* **78 F2** 40 38N 82 14W
Louga, *Senegal* **50 E2** 15 45N 16 5W
Loughborough, *U.K.* **10 E6** 52 47N 1 11W
Loughrea, *Ireland* **13 C3** 53 12N 8 33W
Loughros More B., *Ireland* . **13 B3** 54 48N 8 32W
Louis Trichardt, *S. Africa* . **57 C4** 23 1S 29 43 E
Louis XIV, Pte., *Canada* ... **70 B4** 54 37N 79 45W
Louisa, *U.S.A.* **76 F4** 38 7N 82 36W
Louisbourg, *Canada* **71 C8** 45 55N 60 0W
Louise I., *Canada* **72 C2** 52 55N 131 50W
Louiseville, *Canada* **70 C5** 46 20N 72 56W
Louisiade Arch., *Papua N. G.* **64 J7** 11 10S 153 0 E
Louisiana, *U.S.A.* **80 F9** 39 27N 91 3W
Louisiana □, *U.S.A.* **81 K9** 30 50N 92 0W
Louisville, *Ky., U.S.A.* **76 F3** 38 15N 85 46W
Louisville, *Miss., U.S.A.* ... **81 J10** 33 7N 89 3W
Louisville, *Ohio, U.S.A.* ... **78 F3** 40 50N 81 16W
Loulé, *Portugal* **19 D1** 37 9N 8 0W
Loup City, *U.S.A.* **80 E5** 41 17N 98 58W
Loups Marins, Lacs des,
Canada **70 A5** 56 30N 73 45W
Lourdes, *France* **18 E3** 43 6N 0 3W
Lourenço-Marques =
Maputo, *Mozam.* .... **57 D5** 25 58S 32 32 E
Louth, *Australia* .... **63 E4** 30 30S 145 8 E
Louth, *Ireland* **13 C5** 53 58N 6 32W
Louth, *U.K.* **10 D7** 53 22N 0 1W
Louth □, *Ireland* **13 C5** 53 56N 6 34W
Louvain = Leuven, *Belgium* **15 D4** 50 52N 4 42 E
Louwsburg, *S. Africa* ..... **57 D5** 27 37S 31 7 E
Lovech, *Bulgaria* .... **21 C11** 43 8N 24 42 E
Loveland, *U.S.A.* **80 E2** 40 24N 105 5W
Lovell, *U.S.A.* **82 D9** 44 50N 108 24W
Lovelock, *U.S.A.* **82 F4** 40 11N 118 28W
Loviisa, *Finland* .... **9 F22** 60 28N 26 12 E
Loving, *U.S.A.* **81 J2** 32 17N 104 6W
Lovington, *U.S.A.* **81 J3** 32 57N 103 21W
Lovisa = Loviisa, *Finland* .. **9 F22** 60 28N 26 12 E
Low, L., *Canada* **70 B4** 52 29N 76 17W
Low Pt., *Australia* .... **61 F4** 32 25S 127 25 E
Low Tatra = Nízké Tatry,
Slovak Rep. .... **17 D10** 48 55N 19 30 E
Lowa,
Dem. Rep. of the Congo . **54 C2** 1 25S 25 47 E
Lowa →,
Dem. Rep. of the Congo . **54 C2** 1 24S 25 51 E
Lowell, *U.S.A.* **79 D13** 42 38N 71 19W
Lowellville, *U.S.A.* **78 E4** 41 2N 80 32W
Lower Alkali L., *U.S.A.* **82 F3** 41 16N 120 2W
Lower Arrow L., *Canada* .. **72 D5** 49 40N 118 5W
Lower California = Baja
California, *Mexico* **86 A1** 31 10N 115 12W
Lower Hutt, *N.Z.* .... **59 J5** 41 10S 174 55 E
Lower Lake, *U.S.A.* **84 G4** 38 55N 122 37W
Lower Manitou L., *Canada* . **73 D10** 49 15N 93 0W
Lower Post, *Canada* **72 B3** 59 58N 128 30W
Lower Red L., *U.S.A.* **80 B7** 47 58N 95 0W
Lower Saxony =
Niedersachsen □,
Germany .... **16 B5** 52 50N 9 0 E
Lower Tunguska =
Tunguska, Nizhnyaya →,
Russia .... **27 C9** 65 48N 88 4 E
Lowestoft, *U.K.* .... **11 E9** 52 29N 1 45 E
Łowicz, *Poland* .... **17 B10** 52 6N 19 55 E
Lowville, *U.S.A.* **79 C9** 43 47N 75 29W
Loxton, *Australia* .... **63 E3** 34 28S 140 31 E
Loxton, *S. Africa* .... **56 E3** 31 30S 22 22 E
Loyalton, *U.S.A.* **84 F6** 39 41N 120 14W
Loyalty Is. = Loyauté, Is.,
N. Cal. .... **64 K8** 20 50S 166 30 E
Loyang = Luoyang, *China* . **34 G7** 34 40N 112 26 E
Loyauté, Is., *N. Cal.* ...... **64 K8** 20 50S 166 30 E
Loyev = Loyew, *Belarus* .. **17 C16** 51 56N 30 46 E
Loyew, *Belarus* .... **17 C16** 51 56N 30 46 E
Loyoro, *Uganda* .... **54 B3** 3 22N 34 14 E
Luachimo, *Angola* .... **52 F4** 7 23S 20 48 E
Luajan →, *India* .... **43 G11** 24 44N 85 1 E
Lualaba →,
Dem. Rep. of the Congo . **54 B2** 0 26N 25 20 E
Luampa, *Zambia* .... **55 F1** 15 4S 24 20 E
Luan He →, *China* ...... **35 E10** 39 20N 119 5 E
Luan Xian, *China* .... **35 E10** 39 40N 118 40 E
Luancheng, *China* .... **34 F8** 37 53N 114 40 E
Luanda, *Angola* .... **52 F2** 8 50S 13 15 E
Luang, Thale, *Thailand* .... **39 J3** 7 30N 100 15 E
Luangwa, *Zambia* .... **55 F3** 15 35S 30 16 E
Luangwa →, *Zambia* .... **55 E3** 14 25S 30 25 E
Luangwa Valley, *Zambia* ... **55 E3** 13 30S 31 30 E
Luanne, *China* .... **35 D9** 40 55N 117 40 E
Luanping, *China* .... **35 D9** 40 53N 117 23 E
Luanshya, *Zambia* .... **55 E2** 13 3S 28 28 E
Luapula □, *Zambia* ...... **55 E2** 11 0S 29 0 E
Luapula →, *Africa* ...... **55 D2** 9 26S 28 33 E
Luarca, *Spain* **19 A2** 43 32N 6 32W
Luashi,
Dem. Rep. of the Congo . **55 E1** 10 50S 23 36 E
Luau, *Angola* .... **52 G4** 10 40S 22 10 E
Lubana, Ozero = Lubānas
Ezers, *Latvia* .... **9 H22** 56 45N 27 0 E
Lubānas Ezers, *Latvia* .... **9 H22** 56 45N 27 0 E
Lubang Is., *Phil.* .... **37 B6** 13 50N 120 12 E
Lubango, *Angola* .... **53 G2** 14 55S 13 30 E
Lubbock, *U.S.A.* **81 J4** 33 35N 101 51W
Lübeck, *Germany* .... **16 B6** 53 52N 10 40 E
Lubefu,
Dem. Rep. of the Congo . **54 C1** 4 47S 24 27 E
Lubefu →,
Dem. Rep. of the Congo . **54 C1** 4 10S 23 0 E
Lubero = Luofu,
Dem. Rep. of the Congo . **54 C2** 0 10S 29 15 E
Lubicon L., *Canada* **72 B5** 56 23N 115 56W
Lubilash →,
Dem. Rep. of the Congo . **52 F4** 6 2S 23 45 E
Lubin, *Poland* .... **16 C9** 51 24N 16 11 E
Lublin, *Poland* .... **17 C12** 51 12N 22 38 E
Lubnān, Jabal, *Lebanon* ... **47 B4** 33 45N 35 40 E
Lubny, *Ukraine* .... **26 D4** 50 3N 32 58 E
Lubongola,
Dem. Rep. of the Congo . **54 C2** 2 35S 27 50 E
Lubudi,
Dem. Rep. of the Congo . **52 F5** 9 57S 25 58 E
Lubudi →,
Dem. Rep. of the Congo . **55 D2** 9 0S 25 35 E
Lubuklinggau, *Indonesia* .. **36 E2** 3 15S 102 55 E
Lubuksikaping, *Indonesia* . **36 D2** 0 10N 100 15 E
Lubumbashi,
Dem. Rep. of the Congo . **55 E2** 11 40S 27 28 E
Lubunda,
Dem. Rep. of the Congo . **54 D2** 5 12S 26 41 E
Lubungu, *Zambia* .... **55 E2** 14 35S 26 24 E
Lubutu,
Dem. Rep. of the Congo . **54 C2** 0 45S 26 30 E
Luc An Chau, *Vietnam* .... **38 A5** 22 6N 104 43 E
Lucan, *Canada* **78 C3** 43 11N 81 24W
Lucania, Mt., *Canada* **68 B5** 61 1N 140 29W
Lucapa, *Angola* .... **52 F4** 8 25S 20 45 E
Lucas Channel, *Canada* ... **78 A3** 45 21N 81 45W
Lucca, *Italy* .... **20 C4** 43 50N 10 29 E
Luce Bay, *U.K.* **12 G4** 54 45N 4 48W
Lucea, *Jamaica* **88 C4** 18 25N 78 10W
Lucedale, *U.S.A.* **77 K1** 30 56N 88 35W
Lucena, *Phil.* .... **37 B6** 13 56N 121 37 E
Lucena, *Spain* **19 D3** 37 27N 4 31W
Lučenec, *Slovak Rep.* .... **17 D10** 48 18N 19 42 E
Lucerne = Luzern, *Switz.* .. **18 C8** 47 3N 8 18 E
Lucerne, *U.S.A.* **84 F4** 39 6N 122 48W
Lucerne Valley, *U.S.A.* **85 L10** 34 27N 116 57W
Lucero, *Mexico* **86 A3** 30 49N 106 30W
Lucheng, *China* .... **34 F7** 36 20N 113 11 E
Lucheringo →, *Mozam.* .. **55 E4** 11 43S 36 17 E
Lucia, *U.S.A.* **84 J5** 36 2N 121 33W
Lucinda, *Australia* .... **62 B4** 18 32S 146 20 E
Lucindale, *Australia* ...... **63 F3** 36 58S 140 26 E
Luckenwalde, *Germany* .... **16 B7** 52 5N 13 10 E
Lucknow, *Canada* **78 C3** 43 57N 81 31W
Lucknow, *India* .... **43 F9** 26 50N 81 0 E
Lüda = Dalian, *China* .... **35 E11** 38 50N 121 40 E
Lüderitz, *Namibia* .... **56 D2** 26 41S 15 8 E
Ludhiana, *India* .... **42 D6** 30 57N 75 56 E
Ludington, *U.S.A.* **76 D2** 43 57N 86 27W
Ludlow, *U.K.* **11 E5** 52 22N 2 42W
Ludlow, *Calif., U.S.A.* **85 L10** 34 43N 116 10W
Ludlow, *Pa., U.S.A.* **78 E6** 41 43N 78 56W
Ludlow, *Vt., U.S.A.* **79 C12** 43 24N 72 42W
Ludvika, *Sweden* .... **9 F16** 60 8N 15 14 E
Ludwigsburg, *Germany* .... **16 D5** 48 53N 9 11 E
Ludwigshafen, *Germany* ... **16 D5** 49 29N 8 26 E
Lueki,
Dem. Rep. of the Congo . **54 C2** 3 20S 25 48 E
Luena, *Angola* .... **53 G3** 12 13S 19 51 E
Luena,
Dem. Rep. of the Congo . **55 D2** 9 28S 25 43 E
Luena, *Zambia* .... **55 E3** 10 40S 30 25 E
Lüeyang, *China* .... **34 H4** 33 22N 106 10 E
Lufira →,
Dem. Rep. of the Congo . **55 D2** 9 30S 27 0 E
Lufkin, *U.S.A.* **81 K7** 31 21N 94 44W
Lufupa,
Dem. Rep. of the Congo . **55 E1** 10 37S 24 56 E
Luga, *Russia* .... **24 C4** 58 40N 29 55 E
Lugano, *Switz.* .... **18 C8** 46 1N 8 57 E
Lugansk = Luhansk, *Ukraine* **25 E6** 48 38N 39 15 E
Lugard's Falls, *Kenya* .... **54 C4** 3 6S 38 41 E
Lugela, *Mozam.* .... **55 F4** 16 25S 36 43 E
Lugenda →, *Mozam.* .... **55 E4** 11 25S 38 33 E
Lugh Ganana, *Somali Rep.* . **46 G3** 3 48N 42 34 E
Lugnaquilla, *Ireland* **13 D5** 52 58N 6 28W
Lugo, *Italy* .... **20 B4** 44 25N 11 54 E
Lugo, *Spain* **19 A2** 43 2N 7 35W
Lugoj, *Romania* .... **17 F11** 45 42N 21 57 E
Lugovoy, *Kazakstan* ...... **26 E8** 42 55N 72 43 E
Luhansk, *Ukraine* .... **25 E6** 48 38N 39 15 E
Luiana, *Angola* .... **56 B3** 17 25S 22 59 E
Luimneach = Limerick,
Ireland **13 D3** 52 40N 8 37W
Luing, *U.K.* **12 E3** 56 14N 5 39W
Luís Correia, *Brazil* **93 D10** 3 0S 41 35W
Luitpold Coast, *Antarctica* . **5 D1** 78 30S 32 0W
Luiza,
Dem. Rep. of the Congo . **52 F4** 7 40S 22 30 E
Luizi,
Dem. Rep. of the Congo . **54 D2** 6 0S 27 25 E
Luján, *Argentina* **94 C4** 34 45S 59 5W
Lukanga Swamp, *Zambia* .. **55 E2** 14 30S 27 40 E
Lukenie →,
Dem. Rep. of the Congo . **52 E3** 3 0S 18 50 E
Lukhisaral, *India* .... **43 G12** 25 11N 86 5 E
Lukolela,
Dem. Rep. of the Congo . **54 D1** 5 23S 24 32 E
Lukosi, *Zimbabwe* .... **55 F2** 18 30S 26 30 E
Łuków, *Poland* .... **17 C12** 51 55N 22 23 E
Lule älv →, *Sweden* .... **8 D19** 65 35N 22 10 E
Luleå, *Sweden* .... **8 D20** 65 35N 22 10 E
Lüleburgaz, *Turkey* ...... **21 D12** 41 23N 27 22 E
Luling, *U.S.A.* **81 L6** 29 41N 97 39W
Lulong, *China* .... **35 E10** 39 53N 118 51 E
Lulonga →,
Dem. Rep. of the Congo . **52 D3** 1 0N 18 10 E
Lulua →,
Dem. Rep. of the Congo . **52 E4** 4 30S 20 30 E
Luluabourg = Kananga,
Dem. Rep. of the Congo . **52 F4** 5 55S 22 18 E
Lumajang, *Indonesia* ..... **37 H15** 8 8S 113 13 E
Lumbala N'guimbo, *Angola* **53 G4** 14 18S 21 18 E
Lumberton, *U.S.A.* **77 H6** 34 37N 79 0W
Lumbwa, *Kenya* .... **54 C4** 0 12S 35 28 E
Lumsden, *Canada* **73 C8** 50 39N 104 52W
Lumsden, *N.Z.* .... **59 L2** 45 44S 168 27 E
Lumut, *Malaysia* .... **39 K3** 4 13N 100 37 E
Lumut, Tanjung, *Indonesia* . **36 E3** 3 50S 105 58 E
Luna, *India* .... **42 H3** 23 43N 69 16 E
Lunavada, *India* .... **42 H5** 23 8N 73 37 E
Lund, *Sweden* .... **9 J15** 55 44N 13 12 E
Lundazi, *Zambia* .... **55 E3** 12 20S 33 7 E
Lundi →, *Zimbabwe* .... **55 G3** 21 43S 32 34 E
Lundu, *Malaysia* .... **36 D3** 1 40N 109 50 E
Lundy, *U.K.* **11 F3** 51 10N 4 41W
Lune →, *U.K.* **10 C5** 54 0N 2 51W
Lüneburg, *Germany* ...... **16 B6** 53 15N 10 24 E
Lüneburg Heath =
Lüneburger Heide,
Germany .... **16 B6** 53 10N 10 12 E
Lüneburger Heide, *Germany* **16 B6** 53 10N 10 12 E
Lunenburg, *Canada* **71 D7** 44 22N 64 18W
Lunéville, *France* .... **18 B7** 48 36N 6 30 E
Lunga →, *Zambia* ...... **55 E2** 14 34S 26 25 E
Lunglei, *India* .... **41 H18** 22 55N 92 45 E
Luni, *India* .... **42 G5** 26 0N 73 6 E
Luni →, *India* .... **42 G4** 24 41N 71 14 E
Luninets = Luninyets,
Belarus .... **17 B14** 52 15N 26 50 E
Luning, *U.S.A.* **82 G4** 38 30N 118 11W
Luninyets, *Belarus* ...... **17 B14** 52 15N 26 50 E
Lunkaransar, *India* ...... **42 E5** 28 29N 73 44 E
Lunsemfwa →, *Zambia* .. **55 E3** 14 54S 30 12 E
Lunsemfwa Falls, *Zambia* .. **55 E2** 14 30S 29 6 E
Luo He →, *China* .... **34 G6** 34 35N 110 20 E
Luochuan, *China* .... **34 G5** 35 45N 109 26 E
Luofu,
Dem. Rep. of the Congo . **54 C2** 0 10S 29 15 E
Luohe, *China* .... **34 H8** 33 32N 114 2 E
Luonan, *China* .... **34 G6** 34 5N 110 10 E
Luoning, *China* .... **34 G6** 34 35N 111 40 E
Luoyang, *China* .... **34 G7** 34 40N 112 26 E
Luozigou, *China* .... **35 C16** 43 42N 130 18 E
Lupanshui, *China* .... **32 D5** 26 38N 104 48 E
Lupilichi, *Mozam.* .... **55 E4** 11 47S 35 13 E
Luque, *Paraguay* **94 B4** 25 19S 57 25W
Luray, *U.S.A.* **76 F6** 38 40N 78 28W
Lurgan, *U.K.* **13 B5** 54 28N 6 19W
Lusaka, *Zambia* .... **55 F2** 15 28S 28 16 E
Lusambo,
Dem. Rep. of the Congo . **54 C1** 4 58S 23 28 E
Lusangaye,
Dem. Rep. of the Congo . **54 C2** 4 54S 26 0 E
Luseland, *Canada* **73 C7** 52 5N 109 24W
Lushan, *China* .... **34 H7** 33 45N 112 55 E
Lushi, *China* .... **34 G6** 34 3N 111 3 E
Lushnja, *Albania* .... **21 D8** 40 55N 19 41 E
Lushoto, *Tanzania* .... **54 C4** 4 47S 38 20 E
Lüshun, *China* .... **35 E11** 38 45N 121 15 E
Lusk, *U.S.A.* **80 D2** 42 46N 104 27W
Lūt, Dasht-e, *Iran* .... **45 D8** 31 30N 58 0 E
Luta = Dalian, *China* ..... **35 E11** 38 50N 121 40 E
Lutherstadt Wittenberg,
Germany .... **16 C7** 51 53N 12 39 E
Luton, *U.K.* **11 F7** 51 53N 0 24W
Luton □, *U.K.* **11 F7** 51 53N 0 24W
Lutselke, *Canada* **73 A6** 62 24N 110 44W
Lutsk, *Ukraine* .... **17 C13** 50 50N 25 15 E
Lützow Holmbukta,
Antarctica .... **5 C4** 69 10S 37 30 E
Lutzputs, *S. Africa* ...... **56 D3** 28 3S 20 40 E
Luverne, *Ala., U.S.A.* **77 K2** 31 43N 86 16W
Luverne, *Minn., U.S.A.* ... **80 D6** 43 39N 96 13W
Luvua,
Dem. Rep. of the Congo . **55 D2** 8 48S 25 17 E
Luvua →,
Dem. Rep. of the Congo . **54 D2** 6 50S 27 30 E
Luwegu →, *Tanzania* .... **55 D4** 8 31S 37 23 E
Luwuk, *Indonesia* .... **37 E6** 0 56S 122 47 E
Luxembourg, *Lux.* .... **18 B7** 49 37N 6 9 E
Luxembourg □, *Belgium* ... **15 E5** 49 58N 5 30 E
Luxembourg ■, *Europe* ... **18 B7** 49 45N 6 0 E
Luxi, *China* .... **32 D4** 24 27N 98 36 E
Luxor = El Uqsur, *Egypt* .. **51 C12** 25 41N 32 38 E
Luyi, *China* .... **34 H8** 33 50N 115 35 E
Luza, *Russia* .... **24 B8** 60 39N 47 10 E
Luzern, *Switz.* .... **18 C8** 47 3N 8 18 E
Luzhou, *China* .... **32 D5** 28 52N 105 20 E
Luziânia, *Brazil* **93 G9** 16 20S 48 0W
Luzon, *Phil.* .... **37 A6** 16 0N 121 0 E
Lviv, *Ukraine* .... **17 D13** 49 50N 24 0 E
Lvov = Lviv, *Ukraine* .... **17 D13** 49 50N 24 0 E
Lyakhavichy, *Belarus* .... **17 B14** 53 2N 26 32 E
Lyakhovskiye, Ostrova,
Russia .... **27 B15** 73 40N 141 0 E
Lyal I., *Canada* **78 B3** 44 57N 81 24W
Lyallpur = Faisalabad,
Pakistan .... **42 D5** 31 30N 73 5 E
Lybster, *U.K.* **12 C5** 58 18N 3 15W
Lycksele, *Sweden* .... **8 D18** 64 38N 18 40 E
Lydda = Lod, *Israel* ..... **47 D3** 31 57N 34 54 E
Lydenburg, *S. Africa* ..... **57 D5** 25 10S 30 29 E
Lydia, *Turkey* .... **21 E13** 38 48N 28 19 E
Lyell, *N.Z.* .... **59 J4** 41 48S 172 4 E
Lyell I., *Canada* **72 C2** 52 40N 131 35W
Lyepyel, *Belarus* .... **24 D4** 54 50N 28 40 E
Lykens, *U.S.A.* **79 F8** 40 34N 76 42W
Lyman, *U.S.A.* **82 F8** 41 20N 110 18W
Lyme B., *U.K.* **11 G4** 50 42N 2 53W
Lyme Regis, *U.K.* **11 G5** 50 43N 2 57W
Lymington, *U.K.* **11 G6** 50 45N 1 32W
Łyna →, *Poland* .... **9 J19** 54 37N 21 14 E
Lynchburg, *U.S.A.* **76 G6** 37 25N 79 9W
Lynd →, *Australia* ..... **62 B3** 16 28S 143 18 E
Lynd Ra., *Australia* ..... **63 D4** 25 30S 149 20 E
Lynden, *Canada* **78 C4** 43 14N 80 9W
Lynden, *U.S.A.* **84 B4** 48 57N 122 27W
Lyndhurst, *Australia* ..... **63 E2** 30 15S 138 18 E
Lyndon →, *Australia* .... **61 D1** 23 29S 114 6 E
Lyndonville, *N.Y., U.S.A.* .. **78 C6** 43 20N 78 23W
Lyndonville, *Vt., U.S.A.* ... **79 B12** 44 31N 72 1W
Lyngen, *Norway* .... **8 B19** 69 45N 20 30 E
Lynher Reef, *Australia* ... **60 C3** 15 27S 121 55 E
Lynn, *U.S.A.* **79 D14** 42 28N 70 57W
Lynn Lake, *Canada* **73 B8** 56 51N 101 3W
Lynnwood, *U.S.A.* **84 C4** 47 49N 122 19W
Lynton, *U.K.* **11 F4** 51 13N 3 50W
Lyntupy, *Belarus* .... **9 J22** 55 4N 26 23 E
Lynx L., *Canada* **73 A7** 62 25N 106 15W
Lyon, *France* .... **18 D6** 45 46N 4 50 E
Lyonnais, *France* .... **18 D6** 45 45N 4 15 E
Lyons = Lyon, *France* .... **18 D6** 45 46N 4 50 E
Lyons, *Ga., U.S.A.* **77 J4** 32 12N 82 19W
Lyons, *Kans., U.S.A.* **80 F5** 38 21N 98 12W
Lyons, *N.Y., U.S.A.* **78 C8** 43 5N 77 0W
Lyons →, *Australia* ..... **61 E2** 25 2S 115 9 E
Lyons Falls, *U.S.A.* **79 C9** 43 37N 75 22W
Lys = Leie →, *Belgium* .. **15 C3** 51 2N 3 45 E
Lysva, *Russia* .... **24 C10** 58 7N 57 49 E
Lysychansk, *Ukraine* ..... **25 E6** 48 55N 38 30 E
Lytham St. Anne's, *U.K.* ... **10 D4** 53 45N 3 0W
Lyttelton, *N.Z.* .... **59 K4** 43 35S 172 44 E
Lytton, *Canada* **72 C4** 50 13N 121 31W
Lyubertsy, *Russia* .... **24 C6** 55 39N 37 50 E
Lyuboml, *Ukraine* .... **17 C13** 51 11N 24 4 E

M

M.R. Gomez, Presa, *Mexico* **87 B5** 26 10N 99 0W
Ma →, *Vietnam* .... **38 C5** 19 47N 105 56 E
Ma'adaba, *Jordan* .... **47 E4** 30 43N 35 47 E
Maamba, *Zambia* .... **56 B4** 17 17S 26 28 E
Ma'ān, *Jordan* .... **47 E4** 30 12N 35 44 E
Ma'ān □, *Jordan* .... **47 F5** 30 0N 36 0 E
Maanselkä, *Finland* ...... **8 C23** 63 52N 28 32 E
Ma'anshan, *China* .... **33 C6** 31 44N 118 29 E
Maarianhamina, *Finland* ... **9 F18** 60 5N 19 55 E
Ma'arrat an Nu'mān, *Syria* **44 C3** 35 43N 36 43 E
Maas →, *Neths.* .... **15 C4** 51 45N 4 32 E
Maaseik, *Belgium* .... **15 C5** 51 6N 5 45 E
Maasin, *Phil.* .... **37 B6** 10 8N 124 50 E
Maastricht, *Neths.* .... **18 A6** 50 50N 5 40 E
Maave, *Mozam.* .... **57 C5** 21 4S 34 47 E
Mabel L., *Canada* **72 C5** 50 35N 118 43W
Mabenge,
Dem. Rep. of the Congo . **54 B1** 4 15N 24 12 E
Maberly, *Canada* **79 B8** 44 50N 76 32W
Mablethorpe, *U.K.* .... **10 D8** 53 20N 0 15 E
Maboma,
Dem. Rep. of the Congo . **54 B2** 2 30N 28 10 E
Mac Bac, *Vietnam* .... **39 H6** 9 46N 106 7 E
Macachín, *Argentina* **94 D3** 37 10S 63 43W
Macaé, *Brazil* **95 A7** 22 20S 41 43W
McAlester, *U.S.A.* **81 H7** 34 56N 95 46W
McAllen, *U.S.A.* **81 M5** 26 12N 98 14W
MacAlpine L., *Canada* **68 B9** 66 40N 102 50W
Macamic, *Canada* **70 C4** 48 45N 79 0W
Macao = Macau, *China* ... **33 D6** 22 16N 113 35 E
Macapá, *Brazil* **93 C8** 0 5N 51 4W
McArthur →, *Australia* ... **62 B2** 15 54S 136 40 E
McArthur, Port, *Australia* .. **62 B2** 16 4S 136 23 E
Macau, *Brazil* **93 E11** 5 15S 36 40W
Macau, *China* .... **33 D6** 22 16N 113 35 E
McBride, *Canada* **72 C4** 53 20N 120 19W
McCall, *U.S.A.* **82 D5** 44 55N 116 6W
McCamey, *U.S.A.* **81 K3** 31 8N 102 14W
McCammon, *U.S.A.* **82 E7** 42 39N 112 12W
McCauley I., *Canada* **72 C2** 53 40N 130 15W
McCleary, *U.S.A.* **84 C3** 47 3N 123 16W
Macclenny, *U.S.A.* **77 K4** 30 17N 82 7W
Macclesfield, *U.K.* **10 D5** 53 15N 2 8W
M'Clintock Chan., *Canada* . **68 A9** 72 0N 102 0W
McClintock Ra., *Australia* .. **60 C4** 18 44S 127 38 E
McCloud, *U.S.A.* **82 F2** 41 15N 122 8W
McCluer I., *Australia* ..... **60 B5** 11 5S 133 0 E
McClure, *U.S.A.* **78 F7** 40 42N 77 19W
McClure, L., *U.S.A.* **84 H6** 37 35N 120 16W
M'Clure Str., *Canada* **4 B2** 75 0N 119 0W
McClusky, *U.S.A.* **80 B4** 47 29N 100 27W
McComb, *U.S.A.* **81 K9** 31 15N 90 27W

Mallaig

McConaughy, L., U.S.A. 80 E4 41 14N 101 40W
McCook, U.S.A. 80 E4 40 12N 100 38W
McCreary, Canada 73 C9 50 47N 99 29W
McCullough Mt., U.S.A. 85 K11 35 35N 115 13W
McCusker →, Canada 73 B7 55 32N 108 39W
McDame, Canada 72 B3 59 44N 128 59W
McDermitt, U.S.A. 82 F5 41 59N 117 43W
McDonald, U.S.A. 78 F4 40 22N 80 14W
Macdonald, L., Australia 60 D4 23 30S 129 0 E
McDonald Is., Ind. Oc. 3 G13 53 0S 73 0 E
MacDonnell Ranges, Australia 60 D5 23 40S 133 0 E
MacDowell L., Canada 70 B1 52 15N 92 45W
Macduff, U.K. 12 D6 57 40N 2 31W
Macedonia = Makedhonía □, Greece 21 D10 40 39N 22 0 E
Macedonia, U.S.A. 78 E3 41 19N 81 31W
Macedonia ■, Europe 21 D9 41 53N 21 40 E
Maceió, Brazil 93 E11 9 40S 35 41W
Macerata, Italy 20 C5 43 18N 13 27 E
McFarland, U.S.A. 85 K7 35 41N 119 14W
McFarlane →, Canada 73 B7 59 12N 107 58W
Macfarlane, L., Australia 63 E2 32 0S 136 40 E
McGehee, U.S.A. 81 J9 33 38N 91 24W
McGill, U.S.A. 82 G6 39 23N 114 47W
Macgillycuddy's Reeks, Ireland 13 E2 51 58N 9 45W
McGraw, U.S.A. 79 D8 42 36N 76 8W
McGregor, U.S.A. 80 D9 43 1N 91 11W
McGregor Ra., Australia 63 D3 27 0S 142 45 E
Mach, Pakistan 40 E5 29 50N 67 20 E
Māch Kowr, Iran 45 E9 25 48N 61 28 E
Machado = Jiparaná →, Brazil 92 E6 8 3S 62 52W
Machagai, Argentina 94 B3 26 56S 60 2W
Machakos, Kenya 54 C4 1 30S 37 15 E
Machala, Ecuador 92 D3 3 20S 79 57W
Machanga, Mozam. 57 C6 20 59S 35 0 E
Machattie, L., Australia 62 C2 24 50S 139 48 E
Machava, Mozam. 57 D5 25 54S 32 28 E
Machece, Mozam. 55 F4 19 15S 35 32 E
Machhu →, India 42 H4 23 6N 70 46 E
Machias, Maine, U.S.A. 77 C12 44 43N 67 28W
Machias, N.Y., U.S.A. 78 D6 42 25N 78 30W
Machichi →, Canada 73 B10 57 3N 92 6W
Machico, Madeira 22 D3 32 43N 16 44W
Machilipatnam, India 41 L12 16 12N 81 8 E
Machiques, Venezuela 92 A4 10 4N 72 34W
Machupicchu, Peru 92 F4 13 8S 72 30W
Machynlleth, U.K. 11 E4 52 35N 3 50W
McIlwraith Ra., Australia 62 A3 13 50S 143 20 E
McInnes L., Canada 73 C10 52 13N 93 45W
McIntosh, U.S.A. 80 C4 45 55N 101 21W
McIntosh L., Canada 73 B8 55 45N 105 0W
Macintosh Ra., Australia 61 E4 27 39S 125 32 E
Macintyre →, Australia 63 D5 28 37S 150 47 E
Mackay, Australia 62 C4 21 8S 149 11 E
Mackay, U.S.A. 82 E7 43 55N 113 37W
MacKay →, Canada 72 B6 57 10N 111 38W
Mackay, L., Australia 60 D4 22 30S 129 0 E
McKay Ra., Australia 60 D3 23 0S 122 30 E
McKeesport, U.S.A. 78 F5 40 21N 79 52W
McKellar, Canada 78 A5 45 30N 79 55W
McKenna, U.S.A. 84 D4 46 56N 122 33W
Mackenzie, Canada 72 B4 55 20N 123 5W
McKenzie, U.S.A. 77 G1 36 8N 88 31W
Mackenzie →, Australia 62 C4 23 38S 149 46 E
Mackenzie →, Canada 68 B6 69 10N 134 20W
McKenzie →, U.S.A. 82 D2 44 7N 123 6W
Mackenzie Bay, Canada 4 B1 69 0N 137 30W
Mackenzie City = Linden, Guyana 92 B7 6 0N 58 10W
Mackenzie Mts., Canada 68 B7 64 0N 130 0W
Mackinaw City, U.S.A. 76 C3 45 47N 84 44W
McKinlay, Australia 62 C3 21 16S 141 18 E
McKinlay →, Australia 62 C3 20 50S 141 28 E
McKinley, Mt., U.S.A. 68 B4 63 4N 151 0W
McKinley Sea, Arctic 4 A7 82 0N 0 0 E
McKinney, U.S.A. 81 J6 33 12N 96 37W
Mackinnon Road, Kenya 54 C4 3 40S 39 1 E
McKittrick, U.S.A. 85 K7 35 18N 119 37W
Macklin, Canada 73 C7 52 20N 109 56W
Macksville, Australia 63 E5 30 40S 152 56 E
McLaughlin, U.S.A. 80 C4 45 49N 100 49W
Maclean, Australia 63 D5 29 26S 153 16 E
McLean, U.S.A. 81 H4 35 14N 100 36W
McLeansboro, U.S.A. 80 F10 38 6N 88 32W
Maclear, S. Africa 57 E4 31 2S 28 23 E
Macleay →, Australia 63 E5 30 56S 153 0 E
McLennan, Canada 72 B5 55 42N 116 50W
McLeod →, Canada 72 C5 54 9N 115 44W
MacLeod, B., Canada 73 A7 62 53N 110 0W
McLeod, L., Australia 61 D1 24 9S 113 47 E
MacLeod Lake, Canada 72 C4 54 58N 123 0W
McLoughlin, Mt., U.S.A. 82 E2 42 27N 122 19W
McMechen, U.S.A. 78 G4 39 57N 80 44W
McMinnville, Oreg., U.S.A. 82 D2 45 13N 123 12W
McMinnville, Tenn., U.S.A. 77 H3 35 41N 85 46W
McMurdo Sd., Antarctica 5 D11 77 0S 170 0 E
McMurray = Fort McMurray, Canada 72 B6 56 44N 111 7W
McMurray, U.S.A. 84 B4 48 19N 122 14W
Macodoene, Mozam. 57 C6 23 32S 35 5 E
Macomb, U.S.A. 80 E9 40 27N 90 40W
Mâcon, France 18 C6 46 19N 4 50 E
Macon, Ga., U.S.A. 77 J4 32 51N 83 38W
Macon, Miss., U.S.A. 77 J1 33 7N 88 34W
Macon, Mo., U.S.A. 80 F8 39 44N 92 28W
Macossa, Mozam. 55 F3 17 55S 33 56 E
Macoun L., Canada 73 B8 56 32N 103 40W
Macovane, Mozam. 57 C6 21 30S 35 2 E
McPherson, U.S.A. 80 F6 38 22N 97 40W
McPherson Pk., U.S.A. 85 L7 34 53N 119 53W
McPherson Ra., Australia 63 D5 28 15S 153 15 E
Macquarie →, Australia 63 E4 30 5S 147 30 E
Macquarie Harbour, Australia 62 G4 42 15S 145 23 E
Macquarie Is., Pac. Oc. 64 N7 54 36S 158 55 E
MacRobertson Land, Antarctica 5 D6 71 0S 64 0 E
Macroom, Ireland 13 E3 51 54N 8 57W
MacTier, Canada 78 A5 45 9N 79 46W
Macubela, Mozam. 55 F4 16 53S 37 49 E
Macuiza, Mozam. 55 F3 18 7S 34 29 E
Macusani, Peru 92 F4 14 4S 70 29W
Macuse, Mozam. 55 F4 17 45S 37 10 E
Macuspana, Mexico 87 D6 17 46N 92 36W
Macusse, Angola 56 B3 17 48S 20 23 E
Madadeni, S. Africa 57 D5 27 43S 30 3 E
Madagascar ■, Africa 57 C8 20 0S 47 0 E
Madā'in Sālih, Si. Arabia 44 E3 26 46N 37 57 E
Madama, Niger 51 D8 22 0N 13 40 E
Madame I., Canada 71 C7 45 30N 60 58W
Madaripur, Bangla. 41 H17 23 19N 90 15 E
Madauk, Burma 41 L20 17 56N 96 52 E
Madawaska, Canada 78 A7 45 30N 78 0W
Madawaska →, Canada 78 A8 45 27N 76 21W
Madaya, Burma 41 H20 22 12N 96 10 E
Maddalena, Italy 20 D3 41 16N 9 23 E
Madeira, Atl. Oc. 22 D3 32 50N 17 0W
Madeira →, Brazil 92 D7 3 22S 58 45W
Madeleine, Îs. de la, Canada 71 C7 47 30N 61 40W
Madera, Mexico 86 B3 29 12N 108 7W
Madera, Calif., U.S.A. 84 J6 36 57N 120 3W
Madera, Pa., U.S.A. 78 F6 40 49N 78 26W
Madha, India 40 L9 18 0N 75 30 E
Madhavpur, India 42 J3 21 15N 69 58 E
Madhepura, India 43 F12 26 11N 86 23 E
Madhubani, India 43 F12 26 21N 86 7 E
Madhupur, India 43 G12 24 16N 86 39 E
Madhya Pradesh □, India 42 J8 22 50N 78 0 E
Madidi →, Bolivia 92 F5 12 32S 66 52W
Madikeri, India 40 N9 12 30N 75 45 E
Madill, U.S.A. 81 H6 34 6N 96 46W
Madimba, Dem. Rep. of the Congo 52 E3 4 58S 15 5 E
Ma'din, Syria 44 C3 35 45N 39 36 E
Madingou, Congo 52 E2 4 10S 13 33 E
Madirovalo, Madag. 57 B8 16 26S 46 32 E
Madison, Calif., U.S.A. 84 G5 38 41N 121 59W
Madison, Fla., U.S.A. 77 K4 30 28N 83 25W
Madison, Ind., U.S.A. 76 F3 38 44N 85 23W
Madison, Nebr., U.S.A. 80 E6 41 50N 97 27W
Madison, Ohio, U.S.A. 78 E3 41 46N 81 3W
Madison, S. Dak., U.S.A. 80 D6 44 0N 97 7W
Madison, Wis., U.S.A. 80 D10 43 4N 89 24W
Madison →, U.S.A. 82 D8 45 56N 111 31W
Madison Heights, U.S.A. 76 G6 37 25N 79 8W
Madisonville, Ky., U.S.A. 76 G2 37 20N 87 30W
Madisonville, Tex., U.S.A. 81 K7 30 57N 95 55W
Madista, Botswana 56 C4 21 15S 25 6 E
Madiun, Indonesia 37 G14 7 38S 111 32 E
Madoc, Canada 78 B7 44 30N 77 28W
Madona, Latvia 9 H22 56 53N 26 5 E
Madrakah, Ra's al, Oman 46 D6 19 0N 57 50 E
Madras = Chennai, India 40 N12 13 8N 80 19 E
Madras = Tamil Nadu □, India 40 P10 11 0N 77 0 E
Madras, U.S.A. 82 D3 44 38N 121 8W
Madre, L., Mexico 87 C5 25 0N 97 30W
Madre, Laguna, U.S.A. 81 M6 27 0N 97 30W
Madre, Sierra, Phil. 37 A6 17 0N 122 0 E
Madre de Dios →, Bolivia 92 F5 10 59S 66 8W
Madre de Dios, I., Chile 96 G1 50 20S 75 10W
Madre del Sur, Sierra, Mexico 87 D5 17 30N 100 0W
Madre Occidental, Sierra, Mexico 86 B3 27 0N 107 0W
Madre Oriental, Sierra, Mexico 86 C5 25 0N 100 0W
Madri, India 42 G5 24 16N 73 32 E
Madrid, Spain 19 B4 40 25N 3 45W
Madrid, U.S.A. 79 B9 44 45N 75 8W
Madura, Australia 61 F4 31 55S 127 0 E
Madura, Indonesia 37 G15 7 30S 114 0 E
Madura, Selat, Indonesia 37 G15 7 30S 113 20 E
Madurai, India 40 Q11 9 55N 78 10 E
Madurantakam, India 40 N11 12 30N 79 50 E
Mae Chan, Thailand 38 B2 20 9N 99 52 E
Mae Hong Son, Thailand 38 C2 19 16N 97 56 E
Mae Khlong →, Thailand 38 F3 13 24N 100 0 E
Mae Phrik, Thailand 38 D2 17 27N 99 7 E
Mae Ramat, Thailand 38 D2 16 58N 98 31 E
Mae Rim, Thailand 38 C2 18 54N 98 57 E
Mae Sot, Thailand 38 D2 16 43N 98 34 E
Mae Suai, Thailand 38 C2 19 39N 99 33 E
Mae Tha, Thailand 38 C2 18 28N 99 8 E
Maebashi, Japan 31 F9 36 24N 139 4 E
Maesteg, U.K. 11 F4 51 36N 3 40W
Maestra, Sierra, Cuba 88 B4 20 15N 77 0W
Maevatanana, Madag. 57 B8 16 56S 46 49 E
Mafeking = Mafikeng, S. Africa 56 D4 25 50S 25 38 E
Mafeking, Canada 73 C8 52 40N 101 10W
Mafeteng, Lesotho 56 D4 29 51S 27 15 E
Maffra, Australia 63 F4 37 53S 146 58 E
Mafia I., Tanzania 54 D4 7 45S 39 50 E
Mafikeng, S. Africa 56 D4 25 50S 25 38 E
Mafra, Brazil 95 B6 26 10S 49 55W
Mafra, Portugal 19 C1 38 55N 9 20W
Mafungabusi Plateau, Zimbabwe 55 F2 18 30S 29 8 E
Magadan, Russia 27 D16 59 38N 150 50 E
Magadi, Kenya 54 C4 1 54S 36 19 E
Magadi, L., Kenya 54 C4 1 54S 36 19 E
Magaliesburg, S. Africa 57 D4 26 0S 27 32 E
Magallanes, Estrecho de, Chile 96 G2 52 30S 75 0W
Magangué, Colombia 92 B4 9 14N 74 45W
Magdalen Is. = Madeleine, Îs. de la, Canada 71 C7 47 30N 61 40W
Magdalena, Argentina 94 D4 35 5S 57 30W
Magdalena, Bolivia 92 F6 13 13S 63 57W
Magdalena, Mexico 86 A2 30 50N 112 0W
Magdalena, U.S.A. 83 J10 34 7N 107 15W
Magdalena →, Colombia 92 A4 11 6N 74 51W
Magdalena →, Mexico 86 A2 30 40N 112 25W
Magdalena, B., Mexico 86 C2 24 30N 112 10W
Magdalena, Llano de la, Mexico 86 C2 25 0N 111 30W
Magdeburg, Germany 16 B6 52 7N 11 38 E
Magdelaine Cays, Australia 62 B5 16 33S 150 18 E
Magee, U.S.A. 81 K10 31 52N 89 44W
Magelang, Indonesia 37 G14 7 29S 110 13 E
Magellan's Str. = Magallanes, Estrecho de, Chile 96 G2 52 30S 75 0W
Magenta, L., Australia 61 F2 33 30S 119 2 E
Magerøya, Norway 8 A21 71 3N 25 40 E
Maggiore, Lago, Italy 18 D8 45 57N 8 39 E
Maghâgha, Egypt 51 C12 28 38N 30 50 E
Magherafelt, U.K. 13 B5 54 45N 6 37W
Maghreb, N. Afr. 50 B5 32 0N 4 0W
Magistralnyy, Russia 27 D11 56 16N 107 36 E
Magnetic Pole (North) = North Magnetic Pole, Canada 4 B2 77 58N 102 8W
Magnetic Pole (South) = South Magnetic Pole, Antarctica 5 C9 64 8S 138 8 E
Magnitogorsk, Russia 24 D10 53 27N 59 4 E
Magnolia, Ark., U.S.A. 81 J8 33 16N 93 14W
Magnolia, Miss., U.S.A. 81 K9 31 9N 90 28W
Magog, Canada 79 A12 45 18N 72 9W
Magoro, Uganda 54 B3 1 45N 34 12 E
Magosa = Famagusta, Cyprus 23 D12 35 8N 33 55 E
Magouládhes, Greece 23 A3 39 45N 19 42 E
Magoye, Zambia 55 F2 16 1S 27 30 E
Magozal, Mexico 87 C5 21 34N 97 59W
Magpie, L., Canada 71 B7 51 0N 64 41W
Magrath, Canada 72 D6 49 25N 112 50W
Maguarinho, C., Brazil 93 D9 0 15S 48 30W
Mağusa = Famagusta, Cyprus 23 D12 35 8N 33 55 E
Maguse L., Canada 73 A9 61 40N 95 10W
Maguse Pt., Canada 73 A10 61 20N 93 50W
Magvana, India 42 H3 23 13N 69 22 E
Magwe, Burma 41 J19 20 10N 95 0 E
Maha Sarakham, Thailand 38 D4 16 12N 103 16 E
Mahābād, Iran 44 B5 36 50N 45 45 E
Mahabharat Lekh, Nepal 43 E10 28 30N 82 0 E
Mahabo, Madag. 57 C7 20 23S 44 40 E
Mahadeo Hills, India 43 H8 22 20N 78 30 E
Mahaffey, U.S.A. 78 F6 40 53N 78 44W
Mahagi, Dem. Rep. of the Congo 54 B3 2 20N 31 0 E
Mahajamba →, Madag. 57 B8 15 33S 47 8 E
Mahajamba, Helodranon' i, Madag. 57 B8 15 24S 47 5 E
Mahajan, India 42 E5 28 48N 73 56 E
Mahajanga, Madag. 57 B8 15 40S 46 25 E
Mahajanga □, Madag. 57 B8 17 0S 47 0 E
Mahajilo →, Madag. 57 B8 19 42S 45 22 E
Mahakam →, Indonesia 36 E5 0 35S 117 17 E
Mahalapye, Botswana 56 C4 23 1S 26 51 E
Maḩallāt, Iran 45 C6 33 55N 50 30 E
Māhān, Iran 45 D8 30 5N 57 18 E
Mahan →, India 43 H10 23 30N 82 50 E
Mahanadi →, India 41 J15 20 20N 86 25 E
Mahananda →, India 43 G12 25 12N 87 52 E
Mahanoro, Madag. 57 B8 19 54S 48 48 E
Mahanoy City, U.S.A. 79 F8 40 49N 76 9W
Maharashtra □, India 40 J9 20 30N 75 30 E
Mahari Mts., Tanzania 54 D3 6 20S 30 0 E
Mahasham, W. →, Egypt 47 E3 30 15N 34 10 E
Mahasolo, Madag. 57 B8 19 7S 46 22 E
Mahattat ash Shīdīyah, Jordan 47 F4 29 55N 35 55 E
Mahattat 'Unayzah, Jordan 47 E4 30 30N 35 47 E
Mahaxay, Laos 38 D5 17 22N 105 12 E
Mahbubnagar, India 40 L10 16 45N 77 59 E
Maḩḑah, Oman 45 E7 24 24N 55 59 E
Mahdia, Tunisia 51 A8 35 28N 11 0 E
Mahe, India 43 C8 33 10N 78 32 E
Mahendragarh, India 42 E7 28 17N 76 14 E
Mahenge, Tanzania 55 D4 8 45S 36 41 E
Maheno, N.Z. 59 L3 45 10S 170 50 E
Mahesana, India 42 H5 23 39N 72 26 E
Maheshwar, India 42 H6 22 11N 75 35 E
Mahgawan, India 43 F8 26 29N 78 37 E
Mahi →, India 42 H5 22 15N 72 55 E
Mahia Pen., N.Z. 59 H6 39 9S 177 55 E
Mahilyow, Belarus 17 B16 53 55N 30 18 E
Mahmud Kot, Pakistan 42 D4 30 16N 71 0 E
Mahnomen, U.S.A. 80 B7 47 19N 95 58W
Mahoba, India 43 G8 25 15N 79 55 E
Mahón = Maó, Spain 22 B11 39 53N 4 16 E
Mahone Bay, Canada 71 D7 44 30N 64 20W
Mahopac, U.S.A. 79 E11 41 22N 73 45W
Mahuva, India 42 J4 21 5N 71 48 E
Mai-Ndombe, L., Dem. Rep. of the Congo 52 E3 2 0S 18 20 E
Mai-Sai, Thailand 38 B2 20 20N 99 55 E
Maicurú →, Brazil 93 D8 2 14S 54 17W
Maidan Khula, Afghan. 42 C3 33 36N 69 50 E
Maidenhead, U.K. 11 F7 51 31N 0 42W
Maidstone, Canada 73 C7 53 5N 109 20W
Maidstone, U.K. 11 F8 51 16N 0 32 E
Maiduguri, Nigeria 51 F8 12 0N 13 20 E
Maihar, India 43 G9 24 16N 80 45 E
Maijdi, Bangla. 41 H17 22 48N 91 10 E
Maikala Ra., India 41 J12 22 0N 81 0 E
Mailani, India 43 E9 28 17N 80 21 E
Mailsi, Pakistan 42 E5 29 48N 72 15 E
Main →, Germany 16 C5 50 0N 8 18 E
Main →, U.K. 13 B5 54 48N 6 18W
Maine, France 18 C3 48 20N 0 15W
Maine □, U.S.A. 77 C11 45 20N 69 0W
Maine →, Ireland 13 D2 52 9N 9 45W
Maingkwan, Burma 41 F20 26 15N 96 37 E
Mainit, L., Phil. 37 C7 9 31N 125 30 E
Mainland, Orkney, U.K. 12 C5 58 59N 3 8W
Mainland, Shet., U.K. 12 A7 60 15N 1 22W
Mainoru, Australia 62 A1 14 0S 134 6 E
Mainpuri, India 43 F8 27 18N 79 4 E
Maintirano, Madag. 57 B7 18 3S 44 1 E
Mainz, Germany 16 C5 50 1N 8 14 E
Maipú, Argentina 94 D4 36 52S 57 50W
Maiquetía, Venezuela 92 A5 10 36N 66 57W
Mairabari, India 41 F18 26 30N 92 22 E
Maisi, Cuba 89 B5 20 17N 74 9W
Maisi, Pta. de, Cuba 89 B5 20 10N 74 10W
Maitland, N.S.W., Australia 63 E5 32 33S 151 36 E
Maitland, S. Austral., Australia 63 E2 34 23S 137 40 E
Maitland →, Canada 78 C3 43 45N 81 43W
Maiz, Is. del, Nic. 88 D3 12 15N 83 4W
Maizuru, Japan 31 G7 35 25N 135 22 E
Majalengka, Indonesia 37 G13 6 50S 108 13 E
Majene, Indonesia 37 E5 3 38S 118 57 E
Majorca = Mallorca, Spain 22 B10 39 30N 3 0 E
Makale, Indonesia 37 E5 3 6S 119 51 E
Makamba, Burundi 54 C2 4 8S 29 49 E
Makarikari = Makgadikgadi Salt Pans, Botswana 56 C4 20 40S 25 45 E
Makarovo, Russia 27 D11 57 40N 107 45 E
Makasar = Ujung Pandang, Indonesia 37 F5 5 10S 119 20 E
Makasar, Selat, Indonesia 37 E5 1 0S 118 20 E
Makasar, Str. of = Makasar, Selat, Indonesia 37 E5 1 0S 118 20 E
Makat, Kazakstan 25 E9 47 39N 53 19 E
Makedhonía □, Greece 21 D10 40 39N 22 0 E
Makedonija = Macedonia ■, Europe 21 D9 41 53N 21 40 E
Makena, U.S.A. 74 H16 20 39N 156 27W
Makeyevka = Makiyivka, Ukraine 25 E6 48 0N 38 0 E
Makgadikgadi Salt Pans, Botswana 56 C4 20 40S 25 45 E
Makhachkala, Russia 25 F8 43 0N 47 30 E
Makhmūr, Iraq 44 C4 35 46N 43 35 E
Makian, Indonesia 37 D7 0 20N 127 20 E
Makindu, Kenya 54 C4 2 18S 37 50 E
Makinsk, Kazakstan 26 D8 52 37N 70 26 E
Makiyivka, Ukraine 25 E6 48 0N 38 0 E
Makkah, Si. Arabia 46 C2 21 30N 39 54 E
Makkovik, Canada 71 A8 55 10N 59 10W
Makó, Hungary 17 E11 46 14N 20 33 E
Makokou, Gabon 52 D2 0 40N 12 50 E
Makongo, Dem. Rep. of the Congo 54 B2 3 25N 26 17 E
Makoro, Dem. Rep. of the Congo 54 B2 3 10N 29 59 E
Makrai, India 40 H10 22 2N 77 0 E
Makran Coast Range, Pakistan 40 G4 25 40N 64 0 E
Makrana, India 42 F6 27 2N 74 46 E
Mákriyialos, Greece 23 D7 35 2N 25 59 E
Mākū, Iran 44 B5 39 15N 44 31 E
Makunda, Botswana 56 C3 22 30S 20 7 E
Makurazaki, Japan 31 J5 31 15N 130 20 E
Makurdi, Nigeria 50 G7 7 43N 8 35 E
Makūyeh, Iran 45 D7 28 7N 53 9 E
Makwassie, S. Africa 56 D4 27 17S 26 0 E
Mal B., Ireland 13 D2 52 50N 9 30W
Mala, Pta., Panama 88 E3 7 28N 80 2W
Malabar Coast, India 40 P9 11 0N 75 0 E
Malabo = Rey Malabo, Eq. Guin. 52 D1 3 45N 8 50 E
Malacca, Str. of, Indonesia 39 L3 3 0N 101 0 E
Malad City, U.S.A. 82 E7 42 12N 112 15W
Maladzyechna, Belarus 17 A14 54 20N 26 50 E
Málaga, Spain 19 D3 36 43N 4 23W
Malagarasi, Tanzania 54 D3 5 5S 30 50 E
Malagarasi →, Tanzania 54 D2 5 12S 29 47 E
Malagasy Rep. = Madagascar ■, Africa 57 C8 20 0S 47 0 E
Malahide, Ireland 13 C5 53 26N 6 9W
Malaimbandy, Madag. 57 C8 20 20S 45 36 E
Malakâl, Sudan 51 G12 9 33N 31 40 E
Malakand, Pakistan 42 B4 34 40N 71 55 E
Malakwal, Pakistan 42 C5 32 34N 73 13 E
Malamala, Indonesia 37 E6 3 21S 120 55 E
Malanda, Australia 62 B4 17 22S 145 35 E
Malang, Indonesia 37 G15 7 59S 112 45 E
Malangen, Norway 8 B18 69 24N 18 37 E
Malanje, Angola 52 F3 9 36S 16 17 E
Mälaren, Sweden 9 G17 59 30N 17 10 E
Malargüe, Argentina 94 D2 35 32S 69 30W
Malartic, Canada 70 C4 48 9N 78 9W
Malaryta, Belarus 17 C13 51 50N 24 3 E
Malatya, Turkey 25 G6 38 25N 38 20 E
Malawi ■, Africa 55 E3 11 55S 34 0 E
Malawi, L. = Nyasa, L., Africa 55 E3 12 30S 34 30 E
Malay Pen., Asia 39 J3 7 25N 100 0 E
Malaya Vishera, Russia 24 C5 58 55N 32 25 E
Malaybalay, Phil. 37 C7 8 5N 125 7 E
Malāyer, Iran 45 C6 34 19N 48 51 E
Malaysia ■, Asia 39 K4 5 0N 110 0 E
Malazgirt, Turkey 25 G7 39 10N 42 33 E
Malbon, Australia 62 C3 21 5S 140 17 E
Malbooma, Australia 63 E1 30 41S 134 11 E
Malbork, Poland 17 B10 54 3N 19 1 E
Malcolm, Australia 61 E3 28 51S 121 25 E
Malcolm, Pt., Australia 61 F3 33 48S 123 45 E
Maldah, India 43 G13 25 2N 88 9 E
Maldegem, Belgium 15 C3 51 14N 3 26 E
Malden, Mass., U.S.A. 79 D13 42 26N 71 4W
Malden, Mo., U.S.A. 81 G10 36 34N 89 57W
Malden I., Kiribati 65 H12 4 3S 155 1W
Maldives ■, Ind. Oc. 29 J11 5 0N 73 0 E
Maldonado, Uruguay 95 C5 34 59S 55 0W
Maldonado, Punta, Mexico 87 D5 16 19N 98 35W
Malé, Maldives 29 J11 4 0N 73 28 E
Malé Karpaty, Slovak Rep. 17 D9 48 30N 17 20 E
Maléa, Ákra, Greece 21 F10 36 28N 23 7 E
Malegaon, India 40 J9 20 30N 74 38 E
Malei, Mozam. 55 F4 17 12S 36 58 E
Malek Kandī, Iran 44 B5 37 9N 46 6 E
Malela, Dem. Rep. of the Congo 54 C2 4 22S 26 8 E
Malema, Mozam. 55 E4 14 57S 37 20 E
Máleme, Greece 23 D5 35 31N 23 49 E
Maleny, Australia 63 D5 26 45S 152 52 E
Malerkotla, India 42 D6 30 32N 75 58 E
Máles, Greece 23 D7 35 6N 25 35 E
Malgomaj, Sweden 8 D17 64 40N 16 30 E
Malha, Sudan 51 E11 15 8N 25 10 E
Malhargarh, India 42 G6 24 17N 74 59 E
Malheur →, U.S.A. 82 D5 44 4N 116 59W
Malheur L., U.S.A. 82 E4 43 20N 118 48W
Mali ■, Africa 50 E5 17 0N 3 0W
Mali →, Burma 41 G20 25 40N 97 40 E
Mali Kyun, Burma 38 F2 13 0N 98 20 E
Malibu, U.S.A. 85 L8 34 2N 118 41W
Maliku, Indonesia 37 E6 0 39S 123 16 E
Malili, Indonesia 37 E6 2 42S 121 6 E
Malimba, Mts., Dem. Rep. of the Congo 54 D2 7 30S 29 30 E
Malin Hd., Ireland 13 A4 55 23N 7 23W
Malin Pen., Ireland 13 A4 55 20N 7 17W
Malindi, Kenya 54 C5 3 12S 40 5 E
Malines = Mechelen, Belgium 15 C4 51 2N 4 29 E
Malino, Indonesia 37 D6 1 0N 121 0 E
Malinyi, Tanzania 55 D4 8 56S 36 0 E
Malita, Phil. 37 C7 6 19N 125 39 E
Maliwun, Burma 36 B1 10 17N 98 40 E
Maliya, India 42 H4 23 5N 70 46 E
Malkara, Turkey 21 D12 40 53N 26 53 E
Mallacoota Inlet, Australia 63 F4 37 34S 149 40 E
Mallaig, U.K. 12 D3 57 0N 5 50W

Mehr Jān

Mehr Jān, Iran 45 C7 33 50N 55 6 E
Mehrābād, Iran 44 B5 36 53N 47 55 E
Mehrān, Iran 44 C5 33 7N 46 10 E
Mehrīz, Iran 45 D7 31 35N 54 28 E
Mei Xian, China 34 G4 34 18N 107 55 E
Meiktila, Burma 41 J19 20 53N 95 54 E
Meissen, Germany 16 C7 51 9N 13 29 E
Meizhou, China 33 D6 24 16N 116 6 E
Meja, India 43 G10 25 9N 82 7 E
Mejillones, Chile 94 A1 23 10S 70 30W
Mekele, Ethiopia 46 E2 13 33N 39 30 E
Mekhtar, Pakistan 40 D6 30 30N 69 15 E
Meknès, Morocco 50 B4 33 57N 5 33W
Mekong →, Asia 39 H6 9 30N 106 15 E
Mekongga, Indonesia 37 E6 3 39S 121 15 E
Mekvari = Kür →, Azerbaijan 25 G8 39 29N 49 15 E
Melagiri Hills, India 40 N10 12 20N 77 30 E
Melaka, Malaysia 39 L4 2 15N 102 15 E
Melalap, Malaysia 36 C5 5 10N 116 5 E
Mélambes, Greece 23 D6 35 8N 24 40 E
Melanesia, Pac. Oc. 64 H7 4 0S 155 0 E
Melbourne, Australia 63 F4 37 50S 145 0 E
Melbourne, U.S.A. 77 L5 28 5N 80 37W
Melchor Múzquiz, Mexico 86 B4 27 50N 101 30W
Melchor Ocampo, Mexico 86 C4 24 52N 101 40W
Mélèzes →, Canada 69 C12 57 30N 71 0W
Mélèzes →, Qué., Canada 70 A5 57 40N 69 29W
Melfort, Canada 73 C8 52 50N 104 37W
Melfort, Zimbabwe 55 F3 18 0S 31 25 E
Melhus, Norway 8 E14 63 17N 10 18 E
Melilla, N. Afr. 19 E4 35 21N 2 57W
Melipilla, Chile 94 C1 33 42S 71 15W
Mélissa, Ákra, Greece 23 D6 35 6N 24 33 E
Melita, Canada 73 D8 49 15N 101 0W
Melitopol, Ukraine 25 E6 46 50N 35 22 E
Melk, Austria 16 D8 48 13N 15 20 E
Mellansel, Sweden 8 E18 63 25N 18 17 E
Mellen, U.S.A. 80 B9 46 20N 90 40W
Mellerud, Sweden 9 G15 58 41N 12 28 E
Mellette, U.S.A. 80 C5 45 9N 98 30W
Mellieha, Malta 23 D1 35 57N 14 21 E
Melo, Uruguay 95 C5 32 20S 54 10W
Melolo, Indonesia 37 F6 9 53S 120 40 E
Melouprey, Cambodia 38 F5 13 48N 105 16 E
Melrose, Australia 63 E4 32 42S 146 57 E
Melrose, U.K. 12 F6 55 36N 2 43W
Melrose, Minn., U.S.A. 80 C7 45 40N 94 49W
Melrose, N. Mex., U.S.A. 81 H3 34 26N 103 38W
Melstone, U.S.A. 82 C10 46 36N 107 52W
Melton Mowbray, U.K. 10 E7 52 47N 0 54W
Melun, France 18 B5 48 32N 2 39 E
Melville, Canada 73 C8 50 55N 102 50W
Melville, C., Australia 62 A3 14 11S 144 30 E
Melville, L., Canada 71 B8 53 30N 60 0W
Melville B., Australia 62 A2 12 0S 136 45 E
Melville I., Australia 60 B5 11 30S 131 0 E
Melville I., Canada 4 B2 75 30N 112 0W
Melville Pen., Canada 69 B11 68 0N 84 0W
Memba, Mozam. 55 E5 14 11S 40 30 E
Memboro, Indonesia 37 F5 9 30S 119 30 E
Memel = Klaipėda, Lithuania 9 J19 55 43N 21 10 E
Memel, S. Africa 57 D4 27 38S 29 36 E
Memmingen, Germany 16 E6 47 58N 10 10 E
Mempawah, Indonesia 36 D3 0 30N 109 5 E
Memphis, Mich., U.S.A. 78 D2 42 54N 82 46W
Memphis, Tenn., U.S.A. 81 H10 35 8N 90 3W
Memphis, Tex., U.S.A. 81 H4 34 44N 100 33W
Memphremagog, L., U.S.A. 79 B12 45 0N 72 12W
Mena, U.S.A. 81 H7 34 35N 94 15W
Menai Strait, U.K. 10 D3 53 11N 4 13W
Ménaka, Mali 50 E6 15 59N 2 18 E
Menan = Chao Phraya →, Thailand 38 F3 13 32N 100 36 E
Menarandra →, Madag. 57 D7 25 17S 44 30 E
Menard, U.S.A. 81 K5 30 55N 99 47W
Mendawai →, Indonesia 36 E4 3 30S 113 0 E
Mende, France 18 D5 44 31N 3 30 E
Mendez, Mexico 87 B5 25 7N 98 34W
Mendhar, India 43 C6 33 35N 74 10 E
Mendip Hills, U.K. 11 F5 51 17N 2 40W
Mendocino, U.S.A. 82 G2 39 19N 123 48W
Mendocino, C., U.S.A. 82 F1 40 26N 124 25W
Mendooran, Australia 63 E4 31 50S 149 6 E
Mendota, Calif., U.S.A. 84 J6 36 45N 120 23W
Mendota, Ill., U.S.A. 80 E10 41 33N 89 7W
Mendoza, Argentina 94 C2 32 50S 68 52W
Mendoza □, Argentina 94 C2 33 0S 69 0W
Mene Grande, Venezuela 92 B4 9 49N 70 56W
Menemen, Turkey 21 E12 38 34N 27 3 E
Menen, Belgium 15 D3 50 47N 3 7 E
Menggala, Indonesia 36 E3 4 30S 105 15 E
Mengjin, China 34 G7 34 55N 112 45 E
Mengyin, China 35 G9 35 40N 117 58 E
Mengzi, China 32 D5 23 20N 103 22 E
Menihek, Canada 71 B6 54 28N 56 36W
Menihek L., Canada 71 B6 54 0N 67 0W
Menin = Menen, Belgium 15 D3 50 47N 3 7 E
Menindee, Australia 63 E3 32 20S 142 25 E
Menindee L., Australia 63 E3 32 20S 142 25 E
Meningie, Australia 63 F2 35 50S 139 18 E
Menlo Park, U.S.A. 84 H4 37 27N 122 12W
Menominee, U.S.A. 76 C2 45 6N 87 37W
Menominee →, U.S.A. 76 C2 45 6N 87 36W
Menomonie, U.S.A. 80 C9 44 53N 91 55W
Menongue, Angola 53 G3 14 48S 17 52 E
Menorca, Spain 22 B11 40 0N 4 0 E
Mentakab, Malaysia 39 L4 3 29N 102 21 E
Mentawai, Kepulauan, Indonesia 36 E1 2 0S 99 0 E
Menton, France 18 E7 43 50N 7 29 E
Mentor, U.S.A. 78 E3 41 40N 81 21W
Menzelinsk, Russia 24 C9 55 47N 53 11 E
Menzies, Australia 61 E3 29 40S 121 2 E
Me'ona, Israel 47 B4 33 1N 35 15 E
Meoqui, Mexico 86 B3 28 17N 105 29W
Mepaco, Mozam. 55 F3 15 57S 30 48 E
Meppel, Neths. 15 B6 52 42N 6 12 E
Merabéllou, Kólpos, Greece 23 D7 35 10N 25 50 E
Merak, Indonesia 37 F12 6 10N 106 26 E
Meramangye, L., Australia 61 E5 28 25S 132 13 E
Meran = Merano, Italy 20 A4 46 40N 11 9 E
Merano, Italy 20 A4 46 40N 11 9 E
Merauke, Indonesia 37 F10 8 29S 140 24 E
Merbein, Australia 63 E3 34 10S 142 2 E
Merca, Somali Rep. 46 G3 1 48N 44 50 E
Merced, U.S.A. 84 H6 37 18N 120 29W
Merced →, U.S.A. 84 H6 37 21N 120 59W
Merced Pk., U.S.A. 84 H7 37 36N 119 24W
Mercedes, Buenos Aires, Argentina 94 C4 34 40S 59 30W
Mercedes, Corrientes, Argentina 94 B4 29 10S 58 5W
Mercedes, San Luis, Argentina 94 C2 33 40S 65 21W
Mercedes, Uruguay 94 C4 33 12S 58 0W
Mercedes, U.S.A. 81 M6 26 9N 97 55W
Merceditas, Chile 94 B1 28 20S 70 35W
Mercer, N.Z. 59 G5 37 16S 175 5 E
Mercer, U.S.A. 78 E4 41 14N 80 15W
Mercer Island, U.S.A. 84 C4 47 35N 122 15W
Mercury, U.S.A. 85 J11 36 40N 115 58W
Mercy C., Canada 69 B13 65 0N 63 30W
Mere, U.K. 11 F5 51 6N 2 16W
Meredith, C., Falk. Is. 96 G4 52 15S 60 40W
Meredith, L., U.S.A. 81 H4 35 43N 101 33W
Mergui, Burma 38 F2 12 26N 98 34 E
Mergui Arch. = Myeik Kyunzu, Burma 39 G1 11 30N 97 30 E
Mérida, Mexico 87 C7 20 58N 89 37W
Mérida, Spain 19 C2 38 55N 6 25W
Mérida, Venezuela 92 B4 8 24N 71 8W
Mérida, Cord. de, Venezuela 90 C3 9 0N 71 0W
Meriden, U.K. 11 E6 52 26N 1 38W
Meriden, U.S.A. 79 E12 41 32N 72 48W
Meridian, Calif., U.S.A. 84 F5 39 9N 121 55W
Meridian, Idaho, U.S.A. 82 E5 43 37N 116 24W
Meridian, Miss., U.S.A. 77 J1 32 22N 88 42W
Merimbula, Australia 63 F4 36 53S 149 54 E
Merinda, Australia 62 C4 20 2S 148 11 E
Meringur, Australia 63 E3 34 20S 141 19 E
Merir, Pac. Oc. 37 D8 4 10N 132 30 E
Merirumã, Brazil 93 C8 1 15N 54 50W
Merkel, U.S.A. 81 J5 32 28N 100 1W
Mermaid Reef, Australia 60 C2 17 6S 119 36 E
Merredin, Australia 61 F2 31 28S 118 18 E
Merrick, U.K. 12 F4 55 8N 4 28W
Merrickville, Canada 79 B9 44 55N 75 50W
Merrill, Oreg., U.S.A. 82 E3 42 1N 121 36W
Merrill, Wis., U.S.A. 80 C10 45 11N 89 41W
Merrimack →, U.S.A. 79 D14 42 49N 70 49W
Merriman, U.S.A. 80 D4 42 55N 101 42W
Merritt, Canada 72 C4 50 10N 120 45W
Merritt Island, U.S.A. 77 L5 28 21N 80 42W
Merriwa, Australia 63 E5 32 6S 150 22 E
Merry I., Canada 70 A4 55 29N 77 31W
Merryville, U.S.A. 81 K8 30 45N 93 33W
Mersch, Lux. 15 E6 49 44N 6 7 E
Mersea I., U.K. 11 F8 51 47N 0 58 E
Merseburg, Germany 16 C6 51 22N 11 59 E
Mersey →, U.K. 10 D4 53 25N 3 1W
Merseyside □, U.K. 10 D4 53 31N 3 2W
Mersin, Turkey 25 G5 36 51N 34 36 E
Mersing, Malaysia 39 L4 2 25N 103 50 E
Merta, India 42 F6 26 39N 74 4 E
Merta Road, India 42 F5 26 43N 73 55 E
Merthyr Tydfil, U.K. 11 F4 51 45N 3 22W
Merthyr Tydfil □, U.K. 11 F4 51 46N 3 21W
Mértola, Portugal 19 D2 37 40N 7 40W
Mertzon, U.S.A. 81 K4 31 16N 100 49W
Meru, Kenya 54 B4 0 3N 37 40 E
Meru, Tanzania 54 C4 3 15S 36 46 E
Mesa, U.S.A. 83 K8 33 25N 111 50W
Mesa Verde National Park, U.S.A. 83 H9 37 11N 108 29W
Mesanagrós, Greece 23 C9 36 1N 27 49 E
Mesaoría □, Cyprus 23 D12 35 12N 33 14 E
Mesarás, Kólpos, Greece 23 D6 35 6N 24 47 E
Mesgouez, L., Canada 70 B5 51 20N 75 0W
Meshed = Mashhad, Iran 45 B8 36 20N 59 35 E
Meshoppen, U.S.A. 79 E8 41 36N 76 3W
Mesilinka →, Canada 72 B4 56 6N 124 30W
Mesilla, U.S.A. 83 K10 32 16N 106 48W
Mesolóngion, Greece 21 E9 38 21N 21 28 E
Mesopotamia = Al Jazirah, Iraq 44 C5 33 30N 44 0 E
Mesopotamia, U.S.A. 78 E4 41 27N 80 57W
Mesquite, U.S.A. 83 H6 36 47N 114 6W
Messad, Algeria 50 B6 34 8N 3 30 E
Messalo →, Mozam. 55 E4 12 25S 39 15 E
Messina, Italy 20 E6 38 11N 15 34 E
Messina, S. Africa 57 C5 22 20S 30 5 E
Messina, Str. di, Italy 20 F6 38 15N 15 35 E
Messini, Greece 21 F10 37 4N 22 1 E
Messiniakós Kólpos, Greece 21 F10 36 45N 22 5 E
Messonghi, Greece 23 B3 39 29N 19 56 E
Mesta →, Bulgaria 21 D11 40 54N 24 49 E
Meta →, S. Amer. 92 B5 6 12N 67 28W
Meta Incognita Peninsula, Canada 69 B13 62 40N 68 0W
Metabetchouan, Canada 71 C5 48 26N 71 52W
Metairie, U.S.A. 81 L9 29 58N 90 10W
Metaline Falls, U.S.A. 82 B5 48 52N 117 22W
Metán, Argentina 94 B3 25 30S 65 0W
Metangula, Mozam. 55 E3 12 40S 34 50 E
Metengobalame, Mozam. 55 E3 14 49S 34 30 E
Methven, N.Z. 59 K3 43 38S 171 40 E
Metil, Mozam. 55 F4 16 24S 39 0 E
Metlakatla, U.S.A. 68 C6 55 8N 131 35W
Metropolis, U.S.A. 81 G10 37 9N 88 44W
Mettur Dam, India 40 P10 11 45N 77 45 E
Metu, Ethiopia 46 F2 8 18N 35 35 E
Metz, France 18 B7 49 8N 6 10 E
Meulaboh, Indonesia 36 D1 4 11N 96 3 E
Meureudu, Indonesia 36 C1 5 19N 96 10 E
Meuse →, Europe 18 A6 50 45N 5 41 E
Mexia, U.S.A. 81 K6 31 41N 96 29W
Mexiana, I., Brazil 93 D9 0 0 49 30W
Mexicali, Mexico 85 N11 32 40N 115 30W
Mexican Plateau, Mexico 66 G9 25 0N 104 0W
Mexican Water, U.S.A. 83 H9 36 57N 109 32W
México, Mexico 87 D5 19 20N 99 10W
Mexico, Maine, U.S.A. 79 B14 44 34N 70 33W
Mexico, Mo., U.S.A. 80 F9 39 10N 91 53W
Mexico, N.Y., U.S.A. 79 C8 43 28N 76 18W
México □, Mexico 87 D5 19 20N 99 10W
Mexico ■, Cent. Amer. 86 C4 25 0N 105 0W
Mexico, G. of, Cent. Amer. 87 C7 25 0N 90 0W
Mexico B., U.S.A. 79 C8 43 35N 76 20W
Meydān-e Naftūn, Iran 45 D6 31 56N 49 18 E
Meydani, Ra's-e, Iran 45 E8 25 24N 59 6 E
Meymaneh, Afghan. 40 B4 35 53N 64 38 E
Mezen, Russia 24 A7 65 50N 44 20 E
Mezen →, Russia 24 A7 65 44N 44 22 E
Mézenc, Mt., France 18 D6 44 54N 4 11 E
Mezhdurechenskiy, Russia 26 D7 59 36N 65 56 E
Mezőkövesd, Hungary 17 E11 47 49N 20 35 E
Mezőtúr, Hungary 17 E11 47 1N 20 41 E
Mezquital, Mexico 86 C4 23 29N 104 23W
Mgeta, Tanzania 55 D4 8 22S 36 6 E
Mhlaba Hills, Zimbabwe 55 F3 18 30S 30 30 E
Mhow, India 42 H6 22 33N 75 50 E
Miahuatlán, Mexico 87 D5 16 21N 96 36W
Miami, Fla., U.S.A. 77 N5 25 47N 80 11W
Miami, Okla., U.S.A. 81 G7 36 53N 94 53W
Miami, Tex., U.S.A. 81 H4 35 42N 100 38W
Miami Beach, U.S.A. 77 N5 25 47N 80 8W
Mian Xian, China 34 H4 33 10N 106 32 E
Mianchi, China 34 G6 34 48N 111 48 E
Miāndarreh, Iran 45 C7 35 37N 53 39 E
Miāndowāb, Iran 44 B5 37 0N 46 5 E
Miandrivazo, Madag. 57 B8 19 31S 45 29 E
Miāneh, Iran 44 B5 37 30N 47 40 E
Mianwali, Pakistan 42 C4 32 38N 71 28 E
Miarinarivo, Madag. 57 B8 18 57S 46 55 E
Miass, Russia 24 D11 54 59N 60 6 E
Michalovce, Slovak Rep. 17 D11 48 47N 21 58 E
Michigan □, U.S.A. 76 C3 44 0N 85 0W
Michigan, L., U.S.A. 76 D2 44 0N 87 0W
Michigan City, U.S.A. 76 E2 41 43N 86 54W
Michipicoten I., Canada 70 C2 47 40N 85 40W
Michoacan □, Mexico 86 D4 19 0N 102 0W
Michurin, Bulgaria 21 C12 42 9N 27 51 E
Michurinsk, Russia 24 D7 52 58N 40 27 E
Mico, Pta., Nic. 88 D3 12 0N 83 30W
Micronesia, Pac. Oc. 64 G7 11 0N 160 0 E
Micronesia, Federated States of ■, Pac. Oc. 64 G7 9 0N 150 0 E
Midai, Indonesia 39 L6 3 0N 107 47 E
Midale, Canada 73 D8 49 25N 103 20W
Middelburg, Neths. 15 C3 51 30N 3 36 E
Middelburg, Eastern Cape, S. Africa 56 E4 31 30S 25 0 E
Middelburg, Mpumalanga, S. Africa 57 D4 25 49S 29 28 E
Middelwit, S. Africa 56 C4 24 51S 27 3 E
Middle Alkali L., U.S.A. 82 F3 41 27N 120 5W
Middle Bass I., U.S.A. 78 E2 41 41N 82 49W
Middle East, Asia 28 F7 38 0N 40 0 E
Middle Fork Feather →, U.S.A. 84 F5 38 33N 121 30W
Middle I., Australia 61 F3 34 6S 123 11 E
Middle Loup →, U.S.A. 80 E5 41 17N 98 24W
Middle Sackville, Canada 71 D7 44 47N 63 42W
Middleboro, U.S.A. 79 E14 41 54N 70 55W
Middleburg, Fla., U.S.A. 77 K5 30 4N 81 52W
Middleburg, N.Y., U.S.A. 79 D10 42 36N 74 20W
Middleburg, Pa., U.S.A. 78 F7 40 47N 77 3W
Middlebury, U.S.A. 79 B11 44 1N 73 10W
Middlemount, Australia 62 C4 22 50S 148 40 E
Middleport, N.Y., U.S.A. 78 C6 43 13N 78 29W
Middleport, Ohio, U.S.A. 76 F4 39 0N 82 3W
Middlesboro, U.S.A. 77 G4 36 36N 83 43W
Middlesbrough, U.K. 10 C6 54 35N 1 13W
Middlesbrough □, U.K. 10 C6 54 28N 1 13W
Middlesex, Belize 88 C2 17 2N 88 31W
Middlesex, N.J., U.S.A. 79 F10 40 36N 74 30W
Middlesex, N.Y., U.S.A. 78 D7 42 42N 77 16W
Middleton, Australia 62 C3 22 22S 141 32 E
Middleton, Canada 71 D6 44 57N 65 4W
Middleton Cr. →, Australia 62 C3 22 35S 141 51 E
Middletown, U.K. 13 B5 54 17N 6 51W
Middletown, Calif., U.S.A. 84 G4 38 45N 122 37W
Middletown, Conn., U.S.A. 79 E12 41 34N 72 39W
Middletown, N.Y., U.S.A. 79 E10 41 27N 74 25W
Middletown, Ohio, U.S.A. 76 F3 39 31N 84 24W
Middletown, Pa., U.S.A. 79 F8 40 12N 76 44W
Midhurst, U.K. 11 G7 50 59N 0 44W
Midi, Canal du →, France 18 E4 43 45N 1 21 E
Midland, Canada 78 B5 44 45N 79 50W
Midland, Calif., U.S.A. 85 M12 33 52N 114 48W
Midland, Mich., U.S.A. 76 D3 43 37N 84 14W
Midland, Pa., U.S.A. 78 F4 40 39N 80 27W
Midland, Tex., U.S.A. 81 K3 32 0N 102 3W
Midlands □, Zimbabwe 55 F2 19 40S 29 0 E
Midleton, Ireland 13 E3 51 55N 8 10W
Midlothian, U.S.A. 81 J6 32 30N 97 0W
Midlothian □, U.K. 12 F5 55 51N 3 5W
Midongy, Tangorombohitr' i, Madag. 57 C8 23 30S 47 0 E
Midongy Atsimo, Madag. 57 C8 23 35S 47 1 E
Midway Is., Pac. Oc. 64 E10 28 13N 177 22W
Midway Wells, U.S.A. 85 N11 32 41N 115 7W
Midwest, U.S.A. 75 B9 42 0N 90 0W
Midwest, Wyo., U.S.A. 82 E10 43 25N 106 16W
Midwest City, U.S.A. 81 H6 35 27N 97 24W
Midyat, Turkey 44 B4 37 25N 41 23 E
Midžor, Bulgaria 21 C10 43 24N 22 40 E
Mie □, Japan 31 G8 34 30N 136 10 E
Międzychód, Poland 16 B8 52 35N 15 53 E
Międzyrzec Podlaski, Poland 17 C12 51 58N 22 45 E
Mielec, Poland 17 C11 50 15N 21 25 E
Mienga, Angola 56 B2 17 12S 19 48 E
Miercurea-Ciuc, Romania 17 E13 46 21N 25 48 E
Mieres, Spain 19 A3 43 18N 5 48W
Mifflintown, U.S.A. 78 F7 40 34N 77 24W
Mifraz Hefa, Israel 47 C4 32 52N 35 0 E
Miguel Alemán, Presa, Mexico 87 D5 18 15N 96 40W
Mihara, Japan 31 G6 34 24N 133 5 E
Mikese, Tanzania 54 D4 6 48S 37 55 E
Mikhaylovgrad = Montana, Bulgaria 21 C10 43 27N 23 16 E
Mikhaylovka, Russia 25 D7 50 3N 43 5 E
Mikkeli, Finland 9 F22 61 43N 27 15 E
Mikkwa →, Canada 72 B6 58 25N 114 46W
Míkonos, Greece 21 F11 37 30N 25 25 E
Mikumi, Tanzania 54 D4 7 26S 37 0 E
Mikun, Russia 24 B9 62 20N 50 0 E
Milaca, U.S.A. 80 C8 45 45N 93 39W
Milagro, Ecuador 92 D3 2 11S 79 36W
Milan = Milano, Italy 18 D8 45 28N 9 12 E
Milan, Mo., U.S.A. 80 E8 40 12N 93 7W
Milan, Tenn., U.S.A. 77 H1 35 55N 88 46W
Milang, Australia 63 F2 35 24S 138 58 E
Milange, Mozam. 55 F4 16 3S 35 45 E
Milano, Italy 18 D8 45 28N 9 12 E
Milâs, Turkey 21 F12 37 20N 27 50 E
Milatos, Greece 23 D7 35 18N 25 34 E
Milazzo, Italy 20 E6 38 13N 15 15 E
Milbank, U.S.A. 80 C6 45 13N 96 38W
Milbanke Sd., Canada 72 C3 52 15N 128 35W
Milden, Canada 73 C7 51 29N 107 32W
Mildenhall, U.K. 11 E8 52 21N 0 32 E
Mildmay, Canada 78 B3 44 3N 81 7W
Mildura, Australia 63 E3 34 13S 142 9 E
Miles, Australia 63 D5 26 40S 150 9 E
Miles City, U.S.A. 80 B2 46 25N 105 51W
Milestone, Canada 73 D8 49 59N 104 31W
Miletus, Turkey 21 F12 37 30N 27 18 E
Milford, Calif., U.S.A. 84 E6 40 10N 120 22W
Milford, Conn., U.S.A. 79 E11 41 14N 73 3W
Milford, Del., U.S.A. 76 F8 38 55N 75 26W
Milford, Mass., U.S.A. 79 D13 42 8N 71 31W
Milford, N.H., U.S.A. 79 D13 42 50N 71 39W
Milford, Pa., U.S.A. 79 E10 41 19N 74 48W
Milford, Utah, U.S.A. 83 G7 38 24N 113 1W
Milford Haven, U.K. 11 F2 51 42N 5 7W
Milford Sd., N.Z. 59 L1 44 41S 167 47 E
Milḥ, Baḥr al, Iraq 44 C4 32 40N 43 35 E
Milikapiti, Australia 60 B5 11 26S 130 40 E
Miling, Australia 61 F2 30 30S 116 17 E
Milk →, U.S.A. 82 B10 48 4N 106 19W
Milk River, Canada 72 D6 49 10N 112 5W
Mill I., Antarctica 5 C8 66 0S 101 30 E
Mill Valley, U.S.A. 84 H4 37 54N 122 32W
Millau, France 18 D5 44 8N 3 4 E
Millbridge, Canada 78 B7 44 41N 77 36W
Millbrook, Canada 78 B6 44 10N 78 29W
Millbrook, U.S.A. 79 E11 41 47N 73 42W
Mille Lacs, L. des, Canada 70 C1 48 45N 90 35W
Mille Lacs L., U.S.A. 80 B8 46 15N 93 39W
Milledgeville, U.S.A. 77 J4 33 5N 83 14W
Millen, U.S.A. 77 J5 32 48N 81 57W
Millennium I. = Caroline I., Kiribati 65 H12 9 15S 150 3W
Miller, U.S.A. 80 C5 44 31N 98 59W
Millersburg, Ohio, U.S.A. 78 F3 40 33N 81 55W
Millersburg, Pa., U.S.A. 78 F8 40 32N 76 58W
Millerton, U.S.A. 79 E11 41 57N 73 31W
Millerton L., U.S.A. 84 J7 37 1N 119 41W
Millheim, U.S.A. 78 F7 40 54N 77 29W
Millicent, Australia 63 F3 37 34S 140 21 E
Millington, U.S.A. 81 H10 35 20N 89 53W
Millinocket, U.S.A. 77 C11 45 39N 68 43W
Millmerran, Australia 63 D5 27 53S 151 16 E
Millom, U.K. 10 C4 54 13N 3 16W
Mills L., Canada 72 A5 61 30N 118 20W
Millsboro, U.S.A. 78 G5 40 0N 80 0W
Milltown Malbay, Ireland 13 D2 52 52N 9 24W
Millville, N.J., U.S.A. 76 F8 39 24N 75 2W
Millville, Pa., U.S.A. 79 E8 41 7N 76 32W
Millwood L., U.S.A. 81 J8 33 42N 93 58W
Milne →, Australia 62 C2 21 10S 137 33 E
Milo, U.S.A. 77 C11 45 15N 68 59W
Mílos, Greece 21 F11 36 44N 24 25 E
Milparinka, Australia 63 D3 29 46S 141 57 E
Milton, N.S., Canada 71 D7 44 4N 64 45W
Milton, Ont., Canada 78 C5 43 31N 79 53W
Milton, N.Z. 59 M2 46 7S 169 59 E
Milton, Calif., U.S.A. 84 G6 38 3N 120 51W
Milton, Fla., U.S.A. 77 K2 30 38N 87 3W
Milton, Pa., U.S.A. 78 F8 41 1N 76 51W
Milton, Vt., U.S.A. 79 B11 44 38N 73 7W
Milton-Freewater, U.S.A. 82 D4 45 56N 118 23W
Milton Keynes, U.K. 11 E7 52 1N 0 44W
Milton Keynes □, U.K. 11 E7 52 1N 0 44W
Milverton, Canada 78 C4 43 34N 80 55W
Milwaukee, U.S.A. 76 D2 43 2N 87 55W
Milwaukee Deep, Atl. Oc. 89 C6 19 50N 68 0W
Milwaukie, U.S.A. 84 E4 45 27N 122 38W
Min Jiang →, Fujian, China 33 D6 26 0N 119 35 E
Min Jiang →, Sichuan, China 32 D5 28 45N 104 40 E
Min Xian, China 34 G3 34 25N 104 5 E
Mina Pirquitas, Argentina 94 A2 22 40S 66 30W
Mīnā Su'ud, Si. Arabia 45 D6 28 45N 48 28 E
Mīnā'al Aḥmadī, Kuwait 45 D6 29 5N 48 10 E
Minago →, Canada 73 C9 54 33N 98 59W
Minaki, Canada 73 D10 49 59N 94 40W
Minamata, Japan 31 H5 32 10N 130 30 E
Minami-Tori-Shima, Pac. Oc. 64 E7 24 20N 153 58 E
Minas, Uruguay 95 C4 34 20S 55 10W
Minas, Sierra de las, Guatemala 88 C2 15 9N 89 31W
Minas Basin, Canada 71 C7 45 20N 64 12W
Minas Gerais □, Brazil 93 G9 18 50S 46 0W
Minatitlán, Mexico 87 D6 17 59N 94 31W
Minbu, Burma 41 J19 20 10N 94 52 E
Minchinabad, Pakistan 42 D5 30 10N 73 34 E
Mindanao, Phil. 37 C7 8 0N 125 0 E
Mindanao Sea = Bohol Sea, Phil. 37 C6 9 0N 124 0 E
Mindanao Trench, Pac. Oc. 37 B7 12 0N 126 6 E
Minden, Canada 78 B6 44 55N 78 43W
Minden, Germany 16 B5 52 17N 8 55 E
Minden, La., U.S.A. 81 J8 32 37N 93 17W
Minden, Nev., U.S.A. 84 G7 38 57N 119 46W
Mindiptana, Indonesia 37 F10 5 55S 140 22 E
Mindoro, Phil. 37 B6 13 0N 121 0 E
Mindoro Str., Phil. 37 B6 12 30N 120 30 E
Mine, Japan 31 G5 34 12N 131 7 E
Minehead, U.K. 11 F4 51 12N 3 29W
Mineola, N.Y., U.S.A. 79 F11 40 45N 73 39W
Mineola, Tex., U.S.A. 81 J7 32 40N 95 29W
Mineral King, U.S.A. 84 J8 36 27N 118 36W
Mineral Wells, U.S.A. 81 J5 32 48N 98 7W
Minersville, U.S.A. 79 F8 40 41N 76 16W
Minerva, U.S.A. 78 F3 40 44N 81 6W
Minetto, U.S.A. 79 C8 43 24N 76 28W
Mingäçevir Su Anbarı, Azerbaijan 25 F8 40 57N 46 50 E
Mingan, Canada 71 B7 50 20N 64 0W
Mingechaurskoye Vdkhr. = Mingäçevir Su Anbarı, Azerbaijan 25 F8 40 57N 46 50 E
Mingela, Australia 62 B4 19 52S 146 38 E
Mingenew, Australia 61 E2 29 12S 115 21 E
Mingera Cr. →, Australia 62 C2 20 38S 137 45 E
Mingin, Burma 41 H19 22 50N 94 30 E
Mingo Junction, U.S.A. 78 F4 40 19N 80 37W
Mingyuegue, China 35 C15 43 2N 128 50 E
Minho = Miño →, Spain 19 A2 41 52N 8 40W
Minho, Portugal 19 B1 41 25N 8 20W
Minidoka, U.S.A. 82 E7 42 45N 113 29W

N

North Knife

New Smyrna Beach, U.S.A. **77 L5** 29 1N 80 56W
New South Wales □, Australia **63 E4** 33 0S 146 0 E
New Town, U.S.A. **80 B3** 47 59N 102 30W
New Tredegar, U.K. **11 F4** 51 44N 3 16W
New Ulm, U.S.A. **80 C7** 44 19N 94 28W
New Waterford, Canada **71 C7** 46 13N 60 4W
New Westminster, Canada **84 A4** 49 13N 122 55W
New York, U.S.A. **79 F11** 40 45N 74 0W
New York □, U.S.A. **79 D9** 43 0N 75 0W
New York Mts., U.S.A. **83 J6** 35 0N 115 20W
New Zealand ■, Oceania **59 J6** 40 0S 176 0 E
Newaj →, India **42 G7** 24 24N 76 49 E
Newala, Tanzania **55 E4** 10 58S 39 18 E
Newark, Del., U.S.A. **76 F8** 39 41N 75 46W
Newark, N.J., U.S.A. **79 F10** 40 44N 74 10W
Newark, N.Y., U.S.A. **78 C7** 43 3N 77 6W
Newark, Ohio, U.S.A. **78 F2** 40 3N 82 24W
Newark-on-Trent, U.K. **10 D7** 53 5N 0 48W
Newark Valley, U.S.A. **79 D8** 42 14N 76 11W
Newberg, U.S.A. **82 D2** 45 18N 122 58W
Newberry, Mich., U.S.A. **76 B3** 46 21N 85 30W
Newberry, S.C., U.S.A. **77 H5** 34 17N 81 37W
Newberry Springs, U.S.A. **85 L10** 34 50N 116 41W
Newboro L., Canada **79 B8** 44 38N 76 20W
Newbridge = Droichead Nua, Ireland **13 C5** 53 11N 6 48W
Newburgh, Canada **78 B8** 44 19N 76 52W
Newburgh, U.S.A. **79 E10** 41 30N 74 1W
Newbury, U.K. **11 F6** 51 24N 1 20W
Newbury, N.H., U.S.A. **79 B12** 43 19N 72 3W
Newbury, Vt., U.S.A. **79 B12** 44 5N 72 4W
Newburyport, U.S.A. **77 D10** 42 49N 70 53W
Newcastle, Australia **63 E5** 33 0S 151 46 E
Newcastle, N.B., Canada **71 C6** 47 1N 65 38W
Newcastle, Ont., Canada **70 D4** 43 55N 78 35W
Newcastle, S. Africa **57 D4** 27 45S 29 58 E
Newcastle, U.K. **13 B6** 54 13N 5 54W
Newcastle, Calif., U.S.A. **84 G5** 38 53N 121 8W
Newcastle, Wyo., U.S.A. **80 D2** 43 50N 104 11W
Newcastle Emlyn, U.K. **11 E3** 52 2N 4 28W
Newcastle Ra., Australia **60 C5** 15 45S 130 15 E
Newcastle-under-Lyme, U.K. **10 D5** 53 1N 2 14W
Newcastle-upon-Tyne, U.K. **10 C6** 54 58N 1 36W
Newcastle Waters, Australia **62 B1** 17 30S 133 28 E
Newcastle West, Ireland **13 D2** 52 27N 9 3W
Newcomb, U.S.A. **79 C10** 43 58N 74 10W
Newcomerstown, U.S.A. **78 F3** 40 16N 81 36W
Newdegate, Australia **61 F2** 33 6S 119 0 E
Newell, Australia **62 B4** 16 20S 145 16 E
Newell, U.S.A. **80 C3** 44 43N 103 25W
Newfane, U.S.A. **78 C6** 43 17N 78 43W
Newfield, U.S.A. **79 D8** 42 18N 76 33W
Newfound L., U.S.A. **79 C13** 43 40N 71 47W
Newfoundland, N. Amer. **66 E14** 49 0N 55 0W
Newfoundland, U.S.A. **79 E9** 41 18N 75 19W
Newfoundland □, Canada **71 B8** 53 0N 58 0W
Newhall, U.S.A. **85 L8** 34 23N 118 32W
Newhaven, U.K. **11 G8** 50 47N 0 3 E
Newkirk, U.S.A. **81 G6** 36 53N 97 3W
Newlyn, U.K. **11 G2** 50 6N 5 34W
Newman, Australia **60 D2** 23 18S 119 45 E
Newman, U.S.A. **84 H5** 37 19N 121 1W
Newmarket, Canada **78 B5** 44 3N 79 28W
Newmarket, Ireland **13 D2** 52 13N 9 0W
Newmarket, U.K. **11 E8** 52 15N 0 25 E
Newmarket, N.H., U.S.A. **79 C14** 43 4N 70 56W
Newmarket, N.H., U.S.A. **79 C14** 43 5N 70 56W
Newnan, U.S.A. **77 J3** 33 23N 84 48W
Newport, Ireland **13 C2** 53 53N 9 33W
Newport, I. of W., U.K. **11 G6** 50 42N 1 17W
Newport, Newp., U.K. **11 F5** 51 35N 3 0W
Newport, Ark., U.S.A. **81 H9** 35 37N 91 16W
Newport, Ky., U.S.A. **76 F3** 39 5N 84 30W
Newport, N.H., U.S.A. **79 C12** 43 22N 72 10W
Newport, N.Y., U.S.A. **79 C9** 43 11N 75 1W
Newport, Oreg., U.S.A. **82 D1** 44 39N 124 3W
Newport, Pa., U.S.A. **78 F7** 40 29N 77 8W
Newport, R.I., U.S.A. **79 E13** 41 29N 71 19W
Newport, Tenn., U.S.A. **77 H4** 35 58N 83 11W
Newport, Vt., U.S.A. **79 B12** 44 56N 72 13W
Newport, Wash., U.S.A. **82 B5** 48 11N 117 3W
Newport □, U.K. **11 F4** 51 33N 3 1W
Newport Beach, U.S.A. **85 M9** 33 37N 117 56W
Newport News, U.S.A. **76 G7** 36 59N 76 25W
Newport Pagnell, U.K. **11 E7** 52 5N 0 43W
Newquay, U.K. **11 G2** 50 25N 5 6W
Newry, U.K. **13 B5** 54 11N 6 21W
Newton, Ill., U.S.A. **80 F10** 38 59N 88 10W
Newton, Iowa, U.S.A. **80 E8** 41 42N 93 3W
Newton, Kans., U.S.A. **81 F6** 38 3N 97 21W
Newton, Mass., U.S.A. **79 D13** 42 21N 71 12W
Newton, Miss., U.S.A. **81 J10** 32 19N 89 10W
Newton, N.C., U.S.A. **77 H5** 35 40N 81 13W
Newton, N.J., U.S.A. **79 E10** 41 3N 74 45W
Newton, Tex., U.S.A. **81 K8** 30 51N 93 46W
Newton Abbot, U.K. **11 G4** 50 32N 3 37W
Newton Aycliffe, U.K. **10 C6** 54 37N 1 34W
Newton Falls, U.S.A. **78 E4** 41 11N 80 59W
Newton Stewart, U.K. **12 G4** 54 57N 4 30W
Newtonmore, U.K. **12 D4** 57 4N 4 8W
Newtown, U.K. **11 E4** 52 31N 3 19W
Newtownabbey, U.K. **13 B6** 54 40N 5 56W
Newtownards, U.K. **13 B6** 54 36N 5 42W
Newtownbarry = Bunclody, Ireland **13 D5** 52 39N 6 40W
Newtownstewart, U.K. **13 B4** 54 43N 7 23W
Newville, U.S.A. **78 F7** 40 10N 77 24W
Neya, Russia **24 C7** 58 21N 43 49 E
Neyrīz, Iran **45 D7** 29 15N 54 19 E
Neyshābūr, Iran **45 B8** 36 10N 58 50 E
Nezhin = Nizhyn, Ukraine **25 D5** 51 5N 31 55 E
Nezperce, U.S.A. **82 C5** 46 14N 116 14W
Ngabang, Indonesia **36 D3** 0 23N 109 55 E
Ngabordamlu, Tanjung, Indonesia **37 F8** 6 56S 134 11 E
N'Gage, Angola **52 F3** 7 46S 15 16 E
Ngami Depression, Botswana **56 C3** 20 30S 22 46 E
Ngamo, Zimbabwe **55 F2** 19 3S 27 32 E
Nganglong Kangri, China **41 C12** 33 0N 81 0 E
Ngao, Thailand **38 C2** 18 46N 99 59 E
Ngaoundéré, Cameroon **52 C2** 7 15N 13 35 E
Ngapara, N.Z. **59 L3** 44 57S 170 46 E
Ngara, Tanzania **54 C3** 2 29S 30 40 E
Ngawi, Indonesia **37 G14** 7 24S 111 26 E
Ngoma, Malawi **55 E3** 13 8S 33 45 E
Ngomahura, Zimbabwe **55 G3** 20 26S 30 43 E
Ngomba, Tanzania **55 D3** 8 20S 32 53 E
Ngoring Hu, China **32 C4** 34 55N 97 5 E
Ngorongoro, Tanzania **54 C4** 3 11S 35 32 E
Ngozi, Burundi **54 C2** 2 54S 29 50 E
Ngudu, Tanzania **54 C3** 2 58S 33 25 E
Nguigmi, Niger **51 F8** 14 20N 13 20 E
Nguiu, Australia **60 B5** 11 46S 130 38 E
Ngukurr, Australia **62 A1** 14 44S 134 44 E
Ngulu Atoll, Pac. Oc. **37 C9** 8 0N 137 30 E
Ngunga, Tanzania **54 C3** 3 37S 33 37 E
Nguru, Nigeria **51 F8** 12 56N 10 29 E
Nguru Mts., Tanzania **54 D4** 6 0S 37 30 E
Nha Trang, Vietnam **39 F7** 12 16N 109 10 E
Nhacoongo, Mozam. **57 C6** 24 18S 35 14 E
Nhamaabué, Mozam. **55 F4** 17 25S 35 5 E
Nhamundá →, Brazil **93 D7** 2 12S 56 41W
Nhangutazi, L., Mozam. **57 C5** 24 0S 34 30 E
Nhill, Australia **63 F3** 36 18S 141 40 E
Nhulunbuy, Australia **62 A2** 12 10S 137 20 E
Nia-nia, Dem. Rep. of the Congo **54 B2** 1 30N 27 40 E
Niagara Falls, Canada **78 C5** 43 7N 79 5W
Niagara Falls, U.S.A. **78 C6** 43 5N 79 4W
Niagara-on-the-Lake, Canada **78 C5** 43 15N 79 4W
Niah, Malaysia **36 D4** 3 58N 113 46 E
Niamey, Niger **50 F6** 13 27N 2 6 E
Niangara, Dem. Rep. of the Congo **54 B2** 3 42N 27 50 E
Niantic, U.S.A. **79 E12** 41 20N 72 11W
Nias, Indonesia **36 D1** 1 0N 97 30 E
Niassa □, Mozam. **55 E4** 13 30S 36 0 E
Nibāk, Si. Arabia **45 E7** 24 25N 50 50 E
Nicaragua ■, Cent. Amer. **88 D2** 11 40N 85 30W
Nicaragua, L. de, Nic. **88 D2** 12 0N 85 30W
Nicastro, Italy **20 E7** 38 59N 16 19 E
Nice, France **18 E7** 43 42N 7 14 E
Niceville, U.S.A. **77 K2** 30 31N 86 30W
Nichicun, L., Canada **71 B5** 53 5N 71 0W
Nichinan, Japan **31 J5** 31 38N 131 23 E
Nicholás, Canal, W. Indies **88 B3** 23 30N 80 5W
Nicholasville, U.S.A. **76 G3** 37 53N 84 34W
Nichols, U.S.A. **79 D8** 42 1N 76 22W
Nicholson, Australia **60 C4** 18 2S 128 54 E
Nicholson, U.S.A. **79 E9** 41 37N 75 47W
Nicholson →, Australia **62 B2** 17 31S 139 36 E
Nicholson L., Canada **73 A8** 62 40N 102 40W
Nicholson Ra., Australia **61 E2** 27 15S 116 45 E
Nicholville, U.S.A. **79 B10** 44 41N 74 39W
Nicobar Is., Ind. Oc. **28 J13** 9 0N 93 0 E
Nicola, Canada **72 C4** 50 12N 120 40W
Nicolls Town, Bahamas **88 A4** 25 8N 78 0W
Nicosia, Cyprus **23 D12** 35 10N 33 25 E
Nicoya, Costa Rica **88 D2** 10 9N 85 27W
Nicoya, G. de, Costa Rica **88 E3** 10 0N 85 0W
Nicoya, Pen. de, Costa Rica **88 E2** 9 45N 85 40W
Nidd →, U.K. **10 D6** 53 59N 1 23W
Niedersachsen □, Germany **16 B5** 52 50N 9 0 E
Niekerkshoop, S. Africa **56 D3** 29 19S 22 51 E
Niemba, Dem. Rep. of the Congo **54 D2** 5 58S 28 24 E
Niemen = Neman →, Lithuania **9 J20** 55 25N 21 10 E
Nienburg, Germany **16 B5** 52 39N 9 13 E
Nieu Bethesda, S. Africa **56 E3** 31 51S 24 34 E
Nieuw Amsterdam, Surinam **93 B7** 5 53N 55 5W
Nieuw Nickerie, Surinam **93 B7** 6 0N 56 59W
Nieuwoudtville, S. Africa **56 E2** 31 23S 19 7 E
Nieuwpoort, Belgium **15 C2** 51 8N 2 45 E
Nieves, Pico de las, Canary Is. **22 G4** 27 57N 15 35W
Niğde, Turkey **25 G5** 37 58N 34 40 E
Nigel, S. Africa **57 D4** 26 27S 28 25 E
Niger ■, W. Afr. **50 E7** 17 30N 10 0 E
Niger →, W. Afr. **50 G7** 5 33N 6 33 E
Nigeria ■, W. Afr. **50 G7** 8 30N 8 0 E
Nighasin, India **43 E9** 28 14N 80 52 E
Nightcaps, N.Z. **59 L2** 45 57S 168 2 E
Nii-Jima, Japan **31 G9** 34 20N 139 15 E
Niigata, Japan **30 F9** 37 58N 139 0 E
Niigata □, Japan **31 F9** 37 15N 138 45 E
Niihama, Japan **31 H6** 33 55N 133 16 E
Niihau, U.S.A. **74 H14** 21 54N 160 9W
Niimi, Japan **31 G6** 34 59N 133 28 E
Niitsu, Japan **30 F9** 37 48N 139 7 E
Nijil, Jordan **47 E4** 30 32N 35 33 E
Nijkerk, Neths. **15 B5** 52 13N 5 30 E
Nijmegen, Neths. **15 C5** 51 50N 5 52 E
Nijverdal, Neths. **15 B6** 52 22N 6 28 E
Nik Pey, Iran **45 B6** 36 50N 48 10 E
Nikiniki, Indonesia **37 F6** 9 49S 124 30 E
Nikkō, Japan **31 F9** 36 45N 139 35 E
Nikolayev = Mykolayiv, Ukraine **25 E5** 46 58N 32 0 E
Nikolayevsk, Russia **25 E8** 50 0N 45 35 E
Nikolayevsk-na-Amur, Russia **27 D15** 53 8N 140 44 E
Nikolskoye, Russia **27 D17** 55 12N 166 0 E
Nikopol, Ukraine **25 E5** 47 35N 34 25 E
Nikshahr, Iran **45 E9** 26 15N 60 10 E
Nikšić, Montenegro, Yug. **21 C8** 42 50N 18 57 E
Nîl, Nahr en →, Africa **51 B12** 30 10N 31 6 E
Nîl el Abyad →, Sudan **51 E12** 15 38N 32 31 E
Nîl el Azraq →, Sudan **51 E12** 15 38N 32 31 E
Nila, Indonesia **37 F7** 6 44S 129 31 E
Niland, U.S.A. **85 M11** 33 14N 115 31W
Nile = Nîl, Nahr en →, Africa **51 B12** 30 10N 31 6 E
Niles, Mich., U.S.A. **76 E2** 41 50N 86 15W
Niles, Ohio, U.S.A. **78 E4** 41 11N 80 46W
Nim Ka Thana, India **42 F6** 27 44N 75 48 E
Nimach, India **42 G6** 24 30N 74 56 E
Nimbahera, India **42 G6** 24 37N 74 45 E
Nîmes, France **18 E6** 43 50N 4 23 E
Nimfaíon, Ákra = Pínnes, Ákra, Greece **21 D11** 40 5N 24 20 E
Nimmitabel, Australia **63 F4** 36 29S 149 15 E
Ninawá, Iraq **44 B4** 36 25N 43 10 E
Nindigully, Australia **63 D4** 28 21S 148 50 E
Nineveh = Ninawá, Iraq **44 B4** 36 25N 43 10 E
Ning Xian, China **34 G4** 35 30N 107 58 E
Ning'an, China **35 B15** 44 22N 129 20 E
Ningbo, China **33 D7** 29 51N 121 28 E
Ningcheng, China **35 D10** 41 32N 119 53 E
Ningjin, China **34 F8** 37 35N 114 57 E
Ningjing Shan, China **32 D4** 30 0N 98 20 E
Ningling, China **34 G8** 34 25N 115 22 E
Ningpo = Ningbo, China **33 D7** 29 51N 121 28 E
Ningqiang, China **34 H4** 32 47N 106 15 E
Ningshan, China **34 H5** 33 21N 108 21 E
Ningsia Hui A.R. = Ningxia Huizu Zizhiqu □, China **34 F4** 38 0N 106 0 E
Ningwu, China **34 E7** 39 0N 112 18 E
Ningxia Huizu Zizhiqu □, China **34 F4** 38 0N 106 0 E
Ningyang, China **34 G9** 35 47N 116 45 E
Ninh Giang, Vietnam **38 B6** 20 44N 106 24 E
Ninh Hoa, Vietnam **38 F7** 12 30N 109 7 E
Ninh Ma, Vietnam **38 F7** 12 48N 109 21 E
Ninove, Belgium **15 D4** 50 51N 4 2 E
Nioaque, Brazil **95 A4** 21 5S 55 50W
Niobrara, U.S.A. **80 D6** 42 45N 98 2W
Niobrara →, U.S.A. **80 D6** 42 46N 98 3W
Nioro du Sahel, Mali **50 E4** 15 15N 9 30W
Niort, France **18 C3** 46 19N 0 29W
Nipawin, Canada **73 C8** 53 20N 104 0W
Nipigon, Canada **70 C2** 49 0N 88 17W
Nipigon, L., Canada **70 C2** 49 50N 88 30W
Nipishish L., Canada **71 B7** 54 12N 60 45W
Nipissing, L., Canada **70 C4** 46 20N 80 0W
Nipomo, U.S.A. **85 K6** 35 3N 120 29W
Nipton, U.S.A. **85 K11** 35 28N 115 16W
Niquelândia, Brazil **93 F9** 14 33S 48 23W
Nīr, Iran **44 B5** 38 2N 47 59 E
Nirasaki, Japan **31 G9** 35 42N 138 27 E
Nirmal, India **40 K11** 19 3N 78 20 E
Nirmali, India **43 F12** 26 20N 86 35 E
Niš, Serbia, Yug. **21 C9** 43 19N 21 58 E
Nişab, Si. Arabia **44 D5** 29 11N 44 43 E
Nişāb, Yemen **46 E4** 14 25N 46 29 E
Nishinomiya, Japan **31 G7** 34 45N 135 20 E
Nishino'omote, Japan **31 J5** 30 43N 130 59 E
Nishiwaki, Japan **31 G7** 34 59N 134 58 E
Niskibi →, Canada **70 A2** 56 29N 88 9W
Nisqually →, U.S.A. **84 C4** 47 6N 122 42W
Nissáki, Greece **23 A3** 39 43N 19 52 E
Nissum Bredning, Denmark **9 H13** 56 40N 8 20 E
Nistru = Dnister →, Europe **17 E16** 46 18N 30 17 E
Nisutlin →, Canada **72 A2** 60 14N 132 34W
Nitchequon, Canada **71 B5** 53 10N 70 58W
Niterói, Brazil **95 A7** 22 52S 43 0W
Nith →, Canada **78 C4** 43 12N 80 23W
Nith →, U.K. **12 F5** 55 14N 3 33W
Nitra, Slovak Rep. **17 D10** 48 19N 18 4 E
Nitra →, Slovak Rep. **17 E10** 47 46N 18 10 E
Niuafo'ou, Tonga **59 B11** 15 30S 175 58W
Niue, Cook Is. **65 J11** 19 2S 169 54W
Niut, Indonesia **36 D4** 0 55N 110 6 E
Niuzhuang, China **35 D12** 40 58N 122 28 E
Nivala, Finland **8 E21** 63 56N 24 57 E
Nivelles, Belgium **15 D4** 50 35N 4 20 E
Nivernais, France **18 C5** 47 15N 3 30 E
Niwas, India **43 H9** 23 3N 80 26 E
Nixon, U.S.A. **81 L6** 29 16N 97 46W
Nizamabad, India **40 K11** 18 45N 78 7 E
Nizamghat, India **41 E19** 28 20N 95 45 E
Nizhne Kolymsk, Russia **27 C17** 68 34N 160 55 E
Nizhnekamsk, Russia **24 C9** 55 38N 51 49 E
Nizhneudinsk, Russia **27 D10** 54 54N 99 3 E
Nizhnevartovsk, Russia **26 C8** 60 56N 76 38 E
Nizhniy Novgorod, Russia **24 C7** 56 20N 44 0 E
Nizhniy Tagil, Russia **24 C10** 57 55N 59 57 E
Nizhyn, Ukraine **25 D5** 51 5N 31 55 E
Nizip, Turkey **44 B3** 37 5N 37 50 E
Nízké Tatry, Slovak Rep. **17 D10** 48 55N 19 30 E
Njakwa, Malawi **55 E3** 11 1S 33 56 E
Njanji, Zambia **55 E3** 14 25S 31 46 E
Njinjo, Tanzania **55 D4** 8 48S 38 54 E
Njombe, Tanzania **55 D3** 9 20S 34 50 E
Njombe →, Tanzania **54 D4** 6 56S 35 6 E
Nkana, Zambia **55 E2** 12 50S 28 8 E
Nkayi, Zimbabwe **55 F2** 19 41S 29 20 E
Nkhotakota, Malawi **55 E3** 12 56S 34 15 E
Nkongsamba, Cameroon **52 D1** 4 55N 9 55 E
Nkurenkuru, Namibia **56 B2** 17 42S 18 32 E
Nmai →, Burma **41 G20** 25 30N 97 25 E
Noakhali = Maijdi, Bangla. **41 H17** 22 48N 91 10 E
Nobel, Canada **78 A4** 45 25N 80 6W
Nobeoka, Japan **31 H5** 32 36N 131 41 E
Noblesville, U.S.A. **76 E3** 40 3N 86 1W
Nocera Inferiore, Italy **20 D6** 40 44N 14 38 E
Nocona, U.S.A. **81 J6** 33 47N 97 44W
Noda, Japan **31 G9** 35 56N 139 52 E
Nogales, Mexico **86 A2** 31 20N 110 56W
Nogales, U.S.A. **83 L8** 31 20N 110 56W
Nōgata, Japan **31 H5** 33 48N 130 44 E
Noggerup, Australia **61 F2** 33 32S 116 5 E
Noginsk, Russia **27 C10** 64 30N 90 50 E
Nogoa →, Australia **62 C4** 23 40S 147 55 E
Nogoyá, Argentina **94 C4** 32 24S 59 48W
Nohar, India **42 E6** 29 11N 74 49 E
Nohta, India **43 H8** 23 40N 79 34 E
Noire, Mts., France **18 B2** 48 7N 3 28W
Noirmoutier, Î. de, France **18 C2** 46 58N 2 10W
Nojane, Botswana **56 C3** 23 15S 20 14 E
Nojima-Zaki, Japan **31 G9** 34 54N 139 53 E
Nok Kundi, Pakistan **40 E3** 28 50N 62 45 E
Nokaneng, Botswana **56 B3** 19 40S 22 17 E
Nokia, Finland **9 F20** 61 30N 23 30 E
Nokomis, Canada **73 C8** 51 35N 105 0W
Nokomis L., Canada **73 B8** 57 0N 103 0W
Nola, C.A.R. **52 D3** 3 35N 16 4 E
Noma Omuramba →, Namibia **56 B3** 18 52S 20 53 E
Nombre de Dios, Panama **88 E4** 9 34N 79 28W
Nome, U.S.A. **68 B3** 64 30N 165 25W
Nomo-Zaki, Japan **31 H4** 32 35N 129 44 E
Nonacho L., Canada **73 A7** 61 42N 109 40W
Nonda, Australia **62 C3** 20 40S 142 28 E
Nong Chang, Thailand **38 E2** 15 23N 99 51 E
Nong Het, Laos **38 C4** 19 29N 103 59 E
Nong Khai, Thailand **38 D4** 17 50N 102 46 E
Nong'an, China **35 B13** 44 25N 125 5 E
Nongoma, S. Africa **57 D5** 27 58S 31 35 E
Nonoava, Mexico **86 B3** 27 28N 106 44W
Nonoava →, Mexico **86 B3** 27 29N 106 45W
Nonthaburi, Thailand **38 F3** 13 51N 100 34 E
Noonamah, Australia **60 B5** 12 40S 131 4 E
Noord Brabant □, Neths. **15 C5** 51 40N 5 0 E
Noord Holland □, Neths. **15 B4** 52 30N 4 45 E
Noordbeveland, Neths. **15 C3** 51 35N 3 50 E
Noordoostpolder, Neths. **15 B5** 52 45N 5 45 E
Noordwijk, Neths. **15 B4** 52 14N 4 26 E
Nootka I., Canada **72 D3** 49 32N 126 42W
Nopiming Prov. Park, Canada **73 C9** 50 30N 95 37W
Noralee, Canada **72 C3** 53 59N 126 26W
Noranda = Rouyn-Noranda, Canada **70 C4** 48 20N 79 0W
Norco, U.S.A. **85 M9** 33 56N 117 33W
Nord-Kivu □, Dem. Rep. of the Congo **54 C2** 1 0S 29 0 E
Nord-Ostsee-Kanal, Germany **16 A5** 54 12N 9 32 E
Nordaustlandet, Svalbard **4 B9** 79 14N 23 0 E
Nordegg, Canada **72 C5** 52 29N 116 5W
Norderney, Germany **16 B4** 53 42N 7 9 E
Norderstedt, Germany **16 B5** 53 42N 10 1 E
Nordfjord, Norway **9 F11** 61 55N 5 30 E
Nordfriesische Inseln, Germany **16 A5** 54 40N 8 20 E
Nordhausen, Germany **16 C6** 51 30N 10 47 E
Norðoyar, Færoe Is. **8 E9** 62 17N 6 35W
Nordkapp, Norway **8 A21** 71 10N 25 50 E
Nordkapp, Svalbard **4 A9** 80 31N 20 0 E
Nordkinn = Kinnarodden, Norway **6 A11** 71 8N 27 40 E
Nordkinn-halvøya, Norway **8 A22** 70 55N 27 40 E
Nordrhein-Westfalen □, Germany **16 C4** 51 45N 7 30 E
Nordvik, Russia **27 B12** 74 2N 111 32 E
Nore →, Ireland **13 D4** 52 25N 6 58W
Norfolk, Nebr., U.S.A. **80 D6** 42 2N 97 25W
Norfolk, Va., U.S.A. **76 G7** 36 51N 76 17W
Norfolk □, U.K. **11 E8** 52 39N 0 54 E
Norfolk I., Pac. Oc. **64 K8** 28 58S 168 3 E
Norfork L., U.S.A. **81 G8** 36 15N 92 14W
Norilsk, Russia **27 C9** 69 20N 88 6 E
Norma, Mt., Australia **62 C3** 20 55S 140 42 E
Normal, U.S.A. **80 E10** 40 31N 88 59W
Norman, U.S.A. **81 H6** 35 13N 97 26W
Norman →, Australia **62 B3** 19 18S 141 51 E
Norman Wells, Canada **68 B7** 65 17N 126 51W
Normanby →, Australia **62 A3** 14 23S 144 10 E
Normandie, France **18 B4** 48 45N 0 10 E
Normandin, Canada **70 C5** 48 49N 72 31W
Normandy = Normandie, France **18 B4** 48 45N 0 10 E
Normanhurst, Mt., Australia **61 E3** 25 4S 122 30 E
Normanton, Australia **62 B3** 17 40S 141 10 E
Normétal, Canada **70 C4** 49 0N 79 22W
Norquay, Canada **73 C8** 51 53N 102 5W
Norquinco, Argentina **96 E2** 41 51S 70 55W
Norrbotten □, Sweden **8 C19** 66 30N 22 30 E
Norris Point, Canada **71 C8** 49 31N 57 53W
Norristown, U.S.A. **79 F9** 40 7N 75 21W
Norrköping, Sweden **9 G17** 58 37N 16 11 E
Norrland, Sweden **9 E16** 62 15N 15 45 E
Norrtälje, Sweden **9 G18** 59 46N 18 42 E
Norseman, Australia **61 F3** 32 8S 121 43 E
Norsk, Russia **27 D14** 52 30N 130 5 E
Norte, Pta. del, Canary Is. **22 G2** 27 51N 17 57W
Norte, Serra do, Brazil **92** 11 20S 59 0W
North, C., Canada **71 C7** 47 2N 60 20W
North Adams, U.S.A. **79 D11** 42 42N 73 7W
North Arm, Canada **72 A5** 62 0N 114 30W
North Augusta, U.S.A. **77 J5** 33 30N 81 59W
North Ayrshire □, U.K. **12 F4** 55 45N 4 44W
North Bass I., U.S.A. **78 E2** 41 43N 82 49W
North Battleford, Canada **73 C7** 52 50N 108 17W
North Bay, Canada **70 C4** 46 20N 79 30W
North Belcher Is., Canada **70 A4** 56 50N 79 50W
North Bend, Oreg., U.S.A. **82 E1** 43 24N 124 14W
North Bend, Pa., U.S.A. **78 E7** 41 20N 77 42W
North Bend, Wash., U.S.A. **84 C5** 47 30N 121 47W
North Bennington, U.S.A. **79 D11** 42 56N 73 15W
North Berwick, U.K. **12 E6** 56 4N 2 42W
North Berwick, U.S.A. **79 C14** 43 18N 70 44W
North C., Canada **71 C7** 47 5N 64 0W
North C., N.Z. **59 F4** 34 23S 173 4 E
North Canadian →, U.S.A. **81 H7** 35 16N 95 31W
North Canton, U.S.A. **78 F3** 40 53N 81 24W
North Cape = Nordkapp, Norway **8 A21** 71 10N 25 50 E
North Cape = Nordkapp, Svalbard **4 A9** 80 31N 20 0 E
North Caribou L., Canada **70 B1** 52 50N 90 40W
North Carolina □, U.S.A. **77 H6** 35 30N 80 0W
North Cascades National Park, U.S.A. **82 B3** 48 45N 121 10W
North Channel, Canada **70 C3** 46 0N 83 0W
North Channel, U.K. **12 F3** 55 13N 5 52W
North Charleston, U.S.A. **77 J6** 32 53N 79 58W
North Chicago, U.S.A. **76 D2** 42 19N 87 51W
North Creek, U.S.A. **79 C11** 43 41N 73 59W
North Dakota □, U.S.A. **80 B5** 47 30N 100 15W
North Downs, U.K. **11 F8** 51 19N 0 21 E
North East, U.S.A. **78 D5** 42 13N 79 50W
North East Frontier Agency = Arunachal Pradesh □, India **41 F19** 28 0N 95 0 E
North East Lincolnshire □, U.K. **10 D7** 53 34N 0 2W
North Eastern □, Kenya **54 B5** 1 30N 40 0 E
North Esk →, U.K. **12 E6** 56 46N 2 24W
North European Plain, Europe **6 E10** 55 0N 25 0 E
North Foreland, U.K. **11 F9** 51 22N 1 28 E
North Fork, U.S.A. **84 H7** 37 14N 119 21W
North Fork American →, U.S.A. **84 G5** 38 57N 120 59W
North Fork Feather →, U.S.A. **84 F5** 38 33N 121 30W
North Fork Grand →, U.S.A. **80 C3** 45 47N 102 16W
North Fork Red →, U.S.A. **81 H5** 34 24N 99 14W
North Frisian Is. = Nordfriesische Inseln, Germany **16 A5** 54 40N 8 20 E
North Gower, Canada **79 A9** 45 8N 75 43W
North Hd., Australia **61 F1** 30 14S 114 59 E
North Henik L., Canada **73 A9** 61 45N 97 40W
North Highlands, U.S.A. **84 G5** 38 40N 121 23W
North Horr, Kenya **54 B4** 3 20N 37 8 E
North I., Kenya **54 B4** 4 5N 36 5 E
North I., N.Z. **59 H5** 38 0S 175 0 E
North Kingsville, U.S.A. **78 E4** 41 54N 80 42W
North Knife →, Canada **73 B10** 58 53N 94 45W

O

Oshkosh

Ofotfjorden, Norway 8 B17 68 27N 17 0 E
Ōfunato, Japan 30 E10 39 4N 141 43 E
Oga, Japan 30 E9 39 55N 139 50 E
Oga-Hantō, Japan 30 E9 39 58N 139 47 E
Ogaden, Ethiopia 46 F3 7 30N 45 30 E
Ōgaki, Japan 31 G8 35 21N 136 37 E
Ogallala, U.S.A. 80 E4 41 8N 101 43W
Ogasawara Gunto, Pac. Oc. 28 G18 27 0N 142 0 E
Ogbomosho, Nigeria 50 G6 8 1N 4 11 E
Ogden, U.S.A. 82 F7 41 13N 111 58W
Ogdensburg, U.S.A. 79 B9 44 42N 75 30W
Ogeechee →, U.S.A. 77 K5 31 50N 81 3W
Ogilby, U.S.A. 85 N12 32 49N 114 50W
Oglio →, Italy 20 B4 45 2N 10 39 E
Ogmore, Australia 62 C4 22 37S 149 35 E
Ogoki, Canada 70 B2 51 38N 85 58W
Ogoki →, Canada 70 B2 51 38N 85 57W
Ogoki L., Canada 70 B2 50 50N 87 10W
Ogoki Res., Canada 70 B2 50 45N 88 15W
Ogooué →, Gabon 52 E1 1 0S 9 0 E
Ogowe = Ogooué →, Gabon 52 E1 1 0S 9 0 E
Ogre, Latvia 9 H21 56 49N 24 36 E
Ogurchinskiy, Ostrov, Turkmenistan 45 B7 38 55N 53 2 E
Ohai, N.Z. 59 L2 45 55S 168 0 E
Ohakune, N.Z. 59 H5 39 24S 175 24 E
Ohata, Japan 30 D10 41 24N 141 10 E
Ohau, L., N.Z. 59 L2 44 15S 169 53 E
Ohio □, U.S.A. 78 F2 40 15N 82 45W
Ohio →, U.S.A. 76 G1 36 59N 89 8W
Ohře →, Czech Rep. 16 C8 50 30N 14 10 E
Ohrid, Macedonia 21 D9 41 8N 20 52 E
Ohridsko Jezero, Macedonia 21 D9 41 8N 20 52 E
Ohrigstad, S. Africa 57 C5 24 39S 30 36 E
Oiapoque, Brazil 93 3 50N 51 50W
Oikou, China 35 E9 38 35N 117 42 E
Oil City, U.S.A. 78 E5 41 26N 79 42W
Oil Springs, Canada 78 D2 42 47N 82 7W
Oildale, U.S.A. 85 K7 35 25N 119 1W
Oise →, France 18 B5 49 0N 2 4 E
Ōita, Japan 31 H5 33 14N 131 36 E
Ōita □, Japan 31 H5 33 15N 131 30 E
Oiticica, Brazil 93 E10 5 3S 41 5W
Ojacaliente, Mexico 86 C4 22 34N 102 15W
Ojai, U.S.A. 85 L7 34 27N 119 15W
Ojinaga, Mexico 86 B4 29 34N 104 25W
Ojiya, Japan 31 F9 37 18N 138 48 E
Ojos del Salado, Cerro, Argentina 94 B2 27 0S 68 40W
Oka →, Russia 24 C7 56 20N 43 59 E
Okaba, Indonesia 37 F9 8 6S 139 42 E
Okahandja, Namibia 56 C2 22 0S 16 59 E
Okahukura, N.Z. 59 H5 38 48S 175 14 E
Okanagan L., Canada 72 D5 50 0N 119 30W
Okanogan, U.S.A. 82 B4 48 22N 119 35W
Okanogan →, U.S.A. 82 B4 48 6N 119 44W
Okaputa, Namibia 56 C2 20 5S 17 0 E
Okara, Pakistan 42 D5 30 50N 73 31 E
Okarito, N.Z. 59 K3 43 15S 170 9 E
Okaukuejo, Namibia 56 B2 19 10S 16 0 E
Okavango Swamps, Botswana 56 B3 18 45S 22 45 E
Okaya, Japan 31 F9 36 5N 138 10 E
Okayama, Japan 31 G6 34 40N 133 54 E
Okayama □, Japan 31 G6 35 0N 133 50 E
Okazaki, Japan 31 G8 34 57N 137 10 E
Okeechobee, U.S.A. 77 M5 27 15N 80 50W
Okeechobee, L., U.S.A. 77 M5 27 0N 80 50W
Okefenokee Swamp, U.S.A. 77 K4 30 40N 82 20W
Okehampton, U.K. 11 G4 50 44N 4 0W
Okha, India 42 H3 22 27N 69 4 E
Okha, Russia 27 D15 53 40N 143 0 E
Okhotsk, Russia 27 D15 59 20N 143 10 E
Okhotsk, Sea of, Asia 27 D15 55 0N 145 0 E
Okhotskiy Perevoz, Russia 27 C14 61 52N 135 35 E
Okhtyrka, Ukraine 25 D5 50 25N 35 0 E
Oki-Shotō, Japan 31 F6 36 5N 133 15 E
Okiep, S. Africa 56 D2 29 39S 17 53 E
Okinawa □, Japan 31 L4 26 40N 128 0 E
Okinawa-Guntō, Japan 31 L4 26 40N 128 0 E
Okinawa-Jima, Japan 31 L4 26 32N 128 0 E
Okino-erabu-Shima, Japan 31 L4 27 21N 128 33 E
Oklahoma □, U.S.A. 81 H6 35 20N 97 30W
Oklahoma City, U.S.A. 81 H6 35 30N 97 30W
Okmulgee, U.S.A. 81 H7 35 37N 95 58W
Oknitsa = Ocniţa, Moldova 17 D14 48 25N 27 30 E
Okolo, Uganda 54 B3 2 37N 31 8 E
Okolona, U.S.A. 81 J10 34 0N 88 45W
Okotoks, Canada 72 C6 50 43N 113 58W
Oksibil, Indonesia 37 E10 4 59S 140 35 E
Oksovskiy, Russia 24 B6 62 33N 39 57 E
Oktabrsk = Oktyabrsk, Kazakstan 25 E10 49 28N 57 25 E
Oktyabrsk, Kazakstan 25 E10 49 28N 57 25 E
Oktyabrskiy = Aktsyabrski, Belarus 17 B15 52 38N 28 53 E
Oktyabrskiy, Russia 24 D9 54 28N 53 28 E
Oktyabrskoy Revolyutsii, Ostrov, Russia 27 B10 79 30N 97 0 E
Okuru, N.Z. 59 K2 43 55S 168 55 E
Okushiri-Tō, Japan 30 C9 42 15N 139 30 E
Okwa →, Botswana 56 C3 22 30S 23 0 E
Ola, U.S.A. 81 H8 35 2N 93 13W
Ólafsfjörður, Iceland 8 C4 66 4N 18 39W
Ólafsvík, Iceland 8 D2 64 53N 23 43W
Olancha, U.S.A. 85 J8 36 17N 118 1W
Olancha Pk., U.S.A. 85 J8 36 15N 118 7W
Olanchito, Honduras 88 C2 15 30N 86 30W
Öland, Sweden 9 H17 56 45N 16 38 E
Olary, Australia 63 E3 32 18S 140 19 E
Olascoaga, Argentina 94 D3 35 15S 60 39W
Olathe, U.S.A. 80 F7 38 53N 94 49W
Olavarría, Argentina 94 D3 36 55S 60 20W
Oława, Poland 17 C9 50 57N 17 20 E
Ólbia, Italy 20 D3 40 55N 9 31 E
Olcott, U.S.A. 78 C6 43 20N 78 42W
Old Bahama Chan. = Bahama, Canal Viejo de, W. Indies 88 B4 22 10N 77 30W
Old Baldy Pk. = San Antonio, Mt., U.S.A. 85 L9 34 17N 117 38W
Old Castile = Castilla y Leon □, Spain 19 B3 42 0N 5 0W
Old Crow, Canada 68 B6 67 30N 139 55W
Old Dale, U.S.A. 85 L11 34 8N 115 47W
Old Forge, N.Y., U.S.A. 79 C10 43 43N 74 58W
Old Forge, Pa., U.S.A. 79 E9 41 22N 75 45W
Old Perlican, Canada 71 C9 48 5N 53 1W
Old Shinyanga, Tanzania 54 C3 3 33S 33 27 E
Old Speck Mt., U.S.A. 79 B14 44 34N 70 57W
Old Town, U.S.A. 77 C11 44 56N 68 39W
Old Washington, U.S.A. 78 F3 40 2N 81 27W
Old Wives L., Canada 73 C7 50 5N 106 0W
Oldbury, U.K. 11 F5 51 38N 2 33W
Oldcastle, Ireland 13 C4 53 46N 7 10W
Oldeani, Tanzania 54 C4 3 22S 35 35 E
Oldenburg, Germany 16 B5 53 9N 8 13 E
Oldenzaal, Neths. 15 B6 52 19N 6 53 E
Oldham, U.K. 10 D5 53 33N 2 7W
Oldman →, Canada 72 D6 49 57N 111 42W
Oldmeldrum, U.K. 12 D6 57 20N 2 19W
Olds, Canada 72 C6 51 50N 114 10W
Oldziyt, Mongolia 34 B5 44 40N 109 1 E
Olean, U.S.A. 78 D6 42 5N 78 26W
Olekma →, Russia 27 C13 60 22N 120 42 E
Olekminsk, Russia 27 C13 60 25N 120 30 E
Oleksandriya, Ukraine 17 C14 50 37N 26 19 E
Olema, U.S.A. 84 G4 38 3N 122 47W
Olenegorsk, Russia 24 A5 68 9N 33 18 E
Olenek, Russia 27 C12 68 28N 112 18 E
Olenek →, Russia 27 B13 73 0N 120 10 E
Oléron, Î. d', France 18 D3 45 55N 1 15W
Oleśnica, Poland 17 C9 51 13N 17 22 E
Olevsk, Ukraine 17 C14 51 12N 27 39 E
Olga, Russia 27 E14 43 50N 135 14 E
Olga, L., Canada 70 C4 49 47N 77 15W
Olga, Mt., Australia 61 E5 25 20S 130 50 E
Olhão, Portugal 19 D2 37 3N 7 48W
Olifants →, Africa 57 C5 23 57S 31 58 E
Olifantshoek, S. Africa 56 D3 27 57S 22 42 E
Ólimbos, Óros, Greece 21 D10 40 6N 22 23 E
Olímpia, Brazil 95 A6 20 44S 48 54W
Olinda, Brazil 93 E12 8 1S 34 51W
Oliva, Argentina 94 C3 32 0S 63 38W
Olivehurst, U.S.A. 84 F5 39 6N 121 34W
Olivenza, Spain 19 C2 38 41N 7 9W
Oliver, Canada 72 D5 49 13N 119 37W
Oliver L., Canada 73 B8 56 56N 103 22W
Ollagüe, Chile 94 A2 21 15S 68 10W
Olney, Ill., U.S.A. 76 F1 38 44N 88 5W
Olney, Tex., U.S.A. 81 J5 33 22N 98 45W
Olomane →, Canada 71 B7 50 14N 60 37W
Olomouc, Czech Rep. 17 D9 49 38N 17 12 E
Olonets, Russia 24 B5 61 0N 32 54 E
Olongapo, Phil. 37 B6 14 50N 120 18 E
Olot, Spain 19 A7 42 11N 2 30 E
Olovyannaya, Russia 27 D12 50 58N 115 35 E
Oloy →, Russia 27 C16 66 29N 159 29 E
Olsztyn, Poland 17 B11 53 48N 20 29 E
Olt →, Romania 17 G13 43 43N 24 51 E
Olteniţa, Romania 17 F14 44 7N 26 42 E
Olton, U.S.A. 81 H3 34 11N 102 8W
Olymbos, Cyprus 23 D12 35 21N 33 45 E
Olympia, Greece 21 F9 37 39N 21 39 E
Olympia, U.S.A. 84 D4 47 3N 122 53W
Olympic Dam, Australia 63 E2 30 30S 136 55 E
Olympic Mts., U.S.A. 84 C3 47 55N 123 45W
Olympic Nat. Park, U.S.A. 84 C3 47 48N 123 30W
Olympus, Cyprus 23 E11 34 56N 32 52 E
Olympus, Mt. = Ólimbos, Óros, Greece 21 D10 40 6N 22 23 E
Olympus, Mt. = Uludağ, Turkey 21 D13 40 4N 29 13 E
Olympus, Mt., U.S.A. 84 C3 47 48N 123 43W
Olyphant, U.S.A. 79 E9 41 27N 75 36W
Om →, Russia 26 D8 54 59N 73 22 E
Om Koi, Thailand 38 D2 17 48N 98 22 E
Ōma, Japan 30 D10 41 45N 141 5 E
Ōmachi, Japan 31 F8 36 30N 137 50 E
Omae-Zaki, Japan 31 G9 34 36N 138 14 E
Ōmagari, Japan 30 E10 39 27N 140 29 E
Omagh, U.K. 13 B4 54 36N 7 19W
Omagh □, U.K. 13 B4 54 35N 7 15W
Omaha, U.S.A. 80 E7 41 17N 95 58W
Omak, U.S.A. 82 B4 48 25N 119 31W
Omalos, Greece 23 D5 35 19N 23 55 E
Oman ■, Asia 46 C6 23 0N 58 0 E
Oman, G. of, Asia 45 E8 24 30N 58 30 E
Omaruru, Namibia 56 C2 21 26S 16 0 E
Omaruru →, Namibia 56 C1 22 7S 14 15 E
Omate, Peru 92 G4 16 45S 71 0W
Ombai, Selat, Indonesia 37 F6 8 30S 124 50 E
Omboué, Gabon 52 E1 1 35S 9 15 E
Ombrone →, Italy 20 C4 42 42N 11 5 E
Omdurmân, Sudan 51 E12 15 40N 32 28 E
Omemee, Canada 78 B6 44 18N 78 33W
Omeo, Australia 63 F4 37 6S 147 36 E
Omeonga, Dem. Rep. of the Congo 54 C1 3 40S 24 22 E
Ometepe, I. de, Nic. 88 D2 11 32N 85 35W
Ometepec, Mexico 87 D5 16 39N 98 23W
Ominato, Japan 30 D10 41 17N 141 10 E
Omineca →, Canada 72 B4 56 3N 124 16W
Omitara, Namibia 56 C2 22 16S 18 2 E
Ōmiya, Japan 31 G9 35 54N 139 38 E
Ommen, Neths. 15 B6 52 31N 6 26 E
Ömnögovĭ □, Mongolia 34 C3 43 15N 104 0 E
Omo →, Ethiopia 46 F2 6 25N 36 10 E
Omodhos, Cyprus 23 E11 34 51N 32 48 E
Omolon →, Russia 27 C16 68 42N 158 36 E
Omono-Gawa →, Japan 30 E10 39 46N 140 3 E
Omsk, Russia 26 D8 55 0N 73 12 E
Omsukchan, Russia 27 C16 62 32N 155 48 E
Ōmu, Japan 30 B11 44 34N 142 58 E
Omul, Vf., Romania 17 F13 45 27N 25 29 E
Ōmura, Japan 31 H4 32 56N 129 57 E
Omuramba Omatako →, Namibia 53 H4 17 45S 20 25 E
Ōmuta, Japan 31 H5 33 5N 130 26 E
Onaga, U.S.A. 80 F6 39 29N 96 10W
Onalaska, U.S.A. 80 D9 43 53N 91 14W
Onancock, U.S.A. 76 G8 37 43N 75 45W
Onang, Indonesia 37 E5 3 2S 118 49 E
Onaping L., Canada 70 C3 47 3N 81 30W
Onavas, Mexico 86 B3 28 28N 109 30W
Onawa, U.S.A. 80 D6 42 2N 96 6W
Oncócua, Angola 56 B1 16 30S 13 25 E
Onda, Spain 19 C5 39 55N 0 17W
Ondaejin, N. Korea 35 D15 41 34N 129 40 E
Ondangua, Namibia 56 B2 17 57S 16 4 E
Ondjiva, Angola 56 B2 16 48S 15 50 E
Öndörshil, Mongolia 34 B5 45 13N 108 5 E
Öndverðarnes, Iceland 8 D1 64 52N 24 0W
One Tree, Australia 63 E3 34 11S 144 43 E
Onega, Russia 24 B6 64 0N 38 10 E
Onega →, Russia 24 B6 63 58N 38 2 E
Onega, G. of = Onezhskaya Guba, Russia 24 B6 64 24N 36 38 E
Onega, L. = Onezhskoye Ozero, Russia 24 B6 61 44N 35 22 E
Onehunga, N.Z. 59 G5 36 55S 174 48 E
Oneida, U.S.A. 79 C9 43 6N 75 39W
Oneida L., U.S.A. 79 C9 43 12N 75 54W
O'Neill, U.S.A. 80 D5 42 27N 98 39W
Onekotan, Ostrov, Russia 27 E16 49 25N 154 45 E
Onema, Dem. Rep. of the Congo 54 C1 4 35S 24 30 E
Oneonta, U.S.A. 79 D9 42 27N 75 4W
Oneşti, Romania 17 E14 46 15N 26 45 E
Onezhskaya Guba, Russia 24 B6 64 24N 36 38 E
Onezhskoye Ozero, Russia 24 B6 61 44N 35 22 E
Ongarue, N.Z. 59 H5 38 42S 175 19 E
Ongerup, Australia 61 F2 33 58S 118 28 E
Ongjin, N. Korea 35 F13 37 56N 125 21 E
Ongkharak, Thailand 38 E3 14 8N 101 1 E
Ongniud Qi, China 35 C10 43 0N 118 38 E
Ongoka, Dem. Rep. of the Congo 54 C2 1 20S 26 0 E
Ongole, India 40 M12 15 33N 80 2 E
Ongon = Havirga, Mongolia 34 B7 45 41N 113 5 E
Onida, U.S.A. 80 C4 44 42N 100 4W
Onilahy →, Madag. 57 C7 23 34S 43 45 E
Onitsha, Nigeria 50 G7 6 6N 6 42 E
Onoda, Japan 31 G5 34 2N 131 25 E
Onpyŏng-ni, S. Korea 35 H14 33 25N 126 55 E
Onslow, Australia 60 D2 21 40S 115 12 E
Onslow B., U.S.A. 77 H7 34 20N 77 15W
Ontake-San, Japan 31 G8 35 53N 137 29 E
Ontario, Calif., U.S.A. 85 L9 34 4N 117 39W
Ontario, Oreg., U.S.A. 82 D5 44 2N 116 58W
Ontario □, Canada 70 B2 48 0N 83 0W
Ontario, L., N. Amer. 75 B11 43 20N 78 0W
Ontonagon, U.S.A. 80 B10 46 52N 89 19W
Onyx, U.S.A. 85 K8 35 41N 118 14W
Oodnadatta, Australia 63 D2 27 33S 135 30 E
Ooldea, Australia 61 F5 30 27S 131 50 E
Oombulgurri, Australia 60 C4 15 15S 127 45 E
Oorindi, Australia 62 C3 20 40S 141 1 E
Oost-Vlaanderen □, Belgium 15 C3 51 5N 3 50 E
Oostende, Belgium 15 C2 51 15N 2 54 E
Oosterhout, Neths. 15 C4 51 39N 4 47 E
Oosterschelde →, Neths. 15 C4 51 33N 4 0 E
Oosterwolde, Neths. 15 B6 53 0N 6 17 E
Ootacamund = Udagamandalam, India 40 P10 11 30N 76 44 E
Ootsa L., Canada 72 C3 53 50N 126 2W
Opala, Dem. Rep. of the Congo 54 C1 0 40S 24 20 E
Opanake, Sri Lanka 40 R12 6 35N 80 40 E
Opasatika, Canada 70 C3 49 30N 82 50W
Opasquia Prov. Park, Canada 70 B1 53 33N 93 5W
Opava, Czech Rep. 17 D9 49 57N 17 58 E
Opelika, U.S.A. 77 J3 32 39N 85 23W
Opelousas, U.S.A. 81 K8 30 32N 92 5W
Opémisca, L., Canada 70 C5 49 56N 74 52W
Opheim, U.S.A. 82 B10 48 51N 106 24W
Ophthalmia Ra., Australia 60 D2 23 15S 119 30 E
Opinaca →, Canada 70 B4 52 15N 78 2W
Opinaca, Rés., Canada 70 B4 52 39N 76 20W
Opinnagau →, Canada 70 B3 54 12N 82 25W
Opiscoteo, L., Canada 71 B6 53 10N 68 10W
Opole, Poland 17 C9 50 42N 17 58 E
Oporto = Porto, Portugal 19 B1 41 8N 8 40W
Opotiki, N.Z. 59 H6 38 1S 177 19 E
Opp, U.S.A. 77 K2 31 17N 86 16W
Oppdal, Norway 9 E13 62 35N 9 41 E
Opportunity, U.S.A. 82 C5 47 39N 117 15W
Opua, N.Z. 59 F5 35 19S 174 9 E
Opunake, N.Z. 59 H4 39 26S 173 52 E
Ora, Cyprus 23 E12 34 51N 33 12 E
Oracle, U.S.A. 83 K8 32 37N 110 46W
Oradea, Romania 17 E11 47 2N 21 58 E
Öræfajökull, Iceland 8 D5 64 2N 16 39W
Orai, India 43 G8 25 58N 79 30 E
Oral = Zhayyq →, Kazakstan 25 E9 47 0N 51 48 E
Oral, Kazakstan 25 D9 51 20N 51 20 E
Oran, Algeria 50 A5 35 45N 0 39W
Orange, Australia 63 E4 33 15S 149 7 E
Orange, France 18 D6 44 8N 4 47 E
Orange, Calif., U.S.A. 85 M9 33 47N 117 51W
Orange, Mass., U.S.A. 79 D12 42 35N 72 19W
Orange, Tex., U.S.A. 81 K8 30 6N 93 44W
Orange, Va., U.S.A. 76 F6 38 15N 78 7W
Orange →, S. Africa 56 D2 28 41S 16 28 E
Orange, C., Brazil 93 C8 4 20N 51 30W
Orange Cove, U.S.A. 84 J7 36 38N 119 19W
Orange Free State = Free State □, S. Africa 56 D4 28 30S 27 0 E
Orange Grove, U.S.A. 81 M6 27 58N 97 56W
Orange Walk, Belize 87 D7 18 6N 88 33W
Orangeburg, U.S.A. 77 J5 33 30N 80 52W
Orangeville, Canada 78 C4 43 55N 80 5W
Oranienburg, Germany 16 B7 52 45N 13 14 E
Oranje = Orange →, S. Africa 56 D2 28 41S 16 28 E
Oranje Vrystaat = Free State □, S. Africa 56 D4 28 30S 27 0 E
Oranjemund, Namibia 56 D2 28 38S 16 29 E
Oranjerivier, S. Africa 56 D3 29 40S 24 12 E
Oranjestad, Aruba 89 D5 12 32N 70 2W
Orapa, Botswana 53 J5 21 15S 25 30 E
Oras, Phil. 37 B7 12 9N 125 28 E
Oraşul Stalin = Braşov, Romania 17 F13 45 38N 25 35 E
Orbetello, Italy 20 C4 42 27N 11 13 E
Orbisonia, U.S.A. 78 F7 40 15N 77 54W
Orbost, Australia 63 F4 37 40S 148 29 E
Orcas I., U.S.A. 84 B4 48 42N 122 56W
Orchard City, U.S.A. 83 G10 38 50N 107 58W
Orchila, I., Venezuela 89 D6 11 48N 66 10W
Orcutt, U.S.A. 85 L6 34 52N 120 27W
Ord, U.S.A. 80 E5 41 36N 98 56W
Ord →, Australia 60 C4 15 33S 128 15 E
Ord, Mt., Australia 60 C4 17 20S 125 34 E
Orderville, U.S.A. 83 H7 37 17N 112 38W
Ordos = Mu Us Shamo, China 34 E5 39 0N 109 0 E
Ordu, Turkey 25 F6 40 55N 37 53 E
Ordway, U.S.A. 80 F3 38 13N 103 46W
Ordzhonikidze = Vladikavkaz, Russia 25 F7 43 0N 44 35 E
Ore, Dem. Rep. of the Congo 54 B2 3 17N 29 30 E
Ore Mts. = Erzgebirge, Germany 16 C7 50 27N 12 55 E
Örebro, Sweden 9 G16 59 20N 15 18 E
Oregon, U.S.A. 80 D10 42 1N 89 20W
Oregon □, U.S.A. 82 E3 44 0N 121 0W
Oregon City, U.S.A. 84 E4 45 21N 122 36W
Orekhovo-Zuyevo, Russia 24 C6 55 50N 38 55 E
Orel, Russia 24 D6 52 57N 36 3 E
Orem, U.S.A. 74 B4 40 19N 111 42W
Ören, Turkey 21 F12 37 3N 27 57 E
Orenburg, Russia 24 D10 51 45N 55 6 E
Orense = Ourense, Spain 19 A2 42 19N 7 55W
Orepuki, N.Z. 59 M1 46 19S 167 46 E
Orestiás, Greece 21 D12 41 30N 26 33 E
Orestos Pereyra, Mexico 86 B3 26 31N 105 40W
Orford Ness, U.K. 11 E9 52 5N 1 35 E
Organos, Pta. de los, Canary Is. 22 F2 28 12N 17 17W
Orgaz, Spain 19 C4 39 39N 3 53W
Orgeyev = Orhei, Moldova 17 E15 47 24N 28 50 E
Orhaneli, Turkey 21 E13 39 54N 28 59 E
Orhangazi, Turkey 21 D13 40 29N 29 18 E
Orhei, Moldova 17 E15 47 24N 28 50 E
Orhon Gol →, Mongolia 32 A5 50 21N 106 0 E
Oriental, Cordillera, Colombia 92 B4 6 0N 73 0W
Orientale □, Dem. Rep. of the Congo 54 B2 2 20N 26 0 E
Oriente, Argentina 94 D3 38 44S 60 37W
Orihuela, Spain 19 C5 38 7N 0 55W
Orillia, Canada 78 B5 44 40N 79 24W
Orinoco →, Venezuela 92 B6 9 15N 61 30W
Orion, Canada 73 D6 49 27N 110 49W
Oriskany, U.S.A. 79 C9 43 10N 75 20W
Orissa □, India 41 K14 20 0N 84 0 E
Orissaare, Estonia 9 G20 58 34N 23 5 E
Oristano, Italy 20 E3 39 54N 8 36 E
Oristano, G. di, Italy 20 E3 39 50N 8 29 E
Orizaba, Mexico 87 D5 18 51N 97 6W
Orkanger, Norway 8 E13 63 18N 9 52 E
Orkla →, Norway 8 E13 63 18N 9 51 E
Orkney, S. Africa 56 D4 26 58S 26 40 E
Orkney □, U.K. 12 B5 59 2N 3 13W
Orkney Is., U.K. 12 B6 59 0N 3 0W
Orland, U.S.A. 84 F4 39 45N 122 12W
Orlando, U.S.A. 77 L5 28 33N 81 23W
Orléanais, France 18 C5 48 0N 2 0 E
Orléans, France 18 C4 47 54N 1 52 E
Orleans, U.S.A. 79 B12 44 49N 72 12W
Orléans, I. d', Canada 71 C5 46 54N 70 58W
Ormara, Pakistan 40 G4 25 16N 64 33 E
Ormoc, Phil. 37 B6 11 0N 124 37 E
Ormond, N.Z. 59 H6 38 33S 177 56 E
Ormond Beach, U.S.A. 77 L5 29 17N 81 3W
Ormskirk, U.K. 10 D5 53 35N 2 54W
Ormstown, Canada 79 A11 45 8N 74 0W
Örnsköldsvik, Sweden 8 E18 63 17N 18 40 E
Oro, N. Korea 35 D14 40 1N 127 27 E
Oro →, Mexico 86 B3 25 35N 105 2W
Oro Grande, U.S.A. 85 L9 34 36N 117 20W
Oro Valley, U.S.A. 83 K8 32 26N 110 58W
Orocué, Colombia 92 C4 4 48N 71 20W
Orofino, U.S.A. 82 C5 46 29N 116 15W
Orol Dengizi = Aral Sea, Asia 26 E7 44 30N 60 0 E
Oromocto, Canada 71 C6 45 54N 66 29W
Orono, Canada 78 C6 43 59N 78 37W
Orono, U.S.A. 77 C11 44 53N 68 40W
Oronsay, U.K. 12 E2 56 1N 6 15W
Oroqen Zizhiqi, China 33 A7 50 34N 123 43 E
Oroquieta, Phil. 37 C6 8 32N 123 44 E
Orosháza, Hungary 17 E11 46 32N 20 42 E
Orotukan, Russia 27 C16 62 16N 151 42 E
Oroville, Calif., U.S.A. 84 F5 39 31N 121 33W
Oroville, Wash., U.S.A. 82 B4 48 56N 119 26W
Oroville, L., U.S.A. 84 F5 39 33N 121 29W
Orroroo, Australia 63 E2 32 43S 138 38 E
Orrville, U.S.A. 78 F3 40 50N 81 46W
Orsha, Belarus 24 D5 54 30N 30 25 E
Orsk, Russia 26 D6 51 12N 58 34 E
Orşova, Romania 17 F12 44 41N 22 25 E
Ortaca, Turkey 21 F13 36 49N 28 45 E
Ortegal, C., Spain 19 A2 43 43N 7 52W
Orthez, France 18 E3 43 29N 0 48W
Ortigueira, Spain 19 A2 43 40N 7 50W
Orting, U.S.A. 84 C4 47 6N 122 12W
Ortles, Italy 18 C9 46 31N 10 33 E
Ortón →, Bolivia 92 F5 10 50S 67 0W
Ortonville, U.S.A. 80 C6 45 19N 96 27W
Orūmīyeh, Iran 44 B5 37 40N 45 0 E
Orūmīyeh, Daryācheh-ye, Iran 44 B5 37 50N 45 30 E
Oruro, Bolivia 92 G5 18 0S 67 9W
Orust, Sweden 9 G14 58 10N 11 40 E
Oruzgān □, Afghan. 40 C5 33 30N 66 0 E
Orvieto, Italy 20 C5 42 43N 12 7 E
Orwell, N.Y., U.S.A. 79 C9 43 35N 75 50W
Orwell, Ohio, U.S.A. 78 E4 41 32N 80 52W
Orwell →, U.K. 11 F9 51 59N 1 18 E
Orwigsburg, U.S.A. 79 F8 40 38N 76 6W
Oryakhovo, Bulgaria 21 C10 43 40N 23 57 E
Osa, Russia 24 C10 57 17N 55 26 E
Osa, Pen. de, Costa Rica 88 E3 8 0N 84 0W
Osage, U.S.A. 80 D8 43 17N 92 49W
Osage →, U.S.A. 80 F9 38 35N 91 57W
Osage City, U.S.A. 80 F7 38 38N 95 50W
Ōsaka, Japan 31 G7 34 40N 135 30 E
Osan, S. Korea 35 F14 37 11N 127 4 E
Osawatomie, U.S.A. 80 F7 38 31N 94 57W
Osborne, U.S.A. 80 F5 39 26N 98 42W
Osceola, Ark., U.S.A. 81 H10 35 42N 89 58W
Osceola, Iowa, U.S.A. 80 E8 41 2N 93 46W
Oscoda, U.S.A. 78 B1 44 26N 83 20W
Ösel = Saaremaa, Estonia 9 G20 58 30N 22 30 E
Osgoode, Canada 79 A9 45 8N 75 36W
Osh, Kyrgyzstan 26 E8 40 37N 72 49 E
Oshakati, Namibia 53 H3 17 45S 15 40 E
Oshawa, Canada 78 C6 43 50N 78 50W
Oshkosh, Nebr., U.S.A. 80 E3 41 24N 102 21W
Oshkosh, Wis., U.S.A. 80 C10 44 1N 88 33W

Penn Yan

Penn Yan, U.S.A. 78 D7 42 40N 77 3W
Pennant, Canada 73 C7 50 32N 108 14W
Penner →, India 40 M12 14 35N 80 10 E
Pennines, U.K. 10 C5 54 45N 2 27W
Pennington, U.S.A. 84 F5 39 15N 121 47W
Pennsburg, U.S.A. 79 F9 40 23N 75 29W
Pennsylvania □, U.S.A. 76 E7 40 45N 77 30W
Penny, Canada 72 C4 53 51N 121 20W
Penobscot →, U.S.A. 77 C11 44 30N 68 48W
Penobscot B., U.S.A. 77 C11 44 35N 68 50W
Penola, Australia 63 F3 37 25S 140 48 E
Penong, Australia 61 F5 31 56S 133 1 E
Penonomé, Panama 88 E3 8 31N 80 21W
Penrith, Australia 63 E5 33 43S 150 38 E
Penrith, U.K. 10 C5 54 40N 2 45W
Penryn, U.K. 11 G2 50 9N 5 7W
Pensacola, U.S.A. 77 K2 30 25N 87 13W
Pensacola Mts., Antarctica 5 E1 84 0S 40 0W
Pense, Canada 73 C8 50 25N 104 59W
Penshurst, Australia 63 F3 37 49S 142 20 E
Penticton, Canada 72 D5 49 30N 119 38W
Pentland, Australia 62 C4 20 32S 145 25 E
Pentland Firth, U.K. 12 C5 58 43N 3 10W
Pentland Hills, U.K. 12 F5 55 48N 3 25W
Penza, Russia 24 D8 53 15N 45 5 E
Penzance, U.K. 11 G2 50 7N 5 33W
Penzhino, Russia 27 C17 63 30N 167 55 E
Penzhinskaya Guba, Russia 27 C17 61 30N 163 0 E
Peoria, Ariz., U.S.A. 83 K7 33 35N 112 14W
Peoria, Ill., U.S.A. 80 E10 40 42N 89 36W
Pepacton Reservoir, U.S.A. 79 D10 42 5N 74 58W
Pera Hd., Australia 62 A3 12 55S 141 37 E
Perabumulih, Indonesia 36 E2 3 27S 104 15 E
Perak →, Malaysia 39 K3 4 0N 100 50 E
Pérama, Kérkira, Greece 23 A3 39 34N 19 54 E
Pérama, Kríti, Greece 23 D6 35 20N 24 40 E
Peräpohjola, Finland 8 C22 66 16N 26 10 E
Percé, Canada 71 C7 48 31N 64 13W
Perche, Collines du, France 18 B4 48 30N 0 40 E
Percival Lakes, Australia 60 D4 21 25S 125 0 E
Percy Is., Australia 62 C5 21 39S 150 16 E
Perdido, Mte., Spain 19 A6 42 40N 0 5 E
Perdu, Mt. = Perdido, Mte., Spain 19 A6 42 40N 0 5 E
Pereira, Colombia 92 C3 4 49N 75 43W
Perenjori, Australia 61 E2 29 26S 116 16 E
Pereyaslav-Khmelnytskyy, Ukraine 25 D5 50 3N 31 28 E
Pérez, I., Mexico 87 C7 22 24N 89 42W
Pergamino, Argentina 94 C3 33 52S 60 30W
Pergau →, Malaysia 39 K3 5 23N 102 2 E
Perham, U.S.A. 80 B7 46 36N 95 34W
Perhentian, Kepulauan, Malaysia 36 C2 5 54N 102 42 E
Péribonca →, Canada 71 C5 48 45N 72 5W
Péribonca, L., Canada 71 B5 50 1N 71 10W
Perico, Argentina 94 A2 24 20S 65 5W
Pericos, Mexico 86 B3 25 3N 107 42W
Périgueux, France 18 D4 45 10N 0 42 E
Perijá, Sierra de, Colombia 92 B4 9 30N 73 3W
Peristerona →, Cyprus 23 D12 35 8N 33 5 E
Perito Moreno, Argentina 96 F2 46 36S 70 56W
Perkasie, U.S.A. 79 F9 40 22N 75 18W
Perlas, Arch. de las, Panama 88 E4 8 41N 79 7W
Perlas, Punta de, Nic. 88 D3 12 30N 83 30W
Perm, Russia 24 C10 58 0N 56 10 E
Pernambuco = Recife, Brazil 93 E12 8 0S 35 0W
Pernambuco □, Brazil 93 E11 8 0S 37 0W
Pernatty Lagoon, Australia 63 E2 31 30S 137 12 E
Pernik, Bulgaria 21 C10 42 35N 23 2 E
Peron Is., Australia 60 B5 13 9S 130 4 E
Peron Pen., Australia 61 E1 26 0S 113 10 E
Perow, Canada 72 C3 54 35N 126 10W
Perpendicular Pt., Australia 63 E5 31 37S 152 52 E
Perpignan, France 18 E5 42 42N 2 53 E
Perris, U.S.A. 85 M9 33 47N 117 14W
Perry, Fla., U.S.A. 77 K4 30 7N 83 35W
Perry, Ga., U.S.A. 77 J4 32 28N 83 44W
Perry, Iowa, U.S.A. 80 E7 41 51N 94 6W
Perry, Okla., U.S.A. 81 G6 36 17N 97 14W
Perryton, U.S.A. 81 G4 36 24N 100 48W
Perryville, U.S.A. 81 G10 37 43N 89 52W
Persepolis, Iran 45 D7 29 55N 52 50 E
Pershotravensk, Ukraine 17 C14 50 13N 27 40 E
Persia = Iran ■, Asia 45 C7 33 0N 53 0 E
Persian Gulf = Gulf, The, Asia 45 E6 27 0N 50 0 E
Perth, Australia 61 F2 31 57S 115 52 E
Perth, Canada 79 B8 44 55N 76 15W
Perth, U.K. 12 E5 56 24N 3 26W
Perth & Kinross □, U.K. 12 E5 56 45N 3 55W
Perth Amboy, U.S.A. 79 F10 40 31N 74 16W
Perth-Andover, Canada 71 C6 46 44N 67 42W
Peru, Ind., U.S.A. 76 E2 40 45N 86 4W
Peru, N.Y., U.S.A. 79 B11 44 35N 73 32W
Peru ■, S. Amer. 92 D4 4 0S 75 0W
Peru-Chile Trench, Pac. Oc. 92 G3 20 0S 72 0W
Perúgia, Italy 20 C5 43 7N 12 23 E
Pervomaysk, Ukraine 25 E5 48 10N 30 46 E
Pervouralsk, Russia 24 C10 56 59N 59 59 E
Pésaro, Italy 20 C5 43 54N 12 55 E
Pescara, Italy 20 C6 42 28N 14 13 E
Peshawar, Pakistan 42 B4 34 2N 71 37 E
Peshkopi, Albania 21 D9 41 41N 20 25 E
Peshtigo, U.S.A. 76 C2 45 4N 87 46W
Pesqueira, Brazil 93 E11 8 20S 36 42W
Petah Tiqwa, Israel 47 C3 32 6N 34 53 E
Petaling Jaya, Malaysia 39 L3 3 4N 101 42 E
Petaloudhes, Greece 23 C10 36 18N 28 5 E
Petaluma, U.S.A. 84 G4 38 14N 122 39W
Pétange, Lux. 15 E5 49 33N 5 55 E
Petaro, Pakistan 42 G3 25 31N 68 18 E
Petatlán, Mexico 86 D4 17 31N 101 16W
Petauke, Zambia 55 E3 14 14S 31 20 E
Petawawa, Canada 70 C4 45 54N 77 17W
Petén Itzá, L., Guatemala 88 C2 16 58N 89 50W
Peter I.s Øy, Antarctica 5 C16 69 0S 91 0W
Peter Pond L., Canada 73 B7 55 55N 108 44W
Peterbell, Canada 70 C3 48 36N 83 21W
Peterborough, Australia 63 E2 32 58S 138 51 E
Peterborough, Canada 78 B6 44 20N 78 20W
Peterborough, U.K. 11 E7 52 35N 0 15W
Peterborough, U.S.A. 79 D13 42 53N 71 57W
Peterborough □, U.K. 11 E7 52 35N 0 15W
Peterculter, U.K. 12 D6 57 6N 2 16W
Peterhead, U.K. 12 D7 57 31N 1 48W
Peterlee, U.K. 10 C6 54 47N 1 20W
Petermann Bjerg, Greenland 66 B17 73 7N 28 25W
Petermann Ranges, Australia 60 E5 26 0S 130 30 E
Petersburg, Alaska, U.S.A. 68 C6 56 48N 132 58W
Petersburg, Pa., U.S.A. 78 F6 40 34N 78 3W
Petersburg, Va., U.S.A. 76 G7 37 14N 77 24W
Petersburg, W. Va., U.S.A. 76 F6 39 1N 79 5W
Petersfield, U.K. 11 F7 51 1N 0 56W
Petit Goâve, Haiti 89 C5 18 27N 72 51W
Petit Jardin, Canada 71 C8 48 28N 59 14W
Petit Lac Manicouagan, Canada 71 B6 51 25N 67 40W
Petit-Mécatina →, Canada 71 B8 50 40N 59 30W
Petit-Mécatina, I. du, Canada 71 B8 50 30N 59 25W
Petitcodiac, Canada 71 C6 45 57N 65 11W
Petite Baleine →, Canada 70 A4 56 0N 76 45W
Petite Saguenay, Canada 71 C5 48 15N 70 4W
Petitot →, Canada 72 A4 60 14N 123 29W
Petitsikapau L., Canada 71 B6 54 37N 66 25W
Petlad, India 42 H5 22 30N 72 45 E
Peto, Mexico 87 C7 20 10N 88 53W
Petone, N.Z. 59 J5 41 13S 174 53 E
Petorca, Chile 94 C1 32 15S 70 56W
Petoskey, U.S.A. 76 C3 45 22N 84 57W
Petra, Jordan 47 E4 30 20N 35 22 E
Petra, Spain 22 B10 39 37N 3 6 E
Petra, Ostrova, Russia 4 B13 76 15N 118 30 E
Petra Velikogo, Zaliv, Russia 30 C6 42 40N 132 0 E
Petrich, Bulgaria 21 D10 41 24N 23 13 E
Petrified Forest National Park, U.S.A. 83 J9 35 0N 109 30W
Petrikov = Pyetrikaw, Belarus 17 B15 52 11N 28 29 E
Petrograd = Sankt-Peterburg, Russia 24 C5 59 55N 30 20 E
Petrolândia, Brazil 93 E11 9 5S 38 20W
Petrolia, Canada 78 D2 42 54N 82 9W
Petrolina, Brazil 93 E10 9 24S 40 30W
Petropavl, Kazakstan 26 D7 54 53N 69 13 E
Petropavlovsk = Petropavl, Kazakstan 26 D7 54 53N 69 13 E
Petropavlovsk-Kamchatskiy, Russia 27 D16 53 3N 158 43 E
Petrópolis, Brazil 95 A7 22 33S 43 9W
Petroșani, Romania 17 F12 45 28N 23 20 E
Petrovaradin, Serbia, Yug. 21 B8 45 16N 19 55 E
Petrovsk, Russia 24 D8 52 22N 45 19 E
Petrovsk-Zabaykalskiy, Russia 27 D11 51 20N 108 55 E
Petrozavodsk, Russia 24 B5 61 41N 34 20 E
Petrus Steyn, S. Africa 57 D4 27 38S 28 8 E
Petrusburg, S. Africa 56 D4 29 4S 25 26 E
Peumo, Chile 94 C1 34 21S 71 12W
Peureulak, Indonesia 36 D1 4 48N 97 45 E
Pevek, Russia 27 C18 69 41N 171 19 E
Pforzheim, Germany 16 D5 48 52N 8 41 E
Phagwara, India 40 D9 31 10N 75 40 E
Phaistós, Greece 23 D6 35 2N 24 50 E
Phala, Botswana 56 C4 23 45S 26 50 E
Phalera = Phulera, India 42 F6 26 52N 75 16 E
Phalodi, India 42 F5 27 12N 72 24 E
Phan, Thailand 38 C2 19 28N 99 43 E
Phan Rang, Vietnam 39 G7 11 34N 109 0 E
Phan Ri = Hoa Da, Vietnam 39 G7 11 16N 108 40 E
Phan Thiet, Vietnam 39 G7 11 1N 108 9 E
Phanat Nikhom, Thailand 38 F3 13 27N 101 11 E
Phangan, Ko, Thailand 39 H3 9 45N 100 0 E
Phangnga, Thailand 39 H2 8 28N 98 30 E
Phanom Sarakham, Thailand 38 F3 13 45N 101 21 E
Phaphund, India 43 F8 26 36N 79 28 E
Pharenda, India 43 F10 27 5N 83 17 E
Pharr, U.S.A. 81 M5 26 12N 98 11W
Phatthalung, Thailand 39 J3 7 39N 100 6 E
Phayao, Thailand 38 C2 19 11N 99 55 E
Phelps, U.S.A. 78 D7 42 58N 77 3W
Phelps L., Canada 73 B8 59 15N 103 15W
Phenix City, U.S.A. 77 J3 32 28N 85 0W
Phet Buri, Thailand 38 F2 13 1N 99 55 E
Phetchabun, Thailand 38 D3 16 25N 101 8 E
Phetchabun, Thiu Khao, Thailand 38 E3 16 0N 101 20 E
Phetchaburi = Phet Buri, Thailand 38 F2 13 1N 99 55 E
Phi Phi, Ko, Thailand 39 J2 7 45N 98 46 E
Phiafay, Laos 38 E6 14 48N 106 0 E
Phibun Mangsahan, Thailand 38 E5 15 14N 105 14 E
Phichai, Thailand 38 D3 17 22N 100 10 E
Phichit, Thailand 38 D3 16 26N 100 22 E
Philadelphia, Miss., U.S.A. 81 J10 32 46N 89 7W
Philadelphia, N.Y., U.S.A. 79 B9 44 9N 75 43W
Philadelphia, Pa., U.S.A. 79 G9 39 57N 75 10W
Philip, U.S.A. 80 C4 44 2N 101 40W
Philippeville, Belgium 15 D4 50 12N 4 33 E
Philippi, U.S.A. 76 F5 39 9N 80 3W
Philippi L., Australia 62 C2 24 20S 138 55 E
Philippines ■, Asia 37 B6 12 0N 123 0 E
Philippolis, S. Africa 56 E4 30 15S 25 16 E
Philippopolis = Plovdiv, Bulgaria 21 C11 42 8N 24 44 E
Philipsburg, Canada 79 A11 45 2N 73 5W
Philipsburg, Mont., U.S.A. 82 C7 46 20N 113 18W
Philipsburg, Pa., U.S.A. 78 F6 40 54N 78 13W
Philipstown = Daingean, Ireland 13 C4 53 18N 7 17W
Philipstown, S. Africa 56 E3 30 28S 24 30 E
Phillip I., Australia 63 F4 38 30S 145 12 E
Phillips, U.S.A. 80 C9 45 42N 90 24W
Phillipsburg, Kans., U.S.A. 80 F5 39 45N 99 19W
Phillipsburg, N.J., U.S.A. 79 F9 40 42N 75 12W
Philmont, U.S.A. 79 D11 42 15N 73 39W
Philomath, U.S.A. 82 D2 44 32N 123 22W
Phimai, Thailand 38 E4 15 13N 102 30 E
Phitsanulok, Thailand 38 D3 16 50N 100 12 E
Phnom Dangrek, Thailand 36 B2 14 20N 104 0 E
Phnom Penh, Cambodia 39 G5 11 33N 104 55 E
Phnum Penh = Phnom Penh, Cambodia 39 G5 11 33N 104 55 E
Phoenicia, U.S.A. 79 D10 42 5N 74 14W
Phoenix, Ariz., U.S.A. 83 K7 33 27N 112 4W
Phoenix, N.Y., U.S.A. 79 C8 43 14N 76 18W
Phoenix Is., Kiribati 64 H10 3 30S 172 0W
Phoenixville, U.S.A. 79 F9 40 8N 75 31W
Phon, Thailand 38 E4 15 49N 102 36 E
Phon Tiou, Laos 38 D5 17 53N 104 37 E
Phong →, Thailand 38 D4 16 23N 102 56 E
Phong Tho, Vietnam 38 A4 22 32N 103 21 E
Phonhong, Laos 38 C4 18 30N 102 25 E
Phonum, Thailand 39 H2 8 49N 98 48 E
Phosphate Hill, Australia 62 C2 21 53S 139 58 E
Photharam, Thailand 38 F2 13 41N 99 51 E
Phra Nakhon Si Ayutthaya, Thailand 38 E3 14 25N 100 30 E
Phra Thong, Ko, Thailand 39 H2 9 5N 98 17 E
Phrae, Thailand 38 C3 18 7N 100 9 E
Phrom Phiram, Thailand 38 D3 17 2N 100 12 E
Phu Dien, Vietnam 38 C5 18 58N 105 31 E
Phu Loi, Laos 38 B4 20 14N 103 14 E
Phu Quoc, Dao, Vietnam 39 G4 10 20N 104 0 E
Phuket, Thailand 39 J2 7 52N 98 22 E
Phuket, Ko, Thailand 39 J2 8 0N 98 22 E
Phul, India 42 D6 30 19N 75 14 E
Phulad, India 42 G5 25 38N 73 49 E
Phulchari, Bangla. 43 G13 25 11N 89 37 E
Phulera, India 42 F6 26 52N 75 16 E
Phulpur, India 43 G10 25 31N 82 49 E
Phun Phin, Thailand 39 H2 9 7N 99 12 E
Piacenza, Italy 18 D8 45 1N 9 40 E
Pian Cr. →, Australia 63 E4 30 2S 148 12 E
Pianosa, Italy 20 C4 42 35N 10 5 E
Piapot, Canada 73 D7 49 59N 109 8W
Piatra Neamț, Romania 17 E14 46 56N 26 21 E
Piauí □, Brazil 93 E10 7 0S 43 0W
Piaui →, Brazil 93 E10 6 38S 42 42W
Piave →, Italy 20 B5 45 32N 12 44 E
Pibor Post, Sudan 51 G12 6 47N 33 3 E
Picardie, France 18 B5 49 50N 3 0 E
Picardy = Picardie, France 18 B5 49 50N 3 0 E
Picayune, U.S.A. 81 K10 30 32N 89 41W
Pichhor, India 43 G8 25 58N 78 20 E
Pichilemu, Chile 94 C1 34 22S 72 0W
Pichor, India 42 G8 25 11N 78 11 E
Pickerel L., Canada 70 C1 48 40N 91 25W
Pickering, U.K. 10 C7 54 15N 0 46W
Pickering, Vale of, U.K. 10 C7 54 14N 0 45W
Pickle Lake, Canada 70 B1 51 30N 90 12W
Pickwick L., U.S.A. 77 H1 35 4N 88 15W
Pico Truncado, Argentina 96 F3 46 40S 68 0W
Picos, Brazil 93 E10 7 5S 41 28W
Picton, Australia 63 E5 34 12S 150 34 E
Picton, Canada 78 B7 44 1N 77 9W
Picton, N.Z. 59 J5 41 18S 174 3 E
Pictou, Canada 71 C7 45 41N 62 42W
Picture Butte, Canada 72 D6 49 55N 112 45W
Picún Leufú, Argentina 96 D3 39 30S 69 5W
Pidurutalagala, Sri Lanka 40 R12 7 10N 80 50 E
Piedmont = Piemonte □, Italy 18 D7 45 0N 8 0 E
Piedmont, Ala., U.S.A. 77 J3 33 55N 85 37W
Piedmont, S.C., U.S.A. 75 D10 34 0N 81 30W
Piedras Negras, Mexico 86 B4 28 42N 100 31W
Pieksämäki, Finland 9 E22 62 18N 27 10 E
Piemonte □, Italy 18 D7 45 0N 8 0 E
Piercefield, U.S.A. 79 B10 44 13N 74 35W
Pierceland, Canada 73 C7 54 20N 109 46W
Pierpont, U.S.A. 78 E4 41 45N 80 34W
Pierre, U.S.A. 80 C4 44 22N 100 21W
Piet Retief, S. Africa 57 D5 27 1S 30 50 E
Pietarsaari, Finland 8 E20 63 40N 22 43 E
Pietermaritzburg, S. Africa 57 D5 29 35S 30 25 E
Pietersburg, S. Africa 57 C4 23 54S 29 25 E
Pietrosul, Vf., Maramureș, Romania 17 E13 47 35N 24 43 E
Pietrosul, Vf., Suceava, Romania 17 E13 47 12N 25 18 E
Pigeon L., Canada 78 B6 44 27N 78 30W
Piggott, U.S.A. 81 G9 36 23N 90 11W
Pigüe, Argentina 94 D3 37 36S 62 25W
Pihani, India 43 F9 27 36N 80 15 E
Pihlajavesi, Finland 9 F23 61 45N 28 45 E
Pijijiapan, Mexico 87 D6 15 42N 93 14W
Pikangikum Berens, Canada 73 C10 51 49N 94 0W
Pikes Peak, U.S.A. 80 F2 38 50N 105 3W
Piketberg, S. Africa 56 E2 32 55S 18 40 E
Pikeville, U.S.A. 76 G4 37 29N 82 31W
Pikou, China 35 E12 39 18N 122 22 E
Pikwitonei, Canada 73 B9 55 35N 97 9W
Piła, Poland 17 B9 53 10N 16 48 E
Pilani, India 42 E6 28 22N 75 33 E
Pilar, Paraguay 94 B4 26 50S 58 20W
Pilaya →, Bolivia 92 H6 20 55S 64 4W
Pilbara, Australia 60 D2 23 35S 117 25 E
Pilcomayo →, Paraguay 94 B4 25 21S 57 42W
Pilibhit, India 43 E8 28 40N 79 50 E
Pilica →, Poland 17 C11 51 52N 21 17 E
Pilkhawa, India 42 E7 28 43N 77 42 E
Pilliga, Australia 63 E4 30 21S 148 54 E
Pílos, Greece 21 F9 36 55N 21 42 E
Pilot Mound, Canada 73 D9 49 15N 98 54W
Pilot Point, U.S.A. 81 J6 33 24N 96 58W
Pilot Rock, U.S.A. 82 D4 45 29N 118 50W
Pilsen = Plzeň, Czech Rep. 16 D7 49 45N 13 22 E
Pima, U.S.A. 83 K9 32 54N 109 50W
Pimba, Australia 63 E2 31 18S 136 46 E
Pimenta Bueno, Brazil 92 F6 11 35S 61 10W
Pimentel, Peru 92 E3 6 45S 79 55W
Pinang, Malaysia 39 K3 5 25N 100 15 E
Pinar, C. des, Spain 22 B10 39 53N 3 12 E
Pinar del Río, Cuba 88 B3 22 26N 83 40W
Pınarhisar, Turkey 21 D12 41 37N 27 30 E
Pinatubo, Phil. 37 A6 15 8N 120 21 E
Pincher Creek, Canada 72 D6 49 30N 113 57W
Pinchi L., Canada 72 C4 54 38N 124 30W
Pinckneyville, U.S.A. 80 F10 38 5N 89 23W
Pińczów, Poland 17 C11 50 32N 20 32 E
Pindar, Australia 61 E2 28 30S 115 47 E
Pindi Gheb, Pakistan 42 C5 33 14N 72 21 E
Pindos Óros, Greece 21 E9 40 0N 21 0 E
Pindus Mts. = Pindos Óros, Greece 21 E9 40 0N 21 0 E
Pine →, B.C., Canada 72 B4 56 8N 120 43W
Pine →, Sask., Canada 73 B7 58 50N 105 38W
Pine, C., Canada 71 C9 46 37N 53 32W
Pine Bluff, U.S.A. 81 H9 34 13N 92 1W
Pine Bluffs, U.S.A. 80 E2 41 11N 104 4W
Pine City, U.S.A. 80 C8 45 50N 92 59W
Pine Cr. →, U.S.A. 78 E7 41 10N 77 16W
Pine Creek, Australia 60 B5 13 50S 131 50 E
Pine Falls, Canada 73 C9 50 34N 96 11W
Pine Flat Res., U.S.A. 84 J7 36 50N 119 20W
Pine Grove, U.S.A. 79 F8 40 33N 76 23W
Pine Pass, Canada 72 B4 55 25N 122 42W
Pine Point, Canada 72 A6 60 50N 114 28W
Pine Ridge, U.S.A. 80 D3 43 2N 102 33W
Pine River, Canada 73 C8 51 45N 100 30W
Pine River, U.S.A. 80 B7 46 43N 94 24W
Pine Valley, U.S.A. 85 N10 32 50N 116 32W
Pinecrest, U.S.A. 84 G6 38 12N 120 1W
Pinedale, Calif., U.S.A. 84 J7 36 50N 119 48W
Pinedale, Wyo., U.S.A. 82 E9 42 52N 109 52W
Pinega →, Russia 24 B8 64 30N 44 19 E
Pinehill, Australia 62 C4 23 38S 146 57 E
Pinehouse L., Canada 73 B7 55 32N 106 35W
Pineimuta →, Canada 70 B1 52 8N 88 33W
Pinerolo, Italy 18 D7 44 53N 7 21 E
Pinetop, U.S.A. 83 J9 34 8N 109 56W
Pinetown, S. Africa 57 D5 29 48S 30 54 E
Pineville, U.S.A. 81 K8 31 19N 92 26W
Ping →, Thailand 38 E3 15 42N 100 9 E
Pingaring, Australia 61 F2 32 40S 118 32 E
Pingding, China 34 F7 37 47N 113 38 E
Pingdingshan, China 34 H7 33 43N 113 27 E
Pingdong, Taiwan 33 D7 22 39N 120 30 E
Pingdu, China 35 F10 36 42N 119 59 E
Pingelly, Australia 61 F2 32 32S 117 5 E
Pingliang, China 34 G4 35 35N 106 31 E
Pinglu, China 34 E7 39 31N 112 30 E
Pingluo, China 34 E4 38 52N 106 30 E
Pingquan, China 35 D10 41 1N 118 37 E
Pingrup, Australia 61 F2 33 32S 118 29 E
P'ingtung, Taiwan 33 D7 22 38N 120 30 E
Pingwu, China 34 H3 32 25N 104 30 E
Pingxiang, China 32 D5 22 6N 106 46 E
Pingyao, China 34 F7 37 12N 112 10 E
Pingyi, China 35 G9 35 30N 117 35 E
Pingyin, China 34 F9 36 20N 116 25 E
Pingyuan, China 34 F9 37 10N 116 22 E
Pinhal, Brazil 95 A6 22 10S 46 46W
Pinheiro, Brazil 93 D9 2 31S 45 5W
Pinheiro Machado, Brazil 95 C5 31 34S 53 23W
Pinhel, Portugal 19 B2 40 50N 7 1W
Pini, Indonesia 36 D1 0 10N 98 40 E
Piniós →, Greece 21 E10 39 55N 22 41 E
Pinjarra, Australia 61 F2 32 37S 115 52 E
Pink Mountain, Canada 72 B4 57 3N 122 52W
Pinnacles, U.S.A. 84 J5 36 33N 121 19W
Pinnaroo, Australia 63 F3 35 17S 140 53 E
Pinnes, Ákra, Greece 21 D11 40 5N 24 20 E
Pinon Hills, U.S.A. 85 L9 34 26N 117 39W
Pinos, Mexico 86 C4 22 20N 101 40W
Pinos, Mt., U.S.A. 85 L7 34 49N 119 8W
Pinos Pt., U.S.A. 83 H3 36 38N 121 57W
Pinotepa Nacional, Mexico 87 D5 16 19N 98 3W
Pinrang, Indonesia 37 E5 3 46S 119 41 E
Pins, Pte. aux, Canada 78 D3 42 15N 81 51W
Pinsk, Belarus 17 B14 52 10N 26 1 E
Pintados, Chile 92 H5 20 35S 69 40W
Pinyug, Russia 24 B8 60 5N 48 0 E
Pioche, U.S.A. 83 H6 37 56N 114 27W
Piombino, Italy 20 C4 42 55N 10 32 E
Pioner, Ostrov, Russia 27 B10 79 50N 92 0 E
Piorini, L., Brazil 92 D6 3 15S 62 35W
Piotrków Trybunalski, Poland 17 C10 51 23N 19 43 E
Pip, Iran 45 E9 26 45N 60 10 E
Pipar, India 42 F5 26 25N 73 31 E
Pipar Road, India 42 F5 26 27N 73 27 E
Piparia, Mad. P., India 42 H8 22 45N 78 23 E
Piparia, Mad. P., India 42 J7 21 49N 77 37 E
Pipestone, U.S.A. 80 D6 44 0N 96 19W
Pipestone →, Canada 70 B2 52 53N 89 23W
Pipestone Cr. →, Canada 73 D8 49 38N 100 15W
Piplan, Pakistan 42 C4 32 17N 71 21 E
Piploda, India 42 H6 23 37N 74 56 E
Pipmuacan, Rés., Canada 71 C5 49 45N 70 30W
Pippingarra, Australia 60 D2 20 27S 118 42 E
Piqua, U.S.A. 76 E3 40 9N 84 15W
Piquiri →, Brazil 95 A5 24 3S 54 14W
Pīr Sohrāb, Iran 45 E9 25 44N 60 54 E
Piracicaba, Brazil 95 A6 22 45S 47 40W
Piracuruca, Brazil 93 D10 3 50S 41 50W
Piræus = Piraiévs, Greece 21 F10 37 57N 23 42 E
Piraiévs, Greece 21 F10 37 57N 23 42 E
Piraju, Brazil 95 A6 21 59S 49 29W
Piram I., India 42 J5 21 36N 72 21 E
Pirané, Argentina 94 B4 25 42S 59 6W
Pirapora, Brazil 93 G10 17 20S 44 56W
Pirawa, India 42 G7 24 10N 76 2 E
Pírgos, Greece 21 F9 37 40N 21 27 E
Piribebuy, Paraguay 94 B4 25 26S 57 2W
Pirimapun, Indonesia 37 F9 6 45S 138 0 E
Pirin Planina, Bulgaria 21 D10 41 40N 23 30 E
Pírineos = Pyrénées, Europe 18 E4 42 45N 0 18 E
Piripiri, Brazil 93 D10 4 15S 41 46W
Pirmasens, Germany 16 D4 49 12N 7 36 E
Pirot, Serbia, Yug. 21 C10 43 9N 22 33 E
Piru, Indonesia 37 E7 3 4S 128 12 E
Piru, U.S.A. 85 L8 34 25N 118 48W
Pisa, Italy 20 C4 43 43N 10 23 E
Pisagua, Chile 92 G4 19 40S 70 15W
Pisco, Peru 92 F3 13 50S 76 12W
Pisek, Czech Rep. 16 D8 49 19N 14 10 E
Pishan, China 32 C2 37 30N 78 33 E
Pishin, Iran 45 E9 26 6N 61 47 E
Pishin, Pakistan 42 D2 30 35N 67 0 E
Pishin Lora →, Pakistan 42 E1 29 9N 64 5 E
Pising, Indonesia 37 F6 5 8S 121 53 E
Pismo Beach, U.S.A. 85 K6 35 9N 120 38W
Pissis, Cerro, Argentina 94 B2 27 45S 68 48W
Pissouri, Cyprus 23 E11 34 40N 32 42 E
Pistóia, Italy 20 C4 43 55N 10 54 E
Pistol B., Canada 73 A10 62 25N 92 37W
Pisuerga →, Spain 19 B3 41 33N 4 52W
Pit →, U.S.A. 82 F2 40 47N 122 6W
Pitarpunga, L., Australia 63 E3 34 24S 143 30 E
Pitcairn I., Pac. Oc. 65 K14 25 5S 130 5W
Pite älv →, Sweden 8 D19 65 20N 21 25 E
Piteå, Sweden 8 D19 65 20N 21 25 E
Pitești, Romania 17 F13 44 52N 24 54 E
Pithapuram, India 41 L13 17 10N 82 15 E
Pithara, Australia 61 F2 30 20S 116 35 E
Pithoragarh, India 43 E9 29 35N 80 13 E
Pithoro, Pakistan 42 G3 25 31N 69 23 E
Pitlochry, U.K. 12 E5 56 42N 3 44W

Posong

Pitsilia □, *Cyprus* **23 E12** 34 55N 33 0 E
Pitt I., *Canada* **72 C3** 53 30N 129 50W
Pittsburg, *Calif., U.S.A.* **84 G5** 38 2N 121 53W
Pittsburg, *Kans., U.S.A.* **81 G7** 37 25N 94 42W
Pittsburg, *Tex., U.S.A.* **81 J7** 33 0N 94 59W
Pittsburgh, *U.S.A.* **78 F5** 40 26N 80 1W
Pittsfield, *Ill., U.S.A.* **80 F9** 39 36N 90 49W
Pittsfield, *Maine, U.S.A.* **77 C11** 44 47N 69 23W
Pittsfield, *Mass., U.S.A.* **79 D11** 42 27N 73 15W
Pittsfield, *N.H., U.S.A.* **79 C13** 43 18N 71 20W
Pittston, *U.S.A.* **79 E9** 41 19N 75 47W
Pittsworth, *Australia* **63 D5** 27 41S 151 37 E
Pituri →, *Australia* **62 C2** 22 35S 138 30 E
Piura, *Peru* **92 E2** 5 15S 80 38W
Pixley, *U.S.A.* **84 K7** 35 58N 119 18W
Pizhou, *China* **34 G9** 34 44N 116 55 E
Placentia, *Canada* **71 C9** 47 20N 54 0W
Placentia B., *Canada* **71 C9** 47 0N 54 30W
Placerville, *U.S.A.* **84 G6** 38 44N 120 48W
Placetas, *Cuba* **88 B4** 22 15N 79 44W
Plainfield, *N.J., U.S.A.* **79 F10** 40 37N 74 25W
Plainfield, *Ohio, U.S.A.* **78 F3** 40 13N 81 43W
Plainfield, *Vt., U.S.A.* **79 B12** 44 17N 72 26W
Plains, *Mont., U.S.A.* **82 C6** 47 28N 114 53W
Plains, *Tex., U.S.A.* **81 J3** 33 11N 102 50W
Plainview, *Nebr., U.S.A.* **80 D6** 42 21N 97 47W
Plainview, *Tex., U.S.A.* **81 H4** 34 11N 101 43W
Plainwell, *U.S.A.* **76 D3** 42 27N 85 38W
Plaistow, *U.S.A.* **79 D13** 42 50N 71 6W
Pláka, Ákra, *Greece* **23 D8** 35 11N 26 19 E
Plana Cays, *Bahamas* **89 B5** 22 38N 73 30W
Planada, *U.S.A.* **84 H6** 37 16N 120 19W
Plano, *U.S.A.* **81 J6** 33 1N 96 42W
Plant City, *U.S.A.* **77 M4** 28 1N 82 7W
Plaquemine, *U.S.A.* **81 K9** 30 17N 91 14W
Plasencia, *Spain* **19 B2** 40 3N 6 8W
Plaster City, *U.S.A.* **85 N11** 32 47N 115 51W
Plaster Rock, *Canada* **71 C6** 46 53N 67 22W
Plastun, *Russia* **30 B8** 44 45N 136 19 E
Plata, Río de la, *S. Amer.* **94 C4** 34 45S 57 30W
Plátani →, *Italy* **20 F5** 37 23N 13 16 E
Plátanos, *Greece* **23 D5** 35 28N 23 33 E
Platte, *U.S.A.* **80 D5** 43 23N 98 51W
Platte →, *Mo., U.S.A.* **75 C8** 39 16N 94 50W
Platte →, *Nebr., U.S.A.* **80 E7** 41 4N 95 53W
Platteville, *U.S.A.* **80 D9** 42 44N 90 29W
Plattsburgh, *U.S.A.* **79 B11** 44 42N 73 28W
Plattsmouth, *U.S.A.* **80 E7** 41 1N 95 53W
Plauen, *Germany* **16 C7** 50 30N 12 8 E
Plavinas, *Latvia* **9 H21** 56 35N 25 46 E
Playa Blanca, *Canary Is.* **22 F6** 28 55N 13 37W
Playa Blanca Sur, *Canary Is.* **22 F6** 28 51N 13 50W
Playa de las Americas, *Canary Is.* **22 F3** 28 5N 16 43W
Playa de Mogán, *Canary Is.* **22 G4** 27 48N 15 47W
Playa del Inglés, *Canary Is.* **22 G4** 27 45N 15 33W
Playa Esmerelda, *Canary Is.* **22 F5** 28 8N 14 16W
Playgreen L., *Canada* **73 C9** 54 0N 98 15W
Pleasant Bay, *Canada* **71 C7** 46 51N 60 48W
Pleasant Hill, *U.S.A.* **84 H4** 37 57N 122 4W
Pleasant Mount, *U.S.A.* **79 E9** 41 44N 75 26W
Pleasanton, *Calif., U.S.A.* **84 H5** 37 39N 121 52W
Pleasanton, *Tex., U.S.A.* **81 L5** 28 58N 98 29W
Pleasantville, *N.J., U.S.A.* **76 F8** 39 24N 74 32W
Pleasantville, *Pa., U.S.A.* **78 E5** 41 35N 79 34W
Plei Ku, *Vietnam* **38 F7** 13 57N 108 0 E
Plenty →, *Australia* **62 C2** 23 25S 136 31 E
Plenty, B. of, *N.Z.* **59 G6** 37 45S 177 0 E
Plentywood, *U.S.A.* **80 A2** 48 47N 104 34W
Plesetsk, *Russia* **24 B7** 62 43N 40 20 E
Plessisville, *Canada* **71 C5** 46 14N 71 47W
Plétipi, L., *Canada* **71 B5** 51 44N 70 6W
Pleven, *Bulgaria* **21 C11** 43 26N 24 37 E
Plevlja, *Montenegro, Yug.* **21 C8** 43 21N 19 21 E
Plevna, *Canada* **78 B8** 44 58N 76 59W
Płock, *Poland* **17 B10** 52 32N 19 40 E
Plöckenstein, *Germany* **16 D7** 48 46N 13 51 E
Ploieşti, *Romania* **17 F14** 44 57N 26 5 E
Plonge, Lac la, *Canada* **73 B7** 55 8N 107 20W
Plovdiv, *Bulgaria* **21 C11** 42 8N 24 44 E
Plum, *U.S.A.* **78 F5** 40 29N 79 47W
Plum I., *U.S.A.* **79 E12** 41 11N 72 12W
Plumas, *U.S.A.* **84 F7** 39 45N 120 4W
Plummer, *U.S.A.* **82 C5** 47 20N 116 53W
Plumtree, *Zimbabwe* **55 G2** 20 27S 27 55 E
Plungė, *Lithuania* **9 J19** 55 53N 21 59 E
Plymouth, *U.K.* **11 G3** 50 22N 4 10W
Plymouth, *Calif., U.S.A.* **84 G6** 38 29N 120 51W
Plymouth, *Ind., U.S.A.* **76 E2** 41 21N 86 19W
Plymouth, *Mass., U.S.A.* **79 E14** 41 57N 70 40W
Plymouth, *N.C., U.S.A.* **77 H7** 35 52N 76 43W
Plymouth, *N.H., U.S.A.* **79 C13** 43 46N 71 41W
Plymouth, *Pa., U.S.A.* **79 E9** 41 14N 75 57W
Plymouth, *Wis., U.S.A.* **76 D2** 43 45N 87 59W
Plynlimon = Pumlumon Fawr, *U.K.* **11 E4** 52 28N 3 46W
Plzeň, *Czech Rep.* **16 D7** 49 45N 13 22 E
Po →, *Italy* **20 B5** 44 57N 12 4 E
Po Hai = Bo Hai, *China* **35 E10** 39 0N 119 0 E
Pobeda, *Russia* **27 C15** 65 12N 146 12 E
Pobedy, Pik, *Kyrgyzstan* **26 E8** 42 0N 79 58 E
Pocahontas, *Ark., U.S.A.* **81 G9** 36 16N 90 58W
Pocahontas, *Iowa, U.S.A.* **80 D7** 42 44N 94 40W
Pocatello, *U.S.A.* **82 E7** 42 52N 112 27W
Pochutla, *Mexico* **87 D5** 15 50N 96 31W
Pocito Casas, *Mexico* **86 B2** 28 32N 111 6W
Pocomoke City, *U.S.A.* **76 F8** 38 5N 75 34W
Poços de Caldas, *Brazil* **95 A6** 21 50S 46 33W
Podgorica, *Montenegro, Yug.* **21 C8** 42 30N 19 19 E
Podilska Vysochyna, *Ukraine* **17 D14** 49 0N 28 0 E
Podolsk, *Russia* **24 C6** 55 25N 37 30 E
Podporozhye, *Russia* **24 B5** 60 55N 34 2 E
Pofadder, *S. Africa* **56 D2** 29 10S 19 22 E
Pogranitšnyi, *Russia* **30 B5** 44 25N 131 24 E
Poh, *Indonesia* **37 E6** 0 46S 122 51 E
P'ohang, *S. Korea* **35 F15** 36 1N 129 23 E
Pohjanmaa, *Finland* **8 E20** 62 58N 22 50 E
Pohnpei, *Micronesia* **64 G7** 6 55N 158 10 E
Pohri, *India* **42 G6** 25 32N 77 22 E
Poinsett, C., *Antarctica* **5 C8** 65 42S 113 18 E
Point Arena, *U.S.A.* **84 G3** 38 55N 123 41W
Point Baker, *U.S.A.* **72 B2** 56 21N 133 37W
Point Edward, *Canada* **70 D3** 43 0N 82 30W
Point Hope, *U.S.A.* **68 B3** 68 21N 166 47W
Point L., *Canada* **68 B8** 65 15N 113 4W
Point Pedro, *Sri Lanka* **40 Q12** 9 50N 80 15 E
Point Pleasant, *N.J., U.S.A.* **79 F10** 40 5N 74 4W
Point Pleasant, *W. Va., U.S.A.* **76 F4** 38 51N 82 8W
Pointe-à-Pitre, *Guadeloupe* **89 C7** 16 10N 61 30W
Pointe-Claire, *Canada* **79 A11** 45 26N 73 50W
Pointe-Gatineau, *Canada* **79 A9** 45 28N 75 42W
Pointe-Noire, *Congo* **52 E2** 4 48S 11 53 E
Poisonbush Ra., *Australia* **60 D3** 22 30S 121 30 E
Poissonnier Pt., *Australia* **60 C2** 19 57S 119 10 E
Poitiers, *France* **18 C4** 46 35N 0 20 E
Poitou, *France* **18 C3** 46 40N 0 10W
Pojoaque, *U.S.A.* **83 J11** 35 54N 106 1W
Pokaran, *India* **40 F7** 27 0N 71 50 E
Pokataroo, *Australia* **63 D4** 29 30S 148 36 E
Pokhara, *Nepal* **43 E10** 28 14N 83 58 E
Poko, *Dem. Rep. of the Congo* **54 B2** 3 7N 26 52 E
Pokrovsk = Engels, *Russia* **25 D8** 51 28N 46 6 E
Pokrovsk, *Russia* **27 C13** 61 29N 129 0 E
Pola = Pula, *Croatia* **16 F7** 44 54N 13 57 E
Polacca, *U.S.A.* **83 J8** 35 50N 110 23W
Polan, *Iran* **45 E9** 25 30N 61 10 E
Poland ■, *Europe* **17 C10** 52 0N 20 0 E
Polar Bear Prov. Park, *Canada* **70 A2** 55 0N 83 45W
Polatsk, *Belarus* **24 C4** 55 30N 28 50 E
Polcura, *Chile* **94 D1** 37 17S 71 43W
Polessk, *Russia* **9 J19** 54 50N 21 8 E
Polesye = Pripet Marshes, *Europe* **17 B15** 52 10N 28 10 E
Polevskoy, *Russia* **24 C11** 56 26N 60 11 E
Pŏlgyo-ri, *S. Korea* **35 G14** 34 51N 127 21 E
Police, *Poland* **16 B8** 53 33N 14 33 E
Polillo Is., *Phil.* **37 B6** 14 56N 122 0 E
Polis, *Cyprus* **23 D11** 35 2N 32 26 E
Políyiros, *Greece* **21 D10** 40 23N 23 25 E
Polk, *U.S.A.* **78 E5** 41 22N 79 56W
Pollachi, *India* **40 P10** 10 35N 77 0 E
Pollença, *Spain* **22 B10** 39 54N 3 1 E
Pollença, B. de, *Spain* **22 B10** 39 53N 3 8 E
Polnovat, *Russia* **26 C7** 63 50N 65 54 E
Polonne, *Ukraine* **17 C14** 50 6N 27 30 E
Polonnoye = Polonne, *Ukraine* **17 C14** 50 6N 27 30 E
Polson, *U.S.A.* **82 C6** 47 41N 114 9W
Poltava, *Ukraine* **25 E5** 49 35N 34 35 E
Põltsamaa, *Estonia* **9 G21** 58 41N 25 58 E
Polunochnoye, *Russia* **26 C7** 60 52N 60 25 E
Põlva, *Estonia* **9 G22** 58 3N 27 3 E
Polyarny, *Russia* **24 A5** 69 8N 33 20 E
Polynesia, *Pac. Oc.* **65 J11** 10 0S 162 0W
Polynésie française = French Polynesia ■, *Pac. Oc.* **65 K13** 20 0S 145 0W
Pomaro, *Mexico* **86 D4** 18 20N 103 18W
Pombal, *Portugal* **19 C1** 39 55N 8 40W
Pómbia, *Greece* **23 E6** 35 0N 24 51 E
Pomeroy, *Ohio, U.S.A.* **76 F4** 39 2N 82 2W
Pomeroy, *Wash., U.S.A.* **82 C5** 46 28N 117 36W
Pomézia, *Italy* **20 D5** 41 40N 12 30 E
Pomona, *Australia* **63 D5** 26 22S 152 52 E
Pomona, *U.S.A.* **85 L9** 34 4N 117 45W
Pomorskie, Pojezierze, *Poland* **17 B9** 53 40N 16 37 E
Pomos, *Cyprus* **23 D11** 35 9N 32 33 E
Pomos, C., *Cyprus* **23 D11** 35 10N 32 33 E
Pompano Beach, *U.S.A.* **77 M5** 26 14N 80 8W
Pompeys Pillar, *U.S.A.* **82 D10** 45 59N 107 57W
Pompton Lakes, *U.S.A.* **79 F10** 41 0N 74 17W
Ponape = Pohnpei, *Micronesia* **64 G7** 6 55N 158 10 E
Ponask L., *Canada* **70 B1** 54 0N 92 41W
Ponca, *U.S.A.* **80 D6** 42 34N 96 43W
Ponca City, *U.S.A.* **81 G6** 36 42N 97 5W
Ponce, *Puerto Rico* **89 C6** 18 1N 66 37W
Ponchatoula, *U.S.A.* **81 K9** 30 26N 90 26W
Poncheville, L., *Canada* **70 B4** 50 10N 76 55W
Pond, *U.S.A.* **85 K7** 35 43N 119 20W
Pond Inlet, *Canada* **69 A12** 72 40N 77 0W
Pondicherry, *India* **40 P11** 11 59N 79 50 E
Ponds, I. of, *Canada* **71 B8** 53 27N 55 52W
Ponferrada, *Spain* **19 A2** 42 32N 6 35W
Ponnani, *India* **40 P9** 10 45N 75 59 E
Ponnyadaung, *Burma* **41 J19** 22 0N 94 10 E
Ponoka, *Canada* **72 C6** 52 42N 113 40W
Ponorogo, *Indonesia* **37 G14** 7 52S 111 27 E
Ponoy, *Russia* **24 A7** 67 0N 41 13 E
Ponoy →, *Russia* **24 A7** 66 59N 41 17 E
Ponta do Sol, *Madeira* **22 D2** 32 42N 17 7W
Ponta Grossa, *Brazil* **95 B5** 25 7S 50 10W
Ponta Pora, *Brazil* **95 A4** 22 20S 55 35W
Pontarlier, *France* **18 C7** 46 54N 6 20 E
Pontchartrain L., *U.S.A.* **81 K10** 30 5N 90 5W
Ponte do Pungué, *Mozam.* **55 F3** 19 30S 34 33 E
Ponte Nova, *Brazil* **95 A7** 20 25S 42 54W
Ponteix, *Canada* **73 D7** 49 46N 107 29W
Pontevedra, *Spain* **19 A1** 42 26N 8 40W
Pontiac, *Ill., U.S.A.* **80 E10** 40 53N 88 38W
Pontiac, *Mich., U.S.A.* **76 D4** 42 38N 83 18W
Pontian Kecil, *Malaysia* **39 M4** 1 29N 103 23 E
Pontianak, *Indonesia* **36 E3** 0 3S 109 15 E
Pontine Is. = Ponziane, Ísole, *Italy* **20 D5** 40 55N 12 57 E
Pontine Mts. = Kuzey Anadolu Dağları, *Turkey* **25 F6** 41 30N 35 0 E
Pontivy, *France* **18 B2** 48 5N 2 58W
Pontoise, *France* **18 B5** 49 3N 2 5 E
Ponton →, *Canada* **72 B5** 58 27N 116 11W
Pontypool, *Canada* **78 B6** 44 6N 78 38W
Pontypool, *U.K.* **11 F4** 51 42N 3 2W
Ponziane, Ísole, *Italy* **20 D5** 40 55N 12 57 E
Poochera, *Australia* **63 E1** 32 43S 134 51 E
Poole, *U.K.* **11 G6** 50 43N 1 59W
Poole □, *U.K.* **11 G6** 50 43N 1 59W
Poona = Pune, *India* **40 K8** 18 29N 73 57 E
Pooncarie, *Australia* **63 E3** 33 22S 142 31 E
Poopelloe L., *Australia* **63 E3** 31 40S 144 0 E
Poopó, L. de, *Bolivia* **92 G5** 18 30S 67 35W
Popayán, *Colombia* **92 C3** 2 27N 76 36W
Poperinge, *Belgium* **15 D2** 50 51N 2 42 E
Popilta L., *Australia* **63 E3** 33 10S 141 42 E
Popio L., *Australia* **63 E3** 33 10S 141 52 E
Poplar, *U.S.A.* **80 A2** 48 7N 105 12W
Poplar →, *Canada* **73 C9** 53 0N 97 19W
Poplar Bluff, *U.S.A.* **81 G9** 36 46N 90 24W
Poplarville, *U.S.A.* **81 K10** 30 51N 89 32W
Popocatépetl, Volcán, *Mexico* **87 D5** 19 2N 98 38W
Popokabaka, *Dem. Rep. of the Congo* **52 F3** 5 41S 16 40 E
Poprad, *Slovak Rep.* **17 D11** 49 3N 20 18 E
Porali →, *Pakistan* **42 G2** 25 58N 66 26 E
Porbandar, *India* **40 J6** 21 44N 69 43 E
Porcher I., *Canada* **72 C2** 53 50N 130 30W
Porcupine →, *Canada* **73 B8** 59 11N 104 46W
Porcupine →, *U.S.A.* **68 B5** 66 34N 145 19W
Pordenone, *Italy* **20 B5** 45 57N 12 39 E
Pori, *Finland* **9 F19** 61 29N 21 48 E
Porlamar, *Venezuela* **92 A6** 10 57N 63 51W
Poronaysk, *Russia* **27 E15** 49 13N 143 0 E
Poroshiri-Dake, *Japan* **30 C11** 42 41N 142 52 E
Poroto Mts., *Tanzania* **55 D3** 9 0S 33 30 E
Porpoise B., *Antarctica* **5 C9** 66 0S 127 0 E
Porreres, *Spain* **22 B10** 39 31N 3 2 E
Porsangen, *Norway* **8 A21** 70 40N 25 40 E
Porsgrunn, *Norway* **9 G13** 59 10N 9 40 E
Port Alberni, *Canada* **72 D4** 49 14N 124 50W
Port Alfred, *S. Africa* **56 E4** 33 36S 26 55 E
Port Alice, *Canada* **72 C3** 50 20N 127 25W
Port Allegany, *U.S.A.* **78 E6** 41 48N 78 17W
Port Allen, *U.S.A.* **81 K9** 30 27N 91 12W
Port Alma, *Australia* **62 C5** 23 38S 150 53 E
Port Angeles, *U.S.A.* **84 B3** 48 7N 123 27W
Port Antonio, *Jamaica* **88 C4** 18 10N 76 30W
Port Aransas, *U.S.A.* **81 M6** 27 50N 97 4W
Port Arthur = Lüshun, *China* **35 E11** 38 45N 121 15 E
Port Arthur, *Australia* **62 G4** 43 7S 147 50 E
Port Arthur, *U.S.A.* **81 L8** 29 54N 93 56W
Port au Choix, *Canada* **71 B8** 50 43N 57 22W
Port au Port B., *Canada* **71 C8** 48 40N 58 50W
Port-au-Prince, *Haiti* **89 C5** 18 40N 72 20W
Port Augusta, *Australia* **63 E2** 32 30S 137 50 E
Port Austin, *U.S.A.* **78 B2** 44 3N 83 1W
Port Bell, *Uganda* **54 B3** 0 18N 32 35 E
Port Bergé Vaovao, *Madag.* **57 B8** 15 33S 47 40 E
Port Blandford, *Canada* **71 C9** 48 20N 54 10W
Port Bradshaw, *Australia* **62 A2** 12 30S 137 20 E
Port Broughton, *Australia* **63 E2** 33 37S 137 56 E
Port Burwell, *Canada* **78 D4** 42 40N 80 48W
Port Campbell, *Australia* **63 F3** 38 37S 143 1 E
Port Canning, *India* **43 H13** 22 23N 88 40 E
Port-Cartier, *Canada* **71 B6** 50 2N 66 50W
Port Chalmers, *N.Z.* **59 L3** 45 49S 170 30 E
Port Charlotte, *U.S.A.* **77 M4** 26 59N 82 6W
Port Chester, *U.S.A.* **79 F11** 41 0N 73 40W
Port Clements, *Canada* **72 C2** 53 40N 132 10W
Port Clinton, *U.S.A.* **76 E4** 41 31N 82 56W
Port Colborne, *Canada* **78 D5** 42 50N 79 10W
Port Coquitlam, *Canada* **72 D4** 49 15N 122 45W
Port Credit, *Canada* **78 C5** 43 33N 79 35W
Port Curtis, *Australia* **62 C5** 23 57S 151 20 E
Port d'Alcúdia, *Spain* **22 B10** 39 50N 3 7 E
Port Dalhousie, *Canada* **78 C5** 43 13N 79 16W
Port Darwin, *Australia* **60 B5** 12 24S 130 45 E
Port Darwin, *Falk. Is.* **96 G5** 51 50S 59 0W
Port Davey, *Australia* **62 G4** 43 16S 145 55 E
Port-de-Paix, *Haiti* **89 C5** 19 50N 72 50W
Port de Pollença, *Spain* **22 B10** 39 54N 3 4 E
Port de Sóller, *Spain* **22 B9** 39 48N 2 42 E
Port Dickson, *Malaysia* **39 L3** 2 30N 101 49 E
Port Douglas, *Australia* **62 B4** 16 30S 145 30 E
Port Dover, *Canada* **78 D4** 42 47N 80 12W
Port Edward, *Canada* **72 C2** 54 12N 130 10W
Port Elgin, *Canada* **78 B3** 44 25N 81 25W
Port Elizabeth, *S. Africa* **56 E4** 33 58S 25 40 E
Port Ellen, *U.K.* **12 F2** 55 38N 6 11W
Port Erin, *U.K.* **10 C3** 54 5N 4 45W
Port Essington, *Australia* **60 B5** 11 15S 132 10 E
Port Etienne = Nouâdhibou, *Mauritania* **50 D2** 20 54N 17 0W
Port Ewen, *U.S.A.* **79 E11** 41 54N 73 59W
Port Fairy, *Australia* **63 F3** 38 22S 142 12 E
Port Gamble, *U.S.A.* **84 C4** 47 51N 122 35W
Port-Gentil, *Gabon* **52 E1** 0 40S 8 50 E
Port Germein, *Australia* **63 E2** 33 1S 138 1 E
Port Gibson, *U.S.A.* **81 K9** 31 58N 90 59W
Port Glasgow, *U.K.* **12 F4** 55 56N 4 41W
Port Harcourt, *Nigeria* **50 H7** 4 40N 7 10 E
Port Hardy, *Canada* **72 C3** 50 41N 127 30W
Port Harrison = Inukjuak, *Canada* **69 C12** 58 25N 78 15W
Port Hawkesbury, *Canada* **71 C7** 45 36N 61 22W
Port Hedland, *Australia* **60 D2** 20 25S 118 35 E
Port Henry, *U.S.A.* **79 B11** 44 3N 73 28W
Port Hood, *Canada* **71 C7** 46 0N 61 32W
Port Hope, *Canada* **78 C6** 43 56N 78 20W
Port Hope, *U.S.A.* **78 C2** 43 57N 82 43W
Port Hope Simpson, *Canada* **71 B8** 52 33N 56 18W
Port Hueneme, *U.S.A.* **85 L7** 34 7N 119 12W
Port Huron, *U.S.A.* **78 D2** 42 58N 82 26W
Port Jefferson, *U.S.A.* **79 F11** 40 57N 73 3W
Port Jervis, *U.S.A.* **79 E10** 41 22N 74 41W
Port Kelang = Pelabuhan Kelang, *Malaysia* **39 L3** 3 0N 101 23 E
Port Kenny, *Australia* **63 E1** 33 10S 134 41 E
Port Lairge = Waterford, *Ireland* **13 D4** 52 15N 7 8W
Port Laoise, *Ireland* **13 C4** 53 2N 7 18W
Port Lavaca, *U.S.A.* **81 L6** 28 37N 96 38W
Port Leyden, *U.S.A.* **79 C9** 43 35N 75 21W
Port Lincoln, *Australia* **63 E2** 34 42S 135 52 E
Port Loko, *S. Leone* **50 G3** 8 48N 12 46W
Port Louis, *Mauritius* **49 H9** 20 10S 57 30 E
Port Lyautey = Kenitra, *Morocco* **50 B4** 34 15N 6 40W
Port MacDonnell, *Australia* **63 F3** 38 5S 140 48 E
Port McNeill, *Canada* **72 C3** 50 35N 127 6W
Port Macquarie, *Australia* **63 E5** 31 25S 152 25 E
Port Maria, *Jamaica* **88 C4** 18 25N 76 55W
Port Matilda, *U.S.A.* **78 F6** 40 48N 78 3W
Port Mellon, *Canada* **72 D4** 49 32N 123 31W
Port-Menier, *Canada* **71 C7** 49 51N 64 15W
Port Moody, *Canada* **84 A4** 49 17N 122 51W
Port Morant, *Jamaica* **88 C4** 17 54N 76 19W
Port Moresby, *Papua N. G.* **64 H6** 9 24S 147 8 E
Port Musgrave, *Australia* **62 A3** 11 55S 141 50 E
Port Neches, *U.S.A.* **81 L8** 30 0N 93 59W
Port Nolloth, *S. Africa* **56 D2** 29 17S 16 52 E
Port Nouveau-Québec = Kangiqsualujjuaq, *Canada* **69 C13** 58 30N 65 59W
Port of Spain, *Trin. & Tob.* **89 D7** 10 40N 61 31W
Port Orange, *U.S.A.* **77 L5** 29 9N 80 59W
Port Orchard, *U.S.A.* **84 C4** 47 32N 122 38W
Port Orford, *U.S.A.* **82 E1** 42 45N 124 30W
Port Pegasus, *N.Z.* **59 M1** 47 12S 167 41 E
Port Perry, *Canada* **78 B6** 44 6N 78 56W
Port Phillip B., *Australia* **63 F3** 38 10S 144 50 E
Port Pirie, *Australia* **63 E2** 33 10S 138 1 E
Port Radium = Echo Bay, *Canada* **68 B8** 66 5N 117 55W
Port Renfrew, *Canada* **72 D4** 48 30N 124 20W
Port Roper, *Australia* **62 A2** 14 45S 135 25 E
Port Rowan, *Canada* **78 D4** 42 40N 80 30W
Port Safaga = Bûr Safâga, *Egypt* **44 E2** 26 43N 33 57 E
Port Said = Bûr Sa'îd, *Egypt* **51 B12** 31 16N 32 18 E
Port St. Joe, *U.S.A.* **77 L3** 29 49N 85 18W
Port St. Johns, *S. Africa* **57 E4** 31 38S 29 33 E
Port St. Lucie, *U.S.A.* **77 M5** 27 20N 80 20W
Port Sanilac, *U.S.A.* **78 C2** 43 26N 82 33W
Port Severn, *Canada* **78 B5** 44 48N 79 43W
Port Shepstone, *S. Africa* **57 E5** 30 44S 30 28 E
Port Simpson, *Canada* **72 C2** 54 30N 130 20W
Port Stanley = Stanley, *Falk. Is.* **96 G5** 51 40S 59 51W
Port Stanley, *Canada* **78 D3** 42 40N 81 10W
Port Sudan = Bûr Sûdân, *Sudan* **51 E13** 19 32N 37 9 E
Port Sulphur, *U.S.A.* **81 L10** 29 29N 89 42W
Port Talbot, *U.K.* **11 F4** 51 35N 3 47W
Port Townsend, *U.S.A.* **84 B4** 48 7N 122 45W
Port-Vendres, *France* **18 E5** 42 32N 3 8 E
Port Vila, *Vanuatu* **64 J8** 17 45S 168 18 E
Port Vladimir, *Russia* **24 A5** 69 25N 33 6 E
Port Wakefield, *Australia* **63 E2** 34 12S 138 10 E
Port Washington, *U.S.A.* **76 D2** 43 23N 87 53W
Port Weld = Kuala Sepetang, *Malaysia* **39 K3** 4 49N 100 28 E
Porta Orientalis, *Romania* **17 F12** 45 6N 22 18 E
Portadown, *U.K.* **13 B5** 54 25N 6 27W
Portaferry, *U.K.* **13 B6** 54 23N 5 33W
Portage, *Pa., U.S.A.* **78 F6** 40 23N 78 41W
Portage, *Wis., U.S.A.* **80 D10** 43 33N 89 28W
Portage La Prairie, *Canada* **73 D9** 49 58N 98 18W
Portageville, *U.S.A.* **81 G10** 36 26N 89 42W
Portalegre, *Portugal* **19 C2** 39 19N 7 25W
Portales, *U.S.A.* **81 H3** 34 11N 103 20W
Portarlington, *Ireland* **13 C4** 53 9N 7 14W
Portbou, *Spain* **19 A7** 42 25N 3 9 E
Porter L., *N.W.T., Canada* **73 A7** 61 41N 108 5W
Porter L., *Sask., Canada* **73 B7** 56 20N 107 20W
Porterville, *S. Africa* **56 E2** 33 0S 19 0 E
Porterville, *U.S.A.* **84 J8** 36 4N 119 1W
Porthcawl, *U.K.* **11 F4** 51 29N 3 42W
Porthill, *U.S.A.* **82 B5** 48 59N 116 30W
Porthmadog, *U.K.* **10 E3** 52 55N 4 8W
Portile de Fier, *Europe* **17 F12** 44 44N 22 30 E
Portimão, *Portugal* **19 D1** 37 8N 8 32W
Portishead, *U.K.* **11 F5** 51 29N 2 46W
Portknockie, *U.K.* **12 D6** 57 42N 2 51W
Portland, *N.S.W., Australia* **63 E5** 33 20S 150 0 E
Portland, *Vic., Australia* **63 F3** 38 20S 141 35 E
Portland, *Canada* **79 B8** 44 42N 76 12W
Portland, *Conn., U.S.A.* **79 E12** 41 34N 72 38W
Portland, *Maine, U.S.A.* **69 D12** 43 39N 70 16W
Portland, *Mich., U.S.A.* **76 D3** 42 52N 84 54W
Portland, *Oreg., U.S.A.* **84 E4** 45 32N 122 37W
Portland, *Pa., U.S.A.* **79 F9** 40 55N 75 6W
Portland, *Tex., U.S.A.* **81 M6** 27 53N 97 20W
Portland, I. of, *U.K.* **11 G5** 50 33N 2 26W
Portland B., *Australia* **63 F3** 38 15S 141 45 E
Portland Bill, *U.K.* **11 G5** 50 31N 2 28W
Portland Canal, *U.S.A.* **72 B2** 55 56N 130 0W
Portmadoc = Porthmadog, *U.K.* **10 E3** 52 55N 4 8W
Porto, *Portugal* **19 B1** 41 8N 8 40W
Pôrto Alegre, *Brazil* **95 C5** 30 5S 51 10W
Porto Amboim = Gunza, *Angola* **52 G2** 10 50S 13 50 E
Porto Cristo, *Spain* **22 B10** 39 33N 3 20 E
Pôrto de Móz, *Brazil* **93 D8** 1 41S 52 13W
Porto Empédocle, *Italy* **20 F5** 37 17N 13 32 E
Pôrto Esperança, *Brazil* **92 G7** 19 37S 57 29W
Pôrto Franco, *Brazil* **93 E9** 6 20S 47 24W
Pôrto Mendes, *Brazil* **95 A5** 24 30S 54 15W
Porto Moniz, *Madeira* **22 D2** 32 52N 17 11W
Pôrto Murtinho, *Brazil* **92 H7** 21 45S 57 55W
Pôrto Nacional, *Brazil* **93 F9** 10 40S 48 30W
Porto-Novo, *Benin* **50 G6** 6 23N 2 42 E
Porto Petro, *Spain* **22 B10** 39 22N 3 13 E
Porto Santo, *Madeira* **50 B2** 33 45N 16 25W
Pôrto São José, *Brazil* **95 A5** 22 43S 53 10W
Pôrto Seguro, *Brazil* **93 G11** 16 26S 39 5W
Porto Tórres, *Italy* **20 D3** 40 50N 8 24 E
Pôrto União, *Brazil* **95 B5** 26 10S 51 10W
Pôrto Válter, *Brazil* **92 E4** 8 15S 72 40W
Porto-Vecchio, *France* **18 F8** 41 35N 9 16 E
Pôrto Velho, *Brazil* **92 E6** 8 46S 63 54W
Portobelo, *Panama* **88 E4** 9 35N 79 42W
Portoferráio, *Italy* **20 C4** 42 48N 10 20 E
Portola, *U.S.A.* **84 F6** 39 49N 120 28W
Portoscuso, *Italy* **20 E3** 39 12N 8 24 E
Portoviejo, *Ecuador* **92 D2** 1 7S 80 28W
Portpatrick, *U.K.* **12 G3** 54 51N 5 7W
Portree, *U.K.* **12 D2** 57 25N 6 12W
Portrush, *U.K.* **13 A5** 55 12N 6 40W
Portsmouth, *Domin.* **89 C7** 15 34N 61 27W
Portsmouth, *U.K.* **11 G6** 50 48N 1 6W
Portsmouth, *N.H., U.S.A.* **77 D10** 43 5N 70 45W
Portsmouth, *Ohio, U.S.A.* **76 F4** 38 44N 82 57W
Portsmouth, *R.I., U.S.A.* **79 E13** 41 36N 71 15W
Portsmouth, *Va., U.S.A.* **76 G7** 36 50N 76 18W
Portsmouth □, *U.K.* **11 G6** 50 48N 1 6W
Portsoy, *U.K.* **12 D6** 57 41N 2 41W
Portstewart, *U.K.* **13 A5** 55 11N 6 43W
Porttipahtan tekojärvi, *Finland* **8 B22** 68 5N 26 40 E
Portugal ■, *Europe* **19 C1** 40 0N 8 0W
Portumna, *Ireland* **13 C3** 53 6N 8 14W
Portville, *U.S.A.* **78 D6** 42 3N 78 20W
Porvenir, *Chile* **96 G2** 53 10S 70 16W
Porvoo, *Finland* **9 F21** 60 24N 25 40 E
Posadas, *Argentina* **95 B4** 27 30S 55 50W
Poshan = Boshan, *China* **35 F9** 36 28N 117 49 E
Posht-e-Badam, *Iran* **45 C7** 33 2N 55 23 E
Poso, *Indonesia* **37 E6** 1 20S 120 55 E
Posong, *S. Korea* **35 G14** 34 46N 127 5 E

Râs Timirist

Qal'at al Akhḑar, Si. Arabia 44 E3 28 0N 37 10 E
Qal'at Dīzah, Iraq 44 B5 36 11N 45 7 E
Qal'at Şāliḩ, Iraq 44 D5 31 31N 47 16 E
Qal'at Sukkar, Iraq 44 D5 31 51N 46 5 E
Qal'eh Shaharak, Afghan. 40 B4 34 10N 64 20 E
Qamdo, China 32 C4 31 15N 97 6 E
Qamruddin Karez, Pakistan 42 D3 31 45N 68 20 E
Qandahār, Afghan. 40 D4 31 32N 65 30 E
Qandahār □, Afghan. 40 D4 31 0N 65 0 E
Qapān, Iran 45 B7 37 40N 55 47 E
Qapshaghay, Kazakstan 26 E8 43 51N 77 14 E
Qaqortoq = Julianehåb, Greenland 4 C5 60 43N 46 0W
Qara Qash →, India 43 B8 35 0N 78 30 E
Qarabutaq, Kazakstan 26 E7 49 59N 60 14 E
Qaraghandy, Kazakstan 26 E8 49 50N 73 10 E
Qārah, Si. Arabia 44 D4 29 55N 40 3 E
Qarataū, Kazakstan 26 E8 43 10N 70 28 E
Qareh →, Iran 44 B5 39 25N 47 22 E
Qareh Tekān, Iran 45 B6 36 38N 49 29 E
Qarqan He →, China 32 C3 39 30N 88 30 E
Qarqaraly, Kazakstan 26 E8 49 26N 75 30 E
Qarshi, Uzbekistan 26 F7 38 53N 65 48 E
Qartabā, Lebanon 47 A4 34 4N 35 50 E
Qaryat al Gharab, Iraq 44 D5 31 27N 44 48 E
Qaryat al 'Ulyā, Si. Arabia 44 E5 27 33N 47 42 E
Qasr 'Amra, Jordan 44 D3 31 48N 36 35 E
Qaşr-e Qand, Iran 45 E9 26 15N 60 45 E
Qasr Farâfra, Egypt 51 C11 27 0N 28 1 E
Qatanā, Syria 47 B5 33 26N 36 4 E
Qatar ■, Asia 45 E6 25 30N 51 15 E
Qatlīsh, Iran 45 B8 37 50N 57 19 E
Qattâra, Munkhafed el, Egypt 51 C11 29 30N 27 30 E
Qattâra Depression = Qattâra, Munkhafed el, Egypt 51 C11 29 30N 27 30 E
Qawām al Ḩamzah, Iraq 44 D5 31 43N 44 58 E
Qāyen, Iran 45 C8 33 40N 59 10 E
Qazaqstan = Kazakstan ■, Asia 26 E8 50 0N 70 0 E
Qazimämmäd, Azerbaijan 45 A6 40 3N 49 0 E
Qazvin, Iran 45 B6 36 15N 50 0 E
Qena, Egypt 51 C12 26 10N 32 43 E
Qeqertarsuaq = Disko, Greenland 4 C5 69 45N 53 30W
Qeqertarsuaq = Godhavn, Greenland 4 C5 69 15N 53 38W
Qeshlāq, Iran 44 C5 34 55N 46 28 E
Qeshm, Iran 45 E8 26 55N 56 10 E
Qeys, Iran 45 E7 26 32N 53 58 E
Qezel Owzen →, Iran 45 B6 36 45N 49 22 E
Qezi'ot, Israel 47 E3 30 52N 34 26 E
Qi Xian, China 34 G8 34 40N 114 48 E
Qian Gorlos, China 35 B13 45 5N 124 42 E
Qian Xian, China 34 G5 34 31N 108 15 E
Qianyang, China 34 G4 34 40N 107 8 E
Qibā', Si. Arabia 44 E5 27 24N 44 20 E
Qikiqtarjuaq, Canada 69 B13 67 33N 63 0W
Qila Safed, Pakistan 40 E2 29 0N 61 30 E
Qila Saifullāh, Pakistan 42 D3 30 45N 68 17 E
Qilian Shan, China 32 C4 38 30N 96 0 E
Qin He →, China 34 G7 35 1N 113 22 E
Qin Ling = Qinling Shandi, China 34 H5 33 50N 108 10 E
Qin'an, China 34 G3 34 48N 105 40 E
Qing Xian, China 34 E9 38 35N 116 45 E
Qingcheng, China 35 F9 37 15N 117 40 E
Qingdao, China 35 F11 36 5N 120 20 E
Qingfeng, China 34 G8 35 52N 115 8 E
Qinghai □, China 32 C4 36 0N 98 0 E
Qinghai Hu, China 32 C5 36 40N 100 10 E
Qinghecheng, China 35 D13 41 28N 124 15 E
Qinghemen, China 35 D11 41 48N 121 25 E
Qingjian, China 34 F6 37 8N 110 8 E
Qingjiang = Huaiyin, China 35 H10 33 30N 119 2 E
Qingshui, China 34 G4 34 48N 106 8 E
Qingshuihe, China 34 E6 39 55N 111 35 E
Qingtongxia Shuiku, China 34 F3 37 50N 105 58 E
Qingxu, China 34 F7 37 34N 112 22 E
Qingyang, China 34 F4 36 2N 107 55 E
Qingyuan, China 35 C13 42 10N 124 55 E
Qingyun, China 35 F9 37 45N 117 20 E
Qinhuangdao, China 35 E10 39 56N 119 30 E
Qinling Shandi, China 34 H5 33 50N 108 10 E
Qinshui, China 34 G7 35 40N 112 8 E
Qinyang = Jiyuan, China 34 G7 35 7N 112 57 E
Qinyuan, China 34 F7 36 29N 112 20 E
Qinzhou, China 32 D5 21 58N 108 38 E
Qionghai, China 38 C8 19 15N 110 26 E
Qiongzhou Haixia, China 38 B8 20 10N 110 15 E
Qiqihar, China 27 E13 47 26N 124 0 E
Qiraîya, W. →, Egypt 47 E3 30 27N 34 0 E
Qiryat Ata, Israel 47 C4 32 47N 35 6 E
Qiryat Gat, Israel 47 D3 31 32N 34 46 E
Qiryat Mal'akhi, Israel 47 D3 31 44N 34 44 E
Qiryat Shemona, Israel 47 B4 33 13N 35 35 E
Qiryat Yam, Israel 47 C4 32 51N 35 4 E
Qishan, China 34 G4 34 25N 107 38 E
Qitai, China 32 B3 44 2N 89 35 E
Qixia, China 35 F11 37 17N 120 52 E
Qızılağac Körfäzi, Azerbaijan 45 B6 39 9N 49 0 E
Qojūr, Iran 44 B5 36 12N 47 55 E
Qom, Iran 45 C6 34 40N 51 0 E
Qomolangma Feng = Everest, Mt., Nepal 43 E12 28 5N 86 58 E
Qomsheh, Iran 45 D6 32 0N 51 55 E
Qostanay, Kazakstan 26 D7 53 10N 63 35 E
Quabbin Reservoir, U.S.A. 79 D12 42 20N 72 20W
Quairading, Australia 61 F2 32 0S 117 21 E
Quakertown, U.S.A. 79 F9 40 26N 75 21W
Qualicum Beach, Canada 72 D4 49 22N 124 26W
Quambatook, Australia 63 F3 35 49S 143 34 E
Quambone, Australia 63 E4 30 57S 147 53 E
Quamby, Australia 62 C3 20 22S 140 17 E
Quan Long = Ca Mau, Vietnam 39 H5 9 7N 105 8 E
Quanah, U.S.A. 81 H5 34 18N 99 44W
Quang Ngai, Vietnam 38 E7 15 13N 108 58 E
Quang Tri, Vietnam 38 D6 16 45N 107 13 E
Quantock Hills, U.K. 11 F4 51 8N 3 10W
Quanzhou, China 33 D6 24 55N 118 34 E
Qu'Appelle, Canada 73 C8 50 33N 103 53W
Quaqtaq, Canada 69 B13 60 55N 69 40W
Quaraí, Brazil 94 C4 30 15S 56 20W
Quartu Sant'Elena, Italy 20 E3 39 15N 9 10 E
Quartzsite, U.S.A. 85 M12 33 40N 114 13W
Quatsino Sd., Canada 72 C3 50 25N 127 58W
Quba, Azerbaijan 25 F8 41 21N 48 32 E
Qūchān, Iran 45 B8 37 10N 58 27 E
Queanbeyan, Australia 63 F4 35 17S 149 14 E
Québec, Canada 71 C5 46 52N 71 13W
Québec □, Canada 71 C6 48 0N 74 0W
Queen Alexandra Ra., Antarctica 5 E11 85 0S 170 0 E
Queen Charlotte City, Canada 72 C2 53 15N 132 2W
Queen Charlotte Is., Canada 72 C2 53 20N 132 10W
Queen Charlotte Sd., Canada 72 C3 51 0N 128 0W
Queen Charlotte Strait, Canada 72 C3 50 45N 127 10W
Queen Elizabeth Is., Canada 66 B10 76 0N 95 0W
Queen Elizabeth Nat. Park, Uganda 54 C3 0 0 30 0 E
Queen Mary Land, Antarctica 5 D7 70 0S 95 0 E
Queen Maud G., Canada 68 B9 68 15N 102 30W
Queen Maud Land, Antarctica 5 D3 72 30S 12 0 E
Queen Maud Mts., Antarctica 5 E13 86 0S 160 0W
Queens Chan., Australia 60 C4 15 0S 129 30 E
Queenscliff, Australia 63 F3 38 16S 144 39 E
Queensland □, Australia 62 C3 22 0S 142 0 E
Queenstown, Australia 62 G4 42 4S 145 35 E
Queenstown, N.Z. 59 L2 45 1S 168 40 E
Queenstown, S. Africa 56 E4 31 52S 26 52 E
Queets, U.S.A. 84 C2 47 32N 124 20W
Queguay Grande →, Uruguay 94 C4 32 9S 58 9W
Queimadas, Brazil 93 F11 11 0S 39 38W
Quelimane, Mozam. 55 F4 17 53S 36 58 E
Quellón, Chile 96 E2 43 7S 73 37W
Quelpart = Cheju do, S. Korea 35 H14 33 29N 126 34 E
Quemado, N. Mex., U.S.A. 83 J9 34 20N 108 30W
Quemado, Tex., U.S.A. 81 L4 28 58N 100 35W
Quemú-Quemú, Argentina 94 D3 36 3S 63 36W
Quequén, Argentina 94 D4 38 30S 58 30W
Querétaro, Mexico 86 C4 20 36N 100 23W
Querétaro □, Mexico 86 C5 20 30N 100 0W
Queshan, China 34 H8 32 55N 114 2 E
Quesnel, Canada 72 C4 53 0N 122 30W
Quesnel →, Canada 72 C4 52 58N 122 29W
Quesnel L., Canada 72 C4 52 30N 121 20W
Questa, U.S.A. 83 H11 36 42N 105 36W
Quetico Prov. Park, Canada 70 C1 48 30N 91 45W
Quetta, Pakistan 42 D2 30 15N 66 55 E
Quezaltenango, Guatemala 88 D1 14 50N 91 30W
Quezon City, Phil. 37 B6 14 38N 121 0 E
Qufār, Si. Arabia 44 E4 27 26N 41 37 E
Qui Nhon, Vietnam 38 F7 13 40N 109 13 E
Quibaxe, Angola 52 F2 8 24S 14 27 E
Quibdo, Colombia 92 B3 5 42N 76 40W
Quiberon, France 18 C2 47 29N 3 9W
Quiet L., Canada 72 A2 61 5N 133 5W
Quiindy, Paraguay 94 B4 25 58S 57 14W
Quila, Mexico 86 C3 24 23N 107 13W
Quilán, C., Chile 96 E2 43 15S 74 30W
Quilcene, U.S.A. 84 C4 47 49N 122 53W
Quilimarí, Chile 94 C1 32 5S 71 30W
Quilino, Argentina 94 C3 30 14S 64 29W
Quill Lakes, Canada 73 C8 51 55N 104 13W
Quillabamba, Peru 92 F4 12 50S 72 50W
Quillagua, Chile 94 A2 21 40S 69 40W
Quillaicillo, Chile 94 C1 31 17S 71 40W
Quillota, Chile 94 C1 32 54S 71 16W
Quilmes, Argentina 94 C4 34 43S 58 15W
Quilon, India 40 Q10 8 50N 76 38 E
Quilpie, Australia 63 D3 26 35S 144 11 E
Quilpué, Chile 94 C1 33 5S 71 33W
Quilua, Mozam. 55 F4 16 17S 39 54 E
Quimilí, Argentina 94 B3 27 40S 62 30W
Quimper, France 18 B1 48 0N 4 9W
Quimperlé, France 18 C2 47 53N 3 33W
Quinault →, U.S.A. 84 C2 47 21N 124 18W
Quincy, Calif., U.S.A. 84 F6 39 56N 120 57W
Quincy, Fla., U.S.A. 77 K3 30 35N 84 34W
Quincy, Ill., U.S.A. 80 F9 39 56N 91 23W
Quincy, Mass., U.S.A. 79 D14 42 15N 71 0W
Quincy, Wash., U.S.A. 82 C4 47 22N 119 56W
Quines, Argentina 94 C2 32 13S 65 48W
Quinga, Mozam. 55 F5 15 49S 40 15 E
Quinns Rocks, Australia 61 F2 31 40S 115 42 E
Quintana Roo □, Mexico 87 D7 19 0N 88 0W
Quintanar de la Orden, Spain 19 C4 39 36N 3 5W
Quintero, Chile 94 C1 32 45S 71 30W
Quirihue, Chile 94 D1 36 15S 72 35W
Quirindi, Australia 63 E5 31 28S 150 40 E
Quirinópolis, Brazil 93 G8 18 32S 50 30W
Quissanga, Mozam. 55 E5 12 24S 40 28 E
Quitilipi, Argentina 94 B3 26 50S 60 13W
Quitman, U.S.A. 77 K4 30 47N 83 34W
Quito, Ecuador 92 D3 0 15S 78 35W
Quixadá, Brazil 93 D11 4 55S 39 0W
Quixaxe, Mozam. 55 F5 15 17S 40 4 E
Qul'ân, Jazâ'ir, Egypt 44 E2 24 22N 35 31 E
Qumbu, S. Africa 57 E4 31 10S 28 48 E
Quneitra, Syria 47 B4 33 7N 35 48 E
Qŭnghirot, Uzbekistan 26 E6 43 6N 58 54 E
Quoin I., Australia 60 B4 14 54S 129 32 E
Quoin Pt., S. Africa 56 E2 34 46S 19 37 E
Quorn, Australia 63 E2 32 25S 138 5 E
Qŭqon, Uzbekistan 26 E8 40 30N 70 57 E
Qurnat as Sawdā', Lebanon 47 A5 34 18N 36 6 E
Quşaybā', Si. Arabia 44 E4 26 53N 43 35 E
Qusaybah, Iraq 44 C4 34 24N 40 59 E
Quseir, Egypt 44 E2 26 7N 34 16 E
Qūshchī, Iran 44 B5 37 59N 45 3 E
Quthing, Lesotho 57 E4 30 25S 27 36 E
Qūţīābād, Iran 45 C6 35 47N 48 30 E
Quwo, China 34 G6 35 38N 111 25 E
Quyang, China 34 E8 38 35N 114 40 E
Quynh Nhai, Vietnam 38 B4 21 49N 103 33 E
Quyon, Canada 79 A8 45 31N 76 14W
Quzhou, China 33 D6 28 57N 118 54 E
Quzi, China 34 F4 36 20N 107 20 E
Qyzylorda, Kazakstan 26 E7 44 48N 65 28 E

R

Ra, Ko, Thailand 39 H2 9 13N 98 16 E
Raahe, Finland 8 D21 64 40N 24 28 E
Raalte, Neths. 15 B6 52 23N 6 16 E
Raasay, U.K. 12 D2 57 25N 6 4W
Raasay, Sd. of, U.K. 12 D2 57 30N 6 8W
Raba, Indonesia 37 F5 8 36S 118 55 E
Rába →, Hungary 17 E9 47 38N 17 38 E
Rabai, Kenya 54 C4 3 50S 39 31 E
Rabat, Malta 23 D1 35 53N 14 25 E
Rabat, Morocco 50 B4 34 2N 6 48W
Rabaul, Papua N. G. 64 H7 4 24S 152 18 E
Rābigh, Si. Arabia 46 C2 22 50N 39 5 E
Râbniţa, Moldova 17 E15 47 45N 29 0 E
Rābor, Iran 45 D8 29 17N 56 55 E
Race, C., Canada 71 C9 46 40N 53 5W
Rach Gia, Vietnam 39 G5 10 5N 105 5 E
Rachid, Mauritania 50 E3 18 48N 11 41W
Racibórz, Poland 17 C10 50 7N 18 18 E
Racine, U.S.A. 76 D2 42 41N 87 51W
Rackerby, U.S.A. 84 F5 39 26N 121 22W
Radama, Nosy, Madag. 57 A8 14 0S 47 47 E
Radama, Saikanosy, Madag. 57 A8 14 16S 47 53 E
Rădăuţi, Romania 17 E13 47 50N 25 59 E
Radcliff, U.S.A. 76 G3 37 51N 85 57W
Radekhiv, Ukraine 17 C13 50 25N 24 32 E
Radekhov = Radekhiv, Ukraine 17 C13 50 25N 24 32 E
Radford, U.S.A. 76 G5 37 8N 80 34W
Radhanpur, India 42 H4 23 50N 71 38 E
Radhwa, Jabal, Si. Arabia 44 E3 24 34N 38 18 E
Radisson, Canada 70 B4 53 47N 77 37W
Radisson, Sask., Canada 73 C7 52 30N 107 20W
Radium Hot Springs, Canada 72 C5 50 35N 116 2W
Radnor Forest, U.K. 11 E4 52 17N 3 10W
Radom, Poland 17 C11 51 23N 21 12 E
Radomsko, Poland 17 C10 51 5N 19 28 E
Radomyshl, Ukraine 17 C15 50 30N 29 12 E
Radstock, C., Australia 63 E1 33 12S 134 20 E
Radviliškis, Lithuania 9 J20 55 49N 23 33 E
Radville, Canada 73 D8 49 30N 104 15W
Rae, Canada 72 A5 62 50N 116 3W
Rae Bareli, India 43 F9 26 18N 81 20 E
Rae Isthmus, Canada 69 B11 66 40N 87 30W
Raeren, Belgium 15 D6 50 41N 6 7 E
Raeside, L., Australia 61 E3 29 20S 122 0 E
Raetihi, N.Z. 59 H5 39 25S 175 17 E
Rafaela, Argentina 94 C3 31 10S 61 30W
Rafah, Gaza Strip 47 D3 31 18N 34 14 E
Rafai, C.A.R. 54 B1 4 59N 23 58 E
Rafḩā, Si. Arabia 44 D4 29 35N 43 35 E
Rafsanjān, Iran 45 D8 30 30N 56 5 E
Raft Pt., Australia 60 C3 16 4S 124 26 E
Raga, Sudan 51 G11 8 28N 25 41 E
Ragachow, Belarus 17 B16 53 8N 30 5 E
Ragama, Sri Lanka 40 R11 7 0N 79 50 E
Ragged, Mt., Australia 61 F3 33 27S 123 25 E
Raghunathpalli, India 43 H11 22 14N 84 48 E
Raghunathpur, India 43 H12 23 33N 86 40 E
Raglan, N.Z. 59 G5 37 55S 174 55 E
Ragusa, Italy 20 F6 36 55N 14 44 E
Raha, Indonesia 37 E6 4 55S 123 0 E
Rahaeng = Tak, Thailand 38 D2 16 52N 99 8 E
Rahatgarh, India 43 H8 23 47N 78 22 E
Raḩīmah, Si. Arabia 45 E6 26 42N 50 4 E
Rahimyar Khan, Pakistan 42 E4 28 30N 70 25 E
Rāhjerd, Iran 45 C6 34 22N 50 22 E
Rahon, India 42 D7 31 3N 76 7 E
Raichur, India 40 L10 16 10N 77 20 E
Raiganj, India 43 G13 25 37N 88 10 E
Raigarh, India 41 J13 21 56N 83 25 E
Raijua, Indonesia 37 F6 10 37S 121 36 E
Raikot, India 42 D6 30 41N 75 42 E
Railton, Australia 62 G4 41 25S 146 28 E
Rainbow Lake, Canada 72 B5 58 30N 119 23W
Rainier, U.S.A. 84 D4 46 53N 122 41W
Rainier, Mt., U.S.A. 84 D5 46 52N 121 46W
Rainy L., Canada 73 D10 48 42N 93 10W
Rainy River, Canada 73 D10 48 43N 94 29W
Raippaluoto, Finland 8 E19 63 13N 21 14 E
Raipur, India 41 J12 21 17N 81 45 E
Raisen, India 42 H8 23 20N 77 48 E
Raisio, Finland 9 F20 60 28N 22 11 E
Raj Nandgaon, India 41 J12 21 5N 81 5 E
Raj Nilgiri, India 43 J12 21 28N 86 46 E
Raja, Ujung, Indonesia 36 D1 3 40N 96 25 E
Raja Ampat, Kepulauan, Indonesia 37 E8 0 30S 130 0 E
Rajahmundry, India 41 L12 17 1N 81 48 E
Rajang →, Malaysia 36 D4 2 30N 112 0 E
Rajanpur, Pakistan 42 E4 29 6N 70 19 E
Rajapalaiyam, India 40 Q10 9 25N 77 35 E
Rajasthan □, India 42 F5 26 45N 73 30 E
Rajasthan Canal, India 42 F5 28 0N 72 0 E
Rajauri, India 43 C6 33 25N 74 21 E
Rajgarh, Mad. P., India 42 G7 24 2N 76 45 E
Rajgarh, Raj., India 42 F7 27 14N 76 38 E
Rajgarh, Raj., India 42 E6 28 40N 75 25 E
Rajgir, India 43 G11 25 2N 85 25 E
Rajkot, India 42 H4 22 15N 70 56 E
Rajmahal Hills, India 43 G12 24 30N 87 30 E
Rajpipla, India 40 J8 21 50N 73 30 E
Rajpur, India 42 H6 22 18N 74 21 E
Rajpura, India 42 D7 30 25N 76 32 E
Rajshahi, Bangla. 41 G16 24 22N 88 39 E
Rajshahi □, Bangla. 43 G13 25 0N 89 0 E
Rajula, India 42 J4 21 3N 71 26 E
Rakaia, N.Z. 59 K4 43 45S 172 1 E
Rakaia →, N.Z. 59 K4 43 36S 172 15 E
Rakan, Ra's, Qatar 45 E6 26 10N 51 20 E
Rakaposhi, Pakistan 43 A6 36 10N 74 25 E
Rakata, Pulau, Indonesia 36 F3 6 10S 105 20 E
Rakhiv, Ukraine 17 D13 48 3N 24 12 E
Rakhni, Pakistan 42 D3 30 4N 69 56 E
Rakhni →, Pakistan 42 E3 29 31N 69 36 E
Rakitnoye, Russia 30 B7 45 36N 134 17 E
Rakops, Botswana 56 C3 21 1S 24 28 E
Rakvere, Estonia 9 G22 59 20N 26 25 E
Raleigh, U.S.A. 77 H6 35 47N 78 39W
Raleigh B., U.S.A. 75 D11 34 50N 76 15W
Ralls, U.S.A. 81 J4 33 41N 101 24W
Ralston, U.S.A. 78 E8 41 30N 76 57W
Ram →, Canada 72 A4 62 1N 123 41W
Rām Allāh, West Bank 47 D4 31 55N 35 10 E
Ram Hd., Australia 63 F4 37 47S 149 30 E
Rama, Nic. 88 D3 12 9N 84 15W
Ramakona, India 43 J8 21 43N 78 50 E
Raman, Thailand 39 J3 6 29N 101 18 E
Ramanathapuram, India 40 Q11 9 25N 78 55 E
Ramanetaka, B. de, Madag. 57 A8 14 13S 47 52 E
Ramanujganj, India 43 H10 23 48N 83 42 E
Ramat Gan, Israel 47 C3 32 4N 34 48 E
Ramatlhabama, S. Africa 56 D4 25 37S 25 33 E
Ramban, India 43 C6 33 14N 75 12 E
Rambipuji, Indonesia 37 H15 8 12S 113 37 E
Ramechhap, Nepal 43 F12 27 25N 86 10 E
Ramganga →, India 43 F8 27 5N 79 58 E
Ramgarh, Bihar, India 43 H11 23 40N 85 35 E
Ramgarh, Raj., India 42 F6 27 16N 75 14 E
Ramgarh, Raj., India 42 F4 27 30N 70 36 E
Rāmhormoz, Iran 45 D6 31 15N 49 35 E
Ramīān, Iran 45 B7 37 3N 55 16 E
Ramingining, Australia 62 A2 12 19S 135 3 E
Ramla, Israel 47 D3 31 55N 34 52 E
Ramnad = Ramanathapuram, India 40 Q11 9 25N 78 55 E
Ramnagar, India 43 E8 29 24N 79 7 E
Ramnagar, Jammu & Kashmir, India 43 C6 32 47N 75 18 E
Râmnicu Sărat, Romania 17 F14 45 26N 27 3 E
Râmnicu Vâlcea, Romania 17 F13 45 9N 24 21 E
Ramona, U.S.A. 85 M10 33 2N 116 52W
Ramore, Canada 70 C3 48 30N 80 25W
Ramotswa, Botswana 56 C4 24 50S 25 52 E
Rampur, H.P., India 42 D7 31 26N 77 43 E
Rampur, Mad. P., India 42 H5 23 25N 73 53 E
Rampur, Ut. P., India 43 E8 28 50N 79 5 E
Rampur Hat, India 43 G12 24 10N 87 50 E
Rampura, India 42 G6 24 30N 75 27 E
Ramrama Tola, India 43 J8 21 52N 79 55 E
Ramree I. = Ramree Kyun, Burma 41 K19 19 0N 94 0 E
Ramree Kyun, Burma 41 K19 19 0N 94 0 E
Rāmsar, Iran 45 B6 36 53N 50 41 E
Ramsey, U.K. 10 C3 54 20N 4 22W
Ramsey, U.S.A. 79 E10 41 4N 74 9W
Ramsey L., Canada 70 C3 47 13N 82 15W
Ramsgate, U.K. 11 F9 51 20N 1 25 E
Ramtek, India 40 J11 21 20N 79 15 E
Rana Pratap Sagar Dam, India 42 G6 24 58N 75 38 E
Ranaghat, India 43 H13 23 15N 88 35 E
Ranahu, Pakistan 42 G3 25 55N 69 45 E
Ranau, Malaysia 36 C5 6 2N 116 40 E
Rancagua, Chile 94 C1 34 10S 70 50W
Rancheria →, Canada 72 A3 60 13N 129 7W
Ranchester, U.S.A. 82 D10 44 54N 107 10W
Ranchi, India 43 H11 23 19N 85 27 E
Rancho Cucamonga, U.S.A. 85 L9 34 10N 117 30W
Randalstown, U.K. 13 B5 54 45N 6 19W
Randers, Denmark 9 H14 56 29N 10 1 E
Randfontein, S. Africa 57 D4 26 8S 27 45 E
Randle, U.S.A. 84 D5 46 32N 121 57W
Randolph, Mass., U.S.A. 79 D13 42 10N 71 2W
Randolph, N.Y., U.S.A. 78 D6 42 10N 78 59W
Randolph, Utah, U.S.A. 82 F8 41 40N 111 11W
Randolph, Vt., U.S.A. 79 C12 43 55N 72 40W
Randsburg, U.S.A. 85 K9 35 22N 117 39W
Råne älv →, Sweden 8 D20 65 50N 22 20 E
Rangae, Thailand 39 J3 6 19N 101 44 E
Rangaunu B., N.Z. 59 F4 34 51S 173 15 E
Rangeley, U.S.A. 79 B14 44 58N 70 39W
Rangeley L., U.S.A. 79 B14 44 55N 70 43W
Rangely, U.S.A. 82 F9 40 5N 108 48W
Ranger, U.S.A. 81 J5 32 28N 98 41W
Rangia, India 41 F17 26 28N 91 38 E
Rangiora, N.Z. 59 K4 43 19S 172 36 E
Rangitaiki →, N.Z. 59 G6 37 54S 176 49 E
Rangitata →, N.Z. 59 K3 43 45S 171 15 E
Rangkasbitung, Indonesia 37 G12 6 21S 106 15 E
Rangon →, Burma 41 L20 16 28N 96 40 E
Rangoon, Burma 41 L20 16 45N 96 20 E
Rangpur, Bangla. 41 G16 25 42N 89 22 E
Rangsit, Thailand 38 F3 13 59N 100 37 E
Ranibennur, India 40 M9 14 35N 75 30 E
Raniganj, Ut. P., India 43 F9 27 3N 82 13 E
Raniganj, W. Bengal, India 41 H15 23 40N 87 5 E
Ranikhet, India 43 E8 29 39N 79 25 E
Raniwara, India 40 G8 24 50N 72 10 E
Rāniyah, Iraq 44 B5 36 15N 44 53 E
Ranka, India 43 H10 23 59N 83 47 E
Ranken →, Australia 62 C2 20 31S 137 36 E
Rankin, U.S.A. 81 K4 31 13N 101 56W
Rankin Inlet, Canada 68 B10 62 30N 93 0W
Rankins Springs, Australia 63 E4 33 49S 146 14 E
Rannoch, L., U.K. 12 E4 56 41N 4 20W
Rannoch Moor, U.K. 12 E4 56 38N 4 48W
Ranobe, Helodranon' i, Madag. 57 C7 23 3S 43 33 E
Ranohira, Madag. 57 C8 22 29S 45 24 E
Ranomafana, Toamasina, Madag. 57 B8 18 57S 48 50 E
Ranomafana, Toliara, Madag. 57 C8 24 34S 47 0 E
Ranong, Thailand 39 H2 9 56N 98 40 E
Rānsa, Iran 45 C6 33 39N 48 18 E
Ransiki, Indonesia 37 E8 1 30S 134 10 E
Rantauprapat, Indonesia 36 D1 2 15N 99 50 E
Rantemario, Indonesia 37 E5 3 15S 119 57 E
Rantoul, U.S.A. 76 E1 40 19N 88 9W
Raoyang, China 34 E8 38 15N 115 45 E
Rapa, Pac. Oc. 65 K13 27 35S 144 20W
Rapallo, Italy 18 D8 44 21N 9 14 E
Rapar, India 42 H4 23 34N 70 38 E
Rāpch, Iran 45 E8 25 40N 59 15 E
Raper, C., Canada 69 B13 69 44N 67 6W
Rapid City, U.S.A. 80 D3 44 5N 103 14W
Rapid River, U.S.A. 76 C2 45 55N 86 58W
Rapla, Estonia 9 G21 59 1N 24 52 E
Rapti →, India 43 F10 26 18N 83 41 E
Raquette →, U.S.A. 79 B10 45 0N 74 42W
Raquette Lake, U.S.A. 79 C10 43 49N 74 40W
Rarotonga, Cook Is. 65 K12 21 30S 160 0W
Ra's al 'Ayn, Syria 44 B4 36 45N 40 12 E
Ra's al Khaymah, U.A.E. 45 E8 25 50N 55 59 E
Ra's an Naqb, Jordan 47 F4 30 0N 35 29 E
Ras Dashen, Ethiopia 46 E2 13 8N 38 26 E
Râs Timirist, Mauritania 50 E2 19 21N 16 30W

Rasca, Pta. de la

Rasca, Pta. de la, *Canary Is.* **22 G3** 27 59N 16 41W
Raseiniai, *Lithuania* **9 J20** 55 25N 23 5 E
Rashmi, *India* **42 G6** 25 4N 74 22 E
Rasht, *Iran* **45 B6** 37 20N 49 40 E
Rasi Salai, *Thailand* **38 E5** 15 20N 104 9 E
Rason L., *Australia* **61 E3** 28 45S 124 25 E
Rasra, *India* **43 G10** 25 50N 83 50 E
Rasul, *Pakistan* **42 C5** 32 42N 73 34 E
Rat Buri, *Thailand* **38 F2** 13 30N 99 54 E
Rat Islands, *U.S.A.* **68 C1** 52 0N 178 0 E
Rat L., *Canada* **73 B9** 56 10N 99 40W
Ratangarh, *India* **42 E6** 28 5N 74 35 E
Raţāwī, *Iraq* **44 D5** 30 38N 47 13 E
Ratcatchers L., *Australia* **63 E3** 32 38S 143 10 E
Rath, *India* **43 G8** 25 36N 79 37 E
Rath Luirc, *Ireland* **13 D3** 52 21N 8 40W
Rathdrum, *Ireland* **13 D5** 52 56N 6 14W
Rathenow, *Germany* **16 B7** 52 37N 12 19 E
Rathkeale, *Ireland* **13 D3** 52 32N 8 56W
Rathlin I., *U.K.* **13 A5** 55 18N 6 14W
Rathmelton, *Ireland* **13 A4** 55 2N 7 38W
Ratibor = Racibórz, *Poland* **17 C10** 50 7N 18 18 E
Ratlam, *India* **42 H6** 23 20N 75 0 E
Ratnagiri, *India* **40 L8** 16 57N 73 18 E
Ratodero, *Pakistan* **42 F3** 27 48N 68 18 E
Raton, *U.S.A.* **81 G2** 36 54N 104 24W
Rattaphum, *Thailand* **39 J3** 7 8N 100 16 E
Rattray Hd., *U.K.* **12 D7** 57 38N 1 50W
Ratz, Mt., *Canada* **72 B2** 57 23N 132 12W
Raub, *Malaysia* **39 L3** 3 47N 101 52 E
Rauch, *Argentina* **94 D4** 36 45S 59 5W
Raudales de Malpaso, *Mexico* **87 D6** 17 30N 23 30W
Raufarhöfn, *Iceland* **8 C6** 66 27N 15 57W
Raufoss, *Norway* **9 F14** 60 44N 10 37 E
Raukumara Ra., *N.Z.* **59 H6** 38 5S 177 55 E
Rauma, *Finland* **9 F19** 61 10N 21 30 E
Raurkela, *India* **43 H11** 22 14N 84 50 E
Rausu-Dake, *Japan* **30 B12** 44 4N 145 7 E
Rava-Ruska, *Poland* **17 C12** 50 15N 23 42 E
Rava Russkaya = Rava-Ruska, *Poland* **17 C12** 50 15N 23 42 E
Ravalli, *U.S.A.* **82 C6** 47 17N 114 11W
Ravänsar, *Iran* **44 C5** 34 43N 46 40 E
Rävar, *Iran* **45 D8** 31 20N 56 51 E
Ravena, *U.S.A.* **79 D11** 42 28N 73 49W
Ravenna, *Italy* **20 B5** 44 25N 12 12 E
Ravenna, *Nebr., U.S.A.* **80 E5** 41 1N 98 55W
Ravenna, *Ohio, U.S.A.* **78 E3** 41 9N 81 15W
Ravensburg, *Germany* **16 E5** 47 46N 9 36 E
Ravenshoe, *Australia* **62 B4** 17 37S 145 29 E
Ravensthorpe, *Australia* **61 F3** 33 35S 120 2 E
Ravenswood, *Australia* **62 C4** 20 6S 146 54 E
Ravenswood, *U.S.A.* **76 F5** 38 57N 81 46W
Ravi →, *Pakistan* **42 D4** 30 35N 71 49 E
Rawalpindi, *Pakistan* **42 C5** 33 38N 73 8 E
Rawāndūz, *Iraq* **44 B5** 36 40N 44 30 E
Rawang, *Malaysia* **39 L3** 3 20N 101 35 E
Rawene, *N.Z.* **59 F4** 35 25S 173 32 E
Rawlinna, *Australia* **61 F4** 30 58S 125 28 E
Rawlins, *U.S.A.* **82 F10** 41 47N 107 14W
Rawlinson Ra., *Australia* **61 D4** 24 40S 128 30 E
Rawson, *Argentina* **96 E3** 43 15S 65 5W
Raxaul, *India* **43 F11** 26 59N 84 51 E
Ray, *U.S.A.* **80 A3** 48 21N 103 10W
Ray, C., *Canada* **71 C8** 47 33N 59 15W
Rayadurg, *India* **40 M10** 14 40N 76 50 E
Rayagada, *India* **41 K13** 19 15N 83 20 E
Raychikhinsk, *Russia* **27 E13** 49 46N 129 25 E
Rāyen, *Iran* **45 D8** 29 34N 57 26 E
Rayleigh, *U.K.* **11 F8** 51 36N 0 37 E
Raymond, *Canada* **72 D6** 49 30N 112 35W
Raymond, *Calif., U.S.A.* **84 H7** 37 13N 119 54W
Raymond, *N.H., U.S.A.* **79 C13** 43 2N 71 11W
Raymond, *Wash., U.S.A.* **84 D3** 46 41N 123 44W
Raymond Terrace, *Australia* **63 E5** 32 45S 151 44 E
Raymondville, *U.S.A.* **81 M6** 26 29N 97 47W
Raymore, *Canada* **73 C8** 51 25N 104 31W
Rayna, *India* **43 H12** 23 5N 87 54 E
Rayón, *Mexico* **86 B2** 29 43N 110 35W
Rayong, *Thailand* **38 F3** 12 40N 101 20 E
Rayville, *U.S.A.* **81 J9** 32 29N 91 46W
Raz, Pte. du, *France* **18 C1** 48 2N 4 47W
Razan, *Iran* **45 C6** 35 23N 49 2 E
Razdel'naya = Rozdilna, *Ukraine* **17 E16** 46 50N 30 2 E
Razdolnoye, *Russia* **30 C5** 43 30N 131 52 E
Razeh, *Iran* **45 C6** 32 47N 48 9 E
Razgrad, *Bulgaria* **21 C12** 43 33N 26 34 E
Razim, Lacul, *Romania* **17 F15** 44 50N 29 0 E
Razmak, *Pakistan* **42 C3** 32 45N 69 50 E
Ré, Î. de, *France* **18 C3** 46 12N 1 30W
Reading, *U.K.* **11 F7** 51 27N 0 58W
Reading, *U.S.A.* **79 F9** 40 20N 75 56W
Reading □, *U.K.* **11 F7** 51 27N 0 58W
Realicó, *Argentina* **94 D3** 35 0S 64 15W
Ream, *Cambodia* **39 G4** 10 34N 103 39 E
Reata, *Mexico* **86 B4** 26 8N 101 5W
Reay Forest, *U.K.* **12 C4** 58 22N 4 55W
Rebi, *Indonesia* **37 F8** 6 23S 134 7 E
Rebiana, *Libya* **51 D10** 24 12N 22 10 E
Rebun-Tō, *Japan* **30 B10** 45 23N 141 2 E
Recherche, Arch. of the, *Australia* **61 F3** 34 15S 122 50 E
Rechna Doab, *Pakistan* **42 D5** 31 35N 73 30 E
Rechytsa, *Belarus* **17 B16** 52 21N 30 24 E
Recife, *Brazil* **93 E12** 8 0S 35 0W
Recklinghausen, *Germany* **15 C7** 51 37N 7 12 E
Reconquista, *Argentina* **94 B4** 29 10S 59 45W
Recreo, *Argentina* **94 B2** 29 25S 65 10W
Red →, *La., U.S.A.* **81 K9** 31 1N 91 45W
Red →, *N. Dak., U.S.A.* **68 C10** 49 0N 97 15W
Red Bank, *U.S.A.* **79 F10** 40 21N 74 5W
Red Bay, *Canada* **71 B8** 51 44N 56 25W
Red Bluff, *U.S.A.* **82 F2** 40 11N 122 15W
Red Bluff L., *U.S.A.* **81 K3** 31 54N 103 55W
Red Cliffs, *Australia* **63 E3** 34 19S 142 11 E
Red Cloud, *U.S.A.* **80 E5** 40 5N 98 32W
Red Creek, *U.S.A.* **79 C8** 43 14N 76 45W
Red Deer, *Canada* **72 C6** 52 20N 113 50W
Red Deer →, *Alta., Canada* **73 C7** 50 58N 110 0W
Red Deer →, *Man., Canada* **73 C8** 52 53N 101 1W
Red Deer L., *Canada* **73 C8** 52 55N 101 20W
Red Hook, *U.S.A.* **79 E11** 41 55N 73 53W
Red Indian L., *Canada* **71 C8** 48 35N 57 0W
Red L., *Canada* **73 C10** 51 3N 93 49W
Red Lake, *Canada* **73 C10** 51 3N 93 49W
Red Lake Falls, *U.S.A.* **80 B6** 47 53N 96 16W
Red Lake Road, *Canada* **73 C10** 49 59N 93 25W
Red Lodge, *U.S.A.* **82 D9** 45 11N 109 15W
Red Mountain, *U.S.A.* **85 K9** 35 37N 117 38W
Red Oak, *U.S.A.* **80 E7** 41 1N 95 14W
Red Rock, *Canada* **70 C2** 48 55N 88 15W
Red Rock, L., *U.S.A.* **80 E8** 41 22N 92 59W
Red Rocks Pt., *Australia* **61 F4** 32 13S 127 32 E
Red Sea, *Asia* **46 C2** 25 0N 36 0 E
Red Slate Mt., *U.S.A.* **84 H8** 37 31N 118 52W
Red Sucker L., *Canada* **70 B1** 54 9N 93 40W
Red Tower Pass = Turnu Roşu, P., *Romania* **17 F13** 45 33N 24 17 E
Red Wing, *U.S.A.* **80 C8** 44 34N 92 31W
Redang, *Malaysia* **36 C2** 5 49N 103 2 E
Redange, *Lux.* **15 E5** 49 46N 5 52 E
Redcar, *U.K.* **10 C6** 54 37N 1 4W
Redcar & Cleveland □, *U.K.* **10 C7** 54 29N 1 0W
Redcliff, *Canada* **73 C6** 50 10N 110 50W
Redcliffe, *Australia* **63 D5** 27 12S 153 0 E
Redcliffe, Mt., *Australia* **61 E3** 28 30S 121 30 E
Reddersburg, *S. Africa* **56 D4** 29 41S 26 10 E
Redding, *U.S.A.* **82 F2** 40 35N 122 24W
Redditch, *U.K.* **11 E6** 52 18N 1 56W
Redfield, *U.S.A.* **80 C5** 44 53N 98 31W
Redford, *U.S.A.* **79 B11** 44 38N 73 48W
Redlands, *U.S.A.* **85 M9** 34 4N 117 11W
Redmond, *Oreg., U.S.A.* **82 D3** 44 17N 121 11W
Redmond, *Wash., U.S.A.* **84 C4** 47 41N 122 7W
Redon, *France* **18 C2** 47 40N 2 6W
Redonda, *Antigua* **89 C7** 16 58N 62 19W
Redondela, *Spain* **19 A1** 42 15N 8 38W
Redondo Beach, *U.S.A.* **85 M8** 33 50N 118 23W
Redruth, *U.K.* **11 G2** 50 14N 5 14W
Redvers, *Canada* **73 D8** 49 35N 101 40W
Redwater, *Canada* **72 C6** 53 55N 113 6W
Redwood, *U.S.A.* **79 B9** 44 18N 75 48W
Redwood City, *U.S.A.* **84 H4** 37 30N 122 15W
Redwood Falls, *U.S.A.* **80 C7** 44 32N 95 7W
Redwood National Park, *U.S.A.* **82 F1** 41 40N 124 5W
Ree, L., *Ireland* **13 C3** 53 35N 8 0W
Reed, L., *Canada* **73 C8** 54 38N 100 30W
Reed City, *U.S.A.* **76 D3** 43 53N 85 31W
Reedley, *U.S.A.* **84 J7** 36 36N 119 27W
Reedsburg, *U.S.A.* **80 D9** 43 32N 90 0W
Reedsport, *U.S.A.* **82 E1** 43 42N 124 6W
Reedsville, *U.S.A.* **78 F7** 40 39N 77 35W
Reefton, *N.Z.* **59 K3** 42 6S 171 51 E
Reese →, *U.S.A.* **82 F5** 40 48N 117 4W
Refugio, *U.S.A.* **81 L6** 28 18N 97 17W
Regensburg, *Germany* **16 D7** 49 1N 12 6 E
Réggio di Calábria, *Italy* **20 E6** 38 6N 15 39 E
Réggio nell'Emília, *Italy* **20 B4** 44 43N 10 36 E
Reghin, *Romania* **17 E13** 46 46N 24 42 E
Regina, *Canada* **73 C8** 50 27N 104 35W
Regina Beach, *Canada* **73 C8** 50 47N 105 0W
Registro, *Brazil* **95 A6** 24 29S 47 49W
Rehar →, *India* **43 H10** 23 55N 82 40 E
Rehli, *India* **43 H8** 23 38N 79 5 E
Rehoboth, *Namibia* **56 C2** 23 15S 17 4 E
Rehovot, *Israel* **47 D3** 31 54N 34 48 E
Reichenbach, *Germany* **16 C7** 50 37N 12 17 E
Reid, *Australia* **61 F4** 30 49S 128 26 E
Reidsville, *U.S.A.* **77 G6** 36 21N 79 40W
Reigate, *U.K.* **11 F7** 51 14N 0 12W
Reims, *France* **18 B6** 49 15N 4 1 E
Reina Adelaida, Arch., *Chile* **96 G2** 52 20S 74 0W
Reindeer →, *Canada* **73 B8** 55 36N 103 11W
Reindeer I., *Canada* **73 C9** 52 30N 98 0W
Reindeer L., *Canada* **73 B8** 57 15N 102 15W
Reinga, C., *N.Z.* **59 F4** 34 25S 172 43 E
Reinosa, *Spain* **19 A3** 43 2N 4 15W
Reitz, *S. Africa* **57 D4** 27 48S 28 29 E
Reivilo, *S. Africa* **56 D3** 27 36S 24 8 E
Reliance, *Canada* **73 A7** 63 0N 109 20W
Remarkable, Mt., *Australia* **63 E2** 32 48S 138 10 E
Rembang, *Indonesia* **37 G14** 6 42S 111 21 E
Remedios, *Panama* **88 E3** 8 15N 81 50W
Remeshk, *Iran* **45 E8** 26 55N 58 50 E
Remich, *Lux.* **15 E6** 49 32N 6 22 E
Remscheid, *Germany* **15 C7** 51 11N 7 12 E
Ren Xian, *China* **34 F8** 37 8N 114 40 E
Rendsburg, *Germany* **16 A5** 54 17N 9 39 E
Renfrew, *Canada* **79 A8** 45 30N 76 40W
Renfrewshire □, *U.K.* **12 F4** 55 49N 4 38W
Rengat, *Indonesia* **36 E2** 0 30S 102 45 E
Rengo, *Chile* **94 C1** 34 24S 70 50W
Reni, *Ukraine* **17 F15** 45 28N 28 15 E
Renmark, *Australia* **63 E3** 34 11S 140 43 E
Rennell Sd., *Canada* **72 C2** 53 23N 132 35W
Renner Springs, *Australia* **62 B1** 18 20S 133 47 E
Rennes, *France* **18 B3** 48 7N 1 41W
Rennie L., *Canada* **73 A7** 61 32N 105 35W
Reno, *U.S.A.* **84 F7** 39 31N 119 48W
Reno →, *Italy* **20 B5** 44 38N 12 16 E
Renovo, *U.S.A.* **78 E7** 41 20N 77 45W
Renqiu, *China* **34 E9** 38 43N 116 5 E
Rensselaer, *Ind., U.S.A.* **76 E2** 40 57N 87 9W
Rensselaer, *N.Y., U.S.A.* **79 D11** 42 38N 73 45W
Rentería, *Spain* **19 A5** 43 19N 1 54W
Renton, *U.S.A.* **84 C4** 47 29N 122 12W
Reotipur, *India* **43 G10** 25 33N 83 45 E
Republic, *Mo., U.S.A.* **81 G8** 37 7N 93 29W
Republic, *Wash., U.S.A.* **82 B4** 48 39N 118 44W
Republican →, *U.S.A.* **80 F6** 39 4N 96 48W
Repulse Bay, *Canada* **69 B11** 66 30N 86 30W
Requena, *Peru* **92 E4** 5 5S 73 52W
Requena, *Spain* **19 C5** 39 30N 1 4W
Reşadiye = Datça, *Turkey* **21 F12** 36 46N 27 40 E
Reserve, *U.S.A.* **83 K9** 33 43N 108 45W
Resht = Rasht, *Iran* **45 B6** 37 20N 49 40 E
Resistencia, *Argentina* **94 B4** 27 30S 59 0W
Reşiţa, *Romania* **17 F11** 45 18N 21 53 E
Resolution I., *Canada* **69 B13** 61 30N 65 0W
Resolution I., *N.Z.* **59 L1** 45 40S 166 40 E
Ressano Garcia, *Mozam.* **57 D5** 25 25S 32 0 E
Reston, *Canada* **73 D8** 49 33N 101 6W
Retalhuleu, *Guatemala* **88 D1** 14 33N 91 46W
Retenue, L. de, *Dem. Rep. of the Congo* **55 E2** 11 0S 27 0 E
Retford, *U.K.* **10 D7** 53 19N 0 56W
Réthímnon, *Greece* **23 D6** 35 18N 24 30 E
Réthímnon □, *Greece* **23 D6** 35 23N 24 28 E
Reti, *Pakistan* **42 E3** 28 5N 69 48 E
Réunion ■, *Ind. Oc.* **49 J9** 21 0S 56 0 E
Reus, *Spain* **19 B6** 41 10N 1 5 E
Reutlingen, *Germany* **16 D5** 48 29N 9 12 E
Reval = Tallinn, *Estonia* **9 G21** 59 22N 24 48 E
Revda, *Russia* **24 C10** 56 48N 59 57 E
Revelganj, *India* **43 G11** 25 50N 84 40 E
Revelstoke, *Canada* **72 C5** 51 0N 118 10W
Reventazón, *Peru* **92 E2** 6 10S 80 58W
Revillagigedo, Is. de, *Pac. Oc.* **86 D2** 18 40N 112 0W
Revuè →, *Mozam.* **55 F3** 19 50S 34 0 E
Rewa, *India* **43 G9** 24 33N 81 25 E
Rewari, *India* **42 E7** 28 15N 76 40 E
Rexburg, *U.S.A.* **82 E8** 43 49N 111 47W
Rey, *Iran* **45 C6** 35 35N 51 25 E
Rey, I. del, *Panama* **88 E4** 8 20N 78 30W
Rey Malabo, *Eq. Guin.* **52 D1** 3 45N 8 50 E
Reyðarfjörður, *Iceland* **8 D6** 65 2N 14 13W
Reyes, Pt., *U.S.A.* **84 H3** 38 0N 123 0W
Reykjahlið, *Iceland* **8 D5** 65 40N 16 55W
Reykjanes, *Iceland* **8 E2** 63 48N 22 40W
Reykjavík, *Iceland* **8 D3** 64 10N 21 57W
Reynolds Ra., *Australia* **60 D5** 22 30S 133 0 E
Reynoldsville, *U.S.A.* **78 E6** 41 5N 78 58W
Reynosa, *Mexico* **87 B5** 26 5N 98 18W
Rēzekne, *Latvia* **9 H22** 56 30N 27 17 E
Rezvān, *Iran* **45 E8** 27 34N 56 6 E
Rhayader, *U.K.* **11 E4** 52 18N 3 29W
Rhein →, *Europe* **15 C6** 51 52N 6 2 E
Rhein-Main-Donau-Kanal, *Germany* **16 D6** 49 1N 11 27 E
Rheine, *Germany* **16 B4** 52 17N 7 26 E
Rheinland-Pfalz □, *Germany* **16 C4** 50 0N 7 0 E
Rhin = Rhein →, *Europe* **15 C6** 51 52N 6 2 E
Rhine = Rhein →, *Europe* **15 C6** 51 52N 6 2 E
Rhinebeck, *U.S.A.* **79 E11** 41 56N 73 55W
Rhineland-Palatinate = Rheinland-Pfalz □, *Germany* **16 C4** 50 0N 7 0 E
Rhinelander, *U.S.A.* **80 C10** 45 38N 89 25W
Rhinns Pt., *U.K.* **12 F2** 55 40N 6 29W
Rhino Camp, *Uganda* **54 B3** 3 0N 31 22 E
Rhir, Cap, *Morocco* **50 B4** 30 38N 9 54W
Rhode Island □, *U.S.A.* **79 E13** 41 40N 71 30W
Rhodes = Ródhos, *Greece* **23 C10** 36 15N 28 10 E
Rhodesia = Zimbabwe ■, *Africa* **55 F3** 19 0S 30 0 E
Rhodope Mts. = Rhodopi Planina, *Bulgaria* **21 D11** 41 40N 24 20 E
Rhodopi Planina, *Bulgaria* **21 D11** 41 40N 24 20 E
Rhön = Rhön, *Germany* **16 C5** 50 24N 9 58 E
Rhön, *Germany* **16 C5** 50 24N 9 58 E
Rhondda, *U.K.* **11 F4** 51 39N 3 31W
Rhondda Cynon Taff □, *U.K.* **11 F4** 51 42N 3 27W
Rhône →, *France* **18 E6** 43 28N 4 42 E
Rhum, *U.K.* **12 E2** 57 0N 6 20W
Rhyl, *U.K.* **10 D4** 53 20N 3 29W
Riachão, *Brazil* **93 E9** 7 20S 46 37W
Riasi, *India* **43 C6** 33 10N 74 50 E
Riau □, *Indonesia* **36 E2** 0 0 102 35 E
Riau, Kepulauan, *Indonesia* **36 D2** 0 30N 104 20 E
Riau Arch. = Riau, Kepulauan, *Indonesia* **36 D2** 0 30N 104 20 E
Ribadeo, *Spain* **19 A2** 43 35N 7 5W
Ribas do Rio Pardo, *Brazil* **93 H8** 20 27S 53 46W
Ribble →, *U.K.* **10 D5** 53 52N 2 25W
Ribe, *Denmark* **9 J13** 55 19N 8 44 E
Ribeira Brava, *Madeira* **22 D2** 32 41N 17 4W
Ribeirão Prêto, *Brazil* **95 A6** 21 10S 47 50W
Riberalta, *Bolivia* **92 F5** 11 0S 66 0W
Riccarton, *N.Z.* **59 K4** 43 32S 172 37 E
Rice, *U.S.A.* **85 L12** 34 5N 114 51W
Rice L., *Canada* **78 B6** 44 12N 78 10W
Rice Lake, *U.S.A.* **80 C9** 45 30N 91 44W
Rich, C., *Canada* **78 B4** 44 43N 80 38W
Richards Bay, *S. Africa* **57 D5** 28 48S 32 6 E
Richardson →, *Canada* **73 B6** 58 25N 111 14W
Richardson Lakes, *U.S.A.* **76 C10** 44 46N 70 58W
Richardson Springs, *U.S.A.* **84 F5** 39 51N 121 46W
Riche, C., *Australia* **61 F2** 34 36S 118 47 E
Richey, *U.S.A.* **80 B2** 47 39N 105 4W
Richfield, *U.S.A.* **83 G8** 38 46N 112 5W
Richfield Springs, *U.S.A.* **79 D10** 42 51N 74 59W
Richford, *U.S.A.* **79 B12** 45 0N 72 40W
Richibucto, *Canada* **71 C7** 46 42N 64 54W
Richland, *Ga., U.S.A.* **77 J3** 32 5N 84 40W
Richland, *Wash., U.S.A.* **82 C4** 46 17N 119 18W
Richland Center, *U.S.A.* **80 D9** 43 21N 90 23W
Richlands, *U.S.A.* **76 G5** 37 6N 81 48W
Richmond, *Australia* **62 C3** 20 43S 143 8 E
Richmond, *N.Z.* **59 J4** 41 20S 173 12 E
Richmond, *U.K.* **10 C6** 54 25N 1 43W
Richmond, *Calif., U.S.A.* **84 H4** 37 56N 122 21W
Richmond, *Ind., U.S.A.* **76 F3** 39 50N 84 53W
Richmond, *Ky., U.S.A.* **76 G3** 37 45N 84 18W
Richmond, *Mich., U.S.A.* **78 D2** 42 49N 82 45W
Richmond, *Mo., U.S.A.* **80 F8** 39 17N 93 58W
Richmond, *Tex., U.S.A.* **81 L7** 29 35N 95 46W
Richmond, *Utah, U.S.A.* **82 F8** 41 56N 111 48W
Richmond, *Va., U.S.A.* **76 G7** 37 33N 77 27W
Richmond, *Vt., U.S.A.* **79 B12** 44 24N 72 59W
Richmond Hill, *Canada* **78 C5** 43 52N 79 27W
Richmond Ra., *Australia* **63 D5** 29 0S 152 45 E
Richwood, *U.S.A.* **76 F5** 38 14N 80 32W
Ridder = Leninogorsk, *Kazakstan* **26 D9** 50 20N 83 30 E
Riddlesburg, *U.S.A.* **78 F6** 40 9N 78 15W
Ridgecrest, *U.S.A.* **85 K9** 35 38N 117 40W
Ridgefield, *Conn., U.S.A.* **79 E11** 41 17N 73 30W
Ridgefield, *Wash., U.S.A.* **84 E4** 45 49N 122 45W
Ridgeland, *U.S.A.* **77 J5** 32 29N 80 59W
Ridgetown, *Canada* **78 D3** 42 26N 81 52W
Ridgewood, *U.S.A.* **79 F10** 40 59N 74 7W
Ridgway, *U.S.A.* **78 E6** 41 25N 78 44W
Riding Mountain Nat. Park, *Canada* **73 C9** 50 50N 100 0W
Ridley, Mt., *Australia* **61 F3** 33 12S 122 7 E
Ried, *Austria* **16 D7** 48 14N 13 30 E
Riesa, *Germany* **16 C7** 51 17N 13 17 E
Riet →, *S. Africa* **56 D3** 29 0S 23 54 E
Rieti, *Italy* **20 C5** 42 24N 12 51 E
Riffe L., *U.S.A.* **84 D4** 46 32N 122 26W
Rifle, *U.S.A.* **82 G10** 39 32N 107 47W
Rift Valley □, *Kenya* **54 B4** 0 20N 36 0 E
Rīga, *Latvia* **9 H21** 56 53N 24 8 E
Riga, G. of, *Latvia* **9 H20** 57 40N 23 45 E
Rīgān, *Iran* **45 D8** 28 37N 58 58 E
Rīgas Jūras Līcis = Riga, G. of, *Latvia* **9 H20** 57 40N 23 45 E
Rigaud, *Canada* **79 A10** 45 29N 74 18W
Rigby, *U.S.A.* **82 E8** 43 40N 111 55W
Rigestān □, *Afghan.* **40 D4** 30 15N 65 0 E
Riggins, *U.S.A.* **82 D5** 45 25N 116 19W
Rigolet, *Canada* **71 B8** 54 10N 58 23W
Rihand Dam, *India* **43 G10** 24 9N 83 2 E
Riihimäki, *Finland* **9 F21** 60 45N 24 48 E
Riiser-Larsen-halvøya, *Antarctica* **5 C4** 68 0S 35 0 E
Rijeka, *Croatia* **16 F8** 45 20N 14 21 E
Rijssen, *Neths.* **15 B6** 52 19N 6 31 E
Rikuzentakada, *Japan* **30 E10** 39 0N 141 40 E
Riley, *U.S.A.* **82 E4** 43 32N 119 28W
Rimah, Wadi ar →, *Si. Arabia* **44 E4** 26 5N 41 30 E
Rimbey, *Canada* **72 C6** 52 35N 114 15W
Rimersburg, *U.S.A.* **78 E5** 41 3N 79 30W
Rimini, *Italy* **20 B5** 44 3N 12 33 E
Rimouski, *Canada* **71 C6** 48 27N 68 30W
Rimrock, *U.S.A.* **84 D5** 46 38N 121 10W
Rinca, *Indonesia* **37 F5** 8 45S 119 35 E
Rincón de Romos, *Mexico* **86 C4** 22 14N 102 18W
Rinconada, *Argentina* **94 A2** 22 26S 66 10W
Rind →, *India* **43 G9** 25 53N 80 33 E
Ringas, *India* **42 F6** 27 21N 75 34 E
Ringkøbing, *Denmark* **9 H13** 56 5N 8 15 E
Ringvassøy, *Norway* **8 B18** 69 56N 19 15 E
Ringwood, *U.S.A.* **79 E10** 41 7N 74 15W
Rinjani, *Indonesia* **36 F5** 8 24S 116 28 E
Rio Branco, *Brazil* **92 E5** 9 58S 67 49W
Río Branco, *Uruguay* **95 C5** 32 40S 53 40W
Río Bravo del Norte →, *Mexico* **87 B5** 25 57N 97 9W
Rio Brilhante, *Brazil* **95 A5** 21 48S 54 33W
Rio Claro, *Brazil* **95 A6** 22 19S 47 35W
Rio Claro, *Trin. & Tob.* **89 D7** 10 20N 61 25W
Río Colorado, *Argentina* **96 D4** 39 0S 64 0W
Río Cuarto, *Argentina* **94 C3** 33 10S 64 25W
Rio das Pedras, *Mozam.* **57 C6** 23 8S 35 28 E
Rio de Janeiro, *Brazil* **95 A7** 23 0S 43 12W
Rio de Janeiro □, *Brazil* **95 A7** 22 50S 43 0W
Rio do Sul, *Brazil* **95 B6** 27 13S 49 37W
Río Gallegos, *Argentina* **96 G3** 51 35S 69 15W
Rio Grande = Grande, Rio →, *U.S.A.* **81 N6** 25 58N 97 9W
Río Grande, *Argentina* **96 G3** 53 50S 67 45W
Rio Grande, *Brazil* **95 C5** 32 0S 52 20W
Río Grande, *Mexico* **86 C4** 23 50N 103 2W
Río Grande, *Nic.* **88 D3** 12 54N 83 33W
Rio Grande City, *U.S.A.* **81 M5** 26 23N 98 49W
Río Grande de Santiago →, *Mexico* **86 C3** 21 36N 105 26W
Rio Grande del Norte →, *N. Amer.* **75 E7** 26 0N 97 0W
Rio Grande do Norte □, *Brazil* **93 E11** 5 40S 36 0W
Rio Grande do Sul □, *Brazil* **95 C5** 30 0S 53 0W
Río Hato, *Panama* **88 E3** 8 22N 80 10W
Río Lagartos, *Mexico* **87 C7** 21 36N 88 10W
Rio Largo, *Brazil* **93 E11** 9 28S 35 50W
Río Mulatos, *Bolivia* **92 G5** 19 40S 66 50W
Río Muni = Mbini □, *Eq. Guin.* **52 D2** 1 30N 10 0 E
Rio Negro, *Brazil* **95 B6** 26 0S 49 55W
Rio Pardo, *Brazil* **95 C5** 30 0S 52 30W
Rio Rancho, *U.S.A.* **83 J10** 35 14N 106 38W
Río Segundo, *Argentina* **94 C3** 31 40S 63 59W
Río Tercero, *Argentina* **94 C3** 32 15S 64 8W
Rio Verde, *Brazil* **93 G8** 17 50S 51 0W
Río Verde, *Mexico* **87 C5** 21 56N 99 59W
Rio Vista, *U.S.A.* **84 G5** 38 10N 121 42W
Ríobamba, *Ecuador* **92 D3** 1 50S 78 45W
Ríohacha, *Colombia* **92 A4** 11 33N 72 55W
Riosucio, *Colombia* **92 B3** 7 27N 77 7W
Riou L., *Canada* **73 B7** 59 7N 106 25W
Ripley, *Canada* **78 B3** 44 4N 81 35W
Ripley, *Calif., U.S.A.* **85 M12** 33 32N 114 39W
Ripley, *N.Y., U.S.A.* **78 D5** 42 16N 79 43W
Ripley, *Tenn., U.S.A.* **81 H10** 35 45N 89 32W
Ripley, *W. Va., U.S.A.* **76 F5** 38 49N 81 43W
Ripon, *U.K.* **10 C6** 54 9N 1 31W
Ripon, *Calif., U.S.A.* **84 H5** 37 44N 121 7W
Ripon, *Wis., U.S.A.* **76 D1** 43 51N 88 50W
Rishā', W. ar →, *Si. Arabia* **44 E5** 25 33N 44 5 E
Rishiri-Tō, *Japan* **30 B10** 45 11N 141 15 E
Rishon le Ẕiyyon, *Israel* **47 D3** 31 58N 34 48 E
Rison, *U.S.A.* **81 J8** 33 58N 92 11W
Risør, *Norway* **9 G13** 58 43N 9 13 E
Rita Blanca Cr. →, *U.S.A.* **81 H3** 35 40N 102 29W
Ritter, Mt., *U.S.A.* **84 H7** 37 41N 119 12W
Rittman, *U.S.A.* **78 F3** 40 58N 81 47W
Ritzville, *U.S.A.* **82 C4** 47 8N 118 23W
Riva del Garda, *Italy* **20 B4** 45 53N 10 50 E
Rivadavia, *Buenos Aires, Argentina* **94 D3** 35 29S 62 59W
Rivadavia, *Mendoza, Argentina* **94 C2** 33 13S 68 30W
Rivadavia, *Salta, Argentina* **94 A3** 24 5S 62 54W
Rivadavia, *Chile* **94 B1** 29 57S 70 35W
Rivas, *Nic.* **88 D2** 11 30N 85 50W
River Cess, *Liberia* **50 G4** 5 30N 9 32W
River Jordan, *Canada* **84 B2** 48 26N 124 3W
Rivera, *Argentina* **94 D3** 37 12S 63 14W
Rivera, *Uruguay* **95 C4** 31 0S 55 50W
Riverbank, *U.S.A.* **84 H6** 37 44N 120 56W
Riverdale, *U.S.A.* **84 J7** 36 26N 119 52W
Riverhead, *U.S.A.* **79 F12** 40 55N 72 40W
Riverhurst, *Canada* **73 C7** 50 55N 106 50W
Rivers, *Canada* **73 C8** 50 2N 100 14W
Rivers Inlet, *Canada* **72 C3** 51 42N 127 15W
Riversdale, *S. Africa* **56 E3** 34 7S 21 15 E
Riverside, *U.S.A.* **85 M9** 33 59N 117 22W
Riverton, *Australia* **63 E2** 34 10S 138 46 E
Riverton, *Canada* **73 C9** 51 1N 97 0W
Riverton, *N.Z.* **59 M2** 46 21S 168 0 E
Riverton, *U.S.A.* **82 E9** 43 2N 108 23W
Riverton Heights, *U.S.A.* **84 C4** 47 28N 122 17W
Riviera, *U.S.A.* **85 K12** 35 4N 114 35W
Riviera di Levante, *Italy* **18 D8** 44 15N 9 30 E
Riviera di Ponente, *Italy* **18 D8** 44 10N 8 20 E
Rivière-au-Renard, *Canada* **71 C7** 48 59N 64 23W
Rivière-du-Loup, *Canada* **71 C6** 47 50N 69 30W
Rivière-Pentecôte, *Canada* **71 C6** 49 57N 67 1W

Rzhev

Rivière-Pilote, *Martinique* **89 D7** 14 26N 60 53W
Rivière St. Paul, *Canada* **71 B8** 51 28N 57 45W
Rivne, *Ukraine* **17 C14** 50 40N 26 10 E
Rívoli, *Italy* **18 D7** 45 3N 7 31 E
Rivoli B., *Australia* **63 F3** 37 32S 140 3 E
Riyadh = Ar Riyāḍ, *Si. Arabia* **46 C4** 24 41N 46 42 E
Rize, *Turkey* **25 F7** 41 0N 40 30 E
Rizhao, *China* **35 G10** 35 25N 119 30 E
Rizokarpaso, *Cyprus* **23 D13** 35 36N 34 23 E
Rizzuto, C., *Italy* **20 E7** 38 53N 17 5 E
Rjukan, *Norway* **9 G13** 59 54N 8 33 E
Road Town, *Virgin Is.* **89 C7** 18 27N 64 37W
Roan Plateau, *U.S.A.* **82 G9** 39 20N 109 20W
Roanne, *France* **18 C6** 46 3N 4 4 E
Roanoke, *Ala., U.S.A.* **77 J3** 33 9N 85 22W
Roanoke, *Va., U.S.A.* **76 G6** 37 16N 79 56W
Roanoke →, *U.S.A.* **77 H7** 35 57N 76 42W
Roanoke I., *U.S.A.* **77 H8** 35 55N 75 40W
Roanoke Rapids, *U.S.A.* **77 G7** 36 28N 77 40W
Roatán, *Honduras* **88 C2** 16 18N 86 35W
Robāt Sang, *Iran* **45 C8** 35 35N 59 10 E
Robbins I., *Australia* **62 G4** 40 42S 145 0 E
Robe, *Australia* **63 F2** 37 11S 139 45 E
Robe →, *Australia* **60 D2** 21 42S 116 15 E
Robert Lee, *U.S.A.* **81 K4** 31 54N 100 29W
Robertsdale, *U.S.A.* **78 F6** 40 11N 78 6W
Robertsganj, *India* **43 G10** 24 44N 83 4 E
Robertson, *S. Africa* **56 E2** 33 46S 19 50 E
Robertson I., *Antarctica* **5 C18** 65 15S 59 30W
Robertson Ra., *Australia* **60 D3** 23 15S 121 0 E
Robertstown, *Australia* **63 E2** 33 58S 139 5 E
Roberval, *Canada* **71 C5** 48 32N 72 15W
Robeson Chan., *Greenland* **4 A4** 82 0N 61 30W
Robesonia, *U.S.A.* **79 F8** 40 21N 76 8W
Robinson, *U.S.A.* **76 F2** 39 0N 87 44W
Robinson →, *Australia* **62 B2** 16 3S 137 16 E
Robinson Ra., *Australia* **61 E2** 25 40S 119 0 E
Robinvale, *Australia* **63 E3** 34 40S 142 45 E
Roblin, *Canada* **73 C8** 51 14N 101 21W
Roboré, *Bolivia* **92 G7** 18 10S 59 45W
Robson, *Canada* **72 D5** 49 20N 117 41W
Robson, Mt., *Canada* **72 C5** 53 10N 119 10W
Robstown, *U.S.A.* **81 M6** 27 47N 97 40W
Roca, C. da, *Portugal* **19 C1** 38 40N 9 31W
Roca Partida, I., *Mexico* **86 D2** 19 1N 112 2W
Rocas, I., *Brazil* **93 D12** 4 0S 34 1W
Rocha, *Uruguay* **95 C5** 34 30S 54 25W
Rochdale, *U.K.* **10 D5** 53 38N 2 9W
Rochefort, *Belgium* **15 D5** 50 9N 5 12 E
Rochefort, *France* **18 D3** 45 56N 0 57W
Rochelle, *U.S.A.* **80 E10** 41 56N 89 4W
Rocher River, *Canada* **72 A6** 61 23N 112 44W
Rochester, *U.K.* **11 F8** 51 23N 0 31 E
Rochester, *Ind., U.S.A.* **76 E2** 41 4N 86 13W
Rochester, *Minn., U.S.A.* **80 C8** 44 1N 92 28W
Rochester, *N.H., U.S.A.* **79 C14** 43 18N 70 59W
Rochester, *N.Y., U.S.A.* **78 C7** 43 10N 77 37W
Rock →, *Canada* **72 A3** 60 7N 127 7W
Rock Creek, *U.S.A.* **78 E4** 41 40N 80 52W
Rock Falls, *U.S.A.* **80 E10** 41 47N 89 41W
Rock Hill, *U.S.A.* **77 H5** 34 56N 81 1W
Rock Island, *U.S.A.* **80 E9** 41 30N 90 34W
Rock Rapids, *U.S.A.* **80 D6** 43 26N 96 10W
Rock Sound, *Bahamas* **88 B4** 24 54N 76 12W
Rock Springs, *Mont., U.S.A.* **82 C10** 46 49N 106 15W
Rock Springs, *Wyo., U.S.A.* **82 F9** 41 35N 109 14W
Rock Valley, *U.S.A.* **80 D6** 43 12N 96 18W
Rockall, *Atl. Oc.* **6 D3** 57 37N 13 42W
Rockdale, *Tex., U.S.A.* **81 K6** 30 39N 97 0W
Rockdale, *Wash., U.S.A.* **84 C5** 47 22N 121 28W
Rockefeller Plateau, *Antarctica* **5 E14** 80 0S 140 0W
Rockford, *U.S.A.* **80 D10** 42 16N 89 6W
Rockglen, *Canada* **73 D7** 49 11N 105 57W
Rockhampton, *Australia* **62 C5** 23 22S 150 32 E
Rockingham, *Australia* **61 F2** 32 15S 115 38 E
Rockingham, *U.S.A.* **77 H6** 34 57N 79 46W
Rockingham B., *Australia* **62 B4** 18 5S 146 10 E
Rocklake, *U.S.A.* **80 A5** 48 47N 99 15W
Rockland, *Canada* **79 A9** 45 33N 75 17W
Rockland, *Idaho, U.S.A.* **82 E7** 42 34N 112 53W
Rockland, *Maine, U.S.A.* **77 C11** 44 6N 69 7W
Rockland, *Mich., U.S.A.* **80 B10** 46 44N 89 11W
Rocklin, *U.S.A.* **84 G5** 38 48N 121 14W
Rockport, *Mass., U.S.A.* **79 D14** 42 39N 70 37W
Rockport, *Mo., U.S.A.* **80 E7** 40 25N 95 31W
Rockport, *Tex., U.S.A.* **81 L6** 28 2N 97 3W
Rocksprings, *U.S.A.* **81 K4** 30 1N 100 13W
Rockville, *Conn., U.S.A.* **79 E12** 41 52N 72 28W
Rockville, *Md., U.S.A.* **76 F7** 39 5N 77 9W
Rockwall, *U.S.A.* **81 J6** 32 56N 96 28W
Rockwell City, *U.S.A.* **80 D7** 42 24N 94 38W
Rockwood, *Canada* **78 C4** 43 37N 80 8W
Rockwood, *Maine, U.S.A.* **77 C11** 45 41N 69 45W
Rockwood, *Tenn., U.S.A.* **77 H3** 35 52N 84 41W
Rocky Ford, *U.S.A.* **80 F3** 38 3N 103 43W
Rocky Gully, *Australia* **61 F2** 34 30S 116 57 E
Rocky Harbour, *Canada* **71 C8** 49 36N 57 55W
Rocky Island L., *Canada* **70 C3** 46 55N 83 0W
Rocky Lane, *Canada* **72 B5** 58 31N 116 22W
Rocky Mount, *U.S.A.* **77 H7** 35 57N 77 48W
Rocky Mountain House, *Canada* **72 C6** 52 22N 114 55W
Rocky Mountain National Park, *U.S.A.* **82 F11** 40 25N 105 45W
Rocky Mts., *N. Amer.* **74 C5** 49 0N 115 0W
Rod, *Pakistan* **40 E3** 28 10N 63 5 E
Rødbyhavn, *Denmark* **9 J14** 54 39N 11 22 E
Roddickton, *Canada* **71 B8** 50 51N 56 8W
Rodez, *France* **18 D5** 44 21N 2 33 E
Rodhopoú, *Greece* **23 D5** 35 34N 23 45 E
Ródhos, *Greece* **23 C10** 36 15N 28 10 E
Rodney, *Canada* **78 D3** 42 34N 81 41W
Rodney, C., *N.Z.* **59 G5** 36 17S 174 50 E
Rodriguez, *Ind. Oc.* **3 E13** 19 45S 63 20 E
Roe →, *U.K.* **13 A5** 55 6N 6 59W
Roebling, *U.S.A.* **79 F10** 40 7N 74 47W
Roebourne, *Australia* **60 D2** 20 44S 117 9 E
Roebuck B., *Australia* **60 C3** 18 5S 122 20 E
Roermond, *Neths.* **15 C6** 51 12N 6 0 E
Roes Welcome Sd., *Canada* **69 B11** 65 0N 87 0W
Roeselare, *Belgium* **15 D3** 50 57N 3 7 E
Rogachev = Ragachow, *Belarus* **17 B16** 53 8N 30 5 E
Rogagua, L., *Bolivia* **92 F5** 13 43S 66 50W
Rogatyn, *Ukraine* **17 D13** 49 24N 24 36 E
Rogdhia, *Greece* **23 D7** 35 22N 25 1 E
Rogers, *U.S.A.* **81 G7** 36 20N 94 7W
Rogers City, *U.S.A.* **76 C4** 45 25N 83 49W
Rogersville, *Canada* **71 C6** 46 44N 65 26W
Roggan →, *Canada* **70 B4** 54 24N 79 25W
Roggan L., *Canada* **70 B4** 54 8N 77 50W
Roggeveldberge, *S. Africa* **56 E3** 32 10S 20 10 E
Rogoaguado, L., *Bolivia* **92 F5** 13 0S 65 30W
Rogue →, *U.S.A.* **82 E1** 42 26N 124 26W
Róhda, *Greece* **23 A3** 39 48N 19 46 E
Rohnert Park, *U.S.A.* **84 G4** 38 16N 122 40W
Rohri, *Pakistan* **42 F3** 27 45N 68 51 E
Rohri Canal, *Pakistan* **42 F3** 26 15N 68 27 E
Rohtak, *India* **42 E7** 28 55N 76 43 E
Roi Et, *Thailand* **38 D4** 16 4N 103 40 E
Roja, *Latvia* **9 H20** 57 29N 22 43 E
Rojas, *Argentina* **94 C3** 34 10S 60 45W
Rojo, C., *Mexico* **87 C5** 21 33N 97 20W
Rokan →, *Indonesia* **36 D2** 2 0N 100 50 E
Rokiškis, *Lithuania* **9 J21** 55 55N 25 35 E
Rolândia, *Brazil* **95 A5** 23 18S 51 23W
Rolla, *U.S.A.* **81 G9** 37 57N 91 46W
Rolleston, *Australia* **62 C4** 24 28S 148 35 E
Rollingstone, *Australia* **62 B4** 19 2S 146 24 E
Roma, *Australia* **63 D4** 26 32S 148 49 E
Roma, *Italy* **20 D5** 41 54N 12 29 E
Roma, *Sweden* **9 H18** 57 32N 18 26 E
Roma, *U.S.A.* **81 M5** 26 25N 99 1W
Romain C., *U.S.A.* **77 J6** 33 0N 79 22W
Romaine, *Canada* **71 B7** 50 13N 60 40W
Romaine →, *Canada* **71 B7** 50 18N 63 47W
Roman, *Romania* **17 E14** 46 57N 26 55 E
Romang, *Indonesia* **37 F7** 7 30S 127 20 E
Români, *Egypt* **47 E1** 30 59N 32 38 E
Romania ■, *Europe* **17 F12** 46 0N 25 0 E
Romano, Cayo, *Cuba* **88 B4** 22 0N 77 30W
Romanovka = Basarabeasca, *Moldova* **17 E15** 46 21N 28 58 E
Romans-sur-Isère, *France* **18 D6** 45 3N 5 3 E
Romblon, *Phil.* **37 B6** 12 33N 122 17 E
Rome = Roma, *Italy* **20 D5** 41 54N 12 29 E
Rome, *Ga., U.S.A.* **77 H3** 34 15N 85 10W
Rome, *N.Y., U.S.A.* **79 C9** 43 13N 75 27W
Rome, *Pa., U.S.A.* **79 E8** 41 51N 76 21W
Romney, *U.S.A.* **76 F6** 39 21N 78 45W
Romney Marsh, *U.K.* **11 F8** 51 2N 0 54 E
Rømø, *Denmark* **9 J13** 55 10N 8 30 E
Romorantin-Lanthenay, *France* **18 C4** 47 21N 1 45 E
Romsdalen, *Norway* **9 E12** 62 25N 7 52 E
Romsey, *U.K.* **11 G6** 51 0N 1 29W
Ron, *Vietnam* **38 D6** 17 53N 106 27 E
Rona, *U.K.* **12 D3** 57 34N 5 59W
Ronan, *U.S.A.* **82 C6** 47 32N 114 6W
Roncador, Cayos, *Caribbean* **88 D3** 13 32N 80 4W
Roncador, Serra do, *Brazil* **93 F8** 12 30S 52 30W
Ronda, *Spain* **19 D3** 36 46N 5 12W
Rondane, *Norway* **9 F13** 61 57N 9 50 E
Rondônia □, *Brazil* **92 F6** 11 0S 63 0W
Rondonópolis, *Brazil* **93 G8** 16 28S 54 38W
Rong, Koh, *Cambodia* **39 G4** 10 45N 103 15 E
Ronge, L. la, *Canada* **73 B7** 55 6N 105 17W
Rønne, *Denmark* **9 J16** 55 6N 14 43 E
Ronne Ice Shelf, *Antarctica* **5 D18** 78 0S 60 0W
Ronsard, C., *Australia* **61 D1** 24 46S 113 10 E
Ronse, *Belgium* **15 D3** 50 45N 3 35 E
Roodepoort, *S. Africa* **57 D4** 26 11S 27 54 E
Roof Butte, *U.S.A.* **83 H9** 36 28N 109 5W
Roorkee, *India* **42 E7** 29 52N 77 59 E
Roosendaal, *Neths.* **15 C4** 51 32N 4 29 E
Roosevelt, *U.S.A.* **82 F8** 40 18N 109 59W
Roosevelt →, *Brazil* **92 E6** 7 35S 60 20W
Roosevelt, Mt., *Canada* **72 B3** 58 26N 125 20W
Roosevelt I., *Antarctica* **5 D12** 79 30S 162 0W
Roper →, *Australia* **62 A2** 14 43S 135 27 E
Roper Bar, *Australia* **62 A1** 14 44S 134 44 E
Roque Pérez, *Argentina* **94 D4** 35 25S 59 24W
Roquetas de Mar, *Spain* **19 D4** 36 46N 2 36W
Roraima □, *Brazil* **92 C6** 2 0N 61 30W
Roraima, Mt., *Venezuela* **92 B6** 5 10N 60 40W
Røros, *Norway* **9 E14** 62 35N 11 23 E
Rosa, *Zambia* **55 D3** 9 33S 31 15 E
Rosa, L., *Bahamas* **89 B5** 21 0N 73 30W
Rosa, Monte, *Europe* **18 D7** 45 57N 7 53 E
Rosalia, *U.S.A.* **82 C5** 47 14N 117 22W
Rosamond, *U.S.A.* **85 L8** 34 52N 118 10W
Rosario, *Argentina* **94 C3** 33 0S 60 40W
Rosário, *Brazil* **93 D10** 3 0S 44 15W
Rosario, *Baja Calif., Mexico* **86 B1** 30 0N 115 50W
Rosario, *Sinaloa, Mexico* **86 C3** 23 0N 105 52W
Rosario, *Paraguay* **94 A4** 24 30S 57 35W
Rosario de la Frontera, *Argentina* **94 B3** 25 50S 65 0W
Rosario de Lerma, *Argentina* **94 A2** 24 59S 65 35W
Rosario del Tala, *Argentina* **94 C4** 32 20S 59 10W
Rosário do Sul, *Brazil* **95 C5** 30 15S 54 55W
Rosarito, *Mexico* **85 N9** 32 18N 117 4W
Roscoe, *U.S.A.* **79 E10** 41 56N 74 55W
Roscommon, *Ireland* **13 C3** 53 38N 8 11W
Roscommon □, *Ireland* **13 C3** 53 49N 8 23W
Roscrea, *Ireland* **13 D4** 52 57N 7 49W
Rose →, *Australia* **62 A2** 14 16S 135 45 E
Rose Blanche, *Canada* **71 C8** 47 38N 58 45W
Rose Pt., *Canada* **72 C2** 54 11N 131 39W
Rose Valley, *Canada* **73 C8** 52 19N 103 49W
Roseau, *Domin.* **89 C7** 15 20N 61 24W
Roseau, *U.S.A.* **80 A7** 48 51N 95 46W
Rosebery, *Australia* **62 G4** 41 46S 145 33 E
Rosebud, *S. Dak., U.S.A.* **80 D4** 43 14N 100 51W
Rosebud, *Tex., U.S.A.* **81 K6** 31 4N 96 59W
Roseburg, *U.S.A.* **82 E2** 43 13N 123 20W
Rosedale, *U.S.A.* **81 J9** 33 51N 91 2W
Roseland, *U.S.A.* **84 G4** 38 25N 122 43W
Rosemary, *Canada* **72 C6** 50 46N 112 5W
Rosenberg, *U.S.A.* **81 L7** 29 34N 95 49W
Rosenheim, *Germany* **16 E7** 47 51N 12 7 E
Roses, G. de, *Spain* **19 A7** 42 10N 3 15 E
Rosetown, *Canada* **73 C7** 51 35N 107 59W
Roseville, *Calif., U.S.A.* **84 G5** 38 45N 121 17W
Roseville, *Mich., U.S.A.* **78 D2** 42 30N 82 56W
Rosewood, *Australia* **63 D5** 27 38S 152 36 E
Roshkhvār, *Iran* **45 C8** 34 58N 59 37 E
Rosignano Marittimo, *Italy* **20 C4** 43 24N 10 28 E
Rosignol, *Guyana* **92 B7** 6 15N 57 30W
Roşiori-de-Vede, *Romania* **17 F13** 44 7N 24 59 E
Roskilde, *Denmark* **9 J15** 55 38N 12 3 E
Roslavl, *Russia* **24 D5** 53 57N 32 55 E
Rosmead, *S. Africa* **56 E4** 31 29S 25 8 E
Ross, *Australia* **62 G4** 42 2S 147 30 E
Ross, *N.Z.* **59 K3** 42 53S 170 49 E
Ross I., *Antarctica* **5 D11** 77 30S 168 0 E
Ross Ice Shelf, *Antarctica* **5 E12** 80 0S 180 0 E
Ross L., *U.S.A.* **82 B3** 48 44N 121 4W
Ross-on-Wye, *U.K.* **11 F5** 51 54N 2 34W
Ross River, *Australia* **62 C1** 23 44S 134 30 E
Ross River, *Canada* **72 A2** 62 30N 131 30W
Ross Sea, *Antarctica* **5 D11** 74 0S 178 0 E
Rossall Pt., *U.K.* **10 D4** 53 55N 3 3W
Rossan Pt., *Ireland* **13 B3** 54 42N 8 47W
Rossano, *Italy* **20 E7** 39 36N 16 39 E
Rossburn, *Canada* **73 C8** 50 40N 100 49W
Rosseau, *Canada* **78 A5** 45 16N 79 39W
Rosseau L., *Canada* **78 A5** 45 10N 79 35W
Rosses, The, *Ireland* **13 A3** 55 2N 8 20W
Rossignol, L., *Canada* **70 B5** 52 43N 73 40W
Rossignol Res., *Canada* **71 D6** 44 12N 65 10W
Rossland, *Canada* **72 D5** 49 6N 117 50W
Rosslare, *Ireland* **13 D5** 52 17N 6 24W
Rosso, *Mauritania* **50 E2** 16 40N 15 45W
Rossosh, *Russia* **25 D6** 50 15N 39 28 E
Røssvatnet, *Norway* **8 D16** 65 45N 14 5 E
Røst, *Norway* **8 C15** 67 32N 12 0 E
Rosthern, *Canada* **73 C7** 52 40N 106 20W
Rostock, *Germany* **16 A7** 54 5N 12 8 E
Rostov, *Don, Russia* **25 E6** 47 15N 39 45 E
Rostov, *Yaroslavl, Russia* **24 C6** 57 14N 39 25 E
Roswell, *Ga., U.S.A.* **77 H3** 34 2N 84 22W
Roswell, *N. Mex., U.S.A.* **81 J2** 33 24N 104 32W
Rotan, *U.S.A.* **81 J4** 32 51N 100 28W
Rother →, *U.K.* **11 G8** 50 59N 0 45 E
Rotherham, *U.K.* **10 D6** 53 26N 1 20W
Rothes, *U.K.* **12 D5** 57 32N 3 13W
Rothesay, *Canada* **71 C6** 45 23N 66 0W
Rothesay, *U.K.* **12 F3** 55 50N 5 3W
Roti, *Indonesia* **37 F6** 10 50S 123 0 E
Roto, *Australia* **63 E4** 33 0S 145 30 E
Rotondo Mte., *France* **18 E8** 42 14N 9 8 E
Rotoroa, L., *N.Z.* **59 J4** 41 55S 172 39 E
Rotorua, *N.Z.* **59 H6** 38 9S 176 16 E
Rotorua, L., *N.Z.* **59 H6** 38 5S 176 18 E
Rotterdam, *Neths.* **15 C4** 51 55N 4 30 E
Rotterdam, *U.S.A.* **79 D10** 42 48N 74 1W
Rottnest I., *Australia* **61 F2** 32 0S 115 27 E
Rottumeroog, *Neths.* **15 A6** 53 33N 6 34 E
Rottweil, *Germany* **16 D5** 48 9N 8 37 E
Rotuma, *Fiji* **64 J9** 12 25S 177 5 E
Roubaix, *France* **18 A5** 50 40N 3 10 E
Rouen, *France* **18 B4** 49 27N 1 4 E
Rouleau, *Canada* **73 C8** 50 10N 104 56W
Round Mountain, *U.S.A.* **82 G5** 38 43N 117 4W
Round Mt., *Australia* **63 E5** 30 26S 152 16 E
Round Rock, *U.S.A.* **81 K6** 30 31N 97 41W
Roundup, *U.S.A.* **82 C9** 46 27N 108 33W
Rousay, *U.K.* **12 B5** 59 10N 3 2W
Rouses Point, *U.S.A.* **79 B11** 44 59N 73 22W
Rouseville, *U.S.A.* **78 E5** 41 28N 79 42W
Roussillon, *France* **18 E5** 42 30N 2 35 E
Rouxville, *S. Africa* **56 E4** 30 25S 26 50 E
Rouyn-Noranda, *Canada* **70 C4** 48 20N 79 0W
Rovaniemi, *Finland* **8 C21** 66 29N 25 41 E
Rovereto, *Italy* **20 B4** 45 53N 11 3 E
Rovigo, *Italy* **20 B4** 45 4N 11 47 E
Rovinj, *Croatia* **16 F7** 45 5N 13 40 E
Rovno = Rivne, *Ukraine* **17 C14** 50 40N 26 10 E
Rovuma = Ruvuma →, *Tanzania* **55 E5** 10 29S 40 28 E
Row'ān, *Iran* **45 C6** 35 8N 48 51 E
Rowena, *Australia* **63 D4** 29 48S 148 55 E
Rowley Shoals, *Australia* **60 C2** 17 30S 119 0 E
Roxas, *Phil.* **37 B6** 11 36N 122 49 E
Roxboro, *U.S.A.* **77 G6** 36 24N 78 59W
Roxburgh, *N.Z.* **59 L2** 45 33S 169 19 E
Roxbury, *U.S.A.* **78 F7** 40 6N 77 39W
Roy, *Mont., U.S.A.* **82 C9** 47 20N 108 58W
Roy, *N. Mex., U.S.A.* **81 H2** 35 57N 104 12W
Roy, *Utah, U.S.A.* **82 F7** 41 10N 112 2W
Royal Canal, *Ireland* **13 C4** 53 30N 7 13W
Royal Leamington Spa, *U.K.* **11 E6** 52 18N 1 31W
Royal Tunbridge Wells, *U.K.* **11 F8** 51 7N 0 16 E
Royan, *France* **18 D3** 45 37N 1 2W
Royston, *U.K.* **11 E7** 52 3N 0 0 E
Rozdilna, *Ukraine* **17 E16** 46 50N 30 2 E
Rozhyshche, *Ukraine* **17 C13** 50 54N 25 15 E
Rtishchevo, *Russia* **24 D7** 52 18N 43 46 E
Ruacaná, *Angola* **56 B1** 17 20S 14 12 E
Ruahine Ra., *N.Z.* **59 H6** 39 55S 176 2 E
Ruapehu, *N.Z.* **59 H5** 39 17S 175 35 E
Ruapuke I., *N.Z.* **59 M2** 46 46S 168 31 E
Ruâq, W. →, *Egypt* **47 F2** 30 0N 33 49 E
Rub' al Khālī, *Si. Arabia* **46 D4** 18 0N 48 0 E
Rubeho Mts., *Tanzania* **54 D4** 6 50S 36 25 E
Rubh a' Mhail, *U.K.* **12 F2** 55 56N 6 8W
Rubha Hunish, *U.K.* **12 D2** 57 42N 6 20W
Rubha Robhanais = Lewis, Butt of, *U.K.* **12 C2** 58 31N 6 16W
Rubicon →, *U.S.A.* **84 G5** 38 53N 121 4W
Rubio, *Venezuela* **92 B4** 7 43N 72 22W
Rubtsovsk, *Russia* **26 D9** 51 30N 81 10 E
Ruby L., *U.S.A.* **82 F6** 40 10N 115 28W
Ruby Mts., *U.S.A.* **82 F6** 40 30N 115 20W
Rubyvale, *Australia* **62 C4** 23 25S 147 42 E
Rūd Sar, *Iran* **45 B6** 37 8N 50 18 E
Rudall, *Australia* **63 E2** 33 43S 136 17 E
Rudall →, *Australia* **60 D3** 22 34S 122 13 E
Rudewa, *Tanzania* **55 E3** 10 7S 34 40 E
Rudnyy, *Kazakstan* **26 D7** 52 57N 63 7 E
Rudolfa, Ostrov, *Russia* **26 A6** 81 45N 58 30 E
Rudyard, *U.S.A.* **76 B3** 46 14N 84 36W
Rufiji →, *Tanzania* **54 D4** 7 50S 39 15 E
Rufino, *Argentina* **94 C3** 34 20S 62 50W
Rufunsa, *Zambia* **55 F2** 15 4S 29 34 E
Rugby, *U.K.* **11 E6** 52 23N 1 16W
Rugby, *U.S.A.* **80 A5** 48 22N 100 0W
Rügen, *Germany* **16 A7** 54 22N 13 24 E
Ruhengeri, *Rwanda* **54 C2** 1 30S 29 36 E
Ruhnu, *Estonia* **9 H20** 57 48N 23 15 E
Ruhr →, *Germany* **16 C4** 51 27N 6 43 E
Ruhuhu →, *Tanzania* **55 E3** 10 31S 34 34 E
Ruidoso, *U.S.A.* **83 K11** 33 20N 105 41W
Ruivo, Pico, *Madeira* **22 D3** 32 45N 16 56W
Rujm Tal'at al Jamā'ah, *Jordan* **47 E4** 30 24N 35 30 E
Ruk, *Pakistan* **42 F3** 27 50N 68 42 E
Rukhla, *Pakistan* **42 C4** 32 27N 71 57 E
Ruki →, *Dem. Rep. of the Congo* **52 E3** 0 5N 18 17 E
Rukwa □, *Tanzania* **54 D3** 7 0S 31 30 E
Rukwa, L., *Tanzania* **54 D3** 8 0S 32 20 E
Rulhieres, C., *Australia* **60 B4** 13 56S 127 22 E
Rum = Rhum, *U.K.* **12 E2** 57 0N 6 20W
Rum Cay, *Bahamas* **89 B5** 23 40N 74 58W
Rum Jungle, *Australia* **60 B5** 13 0S 130 59 E
Rumāḥ, *Si. Arabia* **44 E5** 25 29N 47 10 E
Rumania = Romania ■, *Europe* **17 F12** 46 0N 25 0 E
Rumaylah, *Iraq* **44 D5** 30 47N 47 37 E
Rumbêk, *Sudan* **51 G11** 6 54N 29 37 E
Rumford, *U.S.A.* **77 C10** 44 33N 70 33W
Rumia, *Poland* **17 A10** 54 37N 18 25 E
Rumoi, *Japan* **30 C10** 43 56N 141 39 E
Rumonge, *Burundi* **54 C2** 3 59S 29 26 E
Rumson, *U.S.A.* **79 F11** 40 23N 74 0W
Rumuruti, *Kenya* **54 B4** 0 17N 36 32 E
Runan, *China* **34 H8** 33 0N 114 30 E
Runanga, *N.Z.* **59 K3** 42 25S 171 15 E
Runaway, C., *N.Z.* **59 G6** 37 32S 177 59 E
Runcorn, *U.K.* **10 D5** 53 21N 2 44W
Rundu, *Namibia* **53 H3** 17 52S 19 43 E
Rungwa, *Tanzania* **54 D3** 6 55S 33 32 E
Rungwa →, *Tanzania* **54 D3** 7 36S 31 50 E
Rungwe, *Tanzania* **55 D3** 9 11S 33 32 E
Rungwe, Mt., *Tanzania* **52 F6** 9 8S 33 40 E
Runton Ra., *Australia* **60 D3** 23 31S 123 6 E
Ruoqiang, *China* **32 C3** 38 55N 88 10 E
Rupa, *India* **41 F18** 27 15N 92 21 E
Rupar, *India* **42 D7** 31 2N 76 38 E
Rupat, *Indonesia* **36 D2** 1 45N 101 40 E
Rupen →, *India* **42 H4** 23 28N 71 31 E
Rupert, *U.S.A.* **82 E7** 42 37N 113 41W
Rupert →, *Canada* **70 B4** 51 29N 78 45W
Rupert B., *Canada* **70 B4** 51 35N 79 0W
Rupert House = Waskaganish, *Canada* **70 B4** 51 30N 78 40W
Rupsa, *India* **43 J12** 21 37N 87 1 E
Rurrenabaque, *Bolivia* **92 F5** 14 30S 67 32W
Rusambo, *Zimbabwe* **55 F3** 16 30S 32 4 E
Rusape, *Zimbabwe* **55 F3** 18 35S 32 8 E
Ruschuk = Ruse, *Bulgaria* **21 C12** 43 48N 25 59 E
Ruse, *Bulgaria* **21 C12** 43 48N 25 59 E
Rush, *Ireland* **13 C5** 53 31N 6 6W
Rushan, *China* **35 F11** 36 56N 121 30 E
Rushden, *U.K.* **11 E7** 52 18N 0 35W
Rushmore, Mt., *U.S.A.* **80 D3** 43 53N 103 28W
Rushville, *Ill., U.S.A.* **80 E9** 40 7N 90 34W
Rushville, *Ind., U.S.A.* **76 F3** 39 37N 85 27W
Rushville, *Nebr., U.S.A.* **80 D3** 42 43N 102 28W
Russas, *Brazil* **93 D11** 4 55S 37 50W
Russell, *Canada* **73 C8** 50 50N 101 20W
Russell, *Kans., U.S.A.* **80 F5** 38 54N 98 52W
Russell, *N.Y., U.S.A.* **79 B9** 44 27N 75 9W
Russell, *Pa., U.S.A.* **78 E5** 41 56N 79 8W
Russell L., *Man., Canada* **73 B8** 56 15N 101 30W
Russell L., *N.W.T., Canada* **72 A5** 63 5N 115 44W
Russellkonda, *India* **41 K14** 19 57N 84 42 E
Russellville, *Ala., U.S.A.* **77 H2** 34 30N 87 44W
Russellville, *Ark., U.S.A.* **81 H8** 35 17N 93 8W
Russellville, *Ky., U.S.A.* **77 G2** 36 51N 86 53W
Russia ■, *Eurasia* **27 C11** 62 0N 105 0 E
Russian →, *U.S.A.* **84 G3** 38 27N 123 8W
Russkoye Ustie, *Russia* **4 B15** 71 0N 149 0 E
Rustam, *Pakistan* **42 B5** 34 25N 72 13 E
Rustam Shahr, *Pakistan* **42 F2** 26 58N 66 6 E
Rustavi, *Georgia* **25 F8** 41 30N 45 0 E
Rustenburg, *S. Africa* **56 D4** 25 41S 27 14 E
Ruston, *U.S.A.* **81 J8** 32 32N 92 38W
Rutana, *Burundi* **54 C3** 3 55S 30 0 E
Ruteng, *Indonesia* **37 F6** 8 35S 120 30 E
Ruth, *U.S.A.* **78 C2** 43 42N 82 45W
Rutherford, *U.S.A.* **84 G4** 38 26N 122 24W
Rutland, *U.S.A.* **79 C12** 43 37N 72 58W
Rutland □, *U.K.* **11 E7** 52 38N 0 40W
Rutland Water, *U.K.* **11 E7** 52 39N 0 38W
Rutledge →, *Canada* **73 A6** 61 4N 112 0W
Rutledge L., *Canada* **73 A6** 61 33N 110 47W
Rutshuru, *Dem. Rep. of the Congo* **54 C2** 1 13S 29 25 E
Ruvu, *Tanzania* **54 D4** 6 49S 38 43 E
Ruvu →, *Tanzania* **54 D4** 6 23S 38 52 E
Ruvuma □, *Tanzania* **55 E4** 10 20S 36 0 E
Ruvuma →, *Tanzania* **55 E5** 10 29S 40 28 E
Ruwais, *U.A.E.* **45 E7** 24 5N 52 50 E
Ruwenzori, *Africa* **54 B2** 0 30N 29 55 E
Ruyigi, *Burundi* **54 C3** 3 29S 30 15 E
Ružomberok, *Slovak Rep.* **17 D10** 49 3N 19 17 E
Rwanda ■, *Africa* **54 C3** 2 0S 30 0 E
Ryan, L., *U.K.* **12 G3** 55 0N 5 2W
Ryazan, *Russia* **24 D6** 54 40N 39 40 E
Ryazhsk, *Russia* **24 D7** 53 45N 40 3 E
Rybache = Rybachye, *Kazakstan* **26 E9** 46 40N 81 20 E
Rybachiy Poluostrov, *Russia* **24 A5** 69 43N 32 0 E
Rybachye = Ysyk-Köl, *Kyrgyzstan* **28 E11** 42 26N 76 12 E
Rybachye, *Kazakstan* **26 E9** 46 40N 81 20 E
Rybinsk, *Russia* **24 C6** 58 5N 38 50 E
Rybinskoye Vdkhr., *Russia* **24 C6** 58 30N 38 25 E
Rybnitsa = Râbniţa, *Moldova* **17 E15** 47 45N 29 0 E
Rycroft, *Canada* **72 B5** 55 45N 118 40W
Ryde, *U.K.* **11 G6** 50 43N 1 9W
Ryderwood, *U.S.A.* **84 D3** 46 23N 123 3W
Rye, *U.K.* **11 G8** 50 57N 0 45 E
Rye →, *U.K.* **10 C7** 54 11N 0 44W
Rye Bay, *U.K.* **11 G8** 50 52N 0 49 E
Rye Patch Reservoir, *U.S.A.* **82 F4** 40 28N 118 19W
Ryegate, *U.S.A.* **82 C9** 46 18N 109 15W
Ryley, *Canada* **72 C6** 53 17N 112 26W
Rylstone, *Australia* **63 E4** 32 46S 149 58 E
Ryōtsu, *Japan* **30 E9** 38 5N 138 26 E
Rypin, *Poland* **17 B10** 53 3N 19 25 E
Ryūgasaki, *Japan* **31 G10** 35 54N 140 11 E
Ryūkyū Is. = Ryūkyū-rettō, *Japan* **31 M3** 26 0N 126 0 E
Ryūkyū-rettō, *Japan* **31 M3** 26 0N 126 0 E
Rzeszów, *Poland* **17 C11** 50 5N 21 58 E
Rzhev, *Russia* **24 C5** 56 20N 34 20 E

S

Sa, Thailand 38 C3 18 34N 100 45 E
Sa Canal, Spain 22 C7 38 51N 1 23 E
Sa Conillera, Spain 22 C7 38 59N 1 13 E
Sa Dec, Vietnam 39 G5 10 20N 105 46 E
Sa Dragonera, Spain 22 B9 39 35N 2 19 E
Sa Mesquida, Spain 22 B11 39 55N 4 16 E
Sa Savina, Spain 22 C7 38 44N 1 25 E
Sa'ādatābād, Fārs, Iran 45 D7 30 10N 53 5 E
Sa'ādatābād, Hormozgān, Iran 45 D7 28 3N 55 53 E
Sa'ādatābād, Kermān, Iran 45 D7 29 40N 55 51 E
Saale →, Germany 16 C6 51 56N 11 54 E
Saalfeld, Germany 16 C6 50 38N 11 21 E
Saar →, Europe 18 B7 49 41N 6 32 E
Saarbrücken, Germany 16 D4 49 14N 6 59 E
Saaremaa, Estonia 9 G20 58 30N 22 30 E
Saarijärvi, Finland 9 E21 62 43N 25 16 E
Saariselkä, Finland 8 B23 68 16N 28 15 E
Sab 'Ābar, Syria 44 C3 33 46N 37 41 E
Saba, W. Indies 89 C7 17 42N 63 26W
Šabac, Serbia, Yug. 21 B8 44 48N 19 42 E
Sabadell, Spain 19 B7 41 28N 2 7 E
Sabah □, Malaysia 36 C5 6 0N 117 0 E
Sabak Bernam, Malaysia 39 L3 3 46N 100 58 E
Sabalān, Kūhhā-ye, Iran 44 B5 38 15N 47 45 E
Sabalana, Kepulauan, Indonesia 37 F5 6 45S 118 50 E
Sábana de la Mar, Dom. Rep. 89 C6 19 7N 69 24W
Sábanalarga, Colombia 92 A4 10 38N 74 55W
Sabang, Indonesia 36 C1 5 50N 95 15 E
Sabará, Brazil 93 G10 19 55S 43 46W
Sabarmati →, India 42 H5 22 18N 72 22 E
Sabattis, U.S.A. 79 B10 44 6N 74 40W
Saberania, Indonesia 37 E9 2 5S 138 18 E
Sabhah, Libya 51 C8 27 9N 14 29 E
Sabi →, India 42 E7 28 29N 76 44 E
Sabie, S. Africa 57 D5 25 10S 30 48 E
Sabinal, Mexico 86 A3 30 58N 107 25W
Sabinal, U.S.A. 81 L5 29 19N 99 28W
Sabinas, Mexico 86 B4 27 50N 101 10W
Sabinas →, Mexico 86 B4 27 37N 100 42W
Sabinas Hidalgo, Mexico 86 B4 26 33N 100 10W
Sabine →, U.S.A. 81 L8 29 59N 93 47W
Sabine L., U.S.A. 81 L8 29 53N 93 51W
Sabine Pass, U.S.A. 81 L8 29 44N 93 54W
Sabinsville, U.S.A. 78 E7 41 52N 77 31W
Sabkhet el Bardawîl, Egypt 47 D2 31 10N 33 15 E
Sablayan, Phil. 37 B6 12 50N 120 50 E
Sable, Canada 71 A6 55 30N 68 21W
Sable, C., Canada 71 D6 43 29N 65 38W
Sable, C., U.S.A. 75 E10 25 9N 81 8W
Sable I., Canada 71 D8 44 0N 60 0W
Sabrina Coast, Antarctica 5 C9 68 0S 120 0 E
Sabulubbek, Indonesia 36 E1 1 36S 98 40 E
Sabzevār, Iran 45 B8 36 15N 57 40 E
Sabzvārān, Iran 45 D8 28 45N 57 50 E
Sac City, U.S.A. 80 D7 42 25N 95 0W
Săcele, Romania 17 F13 45 37N 25 41 E
Sachigo →, Canada 70 A2 55 6N 88 58W
Sachigo, L., Canada 70 B1 53 50N 92 12W
Sachsen □, Germany 16 C7 50 55N 13 10 E
Sachsen-Anhalt □, Germany 16 C7 52 0N 12 0 E
Sackets Harbor, U.S.A. 79 C8 43 57N 76 7W
Sackville, Canada 71 C7 45 54N 64 22W
Saco, Maine, U.S.A. 77 D10 43 30N 70 27W
Saco, Mont., U.S.A. 82 B10 48 28N 107 21W
Sacramento, U.S.A. 84 G5 38 35N 121 29W
Sacramento →, U.S.A. 84 G5 38 3N 121 56W
Sacramento Mts., U.S.A. 83 K11 32 30N 105 30W
Sacramento Valley, U.S.A. 84 G5 39 30N 122 0W
Sada-Misaki, Japan 31 H6 33 20N 132 1 E
Sadabad, India 42 F8 27 27N 78 3 E
Sadani, Tanzania 54 D4 5 58S 38 35 E
Sadao, Thailand 39 J3 6 38N 100 26 E
Sadd el Aali, Egypt 51 D12 23 54N 32 54 E
Saddle Mt., U.S.A. 84 E3 45 58N 123 41W
Sadimi, Dem. Rep. of the Congo 55 D1 9 25S 23 32 E
Sado, Japan 30 F9 38 0N 138 25 E
Sadon, Burma 41 G20 25 28N 97 55 E
Sadra, India 42 H5 23 21N 72 43 E
Sadri, India 42 G5 25 11N 73 26 E
Sæby, Denmark 9 H14 57 21N 10 30 E
Saegertown, U.S.A. 78 E4 41 43N 80 9W
Şafājah, Si. Arabia 44 E3 26 25N 39 0 E
Säffle, Sweden 9 G15 59 8N 12 55 E
Safford, U.S.A. 83 K9 32 50N 109 43W
Saffron Walden, U.K. 11 E8 52 1N 0 16 E
Safi, Morocco 50 B4 32 18N 9 20W
Şafīābād, Iran 45 B8 36 45N 57 58 E
Safīd Dasht, Iran 45 C6 33 27N 48 11 E
Safīd Kūh, Afghan. 40 B3 34 45N 63 0 E
Safīd Rūd →, Iran 45 B6 37 23N 50 11 E
Safipur, India 43 F9 26 44N 80 21 E
Safwān, Iraq 44 D5 30 7N 47 43 E
Sag Harbor, U.S.A. 79 F12 41 0N 72 18W
Saga, Japan 31 H5 33 15N 130 16 E
Saga □, Japan 31 H5 33 15N 130 20 E
Sagae, Japan 30 E10 38 22N 140 17 E
Sagamore, U.S.A. 78 F5 40 46N 79 14W
Sagar, India 40 M9 14 14N 75 6 E
Sagar, Mad. P., India 43 H8 23 50N 78 44 E
Sagara, L., Tanzania 54 D3 5 20S 31 0 E
Saginaw, U.S.A. 76 D4 43 26N 83 56W
Saginaw →, U.S.A. 76 D4 43 39N 83 51W
Saginaw B., U.S.A. 76 D4 43 50N 83 40W
Saglouc = Salluit, Canada 69 B12 62 14N 75 38W
Sagŏ-ri, S. Korea 35 G14 35 25N 126 49 E
Sagua la Grande, Cuba 88 B3 22 50N 80 10W
Saguache, U.S.A. 83 G10 38 5N 106 8W
Saguaro Nat. Park, U.S.A. 83 K8 32 12N 110 38W
Saguenay →, Canada 71 C5 48 22N 71 0W
Sagunt, Spain 19 C5 39 42N 0 18W
Sagunto = Sagunt, Spain 19 C5 39 42N 0 18W
Sagwara, India 42 H6 23 41N 74 1 E
Sahagún, Spain 19 A3 42 18N 5 2W
Saḩam al Jawlān, Syria 47 C4 32 45N 35 55 E
Sahand, Kūh-e, Iran 44 B5 37 44N 46 27 E
Sahara, Africa 50 D6 23 0N 5 0 E
Saharan Atlas = Saharien, Atlas, Algeria 50 B6 33 30N 1 0 E
Saharanpur, India 42 E7 29 58N 77 33 E
Saharien, Atlas, Algeria 50 B6 33 30N 1 0 E
Saharsa, India 43 G12 25 53N 86 36 E
Sahasinaka, Madag. 57 C8 21 49S 47 49 E
Sahaswan, India 43 E8 28 5N 78 45 E
Sahel, Africa 50 E5 16 0N 5 0 E
Sahibganj, India 43 G12 25 12N 87 40 E
Sāḩilīyah, Iraq 44 C4 33 43N 42 42 E
Sahiwal, Pakistan 42 D5 30 45N 73 8 E
Şaḩneh, Iran 44 C5 34 29N 47 41 E
Sahuaripa, Mexico 86 B3 29 0N 109 13W
Sahuarita, U.S.A. 83 L8 31 57N 110 58W
Sahuayo, Mexico 86 C4 20 4N 102 43W
Sai →, India 43 G10 25 39N 82 47 E
Sai Buri, Thailand 39 J3 6 43N 101 45 E
Sa'id Bundas, Sudan 51 G10 8 24N 24 48 E
Sa'īdābād, Kermān, Iran 45 D7 29 30N 55 45 E
Sa'īdābād, Semnān, Iran 45 B7 36 8N 54 11 E
Sa'īdīyeh, Iran 45 B6 36 20N 48 55 E
Saidpur, Bangla. 41 G16 25 48N 89 0 E
Saidpur, India 43 G10 25 33N 83 11 E
Saidu, Pakistan 43 B5 34 43N 72 24 E
Saigon = Thanh Pho Ho Chi Minh, Vietnam 39 G6 10 58N 106 40 E
Saijō, Japan 31 H6 33 55N 133 11 E
Saikhoa Ghat, India 41 F19 27 50N 95 40 E
Saiki, Japan 31 H5 32 58N 131 51 E
Sailana, India 42 H6 23 28N 74 55 E
Sailolof, Indonesia 37 E8 1 7S 130 46 E
Saimaa, Finland 9 F23 61 15N 28 15 E
Şa'in Dezh, Iran 44 B5 36 40N 46 25 E
St. Abb's Head, U.K. 12 F6 55 55N 2 8W
St. Alban's, Canada 71 C8 47 51N 55 50W
St. Albans, U.K. 11 F7 51 45N 0 19W
St. Albans, Vt., U.S.A. 79 B11 44 49N 73 5W
St. Albans, W. Va., U.S.A. 76 F5 38 23N 81 50W
St. Alban's Head, U.K. 11 G5 50 34N 2 4W
St. Albert, Canada 72 C6 53 37N 113 32W
St. Andrew's, Canada 71 C8 47 45N 59 15W
St. Andrews, U.K. 12 E6 56 20N 2 47W
St-Anicet, Canada 79 A10 45 8N 74 22W
St. Ann B., Canada 71 C7 46 22N 60 25W
St. Ann's Bay, Jamaica 88 C4 18 26N 77 15W
St. Anthony, Canada 71 B8 51 22N 55 35W
St. Anthony, U.S.A. 82 E8 43 58N 111 41W
St. Antoine, Canada 71 C7 46 22N 64 45W
St. Arnaud, Australia 63 F3 36 40S 143 16 E
St-Augustin →, Canada 71 B8 51 16N 58 40W
St-Augustin-Saguenay, Canada 71 B8 51 13N 58 38W
St. Augustine, U.S.A. 77 L5 29 54N 81 19W
St. Austell, U.K. 11 G3 50 20N 4 47W
St. Barbe, Canada 71 B8 51 12N 56 46W
St-Barthélemy, W. Indies 89 C7 17 50N 62 50W
St. Bees Hd., U.K. 10 C4 54 31N 3 38W
St. Bride's, Canada 71 C9 46 56N 54 10W
St. Brides B., U.K. 11 F2 51 49N 5 9W
St-Brieuc, France 18 B2 48 30N 2 46W
St. Catharines, Canada 78 C5 43 10N 79 15W
St. Catherines I., U.S.A. 77 K5 31 40N 81 10W
St. Catherine's Pt., U.K. 11 G6 50 34N 1 18W
St-Chamond, France 18 D6 45 28N 4 31 E
St. Charles, Ill., U.S.A. 76 E1 41 54N 88 19W
St. Charles, Mo., U.S.A. 80 F9 38 47N 90 29W
St. Charles, Va., U.S.A. 76 F7 36 48N 83 4W
St. Christopher-Nevis = St. Kitts & Nevis ■, W. Indies 89 C7 17 20N 62 40W
St. Clair, Mich., U.S.A. 78 D2 42 50N 82 30W
St. Clair, Pa., U.S.A. 79 F8 40 43N 76 12W
St. Clair →, U.S.A. 78 D2 42 38N 82 31W
St. Clair, L., Canada 70 D3 42 30N 82 45W
St. Clair, L., U.S.A. 78 D2 42 27N 82 39W
St. Clairsville, U.S.A. 78 F4 40 5N 80 54W
St. Claude, Canada 73 D9 49 40N 98 20W
St-Clet, Canada 79 A10 45 21N 74 13W
St. Cloud, Fla., U.S.A. 77 L5 28 15N 81 17W
St. Cloud, Minn., U.S.A. 80 C7 45 34N 94 10W
St. Cricq, C., Australia 61 E1 25 17S 113 6 E
St. Croix, Virgin Is. 89 C7 17 45N 64 45W
St. Croix →, U.S.A. 80 C8 44 45N 92 48W
St. Croix Falls, U.S.A. 80 C8 45 24N 92 38W
St. David's, Canada 71 C8 48 12N 58 52W
St. David's, U.K. 11 F2 51 53N 5 16W
St. David's Head, U.K. 11 F2 51 54N 5 19W
St-Denis, France 18 B5 48 56N 2 22 E
St-Dizier, France 18 B6 48 38N 4 56 E
St. Elias, Mt., U.S.A. 68 B5 60 18N 140 56W
St. Elias Mts., Canada 72 A1 60 33N 139 28W
St. Elias Mts., U.S.A. 68 C6 60 0N 138 0W
St-Étienne, France 18 D6 45 27N 4 22 E
St. Eugène, Canada 79 A10 45 30N 74 28W
St. Eustatius, W. Indies 89 C7 17 20N 63 0W
St-Félicien, Canada 70 C5 48 40N 72 25W
St-Flour, France 18 D5 45 2N 3 6 E
St. Francis, U.S.A. 80 F4 39 47N 101 48W
St. Francis →, U.S.A. 81 H9 34 38N 90 36W
St. Francis, C., S. Africa 56 E3 34 14S 24 49 E
St. Francisville, U.S.A. 81 K9 30 47N 91 23W
St-François, L., Canada 79 A10 45 10N 74 22W
St-Gabriel, Canada 70 C5 46 17N 73 24W
St. Gallen = Sankt Gallen, Switz. 18 C8 47 26N 9 22 E
St-Gaudens, France 18 E4 43 6N 0 44 E
St. George, Australia 63 D4 28 1S 148 30 E
St. George, Canada 71 C6 45 11N 66 50W
St. George, S.C., U.S.A. 77 J5 33 11N 80 35W
St. George, Utah, U.S.A. 83 H7 37 6N 113 35W
St. George, C., Canada 71 C8 48 30N 59 16W
St. George, C., U.S.A. 77 L3 29 40N 85 5W
St. George Ra., Australia 60 C4 18 40S 125 0 E
St. George's, Canada 71 C8 48 26N 58 31W
St-Georges, Canada 71 C5 46 8N 70 40W
St. George's, Grenada 89 D7 12 5N 61 43W
St. George's B., Canada 71 C8 48 24N 58 53W
St. Georges Basin, N.S.W., Australia 63 F5 35 7S 150 36 E
St. Georges Basin, W. Austral., Australia 60 C4 15 23S 125 2 E
St. George's Channel, Europe 13 E6 52 0N 6 0W
St. Georges Hd., Australia 63 F5 35 12S 150 42 E
St. Gotthard P. = San Gottardo, P. del, Switz. 18 C8 46 33N 8 33 E
St. Helena, U.S.A. 82 G2 38 30N 122 28W
St. Helena ■, Atl. Oc. 49 H3 15 55S 5 44W
St. Helena, Mt., U.S.A. 84 G4 38 40N 122 36W
St. Helena B., S. Africa 56 E2 32 40S 18 10 E
St. Helens, Australia 62 G4 41 20S 148 15 E
St. Helens, U.K. 10 D5 53 27N 2 44W
St. Helens, U.S.A. 84 E4 45 52N 122 48W
St. Helens, Mt., U.S.A. 84 D4 46 12N 122 12W
St. Helier, U.K. 11 H5 49 10N 2 7W
St-Hubert, Belgium 15 D5 50 2N 5 23 E
St-Hyacinthe, Canada 70 C5 45 40N 72 58W
St. Ignace, U.S.A. 76 C3 45 52N 84 44W
St. Ignace I., Canada 70 C2 48 45N 88 0W
St. Ignatius, U.S.A. 82 C6 47 19N 114 6W
St. Ives, U.K. 11 G2 50 12N 5 30W
St. James, U.S.A. 80 D7 43 59N 94 38W
St-Jean →, Canada 71 B7 50 17N 64 20W
St-Jean, L., Canada 71 C5 48 40N 72 0W
St-Jean-Port-Joli, Canada 71 C5 47 15N 70 13W
St-Jean-sur-Richelieu, Canada 79 A11 45 20N 73 20W
St-Jérôme, Canada 70 C5 45 47N 74 0W
St. John, Canada 71 C6 45 20N 66 8W
St. John, U.S.A. 81 G5 38 0N 98 46W
St. John →, U.S.A. 77 C12 45 12N 66 5W
St. John, C., Canada 71 C8 50 0N 55 32W
St. John's, Antigua 89 C7 17 6N 61 51W
St. John's, Canada 71 C9 47 35N 52 40W
St. Johns, Ariz., U.S.A. 83 J9 34 30N 109 22W
St. Johns, Mich., U.S.A. 76 D3 43 0N 84 33W
St. Johns →, U.S.A. 77 K5 30 24N 81 24W
St. John's Pt., Ireland 13 B3 54 34N 8 27W
St. Johnsbury, U.S.A. 79 B12 44 25N 72 1W
St. Johnsville, U.S.A. 79 D10 43 0N 74 43W
St. Joseph, La., U.S.A. 81 K9 31 55N 91 14W
St. Joseph, Mich., U.S.A. 75 B9 42 6N 86 29W
St. Joseph, Mo., U.S.A. 80 F7 39 46N 94 50W
St. Joseph →, U.S.A. 76 D2 42 7N 86 29W
St. Joseph, I., Canada 70 C3 46 12N 83 58W
St. Joseph, L., Canada 70 B1 51 10N 90 35W
St-Jovite, Canada 70 C5 46 8N 74 38W
St. Kilda, N.Z. 59 L3 45 53S 170 31 E
St. Kitts & Nevis ■, W. Indies 89 C7 17 20N 62 40W
St. Laurent, Canada 73 C9 50 25N 97 58W
St. Lawrence, Australia 62 C4 22 16S 149 31 E
St. Lawrence, Canada 71 C8 46 54N 55 23W
St. Lawrence →, Canada 71 C6 49 30N 66 0W
St. Lawrence, Gulf of, Canada 71 C7 48 25N 62 0W
St. Lawrence I., U.S.A. 68 B3 63 30N 170 30W
St. Leonard, Canada 71 C6 47 12N 67 58W
St. Lewis →, Canada 71 B8 52 26N 56 11W
St-Lô, France 18 B3 49 7N 1 5W
St-Louis, Senegal 50 E2 16 8N 16 27W
St. Louis, U.S.A. 80 F9 38 37N 90 12W
St. Louis →, U.S.A. 80 B8 47 15N 92 45W
St. Lucia ■, W. Indies 89 D7 14 0N 60 50W
St. Lucia, L., S. Africa 57 D5 28 5S 32 30 E
St. Lucia Channel, W. Indies 89 D7 14 15N 61 0W
St. Maarten, W. Indies 89 C7 18 0N 63 5W
St. Magnus B., U.K. 12 A7 60 25N 1 35W
St-Malo, France 18 B2 48 39N 2 1W
St-Marc, Haiti 89 C5 19 10N 72 41W
St. Maries, U.S.A. 82 C5 47 19N 116 35W
St-Martin, W. Indies 89 C7 18 0N 63 0W
St. Martin, L., Canada 73 C9 51 40N 98 30W
St. Mary Pk., Australia 63 E2 31 32S 138 34 E
St. Marys, Australia 62 G4 41 35S 148 11 E
St. Marys, Canada 78 C3 43 20N 81 10W
St. Mary's, Corn., U.K. 11 H1 49 55N 6 18W
St. Mary's, Orkney, U.K. 12 C6 58 54N 2 54W
St. Marys, Ga., U.S.A. 77 K5 30 44N 81 33W
St. Marys, Pa., U.S.A. 78 E6 41 26N 78 34W
St. Mary's, C., Canada 71 C9 46 50N 54 12W
St. Mary's B., Canada 71 C9 46 50N 53 50W
St. Marys Bay, Canada 71 D6 44 25N 66 10W
St-Mathieu, Pte., France 18 B1 48 20N 4 45W
St. Matthew I., U.S.A. 68 B2 60 24N 172 42W
St. Matthews, I. = Zadetkyi Kyun, Burma 39 H2 10 0N 98 25 E
St-Maurice →, Canada 70 C5 46 21N 72 31W
St-Nazaire, France 18 C2 47 17N 2 12W
St. Neots, U.K. 11 E7 52 14N 0 15W
St-Niklaas, Belgium 15 C4 51 10N 4 8 E
St-Omer, France 18 A5 50 45N 2 15 E
St-Pamphile, Canada 71 C6 46 58N 69 48W
St. Pascal, Canada 71 C6 47 32N 69 48W
St. Paul, Canada 72 C6 54 0N 111 17W
St. Paul, Minn., U.S.A. 80 C8 44 57N 93 6W
St. Paul, Nebr., U.S.A. 80 E5 41 13N 98 27W
St-Paul →, Canada 71 B8 51 27N 57 42W
St. Paul, I., Ind. Oc. 3 F13 38 55S 77 34 E
St. Paul I., Canada 71 C7 47 12N 60 9W
St. Peter, U.S.A. 80 C8 44 20N 93 57W
St. Peter Port, U.K. 11 H5 49 26N 2 33W
St. Peters, N.S., Canada 71 C7 45 40N 60 53W
St. Peters, P.E.I., Canada 71 C7 46 25N 62 35W
St. Petersburg = Sankt-Peterburg, Russia 24 C5 59 55N 30 20 E
St. Petersburg, U.S.A. 77 M4 27 46N 82 39W
St-Pie, Canada 79 A12 45 30N 72 54W
St-Pierre, St- P. & M. 71 C8 46 46N 56 12W
St-Pierre, L., Canada 70 C5 46 12N 72 52W
St-Pierre et Miquelon □, St- P. & M. 71 C8 46 55N 56 10W
St-Quentin, Canada 71 C6 47 30N 67 23W
St-Quentin, France 18 B5 49 50N 3 16 E
St. Regis, U.S.A. 82 C6 47 18N 115 6W
St. Sebastien, Tanjon' i, Madag. 57 A8 12 26S 48 44 E
St-Siméon, Canada 71 C6 47 51N 69 54W
St. Simons I., U.S.A. 77 K5 31 12N 81 15W
St. Simons Island, U.S.A. 77 K5 31 9N 81 22W
St. Stephen, Canada 71 C6 45 16N 67 17W
St. Thomas, Canada 78 D3 42 45N 81 10W
St. Thomas I., Virgin Is. 89 C7 18 20N 64 55W
St-Tite, Canada 70 C5 46 45N 72 34W
St-Tropez, France 18 E7 43 17N 6 38 E
St. Troud = St. Truiden, Belgium 15 D5 50 48N 5 10 E
St. Truiden, Belgium 15 D5 50 48N 5 10 E
St. Vincent, G., Australia 63 F2 35 0S 138 0 E
St. Vincent & the Grenadines ■, W. Indies 89 D7 13 0N 61 10W
St. Vincent Passage, W. Indies 89 D7 13 30N 61 0W
St-Vith, Belgium 15 D6 50 17N 6 9 E
St. Walburg, Canada 73 C7 53 39N 109 12W
Ste-Agathe-des-Monts, Canada 70 C5 46 3N 74 17W
Ste-Anne, L., Canada 71 B6 50 0N 67 42W
Ste-Anne-des-Monts, Canada 71 C6 49 8N 66 30W
Ste. Genevieve, U.S.A. 80 G9 37 59N 90 2W
Ste-Marguerite →, Canada 71 B6 50 9N 66 36W
Ste-Marie, Martinique 89 D7 14 48N 61 1W
Ste-Marie de la Madeleine, Canada 71 C5 46 26N 71 0W
Ste-Rose, Guadeloupe 89 C7 16 20N 61 45W
Ste. Rose du Lac, Canada 73 C9 51 4N 99 30W
Saintes, France 18 D3 45 45N 0 37W
Saintes, I. des, Guadeloupe 89 C7 15 50N 61 35W
Saintfield, U.K. 13 B6 54 28N 5 49W
Sainthiya, India 43 H12 23 57N 87 40 E
Saintonge, France 18 D3 45 40N 0 50W
Saipan, Pac. Oc. 64 F6 15 12N 145 45 E
Sairang, India 41 H18 23 50N 92 45 E
Sairecábur, Cerro, Bolivia 94 A2 22 43S 67 54W
Saitama □, Japan 31 F9 36 25N 139 30 E
Saiyid, Pakistan 42 C5 33 7N 73 2 E
Sajama, Bolivia 92 G5 18 7S 69 0W
Sajószentpéter, Hungary 17 D11 48 12N 20 44 E
Sajum, India 43 C8 33 20N 79 0 E
Sak →, S. Africa 56 E3 30 52S 20 25 E
Sakai, Japan 31 G7 34 30N 135 30 E
Sakaide, Japan 31 G6 34 15N 133 50 E
Sakaiminato, Japan 31 G6 35 38N 133 11 E
Sakākah, Si. Arabia 44 D4 30 0N 40 8 E
Sakakawea, L., U.S.A. 80 B4 47 30N 101 25W
Sakami →, Canada 70 B4 53 40N 76 40W
Sakami, L., Canada 70 B4 53 15N 77 0W
Sakania, Dem. Rep. of the Congo 55 E2 12 43S 28 30 E
Sakarya, Turkey 25 F5 40 48N 30 25 E
Sakashima-Guntō, Japan 31 M2 24 46N 124 0 E
Sakata, Japan 30 E9 38 55N 139 50 E
Sakchu, N. Korea 35 D13 40 23N 125 2 E
Sakeny →, Madag. 57 C8 20 0S 45 25 E
Sakha □, Russia 27 C14 66 0N 130 0 E
Sakhalin, Russia 27 D15 51 0N 143 0 E
Sakhalinskiy Zaliv, Russia 27 D15 54 0N 141 0 E
Šakiai, Lithuania 9 J20 54 59N 23 2 E
Sakon Nakhon, Thailand 38 D5 17 10N 104 9 E
Sakrand, Pakistan 42 F3 26 10N 68 15 E
Sakri, India 43 F12 26 13N 86 5 E
Sakrivier, S. Africa 56 E3 30 54S 20 28 E
Sakti, India 43 H10 22 2N 82 58 E
Sakuma, Japan 31 G8 35 3N 137 49 E
Sakurai, Japan 31 G7 34 30N 135 51 E
Sala, Sweden 9 G17 59 58N 16 35 E
Sala Consilina, Italy 20 D6 40 23N 15 36 E
Sala-y-Gómez, Pac. Oc. 65 K17 26 28S 105 28W
Salaberry-de-Valleyfield, Canada 79 A10 45 15N 74 8W
Saladas, Argentina 94 B4 28 15S 58 40W
Saladillo, Argentina 94 D4 35 40S 59 55W
Salado →, Buenos Aires, Argentina 94 D4 35 44S 57 22W
Salado →, La Pampa, Argentina 96 D3 37 30S 67 0W
Salado →, Santa Fe, Argentina 94 C3 31 40S 60 41W
Salado →, Mexico 81 M5 26 52N 99 19W
Salaga, Ghana 50 G5 8 31N 0 31W
Sālah, Syria 47 C5 32 40N 36 45 E
Sálakhos, Greece 23 C9 36 17N 27 57 E
Şalālah, Oman 46 D5 16 56N 53 59 E
Salamanca, Chile 94 C1 31 46S 70 59W
Salamanca, Spain 19 B3 40 58N 5 39W
Salamanca, U.S.A. 78 D6 42 10N 78 43W
Salāmatābād, Iran 44 C5 35 39N 47 50 E
Salamis, Cyprus 23 D12 35 11N 33 54 E
Salamís, Greece 21 F10 37 56N 23 30 E
Salar de Atacama, Chile 94 A2 23 30S 68 25W
Salar de Uyuni, Bolivia 92 H5 20 30S 67 45W
Salatiga, Indonesia 37 G14 7 19S 110 30 E
Salavat, Russia 24 D10 53 21N 55 55 E
Salaverry, Peru 92 E3 8 15S 79 0W
Salawati, Indonesia 37 E8 1 7S 130 52 E
Salaya, India 42 H3 22 19N 69 35 E
Salayar, Indonesia 37 F6 6 7S 120 30 E
Salcombe, U.K. 11 G4 50 14N 3 47W
Saldanha, S. Africa 56 E2 33 0S 17 58 E
Saldanha B., S. Africa 56 E2 33 6S 18 0 E
Saldus, Latvia 9 H20 56 38N 22 30 E
Sale, Australia 63 F4 38 6S 147 6 E
Salé, Morocco 50 B4 34 3N 6 48W
Sale, U.K. 10 D5 53 26N 2 19W
Salekhard, Russia 26 C7 66 30N 66 35 E
Salem, India 40 P11 11 40N 78 11 E
Salem, Ill., U.S.A. 76 F1 38 38N 88 57W
Salem, Ind., U.S.A. 76 F2 38 36N 86 6W
Salem, Mass., U.S.A. 79 D14 42 31N 70 53W
Salem, Mo., U.S.A. 81 G9 37 39N 91 32W
Salem, N.H., U.S.A. 79 D13 42 45N 71 12W
Salem, N.J., U.S.A. 76 F8 39 34N 75 28W
Salem, N.Y., U.S.A. 79 C11 43 10N 73 20W
Salem, Ohio, U.S.A. 78 F4 40 54N 80 52W
Salem, Oreg., U.S.A. 82 D2 44 56N 123 2W
Salem, S. Dak., U.S.A. 80 D6 43 44N 97 23W
Salem, Va., U.S.A. 76 G5 37 18N 80 3W
Salerno, Italy 20 D6 40 41N 14 47 E
Salford, U.K. 10 D5 53 30N 2 18W
Salgótarján, Hungary 17 D10 48 5N 19 47 E
Salgueiro, Brazil 93 E11 8 4S 39 6W
Salibabu, Indonesia 37 D7 3 51N 126 40 E
Salida, U.S.A. 74 C5 38 32N 106 0W
Salihli, Turkey 21 E13 38 28N 28 8 E
Salihorsk, Belarus 17 B14 52 51N 27 27 E
Salima, Malawi 53 G6 13 47S 34 28 E
Salina, Italy 20 E6 38 34N 14 50 E
Salina, Kans., U.S.A. 80 F6 38 50N 97 37W
Salina, Utah, U.S.A. 83 G8 38 58N 111 51W
Salina Cruz, Mexico 87 D5 16 10N 95 10W
Salinas, Brazil 93 G10 16 10S 42 10W
Salinas, Chile 94 A2 23 31S 69 29W
Salinas, Ecuador 92 D2 2 10S 80 58W
Salinas, U.S.A. 84 J5 36 40N 121 39W
Salinas →, Guatemala 87 D6 16 28N 90 31W
Salinas →, U.S.A. 84 J5 36 45N 121 48W
Salinas, B. de, Nic. 88 D2 11 4N 85 45W
Salinas, Pampa de las, Argentina 94 C2 31 58S 66 42W
Salinas Ambargasta, Argentina 94 B3 29 0S 65 0W

159

Solfonn

Sikinos, Greece 21 F11 36 40N 25 8 E
Sikkani Chief →, Canada 72 B4 57 47N 122 15W
Sikkim □, India 41 F16 27 50N 88 30 E
Sikotu-Ko, Japan 30 C10 42 45N 141 25 E
Sil →, Spain 19 A2 42 27N 7 43W
Silacayoapan, Mexico 87 D5 17 30N 98 9W
Silawad, India 42 J6 21 54N 74 54 E
Silchar, India 41 G18 24 49N 92 48 E
Siler City, U.S.A. 77 H6 35 44N 79 28W
Silesia = Śląsk, Poland 16 C9 51 0N 16 30 E
Silgarhi Doti, Nepal 43 E9 29 15N 81 0 E
Silghat, India 41 F18 26 35N 93 0 E
Silifke, Turkey 25 G5 36 22N 33 58 E
Siliguri = Shiliguri, India 41 F16 26 45N 88 25 E
Siling Co, China 32 C3 31 50N 89 20 E
Silistra, Bulgaria 21 B12 44 6N 27 19 E
Silivri, Turkey 21 D13 41 4N 28 14 E
Siljan, Sweden 9 F16 60 55N 14 45 E
Silkeborg, Denmark 9 H13 56 10N 9 32 E
Silkwood, Australia 62 B4 17 45S 146 2 E
Sillajhuay, Cordillera, Chile 92 G5 19 46S 68 40W
Sillamäe, Estonia 9 G22 59 24N 27 45 E
Silloth, U.K. 10 C4 54 52N 3 23W
Siloam Springs, U.S.A. 81 G7 36 11N 94 32W
Silsbee, U.S.A. 81 K7 30 21N 94 11W
Šilutė, Lithuania 9 J19 55 21N 21 33 E
Silva Porto = Kuito, Angola 53 G3 12 22S 16 55 E
Silvani, India 43 H8 23 18N 78 25 E
Silver City, U.S.A. 83 K9 32 46N 108 17W
Silver Cr. →, U.S.A. 82 E4 43 16N 119 13W
Silver Creek, U.S.A. 78 D5 42 33N 79 10W
Silver L., U.S.A. 84 G6 38 39N 120 6W
Silver Lake, Calif., U.S.A. 85 K10 35 21N 116 7W
Silver Lake, Oreg., U.S.A. 82 E3 43 8N 121 3W
Silver Streams, S. Africa 56 D3 28 20S 23 33 E
Silverton, Colo., U.S.A. 83 H10 37 49N 107 40W
Silverton, Tex., U.S.A. 81 H4 34 28N 101 19W
Silvies →, U.S.A. 82 E4 43 34N 119 2W
Simaltala, India 43 G12 24 43N 86 33 E
Simanggang = Bandar Sri Aman, Malaysia 36 D4 1 15N 111 32 E
Simard, L., Canada 70 C4 47 40N 78 40W
Simav, Turkey 21 E13 39 4N 28 58 E
Simba, Tanzania 54 C4 2 10S 37 36 E
Simbirsk, Russia 24 D8 54 20N 48 25 E
Simbo, Tanzania 54 C2 4 51S 29 41 E
Simcoe, Canada 78 D4 42 50N 80 20W
Simcoe, L., Canada 78 B5 44 25N 79 20W
Simdega, India 43 H11 22 37N 84 31 E
Simeria, Romania 17 F12 45 51N 23 1 E
Simeulue, Indonesia 36 D1 2 45N 95 45 E
Simferopol, Ukraine 25 F5 44 55N 34 3 E
Simi, Greece 21 F12 36 35N 27 50 E
Simi Valley, U.S.A. 85 L8 34 16N 118 47W
Simikot, Nepal 43 E9 30 0N 81 50 E
Simla, India 42 D7 31 2N 77 9 E
Simmie, Canada 73 D7 49 56N 108 6W
Simmler, U.S.A. 85 K7 35 21N 119 59W
Simojoki →, Finland 8 D21 65 35N 25 1 E
Simojovel, Mexico 87 D6 17 12N 92 38W
Simonette →, Canada 72 B5 55 9N 118 15W
Simonstown, S. Africa 56 E2 34 14S 18 26 E
Simplonpass, Switz. 18 C8 46 15N 8 3 E
Simpson Desert, Australia 62 D2 25 0S 137 0 E
Simpson Pen., Canada 69 B11 68 34N 88 45W
Simpungdong, N. Korea 35 D15 40 56N 129 29 E
Simrishamn, Sweden 9 J16 55 33N 14 22 E
Simsbury, U.S.A. 79 E12 41 53N 72 48W
Simushir, Ostrov, Russia 27 E16 46 50N 152 30 E
Sin Cowe I., S. China Sea 36 C4 9 53N 114 19 E
Sinabang, Indonesia 36 D1 2 30N 96 24 E
Sinadogo, Somali Rep. 46 F4 5 50N 47 0 E
Sinai = Es Sînâ', Egypt 47 F3 29 0N 34 0 E
Sinai, Mt. = Mûsa, Gebel, Egypt 44 D2 28 33N 33 59 E
Sinai Peninsula, Egypt 47 F3 29 30N 34 0 E
Sinaloa □, Mexico 86 C3 25 0N 107 30W
Sinaloa de Leyva, Mexico 86 B3 25 50N 108 20W
Sinarádhes, Greece 23 A3 39 34N 19 51 E
Sincelejo, Colombia 92 B3 9 18N 75 24W
Sinch'ang, N. Korea 35 D15 40 7N 128 28 E
Sinchang-ni, N. Korea 35 E14 39 24N 126 8 E
Sinclair, U.S.A. 82 F10 41 47N 107 7W
Sinclair Mills, Canada 72 C4 54 5N 121 40W
Sinclair's B., U.K. 12 C5 58 31N 3 5W
Sinclairville, U.S.A. 78 D5 42 16N 79 16W
Sincorá, Serra do, Brazil 93 F10 13 30S 41 0W
Sind, Pakistan 42 G3 26 0N 68 30 E
Sind □, Pakistan 42 G3 26 0N 69 0 E
Sind →, India 43 F8 26 26N 79 13 E
Sind →, Jammu & Kashmir, India 43 B6 34 18N 74 45 E
Sind Sagar Doab, Pakistan 42 D4 32 0N 71 30 E
Sindangan, Phil. 37 C6 8 10N 123 5 E
Sindangbarang, Indonesia 37 G12 7 27S 107 1 E
Sinde, Zambia 55 F2 17 28S 25 51 E
Sindri, India 43 H12 23 45N 86 42 E
Sines, Portugal 19 D1 37 56N 8 51W
Sines, C. de, Portugal 19 D1 37 58N 8 53W
Sineu, Spain 22 B10 39 38N 3 1 E
Sing Buri, Thailand 38 E3 14 53N 100 25 E
Singa, Sudan 51 F12 13 10N 33 57 E
Singapore ■, Asia 39 M4 1 17N 103 51 E
Singapore, Straits of, Asia 39 M5 1 15N 104 0 E
Singaraja, Indonesia 36 F5 8 6S 115 10 E
Singida, Tanzania 54 C3 4 49S 34 48 E
Singida □, Tanzania 54 D3 6 0S 34 30 E
Singitikós Kólpos, Greece 21 D11 40 6N 24 0 E
Singkaling Hkamti, Burma 41 G19 26 0N 95 39 E
Singkang, Indonesia 37 E6 4 8S 120 1 E
Singkawang, Indonesia 36 D3 1 0N 108 57 E
Singkep, Indonesia 36 E2 0 30S 104 25 E
Singleton, Australia 63 E5 32 33S 151 0 E
Singleton, Mt., N. Terr., Australia 60 D5 22 0S 130 46 E
Singleton, Mt., W. Austral., Australia 61 E2 29 27S 117 15 E
Singoli, India 42 G6 25 0N 75 22 E
Singora = Songkhla, Thailand 39 J3 7 13N 100 37 E
Singosan, N. Korea 35 E14 38 52N 127 25 E
Sinhung, N. Korea 35 D14 40 11N 127 34 E
Sînî □, Egypt 47 F3 30 0N 34 0 E
Sinjai, Indonesia 37 F6 5 7S 120 20 E
Sinjār, Iraq 44 B4 36 19N 41 52 E
Sinkat, Sudan 51 E13 18 55N 36 49 E
Sinkiang Uighur = Xinjiang Uygur Zizhiqu □, China 32 C3 42 0N 86 0 E
Sinmak, N. Korea 35 E14 38 25N 126 14 E
Sinnamary, Fr. Guiana 93 B8 5 25N 53 0W
Sinni →, Italy 20 D7 40 8N 16 41 E
Sinop, Turkey 25 F6 42 1N 35 11 E
Sinor, India 42 J5 21 55N 73 20 E
Sinp'o, N. Korea 35 E15 40 0N 128 13 E
Sinsk, Russia 27 C13 61 8N 126 48 E
Sintang, Indonesia 36 D4 0 5N 111 35 E
Sinton, U.S.A. 81 L6 28 2N 97 31W
Sintra, Portugal 19 C1 38 47N 9 25W
Sinŭiju, N. Korea 35 D13 40 5N 124 24 E
Siocon, Phil. 37 C6 7 40N 122 10 E
Siófok, Hungary 17 E10 46 54N 18 3 E
Sioma, Zambia 56 B3 16 25S 23 28 E
Sion, Switz. 18 C7 46 14N 7 20 E
Sion Mills, U.K. 13 B4 54 48N 7 29W
Sioux City, U.S.A. 80 D6 42 30N 96 24W
Sioux Falls, U.S.A. 80 D6 43 33N 96 44W
Sioux Lookout, Canada 70 B1 50 10N 91 50W
Sioux Narrows, Canada 73 D10 49 25N 94 10W
Siping, China 35 C13 43 8N 124 21 E
Sipiwesk L., Canada 73 B9 55 5N 97 35W
Sipra →, India 42 H6 23 55N 75 28 E
Sipura, Indonesia 36 E1 2 18S 99 40 E
Siquia →, Nic. 88 D3 12 10N 84 20W
Siquijor, Phil. 37 C6 9 12N 123 35 E
Siquirres, Costa Rica 88 D3 10 6N 83 30W
Şir Banī Yās, U.A.E. 45 E7 24 19N 52 37 E
Sir Edward Pellew Group, Australia 62 B2 15 40S 137 10 E
Sir Graham Moore Is., Australia 60 B4 13 53S 126 34 E
Sir James MacBrien, Mt., Canada 68 B7 62 8N 127 40W
Sira →, Norway 9 G12 58 23N 6 34 E
Siracusa, Italy 20 F6 37 4N 15 17 E
Sirajganj, Bangla. 43 G13 24 25N 89 47 E
Sirathu, India 43 G9 25 39N 81 19 E
Sīrdān, Iran 45 B6 36 39N 49 12 E
Sirdaryo = Syrdarya →, Kazakstan 26 E7 46 3N 61 0 E
Siren, U.S.A. 80 C8 45 47N 92 24W
Sirer, Spain 22 C7 38 56N 1 22 E
Siret →, Romania 17 F14 45 24N 28 1 E
Sirghāyā, Syria 47 B5 33 51N 36 8 E
Sirmaur, India 43 G9 24 51N 81 23 E
Sirohi, India 42 G5 24 52N 72 53 E
Sironj, India 42 G7 24 5N 77 39 E
Síros, Greece 21 F11 37 28N 24 57 E
Sirretta Pk., U.S.A. 85 K8 35 56N 118 19W
Sirrī, Iran 45 E7 25 55N 54 32 E
Sirsa, India 42 E6 29 33N 75 4 E
Sirsa →, India 43 F8 26 51N 79 4 E
Sisak, Croatia 16 F9 45 30N 16 21 E
Sisaket, Thailand 38 E5 15 8N 104 23 E
Sishen, S. Africa 56 D3 27 47S 22 59 E
Sishui, Henan, China 34 G7 34 48N 113 15 E
Sishui, Shandong, China 35 G9 35 42N 117 18 E
Sisipuk L., Canada 73 B8 55 45N 101 50W
Sisophon, Cambodia 38 F4 13 38N 102 59 E
Sisseton, U.S.A. 80 C6 45 40N 97 3W
Sīstān, Asia 45 D9 30 50N 61 0 E
Sīstān, Daryācheh-ye, Iran 40 D2 31 0N 61 0 E
Sīstān va Balūchestān □, Iran 45 E9 27 0N 62 0 E
Sisters, U.S.A. 82 D3 44 18N 121 33W
Siswa Bazar, India 43 F10 27 9N 83 46 E
Sitamarhi, India 43 F11 26 37N 85 30 E
Sitapur, India 43 F9 27 38N 80 45 E
Siteki, Swaziland 57 D5 26 32S 31 58 E
Sitges, Spain 19 B6 41 17N 1 47 E
Sitia, Greece 23 D8 35 13N 26 6 E
Sitka, U.S.A. 72 B1 57 3N 135 20W
Sitoti, Botswana 56 C3 23 15S 23 40 E
Sittang Myit →, Burma 41 L20 17 20N 96 45 E
Sittard, Neths. 15 C5 51 0N 5 52 E
Sittingbourne, U.K. 11 F8 51 21N 0 45 E
Sittwe, Burma 41 J18 20 18N 92 45 E
Situbondo, Indonesia 37 G16 7 42S 114 0 E
Siuna, Nic. 88 D3 13 37N 84 45W
Siuri, India 43 H12 23 50N 87 34 E
Sīvand, Iran 45 D7 30 5N 52 55 E
Sivas, Turkey 25 G6 39 43N 36 58 E
Siverek, Turkey 44 B3 37 50N 39 19 E
Sivomaskinskiy, Russia 24 A11 66 40N 62 35 E
Sivrihisar, Turkey 25 G5 39 30N 31 35 E
Sîwa, Egypt 51 C11 29 11N 25 31 E
Siwa Oasis, Egypt 48 D6 29 10N 25 30 E
Siwalik Range, Nepal 43 F10 28 0N 83 0 E
Siwan, India 43 F11 26 13N 84 21 E
Siwana, India 42 G5 25 38N 72 25 E
Sixmilebridge, Ireland 13 D3 52 44N 8 46W
Sixth Cataract, Sudan 51 E12 16 20N 32 42 E
Siziwang Qi, China 34 D6 41 25N 111 40 E
Sjælland, Denmark 9 J14 55 30N 11 30 E
Sjumen = Shumen, Bulgaria 21 C12 43 18N 26 55 E
Skadarsko Jezero, Montenegro, Yug. 21 C8 42 10N 19 20 E
Skaftafell, Iceland 8 D5 64 1N 17 0W
Skagafjörður, Iceland 8 D4 65 54N 19 35W
Skagastølstindane, Norway 9 F12 61 28N 7 52 E
Skagaströnd, Iceland 8 D3 65 50N 20 19W
Skagen, Denmark 9 H14 57 43N 10 35 E
Skagerrak, Denmark 9 H13 57 30N 9 0 E
Skagit →, U.S.A. 84 B4 48 23N 122 22W
Skagway, U.S.A. 68 C6 59 28N 135 19W
Skala-Podilska, Ukraine 17 D14 48 50N 26 15 E
Skala Podolskaya = Skala-Podilska, Ukraine 17 D14 48 50N 26 15 E
Skalat, Ukraine 17 D13 49 23N 25 55 E
Skåne, Sweden 9 J15 55 59N 13 30 E
Skaneateles, U.S.A. 79 D8 42 57N 76 26W
Skaneateles L., U.S.A. 79 D8 42 51N 76 22W
Skara, Sweden 9 G15 58 25N 13 30 E
Skardu, Pakistan 43 B6 35 20N 75 44 E
Skarżysko-Kamienna, Poland 17 C11 51 7N 20 52 E
Skeena →, Canada 72 C2 54 9N 130 5W
Skeena Mts., Canada 72 B3 56 40N 128 30W
Skegness, U.K. 10 D8 53 9N 0 20 E
Skeldon, Guyana 92 B7 5 55N 57 20W
Skellefte älv →, Sweden 8 D19 64 45N 21 10 E
Skellefteå, Sweden 8 D19 64 45N 20 50 E
Skelleftehamn, Sweden 8 D19 64 40N 21 9 E
Skerries, The, U.K. 10 D3 53 25N 4 36W
Ski, Norway 9 G14 59 43N 10 52 E
Skíathos, Greece 21 E10 39 12N 23 30 E
Skibbereen, Ireland 13 E2 51 33N 9 16W
Skiddaw, U.K. 10 C4 54 39N 3 9W
Skidegate, Canada 72 C2 53 15N 132 1W
Skien, Norway 9 G13 59 12N 9 35 E
Skierniewice, Poland 17 C11 51 58N 20 10 E
Skikda, Algeria 50 A7 36 50N 6 58 E
Skilloura, Cyprus 23 D12 35 14N 33 10 E
Skipton, U.K. 10 D5 53 58N 2 3W
Skirmish Pt., Australia 62 A1 11 59S 134 17 E
Skíros, Greece 21 E11 38 55N 24 34 E
Skive, Denmark 9 H13 56 33N 9 2 E
Skjálfandafljót →, Iceland 8 D5 65 59N 17 25W
Skjálfandi, Iceland 8 C5 66 5N 17 30W
Skoghall, Sweden 9 G15 59 20N 13 30 E
Skole, Ukraine 17 D12 49 3N 23 30 E
Skópelos, Greece 21 E10 39 9N 23 47 E
Skopí, Greece 23 D8 35 11N 26 2 E
Skopje, Macedonia 21 C9 42 1N 21 26 E
Skövde, Sweden 9 G15 58 24N 13 50 E
Skovorodino, Russia 27 D13 54 0N 124 0 E
Skowhegan, U.S.A. 77 C11 44 46N 69 43W
Skull, Ireland 13 E2 51 32N 9 34W
Skunk →, U.S.A. 80 E9 40 42N 91 7W
Skuodas, Lithuania 9 H19 56 16N 21 33 E
Skvyra, Ukraine 17 D15 49 44N 29 40 E
Skye, U.K. 12 D2 57 15N 6 10W
Skykomish, U.S.A. 82 C3 47 42N 121 22W
Skyros = Skíros, Greece 21 E11 38 55N 24 34 E
Slættaratindur, Færoe Is. 8 E9 62 18N 7 1W
Slagelse, Denmark 9 J14 55 23N 11 19 E
Slamet, Indonesia 37 G13 7 16S 109 8 E
Slaney →, Ireland 13 D5 52 26N 6 33W
Śląsk, Poland 16 C9 51 0N 16 30 E
Slate Is., Canada 70 C2 48 40N 87 0W
Slatina, Romania 17 F13 44 28N 24 22 E
Slatington, U.S.A. 79 F9 40 45N 75 37W
Slaton, U.S.A. 81 J4 33 26N 101 39W
Slave →, Canada 72 A6 61 18N 113 39W
Slave Coast, W. Afr. 50 G6 6 0N 2 30 E
Slave Lake, Canada 72 B6 55 17N 114 43W
Slave Pt., Canada 72 A5 61 11N 115 56W
Slavgorod, Russia 26 D8 53 1N 78 37 E
Slavonski Brod, Croatia 21 B8 45 11N 18 1 E
Slavuta, Ukraine 17 C14 50 15N 27 2 E
Slavyanka, Russia 30 C5 42 53N 131 21 E
Slavyansk = Slovyansk, Ukraine 25 E6 48 55N 37 36 E
Slawharad, Belarus 17 B16 53 27N 31 0 E
Sleaford, U.K. 10 D7 53 0N 0 24W
Sleaford B., Australia 63 E2 34 55S 135 45 E
Sleat, Sd. of, U.K. 12 D3 57 5N 5 47W
Sleeper Is., Canada 69 C11 58 30N 81 0W
Sleepy Eye, U.S.A. 80 C7 44 18N 94 43W
Slemon L., Canada 72 A5 63 13N 116 4W
Slide Mt., U.S.A. 79 E10 42 0N 74 25W
Slidell, U.S.A. 81 K10 30 17N 89 47W
Sliema, Malta 23 D2 35 54N 14 30 E
Slieve Aughty, Ireland 13 C3 53 4N 8 30W
Slieve Bloom, Ireland 13 C4 53 4N 7 40W
Slieve Donard, U.K. 13 B6 54 11N 5 55W
Slieve Gamph, Ireland 13 B3 54 6N 9 0W
Slieve Gullion, U.K. 13 B5 54 7N 6 26W
Slieve Mish, Ireland 13 D2 52 12N 9 50W
Slievenamon, Ireland 13 D4 52 25N 7 34W
Sligeach = Sligo, Ireland 13 B3 54 16N 8 28W
Sligo, Ireland 13 B3 54 16N 8 28W
Sligo, U.S.A. 78 E5 41 6N 79 29W
Sligo □, Ireland 13 B3 54 8N 8 42W
Sligo B., Ireland 13 B3 54 18N 8 40W
Slippery Rock, U.S.A. 78 E4 41 3N 80 3W
Slite, Sweden 9 H18 57 42N 18 48 E
Sliven, Bulgaria 21 C12 42 42N 26 19 E
Sloan, U.S.A. 85 K11 35 57N 115 13W
Sloansville, U.S.A. 79 D10 42 45N 74 22W
Slobodskoy, Russia 24 C9 58 40N 50 6 E
Slobozia, Romania 17 F14 44 34N 27 23 E
Slocan, Canada 72 D5 49 48N 117 28W
Slonim, Belarus 17 B13 53 4N 25 19 E
Slough, U.K. 11 F7 51 30N 0 36W
Slough □, U.K. 11 F7 51 30N 0 36W
Sloughhouse, U.S.A. 84 G5 38 26N 121 12W
Slovak Rep. ■, Europe 17 D10 48 30N 20 0 E
Slovakia = Slovak Rep. ■, Europe 17 D10 48 30N 20 0 E
Slovakian Ore Mts. = Slovenské Rudohorie, Slovak Rep. 17 D10 48 45N 20 0 E
Slovenia ■, Europe 16 F8 45 58N 14 30 E
Slovenija = Slovenia ■, Europe 16 F8 45 58N 14 30 E
Slovenské Rudohorie, Slovak Rep. 17 D10 48 45N 20 0 E
Slovyansk, Ukraine 25 E6 48 55N 37 36 E
Sluch →, Ukraine 17 C14 51 37N 26 38 E
Sluis, Neths. 15 C3 51 18N 3 23 E
Słupsk, Poland 17 A9 54 30N 17 3 E
Slurry, S. Africa 56 D4 25 49S 25 42 E
Slutsk, Belarus 17 B14 53 2N 27 31 E
Slyne Hd., Ireland 13 C1 53 25N 10 10W
Slyudyanka, Russia 27 D11 51 40N 103 40 E
Småland, Sweden 9 H16 57 15N 15 25 E
Smalltree L., Canada 73 A8 61 0N 105 0W
Smallwood Res., Canada 71 B7 54 0N 64 0W
Smara, Morocco 50 B4 32 9N 8 16W
Smarhon, Belarus 17 A14 54 20N 26 24 E
Smartt Syndicate Dam, S. Africa 56 E3 30 45S 23 10 E
Smartville, U.S.A. 84 F5 39 13N 121 18W
Smeaton, Canada 73 C8 53 30N 104 49W
Smederevo, Serbia, Yug. 21 B9 44 40N 20 57 E
Smerwick Harbour, Ireland 13 D1 52 12N 10 23W
Smethport, U.S.A. 78 E6 41 49N 78 27W
Smidovich, Russia 27 E14 48 36N 133 49 E
Smith, Canada 72 B6 55 10N 114 0W
Smith Center, U.S.A. 80 F5 39 47N 98 47W
Smith Sund, Greenland 4 B4 78 30N 74 0W
Smithburne →, Australia 62 B3 17 3S 140 57 E
Smithers, Canada 72 C3 54 45N 127 10W
Smithfield, S. Africa 57 E4 30 9S 26 30 E
Smithfield, N.C., U.S.A. 77 H6 35 31N 78 21W
Smithfield, Utah, U.S.A. 82 F8 41 50N 111 50W
Smiths Falls, Canada 79 B9 44 55N 76 0W
Smithton, Australia 62 G4 40 53S 145 6 E
Smithville, Canada 78 C5 43 6N 79 33W
Smithville, U.S.A. 81 K6 30 1N 97 10W
Smoky →, Canada 72 B5 56 10N 117 21W
Smoky Bay, Australia 63 E1 32 22S 134 13 E
Smoky Hill →, U.S.A. 80 F6 39 4N 96 48W
Smoky Hills, U.S.A. 80 F5 39 15N 99 30W
Smoky Lake, Canada 72 C6 54 10N 112 30W
Smøla, Norway 8 E13 63 23N 8 3 E
Smolensk, Russia 24 D5 54 45N 32 5 E
Smolikas, Óros, Greece 21 D9 40 9N 20 58 E
Smolyan, Bulgaria 21 D11 41 36N 24 38 E
Smooth Rock Falls, Canada 70 C3 49 17N 81 37W
Smoothstone L., Canada 73 C7 54 40N 106 50W
Smorgon = Smarhon, Belarus 17 A14 54 20N 26 24 E
Smyrna = İzmir, Turkey 21 E12 38 25N 27 8 E
Smyrna, U.S.A. 76 F8 39 18N 75 36W
Snæfell, Iceland 8 D6 64 48N 15 34W
Snaefell, U.K. 10 C3 54 16N 4 27W
Snæfellsjökull, Iceland 8 D2 64 49N 23 46W
Snake →, U.S.A. 82 C4 46 12N 119 2W
Snake I., Australia 63 F4 38 47S 146 33 E
Snake Range, U.S.A. 82 G6 39 0N 114 20W
Snake River Plain, U.S.A. 82 E7 42 50N 114 0W
Snåsavatnet, Norway 8 D14 64 12N 12 0 E
Sneek, Neths. 15 A5 53 2N 5 40 E
Sneeuberge, S. Africa 56 E3 31 46S 24 20 E
Snelling, U.S.A. 84 H6 37 31N 120 26W
Sněžka, Europe 16 C8 50 41N 15 50 E
Snizort, L., U.K. 12 D2 57 33N 6 28W
Snøhetta, Norway 9 E13 62 19N 9 16 E
Snohomish, U.S.A. 84 C4 47 55N 122 6W
Snoul, Cambodia 39 F6 12 4N 106 26 E
Snow Hill, U.S.A. 76 F8 38 11N 75 24W
Snow Lake, Canada 73 C8 54 52N 100 3W
Snow Mt., Calif., U.S.A. 84 F4 39 23N 122 45W
Snow Mt., Maine, U.S.A. 79 A14 45 18N 70 48W
Snow Shoe, U.S.A. 78 E7 41 2N 77 57W
Snowbird L., Canada 73 A8 60 45N 103 0W
Snowdon, U.K. 10 D3 53 4N 4 5W
Snowdrift →, Canada 73 A6 62 24N 110 44W
Snowflake, U.S.A. 83 J8 34 30N 110 5W
Snowshoe Pk., U.S.A. 82 B6 48 13N 115 41W
Snowtown, Australia 63 E2 33 46S 138 14 E
Snowville, U.S.A. 82 F7 41 58N 112 43W
Snowy →, Australia 63 F4 37 46S 148 30 E
Snowy Mt., U.S.A. 79 C10 43 42N 74 23W
Snowy Mts., Australia 63 F4 36 30S 148 20 E
Snug Corner, Bahamas 89 B5 22 33N 73 52W
Snyatyn, Ukraine 17 D13 48 27N 25 38 E
Snyder, Okla., U.S.A. 81 H5 34 40N 98 57W
Snyder, Tex., U.S.A. 81 J4 32 44N 100 55W
Soahanina, Madag. 57 B7 18 42S 44 13 E
Soalala, Madag. 57 B8 16 6S 45 20 E
Soan →, Pakistan 42 C4 33 1N 71 44 E
Soanierana-Ivongo, Madag. 57 B8 16 55S 49 35 E
Sobat, Nahr →, Sudan 51 G12 9 22N 31 33 E
Sobhapur, India 42 H8 22 47N 78 17 E
Sobradinho, Représa de, Brazil 93 E10 9 30S 42 0 E
Sobral, Brazil 93 D10 3 50S 40 20W
Soc Trang, Vietnam 39 H5 9 37N 105 50 E
Socastee, U.S.A. 77 J6 33 41N 79 1W
Soch'e = Shache, China 32 C2 38 20N 77 10 E
Sochi, Russia 25 F6 43 35N 39 40 E
Société, Is. de la, Pac. Oc. 65 J12 17 0S 151 0W
Society Is. = Société, Is. de la, Pac. Oc. 65 J12 17 0S 151 0W
Socompa, Portezuelo de, Chile 94 A2 24 27S 68 18W
Socorro, N. Mex., U.S.A. 83 J10 34 4N 106 54W
Socorro, Tex., U.S.A. 83 L10 31 39N 106 18W
Socorro, I., Mexico 86 D2 18 45N 110 58W
Socotra, Ind. Oc. 46 E5 12 30N 54 0 E
Soda L., U.S.A. 83 J5 35 10N 116 4W
Soda Plains, India 43 B8 35 30N 79 0 E
Soda Springs, U.S.A. 82 E8 42 39N 111 36W
Sodankylä, Finland 8 C22 67 29N 26 40 E
Soddy-Daisy, U.S.A. 77 H3 35 17N 85 10W
Söderhamn, Sweden 9 F17 61 18N 17 10 E
Söderköping, Sweden 9 G17 58 31N 16 20 E
Södermanland, Sweden 9 G17 58 56N 16 55 E
Södertälje, Sweden 9 G17 59 12N 17 39 E
Sodiri, Sudan 51 F11 14 27N 29 0 E
Sodus, U.S.A. 78 C7 43 14N 77 4W
Soekmekaar, S. Africa 57 C4 23 30S 29 55 E
Soest, Neths. 15 B5 52 9N 5 19 E
Sofia = Sofiya, Bulgaria 21 C10 42 45N 23 20 E
Sofia →, Madag. 57 B8 15 27S 47 23 E
Sofiya, Bulgaria 21 C10 42 45N 23 20 E
Sōfu-Gan, Japan 31 K10 29 49N 140 21 E
Sogamoso, Colombia 92 B4 5 43N 72 56W
Sogār, Iran 45 E8 25 53N 58 6 E
Sogndalsfjøra, Norway 9 F12 61 14N 7 5 E
Søgne, Norway 9 G12 58 5N 7 48 E
Sognefjorden, Norway 9 F11 61 10N 5 50 E
Sŏgwipo, S. Korea 35 H14 33 13N 126 34 E
Soh, Iran 45 C6 33 26N 51 27 E
Sohâg, Egypt 51 C12 26 33N 31 43 E
Sohagpur, India 42 H8 22 42N 78 12 E
Sŏhori, N. Korea 35 D15 40 7N 128 23 E
Soignies, Belgium 15 D4 50 35N 4 5 E
Soissons, France 18 B5 49 25N 3 19 E
Sōja, Japan 31 G6 34 40N 133 45 E
Sojat, India 42 G5 25 55N 73 45 E
Sokal, Ukraine 17 C13 50 31N 24 15 E
Söke, Turkey 21 F12 37 48N 27 28 E
Sokelo, Dem. Rep. of the Congo 55 D1 9 55S 24 36 E
Sokhumi, Georgia 25 F7 43 0N 41 0 E
Sokodé, Togo 50 G6 9 0N 1 11 E
Sokol, Russia 24 C7 59 30N 40 5 E
Sokółka, Poland 17 B12 53 25N 23 30 E
Sokołów Podlaski, Poland 17 B12 52 25N 22 15 E
Sokoto, Nigeria 50 F7 13 2N 5 16 E
Sol Iletsk, Russia 24 D10 51 10N 55 0 E
Solai, Kenya 54 B4 0 2N 36 12 E
Solan, India 42 D7 30 55N 77 7 E
Solano, Phil. 37 A6 16 31N 121 15 E
Solapur, India 40 L9 17 43N 75 56 E
Soldotna, U.S.A. 68 B4 60 29N 151 3W
Soléa □, Cyprus 23 D12 35 5N 33 4 E
Soledad, Colombia 92 A4 10 55N 74 46W
Soledad, U.S.A. 84 J5 36 26N 121 20W
Soledad, Venezuela 92 B6 8 10N 63 34W
Solent, The, U.K. 11 G6 50 45N 1 25W
Solfonn, Norway 9 F12 60 2N 6 57 E

Sursar

Staten, I. = Estados, I. de Los, Argentina 96 G4 54 40S 64 30W
Staten I., U.S.A. 79 F10 40 35N 74 9W
Statesboro, U.S.A. 77 J5 32 27N 81 47W
Statesville, U.S.A. 77 H5 35 47N 80 53W
Stauffer, U.S.A. 85 L7 34 45N 119 3W
Staunton, Ill., U.S.A. 80 F10 39 1N 89 47W
Staunton, Va., U.S.A. 76 F6 38 9N 79 4W
Stavanger, Norway 9 G11 58 57N 5 40 E
Staveley, N.Z. 59 K3 43 40S 171 32 E
Stavelot, Belgium 15 D5 50 23N 5 55 E
Stavern, Norway 9 G14 59 0N 10 1 E
Stavoren, Neths. 15 B5 52 53N 5 22 E
Stavropol, Russia 25 E7 45 5N 42 0 E
Stavros, Cyprus 23 D11 35 1N 32 38 E
Stavrós, Greece 23 D6 35 12N 24 45 E
Stavros, Ákra, Greece 23 D6 35 26N 24 58 E
Stawell, Australia 63 F3 37 5S 142 47 E
Stawell →, Australia 62 C3 20 20S 142 55 E
Stayner, Canada 78 B4 44 25N 80 5W
Stayton, U.S.A. 82 D2 44 48N 122 48W
Steamboat Springs, U.S.A. 82 F10 40 29N 106 50W
Steele, U.S.A. 80 B5 46 51N 99 55W
Steelton, U.S.A. 78 F8 40 14N 76 50W
Steen River, Canada 72 B5 59 40N 117 12W
Steenkool = Bintuni, Indonesia 37 E8 2 7S 133 32 E
Steens Mt., U.S.A. 82 E4 42 35N 118 40W
Steenwijk, Neths. 15 B6 52 47N 6 7 E
Steep Pt., Australia 61 E1 26 8S 113 8 E
Steep Rock, Canada 73 C9 51 30N 98 48W
Stefanie L. = Chew Bahir, Ethiopia 46 G2 4 40N 36 50 E
Stefansson Bay, Antarctica 5 C5 67 20S 59 8 E
Steiermark □, Austria 16 E8 47 26N 15 0 E
Steilacoom, U.S.A. 84 C4 47 10N 122 36W
Steinbach, Canada 73 D9 49 32N 96 40W
Steinkjer, Norway 8 D14 64 1N 11 31 E
Steinkopf, S. Africa 56 D2 29 18S 17 43 E
Stellarton, Canada 71 C7 45 32N 62 30W
Stellenbosch, S. Africa 56 E2 33 58S 18 50 E
Stendal, Germany 16 B6 52 36N 11 53 E
Steornabhaigh = Stornoway, U.K. 12 C2 58 13N 6 23W
Stepanakert = Xankändi, Azerbaijan 25 G8 39 52N 46 49 E
Stephens Creek, Australia 63 E3 31 50S 141 30 E
Stephens I., Canada 72 C2 54 10N 130 45W
Stephens L., Canada 73 B9 56 32N 95 0W
Stephenville, Canada 71 C8 48 31N 58 35W
Stephenville, U.S.A. 81 J5 32 13N 98 12W
Stepnoi = Elista, Russia 25 E7 46 16N 44 14 E
Steppe, Asia 28 D9 50 0N 50 0 E
Sterkstroom, S. Africa 56 E4 31 32S 26 32 E
Sterling, Colo., U.S.A. 80 E3 40 37N 103 13W
Sterling, Ill., U.S.A. 80 E10 41 48N 89 42W
Sterling, Kans., U.S.A. 80 F5 38 13N 98 12W
Sterling City, U.S.A. 81 K4 31 51N 101 0W
Sterling Heights, U.S.A. 76 D4 42 35N 83 0W
Sterling Run, U.S.A. 78 E6 41 25N 78 12W
Sterlitamak, Russia 24 D10 53 40N 56 0 E
Stérnes, Greece 23 D6 35 30N 24 9 E
Stettin = Szczecin, Poland 16 B8 53 27N 14 27 E
Stettiner Haff, Germany 16 B8 53 47N 14 15 E
Stettler, Canada 72 C6 52 19N 112 40W
Steubenville, U.S.A. 78 F4 40 22N 80 37W
Stevenage, U.K. 11 F7 51 55N 0 13W
Stevens Point, U.S.A. 80 C10 44 31N 89 34W
Stevenson, U.S.A. 84 E5 45 42N 121 53W
Stevenson L., Canada 73 C9 53 55N 96 0W
Stevensville, U.S.A. 82 C6 46 30N 114 5W
Stewart, B.C., Canada 72 B3 55 56N 129 57W
Stewart, N.W.T., Canada 68 B6 63 19N 139 26W
Stewart, U.S.A. 84 F7 39 5N 119 46W
Stewart, C., Australia 62 A1 11 57S 134 56 E
Stewart, I., Chile 96 G2 54 50S 71 15W
Stewart I., N.Z. 59 M1 46 58S 167 54 E
Stewarts Point, U.S.A. 84 G3 38 39N 123 24W
Stewartville, U.S.A. 80 D8 43 51N 92 29W
Stewiacke, Canada 71 C7 45 9N 63 22W
Steynsburg, S. Africa 56 E4 31 15S 25 49 E
Steyr, Austria 16 D8 48 3N 14 25 E
Steytlerville, S. Africa 56 E3 33 17S 24 19 E
Stigler, U.S.A. 81 H7 35 15N 95 8W
Stikine →, Canada 72 B2 56 40N 132 30W
Stilfontein, S. Africa 56 D4 26 51S 26 50 E
Stillwater, N.Z. 59 K3 42 27S 171 20 E
Stillwater, Minn., U.S.A. 80 C8 45 3N 92 49W
Stillwater, N.Y., U.S.A. 79 D11 42 55N 73 41W
Stillwater, Okla., U.S.A. 81 G6 36 7N 97 4W
Stillwater Range, U.S.A. 82 G4 39 50N 118 5W
Stillwater Reservoir, U.S.A. 79 C9 43 54N 75 3W
Stilwell, U.S.A. 81 H7 35 49N 94 38W
Štip, Macedonia 21 D10 41 42N 22 10 E
Stirling, Canada 78 B7 44 18N 77 33W
Stirling, U.K. 12 E5 56 8N 3 57W
Stirling □, U.K. 12 E4 56 12N 4 18W
Stirling Ra., Australia 61 F2 34 23S 118 0 E
Stittsville, Canada 79 A9 45 15N 75 55W
Stjernøya, Norway 8 A20 70 20N 22 40 E
Stjørdalshalsen, Norway 8 E14 63 29N 10 51 E
Stockerau, Austria 16 D9 48 24N 16 12 E
Stockholm, Sweden 9 G18 59 20N 18 3 E
Stockport, U.K. 10 D5 53 25N 2 9W
Stocksbridge, U.K. 10 D6 53 29N 1 35W
Stockton, Calif., U.S.A. 84 H5 37 58N 121 17W
Stockton, Kans., U.S.A. 80 F5 39 26N 99 16W
Stockton, Mo., U.S.A. 81 G8 37 42N 93 48W
Stockton-on-Tees, U.K. 10 C6 54 35N 1 19W
Stockton-on-Tees □, U.K. 10 C6 54 35N 1 19W
Stockton Plateau, U.S.A. 81 K3 30 30N 102 30W
Stoeng Treng, Cambodia 38 F5 13 31N 105 58 E
Stoer, Pt. of, U.K. 12 C3 58 16N 5 23W
Stoke-on-Trent, U.K. 10 D5 53 1N 2 11W
Stoke-on-Trent □, U.K. 10 D5 53 1N 2 11W
Stokes Pt., Australia 62 G3 40 10S 143 56 E
Stokes Ra., Australia 60 C5 15 50S 130 50 E
Stokksnes, Iceland 8 D6 64 14N 14 58W
Stokmarknes, Norway 8 B16 68 34N 14 54 E
Stolac, Bos.-H. 21 C7 43 5N 17 59 E
Stolbovoy, Ostrov, Russia 27 D17 74 44N 135 14 E
Stolbtsy = Stowbtsy, Belarus 17 B14 53 30N 26 43 E
Stolin, Belarus 17 C14 51 53N 26 50 E
Stomíon, Greece 23 D5 35 21N 23 32 E
Stone, U.K. 10 E5 52 55N 2 9W
Stoneboro, U.S.A. 78 E4 41 20N 80 7W
Stonehaven, U.K. 12 E6 56 59N 2 12W
Stonehenge, Australia 62 C3 24 22S 143 17 E
Stonehenge, U.K. 11 F6 51 9N 1 45W
Stonewall, Canada 73 C9 50 10N 97 19W
Stony L., Man., Canada 73 B9 58 51N 98 40W
Stony L., Ont., Canada 78 B6 44 30N 78 5W
Stony Point, U.S.A. 79 E11 41 14N 73 59W
Stony Pt., U.S.A. 79 C8 43 50N 76 18W
Stony Rapids, Canada 73 B7 59 16N 105 50W
Stony Tunguska = Tunguska, Podkamennaya →, Russia 27 C10 61 50N 90 13 E
Stonyford, U.S.A. 84 F4 39 23N 122 33W
Stora Lulevatten, Sweden 8 C18 67 10N 19 30 E
Storavan, Sweden 8 D18 65 45N 18 10 E
Stord, Norway 9 G11 59 52N 5 23 E
Store Bælt, Denmark 9 J14 55 20N 11 0 E
Storm B., Australia 62 G4 43 10S 147 30 E
Storm Lake, U.S.A. 80 D7 42 39N 95 13W
Stormberge, S. Africa 56 E4 31 16S 26 17 E
Stormsrivier, S. Africa 56 E3 33 59S 23 52 E
Stornoway, U.K. 12 C2 58 13N 6 23W
Storozhinets = Storozhynets, Ukraine 17 D13 48 14N 25 45 E
Storozhynets, Ukraine 17 D13 48 14N 25 45 E
Storrs, U.S.A. 79 E12 41 49N 72 15W
Storsjön, Sweden 8 E16 63 9N 14 30 E
Storuman, Sweden 8 D17 65 5N 17 10 E
Storuman, sjö, Sweden 8 D17 65 13N 16 50 E
Stouffville, Canada 78 C5 43 58N 79 15W
Stoughton, Canada 73 D8 49 40N 103 0W
Stour →, Dorset, U.K. 11 G6 50 43N 1 47W
Stour →, Kent, U.K. 11 F9 51 18N 1 22 E
Stour →, Suffolk, U.K. 11 F9 51 57N 1 4 E
Stourbridge, U.K. 11 E5 52 28N 2 8W
Stout L., Canada 73 C10 52 0N 94 40W
Stove Pipe Wells Village, U.S.A. 85 J9 36 35N 117 11W
Stow, U.S.A. 78 E3 41 10N 81 27W
Stowbtsy, Belarus 17 B14 53 30N 26 43 E
Stowmarket, U.K. 11 E9 52 12N 1 0 E
Strabane, U.K. 13 B4 54 50N 7 27W
Strahan, Australia 62 G4 42 9S 145 20 E
Stralsund, Germany 16 A7 54 18N 13 4 E
Strand, S. Africa 56 E2 34 9S 18 48 E
Stranda, Møre og Romsdal, Norway 9 E12 62 19N 6 58 E
Stranda, Nord-Trøndelag, Norway 8 E14 63 33N 10 14 E
Strangford L., U.K. 13 B6 54 30N 5 37W
Stranraer, U.K. 12 G3 54 54N 5 1W
Strasbourg, Canada 73 C8 51 4N 104 55W
Strasbourg, France 18 B7 48 35N 7 42 E
Stratford, Canada 78 C4 43 23N 81 0W
Stratford, N.Z. 59 H5 39 20S 174 19 E
Stratford, Calif., U.S.A. 84 J7 36 11N 119 49W
Stratford, Conn., U.S.A. 79 E11 41 12N 73 8W
Stratford, Tex., U.S.A. 81 G3 36 20N 102 4W
Stratford-upon-Avon, U.K. 11 E6 52 12N 1 42W
Strath Spey, U.K. 12 D5 57 9N 3 49W
Strathalbyn, Australia 63 F2 35 13S 138 53 E
Strathaven, U.K. 12 F4 55 40N 4 5W
Strathcona Prov. Park, Canada 72 D3 49 38N 125 40W
Strathmore, Canada 72 C6 51 5N 113 18W
Strathmore, U.K. 12 E5 56 37N 3 7W
Strathmore, U.S.A. 84 J7 36 9N 119 4W
Strathnaver, Canada 72 C4 53 20N 122 33W
Strathpeffer, U.K. 12 D4 57 35N 4 32W
Strathroy, Canada 78 D3 42 58N 81 38W
Strathy Pt., U.K. 12 C4 58 36N 4 1W
Strattanville, U.S.A. 78 E5 41 12N 79 19W
Stratton, U.S.A. 79 A14 45 8N 70 26W
Stratton Mt., U.S.A. 79 C12 43 4N 72 55W
Straubing, Germany 16 D7 48 52N 12 34 E
Straumnes, Iceland 8 C2 66 26N 23 8W
Strawberry →, U.S.A. 82 F8 40 10N 110 24W
Streaky B., Australia 63 E1 32 48S 134 13 E
Streaky Bay, Australia 63 E1 32 51S 134 18 E
Streator, U.S.A. 80 E10 41 8N 88 50W
Streetsboro, U.S.A. 78 E3 41 14N 81 21W
Streetsville, Canada 78 C5 43 35N 79 42W
Strelka, Russia 27 D10 58 5N 93 3 E
Streng →, Cambodia 38 F4 13 12N 103 37 E
Streymoy, Færoe Is. 8 E9 62 8N 7 5W
Strezhevoy, Russia 26 C8 60 42N 77 34 E
Strimón →, Greece 21 D10 40 46N 23 51 E
Strimonikós Kólpos, Greece 21 D11 40 33N 24 0 E
Stroma, U.K. 12 C5 58 41N 3 7W
Strómboli, Italy 20 E6 38 47N 15 13 E
Stromeferry, U.K. 12 D3 57 21N 5 33W
Stromness, U.K. 12 C5 58 58N 3 17W
Stromsburg, U.S.A. 80 E6 41 7N 97 36W
Strömstad, Sweden 9 G14 58 56N 11 10 E
Strömsund, Sweden 8 E16 63 51N 15 33 E
Strongsville, U.S.A. 78 E3 41 19N 81 50W
Stronsay, U.K. 12 B6 59 7N 2 35W
Stroud, U.K. 11 F5 51 45N 2 13W
Stroud Road, Australia 63 E5 32 18S 151 57 E
Stroudsburg, U.S.A. 79 F9 40 59N 75 12W
Stroumbi, Cyprus 23 E11 34 53N 32 29 E
Struer, Denmark 9 H13 56 30N 8 35 E
Strumica, Macedonia 21 D10 41 28N 22 41 E
Struthers, Canada 70 C2 48 41N 85 51W
Struthers, U.S.A. 78 E4 41 4N 80 39W
Stryker, U.S.A. 82 B6 48 41N 114 46W
Stryy, Ukraine 17 D12 49 16N 23 48 E
Strzelecki Cr. →, Australia 63 D2 29 37S 139 59 E
Stuart, Fla., U.S.A. 77 M5 27 12N 80 15W
Stuart, Nebr., U.S.A. 80 D5 42 36N 99 8W
Stuart →, Canada 72 C4 54 0N 123 35W
Stuart Bluff Ra., Australia 60 D5 22 50S 131 52 E
Stuart L., Canada 72 C4 54 30N 124 30W
Stuart Ra., Australia 63 D1 29 10S 134 56 E
Stull, L., Canada 70 B1 54 24N 92 34W
Stung Treng = Stoeng Treng, Cambodia 38 F5 13 31N 105 58 E
Stupart →, Canada 70 A1 56 0N 93 25W
Sturgeon B., Canada 73 C9 52 0N 97 50W
Sturgeon Bay, U.S.A. 76 C2 44 50N 87 23W
Sturgeon Falls, Canada 70 C4 46 25N 79 57W
Sturgeon L., Alta., Canada 72 B5 55 6N 117 32W
Sturgeon L., Ont., Canada 70 C1 50 0N 90 45W
Sturgeon L., Ont., Canada 78 B6 44 28N 78 43W
Sturgis, Canada 73 C8 51 56N 102 36W
Sturgis, Mich., U.S.A. 76 E3 41 48N 85 25W
Sturgis, S. Dak., U.S.A. 80 C3 44 25N 103 31W
Sturt Cr. →, Australia 60 C4 19 8S 127 50 E
Stutterheim, S. Africa 56 E4 32 33S 27 28 E
Stuttgart, Germany 16 D5 48 48N 9 11 E
Stuttgart, U.S.A. 81 H9 34 30N 91 33W
Stuyvesant, U.S.A. 79 D11 42 23N 73 45W
Stykkishólmur, Iceland 8 D2 65 2N 22 40W
Styria = Steiermark □, Austria 16 E8 47 26N 15 0 E
Su Xian = Suzhou, China 34 H9 33 41N 116 59 E
Suakin, Sudan 51 E13 19 8N 37 20 E
Suan, N. Korea 35 E14 38 42N 126 22 E
Suaqui, Mexico 86 B3 29 12N 109 41W
Suar, India 43 E8 29 2N 79 3 E
Subang, Indonesia 37 G12 6 34S 107 45 E
Subansiri →, India 41 F18 26 48N 93 50 E
Subarnarekha →, India 43 H12 22 34N 87 24 E
Subayhah, Si. Arabia 44 D3 30 2N 38 50 E
Subi, Indonesia 39 L7 2 58N 108 50 E
Subotica, Serbia, Yug. 21 A8 46 6N 19 39 E
Suceava, Romania 17 E14 47 38N 26 16 E
Suchan, Russia 30 C6 43 8N 133 9 E
Suchitoto, El Salv. 88 D2 13 56N 89 0W
Suchou = Suzhou, China 33 C7 31 19N 120 38 E
Süchow = Xuzhou, China 35 G9 34 18N 117 10 E
Suck →, Ireland 13 C3 53 17N 8 3W
Sucre, Bolivia 92 G5 19 0S 65 15W
Sucuriú →, Brazil 93 H8 20 47S 51 38W
Sud, Pte. du, Canada 71 C7 49 3N 62 14W
Sud-Kivu □, Dem. Rep. of the Congo 54 C2 3 30S 28 0 E
Sud-Ouest, Pte. du, Canada 71 C7 49 23N 63 36W
Sudan, U.S.A. 81 H3 34 4N 102 32W
Sudan ■, Africa 51 E11 15 0N 30 0 E
Sudbury, Canada 70 C3 46 30N 81 0W
Sudbury, U.K. 11 E8 52 2N 0 45 E
Sûdd, Sudan 51 G12 8 20N 30 0 E
Sudeten Mts. = Sudety, Europe 17 C9 50 20N 16 45 E
Sudety, Europe 17 C9 50 20N 16 45 E
Suðuroy, Færoe Is. 8 F9 61 32N 6 50W
Sudi, Tanzania 55 E4 10 11S 39 57 E
Sudirman, Pegunungan, Indonesia 37 E9 4 30S 137 0 E
Sueca, Spain 19 C5 39 12N 0 21W
Suemez I., U.S.A. 72 B2 55 15N 133 20W
Suez = El Suweis, Egypt 51 C12 29 58N 32 31 E
Suez, G. of = Suweis, Khalîg el, Egypt 51 C12 28 40N 33 0 E
Suez Canal = Suweis, Qanâ es, Egypt 51 B12 31 0N 32 20 E
Suffield, Canada 72 C6 50 12N 111 10W
Suffolk, U.S.A. 76 G7 36 44N 76 35W
Suffolk □, U.K. 11 E9 52 16N 1 0 E
Sugargrove, U.S.A. 78 E5 41 59N 79 21W
Sugarive →, India 43 F12 26 16N 86 24 E
Sugluk = Salluit, Canada 69 B12 62 14N 75 38W
Şuḩār, Oman 45 E8 24 20N 56 40 E
Sühbaatar □, Mongolia 34 B8 45 30N 114 0 E
Suhl, Germany 16 C6 50 36N 10 42 E
Sui, Pakistan 42 E3 28 37N 69 19 E
Sui Xian, China 34 G8 34 25N 115 2 E
Suide, China 34 F6 37 30N 110 12 E
Suifenhe, China 35 B16 44 25N 131 10 E
Suihua, China 33 B7 46 32N 126 55 E
Suining, China 35 H9 33 56N 117 58 E
Suiping, China 34 H7 33 10N 113 59 E
Suir →, Ireland 13 D4 52 16N 7 9W
Suisun City, U.S.A. 84 G4 38 15N 122 2W
Suiyang, China 35 B16 44 30N 130 56 E
Suizhong, China 35 D11 40 21N 120 20 E
Sujangarh, India 42 F6 27 42N 74 31 E
Sukabumi, Indonesia 37 G12 6 56S 106 50 E
Sukadana, Indonesia 36 E4 1 10S 110 0 E
Sukagawa, Japan 31 F10 37 17N 140 23 E
Sukaraja, Indonesia 36 E4 2 28S 110 25 E
Sukarnapura = Jayapura, Indonesia 37 E10 2 28S 140 38 E
Sukch'ŏn, N. Korea 35 E13 39 22N 125 35 E
Sukhona →, Russia 24 C6 61 15N 46 39 E
Sukhothai, Thailand 38 D2 17 1N 99 49 E
Sukhumi = Sokhumi, Georgia 25 F7 43 0N 41 0 E
Sukkur, Pakistan 42 F3 27 42N 68 54 E
Sukkur Barrage, Pakistan 42 F3 27 40N 68 50 E
Sukri →, India 42 G4 25 4N 71 43 E
Sukumo, Japan 31 H6 32 56N 132 44 E
Sukunka →, Canada 72 B4 55 45N 121 15W
Sula, Kepulauan, Indonesia 37 E7 1 45S 125 0 E
Sulaco →, Honduras 88 C2 15 2N 87 44W
Sulaiman Range, Pakistan 42 D3 30 30N 69 50 E
Sūlār, Iran 45 D6 31 53N 51 54 E
Sulawesi □, Indonesia 37 E6 2 0S 120 0 E
Sulawesi Sea = Celebes Sea, Indonesia 37 D6 3 0N 123 0 E
Sulawesi Selatan □, Indonesia 37 E6 2 30S 120 0 E
Sulawesi Utara □, Indonesia 37 D6 1 0N 122 30 E
Sulima, S. Leone 50 G3 6 58N 11 32W
Sulina, Romania 17 F15 45 10N 29 40 E
Sulitjelma, Norway 8 C17 67 9N 16 3 E
Sullana, Peru 92 D2 4 52S 80 39W
Sullivan, Ill., U.S.A. 80 F10 39 36N 88 37W
Sullivan, Ind., U.S.A. 76 F2 39 6N 87 24W
Sullivan, Mo., U.S.A. 80 F9 38 13N 91 10W
Sullivan Bay, Canada 72 C3 50 55N 126 50W
Sullivan I. = Lambi Kyun, Burma 39 G2 10 50N 98 20 E
Sulphur, La., U.S.A. 81 K8 30 14N 93 23W
Sulphur, Okla., U.S.A. 81 H6 34 31N 96 58W
Sulphur Pt., Canada 72 A6 60 56N 114 48W
Sulphur Springs, U.S.A. 81 J7 33 8N 95 36W
Sultan, Canada 70 C3 47 36N 82 47W
Sultan, U.S.A. 84 C5 47 52N 121 49W
Sultanpur, India 43 F10 26 18N 82 4 E
Sultanpur, Mad. P., India 42 H8 23 9N 77 56 E
Sultanpur, Punjab, India 42 D6 31 13N 75 11 E
Sulu Arch., Phil. 37 C6 6 0N 121 0 E
Sulu Sea, E. Indies 37 C6 8 0N 120 0 E
Suluq, Libya 51 B10 31 44N 20 14 E
Sulzberger Ice Shelf, Antarctica 5 D10 78 0S 150 0 E
Sumalata, Indonesia 37 D6 1 0N 122 31 E
Sumampa, Argentina 94 B3 29 25S 63 29W
Sumatera □, Indonesia 36 D2 0 40N 100 20 E
Sumatera Barat □, Indonesia 36 E2 1 0S 101 0 E
Sumatera Utara □, Indonesia 36 D1 2 30N 98 0 E
Sumatra = Sumatera □, Indonesia 36 D2 0 40N 100 20 E
Sumba, Indonesia 37 F5 9 45S 119 35 E
Sumba, Selat, Indonesia 37 F5 9 0S 118 40 E
Sumbawa, Indonesia 36 F5 8 26S 117 30 E
Sumbawa Besar, Indonesia 36 F5 8 30S 117 26 E
Sumbawanga □, Tanzania 52 F6 8 0S 31 30 E
Sumbe, Angola 52 G2 11 10S 13 48 E
Sumburgh Hd., U.K. 12 B7 59 52N 1 17W
Sumdeo, India 43 D8 31 26N 78 44 E
Sumdo, India 43 B8 35 6N 78 41 E
Sumedang, Indonesia 37 G12 6 52S 107 55 E
Šumen = Shumen, Bulgaria 21 C12 43 18N 26 55 E
Sumenep, Indonesia 37 G15 7 1S 113 52 E
Sumgait = Sumqayıt, Azerbaijan 25 F8 40 34N 49 38 E
Summer L., U.S.A. 82 E3 42 50N 120 45W
Summerland, Canada 72 D5 49 32N 119 41W
Summerside, Canada 71 C7 46 24N 63 47W
Summersville, U.S.A. 76 F5 38 17N 80 51W
Summerville, Ga., U.S.A. 77 H3 34 29N 85 21W
Summerville, S.C., U.S.A. 77 J5 33 1N 80 11W
Summit Lake, Canada 72 C4 54 20N 122 40W
Summit Peak, U.S.A. 83 H10 37 21N 106 42W
Sumner, Iowa, U.S.A. 80 D8 42 51N 92 6W
Sumner, Wash., U.S.A. 84 C4 47 12N 122 14W
Sumoto, Japan 31 G7 34 21N 134 54 E
Šumperk, Czech Rep. 17 D9 49 59N 16 59 E
Sumqayıt, Azerbaijan 25 F8 40 34N 49 38 E
Sumter, U.S.A. 77 J5 33 55N 80 21W
Sumy, Ukraine 25 D5 50 57N 34 50 E
Sun City, Ariz., U.S.A. 83 K7 33 36N 112 17W
Sun City, Calif., U.S.A. 85 M9 33 42N 117 11W
Sun City Center, U.S.A. 77 M4 27 43N 82 18W
Sun Lakes, U.S.A. 83 K8 33 10N 111 52W
Sun Valley, U.S.A. 82 E6 43 42N 114 21W
Sunagawa, Japan 30 C10 43 29N 141 55 E
Sunan, N. Korea 35 E13 39 15N 125 40 E
Sunart, L., U.K. 12 E3 56 42N 5 43W
Sunburst, U.S.A. 82 B8 48 53N 111 55W
Sunbury, Australia 63 F3 37 35S 144 44 E
Sunbury, U.S.A. 79 F8 40 52N 76 48W
Sunchales, Argentina 94 C3 30 58S 61 35W
Suncho Corral, Argentina 94 B3 27 55S 63 27W
Sunch'ŏn, S. Korea 35 G14 34 52N 127 31 E
Suncook, U.S.A. 79 C13 43 8N 71 27W
Sunda, Selat, Indonesia 36 F3 6 20S 105 30 E
Sunda Is., Indonesia 28 K14 5 0S 105 0 E
Sunda Str. = Sunda, Selat, Indonesia 36 F3 6 20S 105 30 E
Sundance, Canada 73 B10 56 32N 94 4W
Sundance, U.S.A. 80 C2 44 24N 104 23W
Sundar Nagar, India 42 D7 31 32N 76 53 E
Sundarbans, The, Asia 41 J16 22 0N 89 0 E
Sundargarh, India 41 H14 22 4N 84 5 E
Sundays = Sondags →, S. Africa 56 E4 33 44S 25 51 E
Sunderland, Canada 78 B5 44 16N 79 4W
Sunderland, U.K. 10 C6 54 55N 1 23W
Sundre, Canada 72 C6 51 49N 114 38W
Sundsvall, Sweden 9 E17 62 23N 17 17 E
Sung Hei, Vietnam 39 G6 10 20N 106 2 E
Sungai Kolok, Thailand 39 J3 6 2N 101 58 E
Sungai Lembing, Malaysia 39 L4 3 55N 103 3 E
Sungai Petani, Malaysia 39 K3 5 37N 100 30 E
Sungaigerong, Indonesia 36 E2 2 59S 104 52 E
Sungailiat, Indonesia 36 E3 1 51S 106 8 E
Sungaipenuh, Indonesia 36 E2 2 1S 101 20 E
Sungari = Songhua Jiang →, China 33 B8 47 45N 132 30 E
Sunghua Chiang = Songhua Jiang →, China 33 B8 47 45N 132 30 E
Sunland Park, U.S.A. 83 L10 31 50N 106 40W
Sunndalsøra, Norway 9 E13 62 40N 8 33 E
Sunnyside, U.S.A. 82 C3 46 20N 120 0W
Sunnyvale, U.S.A. 84 H4 37 23N 122 2W
Suntar, Russia 27 C12 62 15N 117 30 E
Suomenselkä, Finland 8 E21 62 52N 24 0 E
Suomussalmi, Finland 8 D23 64 54N 29 10 E
Suoyarvi, Russia 24 B5 62 3N 32 20 E
Supai, U.S.A. 83 H7 36 15N 112 41W
Supaul, India 43 F12 26 10N 86 40 E
Superior, Ariz., U.S.A. 83 K8 33 18N 111 6W
Superior, Mont., U.S.A. 82 C6 47 12N 114 53W
Superior, Nebr., U.S.A. 80 E5 40 1N 98 4W
Superior, Wis., U.S.A. 80 B8 46 44N 92 6W
Superior, L., N. Amer. 70 C2 47 0N 87 0W
Suphan Buri, Thailand 38 E3 14 14N 100 10 E
Suphan Dağı, Turkey 44 B4 38 54N 42 48 E
Supiori, Indonesia 37 E9 1 0S 136 0 E
Supung Shuiku, China 35 D13 40 35N 124 50 E
Sūq Suwayq, Si. Arabia 44 E3 24 23N 38 27 E
Suqian, China 35 H10 33 54N 118 8 E
Sūr, Lebanon 47 B4 33 19N 35 16 E
Sūr, Oman 46 C6 22 34N 59 32 E
Sur, Pt., U.S.A. 84 J5 36 18N 121 54W
Sura →, Russia 24 C8 56 6N 46 0 E
Surab, Pakistan 42 E2 28 25N 66 15 E
Surabaja = Surabaya, Indonesia 37 G15 7 17S 112 45 E
Surabaya, Indonesia 37 G15 7 17S 112 45 E
Surakarta, Indonesia 37 G14 7 35S 110 48 E
Surat, Australia 63 D4 27 10S 149 6 E
Surat, India 40 J8 21 12N 72 55 E
Surat Thani, Thailand 39 H2 9 6N 99 20 E
Suratgarh, India 42 E5 29 18N 73 55 E
Surendranagar, India 42 H4 22 45N 71 40 E
Surf, U.S.A. 85 L6 34 41N 120 36W
Surgut, Russia 26 C8 61 14N 73 20 E
Suriapet, India 40 L11 17 10N 79 40 E
Surigao, Phil. 37 C7 9 47N 125 29 E
Surin, Thailand 38 E4 14 50N 103 34 E
Surin Nua, Ko, Thailand 39 H1 9 30N 97 55 E
Surinam ■, S. Amer. 93 C7 4 0N 56 0W
Suriname = Surinam ■, S. Amer. 93 C7 4 0N 56 0W
Suriname →, Surinam 93 B7 5 50N 55 15W
Sūrmaq, Iran 45 D7 31 3N 52 48 E
Surrey □, U.K. 11 F7 51 15N 0 31W
Sursand, India 43 F11 26 39N 85 43 E
Sursar →, India 43 F12 26 14N 87 3 E

Tha Sala

Tanout, *Niger* 50 F7 14 50N 8 55 E
Tanta, *Egypt* 51 B12 30 45N 30 57 E
Tantoyuca, *Mexico* 87 C5 21 21N 98 10W
Tantung = Dandong, *China* 35 D13 40 10N 124 20 E
Tanunda, *Australia* 63 E2 34 30S 139 0 E
Tanzania ■, *Africa* 54 D3 6 0S 34 0 E
Tanzilla →, *Canada* 72 B2 58 8N 130 43W
Tao, Ko, *Thailand* 39 G2 10 5N 99 52 E
Tao'an = Taonan, *China* 35 B12 45 22N 122 40 E
Tao'er He →, *China* 35 B13 45 45N 124 5 E
Taolanaro, *Madag.* 57 D8 25 2S 47 0 E
Taole, *China* 34 E4 38 48N 106 40 E
Taonan, *China* 35 B12 45 22N 122 40 E
Taos, *U.S.A.* 83 H11 36 24N 105 35W
Taoudenni, *Mali* 50 D5 22 40N 3 55W
Tapa, *Estonia* 9 G21 59 15N 25 50 E
Tapa Shan = Daba Shan, *China* 33 C5 32 0N 109 0 E
Tapachula, *Mexico* 87 E6 14 54N 92 17W
Tapah, *Malaysia* 39 K3 4 12N 101 15 E
Tapajós →, *Brazil* 93 D8 2 24S 54 41W
Tapaktuan, *Indonesia* 36 D1 3 15N 97 10 E
Tapanahoni →, *Surinam* 93 C8 4 20N 54 25W
Tapanui, *N.Z.* 59 L2 45 56S 169 18 E
Tapauá →, *Brazil* 92 E6 5 40S 64 21W
Tapes, *Brazil* 95 C5 30 40S 51 23W
Tapeta, *Liberia* 50 G4 6 29N 8 52W
Taphan Hin, *Thailand* 38 D3 16 13N 100 26 E
Tapirapecó, Serra, *Venezuela* 92 C6 1 10N 65 0W
Tapuaenuku, Mt., *N.Z.* 59 K4 42 0S 173 39 E
Tapul Group, *Phil.* 37 C6 5 35N 120 50 E
Tapurucuará, *Brazil* 92 D5 0 24S 65 2W
Ṭaqṭaq, *Iraq* 44 C5 35 53N 44 35 E
Taquara, *Brazil* 95 B5 29 36S 50 46W
Taquari →, *Brazil* 92 G7 19 15S 57 17W
Tara, *Australia* 63 D5 27 17S 150 31 E
Tara, *Canada* 78 B3 44 28N 81 9W
Tara, *Russia* 26 D8 56 55N 74 24 E
Tara, *Zambia* 55 F2 16 58S 26 45 E
Tara →, *Montenegro, Yug.* 21 C8 43 21N 18 51 E
Tarabagatay, Khrebet, *Kazakstan* 26 E9 48 0N 83 0 E
Tarābulus, *Lebanon* 47 A4 34 31N 35 50 E
Tarābulus, *Libya* 51 B8 32 49N 13 7 E
Taradehi, *India* 43 H8 23 18N 79 21 E
Tarajalejo, *Canary Is.* 22 F5 28 12N 14 7W
Tarakan, *Indonesia* 36 D5 3 20N 117 35 E
Tarakit, Mt., *Kenya* 54 B4 2 2N 35 10 E
Tarama-Jima, *Japan* 31 M2 24 39N 124 42 E
Taran, Mys, *Russia* 9 J18 54 56N 19 59 E
Taranagar, *India* 42 E6 28 43N 74 50 E
Taranaki □, *N.Z.* 59 H5 39 25S 174 30 E
Tarancón, *Spain* 19 B4 40 1N 3 0W
Taranga Hill, *India* 40 H8 24 0N 72 40 E
Taransay, *U.K.* 12 D1 57 54N 7 0W
Táranto, *Italy* 20 D7 40 28N 17 14 E
Táranto, G. di, *Italy* 20 D7 40 8N 17 20 E
Tarapacá, *Colombia* 92 D5 2 56S 69 46W
Tarapacá □, *Chile* 94 A2 20 45S 69 30W
Tarapoto, *Peru* 92 E3 6 30S 76 20W
Tararua Ra., *N.Z.* 59 J5 40 45S 175 25 E
Tarashcha, *Ukraine* 17 D16 49 30N 30 31 E
Tarauacá, *Brazil* 92 E4 8 6S 70 48W
Tarauacá →, *Brazil* 92 E5 6 42S 69 48W
Tarawa = Bairiki, *Kiribati* 64 G9 1 30N 173 0 E
Tarawera, *N.Z.* 59 H6 39 2S 176 36 E
Tarawera L., *N.Z.* 59 H6 38 13S 176 27 E
Taraz = Zhambyl, *Kazakstan* 26 E8 42 54N 71 22 E
Tarazona, *Spain* 19 B5 41 55N 1 43W
Tarbat Ness, *U.K.* 12 D5 57 52N 3 47W
Tarbela Dam, *Pakistan* 42 B5 34 8N 72 52 E
Tarbert, *Arg. & Bute, U.K.* 12 F3 55 52N 5 25W
Tarbert, *W. Isles, U.K.* 12 D2 57 54N 6 49W
Tarbes, *France* 18 E4 43 15N 0 3 E
Tarboro, *U.S.A.* 77 H7 35 54N 77 32W
Tarcoola, *Australia* 63 E1 30 44S 134 36 E
Tarcoon, *Australia* 63 E4 30 15S 146 43 E
Taree, *Australia* 63 E5 31 50S 152 30 E
Tarfaya, *Morocco* 50 C3 27 55N 12 55W
Târgovişte, *Romania* 17 F13 44 55N 25 27 E
Târgu-Jiu, *Romania* 17 F12 45 5N 23 19 E
Târgu Mureş, *Romania* 17 E13 46 31N 24 38 E
Ṭarif, *U.A.E.* 45 E7 24 3N 53 46 E
Tarifa, *Spain* 19 D3 36 1N 5 36W
Tarija, *Bolivia* 94 A3 21 30S 64 40W
Tarija □, *Bolivia* 94 A3 21 30S 63 30W
Tariku →, *Indonesia* 37 E9 2 55S 138 26 E
Tarim Basin = Tarim Pendi, *China* 32 B3 40 0N 84 0 E
Tarim He →, *China* 32 C3 39 30N 88 30 E
Tarim Pendi, *China* 32 B3 40 0N 84 0 E
Taritatu →, *Indonesia* 37 E9 2 54S 138 27 E
Tarka →, *S. Africa* 56 E4 32 10S 26 0 E
Tarkastad, *S. Africa* 56 E4 32 0S 26 16 E
Tarkhankut, Mys, *Ukraine* 25 E5 45 25N 32 30 E
Tarko Sale, *Russia* 26 C8 64 55N 77 50 E
Tarkwa, *Ghana* 50 G5 5 20N 2 0W
Tarlac, *Phil.* 37 A6 15 29N 120 35 E
Tarma, *Peru* 92 F3 11 25S 75 45W
Tarn →, *France* 18 E4 44 5N 1 6 E
Târnăveni, *Romania* 17 E13 46 19N 24 13 E
Tarnobrzeg, *Poland* 17 C11 50 35N 21 41 E
Tarnów, *Poland* 17 C11 50 3N 21 0 E
Tarnowskie Góry, *Poland* 17 C10 50 27N 18 54 E
Ṭārom, *Iran* 45 D7 28 11N 55 46 E
Taroom, *Australia* 63 D4 25 36S 149 48 E
Taroudannt, *Morocco* 50 B4 30 30N 8 52W
Tarpon Springs, *U.S.A.* 77 L4 28 9N 82 45W
Tarragona, *Spain* 19 B6 41 5N 1 17 E
Tarraleah, *Australia* 62 G4 42 17S 146 26 E
Tarrasa = Terrassa, *Spain* 19 B7 41 34N 2 1 E
Tarrytown, *U.S.A.* 79 E11 41 4N 73 52W
Tarshiha = Me'ona, *Israel* 47 B4 33 1N 35 15 E
Tarso Emissi, *Chad* 51 D9 21 27N 18 36 E
Tarsus, *Turkey* 25 G5 36 58N 34 55 E
Tartagal, *Argentina* 94 A3 22 30S 63 50W
Tartu, *Estonia* 9 G22 58 20N 26 44 E
Ṭarṭūs, *Syria* 44 C2 34 55N 35 55 E
Tarumizu, *Japan* 31 J5 31 29N 130 42 E
Tarutao, Ko, *Thailand* 39 J2 6 33N 99 40 E
Tarutung, *Indonesia* 36 D1 2 0N 98 54 E
Taseko →, *Canada* 72 C4 52 8N 123 45W
Tash-Kömür, *Kyrgyzstan* 26 E8 41 40N 72 10 E
Tash-Kumyr = Tash-Kömür, *Kyrgyzstan* 26 E8 41 40N 72 10 E
Tashauz = Dashhowuz, *Turkmenistan* 26 E6 41 49N 59 58 E
Tashi Chho Dzong = Thimphu, *Bhutan* 41 F16 27 31N 89 45 E
Ţashk, Daryācheh-ye, *Iran* 45 D7 29 45N 53 35 E
Tashkent = Toshkent, *Uzbekistan* 26 E7 41 20N 69 10 E
Tashtagol, *Russia* 26 D9 52 47N 87 53 E
Tasikmalaya, *Indonesia* 37 G13 7 18S 108 12 E
Tåsjön, *Sweden* 8 D16 64 15N 15 40 E
Taskan, *Russia* 27 C16 62 59N 150 20 E
Tasman B., *N.Z.* 59 J4 40 59S 173 25 E
Tasman Mts., *N.Z.* 59 J4 41 3S 172 25 E
Tasman Pen., *Australia* 62 G4 43 10S 148 0 E
Tasman Sea, *Pac. Oc.* 64 L8 36 0S 160 0 E
Tasmania □, *Australia* 62 G4 42 0S 146 30 E
Tassili n'Ajjer, *Algeria* 50 C7 25 47N 8 1 E
Tatabánya, *Hungary* 17 E10 47 32N 18 25 E
Tatahouine, *Tunisia* 51 B8 32 56N 10 27 E
Tatar Republic = Tatarstan □, *Russia* 24 C9 55 30N 51 30 E
Tatarbunary, *Ukraine* 17 F15 45 50N 29 39 E
Tatarsk, *Russia* 26 D8 55 14N 76 0 E
Tatarstan □, *Russia* 24 C9 55 30N 51 30 E
Tateyama, *Japan* 31 G9 35 0N 139 50 E
Tathlina L., *Canada* 72 A5 60 33N 117 39W
Tathra, *Australia* 63 F4 36 44S 149 59 E
Tati →, *India* 40 J8 21 8N 72 41 E
Tatinnai L., *Canada* 73 A9 60 55N 97 40W
Tatla L., *Canada* 72 C4 52 0N 124 20W
Tatnam, C., *Canada* 73 B10 57 16N 91 0W
Tatra = Tatry, *Slovak Rep.* 17 D11 49 20N 20 0 E
Tatry, *Slovak Rep.* 17 D11 49 20N 20 0 E
Tatshenshini →, *Canada* 72 B1 59 28N 137 45W
Tatsuno, *Japan* 31 G7 34 52N 134 33 E
Tatta, *Pakistan* 42 G2 24 42N 67 55 E
Tatuī, *Brazil* 95 A6 23 25S 47 53W
Tatum, *U.S.A.* 81 J3 33 16N 103 19W
Tat'ung = Datong, *China* 34 D7 40 6N 113 18 E
Tatvan, *Turkey* 25 G7 38 31N 42 15 E
Taubaté, *Brazil* 95 A6 23 0S 45 36W
Tauern, *Austria* 16 E7 47 15N 12 40 E
Taumarunui, *N.Z.* 59 H5 38 53S 175 15 E
Taumaturgo, *Brazil* 92 E4 8 54S 72 51W
Taung, *S. Africa* 56 D3 27 33S 24 47 E
Taungdwingyi, *Burma* 41 J19 20 1N 95 40 E
Taunggyi, *Burma* 41 J20 20 50N 97 0 E
Taungup, *Burma* 41 K19 18 51N 94 14 E
Taungup Pass, *Burma* 41 K19 18 40N 94 45 E
Taungup Taunggya, *Burma* 41 K18 18 20N 93 40 E
Taunsa, *Pakistan* 42 D4 30 42N 70 39 E
Taunsa Barrage, *Pakistan* 42 D4 30 42N 70 50 E
Taunton, *U.K.* 11 F4 51 1N 3 5W
Taunton, *U.S.A.* 79 E13 41 54N 71 6W
Taunus, *Germany* 16 C5 50 13N 8 34 E
Taupo, *N.Z.* 59 H6 38 41S 176 7 E
Taupo, L., *N.Z.* 59 H5 38 46S 175 55 E
Tauragė, *Lithuania* 9 J20 55 14N 22 16 E
Tauranga, *N.Z.* 59 G6 37 42S 176 11 E
Tauranga Harb., *N.Z.* 59 G6 37 30S 176 5 E
Taureau, Rés., *Canada* 70 C5 46 46N 73 50W
Taurianova, *Italy* 20 E7 38 21N 16 1 E
Taurus Mts. = Toros Dağları, *Turkey* 25 G5 37 0N 32 30 E
Tavda, *Russia* 26 D7 58 7N 65 8 E
Tavda →, *Russia* 26 D7 57 47N 67 18 E
Taveta, *Tanzania* 54 C4 3 23S 37 37 E
Taveuni, *Fiji* 59 C9 16 51S 179 58W
Tavira, *Portugal* 19 D2 37 8N 7 40W
Tavistock, *Canada* 78 C4 43 19N 80 50W
Tavistock, *U.K.* 11 G3 50 33N 4 9W
Tavoy = Dawei, *Burma* 38 E2 14 2N 98 12 E
Taw →, *U.K.* 11 F3 51 4N 4 4W
Tawa →, *India* 42 H8 22 48N 77 48 E
Tawas City, *U.S.A.* 76 C4 44 16N 83 31W
Tawau, *Malaysia* 36 D5 4 20N 117 55 E
Tawitawi, *Phil.* 37 C6 5 10N 120 0 E
Taxco de Alarcón, *Mexico* 87 D5 18 33N 99 36W
Taxila, *Pakistan* 42 C5 33 42N 72 52 E
Tay →, *U.K.* 12 E5 56 37N 3 38W
Tay, Firth of, *U.K.* 12 E5 56 25N 3 8W
Tay, L., *Australia* 61 F3 32 55S 120 48 E
Tay, L., *U.K.* 12 E4 56 32N 4 8W
Tay Ninh, *Vietnam* 39 G6 11 20N 106 5 E
Tayabamba, *Peru* 92 E3 8 15S 77 16W
Taylakova, *Russia* 26 D8 59 13N 74 0 E
Taylakovy = Taylakova, *Russia* 26 D8 59 13N 74 0 E
Taylor, *Canada* 72 B4 56 13N 120 40W
Taylor, *Nebr., U.S.A.* 80 E5 41 46N 99 23W
Taylor, *Pa., U.S.A.* 79 E9 41 23N 75 43W
Taylor, *Tex., U.S.A.* 81 K6 30 34N 97 25W
Taylor, Mt., *U.S.A.* 83 J10 35 14N 107 37W
Taylorville, *U.S.A.* 80 F10 39 33N 89 18W
Taymā, *Si. Arabia* 44 E3 27 35N 38 45 E
Taymyr, Oz., *Russia* 27 B11 74 20N 102 0 E
Taymyr, Poluostrov, *Russia* 27 B11 75 0N 100 0 E
Tayport, *U.K.* 12 E6 56 27N 2 52W
Tayshet, *Russia* 27 D10 55 58N 98 1 E
Taytay, *Phil.* 37 B5 10 45N 119 30 E
Taz →, *Russia* 26 C8 67 32N 78 40 E
Taza, *Morocco* 50 B5 34 16N 4 6W
Tāzah Khurmātū, *Iraq* 44 C5 35 18N 44 20 E
Tazawa-Ko, *Japan* 30 E10 39 43N 140 40 E
Tazin, *Canada* 73 B7 59 48N 109 55W
Tazin L., *Canada* 73 B7 59 44N 108 42W
Tazovskiy, *Russia* 26 C8 67 30N 78 44 E
Tbilisi, *Georgia* 25 F7 41 43N 44 50 E
Tchad = Chad ■, *Africa* 51 F8 15 0N 17 15 E
Tchad, L., *Chad* 51 F8 13 30N 14 30 E
Tch'eng-tou = Chengdu, *China* 32 C5 30 38N 104 2 E
Tchentlo L., *Canada* 72 B4 55 15N 125 0W
Tchibanga, *Gabon* 52 E2 2 45S 11 0 E
Tch'ong-k'ing = Chongqing, *China* 32 D5 29 35N 106 25 E
Tczew, *Poland* 17 A10 54 8N 18 50 E
Te Anau, L., *N.Z.* 59 L1 45 15S 167 45 E
Te Aroha, *N.Z.* 59 G5 37 32S 175 44 E
Te Awamutu, *N.Z.* 59 H5 38 1S 175 20 E
Te Kuiti, *N.Z.* 59 H5 38 20S 175 11 E
Te Puke, *N.Z.* 59 G6 37 46S 176 22 E
Te Waewae B., *N.Z.* 59 M1 46 13S 167 33 E
Teague, *U.S.A.* 81 K6 31 38N 96 17W
Teapa, *Mexico* 87 D6 18 35N 92 56W
Tebakang, *Malaysia* 36 D4 1 6N 110 30 E
Tébessa, *Algeria* 50 A7 35 22N 8 8 E
Tebicuary →, *Paraguay* 94 B4 26 36S 58 16W
Tebingtinggi, *Indonesia* 36 D1 3 20N 99 9 E
Tebintingii, *Indonesia* 36 E2 1 0N 102 45 E
Tecate, *Mexico* 85 N10 32 34N 116 38W
Tecka, *Argentina* 96 E2 43 29S 70 48W
Tecomán, *Mexico* 86 D4 18 55N 103 53W
Tecopa, *U.S.A.* 85 K10 35 51N 116 13W
Tecoripa, *Mexico* 86 B3 28 37N 109 57W
Tecuala, *Mexico* 86 C3 22 23N 105 27W
Tecuci, *Romania* 17 F14 45 51N 27 27 E
Tecumseh, *Canada* 78 D2 42 19N 82 54W
Tecumseh, *Mich., U.S.A.* 76 D4 42 0N 83 57W
Tecumseh, *Okla., U.S.A.* 81 H6 35 15N 96 56W
Tedzhen = Tejen, *Turkmenistan* 26 F7 37 23N 60 31 E
Tees →, *U.K.* 10 C6 54 37N 1 10W
Tees B., *U.K.* 10 C6 54 40N 1 9W
Teeswater, *Canada* 78 C3 43 59N 81 17W
Tefé, *Brazil* 92 D6 3 25S 64 50W
Tegal, *Indonesia* 37 G13 6 52S 109 8 E
Tegid, L. = Bala, L., *U.K.* 10 E4 52 53N 3 37W
Tegucigalpa, *Honduras* 88 D2 14 5N 87 14W
Tehachapi, *U.S.A.* 85 K8 35 8N 118 27W
Tehachapi Mts., *U.S.A.* 85 L8 35 0N 118 30W
Tehoru, *Indonesia* 37 E7 3 19S 129 37 E
Tehrān, *Iran* 45 C6 35 44N 51 30 E
Tehri, *India* 43 D8 30 23N 78 29 E
Tehuacán, *Mexico* 87 D5 18 30N 97 30W
Tehuantepec, *Mexico* 87 D5 16 21N 95 13W
Tehuantepec, G. de, *Mexico* 87 D5 15 50N 95 12W
Tehuantepec, Istmo de, *Mexico* 87 D6 17 0N 94 30W
Teide, *Canary Is.* 22 F3 28 15N 16 38W
Teifi →, *U.K.* 11 E3 52 5N 4 41W
Teign →, *U.K.* 11 G4 50 32N 3 32W
Teignmouth, *U.K.* 11 G4 50 33N 3 31W
Tejam, *India* 43 E9 29 57N 80 11 E
Tejen, *Turkmenistan* 26 F7 37 23N 60 31 E
Tejen →, *Turkmenistan* 45 B9 37 24N 60 38 E
Tejo →, *Europe* 19 C1 38 40N 9 24W
Tejon Pass, *U.S.A.* 85 L8 34 49N 118 53W
Tekamah, *U.S.A.* 80 E6 41 47N 96 13W
Tekapo, L., *N.Z.* 59 K3 43 53S 170 33 E
Tekax, *Mexico* 87 C7 20 11N 89 18W
Tekeli, *Kazakstan* 26 E8 44 50N 79 0 E
Tekirdağ, *Turkey* 21 D12 40 58N 27 30 E
Tekkali, *India* 41 K14 18 37N 84 15 E
Tekoa, *U.S.A.* 82 C5 47 14N 117 4W
Tel Aviv-Yafo, *Israel* 47 C3 32 4N 34 48 E
Tel Lakhish, *Israel* 47 D3 31 34N 34 51 E
Tel Megiddo, *Israel* 47 C4 32 35N 35 11 E
Tela, *Honduras* 88 C2 15 40N 87 28W
Telanaipura = Jambi, *Indonesia* 36 E2 1 38S 103 30 E
Telavi, *Georgia* 25 F8 42 0N 45 30 E
Telde, *Canary Is.* 22 G4 27 59N 15 25W
Telegraph Creek, *Canada* 72 B2 58 0N 131 10W
Telekhany = Tsyelyakhany, *Belarus* 17 B13 52 30N 25 46 E
Telemark, *Norway* 9 G12 59 15N 7 40 E
Telén, *Argentina* 94 D2 36 15S 65 31W
Teleng, *Iran* 45 E9 25 47N 61 3 E
Teles Pires →, *Brazil* 92 E7 7 21S 58 3W
Telescope Pk., *U.S.A.* 85 J9 36 10N 117 5W
Telfer Mine, *Australia* 60 C3 21 40S 122 12 E
Telford, *U.K.* 11 E5 52 40N 2 27W
Telford and Wrekin □, *U.K.* 10 E5 52 45N 2 27W
Telkwa, *Canada* 72 C3 54 41N 127 5W
Tell City, *U.S.A.* 76 G2 37 57N 86 46W
Tellicherry, *India* 40 P9 11 45N 75 30 E
Telluride, *U.S.A.* 83 H10 37 56N 107 49W
Teloloapán, *Mexico* 87 D5 18 21N 99 51W
Telpos Iz, *Russia* 24 B10 63 16N 59 13 E
Telsen, *Argentina* 96 E3 42 30S 66 50W
Telšiai, *Lithuania* 9 H20 55 59N 22 14 E
Teluk Anson = Teluk Intan, *Malaysia* 39 K3 4 3N 101 0 E
Teluk Betung = Tanjungkarang Telukbetung, *Indonesia* 36 F3 5 20S 105 10 E
Teluk Intan, *Malaysia* 39 K3 4 3N 101 0 E
Telukbutun, *Indonesia* 39 K7 4 13N 108 12 E
Telukdalem, *Indonesia* 36 D1 0 33N 97 50 E
Tema, *Ghana* 50 G5 5 41N 0 0W
Temax, *Mexico* 87 C7 21 10N 88 50W
Temba, *S. Africa* 57 D4 25 20S 28 17 E
Tembagapura, *Indonesia* 37 E9 4 20S 137 0 E
Tembe, *Dem. Rep. of the Congo* 54 C2 0 16S 28 14 E
Temblor Range, *U.S.A.* 85 K7 35 20N 119 50W
Teme →, *U.K.* 11 E5 52 11N 2 13W
Temecula, *U.S.A.* 85 M9 33 30N 117 9W
Temerloh, *Malaysia* 36 D2 3 27N 102 25 E
Teminabuan, *Indonesia* 37 E8 1 26S 132 1 E
Temir, *Kazakstan* 25 E10 49 1N 57 14 E
Temirtau, *Kazakstan* 26 D8 50 5N 72 56 E
Temirtau, *Russia* 26 D9 53 10N 87 30 E
Temiscamie →, *Canada* 71 B5 50 59N 73 5W
Témiscaming, *Canada* 70 C4 46 44N 79 5W
Témiscamingue, L., *Canada* 70 C4 47 10N 79 25W
Temosachic, *Mexico* 86 B3 28 58N 107 50W
Tempe, *U.S.A.* 83 K8 33 25N 111 56W
Tempiute, *U.S.A.* 84 H11 37 39N 115 38W
Temple, *U.S.A.* 81 K6 31 6N 97 21W
Temple B., *Australia* 62 A3 12 15S 143 3 E
Templemore, *Ireland* 13 D4 52 47N 7 51W
Templeton, *U.S.A.* 84 K6 35 33N 120 42W
Templeton →, *Australia* 62 C2 21 0S 138 40 E
Tempoal, *Mexico* 87 C5 21 31N 98 23W
Temuco, *Chile* 96 D2 38 45S 72 40W
Temuka, *N.Z.* 59 L3 44 14S 171 17 E
Tenabo, *Mexico* 87 C6 20 2N 90 12W
Tenaha, *U.S.A.* 81 K7 31 57N 94 15W
Tenakee Springs, *U.S.A.* 72 B1 57 47N 135 13W
Tenali, *India* 40 L12 16 15N 80 35 E
Tenancingo, *Mexico* 87 D5 19 0N 99 33W
Tenango, *Mexico* 87 D5 19 7N 99 33W
Tenasserim, *Burma* 39 F2 12 6N 99 3 E
Tenasserim □, *Burma* 38 F2 14 0N 98 30 E
Tenby, *U.K.* 11 F3 51 40N 4 42W
Tenda, Colle di, *France* 18 D7 44 7N 7 36 E
Tendaho, *Ethiopia* 46 E3 11 48N 40 54 E
Tendukhera, *India* 43 H8 23 24N 79 33 E
Ténéré, *Niger* 50 E7 19 0N 10 30 E
Tenerife, *Canary Is.* 22 F3 28 15N 16 35W
Tenerife, Pico, *Canary Is.* 22 G1 27 43N 18 1W
Teng Xian, *China* 35 G9 35 5N 117 10 E
Tengah □, *Indonesia* 37 E6 2 0S 122 0 E
Tengah, Kepulauan, *Indonesia* 36 F5 7 5S 118 15 E
Tengchong, *China* 32 D4 25 0N 98 28 E
Tengchowfu = Penglai, *China* 35 F11 37 48N 120 42 E
Tenggara □, *Indonesia* 37 E6 3 0S 122 0 E
Tenggarong, *Indonesia* 36 E5 0 24S 116 58 E
Tenggol, Pulau, *Malaysia* 39 K4 4 48N 103 41 E
Tengiz, Ozero, *Kazakstan* 26 D7 50 30N 69 0 E
Tenino, *U.S.A.* 84 D4 46 51N 122 51W
Tenkasi, *India* 40 Q10 8 55N 77 20 E
Tenke, *Katanga, Dem. Rep. of the Congo* 55 E2 11 22S 26 40 E
Tenke, *Katanga, Dem. Rep. of the Congo* 55 E2 10 32S 26 7 E
Tennant Creek, *Australia* 62 B1 19 30S 134 15 E
Tennessee □, *U.S.A.* 77 H2 36 0N 86 30W
Tennessee →, *U.S.A.* 76 G1 37 4N 88 34W
Teno, Pta. de, *Canary Is.* 22 F3 28 21N 16 55W
Tenom, *Malaysia* 36 C5 5 4N 115 57 E
Tenosique, *Mexico* 87 D6 17 30N 91 24W
Tenryū-Gawa →, *Japan* 31 G8 35 39N 137 48 E
Tenterden, *U.K.* 11 F8 51 4N 0 42 E
Tenterfield, *Australia* 63 D5 29 0S 152 0 E
Teófilo Otoni, *Brazil* 93 G10 17 50S 41 30W
Tepa, *Indonesia* 37 F7 7 52S 129 31 E
Tepalcatepec →, *Mexico* 86 D4 18 35N 101 59W
Tepehuanes, *Mexico* 86 B3 25 21N 105 44W
Tepetongo, *Mexico* 86 C4 22 28N 103 9W
Tepic, *Mexico* 86 C4 21 30N 104 54W
Teplice, *Czech Rep.* 16 C7 50 40N 13 48 E
Tepoca, C., *Mexico* 86 A2 30 20N 112 25W
Tequila, *Mexico* 86 C4 20 54N 103 47W
Ter →, *Spain* 19 A7 42 2N 3 12 E
Ter Apel, *Neths.* 15 B7 52 53N 7 5 E
Teraina, *Kiribati* 65 G11 4 43N 160 25W
Téramo, *Italy* 20 C5 42 39N 13 42 E
Terang, *Australia* 63 F3 38 15S 142 55 E
Tercero →, *Argentina* 94 C3 32 58S 61 47W
Terebovlya, *Ukraine* 17 D13 49 18N 25 44 E
Terek →, *Russia* 25 F8 44 0N 47 30 E
Teresina, *Brazil* 93 E10 5 9S 42 45W
Terewah, L., *Australia* 63 D4 29 52S 147 35 E
Teridgerie Cr. →, *Australia* 63 E4 30 25S 148 50 E
Termez = Termiz, *Uzbekistan* 26 F7 37 15N 67 15 E
Términi Imerese, *Italy* 20 F5 37 59N 13 42 E
Términos, L. de, *Mexico* 87 D6 18 35N 91 30W
Termiz, *Uzbekistan* 26 F7 37 15N 67 15 E
Térmoli, *Italy* 20 C6 42 0N 15 0 E
Ternate, *Indonesia* 37 D7 0 45N 127 25 E
Terneuzen, *Neths.* 15 C3 51 20N 3 50 E
Terney, *Russia* 27 E14 45 3N 136 37 E
Terni, *Italy* 20 C5 42 34N 12 37 E
Ternopil, *Ukraine* 17 D13 49 30N 25 40 E
Ternopol = Ternopil, *Ukraine* 17 D13 49 30N 25 40 E
Terowie, *Australia* 63 E2 33 8S 138 55 E
Terra Bella, *U.S.A.* 85 K7 35 58N 119 3W
Terra Nova Nat. Park, *Canada* 71 C9 48 33N 53 55W
Terrace, *Canada* 72 C3 54 30N 128 35W
Terrace Bay, *Canada* 70 C2 48 47N 87 5W
Terracina, *Italy* 20 D5 41 17N 13 15 E
Terralba, *Italy* 20 E3 39 43N 8 39 E
Terranova = Ólbia, *Italy* 20 D3 40 55N 9 31 E
Terrassa, *Spain* 19 B7 41 34N 2 1 E
Terre Haute, *U.S.A.* 76 F2 39 28N 87 25W
Terrebonne B., *U.S.A.* 81 L9 29 5N 90 35W
Terrell, *U.S.A.* 81 J6 32 44N 96 17W
Terrenceville, *Canada* 71 C9 47 40N 54 44W
Terry, *U.S.A.* 80 B2 46 47N 105 19W
Terryville, *U.S.A.* 79 E11 41 41N 73 3W
Terschelling, *Neths.* 15 A5 53 25N 5 20 E
Teruel, *Spain* 19 B5 40 22N 1 8W
Tervola, *Finland* 8 C21 66 6N 24 49 E
Teryaweyna L., *Australia* 63 E3 32 18S 143 22 E
Teshio, *Japan* 30 B10 44 53N 141 44 E
Teshio-Gawa →, *Japan* 30 B10 44 53N 141 45 E
Tesiyn Gol →, *Mongolia* 32 A4 50 40N 93 20 E
Teslin, *Canada* 72 A2 60 10N 132 43W
Teslin →, *Canada* 72 A2 61 34N 134 35W
Teslin L., *Canada* 72 A2 60 15N 132 57W
Tessalit, *Mali* 50 D6 20 12N 1 0 E
Test →, *U.K.* 11 G6 50 56N 1 29W
Testigos, Is. Las, *Venezuela* 89 D7 11 23N 63 7W
Tetachuck L., *Canada* 72 C3 53 18N 125 55W
Tetas, Pta., *Chile* 94 A1 23 31S 70 38W
Tete, *Mozam.* 55 F3 16 13S 33 33 E
Tete □, *Mozam.* 55 F3 15 15S 32 40 E
Teterev →, *Ukraine* 17 C16 51 1N 30 5 E
Teteven, *Bulgaria* 21 C11 42 58N 24 17 E
Tethul →, *Canada* 72 A6 60 35N 112 12W
Tetiyev, *Ukraine* 17 D15 49 22N 29 38 E
Teton →, *U.S.A.* 82 C8 47 56N 110 31W
Tétouan, *Morocco* 50 A4 35 35N 5 21W
Tetovo, *Macedonia* 21 C9 42 1N 20 59 E
Teuco →, *Argentina* 94 B3 25 35S 60 11W
Teulon, *Canada* 73 C9 50 23N 97 16W
Teun, *Indonesia* 37 F7 6 59S 129 8 E
Teutoburger Wald, *Germany* 16 B5 52 5N 8 22 E
Tevere →, *Italy* 20 D5 41 44N 12 14 E
Teverya, *Israel* 47 C4 32 47N 35 32 E
Teviot →, *U.K.* 12 F6 55 29N 2 38W
Tewantin, *Australia* 63 D5 26 27S 153 3 E
Tewkesbury, *U.K.* 11 F5 51 59N 2 9W
Texada I., *Canada* 72 D4 49 40N 124 25W
Texarkana, *Ark., U.S.A.* 81 J8 33 26N 94 2W
Texarkana, *Tex., U.S.A.* 81 J7 33 26N 94 3W
Texas, *Australia* 63 D5 28 49S 151 9 E
Texas □, *U.S.A.* 81 K5 31 40N 98 30W
Texas City, *U.S.A.* 81 L7 29 24N 94 54W
Texel, *Neths.* 15 A4 53 5N 4 50 E
Texline, *U.S.A.* 81 G3 36 23N 103 2W
Texoma, L., *U.S.A.* 81 J6 33 50N 96 34W
Tezin, *Afghan.* 42 B3 34 24N 69 30 E
Teziutlán, *Mexico* 87 D5 19 50N 97 22W
Tezpur, *India* 41 F18 26 40N 92 45 E
Tezzeron L., *Canada* 72 C4 54 43N 124 30W
Tha-anne →, *Canada* 73 A10 60 31N 94 37W
Tha Deua, *Laos* 38 D4 17 57N 102 53 E
Tha Deua, *Laos* 38 C3 19 26N 101 50 E
Tha Pla, *Thailand* 38 D3 17 48N 100 32 E
Tha Rua, *Thailand* 38 E3 14 34N 100 44 E
Tha Sala, *Thailand* 39 H2 8 40N 99 56 E

Tha Song Yang

Tha Song Yang, *Thailand* 38 D1 17 34N 97 55 E
Thaba Putsoa, *Lesotho* 57 D4 29 45S 28 0 E
Thabana Ntlenyana, *Lesotho* 57 D4 29 30S 29 16 E
Thabazimbi, *S. Africa* 57 C4 24 40S 27 21 E
Thādiq, *Si. Arabia* 44 E5 25 18N 45 52 E
Thai Muang, *Thailand* 39 H2 8 24N 98 16 E
Thailand ■, *Asia* 38 E4 16 0N 102 0 E
Thailand, G. of, *Asia* 39 G3 11 30N 101 0 E
Thakhek, *Laos* 38 D5 17 25N 104 45 E
Thal, *Pakistan* 42 C4 33 28N 70 33 E
Thal Desert, *Pakistan* 42 D4 31 10N 71 30 E
Thala La, *Burma* 41 E20 28 25N 97 23 E
Thalabarivat, *Cambodia* 38 F5 13 33N 105 57 E
Thallon, *Australia* 63 D4 28 39S 148 49 E
Thames, *N.Z.* 59 G5 37 7S 175 34 E
Thames →, *Canada* 78 D2 42 20N 82 25W
Thames →, *U.K.* 11 F8 51 29N 0 34 E
Thames →, *U.S.A.* 79 E12 41 18N 72 5W
Thames Estuary, *U.K.* 11 F8 51 29N 0 52 E
Thamesford, *Canada* 78 C4 43 4N 81 0W
Thamesville, *Canada* 78 D3 42 33N 81 59W
Than, *India* 42 H4 22 34N 71 11 E
Than Uyen, *Vietnam* 38 B4 22 0N 103 54 E
Thana Gazi, *India* 42 F7 27 25N 76 19 E
Thandla, *India* 42 H6 23 0N 74 34 E
Thane, *India* 40 K8 19 12N 72 59 E
Thanesar, *India* 42 D7 30 1N 76 52 E
Thanet, I. of, *U.K.* 11 F9 51 21N 1 20 E
Thangool, *Australia* 62 C5 24 38S 150 42 E
Thanh Hoa, *Vietnam* 38 C5 19 48N 105 46 E
Thanh Hung, *Vietnam* 39 H5 9 55N 105 43 E
Thanh Pho Ho Chi Minh, *Vietnam* 39 G6 10 58N 106 40 E
Thanh Thuy, *Vietnam* 38 A5 22 55N 104 51 E
Thanjavur, *India* 40 P11 10 48N 79 12 E
Thano Bula Khan, *Pakistan* 42 G2 25 22N 67 50 E
Thaolinta L., *Canada* 73 A9 61 30N 96 25W
Thap Sakae, *Thailand* 39 G2 11 30N 99 37 E
Thap Than, *Thailand* 38 E2 15 27N 99 54 E
Thar Desert, *India* 42 F5 28 0N 72 0 E
Tharad, *India* 42 G4 24 30N 71 44 E
Thargomindah, *Australia* 63 D3 27 58S 143 46 E
Tharrawaddy, *Burma* 41 L19 17 38N 95 48 E
Tharthār, Mileh, *Iraq* 44 C4 34 0N 43 15 E
Tharthār, W. ath →, *Iraq* 44 C4 33 59N 43 12 E
Thásos, *Greece* 21 D11 40 40N 24 40 E
Thatcher, *Ariz., U.S.A.* 83 K9 32 51N 109 46W
Thatcher, *Colo., U.S.A.* 81 G2 37 33N 104 7W
Thaton, *Burma* 41 L20 16 55N 97 22 E
Thaungdut, *Burma* 41 G19 24 30N 94 40 E
Thayer, *U.S.A.* 81 G9 36 31N 91 33W
Thayetmyo, *Burma* 41 K19 19 20N 95 10 E
Thazi, *Burma* 41 J20 21 0N 96 5 E
The Alberga →, *Australia* 63 D2 27 6S 135 33 E
The Bight, *Bahamas* 89 B4 24 19N 75 24W
The Coorong, *Australia* 63 F2 35 50S 139 20 E
The Dalles, *U.S.A.* 82 D3 45 36N 121 10W
The English Company's Is., *Australia* 62 A2 11 50S 136 32 E
The Frome →, *Australia* 63 D2 29 8S 137 54 E
The Great Divide = Great Dividing Ra., *Australia* 62 C4 23 0S 146 0 E
The Hague = 's-Gravenhage, *Neths.* 15 B4 52 7N 4 17 E
The Hamilton →, *Australia* 63 D2 26 40S 135 19 E
The Macumba →, *Australia* 63 D2 27 52S 137 12 E
The Neales →, *Australia* 63 D2 28 8S 136 47 E
The Officer →, *Australia* 61 E5 27 46S 132 30 E
The Pas, *Canada* 73 C8 53 45N 101 15W
The Range, *Zimbabwe* 55 F3 19 2S 31 2 E
The Rock, *Australia* 63 F4 35 15S 147 2 E
The Salt L., *Australia* 63 E3 30 6S 142 8 E
The Sandheads, *India* 43 J13 21 10N 88 20 E
The Stevenson →, *Australia* 63 D2 27 6S 135 33 E
The Warburton →, *Australia* 63 D2 28 4S 137 28 E
The Woodlands, *U.S.A.* 81 K7 30 9N 95 27W
Thebes = Thívai, *Greece* 21 E10 38 19N 23 19 E
Thebes, *Egypt* 51 C12 25 40N 32 35 E
Thedford, *Canada* 78 C3 43 9N 81 51W
Thedford, *U.S.A.* 80 E4 41 59N 100 35W
Theebine, *Australia* 63 D5 25 57S 152 34 E
Thekulthili L., *Canada* 73 A7 61 3N 110 0W
Thelon →, *Canada* 73 A8 62 35N 104 3W
Theodore, *Australia* 62 C5 24 55S 150 3 E
Theodore, *Canada* 73 C8 51 26N 102 55W
Theodore, *U.S.A.* 77 K1 30 33N 88 10W
Theodore Roosevelt National Memorial Park, *U.S.A.* 80 B3 47 0N 103 25W
Theodore Roosevelt Res., *U.S.A.* 83 K8 33 46N 111 0W
Thepha, *Thailand* 39 J3 6 52N 100 58 E
Theresa, *U.S.A.* 79 B9 44 13N 75 48W
Thermaïkós Kólpos, *Greece* 21 D10 40 15N 22 45 E
Thermopolis, *U.S.A.* 82 E9 43 39N 108 13W
Thermopylae P., *Greece* 21 E10 38 48N 22 35 E
Thessalon, *Canada* 70 C3 46 20N 83 30W
Thessaloníki, *Greece* 21 D10 40 38N 22 58 E
Thessaloniki, Gulf of = Thermaïkós Kólpos, *Greece* 21 D10 40 15N 22 45 E
Thetford, *U.K.* 11 E8 52 25N 0 45 E
Thetford Mines, *Canada* 71 C5 46 8N 71 18W
Theun →, *Laos* 38 C5 18 19N 104 0 E
Theunissen, *S. Africa* 56 D4 28 26S 26 43 E
Thevenard, *Australia* 63 E1 32 9S 133 38 E
Thibodaux, *U.S.A.* 81 L9 29 48N 90 49W
Thicket Portage, *Canada* 73 B9 55 19N 97 42W
Thief River Falls, *U.S.A.* 80 A6 48 7N 96 10W
Thiel Mts., *Antarctica* 5 E16 85 15S 91 0W
Thiers, *France* 18 D5 45 52N 3 33 E
Thiès, *Senegal* 50 F2 14 50N 16 51W
Thika, *Kenya* 54 C4 1 1S 37 5 E
Thikombia, *Fiji* 59 B9 15 44S 179 55W
Thimphu, *Bhutan* 41 F16 27 31N 89 45 E
þingvallavatn, *Iceland* 8 D3 64 11N 21 9W
Thionville, *France* 18 B7 49 20N 6 10 E
Thíra, *Greece* 21 F11 36 23N 25 27 E
Third Cataract, *Sudan* 51 E12 19 49N 30 19 E
Thirsk, *U.K.* 10 C6 54 14N 1 19W
Thisted, *Denmark* 9 H13 56 58N 8 40 E
Thistle I., *Australia* 63 F2 35 0S 136 8 E
Thívai, *Greece* 21 E10 38 19N 23 19 E
þjórsá →, *Iceland* 8 E3 63 47N 20 48W
Thlewiaza →, *Man., Canada* 73 B8 59 43N 100 5W
Thlewiaza →, *N.W.T., Canada* 73 A10 60 29N 94 40W
Thmar Puok, *Cambodia* 38 F4 13 57N 103 4 E
Tho Vinh, *Vietnam* 38 C5 19 16N 105 42 E
Thoa →, *Canada* 73 A7 60 31N 109 47W
Thoen, *Thailand* 38 D2 17 43N 99 12 E
Thoeng, *Thailand* 38 C3 19 41N 100 12 E
Thohoyandou, *S. Africa* 53 J6 22 58S 30 29 E
Tholdi, *Pakistan* 43 B7 35 5N 76 6 E
Thomas, *U.S.A.* 81 H5 35 45N 98 45W
Thomas, L., *Australia* 63 D2 26 4S 137 58 E
Thomaston, *U.S.A.* 77 J3 32 53N 84 20W
Thomasville, *Ala., U.S.A.* 77 K2 31 55N 87 44W
Thomasville, *Ga., U.S.A.* 77 K4 30 50N 83 59W
Thomasville, *N.C., U.S.A.* 77 H5 35 53N 80 5W
Thompson, *Canada* 73 B9 55 45N 97 52W
Thompson, *U.S.A.* 79 E9 41 52N 75 31W
Thompson →, *Canada* 72 C4 50 15N 121 24W
Thompson →, *U.S.A.* 80 F8 39 46N 93 37W
Thompson Falls, *U.S.A.* 82 C6 47 36N 115 21W
Thompson Pk., *U.S.A.* 82 F2 41 0N 123 0W
Thompson Springs, *U.S.A.* 83 G9 38 58N 109 43W
Thompsontown, *U.S.A.* 78 F7 40 33N 77 14W
Thomson, *U.S.A.* 77 J4 33 28N 82 30W
Thomson →, *Australia* 62 C3 25 11S 142 53 E
Thomson's Falls = Nyahururu, *Kenya* 54 B4 0 2N 36 27 E
þórisvatn, *Iceland* 8 D4 64 20N 18 55W
Thornaby on Tees, *U.K.* 10 C6 54 33N 1 18W
Thornbury, *Canada* 78 B4 44 34N 80 26W
Thorne, *U.K.* 10 D7 53 37N 0 57W
Thornhill, *Canada* 72 C3 54 31N 128 32W
Thorold, *Canada* 78 C5 43 7N 79 12W
þórshöfn, *Iceland* 8 C6 66 12N 15 20W
Thouin, C., *Australia* 60 D2 20 20S 118 10 E
Thousand Oaks, *U.S.A.* 85 L8 34 10N 118 50W
Thrace, *Turkey* 21 D12 41 0N 27 0 E
Three Forks, *U.S.A.* 82 D8 45 54N 111 33W
Three Hills, *Canada* 72 C6 51 43N 113 15W
Three Hummock I., *Australia* 62 G3 40 25S 144 55 E
Three Points, C., *Ghana* 50 H5 4 42N 2 6W
Three Rivers, *Calif., U.S.A.* 84 J8 36 26N 118 54W
Three Rivers, *Tex., U.S.A.* 81 L5 28 28N 98 11W
Three Sisters, *U.S.A.* 82 D3 44 4N 121 51W
Three Springs, *Australia* 61 E2 29 32S 115 45 E
Throssell, L., *Australia* 61 E3 27 33S 124 10 E
Throssell Ra., *Australia* 60 D3 22 3S 121 43 E
Thuan Hoa, *Vietnam* 39 H5 8 58N 105 30 E
Thubun Lakes, *Canada* 73 A6 61 30N 112 0W
Thuin, *Belgium* 15 D4 50 20N 4 17 E
Thule, *Greenland* 4 B4 77 40N 69 0W
Thun, *Switz.* 18 C7 46 45N 7 38 E
Thunder B., *U.S.A.* 78 B1 45 0N 83 20W
Thunder Bay, *Canada* 70 C2 48 20N 89 15W
Thung Song, *Thailand* 39 H2 8 10N 99 40 E
Thunkar, *Bhutan* 41 F17 27 55N 91 0 E
Thuong Tra, *Vietnam* 38 D6 16 2N 107 42 E
Thüringer Wald, *Germany* 16 C6 50 35N 11 0 E
Thurles, *Ireland* 13 D4 52 41N 7 49W
Thurrock □, *U.K.* 11 F8 51 31N 0 23 E
Thursday I., *Australia* 62 A3 10 30S 142 3 E
Thurso, *Canada* 70 C4 45 36N 75 15W
Thurso, *U.K.* 12 C5 58 36N 3 32W
Thurso →, *U.K.* 12 C5 58 36N 3 32W
Thurston I., *Antarctica* 5 D16 72 0S 100 0W
Thutade L., *Canada* 72 B3 57 0N 126 55W
Thyolo, *Malawi* 55 F4 16 7S 35 5 E
Thysville = Mbanza Ngungu, *Dem. Rep. of the Congo* 52 F2 5 12S 14 53 E
Ti Tree, *Australia* 62 C1 22 5S 133 22 E
Tian Shan, *Asia* 32 B3 42 0N 76 0 E
Tianjin, *China* 35 E9 39 8N 117 10 E
Tianshui, *China* 34 G3 34 32N 105 40 E
Tianzhen, *China* 34 D8 40 24N 114 5 E
Tianzhuangtai, *China* 35 D12 40 43N 122 5 E
Tiaret, *Algeria* 50 A6 35 20N 1 21 E
Tibagi, *Brazil* 95 A5 24 30S 50 24W
Tibagi →, *Brazil* 95 A5 22 47S 51 1W
Tiber = Tevere →, *Italy* 20 D5 41 44N 12 14 E
Tiberias = Teverya, *Israel* 47 C4 32 47N 35 32 E
Tiberias, L. = Yam Kinneret, *Israel* 47 C4 32 45N 35 35 E
Tibesti, *Chad* 51 D9 21 0N 17 30 E
Tibet = Xizang Zizhiqu □, *China* 32 C3 32 0N 88 0 E
Tibet, Plateau of, *Asia* 28 F12 32 0N 86 0 E
Tibnī, *Syria* 44 C3 35 36N 39 50 E
Tibooburra, *Australia* 63 D3 29 26S 142 1 E
Tiburón, I., *Mexico* 86 B2 29 0N 112 30W
Ticino →, *Italy* 18 D8 45 9N 9 14 E
Ticonderoga, *U.S.A.* 79 C11 43 51N 73 26W
Ticul, *Mexico* 87 C7 20 20N 89 31W
Tidaholm, *Sweden* 9 G15 58 12N 13 58 E
Tiddim, *Burma* 41 H18 23 28N 93 45 E
Tidioute, *U.S.A.* 78 E5 41 41N 79 24W
Tidjikja, *Mauritania* 50 E3 18 29N 11 35W
Tidore, *Indonesia* 37 D7 0 40N 127 25 E
Tiel, *Neths.* 15 C5 51 53N 5 26 E
Tieling, *China* 35 C12 42 20N 123 55 E
Tielt, *Belgium* 15 C3 51 0N 3 20 E
Tien Shan = Tian Shan, *Asia* 32 B3 42 0N 76 0 E
Tien-tsin = Tianjin, *China* 35 E9 39 8N 117 10 E
Tien Yen, *Vietnam* 38 B6 21 20N 107 24 E
T'ienching = Tianjin, *China* 35 E9 39 8N 117 10 E
Tienen, *Belgium* 15 D4 50 48N 4 57 E
Tientsin = Tianjin, *China* 35 E9 39 8N 117 10 E
Tieri, *Australia* 62 C4 23 2S 148 21 E
Tierra Amarilla, *Chile* 94 B1 27 28S 70 18W
Tierra Amarilla, *U.S.A.* 83 H10 36 42N 106 33W
Tierra Colorada, *Mexico* 87 D5 17 10N 99 35W
Tierra de Campos, *Spain* 19 A3 42 10N 4 50W
Tierra del Fuego, I. Gr. de, *Argentina* 96 G3 54 0S 69 0W
Tiétar →, *Spain* 19 C3 39 50N 6 1W
Tieté →, *Brazil* 95 A5 20 40S 51 35W
Tiffin, *U.S.A.* 76 E4 41 7N 83 11W
Tiflis = Tbilisi, *Georgia* 25 F7 41 43N 44 50 E
Tifton, *U.S.A.* 77 K4 31 27N 83 31W
Tifu, *Indonesia* 37 E7 3 39S 126 24 E
Tighina, *Moldova* 17 E15 46 50N 29 30 E
Tigil, *Russia* 27 D16 57 49N 158 40 E
Tignish, *Canada* 71 C7 46 58N 64 2W
Tigre →, *Peru* 92 D4 4 30S 74 10W
Tigre →, *Venezuela* 92 B6 9 20N 62 30W
Tigris = Dijlah, Nahr →, *Asia* 44 D5 31 0N 47 25 E
Tigyaing, *Burma* 41 H20 23 45N 96 10 E
Tijara, *India* 42 F7 27 56N 76 31 E
Tijuana, *Mexico* 85 N9 32 30N 117 10W
Tikal, *Guatemala* 88 C2 17 13N 89 24W
Tikamgarh, *India* 43 G8 24 44N 78 50 E
Tikhoretsk, *Russia* 25 E7 45 56N 40 5 E
Tikhvin, *Russia* 24 C5 59 35N 33 30 E
Tikrīt, *Iraq* 44 C4 34 35N 43 37 E
Tiksi, *Russia* 27 B13 71 40N 128 45 E
Tilamuta, *Indonesia* 37 D6 0 32N 122 23 E
Tilburg, *Neths.* 15 C5 51 31N 5 6 E
Tilbury, *Canada* 78 D2 42 17N 82 23W
Tilbury, *U.K.* 11 F8 51 27N 0 22 E
Tilcara, *Argentina* 94 A2 23 36S 65 23W
Tilden, *U.S.A.* 80 D6 42 3N 97 50W
Tilhar, *India* 43 F8 28 0N 79 45 E
Tilichiki, *Russia* 27 C17 60 27N 166 5 E
Tilissos, *Greece* 23 D7 35 20N 25 1 E
Till →, *U.K.* 10 B5 55 41N 2 13W
Tillamook, *U.S.A.* 82 D2 45 27N 123 51W
Tillsonburg, *Canada* 78 D4 42 53N 80 44W
Tillyeria □, *Cyprus* 23 D11 35 6N 32 40 E
Tílos, *Greece* 21 F12 36 27N 27 27 E
Tilpa, *Australia* 63 E3 30 57S 144 24 E
Tilsit = Sovetsk, *Russia* 9 J19 55 6N 21 50 E
Tilt →, *U.K.* 12 E5 56 46N 3 51W
Tilton, *U.S.A.* 79 C13 43 27N 71 36W
Tiltonsville, *U.S.A.* 78 F4 40 10N 80 41W
Timagami, L., *Canada* 70 C3 47 0N 80 10W
Timanskiy Kryazh, *Russia* 24 A9 65 58N 50 5 E
Timaru, *N.Z.* 59 L3 44 23S 171 14 E
Timau, *Kenya* 54 B4 0 4N 37 15 E
Timbákion, *Greece* 23 D6 35 4N 24 45 E
Timber Creek, *Australia* 60 C5 15 40S 130 29 E
Timber Lake, *U.S.A.* 80 C4 45 26N 101 5W
Timber Mt., *U.S.A.* 84 H10 37 6N 116 28W
Timbuktu = Tombouctou, *Mali* 50 E5 16 50N 3 0W
Timi, *Cyprus* 23 E11 34 44N 32 31 E
Timimoun, *Algeria* 50 C6 29 14N 0 16 E
Timişoara, *Romania* 17 F11 45 43N 21 15 E
Timmins, *Canada* 70 C3 48 28N 81 25W
Timok →, *Serbia, Yug.* 21 B10 44 10N 22 40 E
Timor, *Indonesia* 37 F7 9 0S 125 0 E
Timor Sea, *Ind. Oc.* 60 B4 12 0S 127 0 E
Timor Timur = East Timor □, *Indonesia* 37 F7 9 0S 125 0 E
Tin Can Bay, *Australia* 63 D5 25 56S 153 0 E
Tin Mt., *U.S.A.* 84 J9 36 50N 117 10W
Tinaca Pt., *Phil.* 37 C7 5 30N 125 25 E
Tinajo, *Canary Is.* 22 E6 29 4N 13 42W
Tindal, *Australia* 60 B5 14 31S 132 22 E
Tindouf, *Algeria* 50 C4 27 42N 8 10W
Tinggi, Pulau, *Malaysia* 39 L5 2 18N 104 7 E
Tingo Maria, *Peru* 92 E3 9 10S 75 54W
Tingrela, *Ivory C.* 50 F4 10 27N 6 25W
Tinh Bien, *Vietnam* 39 G5 10 36N 104 57 E
Tinnevelly = Tirunelveli, *India* 40 Q10 8 45N 77 45 E
Tinogasta, *Argentina* 94 B2 28 5S 67 32W
Tinos, *Greece* 21 F11 37 33N 25 8 E
Tinpahar, *India* 43 G12 24 59N 87 44 E
Tintina, *Argentina* 94 B3 27 2S 62 45W
Tintinara, *Australia* 63 F3 35 48S 140 2 E
Tioga, *N. Dak., U.S.A.* 80 A3 48 23N 102 56W
Tioga, *Pa., U.S.A.* 78 E7 41 55N 77 8W
Tioman, Pulau, *Malaysia* 39 L5 2 50N 104 10 E
Tionesta, *U.S.A.* 78 E5 41 30N 79 28W
Tipongpani, *India* 41 F19 27 20N 95 55 E
Tipperary, *Ireland* 13 D3 52 28N 8 10W
Tipperary □, *Ireland* 13 D4 52 37N 7 55W
Tipton, *Calif., U.S.A.* 84 J7 36 4N 119 19W
Tipton, *Iowa, U.S.A.* 80 E9 41 46N 91 8W
Tipton Mt., *U.S.A.* 85 K12 35 32N 114 12W
Tiptonville, *U.S.A.* 81 G10 36 23N 89 29W
Tīrān, *Iran* 45 C6 32 45N 51 8 E
Tirana, *Albania* 21 D8 41 18N 19 49 E
Tiranë = Tirana, *Albania* 21 D8 41 18N 19 49 E
Tiraspol, *Moldova* 17 E15 46 55N 29 35 E
Tire, *Turkey* 21 E12 38 5N 27 45 E
Tirebolu, *Turkey* 25 F6 40 58N 38 45 E
Tiree, *U.K.* 12 E2 56 31N 6 55W
Tiree, Passage of, *U.K.* 12 E2 56 30N 6 30W
Tîrgovişte = Târgovişte, *Romania* 17 F13 44 55N 25 27 E
Tîrgu-Jiu = Târgu-Jiu, *Romania* 17 F12 45 5N 23 19 E
Tîrgu Mureş = Târgu Mureş, *Romania* 17 E13 46 31N 24 38 E
Tirich Mir, *Pakistan* 40 A7 36 15N 71 55 E
Tirnavos, *Greece* 21 E10 39 45N 22 18 E
Tirodi, *India* 40 J11 21 40N 79 44 E
Tirol □, *Austria* 16 E6 47 3N 10 43 E
Tirso →, *Italy* 20 E3 39 53N 8 32 E
Tiruchchirappalli, *India* 40 P11 10 45N 78 45 E
Tirunelveli, *India* 40 Q10 8 45N 77 45 E
Tirupati, *India* 40 N11 13 39N 79 25 E
Tiruppur, *India* 40 P10 11 5N 77 22 E
Tiruvannamalai, *India* 40 N11 12 15N 79 5 E
Tisa, *India* 42 C7 32 50N 76 9 E
Tisa →, *Serbia, Yug.* 21 B9 45 15N 20 17 E
Tisdale, *Canada* 73 C8 52 50N 104 0W
Tishomingo, *U.S.A.* 81 H6 34 14N 96 41W
Tisza = Tisa →, *Serbia, Yug.* 21 B9 45 15N 20 17 E
Tit-Ary, *Russia* 27 B13 71 55N 127 2 E
Tithwal, *Pakistan* 43 B5 34 21N 73 50 E
Titicaca, L., *S. Amer.* 92 G5 15 30S 69 30W
Titograd = Podgorica, *Montenegro, Yug.* 21 C8 42 30N 19 19 E
Titule, *Dem. Rep. of the Congo* 54 B2 3 15N 25 31 E
Titusville, *Fla., U.S.A.* 77 L5 28 37N 80 49W
Titusville, *Pa., U.S.A.* 78 E5 41 38N 79 41W
Tivaouane, *Senegal* 50 F2 14 56N 16 45W
Tiverton, *U.K.* 11 G4 50 54N 3 29W
Tivoli, *Italy* 20 D5 41 58N 12 45 E
Tizi-Ouzou, *Algeria* 50 A6 36 42N 4 3 E
Tizimín, *Mexico* 87 C7 21 0N 88 1W
Tjeggelvas, *Sweden* 8 C17 66 37N 17 45 E
Tjirebon = Cirebon, *Indonesia* 37 G13 6 45S 108 32 E
Tjörn, *Sweden* 9 G14 58 0N 11 35 E
Tlacotalpan, *Mexico* 87 D5 18 37N 95 40W
Tlahualilo, *Mexico* 86 B4 26 20N 103 30W
Tlaquepaque, *Mexico* 86 C4 20 39N 103 19W
Tlaxcala, *Mexico* 87 D5 19 20N 98 14W
Tlaxcala □, *Mexico* 87 D5 19 30N 98 20W
Tlaxiaco, *Mexico* 87 D5 17 18N 97 40W
Tlemcen, *Algeria* 50 B5 34 52N 1 21W
To Bong, *Vietnam* 38 F7 12 45N 109 16 E
Toad →, *Canada* 72 B4 59 25N 124 57W
Toad River, *Canada* 72 B3 58 51N 125 14W
Toamasina, *Madag.* 57 B8 18 10S 49 25 E
Toamasina □, *Madag.* 57 B8 18 0S 49 0 E
Toay, *Argentina* 94 D3 36 43S 64 38W
Toba, *Japan* 31 G8 34 30N 136 51 E
Toba, Danau, *Indonesia* 36 D1 2 30N 97 30 E
Toba Kakar, *Pakistan* 42 D3 31 30N 69 0 E
Toba Tek Singh, *Pakistan* 42 D5 30 55N 72 25 E
Tobago, *W. Indies* 89 D7 11 10N 60 30W
Tobelo, *Indonesia* 37 D7 1 45N 127 56 E
Tobermory, *Canada* 78 A3 45 12N 81 40W
Tobermory, *U.K.* 12 E2 56 38N 6 5W
Tobi, *Pac. Oc.* 37 D8 2 40N 131 10 E
Tobin, *U.S.A.* 84 F5 39 55N 121 19W
Tobin, L., *Australia* 60 D4 21 45S 125 49 E
Tobin L., *Canada* 73 C8 53 35N 103 30W
Toboali, *Indonesia* 36 E3 3 0S 106 25 E
Tobol →, *Russia* 26 D7 58 10N 68 12 E
Toboli, *Indonesia* 37 E6 0 38S 120 5 E
Tobolsk, *Russia* 26 D7 58 15N 68 10 E
Tobruk = Tubruq, *Libya* 51 B10 32 7N 23 55 E
Tobyhanna, *U.S.A.* 79 E9 41 11N 75 25W
Tobyl = Tobol →, *Russia* 26 D7 58 10N 68 12 E
Tocantinópolis, *Brazil* 93 E9 6 20S 47 25W
Tocantins □, *Brazil* 93 F9 10 0S 48 0W
Tocantins →, *Brazil* 93 D9 1 45S 49 10W
Toccoa, *U.S.A.* 77 H4 34 35N 83 19W
Tochi →, *Pakistan* 42 C4 32 49N 70 41 E
Tochigi, *Japan* 31 F9 36 25N 139 45 E
Tochigi □, *Japan* 31 F9 36 45N 139 45 E
Toconao, *Chile* 94 A2 23 11S 68 1W
Tocopilla, *Chile* 94 A1 22 5S 70 10W
Tocumwal, *Australia* 63 F4 35 51S 145 31 E
Tocuyo →, *Venezuela* 92 A5 11 3N 68 23W
Todd →, *Australia* 62 C2 24 52S 135 48 E
Todeli, *Indonesia* 37 E6 1 38S 124 34 E
Todenyang, *Kenya* 54 B4 4 35N 35 56 E
Todgarh, *India* 42 G5 25 42N 73 58 E
Todos os Santos, B. de, *Brazil* 93 F11 12 48S 38 38W
Todos Santos, *Mexico* 86 C2 23 27N 110 13W
Toe Hd., *U.K.* 12 D1 57 50N 7 8W
Tofield, *Canada* 72 C6 53 25N 112 40W
Tofino, *Canada* 72 D3 49 11N 125 55W
Tofua, *Tonga* 59 D11 19 45S 175 5W
Tōgane, *Japan* 31 G10 35 33N 140 22 E
Togian, Kepulauan, *Indonesia* 37 E6 0 20S 121 50 E
Togliatti, *Russia* 24 D8 53 32N 49 24 E
Togo ■, *W. Afr.* 50 G6 8 30N 1 35 E
Togtoh, *China* 34 D6 40 15N 111 10 E
Tōhoku □, *Japan* 30 E10 39 50N 141 45 E
Töhöm, *Mongolia* 34 B5 44 27N 108 2 E
Toinya, *Sudan* 51 G11 6 17N 29 46 E
Toiyabe Range, *U.S.A.* 82 G5 39 30N 117 0W
Tojikiston = Tajikistan ■, *Asia* 26 F8 38 30N 70 0 E
Tojo, *Indonesia* 37 E6 1 20S 121 15 E
Tōjō, *Japan* 31 G6 34 53N 133 16 E
Tok, *U.S.A.* 68 B5 63 20N 142 59W
Tok-do, *Japan* 31 F5 37 15N 131 52 E
Tokachi-Dake, *Japan* 30 C11 43 17N 142 5 E
Tokachi-Gawa →, *Japan* 30 C11 42 44N 143 42 E
Tokala, *Indonesia* 37 E6 1 30S 121 40 E
Tōkamachi, *Japan* 31 F9 37 8N 138 43 E
Tokanui, *N.Z.* 59 M2 46 34S 168 56 E
Tokara-Rettō, *Japan* 31 K4 29 37N 129 43 E
Tokarahi, *N.Z.* 59 L3 44 56S 170 39 E
Tokashiki-Shima, *Japan* 31 L3 26 11N 127 21 E
Tokat □, *Turkey* 25 F6 40 15N 36 30 E
Tŏkch'ŏn, *N. Korea* 35 E14 39 45N 126 18 E
Tokeland, *U.S.A.* 84 D3 46 42N 123 59W
Tokelau Is., *Pac. Oc.* 64 H10 9 0S 171 45W
Tokmak, *Kyrgyzstan* 26 E8 42 49N 75 15 E
Toko Ra., *Australia* 62 C2 23 5S 138 20 E
Tokoro-Gawa →, *Japan* 30 B12 44 7N 144 5 E
Tokuno-Shima, *Japan* 31 L4 27 56N 128 55 E
Tokushima, *Japan* 31 G7 34 4N 134 34 E
Tokushima □, *Japan* 31 H7 33 55N 134 0 E
Tokuyama, *Japan* 31 G5 34 3N 131 50 E
Tōkyō, *Japan* 31 G9 35 45N 139 45 E
Tolaga Bay, *N.Z.* 59 H7 38 21S 178 20 E
Tolbukhin = Dobrich, *Bulgaria* 21 C12 43 37N 27 49 E
Toledo, *Brazil* 95 A5 24 44S 53 45W
Toledo, *Spain* 19 C3 39 50N 4 2W
Toledo, *Ohio, U.S.A.* 76 E4 41 39N 83 33W
Toledo, *Oreg., U.S.A.* 82 D2 44 37N 123 56W
Toledo, *Wash., U.S.A.* 82 C2 46 26N 122 51W
Toledo, Montes de, *Spain* 19 C3 39 33N 4 20W
Toledo Bend Reservoir, *U.S.A.* 81 K8 31 11N 93 34W
Tolga, *Australia* 62 B4 17 15S 145 29 E
Toliara, *Madag.* 57 C7 23 21S 43 40 E
Toliara □, *Madag.* 57 C8 21 0S 45 0 E
Tolima, *Colombia* 92 C3 4 40N 75 19W
Tolitoli, *Indonesia* 37 D6 1 5N 120 50 E
Tollhouse, *U.S.A.* 84 H7 37 1N 119 24W
Tolo, Teluk, *Indonesia* 37 E6 2 20S 122 10 E
Toluca, *Mexico* 87 D5 19 20N 99 40W
Tom Burke, *S. Africa* 57 C4 23 5S 28 0 E
Tom Price, *Australia* 60 D2 22 40S 117 48 E
Tomah, *U.S.A.* 80 D9 43 59N 90 30W
Tomahawk, *U.S.A.* 80 C10 45 28N 89 44W
Tomakomai, *Japan* 30 C10 42 38N 141 36 E
Tomales, *U.S.A.* 84 G4 38 15N 122 53W
Tomales B., *U.S.A.* 84 G3 38 15N 123 58W
Tomar, *Portugal* 19 C1 39 36N 8 25W
Tomaszów Mazowiecki, *Poland* 17 C10 51 30N 20 2 E
Tomatlán, *Mexico* 86 D3 19 56N 105 15W
Tombador, Serra do, *Brazil* 92 F7 12 0S 58 0W
Tombigbee →, *U.S.A.* 77 K2 31 8N 87 57W
Tombouctou, *Mali* 50 E5 16 50N 3 0W
Tombstone, *U.S.A.* 83 L8 31 43N 110 4W
Tombua, *Angola* 56 B1 15 55S 11 55 E

Tukums

Tomé, *Chile* 94 D1 36 36S 72 57W
Tomelloso, *Spain* 19 C4 39 10N 3 2W
Tomini, *Indonesia* 37 D6 0 30N 120 30 E
Tomini, Teluk, *Indonesia* 37 E6 0 10S 122 0 E
Tomintoul, *U.K.* 12 D5 57 15N 3 23W
Tomkinson Ranges, *Australia* 61 E4 26 11S 129 5 E
Tommot, *Russia* 27 D13 59 4N 126 20 E
Tomnop Ta Suos, *Cambodia* 39 G5 11 20N 104 15 E
Tomo →, *Colombia* 92 B5 5 20N 67 48W
Toms Place, *U.S.A.* 84 H8 37 34N 118 41W
Toms River, *U.S.A.* 79 G10 39 58N 74 12W
Tomsk, *Russia* 26 D9 56 30N 85 5 E
Tonalá, *Mexico* 87 D6 16 8N 93 41W
Tonantins, *Brazil* 92 D5 2 45S 67 45W
Tonasket, *U.S.A.* 82 B4 48 42N 119 26W
Tonawanda, *U.S.A.* 78 D6 43 1N 78 53W
Tonbridge, *U.K.* 11 F8 51 11N 0 17 E
Tondano, *Indonesia* 37 D6 1 35N 124 54 E
Tone →, *Australia* 61 F2 34 25S 116 25 E
Tone-Gawa →, *Japan* 31 F9 35 44N 140 51 E
Tonekābon, *Iran* 45 B6 36 45N 51 12 E
Tong Xian, *China* 34 E9 39 55N 116 35 E
Tonga ■, *Pac. Oc.* 59 D11 19 50S 174 30W
Tonga Trench, *Pac. Oc.* 64 J10 18 0S 173 0W
Tongaat, *S. Africa* 57 D5 29 33S 31 9 E
Tongareva, *Cook Is.* 65 H12 9 0S 158 0W
Tongatapu, *Tonga* 59 E12 21 10S 174 0W
Tongchŏn-ni, *N. Korea* 35 E14 39 50N 127 25 E
Tongchuan, *China* 34 G5 35 6N 109 3 E
Tongeren, *Belgium* 15 D5 50 47N 5 28 E
Tongguan, *China* 34 G6 34 40N 110 25 E
Tonghua, *China* 35 D13 41 42N 125 58 E
Tongjosŏn Man, *N. Korea* 35 E15 39 30N 128 0 E
Tongking, G. of, *Asia* 32 E5 20 0N 108 0 E
Tongliao, *China* 35 C12 43 38N 122 18 E
Tongling, *China* 33 C6 30 55N 117 48 E
Tongnae, *S. Korea* 35 G15 35 12N 129 5 E
Tongobory, *Madag.* 57 C7 23 32S 44 20 E
Tongoy, *Chile* 94 C1 30 16S 71 31W
Tongres = Tongeren, *Belgium* 15 D5 50 47N 5 28 E
Tongsa Dzong, *Bhutan* 41 F17 27 31N 90 31 E
Tongue, *U.K.* 12 C4 58 29N 4 25W
Tongue →, *U.S.A.* 80 B2 46 25N 105 52W
Tongwei, *China* 34 G3 35 0N 105 5 E
Tongxin, *China* 34 F3 36 59N 105 58 E
Tongyang, *N. Korea* 35 E14 39 9N 126 53 E
Tongyu, *China* 35 B12 44 45N 123 4 E
Tonj, *Sudan* 51 G11 7 20N 28 44 E
Tonk, *India* 42 F6 26 6N 75 54 E
Tonkawa, *U.S.A.* 81 G6 36 41N 97 18W
Tonkin = Bac Phan, *Vietnam* 38 B5 22 0N 105 0 E
Tonle Sap, *Cambodia* 38 F5 13 0N 104 0 E
Tono, *Japan* 30 E10 39 19N 141 32 E
Tonopah, *U.S.A.* 83 G5 38 4N 117 14W
Tonosí, *Panama* 88 E3 7 20N 80 20W
Tons →, *Haryana, India* 42 D7 30 30N 77 39 E
Tons →, *Ut. P., India* 43 F10 26 1N 83 33 E
Tønsberg, *Norway* 9 G14 59 19N 10 25 E
Toobanna, *Australia* 62 B4 18 42S 146 9 E
Toodyay, *Australia* 61 F2 31 34S 116 28 E
Tooele, *U.S.A.* 82 F7 40 32N 112 18W
Toompine, *Australia* 63 D3 27 15S 144 19 E
Toora, *Australia* 63 F4 38 39S 146 23 E
Toora-Khem, *Russia* 27 D10 52 28N 96 17 E
Toowoomba, *Australia* 63 D5 27 32S 151 56 E
Top-ozero, *Russia* 24 A5 65 35N 32 0 E
Top Springs, *Australia* 60 C5 16 37S 131 51 E
Topaz, *U.S.A.* 84 G7 38 41N 119 30W
Topeka, *U.S.A.* 80 F7 39 3N 95 40W
Topley, *Canada* 72 C3 54 49N 126 18W
Topocalma, Pta., *Chile* 94 C1 34 10S 72 2W
Topock, *U.S.A.* 85 L12 34 46N 114 29W
Topoľčany, *Slovak Rep.* 17 D10 48 35N 18 12 E
Topolobampo, *Mexico* 86 B3 25 40N 109 4W
Toppenish, *U.S.A.* 82 C3 46 23N 120 19W
Toraka Vestale, *Madag.* 57 B7 16 20S 43 58 E
Torata, *Peru* 92 G4 17 23S 70 1W
Torbalı, *Turkey* 21 E12 38 10N 27 21 E
Torbat-e Heydārīyeh, *Iran* 45 C8 35 15N 59 12 E
Torbat-e Jām, *Iran* 45 C9 35 16N 60 35 E
Torbay, *Canada* 71 C9 47 40N 52 42W
Torbay □, *U.K.* 11 G4 50 26N 3 31W
Tordesillas, *Spain* 19 B3 41 30N 5 0W
Torfaen □, *U.K.* 11 F4 51 43N 3 3W
Torgau, *Germany* 16 C7 51 34N 13 0 E
Torhout, *Belgium* 15 C3 51 5N 3 7 E
Tori-Shima, *Japan* 31 J10 30 29N 140 19 E
Torin, *Mexico* 86 B2 27 33N 110 15W
Torino, *Italy* 18 D7 45 3N 7 40 E
Torit, *Sudan* 51 H12 4 27N 32 31 E
Torkamān, *Iran* 44 B5 37 35N 47 23 E
Tormes →, *Spain* 19 B2 41 18N 6 29W
Tornado Mt., *Canada* 72 D6 49 55N 114 40W
Torne älv →, *Sweden* 8 D21 65 50N 24 12 E
Torneå = Tornio, *Finland* 8 D21 65 50N 24 12 E
Torneträsk, *Sweden* 8 B18 68 24N 19 15 E
Tornio, *Finland* 8 D21 65 50N 24 12 E
Tornionjoki →, *Finland* 8 D21 65 50N 24 12 E
Tornquist, *Argentina* 94 D3 38 8S 62 15W
Toro, *Spain* 22 B11 39 59N 4 8 E
Toro, Cerro del, *Chile* 94 B2 29 10S 69 50W
Toro Pk., *U.S.A.* 85 M10 33 34N 116 24W
Toroníios Kólpos, *Greece* 21 D10 40 5N 23 30 E
Toronto, *Canada* 78 C5 43 39N 79 20W
Toronto, *U.S.A.* 78 F4 40 28N 80 36W
Toropets, *Russia* 24 C5 56 30N 31 40 E
Tororo, *Uganda* 54 B3 0 45N 34 12 E
Toros Dağlan, *Turkey* 25 G5 37 0N 32 30 E
Torpa, *India* 43 H11 22 57N 85 6 E
Torquay, *Australia* 63 F3 38 20S 144 19 E
Torquay, *U.K.* 11 G4 50 27N 3 32W
Torrance, *U.S.A.* 85 M8 33 50N 118 19W
Torre de Moncorvo, *Portugal* 19 B2 41 12N 7 8W
Torre del Greco, *Italy* 20 D6 40 47N 14 22 E
Torrejón de Ardoz, *Spain* 19 B4 40 27N 3 29W
Torrelavega, *Spain* 19 A3 43 20N 4 5W
Torremolinos, *Spain* 19 D3 36 38N 4 30W
Torrens, L., *Australia* 63 E2 31 0S 137 50 E
Torrens Cr. →, *Australia* 62 C4 22 23S 145 9 E
Torrens Creek, *Australia* 62 C4 20 48S 145 3 E
Torrent, *Spain* 19 C5 39 27N 0 28W
Torreón, *Mexico* 86 B4 25 33N 103 26W
Torres, *Brazil* 95 B5 29 21S 49 44W
Torres, *Mexico* 86 B2 28 46N 110 47W
Torres Strait, *Australia* 64 H6 9 50S 142 20 E
Torres Vedras, *Portugal* 19 C1 39 5N 9 15W
Torrevieja, *Spain* 19 D5 37 59N 0 42W
Torrey, *U.S.A.* 83 G8 38 18N 111 25W
Torridge →, *U.K.* 11 G3 51 0N 4 13W
Torridon, L., *U.K.* 12 D3 57 35N 5 50W
Torrington, *Conn., U.S.A.* 79 E11 41 48N 73 7W
Torrington, *Wyo., U.S.A.* 80 D2 42 4N 104 11W
Tórshavn, *Færoe Is.* 8 E9 62 5N 6 56W
Tortola, *Virgin Is.* 89 C7 18 19N 64 45W
Tortosa, *Spain* 19 B6 40 49N 0 31 E
Tortosa, C., *Spain* 19 B6 40 41N 0 52 E
Tortue, I. de la, *Haiti* 89 B5 20 5N 72 57W
Torūd, *Iran* 45 C7 35 25N 55 5 E
Toruń, *Poland* 17 B10 53 2N 18 39 E
Tory I., *Ireland* 13 A3 55 16N 8 14W
Tosa, *Japan* 31 H6 33 24N 133 23 E
Tosa-Shimizu, *Japan* 31 H6 32 52N 132 58 E
Tosa-Wan, *Japan* 31 H6 33 15N 133 30 E
Toscana □, *Italy* 20 C4 43 25N 11 0 E
Toshkent, *Uzbekistan* 26 E7 41 20N 69 10 E
Tostado, *Argentina* 94 B3 29 15S 61 50W
Tostón, Pta. de, *Canary Is.* 22 F5 28 42N 14 2W
Tosu, *Japan* 31 H5 33 22N 130 31 E
Toteng, *Botswana* 56 C3 20 22S 22 58 E
Totma, *Russia* 24 C7 60 0N 42 40 E
Totnes, *U.K.* 11 G4 50 26N 3 42W
Totness, *Surinam* 93 B7 5 53N 56 19W
Totonicapán, *Guatemala* 88 D1 14 58N 91 12W
Totten Glacier, *Antarctica* 5 C8 66 45S 116 10 E
Tottenham, *Australia* 63 E4 32 14S 147 21 E
Tottenham, *Canada* 78 B5 44 1N 79 49W
Tottori, *Japan* 31 G7 35 30N 134 15 E
Tottori □, *Japan* 31 G7 35 30N 134 12 E
Toubkal, Djebel, *Morocco* 50 B4 31 0N 8 0W
Tougan, *Burkina Faso* 50 F5 13 11N 2 58W
Touggourt, *Algeria* 50 B7 33 6N 6 4 E
Toul, *France* 18 B6 48 40N 5 53 E
Toulon, *France* 18 E6 43 10N 5 55 E
Toulouse, *France* 18 E4 43 37N 1 27 E
Toummo, *Niger* 51 D8 22 45N 14 8 E
Toungoo, *Burma* 41 K20 19 0N 96 30 E
Touraine, *France* 18 C4 47 20N 0 30 E
Tourane = Da Nang, *Vietnam* 38 D7 16 4N 108 13 E
Tourcoing, *France* 18 A5 50 42N 3 10 E
Touriñán, C., *Spain* 19 A1 43 3N 9 18W
Tournai, *Belgium* 15 D3 50 35N 3 25 E
Tournon-sur-Rhône, *France* 18 D6 45 4N 4 50 E
Tours, *France* 18 C4 47 22N 0 40 E
Tousidé, Pic, *Chad* 51 D9 21 1N 16 29 E
Toussora, Mt., *C.A.R.* 52 C4 9 7N 23 14 E
Touwsrivier, *S. Africa* 56 E3 33 20S 20 2 E
Towada, *Japan* 30 D10 40 37N 141 13 E
Towada-Ko, *Japan* 30 D10 40 28N 140 55 E
Towanda, *U.S.A.* 79 E8 41 46N 76 27W
Towang, *India* 41 F17 27 37N 91 50 E
Tower, *U.S.A.* 80 B8 47 48N 92 17W
Towerhill Cr. →, *Australia* 62 C3 22 28S 144 35 E
Towner, *U.S.A.* 80 A4 48 21N 100 25W
Townsend, *U.S.A.* 82 C8 46 19N 111 31W
Townshend I., *Australia* 62 C5 22 10S 150 31 E
Townsville, *Australia* 62 B4 19 15S 146 45 E
Towson, *U.S.A.* 76 F7 39 24N 76 36W
Towuti, Danau, *Indonesia* 37 E6 2 45S 121 32 E
Toya-Ko, *Japan* 30 C10 42 35N 140 51 E
Toyama, *Japan* 31 F8 36 40N 137 15 E
Toyama □, *Japan* 31 F8 36 45N 137 30 E
Toyama-Wan, *Japan* 31 F8 37 0N 137 30 E
Toyohashi, *Japan* 31 G8 34 45N 137 25 E
Toyokawa, *Japan* 31 G8 34 48N 137 27 E
Toyonaka, *Japan* 31 G7 34 50N 135 28 E
Toyooka, *Japan* 31 G7 35 35N 134 48 E
Toyota, *Japan* 31 G8 35 3N 137 7 E
Tozeur, *Tunisia* 50 B7 33 56N 8 8 E
Trá Li = Tralee, *Ireland* 13 D2 52 16N 9 42W
Tra On, *Vietnam* 39 H5 9 58N 105 55 E
Trabzon, *Turkey* 25 F6 41 0N 39 45 E
Tracadie, *Canada* 71 C7 47 30N 64 55W
Tracy, *Calif., U.S.A.* 84 H5 37 44N 121 26W
Tracy, *Minn., U.S.A.* 80 C7 44 14N 95 37W
Trafalgar, C., *Spain* 19 D2 36 10N 6 2W
Trail, *Canada* 72 D5 49 5N 117 40W
Trainor L., *Canada* 72 A4 60 24N 120 17W
Trákhonas, *Cyprus* 23 D12 35 12N 33 21 E
Tralee, *Ireland* 13 D2 52 16N 9 42W
Tralee B., *Ireland* 13 D2 52 17N 9 55W
Tramore, *Ireland* 13 D4 52 10N 7 10W
Tramore B., *Ireland* 13 D4 52 9N 7 10W
Tran Ninh, Cao Nguyen, *Laos* 38 C4 19 30N 103 10 E
Tranås, *Sweden* 9 G16 58 3N 14 59 E
Trancas, *Argentina* 94 B2 26 11S 65 20W
Trang, *Thailand* 39 J2 7 33N 99 38 E
Trangahy, *Madag.* 57 B7 19 7S 44 31 E
Trangan, *Indonesia* 37 F8 6 40S 134 20 E
Trangie, *Australia* 63 E4 32 4S 148 0 E
Trani, *Italy* 20 D7 41 17N 16 25 E
Tranoroa, *Madag.* 57 C8 24 42S 45 4 E
Tranqueras, *Uruguay* 95 C4 31 13S 55 45W
Transantarctic Mts., *Antarctica* 5 E12 85 0S 170 0W
Transilvania, *Romania* 17 E12 46 30N 24 0 E
Transilvanian Alps = Carpaţii Meridionali, *Romania* 17 F13 45 30N 25 0 E
Transvaal □, *S. Africa* 53 K5 25 0S 29 0 E
Transylvania = Transilvania, *Romania* 17 E12 46 30N 24 0 E
Trápani, *Italy* 20 E5 38 1N 12 29 E
Trapper Pk., *U.S.A.* 82 D6 45 54N 114 18W
Traralgon, *Australia* 63 F4 38 12S 146 34 E
Trasimeno, L., *Italy* 20 C5 43 8N 12 6 E
Trat, *Thailand* 39 F4 12 14N 102 33 E
Tratani →, *Pakistan* 42 E3 29 19N 68 20 E
Traun, *Austria* 16 D8 48 14N 14 15 E
Travellers L., *Australia* 63 E3 33 20S 142 0 E
Travemünde, *Germany* 16 B6 53 57N 10 52 E
Travers, Mt., *N.Z.* 59 K4 42 1S 172 45 E
Traverse City, *U.S.A.* 76 C3 44 46N 85 38W
Travis, L., *U.S.A.* 81 K5 30 24N 97 55W
Travnik, *Bos.-H.* 21 B7 44 17N 17 39 E
Trébbia →, *Italy* 18 D8 45 4N 9 41 E
Třebíč, *Czech Rep.* 16 D8 49 14N 15 55 E
Trebinje, *Bos.-H.* 21 C8 42 44N 18 22 E
Trebonne, *Australia* 62 B4 18 37S 146 5 E
Tregaron, *U.K.* 11 E4 52 14N 3 56W
Tregrosse Is., *Australia* 62 B5 17 41S 150 43 E
Treherne, *Canada* 73 D9 49 38N 98 42W
Treinta y Tres, *Uruguay* 95 C5 33 16S 54 17W
Trelew, *Argentina* 96 E3 43 10S 65 20W
Trelleborg, *Sweden* 9 J15 55 20N 13 10 E
Tremadog Bay, *U.K.* 10 E3 52 51N 4 18W
Tremonton, *U.S.A.* 82 F7 41 43N 112 10W
Tremp, *Spain* 19 A6 42 10N 0 52 E
Trenche →, *Canada* 70 C5 47 46N 72 53W
Trenčín, *Slovak Rep.* 17 D10 48 52N 18 4 E
Trenggalek, *Indonesia* 37 H14 8 3S 111 43 E
Trenque Lauquen, *Argentina* 94 D3 36 5S 62 45W
Trent →, *Canada* 78 B7 44 6N 77 34W
Trent →, *U.K.* 10 D7 53 41N 0 42W
Trento, *Italy* 20 A4 46 4N 11 8 E
Trenton, *Canada* 78 B7 44 10N 77 34W
Trenton, *Mo., U.S.A.* 80 E8 40 5N 93 37W
Trenton, *N.J., U.S.A.* 79 F10 40 14N 74 46W
Trenton, *Nebr., U.S.A.* 80 E4 40 11N 101 1W
Trepassey, *Canada* 71 C9 46 43N 53 25W
Tres Arroyos, *Argentina* 94 D3 38 26S 60 20W
Três Corações, *Brazil* 95 A6 21 44S 45 15W
Três Lagoas, *Brazil* 93 H8 20 50S 51 43W
Tres Lomas, *Argentina* 94 D3 36 27S 62 51W
Tres Marías, Islas, *Mexico* 86 C3 21 25N 106 28W
Tres Montes, C., *Chile* 96 F1 46 50S 75 30W
Tres Pinos, *U.S.A.* 84 J5 36 48N 121 19W
Três Pontas, *Brazil* 95 A6 21 23S 45 29W
Tres Puentes, *Chile* 94 B1 27 50S 70 15W
Tres Puntas, C., *Argentina* 96 F3 47 0S 66 0W
Três Rios, *Brazil* 95 A7 22 6S 43 15W
Tres Valles, *Mexico* 87 D5 18 15N 96 8W
Tresco, *U.K.* 11 H1 49 57N 6 20W
Treviso, *Italy* 20 B5 45 40N 12 15 E
Triabunna, *Australia* 62 G4 42 30S 147 55 E
Triánda, *Greece* 23 C10 36 25N 28 10 E
Tribulation, C., *Australia* 62 B4 16 5S 145 29 E
Tribune, *U.S.A.* 80 F4 38 28N 101 45W
Trichinopoly = Tiruchchirappalli, *India* 40 P11 10 45N 78 45 E
Trichur, *India* 40 P10 10 30N 76 18 E
Trida, *Australia* 63 E4 33 1S 145 1 E
Trier, *Germany* 16 D4 49 45N 6 38 E
Trieste, *Italy* 20 B5 45 40N 13 46 E
Triglav, *Slovenia* 16 E7 46 21N 13 50 E
Tríkkala, *Greece* 21 E9 39 34N 21 47 E
Trikomo, *Cyprus* 23 D12 35 17N 33 52 E
Trikora, Puncak, *Indonesia* 37 E9 4 15S 138 45 E
Trim, *Ireland* 13 C5 53 33N 6 48W
Trincomalee, *Sri Lanka* 40 Q12 8 38N 81 15 E
Trindade, *Brazil* 93 G9 16 40S 49 30W
Trindade, I., *Atl. Oc.* 2 F8 20 20S 29 50W
Trinidad, *Bolivia* 92 F6 14 46S 64 50W
Trinidad, *Cuba* 88 B4 21 48N 80 0W
Trinidad, *Uruguay* 94 C4 33 30S 56 50W
Trinidad, *U.S.A.* 81 G2 37 10N 104 31W
Trinidad, *W. Indies* 89 D7 10 30N 61 15W
Trinidad →, *Mexico* 87 D5 17 49N 95 9W
Trinidad & Tobago ■, *W. Indies* 89 D7 10 30N 61 20W
Trinity, *Canada* 71 C9 48 59N 53 55W
Trinity, *U.S.A.* 81 K7 30 57N 95 22W
Trinity →, *Calif., U.S.A.* 82 F2 41 11N 123 42W
Trinity →, *Tex., U.S.A.* 81 L7 29 45N 94 43W
Trinity B., *Canada* 71 C9 48 20N 53 10W
Trinity Is., *U.S.A.* 68 C4 56 33N 154 25W
Trinity Range, *U.S.A.* 82 F4 40 15N 118 45W
Trinkitat, *Sudan* 51 E13 18 45N 37 51 E
Trinway, *U.S.A.* 78 F2 40 9N 82 1W
Tripoli = Tarābulus, *Lebanon* 47 A4 34 31N 35 50 E
Tripoli = Tarābulus, *Libya* 51 B8 32 49N 13 7 E
Trípolis, *Greece* 21 F10 37 31N 22 25 E
Tripolitania, *Libya* 48 C5 31 0N 12 0 E
Tripolitania, *N. Afr.* 51 B8 31 0N 13 0 E
Tripura □, *India* 41 H18 24 0N 92 0 E
Tripylos, *Cyprus* 23 E11 34 59N 32 41 E
Tristan da Cunha, *Atl. Oc.* 49 K2 37 6S 12 20W
Trisul, *India* 43 D8 30 19N 79 47 E
Trivandrum, *India* 40 Q10 8 41N 77 0 E
Trnava, *Slovak Rep.* 17 D9 48 23N 17 35 E
Trochu, *Canada* 72 C6 51 50N 113 13W
Trodely I., *Canada* 70 B4 52 15N 79 26W
Troglav, *Croatia* 20 C7 43 56N 16 36 E
Troilus, L., *Canada* 70 B5 50 50N 74 35W
Trois-Pistoles, *Canada* 71 C6 48 5N 69 10W
Trois-Rivières, *Canada* 70 C5 46 25N 72 34W
Troitsk, *Russia* 26 D7 54 10N 61 35 E
Troitsko Pechorsk, *Russia* 24 B10 62 40N 56 10 E
Trölladyngja, *Iceland* 8 D5 64 54N 17 16W
Trollhättan, *Sweden* 9 G15 58 17N 12 20 E
Trollheimen, *Norway* 8 E13 62 46N 9 1 E
Trombetas →, *Brazil* 93 D7 1 55S 55 35W
Tromsø, *Norway* 8 B18 69 40N 18 56 E
Trona, *U.S.A.* 85 K9 35 46N 117 23W
Tronador, Mte., *Argentina* 96 E2 41 10S 71 50W
Trøndelag, *Norway* 8 D14 64 17N 11 50 E
Trondheim, *Norway* 8 E14 63 36N 10 25 E
Trondheimsfjorden, *Norway* 8 E14 63 35N 10 30 E
Troodos, *Cyprus* 23 E11 34 55N 32 52 E
Troon, *U.K.* 12 F4 55 33N 4 39W
Tropic, *U.S.A.* 83 H7 37 37N 112 5W
Trostan, *U.K.* 13 A5 55 3N 6 10W
Trout →, *Canada* 72 A5 61 19N 119 51W
Trout L., *N.W.T., Canada* 72 A4 60 40N 121 14W
Trout L., *Ont., Canada* 73 C10 51 20N 93 15W
Trout Lake, *Canada* 72 B6 56 30N 114 32W
Trout Lake, *U.S.A.* 84 E5 46 0N 121 32W
Trout River, *Canada* 71 C8 49 29N 58 8W
Trout Run, *U.S.A.* 78 E7 41 23N 77 3W
Trouville-sur-Mer, *France* 18 B4 49 21N 0 5 E
Trowbridge, *U.K.* 11 F5 51 18N 2 12W
Troy, *Turkey* 21 E12 39 57N 26 12 E
Troy, *Ala., U.S.A.* 77 K3 31 48N 85 58W
Troy, *Kans., U.S.A.* 80 F7 39 47N 95 5W
Troy, *Mo., U.S.A.* 80 F9 38 59N 90 59W
Troy, *Mont., U.S.A.* 82 B6 48 28N 115 53W
Troy, *N.Y., U.S.A.* 79 D11 42 44N 73 41W
Troy, *Ohio, U.S.A.* 76 E3 40 2N 84 12W
Troy, *Pa., U.S.A.* 79 E8 41 47N 76 47W
Troyes, *France* 18 B6 48 19N 4 3 E
Truchas Peak, *U.S.A.* 81 H2 35 58N 105 39W
Trucial States = United Arab Emirates ■, *Asia* 45 F7 23 50N 54 0 E
Truckee, *U.S.A.* 84 F6 39 20N 120 11W
Trudovoye, *Russia* 30 C6 43 17N 132 5 E
Trujillo, *Honduras* 88 C2 16 0N 86 0W
Trujillo, *Peru* 92 E3 8 6S 79 0W
Trujillo, *Spain* 19 C3 39 28N 5 55W
Trujillo, *U.S.A.* 81 H2 35 32N 104 42W
Trujillo, *Venezuela* 92 B4 9 22N 70 38W
Truk, *Micronesia* 64 G7 7 25N 151 46 E
Trumann, *U.S.A.* 81 H9 35 41N 90 31W
Trumansburg, *U.S.A.* 79 D8 42 33N 76 40W
Trumbull, Mt., *U.S.A.* 83 H7 36 25N 113 8W
Trundle, *Australia* 63 E4 32 53S 147 35 E
Trung-Phan = Annam, *Vietnam* 38 E7 16 0N 108 0 E
Truro, *Canada* 71 C7 45 21N 63 14W
Truro, *U.K.* 11 G2 50 16N 5 4W
Truskavets, *Ukraine* 17 D12 49 17N 23 30 E
Trutch, *Canada* 72 B4 57 44N 122 57W
Truth or Consequences, *U.S.A.* 83 K10 33 8N 107 15W
Trutnov, *Czech Rep.* 16 C8 50 37N 15 54 E
Truxton, *U.S.A.* 79 D8 42 45N 76 2W
Tryonville, *U.S.A.* 78 E5 41 42N 79 48W
Tsaratanana, *Madag.* 57 B8 16 47S 47 39 E
Tsaratanana, Mt. de, *Madag.* 57 A8 14 0S 49 0 E
Tsarevo = Michurin, *Bulgaria* 21 C12 42 9N 27 51 E
Tsau, *Botswana* 56 C3 20 8S 22 22 E
Tselinograd = Astana, *Kazakstan* 26 D8 51 10N 71 30 E
Tsetserleg, *Mongolia* 32 B5 47 36N 101 32 E
Tshabong, *Botswana* 56 D3 26 2S 22 29 E
Tshane, *Botswana* 56 C3 24 5S 21 54 E
Tshela, *Dem. Rep. of the Congo* 52 E2 4 57S 13 4 E
Tshesebe, *Botswana* 57 C4 21 51S 27 32 E
Tshibeke, *Dem. Rep. of the Congo* 54 C2 2 40S 28 35 E
Tshibinda, *Dem. Rep. of the Congo* 54 C2 2 23S 28 43 E
Tshikapa, *Dem. Rep. of the Congo* 52 F4 6 28S 20 48 E
Tshilenge, *Dem. Rep. of the Congo* 54 D1 6 17S 23 48 E
Tshinsenda, *Dem. Rep. of the Congo* 55 E2 12 20S 28 0 E
Tshofa, *Dem. Rep. of the Congo* 54 D2 5 13S 25 16 E
Tshwane, *Botswana* 56 C3 22 24S 22 1 E
Tsigara, *Botswana* 56 C4 20 22S 25 54 E
Tsihombe, *Madag.* 57 D8 25 10S 45 41 E
Tsiigehtchic, *Canada* 68 B6 67 15N 134 0W
Tsimlyansk Res. = Tsimlyanskoye Vdkhr., *Russia* 25 E7 48 0N 43 0 E
Tsimlyanskoye Vdkhr., *Russia* 25 E7 48 0N 43 0 E
Tsinan = Jinan, *China* 34 F9 36 38N 117 1 E
Tsineng, *S. Africa* 56 D3 27 5S 23 5 E
Tsinghai = Qinghai □, *China* 32 C4 36 0N 98 0 E
Tsingtao = Qingdao, *China* 35 F11 36 5N 120 20 E
Tsinjomitondraka, *Madag.* 57 B8 15 40S 47 8 E
Tsiroanomandidy, *Madag.* 57 B8 18 46S 46 2 E
Tsivory, *Madag.* 57 C8 24 4S 46 5 E
Tskhinvali, *Georgia* 25 F7 42 14N 44 1 E
Tsna →, *Russia* 24 D7 54 55N 41 58 E
Tso Moriri, L., *India* 43 C8 32 50N 78 20 E
Tsodilo Hill, *Botswana* 56 B3 18 49S 21 43 E
Tsogttsetsiy = Baruunsuu, *Mongolia* 34 C3 43 43N 105 35 E
Tsolo, *S. Africa* 57 E4 31 18S 28 37 E
Tsomo, *S. Africa* 57 E4 32 0S 27 42 E
Tsu, *Japan* 31 G8 34 45N 136 25 E
Tsu L., *Canada* 72 A6 60 40N 111 52W
Tsuchiura, *Japan* 31 F10 36 5N 140 15 E
Tsugaru-Kaikyō, *Japan* 30 D10 41 35N 141 0 E
Tsumeb, *Namibia* 56 B2 19 9S 17 44 E
Tsumis, *Namibia* 56 C2 23 39S 17 29 E
Tsuruga, *Japan* 31 G8 35 45N 136 2 E
Tsurugi-San, *Japan* 31 H7 33 51N 134 6 E
Tsuruoka, *Japan* 30 E9 38 44N 139 50 E
Tsushima, *Gifu, Japan* 31 G8 35 10N 136 43 E
Tsushima, *Nagasaki, Japan* 31 G4 34 20N 129 20 E
Tsuyama, *Japan* 31 G7 35 3N 134 0 E
Tsyelyakhany, *Belarus* 17 B13 52 30N 25 46 E
Tual, *Indonesia* 37 F8 5 38S 132 44 E
Tuam, *Ireland* 13 C3 53 31N 8 51W
Tuamotu Arch. = Tuamotu Is., *Pac. Oc.* 65 J13 17 0S 144 0W
Tuamotu Is., *Pac. Oc.* 65 J13 17 0S 144 0W
Tuamotu Ridge, *Pac. Oc.* 65 K14 20 0S 138 0W
Tuao, *Phil.* 37 A6 17 55N 121 22 E
Tuapse, *Russia* 25 F6 44 5N 39 10 E
Tuatapere, *N.Z.* 59 M1 46 8S 167 41 E
Tuba City, *U.S.A.* 83 H8 36 8N 111 14W
Tuban, *Indonesia* 37 G15 6 54S 112 3 E
Tubarão, *Brazil* 95 B6 28 30S 49 0W
Tūbās, *West Bank* 47 C4 32 20N 35 22 E
Tübingen, *Germany* 16 D5 48 31N 9 4 E
Tubruq, *Libya* 51 B10 32 7N 23 55 E
Tubuai Is., *Pac. Oc.* 65 K13 25 0S 150 0W
Tuc Trung, *Vietnam* 39 G6 11 1N 107 12 E
Tucacas, *Venezuela* 92 A5 10 48N 68 19W
Tuchodi →, *Canada* 72 B4 58 17N 123 42W
Tuckanarra, *Australia* 61 E2 27 7S 118 5 E
Tucson, *U.S.A.* 83 K8 32 13N 110 58W
Tucumán □, *Argentina* 94 B2 26 48S 66 2W
Tucumcari, *U.S.A.* 81 H3 35 10N 103 44W
Tucupita, *Venezuela* 92 B6 9 2N 62 3W
Tucuruí, *Brazil* 93 D9 3 42S 49 44W
Tucuruí, Reprêsa de, *Brazil* 93 D9 4 0S 49 30W
Tudela, *Spain* 19 A5 42 4N 1 39W
Tudmur, *Syria* 44 C3 34 36N 38 15 E
Tudor, L., *Canada* 71 A6 55 50N 65 25W
Tugela →, *S. Africa* 57 D5 29 14S 31 30 E
Tuguegarao, *Phil.* 37 A6 17 35N 121 42 E
Tugur, *Russia* 27 D14 53 44N 136 45 E
Tui, *Spain* 19 A1 42 3N 8 39W
Tuineje, *Canary Is.* 22 F5 28 19N 14 3W
Tukangbesi, Kepulauan, *Indonesia* 37 F6 6 0S 124 0 E
Tukarak I., *Canada* 70 A4 56 15N 78 45W
Tukayyid, *Iraq* 44 D5 29 47N 45 36 E
Tuktoyaktuk, *Canada* 68 B6 69 27N 133 2W
Tukums, *Latvia* 9 H20 56 58N 23 10 E

U

Vestfjorden

Vestfjorden, Norway 8 C15 67 55N 14 0 E
Vestmannaeyjar, Iceland 8 E3 63 27N 20 15W
Vestspitsbergen, Svalbard 4 B8 78 40N 17 0 E
Vestvågøy, Norway 8 B15 68 18N 13 50 E
Vesuvio, Italy 20 D6 40 49N 14 26 E
Vesuvius, Mt. = Vesuvio, Italy 20 D6 40 49N 14 26 E
Veszprém, Hungary 17 E9 47 8N 17 57 E
Vetlanda, Sweden 9 H16 57 24N 15 3 E
Vetlugu →, Russia 24 C8 56 36N 46 4 E
Vettore, Mte., Italy 20 C5 42 49N 13 16 E
Veurne, Belgium 15 C2 51 5N 2 40 E
Veys, Iran 45 D6 31 30N 49 0 E
Vezhen, Bulgaria 21 C11 42 50N 24 20 E
Vi Thanh, Vietnam 39 H5 9 42N 105 26 E
Viacha, Bolivia 92 G5 16 39S 68 18W
Viamão, Brazil 95 C5 30 5S 51 0W
Viana, Brazil 93 D10 3 13S 44 55W
Viana do Alentejo, Portugal 19 C2 38 17N 7 59W
Viana do Castelo, Portugal 19 B1 41 42N 8 50W
Vianden, Lux. 15 E6 49 56N 6 12 E
Vianópolis, Brazil 93 G9 16 40S 48 35W
Viaréggio, Italy 20 C4 43 52N 10 14 E
Vibo Valéntia, Italy 20 E7 38 40N 16 6 E
Viborg, Denmark 9 H13 56 27N 9 23 E
Vic, Spain 19 B7 41 58N 2 19 E
Vicenza, Italy 20 B4 45 33N 11 33 E
Vich = Vic, Spain 19 B7 41 58N 2 19 E
Vichada →, Colombia 92 C5 4 55N 67 50W
Vichy, France 18 C5 46 9N 3 26 E
Vicksburg, Ariz., U.S.A. 85 M13 33 45N 113 45W
Vicksburg, Miss., U.S.A. 81 J9 32 21N 90 53W
Victor, India 42 J4 21 0N 71 30 E
Victor, U.S.A. 78 D7 42 58N 77 24W
Victor Harbor, Australia 63 F2 35 30S 138 37 E
Victoria = Labuan, Malaysia 36 C5 5 20N 115 14 E
Victoria, Argentina 94 C3 32 40S 60 10W
Victoria, Canada 72 D4 48 30N 123 25W
Victoria, Chile 96 D2 38 13S 72 20W
Victoria, Malta 23 C1 36 2N 14 14 E
Victoria, Kans., U.S.A. 80 F5 38 52N 99 9W
Victoria, Tex., U.S.A. 81 L6 28 48N 97 0W
Victoria □, Australia 63 F3 37 0S 144 0 E
Victoria →, Australia 60 C4 15 10S 129 40 E
Victoria, Grand L., Canada 70 C4 47 31N 77 30W
Victoria, L., Africa 54 C3 1 0S 33 0 E
Victoria, L., Australia 63 E3 33 57S 141 15 E
Victoria Beach, Canada 73 C9 50 40N 96 35W
Victoria de Durango = Durango, Mexico 86 C4 24 3N 104 39W
Victoria de las Tunas, Cuba 88 B4 20 58N 76 59W
Victoria Falls, Zimbabwe 55 F2 17 58S 25 52 E
Victoria Harbour, Canada 78 B5 44 45N 79 45W
Victoria I., Canada 68 A8 71 0N 111 0W
Victoria L., Canada 71 C8 48 20N 57 27W
Victoria Ld., Antarctica 5 D11 75 0S 160 0 E
Victoria Nile →, Uganda 54 B3 2 14N 31 26 E
Victoria River, Australia 60 C5 16 25S 131 0 E
Victoria Str., Canada 68 B9 69 30N 100 0W
Victoria Taungdeik, Burma 41 J18 21 15N 93 55 E
Victoria West, S. Africa 56 E3 31 25S 23 4 E
Victoriaville, Canada 71 C5 46 4N 71 56W
Victorica, Argentina 94 D2 36 20S 65 30W
Victorville, U.S.A. 85 L9 34 32N 117 18W
Vicuña, Chile 94 C1 30 0S 70 50W
Vicuña Mackenna, Argentina 94 C3 33 53S 64 25W
Vidal, U.S.A. 85 L12 34 7N 114 31W
Vidal Junction, U.S.A. 85 L12 34 11N 114 34W
Vidalia, U.S.A. 77 J4 32 13N 82 25W
Vídho, Greece 23 A3 39 38N 19 55 E
Vidin, Bulgaria 21 C10 43 59N 22 50 E
Vidisha, India 42 H7 23 28N 77 53 E
Vidzy, Belarus 9 J22 55 23N 26 37 E
Viedma, Argentina 96 E4 40 50S 63 0W
Viedma, L., Argentina 96 F2 49 30S 72 30W
Vielsalm, Belgium 15 D5 50 17N 5 54 E
Vienna = Wien, Austria 16 D9 48 12N 16 22 E
Vienna, Ill., U.S.A. 81 G10 37 25N 88 54W
Vienna, Mo., U.S.A. 80 F9 38 11N 91 57W
Vienne, France 18 D6 45 31N 4 53 E
Vienne →, France 18 C4 47 13N 0 5 E
Vientiane, Laos 38 D4 17 58N 102 36 E
Vientos, Paso de los, Caribbean 89 C5 20 0N 74 0W
Vierzon, France 18 C5 47 13N 2 5 E
Vietnam ■, Asia 38 C6 19 0N 106 0 E
Vigan, Phil. 37 A6 17 35N 120 28 E
Vigévano, Italy 18 D8 45 19N 8 51 E
Vigia, Brazil 93 D9 0 50S 48 5W
Vigía Chico, Mexico 87 D7 19 46N 87 35W
Víglas, Ákra, Greece 23 D9 35 54N 27 51 E
Vigo, Spain 19 A1 42 12N 8 41W
Vihowa, Pakistan 42 D4 31 8N 70 30 E
Vihowa →, Pakistan 42 D4 31 8N 70 41 E
Vijayawada, India 41 L12 16 31N 80 39 E
Vík, Iceland 8 E4 63 25N 19 1W
Vikeke, Indonesia 37 F7 8 52S 126 23 E
Viking, Canada 72 C6 53 7N 111 50W
Vikna, Norway 8 D14 64 55N 10 58 E
Vila da Maganja, Mozam. 55 F4 17 18S 37 30 E
Vila de João Belo = Xai-Xai, Mozam. 57 D5 25 6S 33 31 E
Vila do Bispo, Portugal 19 D1 37 5N 8 53W
Vila do Chibuto, Mozam. 57 C5 24 40S 33 33 E
Vila Franca de Xira, Portugal 19 C1 38 57N 8 59W
Vila Gamito, Mozam. 55 E3 14 12S 33 0 E
Vila Gomes da Costa, Mozam. 57 C5 24 20S 33 37 E
Vila Machado, Mozam. 55 F3 19 15S 34 14 E
Vila Mouzinho, Mozam. 55 E3 14 48S 34 25 E
Vila Nova de Gaia, Portugal 19 B1 41 8N 8 37W
Vila Real, Portugal 19 B2 41 17N 7 48W
Vila-real de los Infantes, Spain 19 C5 39 55N 0 3W
Vila Real de Santo António, Portugal 19 D2 37 10N 7 28W
Vila Vasco da Gama, Mozam. 55 E3 14 54S 32 14 E
Vila Velha, Brazil 95 A7 20 20S 40 17W
Vilagarcía de Arousa, Spain 19 A1 42 34N 8 46W
Vilaine →, France 18 C2 47 30N 2 27W
Vilanandro, Tanjona, Madag. 57 B7 16 11S 44 27 E
Vilanculos, Mozam. 57 C6 22 1S 35 17 E
Vilanova i la Geltrú, Spain 19 B6 41 13N 1 40 E
Vileyka, Belarus 17 A14 54 30N 26 53 E
Vilhelmina, Sweden 8 D17 64 35N 16 39 E
Vilhena, Brazil 92 F6 12 40S 60 5W
Viliga, Russia 27 C16 61 36N 156 56 E
Viliya →, Lithuania 9 J21 55 8N 24 16 E
Viljandi, Estonia 9 G21 58 28N 25 30 E
Vilkitskogo, Proliv, Russia 27 B11 78 0N 103 0 E
Vilkovo = Vylkove, Ukraine 17 F15 45 28N 29 32 E
Villa Abecia, Bolivia 94 A2 21 0S 68 18W
Villa Ahumada, Mexico 86 A3 30 38N 106 30W
Villa Ana, Argentina 94 B4 28 28S 59 40W
Villa Ángela, Argentina 94 B3 27 34S 60 45W
Villa Bella, Bolivia 92 F5 10 25S 65 22W
Villa Bens = Tarfaya, Morocco 50 C3 27 55N 12 55W
Villa Cañás, Argentina 94 C3 34 0S 61 35W
Villa Cisneros = Dakhla, W. Sahara 50 D2 23 50N 15 53W
Villa Colón, Argentina 94 C2 31 38S 68 20W
Villa Constitución, Argentina 94 C3 33 15S 60 20W
Villa de María, Argentina 94 B3 29 55S 63 43W
Villa Dolores, Argentina 94 C2 31 58S 65 15W
Villa Frontera, Mexico 86 B4 26 56N 101 27W
Villa Guillermina, Argentina 94 B4 28 15S 59 29W
Villa Hayes, Paraguay 94 B4 25 5S 57 20W
Villa Iris, Argentina 94 D3 38 12S 63 12W
Villa Juárez, Mexico 86 B4 27 37N 100 44W
Villa María, Argentina 94 C3 32 20S 63 10W
Villa Mazán, Argentina 94 B2 28 40S 66 30W
Villa Montes, Bolivia 94 A3 21 10S 63 30W
Villa Ocampo, Argentina 94 B4 28 30S 59 20W
Villa Ocampo, Mexico 86 B3 26 29N 105 30W
Villa Ojo de Agua, Argentina 94 B3 29 30S 63 44W
Villa San José, Argentina 94 C4 32 12S 58 15W
Villa San Martín, Argentina 94 B3 28 15S 64 9W
Villa Unión, Mexico 86 C3 23 12N 106 14W
Villacarlos, Spain 22 B11 39 53N 4 17 E
Villacarrillo, Spain 19 C4 38 7N 3 3W
Villach, Austria 16 E7 46 37N 13 51 E
Villafranca de los Caballeros, Spain 22 B10 39 34N 3 25 E
Villagrán, Mexico 87 C5 24 29N 99 29W
Villaguay, Argentina 94 C4 32 0S 59 0W
Villahermosa, Mexico 87 D6 17 59N 92 55W
Villajoyosa, Spain 19 C5 38 30N 0 12W
Villalba, Spain 19 A2 43 26N 7 40W
Villanueva, U.S.A. 81 H2 35 16N 105 22W
Villanueva de la Serena, Spain 19 C3 38 59N 5 50W
Villanueva y Geltrú = Vilanova i la Geltrú, Spain 19 B6 41 13N 1 40 E
Villarreal = Vila-real de los Infantes, Spain 19 C5 39 55N 0 3W
Villarrica, Chile 96 D2 39 15S 72 15W
Villarrica, Paraguay 94 B4 25 40S 56 30W
Villarrobledo, Spain 19 C4 39 18N 2 36W
Villavicencio, Argentina 94 C2 32 28S 69 0W
Villavicencio, Colombia 92 C4 4 9N 73 37W
Villaviciosa, Spain 19 A3 43 32N 5 27W
Villazón, Bolivia 94 A2 22 0S 65 35W
Ville-Marie, Canada 70 C4 47 20N 79 30W
Ville Platte, U.S.A. 81 K8 30 41N 92 17W
Villena, Spain 19 C5 38 39N 0 52W
Villeneuve-d'Ascq, France 18 A5 50 38N 3 9 E
Villeneuve-sur-Lot, France 18 D4 44 24N 0 42 E
Villiers, S. Africa 57 D4 27 2S 28 36 E
Villingen-Schwenningen, Germany 16 D5 48 3N 8 26 E
Vilna, Canada 72 C6 54 7N 111 55W
Vilnius, Lithuania 9 J21 54 38N 25 19 E
Vilvoorde, Belgium 15 D4 50 56N 4 26 E
Vilyuy →, Russia 27 C13 64 24N 126 26 E
Vilyuysk, Russia 27 C13 63 40N 121 35 E
Viña del Mar, Chile 94 C1 33 0S 71 30W
Vinarós, Spain 19 B6 40 30N 0 27 E
Vincennes, U.S.A. 76 F2 38 41N 87 32W
Vincent, U.S.A. 85 L8 34 33N 118 11W
Vinchina, Argentina 94 B2 28 45S 68 15W
Vindelälven →, Sweden 8 E18 63 55N 19 50 E
Vindeln, Sweden 8 D18 64 12N 19 43 E
Vindhya Ra., India 42 H7 22 50N 77 0 E
Vineland, U.S.A. 76 F8 39 29N 75 2W
Vinh, Vietnam 38 C5 18 45N 105 38 E
Vinh Linh, Vietnam 38 D6 17 4N 107 2 E
Vinh Long, Vietnam 39 G5 10 16N 105 57 E
Vinita, U.S.A. 81 G7 36 39N 95 9W
Vinkovci, Croatia 21 B8 45 19N 18 48 E
Vinnitsa = Vinnytsya, Ukraine 17 D15 49 15N 28 30 E
Vinnytsya, Ukraine 17 D15 49 15N 28 30 E
Vinton, Calif., U.S.A. 84 F6 39 48N 120 10W
Vinton, Iowa, U.S.A. 80 D8 42 10N 92 1W
Vinton, La., U.S.A. 81 K8 30 11N 93 35W
Virac, Phil. 37 B6 13 30N 124 20 E
Virachei, Cambodia 38 F6 13 59N 106 49 E
Virago Sd., Canada 72 C2 54 0N 132 30W
Viramgam, India 42 H5 23 5N 72 0 E
Viranşehir, Turkey 44 B3 37 13N 39 45 E
Virawah, Pakistan 42 G4 24 31N 70 46 E
Virden, Canada 73 D8 49 50N 100 56W
Vire, France 18 B3 48 50N 0 53W
Virgenes, C., Argentina 96 G3 52 19S 68 21W
Virgin →, U.S.A. 83 H6 36 28N 114 21W
Virgin Gorda, Virgin Is. 89 C7 18 30N 64 26W
Virgin Is. (British) ■, W. Indies 89 C7 18 30N 64 30W
Virgin Is. (U.S.) ■, W. Indies 89 C7 18 20N 65 0W
Virginia, S. Africa 56 D4 28 8S 26 55 E
Virginia, U.S.A. 80 B8 47 31N 92 32W
Virginia □, U.S.A. 76 G7 37 30N 78 45W
Virginia Beach, U.S.A. 76 G8 36 51N 75 59W
Virginia City, Mont., U.S.A. 82 D8 45 18N 111 56W
Virginia City, Nev., U.S.A. 84 F7 39 19N 119 39W
Virginia Falls, Canada 72 A3 61 38N 125 42W
Virginiatown, Canada 70 C4 48 9N 79 36W
Viroqua, U.S.A. 80 D9 43 34N 90 53W
Virovitica, Croatia 20 B7 45 51N 17 21 E
Virpur, India 42 J4 21 51N 70 42 E
Virton, Belgium 15 E5 49 35N 5 32 E
Virudunagar, India 40 Q10 9 30N 77 58 E
Vis, Croatia 20 C7 43 4N 16 10 E
Visalia, U.S.A. 84 J7 36 20N 119 18W
Visayan Sea, Phil. 37 B6 11 30N 123 30 E
Visby, Sweden 9 H18 57 37N 18 18 E
Viscount Melville Sd., Canada 4 B2 74 10N 108 0W
Visé, Belgium 15 D5 50 44N 5 41 E
Višegrad, Bos.-H. 21 C8 43 47N 19 17 E
Viseu, Brazil 93 D9 1 10S 46 5W
Viseu, Portugal 19 B2 40 40N 7 55W
Vishakhapatnam, India 41 L13 17 45N 83 20 E
Visnagar, India 42 H5 23 45N 72 32 E
Viso, Mte., Italy 18 D7 44 38N 7 5 E
Visokoi I., Antarctica 5 B1 56 43S 27 15W
Vista, U.S.A. 85 M9 33 12N 117 14W
Vistula = Wisła →, Poland 17 A10 54 22N 18 55 E
Vitebsk = Vitsyebsk, Belarus 24 C5 55 10N 30 15 E
Viterbo, Italy 20 C5 42 25N 12 6 E
Viti Levu, Fiji 59 C7 17 30S 177 30 E
Vitigudino, Spain 19 B2 41 1N 6 26W
Vitim, Russia 27 D12 59 28N 112 35 E
Vitim →, Russia 27 D12 59 26N 112 34 E
Vitória, Brazil 93 H10 20 20S 40 22W
Vitória da Conquista, Brazil 93 F10 14 51S 40 51W
Vitória de São Antão, Brazil 93 E11 8 10S 35 20W
Vitoria-Gasteiz, Spain 19 A4 42 50N 2 41W
Vitsyebsk, Belarus 24 C5 55 10N 30 15 E
Vittória, Italy 20 F6 36 57N 14 32 E
Vittório Véneto, Italy 20 B5 45 59N 12 18 E
Viveiro, Spain 19 A2 43 39N 7 38W
Vivian, U.S.A. 81 J8 32 53N 93 59W
Vizcaíno, Desierto de, Mexico 86 B2 27 40N 113 50W
Vizcaíno, Sierra, Mexico 86 B2 27 30N 114 0W
Vize, Turkey 21 D12 41 34N 27 45 E
Vizianagaram, India 41 K13 18 6N 83 30 E
Vjosa →, Albania 21 D8 40 37N 19 24 E
Vlaardingen, Neths. 15 C4 51 55N 4 21 E
Vladikavkaz, Russia 25 F7 43 0N 44 35 E
Vladimir, Russia 24 C7 56 15N 40 30 E
Vladimir Volynskiy = Volodymyr-Volynskyy, Ukraine 17 C13 50 50N 24 18 E
Vladivostok, Russia 27 E14 43 10N 131 53 E
Vlieland, Neths. 15 A4 53 16N 4 55 E
Vlissingen, Neths. 15 C3 51 26N 3 34 E
Vlóra, Albania 21 D8 40 32N 19 28 E
Vltava →, Czech Rep. 16 D8 50 21N 14 30 E
Vo Dat, Vietnam 39 G6 11 9N 107 31 E
Voe, U.K. 12 A7 60 21N 1 16W
Vogelkop = Doberai, Jazirah, Indonesia 37 E8 1 25S 133 0 E
Vogelsberg, Germany 16 C5 50 31N 9 12 E
Voghera, Italy 18 D8 44 59N 9 1 E
Vohibinany, Madag. 57 B8 18 49S 49 4 E
Vohimarina = Iharana, Madag. 57 A9 13 25S 50 0 E
Vohimena, Tanjon' i, Madag. 57 D8 25 36S 45 8 E
Vohipeno, Madag. 57 C8 22 22S 47 51 E
Voi, Kenya 54 C4 3 25S 38 32 E
Voiron, France 18 D6 45 22N 5 35 E
Voisey B., Canada 71 A7 56 15N 61 50W
Vojmsjön, Sweden 8 D17 64 55N 16 40 E
Vojvodina □, Serbia, Yug. 21 B9 45 20N 20 0 E
Volborg, U.S.A. 80 C2 45 51N 105 41W
Volcano Is. = Kazan-Rettō, Pac. Oc. 64 E6 25 0N 141 0 E
Volda, Norway 9 E12 62 9N 6 5 E
Volga →, Russia 25 E8 46 0N 48 30 E
Volga Hts. = Privolzhskaya Vozvyshennost, Russia 25 D8 51 0N 46 0 E
Volgodonsk, Russia 25 E7 47 33N 42 5 E
Volgograd, Russia 25 E7 48 40N 44 25 E
Volgogradskoye Vdkhr., Russia 25 D8 50 0N 45 20 E
Volkhov →, Russia 24 B5 60 8N 32 20 E
Volkovysk = Vawkavysk, Belarus 17 B13 53 9N 24 30 E
Volksrust, S. Africa 57 D4 27 24S 29 53 E
Volochanka, Russia 27 B10 71 0N 94 28 E
Volodymyr-Volynskyy, Ukraine 17 C13 50 50N 24 18 E
Vologda, Russia 24 C6 59 10N 39 45 E
Vólos, Greece 21 E10 39 24N 22 59 E
Volovets, Ukraine 17 D12 48 43N 23 11 E
Volozhin = Valozhyn, Belarus 17 A14 54 3N 26 30 E
Volsk, Russia 24 D8 52 5N 47 22 E
Volta →, Ghana 48 F4 5 46N 0 41 E
Volta, L., Ghana 50 G6 7 30N 0 0 E
Volta Redonda, Brazil 95 A7 22 31S 44 5W
Voltaire, C., Australia 60 B4 14 16S 125 35 E
Volterra, Italy 20 C4 43 24N 10 51 E
Volturno →, Italy 20 D5 41 1N 13 55 E
Volzhskiy, Russia 25 E7 48 56N 44 46 E
Vondrozo, Madag. 57 C8 22 49S 47 20 E
Vopnafjörður, Iceland 8 D6 65 45N 14 50W
Vóriai Sporádhes, Greece 21 E10 39 15N 23 30 E
Vorkuta, Russia 24 A11 67 48N 64 20 E
Vormsi, Estonia 9 G20 59 1N 23 13 E
Voronezh, Russia 25 D6 51 40N 39 10 E
Voroshilovgrad = Luhansk, Ukraine 25 E6 48 38N 39 15 E
Voroshilovsk = Alchevsk, Ukraine 25 E6 48 30N 38 45 E
Võrts Järv, Estonia 9 G22 58 16N 26 3 E
Võru, Estonia 9 H22 57 48N 26 54 E
Vosges, France 18 B7 48 20N 7 10 E
Voss, Norway 9 F12 60 38N 6 26 E
Vostok I., Kiribati 65 J12 10 5S 152 23W
Votkinsk, Russia 24 C9 57 0N 53 55 E
Votkinskoye Vdkhr., Russia 24 C10 57 22N 55 12 E
Votsuri-Shima, Japan 31 M1 25 45N 123 29 E
Vouga →, Portugal 19 B1 40 41N 8 40W
Voúxa, Ákra, Greece 23 D5 35 37N 23 32 E
Vozhe, Ozero, Russia 24 B6 60 45N 39 0 E
Voznesensk, Ukraine 25 E5 47 35N 31 21 E
Voznesenye, Russia 24 B6 61 0N 35 28 E
Vrangelya, Ostrov, Russia 27 B19 71 0N 180 0 E
Vranje, Serbia, Yug. 21 C9 42 34N 21 54 E
Vratsa, Bulgaria 21 C10 43 15N 23 30 E
Vrbas →, Bos.-H. 20 B7 45 8N 17 29 E
Vrede, S. Africa 57 D4 27 24S 29 6 E
Vredefort, S. Africa 56 D4 27 0S 27 22 E
Vredenburg, S. Africa 56 E2 32 56S 18 0 E
Vredendal, S. Africa 56 E2 31 41S 18 35 E
Vrindavan, India 42 F7 27 37N 77 40 E
Vrises, Greece 23 D6 35 23N 24 13 E
Vršac, Serbia, Yug. 21 B9 45 8N 21 20 E
Vryburg, S. Africa 56 D3 26 55S 24 45 E
Vryheid, S. Africa 57 D5 27 45S 30 47 E
Vu Liet, Vietnam 38 C5 18 43N 105 23 E
Vukovar, Croatia 21 B8 45 21N 18 59 E
Vulcan, Canada 72 C6 50 25N 113 15W
Vulcan, Romania 17 F12 45 23N 23 17 E
Vulcaneşti, Moldova 17 F15 45 41N 28 18 E
Vulcano, Italy 20 E6 38 24N 14 58 E
Vulkaneshty = Vulcaneşti, Moldova 17 F15 45 41N 28 18 E
Vunduzi →, Mozam. 55 F3 18 56S 34 1 E
Vung Tau, Vietnam 39 G6 10 21N 107 4 E
Vyatka = Kirov, Russia 24 C8 58 35N 49 40 E
Vyatka →, Russia 24 C9 55 37N 51 28 E
Vyatskiye Polyany, Russia 24 C9 56 14N 51 5 E
Vyazemskiy, Russia 27 E14 47 32N 134 45 E
Vyazma, Russia 24 C5 55 10N 34 15 E
Vyborg, Russia 24 B4 60 43N 28 47 E
Vychegda →, Russia 24 B8 61 18N 46 36 E
Vychodné Beskydy, Europe 17 D11 49 20N 22 0 E
Vyg-ozero, Russia 24 B5 63 47N 34 29 E
Vylkove, Ukraine 17 F15 45 28N 29 32 E
Vynohradiv, Ukraine 17 D12 48 9N 23 2 E
Vyrnwy, L., U.K. 10 E4 52 48N 3 31W
Vyshniy Volochek, Russia 24 C5 57 30N 34 30 E
Vyškov, Czech Rep. 17 D9 49 17N 17 0 E
Vytegra, Russia 24 B6 61 0N 36 27 E

W

W.A.C. Bennett Dam, Canada 72 B4 56 2N 122 6W
Waal →, Neths. 15 C5 51 37N 5 0 E
Waalwijk, Neths. 15 C5 51 42N 5 4 E
Wabana, Canada 71 C9 47 40N 53 0W
Wabasca →, Canada 72 B5 58 22N 115 20W
Wabasca-Desmarais, Canada 72 B6 55 57N 113 56W
Wabash, U.S.A. 76 E3 40 48N 85 49W
Wabash →, U.S.A. 76 G1 37 48N 88 2W
Wabigoon L., Canada 73 D10 49 44N 92 44W
Wabowden, Canada 73 C9 54 55N 98 38W
Wabuk Pt., Canada 70 A2 55 20N 85 5W
Wabush, Canada 71 B6 52 55N 66 52W
Waco, U.S.A. 81 K6 31 33N 97 9W
Waconichi, L., Canada 70 B5 50 8N 74 0W
Wad Hamid, Sudan 51 E12 16 30N 32 45 E
Wâd Medanî, Sudan 51 F12 14 28N 33 30 E
Wad Thana, Pakistan 42 F2 27 22N 66 23 E
Wadai, Africa 48 E5 12 0N 19 0 E
Wadayama, Japan 31 G7 35 19N 134 52 E
Waddeneilanden, Neths. 15 A5 53 20N 5 10 E
Waddenzee, Neths. 15 A5 53 6N 5 10 E
Waddington, U.S.A. 79 B9 44 52N 75 12W
Waddington, Mt., Canada 72 C3 51 23N 125 15W
Waddy Pt., Australia 63 C5 24 58S 153 21 E
Wadebridge, U.K. 11 G3 50 31N 4 51W
Wadena, Canada 73 C8 51 57N 103 47W
Wadena, U.S.A. 80 B7 46 26N 95 8W
Wadeye, Australia 60 B4 14 28S 129 52 E
Wadhams, Canada 72 C3 51 30N 127 30W
Wādī as Sīr, Jordan 47 D4 31 56N 35 49 E
Wadi Halfa, Sudan 51 D12 21 53N 31 19 E
Wadsworth, Nev., U.S.A. 82 G4 39 38N 119 17W
Wadsworth, Ohio, U.S.A. 78 E3 41 2N 81 44W
Waegwan, S. Korea 35 G15 35 59N 128 23 E
Wafangdian, China 35 E11 39 38N 121 58 E
Wafrah, Si. Arabia 44 D5 28 33N 47 56 E
Wageningen, Neths. 15 C5 51 58N 5 40 E
Wager B., Canada 69 B11 65 26N 88 40W
Wagga Wagga, Australia 63 F4 35 7S 147 24 E
Waghete, Indonesia 37 E9 4 10S 135 50 E
Wagin, Australia 61 F2 33 17S 117 25 E
Wagner, U.S.A. 80 D5 43 5N 98 18W
Wagon Mound, U.S.A. 81 G2 36 1N 104 42W
Wagoner, U.S.A. 81 H7 35 58N 95 22W
Wah, Pakistan 42 C5 33 45N 72 40 E
Wahai, Indonesia 37 E7 2 48S 129 35 E
Wahiawa, U.S.A. 74 H15 21 30N 158 2W
Wâḥid, Egypt 47 E1 30 48N 32 21 E
Wahnai, Afghan. 42 C1 32 40N 65 50 E
Wahoo, U.S.A. 80 E6 41 13N 96 37W
Wahpeton, U.S.A. 80 B6 46 16N 96 36W
Wai, Koh, Cambodia 39 H4 9 55N 102 55 E
Waiau →, N.Z. 59 K4 42 47S 173 22 E
Waibeem, Indonesia 37 E8 0 30S 132 59 E
Waigeo, Indonesia 37 E8 0 20S 130 40 E
Waihi, N.Z. 59 G5 37 23S 175 52 E
Waihou →, N.Z. 59 G5 37 15S 175 40 E
Waika, Dem. Rep. of the Congo 54 C2 2 22S 25 42 E
Waikabubak, Indonesia 37 F5 9 45S 119 25 E
Waikari, N.Z. 59 K4 42 58S 172 41 E
Waikato →, N.Z. 59 G5 37 23S 174 43 E
Waikerie, Australia 63 E3 34 9S 140 0 E
Waikokopu, N.Z. 59 H6 39 3S 177 52 E
Waikouaiti, N.Z. 59 L3 45 36S 170 41 E
Wailuku, U.S.A. 74 H16 20 53N 156 30W
Waimakariri →, N.Z. 59 K4 43 24S 172 42 E
Waimate, N.Z. 59 L3 44 45S 171 3 E
Wainganga →, India 40 K11 18 50N 79 55 E
Waingapu, Indonesia 37 F6 9 35S 120 11 E
Waini →, Guyana 92 B7 8 20N 59 50W
Wainwright, Canada 73 C6 52 50N 110 50W
Waiouru, N.Z. 59 H5 39 28S 175 41 E
Waipara, N.Z. 59 K4 43 3S 172 46 E
Waipawa, N.Z. 59 H6 39 56S 176 38 E
Waipiro, N.Z. 59 H7 38 2S 178 22 E
Waipu, N.Z. 59 F5 35 59S 174 29 E
Waipukurau, N.Z. 59 J6 40 1S 176 33 E
Wairakei, N.Z. 59 H6 38 37S 176 6 E
Wairarapa, L., N.Z. 59 J5 41 14S 175 15 E
Wairoa, N.Z. 59 H6 39 3S 177 25 E
Waitaki →, N.Z. 59 L3 44 56S 171 7 E
Waitara, N.Z. 59 H5 38 59S 174 15 E
Waitsburg, U.S.A. 82 C5 46 16N 118 9W
Waiuku, N.Z. 59 G5 37 15S 174 45 E
Wajima, Japan 31 F8 37 30N 137 0 E
Wajir, Kenya 54 B5 1 42N 40 5 E
Wakasa, Japan 31 G7 35 20N 134 24 E
Wakasa-Wan, Japan 31 G7 35 40N 135 30 E
Wakatipu, L., N.Z. 59 L2 45 5S 168 33 E
Wakaw, Canada 73 C7 52 39N 105 44W
Wakayama, Japan 31 G7 34 15N 135 15 E
Wakayama □, Japan 31 H7 33 50N 135 30 E
Wake Forest, U.S.A. 77 H6 35 59N 78 30W

West Ice Shelf

Wake I., Pac. Oc. 64 F8 19 18N 166 36 E
WaKeeney, U.S.A. 80 F5 39 1N 99 53W
Wakefield, N.Z. 59 J4 41 24 S 173 5 E
Wakefield, U.K. 10 D6 53 41N 1 29W
Wakefield, Mass., U.S.A. 79 D13 42 30N 71 4W
Wakefield, Mich., U.S.A. 80 B10 46 29N 89 56W
Wakema, Burma 41 L19 16 30N 95 11 E
Wakkanai, Japan 30 B10 45 28N 141 35 E
Wakkerstroom, S. Africa 57 D5 27 24 S 30 10 E
Wakool, Australia 63 F3 35 28 S 144 23 E
Wakool →, Australia 63 F3 35 5 S 143 33 E
Wakre, Indonesia 37 E8 0 19 S 131 5 E
Wakuach, L., Canada 71 A6 55 34N 67 32W
Walamba, Zambia 55 E2 13 30 S 28 42 E
Wałbrzych, Poland 16 C9 50 45N 16 18 E
Walbury Hill, U.K. 11 F6 51 21N 1 28W
Walcha, Australia 63 E5 30 55 S 151 31 E
Walcheren, Neths. 15 C3 51 30N 3 35 E
Walcott, U.S.A. 82 F10 41 46N 106 51W
Wałcz, Poland 16 B9 53 17N 16 27 E
Waldburg Ra., Australia 61 D2 24 40 S 117 35 E
Walden, Colo., U.S.A. 82 F10 40 44N 106 17W
Walden, N.Y., U.S.A. 79 E10 41 34N 74 11W
Waldport, U.S.A. 82 D1 44 26N 124 4W
Waldron, U.S.A. 81 H7 34 54N 94 5W
Walebing, Australia 61 F2 30 41 S 116 13 E
Wales □, U.K. 11 E3 52 19N 4 43W
Walgett, Australia 63 E4 30 0 S 148 5 E
Walgreen Coast, Antarctica 5 D15 75 15 S 105 0W
Walker, U.S.A. 80 B7 47 6N 94 35W
Walker, L., Canada 71 B6 50 20N 67 11W
Walker L., Canada 73 C9 54 42N 95 57W
Walker L., U.S.A. 82 G4 38 42N 118 43W
Walkerston, Australia 62 C4 21 11 S 149 8 E
Walkerton, Canada 78 B3 44 10N 81 10W
Wall, U.S.A. 80 D3 44 0N 102 8W
Walla Walla, U.S.A. 82 C4 46 4N 118 20W
Wallace, Idaho, U.S.A. 82 C6 47 28N 115 56W
Wallace, N.C., U.S.A. 77 H7 34 44N 77 59W
Wallaceburg, Canada 78 D2 42 34N 82 23W
Wallachia = Valahia, Romania 17 F13 44 35N 25 0 E
Wallal, Australia 63 D4 26 32 S 146 7 E
Wallam Cr. →, Australia 63 D4 28 40 S 147 20 E
Wallambin, L., Australia 61 F2 30 57 S 117 35 E
Wallan, Australia 63 F3 37 26 S 144 59 E
Wallangarra, Australia 63 D5 28 56 S 151 58 E
Wallaroo, Australia 63 E2 33 56 S 137 39 E
Wallenpaupack, L., U.S.A. 79 E9 41 25N 75 15W
Wallingford, U.S.A. 79 E12 41 27N 72 50W
Wallis & Futuna, Is., Pac. Oc. 64 J10 13 18 S 176 10W
Wallowa, U.S.A. 82 D5 45 34N 117 32W
Wallowa Mts., U.S.A. 82 D5 45 20N 117 30W
Walls, U.K. 12 A7 60 14N 1 33W
Wallula, U.S.A. 82 C4 46 5N 118 54W
Wallumbilla, Australia 63 D4 26 33 S 149 9 E
Walmsley, L., Canada 73 A7 63 25N 108 36W
Walney, I. of, U.K. 10 C4 54 6N 3 15W
Walnut Creek, U.S.A. 84 H4 37 54N 122 4W
Walnut Ridge, U.S.A. 81 G9 36 4N 90 57W
Walpole, Australia 61 F2 34 58 S 116 44 E
Walpole, U.S.A. 79 D13 42 9N 71 15W
Walsall, U.K. 11 E6 52 35N 1 58W
Walsenburg, U.S.A. 81 G2 37 38N 104 47W
Walsh, U.S.A. 81 G3 37 23N 102 17W
Walsh →, Australia 62 B3 16 31 S 143 42 E
Walterboro, U.S.A. 77 J5 32 55N 80 40W
Walters, U.S.A. 81 H5 34 22N 98 19W
Waltham, U.S.A. 79 D13 42 23N 71 14W
Waltman, U.S.A. 82 E10 43 4N 107 12W
Walton, U.S.A. 79 D9 42 10N 75 8W
Walton-on-the-Naze, U.K. 11 F9 51 51N 1 17 E
Walvis Bay, Namibia 56 C1 23 0 S 14 28 E
Walvisbaai = Walvis Bay, Namibia 56 C1 23 0 S 14 28 E
Wamba, Dem. Rep. of the Congo 54 B2 2 10N 27 57 E
Wamba, Kenya 54 B4 0 58N 37 19 E
Wamego, U.S.A. 80 F6 39 12N 96 18W
Wamena, Indonesia 37 E9 4 4 S 138 57 E
Wamsutter, U.S.A. 82 F9 41 40N 107 58W
Wamulan, Indonesia 37 E7 3 27 S 126 7 E
Wan Xian, China 34 E8 38 47N 115 7 E
Wana, Pakistan 42 C3 32 20N 69 32 E
Wanaaring, Australia 63 D3 29 38 S 144 9 E
Wanaka, N.Z. 59 L2 44 42 S 169 9 E
Wanaka L., N.Z. 59 L2 44 33 S 169 7 E
Wanapitei L., Canada 70 C3 46 45N 80 40W
Wandel Sea = McKinley Sea, Arctic 4 A7 82 0N 0 0 E
Wanderer, Zimbabwe 55 F3 19 36 S 30 1 E
Wandhari, Pakistan 42 F2 27 42N 66 48 E
Wandoan, Australia 63 D4 26 5 S 149 55 E
Wanfu, China 35 D12 40 8N 122 38 E
Wang →, Thailand 38 D2 17 8N 99 2 E
Wang Noi, Thailand 38 E3 14 13N 100 44 E
Wang Saphung, Thailand 38 D3 17 18N 101 46 E
Wang Thong, Thailand 38 D3 16 50N 100 26 E
Wanga, Dem. Rep. of the Congo 54 B2 2 58N 29 12 E
Wangal, Indonesia 37 F8 6 8 S 134 9 E
Wanganella, Australia 63 F3 35 6 S 144 49 E
Wanganui, N.Z. 59 H5 39 56 S 175 3 E
Wangaratta, Australia 63 F4 36 21 S 146 19 E
Wangary, Australia 63 E2 34 35 S 135 29 E
Wangdu, China 34 E8 38 40N 115 7 E
Wangerooge, Germany 16 B4 53 47N 7 54 E
Wangi, Kenya 54 C5 1 58 S 40 58 E
Wangiwangi, Indonesia 37 F6 5 22 S 123 37 E
Wangqing, China 35 C15 43 12N 129 42 E
Wankaner, India 42 H4 22 35N 71 0 E
Wanless, Canada 73 C8 54 11N 101 21W
Wanning, Taiwan 38 C8 23 15N 121 17 E
Wanon Niwat, Thailand 38 D4 17 38N 103 46 E
Wanquan, China 34 D8 40 50N 114 40 E
Wanrong, China 34 G6 35 25N 110 50 E
Wantage, U.K. 11 F6 51 35N 1 25W
Wanxian, China 33 C5 30 42N 108 20 E
Wapakoneta, U.S.A. 76 E3 40 34N 84 12W
Wapato, U.S.A. 82 C3 46 27N 120 25W
Wapawekka L., Canada 73 C8 54 55N 104 40W
Wapikopa L., Canada 70 B2 52 56N 87 53W
Wapiti →, Canada 72 B5 55 5N 118 18W
Wappingers Falls, U.S.A. 79 E11 41 36N 73 55W
Wapsipinicon →, U.S.A. 80 E9 41 44N 90 19W
Warangal, India 40 L11 17 58N 79 35 E
Waraseoni, India 43 J9 21 45N 80 2 E
Waratah, Australia 62 G4 41 30 S 145 30 E
Waratah B., Australia 63 F4 38 54 S 146 5 E
Warburton, Vic., Australia 63 F4 37 47 S 145 42 E
Warburton, W. Austral., Australia 61 E4 26 8 S 126 35 E
Warburton Ra., Australia 61 E4 25 55 S 126 28 E
Ward, N.Z. 59 J5 41 49 S 174 11 E
Ward →, Australia 63 D4 26 28 S 146 6 E
Ward Mt., U.S.A. 84 H8 37 12N 118 54W
Warden, S. Africa 57 D4 27 50 S 29 0 E
Wardha, India 40 J11 20 45N 78 39 E
Wardha →, India 40 K11 19 57N 79 11 E
Ware, Canada 72 B3 57 26N 125 41W
Ware, U.S.A. 79 D12 42 16N 72 14W
Waregem, Belgium 15 D3 50 53N 3 27 E
Wareham, U.S.A. 79 E14 41 46N 70 43W
Waremme, Belgium 15 D5 50 43N 5 15 E
Warialda, Australia 63 D5 29 29 S 150 33 E
Wariap, Indonesia 37 E8 1 30 S 134 5 E
Warin Chamrap, Thailand 38 E5 15 12N 104 53 E
Warkopi, Indonesia 37 E8 1 12 S 134 9 E
Warm Springs, U.S.A. 83 G5 38 10N 116 20W
Warman, Canada 73 C7 52 19N 106 30W
Warmbad, Namibia 56 D2 28 25 S 18 42 E
Warmbad, S. Africa 57 C4 24 51 S 28 19 E
Warminster, U.K. 11 F5 51 12N 2 10W
Warminster, U.S.A. 79 F9 40 12N 75 6W
Warner Mts., U.S.A. 82 F3 41 40N 120 15W
Warner Robins, U.S.A. 77 J4 32 37N 83 36W
Waroona, Australia 61 F2 32 50 S 115 58 E
Warracknabeal, Australia 63 F3 36 9 S 142 26 E
Warragul, Australia 63 F4 38 10 S 145 58 E
Warrego →, Australia 63 E4 30 24 S 145 21 E
Warrego Ra., Australia 62 C4 24 58 S 146 0 E
Warren, Australia 63 E4 31 42 S 147 51 E
Warren, Ark., U.S.A. 81 J8 33 37N 92 4W
Warren, Mich., U.S.A. 76 D4 42 30N 83 0W
Warren, Minn., U.S.A. 80 A6 48 12N 96 46W
Warren, Ohio, U.S.A. 78 E4 41 14N 80 49W
Warren, Pa., U.S.A. 78 E5 41 51N 79 9W
Warrenpoint, U.K. 13 B5 54 6N 6 15W
Warrensburg, Mo., U.S.A. 80 F8 38 46N 93 44W
Warrensburg, N.Y., U.S.A. 79 C11 43 29N 73 46W
Warrenton, S. Africa 56 D3 28 9 S 24 47 E
Warrenton, U.S.A. 84 D3 46 10N 123 56W
Warri, Nigeria 50 G7 5 30N 5 41 E
Warrina, Australia 63 D2 28 12 S 135 50 E
Warrington, U.K. 10 D5 53 24N 2 35W
Warrington, U.S.A. 77 K2 30 23N 87 17W
Warrington □, U.K. 10 D5 53 24N 2 35W
Warrnambool, Australia 63 F3 38 25 S 142 30 E
Warroad, U.S.A. 80 A7 48 54N 95 19W
Warruwi, Australia 62 A1 11 36 S 133 20 E
Warsa, Indonesia 37 E9 0 47 S 135 55 E
Warsak Dam, Pakistan 42 B4 34 11N 71 19 E
Warsaw = Warszawa, Poland 17 B11 52 13N 21 0 E
Warsaw, Ind., U.S.A. 76 E3 41 14N 85 51W
Warsaw, N.Y., U.S.A. 78 D6 42 45N 78 8W
Warsaw, Ohio, U.S.A. 78 F3 40 20N 82 0W
Warszawa, Poland 17 B11 52 13N 21 0 E
Warta →, Poland 16 B8 52 35N 14 39 E
Warthe = Warta →, Poland 16 B8 52 35N 14 39 E
Waru, Indonesia 37 E8 3 30 S 130 36 E
Warwick, Australia 63 D5 28 10 S 152 1 E
Warwick, U.K. 11 E6 52 18N 1 35W
Warwick, N.Y., U.S.A. 79 E10 41 16N 74 22W
Warwick, R.I., U.S.A. 79 E13 41 42N 71 28W
Warwickshire □, U.K. 11 E6 52 14N 1 38W
Wasaga Beach, Canada 78 B4 44 31N 80 1W
Wasagaming, Canada 73 C9 50 39N 99 58W
Wasatch Ra., U.S.A. 82 F8 40 30N 111 15W
Wasbank, S. Africa 57 D5 28 15 S 30 9 E
Wasco, Calif., U.S.A. 85 K7 35 36N 119 20W
Wasco, Oreg., U.S.A. 82 D3 45 36N 120 42W
Waseca, U.S.A. 80 C8 44 5N 93 30W
Wasekamio L., Canada 73 B7 56 45N 108 45W
Wash, The, U.K. 10 E8 52 58N 0 20 E
Washago, Canada 78 B5 44 45N 79 20W
Washburn, N. Dak., U.S.A. 80 B4 47 17N 101 2W
Washburn, Wis., U.S.A. 80 B9 46 40N 90 54W
Washim, India 40 J10 20 3N 77 0 E
Washington, U.K. 10 C6 54 55N 1 30W
Washington, D.C., U.S.A. 76 F7 38 54N 77 2W
Washington, Ga., U.S.A. 77 J4 33 44N 82 44W
Washington, Ind., U.S.A. 76 F2 38 40N 87 10W
Washington, Iowa, U.S.A. 80 E9 41 18N 91 42W
Washington, Mo., U.S.A. 80 F9 38 33N 91 1W
Washington, N.C., U.S.A. 77 H7 35 33N 77 3W
Washington, N.J., U.S.A. 79 F10 40 46N 74 59W
Washington, Pa., U.S.A. 78 F4 40 10N 80 15W
Washington, Utah, U.S.A. 83 H7 37 8N 113 31W
Washington □, U.S.A. 82 C3 47 30N 120 30W
Washington, Mt., U.S.A. 79 B13 44 16N 71 18W
Washington Court House, U.S.A. 76 F4 39 32N 83 26W
Washington I., U.S.A. 76 C2 45 23N 86 54W
Washougal, U.S.A. 84 E4 45 35N 122 21W
Wasian, Indonesia 37 E8 1 47 S 133 19 E
Wasilla, U.S.A. 68 B5 61 35N 149 26W
Wasior, Indonesia 37 E8 2 43 S 134 30 E
Waskaganish, Canada 70 B4 51 30N 78 40W
Waskaiowaka, L., Canada 73 B9 56 33N 96 23W
Waskesiu Lake, Canada 73 C7 53 55N 106 5W
Wasserkuppe, Germany 16 C5 50 29N 9 55 E
Waswanipi, Canada 70 C4 49 40N 76 29W
Waswanipi, L., Canada 70 C4 49 35N 76 40W
Watampone, Indonesia 37 E6 4 29 S 120 25 E
Water Park Pt., Australia 62 C5 22 56 S 150 47 E
Water Valley, U.S.A. 81 H10 34 10N 89 38W
Waterberge, S. Africa 57 C4 24 10 S 28 0 E
Waterbury, Conn., U.S.A. 79 E11 41 33N 73 3W
Waterbury, Vt., U.S.A. 79 B12 44 20N 72 46W
Waterbury L., Canada 73 B8 58 10N 104 22W
Waterdown, Canada 78 C5 43 20N 79 53W
Waterford, Canada 78 D4 42 56N 80 17W
Waterford, Ireland 13 D4 52 15N 7 8W
Waterford, Calif., U.S.A. 84 H6 37 38N 120 46W
Waterford, Pa., U.S.A. 78 E5 41 57N 79 59W
Waterford □, Ireland 13 D4 52 10N 7 40W
Waterford Harbour, Ireland 13 D5 52 8N 6 58W
Waterhen L., Canada 73 C9 52 10N 99 40W
Waterloo, Belgium 15 D4 50 43N 4 25 E
Waterloo, Ont., Canada 78 C4 43 30N 80 32W
Waterloo, Qué., Canada 79 A12 45 22N 72 32W
Waterloo, Ill., U.S.A. 80 F9 38 20N 90 9W
Waterloo, Iowa, U.S.A. 80 D8 42 30N 92 21W
Waterloo, N.Y., U.S.A. 78 D8 42 54N 76 52W
Watersmeet, U.S.A. 80 B10 46 16N 89 11W
Waterton Nat. Park, U.S.A. 82 B7 48 45N 115 0W
Watertown, Conn., U.S.A. 79 E11 41 36N 73 7W
Watertown, N.Y., U.S.A. 79 C9 43 59N 75 55W
Watertown, S. Dak., U.S.A. 80 C6 44 54N 97 7W
Watertown, Wis., U.S.A. 80 D10 43 12N 88 43W
Waterval-Boven, S. Africa 57 D5 25 40 S 30 18 E
Waterville, Canada 79 A13 45 16N 71 54W
Waterville, Maine, U.S.A. 77 C11 44 33N 69 38W
Waterville, N.Y., U.S.A. 79 D9 42 56N 75 23W
Waterville, Pa., U.S.A. 78 E7 41 19N 77 21W
Waterville, Wash., U.S.A. 82 C3 47 39N 120 4W
Watervliet, U.S.A. 79 D11 42 44N 73 42W
Wates, Indonesia 37 G14 7 51 S 110 10 E
Watford, Canada 78 D3 42 57N 81 53W
Watford, U.K. 11 F7 51 40N 0 24W
Watford City, U.S.A. 80 B3 47 48N 103 17W
Wathaman →, Canada 73 B8 57 16N 102 59W
Wathaman L., Canada 73 B8 56 58N 103 44W
Watheroo, Australia 61 F2 30 15 S 116 0 E
Wating, China 34 G4 35 40N 106 38 E
Watkins Glen, U.S.A. 78 D8 42 23N 76 52W
Watling I. = San Salvador I., Bahamas 89 B5 24 0N 74 40W
Watonga, U.S.A. 81 H5 35 51N 98 25W
Watrous, Canada 73 C7 51 40N 105 25W
Watrous, U.S.A. 81 H2 35 48N 104 59W
Watsa, Dem. Rep. of the Congo 54 B2 3 4N 29 30 E
Watseka, U.S.A. 76 E2 40 47N 87 44W
Watson, Australia 61 F5 30 29 S 131 31 E
Watson, Canada 73 C8 52 10N 104 30W
Watson Lake, Canada 72 A3 60 6N 128 49W
Watsontown, U.S.A. 78 E8 41 5N 76 52W
Watsonville, U.S.A. 84 J5 36 55N 121 45W
Wattiwarriganna Cr. →, Australia 63 D2 28 57 S 136 10 E
Watuata = Batuata, Indonesia 37 F6 6 12 S 122 42 E
Watubela, Kepulauan, Indonesia 37 E8 4 28 S 131 35 E
Watubela Is. = Watubela, Kepulauan, Indonesia 37 E8 4 28 S 131 35 E
Wau, Sudan 49 F6 7 45N 28 1 E
Waubamik, Canada 78 A4 45 27N 80 1W
Waubay, U.S.A. 80 C6 45 20N 97 18W
Wauchope, N.S.W., Australia 63 E5 31 28 S 152 45 E
Wauchope, N. Terr., Australia 62 C1 20 36 S 134 15 E
Waukarlycarly, L., Australia 60 D3 21 18 S 121 56 E
Waukegan, U.S.A. 75 B9 42 22N 87 50W
Waukesha, U.S.A. 76 D1 43 1N 88 14W
Waukon, U.S.A. 80 D9 43 16N 91 29W
Waupaca, U.S.A. 80 C10 44 21N 89 5W
Waupun, U.S.A. 80 D10 43 38N 88 44W
Waurika, U.S.A. 81 H6 34 10N 98 0W
Wausau, U.S.A. 80 C10 44 58N 89 38W
Wautoma, U.S.A. 80 C10 44 4N 89 18W
Wauwatosa, U.S.A. 76 D2 43 3N 88 0W
Waveney →, U.K. 11 E9 52 35N 1 39 E
Waverley, N.Z. 59 H5 39 46 S 174 37 E
Waverly, Iowa, U.S.A. 80 D8 42 44N 92 29W
Waverly, N.Y., U.S.A. 79 E8 42 1N 76 32W
Wavre, Belgium 15 D4 50 43N 4 38 E
Wâw, Sudan 51 G11 7 45N 28 1 E
Wāw al Kabīr, Libya 51 C9 25 20N 16 43 E
Wawa, Canada 70 C3 47 59N 84 47W
Wawanesa, Canada 73 D9 49 36N 99 40W
Wawona, U.S.A. 84 H7 37 32N 119 39W
Waxahachie, U.S.A. 81 J6 32 24N 96 51W
Way, L., Australia 61 E3 26 45 S 120 16 E
Waycross, U.S.A. 77 K4 31 13N 82 21W
Wayland, U.S.A. 78 D7 42 34N 77 35W
Wayne, Nebr., U.S.A. 80 D6 42 14N 97 1W
Wayne, W. Va., U.S.A. 76 F4 38 13N 82 27W
Waynesboro, Ga., U.S.A. 77 J4 33 6N 82 1W
Waynesboro, Miss., U.S.A. 77 K1 31 40N 88 39W
Waynesboro, Pa., U.S.A. 76 F7 39 45N 77 35W
Waynesboro, Va., U.S.A. 76 F6 38 4N 78 53W
Waynesburg, U.S.A. 76 F5 39 54N 80 11W
Waynesville, U.S.A. 77 H4 35 28N 82 58W
Waynoka, U.S.A. 81 G5 36 35N 98 53W
Wazirabad, Pakistan 42 C6 32 30N 74 8 E
We, Indonesia 36 C1 5 51N 95 18 E
Weald, The, U.K. 11 F8 51 4N 0 20 E
Wear →, U.K. 10 C6 54 55N 1 23W
Weatherford, Okla., U.S.A. 81 H5 35 32N 98 43W
Weatherford, Tex., U.S.A. 81 J6 32 46N 97 48W
Weaverville, U.S.A. 82 F2 40 44N 122 56W
Webb City, U.S.A. 81 G7 37 9N 94 28W
Webequie, Canada 70 B2 52 59N 87 21W
Webster, Mass., U.S.A. 79 D13 42 3N 71 53W
Webster, N.Y., U.S.A. 78 C7 43 13N 77 26W
Webster, S. Dak., U.S.A. 80 C6 45 20N 97 31W
Webster City, U.S.A. 80 D8 42 28N 93 49W
Webster Springs, U.S.A. 76 F5 38 29N 80 25W
Weda, Indonesia 37 D7 0 21N 127 50 E
Weda, Teluk, Indonesia 37 D7 0 30N 127 50 E
Weddell I., Falk. Is. 96 G4 51 50 S 61 0W
Weddell Sea, Antarctica 5 D1 72 30 S 40 0W
Wedderburn, Australia 63 F3 36 26 S 143 33 E
Wedgeport, Canada 71 D6 43 44N 65 59W
Wedza, Zimbabwe 55 F3 18 40 S 31 33 E
Wee Waa, Australia 63 E4 30 11 S 149 26 E
Weed, U.S.A. 82 F2 41 25N 122 23W
Weed Heights, U.S.A. 84 G7 38 59N 119 13W
Weedsport, U.S.A. 79 C8 43 3N 76 35W
Weedville, U.S.A. 78 E6 41 17N 78 30W
Weenen, S. Africa 57 D5 28 48 S 30 7 E
Weert, Neths. 15 C5 51 15N 5 43 E
Wei He →, Hebei, China 34 F8 36 10N 115 45 E
Wei He →, Shaanxi, China 34 G6 34 38N 110 15 E
Weichang, China 35 D9 41 58N 117 49 E
Weichuan, China 34 G7 34 20N 113 59 E
Weiden, Germany 16 D7 49 41N 12 10 E
Weifang, China 35 F10 36 44N 119 7 E
Weihai, China 35 F12 37 30N 122 6 E
Weimar, Germany 16 C6 50 58N 11 19 E
Weinan, China 34 G5 34 31N 109 29 E
Weipa, Australia 62 A3 12 40 S 141 50 E
Weir →, Australia 63 D4 28 20 S 149 50 E
Weir →, Canada 73 B10 56 54N 93 21W
Weir River, Canada 73 B10 56 49N 94 6W
Weirton, U.S.A. 78 F4 40 24N 80 35W
Weiser, U.S.A. 82 D5 44 10N 117 0W
Weishan, China 35 G9 34 47N 117 5 E
Weiyuan, China 34 G3 35 7N 104 10 E
Wejherowo, Poland 17 A10 54 35N 18 12 E
Wekusko L., Canada 73 C9 54 40N 99 50W
Welch, U.S.A. 76 G5 37 26N 81 35W
Welkom, S. Africa 56 D4 28 0 S 26 46 E
Welland, Canada 78 D5 43 0N 79 15W
Welland →, U.K. 11 E7 52 51N 0 5W
Wellesley Is., Australia 62 B2 16 42 S 139 30 E
Wellingborough, U.K. 11 E7 52 19N 0 41W
Wellington, Australia 63 E4 32 35 S 148 59 E
Wellington, Canada 78 C7 43 57N 77 20W
Wellington, N.Z. 59 J5 41 19 S 174 46 E
Wellington, S. Africa 56 E2 33 38 S 19 1 E
Wellington, Somst., U.K. 11 G4 50 58N 3 13W
Wellington, Telford & Wrekin, U.K. 11 E5 52 42N 2 30W
Wellington, Colo., U.S.A. 80 E2 40 42N 105 0W
Wellington, Kans., U.S.A. 81 G6 37 16N 97 24W
Wellington, Nev., U.S.A. 84 G7 38 45N 119 23W
Wellington, Ohio, U.S.A. 78 E2 41 10N 82 13W
Wellington, Tex., U.S.A. 81 H4 34 51N 100 13W
Wellington, I., Chile 96 F2 49 30 S 75 0W
Wellington, L., Australia 63 F4 38 6 S 147 20 E
Wells, U.K. 11 F5 51 13N 2 39W
Wells, Maine, U.S.A. 79 C14 43 20N 70 35W
Wells, N.Y., U.S.A. 79 C10 43 24N 74 17W
Wells, Nev., U.S.A. 82 F6 41 7N 114 58W
Wells, L., Australia 61 E3 26 44 S 123 15 E
Wells, Mt., Australia 60 C4 17 25 S 127 8 E
Wells Gray Prov. Park, Canada 72 C4 52 30N 120 15W
Wells-next-the-Sea, U.K. 10 E8 52 57N 0 51 E
Wells River, U.S.A. 79 B12 44 9N 72 4W
Wellsboro, U.S.A. 78 E7 41 45N 77 18W
Wellsburg, U.S.A. 78 F4 40 16N 80 37W
Wellsville, N.Y., U.S.A. 78 D7 42 7N 77 57W
Wellsville, Ohio, U.S.A. 78 F4 40 36N 80 39W
Wellsville, Utah, U.S.A. 82 F8 41 38N 111 56W
Wellton, U.S.A. 83 K6 32 40N 114 8W
Wels, Austria 16 D8 48 9N 14 1 E
Welshpool, U.K. 11 E4 52 39N 3 8W
Welwyn Garden City, U.K. 11 F7 51 48N 0 12W
Wem, U.K. 10 E5 52 52N 2 44W
Wembere →, Tanzania 54 C3 4 10 S 34 15 E
Wemindji, Canada 70 B4 53 0N 78 49W
Wen Xian, China 34 G7 34 55N 113 5 E
Wenatchee, U.S.A. 82 C3 47 25N 120 19W
Wenchang, China 38 C8 19 38N 110 42 E
Wenchi, Ghana 50 G5 7 46N 2 8W
Wenchow = Wenzhou, China 33 D7 28 0N 120 38 E
Wenden, U.S.A. 85 M13 33 49N 113 33W
Wendeng, China 35 F12 37 15N 122 5 E
Wendesi, Indonesia 37 E8 2 30 S 134 17 E
Wendover, U.S.A. 82 F6 40 44N 114 2W
Wenlock →, Australia 62 A3 12 2 S 141 55 E
Wenshan, China 32 D5 23 20N 104 18 E
Wenshang, China 34 G9 35 45N 116 30 E
Wenshui, China 34 F7 37 26N 112 1 E
Wensleydale, U.K. 10 C6 54 17N 2 0W
Wensu, China 32 B3 41 15N 80 10 E
Wensum →, U.K. 10 E8 52 40N 1 15 E
Wentworth, Australia 63 E3 34 2 S 141 54 E
Wentzel L., Canada 72 B6 59 2N 114 28W
Wenut, Indonesia 37 E8 3 11 S 133 19 E
Wenxi, China 34 G6 35 20N 111 10 E
Wenxian, China 34 H3 32 43N 104 36 E
Wenzhou, China 33 D7 28 0N 120 38 E
Weott, U.S.A. 82 F2 40 20N 123 55W
Wepener, S. Africa 56 D4 29 42 S 27 3 E
Werda, Botswana 56 D3 25 24 S 23 15 E
Weri, Indonesia 37 E8 3 10 S 132 38 E
Werra →, Germany 16 C5 51 24N 9 39 E
Werrimull, Australia 63 E3 34 25 S 141 38 E
Werris Creek, Australia 63 E5 31 18 S 150 38 E
Weser →, Germany 16 B5 53 36N 8 28 E
Wesiri, Indonesia 37 F7 7 30 S 126 30 E
Weslemkoon L., Canada 78 A7 45 2N 77 25W
Wesleyville, Canada 71 C9 49 8N 53 36W
Wesleyville, U.S.A. 78 D4 42 9N 80 0W
Wessel, C., Australia 62 A2 10 59 S 136 46 E
Wessel Is., Australia 62 A2 11 10 S 136 45 E
Wessington Springs, U.S.A. 80 C5 44 5N 98 34W
West, U.S.A. 81 K6 31 48N 97 6W
West →, U.S.A. 79 D12 42 52N 72 33W
West Baines →, Australia 60 C4 15 38 S 129 59 E
West Bank □, Asia 47 C4 32 6N 35 13 E
West Bend, U.S.A. 76 D1 43 25N 88 11W
West Bengal □, India 43 H13 23 0N 88 0 E
West Berkshire □, U.K. 11 F6 51 25N 1 17W
West Beskids = Západné Beskydy, Europe 17 D10 49 30N 19 0 E
West Branch, U.S.A. 76 C3 44 17N 84 14W
West Branch Susquehanna →, U.S.A. 79 F8 40 53N 76 48W
West Bromwich, U.K. 11 E6 52 32N 1 59W
West Burra, U.K. 12 A7 60 5N 1 21W
West Canada Cr. →, U.S.A. 79 C10 43 1N 74 58W
West Cape Howe, Australia 61 G2 35 8 S 117 36 E
West Chazy, U.S.A. 79 B11 44 49N 73 28W
West Chester, U.S.A. 79 G9 39 58N 75 36W
West Columbia, U.S.A. 81 L7 29 9N 95 39W
West Covina, U.S.A. 85 L9 34 4N 117 54W
West Des Moines, U.S.A. 80 E8 41 35N 93 43W
West Dunbartonshire □, U.K. 12 F4 55 59N 4 30W
West End, Bahamas 88 A4 26 41N 78 58W
West Falkland, Falk. Is. 96 G5 51 40 S 60 0W
West Fargo, U.S.A. 80 B6 46 52N 96 54W
West Farmington, U.S.A. 78 E4 41 23N 80 58W
West Fjord = Vestfjorden, Norway 8 C15 67 55N 14 0 E
West Fork Trinity →, U.S.A. 81 J6 32 48N 96 54W
West Frankfort, U.S.A. 80 G10 37 54N 88 55W
West Hartford, U.S.A. 79 E12 41 45N 72 44W
West Haven, U.S.A. 79 E12 41 17N 72 57W
West Hazleton, U.S.A. 79 F9 40 58N 76 0W
West Helena, U.S.A. 81 H9 34 33N 90 38W
West Hurley, U.S.A. 79 E10 41 59N 74 7W
West Ice Shelf, Antarctica 5 C7 67 0 S 85 0 E

West Indies

World: Regions in the News

YUGOSLAVIA
Population 10,761,000
(Serb 62.6%, Albanian 16.5%,
Montenegrin 5%, Hungarian 3.3%,
Muslim 3.2%)
Serbia Population: 5,799,800
(Serb 87.7%, excluding the
provinces of Kosovo and
Vojvodina)
Kosovo Population: 2,084,4000
(Albanian 81.6%, Serb 9.9%)
Vojvodena Population: 1,980,800
(Serb 56.8%, Hungarian 16.9%)
Montenegro Population: 635,000
(Montenegrin 61.9%, Muslim
14.6%, Albanian 7%)

CROATIA
Population: 4,960,000
(Croat 78.1%, Serb 12.2%)

SLOVENIA
Population: 2,055,000
(Slovene 88%, Croat 3%, Serb 2%)

MACEDONIA (F. Y. R. O. M.)
Population: 2,157,000
(Macedonian 64%, Albanian 21.7%,
Turkish 5%, Romanian 3%,
Serb 2%)

BOSNIA-HERZEGOVINA
Population: 4,601,000
(Muslim 49%, Serb 31.2%,
Croat 17.2%)

FORMER YUGOSLAVIA AND KOSOVO

The former Yugoslavia, a federation of six republics, split apart in 1991–2.
Fearing Serb domination, Croatia, Slovenia, Macedonia and Bosnia-
Herzegovina declared themselves independent. This left two states, Serbia and
Montenegro, to continue as Yugoslavia. The presence in Croatia and Bosnia-
Herzegovina of Orthodox Christian Serbs, Roman Catholic Croats, and Muslims
led to civil war and 'ethnic cleansing'. In 1995, the war ended when the Dayton
Peace Accord affirmed Bosnia-Herzegovina as a single state partitioned into a
Muslim–Croat Federation and a Serbian Republic.

But the status of Kosovo, a former autonomous Yugoslav region, remained
unresolved. Kosovo's autonomy had been abolished in 1989 and the Albanian-
speaking, Muslim Kosovars were forced to accept direct Serbian rule. After
1995, support grew for the rebel Kosovo Liberation Army. The Serbs hit back and
thousands of Kosovars were forced to flee their homes. In March 1999, NATO
launched an aerial offensive against Serbia in an attempt to halt the 'ethnic
cleansing'. A Serb military withdrawal from Kosovo was agreed in June 1999.

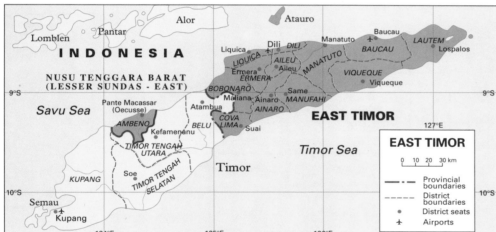

**COUNTRIES AND REPUBLICS
OF THE CAUCASUS REGION**

**RUSSIAN REPUBLICS IN THE
NEWS**
North Ossetia (Alania)
Population: 695,000
(Ossetian 53%, Russian 29%,
Chechen 5.2%, Armenian 1.9%)
Chechenia Population: 1,308,000
(Chechen and Ingush 70.7%,
Russian 23.1%, Armenian 1.2%)
Ingushetia (Split from Chechenia
in June 1993) Population: 250,000

GEORGIA
Population: 5,777,000
(Georgian 70.1%, Armenian 8.1%,
Russian 6.3%, Azerbaijani 5.7%,
Ossetian 3%, Greek 2%,
Abkhazian 2%)
Abkhazia Population: 537,500
(Georgian 45.7%, Abkhazian 17.8%,
Armenian 14.6%, Russian 14.3%)
Ajaria Population: 382,000
(Georgian 82.8%, Russian 7.7%,
Armenian 4%)

ARMENIA
Population: 3,968,000
(Armenian 93%, Azerbaijani 3%)
Nagorno-Karabakh
Population: 192,400 (Armenian
76.9%, Azerbaijani 21.5%)

AZERBAIJAN
Population: 8,324,000
(Azerbaijani 83%, Russian 6%,
Armenian 6%, Lezgin 2%)

Naxçivan Population: 300,400

Georgia, Armenia and Azerbaijan
achieved independence in 1991.
Abkhazia, Ajaria and South Ossetia
seek independence from Georgia.
Chechenia has been trying to break
away from Russia since 1991, but
Russia has resisted with military force.
Hostility also continues between
Armenia and Azerbaijan over the
enclave of Nagorno-Karabakh.

ISRAEL
Population: 5,321,000 (inc. East
Jerusalem and Jewish settlers in the
areas under Israeli administration.
Jewish 82%, Arab Muslim 13.8%,
Arab Christian 2.5%, Druze 1.7%)

West Bank
Population: 1,122,900 (Palestinian
Arabs 97% [of whom Arab Muslim
85%, Jewish 7%, Christian 8%])

Gaza Strip
Population: 748,400 (Arab 98%)

JORDAN
Population: 5,558,000 (Arab 99% [of
whom about 50% are Palestinian Arab])

LEBANON
Population: 3,327,000 (Arab 93% [of
whom 83% are Lebanese Arab and
10% Palestinian Arab])

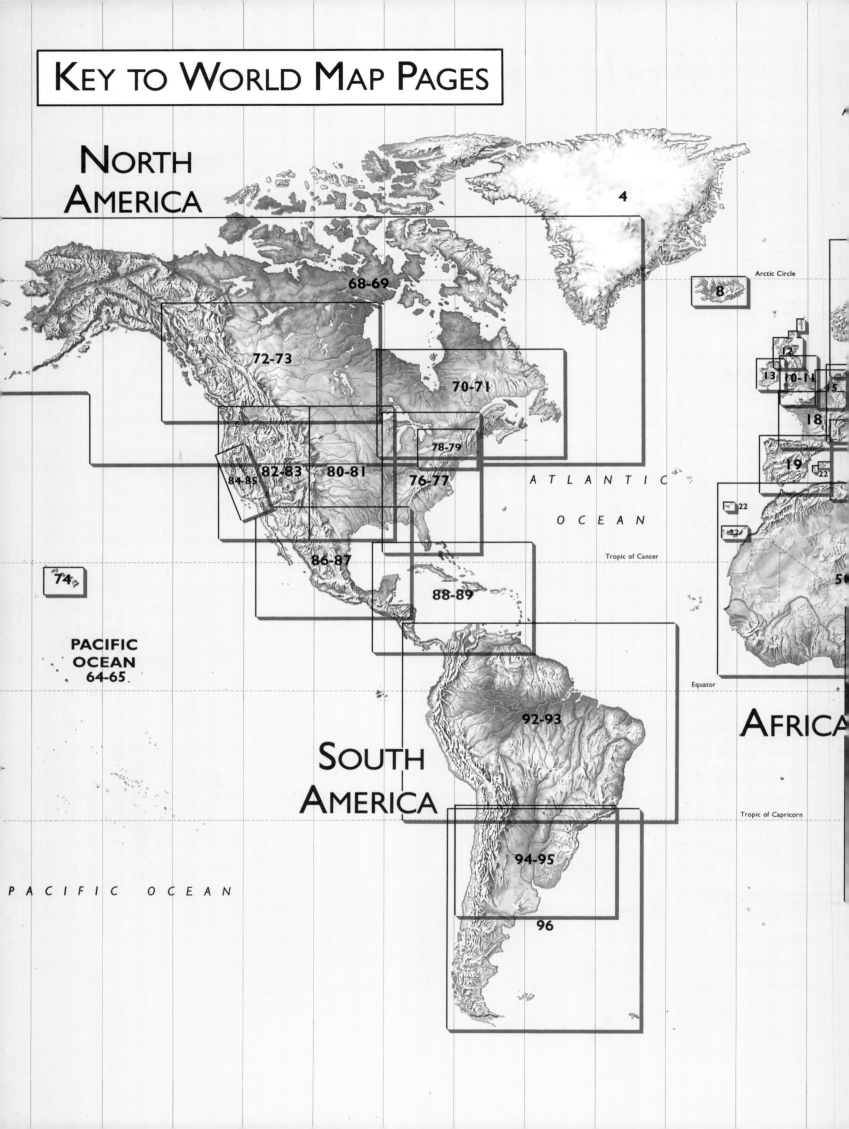

KEY TO WORLD MAP PAGES

NORTH AMERICA

4

8

Arctic Circle

68-69

72-73

70-71

12

13 **10-11**

15

18

78-79

82-83 **80-81**

76-77

ATLANTIC

19

22

84-85

OCEAN

22

86-87

Tropic of Cancer

22

50

74

88-89

PACIFIC
OCEAN
64-65

Equator

92-93

SOUTH

AFRICA

AMERICA

PACIFIC OCEAN

Tropic of Capricorn

94-95

96